Uppers, Downers,
All Arounders

Physical and Mental Effects
of Psychoactive Drugs

Sixth Edition

Darryl S. Inaba, Pharm.D., CADC III

Director of Clinical and Behavioral Health, Addictions Recovery Services,
   Medford, Oregon
Director of Research and Education, CNS Productions, Inc., Medford, Oregon
Associate Clinical Professor of Pharmacology, University of California
   Medical Center, San Francisco
Consultant/Instructor, University of Utah, School on Alcoholism and Other
   Drug Dependencies, Salt Lake City, UT

William E. Cohen, CGAC I

President, CNS Productions, Inc., Medford, Oregon

CNS Publications, Inc.™
Medford, Oregon

CNS Productions, Inc.™
Owner; **Paul J. Steinbroner**
11 Almond Street
Medford, Oregon, 97504
Tel: (800) 888-0617 Fax: (541) 773-5905
Web Site: www.cnsproductions.com
Email: info@cnsproductions.com

Uppers, Downers, All Arounders, Sixth Edition - 4th Printing
© 2007, William E. Cohen & Darryl S. Inaba

First Edition	© 1989
Second Edition	© 1993
Third Edition	© 1997
Fourth Edition	© 2000
Fifth Edition	© 2004

Editor: **Elizabeth von Radics**

Book Design: **Data Management, Inc./Connie Wolfe,** Cedar Rapids, Iowa

Illustrations: **Impact Publications/David Ruppe,** Medford, Oregon

Acquisitions Editor: **Paul J. Steinbroner**

Marketing Director: **Ellen Cholewa**

Cover Design: **Don Thomas Illustration,** Medford, Oregon

Printing and Color Separations: **Cedar Graphics,** Cedar Rapids, Iowa

Study Guide CD-ROM Design: **Sharp Design/Robert Sharp,** Medford, Oregon

Co-writer, Chapter 10: **Pablo Stewart, M.D.,** Clinical Professor of Psychiatry, University of California, San Francisco, School of Medicine

Special thanks to:
Michael Aldrich, Ph.D., Curator, Fitz Hugh Ludlow Memorial Library, San Francisco, California
Sterling K. Clarren, M.D., Children's Hospital, Seattle, Washington
Genesis Recovery and Mental Health Services, Central Point, Oregon

DISCLAIMER: Information in this book is in no way meant to replace professional medical advice or professional counseling and treatment.

Publisher's Cataloging-in-Publication
Inaba, Darryl S.
   Uppers, downers, all arounders: physical and mental
effects of psychoactive drugs/Darryl S. Inaba,
William E. Cohen —6th ed.
   p. cm.
   Includes bibliographical references, glossary, and index
   LCCN: 2007930154
   ISBN: 978-0-926544-28-4
   Psychoactive drugs—Side effects. 2. Drug abuse—
Complications. I. Cohen, William E., 1941-II. Title

Printed in the United States of America

T he Sixth Edition of Uppers, Downers, All Arounders is dedicated to the thousands of recovery professionals who provide drug abuse treatment, aftercare, education, and prevention services and whose passion can be measured by the miracles they facilitate on a daily basis.

The authors also acknowledge a debt of gratitude to those clients in treatment who so generously shared the stories of their one-day-at-a-time courageous battles with addiction and their willing entry into recovery so that others may learn from their experiences.

PREFACE

This edition incorporates the most current and comprehensive information on the physiology, neurochemistry, and sociology of drugs and compulsive behaviors.

Throughout each chapter, **key phrases emphasizing the most significant concepts are highlighted** to help the reader prioritize the information. A Study Guide CD accompanies the book and includes chapter outlines, guided reviews, key word and drug identification exercises, sample tests, and a glossary. The CD is cross-platform and does not require an internet connection.

Additional content can be found online at www.cnsproductions.com. This interactive web site includes access to an author's blog, the reader forum, on-line video, and links to the most up-to-date information on substance abuse and treatment.

Note: the trademark symbol ® distinguishes trade (brand) name prescription and over-the-counter drugs from chemical (generic) names.

CONTENTS

Psychoactive Drugs:
History & Classification

*T*his Currier & Ives lithograph from 1874 was the artist's reaction to the ax-wielding, saloon-busting Carrie Nation and her Woman's Christian Temperance Union (WCTU). In truth it wasn't temperance that the WCTU was aiming for but prohibition. Nation's tombstone even read, "Faithful to the cause of prohibition. She hath done what she could."

Courtesy of the National Library of Medicine, Bethesda, MD

INTRODUCTION

- **Five Historical Themes of Drug Use:**
    1. the basic need of human beings to cope with their environment and enhance their existence;
    2. the vulnerability of brain chemistry to psychoactive drugs, behavioral addictions, and mental illness;
    3. the involvement of ruling classes, governments, and businesses in growing, manufacturing, distributing, taxing, and prohibiting drugs;
    4. technological advances in refining and synthesizing drugs; and
    5. the development of faster and more efficient methods of putting drugs into the body.

HISTORY OF PSYCHOACTIVE DRUGS

- **Prehistory & the Neolithic Period (8500–4000 B.C.).** The earliest human uses of psychoactive drugs involved plants and fruits whose mood-altering qualities were accidentally discovered and then deliberately cultivated.
- **Ancient Civilizations (4000 B.C.–A.D. 400).** Sumerian, Egyptian, Indian, Chinese, South American, and other ancient cultures used opium, alcohol, *Cannabis* (marijuana), peyote, psychedelic mushrooms, and coca leaves.
- **Middle Ages (400–1400).** Psychoactive plants, such as belladonna and psilocybin mushrooms, were used by witches and shamans for healing and spiritual purposes; distilled alcohol and coffee were added to the list of available psychoactive drugs.
- **Renaissance & the Age of Discovery (1400–1700).** Tobacco, coffee, tea, distilled alcohol, and opium spread along the trade routes. The ruling classes, governments, and merchants controlled much of the trade.
- **Age of Enlightenment & the Early Industrial Revolution (1700–1900).** New refinement techniques (e.g., morphine from opium), new methods of use (e.g., hypodermic needle), and new manufacturing techniques (e.g., cigarette-rolling machines) increased use, abuse, and addiction liability. Temperance and prohibition movements also spread.
- **Twentieth Century.** Wider distribution channels, new synthetic drugs, and extensive drug regulations (including alcohol prohibition/repeal and marijuana exclusion) generally increased illegal and legal use. Defining addiction as a disease and researching biochemical roots of addiction helped expand treatment options.
- **Today & Tomorrow.** The huge amounts of money involved in the drug trade coupled with the 9/11 attacks on the Pentagon and the World Trade Center; the wars in Afghanistan and Iraq; the bombings of Spanish, British, and Indian trains; and other acts of terrorism have emphasized the geopolitics of growing, refining, smuggling, and selling drugs. At the beginning of the twenty-first century, while the use of club drugs (e.g., ecstasy and GHB) declines, alcohol, tobacco, marijuana, and methamphetamines are still the drugs of choice. A recent increase in the abuse of prescription drugs, especially opioid pain medications, has raised their abuse by teenagers. HIV and AIDS have decreased, but the instances of hepatitis C, predominantly in substance abusers, continue to grow. Finally, federal and state drug policies are trying to shift from supply reduction to demand reduction and from a focus on drug addiction alone to a new focus on co-occurring disorders (drug addiction and a mental health disorder).
- **Conclusions.** The history of man reflects the integral part that psychoactive drugs have played in the social, economic, and emotional development of civilizations; and though the current drug of choice often changes, the reasons for drug use remain the same.

CLASSIFICATION OF PSYCHOACTIVE DRUGS

- **What Is a Psychoactive Drug?** Psychoactive drugs can be identified by their street name, chemical name, or trade name. This book classifies most drugs by their general effects.
- **Major Drugs:**
    ◇ **Uppers.** Stimulants, such as cocaine, methamphetamine, caffeine, and nicotine, force the release of energy chemicals. The strongest stimulants—cocaine and methamphetamine—can produce an intense rush and, in the case of methamphetamines, more-prolonged highs.
    ◇ **Downers.** Depressants include opioids (e.g., heroin), sedative-hypnotics, and alcohol. They depress circulatory, respiratory, and muscular systems; they also control pain, reduce anxiety, promote sleep, and lower inhibitions; they can also induce euphoria.
    ◇ **All Arounders.** Psychedelics (e.g., marijuana, LSD, and MDMA) can cause some stimulation but mostly they alter sensory input and can cause illusions, delusions, and hallucinations.
- **Other Drugs & Addictions**
    ◇ **Inhalants** include organic solvents, volatile nitrites, and nitrous oxide ("laughing gas") and can induce the full range of upper, downer, or psychedelic effects, depending on the specific substance and the amount used.
    ◇ **Anabolic steroids** and other sports drugs are used to enhance athletic performance by increasing endurance, muscle size, and aggression.
    ◇ **Psychiatric medications** include antidepressants, antipsychotics, mood stabilizers, and antianxiety drugs. They are prescribed to rebalance brain chemistry when there are mental health problems.
    ◇ **Compulsive behaviors**, such as binge-eating, anorexia, bulimia, compulsive gambling, sexual compulsion, Internet addiction, compulsive shopping, and even codependency, affect many of the same areas of the brain that are influenced by psychoactive drugs.

HARDING'S PEN SPEEDS DRIVE AGAINST DRUGS

President Signs Congress Re-solution to Join with Other Nations in Limiting Supply

Negotiations, to Open at Once with Land the Bases of Cocai Grow

COOLIDGE SIGNS BILL FOR DOPE-CURE FARMS

NEW U.S. LAW WILL HELP END NARCOTIC EVIL, SAVE ADDICTS

JANUARY, 20, 1929
All Drug Slave" Convicts Will

HOOVER BACKS U.S. IN DOPE WAR

WASHINGTON, Jan 21 - President Hoover today sent a message to Congress rec-

Reagan, Congress Call for Drug War

Clinton to Announce New Drug Plan

volved in educating youths about

gress, Clinton's budget for the 1999 fiscal year calls for spending $1.1 more for drug-control mea- across all departments, rep- ting slightly less than a 7 per-

Bush, in Colombia, pledges to fight drugs

INTRODUCTION

"All states are required to raise their minimum age for purchase and public possession of alcohol to age 21. States that do not comply face a reduction in federal highway funds. The term 'public possession' does not apply to the use of alcohol for an established religious purpose, prescribed medical purposes, and in private clubs, establishments, or at home."
The U.S. National Minimum Drinking Age Act of 1984

"Let us not then simply censure the gift of Dionysus as bad and unfit to be received into the State. For wine has many excellences.... Shall we begin by enacting that boys shall not taste wine at all until they are eighteen years of age; we will tell them that fire must not be poured upon fire, whether in the body or in the soul."
Athenian Stranger in The Laws by Plato, 360 B.C.

More than 2,367 years later, the question of who can handle their alcohol (or other psychoactive drug) and when it's all right to drink or use still concerns societies. Whether it has been to alter states of consciousness, reduce pain, forget harsh surroundings, alter a mood, medicate a mental illness, or enhance the senses, **throughout history some people have chosen to alter their perception of reality with substances**. Which drugs are used, how they are used, and how abuse is punished, treated, or prevented have varied from culture to culture and from century to century. There are currently many different issues involving psychoactive drugs and other compulsive behaviors:

◊ debate over the legalization of medical marijuana;

◊ explosive growth of crystal methamphetamines in all regions of the United States, in Europe, and in Asia (where it's called "yaa baa");

◊ unexpected epidemic of prescription drug abuse, especially by teens;

◊ increasing legal limitations of where one can smoke;

◊ attempts to eliminate steroids and other performance-enhancing drugs from sports;

◊ use of buprenorphine in doctors' offices to treat opioid addiction;

◊ continued growth of hepatitis C, transmitted through intravenous (IV) drug use;

◊ high cost of treating the medical consequences of abuse and addiction;

◊ expansion of the use of psychiatric medications for everything from treating addiction and controlling depression to calming children with attention-deficit/hyperactivity disorder (ADHD);

◊ immense growth of computer games, cell phones, and online addictions; and

◊ continued legalization and expansion of all forms of gambling.

Whether the drugs were used and abused 5,000 years ago in Mesopotamia or yesterday in New York, certain themes seem to transcend time and cultural makeup.

FIVE HISTORICAL THEMES OF DRUG USE

1. Human beings have a basic need to cope with their environment and enhance their existence.

Early man lived in a dangerous and mysterious environment that could inflict pain and death in an instant. Brutal weather, carnivorous predators, life-threatening physical diseases, aggressive enemies, and even abusive parents or siblings could wound, maim, or kill. Primitive and eventually civilized human beings have continuously searched for ways to control these dangers. They drew cave pictures of animals 20,000 years ago in France to help in the hunt. They built the city of Jericho 10,000 years ago so they could grow and control their food supply and protect themselves from their enemies. They worshipped hundreds of gods, praying for divine intervention that would let them survive. They fasted, chanted, meditated, danced incessantly, practiced self-hypnosis, inflicted pain on themselves, went without sleep, and used other nondrug methods so they could receive revelations from the gods (La Barre, 1979A; Furst, 1976). By chance and by experimentation, **they found that ingesting certain plants could ease fear and anxiety, reduce pain, treat some illnesses, give pleasure, and let them talk to their gods**. Our modern environment also has uncertainties, pains, illnesses, and fears that can compel a person to use psychoactive drugs.

A payé (modern shaman) in Rio Popeyaká, Amazonas, lights a resin-covered torch to help produce true hallucinations during the ayahuasca ceremony, which is used for prophecy, divination, sorcery, and medical purposes. The ayahuasca plant, known as the "vine of the soul," is boiled in water, and the resulting mixture is drunk to help the payé free his soul and see visions.

2. Human brain chemistry can be affected by psychoactive drugs, behavioral addictions, and mental illness to induce an altered state of consciousness.

If psychoactive drugs and behavioral addictions did not affect human brain chemistry in a desirable manner, they would not be used voluntarily. They are used to affect the primitive, or "old," part of the brain that controls emotions, instincts, natural physiological functions (e.g., breathing and heart rate), emotional memories, sensory perception, and physical and emotional pain. They also affect the reasoning and memory centers of the "new" brain, called the *neocortex*. In addition, because mental illnesses are caused by unbalanced brain chemistry, psychoactive drugs can be used to try to control illnesses such as depression and schizophrenia. These neurochemicals and brain structures evolved over hundreds of millions of years, starting in invertebrate creatures such as insects and snails and growing in complexity in vertebrate creatures, especially Homo sapiens (Nesse & Berridge, 1997).

3. The ruling classes, governments, and businesses as well as criminal organizations have been involved in growing, manufacturing, distributing, taxing, and prohibiting drugs.

The intensity of the demand for substances that could relieve pain and induce pleasure has matched the **struggles for control of the supplies**. The desire for control of the supplies has resulted in the:

© 2002 Benita Epstein. Printed by permission of Creators Syndicate, Inc.

◊◊◊◊◊◊◊◊◊◊◊◊◊◊◊◊◊◊◊◊◊◊◊◊

◊ use of opium by the medicine men of ancient Sumeria for their secret medicines;

◊ doling out of beer by the pharaohs of Egypt to keep their laborers building pyramids;

◊ **monopolization** of coca leaf growing by the conquistadors in Peru to increase tax revenues for Spain;

◊ exportation of and **excise taxes** on whiskey, hemp, and tobacco to finance the American Revolution;

◊ sale of opium to China by Britain, France, Japan, and other imperial powers to **support their colonies**;

◊ trading in drugs by Al Qaeda to **finance the terrorist bombings of trains in Spain** in 2004 and probably London in 2005; and

◊ **prohibition or restriction** of alcohol, tobacco, opium, and most every other psychoactive drug by virtually every country at one time or another to control drug abuse.

4. Technological advances in refining, synthesizing, and manufacturing drugs have increased the potency of these substances.

Over the centuries various cultures have learned how to:

◊ **distill** alcoholic beverages to higher potency (Arabia, tenth century);

◊ **refine** morphine from opium (Germany, 1804);

◊ **refine** cocaine from coca leaves (Germany, 1859);

◊ **invent** the automatic cigarette-rolling machine (United States, 1881);

◊ **synthesize** the stimulant amphetamine to create a replacement for ephedra (Germany, 1887, and Japan, 1919);

◊ **synthesize** LSD (Switzerland, 1938);

◊ **use the sinsemilla growing technique** to increase the THC content of marijuana (United States, 1960–present); and

◊ **modify** the amphetamine molecule to produce designer drugs like MDMA (ecstasy) (United States, 1910–present).

These and other techniques have enabled drug users to put more of the active psychoactive ingredients into the body at one time. For example, coca leaves contain only 0.5% to 2.0% cocaine, whereas street cocaine is often 60% to 70% pure. Marijuana in 2007 has up to 14 times as much THC (delta-9-tetrahydrocannabinol—the main active ingredient) as the average street marijuana had in the 1970s. Research shows that the more potent the psy-choactive drug, the more rapid the development of addiction. **It is hard to overemphasize the importance of the increased potency of drugs in the development of a growing population of abusers and addicts in societies throughout the world.**

5. The development of faster and more efficient methods of putting drugs into the body has intensified the effects.

Technological and pragmatic discoveries have taught users to:

◊ **mix** alcohol and opium for stronger effects (Sumeria, 4000 B.C.);

◊ **absorb** more juice from the chewed coca leaf by mixing it with charred oyster shell (Peru, 1450);

◊ **inhale** nitrous oxide to become giddy and high (England, 1800);

◊ **inject** morphine to put the drug directly into the bloodstream (England, 1855);

◊ **snort** cocaine to absorb the drug more quickly (Europe, 1900);

◊ **smoke** crack cocaine to intensify the high (United States, 1975–1985); and

◊ **crush and inject time-release medications**, such as the pain reliever OxyContin,® for a bigger rush (United States, 2003).

In behavioral addictions the development and the subsequent availability of rapid-play poker machines increased the number of problem and pathological gamblers in a state like Oregon from 20,000 to well over 75,000 (Moore, 2006).

When the history of substance use is closely examined, the five themes identified here appear time and time again. By studying this recurrent yet progressive nature of drug use and abuse, it becomes clear that solutions must change and adapt as society changes and as science gives us a clearer picture of the reasons for craving and addiction.

"Most of the crime in our city is caused by cocaine."
Police chief of Atlanta, GA, 1911

HISTORY OF PSYCHOACTIVE DRUGS

PREHISTORY & THE NEOLITHIC PERIOD (8500–4000 B.C.)

Many of the drugs available today have antecedents in psychoactive plants that have been around for millions of years. It has been estimated that **4,000 plants yield psychoactive substances**, although only about 60 of those plants have been in continuous use somewhere in the world throughout history. Opium poppies, marijuana tops, coca leaves, tea leaves, betel nuts, khat leaves, coffee beans, tobacco leaves, and fruits or other plants that ferment into alcohol have been the most popular over the centuries (Austin, 1979).

Evidence exists that 50,000 years ago Neanderthals in Europe and Asia used medicinal and psychedelic plants such as the fly-agaric mushroom in shamanistic religions as a way to deal with their environment and inner turmoil. Shamanism holds beliefs in an unseen world of external and internal demons, gods, and ancestral spirits who listen only to the shaman. **The shaman, a combination priest–medicine man, was the key figure in these religions and functioned as a conduit to the supernatural**, using both naturally induced (e.g., fasting and dancing) and drug-induced altered states of consciousness. The shaman would also perform the equivalent of an exorcism or use some natural plant preparation to expel what he perceived to be inner demons in his patient. In those days the "demon" might have been a mental illness, especially schizophrenia (Wikipedia, 2006).

The use of psychoactive substances spread through tribal migration. One hypothesis maintains that the earliest Native Americans were Eurasians who migrated to the Americas 10,000 to 15,000 years ago over the frozen Aleutian Islands chain, bringing their customs, religions, and psychoactive substances, like the hallucinogenic mescal bean and sophora seeds (Furst, 1976; La Barre, 1979A). Recent archeological finds of 30,000-year-old tools in the Asian Arctic's Yana River Valley suggest that the migration could have occurred thousands of years earlier (Wilford, 2004).

Alcohol has been the most popular psychoactive substance over the millennia. This food/medicine/drug has been with us since prehistoric times. Perhaps hunger, thirst, or curiosity made early humans eat or drink fruits that had begun to *ferment* (chemically change into alcohol due to airborne yeast). They also discovered that chewing starchy vegetation would provide the catalyst, found in saliva, to convert the more complex carbohydrates into alcohol. Liking the taste, the nutrition, and the psychoactive effects, particularly the drunken states that made them feel closer to their gods, they learned how to produce fermented beverages themselves (O'Brien & Chafetz, 1991). They collected honey to ferment into mead, an alcoholic beverage; they cultivated grains to ferment starchy foods into beer; and they cultivated grapes and other fruits to make wine. These agricultural experiments are the earliest signs of organized efforts to guarantee a steady supply of a desirable psychoactive substance.

ANCIENT CIVILIZATIONS (4000 B.C.–A.D. 400)

Nomadic tribes began settling into small agricultural communities 10,000 to 20,000 years ago; over the millennia they gradually grew, accumulating power and influence. Great civilizations arose where the land was fertile, usually next to rivers such as the Tigris and the Euphrates in the Middle East and the Nile in Egypt. **The earliest crops were wheat and barley, used to make bread and beer** (beer was much more nutritious than it is today) (Ganeri, Martell & Williams, 1998). Asian civilizations used rice as a staple food and to make wine (sake). **Some ancient cultures also cultivated the opium poppy and the hemp plant (*Cannabis*).**

ALCOHOL

In 2004 and 2005 in Jiahu, China, archeologists uncovered evidence of the use of alcoholic drinks 9,000 years ago. Residue in ancient pottery vessels from this Stone Age village in China's Henan province indicated a fermented beverage of rice, honey, and fruit at approximately the same time that barley beer and grape wine were being made in the Middle East (McGovern, Zhang, Tang, et al., 2004).

The **first written references to alcohol are Sumerian clay tablets from 4000 B.C.** found in ancient Mesopotamia (now Iraq and Iran). They contained recipes for using wine as a solvent for medications, including opium.

Many ancient cultures considered alcohol, particularly wine, a gift from the gods. In legends Osiris gave alcohol to the Egyptians as did Dionysus to the Greeks and Bacchus to the Romans (Frazer, 1922). In ancient Egypt a barley beer called *hek* was given as a reward to laborers building the great pyramids. The value of *hek* was such that bureaucrats were appointed to control its production. Beer was the drink of the workers, and wine was the privilege of the pharaohs as evidenced by earthen jars in King Tut's tomb, which noted the vintage (year) of the wine and the location of the vineyard.

Rice wine was the drink of the masses in ancient China and later Japan, but grape wine was more highly prized. In about 180 B.C., a gift of grape wine was sufficient to serve as a bribe to get a civil service job (Lee, 1987). The Jewish people have historically used wine as part of their religious and secular celebrations, including circumcisions, weddings, and the Sabbath.

The reaction of the human brain and body to alcohol caused not only the desired effects but also side effects capable of creating social and health problems. As a result, most **civilizations throughout history have placed religious, social, and legal controls on the use of alcohol and other drugs**. In fact, there are 150 biblical references to alcohol, often warnings.

Make not thyself helpless in drinking in the beer shop. For will not the words of [thy] report repeated slip out from { thy mouth } without { thy knowing } { that thou hast uttered them ? } Falling down thy limbs will be broken, [and] no one will give thee { a hand [to help] thee up } as for thy companions in the swilling of beer, they will get up and say, " Outside with this drunkard."

This Egyptian hieroglyphic from 1500 B.C. advised moderation in barley beer drinking as well as avoidance of other compulsive behaviors. Written Egyptian references to alcohol have been unearthed that date back to 3500 B.C.

Translation from *Precepts of Ani,* World Health Organization

• •

"Give strong drink to him who is perishing, and wine to those in bitter distress; let them drink and forget their poverty, and remember their misery no more."

Proverbs, 31:6—7

One of the **earliest attempts at** *temperance* **(limiting drinking)** occurred in China around 2200 B.C. when the legendary Emperor Yu levied a tax on wine to curtail consumption. Centuries later, during the Chu Dynasty (1122–249 B.C.), the penalties for drunkenness were extremely severe for the lower classes while the upper classes were given a chance at recovery, not unlike current realities (Cherrington, 1924).

"As to the ministers and officers who have been . . . addicted to drink, it is not necessary to put them to death; let them be taught for a time. . . . If you disregard my lessons, then I . . . will show you no pity."

Emperor Wu Wang, founder of Chu Dynasty, 1120 B.C.

In ancient religious hymns (*Vedas*) **in India, alcohol was believed to cause falsity, misery, and darkness** while its favorable aspects were dismissed. And

though many ancient Greek poets, philosophers, and writers, including Plato, Homer, and Aeschylus, drank wine all day, every day, warnings about excess use abounded in Greek literature. This was reinforced with cautionary tales of battles lost due to drunkenness (O'Brien & Chafetz, 1991). The temperance of later Greek society embodied in **Dionysus (god of wine and ecstasy)** gave way to binge drinking in Roman society, encouraged by **Bacchus,** a more liberal version of Dionysus.

Orgiastic drinking became such a problem in the Roman Empire that in A.D. 81 the Emperor Comitian destroyed half the nation's vineyards and prohibited the planting of new ones (Keller, 1984). By the fourth century A.D., heavy drinkers were led through town

by a cord strung through their noses. Habitual offenders were tied with the nose cord and left for ridicule in the public square. The conflicts among heavy consumption, temperance, and abstinence have continued to this day.

OPIUM

Remnants of ancient poppy plantations in Spain, Greece, northeast Africa, Egypt, and Mesopotamia give evidence of the widespread early use of opium (Escohotado, 1999). For example, around 4000 B.C. the Sumerians in southern **Mesopotamia cultivated the opium poppy in addition to barley and wheat,** their basic agricultural crops. They named it *hul gil*—the plant of joy. The milky white fluid from the dried bulb was boiled to a sticky gum and chewed. It could also be burned and inhaled or mixed with fermented liquids and drunk. It was **used both for its medicinal properties of pain relief, cough suppression, and diarrhea control as well as for its mental properties of sedation and euphoria** (Hoffman, 1990). Because it was only ingested (and not smoked as in later centuries), its bitter taste and the moderate concentration of active ingredients limited the abuse potential (Scarborough, 1995).

In ancient civilizations opium was used in many ways. Early Egyptian medical texts referred to it as both a medicine and a poison. In Egypt it was fed to crying babies to calm their discomfort and fears. Almost 5,000 years ago at the Temple of Imhotep, a center for treating mental illness, opium was used in an attempt to cure the mentally ill by inducing visions, performing rituals, and praying to the gods. So drugs were used both to

Morpheus, the son of Hypnos, the Greek god of sleep, is shown with opium poppies strewn at his feet. The word morphine *comes from Morpheus.*

Sculpture by Jean Antoine Houdon, Louvre Museum, Paris. Photo © 1995 CNS Productions, Inc.

• • • • • • • • • • • • • • • • • • • •

get in contact with spirits and to get rid of them. This **close relationship between drugs and mental illness** has been noted, researched, and utilized in treatment throughout history.

Other ancient civilizations also employed opium to alter mental states (to self-medicate). In *The Odyssey* Homer spoke about an opium mixture, called *nepenthe,* given by Helen of Troy to Telemachus to banish unwanted feelings.

"[Helen] drugged the wine with an herb that banishes all care, sorrow, and ill humour. Whoever drinks wine thus drugged cannot shed a single tear all the rest of the day, not even though his father and mother both of them drop down dead, or he sees a brother or a son hewn in pieces before his very eyes."
Homer, The Odyssey, IV, 221–226, 700 B.C.

Hippocrates, the "father of medicine," recommended opium as a painkiller and as a treatment for female hysteria. Centuries later in the Roman Empire, Marcus Aurelius (A.D. 121–180), writer, philosopher, and emperor, would drink a potion of opium mixed with wine as a daily balm.

In A.D. 312 in Rome, 793 stores sold opium, and the **excise tax on the drug provided 15% of the city's revenue** (Escohotado, 1999). The best opium was "thick and heavy and soporific to the smell, bitter to the taste, easily diluted in water, smooth, white, neither rough nor full of lumps" (Dioscorides, A.D. 70).

CANNABIS (MARIJUANA)

Historically, *Cannabis* was known in many countries and languages: *kannabis* (Greek), *qunubu* (Assyrian), *qanneb* (Hebrew), and *qannob* (Arabic) (Booth, 2003). *Cannabis* was prized as **a source of oil and fiber, for its edible seeds, as a medicine, and as a psychedelic**. Archaeologists have found traces of hemp fibers in clothes, shoes, paper, and rope dating to 4000 B.C. in Taiwan, although it was probably cultivated since Neolithic times around 9000 B.C. (Schultes & Hofmann, 1992; Stafford, 1982). According to legend, in 2737 B.C. the Chinese Emperor Shen-Nung studied,

experimented on himself, and recorded his efforts to use *Cannabis* (*ma-fen*) as a medicine. In a medical herbal encyclopedia called the *Pen-tsao,* written in A.D. 100 but referring back to Shen-Nung's study of 364 drugs (including ephedra and ginseng), *Cannabis* is referred to not only as a medication but also as **a substance with stupefying and hallucinogenic properties** (Schultes & Hofmann, 1992).

Medically, over the centuries *Cannabis* has been recommended for constipation, dysentery, rheumatism, absent-mindedness, female disorders, malaria, and beriberi; for the treatment of wasting diseases; and for dozens of other maladies. The Chinese physician

This saddhu *(Hindu ascetic) is making a beverage from* Cannabis indica. *He grinds the leaves into a paste, filters out the remains of the plant by pouring water through cheesecloth, then drinks the resulting infusion. He uses the drink as part of his religious belief system for meditation and concentration. He is a follower of the Hindu god Shiva. Shivites believe in the use of this intoxicant, though many other Hindus do not endorse the use of* Cannabis.
© 2000 CNS Productions, Inc.

Hua T'o, in A.D. 200, recommended *Cannabis* as **an analgesic or painkiller for surgery** (Li, 1974).

India had an even more benevolent view of the psychoactive properties of *Cannabis*. Almost 1,500 years before the birth of Christ, the *Atharva-Veda* (sacred psalms) sang of *Cannabis* (*bhang*) as one of five sacred plants that gave a long life, visions (hallucinations), and freedom from distress. Other texts from India listed dozens of medicinal uses for the drug (Aldrich, 1977, 1997). Initially, *Cannabis* **and its psychoactive resin were reserved for the ruling classes**; the lower classes were allowed to use it only at significant religious festivals. Later it was found to calm soldiers' nerves in battle, and eventually it was used at weddings and other social occasions.

About 500 B.C. the Scythians, whose territory ranged from the Danube to the Volga in eastern Europe, threw *Cannabis* on hot stones placed in small tents and inhaled the vapors (Brunner, 1977).

"The Scythians then take the seed of this hemp and, crawling in under the mats, throw it on the red-hot stones, where it smolders and sends forth such fumes that no Greek vapor bath could surpass it. The Scythians, transported with the vapor, shout for joy."
Herodotus, The Histories, 4.75.1, 460 B.C.

Around A.D. 200 the **Greek physician Galen** wrote about hosts offering hemp to guests to stimulate enjoyment and promote hilarity. The hemp was possibly mixed with wine to increase its potency. For most ancient civilizations, however, including Greece, Rome, and England, hemp was used predominantly as a fiber.

MESCAL BEAN, SAN PEDRO & PEYOTE CACTI (MESCALINE) IN MESOAMERICA

The presence of **dozens of hallucinatory plants in North and South America gave rise to complex ceremonies overseen by shamans**, who

These are a few of the 200 psilocybe mushroom stone gods that survived the concerted efforts of Catholic missionaries to wipe out the culture that used psychedelic mushrooms in sacred ceremonies. Some date back to A.D. 100.

came to positions of spiritual influence as did those in Neolithic times in Asia. The psychoactive mescal beans they brought with them were roasted and eaten during sacred rites, causing a sleepy delirium that lasted for days. Later, cacti containing mescaline became another ceremonial hallucinogen of choice. Stone carvings and textiles depicting images of this plant (**San Pedro cactus**) were found at a Chavin temple in the Peruvian highlands and date back to 1300 B.C. Other South American cultures, including the Nazca and Chimu peoples, boiled the cacti for up to seven hours and drank the potion to **produce hallucinations and communicate with the supernatural** (La Barre, 1979B). Evidence found in caves in what is now Texas implies ceremonial use of the *peyotl,* or peyote cactus (which also contains mescaline), 3,000 years ago (Schultes & Hofmann, 1992).

PSYCHEDELIC MUSHROOMS IN INDIA, SIBERIA & MESOAMERICA

Archeology has suggested that the **sacramental use of mushrooms has been around since Paleolithic times**, about 7,000 years ago. Cave drawings

from that era discovered in Algeria show shamanic figures enmeshed in mushrooms (possibly *Psilocybe mairei*), suggesting their early sacramental use (Stamets, 1996). In 1500 B.C. the *Vedas* of ancient India sang of a holy inebriant that proved to be an extract of the **Amanita muscaria mushroom**, also called the *fly-agaric* mushroom. The active ingredients are ibotenic acid and the alkaloid muscimole. In fact, **Soma**, their name for the hallucinogen, was also one of their most important gods. More than 100 holy hymns from the *Rig-Veda* are devoted to Soma.

"It is drunk by the sick man as medicine at sunrise; partaking of it strengthens the limbs, preserves the legs from breaking, wards off all disease, and lengthens life. Then need and trouble vanish away."
Rig-Veda, 1500 B.C. (McKenna, 1992)

Though the *Amanita muscaria* also grows in North America, **it was the Psilocybe mushroom that was preferred by Aztec and Mayan cultures** in pre-Columbian Mexico (Schultes & Hofmann, 1992). Although there are more

than 30,000 different identified species of mushroom, only 80 produce psilocybin and psilocin, the main active hallucinogenic ingredients. Of the many psychedelic mushrooms, *Psilocybe cubensis* is grown most widely (Borhegi, 1961; Stamets, 1996).

TOBACCO & COCA LEAF IN MESOAMERICA

The genesis of **plants containing stimulant alkaloids (e.g., tobacco [nicotine] and coca leaves [cocaine])** occurred 65 million to 250 million years ago. The bitter alkaloids were the plants' way of repelling dinosaurs, other herbivores, and insects. It wasn't until approximately 5000 B.C. that humans on a regular basis started drinking (in solution), chewing, snorting, and smoking tobacco for religious ceremonies and for stimulation. At about the same time, they started chewing the coca leaf for stimulation, for nutrition, and to control their appetite when food was scarce (Siegel, 1982).

Burial sites unearthed on the north coast of Peru and dating back to 2500 B.C. contained bags that held coca leaves, flowers, and occasionally a wad of coca leaves and soda lime formed

This Colombian carving depicts a user's cheek stuffed with cocada—coca leaf mixed with powdered lime.
Courtesy of the Fitz Hugh Ludlow Memorial Library

into a ball for chewing, called *cocada.* The coca was used to facilitate the deceased's journey through the afterlife. *Cocada* chewing rose to such prominence in ancient Peruvian culture that it also became a standard unit of time and of distance: one *cocada* equaled the distance a person could walk before the effects of a single wad wore off (about 45 minutes). Recent discoveries in the Andes dating to 3000 B.C. have uncovered even older complex societies that employed the chewing of coca leaves for spiritual and even medical practices (Maugh, 2004). The use of coca has persisted to the present day as evidenced by the existence (since the third century B.C.) of hundreds of stone and wood sculptures of heads with cheeks enlarged due to a wad of coca leaves.

MIDDLE AGES (400–1400)

PSYCHEDELIC "HEXING HERBS"

Other psychedelics used over the centuries include **members of the nightshade family *Solanaceae* that contain the psychoactive chemicals atropine and scopolamine**. In the Middle Ages, the nightshade varietals were sometimes used by medicine men and women who were later accused of witchcraft.

◇ **Datura** (thornapple) was often made into a salve and absorbed through the skin (McKenna, 1992).

◇ **Henbane** was referred to as early as 1500 B.C. in Egyptian medical texts. It was used as a painkiller and a poison. It was also used to mimic insanity, produce hallucinations, and generate prophecies.

◇ **Belladonna,** also known as witch's berry and devil's herb, dilates pupils, inebriates the user, and can cause hallucinations and delirium.

◇ **Mandrake,** or mandragora, a root that often grows in the shape of a human body, was used in ancient Greece as well as in medieval times. Its properties, similar to those of henbane and belladonna, cause dis-

This fifteenth-century engraving by Martin Schongauer shows Saint Anthony being assaulted by visions of sexual licentiousness and savage animals—visions similar to those caused by the ergot fungus found on spoiled rye or wheat cereal grasses. Ergotism was often fatal because it led to gangrene and extreme delirium.

Museum of Fine Arts, Budapest, Hungary. EMB Services for Publishers. Reprinted by permission. All rights reserved.

orientation and delirium. Mandrake was considered an aphrodisiac in the 1400s in Italy, and a century later Niccolò Machiavelli wrote a risqué comedy called *Mandragola* about seduction and infidelity.

PSYCHEDELIC MOLD— ERGOT (SAINT ANTHONY'S FIRE)

Another psychedelic that has persisted through the ages is found in ergot, a brownish purple fungus named *Claviceps purpurea,* which **grows on infected rye and wheat plants. The active ingredient is lysergic acid diethylamide**, the natural form of the modern hallucinogen LSD. Ergot and its effects are referred to in ancient Greek and medieval European literature. It was recognized as a poison and a psychedelic as early as 600 B.C. Ergot in small doses was even used as a medication in the Middle Ages to induce childbirth.

Over the centuries there have been **numerous outbreaks of ergot poisoning** when whole towns, particularly in rye-consuming areas of eastern Europe, seemed to go mad, occasion-

ally with great loss of life. In A.D. 944 in France, 40,000 people are estimated to have died from an ergotism epidemic. There were outbreaks as recently as 1953 in France and Belgium. **Hallucinations, convulsions, possibly permanent insanity, a burning sensation in the feet and hands, and gangrene** that occasionally caused a loss of extremities—toes, feet, fingers, and nose—were common. One of the outbreaks in A.D. 1039 gave the name *Saint Anthony's Fire* to the affliction when a wealthy Frenchman and his son, who were afflicted with ergot poisoning, prayed to Saint Anthony, a fourth-century saint who protects supplicants against fire, epilepsy, and infection. His and his son's recoveries inspired the father to build a hospital in Dauphiné, France (where Saint Anthony was buried) for the care of sufferers of ergotism.

FROM MEDICINE, TO PSYCHOACTIVE DRUG, TO POISON

Theophrastus, a Greek philosopher and naturalist, emphasized that the plant datura can be a **medicine at a low** dose, a psychoactive drug at a moderate dose, and a deadly poison at a high dose.

"One administers one drachma [of datura], if the patient must only be animated and made to think well of himself; double that, if he must enter delirium and see hallucinations; triple it, if he must become permanently deranged; give a quadruple dose if he is to die."

Theophrastus, Inquiry into Plants, 323 B.C.

Not only datura but also ergot, opium, and most other psychoactive drugs follow this pattern. Opium sedates and suppresses pain at a low dose, causes euphoria at a higher dose, and depresses breathing to dangerous levels at a very high dose.

Healers and shamans were well aware of the dose-dependent dangers of most drugs and so would experiment with various substances to find the correct dose to heal a patient or induce a trance state. They lost quite a few patients in the process.

ALCOHOL & DISTILLATION

Even though techniques for the distillation of seawater and alcohol had been around for thousands of years (e.g., boiling mead under a cloth that catches the evaporating alcohol and is wrung out), it wasn't until the eighth to fourteenth centuries that knowledge of the techniques became widespread. This evaporation process was used to **raise the alcohol content of beverages from 14% to 40%** (McKenna, 1992). In one version of history, an Arabian alchemist named Geber is credited with perfecting a wine distillation method in the eighth century A.D. In another version an Arabian physician, Rhazes, discovered distilled spirits. Whiskey distillation in Ireland was popular by the twelfth century (O'Brien & Chafetz, 1991).

Technical advances in cultivation as well as in distillation during the Middle Ages made a difference in consumption. The increased strength of alcoholic beverages forced **cultural attitudes to shift among abstention, temperance, and bingeing**. Christians

in the early days celebrated their faith with banquets of wine and bread; but as problems with alcohol increased, the Eucharist ceremony used less and less wine until it was used only symbolically. Inevitably, **controlling drinking became a moral cause**. Saint Paul and others condemned the relaxed behavior caused by excessive drinking because it led users away from God. **Paganism and the use of psychoactive substances to communicate with the supernatural gave way to a demand that faith alone be used to understand God.**

ISLAMIC SUBSTITUTES FOR ALCOHOL

Yusaf Ali: "O ye who believe! Intoxicants and gambling, [dedication of] stones, and [divination by] arrows, are an abomination—of Satan's handwork: eschew such [abomination], that ye may prosper."

Qur'an, 590

"A parable of the garden which those guarding [against evil] are promised: Therein are rivers of water that does not alter, and rivers of milk the taste whereof does not change, and rivers of drink [or wine, (depending on the translation)] delicious to those who drink, and rivers of honey clarified and for them."

Qur'an, 4715

In the Qur'an (Koran), the holy book of Islam, a few references are made to wine and intoxicants. Wine was not used as a sacrament in Islam, and the **drinking of wine was frowned upon**. The prophet Mohammed did not mention wine, only that he chastised a drunkard for not performing his duties. Mohammed's brother-in-law, Ali, set the tone for alcohol in later Muslim societies.

"He who drinks gets drunk, he who is drunk, does nonsensical things, he who acts nonsensically says lies, and he who lies must be punished."

Ali (Escohotado, 1999)

So it was not alcohol per se that was shunned but what alcohol made a drinker do. Through the centuries, however, temperance gave way to prohibition; and objections to the debilitating effects of alcohol and other psychoactive drugs gave way to bans on any substance that could make one forget religious and moral duties. A few sects such as the Alawites permit wine but shun getting drunk.

The reasons that drew people to psychoactive substances remained, so some Muslims searched for alternatives. **Opium for the relief of pain**, both physical and mental, was seen as an acceptable substitute. It was used in Arab society as a general tonic much as Roman nobility had used it. Among other qualities, it was supposed to ease the transition to old age. In later centuries **tobacco, hashish (concentrated *Cannabis*), and particularly coffee were employed as substitutes for alcohol** to provide stimulation, induce sedation, or alter consciousness. These substances were also used medicinally.

Khat, a stimulant that was permissible in some Islamic cultures, was originally cultivated in the southern Arabian peninsula and the Horn of Africa. It was used during long prayer ceremonies to help the congregation stay awake (much as coffee). In A.D. 1238 Arab physician Naguib Ad-Din distributed khat to soldiers to prevent hunger and fatigue; an Arab king, Sabr Ad-Din, gave it freely to subjects he had recently conquered to placate them and quell their revolutionary tendencies (Giannini, Burge, Shaheen, et al., 1986).

COFFEE, TEA & CHOCOLATE (caffeine)

Centuries after the **coffee plant *Coffea Arabica* was found growing wild in Ethiopia**, about A.D. 850, it was imported and intensely cultivated in Arabia (around the fourteenth century). At first coffee was consumed by chewing the beans or by infusing them in water. During the later Middle Ages, coffee was **made more potent when people learned how to roast and grind the beans**, producing a tastier version. It was also used medicinally (e.g., as a diuretic and an asthma treatment and for headache relief). It took 500 more years (1820) before caffeine, the active alkaloid in coffee and tea, was finally identified.

Tea from the leaves of the ***Thea sinensis*** (*chinensis*) bush was supposedly used in China 4,700 years ago, but the first written evidence of its use didn't appear until approximately A.D. 350. The fact that boiling water killed germs made tea a popular drink. The cultivation of tea in Japan and the development of tea ceremonies occurred about A.D. 800. Tea remains at the heart of social and religious ceremonies in Japan and a number of other countries to the present day (Harler, 1984).

Approximately **60 plants contain caffeine, including guarana, maté, yoco, kola, and cacao.** Chocolate, refined from the cacao tree's bean (cocoa bean), has been traced back to the Olmecs of Mexico (1500 to 400 B.C.). The Mayans (1000 B.C. to A.D. 900) were the second people to cultivate cacao on plantations throughout their empire in Mexico and the Yucatan peninsula. The Toltecs and then the Aztecs continued to grow cacao. The beans, which were ground and used to make a stimulating, highly desirable though bitter chocolate drink (with foam), were highly prized. For example, 4 beans would buy a squash; 8 to 10, a rabbit; and 100 was the average daily wage of a porter in central Mexico (Weinberg & Bealer, 2001).

RENAISSANCE & THE AGE OF DISCOVERY (1400–1700)

Two developments spread the use of psychoactive substances worldwide. First, exploration, trade, and colonization by Portugal, Spain, England, France, and the Netherlands put **Europeans in contact with diverse cultures and unfamiliar psychoactive plants that they then brought home.** The most notable substances were coffee from Turkey and Arabia, tobacco and coca from the New World, tea from China, and the kola nut from Africa. Second, these European explorers, sol-

diers, merchants, traders, and missionaries **carried their own culture's drugs and drug-using customs to the rest of the world.** Urbanization, spreading wealth, growing personal freedom, and greater secularization of life (less control by churches) increased use.

ALCOHOL

Laws limiting the use of alcohol were based mostly on the effects of overuse, particularly of high-potency beverages. Those in power wanted to limit the toxic effects and confront the moral issues regarding lowered inhibitions that made the drinker forget his or her "duties." Switzerland and England passed closing-time laws in the thirteenth century. Even Scotland and Germany limited sales on religious days in the fifteenth century (O'Brien & Chafetz, 1991). But because the medicinal and recreational values of drinking were well established, laws were aimed more at temperance than at prohibition, particularly since the increasing availability of **distilled beverages produced hefty tax revenues.**

It wasn't only European countries that had well-established drinking patterns. For example, many African cultures brewed wine from palm trees or beer from maize and used it for rituals,

as a foodstuff, and for social interaction. When slavers ripped many Africans from their villages and sent them to America starting in the 1500s, tribes such as the Whidahs, Eboes, Congoes, and Mandingoes brought many of their brewing techniques and drinking rituals with them (James & Johnson, 1996). Some rituals remained, but more often the changed power structure disrupted those patterns. In addition, the **ships involved in the slave trade or bringing missionaries to non-Christian countries also brought rum to tribes that were used to beer and wine.** The higher alcohol content often led to a disruption in drinking patterns that had developed over centuries. These customs contained the abuse of alcohol.

COCA & THE CONQUISTADORS

One example of how the **economic and political needs of a country transformed the way a substance was used** was the interaction between the Spanish conquistadors who colonized Peru in the 1500s and the native tribes' use of the coca leaf. When the explorers/invaders arrived, coca leaf was used as a mild stimulant, as a reward, and as a way to suppress hunger and thirst. Some people chewed throughout the

In Cusco, Peru, in the Andes Mountains, a campesino *uses a stick to add lime from a* poporo *to the coca leaf juice in his mouth to help absorption and increase the effects.*
Courtesy of the Fitz Hugh Ludlow Memorial Library

day, much as Americans drink coffee nowadays; but because the leaf was only 0.5% to 2% cocaine, it was not toxic.

"They carry them [coca leaves] from some high mountains, to others, as merchandise to be sold, and they barter and change them for mantillas, and cattle, and salt, and other things."
Monardes, 1577

When the conquistadors started exploiting the silver mines that they had discovered at extremely high altitudes in the Andes, they needed to find ways to keep the subjugated Indians working. The **Spanish started appropriating the Incan coca plantations** so they could keep the natives chewing (and working throughout the day). They planted so many coca shrubs that at times there was a glut on the market (Cleza de Leon, 1959). **Coca chewing increased dramatically as did revenue from the trade.** About 8% of the Spaniards living in Peru during the sixteenth century were involved in the coca trade and even had their own lobby back in Spain (Gagliano, 1994). Although the **tax revenues from coca helped pay for the colony**, many Spaniards opposed the use of coca (Acosta, 1588). Even the Church was torn: it needed the revenue to pay for its missionary activities, but it was also repulsed at the way the Incas were exploited and it doubted that someone chewing coca could be converted to Christianity (Karch, 1997).

TOBACCO CROSSES THE OCEANS

In 1492 Christopher Columbus crossed the Atlantic and landed on a number of islands in the West Indies, including San Salvador and Cuba. He noted the natives' use of tobacco, or, as he referred to it in his journal, "certain dried leaves." **Tobacco was smoked in pipes, cigars, and cigarettes as well as put in contact with mucosal tissues as snuff and chew** (Heiman, 1960). In North America straight pipes (war pipes, peace pipes, and pleasure pipes, later called *calumets*) were common. The Quiche Mayans and the Cuban natives preferred cigars.

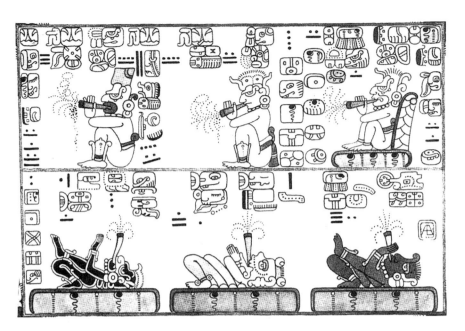

The use of tobacco in a number of forms predated the arrival of Columbus in the Americas in 1492. This watercolor of reclining Aztec smokers who seem to be getting high from their cigars was done by Ariel Baynes, after the originals reproduced in Lord Kingsborough's Antiquities of Mexico *(1843–1848).*
Courtesy of the Arents Collection, New York Public Library

Tobacco was widely used in rituals, such as for planting, fertility, good fishing, consulting the spirits, and preparing magical cures. Shamans in South America **used the toxicity of tobacco to induce trancelike states** to awe their tribesmen (Benowitz & Fredericks, 1995). Tobacco was also **used as a medicine for a wide variety of ailments**, including headache, toothache, snakebite, skin diseases, and stomach and heart pains.

Soon the Spaniards and the British were exporting tobacco from their North American colonies to Europe, where it was received enthusiastically, originally as a medicine and later as a stimulant, mild relaxant, and mild euphoriant. **Sir Walter Raleigh brought "tobacco smoking for recreation" to the court of Queen Elizabeth** (Benowitz & Fredericks, 1995). In France tobacco was called *nicotiana* after Jean Nicot, who described its medicinal properties. **Portuguese sailors introduced tobacco to Japan**, where its cultivation began about 1605. The **Portuguese also introduced tobacco to China**, where it was highly regarded as a medicine. It was carried throughout China by soldiers, then banned, and then taxed. It was in vogue at the emperor's court, then among the people, and then actively propagated throughout Asia. Despite sporadic attempts at prohibition by rulers, governments, and churches that thought it harmful to society, tobacco use spread.

"The use of tobacco is growing greater and conquers men with a certain secret pleasure, so that those who have once become accustomed thereto can later hardly be restrained therefrom."
Sir Francis Bacon, 1620

Back in Europe the dangers of fire, the congregation of smokers in tobacco houses where radical ideas and politics were discussed, and the abuse of tobacco by the clergy led to **vigorous attacks by various authorities, including King James I of England**.

"[Smoking is] a custome lothsome to the eye, hateful to the Nose, harmefull to the braine, dangerous to the Lungs, and the blacke stinking fume thereof, neerest resembling the horrible Stigian smoke of the pit that is bottomless."
James I, 1604

Pope Urban VIII forbade smoking under the threat of excommunication. It was also forbidden in Turkey under pain of torture and death and banned by Czars Michael and Alexis in Russia under similar penalties (Benowitz & Fredericks, 1995). But smuggling and widespread covert use by clergy, commoners, and nobility defeated all attempts at prohibition. Over the centuries the **craving for tobacco and the addictive qualities of nicotine have overwhelmed most calls for prohibition**.

From the beginning the economic power of trade in a substance that was both pleasurable and habit-forming was recognized. Eventually, **tobacco became a large source of revenue for many governments, especially Spain and later England and America.**

COFFEE & TEA

From the beginning **coffee and tea were perceived as drugs and medications and then as social lubricants**. An early English coffee advertisement promised that the drink "closes the Orifice of the Stomack, fortifies the heat within, helpeth Digestion, quickneth the Spirits, maketh the Heart lightsom, is good against Eye-sores, Coughs, or Colds, Head-ache . . ." (Weinberg & Bealer, 2001). As with many psychoactive drugs, such as marijuana and opiates, **it is hard to separate the actual medicinal benefits from the desirable feelings engendered by the substance.**

Coffee drinking became widespread in Europe, first among the wealthy classes, then, as supply increased and prices declined, among the middle and lower classes. Coffee became a favorite alternative to alcohol. In cities such as Amsterdam and London, and later Paris, New York, and Boston, it was drunk in coffeehouses that became popular centers of intellectual, political, and literary discussion and news circulation.

Tea wasn't popular outside of Asia until Dutch traders introduced it in Europe in 1610 and in America 40 years later. Its popularity grew until it **became the center of social interaction and a ritualistic part of family life (e.g., afternoon tea)** (Weinberg & Bealer, 2001).

The preparation of theriac, the ancient cure-all, is depicted in this sixteenth-century woodcut. From H. Brunschwig, Das Neu Distiller Buch, *Strasbourg, 1537.*
Courtesy of the National Library of Medicine, Bethesda, MD

The other major source of caffeine, **chocolate, made from the cacao or cocoa bean, was brought to Europe by Cortés**, who had sampled the beverage in Montezuma II's court back in the Aztec's Mexican Empire. The bitter brew of crushed, roasted, and steeped cacao beans was thickened with corn flour and flavored with vanilla, spices, and honey. The Spaniards began cultivating their own cacao plantations in Haiti and Trinidad.

OPIUM RETURNS

During the Renaissance in the fifteenth and sixteenth centuries, the use of opium in medicinal concoctions returned to favor when the works of the second-century **Greek physician Galen and the eleventh-century Moorish physician Avicenna** became widely taught in medical education (Acker, 1995). **Theriac, one of the opium preparations mentioned by both physicians, became popular again**. First described by Andromachus, physician to Emperor Nero in A.D. 15, theriac originally contained more than 70 ingredients in addition to opium, and Galen added more than 30 more. It was prescribed for an incre-

dible variety of illnesses, including inflammation, diarrhea, madness, melancholy, headaches, pestilence, anything involving pain, and even nosebleeds. As usual many look-alike theriac preparations were hawked in the marketplaces of Europe and the Middle East in later centuries. These bogus versions, called *treacle,* were sold to the poor, letting them feel they could share in what seventeenth-century physician George Bartisch called "a highly praiseworthy, imperial, royal, and princely medicine" (Blanchard, 2000).

"This Theriac used daily serves old, cold, and enfeebled men. It awakens sexual appetite and intercourse. It strengthens and increases the manly nature and brings joy and desire."
Bartisch, 1602

In 1524 **Paracelsus** (Theophrastus von Hohenheim) returned from Constantinople to western Europe with the **secret of laudanum**, a tincture of opium in alcohol (with henbane juice, crushed pearls, coral, amber, musk, and essential oils added). It was employed as a *panacea,* or cure-all medication, and for many was a simple way to soothe a crying child. Inexpensive and readily available, it was soon widely used (and abused) in all strata of society, unlike theriac, which for centuries was reserved for the nobility and the wealthy. Laudanum was found in most home remedy chests. Paracelsus believed and widely promoted the idea that pain relief and sleep were part of the cure for any disease, so he medicated many of his patients with preparations containing opium (Karch, 1997). **A medicine that could kill pain and make one feel euphoric was highly prized in any society.**

AGE OF ENLIGHTEN-MENT & THE EARLY INDUSTRIAL REVOLUTION (1700–1900)

The development of refined forms of psychoactive drugs, new methods of use, and improved production techniques, along with governments' and merchants' economic motives, led to not only more users but also more mental and physical problems, including abuse and addiction.

DISTILLED LIQUORS & THE GIN EPIDEMIC

In addition to making one feel better, beer and wine had long been part of the European diet. Beer was much thicker than modern brews, contributing B vitamins and other nutrients to Europeans' daily intake. Wine used moderately was considered beneficial to health and had some food value. Distilled spirits (about 40% alcohol) had little nutritional content and were most often used just to feel better and to get drunk.

Gin was first made in Holland during the 1600s from fermented mixtures of grains flavored with juniper berries. It became popular throughout Europe; and when the **English Parliament encouraged the production and the consumption of gin**, urban alcoholism and the mortality rate skyrocketed. During the **London Gin Epidemic from 1710 to 1750**, novelist Henry Fielding said that gin was the principal sustenance of more than 100,000 Londoners, and he predicted:

"Should the drinking of this poison be continued at its present height, during the next 20 years, there will be by that time very few of the common people left to drink it."

Henry Fielding, <u>Enquiry,</u> 1740

It was estimated that one house in six in London was a gin house. Production went from 1.23 million gallons in 1700, to 6.4 million gallons in 1735, to 7 million gallons by 1751. The passage of the Tippling Act in 1751 prohibited distillers from selling gin. Prices rose and consumption declined to about 2 million gallons. **The epidemic showed how unlimited availability of a desirable substance causes excess use. Only stiff taxes and the strict regulation of sales brought epidemic consumption under control.** One of the main objections to the availability of gin by the class-conscious British was that it hindered the production capabilities of the lower classes, who were the producers of England's wealth (Abel, 2001). The upper class also felt that women who drank heavily gave birth to weak children, therefore threatening the supply of strong young men for the army and the navy.

During the latter half of the eighteenth century, **rum was the chief medium of exchange in the slave trade and, along with whiskey, one of the mainstays of the economy of colonial America.** A farmer using a 25¢ bushel of corn could produce 2.5 gallons of whiskey valued at $1.25 that

The Gin Epidemic devastated London from 1710 to 1750. This engraving by William Hogarth depicts Gin Lane, *c. 1751. A companion engraving,* Beer Street, *showed a happier group of drinkers and recommended beer as a way to drive gin out of vogue.*

Courtesy of the National Library of Medicine, Bethesda, MD

could be shipped easily and not spoil (Skolnick, 1997). Around 1790 per-capita consumption was three to four times what it is today. When the federal government enacted a tax on liquor, the farmers in western Pennsylvania led **the Whiskey Rebellion** that was broken up when George Washington sent troops.

TOBACCO, HEMP & THE AMERICAN REVOLUTION

Tobacco was introduced to the Jamestown colony in 1612. The first shipment of *Nicotiana tabacum* **(Virginia leaf)** was sent to England by John Rolf, husband of the Indian princess Pocahontas. **It became a financial mainstay for the southern colonies.** Virtually all of **it was chewed or smoked in cigars and pipes.** Tobacco was so important to America that sculptures of tobacco leaves and flowers were used to decorate the columns supporting the dome of the U.S. Capitol building, which was built in 1818 (Slade, 1989). Tobacco, along with rum (and continental currency, or "continentals," which wasn't worth much), helped finance much of the U.S. Revolutionary War. A lottery was also used to partially fund the Continental Army; George Washington was the first American to buy a government-sponsored lottery ticket.

Before the war **King George III of England sent a proclamation to America in 1764 to encourage the planting of hemp** (another important crop in the new American colonies) to send to England. *Hemp* is the word used to describe *Cannabis sativa* plants that are high in fiber content and generally low in psychoactive components. In later centuries *marijuana* was used to describe *Cannabis sativa* plants that were high in psychoactive ingredients. A single ship of that era used 1,000 yards of hemp rope to rig the sails and secure the cargo. George Washington cultivated hemp at his Mount Vernon plantation and encouraged its production as a domestic source of rope and sails for the fledgling U.S. Navy. There is no convincing evidence that *Cannabis* plants were used for their psychoactive effects in the American colonies. Until the Civil War, hemp was the South's second-largest crop, behind cotton. But **because hemp was de-** pendent on slave labor, it was no longer profitable after the slaves were freed.

ETHER, NITROUS OXIDE, OTHER ANESTHETICS & OTHER INHALANTS

Ether (called "sweet vitriol") was discovered in 1275 by Spanish chemist Raymundus Lullius, but it took almost 300 years for Paracelsus to discover the drug's hypnotic effects and another 200 years for a German physician, Frederick Hofmann, to **develop and use a liquid form of ether, called *anodyne,* as an anesthetic (in 1730).** It was also used as a medicine, a drink, and an inhalant, often for intoxication because it was thought to be less harmful than alcohol.

Inhaling a gas (as opposed to smoking a drug) became more popular after Joseph Priestly discovered **nitrous oxide, or "laughing gas,"** in 1776. Its popularity was encouraged in the early 1800s by Sir Humphry Davy, who suggested a nitrous oxide tavern as an alternative to saloons (Agnew, 1968). Several other gases used for anesthesia were also developed, including **chloroform** in 1831. Both men and women participated in "gas frolics" in the 1830s. Later in the nineteenth century, the refinement of various hydrocarbons (fossil fuels) into **volatile solvents** increased the range of psychoactive substances that could be inhaled.

OPIUM TO MORPHINE TO HEROIN

For thousands of years, opium had been used mostly as a medicine and a tonic, but as the Age of Enlightenment and the Industrial Revolution brought forth **scientific developments, changes in methods of use, economic innovation, and political expediency**, the use of opiates spread and often escalated into habituation, abuse, and addiction.

◇ The scientific developments were the refinement of morphine from opium and the modification of morphine into heroin.

◇ The changes in methods of use were the spread of smoking as a means of using opium plus the invention of the hypodermic needle so that mor-

A GRAND
EXHIBITION
OF THE EFFECTS PRODUCED BY INHALING
NITROUS OXIDE, EXHILERATING, OR
LAUGHING GAS
WILL BE GIVEN AT THE MASONIC HALL
SATURDAY EVENING, 5 PM, 1845

30 GALLONS OF GAS will be prepared and administered to all in the audience who desire to inhale it.

MEN will be invited from the audience to protect those under the influence of the Gas from injuring themselves or others. This course is adopted that no apprehension of danger may be entertained. Probably no one will attempt to fight.

THE EFFECT OF THE GAS IS TO MAKE THOSE WHO INHALE IT, EITHER
LAUGH, SING, DANCE, SPEAK OR FIGHT, &c. &c.
according to the leading trait of their character. They seem to retain consciousness enough not to say or do that which they would have occasion to regret.

N.B. The Gas will be administered only to gentlemen of the first respectability. The object is to make The entertainment in every respect, a genteel affair.

This reproduction of an 1845 poster shows the excitement that accompanied a new mood-altering substance. A whiff of the gas could be bought for 25¢. Inhalants and other substances were often considered alternatives to alcohol, which was the substance that caused the most problems.

phine and later heroin could be injected directly into the body.

◇ The economic and political developments stemmed from recognition that **huge profits could be made from the opium drug trade**. That money could then finance other activities (e.g., excise taxes to finance exploration or wars of conquest). Under the British East India Company, the export of opium from its fields in India to the smokers in China increased from 13 tons in 1729 to 2,558 tons in 1839.

Scientific Developments

In 1804 a German pharmacist, Friedrich W. Serturner, discovered how to refine *morphium* (morphine) from opium. **Morphine is about 10 times more powerful than opium** and therefore a more effective pain reliever. Opium had been used during the American Revolutionary War in the eighteenth century, but it was morphine that was used in the nineteenth century, most notably during the Crimean War (1853–1856) and the U.S. Civil War (1861–1865). The higher potency of the preparation caused greater changes in the human body, leading to **more-rapid development of tolerance to the drug and therefore greater dependence**. The increased wartime use of morphine and the subsequent creation of dependent users generated the phrase "the soldier's disease." Some historians felt that the scope of the problem was overstated. When opium was ingested (not smoked) and partly metabolized before reaching the brain, overdose was rarely a problem, but the greater potency of morphine made overdose more common (Hoffman, 1990; Karch, 1996).

The other result of Serturner's refinement of morphine was the **discovery of active alkaloids in many other plants** (e.g., cocaine in the coca leaf), leading to more-concentrated forms of a number of drugs.

In 1874 morphine was chemically altered into **diacetyl morphine, better known as *heroin***, at St. Mary's Hospital in London by C. R. Alder Wright. Heroin was two to five times stronger than morphine, but it wasn't until 1898 that the German Bayer Company began marketing Heroin® as a remedy for coughs, chest pain, and tuberculosis. At one time it was considered a possible cure for morphine addiction and alcoholism. The company brochure promised that "Morphine addicts treated with this substance immediately lose all interest in morphine." Of course the greater intensity of the heroin high caused a **more rapid progression to abuse and addiction**, but it wasn't until the twentieth century that heroin became a large problem on the world stage.

Changes in Methods of Use

Opium smoking was first introduced to China around 1500 by Portuguese traders, but it didn't become popular for 200 more years. **Smoking put greater amounts of opium into the blood (via the lungs) and therefore into the brain sooner, thus increasing the intensity of the effects.** Because the lungs have such a large surface area, excessive amounts could be absorbed rapidly. Smoking also bypassed the distasteful flavor of ingested opium. Repeated use and dependence developed more quickly through smoking, causing a vast increase in opium use in China.

Injection and infusion had been tried since the 1600s, when several experimenters noticed that injecting an opium solution into a dog stupefied the animal quite quickly (Boyle, 1744). But it wasn't until **1855 that the reusable hypodermic needle was invented**. Some say that Frenchman Charles Gabriel Pravaz invented it, but most credit the revolutionary development to Scottish physician Alexander Wood. **Drugs could easily be put directly into the bloodstream, causing more-intense effects.** It also made it easier to overload the brain. Unfortunately, Wood, through self-experimentation, managed to addict himself and his wife to morphine (Karch, 1998). The use of **the hypodermic needle also bypassed the natural barriers that protected the body from infection**—such as skin, mucous membranes, lung tissue, stomach acids, and intestinal walls. By the time of the Civil War, morphine injection was common, and by 1868 both opium and morphine had become cheaper than alcohol.

Economic & Political Developments

An obvious example of the effects of economic and political developments on drug use were the **Opium Wars**. By the late 1700s, China was considered a potentially lucrative trading partner, with many national riches, such as silk, jade, porcelains, and especially tea, all ripe for exploitation. **Colonial powers vied for the right to sell opium in China.** Because of the English obsession with tea, **the British government, through the East India Trading Company, grew opium in India to trade to China for silver to buy tea**. This complicated method of trade occurred because the Chinese government, which controlled the tea trade, would accept only silver as payment.

By the early 1800s, China had banned the use and the import of opium because the dramatic growth in smoking had led to increases in crime, corruption, and addiction. Burdened by an unfavorable trade deficit due to massive tea imports, the British insisted on their "right" of free trade. In 1839 Commissioner Lin Tse-hau, who had been appointed by the Manchu emperor (Ch'ing Dynasty) to stop the opium trade, demanded that the traders surrender the tons of opium stored in their warehouses. "The Wars for Free Trade," as the British called them, or the **"Opium Wars" (1839–1842, 1856–1860)**, as the rest of the world named them, were fought to enforce the British right to sell opium to Chinese traders. They, in turn, bribed government officials so they could sell the drug to all classes (Hodgson, 1999; Wallbank & Taylor, 1992). England and other countries that won both wars were **granted greater trade concessions and the unacknowledged right to sell opium. England was also granted Hong Kong.**

The resulting addiction of many Chinese, the indignities of China's defeat, and the unequal treaties imposed by Western countries after the Opium Wars continue to complicate China's relations with the West even today (Latimer & Goldberg, 1981).

FROM COCA TO COCAINE

A parallel story of how refinement of a substance changed its use and addiction liability is the history of the coca leaf's transformation from a bracing tonic to a powerful stimulant. Until 1859, when **Albert Niemann isolated the alkaloid cocaine from the coca leaf**, the drug was chewed or chopped and absorbed on the gums, so the stimulatory effect was similar to several cups of espresso. Once refined cocaine was available, the mild excitement became an intense rush followed by ecstatic feelings and a powerful physical stimulation particularly when injected, smoked, or snorted. It could also be absorbed on the gums or drunk. Various medical and commercial developments popularized the powerful stimulant:

◇ Physician Karl Koller found that cocaine was a strong **topical anesthetic** that made eye surgery possible; he was nicknamed "Dr. Coca Koller" for his discovery.
◇ A French chemist, Angelo Mariani, popularized his **cocaine wine** (Vin Mariani) as a medicinal tonic;
◇ **Sigmund Freud published his treatise, *Über Coca*,** and suggested cocaine's use for a number of ailments: to control asthma, to calm gastric disorders, as an aphrodisiac, and to treat morphine and alcohol addicts (Freud, 1884). Freud and others also used cocaine to feel better and relieve depression.

There is evidence that the "father of psychiatry" became addicted for a while even though he denied that he had a problem. His writings in *Über Coca* about his craving for the drug and his fear of being without it belied his denial. Though the manufacture and sale of coca wine and patent medicines spread rapidly, along with widespread binge use and dependency, the **possibility of negative consequences was minimized**.

"As, at present, many authorities seem to harbor unjustified fears with regard to the internal use of cocaine. For humans the toxic dose is very high, and there seems to be no lethal dose."
Sigmund Freud, 1884 (Scrivener, 1871)

It was only through the hindsight of a generation of abuse that the addictive nature of cocaine was recognized and its widespread availability curtailed. Unfortunately, new generations often forget the lessons of the past.

TEMPERANCE & PROHIBITION MOVEMENTS

The widespread availability of rum and whiskey in the United States in the eighteenth and nineteenth centuries led to increased bouts of drunkenness, violence, and public disruption. As a result, the **first temperance movement in the United States was started around 1785 by Dr. Benjamin Rush**, a noted physician and reformer who warned against overuse of alcohol but praised limited amounts for health reasons. The disease concept of alcohol was suggested by the early writings of Rush (Goodwin & Gabrielli, 1997).

"Strong liquor is more destructive than the sword. The destruction of war is periodic, whereas alcohol exerts its influence upon human life at all times and in all seasons."
Benjamin Rush, 1788

The first national temperance organization, **the American Temperance Society, was created in 1826**; it was supported by businessmen who needed sober and industrious workers (Langton, 1995). The proliferation of these societies to more than 1,000 four years later did not stem the increased use of alcohol. Consumption peaked in 1830 in the United States with a yearly per capita consumption of 7.1 gallons of pure alcohol vs. 1.8 gallons today. In fact, at Andrew Jackson's inauguration in 1833 the new president's staff stopped serving alcohol because they were afraid that drunken revelers would destroy the White House.

It wasn't until 1851 that Maine passed the first prohibition law. Within four years one-third of the states had laws controlling the sale and the use of alcohol, and consumption fell by two-thirds. The Civil War stalled and in some cases reversed the Prohibition movement, but after the war **the Women's Crusade, the Woman's Christian Temperance Union, and the Anti-Saloon League (1893)** led

Opium was the usual active ingredient in diarrhea medications. It was also prescribed for almost every other illness because it could relieve pain. It was used mostly to treat symptoms rather than correct the disease state.

Courtesy of the National Library of Medicine, Bethesda, MD

the Temperance movement (which later became the Prohibition movement) into the twentieth century. The first facility that treated alcoholism rather than just condemning it opened in 1841 in Massachusetts.

OPIATES & COCAINE IN PATENT MEDICINES & PRESCRIPTION DRUGS

With the rising use of science to explain illness (physical and mental), the rush to formulate treatments and cures became a priority. As in centuries and millennia past, hundreds of medications were offered. Over-the-counter (OTC) medicines sold at the turn of the twentieth century had imaginative names, such as Mrs. Winslow's Soothing Syrup, Roger's Cocaine Pile Remedy, Lloyd's Cocaine Toothache Drops, and McMunn's Elixir of Opium—all **loaded with opium, morphine, cocaine, *Cannabis,* and usually alcohol** (Armstrong & Armstrong, 1991).

Needless to say, patent medicines were very popular in all strata of society and were used as a cure for any illness from lumbago to depression, much like nepenthe, theriac, and laudanum centuries before. The **manufacturers of these tonics did not need to list ingredients or back up their claims** regarding the medical usefulness of their products, so many people took tonics thinking they were benign medicines rather than potentially dangerous substances.

"It may strike you as strange that I who have had no pain—should need opium in any shape. But I have had restlessness till it made me almost mad ... So the medical people gave me opium—a preparation of it, called morphine, and ether—and ever since I have been calling it my amreeta ... my elixir."

Elizabeth Barrett Browning, 1837 (Aldrich, 1994)

One of the finest poets of the nineteenth century, Elizabeth Barrett Browning, became dependent on opium and morphine in much the same way that other middle- and upper-class European and American women of that era did, through their male **physicians' overprescribing psychoactive medications (iatrogenic addiction)**. In fact, the **majority of addicts in the Victorian era were women** (Courtwright, 1982). Some of the more well-known female addicts were the writers Louisa May Alcott and Charlotte Brontë and the actress Sarah Bernhardt. Laudanum compounds and patent medicines were prescribed for anemia, angina, depression, menopause, and the vague complaint of neurasthenia or nervous weakness. Between 1860 and 1901, U.S. imports of opium rose from 131,000 to 628,000 pounds. In the mid-1880s there were an estimated 150,000 to 200,000 chronic opium users in the United States (Kandall, 1996).

Cocaine was almost as popular a patent medicine ingredient as opium. Its ability to counteract depression made it a common recommendation from doctors. In 1887 the Hay Fever Association even declared cocaine its

official remedy. It was offered for sale in drugstores, by mail order, and in catalogs. From its formulation in 1886 until 1903, **Coca-Cola® contained about 5 mg of cocaine**, or one-third to one-half of a "line." Today the beverage contains caffeine and a coca extract from which the cocaine has been removed (Karch, 1998). In fact, Coca-Cola® continues to this day to be the largest single buyer of Trujillo coca leaf.

TWENTIETH CENTURY

FROM PIPES & SMOKELESS TOBACCO TO CIGARETTES

As governments and businesses exploited psychoactive substances, especially **tea, coffee, alcohol, and tobacco, they became more readily available to the public at large**. Adding to this trend was the increased recreational use of these stimulants and depressants spurred by democratic governments that allowed greater personal freedom and the growth of a middle class (Matthee, 1995).

Tobacco use is an excellent example of this shift. Historically, only small to moderate amounts of tobacco had been used—a pinch of snuff for the upper classes and some chopped leaf in the cheek or in a pipe for the lower classes. At the beginning of the twentieth century, automation (particularly the Bonsack **automatic cigarette-rolling machine** in 1884) that lowered prices, **a milder strain of tobacco** that enabled smokers to inhale deeply, **ad-**

vertising, and **a more plentiful supply of the leaf** vastly expanded the market for cigarettes. J. B. Duke, a North Carolina cigarette manufacturer, exploited these and many other innovations to increase sales. In his fifth year of automated manufacturing, his annual sales went from 10 million cigarettes to 744 million. Other manufacturers such as J. B. Reynolds joined forces with Duke, and they created a monopoly. By 1910 the cartel controlled 86% of the cigarette trade, leading to a breakup of the tobacco juggernaut into its component parts: American Tobacco, Reynolds, Liggett & Meyers, and Lorillard.

The pioneer of the "mild" cigarette was the Camel® brand produced by R. J. Reynolds. During the 1920s this brand was actively **marketed to women, young people, and those who wanted to lose weight**. Although sales continued to skyrocket, smoking cigarettes was recognized as harmful. The reaction to cigarettes was often fierce, and the facts were distorted by passion.

"The cigarette has a violent action in the nerve centers, producing degeneration of the brain, which is quite rapid among boys. Unlike most narcotics, this degeneration is permanent and uncontrollable. I employ no person who smokes cigarettes."

Thomas A. Edison, 1914

Inspired by the success of Prohibition, antismoking forces redoubled their efforts. State laws prohibiting cigarettes were passed, but they were

This ad for a French tonic wine made with coca leaf extract promised to help the user's digestion and disposition (c. 1896 by Alphonse Mucha).

Courtesy of the estate of Timothy C. Plowman

largely unenforceable and were repealed by the late 1920s. By the 1930s **taxes on cigarettes were providing a rich source of revenue for state and federal governments**, money that was sorely needed during the Depression and World War II.

As in decades past, intense marketing and promotion campaigns were employed to increase sales; **cigarette packs were distributed free to soldiers** during World War II and the Korean War. By the end of World War II, demand for cigarettes sometimes exceeded supply and **smoking had become socially acceptable**.

By midcentury smoking was entrenched in American society. It was a source of revenue for advertisers, retailers, the media, tobacco farmers, and government treasuries. Warnings of the health hazards of smoking were issued as early as 1945 by the Mayo Clinic and were echoed by the American Cancer Society and various heart and physicians' organizations throughout the 1950s. The tobacco industry ridiculed health concerns and responded to health warnings with slogans such as "Old Golds: for a treat instead of a treatment." They also formed the Tobacco Institute, the industry's chief political lobby. **In 1964 and 1967, the U.S. Surgeon General issued reports that concluded, "Cigarette smoking is a health hazard."** Smoking in the United States generally decreased through the 1960s, rose during the

1970s, and finally went into the long decline that continues into the present.

DRUG REGULATION

As societies' attitudes toward drugs and alcohol varied from total acceptance to temperance to prohibition, so did the laws and legislation. And though physicians understood the addictive and health liabilities of opiates and cocaine in the late 1800s, it took another two decades before serious U.S. regulation began. The **Pure Food and Drug Act (1906)** prohibited interstate commerce in misbranded and adulterated foods, drinks, and drugs, and it required accurate labeling of ingredients. The **Opium Exclusion Act (1909)** encouraged the gradual reduction in worldwide opium production and an eventual ban on smoking. That same year Congress banned the importation of opium not intended for medical use. The **Harrison Narcotic Act (1914)** controlled the sale of opium, which could then be monitored by the federal government (Acker, 1995). Although these acts and others did, in fact, eliminate the over-the-counter availability of opiates and cocaine in the United States, **the tight control of all supplies encouraged prescription drug diversion and the development of a huge illicit-drug trade**.

It wasn't only the expanding importation of opiates and cocaine and the attendant health and social liabilities of

the substances that spurred attempts at drug regulation. When cocaine and opiates made their way to minority and poor urban populations, they became a matter of great political concern. Headlines about "drug-crazed Negroes" and the "Yellow Peril" (in regard to the Chinese immigrant use of opiates) along with warnings about rape and sexual promiscuity moved national and state legislatures to enact more laws (Kandall, 1996). Even at the end of the twentieth century, there was bias in the legislation. For example, the federal penalties for crack cocaine, which was regarded as a ghetto drug, were much more severe than for powdered cocaine, which was considered a middle- and upper-class drug.

The intent of drug legislation varies from trying to control the supply to providing treatment. Numerous other laws have been passed over the years:

1920   Volstead Act implemented the Eighteenth Amendment **prohibiting the manufacture and the sale of any alcoholic beverage**.

1933   **Prohibition and the Volstead Act were repealed.**

1937   Marijuana Tax Act **banned the cultivation and the use of *Cannabis* sativa (marijuana)**.

1963   Community Mental Health Centers Act provided the first federal assistance for local **treatment of addiction under the cover of mental illness**.

1965   Drug Abuse Control Amendments **prohibited the illicit manufacture of stimulants and depressants**.

1970   Comprehensive Drug Abuse Prevention and Control Act of 1970 **combined all previous drug legislation, created schedules to rate drugs**, and devised a new penalty schedule.

1984   **Drinking age was raised to 21 years.**

1986   Anti–Drug Abuse Act strengthened federal efforts to encourage **foreign cooperation in eradicating drug crops**.

1990   Crime Control Act of 1990 **regulated precursor chemicals**, allowed the seizure of drug traffickers' assets, and controlled

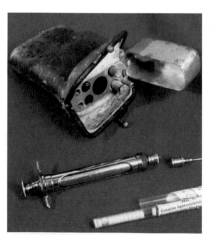

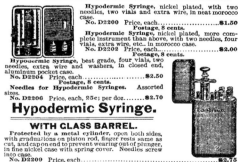

SEARS, ROEBUCK & CO., (Incorporated), Cl

HYPODERMIC SYRINGES.

Hypodermic Syringe, nickel plated, with two needles, two vials and extra wire, in neat morocco case.
No. D2200 Price, each........................**$1.50**
Postage, 8 cents.
Hypodermic Syringe, nickel plated, more complete instrument than above, with two needles, four vials, extra wire, etc., in morocco case.
No. D2202 Price, each........................**$2.00**
Postage, 8 cents.
Hypodermic Syringe, best grade, four vials, two needles, extra wire and washers, in closed end, aluminum pocket case.
No. D2204 Price, each........................**$2.50**
Postage, 8 cents.
Needles for Hypodermic Syringes. Assorted sizes.
No. D2206 Price, each, 25c; per doz........**$2.70**

Hypodermic Syringe.

WITH GLASS BARREL.

Protected by a metal cylinder, open both sides, with graduations on piston rod, finger rests same as cut, and cap on end to prevent wearing out of plunger, in fine nickel case with spring cover. Needles screw into case.
No. D2209 Price, each........................**$2.75**

Drug kits that often included vials of cocaine and heroin and a reusable syringe were advertised in the drug section of the 1897 Sears Roebuck catalog along with dozens of patent medicines that also contained opium, cocaine, and marijuana.
Courtesy of the Fitz Hugh Ludlow Memorial Library

drug paraphernalia and money laundering.

2000 Proposition 36 in California required a **treatment option for first-time nonviolent drug offenders.**

2005 The U.S. Supreme Court said that **federal authorities may prosecute individuals who grow or use marijuana for medicinal purposes.**

1996–present   More than 36 states passed laws **legalizing the medical use of marijuana.**

ALCOHOL PROHIBITION & TREATMENT

Between 1870 and 1915, one-half to two-thirds of the U.S. budget came from the liquor tax. The new era in American politics, the Progressive Era, however, eliminated moderation or temperance as a viable choice. The anti-alcohol movement claimed that there could be no compromise with the "forces of evil." There was great debate over whether alcohol abuse was the result or the cause of poverty; the majority called it the cause.

It took 13 months to ratify the **Eighteenth Amendment (Prohibition) in 1920**, prohibiting the manufacture and the sale of any beverage with an alcohol content greater than 0.5%. **The Volstead Act implemented the provisions of the amendment.** Prohibition was called "the noble experiment," but not only the United States tried it. Shorter so-called noble experiments were enacted in Iceland, Russia, parts of Canada, India, and Finland among others (Heath, 1995).

It took 10 months of political wrangling to **repeal Prohibition 13 years later.** Americans hadn't changed their feelings about the benefits or liabilities of alcohol; they had simply discovered that Prohibition created other serious problems in spite of the fact that **it did help control a number of serious health and social issues.** Cirrhosis of the liver and other alcohol-related diseases declined dramatically; domestic violence fell; violent crime dropped by two-thirds; and public drunkenness almost disappeared even though people still disregarded the law and drank in speakeasies or made bathtub gin and beer.

This illustration of the founders of Alcoholics Anonymous (Bill W. and Doctor Bob) making a call on an alcoholic who still suffers has been used in AA literature over the years. At present there are more than 2 million members of Alcoholics Anonymous in more than 100,000 groups around the world. Almost half the members are outside the United States.

Courtesy of Alcoholics Anonymous. All rights reserved.

During the tenure of the Eighteenth Amendment, a new coalition of smugglers, strong-arm thieves, Mafiosi, corrupt politicians, and crooked police had developed a lucrative trade in the distribution and the sale of illicit alcohol. With the return of alcohol to legal status, this coalition turned to other illicit enterprises, including the expansion of the drug trade that handled heroin and cocaine.

With the end of Prohibition, alcoholism again increased, though it took 20 years for per-capita drinking in the United States to reach pre-Prohibition levels. Higher levels of alcoholism were partly answered by the creation of an organization to help alcoholics recover. **Alcoholics Anonymous (AA), a spiritual program that teaches 12 steps to recovery**, was founded in 1934 by two alcoholics, Bill Wilson and Dr. Bob Smith (Alcoholics Anonymous, 1934, 1976). Over the years AA has proved itself to be the most successful support/recovery program in history (Trice, 1995). Today there are **52,050 groups in the United States** with a membership of 1,068,516. In Canada and overseas, there are another 51,625 groups with 732,537 members (Alcoholics Anonymous, 2006). Other programs used the 12-step model to help narcotics addicts (NA), marijuana addicts (MA), overeaters (OA), gamblers (GA), adult children of alcoholics (ACoA), and even sex addicts (SA). There are more than 50 other major 12-step groups operating throughout the world.

The success of Alcoholics Anonymous and its cooperation with researchers, physicians, and organizations like the National Council on Alcoholism under Marty Mann were instrumental in convincing the public, and hence the politicians, that **alcoholism is a disease and not a moral weakness.**

MARIJUANA: FROM DITCHWEED TO SINSEMILLA

Though *Cannabis* had been widely used in patent medicines that were ingested, **marijuana smoking wasn't really noticed in the United States until it was seen in Texas around 1910.** Gradually, it spread to the Southwest and the West. Another reason why it was eventually listed as a narcotic and banned was due to an anti-marijuana campaign by the Hearst newspapers in the 1930s. Publisher William Randolph Hearst had his papers popularize the Mexican word *marijuana* to make the drug sound more foreign and menacing. The fear of Mexican marijuana smokers was used to rail against immigration. In addition, when Prohibition ended, a large number of federal drug-regulatory employees, particularly their boss **Harry Anslinger, needed a new mission.** Marijuana seemed a likely target. Anslinger used the fear of rape and debauchery to bolster his opposition to marijuana. In 1937 he was quoted in the *Washington Herald* as saying, "If the hideous monster

Frankenstein came face to face with the monster marijuana, he would die of fright" (Booth, 2003).

Under pressure to ban the drug, 38 states added marijuana to their "most dangerous drugs" lists by 1936. The federal response was the **1937 Marijuana Tax Act, which banned *Cannabis sativa*.** The ban on growing and using marijuana occurred despite its use in numerous medicines for more than 5,000 years, though the discovery of newer medications lowered much of its unique medicinal value. The growing of *Cannabis* in the United States for economic uses (e.g., hemp fiber for rope, paper, and oil) were also effectively prohibited except for a brief period during World War II when it was needed by the military.

During the 1950s marijuana use was found mainly in rural areas and inner cities. It was glamorized by jazz musicians and in the works of the beat generation poets and writers, chiefly Allen Ginsberg, Jack Kerouac, and Gregory Corso. **By the 1960s a new generation began defying prohibitions against marijuana,** in part because they discovered that it was not as demonic a drug as portrayed by the government and the media. It was also a **symbol of youthful rebellion** against parents, authority, and the war in Vietnam.

As marijuana became popular, people started practicing different growing techniques. Bags of fertilizer, watering pipes and tubing, window boxes, and grow lights became hot items. The price of marijuana in the 1960s was low ($50 to $100 per pound) as was the concentration of THC, the active psychedelic ingredient, although stronger concentrations were grown but not readily available. It wasn't until the 1970s that the **sinsemilla growing technique** (which increased the concentration of THC) was widespread and the price skyrocketed (*see Chapter 6*). It is estimated that 160 million people use marijuana worldwide and more than 120 countries cultivate it (United Nations Office on Drugs and Crime, 2005).

AMPHETAMINES IN WAR & WEIGHT LOSS

In a search for medications to treat asthma and respiratory problems, **am-phetamine was first synthesized in 1887 in Germany, and methamphetamine was created in 1919 in Japan**, but it wasn't until the 1930s that they were used therapeutically. Amphetamine was first marketed **under the trade name Benzedrine®** as a decongestant in an inhaler. In other forms amphetamines were tried for the treatment of low blood pressure, narcolepsy, epilepsy, schizophrenia, alcoholism, and barbiturate intoxication (Grinspoon & Hedblom, 1975). Its **appetite-suppressant qualities were soon recognized** along with its calming and focusing effect on children diagnosed with what came to be known as ADHD.

It also took until the 1930s for **amphetamine's stimulating effects on the central nervous system** (CNS) to become widely known and exploited. The drug was often used nonmedically to stay awake, to increase confidence, or to induce a high. These qualities were exploited during **World War II**, when American, British, German, and Japanese army doctors routinely dispensed amphetamines (speed) **to fight fatigue, heighten en-durance, and "elevate the fighting spirit"** (Marnell, 2005). Illicit amphetamine abuse increased during the 1940s and 1950s among truck drivers and workers engaged in monotonous factory jobs and among college students who needed to cram for exams. A popular song of the times was "Who Put the Benzedrine in Mrs. Murphy's Ovaltine?" People would even swallow the wad of propylhexadrine-soaked cotton in the inhalers to concentrate the effect.

Internationally, **excessive amphetamine use in Japan after the war led to widespread abuse and thousand of cases of drug-induced psychosis.** By 1955, when there were 2 million users, the Japanese government mounted an extensive prevention and treatment campaign to stem the epidemic (Blum, 1984; Courtwright, 2001). Massive amounts of amphetamines were dispensed during the Vietnam War—almost 225 million tablets of Dexedrine.® The publicity about marijuana and heroin use in Vietnam obscured information concerning the widespread use of amphetamines (Grinspoon & Hedblom, 1975).

The 1950s saw dozens of pulp novels warning of the dangers of drugs. The beat poets and counterculture writers of the 1960s reversed this trend by praising the use of psychoactive substances.

The appetite-suppressant (anorexic) effects led to the **massive use of amphetamines as diet drugs in the fifties and sixties**. In 1970 it was estimated that 6% to 8% of the American population was using 12 billion pills, tablets, and capsules containing legal amphetamines.

Amphetamines and methamphetamines were also the **fuel for the hippie movement and the "Summer of Love" in 1967**. As a reaction to the suddenly expanded use of these drugs, Congress passed the **Comprehensive Drug Abuse Prevention and Control Act of 1970**. Initially, the legislation made it harder to manufacture and prescribe amphetamines in the United States, but the street market expanded to fill the need. "Crosstops," smuggled from Mexico, were the most popular, but methamphetamines in powder or crystal form ("crank" or "crystal") were also available.

SPORTS & DRUGS

The 2004 Olympics and the 2005 baseball steroid hearings made for endless headlines about the use of performance-enhancing drugs in sports, but even in ancient Greece and Rome the rewards of success in sports were quite large and led athletes to try anything to improve performance. Plato noted that victory could bring homes, tax exemptions, large sums of money, and even deferment from serving in the army, leading many athletes to try such substances as extracts of mushrooms, donkey hooves, and certain plant seeds to win. Such "doping" fell out of favor until the nineteenth and twentieth centuries, when sports once again became a rewarding endeavor. As the rewards increased, so did the win-at-any-cost attitude.

The Cold War inflamed athletic competition between the Free World and the Communist-bloc countries. This was very evident at the **Olympics** and other international sporting events during the 1950s and 1960s. The use of **anabolic androgenic steroids, stimulants, and other performance-enhancing drugs** became widespread.

"The athletes themselves came out and told that their coaches and scientists forced these drugs on them. And then they found the records that proved it. I've seen these [East] German girls; swimmers with their beards growing out. We used to dance with them after the meet. And their great strength— you didn't want to mess with any of them. They had muscles. They could knock you out."

Su Haa, Turkish Olympic Swim Team, 1972

By 1968 the **International Olympic Committee** had defined performance-enhancing drug use, made a list of banned substances, and **began drug testing** (Australian Drug Foundation, 1999). The **National Collegiate Athletic Association** began drug testing 18 years later. By that time the proliferation of various steroids, the expansion of an underground steroid network in weightlifting gyms, the growing sophistication of street chemists, and the growth of OTC nutritional supplements—including androstenedione, gamma-hydroxybutyrate (GHB), and creatine—had multiplied.

SEDATIVE-HYPNOTICS & PSYCHIATRIC MEDICATIONS

As the scientific transformation in pharmacology took advantage of new technologies, drug companies found that they could **synthesize medications rather than rely on extracts from natural products**. Sedatives, such as bromides, chloral hydrate, and paraldehyde, gave way to barbiturates. The first to be marketed was Veronal® (barbital) in 1903; phenobarbital came 10 years later, and **eventually 50 barbiturates were used to induce sleep and calm anxiety**. Their use peaked in the 1930s and 1940s. The overprescribing of these drugs plus their addiction and overdose liability led to the development of Miltown® and other milder tranquilizers in the 1950s and 1960s (Hollister, 1983). Quickly thereafter **benzodiazepines came to dominate the prescription downer market because of potentially much lower overdose liability**. Benzodiazepine sedatives include Librium,® Valium,® Xanax,® Klonopin,® and Halcion.® At one point in the 1980s, 100 million prescriptions were written each year for sedative-hypnotics (sedatives are generally used to calm anxiety whereas hypnotics are mostly used to induce sleep).

The recognition of **brain chemical imbalances as the cause of almost all mental illnesses** spurred the development of **psychiatric medications** other than sedatives and hypnotics. The development of **antipsychotics (e.g., Thorazine®)**, (e.g., benzodiazepines), mood stabilizers (e.g. lithium), **antianxiety drugs, and antidepressants** (e.g., tricyclics, MAO inhibitors, and, later, **selective serotonin reuptake inhibitors [SSRIs] such as Prozac®**) led to a drastic change in the treatment of mental illness. And as medical researchers came to realize the intimate connection between the neurological imbalances of mental illness and those caused by psychoactive drugs, concepts such as self-medication, methamphetamine-induced psychoses, alcohol-induced depression, and steroid-induced mania became clearer.

Research into the connection between mental illness and psychoactive drugs also led to the **development of medications to treat drug abuse and addiction**, including aids for **detoxification, long-term abstinence, and relapse prevention**. This pharmacologic evolution of psychiatric medications became much more common because they have a much lower addiction liability than standard sedative-hypnotics. Unfortunately, they also have significant side effects.

LSD & THE NEW PSYCHEDELICS

Pharmacological developments led not only to synthetic depressants, stimulants, and psychiatric medications but also to new hallucinogenic drugs, or *psychedelics*. For example, the active ingredient in **ergot fungus, called *LSD* (lysergic acid diethylamide), was isolated and extracted in 1938** in Switzerland by Albert Hoffman of Sandoz Pharmaceuticals; its hallucinogenic properties weren't discovered for five more years, when he accidentally dosed himself with 250 micrograms—about two and a half times a normal dose.

"My visual field wavered and everything appeared deformed as in a faulty mirror. Space and time became more and more disorganized and I was overcome by a fear that I was going out of my mind, the worst part of it being that I was clearly aware of my condition."

Albert Hoffman, 1943

Due to Hoffman's findings, various groups, including the psychiatric community, started experimenting with LSD and other psychedelic drugs, seeing them as a potential treatment for mental illness, particularly schizophrenia, and as a way to examine and possibly gain insight into hidden memories and emotions. **The army and the Central Intelligence Agency experimented with them as mind-control drugs**, as truth serums, and as chemical weapons to disrupt the enemy's thought processes. Still others thought it would enhance human thought, emotions, and spirituality (Julien, 2005).

Dr. Timothy Leary encouraged the youth of the sixties to "turn on, tune in, and drop out" to the apprehension and outrage of older generations, including his bosses at Harvard University and even Albert Hoffman, who called LSD his "problem child." Leary, the so-called guru of LSD, advocated drug experimentation to alter the mind and to gain insight. Other psychedelics such as marijuana, MDA, peyote, and psilocybin mushrooms were also employed in this quest.

In the 1960s and thereafter, a flood of **synthetic psychedelic drugs and rediscovered natural psychedelic substances like MDA, DOB, DMT, PCP, 2CB, CBR (nexus), peyote, psilocybin, *salvia divinorum,* and particularly MDMA (ecstasy) were tried**. These drugs, combined with the counter-cultural attitude of the times, made many live the slogan *Better living through chemistry.*

PREVENTING & TREATING DRUG ABUSE

Attempts to address the problems of abuse, addiction, and crime brought on by the misuse of drugs focused on:

◇ **demand reduction**—prevention coupled with treatment;

◇ **supply reduction**—interdiction plus stricter laws concerning use; and

◇ **harm reduction**—medical or social techniques to reduce the physical and social damage caused by abuse and dependence (e.g., methadone maintenance, free needle distribution, and temperance).

As research findings were compiled, including the **discovery of brain chemicals (endorphins) that acted like psychoactive drugs** (opiates), understanding of the process of addiction grew and treatment facilities expanded. Alcoholism and other addictions were defined and, to a certain extent, accepted as illnesses. **The treatment of addiction became a medical as well as a social science.** Some of the treatment protocols developed for addiction consisted of therapeutic communities, new medical treatments in hospitals, free-clinic approaches, outpatient clinics, and 12-step fellowships.

METHADONE

In the early part of the twentieth century, physicians prescribed morphine or other drugs to control opiate craving in an effort to treat heroin addiction. By 1918 the federal government considered drug use a criminal activity and prosecuted physicians who tried this kind of treatment. It wasn't until the 1960s in New York that this method was tried again, using a long-acting opioid called methadone. This drug, developed in Germany in the early 1940s, was the keystone of the program called "methadone maintenance." It was designed to **substitute a legal opiate (methadone) for an illegal one (heroin)**. Methadone isn't as intense as heroin, and it keeps the user on a more even keel, though it too is addictive. According to the American Methadone Treatment Association, methadone clinics spread throughout the United States; there are now more than 1,292 clinics that supply methadone to about 228,000 heroin addicts, 48,000 in New York City alone (N-SSATS, 2006). In 2004, 47 other countries had methadone maintenance pro-

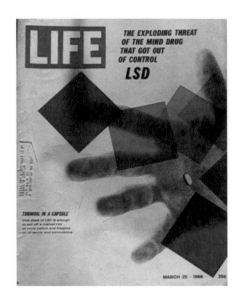

The hallucinogen LSD made a media splash in the 1960s as the public debated whether to accept it as a possible psychotherapeutic medication or to condemn it as a dangerous mind-altering drug.

grams with an enrollment of more than 500,000. The original goals of methadone maintenance were to control the illegal activities and the addictive behavior of the heroin addict population. It was an early example of a **harm reduction goal that was targeted to benefit society** as well as the addict. Because methadone is administered orally, it has had great success in decreasing the problems associated with needle injection of heroin, such as HIV/AIDS, hepatitis C, and bacterial infections of the heart, veins, and other body tissues.

HEROIN & VIETNAM

In the late 1960s and 1970s, an unpopular war in Vietnam, along with a flood of opium from the Golden Triangle (Myanmar [Burma], Laos, and Thailand), encouraged the use of heroin. **A new group of heroin addicts both at home and abroad was created during the years of America's involvement in the war**. Though half the soldiers in Vietnam experimented with heroin and 20% of those had been addicted during their tour of duty, only 5% continued their heroin use after the war (Robins & Slobodyan, 2003).

COCAINE, THE CRACK EPIDEMIC & ICE

After the **two earlier eras of heavy cocaine use (1880–1905 and 1920–1930)**, snorting and shooting the drug was more limited. It wasn't until the late seventies and early eighties that more-plentiful supplies, an excess of publicity, social amnesia about earlier problems, and the development of **new ways of preparing and using the drug made cocaine fashionable once again** (Siegel, 1982).

Snorting and injecting, the traditional methods for using cocaine, were supplemented by smoking a new street form of the drug. This new form of cocaine use was made possible by chemically altering cocaine hydrochloride into cocaine freebase, a form of the drug that could be vaporized without destroying its psychoactive properties. Developed in the 1970s, it was **originally known as "freebase." Later an easier method of making freebase was developed. The smokable crystals were called "crack."** Use went from after-hours clubs, to freebase parlors, to crack houses and individuals' apartments, and finally to street dealers (Hamid, 1992).

The ensuing crack epidemic in the mid- and late 1980s was partly fueled by the media's heavy-handed news coverage but mostly by the rapid stimulating effects of the drug itself. The other main reasons for crack's surge in use were the low cost of a "hit" and various socioeconomic forces in the inner city, including the dissolution of family structures and a lack of economic opportunities (Dunlop & Johnson, 1992). Experimentation and binge use were common in the suburbs, but as the glamour of crack faded, it **moved to the inner city, and heavy use became more prevalent among minorities**. Because the middle and upper classes began avoiding crack cocaine, newspaper coverage faded and all that was left were severe legal penalties for possession and use.

In the late 1980s, perhaps in response to the popularity of smoked cocaine, a slightly altered **smokable methamphetamine called "ice"** came onto the scene. Also called "L.A. glass" and "peanut butter," its mental effects were stronger and lasted longer than the common methamphetamines. The initial center of "ice" abuse was Hawaii. By the beginning of the 1990s and even into the 2000s, people thought its use hadn't spread as rapidly as had been feared, but **most of the methamphetamine confiscated by the Drug Enforcement Administration (DEA) during the past decade has been this slightly different form of the drug, which is most often called "crystal meth."**

TODAY & TOMORROW

Worldwide more than 1.5 billion people drink alcohol and, of that figure, at least **76 million have an alcohol use disorder**. Added to that are the **180 million who abuse illicit drugs, the 1 billion who use tobacco, and the 160 million who smoke marijuana each year** (World Health Organization [WHO], 2005). Psychoactive drugs have an enormous social impact on all aspects of society. For example, depending on the estimates, 20% to 60% of hospital beds are filled with the medical consequences of drug abuse. If food addiction is included, that percentage is probably closer to 80%. In fact, **there are 72 major medical illnesses in which substance abuse, in all of its forms, is the primary contributor**, especially heart disease, cirrhosis of the liver, lung cancer, emphysema, hepatitis C, and AIDS.

GEOPOLITICS OF DRUGS

The monetary value of drugs has often been part of legitimate and illegitimate governments' economic plans. Whether it was the profit on opium sales to China, the excise taxes on whiskey and tobacco, a government-run monopoly on coca (conquistadors), state-sponsored gambling in the form of lotteries and slot machines, or an insurgency-controlled drug trade to support terrorist and revolutionary activities, the link is clear. For insurgencies heroin, cocaine, and, to a lesser extent, marijuana have been the media of exchange. Lately, MDMA (ecstasy) and methamphetamine have been added to that list.

Heroin

Four regions grow and export almost all of the world's opium and heroin: the Golden Crescent (southwest Asia: Afghanistan, Iran, and Pakistan), the Golden Triangle (Southeast Asia: Thailand, Myanmar, and Laos), Mexico, and Colombia. Each of these areas at one time or another has been the main supplier of heroin to the United States.

Currently **in the United States, Colombian white heroin, Mexican black tar and brown heroin, and Afghani white are the most common**, although recently exports from Colombia have dropped significantly. According to congressional testimony by DEA representatives, much of the heroin is smuggled across the U.S.-Mexico border. Because of the increased supply, the price of heroin has dropped while its purity has risen from 7% about 20 years ago to 36.8% today (Drug Enforcement Administration [DEA], 2006). Only a small amount of this trade supports insurgency activities. Most is driven strictly by the great individual profits made in heroin trafficking.

Internationally, the biggest influence on the opium/heroin trade has been the rising and falling fortunes of Afghanistan's opium crop in the Golden Crescent. **Afghanistan had been the largest grower of opium for many years, providing 6,000 tons, or about 90% of the world's illicit supply, in 2006.** Various groups, including the Taliban and members of the Northern Alliance, **used the profits to fund insurgencies and/or terrorist activities**. The Taliban eventually destroyed most of the crops, but when it was thrown from power by the United States in 2002, the fields were replanted. The new Afghan government has pledged to wage war on opium growing, but **in 2006 the acreage of opium poppies under cultivation had grown by another 50%**. Only time will tell if the crop, which supplies 60% of the country's income, can be replaced with legal crops. Most of the opium grown in Afghanistan is used to supply Europe's heroin market. Since 2001, however, the amount of Afghani heroin on U.S. streets has grown from 7% of the supply to more than 14%.

An Afghani woman tends a poppy field. In 2006 the United Nations estimated that Afghanistan supplies 90% of the world's opium.
© 1990 Alain Labrousse

• •

In addition, it is a purer heroin, thus increasing the number of overdoses (Therolf, 2006).

Since the 1991 collapse of the Soviet Union, Russia has become a major transit route for heroin from Afghanistan and the number of drug addicts (heroin and other drugs) inside Russia has exploded. The result has been 6 million addicts, a younger age of first use, 70,000 drug overdoses each year, 300,000 people infected with the HIV virus, and increased corruption (U.S. Embassy, 2006). This is in addition to a staggering alcoholism rate: alcohol intake per Russian male increased by four times between 1991 and 2000.

Changes in Southeast Asia, particularly in Myanmar, the largest producer of opium in the **Golden Triangle, have cut production levels to half those of the 1990s.** Unfortunately, so long as there is a market, others are always willing to take up the slack. Though there is an expanding internal market for heroin in the Asian countries that grow and smuggle the drug (about one-fourth of the total crop), the profits still lie in selling to users in wealthier countries.

A past example of using the huge profits from the opium/heroin trade to buy guns, bombs, and bribes occurred after World War II when the Kuomintang under **Chiang Kai Shek** fled from mainland China to Taiwan and Burma (now Myanmar). They had been involved with the Green Gang, the leading criminal group in Shanghai that handled heroin among their other illegal activities. The United States turned a blind eye when the Kuomintang continued growing opium along the Thailand-Burma border with China because they acted as a buffer between Southeast Asia and the Chinese Communists. The drug gangs had extensive militias composed mostly of Kuomintang soldiers.

During the Vietnam War, the United States again disregarded the drug growing and trafficking by the hill tribesmen (Hmong) so that they would support the effort against the North Vietnamese and the Viet Cong. Now that the Cold War is a thing of the past, the United States is applying pressure to Thailand and other former "frontline" buffers to Communism to control their drug trafficking (Observatoire Geopolitique des Drogues, 1996; United Nations Office on Drugs and Crime, 2005).

Cocaine

Geopolitics is also important in cocaine production and smuggling. **Virtually all cocaine is grown in South America,** specifically Colombia, Peru, and Bolivia; and the traffickers continue to infiltrate the economic, political, law enforcement, and military institutions of those countries. Colombia has been in a state of civil war for more than half a century. The unrest was originally because of insurgency movements, but over the past 25 years cocaine has been the catalyst. In addition, countries and territories that are transit routes for smuggling, especially Mexico but also the Dominican Republic, the Bahamas, and Puerto Rico, are necessarily vulnerable to corruption and bribery. About **65% of the cocaine smuggled into the United States comes across the U.S.-Mexico border**. In 2005 the *National Survey on Drug Use and Health* documented that at least 2.6 million Americans used cocaine in the past month (Substance Abuse and Mental Health Services Administration [SAMHSA], 2006).

The Mexican cocaine trade has spawned an increasing population of crack addicts within Mexico itself as lower-level members of the cartels, who are often paid with drugs, develop their own marketing networks in cities such as Nuevo Laredo. *Tienditas* (drug shops) have sprung up everywhere, fueling an increase in violence, corruption, and addiction. The local drug clinics have been overwhelmed with crack addicts seeking treatment (Grillo, 2005).

HIV, AIDS & HEPATITIS C

The HIV virus that causes AIDS has been around for more than 25 years. Societies have gone through a number of phases, including ignorance, bewilderment, alarm, and complacency, until today, when governments and health agencies are more alarmed than ever over the sheer numbers of the epidemic. **Worldwide more than 25 million people have died of AIDS while over 40 million are living with the disease,** the majority in sub-Saharan Africa with growing numbers in Asia. Each year more than 5 million people are newly infected and 3 million die.

In the United States, more than 500,000 have died while 850,000 to

950,000 are living with HIV/AIDS (UNAIDS, 2006). Initially in the United States, the HIV virus was spread by unsafe sex, mostly in the gay community, but as more people became infected, transmission by **contaminated needles fueled a new surge of infections**; 25% of new cases are caused by injection drug use. Overseas, AIDS is spread primarily by unsafe heterosexual sex and secondarily by contaminated needles.

Unfortunately, HIV/AIDS isn't the only major infection caused by the consequences of drug use, particularly injection drug use. **More than 4 million Americans suffer from hepatitis C (HCV), a liver infection** that can be fatal. The prevalence among injection drug users is an astonishing 85% to 90%. Until 1992 there was no test for hepatitis C, so the rate of new infections was extremely high, about 240,000 per year. New infections currently average 30,000 per year. Drug use can also **spread HIV and to a lesser extent HCV through high-risk sexual practices** that often occur when inhibitions are lowered by the drug's effects or by the need to trade sex for drugs (Centers for Disease Control [CDC], 2006).

CLUB DRUGS

The reemergence of the psychedelic clubs and rock music events of the 1960s and 1970s, now called **"rave clubs," "raves," or just "music parties,"** has kept alive the tradition of mixing music and psychoactive drugs. In the 1920s it was jazz, cocaine, and bootleg liquor; in the fifties it was the blues, heroin, and whiskey; in the sixties and seventies, it was hard rock, LSD, speed, marijuana, and wine; and in the 2000s, it's techno or electronic trance music, ecstasy, marijuana, nitrous oxide, ketamine, GHB, and beer (although many commercial rave parties for teenagers ban alcohol and drugs).

The most common drug used at these parties, **MDMA (ecstasy, "X," "E," "Adam," and "rave"), is a psychedelic, also referred to as a psychostimulant**. One dose can cost $20 to $30. MDMA users claim that it promotes closeness and empathy along

These three advertisements for rave parties use cartoon icons and try to keep alcohol out of the events, but many club drugs are available through individuals and dealers who handle ecstasy, nitrous oxide, GHB, and a few other substances. Only about half of the drugs purported to be ecstasy have any of the real drug. A number of DJs supply the music for these events.

with a loss of inhibitions that can trigger a strong urge to dance, socialize, and keep active. Dilution and adulteration are common with MDMA; PMA (paramethoxyamphetamine) and other stimulants are often found in bogus "E" tablets sold at raves as are totally inactive ingredients. "Molly" is a new street name for supposedly pure, or "molecular," MDMA. As with the purchase of any street drug, relying on this to be safe would be foolhardy. Some tablets sold as "Molly" were analyzed and found to actually be BZP (benzylpiperazine) or TFMPP (trifluoromethylphenyl piperazine), drugs with more-toxic effects than real MDMA. Less than 50% of the tablets sold as ecstasy actually contained MDMA, and only one-third of those contained only MDMA as an active ingredient.

Another drug that has seen more abuse in recent years is **GHB (gamma-hydroxybutyrate), a sedative**. This drug was originally developed as an anesthetic. It was banned in the United States because youths were using it as a sedative, to induce euphoria, and for its anabolic or muscle-building effects. It has also been used by sexual predators to induce amnesia in their victims.

Dextromethorphan (DXM), found in many nonprescription cough and cold medications, can induce psychedelic effects when used in large quantities (10 to 30 times the normal dose). The other ingredients found in these combination cold medications can also cause problems when used to excess (e.g., chlorpheniramine maleate and other ingredients in Coricidin Cough and Cold® can be deadly). Because of abuse, many states require drugs containing dextromethorphan to be sold at the counter to limit shoplifting and the purchase of large amounts.

MARIJUANA (*Cannabis*) & HEALTH

The biggest story regarding marijuana still has to do with **the legalization of medical marijuana**. On June 6, 2005, in a 6-to-3 decision, the U.S. Supreme Court ruled that federal authorities may prosecute individuals who grow or use marijuana for medicinal purposes. Before the ruling (in a case involving two California women who used marijuana for medical purposes), there were more than 37 cannabis clubs in San Francisco alone, with about 8,000 licensed users; there were more than 135 clubs statewide. In addition, an increasing number of states had legalized the drug for medical purposes; as of 2006 they were **Alaska, Arkansas, California, Colorado, Hawaii, Maine, Maryland, Montana, Nevada, Oregon, Rhode Island, Vermont, and Washington**. The ruling prompted almost all of those states to stop issuing permits for medical marijuana use, putting a damper on the growth of medical use of the drug. Outside of the United States, a few countries allow medical marijuana, most notably Australia, Canada, Germany, and the Netherlands. A few other countries are studying the possibility of legalization.

At the start of the twenty-first century, marijuana is the most widely used illicit drug in the United States, Australia, Canada, Mexico, South Africa, and dozens of other countries. **High-potency marijuana continues to be widely available** (up to 14 times as strong as varieties readily available in the 1970s). High-potency marijuana was always available, but it was not very plentiful. Just as the refinement of coca leaves into cocaine and of opium into morphine and heroin led to greater abuse and addiction liability with those drugs, **improved sinsemilla cultivation techniques have increased the compulsive liability of marijuana**. Almost 300,000 clients (16% of all admissions) entering treatment in 2004 in the United States listed marijuana as their primary drug (SAMHSA, 2006). As with cocaine and heroin, the higher-potency marijuana commands a much steeper price, a 10- to 30-fold increase since the early 1970s. For example, the $50 to $80 that an eighth of an ounce would cost today could have purchased a pound of marijuana in the early 1970s.

TOBACCO, HEALTH & THE LAW

Worldwide many countries and their health agencies have become involved in smoking prevention. For example, the European health ministers in 2002 passed a tough new law banning tobacco advertising on the radio, in print, and on the Internet to add to its ban on TV advertising; in 2004 Ireland banned smoking in pubs; even Cuba banned smoking in public places.

In the United States, after a rise in smoking among junior high and high school students in the 1990s, smoking is declining again. Among the 18-and-above age groups, it has continued to decline. **Between 1966 and 2005, the percentage of Americans who smoked regularly dropped from 42.6% of the population to 22.5%** (SAMHSA, 2006). This decline began soon after the 1964 U.S. Surgeon General's Report on the dangers of smoking. Since then antismoking campaigns, printed warnings on packaging, legislation prohibiting smoking in public places, lawsuits against tobacco companies, restrictions on tobacco advertising, and of course continuing research on the dangerous health effects from smoking—all have had an impact.

Although each day in the United States, 3,500 cigarette smokers do quit, approximately 1,178 others die prematurely from the effects of smoking. Increased smoking among women worldwide **propelled lung cancer deaths past those from breast cancer**, although in the past two years those numbers have finally begun to decline in the United States (CDC, 2006; Konietzko, 2001). A 50-year longitudinal study in England showed that smoking takes 10 years off the life of the average user (Doll, Boreham & Sutherland, 2004).

The tobacco companies have tried to keep their revenues up by **developing foreign markets mostly in third world countries**. Smoking in developing countries is increasing at a rate of 3.4% per year, although even those countries recognize the danger. China has recently initiated a rigorous antismoking campaign. Worldwide about one-third of all adults smoke, although the percentage is much higher among males (e.g., 70% of Indonesian males smoke). Tobacco companies have tried to sustain the U.S. market by advertising generic brands, cutting prices, and targeting female, minority, and younger smokers.

In 1998 in the biggest class-action lawsuit settlement ever, the **major tobacco companies agreed to pay $246 billion over a period of 25 years** to the various states. The settlement money was to be used to develop programs to prevent teenagers from smoking and to help defray the medical costs associated with diseases caused by smoking or chewing tobacco. Many of the states,

however, used the largest percentage of the money to defray the costs of other programs rather than for its stated purposes. This is unfortunate because prevention programs and antismoking advertising do work. In Washington, where the lawsuit money was used for its intended purpose, the smoking rate dropped 12% in just four years. **Recent lawsuits have focused on secondhand smoke, smoking in public places, and false claims from tobacco companies about the greater safety of low-tar/low-nicotine cigarettes.** In an attempt to control medical costs, more and more companies are firing employees who smoke, after giving them a chance to quit and even paying for treatment.

AMPHETAMINES & METHAMPHETAMINES

Over the past few years there has been an **intense focus on amphetamine-type stimulants (ATSs)**, not just in the United States but throughout the world. An estimated **33 million people use ATSs worldwide** compared with half that number who use cocaine. Even though the actual numbers of users are low compared with marijuana, the impact on the environment, law enforcement, and treatment centers has been large.

In 2005 U.S. law enforcement agencies raided nearly 12,500 meth laboratories, many of them in the Midwest (e.g., Missouri, Iowa, and Indiana). This figure is down from 16,000 in 2004 due in part to a crackdown on precursor chemicals, particularly pseudoephedrine and ephedrine, much of it sold over the counter in drugstores. One reason for the explosive growth in the early 2000s was that street chemists had developed **newer, cheaper, somewhat safer, and more-effective ways of manufacturing illicit methamphetamines**. Sold in the past as "crank," "meth," and "speed," lately most of the seizures have been of "crystal meth," a more readily smokable form of the drug. One pound of meth, with an average purity of about 40%, sells for anywhere from $3,500 in California to $21,000 in the southeastern and northeastern regions of the country. Retail prices range from $400 to $3,000 per ounce (DEA, 2006).

A large number of the meth labs

were small, mom-and-pop stovetop operations called "user labs," but a significant portion of the manufacturing and wholesaling is done by Mexican trafficking organizations or independent gangs in Mexico and the United States. Methamphetamine is either manufactured in Mexico and smuggled into the United States, or the personnel and raw materials are supplied to set up meth labs in the United States, many in California. Because there are fewer restrictions in Mexico on **precursor chemicals like ephedrine and pseudoephedrine, drugs needed to manufacture speed**, the Mexican nationals have an advantage over the biker gangs and independents that used to manufacture most of the street meth in the 1960s and 1970s. International efforts to limit the availability of precursor chemicals have lowered the purity of street meth by half and have cut the number of major lab seizures.

A recent development has been the expansion by Asian crime organizations into Canada, particularly British Columbia. They are smuggling pseudoephedrine and ephedrine from other countries, setting up crystal meth laboratories, and smuggling the finished drug into the United States and even as far as Japan. Canada has also displaced Europe as the main supplier of ecstasy in the United States. The Royal Canadian Mounted Police have noted, however, that 70% of the ecstasy pills seized in Canada contained some quantity of crystal meth (Suo, 2006).

In a further attempt to limit the availability of ephedrine and pseudoephedrine, a number of states, including Hawaii, Idaho, Iowa, and Oregon, have **restricted OTC sales of cold medications containing these ingredients**. This has cut down on the number of small meth operations, but the larger organizations still provide the greatest percentage of the U.S. meth supply.

From 1993 to 2004, admissions to drug treatment facilities for amphetamines, mainly methamphetamines, rose from 21,000 to 151,000 (SAMHSA, 2006). Many prisons and treatment centers are being overwhelmed by the surge in methamphetamine abusers (Sanello, 2005).

In addition, methamphetamine

Jeff Sweetin, DEA special agent in charge of the Rocky Mountain Field Division, displays one of a number of Tickle Me Elmo® dolls that were used to smuggle coke and meth from Colorado to various locations in the United States.
Courtesy of the U.S. DEA Enforcement Division

abuse has spread to a number of other countries, including the Philippines and Thailand, where **small methamphetamine pills called "yaa baa" have become extremely popular**, particularly among young people. Much of the "yaa baa" is made in Myanmar and smuggled throughout Asia. In 2002 and 2003, the Thai government made a concerted effort to crush the "yaa baa" trade. Officials arrested 92,500 drug addicts, 43,000 dealers, and 756 producers/importers. About 2,500 others involved in the trade died under mysterious circumstances during the campaign. The number of drug cases that reached the courts dropped by half, but only time will tell if the reduction in arrests holds up particularly because the main manufacturers in Myanmar were untouched (Chouvy & Meissonnier, 2004). Exacerbating the problem is North Korea, which supplemented its opium growing with "yaa baa" manufacturing and smuggling, much of it to eastern Russia.

OTHER STIMULANTS

Human beings' desire for stimulation has historically involved tobacco, caffeine, betel nuts, khat, and a few other plant stimulants. In the twenty-first century, it is the **expansion of coffee outlets, caffeinated soft drinks, and most recently energy drinks that has been most remarkable**. The desire for caffeine in triple espressos and 20-ounce lattes is reflected in the more than 23,000 coffee shops and kiosks in operation, just in the United States, in 2007, with the numbers growing by the day. Starbucks, with 11,000 outlets

worldwide, is aiming toward 40,000 outlets over the next 10 years.

With names like Red Bull,® Rockstar,® Full Throttle,® and even Cocaine,® the explosion of energy drinks has been as dramatic as the growth of coffee purveyors. More than 200 new drinks entered the marketplace in 2006 alone. The drinks, laced with caffeine, sugar, vitamins, minerals, amino acids (e.g., taurine), herbs, and dietary supplements (e.g., ginseng and glucosamine), generated $3.7 billion in sales in 2006. They contain about twice the caffeine as an average cup of coffee and, coupled with the other ingredients, give a stronger buzz than coffee alone. In addition, many users consume 3, 4, and even 5 or more per day, often exaggerating the stimulatory effects, leading to jitteriness and extreme anxiety (Mason, 2006).

Even **the use of khat has expanded**. The leaves from this evergreen shrub (*Catha edulis*), native to eastern Africa and the Arabian Peninsula, are being smuggled into the United States in increasing amounts. In July 2006 federal prosecutors arrested 62 people involved in smuggling bundles of the plant (more than 25 tons) from Africa through Europe into immigrant communities in the United States (Operation Somalia Express, 2006). Cathinone, the active stimulant alkaloid in khat, can be as powerful as methamphetamine when purified from the leaf or synthesized in the laboratory (methcathinone).

PRESCRIPTION DRUG ABUSE

By 2006 several studies of U.S. drug-abuse trends reported that despite

TABLE 1-A PERCENTAGE OF TEENS WHO HAVE USED A NONPRESCRIBED SUBSTANCE

Marijuana	37%
Inhalants	19%
Vicodin® (hydrocodone)	18%
OxyContin® (oxycodone)	10%
Ritalin® or Adderall®	10%
Cough medicine (dextromethorphan [DXM])	10%
Cocaine or crack	9%
Ecstasy (MDMA)	9%
Methamphetamine	8%
LSD	6%
Ketamine	5%
Heroin	4%

(PATS, 2005B; Monitoring the Future, 2006)

a decrease in abuse of most street drugs, **there was an alarming increase in the abuse of prescription and over-the-counter medications especially by adolescents** (Center on Addictions and Substance Abuse [CASA], 2005; Partnership for a Drug Free America [PATS], 2005A; SAMHSA, 2006). This trend has been dubbed a **shift from the "Generation X" of the rave and club drug scene to "Generation Rx,"** cohorts who share and mix their diverted prescription and OTC drugs at "pharming parties" (Critser, 2005). Prescription drugs are now involved in 30% of all hospital emergency room deaths and 80% of drug mentions during an emergency room encounter (CASA, 2005).

Approximately 15 million to 17 million Americans now admit to abusing prescription drugs, doubling the number of a decade earlier. Abuse of prescriptions drugs has risen even more rapidly among teens, tripling during the same period. Teen abuse of prescription opioid pain medications increased more than 540% in the past few years alone (CASA, 2005). Abuse of prescription and OTC medications by teens now exceeds abuse levels for many of the media-hyped street drugs like ecstasy and methamphetamine (Critser, 2005). Adolescent abuse of prescription

sedatives like Valium® and Xanax® as well as prescription anabolic-androgenic steroids, or "roids," like Anadrol® and Equipoise® has also increased greatly in recent years (CASA, 2005).

A strong association between the abuse of street drugs and of alcohol has been noted in those teens who abuse prescription drugs. The 2004 Partnership Attitude Tracking Study found that teens who abused prescription drugs were 21 times more likely than those who didn't to abuse cocaine, 12 times more likely to do heroin, 5 times more likely to abuse marijuana, and twice as likely to use alcohol (CASA, 2005).

A number of reasons for the recent increase in prescription drug abuse have been suggested:

◇ **Increased airport and U.S. entry-point security** since 9/11 has slowed the influx of ecstasy and other club drugs (Leinwand, 2005).

◇ **The availability of abusable prescription drugs to adults** in the past decade has increased 150%, and the number of people abusing them has risen seven times faster than the U.S. population growth (CASA, 2005).

◇ **The tremendous increase in the availability of prescription drugs over the Internet** has enabled teens to sidestep normal precautions taken by pharmacies and physicians.

◇ Youth and adults gain access to these medications through "grazing"—raiding medication cabinets for controlled-substance prescriptions during visits to the homes of others.

◇ Increased prescribing of controlled substances to youth has resulted in greater diversion of these medications for abuse both by those who take them for nonmedical purposes and by the sharing of the medications with others.

◇ Increased awareness of the dangers of street drugs, drug-abuse prevention campaigns, ubiquitous television advertising of prescription drugs, and especially the Internet have made pharmaceuticals a seemingly safer and more attractive alternative for altering states of consciousness.

◇ Abusable prescription drugs are more reliable, more available, and more affordable than street drugs.

◇ A July 2005 survey conducted by the National Center on Addictions and Substance Abuse at Columbia University found that 75% of physicians and 50% of pharmacists had received no training since professional school in identifying prescription drug abuse or diversion of prescription drugs.

The most rapid increase in diversion of prescription drugs for abuse has occurred with prescription opioid pain medications like OxyContin® and Vicodin.®

◇ By 2004, 4.3 million teens (18%) had abused Vicodin® (hydrocodone) and 2.3 million had abused OxyContin® (oxycodone) at some time in their lives (PATS, 2005B).

◇ In 2005, 13% of people age 12 or older (almost 33 million Americans) had used prescription pain relievers nonmedically in their lifetime, 4.7 million in the past month (SAMHSA, 2006).

The continuing abuse of OxyContin® shows how a technological change can increase problems with an existing drug. OxyContin® is a time-release version of oxycodone, an opiate originally sold as Percodan.® Opiate addicts discovered that **the drug, when crushed, loses its time-release capabilities; and when swallowed or injected thereafter, it gives a powerful, almost heroin-like high.** A rash of pharmacy robberies, forged prescriptions, and overdoses caused the DEA to issue warnings. In response the manufacturer, Purdue Pharma, is developing new formulations that would decrease this form of abuse and is placing tracking labels on all wholesale shipments.

Hydrocodone (Vicodin,® Lortab,® Norco,® Anexsia,® Hycodan,® and Tylox®) is the most widely used and abused prescription opiate, a distinction that used to belong to codeine-based prescriptions. Hydrocodone causes less nausea but has the same pain-diminishing effect as well as the addictive potential of codeine. Since 1990 there has been a 500% increase in the number of emergency department visits due to hydrocodone. Because it is often co-formulated with acetaminophen, the abuse of the combination for the psychic effects of the opioid can cause liver damage from the acetaminophen.

A recent trend has been the increased abuse and diversion of prescription methadone, mostly in states (such as Oregon) where methadone is used extensively for pain control rather than exclusively for methadone maintenance; the number of methadone overdoses is approaching that of heroin.

BUPRENORPHINE

One of the more significant changes in drug treatment has been the trend to get general practitioners and other physicians more involved in the process. **The use of buprenorphine in a doctor's office rather than exclusively in a drug clinic is one such technique.** Buprenorphine is a drug that can block craving for heroin, OxyContin,® Vicodin,® and other opioids. When physicians prescribe buprenorphine, they are also supposed to direct the patient to a drug treatment facility or counselor for further help. This produces more treatment referrals by physicians. Special training is required for prescribing physicians. A minimum eight-hour course seems to be helpful, although some physicians are nervous about cross-reactions with HIV drugs and other medications (Sullivan, Tetrault, Bangalore, et al., 2006). Trials of buprenorphine in opioid-dependent adolescents found better results than treatment with clonidine. More patients were also likely to continue aftercare treatment with naltrexone, especially when the buprenorphine was combined with behavioral interventions (Marsch, Bickel, Badger, et al., 2005). Only time will tell if this expansion of treatment options proves successful.

ALCOHOL HANGS ON

Over the past few years, hard-liquor advertising has reappeared on television in the United States, emphasizing the way alcohol rises and falls in public favor. It is still widely used by every age group and in every country (except Muslim nations) in a variety of ways: as a food, to go with meals, for intoxication, for socialization, for rituals, and to self-medicate. It is ingrained in the social fabric of most cultures, but, unfortunately, in a percentage of the population it still leads to overuse, abuse, and dependence. Used separately or in combination with other psychoactive drugs, **alcohol still directly kills more than 75,000 people a year in the United States and 1.8 million worldwide** (WHO, 2005). An estimated **17.6 million Americans have an alcohol use disorder**; and though that figure is just 8.5% of the adult population, alcoholics make up 10% to 15% of those in hospitals and 10% to 20% of those in nursing homes (SAMHSA, 2006). Alcohol abuse costs the United States an estimated $185 billion per year in health and legal costs, absenteeism, and crime.

Research into the causes and the treatment of alcoholism and addiction in general has intensified in the past 10 years. The areas of focus include **genetic components of susceptibility, neurobiology of satiation, pharmacological interventions to reduce cravings, and refinement of treatment techniques** such as brief intervention and getting the primary physician more involved in diagnosing at-risk patients.

STEROIDS & SPORTS

In 2006 Floyd Landis tested positive for elevated levels of testosterone after his triumph in the Tour de France bicycle race. This was just the latest in a series of allegations and suspensions that has plagued professional bicycle racing (Pound, 2006).

A year earlier, on March 8, 2005, Major League Baseball stars Mark McGwire, Jose Canseco, Rafael Palmeiro, Curt Schilling, and Sammy Sosa, as well as baseball commissioner Allan H. (Bud) Selig and others, testified before Congress about the **increasing use of steroids, stimulants, and other performance-enhancing drugs in baseball**. In his tell-all book, Canseco admitted to using steroids when he played and said that the use of steroids, stimulants, and other drugs was rampant in baseball. Palmeiro, Schilling, and Sosa said that they had not used drugs, but subsequent events (including a positive test for Palmeiro) seemed to raise doubts about those assertions. As a result of previous problems and congressional threats, baseball updated its drug-testing policy to avoid federal legislation. The effectiveness of these new testing policies will have to be carefully evaluated. Football and basketball have their own policies, but continuing research and new compounds developed by unethical street chemists who are constantly looking for ways to bypass or fool drug-testing techniques and restrictions make enforcement difficult. The use of steroids has increased not only in professional and Olympic sports but also among high school athletes as much for improvements in physical appearance as for athletic performance enhancement. Attempts to alter the genetics of athletes through gene splicing has become a recent battleground in the search for an edge in athletic competition. Dick Pound of the World Anti-Doping Agency feels that this time science will stay ahead of scientific developments by perfecting a test for gene doping (Pound, 2006; Ruibal, 2006).

BEHAVIORAL ADDICTIONS (e.g., compulsive gambling, eating disorders, and Internet addictions)

"If I won all the money in the world, I'd have to move to a different world. If I won all the money in the world, there'd be no action, there'd be no game because there'd be no other players."
45-year-old compulsive gambler

At one point in 2006, there were at least 12 different Texas Holdem poker shows on television. Teenagers are having poker parties at their houses with their parents' blessing. If you type *online gambling* on an Internet search engine, you have a choice of more than 36 million sites. By 2007 the annual amount spent on online gambling was $18.7 billion. This newest growth in legalized gambling is in addition to the 48 states that sponsor or allow legalized lotteries, poker machines, and off-track betting and the 300-plus Indian casinos throughout the United States. Overseas, casino and online gambling are showing the same explosive growth (Schwartz, 2006). **Gambling is an addiction just as alcoholism and other drug abuse are addictions.** In fact, a study of MRI (magnetic resonance imaging) brain scans of gamblers showed that the areas of the brain activated by winning or losing are the same as those activated by cocaine. In addition, sweating and blood flow increase, and the heart rate goes up. In states where gambling is legal, 2.5 million people are classified as pathological gamblers, 3 million are considered problem gamblers, and another 15 million are at risk for problem gambling (National Opinion Research Center, 1999). In one study in Minnesota, 1% of the gamblers accounted for 50% of the wagers. In Illinois 10% of riverboat gamblers accounted for 80% of revenues (Grinols, 2004).

Other behavioral addictions that are similar to substance addictions are compulsive overeating, bulimia, anorexia, sexual addiction, Internet addiction, excessive TV watching, and even compulsive shopping. A recent study at Hammersmith Hospital in London that measured the release of dopamine found that playing video games doubled the release of dopamine in the brain.

Nielsen Media Research found that the average American spends 4.5 hours per day, or 1,555 hours per year, watching television; 974 hours per year listening to the radio; 195 hours using the Internet; 175 hours reading daily newspapers; 122 hours reading magazines; and 86 hours playing video games (Associated Press, 2006). That's 9.5 hours per day spent on various media—more hours than we spend working and certainly more than we spend talking to our spouse, children, or friends. The newest addiction is the cell phone and text messaging. Some users send 20 to 100 messages and/or calls per day.

A recent study of obesity found that, globally, as many people are overweight as are underweight. The obesity rates in Germany and Italy are higher than those in the United States. The health consequences of eating disorders are of a greater magnitude than many caused by substance abuse.

Besides genetic components, the environmental factors such as fast-food restaurants with high-fat/high-sugar foods, the growth of the Internet, shopping networks, easily accessible pornography, and the explosion of gambling establishments have greatly increased the opportunities to indulge these addictions.

COURT-REFERRED TREATMENT

Drug policy has shifted in the past 25 years from a heavy emphasis on supply reduction (legislation, raiding laboratories, and stopping drugs at the borders) to an **increased emphasis on demand reduction** (prevention, drug courts, and treatment on demand). For example, in 2000, 61% of Californian voters passed Proposition 36, which requires a treatment option for nonviolent drug users on their first and second offenses. In its second year, about 35,947 users entered treatment. The budget is around $120 million per year, but the state estimates that $250 million per year will be saved by keeping thousands out of jail. About one-third (34.4%) of offenders who had entered treatment through Prop 36 completed their treatment; another 8% were rated as satisfactory progress at discharge; and almost a third more (29.8%) received a "standard dose" of treatment, meaning they had spent the same amount of time in treatment as those who completed treatment. Thus 72.2% of those treated for substance abuse through California's Prop 36 legislation have been evaluated to have benefited from the experience. Results were proportional to matching people to the proper treatment, but those outcomes fared favorably with drug court outcomes in California that had a statewide 41.8% completion rate during the same time frame. Treatment funding allocations for Prop 36 expired on June 30, 2006, and law enforcement personnel feel that more accountability (making sure that users finish treatment) should be emphasized in the future. The treatment community feels that treatment periods should be expanded to include aftercare treatment, and funding for drug testing should be added to future allocations. It is encouraging to note that both law enforcement and substance-abuse treatment professionals are advocating the continuation of the treatment option for drug offenders in California (CSAM News, 2005; Longshore, Urada, Evans, et al., 2004).

About 40 states already use **drug courts, where a first-time offender can be diverted from jail time to treatment**. From the first one started in 1989 in Dade County, Florida, the number has grown to more than **1,600 drug courts nationwide** (National Association of Drug Court Professionals, 2005). There is controversy over a number of aspects of drug courts, but most agree that if they are successful, the savings to society (financially and socially) are significant. The recidivism rate (individuals who are rearrested after release) is 4% to 29% for those who complete a drug court program compared with 48% for those who do not participate. This direction in treatment is known as "coerced treatment" because many addicts would not have voluntarily entered treatment had it not been legally mandated. Coerced treatment has demonstrated better outcomes than voluntary treatment, according to David Deitch, director of the Pacific Southwest Addiction Technology Transfer Center at the University of California at San Diego.

CO-OCCURRING DISORDERS

In recent years there has been an **increased emphasis on recognizing and treating the high incidence of co-occurring disorders** (a substance-abuse disorder and a serious mental illness, or SMI). **About 23% of those with an SMI also have a substance-abuse or dependence disorder compared with only 8% of those without an SMI. Conversely, 19% of those with alcohol or drug dependence have an SMI** (SAMHSA, 2003). If one includes less serious mental illnesses, the incidence of co-occurring disorders greatly increases. The incidence of substance-abuse disorders also increases dramatically with the type of mental illness; those with a bipolar disorder have an incidence of co-occurring disorders approaching 75%. The Substance Abuse and Mental Health Services Administration is increasing the emphasis on not restricting funding to either substance abuse or mental health but rather creating an "'any door is the right door' treatment access policy" so that those with co-occurring disorders can find help for both of their conditions no matter where they enter the system.

"We're hoping to set the stage at the federal level with our blueprint to Congress to educate both public and private funders that co-occurring disorders is more of an expectation and not an exception in case loads, so we think this is very critical that we think about funding not being a barrier. I don't think the solution is just bringing all the funding together at the federal or state level. I do believe you need to continue to be able to keep track of and keep count of the dollars going into the drug and alcohol field and the mental health field, but that should not get in the way of coming up with various models of integrated financing at the provider level."
James Curie, administrator, Substance Abuse and Mental Health Services Administration

There is continuing concern about the overuse of psychiatric medications, especially among children. The federal Food and Drug Administration has suggested suicide warnings on a number of medications even though the actual incidence is extremely small. Warnings that antidepressants, such as Celexa,® Paxil,® Prozac,® Wellbutrin,® and Zoloft,® can increase suicidal behavior in children commenced in 2005. The larger concern is the possibility that dependence on psychiatric medications to handle so many personality traits may limit the amount of behavioral training that is available for such cases.

CONCLUSIONS

Looking at the span of history and the influence of psychoactive drugs and compulsive behaviors on every culture, one is struck by the variety of ways that **abuse and addiction have altered governmental policies, created new social structures, and hijacked personal priorities**. Current research is examining and imaging brain structure and chemistry to find answers. Other research is examining the possibilities of manipulating the genetic components of addiction. Some historians have suggested that **the drive to alter states of consciousness is as essential to human nature as the drive to survive and procreate** (Siegel, 1982). This concept is possible if one understands that the use of psychoactive substances can create a drive or compulsion to continue using that supersedes many survival instincts. Botanical, pharmacological, and technological advances along with improved delivery methods have increased the concentration of these drugs such that they overwhelm the brain's ability to rebalance itself. It is crucial not only to continue this neurochemical research but also to refine various treatment methods such as motivational interviewing, stages of change, and behavioral modification to decrease the burden that drug and behavioral abuse and dependence place on society.

CLASSIFICATION OF PSYCHOACTIVE DRUGS

WHAT IS A PSYCHOACTIVE DRUG?

◇ In ancient Egypt the pharaoh Ramses might have defined a psychoactive drug as the beer he gave his pyramid workers to keep them happy.

◇ A poisoned Frenchman in the Middle Ages could have defined it as the infected rye grain (ergot) he accidentally ate.

◇ About A.D. 1550 Spanish conquistadors in Peru would have defined it as the coca leaves they gave to the native laborers to keep them working in the silver mines.

◇ A wounded soldier in the U.S. Civil War might say it was the injection of morphine that relieved his pain and caused euphoria.

◇ A pilot in World War II would have defined it as the amphetamine the medic gave him to stay awake on a night bombing run.

◇ In the 1990s an AIDS patient might define a psychoactive drug as a joint of marijuana that controls nausea.

◇ A law enforcement officer might define a psychoactive drug by its legal classification as a Schedule I, II, III, or IV substance whose illegal use and sale carry legal penalties.

◇ A member of Gamblers Anonymous might define a psychoactive drug metaphorically as a video poker machine available at the local tavern.

◇ A compulsive overeater might define a psychoactive drug as a quart of Ben & Jerry's Cherry Garcia® ice cream.

"A psychoactive drug is any substance that when injected into a rat gives rise to a scientific paper."
Darryl Inaba, Pharm.D.

Each culture, each generation, each profession, and particularly each user has a definition of what constitutes a psychoactive drug. To complicate matters, most people who take psychoactive drugs on a regular basis use more than one substance.

DEFINITION

Our definition of **a psychoactive drug is any substance that directly alters the normal functioning of the central nervous system**. As the understanding of addictive brain processes increases, this definition might be expanded to include **any behaviors (e.g., gambling) that directly activate the brain's alcohol and drug addiction pathways**. Today there are more psychoactive drugs to choose from than at any time in history. Modern transportation; a more open society; the ability to purchase drugs over the Internet; greater financial incentives for drug

A drug such as marijuana can be examined theoretically as a molecule (a), under magnification as an exotic plant (b), or sociologically as a source of financing for insurgencies (c).

Molecular graphic image produced using the MidasPlus® package from the Computer Graphics Laboratory, University of California at San Francisco (supported by NIH P41 RR-01081). Microphotograph of a marijuana bud courtesy of the U.S. Drug Enforcement Administration. Uzbekistan marijuana field. © 1990 Alain Labrousse.

"blunts," "chronic," and "bammer" for marijuana; "boulya," "24/7," and "beamers" for crack cocaine; ecstasy and "E" for MDMA; and "chiva," "H," and "shit" for heroin evolve almost daily among drug users. Each commonly used and abused substance may have 20 or more informal names. Just as confusing is the continued synthesis of newer psychoactive drugs with **chemical names** such as methylenedioxymethamphetamine (MDMA) and 4-bromo 2,5 dimethoxyphenethylamine (2CB). **Trade names** such as Zoloft® instead of its chemical name sertraline, or OxyContin® instead of oxycodone, further confuse the issue of how to refer to psychoactive drugs.

CLASSIFICATION BY EFFECTS

A more practical way to classify these substances is by their *overall effects.* Thus the terms **"uppers" for stimulants, "downers" for depressants, and "all arounders" for psychedelics** have been chosen to describe the most commonly abused psychoactive drugs. Then there are other drugs that don't fit neatly into one of these categories but that can be defined by their *purpose,* such as performance-enhancing **sports drugs, inhalants, and psychiatric medications**.

Disclaimer warning: *Because drug effects depend on amount, frequency, and duration of use as well as the makeup of the user and the setting in which the drug is taken, reactions to psychoactive substances can vary radically from person to person and even from dose to dose. The information herein about the action of drugs on the body should be used only as general guidelines and not absolutes. It should not in any way be construed as medical advice.*

MAJOR DRUGS

UPPERS (STIMULANTS)

Uppers, or CNS stimulants, include **cocaine** (freebase, crack), **amphetamines** (Adderall,® meth, "crystal meth," speed, "crank," "ice"), **amphetamine congeners** (Ritalin,® diet pills),

dealing; easy access to legal psychoactive drugs like tobacco, alcohol, caffeine, and prescription medications; and new refinement and synthesis techniques—all have come together to increase the availability of these chemicals to all strata of society.

CHEMICAL, TRADE & STREET NAMES

The difficulty categorizing psychoactive drugs is that they have chemical names, trade names, and street names. For example, **street names** like

plant stimulants (khat, betel nuts, ephedra, yohimbe), **look-alike stimulants, caffeine, and nicotine.**

Physical Effects

The usual effect of a small-to-moderate dose is excessive **stimulation of the central nervous system**, creating insomnia, energized muscles, increased heart rate and blood pressure, and decreased appetite. Frequent use of the stronger stimulants (cocaine and amphetamines) over a period of a few days will deplete the body's energy chemicals and exhaust the user. If large amounts are used or if the user is extrasensitive, heart, blood vessel, and seizure problems can occur. Although tobacco is a comparatively weak stimulant, its long-term health effects can be dangerous (e.g., cancer, emphysema, and heart disease).

Mental/Emotional Effects

A small-to-moderate dose of the stronger stimulants can make someone **feel more confident**, excited, outgoing, and eager to perform. It can also **cause a certain rush** or an ecstatic feeling, depending on the specific drug and the physiology of the user. Larger doses can cause **jitteriness, anxiety, anger,** rapid speech, and aggressiveness. Prolonged use of the stronger stimulants can cause extreme anxiety, **paranoia,** anhedonia (inability to experience pleasure), and mental confusion. Overuse of strong stimulants can even mimic a **psychosis.**

DOWNERS (depressants)

Downers, or CNS depressants, are divided into four main categories:

◇ **Opiates and opioids**: opium, morphine, codeine, heroin, oxycodone (OxyContin®), hydrocodone (Vicodin®), methadone, hydromorphone (Dilaudid®), meperidine (Demerol®), propoxyphene (Darvon®), and buprenorphine (Subutex® and Suboxone®).

◇ **Sedative-hypnotics**: benzodiazepines such as alprazolam (Xanax®), diazepam (Valium®), clonazepam (Klonopin®), and flunitrazepam (Rohypnol®); Z-hypnotics such as zolpidem (Ambien®); barbi-turates such as butalbital, and meprobamate (Miltown®).

◇ **Alcohol**: beer, wine, and hard liquors.

◇ **Others**: antihistamines, skeletal muscle relaxants, look-alike sedatives, and bromides.

Physical Effects

Small doses of downers **depress the central nervous system,** which slows heart rate and respiration, relaxes muscles, decreases coordination, induces sleep, dulls the senses, and, most important especially with opiates and opioids, **diminishes pain**. Opiates and opioids can also cause constipation, so they are used to control diarrhea. They can also cause nausea and pinpoint pupils. Excessive drinking or sedative-hypnotic use can slur speech and cause digestive problems. Sedative-hypnotics and alcohol in large doses or in combination with other depressants **can cause dangerous respiratory depression** and coma. High-dose or prolonged use of any depressant can cause sexual dysfunction and tissue dependence.

Mental/Emotional Effects

Initially, small doses (particularly with alcohol) seem to act like stimulants because **they lower inhibitions, thus inducing freer behavior**. But as more of the drug is taken, the overall depressant effect begins to dominate, relaxing and dulling the mind, diminishing anxiety, and controlling some neuroses. Certain downers can also **induce euphoria** or a sense of well-being. Long-term use of any depressant can **cause psychological as well as physical dependence.**

ALL AROUNDERS (psychedelics)

All arounders—hallucinogens or psychedelics—are substances that can distort perceptions and induce illusions, delusions, or hallucinations. There are five classifications for psychedelics:

◇ Ergots/indoles: **LSD, psilocybin mushrooms,** ayahuasca, and DMT.

◇ Phenylalkylamines: **peyote (mescaline), ibogaine, MDMA** (ecstasy), MDA, and 2CB. (MDMA, MDA, and 2CB are also referred to as *psychostimulants* or *entactogens.*)

◇ Cannabinoids: **marijuana** and hashish.

◇ Others: **ketamine, PCP,** *Salvia Divinorum,* dextromethorphan, nutmeg, and *Amanita* mushrooms.

Physical Effects

Most hallucinogenic plants, particularly cacti and some mushrooms, **cause nausea and dizziness.** Marijuana increases appetite and makes the eyes bloodshot. LSD raises the blood pressure and causes sweating. **MDMA and even LSD act like stimulants.** Generally (except for PCP and ketamine, which act as anesthetics), the physical effects are not as dominant as the mental effects in this class of substances.

Mental/Emotional Effects

Most often psychedelics **distort sensory messages** to and from the brainstem—the sensory switchboard for the mind—so many external stimuli, particularly the visual, tactile, and auditory ones, are intensified or altered (**illusions**). This process is also called *synesthesia,* where the brain causes sounds to become visual and sight to be perceived as sound. The brain can also trigger imaginary sensory messages (**hallucinations**) along with distorted thinking (**delusions**).

OTHER DRUGS & ADDICTIONS

There are three other groups of drugs that can stimulate, depress, or confuse the user: inhalants, anabolic steroids and other sports drugs, and psychiatric medications.

INHALANTS (deliriants)

Inhalants are gaseous or liquid substances that are inhaled and absorbed through the lungs. They include **organic solvents,** such as glue, gasoline, metallic paints, gasoline additives (STP®), and household sprays; **volatile nitrites,** such as amyl, butyl, or cyclohexyl nitrite (also called "poppers");

and **anesthetics**, especially nitrous oxide ("laughing gas").

Physical Effects

Most often there is **CNS depression**. Dizziness, slurred speech, unsteady gait, and drowsiness are seen early on. Some inhalants **lower blood pressure**, causing the user to faint or lose balance. Because they are depressants, they can cause drowsiness, stupor, coma, and asphyxiation. The organic solvents can be quite **toxic to cells** in the lung, brain, liver, kidney tissues, and even blood.

Mental/Emotional Effects

With small amounts **impulsiveness, excitement, mental confusion, and irritability** are common. Some inhalants cause a rush through a variety of mechanisms. Larger amounts can cause **delirium and hallucinations**.

ANABOLIC STEROIDS & OTHER SPORTS DRUGS

Anabolic-androgenic steroids are the most common **performance-enhancing drugs**. Others include stimulants (e.g., amphetamines, ephedrine, and caffeine), human growth hormone (HGH), human chorionic gonadotropin (hCG), herbal/nutritional supplements (e.g., creatine and androstenedione), and some therapeutic drugs (e.g., painkillers, beta blockers, and diuretics).

Physical Effects

Anabolic steroids **increase muscle mass and strength**. Prolonged use can cause acne, high blood pressure, shrunken testes, and masculinization in women.

Mental/Emotional Effects

Anabolic steroids often cause a **stimulant-like high, increased confidence, and increased aggression**. Prolonged large-dose use can be accompanied by outbursts of anger known as "roid rage."

PSYCHIATRIC MEDICATIONS

Psychiatric medications are used by psychiatrists and others in an expanding field known as *psychopharmacology* to try to **rebalance irregular brain chem-**

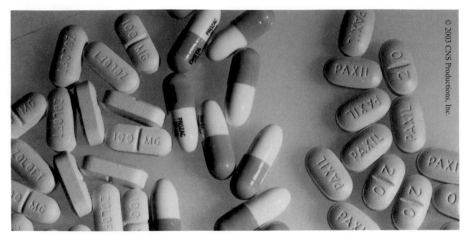

Over the past few years, the number of available psychiatric drugs has increased. The most popular have been the new SSRIs such as Zoloft,® Prozac,® and Paxil.®
© 2003 CNS Productions, Inc.

istry that has caused mental problems, drug addiction, and other compulsive disorders. The most common are **antidepressants** (e.g., Tofranil,® Prozac,® Luvox,® and Zoloft®), **antipsychotics** (e.g., Abilify,® Resperidol,® and Zyprexa®), mood stabilizers (e.g. lithium, Depakote,® and Seroquel®) and **antianxiety** drugs (e.g., Xanax® and BuSpar®) including panic disorder drugs (e.g., Inderal®). These drugs are being prescribed more and more frequently despite the fact that the national incidence of the disorders has remained fairly constant over the past 30 years.

Physical Effects

Psychiatric medications are accompanied by a **wide variety of physical side effects**, particularly on the heart, blood, and skeleto-muscular systems, but their mental and emotional effects are the most important. Side effects, adverse reactions, and toxic effects are especially severe with antipsychotic drugs (also called *neuroleptic drugs*).

Mental/Emotional Effects

Antidepressants counteract depression by manipulating brain chemicals (e.g., serotonin) that **elevate mood**. Antipsychotics manipulate dopamine to **control schizophrenic mood swings and hallucinations**. The mood stabilizers are thought to manipulate glutamate and GABA. Antianxiety drugs also manipulate brain chemicals, such as GABA, to **inhibit anxiety-producing thoughts**.

COMPULSIVE BEHAVIORS

Behaviors such as **eating disorders** (compulsive overeating, anorexia, and bulimia), **compulsive gambling, sexual compulsion, Internet addiction, compulsive shopping, and even codependency** affect many of the same areas of the brain that are affected by the compulsive use of psychoactive drugs.

Physical Effects

The major physical effects of compulsive behaviors are generally confined to **neurological and chemical changes in the brain's reward pathway**. The exception is eating disorders, when excessive or extremely limited food intake can lead to cardiovascular problems, diabetes, nutritional diseases, and obesity.

Mental/Emotional Effects

The development of tolerance, psychological dependence, and even withdrawal symptoms exists with compulsive behaviors as with substance abuse and addiction. The compulsion to gamble or overeat is every bit **as strong as drug-seeking behavior**.

CONTROLLED SUBSTANCES ACT OF 1970

The Comprehensive Drug Abuse Prevention and Control Act of 1970, better known as the Controlled Substances Act, was enacted to **reduce the burgeoning availability and abuse of psychoactive drugs** that occurred in the 1960s in the United States. The act consolidated and updated most drug laws that had been passed in the twentieth century. The **Drug Enforcement Administration** was made responsible for enforcing the provisions of the legislation. The key provisions were to classify all psychoactive drugs; to control their manufacture, sale, and use; to limit imports and exports; and to define criminal penalties. Five levels, or schedules, were defined based on a drug's abuse liability, its value as a medication, its history of use and abuse, the risk to public health, and, in a few cases, political considerations.

◇ Schedule I includes heroin, LSD, marijuana, peyote, psilocybin, mescaline, and MDMA. These drugs have a high abuse potential and supposedly no accepted medical use.

◇ Schedule II substances have a high abuse potential with severe psychological or physical dependence liability even though they have medical uses. These include cocaine, methamphetamine, opium, morphine, hydromorphone, codeine, meperidine, oxycodone, and methylphenidate (Ritalin®).

◇ Schedule III substances have less abuse potential and include Schedule II drugs when used in compounds with other drugs. Schedule III drugs include Tylenol®

with codeine, some barbiturate compounds, and paregoric.

◇ Schedule IV drugs have even less abuse potential and include chloral hydrate, meprobamate, fenfluramine, diazepam (Valium®) and the other benzodiazepines, and phenobarbital.

◇ Schedule V substances have very low abuse potential because they contain very limited quantities of narcotic and stimulant drugs. Examples of Schedule V drugs are Robitussin AC® and Lomotil.® Some of these drugs are sold over the counter.

The 1970 act also scheduled and controlled immediate chemical precurors to the listed drugs.

CHAPTER SUMMARY

INTRODUCTION

1. Psychoactive drugs and drug-seeking behaviors have always been extremely influential in all aspects of human endeavors. Current problems regarding psychoactive drugs and compulsive behaviors include medical marijuana, the growth of methamphetamine use, steroid use in professional sports, and the growth of gambling and online addictions. And though some of the problems are unique to the modern age, historically five themes have affected the use and the abuse of these substances:

◇ the basic need of human beings to cope with their environment;

◇ a brain chemistry that can be affected by certain substances and mental illnesses to induce an altered state of consciousness;

◇ the involvement of ruling classes, governments, and businesses in growing, manufacturing, distributing, taxing, and prohibiting drugs;

◇ technological advances in refining and synthesizing drugs;

◇ the development of faster and more efficient methods of putting drugs into the body.

HISTORY OF PSYCHOACTIVE DRUGS

Prehistory & the Neolithic Period (8500–4000 B.C.)

2. More than 4,000 plants yield psychoactive substances. Their use dates back 50,000 years or more.

3. Psychoactive drugs have been used throughout history as a shortcut to an altered consciousness, to relieve pain, and for spiritual rituals.

Ancient Civilizations (4000 B.C.–A.D. 400)

4. Drugs and methods of use gradually spread as contact among different cultures increased.

5. Alcohol (beer and wine), opium, *Cannabis,* peyote cacti, psychedelic mushrooms, coca, and tobacco were the earliest psychoactive drugs employed by ancient civilizations.

6. Alcohol was considered a gift from the gods; it was used as a food, a reward, and a medicine and

for sacred or shamanic rituals. It is often mentioned in the Bible with warnings about overindulgence.

7. Opium has been used to stop pain, control diarrhea, suppress coughs, lessen anxiety, promote sleep, and induce euphoria.

8. *Cannabis* was used in China and India as a medicine, a food, a fiber, and a euphoriant.

9. *Amanita* mushrooms were used in Asia and Mesoamerica for visions and sacred ceremonies.

10. The peyote and San Pedro cacti (mescaline), the coca leaf (cocaine), the *Psilocybe* mushroom (psilocybin), and tobacco (nicotine) were used in Mesoamerica before the birth of Christ, and that use continues to this day. Other stimulant alkaloids from plants include betel nut, coffee, khat, and ephedra.

Middle Ages (400–1400)

11. Psychedelic plants from the nightshade family (e.g., datura, belladonna, henbane, and mandrake) were employed in religious, magic, or social ceremonies throughout history and especially in the

Middle Ages. Their active ingredients include scopolamine and atropine.

12. Psychedelic mold on infected rye plants (which produced LSD-like symptoms) caused ergot poisonings in the Middle Ages and beyond.

13. A psychoactive substance can be a medicine, a drug, and a poison, depending on the dose. Sometimes it can be a food or drink.

14. The advent of distillation increased the alcoholic content of beverages through evaporation and condensation. Before distillation about 14% alcohol was the strongest alcohol available.

15. In many Islamic countries, tobacco, hashish, and especially coffee were employed as substitutes for alcohol, which is forbidden by the Qur'an, the holy book of Islam.

16. The use of coffee and tea spread to Europe and became extremely popular. Sixty other plants contain caffeine.

17. The coca leaf, peyote cactus, and the *Psilocybe* mushroom were used in the Americas in pre-Columbian times, mostly by the ruling classes.

Renaissance & the Age of Discovery (1400–1700)

18. Exploration, trade, and colonization by European explorers brought various drugs to Europe and carried European drugs, principally alcohol and the newly discovered tobacco, to other peoples.

19. Laws limiting alcohol use, as well as taxes for use, were tried in most countries, but the medicinal and recreational uses along with high tax revenues were so widespread that the laws often failed.

20. In South America, Spanish conquistadors defeated the Incas and took control of coca leaf production. They grew it for profit, to pay workers, and to stimulate the peasants to work longer in the silver mines.

21. Tobacco, which was used in the Americas as a medicine, for rituals, and to induce trancelike states, was introduced to Europe and back to the colonized Americas in the 1500s. Tobacco and hemp production helped support many colonies.

22. Coffeehouses and afternoon tea rituals helped spread the popularity of coffee and tea drinking.

23. Opium was used as a cure-all throughout history. Scientists and physicians such as Galen in the second century, Avicenna in the eleventh century, and Paracelsus in the sixteenth century introduced theriac and laudanum to succeeding generations.

Age of Enlightenment & the Early Industrial Revolution (1700–1900)

24. New refinement techniques and new methods of use were developed.

25. Consumption of distilled liquors like rum, gin, and whiskey increased alcohol abuse, sometimes to epidemic proportions as in the Gin Epidemic in London (1710–1750). Consumption had been encouraged and then discouraged by the British Parliament.

26. The American Revolution was supported by the export of and taxes on tobacco (Virginia leaf mostly), hemp (textile/rope industry), and rum.

27. In the nineteenth century, nitrous oxide ("laughing gas"), an anesthetic, was used at inhalant parties as an intoxicant. Other anesthetics that came into use were chloroform and ether. Later hydrocarbon distillates were also inhaled.

28. The refinement of morphine from opium (1804) and heroin from morphine (1874) along with the invention of the hypodermic needle (1855) and the widespread use of morphine in wartime to control pain expanded the addictive use of opiates.

29. The Opium Wars between England and China in the early to mid-1800s were fought for the right of the British (actually, the East India Trading Company) to sell opium to China (under the Manchus) to improve the British balance of trade. Other European powers also took part.

30. In the second half of the nineteenth century, the refinement of cocaine from coca, its use as a topical anesthetic, the popularization of cocaine by Freud, and the manufacture of stimulant wines (such as Vin Mariani) led to the first cocaine epidemic.

31. The Temperance movement, begun in the eighteenth century by Dr. Benjamin Rush and others in the United States, led to state prohibition laws and temperance societies.

32. Patent medicines at the turn of the twentieth century frequently contained opium, cocaine, and alcohol as their active ingredients. Overprescribing by physicians, usually to women, often led to abuse (iatrogenic addiction).

Twentieth Century

33. Cigarettes gradually replaced cigars and chewing tobacco as the most popular method of nicotine consumption due to automatic cigarette-rolling machines, advertising, a milder strain of tobacco, and plentiful supplies. Women, young people, soldiers, and dieters were often targeted. Use (and taxes) increased through the first half of the century and then began to decline following public health campaigns and legal restrictions.

34. The Pure Food and Drug Act (1906), the Opium Exclusion Act (1909), and the Harrison Narcotic Act (1914) were passed to control opiates and cocaine. Racial biases often influenced legislation.

35. The Eighteenth Amendment (alcohol prohibition) and the supporting Volstead Act lasted from 1920 to 1933. They helped create the multibillion-dollar illegal drug business. The widespread abuse of alcohol encouraged the creation of Alcoholics Anonymous (AA) in 1934, the most successful drug treatment program in history.

36. Marijuana smoking was banned in 1937 by the Marijuana Tax Act.

Marijuana became a symbol of the beat generation in the 1950s and the hippie generation in the 1960s. The sinsemilla growing technique increased the psychoactive properties of marijuana starting in the 1970s.

37. Amphetamines, first popularized in the 1930s as a decongestant, were used by soldiers on both sides in World War II to fight fatigue. They were used and abused as diet drugs in the 1950s and 1960s. Methamphetamines such as "crank," "crystal," and "ice" became the drugs of choice.

38. Anabolic steroids and other performance-enhancing drugs (stimulants) became widely used in the Olympics and other sports competitions due to the Cold War and the large amounts of money involved in winning. Drug testing by the International Olympic Committee and the National Collegiate Athletic Association curbed many of the abuses.

39. Sedative-hypnotics and tranquilizers started with bromides and barbiturates and switched to Miltown® and benzodiazepines, such as Valium® and Xanax,® in the 1950s and 1960s. Because brain chemical imbalances cause most mental illnesses, psychiatric medications, including antipsychotics, antianxiety drugs, mood stabilizers, and antidepressants (SSRIs) that manipulated brain chemistry, became common in the 1950s and their use has continued to grow. Drugs were also developed to aid in detoxification, abstinence, and recovery.

40. LSD (found in the ergot fungus and synthesized) and other hallucinogenic drugs, especially designer psychedelics and psychostimulants, including MDA, DMT, and MDMA, were developed in the 1940s and their use exploded in the 1960s.

41. Supply reduction, demand reduction, and harm reduction were attempted to limit the growth of illegal and legal drugs. Treatment of addiction became a medical as well as a social science.

42. Methadone maintenance was developed as a harm-reduction technique to control heroin use by substituting a legal slow-acting opiate for an illegal one. The Vietnam War expanded heroin use although not as much as experts thought it would.

43. Regular cocaine use and smokable cocaine (freebase, crack) use became popular in the late 1970s and 1980s. A few years later, a smokable form of methamphetamine, called "ice" or "crystal meth," became popular.

44. Sexually transmitted diseases and contaminated-needle diseases, especially HIV/AIDS and hepatitis C, became endemic in the drug-using community. Besides dirty needles, drug-induced high-risk sexual practices encouraged the spread.

Today & Tomorrow

45. Worldwide, 76 million people have an alcohol use disorder, 180 million abuse illicit drugs, 1 billion use tobacco, and 160 million smoke marijuana; all of this use is the primary contributor to at least 72 major medical illnesses, filling our hospitals.

46. The geopolitics of drugs has seen countries corrupted and revolutions supported by the sale of heroin and cocaine. Afghani, Mexican tar, Colombian white, and China white heroin have flooded the world market. Afghanistan grows 90% of the world's illicit opium. The Cold War as well as recent conflicts made countries turn a blind eye to drug trafficking as a way to finance revolutions and civil wars. The amount of cocaine and heroin entering the United States has risen, thus forcing the price down.

47. Worldwide 40 million people are living with HIV/AIDS infections; 25 million have died since 1980. Hepatitis C has reached epidemic proportions, with 4 million infected in the United States, most from IV drug use with infected needles.

48. The rave clubs and music parties of the 2000s are the latest version of the psychedelic clubs of the sixties and seventies. LSD, methamphetamine, nitrous oxide, and marijuana are still around, but MDA is now MDMA, Quaaludes® are GHB, and live acid-rock bands are technorave and rap DVDs and CDs played by club disc jockeys.

49. The big battles in the 2000s over *Cannabis* concern the legalization of medical marijuana sold through *Cannabis* clubs. Marijuana use has remained fairly constant, although the potency of commonly available "pot" has greatly increased due to sinsemilla cultivation techniques.

50. Worldwide many countries and their health agencies have become involved in smoking prevention. Tobacco remains the target of many class-action lawsuits. Smoking in the United States has declined, although marketing pushes by tobacco companies have increased smoking throughout the world. Lung cancer deaths among women have increased due to increased smoking.

51. The use of amphetamine-type stimulants has exploded worldwide, with a user population of more than 33 million. Newer methods of manufacturing methamphetamine have increased the availability of the drug, particularly crystal meth. Recent limitations of precursor drugs have had some effect on the availability, but Mexican gangs are still the main suppliers to the United States. Treatment for methamphetamine dependence has increased U.S. hospital admissions seven-fold in the past 12 years. Meth use is also exploding in Asia in a form called "yaa baa."

52. Other stimulants that have grown in popularity are coffee, fueled by an explosion of coffee shops and kiosks; energy drinks filled with caffeine, herbs, amino acids, and vitamins; and khat, a plant stimulant popular in eastern Africa and the Arabian Peninsula.

53. Prescription drug abuse has shown an alarming increase in the 2000s

especially by adolescents ("Generation Rx"). Abused drugs include painkillers and sedative hypnotics. The painkiller OxyContin,® a time-release opioid, has been abused since its release, when addicts learned to crush the tablets for a heroin-like high. Hydrocodone (Vicodin®) is the most widely abused prescription opioid.

54. Buprenorphine is being used in treatment centers and doctors' offices to treat heroin, OxyContin,® hydrocodone, and other opioid addiction.

55. Alcohol remains the number one drug problem in most of the world, responsible for 1.8 million deaths per year. More than 17.6 million Americans have a drinking problem.

56. The increasing use of steroids, stimulants, and other performance-enhancing drugs in the Olympics, baseball, professional cycling, and other sports has led to more stringent controls and sophisticated testing methods.

57. There is growing recognition that behavioral addictions, such as eating disorders, compulsive gambling, Internet addiction, sexual addiction, television addiction, and even compulsive shopping, are very similar to drug addictions in the way they affect the reward/reinforcement pathway of the brain.

58. Drug policy has shifted from supply reduction to demand reduction. Drug courts and laws like California's Proposition 36, which mandates the availability of treatment to nonviolent drug offenders, has the support of the public and the drug treatment community.

59. There is increased emphasis on recognizing and treating the high incidence of co-occurring disorders instead of focusing on just the addiction or just the mental illness.

Conclusions

60. Abuse and addiction have altered government policies, created new social structures, and hijacked personal priorities. The drive to alter one's state of consciousness seems an essential drive in human beings.

CLASSIFICATION OF PSYCHOACTIVE DRUGS

What Is a Psychoactive Drug?

61. Although people define psychoactive substances in a variety of ways, our definition is *a psychoactive drug is any substance that directly alters the normal functioning of the central nervous system.*

62. A psychoactive drug can be called by its chemical name, trade name, or street name.

63. Drugs can be classified by their effects: uppers (stimulants), downers (depressants), and all arounders (psychedelics). The other psychoactive drug groups can be defined by their purpose; these are inhalants, anabolic steroids and other sports drugs, and psychiatric medications.

Major Drugs

64. Uppers include cocaine, amphetamines, diet pills, and the plant stimulants (e.g., khat, betel nuts, caffeine, and tobacco). Major effects are increased energy, feelings of confidence, raised heart rate and blood pressure, and euphoria with stronger stimulants. Overuse can cause jitteriness, anger, depletion of energy, anhedonia (lack of ability to feel pleasure), and paranoia, along with damage to the heart, lungs, and blood vessels.

65. Downers include opiates and opioids (e.g., heroin and codeine), sedative-hypnotics (e.g., benzodiazepines and barbiturates), and alcohol (beer, wine, and distilled liquor). These drugs depress circulatory, respiratory, and muscular systems. The stronger opiates and sedative-hypnotics can initially cause euphoria. Prolonged use can cause health problems and dependence. Other downers include antihistamines, skeletal muscle relaxants, look-alike sedatives, and bromides.

66. All arounders include marijuana, LSD, MDMA (ecstasy), PCP, psilocybin mushrooms, and peyote. Major mental effects are illusions, hallucinations, delusions, and confused sensations. Physically, many psychedelics cause stimulation, but marijuana usually causes relaxation.

Other Drugs & Addictions

67. Other psychoactive drugs include:
    ◇ inhalants, which are depressants that also cause dizziness and delirium accompanied by confusion;
    ◇ anabolic steroids and other sports drugs, which are used to enhance performance through muscle growth or increased endurance;
    ◇ psychiatric drugs, which help rebalance brain chemistry disrupted by mental illness (e.g., antipsychotics and antianxiety drugs).

68. Certain compulsive behaviors, including overeating, anorexia, bulimia, gambling, sexual compulsion, Internet addiction, compulsive shopping, and even codependency, cause neurological and chemical changes in much the same way as drug addictions.

Controlled Substances Act of 1970

69. The Comprehensive Drug Abuse Prevention and Control Act of 1970 (Controlled Substances Act of 1970) was enacted to limit the availability, use, and abuse of psychoactive substances. Through the Drug Enforcement Administration (DEA), the act categorized dangerous substances into five schedules. Schedules I and II include the major psychoactive drugs (e.g., heroin, cocaine, marijuana, and methamphetamine—drugs with a high abuse potential) and define criminal penalties for possession, intent to sell, and use. The act also controls the availability of precursors.

REFERENCES

Abel, E. L. (2001). The Gin Epidemic: Much Ado About What? *Alcohol & Alcoholism, 36*(5), 401–5.

Acker, C. J. (1995). Opioids and opioid control: History. In J. H. Jaffe, ed. *Encyclopedia of Drugs and Alcohol* (Vol. II, pp. 763–69). New York: Simon & Shuster Macmillan.

Acosta, J. (1588). *Historia Natural y Moral de las Indias.* English translation by C. R. Markham. London: Hakluyt Society, 1880.

Agnew, L. R. (1968). On blowing one's mind (19th century style). *JAMA, 204*(1), 61–62.

Alcoholics Anonymous. (1934, 1976). *Alcoholics Anonymous.* New York: Alcoholics Anonymous World Services, Inc.

Alcoholics Anonymous World Service. (2006). *Estimates of AA Groups and Members.* http://www.aa.org/en_media_resources.cfm?PageID=74 (accessed November 28, 2006).

Aldrich, M. R. (1977). Tantric cannabis use in India. *Journal of Psychoactive Drugs, 9*(3), 227–33.

Aldrich, M. R. (1994). Historical notes on women addicts. *Journal of Psychoactive Drugs, 26*(1), 61–64.

Aldrich, M. R. (1997). History of therapeutic cannabis. In M. L. Mathre, ed. *Cannabis in Medical Practice.* Jefferson, NC: McFarland & Company, Inc.

Armstrong, D. & Armstrong, E. M. (1991). *The Great American Medicine Show.* New York: Prentice Hall.

Associated Press. (2006). If we could take your attention away from the TV for a moment. *Medford Mail Tribune,* p. 7C.

Austin, G. A. (1979). *Perspectives on the History of Psychoactive Substance Use.* DHEW Publication No. (ADM), 79–81.

Australian Drug Foundation. (1999). *The history of drug use in sport.* http://www.adf.org.au/archive/asda/history.html (accessed December 4, 2005).

Benowitz, N. & Fredericks, A. (1995). History of tobacco use. In J. H. Jaffe, ed. *Encyclopedia of Drugs and Alcohol* (Vol. III, pp. 1032–36). New York: Simon & Schuster Macmillan.

Blanchard, D. (2000). *Theriac: George Bartisch.* Portland, OR: Blanchard's Books.

Blum, K. (1984). *Handbook of Abusable Drugs.* New York: Gardner Press, Inc.

Booth, M. (2003). *Cannabis: A History.* New York: Thomas Dunne Books, St. Martin's Press.

Borhegi, S. F. (1961). Miniature mushroom stones from Guatemala. *American Antiquity, 26*(4), 498–504.

Boyle, R. (1744). *The Works: Of the Usefulness of Natural Philosophy.* London (out of print).

Brunner, T. F. (1977). Marijuana in ancient Greece and Rome? The literary evidence. *Journal of Psychoactive Drugs, 9*(3).

Center on Addictions and Substance Abuse [CASA]. (2005). *Under the Counter: The Diversion and Abuse of Controlled Prescription Drugs in the U.S.* http://www.casacolumbia.org/Absolutenm/articlefiles/380-final_report.pdf (accessed December 29, 2006).

Centers for Disease Control [CDC]. (2006). *AIDS Statistics from the Centers for Disease Control.* http://www.cdc.gov/hiv/topics/surveillance/resources/reports/index.htm#surveillance (accessed January 5, 2007).

Cherrington, E. H., ed. (1924). *Standard Encyclopedia of the Alcohol Problem* (Vol. II). Westerville, OH: American Issue Publishing.

Chouvy, P. & Meissonnier, J. (2004). *Yaa Baa: Production, Traffic, and Consumption of Methamphetamine in Mainland Southeast Asia.* Singapore: Singapore University Press.

Cleza de Leon. (1959). *The Incas.* Translated by Harriet de Onis. The Civilization of the American Indian Series (Vol. 53). Tulsa, OK: University of Oklahoma Press.

Courtwright, D. (1982). *Dark Paradise: Opiate Addiction in America Before 1940.* Cambridge, MA: Harvard University Press.

Courtwright, D. (2001). *Forces of Habit.* Cambridge, MA: Harvard University Press.

Critser, G. (2005). *Generation Rx: How Prescription Drugs Are Altering American Lives, Minds, and Bodies.* Boston: Houghton Mifflin Company.

CSAM News. (2005). Proposition 36 Revisited. *CSAM Newsletter 1, 6.* http://www.csam-asam.org/pdf/misc/Spring2005.pdf (accessed January 5, 2007).

Dioscorides. (A.D. 70). In M. Wellman, ed. (1906–14, 1958). *Pedanii Dioscuridis Anazarbei De materia medica* (3 volumes).

Doll, R. P., Boreham, J. & Sutherland, I. (2004). Mortality in relation to smoking: 50 years' observations on male British doctors. *British Medical Journal, 328,* 1519.

Drug Enforcement Administration [DEA]. (2006). *National Drug Threat Assessment 2007.* http://www.usdoj.gov/dea/concern/18862/index.htm#Contents (accessed December 29, 2006).

Dunlop, E. & Johnson, B. D. (1992). The setting for the crack era: Macro forces, micro consequences (1960–1992). *Journal of Psychoactive Drugs, 24*(4), 307–22.

Escohotado, A. (1999). *A Brief History of Drugs.* Rochester, VT: Park Street Press.

Frazer, J. G. (1922). *The Golden Bough* (pp. 0–0). New York: Touchstone.

Freud, S. (1884). *Über Coca.* In R. Byck, ed. (1974). *The Cocaine Papers of Sigmund Freud.* New York: Stonehill.

Furst, P. T. (1976). *Hallucinogens and Culture.* San Francisco: Chandler & Sharp Publishers, Inc.

Gagliano, J. (1994). *Coca Production in Peru: The Historical Debates.* Tucson: University of Arizona Press.

Ganeri, A., Martell, H. M. & Williams, B. (1998). Beer. *World History Encyclopedia.* New York: Barnes & Noble.

Giannini, A. J., Burge, H., Shaheen, J. M. & Price, W. A. (1986). Khat: Another drug of abuse. *Journal of Psychoactive Drugs, 18*(2), 155–58.

Goodwin, D. W. & Gabrielli, W. F. (1997). Alcohol: Clinical aspects. In J. H. Lowinson, P. Ruiz, R. B. Millman & J. G. Langrod, eds. *Substance Abuse: A Comprehensive Textbook* (3rd ed., pp. 142–47). Baltimore: Williams & Wilkins.

Grillo, J. (July 30, 2005). The worst of both worlds: Mexico street drugs. *Houston Chronicle,* p. 1A.

Grinols, E. L. (2004). *Gambling in America: Costs and Benefits.* Cambridge, England: Cambridge University Press.

Grinspoon, L. & Hedblom, P. (1975). *The Speed Culture: Amphetamine Use and Abuse in America.* Cambridge, MA: Harvard University Press.

Hamid, A. (1992). The developmental cycle of a drug epidemic: The cocaine-smoking epidemic of 1981–91. *Journal of Psychoactive Drugs, 24*(4), 337–48.

Harler, C. R. (1984). Tea production. In *Encyclopaedia Britannica* (Vol. 18, pp. 16–19). Chicago: Encyclopaedia Britannica.

Heath, D. B. (1995). Alcohol: History. In J. H. Jaffe, ed. *Encyclopedia of Drugs and*

Alcohol (Vol. I, pp. 70–78). New York: Simon & Schuster Macmillan.

Heiman, R. K. (1960). *Tobacco and Americans*. New York: McGraw-Hill Book Company, Inc.

Hodgson, B. (1999). *Opium: A Portrait of the Heavenly Demon*. San Francisco: Chronicle Books.

Hoffman, J. P. (1990). The historical shift in the perception of opiates: From medicine to social medicine. *Journal of Psychoactive Drugs, 22*(1), 53–62.

Hollister, L. E. (1983). The pre-benzodiazepine era. *Journal of Psychoactive Drugs, 15*(1–2), 9–13.

James I. (1604, 1954). *A Counter-Blaste to Tobacco*. London: The Rodale Press.

James, W. H. & Johnson, S. L. (1996). *Doin' Drugs: Patterns of African American Addiction*. Austin: University of Texas Press.

Julien, R. M. (2005). *A Primer of Drug Action*. New York: W. H. Freeman and Company.

Kandall, S. R. (1996). *Substance and Shadow: Women and Addiction in the United States*. Cambridge, MA: Harvard University Press.

Karch, S. B. (1996). *The Pathology of Drug Abuse*. Boca Raton, FL: CRC Press.

Karch, S. B. (1997). *A Brief History of Cocaine*. Boca Raton, FL: CRC Press.

Karch, S. B. (1998). *Drug Abuse Handbook*. Boca Raton, FL: CRC Press.

Keller, M. (1984). Alcohol consumption. In *Encyclopaedia Britannica* (Vol. 1, pp. 437–50). Chicago: Encyclopaedia Britannica.

Konietzko, N. (September 24, 2001). *Report at 11th Annual Congress of the European Respiratory Society*.

La Barre, W. (1979A). Shamanic origins of religion and medicine. *Journal of Psychoactive Drugs, 11*(1–2), 7–11.

La Barre, W. (1979B). Peyotl and mescaline. *Journal of Psychoactive Drugs, 11*(1–2), 33–39.

Langton, P. A. (1995). Temperance movement. In J. H. Jaffe, ed. *Encyclopedia of Drugs and Alcohol* (Vol. III, pp. 1019–23). New York: Simon & Schuster Macmillan.

Latimer, D. & Goldberg, J. (1981). *Flowers in the Blood: The Story of Opium*. New York: Franklin Watts.

Lee, J. A. (1987). Chinese, alcohol and flushing: Sociohistorical and bio-behavioral considerations. *Journal of Psychoactive Drugs, 19*(4), 319–27.

Leinwand, D. (April 22, 2005). Post-911 security cuts into ecstasy: Youth turning to prescription drugs. *USA Today*, p. 1A.

Li, H. L. (1974). An archeological and historical account of *Cannabis* in China. *Economic Botany, 28*, 437–38.

Longshore, D., Urada, D., Evans, E., Hser, Y., Prendergast, M., Hawken, A., et al. (2004). *Evaluation of the Substance Abuse and Crime Prevention Act: 2003 Report*. UCLA: Integrated Substance Abuse Programs. http://www.court info.ca.gov/programs/collab/documents/2003Prop36Report.pdf (accessed September 8, 2006).

Marnell, T., ed. (2005). *Drug Identification Bible*. Denver: Drug Identification Bible.

Marsch, L. A., Bickel, W. K., Badger, G. J., Stothart, M. E., Quesnel, K. J., Stanger, C., et al. (2005). Comparison of pharmacological treatment for opioid-dependent adolescents: A randomized controlled trial. *Archives of General Psychiatry, 62*(10), 1157–64.

Mason, M. (December 12, 2006). The energy-drink buzz is unmistakable. The health impact unknown. *New York Times*, p. D5.

Matthee, R. (1995). Exotic substances: The introduction and global spread of tobacco, coffee, cocoa, tea, and distilled liquor, sixteenth to eighteenth centuries. In R. Porter & M. Teich, eds. *Drugs and Narcotics in History*. Cambridge, England: Cambridge University Press.

Maugh, T. H. (December 24, 2004). Ancient Andean civilization arose before the pyramids. *L.A. Times*.

McGovern, P., Zhang, J., Tang, J., Zhang, Z., Hall, G. R., Moreau, R. A., et al. (2004). Fermented beverages of pre- and proto-historic China. *Proceedings of the National Academy of Sciences, 101*, 17593–98.

McKenna, T. (1992). *Food of the Gods*. New York: Bantam Books.

Monardes, N. (1577). *Joyfull Newes Out of the Newe Founde Worlde*. Translated by J. Frampton. (1967). New York: AMS Press, Inc.

Monitoring the Future. (2006). http:// monitoringthefuture.org (accessed January 2, 2007.)

Moore, T. L. (2006). *The Prevalence of Disordered Gambling Among Adults in Oregon: A Replication Study*. http:// www.gamblingaddiction.org/PREV200 6/ogatfprevalencestudy2006_072506 .pdf (accessed December 29, 2006).

National Association of Drug Court Professionals. (2005). *What Is a Drug Court?* http://www.nadcp.org/whatis (accessed September 8, 2006).

National Opinion Research Center. (1999). *Gambling Impact and Behavior Study*. http://govinfo.library.unt.edu/ngisc/ reports/gibstdy.pdf (accessed September 8, 2006).

Nesse, R. A. & Berridge, K. C. (1997). Psychoactive drug use in evolutionary perspective. *Science, 278*, 63–65.

N-SSATS. (2005). *National Survey of Substance Abuse Treatment Services (N-SSATS): 2005*. http://wwwdasis.samhsa. gov/05nssats/nssats2k5web.pdf (accessed January 8, 2007).

O'Brien, R. & Chafetz, M. (1991). *The Encyclopedia of Alcoholism* (2nd ed.). New York: Facts On File.

Observatoire Geopolitique des Drogues. (1996). *The Geopolitics of Drugs*. Boston: Northeastern University Press.

Operation Somalia Express. (July 26, 2006). *DEA; Largest Khat Enforcement Ever*. http://www.dea.gov/pubs/press rel/pr072606.html (accessed December 29, 2006).

Partnership for a Drug Free America [PATS]. (2005A). *Partnership Attitude Tracking Study, Winter 2004*. http:// www.drugfree.org/Files/PATS_Parents_ Full_Report (accessed September 8, 2006).

Partnership for a Drug Free America. (2005B). http://www.drugfree.org/ Portal (accessed September 6, 2006).

Plato. (360 B.C.) The Symposium, The Republic, The Laws. In L. R. Loomis, ed. *Plato, Five Great Dialogues*. New York: Gramercy Books.

Pound, D. (2006). *Inside Dope*. Mississauga, Ontario: John Wiley & Sons Canada, Ltd.

Robins, L. N. & Slobodyan, S. (2003). Post-Vietnam heroin use and injection by returning US veterans: Clues to preventing injection today. *Addiction, 98*(8), 1053–60.

Ruibal, S. (December 5, 2006). A new tool to catch sports cheats. *USA Today*, p. A1.

Sanello, F. (2005). *Tweakers: How Crystal Meth Is Ravaging Gay America*. Los Angeles: Alyson Books.

Scarborough, J. (1995). The opium poppy in Hellenistic and Roman medicine. In R. Porter & M. Teich, eds. *Drugs and Narcotics in History*. Cambridge, England: Cambridge University Press.

Schultes, R. E. & Hofmann, A. (1992). *Plants of the Gods*. Rochester, VT: Healing Arts Press.

Schultes, R. E. & Raffauf, R. F. (2004). *Vine of the Soul*. New Mexico: Synergetic Press.

Schwartz, D. G. (2006). *Roll the Bones: The History of Gambling*. New York: Gotham Books.

Scrivener (1871). On the coca leaf and its use in diet and medicine. *Medical Times and Gazette*. In R. Byck, ed. (1974), *The Cocaine Papers of Sigmund Freud*. New York: Stonehill.

Siegel, R. K. (1982). History of cocaine smoking. *Journal of Psychoactive Drugs, 14*(4), 277–97.

Skolnik, A. A. (1997). Lessons from U.S. history of drug use. *JAMA, 277*(24), 1919–21.

Slade, J. (1989). The tobacco epidemic: Lessons from history. *Journal of Psychoactive Drugs, 21*(3), 281–91.

Stafford, P. (1982). *Psychedelics Encyclopedia* (Vol. 1, p. 157). Berkeley, CA: Ronin Publishing.

Stamets, P. (1996). *Psilocybin Mushrooms of the World.* Berkeley: Ten Speed Press.

Substance Abuse and Mental Health Services Administration [SAMHSA]. (2003). *Serious Mental Illness and its Co-occurrence with Substance Use Disorders, 2002.* http://oas.samhsa.gov/CoD/CoD .htm (accessed September 9, 2006).

Substance Abuse and Mental Health Services Administration (2006A). *2005 National Survey on Drug Use and Health: National Findings.* http:// www.oas.samhsa.gov/NSDUH/2k5NSD UH/2k5results.htm (accessed December 29, 2006).

Substance Abuse and Mental Health Services Administration. (2006). *Treatment Episode Data Sets (TEDS).* http://www.DrugAbuseStatistics.SAMH SA.gov (accessed January 7, 2007).

Sullivan, L. E., Tetrault, J., Bangalore, D. & Fiellin, D. A. (2006). Training HIV physicians to prescribe buprenorphine for opioid dependence. *Substance Abuse, 27*(3), 13–18.

Suo, S. (December 4, 2006). B.C. drug traffickers expanding into meth. *Portland Oregonian,* p. A1.

Therolf, G. (December 27, 2006). Afghan heroin surges through United States. *Medford Mail Tribune,* p. 4A.

Trice, H. M. (1995). Alcoholics Anonymous. In J. H. Jaffe, ed. *Encyclopedia of Drugs and Alcohol* (Vol. I, pp. 85–92). New York: Simon & Schuster Macmillan.

UNAIDS. (2006). *AIDS Epidemic Update.* http://www.unaids.org//pub/EpiReport/ 2006/2006_EpiUpdate_en.pdf (accessed December 2, 2006).

United Nations Office on Drugs and Crime. (2005). *2005 World Drug Report.* http://www.unodc.org/pdf/WDR_2005/ volume_1_web.pdf (accessed September 9, 2006).

U.S. Embassy, Moscow. (2006). *International Narcotics Control Strategy Report—2006.* http://moscow. usembassy.gov/embassy/section.php?re cord_id=report_narcotics_2005 (accessed December 29, 2006).

Wallbank, T. W. & Taylor, A. M. (1992). *A Short History of the Opium Wars.* New York: Addison-Wesley Publishing Co.

Weinberg, B. A. & Bealer, B. K. (2001). *The World of Caffeine.* New York: Routledge.

Wikipedia. (2006). *History of Mental Illness.* http://en.wikipedia.org/wiki/ History_of_mental_illness (accessed January 6, 2007).

Wilford, J. N. (January 6, 2004). Discovery may bring new clues into peopling of the Americas. *New York Times,* p. C1.

World Health Organization [WHO]. (2005). *Global Status Report on Alcohol 2004.* http://www.who.int/substance_abuse/ publications/en/global_status_report_ 2004_overview.pdf (accessed September 9, 2006).

Heredity, Environment, Psychoactive Drugs

Joseph stumbles across his brain's pleasure center.

The Neighborhood by
Jerry Van Amerongen
© 1986 Jerry Van Amerongen.
Reprinted by permission of Cowles
Syndicate Inc.

HOW PSYCHOACTIVE DRUGS AFFECT PEOPLE

- **How Drugs Get to the Brain.** A psychoactive drug is absorbed into the body's circulatory system and distributed via the blood to other tissues and organs.
  - ◇ **Routes of Administration & Drug Absorption.** Drugs can be absorbed through inhaling, injecting, mucous membrane absorption, oral ingestion, or contact absorption.
  - ◇ **Drug Distribution.** Psychoactive drugs traveling through the bloodstream finally cross the blood-brain barrier, to the central nervous system. The drugs will cause an effect, be ignored, be absorbed, or be transformed. They will also cross the blood-brain, blood-cerebral spinal fluid, and placental barriers.
  - ◇ **Metabolism & Excretion.** Drugs are metabolized principally by the liver and eliminated through the kidneys, sweat glands, and lungs.
- **The Nervous System.** The two main parts of the nervous system are the peripheral nervous system (autonomic and somatic systems) and the central nervous system (brain and spinal cord).
  - ◇ **Peripheral Nervous System.** This two-part system (autonomic and somatic systems) controls involuntary body functions, relays sensory information, and sends instructions to muscles and organs.
  - ◇ **Central Nervous System.** The brain and the spinal cord receive information from the peripheral nervous system, analyze it, and then send appropriate action messages back through the peripheral nervous system.
  - ◇ **Old Brain–New Brain.** The evolutionary perspective looks at physiological changes and drug cravings in the brain, particularly the old brain, as survival adaptations. In drug users the cravings of the old brain will usually override the common sense of the new brain.
  - ◇ **The Reward/Reinforcement Pathway.** This circuit has a "more" switch and a "stop" switch. These areas of the brain, particularly the nucleus accumbens, give a surge of satisfaction when a physical or emotional need is met or when pain is relieved. They also imprint the message to do it again. The three phases of brain activity when a drug is used include: craving and initial stimulus; activation of the nucleus accumbens and the do-it-again signals; and the transmission of reinforcement signals and the disabling of the stop switch.
  - ◇ **On/Off Switches.** The main "off" switch resides in the prefrontal cortex, whereas craving resides in the reward/reinforcement pathway of the brain; current research on addiction is focusing on these areas in an effort to find a way to control drug hunger.
  - ◇ **Morality & the Reward/Reinforcement Pathway.** The conflict between drug cravings that develop powerfully in the addict's brain and the societal restraints and inhibitions mediated by the neocortex (new brain) are as old as civilization.
  - ◇ **Neuroanatomy.** Psychoactive drugs affect the nerve cells and the neurochemistry of the brain and the spinal cord while altering the way messages are received, processed, and transmitted.
  - ◇ **Neurotransmitters & Receptors.** Neurochemicals called *neurotransmitters* relay messages across the tiny space (synaptic cleft or gap) between nerve cells. When psychoactive drugs modify or mimic the way these neurotransmitters function, they cause physical, mental, and emotional effects.
- **Physiological Responses to Drugs.** In addition to direct effects, phenomena such as tolerance, tissue dependence, psychological dependence, and withdrawal determine a user's reaction to psychoactive drugs.

FROM EXPERIMENTATION TO ADDICTION

- **Desired Effects vs. Side Effects.** People use psychoactive drugs to change their mood, to get high, to self-medicate, to socialize, and for any number of other reasons. These drugs can also cause undesired physical, mental, and social effects (adverse reactions, toxic effects, dependency, isolation, and crime), particularly with prolonged or high-dose use.
- **Polydrug Abuse.** Using drugs to supplement, negate, temper, or replace one's drug of choice is extremely common among drug abusers.
- **Levels of Use.** The amount, frequency, and duration of drug use and the effects on the user's behavior help indicate levels of use, which are abstinence, experimentation, social/recreational use, habituation, abuse, and addiction.
- **Theories of Addiction.** Theories of addiction emphasize a combination of genetic factors, environmental influences, and excessive use of psychoactive drugs or compulsive behaviors as the roots of addiction. The main theories are the addictive disease model, the behavioral/environmental model, the academic model, and the diathesis-stress theory of addiction.
- **Heredity, Environment & Psychoactive Drugs or Compulsive Behaviors.** These factors determine at what level a person might use psychoactive drugs.
  - ◇ **Heredity.** Family history can indicate a genetic susceptibility to compulsive drug use.
  - ◇ **Environment.** The pressures and the stress of growing up, particularly if there is abuse, can make people more susceptible to addiction especially if there is a strong hereditary component. Environmental stress and even poor nutrition can alter the brain's chemistry and function to make one more vulnerable to compulsive drug use. Availability of the drug and peer pressure are also strong environmental factors.
  - ◇ **Psychoactive Drugs.** Drugs can activate a genetic/environmental susceptibility to drug abuse and addiction. They cause alterations in brain chemistry, structure, and function, which can intensify drug-using behavior.
  - ◇ **Compulsive Behaviors.** Compulsive gambling or shopping, eating disorders, hypersexuality, excess Internet use, and other uncontrolled behaviors can cause changes in brain function and neurochemistry.
- **Alcoholic Mice & Sober Mice.** Classic experiments with mice strongly confirm the interrelationship between heredity, environment, psychoactive drugs, and levels of use.
- **Compulsion Curves.** The way heredity, environment, and regular drug use combine to increase susceptibility to addiction can be visualized with compulsion graphs.
- **Conclusions.** Any examination of drug or behavioral addiction should focus on the totality of one's life, not just on the specific drug or behavior problem.

The Unconscious Mind: A Great Decision Maker

and then make astute judgments

Brain study illustrates intense pull of cocaine

Addiction has many fathers, science finds

Genetics, home environment are big factors

Dopamine levels linked to obesity, addiction

By JAMIE TALAN

Craving rats mimic addicted humans

Teenagers' brains really are different

By JAMIE TALAN
Newsday

If you're a teenager, don't read this. Federal scientists may have discovered a biological excuse for laziness.

Environment Beats Genes In Forming IQ, Study Finds

Associated Press

New York

enough below the figure cited by the controversial 1994 book "The Bell Curve" to undercut its authors' main conclusions.

In Chronic Drug Abuse, Acute Dopamine Surge May Erode Resolve To Abstain

Compulsions Tracked in Images of Brain

Psychiatrists able
The approach is adding a new

Mouse gene change leads to anxiety, taste for alcohol

Conference focuses on brain, pleasure

Experiments seek to find why some quit drugs at will

Brain 'switch' zapped urge to smoke

OHSU scientists find gene tied to alcohol, drug reaction

A 38-year-old's stroke points researchers in a new direction

By LAURAN NEERGAARD
The Associated Press

to quit. "My body forgot the urge to smoke," he told his doctor nonchalantly.

His comment inspired research that suggests damage to a silver dollar-sized spot deep in the brain can wipe out the urge to smoke. The surprising discovery may shed

smokers to pinpoint the region invo

Mental abuse as traumatic as physical torture, study says

By Alan Zarembo
LOS ANGELES TIMES

Degrading treatment and psychological manipulation cause as much emotional suffering and

stress disorder. The victims themselves rated the psychological tactics on par with the physical abuses they suffered.

The study, published in the Archives of General Psychiatry, grew

ics, who was not involved in the research.

The researchers, led by Dr. Metin Basoglu, a psychiatrist at King's College in London, interviewed 279 people who suffered various

forced standing, cold showers and blindfolding.

The subjects were asked to rank each abuse on a scale of zero to four in terms of the distress it caused.

The worst physical tortures av-

physical pain," Basoglu said.

The interviews were conducted an average of eight years after the mistreatment.

More than 55 percent of the subjects were suffering from post-

HOW PSYCHOACTIVE DRUGS AFFECT PEOPLE

"To develop more-effective prevention and treatment strategies, we must deepen our understanding of how drugs affect the complex inner workings of the brain. Thanks to remarkable advances in bioscience, and particularly in the neurosciences over the past decade, this is a realistic goal. The challenge is to create from the avalanche of new data a coherent picture of biological events interacting with environmental factors and eventuating in the dysfunction we call addiction."

Nora D. Volkow, M.D., director of the National Institute on Drug Abuse

Over the years drug abuse and dependence have been examined from historical, sociological, psychological, and moralistic perspectives. The intense interest over the past 15 years in the neurological and biochemical aspects of drug use stems in part from a variety of animal and human studies starting more than 50 years ago that have focused on the **reward/reinforcement brain circuitry present in all animals**.

"Why is it that laboratory animals on whom social, economic, and educational variables are inoperative, voluntarily (indeed avidly) self-administer the same drugs that human beings use and abuse and

will not self-administer other drugs? This argues compellingly for a profoundly important biologic basis for substance abuse."

Eliot L. Gardner, Ph.D., National Institute of Drug Abuse, Behavioral Neuroscience Research Branch

Even if the reasons for continued use of psychoactive drugs have more to do with early environmental influences than hereditary ones, the nervous system is still intimately involved because environment can alter the brain as radically as do psychoactive drugs themselves. Before studying in detail the neurochemistry of craving, satiation, and addiction, it is important to understand how drugs get to the brain.

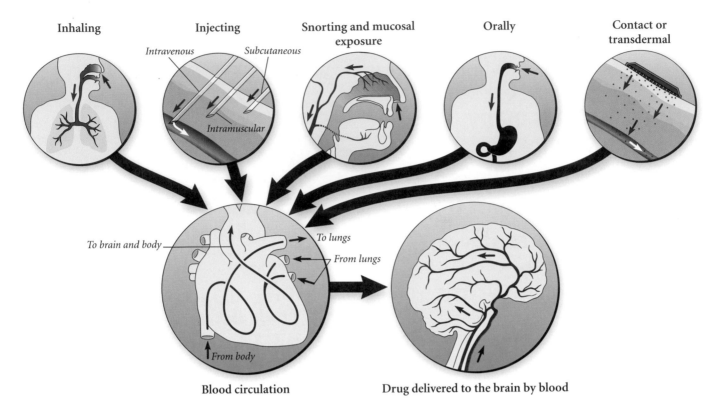

Inhaling

Injecting

Intravenous   *Subcutaneous*

Intramuscular

Snorting and mucosal exposure

Orally

Contact or transdermal

To brain and body   *To lungs*

From lungs

From body

Blood circulation

Drug delivered to the brain by blood

Figure 2-1 •

Whether inhaled (and absorbed in the lungs), injected (in a vein, muscle, or under the skin), snorted (through the nasal or buccal mucosa), drunk (and absorbed by the small intestines), or absorbed by contact (with the skin), the drug enters the bloodstream and eventually makes its way to the brain.

© 2006 CNS Productions, Inc.

HOW DRUGS GET TO THE BRAIN

Psychoactive drugs are natural and synthetic substances that directly affect the central nervous system (the brain and the spinal cord) and cause mental and physical changes. Factors that determine their effects and abuse potential include the drug's **pharmokinetics**—the process by which a drug is absorbed, distributed, metabolized, and eliminated in the body. Key elements with psychoactive drugs are:

◊ **route of administration,**
◊ **speed of transit to the brain, and**
◊ **affinity for nerve cells and neurotransmitters**.

The more rapidly a psychoactive drug reaches its target in the central nervous system, the greater its reinforcing effect (Karan, Zajicek & Pating, 2003).

ROUTES OF ADMINISTRATION & DRUG ABSORPTION

There are five common ways that drugs enter the body: **inhaling, injecting, mucous membrane absorption, oral ingestion,** and **contact absorption** (Figure 2-1). The methods are arranged here in the order of the speed with which they reach the brain and begin to have an effect.

Inhaling

When a person smokes marijuana or inhales nitrous oxide, the vaporized drug enters the lungs and is **rapidly absorbed through capillaries lining the air sacs (alveoli) of the bronchi (air passages)**. From the capillaries (minute blood vessels that connect the arterioles and venules of the lungs), the drug-laden blood travels back to the veins and then to the heart, where it is pumped directly to the brain and other organs and tissues of the body.

Inhaling acts more quickly than any other method of use (**seven to 10 seconds before the drug reaches the brain** and begins to cause changes). The physical characteristics of the inhaled substance (volatility, particle size, and fat solubility) have an effect on the absorption.

Because the effects are felt so quickly and only a small amount of the drug is absorbed with each puff or breath, users can regulate the amount of drug they are receiving (*titration*). For example, cigarette smokers titrate the amount of nicotine they put in their bloodstream by controlling how often they smoke and how deeply they inhale. Because more than 60% of the THC in a marijuana joint is lost when smoked, medical-marijuana researchers are developing a deep lung aerosol spray and a nasal spray as delivery systems for the purified form of the drug called Marinol® (dronabinol). This would avoid the damaging effects of the tar and other toxic substances in marijuana smoke.

Injecting

Substances such as methamphetamine, heroin, and cocaine can be injected directly into the body with a hypodermic syringe by three methods:

◊ **intravenous** (IV, or "slamming")—directly into the bloodstream by way of a vein;

◊ **intramuscular** (IM, or "muscling")—into a muscle mass; and

◊ **subcutaneous** ("skin popping")—under the skin.

Injection is a quick and potent way to absorb a drug (**15 to 30 seconds intravenously or three to five minutes in a muscle or under the skin**). Because a large amount of the drug enters the blood at one time, injecting a strong psychoactive drug intravenously is **most likely to produce an intense rush** (a brief and very intense feeling of excitation and mental electricity), exaggerated sensations, or a strong feeling of well-being. The slower routes of administration will produce euphoria or a high but will not cause a rush. The drug effects will build up more slowly (Jaffe, Knapp & Ciraulo, 2005). This rush is the main reason why some users prefer IV use of heroin, cocaine, and methamphetamine. In addition, none of the drug is wasted as occurs with sidestream smoke, poor nasal absorption, or destruction by body fluids and liver metabolism when taken orally.

The large bolus (concentrated mass) of drugs from injecting can cause exaggerated reactions and even an overdose because the user is often not sure of the purity or identity of the drug. Once injected there is no turning back because the drugs are in an enclosed system and the effects will inevitably take their course. **Injecting is the most dangerous method of use because it bypasses most of the body's natural defenses,** thereby exposing the user to many health problems, such as hepatitis B and C, abscesses, HIV infection, and undissolved particles or additives that can cause embolisms, infections, or other illnesses.

A number of drugs are reformulated so that they can be injected intramuscularly and be released into the bloodstream over time. Drugs such as Haldol® Decanoate (an antipsychotic medication), and Depo-Provera® (a birth control medication), DepoCyt® (an anticancer chemotherapy drug), and Vivitrol® (naltrexone to suppress cravings for alcohol) need be injected only once a month but they continue to work for up to 30 days.

Mucous Membrane Absorption

Certain drugs in powdered form, especially cocaine, heroin, methamphetamine, and even ground OxyContin,® can be **snorted into the nose (insufflation) and absorbed by the capillaries enmeshed in the mucous membranes** lining the nasal passages. The effects are usually more intense and occur more quickly than with the oral route because the drug initially bypasses digestive acids, enzymes, and the liver. A nasal spray containing a tranquilizer has been used in Sweden to calm cancer-stricken children undergoing chemotherapy (Ljungman, Kreuger, Andreasson, et al., 2000). An older method of mucosal absorption involves placing a drug, such as crushed coca leaves (mixed with ash or soda lime) or tobacco, on the **mucous membranes under the tongue (sublingually) or between the gums and cheek (buccally) (three to five minutes for effects to begin** for these two methods). Trials with a marijuana nasal gel or sublingual preparation for mucosal absorption are under review. In hospices for terminally ill patients too weak for an oral dose of a painkiller, they use **morphine suppositories (10 to 15 minutes for effects to begin).** The drug is absorbed through mucosal tissues lining the rectum. Vaginal absorption of drugs is also occasionally employed. Some users employ these last two methods for recreational/abusive/addictive drug use.

Oral Ingestion

When someone swallows an ecstasy tablet or drinks a beer, **the drug passes through the esophagus and the stomach to the small intestine, where it is absorbed into the capillaries enmeshed in the intestinal walls.**

The capillaries feed the drug into the veins that carry it to the liver, where it is partly metabolized (first-pass metabolism). It is then pumped back to the heart and subsequently to the rest of the body. **The effects of drugs taken by this method are delayed (20 to 30 minutes).** About 10% to 20% of alcohol is metabolized by the stomach in men (who have more gastric metabolizing enzymes), so women will generally have higher blood alcohol levels for the same amount consumed.

Drugs enter the capillaries lining the walls of the small intestine through passive transport (absorption). This occurs because many drugs move from an area of high concentration of that drug to areas of low concentration of that same drug. Fat-soluble drugs, which include most psychoactive drugs, move readily across most biological barriers (membranes). Alcohol is both water- and fat-soluble (Wilkinson, 2001).

Contact Absorption

Drugs can be applied to the skin through **saturated adhesive patches** that allow measured quantities of the drug to be passively absorbed over a long period of time (up to seven days). It sometimes takes one or two days for therapeutic effects to begin. This noninvasive **transdermal absorption** method is used with nicotine patches to help smokers quit, fentanyl patches to control pain, clonidine patches to reduce drug withdrawal symptoms or reduce blood pressure, and heart medication patches to control angina (heart pain). Some opioid addicts will chew morphine or fentanyl patches to get a maximum rush from the drug, although an overdose often results from a miscalculation of how much drug there really is.

DRUG DISTRIBUTION

No matter how a drug enters the circulatory system, it is eventually **distributed by the bloodstream to the rest of the body**. The actual amount of drug that reaches the brain depends, among other things, on the bioavailability of the drug. The **bioavailability is defined as the degree to which a drug becomes available to the target tissue after administration** (Dorland,

2003). The drug may be carried inside the blood cells or in the plasma outside the cells, or it might hitch a ride on protein molecules in the bloodstream. The drug molecules then circulate and travel to and through every organ, fluid, and tissue in the body, where they will either **cause a direct effect**, **be ignored**, **be stored** (usually in fat cells), or **be biotransformed** into metabolites or chemical variations of the original drug, some of which can also cause psychoactive effects (Karan, Zajicek & Pating, 2003).

The distribution of a drug within the body depends not only on the characteristics of the drug but also on blood volume. The lighter the person, the less blood volume there is, so a **child of 12 might have only 3 or 4 quarts of blood to dilute the drug** instead of the

6 to 8 quarts of blood in a large adult's circulatory system. The effect of a drug on a specific organ or tissue also depends on the number of blood vessels reaching that site. For example, veins and arteries saturate the heart muscles, and because all drugs pass through these vessels, a drug such as cocaine can have a direct effect on heart function. Bones have fewer blood vessels, so most drugs will have less effect on these sites.

Most important, within only 10 to 15 seconds after entering the bloodstream, the drug will reach the gateway to the central nervous system: the protective blood-brain and blood-cerebral spinal fluid barriers. On the other side of these barriers, the drug will have its greatest effects on the brain and the spinal cord.

The Blood-Brain, Blood-Cerebral Spinal Fluid & Placental Barriers

The drug-laden blood flows through the internal carotid arteries in the neck toward the **blood-brain barrier** and the central nervous system. The walls of the capillaries of this barrier consist of **tightly sealed epithelial cells that allow only certain substances to penetrate** (Figure 2-3). Blood plasma carries oxygen, glucose, and amino acids to the brain and carries away carbon dioxide and other waste products. Generally, dangerous substances such as toxins, viruses, and bacteria can't cross this barrier. **One class of drugs that can infiltrate this blood-brain barrier is psychoactive drugs** (stimulants, depressants, psychedelics, and inhalants). Psychotropic drugs, such as antipsychotics or antidepressants, also cross this barrier, as do most steroids and some muscle relaxants. Interestingly, stress can dramatically increase the ability of drugs to cross this barrier. The fact that psychoactive drug use often involves stressful or emotionally charged situations would tend to speed absorption of the substance and perhaps exaggerate the effects (Hanin, 1996).

A key reason why many psychoactive drugs, including nicotine, alcohol, and marijuana, cross this barrier is that they are fat-soluble (*lipophilic*); and **because the brain is essentially fatty, it readily absorbs fat-soluble substances**. When lipid-soluble drugs pass from an area of higher concentration of a drug to an area of lower concentration, it is called *passive transport*. For example, morphine is partly fat-soluble, so it takes somewhat longer to cross the barrier than the more fat-soluble heroin (Meyer & Quenzer, 2005). Cocaine hydrochloride and other drugs that are water-soluble hitchhike across the blood-brain barrier by attaching to protein molecules going across. This method is known as **active transport** (Wilkinson, 2001). Most substances that are **water-soluble** (*hydrophilic*), such as antibiotics, are prevented from entering the brain. Alcohol is both lipophilic and hydrophilic, so it enters the brain easily.

Very much like the blood-brain

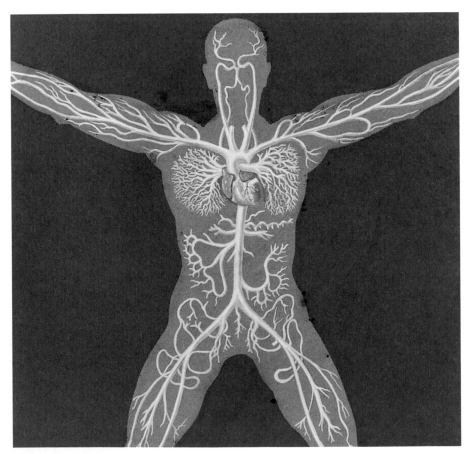

Figure 2-2 •

This drawing shows a small fraction of the veins and the arteries of the circulatory system that, in an adult, carry an average of 5 liters (about 6 quarts) of blood to every part of the body. Miles of tiny capillaries then deliver the drug-laden blood to tissues, especially the nerve cells of the central nervous system. The circulatory system also carries the drug and its metabolites away from the brain and other tissues by filtering 500 gallons of blood a day through the kidneys.

The Blood–Brain Barrier

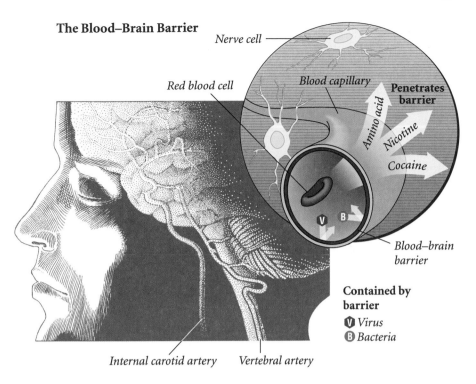

Figure 2-3 •

The inset shows the wall of a capillary in the brain whose tightly sealed epithelial cells with no clefts, pores, or gaps, act as a barrier to most substances. Psychoactive substances, which are fat-soluble, cross this barrier.

© 2006 CNS Productions, Inc.

barrier, the **blood-cerebral spinal fluid barrier** helps prevent unwanted substances from entering the areas of the central nervous system where this fluid flows (subarachnoid space, ventricles, and spinal cord).

The **blood-brain barrier is not completely formed in humans at birth** and does not become fully functional until a child is one to two years old, so ingesting toxic chemicals can be especially dangerous to the fetus during pregnancy. There is also a **placental barrier that provides some protection to the developing fetus**, but it is mostly a barrier to water-soluble chemicals and generally not to fat-soluble ones; and because most psychoactive drugs are fat-soluble, if the mother uses, the baby uses (Finnegan & Kandall, 2005).

METABOLISM & EXCRETION

After the drug has had its effect, it is eliminated from the body through metabolism or excretion.

◇ **Metabolism is the body's mechanism for processing, using, and inactivating a foreign substance that has been taken into the body.**

◇ **Excretion is the process of eliminating those foreign substances and their metabolites from the body.**

As a drug exerts its influence on the body, it is gradually broken down and inactivated (metabolized), primarily by the liver. It can also be metabolized in the blood, in the lymph fluid, by brain enzymes and chemicals, and by a number of body tissues. Drugs can also be inactivated by diverting them to storage in body fat or proteins that absorb and hold the substances to prevent them from acting on body organs. The **liver is the key metabolic organ** because it is able to break down or alter the chemical structure of drugs, making them less active or completely inert.

The **kidneys are the key excretory organs** because they filter the metabolites, water, and other waste from the blood and send the resulting urine through the ureter, bladder, and urethra. Drugs can also be excreted out of the body in exhaled breath, in sweat, or in feces.

Metabolic processes generally decrease (but occasionally increase) the effects of psychoactive drugs. For instance, the liver's enzymes help convert alcohol to water and carbon dioxide that are then excreted from the body through the kidneys and the urethra, the sweat glands, and the lungs. Some

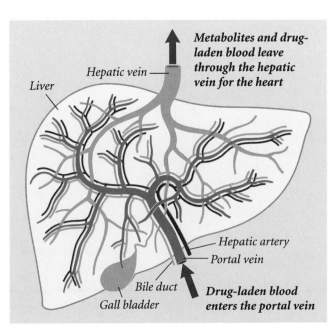

Figure 2-4 •

The liver deactivates a portion of the drug with each recirculation through the circulatory system.

© 2003 CNS Productions, Inc.

drugs, such as Valium,® are **known as "prodrugs" because they are transformed by the liver's enzymes into three or four metabolites that are themselves active and cause major effects in the brain and the body**.

If a drug is eliminated slowly, as with Valium,® it can affect the body for hours or even days. If it is eliminated quickly, as with smokable cocaine or nitrous oxide, the major actions might last just a few minutes, though other subtle side effects last for days, weeks, or longer. **One measure of the time it takes a drug to be inactivated or eliminated by the body is called the half-life**. It generally takes about six half-lives for the drug to be hard to detect. So, if the half-life of a drug is 1 hour, it would take 6 hours to get to one-sixty-fourth of a dose in the blood. Some examples: the half-life of cocaine is 30 to 90 minutes; methadone is 15 to 60 hours; the THC in marijuana is 20 to 30 hours; and fluoxetine (Prozac®) is 1 to 6 days, although the metabolites of these drugs can last much longer. The metabolite of fluoxetine can have a half-life of 4 to 16 days. Cocaethylene, a metabolite of cocaine that is formed when alcohol and cocaine are used together, has a half-life of about 2.5 hours.

Many drug users have learned through word of mouth and experimentation to create metabolites to **extend the effects of many drugs by using them in combination with other drugs** (Karan, Zajicek & Pating, 2003). For a drug and its metabolites to become undetectable in the body takes much longer than many half-lives because minute amounts can be detected by urine, blood, hair, sweat, saliva, and other testing methods. Urine tests for cocaine can be positive for 2 to 4 days, amphetamines for 1 to 2 days, heroin or OxyContin® for 2 to 4 days, and marijuana (1 joint) for 2 to 3 days or even longer depending on drug potency or how much is used. It is important to remember that the half-life as well as the bioavailability of any drug can vary widely.

The following are some other factors that affect the metabolism (and the half-life) of drugs.

◊ **Age.** After the age of 30 and with each subsequent year, the liver pro-

duces fewer and fewer enzymes capable of metabolizing certain drugs; thus the older the person, the greater the effect. This is especially true with drugs like alcohol and sedative-hypnotics.

◊ **Race.** Different ethnic groups have different types and levels of enzymes. More than 50% of Asians break down alcohol more slowly than do Caucasians. They suffer more side effects, such as redness of the face, than many other ethnic groups.

◊ **Heredity.** Individuals pass certain traits to their offspring that affect the metabolism of drugs. They can have a low level of enzymes that metabolize the drug; they can have more body fat that will store certain drugs like Valium® or marijuana; or they can have a high metabolic rate that will eliminate drugs more quickly from the body.

◊ **Gender.** Males and females have different body chemistries, and different body water volumes. Drugs

such as alcohol and barbiturates generally have greater effects in women than in men.

◊ **Health.** Certain medical conditions affect metabolism. Alcohol in a drinker with severe liver damage (hepatitis or cirrhosis) causes more problems than in a drinker with a healthy liver.

◊ **Emotional State.** Anxiety, anger, and other **emotions can exaggerate the effects** of a drug. For example, methamphetamine in an angry person can lead to lashing out and violence.

◊ **Other Drugs. The presence of two or more drugs can exaggerate the effects** by keeping the body so busy metabolizing one drug that metabolism of the second drug is delayed. For example, the presence of alcohol keeps the liver so busy that Xanax® will remain in the body two or three times longer than normal. This exaggeration of effects when two or more drugs are taken together is called **drug synergism**.

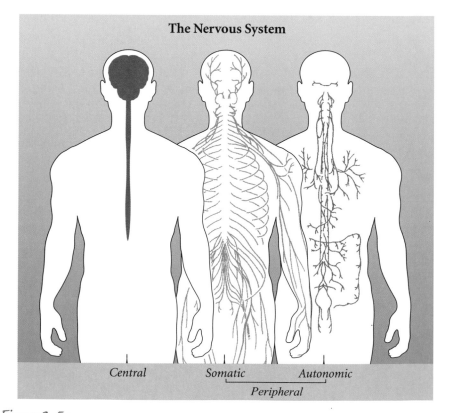

The Nervous System

Central   *Somatic*   *Autonomic*

Peripheral

Figure 2-5 •

The three parts of the complete nervous system function together to transmit, interpret, store, and respond to information from the internal and external environments.

© 2007 CNS Productions, Inc.

◇ **Exaggerated Reaction.** In some cases the reaction to a drug will be out of proportion to the amount taken. Perhaps the user has an **allergy to the drug** in much the same way a person can go into shock from a single bee sting. For example, a person who lacks the enzyme that metabolizes cocaine can die from exposure to just a tiny amount.

◇ **Other Factors.** In addition, factors such as the weight of the user, the level of tolerance, the monthly hormonal cycle for women, enzyme induction, enzyme inhibition, and even the weather can affect metabolism of a psychoactive drug.

THE NERVOUS SYSTEM

Because the principal target of psychoactive drugs is the central nervous system, it is important to understand how this network of **100 billion nerve cells and 100 trillion connections** works.

◇ The **central nervous system (CNS)** is half of the complete nervous system. It contains the brain and the spinal cord. It is better protected (the skull and the spine) than most of the peripheral nervous system.

◇ The **peripheral nervous system (PNS)** is the other half of the nervous system. It connects the CNS with its internal and external environments. The peripheral nervous system is further divided into the **autonomic and the somatic systems**.

PERIPHERAL NERVOUS SYSTEM

Autonomic System. The **autonomic part of the peripheral nervous system controls involuntary internal functions such as circulation, digestion, respiration,** glandular output, and genital reactions. It consists of the:

◇ **sympathetic division**, which helps the body respond to stress;

◇ **parasympathetic division**, which conserves the body's resources and restores homeostasis (physiological balance); and

◇ **enteric division**, which controls smooth muscles in the gut.

The autonomic system automatically helps us breathe, sweat, pump blood, release adrenaline, and so forth to preserve a stable internal environment. For example, sympathetic nerves speed up the heart in response to stress, whereas parasympathetic nerves slow it down when the threat passes.

Though many cell bodies of the autonomic system are located in the brain (hypothalamus) and the spinal cord, they reach out to the affected organs and muscles via the peripheral nervous system. This means that because psychoactive drugs cross the blood-brain barrier, they can also speed up, slow down, and disrupt these involuntary functions in addition to triggering emotional and mental effects. This is why cocaine can raise the heart rate, constrict blood vessels, and cause heightened sexual sensations.

Somatic System. The **somatic part of the peripheral nervous system transmits sensory information** through sensory neurons that reach the skin, muscles, and joints. It tells the central nervous system about the environment and about limb and muscle position. It then transmits any instructions from the CNS back to skeletal muscles, allowing the body to respond.

CENTRAL NERVOUS SYSTEM

The central nervous system receives messages from the peripheral nervous system, analyzes those messages, and then sends responses via the peripheral nervous circuitry to the appropriate systems of the body: nervous, muscular, skeletal, circulatory, respiratory, digestive, lymphatic, urinary, endocrine, integumentary, and/or reproductive. The CNS also enables us to reason and make judgments about our environment. The brain and the spinal cord act as a combination switchboard and computer.

Psychoactive drugs can alter information sent to our brain from our environment, they can disrupt messages sent back to the various parts of the body, and they can disrupt thinking. Psychoactive drugs affect not only the nervous system but every other system as well. They can affect them directly while passing through the organ or tissue, and they can affect them indirectly by manipulating neurochemistry in the CNS that then sends distorted messages back to the organ. For example, alcohol can directly irritate the lining of the stomach and directly damage liver cells. Alcohol can indirectly slow respiration through its effect on the medulla oblongata in the brainstem, located at the top of the spinal cord.

OLD BRAIN–NEW BRAIN

The brain can be described several ways:

◇ It can be anatomically divided into its component parts (spinal cord, brainstem [medulla, pons, cerebellum], midbrain, diencephalon, and the two cerebral hemispheres).

◇ It can be described by function (e.g., vision center, motor cortex, somatosensory cortex, and hearing centers).

◇ It can be divided by location (hindbrain, midbrain, and forebrain).

For the purposes of understanding how psychoactive drugs work and what causes addiction, we have found it valuable to look at the brain in an evolutionary sense. **The evolutionary perspective looks at physiological changes in the brain as survival adaptations** (Allman, 2000; Evans, Gilbert, Mekel-Bobrov, et al., 2005; Nesse, 1994; Nesse & Berridge, 1997). For example, the evolutionary development of a desire for sweet-tasting substances helped survival by identifying food that could supply quick energy for fight-or-flight responses. The instinctual desire for sex ensured offspring who could guarantee the survival of the species.

The evolutionary perspective also theorizes that **psychoactive drugs have an affinity for natural survival mechanisms and initially cause desirable effects**. The problem is that because refined and potent psychoactive drugs are so new in the evolutionary time scale and are more powerful than naturally occurring substances, the body and the brain have not had time to adapt to their effects. The net effect is that **psychoactive drugs hijack and subvert the brain's survival mechanisms** and, for some, can end up being antisurvival. Using the evolutionary perspective, the two major parts of the brain are defined as the "old brain" and the "new brain."

Old Brain

The old brain, also called the primal brain or primitive brain, consists of the **brainstem, cerebellum, and mesocortex or midbrain, which contains the limbic system (the emotional center)**. The spinal cord is considered part of this old-brain system. The old brain exists in all animals from a fish to a human being (Figure 2-6). The three main functions of the old brain are:

◇ **regulating physiological functions** of the body (e.g., respiration, heartbeat, body temperature, hormone release, and muscle movement);

◇ **experiencing basic emotions and cravings** (e.g., anger, fear, hunger, thirst, lust, pain, and pleasure); and

◇ **imprinting survival memories** (e.g., that green plant tastes good, this bad smell signifies danger).

The old brain responds to internal changes and memories or external influences from the environment. For example, if a person has not had enough liquid, the old brain recognizes the body's thirst and triggers a craving for water. If a deer hears a twig snap in the woods, its old brain registers fear and triggers a desire to escape from that danger. If a man and a woman are in a sensual situation, they will usually desire sex.

When anyone uses psychoactive drugs, most often it is the old brain that is involved in craving and addiction. **It is the old brain that orchestrates euphoric recall that becomes addiction memories**—memories of the experience of drug use and of how it felt; these memories can be triggered repeatedly, encouraging continued drug use (Boening, 2001; Gardner, 2005; Nestler, 2001). The emotions, rather than objective reasoning, are often the deciding factor in making many decisions, such as whether to take a certain drug (McGaugh, 2003; Vergano, 2006).

New Brain

The new brain, also called the **neocortex (cerebrum and cerebral cortex), processes information** that is received from the old brain, from different areas of the new brain, or from the senses via the peripheral nervous system. If a human being is thirsty and craves water, the new brain can help locate the nearest water source. If there is danger, the new brain might figure out a smarter way of avoiding it instead of just running away. If an executive decision has to be made about the relative importance or danger of several courses of action, the new brain will decide. **The new brain allows us to speak, reason, create, and remember.** Over millions of years, but particularly the past 200,000 years, the new brain in humans has grown over the old brain until it has folded in on itself to make room for all the billions of new cells (Pollard, Salama, Lambert, et al., 2006; Suzuki, 1994). The farther along the evolutionary scale, the larger and more complex the new brain (Figure 2-6).

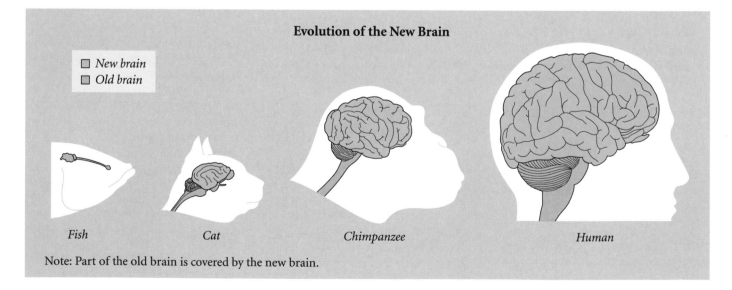

Figure 2-6 •

On the evolutionary scale, from a fish, to a cat, to a chimpanzee, and finally to a human being, the new brain has grown in proportion to the old brain. Though the new brain is much larger, the old brain tends to override it, particularly in times of stress. Only mammals have developed a new brain (cerebrum and cerebral cortex) of any size. The complete brain of an adult human weighs about 3 pounds.

© 2007 CNS Productions, Inc.

The old brain is the senior partner; the new brain is the latecomer. Whenever the two brains are challenged by a crisis, such as fear or anger, there's an automatic tendency to revert to the more established old-brain function. And because the **craving to use a psychoactive drug almost always resides in the old brain**, the desire for the pleasure, pain relief, and excitement that drugs promise can be very powerful. That **craving can override the new brain's rational arguments** that say things like, "too expensive," or "bad side effects," or "there's a midterm exam in the morning, so no partying tonight."

"The impact of that drug, the impact of that sensation and how it immobilized me and made me incapable of dealing with the simplest realities of walking to the bus, of going into my office, of getting on the phone, and of picking up my children was so frightening to me that I did not want to repeat it. I was however very compelled to repeat the use of methamphetamine, which I did for years."
Recovering meth abuser

THE REWARD/ REINFORCEMENT PATHWAY

The specific area of the brain that encourages a human being (or an animal) to perform or repeat an action that promotes survival is called the reward/reinforcement pathway. It is also the part of the brain that is most affected by psychoactive drugs. Technically, this circuit is referred to as the *mesolimbic dopaminergic reward pathway* (Figure 2-8). The pathway is divided into two functional parts: a "more" switch and a "stop" switch. The "more" switch consists of four brain sections: nucleus accumbens septi (NAc), ventral tegmental area (VTA), lateral hypothalamus, and amygdala. The "stop" switch is found mainly in the orbitofrontal cortex.

The **"more" part** of this circuit

◇ **gives animals and human beings a feeling of satisfaction when they**

fulfill a need or even anticipate fulfilling a need or craving that has been triggered by an instinct, a physical imbalance, or an emotional memory (Bassareo & Di Chiara, 1999).

◇ and, just as important, it **gives a surge of relief similar to the intense satisfaction of reward when pain is diminished** (Goldstein, 2001; Nestler, 2005).

Normally, when this center is activated by a substance or an action, it tells the person, "Do more of whatever you did . . . do it again, do it again." The **"stop," or satiation part** of this circuit, then normally:

◇ signals when the craving has been satisfied, and
◇ shuts down the "more" messaging (Koob & Le Moal, 2001; Nestler, Barrot & Self, 2001).

When a psychoactive drug activates this circuit, the person also feels satisfaction or pain relief, and the circuit says to "do it again, do it again," but, unfortunately, **for many substance abusers who have altered their brain chemistry, the "more" switch becomes overactive and the "stop" switch does not shut off, so the person feels an intense need to continue use**. In susceptible individuals, the craving actually increases; the more they use, the greater the craving.

"Crack tastes like more, that's all I can say. You take one hit, it's not enough, and a thousand is not enough. You just want to keep going on and on because it's like a 10-second head rush right after you let the smoke out and you don't get that effect again unless you take another hit."
32-year-old recovering crack addict

Research has defined **three phases of brain activity that compose the reward/reinforcement pathway** when psychoactive drugs are used (Doyon, Anders, Ramachandra, et al., 2005; Gardner, 2005; Volkow, Fowler & Wang, 2004).

1. **Craving and initial stimulus, especially anticipation of drug use**

or compulsive behavior. When an internal or external drug-related cue is received, it activates the amygdala, which then searches for memories connected to that cue (e.g., the sight of a bar triggers memories of taking a drink; seeing white powder of any type triggers memories of snorting cocaine). The anticipation of using and activation of the amygdala by themselves cause a release of dopamine from the ventral tegmental area. The dopamine then activates the shell of the nucleus accumbens, causing craving in some, which often leads to actual use (Di Chiara, 2002).

2. **Activation of the nucleus accumbens and the do-it-again signals.** This is caused when the drug is then taken, and it releases more dopamine in the ventral tegmental area, which then activates the core of the nucleus accumbens—a vital part of the reward/reinforcement pathway (Di Chiara & Bassareo, 2007). The do-it-again signals are triggered. Because addictive drugs preferentially increase extracellular dopamine in the nucleus accumbens, when dopamine is blockaded it blocks the craving for cocaine, amphetamine, and nicotine (Di Chiara, Bassareo, Fenu, et al., 2004). The dopamine release can also result in endorphin or GABA activity at the lateral hypothalamus.

3. **Transmission of reinforcement signals from the nucleus accumbens to the orbitofrontal cortex** (part of the medial prefrontal cortex) that in normal people judges the value or danger of the reward and signals back a "more" or "stop" message. In drug abusers and addicts, that stop/satiation message is weakened, resulting in disruption of the "stop" switch. In addition, the decision-making, or executive function, area of the brain (also in the prefrontal cortex), which normally cautions the abuser about the consequences of using, is severely weakened (Schoenbaum, Roesch & Stalnaker, 2006). Essentially, when an addict' brain is exposed to an addictive substance, it gets stuck on a more intense **do-it-again message**

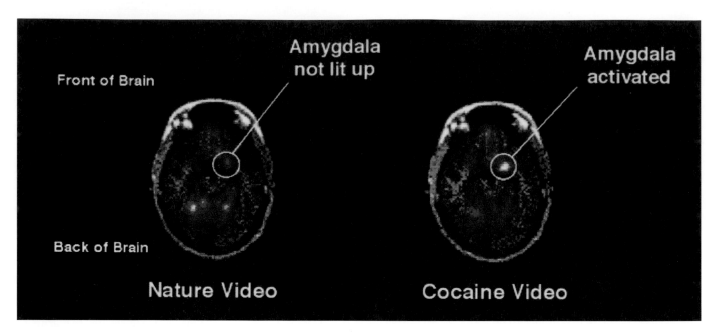

The memory of drugs. *In these PET scans of the brain, the emotional center (amygdala) of the brains of addicts who watched nature videos did not light up or get excited. When they watched a video of cocaine and drug paraphernalia, their amygdalas lit up, most likely signifying phase I of craving. The amygdala is the emotional control center.*
Courtesy of Anna Rose Childress, Ph.D.

that cannot turn itself off no matter how much drug is used.

When the reward/reinforcement pathway is activated by addictive psychoactive drugs, the impact is so strong that the drugs can **imprint the emotional memory of euphoria or pain relief more deeply than most natural survival memories**. Experiments showed that rats learned behaviors more rapidly when they were coupled with drug acquisition and that unlearning a bad behavior took longer (Di Ciano & Everitt, 2004). To test the strength of the emotional memories of drug use and their ability to trigger craving in humans, researchers had a number of cocaine users watch a video about using cocaine. Magnetic resonance imaging (MRI) scans of their brains showed activation of the memories and subsequent craving in the brain as did subjective reports of their feelings. When shown nature videos, the craving and activation of the brain did not appear. Conversely, a control group of nonaddicts showed no such activation or craving when shown any of the visual drug cues (Childress, Mozley, McElgin, et al., 1999).

"When I started drinking, everything went blank in my mind as far as thinking, feelings, emotions. So I like kind of started getting used to it. I said, 'Well that numbed me the first time.' I didn't think of how I was abused or the sexual molestation, so I just continued on, every day, and then I got used to the alcohol."
42-year-old recovering polydrug abuser

The reward center can be activated by psychoactive drugs at several locations on the reward/reinforcement pathway, often through different mechanisms (depending on the substance used). Alcohol might activate the nucleus accumbens via the globus pallidus, heroin through the VTA, and cocaine directly through the NAc (Fields, Hjelmstad, Margolis, et al., 2007; Stahl, 2000).

The **changes in the orbitofrontal cortex** also reinforce the memory that the drug or activity is more pleasurable than other activities. **This alteration of neurochemistry causes normal activities to become even less pleasurable**, leading the user to depend more on the substance or the specific behavior than

on other, less damaging activities for intense experiences (Volkow, Chang, Wang, et al., 2001). For example, methamphetamine will come to have a greater saliency (prominence) in a meth addict's brain than relationships with her children, and gambling will come to have a greater prominence in the compulsive gambler's brain than food or sex.

Part of the reward/reinforcement pathway in the old brain is intimately connected with the physiological regulatory centers of the body (autonomic system). Thus **when drugs are used for intoxication or pleasure, they necessarily affect physiological functions**, especially heart rate and respiration; stimulants speed up these functions, whereas depressants slow them down. **It is the effect on respiration that causes most drug overdose emergencies and deaths.** Psychedelics seem to have a greater effect on the new brain, although they will also affect physiological functions in the old brain (e.g., LSD stimulates, and marijuana sedates). Most drugs also affect memory in one way or another because emotionally tinged memories involve the amygdala and the hippocampus in the old brain.

What makes human beings unique is that starting around the age of three or four years, the neocortex (new brain) becomes more complex and capable. Its value comes from survival lessons and problem-solving skills taught from birth by parents, relatives, schoolteachers, neighbors, and peers.

In most cases, as people continue to grow up they learn how to **integrate the drives of the old brain and the common sense of the new brain**. Some people, however, lose full use of this ability (usually due to genetic abnormalities, a chaotic or abusive childhood, and/or psychoactive drugs or compulsive behaviors). **Psychoactive drugs subvert the survival mechanism away from the commonsense integration of the new and old brains, resulting in the irrational behavior of addiction** (Hyman, Malenka & Nestler, 2006).

"You keep thinking your best thinking got you into this. So then you start to question your own thinking, and then you think, 'Well, I think I'm pretty smart. My best thinking got me to do this.' So that's pretty scary for you right there."

38-year-old compulsive gambler

Nucleus Accumbens

The most important part of the reward/reinforcement pathway is the small group of nerve cells called the *medial forebrain bundle,* which contains the nucleus accumbens septi (Gardner, 2005). This area of the brain was first pinpointed in 1954 by Canadian biologist Dr. James Olds (Olds & Milner, 1954). What Dr. Olds and others have hypothesized, and to a large extent proven, is that **the nucleus accumbens is a powerful motivator (reinforcer)**. It drives people to action. Experimentally, a rat had an electrode attached to its NAc and then connected to an electric switch. When the rat began pressing the switch, activating that part of its brain, it wouldn't stop. In fact, it was so powerful a reinforcer that the rat would press the switch 5,000 times per hour. It wouldn't eat, it wouldn't sleep, it would just keep pushing the switch. The ex-

periment was then tried on human beings. An electrode was implanted in the NAc, and the subjects were given a switch that stimulated that part of the brain. Just as the rats had, the humans pushed it again and again. They talked about how good it made them feel. But most often they simply felt this need to push the switch repeatedly.

Dr. Olds, Dr. Robert Heath, and other researchers found that **many psychoactive drugs also stimulate the NAc** (Olds, 1956). For example, when they had the rat push a lever that gave it a shot of cocaine, the rat would push that lever in much the same way it pushed the switch for the electrical stimulation. In fact, the rats would keep pushing the lever to the exclusion of everything else. They would push it until they died of thirst or starvation.

The actions of the rats were similar to those of human beings who use certain psychoactive drugs. People also respond to the message to do it again, do it again, do it again. **The longer they use, the stronger the do-it-again message becomes.**

What is most interesting about the similarity between the rats' and the humans' reactions is that they respond to the same psychoactive drugs. And, amazingly, the order of preference is also the same; that is, the more intense the drug is in rats, the more intense it is in human beings. This means that the brain reacts in a certain way not because of a bad environment or an abusive childhood or peer pressure but because of the way the brain is designed, especially the reward/reinforcement pathway. This is not to say that in human beings environmental surroundings, emotional states, and peer pressure have no effect. The **effect of social factors has mostly to do with the obsession to use**. The effect of the **alteration in the brain chemistry has to do with the reaction to the drug itself** and even to the anticipation of using. This concept of a susceptible brain and body (coupled with a mental obsession to use) was expressed and disseminated widely by Alcoholics Anonymous (AA) in the 1930s as "The Doctor's Opinion" in AA's *Big Book.*

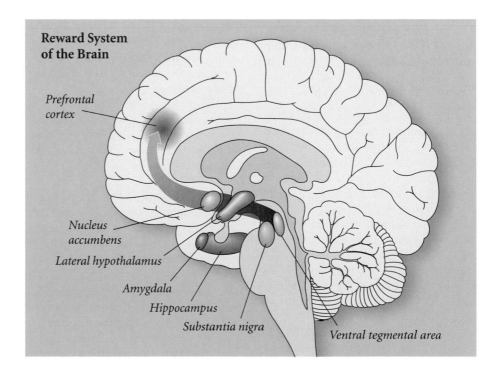

Reward System of the Brain

Prefrontal cortex

Nucleus accumbens

Lateral hypothalamus

Amygdala

Hippocampus

Substantia nigra

Ventral tegmental area

Figure 2-8 •

The reward/reinforcement pathway is really a combination of several structures in the old brain that are activated when the person fulfills some emotion or feeling that has arisen, such as hunger, thirst, or sexual desire. The principal parts are the ventral tegmental area, the nucleus accumbens, the lateral hypothalamus, the amygdala, and the prefrontal cortex.

Courtesy of Kenneth Blum, John Cull, Eric Braverman, and David Comings

William D. Silkworth had worked for years at a hospital specializing in the treatment of alcoholics.

"All these [alcoholics], and many others, have one symptom in common: they cannot start drinking without developing the phenomenon of craving. This phenomenon, as we have suggested, may be the manifestation of an allergy which differentiates these people, and sets them apart as a distinct entity. It has never been, by any treatment with which we are familiar, permanently eradicated. The only relief we have to suggest is entire abstinence."

William D. Silkworth, M.D., in Alcoholics Anonymous Big Book, *1939*

What is remarkable about this statement is that the science of addiction was in its infancy, but since then Dr. Silkworth's observations and conclusions have been validated by modern neuroscience, psychological studies, and brain-imaging techniques. Most of all they have been validated by the behaviors of those afflicted with a substance use disorder.

"Stop" (Satiation) Switch

This stop/satiation center is crucial in keeping craving and satiation in balance. Several areas of the brain are involved in both craving and satiation, although in general satiation involves fewer areas. For example, thirst seems to involve 22 areas of the brain, whereas satiation of that thirst involves just three areas in the cingulate gyrus (Denton, Shade, Zamarippa, et al., 1999). As mentioned, drug craving ("more") involves four areas, and the satiation signal ("stop") usually involves just one area.

What happens to the reward/reinforcement pathway after craving has been activated? Are the changes to the on/off switches that govern craving and satiation permanent or reversible?

"There are switches that allow there to be changes in the way genes work, that they can be turned on or turned off.

One of the things that alcohol does is it turns on and turns off some genes. And as it does this it changes the proteins in those cells and the enzymes that those proteins function as, and that changes the communication between the cells, ultimately leading to a change in the network of the cells and you get a different kind of behavior."

Dr. Ivan Diamond, director, Gallo Research Institute

Neuroscience has discovered that **brain cells change as addiction develops**. Long-term memories are imprinted by the activity of glutamate as well as transcription factors—substances that switch on genes that manufacture proteins. A key factor is deltaFosB, which encourages the growth of new neural connections and strengthens old ones (McDaid, Graham & Napier, 2006). If an action is repeated three or more times, the synapses are sensitized and are more likely to be encoded. An intense stimulus will cause the sensitization with just one encounter (Fields, 2005). **This increase in neural connections results in heightened sensitivity to the drug, thus increasing the risk of relapse even after drug use stops.**

There are a number of theories or ideas about how psychoactive drugs disrupt the on/off switches of the reward/reinforcement pathway and the satiation circuits of the brain:

◇ One concept is that because the feeling of reward did not originate from an essential need of the body, **there is no satiation point**, so the on/off switches do not come into play.
◇ Another concept is that the **on/off switches become stuck**. The mechanism that normally informs the brain that a craving has been satisfied becomes damaged by the use of powerful addictive substances. It becomes stuck in the "on" position, so the person never reacts to the fact that the task has been completed. The use of the drug then continues until the drug runs out or the user hits bottom (Koob & Le Moal, 1997).

◇ Another theory postulates that the **on/off switches are ignored or overridden** because the user wants to continue the euphoria or pain-relief experience from the psychoactive drug's effect on the reward/reinforcement pathway.
◇ A fourth idea is that **psychoactive substances disrupt communication between the two brains** directly (Hyman, 1996). They incapacitate areas of the new brain (thinking and insight) and disconnect its control of the instinctive or automatic old brain.

"I don't like being stuck on stupid, like tweaking all the time. When I'm doing speed, I'm just in this whole little world (can't get me out of it), finding something, nothing, and everything in the dirt."

24-year-old polydrug addict

◇ Finally, certain behaviors, such as compulsive sex, gambling, and risk-taking, also activate the reward/reinforcement pathway of the primitive brain and so are subject to addictive behavioral patterns. This **disruption of the on/off switches due to a behavioral addiction** is identical to drug addiction.

The longer the drug is used or the behavior is practiced, the more the brain changes and the harder it becomes to restore it to healthy functioning.

MORALITY & THE REWARD/ REINFORCEMENT PATHWAY

Throughout human history primal urges, intense emotional memories, and desires that mostly reside in the old brain have been pitted against reason, common sense, and morality that mostly resides in the new brain. In the 1880s Sigmund Freud wrote about how the superego tries to rein in the primal urges of the id and that this conflict causes many of the mental abnormalities in human beings (Freud, 1884, 1995). In many addicts this conflict is more pronounced, but "the old brain rules!"

"Get addicts together and everyone's like, 'Me first,' even me. You know, we fight about who's going to go first. It's always about me, me, me, you know. It's just about the selfishness of it and wanting to feel good."

31-year-old polydrug abuser

But if these primal urges are activated by abnormal biology aggravated by drug use or behavioral addictions rather than normal desires, is it fair to cast addicts as merely being morally weak (Dackis & O'Brien, 2005)?

"It was like I was two people. My inner self would try to communicate to me that, This is not you, you know what I mean? My outer self would communicate to me, This is who you have to be. So I was caught in between two entities, you know, the entities of what is good to you or what is good for you."

44-year-old recovering heroin addict

The Trappist monk Thomas Merton wrote about the conflict between desire and common sense in more poetic terms than old brain vs. new brain:

"As long as pleasure is our end, we will be dishonest with ourselves and with those we love. We will not seek their good but only our own pleasure. Authentic love requires times of self-sacrifice. It requires that people monitor the sensations and feelings and moods of others, not just those of themselves."

Thomas Merton (Merton, 1955)

Because the reward/reinforcement pathway and the rest of the old brain react more quickly and intensely than the neocortex, **it takes a powerful conscious effort to override cravings and desires from the old brain even when reason tells us those feelings are anti-survival.** Greek philosopher Plato wrote almost 2,400 years ago that:

"Passions, and desires, and fears make it impossible for us to think."

Plato, 400 B.C.

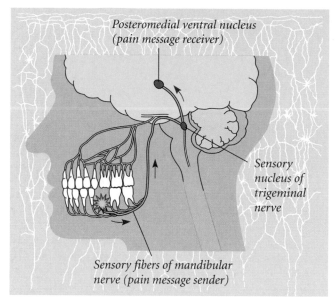

Figure 2-9 •
View of the nerves that would transmit a message of pain from a drilled left molar through the trigeminal nerve to the thalamus.
© 2003 CNS Productions, Inc.

Christian, Buddhist, Islamic, and **almost all theologies (and even atheistic ethical structures) teach that one must resist most primal cravings (including psychoactive drugs) to live a moral or fulfilling life**. Even the idea of original sin can be looked at as the existence of primal urges in a newborn. Some religions look at these urges as sins that must be controlled and their existence forgiven for that person to grow fully and be saved.

The need to balance natural urges with society's restraints and cultural mores will continue to challenge drug treatment facilities and personnel.

NEUROANATOMY

Nerve Cells

Understanding the precise way messages are transmitted by the nervous system is crucial to understanding how psychoactive drugs affect a user's physical, emotional, and mental functioning. For example, if a dentist drills into a lower left molar, the damaged sensory fibers of the mandibular nerve of the peripheral nervous system (Figure 2-9) send tiny electrical pain signals via the trigeminal nerve to the sensory nucleus in the spinal cord. **A rapid signal is immediately relayed to the old brain** and cerebellum in the central nervous system, where a reflex action might jerk the head away from the drill. **A slower signal continues to the thalamus at the top of the brain-**

stem, which identifies the signals as painful and then forwards them to the sensory cortex, where the intensity and the location of the pain is identified. The signal is also forwarded to the frontal cortex, where the cause of the pain is identified and a possible course of action decided. The brain might tell the patient's neck muscles to continue to move the head away from the drill, it might instruct the jaw to bite the dentist's finger, or it might tell the vocal muscles to ask the dentist to prescribe a painkiller. **Nerve impulses might fire up to 1,000 pulses per second** at speeds approaching 270 miles per hour, depending on the size of the nerve (Diagram Group, 1991).

The building blocks of the nervous system, the **nerve cells, are called neurons** (Figure 2-10). Each neuron has four essential parts: **dendrites**, which receive signals from other nerve cells and relay them through the cell body; **the cell body** (soma), which nourishes the cell and keeps it alive; **the axon**, which carries the message from the cell body to the terminals; and **terminals**, which then relay the message to the dendrites, cell body, or even terminals of the next nerve cell. A single cell might have anywhere from a few contacts to up to 150,000 contacts with other cells' dendrites. For example, a spinal motor cell might receive 8,000 messages on its dendrites and 2,000 on its cell body. A Purkinje cell in the cerebellum might have as many

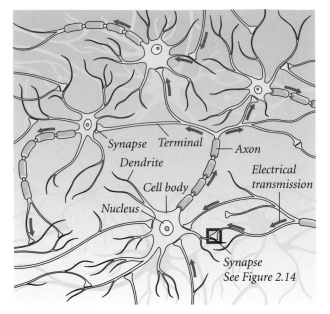

Figure 2-10 •
Stylized depiction of how nerve cells connect with each other. The dendrites, cell bodies, and even terminals receive signals from the terminals of other nerve cells. The transmitted signal then travels through the axon to the next set of terminals, and the message is retransmitted. The process continues until the appropriate part of the nervous system is reached.
© 2003 CNS Productions, Inc.

as 150,000 communication sites available (Figure 2-11). It is estimated that there are 100 trillion to 500 trillion connections among nerve cells. Of course, only a fraction of the synapses will fire at any given time (Kandel, Schwartz & Jessell, 2000; Purves, Augustine, Fitzpatrick, et al., 1997).

The length of a neuron is determined by the length of the cell body, dendrites, terminals, and particularly the axon, which varies from a fraction of a millimeter between brain cells, to 12 inches between a tooth and the brain, to a meter between the spinal cord and a toe. Terminals of one nerve

cell do not touch the adjoining nerve cell because a microscopic gap, called a **synaptic gap**, or **synaptic cleft**, exists between them. This gap is 15 to 50 nanometers (nm) wide. (A *nanometer* is one billionth of a meter.) A million synaptic gap widths added together barely total 1 inch.

The message is transmitted electrically within the neuron, but when it arrives at the synaptic cleft it almost always jumps this gap from the presynaptic terminal to the postsynaptic receptor, not as an electrical signal but as **molecular bits of messenger chemicals called neurotransmitters** (Figure 2-12). These bits of chemicals have been **synthesized within the neuron and stored in tiny sacs called vesicles.** When the neurotransmitters synapse (slot into appropriate postsynaptic receptors), the chemical signal is then converted back to an electrical signal and travels to the next synapse, where it's again converted into a chemical signal for the next synapse (Figure 2-13). **Each synapse transmits the message between neurons until the message reaches the appropriate section of the brain or body for which it was intended.** Though not as common, some synaptic gaps are one-tenth the width of normal synapses. At these junctures the signal is transmitted electrically without the involvement of neurotransmitters. Our focus is on the synapses that need neurotransmitters to jump the gap.

NEUROTRANSMITTERS & RECEPTORS

Although the first neurotransmitters were discovered in the 1920s (acetylcholine) and 1930s (norepinephrine), it was the discovery in the mid-1970s of endorphins and enkephalins that finally **gave an understanding of how psychoactive drugs work in the brain and the body**. For the first time, reaction and addiction to psychoactive drugs could be described in terms of specific naturally occurring chemical and biological processes.

◇ **Endorphins and enkephalins are called endogenous opioids.** *Endogenous* means "originating or produced within the body or organism."

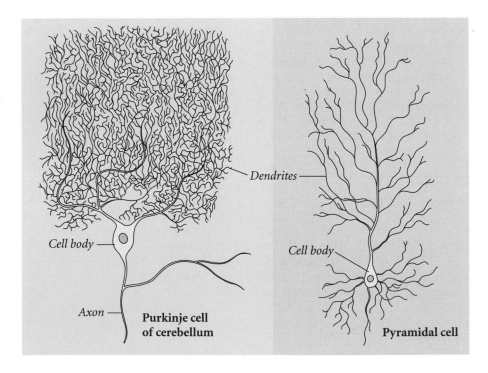

Figure 2-11 •
A two-dimensional tracing of a Purkinje and a Pyramidal cell shows just a fraction of the dendrites that receive signals from other cells. A three-dimensional view of the Purkinje cell would show tens of thousands of contacts.
© 2003 CNS Productions, Inc.

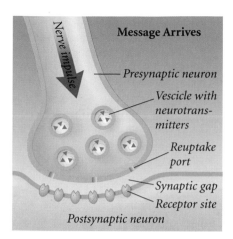

Figure 2-12 •

This is a simplified version of the synapse between nerve cells. The electrical message (nerve impulse) arrives at the junction of two nerve cells, the synaptic gap or cleft.
© 2003 CNS Productions, Inc.

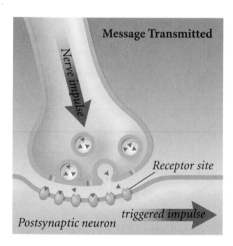

Figure 2-13 •

The electrical message is retriggered in the postsynaptic neuron by neurotransmitters slotting into specialized receptors.
© 2003 CNS Productions, Inc.

◊ **Morphine, heroin, and other opium derivatives or synthetics are called exogenous opioids.** *Exogenous* means "originating or produced outside the organism."

Once the existence of endorphins and enkephalins was confirmed, the search for other natural neurochemicals that mimic psychoactive drugs began in earnest. Over the next 20 to 30, years researchers were able to identify and

then correlate dozens of psychoactive drugs with the neurotransmitters they affect (Table 2-1).

One implication of the research implies that virtually any psychoactive drug works because it mimics or disrupts naturally occurring chemicals in the body that have specific receptor sites. It means that **psychoactive drugs cannot create sensations or feelings that don't have a natural counterpart in the body**. It also implies that human beings can naturally create virtually all of the sensations and feelings they try to get through drugs, although many of them are not as intense as those received through highly concentrated drugs. Here are some examples:

◊ A genuine scare will force the release of adrenaline that will mimic part of a cocaine rush.

◊ Prolonged running produces a "runner's high" through the release of endorphins and enkephalins, similar to a modified heroin rush.

◊ Sleep or sensory deprivation can produce true hallucinations through the same neurotransmitters and mechanisms affected by peyote.

◊ Relaxation and stress-reduction exercises can calm restlessness through glycine and GABA modulation, similar to the effects of benzodiazepines.

One big difference between natural sensations and drug-induced sensations is that **drugs have side effects**, particularly if used to excess, whereas the **natural methods of producing the desired result usually have no side effects**. In addition, the more a drug is used, the weaker the effects become (due to tolerance) and the harder it is to reproduce the desired sensations. Increased doses to achieve the same desired result increase the toxicity of side effects. With natural sensations the opposite is usually true: the desired effects become easier to reproduce with practice. Another key difference is that natural biochemical responses return to a normal state after the response is completed, whereas drugs continue to affect the user's biochemistry until they have been metabolized.

Neurotransmitter research seems to indicate that **some people are drawn to certain drugs because they have an imbalance of one or more neurotransmitters**. These people have discovered through experimentation and self-medication that a specific drug or **drugs would help correct that imbalance temporarily**. For example, people who are born with low endorphin/enkephalin levels or who have damaged their ability to make these chemicals might have a propensity for opioid and alcohol use. Similarly, those with low epinephrine and norepineph-

TABLE 2–1 PSYCHOACTIVE DRUG/NEUROTRANSMITTER RELATIONSHIPS

Drug	Neurotransmitters Directly Affected
Alcohol	GABA (gamma-aminobutyric acid), met-enkephalin, serotonin
Benzodiazepines	GABA, glycine
Marijuana	Anandamide, arachidonylglycerol (2AG), acetylcholine, dynorphin
Heroin	Endorphin, enkephalin, dopamine
LSD	Acetylcholine, dopamine, serotonin
Nicotine	Epinephrine, endorphin, acetylcholine
Cocaine and amphetamines	Dopamine, epinephrine, norepinephrine, serotonin, acetylcholine
MDA, MDMA	Serotonin, dopamine, epinephrine, norepinephrine
PCP	Dopamine, acetylcholine, alpha-endopsychosin

rine (natural stimulants) may be predisposed to amphetamine or cocaine use. This is because those drugs mimic the deficient neurotransmitters and make the user feel normal, satisfied, and in control.

"After I got PMA [para methoxy amphetamine] like down, I never went back to ecstasy again because PMA was like such like a better feeling. It's the derivative of MDMA [ecstasy], that's the feeling that releases all your serotonin. That's what I wanted."

17-year-old recovering meth addict

Major Neurotransmitters

Three groupings of neurotransmitters have been identified:

◇ **monoamines and acetylcholine;**
◇ **amino acids; and**
◇ **peptides, hormones, and nitric oxide.**

Monoamines (e.g., catecholamines) & Acetylcholine

◇ **Acetylcholine (ACh)** is the first known neurotransmitter. It is mostly active at nerve/muscle junctions (e.g., cardiac inhibition and vasodilation), and it also helps control mental acuity, memory, and learning. Acetylcholine imbalance has been implicated in Alzheimer's disease.

◇ **Norepinephrine (NE)** and **epinephrine (E)** are the second two neurotransmitters to be discovered. They are classified as catecholamines and function as stimulants when activated by a demand from the body for energy. Besides stimulating the autonomic system, they also affect motivation, hunger, attention span, confidence, and alertness. Epinephrine has a greater effect on energy, norepinephrine on confidence and feelings of well-being. These neurotransmitters are also known as "adrenaline" and "noradrenaline."

◇ **Dopamine (DA)** was discovered in 1958. This catecholamine helps regulate fine motor muscular activity, emotional stability, satiation,

and the reward/reinforcement pathway. **Dopamine is the most crucial neurotransmitter involved in drug use and abuse.** It is often called the "reward chemical." Parkinson's disease destroys dopamine-producing areas of the brain, thereby inducing erratic and limited motor movements. Excess dopamine causes many of the effects of schizophrenia.

◇ **Histamine** controls inflammation of tissues and allergic response. It also helps regulate emotional behavior and sleep.

◇ **Serotonin** helps control mood stability, including depression and anxiety, appetite, sleep, and sexual activity. MDMA (ecstasy) forces the release of this neurotransmitter. Many antidepressant drugs, including fluoxetine (Prozac®) and paroxetine (Paxil®), are aimed at increasing the amount of serotonin in the synaptic gaps by blocking their reabsorption, thus elevating mood.

Opioid Peptides

◇ **Enkephalins, endorphins, and dynorphins** were discovered in 1973. A number of these opioid peptides are involved in the regulation of pain, the mitigation of stress (emotional and physical), the immune response, stomach activity, and a number of other physiological functions.

Amino Acids

◇ **GABA** (gamma amino butyric acid) is the brain's main inhibitory neurotransmitter and is involved in 25% to 40% of all synapses in the brain. It controls impulses, muscle relaxation, and arousal and generally slows down the brain. Alcohol has a strong effect on GABA.

◇ **Glycine**, an inhibitory neurotransmitter, is found mostly in the spinal cord and the brainstem. It is also prominent in protein synthesis and slows down the brain.

◇ **Glutamic acid (glutamate, glutamine)**, an important excitatory neurotransmitter, is one of the major amino acids and plays a major role in cognition, motor function, and sensory function. It is also impor-

tant in memory reinforcement. Strangely, it is also a precursor for GABA, an inhibitory neurotransmitter.

Tachykinin

◇ **Substance P, a peptide** found in sensory neurons, was first discovered in 1931. It conveys pain impulses from the peripheral nervous system to the central nervous system. Enkephalins block release of substance P.

Lipid Neurotransmitter

◇ **Anandamide**, discovered in 1995, has an affinity for receptor sites, discovered three years earlier, that accommodate THC, the main active ingredient in marijuana. It is found in the limbic system and the areas responsible for integration of sensory experiences with emotions as well as those controlling learning, motor coordination, and memory. It also can act as an analgesic or pain reliever. There are many more cannabinoid receptors in the brain than there are opioid receptors.

Pituitary Peptide

◇ **Corticotropin (ACTH, cortisone)** aids the immune system, healing, and stress control.

Gas

◇ **Nitric oxide** is involved in message transmission to the intestines and other organs, including the penis (erectile function). It also plays a part in regulation of emotions. When mice are bred without nitric oxide, they exhibit aggression along with bizarre and excessive sexual behavior (Snyder, 1996). Nitric oxide (NO) is often confused with the anesthetic nitrous oxide (N_2O).

Hormones

◇ **Adenosine** functions as an autoregulatory local hormone. Most cells contain adenosine receptors that when activated inhibit some cell functions.

Besides the 17 listed above, at least 100 more neurotransmitters have been discovered.

Receptors for Neurotransmitters

Researchers have also discovered hundreds of receptor types, each with a different molecular composition of proteins. **A receptor is designed to receive a compatible neurotransmitter.** There are often multiple receptors on a dendrite or cell body that can accommodate a single type of neurotransmitter. The neurotransmitter serotonin has at least seven types of serotonin receptor sites (e.g., 5-HT1A, 5-HT4) in the brain, each one causing a slightly different effect. There are also at least five dopamine receptors (D_1 to D_5), the most crucial for drug use and abuse is the D_2 receptor.

Each nerve cell produces and sends only one type of neurotransmitter, one exception being some epinephrine nerve cells that also produce norepinephrine. On the other hand, **a single nerve cell can have receptors for several different types of neurotransmitters.** A serotonin receptor will not accommodate dopamine, but a single nerve cell can contain dopamine and serotonin receptors. In addition, the release of one neurotransmitter usually has a cascade effect. For example, the release of serotonin from one neuron will trigger the release of enkephalin in another neuron that then triggers dopamine from a third neuron in the brain's emotional center, which will result in a feeling of well-being.

Advanced Neurochemistry

Message transmission (Figure 2-14) occurs when the incoming electrical signal (1) forces the release of neurotransmitters (2) from the vesicles (3) and sends them across the synaptic gap (4). On the other side of the gap, the neurotransmitters will slot into precise and complex receptor sites (5). These receptor sites are structural protein molecules that when activated by a neurotransmitter cause an ion molecular gate (6) to open, allowing sodium (7), potassium, or chloride ionic electrical charges in or out.

◇ **Excitatory neurotransmitters increase cell firings** by opening the gate and allowing positive sodium ions in.

◇ **Inhibitory neurotransmitters reduce cell firings** by allowing negative chloride ions in and pushing positive potassium ions out.

When enough excitatory neurotransmitters cause sufficient movement of the positively charged sodium ions and the **total voltage reaches a certain action potential** (about 40 to 60 millivolts), it depolarizes and fires the signal (8). The electrical-charge sum of all of the activated receptor sites can cause the cell to reach its action potential and fire off the signal. If enough inhibitory neurotransmitters keep the voltage below the action potential, the cell is inhibited from firing.

◇ The process whereby the neurotransmitter directly affects electrical transmission in the receiving neuron is called the **first messenger system**.

◇ If the received neurotransmitters cause other biological and chemical changes that then affect the electrical transmission, it is called a **second messenger system**. The same neurotransmitter can be a first messenger in one part of the nervous system and a second messenger in another. Second messengers use G-protein-coupled receptors to synthesize neurotransmitters

(Hoffman & Taylor, 2001; Stahl, 2000).

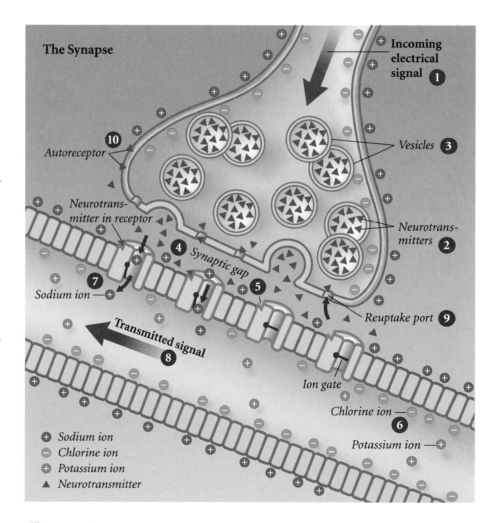

Figure 2-14 •

This is a more complex illustration of what occurs neurochemically and electrically at the synaptic gap. To truly depict the complexity of what happens at the synaptic gap would require dozens of illustrations.

© 2003 CNS Productions, Inc.

As neurotransmitters complete their job in the receptors, they are released back into the synaptic gap and are reabsorbed by the sending nerve cell membrane (reuptake ports [9]) and returned to the vesicles, ready to fire again. The reuptake ports use special molecules (transport carriers, or transporters) as part of **active transport pumps** to move the neurotransmitters through these membranes. Some of the neurotransmitters don't make it back to the reuptake ports of the sending neurons and are metabolized by enzymes surrounding the nerve cells.

The amount of neurotransmitters available for message transmission is constantly monitored by autoreceptors (10) on the sending neuron. If there are too many neurotransmitters, the cell slows their synthesis and release. If there are too few, it speeds up the process. In addition, the number of receptor sites is altered to compensate for variations in the number of neurotransmitters. Two other processes are vital:

◇ **Down regulation. If the cell senses that there are too many neurotransmitters (as there are with drug use), it will retract many of the receptor sites into the cell, causing a slowdown of the message transmission** (Figure 2-15). This causes the person to increase drug intake to try to make the few remaining receptor sites fire faster to restore the original reaction. When drug use is stopped, most of the receptors will be restored. Excessive use however, can cause a permanent decrease in receptor sites. (This process is also known as *pharmacodynamic tolerance*).

◇ **Up regulation.** If there are too few neurotransmitters available to trigger the message, the receiving neuron will increase the number of receptor sites so that the few neurotransmitters remaining can have more receptors to activate.

This information will be crucial later in this section to understand how tolerance, dependence, withdrawal, and addiction occur due to psychoactive drug use.

Although this description of the normal process of neural transmission

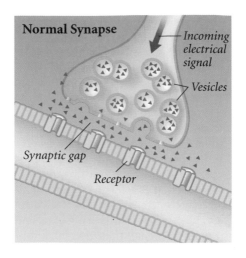 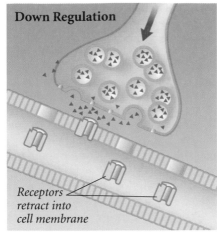

Figure 2-15 •

Down regulation is a process that occurs with excess use of drugs. When a drug such as ecstasy is used, it forces the release of serotonin (A). As the person uses it to excess and over a period of time, the constant bombardment of the serotonin receptors causes them to retreat and retract into the cell membrane (B). This means that the person will not be as sensitive to the drug and will have to use more to get the same effect.

© 2007 CNS Productions, Inc.

is greatly simplified, it is possible to see that it would be easy to induce significant changes in brain functioning by making small changes at this molecular level.

Agonist & Antagonist

Psychoactive drugs are used because they alter the process of message transmission. The two most common ways drugs act are as agonists and as antagonists. Drugs that bind to receptors and:

◇ **mimic or facilitate the effects of neurotransmitters are called** *agonists*;

◇ **don't activate them and thereby block neurotransmitters are called** *antagonists*;

◇ partly mimic the effects of neurotransmitters are called *partial agonists*; and

◇ stabilize the receptor in its inactive state so that it cannot react are called *inverse agonists.*

A drug will sometimes disrupt communication in more than one of the above ways (e.g., acting as an agonist at low doses and as an antagonist at high doses). Drugs can alter the effects of

neurotransmitters through a number of processes:

◇ They can **block the release of neurotransmitters** from the vesicles. Heroin works this way on substance P.

◇ They can **force the release of neurotransmitters** by entering the presynaptic neurons, causing more to be released than occurs naturally. Cocaine works this way on norepinephrine and dopamine; ecstasy works this way on serotonin.

◇ They can **prevent neurotransmitters from being reabsorbed** into the sending neuron, thereby causing them to remain in the synapse to slot into receptors again to induce more-intense effects (e.g., SSRI antidepressants, such as Prozac,® prevent the reuptake of serotonin, thus elevating mood).

◇ They can **inhibit an enzyme that helps synthesize neurotransmitters** to slow the nerve cell's production of neurotransmitters (e.g., heart medications that lower blood pressure by blocking production of norepinephrine, which can raise blood pressure).

◇ They can **inhibit enzymes that metabolize neurotransmitters** in the synaptic gap, thus increasing the number of active neurotransmitters. Methamphetamine inhibits monoamine oxidase and catechol-O-methyltransferase enzymes that metabolize norepinephrine and epinephrine.

◊ They can **interfere with the storage of neurotransmitters**, allowing them to seep out of vesicles and become degraded, thus causing a shortage of those neurotransmitters.

◊ They can **do a combination of these interactions** (Snyder, 1996).

Sometimes the disruption of neurotransmitters is useful (blocking pain messages), sometimes desirable (releasing stimulatory chemicals), and sometimes extremely dangerous (blocking inhibitory neurotransmitters that control violent behavior). For example, a stimulant such as **cocaine will force the release of norepinephrine** (a stimulatory chemical) **and dopamine** (a pleasure-inducing chemical) from the vesicles and then prevent them from being reabsorbed. The net result is that more of both of those neurotransmitters are available to exaggerate existing messages and stimulate new ones (Figure 2-16). The user will stay up past

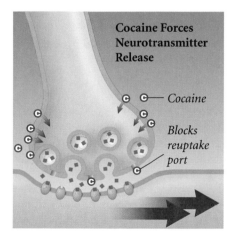

Figure 2-16 •
Cocaine forces the release of extra neurotransmitters and blocks their reabsorption, thus increasing the frequency and therefore the intensity of the electrical signal in the postsynaptic neuron.

© 2007 CNS Productions, Inc.

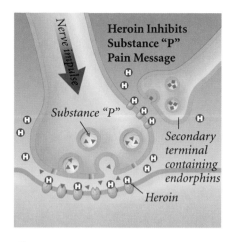

Figure 2-17 •
Acting as a first messenger, heroin inhibits the release of substance P and also blocks most of the neurotransmitter that does get through, so the electrical signal is greatly weakened and the pain controlled.

© 2007 CNS Productions, Inc.

normal exhaustion and feel alert until the neurotransmitters are depleted.

A depressant such as **heroin will act like a second messenger** by mimicking enkephalins and slot into opioid (enkephalin) receptors, thus **inhibiting the release of substance P**, a pain-transmitting neurotransmitter (Figure 2-17). This is the reason why heroin and opioids lessen pain. Heroin **also acts as a first messenger by slotting into substance P receptor sites** on the receiving neurons, thus blocking the pain-causing substance P. Finally, it attaches itself to certain receptor sites in the reward/reinforcement pathway, inducing a euphoric sensation. This too is a desired effect. It also attaches itself to the breathing center, however, thereby depressing respiration. This is a dangerous effect (O'Brien, 2001; Schuckit, 2000B).

An all arounder (psychedelic or hallucinogen) such as LSD will release some stimulatory neurotransmitters but mostly will **alter the user's perception of messages from the external environment**; sounds may become visual distortions, and visual images may become distorted sounds. This intermixing of senses is known as *synesthesia.* Other psychedelics create hallucinations by blocking the action of acetylcholine.

PHYSIOLOGICAL RESPONSES TO DRUGS

Factors such as **tolerance, tissue dependence, psychological dependence, withdrawal, and drug metabolism** can moderate or intensify the effects of psychoactive drugs. These physiological responses are determined by how the drugs interact with neurotransmitters, nerve cells, and other tissues.

TOLERANCE

"If you want to explain any poison properly, then remember, all things are poison. Nothing is without poison; the dose alone causes a thing to be a poison."
Theophrastus von Hohenhein, aka Paracelsus, 1535

The body regards any drug it takes as a poison. Various organs, especially the liver and the kidneys, try to eliminate the chemical before it does too much damage. But if the use continues over a long period of time, **the body is forced to change and adapt** to develop tolerance to the continued input of a foreign substance. The net result is that **the user has to take larger and larger amounts to achieve the same effect**.

"It got to the point where it wasn't working anymore. You know, I'd drink and I'd still be sad, and I'd drink more . . . it got to the point where I had to drink so much more to not feel anything. You know, it was like I was drunk all day long."
17-year-old recovering alcoholic

The body adapts to an upper, such as methamphetamine, to minimize the stimulant's effect on the heart and other systems, so the drug appears to weaken with each succeeding dose if it's used frequently. One dose of meth on the first day of use will energize a user and trigger euphoria that can be matched only by 20 doses on the hundredth day of use.

"When I first started, I remember having a huge reaction to a small amount of speed. Inside of a year, I could shoot a spoon of it easily, which is a pretty fair amount, and it finally got to a point where I couldn't even sleep unless I'd done some."

34-year-old recovering meth user

Although **some tolerance develops with the use of any drug**, a user needs to cross a certain level of use for the development of tolerance to accelerate. For example, if a user takes 5 or 10 milligrams (mg) of diazepam, a sedative, every few days, the development of tolerance is minimal. But if he starts taking two or three times that amount every day, within two or three years he may need to increase the dosage up to 100 mg or more per day to achieve the same effect. Cases of 1,000 mg per day—100 to 200 times the standard dose—have been recorded (O'Brien, 2001).

In experiments with rats, one hour of access to self-administered cocaine per session did not increase intake or tolerance. Six hours of access, however, escalated tolerance and **increased the hedonic set point that is defined as "an individual's preferred level of pharmacological effects from a drug"** (Ahmed & Koob, 1998). The development of tolerance varies widely, depending primarily on the qualities of the drug itself. But it also depends on the amount, frequency, and duration of use, the chemistry of the user, and the psychological state of mind. Generally, **tolerance returns to normal if one stops using the drug**, but reestablishment of tolerance seems to develop more quickly the next time excess amounts are used (Meyer & Quenzer, 2005). There are several different kinds of tolerance.

Kinds of Tolerance

Dispositional Tolerance. The body speeds up the breakdown (metabolism) of the drug to eliminate it. This is particularly the case with alcohol and barbiturates. An example of this biological adaptation can be seen with alcohol. It increases the amount of cytocells and mitochondria in the liver

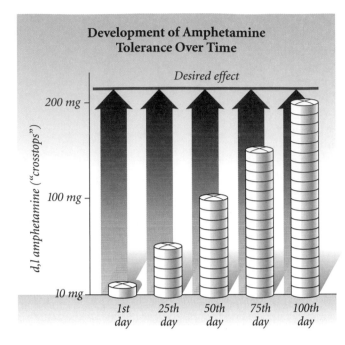

Development of Amphetamine Tolerance Over Time

Figure 2-18 •
This graph shows the gradually increasing amounts of amphetamine needed to produce stimulation or euphoria over time.
© 2007 CNS Productions, Inc.

that are then available to produce more enzymes to break down and deactivate the drug; therefore more has to be drunk to reach the same level of intoxication.

Pharmacodynamic Tolerance. **Nerve cells become less sensitive** to the effects of the drug and even produce an antidote or antagonist to it. With opioids the brain will generate more opioid receptor sites, downregulate them, and produce its own antagonist, cholecystokinin.

Behavioral Tolerance. **The brain learns to compensate** for the effects of the drug by using parts of the brain not affected. A drunken person can make himself appear sober when confronted by police but might be staggering again a few minutes later.

Reverse Tolerance. Initially, one becomes less sensitive to the drug (regular tolerance); but as it destroys certain tissues and/or as one grows older, the trend is reversed and **the user becomes more sensitive and therefore less able to handle even moderate amounts**. This is particularly true in alcoholics when, as the liver is destroyed, it loses the ability to metabolize the drug. An alcoholic with cirrhosis of the liver can stay drunk all day long on a pint of wine because the raw alcohol is passing

through the body repeatedly, unchanged.

"At first I could drink a lot, for about eight or nine years. They'd say I finished 10 or more highballs in the bar, but I'd never get falling down drunk. I'd be pretty high but never passed out. Now, especially since my liver is only slightly smaller than a Volkswagen and not doing its job, if I drink over about four drinks, I can't walk one of those white lines a cop makes you walk if he thinks you're DUI."

43-year-old alcohol user

Acute Tolerance (tachyphylaxis). In these cases **the brain and the body begin to adapt almost instantly** to the toxic effects of the drug. With tobacco, for example, tolerance and adaptation begin with the first puff. Someone who tries suicide with barbiturates can develop an acute tolerance and survive the attempt. They could be awake and alert even with twice the lethal dose in their systems, even if they've never taken barbiturates before.

Select Tolerance. The body develops tolerance to mental and physical effects at different rates. With opiates and depressants, the dose needed to achieve an emotional high comes closer to the lethal physical dose of that drug (Figure 2-19). For example, a barbiturate induces sleep and causes slight euphoria on the first day it is taken. Within a few months, it still induces sleep but no longer causes euphoria, so the user needs five pills to feel good. The user has not developed tolerance to the respiratory depression effects of the barbiturate, however, so that effect is more severe and can be potentially lethal.

"As many pills as I had, I would take. I didn't really care about overdose, which I did many times."
Former barbiturate user

Inverse Tolerance (kindling). **The person becomes more sensitive to the effects of the drug** as the brain chemistry changes. Initially, a marijuana or cocaine user after months of getting a minimal effect from the drug will suddenly get an intense reaction. A cocaine or meth addict becomes more sensitive to the toxic effects after continued use, thus developing a greater risk of heart attack or stroke.

Cross-Tolerance. **As a person develops tolerance to one drug, he develops tolerance to other drugs as well.** A heroin addict will also be tolerant to doses of morphine, codeine, or methadone even if he has never taken those other opioids, because the same biologic mechanisms that establish tolerance to one opioid will be in place to provide tolerance to others as well. Someone tolerant to the effects of alprazolam (Xanax®) will also have a tolerance to the effects of other benzodiazepine sedatives and even alcohol. Cross-tolerance can also occur between drugs of different chemical compositions. A person tolerant to the effects of barbiturates will also be tolerant to benzodiazepines.

TISSUE DEPENDENCE

Tissue dependence is the **biological adaptation of the body** due to prolonged use of drugs. It is often quite extensive, particularly with downers. In fact, with certain drugs the body can change so much that the **tissues and the organs come to depend on the drug just to stay functional (allostasis).** For example, the number of cytocells and mitochondria in the liver of an alcohol user increase with repeated use to keep the drug from poisoning the drinker. This is a form of tissue dependence. Tissue dependence of brain cells has more-severe consequences, but once tissue dependence has set in, abrupt cessation of the drug can trigger dramatic and dangerous withdrawal reactions.

"I would start to feel very abnormal after two or three hours, and it was like trying to maintain until I could begin to feel normal. And that was the only kind of normal that I knew, Darvon-induced normality."
Recovering Darvon® user

Cross-Dependence. As with cross-tolerance, when one develops tissue dependence to a drug, he will also develop it to other drugs. This is why buprenorphine can be used to treat heroin addiction.

PSYCHOLOGICAL DEPENDENCE & THE REWARD-REINFORCING ACTION OF DRUGS

In the past a drug was called addicting only if clear-cut tissue dependence developed, as evidenced by objective physical signs of withdrawal; but with breakthroughs in modern neurochemical research, more-subtle changes in body chemistry can be measured. In addition, **psychological dependence has been recognized in recent years as an important factor in the development of addictive behavior.** Researchers such as Dr. Anna Rose Childress at Veterans Hospital in Philadelphia have shown that psychological dependence actually produces many physical effects, meaning that defining drug dependence as strictly physical or strictly mental is not accurate (Robbins, Ehrman, Childress, et al., 2000).

Drugs cause an altered state of consciousness and distorted perceptions pleasurable to the user. These reinforce continued use of the drug. Psychological dependence can therefore result from the continued misuse of drugs to avoid life's problems and boredom or from their continued use to compensate for inherited deficiencies in brain-reward neurotransmitters.

"I have a choice about the first snort of cocaine I take. I have no choice about the second."
Recovering cocaine user

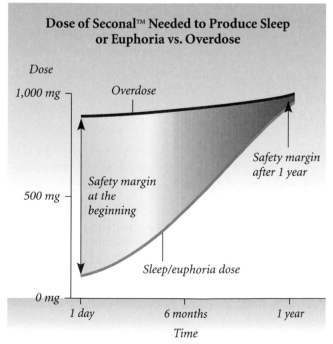

Dose of Seconal™ Needed to Produce Sleep or Euphoria vs. Overdose

Dose

1,000 mg — Overdose

Safety margin at the beginning

Safety margin after 1 year

500 mg —

Sleep/euphoria dose

0 mg —

1 day   6 months   1 year

Time

Figure 2-19 •
With many drugs, tolerance to mental effects develops at a different rate than tolerance to physical effects. If a user increases the amount of barbiturate to continue the high, tolerance to the respiratory depressant effects doesn't increase as quickly as tolerance to the mental effects, so an overdose (potentially fatal physical effects) becomes more likely.
© 2007 CNS Productions, Inc.

Drugs also have the innate ability to guide and **virtually hypnotize the user into continual use (called the "positive reward-reinforcing action of drugs")**. In animal experiments in which rats were trained to press a lever that would feed them heroin or other drugs intravenously, they would continue to press the lever even before physical dependence had developed, showing that a psychoactive drug in and of itself can reinforce the desire to continue use.

There are additional ways that addictive drug taking is reinforced:

◊ **Drug Automatism.** These **substances can induce an aimless, unconscious, repetitive drug-taking behavior** whereby individuals continue taking the substance seemingly without knowing that they are doing so.

◊ **Negative Reinforcement. Benefits obtained by the termination of an unpleasant state also encourage drug use.** Nicotine addicts will wake up to smoke in the middle of the night to terminate the development of nicotine withdrawal.

◊ **Social Reinforcement.** Peer pressure, the desire or need for social inclusion, and other **social factors may encourage the continued use of an addictive psychoactive substance**.

WITHDRAWAL

When a user stops taking a drug that has created tolerance and tissue dependence, the body is left with an altered chemistry. There might be an overabundance of enzymes, receptor sites, or neurotransmitters. Without the drug to support this altered chemistry, the body suddenly tries to return to normal. *Withdrawal* is defined as the "**body's attempt to rebalance itself after cessation of prolonged use of a psychoactive drug.**" All of the things the body was prevented from doing while taking the drug it does to excess while in withdrawal. For example, consider how the desired effects of heroin are quickly replaced by unpleasant withdrawal symptoms once a longtime user stops taking the drug (Table 2-2).

TABLE 2–2   OPIOID EFFECTS VS. WITHDRAWAL SYMPTOMS

Withdrawal effects are often the opposite of the drug's direct effects.

Effects	Withdrawal Symptoms
Numbness	becomes pain
Euphoria	becomes anxiety, depression, or craving
Dryness of mouth	becomes sweating, runny nose, tearing, and increased salivation
Constipation	becomes diarrhea
Slow pulse	becomes rapid pulse
Low blood pressure	becomes high blood pressure
Shallow breathing and suppressed cough	become coughing
Pinpoint pupils	become dilated pupils
Sluggishness	becomes severe hyper-reflexes and muscle cramps

In fact, with many compulsive users the **fear of withdrawal is one reason why they keep using**. They dread the aches, pains, insomnia, vomiting, cramps, and occasional convulsions that accompany withdrawal as the body struggles to achieve homeostasis.

"Your muscles are like wrenching; your entire digestive tract is going crazy. Stomach cramps. Not just stomach cramps, diarrhea . . . everything that can go wrong with your intestinal tract happens. Your legs, you kick constantly at night; that's why I think they call it kicking. Your legs will jerk and kick uncontrollably. You have insomnia. You vomit, sweat, what else, and what else, oh yeah, the craziness. Delirium."
23-year-old female recovering heroin addict

Because the withdrawal can be so severe, many treatment programs use medications to temper the symptoms. Withdrawal from opiates, alcohol, many sedatives, and even nicotine seems to be triggered by an area of the brainstem known as the *locus ceruleus*. Drugs like Catapres,® Vasopressin,® and Baclofen,® which act to quiet down this part of the brain, partially block out the withdrawal symptoms of these drugs.

Kinds of Withdrawal

There are four distinct types of withdrawal symptoms: nonpurposive, purposive, protracted, and post-acute withdrawal symptoms (PAWS).

Nonpurposive Withdrawal. Nonpurposive withdrawal consists of **objective physical signs** that are a direct result of the tissue dependence and are directly observable upon cessation of drug use by an addict. These include seizures, sweating, goose bumps, vomiting, diarrhea, and tremors.

"When I ran out, it was severe. I mean body convulsions, long memory lapses, cramps that were just enough to—you couldn't stand them. And it lasted for about five days—the actual convulsions, the cramps, and the pain and stuff. And then it took another couple of weeks before I ever felt anywhere near normal."
18-year-old recovering heroin user

Purposive Withdrawal. Purposive withdrawal results either from **addict manipulation** (hence purposive, or "with purpose") or from a psychic conversion reaction from the expectation of the withdrawal process. Psychic conversion is an **emotional expectation of physical effects** that have no biological explanation. Because a common behavior of most addicts is malingering or manipulation in an effort to secure more drugs, sympathy, or money, they may claim to have withdrawal symptoms that are very obscure and difficult to verify (e.g., "My nerves are in an uproar. You've got to give me something, Doc!"). Physicians and pharmacists have to be very aware of this type of manipulation.

"It takes a doctor 30 minutes to say no, but it only takes him five minutes to say yes. We used to share doctors that we could scam. We called them 'croakers.'"
33-year-old recovering heroin user

Within the past few decades, the portrayal of drug addiction by the media, books, movies, and television has resulted in another kind of purposive withdrawal. When they run out of drugs, younger addiction-naive drug users expect to suffer withdrawal symptoms similar to those portrayed in the media. They experience a wide range of reactions even though tissue dependence has not truly developed. Treatment personnel must avoid overreacting to these symptoms. Further, as previously mentioned, Dr. Childress has demonstrated that psychological dependence can cause many physical symptoms not directly attributable to biological changes in the body.

Protracted Withdrawal (environmental triggers & cues). A major danger to maintaining recovery and preventing a drug overdose during relapse is protracted withdrawal. This is a **flashback or recurrence of the addiction withdrawal symptoms** and a triggering of heavy craving for the drug long after an

addict has been detoxified. The cause of this reaction (similar to a post-traumatic stress phenomenon) often happens when some sensory input (odor, sight, or noise) stimulates the memories experienced during drug use or withdrawal that evokes a desire for the drug. For instance, the odor of burnt matches or burning metal (smells that occur when cooking heroin) several months after detoxification may cause a heroin addict to suffer some withdrawal symptoms. Any white powder may cause craving in a cocaine addict; a blue pill may do it to a Valium® addict, and a barbecue can cause a recovering alcoholic to crave a beer.

"I had just got a disability check, and that check was like a trigger for me. It just sent me into a state of nervousness or anxiety, and I didn't know what to do. Today I may not even walk on the same block that I used to walk on because I know if I'm feeling shaky, there could be a possibility that I'll run into somebody I want to use with, so I have to stay away from those areas."
32-year-old recovering crack cocaine abuser

Protracted withdrawal often causes recovering addicts to slip or renew their drug use, generally leading to a full relapse (O'Malley & Volpicelli, 1995). These slips are associated with a greater chance of drug overdose because users are prone to taking the same dose they were injecting, smoking, or snorting when they quit. They often forget that their last dose was probably a very high one that they could handle only because tolerance

had developed. They don't remember that abstinence allowed their bodies to return to a less-tolerant state.

"We cleaned up because we didn't have any connections when we moved. We had about 15 clonidine pills to help us through, and I was drinking. Then we shared one bag, one $20 bag of 'cut,' and both of us were on the floor."
33-year-old husband-and-wife heroin users

Research with animals and interviews with addicts demonstrate that once abstinence is interrupted, both tolerance and tissue dependence develop at a much faster rate than before.

Post-Acute Withdrawal Symptoms. PAWS is the persistence of subtle yet significant emotional and physical problems that can last for three to six months into recovery. Six major symptoms have been identified:

◇ unclear thinking and cognitive impairment,
◇ memory problems,
◇ emotional overreaction,
◇ sleep disturbances,
◇ motor coordination/dizziness problems, and
◇ difficulty managing stress.

Drug craving is also part of the PAWS syndrome. PAWS has been documented to occur in many addicts during early recovery from different substances. Symptoms can be severe enough to cause relapse if not adequately treated (Gorski, 2003).

FROM EXPERIMENTATION TO ADDICTION

People take psychoactive drugs for the mental, emotional, and even physical effects they induce. **Most often it is the memory of what that drug did in specific emotional situations that prompts them to use.** It could be that marijuana countered boredom, alcohol reversed shyness, a benzodiazepine erased unwanted memories, crystal meth gave energy, and tobacco eased tension.

DESIRED EFFECTS VS. SIDE EFFECTS

"Let's not kid ourselves. People initially do get something from drugs. They don't say, 'Well, I want to feel miserable so I think I'll swallow this.' They

don't think, I'm gonna make myself cough by smoking a joint until my eyes become bloodshot. They don't plan to get hepatitis or AIDS from a shared needle. They get something out of the drug, something desirable enough to throw caution to the wind."
Authors of Uppers, Downers, All Arounders

Drugs are taken for their desired effects. It's a package deal, however, and the more that is taken for a desired effect, the more the side effects accumulate.

DESIRED EFFECTS

Curiosity & Availability

"She asked me if I'd ever done it, and I told her no, and she was doing it right in front of me, and I just wanted to try it just to see what it was like on it. I did cheerleading in between that, and then when I quit cheerleading, I started smoking weed again."

17-year-old marijuana smoker

To Get High

"It's kind of like life without a coherent thought. It's kind of like an escape. It's like when you go to sleep, you kind of forget about things in your sleep. It's like everything's dreamlike and there's no restraints on anything."

17-year-old heroin user

Self-Medication

"I was very hyperactive, you know. Just always getting into trouble doing things, getting hurt, falling off of things, getting in fights, getting in arguments. And the more I smoked as the years went on, the mellower I got. I stopped getting into trouble."

23-year-old marijuana user

Confidence

"I felt like I was on top of the world and I could accomplish anything. Just the physical part of staying up so long and being able to feel the freedom of staying up so long was great."

22-year-old recovering meth addict

Energy

"I felt really tingly, excited, sexy. I felt that I had all this energy. I felt like I could do anything. I felt really powerful

and I enjoyed that feeling. It made me feel good."*

19-year-old male recovering meth addict

Psychological Pain Relief

"I remember being beat up physically and being emotionally abused and drinking a gallon of wine and feeling like I just wanted to be out of it. And for me that was the way to deal with the pain. I think women tend to do those things; either they'll take drugs with the perpetrator to have some kind of relationship, or after they've been beat up use alcohol or drugs as a way not to deal with the pain."

39-year-old ex-wife of abuser

Anxiety Control

"It relieved certain anxieties. It alleviated depression, which I had. Lots of depression. You tell the doctor, 'I'm depressed.' 'Okay, take some Valium.®' Now they try to give you antidepressant medications prescribed by the doctor. I'll take the Valium.®"

44-year-old Valium® user

To Oblige Friends (internal & external peer pressure)

"If your friends are all getting stoned, then you don't want to just sit there, you know. They're all going to be like having supposedly even more fun because they're stoned, you know. And then they make you look stupid because you feel stupid if you're not."

15-year-old marijuana smoker

Disinhibition

"If you are doing like ecstasy or something, you can just spill your guts to anyone you are with; and if you are with a friend or somebody you're dating, you can just say whatever you want. It changes everything because you just wake up the next morning

and be like, 'Oh God, what did I say last night?' but you remember it."*

17-year-old MDMA (ecstasy) user

Boredom Relief

"They tell you you're going to school to get an education so you can get a good job, okay? They told me how to get a job, so that's 8 hours a day. I knew how to sleep, that's 8 hours a day. I had another 8 hours a day that I didn't know how to fill, and I used marijuana to fill those 8 hours. Period."

35-year-old recovering marijuana user

Altered Consciousness

"Acid put me in a whole other world, like I don't know, it's hard to explain what it was like. Of course, there was the visuals, where like everything seemed to either be dripping or like everything would turn into patterns and like I could look at the carpet and just like see like spirals everywhere in it, but more so I used it for kind of a mental and a body high."

18-year-old LSD user

To Deal with Isolation or Life Problems

"When I got addicted to the cocaine, it was because I was being battered and I used that to hide. When I left the cocaine, I used the drinking to hide. When I left the drinking, the cigarettes kicked in. When I left the cigarettes, I began to overeat. It was like I had to fill up that hole with something."

28-year-old recovering compulsive overeater

Oblivion

"On one occasion I was with my friend; we were just sitting in my house just hitting End Dust,® like three cans we killed and then I couldn't, I didn't know what I was doing. I was just sitting there drooling on myself and I

passed out. When I woke up I saw him, and then he was talking to himself, and then he spit at me, and then he's like, 'Oh, I thought you were somebody else.'"

17-year-old recovering inhalant abuser

Competitive Edge

"I was 125 pounds, not big enough for the team. I started taking steroids, injecting them, that I got from a weightlifter friend down at the gym so I could bulk up. I also started eating like a hungry hog."

19-year-old steroid user

SIDE EFFECTS

"I don't think that a drug is evil in and of itself, but just as drugs can be used to help heal a person, they can result in destroying a life as they did to me. So it really depends on the individual— what and how he chooses and how wisely he uses or chooses not to use medications and drugs."

28-year-old recovering sedative-hypnotic abuser

If drugs did only what people wanted them to and they weren't used to excess, they wouldn't be much of a problem. But drugs not only generate desired emotional and physical effects; they also **trigger mild, moderate, dangerous, and sometimes fatal side effects**. This conflict between the emotional/physical effects that users want and those they don't want is the main problem with using psychoactive drugs.

A physician can prescribed a psychoactive drug such as codeine (an opioid downer) to relieve pain, to suppress a cough, or to treat severe diarrhea. The drug also acts as a sedative, gives a feeling of well-being, and induces an emotional numbness. People who self-prescribe hydrocodone or OxyContin® just for the feeling of well-being or numbness will have slower reaction time and often become constipated. With moderate use they can also be subject to nausea, pinpoint pupils, dry

skin, and slowed respiration. And if users keep using to recapture that feeling of well-being over a long period of time, they can become lethargic, lose sexual desire, and even become compulsive users of the drug, leading to abuse and addiction. In addition to physical and psychological side effects of drug use, **social side effects, including legal, relationship, financial, and work difficulties, can be equally damaging.**

Side effects can be aggravated by a number of other factors, including polydrug abuse and the level of use.

POLYDRUG ABUSE

Drug abuse and the practice of compulsive behaviors can sometimes be considered symptoms of underlying problems rather than the cause; so if addicts can't get the desired effect from one drug, they will try almost any other substance and behavior to attain that change of mood they seek.

Virtually every client who comes in for treatment has practiced polydrug abuse. For this reason treatment is more complex than just getting a person off one drug (*see Chapters 9 and 10*). There are a number of ways a person will resort to polydrug use.

◇ **Replacement.** Some will use another drug when the desired drug is not available (e.g., drinking alcohol when heroin is unavailable).

◇ **Multiple Drug Use.** Some use several drugs to attain different feelings (e.g., taking methamphetamine for stimulation and becoming bored with it, then using ketamine for a different effect).

◇ **Cycling.** This involves using drugs intensely for a period of time, abstaining or using another drug to rest the body or lower tolerance, and then using again (e.g., taking an anabolic steroid for 2 weeks, then a different steroid for 2 weeks, then nothing for 2 weeks, then back to the original steroid).

◇ **Stacking.** This is using two or more similar drugs at one time to enhance a specific desired effect (e.g.,

using alcohol and a benzodiazepine to get to sleep, or using MDMA (ecstasy) with meth to enhance the ecstasy high).

◇ **Mixing.** Somewhat similar to stacking, mixing uses drug combinations to induce different effects (e.g., speedballs [cocaine with heroin]; lacing a marijuana joint with cocaine; X and L [ecstasy and LSD] to prolong the effects of each; methadone with Klonopin® to mimic the effect of heroin; or an antihistamine and a sedative to intensify the downer effects). Some of these combinations are taken intentionally; others are unintentional, as when a dealer spikes his drug with a cheaper drug (e.g., PCP is used to spike a marijuana cigarette to mimic a high THC content).

◇ **Sequentialing.** This is using one drug in an abusive or addictive manner and then later switching to another drug addiction (e.g., a recovering heroin addict who starts using alcohol compulsively, or a cocaine addict who switches to methamphetamine). The sequence can also include behavioral addictions (e.g., a recovering alcoholic who becomes a compulsive gambler, or a compulsive marijuana smoker who switches to compulsive eating).

◇ **Morphing.** This involves the use of one drug to counteract the unwanted effects of another drug (e.g., a cocaine user so wired that she has to drink alcohol to come down; a drunk who drinks coffee in an effort to wake up; a heroin addict who uses methamphetamine simply to function).

LEVELS OF USE

It is important to determine the level at which a person uses drugs and thereby have a benchmark by which to judge whether drug use is accelerating and becoming increasingly problematic. To determine level of use, it is **necessary to know the amount, frequency, and duration of psychoactive drug use**. These three factors by themselves, however, are not enough to make the determination. The second key element is to **know the impact the drug use has on the individual's life**. For example, a man might drink a six-pack of lager beer (amount) twice a week (frequency) and keep it up for 12 years (duration) without developing any problems. Another man might drink only on Fridays but doesn't stop until he passes out. The second man might have more problems regarding relationships, health, the law, or money than the first man, who drinks more frequently but functions well on the job and works at his relationships.

The following categories can help people judge their level of use:

◇ Abstinence
◇ Experimentation
◇ Social/recreational use
◇ Habituation
◇ Abuse
◇ Addiction

The levels of use are presented as distinct categories, although the transition from experimentation to habituation or from habituation to addiction does not happen so neatly. It is a continuous process that can ebb and flow. With most psychoactive drugs, **a point is passed where it becomes harder and harder for the person to choose the level of drug use at which they want to remain—their hedonic set point**. That point can vary radically from person to person.

ABSTINENCE

Abstinence means people do not use a psychoactive substance except accidentally (e.g., when they drink some alcohol-laced punch, take prescribed medication that has a psychoactive component they don't know about, or are in an unventilated room with smokers). The important fact to remember about abstinence is that **even if people have a very strong hereditary and environmental susceptibility to use drugs compulsively, they will never have a problem if they never begin to use**. If they never use, there is no possibility of developing drug craving. They might, however,

have a problem with compulsive behaviors, such as gambling, overeating, excessive Internet use, or compulsive sexual behavior.

Those who experiment with alcohol, nicotine, and marijuana between the ages of 10 and 12 are much more likely to become heroin or cocaine abusers than those who wait until they are 18 or especially those who wait even later in their life before experimenting with drugs of abuse. Further, research demonstrates that those individuals who never try nicotine before the age of 21 are almost never addicted to tobacco later in life. The same goes for people who don't try any drug until their mid-twenties; significantly fewer of them get addicted (Office of National Drug Control Policy, 2001).

Researchers have long believed that a spurt of overproduction of gray matter—the working tissue of the brain's cortex—during the first 18 months of life was followed by a steady decline as unused brain circuitry was discarded. Then, in the late 1990s, the National Institute of Mental Health's Dr. Jay Giedd and his colleagues discovered a second wave of overproduction of gray matter just prior to puberty, followed by a second bout of "use it or lose it" pruning during the teen years. The study followed 13 teenagers for 10 years with MRI scans that showed the ebb and flow of gray matter. They found that the more advanced functions such as integrating information from the senses, reasoning, and other executive functions mature last (Bergstrom & Langstrom, 2005; Giedd, Blumenthal, Jeffries, et al., 1999; McDonald, Daily, Bergstrom, et al., 2005; Sowell, Thompson, Holmes, et al., 1999; Thompson, Giedd, Woods, et al., 2000). Additionally, the part of the brain that blocks risk-taking behavior isn't fully developed until the age of 25 or so.

"My brother died of alcoholism, so I have never had a drink of alcohol or, for that matter, a puff on a cigarette."
Financier Donald Trump, 1999

EXPERIMENTATION

With experimentation **people become curious about the effects of a drug** or are influenced by peers, friends, relatives, advertising, or other

media and take some when it becomes available. The feature that distinguishes experimentation from abstinence is the curiosity about drug use and the willingness to act on that curiosity. With experimentation, drug use is limited to only a few exposures. **No pattern of use develops, and there are only limited negative consequences in the person's life except if:**

◇ large amounts are used at one time, leading to accident, injury, or illness;
◇ the person has an exaggerated reaction to a small amount (e.g., cocaine allergy);
◇ a pre-existing physical or mental condition is aggravated (e.g., schizophrenia);
◇ the user is pregnant (e.g., fetal damage);
◇ legal troubles arise (e.g., drug test or possession arrest);
◇ there is a high genetic and/or environmental susceptibility that can lead to compulsive use and addiction; or
◇ there is a prior history of addictive behavior with other psychoactive drugs that can lead to a relapse.

Then experimentation can rapidly become a more serious level of drug use.

"A lot of my friends did heroin. I just wanted to try it. It was an experiment. I just wanted to see what it was like. It felt good for a little while; you nod off and you are half-dreaming."
22-year-old polydrug user

SOCIAL/RECREATIONAL USE

Whether it's a legal six-pack at a party, a bowl of "bud" with a friend, or a couple of lines of cocaine at home, with social/recreational use the person **seeks out a known drug and wants to experience a known effect, but there is no established pattern**. Drug use is irregular, not too frequent, and has a relatively small impact on the person's life except if it triggers exaggerated reactions, preexisting mental and physical conditions, an existing addiction, genetic/environmental susceptibility, or legal troubles. Social/recreational use is therefore distinguished from experimental use by the **establishment of drug-seeking behavior**.

"The friends I started hanging out with in school were pretty much the ones that were really rebelling and already knew about cigarettes and pot, and so we just started sneaking off and someone would have a joint or something that their dad left around."
24-year-old marijuana smoker

HABITUATION

With habituation **there is a definite pattern of use** (e.g., the TGIF high, the five cups of coffee every day, or the half gram of cocaine most weekends). No matter what happens that day or that week, the person will use that drug. So long as it doesn't affect that person's life in a really negative way, it could be called *habituation*. Regardless of how frequently or infrequently a drug is used, a definite pattern of use indicates that there is a stronger craving for the drug. Despite the development of patterned use, the drug must still have a relatively small impact on the user's life for this behavior to be habitual use.

"You would say that I was a habitual user, but I don't really think that's the case. So it is a habit. I like a drink. And the question, you know, the question is could I go a day without having a drink? I think so but I've never had a reason to try."
42-year-old habitual drinker

ABUSE

The definition of drug abuse is **the continued use of a drug despite negative consequences**. It's the use of cocaine in spite of high blood pressure, the use of LSD though there's a history of mental instability, the alcoholic with diabetes, the two-pack-a-day smoker with emphysema, and the user with a series of arrests for possession. No matter how often a person uses a drug, if negative consequences develop in re-

lationships, social life, finances, legal status, health, work, school, or emotional well-being and drug use continues on a regular basis, that behavior could be classified as drug abuse.

"I had an EEG [electroencephalogram] a CAT [computerized axial tomography] scan, and I was told that I had lowered my seizure threshold by doing so many stimulants, but that's not the reason I stopped using them. The reason I actually stopped was because I discovered heroin and I liked it better. I would probably have continued using speed even with the seizures."
36-year-old speed user

ADDICTION

The step between abuse and addiction has to do with compulsion. Users would be classified as addicted if they:

◊ often use the drug in larger amounts or for longer periods of time than was intended;

◊ unsuccessfully try to cut down or control the drug use;

◊ spend a great deal of time in activities to obtain the substance or recover from its use;

◊ give up or reduce important social, occupational, or recreational activities because of the drug use;

◊ continue drug use despite knowledge that it is causing physical, relationship, social, or psychological problems;

◊ need a hit of their drug to start off the day;

◊ get angry and even enraged defending their drug use;

◊ experience withdrawal when unable to obtain their drug; and/or

◊ continue to increase the amount of drug taken to obtain desirable effects.

Such users have lost control of their use of drugs, and those substances have become the most important thing in their lives (American Psychiatric Association [APA], 2000).

The authors have found that **addiction comprises the four *C*s**, or the cornerstones of addictive behavior: **loss of *control, compulsive* drug use, *cravings* for drugs, and *continued* use** despite increasing negative consequences associated with use.

"The craving was just continuous. It was just like if I was coming off speed, I wanted heroin. If I was coming off heroin, I wanted to snort cocaine. And if I was coming off that, I wanted to stay numb. I wanted to go from one drug to another. If I wanted to stay up all night, I would do speed."
38-year-old recovering polydrug addict

THEORIES OF ADDICTION

For many years there has been an attempt to classify mental and emotional disorders and illnesses. In 1952 the first edition of the American Psychiatric Association's (APA's) *Diagnostic and Statistical Manual of Mental Disorders* (*DSM*) was published. Besides the standard mental illnesses, such as schizophrenia, depression, and manic-depression (bipolar illness), the manual included classifications of substance-related disorders. These classifications have changed over the years to reflect new research and ideas. In the latest edition, *DSM-IV-TR,* **substance-related disorders** are divided into two general categories: substance use disorders and substance-induced disorders.

◊ **Substance use disorders (SUD)** involve patterns of drug use and are divided into substance dependence and substance abuse. Note that the word *dependence,* not *addiction,* is used.

◊ **Substance dependence** is defined in the *DSM-IV-TR* as "a cluster of cognitive, behavioral, and physiological symptoms indicating that the individual continues use of the substance despite significant substance-related problems. There is a pattern of repeated self-administration that can result in tolerance, withdrawal, and compulsive drug-taking behavior."

◇ **Substance abuse** is defined as "a maladaptive pattern of substance use leading to clinically significant impairment or distress" that results in disruption of work, school, or home obligations; recurrent use in physically hazardous situations; recurrent legal problems; and continued use despite adverse consequences.

◇ **Substance-induced disorders** include conditions that are **caused by use of specific substances**. Most of these conditions usually disappear after a period of abstinence; however, some of the damage can last weeks, months, years, and even a lifetime. Substance-induced disorders include **intoxication, withdrawal, and certain mental disorders** (e.g., delirium, dementia, anxiety disorder, sexual dysfunction, and sleep disorder). The substances specifically defined in the *DSM-IV-TR* include alcohol, amphetamines, *Cannabis,* cocaine, hallucinogens, inhalants, opioids, PCP, sedative-hypnotics, and even caffeine and nicotine. Polysubstance-related disorders are also included and probably constitute the drug use patterns of the majority of substance abusers (APA, 2000).

For thousands of years before the classification of mental illnesses and substance-related disorders by the APA's *DSM* in the United States and the World Health Organization's International Classification of Diseases (ICD), **addiction was most often looked at as a moral failure**. Over the past five decades, however, biological research aided by new brain-imaging techniques, sophisticated epidemiological studies, and careful examination of users' genetic, environmental, and drug use histories has enabled society to understand addiction in an objective biological, psychological, and environmental perspective that is being validated by continuing research into its etiology.

"It's just not a physical addiction; it's a spiritual and emotional problem, too. It just doesn't encompass your body; your mind is totally off-key. You're just so involved in whatever the addiction is, you're not living your life—you're living for the addiction."
43-year-old recovering addict

In addition to a number of psychodynamic concepts of compulsive behaviors, including "regressive behavior caused by unconscious conflicts" and "ego conflicts regarding the environment and inner drives" (Khantzian, Dodes & Brehm, 2005), there have been three major schools of thought about addiction; some influence the *DSM* and ICD categories, and some are influenced by those categories. One school emphasizes the influence of heredity (**addictive disease model**), another the influence of environment and behavior (**behavioral/environmental model**), and the third the influence of the physiological effects of psychoactive drugs (**academic model**).

ADDICTIVE DISEASE MODEL

"Drug addiction is without doubt a brain disease—a disease that disrupts the mechanisms responsible for generating, modulating, and controlling cognitive, emotional, and social behavior."
Alan Leshner, Ph.D. (Leshner, 2003)

The addictive disease model, sometimes called the **"medical model,"** maintains that the disease of addiction is a chronic, progressive, relapsing, incurable, and potentially fatal condition that is mostly a consequence of genetic irregularities in brain chemistry and anatomy that may be activated by the particular drugs that are abused. It also maintains that addiction is set into motion by experimentation with the **agent** (drug) by a susceptible **host** in an **environment** that is conducive to drug misuse. The susceptible user quickly experiences a compulsion to use, a loss of control, and a determination to continue the use despite negative physical, emotional, or life consequences (Smith & Seymour, 2001).

"The first time I tried it and I got high, I said, 'I think I want to use some of this for the rest of my life if I could afford it.' If I could afford this, I would do this every day for the rest of my life."
43-year-old recovering heroin addict

Studies of twins in many countries throughout the world, along with other human and animal studies, strongly support the view that **heredity is a powerful influence on uncontrolled compulsive drug use and behavioral addictions**. Some studies place the influence of genetics at anywhere from 40% to 60% (Bierut, Dinwiddie, Begleiter, et al., 1998; Blum, Cull, Braverman, et al., 1996; Eisen, Lin, Lyons, et al., 1998; Kendler, Aggen, Tambs, et al., 2006; Lynskey, Agrawal, Bucholz, et al., 2006; Schuckit, 1986, 2000A).

Under the addictive disease model, addiction (dependence) is characterized by:

◇ compulsive drug abuse marked by use or **intoxication throughout the day and an overwhelming need to continue use**;

◇ **loss of control** over the use of a drug with an inability to reduce intake or stop use;

◇ **continuation of abuse despite the progressive development of serious physical, mental, or social disorders** aggravated by the use;

◇ **repeated attempts to control use** with periods of temporary abstinence interrupted by relapse into compulsive continual drug use;

◇ **a progressive escalation of intake and problems** (even in remission, the disease becomes more severe and can be fatal due to overdose, physical deterioration, infected drugs or needles, and a high-risk lifestyle);

◇ **being incurable** once the user has crossed the line into addictive use (remission is the object of treatment, not cure); and

◇ **pathological reaction to initial drug use, such as increased tolerance**, blackouts or brownouts, and/or dramatic personality and lifestyle changes
(APA, 2000; Smith & Seymour, 2001).

BEHAVIORAL/ ENVIRONMENTAL MODEL

This theory emphasizes the overriding significance of environmental and developmental influences in leading a user to progress into addictive behavior. As seen in animal and human studies, **environmental factors can change brain chemistry** as surely as drug use or heredity. As mentioned earlier, environmentally induced emotional memories have a lifelong influence on people (LeDoux, 1996; McGaugh, 2003). Many studies, supported by scans that show brain function, suggest that physical/emotional stress resulting from abuse, anger, peer pressure, and other environmental factors causes people to seek, use, and sustain their continued dependence on drugs (Griffiths, Bigelow & Liebson, 1978; Schroeder, Holahan, Landry, et al., 2000). For example, chronic stress can decrease brain levels of met-enkephalin (a neurotransmitter) in mice, making normal alcohol-avoiding mice more susceptible to alcohol use (Covington & Miczek, 2005). Many other studies have focused on environment in combination with heredity as critical influences (Ciccocioppo, Sanna & Weiss, 2001; Peele & Brodsky, 1991; Swaim, Oetting, Edwards, et al., 1989; Zinberg, 1984). Even religious affiliation or a lack thereof have been shown to have an influence on susceptibility and relapse (Heath, Bucholz, Madden, et al., 1997).

The behavioral/environmental model delineates the six levels of drug use—abstinence, experimentation, social/recreational use, habituation, abuse, and addiction—and emphasizes the progressive nature of the disease.

ACADEMIC MODEL

In this model addiction occurs when the **body adapts to the toxic effects of drugs at the biochemical and cellular levels** (Spragg, 1940; Tsai, Gastfriend & Coyle, 1995; Wickelgren, 1998). First proposed by C. K. Himmelsbach in 1941, the theory is that psychoactive drugs disrupt the homeostasis (natural balance) of brain chemistry. The principle is that, given sufficient quantities of drugs for an appropriate duration of time, changes in body/brain cells will occur that will lead to addiction. Four physiological changes characterize this process:

◊ **tolerance**—resistance to the drug's effects increase, necessitating larger and larger doses;

◊ **tissue dependence**—actual changes in body cells occur because of excessive use, so the body needs the drug to stay in its adapted abnormal balance;

◊ **withdrawal syndrome**—physical signs and symptoms appear when drug use is stopped as the body tries to return to normal; and

◊ **psychological dependence**—the effects of the drug are desired by the user and thus reinforce the desire to keep using.

(Also see Physiological Responses to Drugs earlier in this chapter.)

DIATHESIS-STRESS THEORY OF ADDICTION

All of the existing theories of addiction are true in their own right. It is beneficial, however, to **integrate these theories and look at addiction as a process that often encompasses a user's life from birth to death**. We have used as a model the diathesis-stress theory of psychological disorders (not addictions).

◊ A *diathesis* is a constitutional predisposition or vulnerability to develop a given disorder under certain conditions. The genotype may provide a diathesis within the person that leads to the development of the disorder if the person encounters a level of stress that exceeds his or her stress threshold or coping abilities. The diathesis may be so potent that the person will develop the disorder even in the most benign of environments (Nevid, Rathus & Greene, 1997).

The above theory was originally developed to help explain the causes of schizophrenia (Gottesman, McGuffin & Farmer, 1987; Meehl, 1962). Our diathesis-stress theory of addiction is similar to the addictive disease model but gives somewhat more flexibility in determining the influence of each of the factors: heredity, environment, and psychoactive drugs.

◊ **A diathesis, or predisposition to addiction, is the result of genetic**

and environmental influences, such as stress. When a person is further stressed or challenged by the use of psychoactive drugs or the practice of certain behaviors, neurochemistry and brain function are further changed to the point that a return to normal use or normal behavior is extremely difficult. The stronger the diathesis, the fewer drugs or less acting out is needed to push the person into addiction; conversely, the weaker the diathesis, the more drugs or behaviors are needed to force a person into addiction (Inaba & Cohen, 2004). *(See Compulsion Curves at the end of this chapter.)*

HEREDITY, ENVIRONMENT, PSYCHOACTIVE DRUGS & COMPULSIVE BEHAVIORS

Currently, increasingly more researchers in the field of addictionology believe that **the reasons for drug addiction are indeed a combination of the three factors of heredity, environment, and the use of psychoactive drugs** (DuPont, 1997; Hoffman & Froemke, 2007; Koob, 1998). Because individual personalities, physiology, and lifestyles vary, each person's resistance or susceptibility to excessive drug use also varies. It is therefore necessary to study the determining factors more closely to understand why one person might remain abstinent, another might use drugs sparingly, a third will use for a lifetime and never have problems, and someone else will use and accelerate to addiction within a few months.

HEREDITY

As mentioned in the context of the addictive disease model above, heredity has a powerful influence on compulsive drug use. For years scientists have known that **many traits are passed on through generations by genes**, features such as eye and hair color, nose shape, bone structure, and, most important, the initial structure and chemistry of the nervous system. In recent years scientists have expanded that list of genetically influenced traits to include more-complex physical reactions and diseases, such as juvenile diabetes, some forms of Alzheimer's disease, schizophrenia, some forms of depression, and even a tendency to certain cancers. Most surprisingly, **many behaviors seem to have an inheritable component** as well, whether it's simply a brain chemistry that results in an exaggerated anger reaction to relatively benign situations or a personality that gets a charge from gambling (Scherrer, Xian, Kapp, et al., 2007; Shaffer, 1998).

What is important to remember is that **there isn't just one gene that affects addiction. There are more than 100 that have been associated with drug abuse,** though some are more significant than others. These genes can affect receptors, gene transcription factors, enzymes, neuropeptides, G proteins, and transporters, among others (Ikemoto, Glazier, Murphy, et al., 1997; Kuhar, Joyce & Dominguez, 2001). If a person has few of these genes, he might have a low propensity to drug dependence; whereas if he has a few dozen, he may have a high propensity to addiction. Marc Schuckit, a major researcher in this field, suggests that up to 60% of dependence and addiction to alcohol is due to genetics.

Twin & Retrospective Studies

One set of indicators that a tendency to addiction has an inheritable component is twin studies that have been done in several countries over several decades. Dr. Donald Goodwin of the Washington University School of Medicine in St. Louis **looked at identical twins who were adopted into separate foster families** shortly after birth. Regardless of the foster parents' family environment, adopted children developed alcohol abuse or abstinence patterns similar to their biological parent's use of alcohol (Goodwin, 1976; Nurnberger, Foroud, Flury, et al., 2001).

Other studies have **compared genetic twins (nearly identical genes) and fraternal twins (similar genes)** who are raised in identical environments. In one survey genetics contributed 61% to nicotine dependence

and 55% to alcohol dependence (True, Xian, Scherrer, et al., 1999).

Other evidence of genetic predisposition to alcoholism comes from a **review of the biological family records of alcoholics** in various treatment programs across the United States (Cloninger, 1987). The data showed that if one biological parent was an alcoholic, a male child was about 34% more likely to be an alcoholic than the male child of nonalcoholics. If both biological parents were alcoholics, the child was about 400% more likely to be an alcoholic. If both parents and a grandfather were alcoholics, the child was about 900% more likely to develop alcoholism. About 28 million Americans have at least one alcoholic parent (Schuckit, 1986).

"I didn't like the way my father fought with my mother when he drank, so I never drank a drop, not a drop, until I was 27. Then it was like a light got turned on and I tried to make up for lost time."

37-year-old drinker

Addiction-Associated Genes

Another breakthrough in this line of inquiry came in 1990 when **a specific gene associated with alcoholism was identified** by Ernest Nobel and Ken Blum, researchers at the University of California at Los Angeles and the University of Texas at San Antonio, respectively (Noble, Blum, Ritchie, et al., 1991). Many researchers believe that this gene helps indicate a person's susceptibility to compulsive drinking. In some studies this **$DRD_2 A_1$ allele gene was found in more than 70% of severe alcoholics** in treatment but in less than 30% of people who were assessed to be social drinkers or abstainers (Feingold, Ball, Kranzler, et al., 1996). This gene indicates a scarcity of dopamine receptors in the brain, particularly in the nucleus accumbens. A shortage of reward/reinforcement dopamine D_2 receptors **means the person will need a more intense sensory or emotional input to feel satisfaction** (Volkow, Fowler, Wang, et al., 1993). Excess amounts of alcohol fill this need. Someone without this anomaly will get

a feeling of reward and satisfaction through a less intense activity or simply a mildly psychoactive substance such as coffee instead of excess amounts of methamphetamine. Recent research indicates that a normal or even excess amount of D_2 receptors acts as a protective factor against alcoholism even when the family of origin has a history of alcoholism (Volkow, Wang, Begleiter, et al, 2006).

What the presence of this $DRD_2 A_1$ allele gene and other yet-to-be discovered ones means is that when people with these hereditary markers do use alcohol (or any psychoactive drug), they are at a much higher risk of becoming alcoholics (or drug addicts) than those in the general population (Gordis, 2003). If they never drink, however, problems with alcohol will never occur. Research seems to confirm the role that this gene also plays in cocaine addiction (Zhang, Walsh & Xu, 2000).

Blum and fellow researchers believe that **this gene indicates a tendency to any drug addiction and some problematic behaviors,** including gambling, attention-deficit disorder, aberrant sexual behavior, overeating, antisocial personality, and even Tourette's syndrome, not just drinking. **They refer to it as a "compulsivity gene" and call the process "the reward deficiency syndrome"** (Blum, Cull, Braverman, et al., 1996; Blum, Braverman, Holder, et al., 2000).

In practical terms what genetic markers mean is that people with one or more marker genes are more susceptible to developing alcoholism (or other compulsive drug use) and that when they begin drinking or using other drugs, they are more likely to do it at a more rapid rate than people without that susceptibility. For example, though many susceptible people receive an intense reaction from alcohol with their first drinking experience, they also seem to need larger amounts of alcohol than others do to get drunk. So, **when they reach that intoxicated state, it is much more intense than most anything they've felt before and causes greater dysfunction (and craving)** (Cloninger, 1987; Cloninger, Bohman & Sigvardson, 1986; Lin & Anthenelli, 2005). Many have blackouts, starting with the first few times they use, where they don't remember what happened to them while drunk; or they experience brownouts, where they can remember only parts of their drunken experience (Schuckit & Smith, 2001).

Genes can also help prevent dependence from developing. The DRD_4 gene, which signifies an excess of dopamine, has been shown to play a role in the personality trait of spiritual acceptance, a temperament that helps a person develop a lifestyle that doesn't include addiction (Comings, Gonzales, Saucier, et al., 2000).

There are a number of other genes implicated in alcohol and other drug dependency.

Alcohol. The CREB, $CHRM_2$, Leu_7Pro allele, $GABRA_2$, and NQD_2 along with the DRD_2A_1 allele genes are associated with increased predisposition to alcoholism, whereas the atypical ADH_4, $KMALDH_1$, and COMT $met_{158}met$ genes are associated with decreased alcohol use and may protect a person against developing alcoholism. Some additional genes involved are $GABRG_3$, TAS_2R_{16}, SNCA, $OPRK_1$, and PDYN (Crabbe, Phillips, Harris, et al., 2006; Edenberg & Foroud, 2006).

Opioids. CYP_2D_6, the Epstein novelty-seeking gene and polymorphism of gene encoding the opioid mu receptor, is associated with increased potential for opioid addiction.

Cocaine. The DRD_2A_1 allele is associated with increased addiction potential for both alcohol and cocaine. Also associated with cocaine dependence are the $Homer_1$ and $Homer_2$ genes.

Nicotine. The $CYP_2A_6*_3$ and $CHRNA_4$ genes are associated with increased nicotine use, whereas $CYP_2A_6*_2$ and $*_4$ are associated with decreased use.

Increased Sensitivity to All Drug Addictions or Polydrug Use. DeltaFosB, DRD_2A_1 taq_1A, and polymorphism of fatty acid amide hydrolase gene are associated with increased susceptibility to compulsion for a wide variety of drugs (Hayner, 2005).

Another marker for a propensity to alcohol addiction is the **P300 ERP (event-related potential) wave that** relates to a person's cognition, decision-making, and processing of short-term memory. In alcoholics the voltage of this wave is reduced as it is in their sons, suggesting yet another genetic connection (Begleiter, 1980; Blum, Braverman, Holder, et al., 2000; Enoch, White, Harris, et al., 2001).

ENVIRONMENT

The environmental influences that help determine the level at which a person uses drugs can be positive or negative and as varied as **sexual/physical/emotional abuse, stress, love, poverty, living conditions, family relationships, nutritional balance, healthcare, neighborhood safety, school quality, peer pressure, the Internet, and television**. Interactions with the environment, particularly the home environment, actually **make new nerve cell connections and alter the neurochemistry a person is born with**, thereby helping determine how that person will use psychoactive drugs.

Environment, Brain Development & Memory Networks

Environmental influences have the greatest impact on the development of the brain. Though we are born with most of the nerve cells we will ever have, about 100 billion neurons in the brain alone, **environment influences the 100 trillion connections (synapses) that develop among nerve cells**. In this way environment helps mold the brain's architecture and neurochemistry, thus altering the way the brain reacts to outside influences. The growth and the alteration are especially influential in the first 10 years of life.

"My mother was addicted to speed and heroin, and I grew up with it. Then I was taken away from her. I'd go and visit her, seeing her high, seeing her not high, seeing her high again, coming down the next time, back and forth. And then when I was 11 years old, she was shot and killed on Valentine's Day. After that I didn't have anything to look forward to, so I didn't care anymore."
24-year-old heroin addict

The process of making new connections and altering brain chemistry continues after the first 10 years but at a progressively slower rate. Because the brain develops from the rear to the front (the last part being the prefrontal cortex), adolescents are more vulnerable than adults to poor decisions and poor impulse-control behaviors like substance abuse. Current evidence indicates that **it takes at least 20 years for the brain to get "hardwired,"** or to form all its major and vital connections, although recent research shows that the frontal lobe volume increases until age 44 and the temporal lobe until age 47 (Bartzokis, Beckson, Lu, et al., 2001). On the other hand, we keep making and losing connections until the day we die, but the older we are, the more difficult the process.

"Every experience you have matters to your brain. And if you are being bathed with repetitive stress hormones and stress chemicals in your brain, it changes your brain in a negative way and can actually cause your brain to become more at risk for these disorders."
Daniel Amen, M.D., 1998

In general, **memories exist because when we learn anything, the memory is encoded in the nerve cells by a neurochemical process** mainly involving noradrenaline (norepinephrine), serotonin, acetylcholine, and dopamine (Govindarajan, Kelleher & Tonegawa, 2006; LeDoux, 1996; McGaugh, 2003). Each memory is stored in several sites (such as the hippocampus or temporal lobes) that are connected by dendrites, terminals, axons, and cell bodies. Through a process called *long-term potentiation* (LTP) that alters neurons, the more an action is repeated or the more that memory is triggered, the easier it becomes to recall (Pliszka, 2003). **In addition, the more emotionally intense the event, the stronger the memory network (e.g., post-traumatic stress disorder, where a trauma is embedded for a lifetime)** (DiCiano & Everitt, 2004; Meyer & Quenzer, 2005).

"I broke down after about six months over in Vietnam and I was in charge of

a gun crew. I didn't respond to my duty of opening up an M-60, and some people's lives were lost in my outfit and I'm responsible. They flew me out to the States, and I immediately jumped into alcohol and heroin."

Vietnam veteran

Children who are subject to **excessive emotional pain** while growing up in a chaotic household remember that pain and may try different ways to deal with it (Nelson, Heath, Lynskey, et al., 2006). They can try to understand why it happened, learn how to face it, find people to help them, and accept what happened, or they can run away, become hyperactive, make jokes, **use drugs, gamble, or overeat—anything to temper the pain or discomfort**. If stress continues long enough, the counterbehavior that the child learned also becomes ingrained in the brain (Fields, Hjelmstad, Margolis, et al., 2007; Nestler & Aghajanian, 1997). **The brain remembers the counterbehavior just as it remembers the stress and the pain.** That addiction memory becomes part of the user's personality (Boening, 2001). Once connections are made and chemistry is altered in response to environmental challenges, they are very difficult to change though not impossible (Bierman, 1995). So when any unwanted emotion arises in childhood as well as adulthood, the brain is often drawn to the simplest, quickest solution.

"My grandfather was a drunk, and my father was a drunk. That is who basically beat me up. I figured the more pain he caused me, the more pot I could smoke. Being abused as a kid really scars you for life. So the more pot I could smoke, the more relief I got from the pressure of being abused."

35-year-old male in recovery

Emotional events that become imprinted on the brain can be pleasurable or painful, and this usually involves the amygdala, the emotional center of the CNS.

"I had $600, put down $240, and did nothing but win. At five minutes after

8 o'clock, I walked away with over $12,000. Gee this is it. This is what I've been waiting for. This is my lucky day. That was the big win that triggered me. I can do this. I don't have to work anymore."

45-year-old recovering compulsive gambler

James L. McGaugh, in his excellent book *Memory & Emotion*, talks of how memories were recorded in medieval times. When an important event such as a wedding, a treaty, or a large transaction had to be recorded, adults took a young child about seven years old, had him carefully witness the event, and then quickly threw him in a cold river to shock his body so the memory would be imprinted for a lifetime (McGaugh, 2003). The cold water probably released excess adrenaline, cortisol, and other neurochemicals, which in turn deeply imprinted the memories on the child's brain (Reuter, Netter, Roqausch, 2002).

"As a child I used to lay in my bedroom, my mother bringing men in off the street to do things to try to help support us. That would kill me. That would kill me. All I could think about, I got to get a job. I got to help my mother. So I was eager to use anything I could do to free myself of that pain."

55-year-old male recovering heroin addict

In summary, environment can make a person more liable to abuse psychoactive substances if:

◇ **stress is common in the home;**
◇ **physical, emotional, or sexual abuse occurs;**
◇ **drinking or other drug use is common in the home or among peers;**
◇ **healthy ways of reacting to stress or anger aren't learned** and self-medication becomes the only solution;
◇ **society tells them in word and deed that drinking, smoking, and using drugs to solve all problems are a normal part of life;**

◇ **living in a community where access to legal and illegal drugs is easy;**
◇ there are pre-existing mental health problems aggravated by the home environment;
◇ one's diet lacks sufficient vitamins and proteins needed to synthesize neurotransmitters and maintain a healthy brain chemistry (e.g., being underweight reduces dopamine levels, possibly leading to amphetamine use to artificially rebalance brain chemistry) (Pothos, 2001);
◇ massive advertising campaigns for tobacco or alcohol fill the airwaves and other media; or
◇ one belongs to a social, business, or peer group in which excessive drinking or drug use is considered normal.

"My parents have a glass of wine after they come home from work to relax and unwind. I'm the same way, just with marijuana. It's just kind of a regular thing that I do instead of alcohol or anything else."

23-year-old marijuana smoker

PSYCHOACTIVE DRUGS

The hereditary and environmental influences mean nothing in terms of drug addiction unless the person actually uses psychoactive substances, so the final factors that determine the level at which a person might use drugs are the drugs themselves. Drugs can affect not only susceptible individuals but also those with no predisposing factors. This occurs because, by definition, psychoactive drugs are substances that affect the functioning of the central nervous system. **Excessive, frequent, or prolonged use of alcohol or other drugs inevitably modifies many of the same nerve cells and neurochemistry that are affected by heredity and environment.** This influences not only the person's reaction to those substances when they are used but also the level at which they are used. **Behavioral addictions also alter brain chemistry.**

The development of **tolerance, tissue dependence, withdrawal, and** psychological dependence are signs that the drugs themselves are causing physical and chemical changes in the body that tend to increase use. Excessive drug use increases not only vulnerability to the drug of choice but also, through a variety of mechanisms, vulnerability to other drugs. For example, in animal experiments the chronic use of THC (the active ingredient in marijuana) increased their vulnerability to amphetamine and heroin (Lamarque, Taghzouti & Simon, 2001). Another mechanism whereby drug use increases vulnerability is the fact that several drugs, particularly methamphetamine, kill brain cells through a process called *apoptosis*, whereby damaged cells are programmed to kill themselves (Cadet, Ordonez & Ordonez, 1997). Nicotine produces immediate and long-term changes in neurotransmitter levels, particularly dopamine and norepinephrine, leading to a faster development of tolerance and dependence (Trauth, Seidler, Ali, et al., 2001).

Finally, animal studies confirm that **some drugs have greater power to compel continued use than other drugs** (positive reinforcement). For example, cocaine and heroin have a tremendous hypnotizing effect to continue their use, whereas Thorazine® or Tofranil® have no positive reinforcing effects.

Psychoactive drugs cause both temporary and permanent changes in various parts of the brain that can be imaged. In the past simple X-rays and EEGs were the only way to examine the brain, but over the past 30 years a wide variety of technologies and techniques have been developed. A **SPECT scan** (single photon emission computed tomography) is a very sophisticated nuclear medicine imaging technique that looks at blood flow and metabolic activity in the brain to show how the brain functions during a given activity, such as taking a psychoactive drug. **PET scans** (positron emission tomography) also show brain function by imaging radioactively labeled chemicals that are injected. A **CAT scan** (computerized axial tomography), which uses X-rays, and an **MRI** (magnetic resonance imaging), which uses magnetic fields and radio waves, produce anatomical studies of the brain

Your Brain on Drugs

1-2 Min   3-4   5-6

6-7   7-8   8-9

9-10   10-20   20-30

These are PET scans of a person's brain on cocaine. The yellow areas are where cocaine is attaching itself (binding) to affected areas of the brain. After 3 or 4 minutes the cocaine is binding to the striatum; at 6 to 8 minutes there is maximum involvement in all areas and then it starts to diminish. At 20 to 30 minutes it has spent its major effect, particularly the high. This rapid up-down cycle is the reason for the binge pattern of use of the drug and the inevitable depletion of dopamine and norepinephrine.
Photo courtesy of Nora Volkow (Volkow, Fowler, Wang, et al., 1993)

but don't show brain functioning. There is also an **fMRI** (functional MRI), which traces blood flow to different regions of the brain, yielding information about motor, sensory, visual, and auditory functions.

COMPULSIVE BEHAVIORS

There is a growing acceptance among many researchers that **certain behaviors, such as gambling, eating, shopping, sexual activity, video games, and the Internet, can become compulsive** in a way that mimics compulsive drug use and that they affect the anatomy and the chemistry of brain cells in the same way addictive drugs

do. For example, from various studies it seems that environment, particularly availability of gambling outlets and parental gambling, has a greater influence on the development of pathological gambling than does heredity (Petry, 2005). Many believe that **gambling, like drug addiction, causes the brain to be rewired**, particularly the reward/reinforcement pathway. People can experience the loss of control and increased craving and will continue to gamble despite devastating adverse consequences (Shaffer, 1998).

"I had given most of the money away, and the only money I really did have at

that point was our daughter's money; and I remember one night—nine months to the night that my husband died—saying, 'screw it, I'm outta here,' and I sat down in front of a $25 video poker machine and I imagine in 24 hours I went through $10,000. It just happened to be her college money, but, uh, I was always going to get it back."

43-year-old compulsive gambler

Research on video game compulsion has demonstrated that **an equivalent amount of dopamine is released in the reward/reinforcement circuitry of the brain of a compulsive video game player** as is released by methamphetamine or Ritalin® injection (Koepp, Gunn, Lawrence, et al., 1998). PET scans of the brains of compulsive overeaters have shown a lack of dopamine (D_2) receptor sites in the nucleus accumbens, part of the reward/reinforcement pathway. This is the same area activated by psychoactive drugs (Wang, Volkow, Logan, et al., 2001).

Whether compulsive sexual behavior, eating disorders, or other behavioral addictions are mostly the result of heredity, environment, or the intense practice of the compulsion, the reward system reacts in a similar way to a drug or alcohol addiction.

"If you have a decrease in dopamine receptors that transmit pleasurable feelings, you become less responsive to the stimuli, such as food or sex, that normally activate them. When you don't reward yourself enough, your brain signals you to do something that will stimulate the circuits sufficiently to create a sense of well-being. Thus an individual who has low sensitivity to normal stimuli learns behaviors, such as abusing drugs or overeating, that will activate them."

Dr. Nora Volkow, Brookhaven National Laboratories
(National Institute of Drug Abuse Notes, 2001)

Behavioral compulsions often accompany or follow drug addictions. For example, 25% to 63% of all compul-sive gamblers (depending on the study) have been alcohol or drug dependent (National Research Council, 1999). Many recovering addicts switched to gambling to pass the time because they thought it was harmless. It is now recognized that **gambling and other compulsive behaviors are actual dysfunctions of brain chemistry in the same way that drugs disrupt brain chemistry** (Koepp, Gunn, Lawrence, et al., 1998; Potenza, 2001). Psychological and social treatment for these compulsive behaviors are evolving along the same lines and using the same interventions utilized in the treatment of drug addiction (Petry, 2005).

These compulsive behaviors are different from **obsessive-compulsive disorder** (OCD) (e.g., repetitive hand washing, repeated and excessive checking to ensure that the door is locked or the stove is turned off, and compulsive ordering like arranging magazines, books, or objects into a certain order and being upset if they are not in the expected place). OCD has been shown to occur along a different brain and neurotransmitter pathway than that associated with compulsive behaviors. With compulsive behaviors there is an experience of pleasure associated with the action, whereas OCD actions are not associated with a pleasurable experience. The repetitive behaviors of OCD patients, however, have been observed to reduce their level of stress. (OCD is also different from **obsessive-compulsive personality disorder**, where a person is preoccupied with details, rules, lists, order, organization, control, and doing things "just right" to the point that less gets done.)

ALCOHOLIC MICE & SOBER MICE

To better understand the close connections among heredity, environment, psychoactive drugs, and compulsive behaviors and to further visualize the diathesis-stress theory of addiction, it might be helpful to examine a series of classic animal studies done over the past 40 years by Gerald McLaren, T. K. Li, Horace Lo, D. S. Cannon, and other researchers (Li, Lumeng, McBride, et al., 1986). Animal experiments are often used to help us understand what the effects of a drug would be on human beings. They were first used scientifically in the 1600s by Johann Jakob Wepfer, a German physician, and in the 1800s by Claude Bernard, a French physiologist.

The basic experiments are as follows. Years ago researchers developed **two genetic strains of mice** (Figure 2-20a) to help researchers understand alcoholism. **One of the strains of mice loved alcohol.** When given the choice between water and even 70% concentrations of alcohol, these mice went for the alcohol every time. If all they had was water, they would grudgingly drink water. **The other strain of mice hated alcohol**. Given the same choice, even with concentrations as low as 2% alcohol, the mice always chose the pure water (Cannon & Carrell, 1987).

In one experiment researchers first took a group of the alcohol-hating mice and injected them with high levels of alcohol, the equivalent of what adult human beings would drink if they were heavy drinkers. Within a few weeks, these **once-sober mice came to prefer alcohol through overexposure to the drug**. In fact, if not stopped, they would drink themselves to death (Figure 2-20b).

Researchers then took another group of the alcohol-hating mice and subjected them to stress by putting them in very small constrictive tubes for intermittent periods. Within a few weeks, this group of sober mice also came to prefer higher and higher concentrations of alcohol to pure water because it relieved the stress. In essence **sober mice had been turned into alcoholic mice by applying stress (environment) and providing access to alcohol** (exposure to psychoactive drugs) (Figure 2-20c).

Furthermore, researcher Dr. Jorge Mardones, a nutritionist, took another group of alcohol-hating mice and from their diet subtracted vitamin B and some proteins that are essential for their brains' production of neurotransmitters like dopamine. This **limited nutrition also resulted in increased alcohol use** after several months (Mardones, 1951) (Figure 2-20d).

Finally, **once the mice whose genetics made them prefer alcohol were**

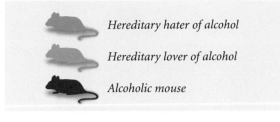

Hereditary hater of alcohol

Hereditary lover of alcohol

Alcoholic mouse

Figure 2-20a • Two strains of mice have been bred to help test theories of addiction, an alcohol-hating mouse and an alcohol-loving mouse.

Figure 2-20b • Alcohol-hating mouse is force-fed large quantities of alcohol.

Figure 2-20c • Alcohol-hating mouse is subjected to stress, and alcohol is made available.

Figure 2-20d • Alcohol-hating mouse is nutritionally deprived, and alcohol is made available.

Figure 2-20e • Alcohol is made available to alcohol-loving mouse.

© 2003 CNS Productions, Inc.

psychoactive drugs, nutritional deficiency, or a combination of several factors, they can all lead to serious addiction (Li & Lumeng, 1984; Li, Lumeng, McBride, et al., 1986).

COMPULSION CURVES

Human beings, of course, are different from mice. We are more complex, our brains are more intricate, and our social patterns are extremely diverse. We have the power of reason, we have more control over our environment, and we have self-awareness. Yet research, especially over the past 15 years, shows that the **basic drug-craving mechanisms in humans, which reside mostly in the old brain, are similar to those of most other mammals—even mice**. The difference is that in humans it usually takes a combination of heredity, environment, and psychoactive drug use to induce compulsive use.

To help understand the interrelationship of heredity, environment, and the use of psychoactive drugs in human beings, we have developed a graphic representation of the ways a user might advance from experimentation to addiction.

given access to alcohol, they drank themselves to death. Even when they were subjected to electric shocks aimed at preventing them from drinking the alcohol (aversive therapy), they continued to drink even when the shocks came close to being fatal (Figure 2-20e). It is important to remember that none of the mice would become alcoholic if they were never given alcohol, even those mice with the highest susceptibility to compulsive drinking.

What was most interesting was that **when the forced drinking, stress induction, and nutritional restrictions were stopped, the once genetically sober alcohol-hating mice did not return to their normal nondrinking habits**. They had been transformed into alcohol-loving mice and if given the chance to drink would be alcoholic mice.

When the brains of the four groups of mice were examined (the hereditary alcoholic mice, the stress-induced alcoholic mice, the alcohol-induced alcoholic mice, and the nutritionally restricted alcoholic mice), **all had similar brain cell changes and neurotransmitter imbalances that made**

them prefer alcohol even though they started with different neurochemical balances. This research suggests that whether the neurochemical disruption is caused by heredity, environment,

Because everyone is unique, **each person starts with a different genetic susceptibility**. Those with low genetic susceptibility or predisposition have more room for drug experimentation or environmental stressors than those with high genetic predisposition. The susceptibility is most often reflected by the brain's structure, neurochemical composition, and the presence of certain genes. The important point is that increasingly more studies confirm that there is at least some heredity influence to any addiction, even compulsive overeating, smoking, and gambling (Eisen, Lin, Lyons, et al., 1998; Petry, 2005). **The contribution of heredity** to drug addiction in our society is only an educated guess, but researchers have estimated figures of **anywhere from 30% to 60%** (Figure 2-21). The wide variation is because of the uniqueness of each individual.

Once a person is born with his or her genetic makeup, environmental influences, particularly stressors, have the greatest effect on susceptibility. These influences include lack of bonding with a caregiver, physical/emotional/sexual abuse (especially during adolescence), poor nutrition, or societal attitudes that permit drug use. Again, **a person may have experienced low, medium, or high environmental contributions toward susceptibility to drug addiction** (Figure 2-22).

The **final factor that will push a person to addiction is the use of psychoactive drugs**. The practice of compulsive behaviors, such as gambling, can also push one along the curve (Figure 2-23). Therefore a person who starts with low inherited susceptibility and low environmental stress might need intense use of drugs or behaviors to push him or her into addiction. The greater the environmental stress, the fewer drugs or behaviors needed to cross the line. The ability of drugs to create compulsive use is not determined just by frequency or amount of drug used; drugs have different potencies (heroin vs. alcohol), different addiction potentials (methamphetamine vs. LSD), and different routes of administration (smoking crack cocaine vs. snorting cocaine hydrochloride) that propel their users toward dependency.

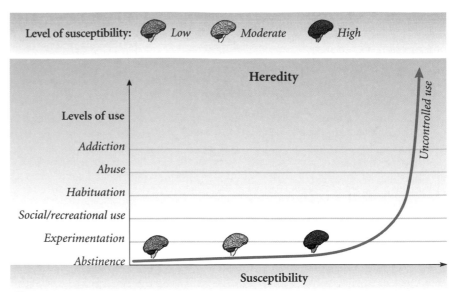

Figure 2-21 • *Initial susceptibility is inherited. If one or more close relatives are drug or alcohol dependent, the chance of heritability increases.*
© 2007 CNS Productions, Inc.

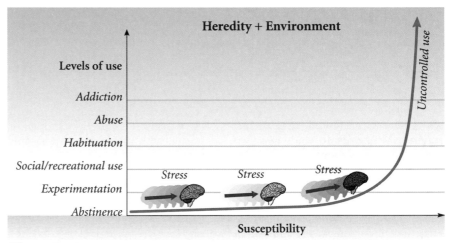

Figure 2-22 • *Susceptibility increases due to environmental stressors, such as abuse, peer pressure, or drug and alcohol use at home.*
© 2007 CNS Productions, Inc.

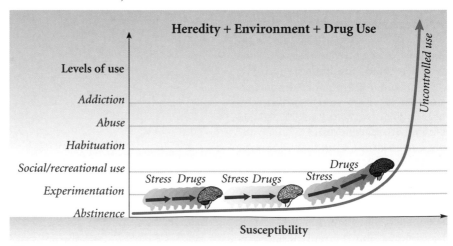

Figure 2-23 • *Susceptibility to abuse and dependence increases due to drug use or practice of certain behaviors. Without drug use, the susceptibility will not be triggered.*
© 2007 CNS Productions, Inc.

The drugs that push the hardest and the quickest toward addiction are, in order from fastest to slowest:

> **smoking tobacco,**
> **smoking crack cocaine,**
> **smoking or injecting heroin,**
> **injecting methamphetamine,**
> **snorting cocaine,**
> **ingesting opioid painkillers,**
> ingesting any amphetamine,
> ingesting sedative hypnotics,
> drinking alcohol,
> smoking marijuana,
> ingesting PCP,
> ingesting caffeine,
> ingesting MDMA (ecstasy),
> ingesting LSD,
> ingesting peyote.

A person with low or even moderate inherited susceptibility will require larger amounts of environmental influences and/or drug exposure to push him or her close to the level of critical susceptibility and addiction than will someone with high inherited susceptibility (Figure 2-24). If both heredity and environmental susceptibility are low or moderately so, it will take a lot more drug exposure or acting-out behavior to push someone into drug dependency or into uncontrolled behaviors like video game playing than someone with high inherited susceptibility.

It might take those with low susceptibility 10 years of drinking to become alcoholics, or it might never occur. It might take them 2 years of occasional injection to become a heroin addict or 6 months of smoking to get to a pack of cigarettes a day. People in the middle of the scale, with moderate inherited susceptibility, might need just 2 or 3 years of use to slip into alcohol addiction or 6 months of heroin use to graduate to a $200-a-day habit. People with high susceptibility might slip into compulsive heavy drinking after just 1 or 2 months of bingeing or heavy drinking because their bodies are primed for compulsive use.

What happens to addicts when they stop using cocaine or stop gambling (Figure 2-25)? They drop below critical susceptibility but not back to the level they were at before they started using drugs or practicing their behavior. This is because their **addiction, aggravated**

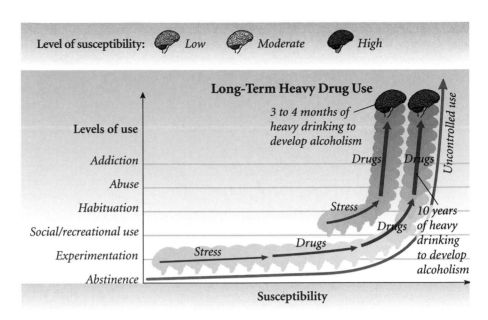

Figure 2-24 • *Addiction develops at different rates. High genetic and environmental susceptibilities will need less drug use to push the person to abuse and addiction.*
© 2007 CNS Productions, Inc.

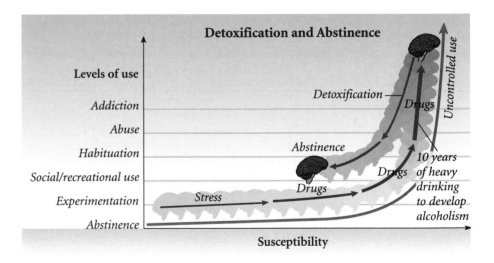

Figure 2-25 • *Susceptibility doesn't return to its starting point after detoxification and abstinence. Some neurochemistry, anatomy, and even some genes are permanently altered.*
© 2007 CNS Productions, Inc.

by the development of tolerance and tissue dependence, has permanently altered their brain cells and circuitry, making them forever liable to trigger uncontrolled use or behavior more quickly than before. Note that their level of use may return to abstinence, but their brain susceptibility remains extremely high, prompting slips that quickly become full-blown relapses (continuous or binge use).

If their environment continues to pile stress on them, they will move to a level of susceptibility where they can and most probably will return to uncontrolled addictive use (e.g., alcoholism) or behavior with just one drink, one snort, one piece of cake, or one bet (Clark, Moss, Kirisci, et al., 1997) (Figure 2-26). If, however, they reduce stress in their environment by staying away from environmental cues, learn

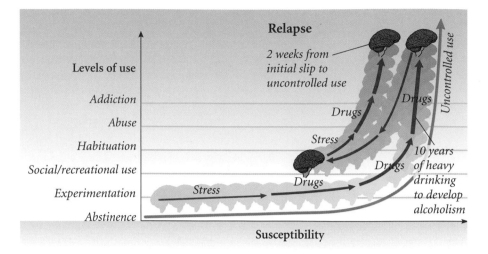

Figure 2-26 • Users return to addictive use more quickly after relapse because of strengthening of memories associated with the addiction and the sensitization of the reward/reinforcement pathway to that drug use or behavior.

© 2007 CNS Productions, Inc.

how to relax, have counseling and support, attend self-help groups, continue to learn, and overcome stressful thoughts, memories, and mental conflicts, they have a chance at continued recovery and positive life gains.

CONCLUSIONS

There has been **discussion in recent years about reclassifying and redefining addiction as an impulse control disorder**, implying that the addict can be taught to make the right choices and stop the behavior. This minimizes much of the recent research that shows, through brain imaging and a variety of other research techniques, that **there are actual chemical and anatomical changes that literally force the person into compulsive behavior**, particularly those who became susceptible through hereditary and environmental influences. One example is the overactivation of the "more" switch and the deactivation of the "stop" switch, which disrupts the ability of those who have altered their brain chemistry to cease use once a drink of alcohol or a hit of a drug has been taken. The excessive stimulation of the nucleus accumbens has exploited the survival mechanisms in the old brain and sends a message that essentially says, "If you don't take this drug or participate in this behavior, you will die." These irresistible cravings and messages are permanently imprinted on the brain in emotionally charged addiction memories created by the excessive use of psychoactive drugs over a period of time. They cause the person to react at a subconscious level.

Think of the disease of addiction as an allergy where, if the specific allergen is present, certain inevitable physical and mental reactions are triggered. For example, if someone who is allergic to bee stings gets stung, it won't matter how moral or kind or empathetic the person is: the body (and the brain) will react automatically to the insult. Remember how mice that were exposed to the same psychoactive drugs as humans reacted in a similar way: once begun, they could not stop use either. So the human condition must take into account not only the disease/allergy part of the addiction but also the mental obsession to use, which has developed in human beings with a variety of social factors.

It is necessary to understand these physiological and psychological changes and devise strategies that take these neurochemical changes into account; however, **any study of addiction should focus on the totality of people's lives**: their personality, thinking patterns, relationships, how they live, what they eat, and their family history (Dackis & O'Brien, 2005). In subsequent chapters this book will not only explore stimulants, depressants, psychedelics, inhalants, and other drugs but will also look at compulsive behaviors and the role of social factors to develop a full view of drug use, abuse, and addiction.

CHAPTER SUMMARY

HOW PSYCHOACTIVE DRUGS AFFECT PEOPLE

1. Advances in neuroscience and brain imaging have yielded an avalanche of data, giving new insight into the dysfunction of addiction. All animals respond to psychoactive drugs, not just human beings.

How Drugs Get to the Brain

2. Method of intake, speed of transit, and affinity for nerve cells and interaction with neurotransmitters determine a drug's effects. The faster it reaches its target, the greater the reinforcing effects.

3. Drugs are absorbed into the body in five ways: inhaling (including smoking), injecting (intravenous, intramuscular, or subcutaneous), mucous membrane absorption (snorting, under the tongue, next to the cheek, rectally, or vaginally), eating or drinking, and contact absorption (e.g., transdermal skin patches).

4. Drugs enter the body and are distributed through the bloodstream,

where they cause a direct effect, are ignored, are stored, or are bio-transformed.

5. Psychoactive drugs must cross the blood-brain and blood-cerebral spinal fluid barriers to reach the fatty nerve cells of the brain.

6. Eventually, the drug molecules reach the central nervous system (CNS, or brain and spinal cord), where they have the greatest effect. The drug molecules also pass through the cerebral/spinal fluid barrier and through the placental barrier in pregnant women who use drugs.

7. Metabolism, the body's mechanism for processing, using, and inactivating foreign substances, primarily involves the liver. Excretion, the body's processes to eliminate waste, involves the kidneys, which filter drugs from the blood and excrete them in the urine. The lungs and the skin are also involved in excretion.

8. Pharmacokinetic factors such as the bioavailability and the half-life affect the impact of a drug on the body.

9. A variety of other factors, such as age, race, health, and gender, help determine how fast a drug is metabolized.

The Nervous System

10. The nervous system, with 100 billion nerve cells and 100 trillion connections, consists of the central nervous system and the peripheral nervous system (PNS, which comprises the autonomic and somatic systems).

11. The peripheral nervous system connects the brain to sensory organs of the body that provide information about the outside world. It also connects the central nervous system to the other body systems to regulate involuntary functions, such as respiration and heart rate, and controls voluntary reactions to stimuli.

12. The central nervous system receives, analyzes, and responds to messages from the peripheral nervous system. Psychoactive drugs can alter incoming information, disrupt messages, and disrupt thinking.

13. The evolutionary perspective divides the brain into the old brain and the new brain. It looks on physiological changes as survival adaptations. Psychoactive drugs have an affinity for survival mechanisms. They hijack and subvert these mechanisms and initially cause desired effects.

14. The old brain controls physiological functions and emotions/feelings/cravings and imprints survival memories. Drug craving and addiction memories reside here.

15. The new brain (neocortex) processes information and controls speech, reasoning, creativity, and other memories. Old-brain craving usually overrides new-brain rational thoughts.

16. A survival mechanism called the reward/reinforcement pathway gives a surge of pleasure when a need is filled or pain is diminished. It is also the part of the brain most affected by psychoactive drugs.

17. The reward/reinforcement pathway has a "more" switch and a "stop" switch. It imprints the memories of pleasure/satisfaction as well as the memories of pain relief. This reward system also says, "Do it again, do it again" when activated by survival needs.

18. The "stop" switch signals when the need has been fulfilled and then turns off the do-it-again message.

19. For substance abusers, drugs also activate the feeling of satisfaction and the "more" circuit, but the "stop" switch does not shut off, so the person continues to use.

20. The key part of the system is called the nucleus accumbens septi.

21. The three phases of brain activity that occur with compulsive drug use are: craving and initial stimulus, especially anticipation of drug use; activation of the nucleus accumbens and the do-it-again signals; and transmission of reinforcement signals from the nucleus accumbens to the orbitofrontal cortex that in normal people says "stop."

22. In drug abusers and addicts, the "stop" or satiation switch, which normally turns off the do-it-again message and stops the craving, does not operate effectively.

23. Psychoactive drugs imprint the emotional memory of euphoria or pain relief more deeply than most natural survival memories.

24. The alteration of neurochemistry causes normal activities to become even less pleasurable for abusers and addicts.

25. Psychoactive drugs affect physiological functions such as respiration and heart beat as well as emotions and feelings.

26. The nucleus accumbens septi is a powerful motivator and reinforcer. The longer psychoactive drugs are used, the stronger the do-it-again message becomes.

27. Animals' reactions to psychoactive drugs are very similar to human beings' reactions.

28. Social factors also have an effect on the obsession to use, whereas alteration of the "more" and "stop" switches has to do with reaction to the drug itself.

29. The "stop" switch is crucial in keeping craving and satiation in balance, but brain cells change as addiction develops. There are several theories about why the "stop" switch becomes dysfunctional.

30. The conflict between doing what our old brain tells us and the common sense and the morality of our new brain is found in the writings and the beliefs of religions and social systems throughout history. It takes a powerful conscious effort to override cravings and desires from the old brain.

31. Messages are transmitted by nerve cells (up to 1,000 impulses per second).

32. A nerve cell (neuron) consists of dendrites, cell body, axon, and terminals. Spaces between nerve cell junctions are called synaptic gaps.

33. Messages travel within a nerve cell as electrical signals. At the junc-

tion between most nerve cells, there is a synaptic gap or cleft. Messages cross this gap as neurochemicals called neurotransmitters, which slot into specific receptor sites, where the messages are then converted back to electrical signals.

34. Endogenous chemicals (e.g., endorphins) are those produced within the body. Exogenous chemicals (e.g., heroin) are those originating outside the organism.

35. Psychoactive drugs cannot create sensations or feelings that don't have a natural counterpart in the body (e.g., because endorphins exist in the brain, heroin can affect the brain).

36. The major neurotransmitters, particularly when psychoactive drugs are involved, are endorphins, dopamine, serotonin, GABA, glutamate, acetylcholine, norepinephrine, anandamide, and substance P.

37. There are receptor sites for each type of neurotransmitter.

38. Neurotransmitters intensify signals (excitatory), inhibit signals (inhibitory), or a combination of the two.

39. Excessive use of drugs can decrease the number of receptor sites (down regulation), forcing the user to use more of the drug to receive the same satisfaction.

40. Psychoactive drugs affect natural functions by mimicking (agonist), blocking (antagonist), or otherwise disrupting the release of these neurotransmitters, thereby affecting their normal functions.

41. Neurotransmitters can act directly on neurotransmitters and receptor sites (first messengers) or indirectly by affecting the release of other neurotransmitters.

Physiological Responses to Drugs

42. When a person takes certain drugs over a long period of time, the body becomes used to their effects, so more is needed to achieve the same high. Tolerance develops with all psychoactive drugs. They also alter an individual's hedonic set point for the drug.

43. There are different kinds of tolerance: dispositional, pharmacodynamic, behavioral, reverse, acute (tachyphylaxis), select, inverse (kindling), and cross-tolerance.

44. The tolerance to physical effects can develop at a different rate than the tolerance to psychological effects (select tolerance). This can cause serious physical effects such as respiratory depression.

45. The brain and the body try to biologically adapt to the increased quantities of drugs by changing their chemical balance and the cellular composition of organs such as the liver. This results in physical or tissue dependence. The person's brain and body can come to depend on the drug just to maintain basic functioning (allostasis).

46. The pleasurable effects of drugs cause an altered state of consciousness and virtually hypnotize the user into continued use (psychological dependence). Drug automatism, negative reinforcement, and social reinforcement also increase drug dependence.

47. When a user stops taking a drug after tissue dependence has developed (mostly with opiates, alcohol, and sedative-hypnotics), the body experiences many of the unpleasant sensations and physical changes it was kept from feeling while taking the drug. This backlash and subsequent attempt by the body to rebalance itself is known as withdrawal.

48. There are four types of withdrawal: nonpurposive withdrawal (objective signs of withdrawal), purposive withdrawal (addict manipulation for drugs or manifestations of expected withdrawal symptoms), protracted withdrawal (remembrance or recurrence of past drug experiences that can cause a person to keep using), and post-acute withdrawal symptoms (persistence of emotional and physical problems three to six months in recovery). All of these types of withdrawal can lead to relapse.

FROM EXPERIMENTATION TO ADDICTION

Desired Effects vs. Side Effects

49. People take drugs for a variety of reasons, including getting high, self-medicating, building confidence, increasing energy, satisfying curiosity, obliging friends (peer pressure), and avoiding problems.

50. Side effects can be mild, moderate, dangerous, or even fatal and can involve legal, relationship, financial, and work problems.

Polydrug Abuse

51. Polydrug abuse is very common. Drug abusers take other drugs to enhance the effect of their primary drug, to counteract unwanted side effects, to act as a substitute for an unavailable drug, and for a number of other reasons.

Levels of Use

52. The level of drug use is judged first by the amount, frequency, and duration of use, then by the effect use has on the individual's life.

53. The six levels of use are abstinence, experimentation, social/recreational use, habituation, abuse, and addiction.

54. The hallmark of drug abuse is continued use despite adverse consequences.

55. The hallmarks of addiction are a loss of control over use, a compulsion to use, cravings to use, and continued use despite adverse consequences.

Theories of Addiction

56. The *DSM-IV-TR* diagnosis manual classifies substance-related disorders into two categories: substance use disorders (substance dependence and substance abuse) and substance-induced disorders (intoxication, withdrawal, and certain mental disorders).

57. The addictive disease model (medical model) says that addiction is a chronic, progressive, relapsing, incurable, and potentially fatal con-

dition that is mostly a consequence of genetic irregularities.

58. The behavioral/environmental model says that certain environmental factors can change brain chemistry (e.g., stress, nutrition, abuse, anger, and peer pressure).

59. The academic model says that it's the adaptation to toxic effects of psychoactive drugs that causes the development of tolerance, tissue dependence, withdrawal, psychological dependence, and ultimately addiction.

60. The diathesis-stress theory states that the combination of heredity and environment creates a predisposition or susceptibility to chemical or behavioral dependency that can be triggered and aggravated by using psychoactive drugs and/or by acting out certain behaviors.

Heredity, Environment, Psychoactive Drugs & Compulsive Behaviors

61. The reasons for drug addiction are a combination of heredity, environment, and the use of psychoactive drugs or compulsive behaviors.

62. Heredity gives people their starting point in life. They begin with a certain inherited susceptibility to use or not use drugs. Twin studies, biological family studies, and the discovery of alcoholism-associated genes reinforce these theories. A number of genes associated with other drug addictions involving nicotine, opiates, and cocaine have also been identified. One of the main genes involved is the DRD_2A_1 allele gene. This gene and several others involve the neurotransmitter dopamine. Different genes involve other neurotransmitters, chemicals, and even brain waves.

63. Environment influences the 100 trillion connections that signify brain development. Emotional memories, which have a strong effect on drug use, are imprinted on the brain, especially sexual/physical/emotional memories. It takes until the age of 20 or so to "hardwire" the brain, so drug use in adolescence has an enormous effect on brain development.

64. The more often a drug is taken, the stronger the memories associated with that use and the more likely it is to influence subsequent behavior. The more emotionally intense the memory (e.g. abuse trauma, first drug use), the more imprinted it is.

65. Excessive, frequent, or prolonged use of psychoactive drugs modifies brain chemistry and triggers preexisting hereditary/environmental susceptibility to abuse and addiction through tolerance and other physiological mechanisms.

66. Various brain-imaging techniques (SPECT, PET, CAT, MRI, and fMRI) confirm many of the changes in brain structure, chemistry, and function associated with substance use disorders.

67. Compulsive behaviors, such as compulsive gambling, overeating, compulsive sexual activity, and Internet obsession, are similar to drug addictions in that they disrupt the brain chemistry and functioning of the reward/reinforcement circuitry and can become addictive.

Alcoholic Mice & Sober Mice

68. Animal experiments with alcohol-loving and alcohol-hating mice demonstrate that compulsive use can be induced through heredity, stress, nutritional restriction, or ingestion of large amounts of alcohol or other drugs. All can cause similar neurological changes in the central nervous system that force the continuation of the addiction.

Compulsion Curves

69. Addiction is not just a matter of learning to make the right choices. There must be an understanding that addiction is indeed a disease (similar to an allergy) and that the neurochemical changes brought on by the combination of heredity, environment, and use of psychoactive drugs, or the practice of compulsive behaviors, are imbedded in the brain and take from the user part of the ability to choose.

Conclusions

70. To understand addiction one has to look at the totality of people's lives and not just their drug-seeking behavior.

REFERENCES

Ahmed, S. H. & Koob, G. F. (1998). Transition from moderate to excessive drug intake: Change in hedonic set point. *Science, 282* (5387), 298-300.

Allman, J. (2000). *Evolving Brains*. New York: W. H. Freeman and Company.

American Psychiatric Association [APA]. (2000). *Diagnostic and Statistical Manual of Mental Disorders* (4th ed., text revision [*DSM-IV-TR*]). Washington, DC: Author.

Bartzokis, G., Beckson, M., Lu, P. H., Nuechterlein, K. H., Edwards, N. & Mintz, J. (2001). Age-related changes in frontal and temporal lobe volumes in men. *Archives of General Psychiatry, 58*(5), 461-65.

Bassareo, V. & Di Chiara, G. (1999). Differential responsiveness of dopamine transmission to food-stimuli in nucleus accumbens shell/core compartments. *Neuroscience, 89*(3), 637-41.

Begleiter, H. (1980). *Biological Effects of Alcohol.* New York: Plenum Press.

Bergstrom, M. & Langstrom, B. (2005). Pharmacokinetic studies with PET. *Progress in Drug Research, 62*, 279-317.

Bierman, K. (October 3, 1995). Early violence leaves its mark on the brain. *New York Times.*

Bierut, L. J., Dinwiddie, S. H., Begleiter, H., Crowe, R. R., Hesselbrock, V., Nurnberger, J. I., Jr., et al. (1998). Familial transmission of substance dependence: Alcohol, marijuana, cocaine, and habitual smoking: A report from the Collaborative Study on the Genetics of Alcoholism. *Archives of General Psychiatry, 55*(11), 982-88.

Blum, K., Braverman, E. R., Holder, J. M., Lubar, J. F., Monastra, V. J., Miller, D., et al. (2000). Reward deficiency syndrome: A biogenetic model for the diagnosis and treatment of impulsive, addictive, and compulsive behaviors. *Journal of Psychoactive Drugs, 32*(suppl. i-iv), 1-112.

Blum, K., Cull, J. G., Braverman, E. R. & Comings, D. E. (1996). Reward deficiency syndrome. *American Scientist, 84,* 132-45.

Boening, J. A. (2001). Neurobiology of an addiction memory. *Journal of Neural Transmission, 108*(6), 755-65.

Cadet, J. L., Ordonez, S. V. & Ordonez, J. V. (1997). Methamphetamine induces apoptosis in immortalized neural cells: Protection by the proto-oncogene, bcl-2. *Synapse, 25*(2), 176-84.

Cannon, D. S. & Carrell, L. E. (1987). Rat strain differences in ethanol self-administration and taste aversion learning. *Pharmacology Biochemistry, and Behavior, 28*(1), 57-63.

Childress, A. R., Mozley, P. D., McElgin, W., Fitzgerald, J., Reivich, M. & O'Brien, C. P. (1999). Limbic activation during cue-induced cocaine craving. *American Journal of Psychiatry, 156*(1), 11-18.

Ciccocioppo, R., Sanna, P. P. & Weiss, F. (2001). Cocaine-predictive stimulus induces drug-seeking behavior and neural activation in limbic brain regions after multiple months of abstinence: Reversal by D(1) antagonists. *Proceedings of the National Academy of Sciences, 98*(4), 1976-81.

Clark, D. B., Moss, H. B., Kirisci, L., Mezzich, A. C., Miles, R. & Ott, P. (1997). Psychopathology in preadolescent sons of fathers with substance use disorders. *Journal of the American Academy of Child and Adolescent Psychiatry, 36*(4), 495-502.

Cloninger, C. R. (1987). Neurogenetic adaptive mechanisms in alcoholism. *Science, 236*(4800), 410-16.

Cloninger, C. R., Bohman, M. & Sigvardson, S. (1986). Inheritance of risk to develop alcoholism. In M. C. Braude & H. M. Chao, eds. *Genetic and Biological Markers in Drug Abuse and Alcoholism.* NIDA Research Monograph 66. Rockville, MD: Department of Health and Human Services.

Comings, D. E., Gonzales, N., Saucier, G., Johnson, J. P. & MacMurray, J. P. (2000). The DRD₄ gene and the spiritual transcendence scale of the character temperament index. *Psychiatric Genetics, 10*(4), 185-89.

Covington, H. E. 3rd & Miczek, K. A. (2005). Intense cocaine self-administration after episodic social defeat stress but not after aggressive behavior. *Psychopharmacology 183*(3), 331-40.

Crabbe, J. C., Phillips, T. J., Harris, R. A., Arends, M. A. & Koob, G. F. (2006). Alcohol-related genes: Contributions from studies with genetically engineered mice. *Addiction Biology, 11*(3-4), 195-269.

Dackis, C. & O'Brien, C. (2005). Neurobiology of addiction: Treatment and public policy ramifications. *Nature Neuroscience, 8*(11), 1431-36.

Denton, D., Shade, R., Zamarippa, F., Egan, G., Blair-West, J., McKinley, M., et al. (1999). Neuroimaging of genesis and satiation of thirst and an interceptor-driven theory of origins of primary consciousness. *Proceedings of the National Academy of Sciences, 96*(9), 5304-9.

Diagram Group. (1991). *The Brain: A User's Manual.* Rockville Centre, NY: Berkley Press.

Di Ciano, P. & Everitt, B. J. (2004). Conditioned reinforcing properties of stimuli paired with self-administered cocaine, heroin or sucrose: Implications for the persistence of addictive behaviour. *Neuropharmacology, 47*(suppl. 1), 202-13.

Di Chiara, G. (2002). Nucleus accumbens shell and core dopamine: Differential role in behavior and addiction. *Behavioural Brain Research, 137*(1-2), 75-114.

Di Chiara, G. & Bassareo, V. (2007). Reward system and addiction: What dopamine does and doesn't do. *Current Opinion in Pharmacology, 7*(1), 69-76.

Di Chiara, G., Bassareo V., Fenu, S., De Luca, M. A., Spina, L., Cadoni, D., et al. (2004). Dopamine and drug addiction: The nucleus accumbens shell connection. *Neuropharmacology, 47*(suppl. 1), 227-41.

Dorland. (2003). *Dorland's Illustrated Medical Dictionary* (30th ed.). Philadelphia: Saunders.

Doyon, W. M., Anders, S. K., Ramachandra, V. S., Czachowski, C. L. & Gonzales, R. A. (2005). Effect of operant self-administration of 10% ethanol plus 10% sucrose on dopamine and ethanol concentrations in the nucleus accumbens. *Journal of Neurochemistry 93*(6), 1469-81.

DuPont, R. L. (1997). *The Selfish Brain: Learning from Addiction.* Washington, DC: American Psychiatric Press, Inc.

Edenberg, H. J. & Foroud, T. (2006). The genetics of alcoholism: Identifying specific genes through family studies. *Addiction Biology, 11*(3-4), 386-96.

Eisen, S. A., Lin, N., Lyons, M. J., Scherrer, J. F., Griffith, K., True, W. R., et al. (1998). Familial influences on gambling behavior. *Addiction, 93*(9), 1375-84.

Enoch, M., White, K. V., Harris, C. R., Rohrbaugh, J. W. & Goldman, D. (2001). Alcohol use disorders and anxiety disorders: Relation to the P300 event-related potential. *Alcoholism: Clinical and Experimental Research, 25*(9), 1293-300.

Evans, P. D., Gilbert, S. L., Mekel-Bobrov, N., Vallender, E. J., Anderson, J. R., Vaez-Azizi, L. M., et al. (2005). Microcephalin, a gene regulating brain size, continues to evolve adaptively in humans. *Science, 309*(5741), 1717-20.

Feingold, A., Ball, S. A., Kranzler, H. R. & Rounsaville, B. J. (1996). Generalizability of the type A/type B distinction across different psychoactive substances. *American Journal of Drug and Alcohol Abuse, 22*(3), 449-62.

Fields, H. L., Hjelmstad, G. O., Margolis, E. B. & Nicola, S. M. (2007). Ventral tegmental area neurons in learned appetitive behavior and positive reinforcement. *Annual Review of Neuroscience.* Prepublication.

Fields, R. D. (2005). Making memories stick. *Scientific American, 292*(2) 75-81.

Finnegan, L. P. & Kandall, S. R. (2005). Maternal and neonatal effects of alcohol and drugs. In J. H. Lowinson, P. Ruiz, R. B. Millman & J. G. Langrod, eds. *Substance Abuse: A Comprehensive Textbook* (4th ed., pp. 805-39). Baltimore: Williams & Wilkins.

Freud, S. 1884, 1995). *The Complete Letters of Sigmund Freud to Wilhelm Fleiss.* Cambridge: Harvard University Press.

Gardner, E. L. (2005). Brain reward mechanisms. In J. H. Lowinson, P. Ruiz, R. B. Millman & J. G. Langrod, eds. *Substance Abuse: A Comprehensive Textbook* (4th ed., pp. 48-97). Baltimore: Williams & Wilkins.

Giedd, J. N., Blumenthal, J., Jeffries, N. O., Castellanos, F. X., Liu, H., Zijdenbos, A., et al. (1999). Brain development during childhood and adolescence: A longitudinal MRI study. *Nature Neuroscience, 2*(10), 861-63.

Goldstein, A. (2001). *Addiction: From Biology to Drug Policy.* New York: Oxford University Press.

Goodwin, D. W. (1976). *Is Alcoholism Hereditary?* New York: Oxford University Press.

Gordis, E. (2003). Understanding alcoholism: Insights from the research. In A. W. Graham, T. K. Schultz, M. F. Mayo-Smith, R. K. Ries & B. B. Wilford, eds. *Principles of Addiction Medicine* (3rd ed., pp. 33-46). Chevy Chase, MD: American Society of Addiction Medicine, Inc.

Gorski, T. T. (2003). *Best Practice Principles in the Treatment of Substance*

Use Disorders. Spring Hill, FL: Gorski-Cenaps Web Productions.

Gottesman, I. I., McGuffin, P. & Farmer, A. E. (1987). Clinical genetics as clues to the "real" genetics of schizophrenia. *Schizophrenia Bulletin, 13*(1), 23-47.

Govindarajan, A., Kelleher, R. J. & Tonegawa, S. (2006). A clustered plasticity model of long-term memory engrams. *Nature Reviews: Neuroscience, 7*(7), 575-83.

Griffiths, R. R., Bigelow, G. E. & Liebson, I. (1978). Experimental drug self-administration: Generality across species and type of drug. *NIDA Research Monograph, 20,* 24-43.

Hanin, I. (1996). The Gulf War, stress and a leaky blood-brain barrier. *Nature Medicine, 2*(12), 1307-8.

Hayner, G. N. (2005). The pathogenesis of addiction. *California Pharmacist, LII*(1), 14-16.

Heath, A. C., Bucholz, K. K., Madden, P. A., Dinwiddie, S. H., Slutske, W. S., Bierut, I. J., et al. (1997). Genetic and environmental contributions to alcohol dependence risk in a national twin sample: Consistency of findings in women and men. *Psychological Medicine, 27*(6), 1381-96.

Hoffman, B. B. & Taylor, P. (2001). Neurotransmission. In J. G. Hardman, L. E. Limbird & A. G. Gilman, eds. *Goodman & Gilman's: The Pharmacological Basis of Therapeutics* (10th ed., pp. 115-53). New York: McGraw-Hill.

Hoffman, J. & Froemke, S. (2007). *Addiction: Why Can't They Just Stop?* New York: Rodale.

Hyman, S. E. (1996). Shaking out the cause of addiction. *Science, 273*(5275), 611-12.

Hyman, S. E., Malenka, R. C. & Nestler, E. J. (2006). Neural mechanisms of addiction: The role of reward-related learning and memory. *Annual Review of Neuroscience, 29,* 565-98.

Ikemoto, S., Glazier, B. S., Murphy, J. M. & McBride, W. J. (1997). Role of dopamine D_1 and D_2 receptors in the nucleus accumbens in mediating reward. *Journal of Neuroscience, 17*(21), 8580-87.

Inaba, D. & Cohen, W. E. (2004). *Uppers, Downers, All Arounders.* Medford, OR: CNS Productions, Inc.

Jaffe, J. H., Knapp, C. M. & Ciraulo, D. A. (2005). Opiates: Clinical aspects. In J. H. Lowinson, P. Ruiz, R. B. Millman & J. G. Langrod, eds. *Substance Abuse: A Comprehensive Textbook* (4th ed., pp. 180-94). Baltimore: Williams & Wilkins.

Kandel, E. R., Schwartz, J. H. & Jessell, T. M., eds. (2000). *Principles of Neural Science* (3rd ed.). New York: McGraw-Hill.

Karan, L. D., Zajicek, A. & Pating, D. R. (2003). Pharmacokinetic and pharmacodynamic principles. In A. W. Graham, T. K. Schultz, M. F. Mayo-Smith, R. K. Ries & B. B. Wilford, eds. *Principles of Addiction Medicine* (3rd ed., pp. 83-100). Chevy Chase, MD: American Society of Addiction Medicine, Inc.

Kendler, K. S., Aggen, S. H., Tambs, K. & Reichborn-Kjennerud, T. (2006). Illicit psychoactive substance use, abuse and dependence in a population-based sample of Norwegian twins. *Psychological Medicine, 36*(7), 955-62.

Khantzian, E. J., Dodes, L. & Brehm, N. M. (2005). Psychodynamics. In J. H. Lowinson, P. Ruiz, R. B. Millman & J. G. Langrod, eds. *Substance Abuse: A Comprehensive Textbook* (4th ed., pp. 97-107). Baltimore: Williams & Wilkins.

Koepp, M. J., Gunn, R. N., Lawrence, A. D., Cunningham, V. J., Dagher, A., Jones, T., et al. (1998). Evidence for striatal dopamine release during a video game. *Nature*, 393(6682), 266-68.

Koob, G. F. (March 30, 1998). *An Interview with George Koob, M.D. Close to Home.* http://www.pbs.org/wnet/closetohome/science/html/koob.html (accessed April 21, 2007).

Koob, G. F. & Le Moal, M. (1997). Drug abuse: Hedonic homeostatic dysregulation. *Science, 278*(5335), 52-58.

Koob, G. F. & Le Moal, M. (2001). Drug addiction, dysregulation of reward, and allostasis. *Neuropsychopharmacology, 24*(2), 97-129.

Kuhar, M. J., Joyce, A. & Dominguez, G. (2001). Genes in drug abuse. *Drug and Alcohol Dependence, 62*(3), 157-62.

Lamarque, S., Taghzouti, K. & Simon, H. (2001). Chronic treatment with Delta(9)-tetrahydrocannabinol enhances the locomotor response to amphetamine and heroin. Implications for vulnerability to drug addiction. *Neuropharmacology, 41*(1), 118-29.

LeDoux, J. E. (1996). *The Emotional Brain.* New York: Simon & Schuster.

Leshner, A. I. (2003). Understanding drug addiction: Insights from research. In A. W. Graham, T. K. Schultz, M. F. Mayo-Smith, R. K. Ries & B. B. Wilford, eds. *Principles of Addiction Medicine* (3rd ed., pp. 47-56). Chevy Chase, MD: American Society of Addiction of Addiction Medicine, Inc.

Li, T. K. & Lumeng, L. (1984). Alcohol preference and voluntary alcohol intakes of inbred rat strains and the National Institutes of Health heterogeneous stock of rats. *Alcoholism, 8*(5), 485-86.

Li, T. K., Lumeng, L., McBride, W. J., Waller, M. B. & Murphy, J. M. (1986).

Studies on an animal model of alcoholism. In M. C. Braude & H. M. Chao, eds. *Genetic and Biological Markers in Drug Abuse and Alcoholism.* NIDA Research Monograph 66. Rockville, MD: Department of Health and Human Services.

Lin, S. W. & Anthenelli, R. M. (2005). Genetic factors in the risk for substance use disorders. In J. H. Lowinson, P. Ruiz, R. B. Millman & J. G. Langrod, eds. *Substance Abuse: A Comprehensive Textbook* (4th ed., pp. 33-47). Baltimore: Williams & Wilkins.

Ljungman, G., Kreuger, A., Andreasson, S., Gordh, T. & Sorensen, S. (2000). Midazolam nasal spray reduces procedural anxiety in children. *Pediatrics, 105*(1 pt. 1), 73-78.

Lynskey, M. T., Agrawal, A., Bucholz, K. K., Nelson, E. C., Madden, P. A., Todorov, A. A., et al. (2006). Subtypes of illicit drug users: A latent class analysis of data from an Australian twin sample. *Twin Research & Human Genetics, 9*(4), 523-30.

Mardones, J. (1951). On the relationship between deficiency of B vitamins and alcohol intake in rats. *Quarterly Journal of Studies on Alcohol, 12*(4), 563-75.

McDaid, J., Graham, M. P. & Napier, T. C. (2006). Methamphetamine-induced sensitization differentially alters pCREB and DeltaFosB throughout the limbic circuit of the mammalian brain. *Molecular Pharmacology, 70*(6), 2064-74.

McDonald C. G., Dailey, V. K., Bergstrom H. C., Wheeler, T. L., Eppolito, A. K., Smith L. N. & Smith R. F. (2005). Periadolescent nicotine administration produces enduring changes in dendritic morphology of medium spiny neurons from nucleus accumbens. *Neuroscience Letters, 385*(2), 163-67.

McGaugh, J. L. (2003). *Memory and Emotion.* New York: Columbia University Press.

Meehl, P. E. (1962). Schizotoma, schizolyphy, schizophrenia. *American Psychologist, 17,* 827-38.

Merton, T. (1955). *No Man Is an Island.* New York: Harcourt, Brace & Company.

Meyer, J. S. & Quenzer. (2005). *Psychopharmacology: Drugs, The Brain, and Behavior.* Sunderland, MA: Sinauer Associates, Inc.

National Institute of Drug Abuse. (2001). Pathological obesity and drug addiction share common brain characteristics. *NIDA Notes,* 16(4).

National Research Council. (1999). *Pathological Gambling: A Critical Review.* Washington, DC: National Research Council.

Nelson, E. C., Heath, A. C., Lynskey, M. T., Bucholz, K. K., Madden, P. A., Statham, D. J., et al. (2006). Childhood sexual abuse and risks for licit and illicit drug-related outcomes: A twin study. *Psychological Medicine, 36*(10), 1473-83.

Nesse, R. M. (1994). An evolutionary perspective on substance abuse. *Etiology and Sociobiology, 15,* (339-48). New York: Elsevier Science, Inc.

Nesse, R. M. & Berridge, K. C. (1997). Psychoactive drug use in evolutionary perspective. *Science, 278,* (5335), 63-66.

Nestler, E. J. & Aghajanian, G. K. (1997). Molecular and cellular basis of addiction. *Science, 278*(5335), 58-63.

Nestler, E. J. (2001). Total recall-the memory of addiction. *Science, 292*(5525), 2266-67.

Nestler, E. J. (2005). Is there a common molecular pathway for addiction? *Nature Neuroscience, 8*(11), 1445-49.

Nestler, E. J., Barrot, M. & Self, D. W. (2001). DeltaFosB: A sustained molecular switch for addiction. *Proceedings of the National Academy of Sciences, 98*(20), 11042-46.

Nevid, J. S., Rathus, S. A. & Greene, B. (1997). *Abnormal Psychology in a Changing World.* Upper Saddle River, NJ: Prentice-Hall.

Noble, E. P., Blum, K., Ritchie, T., Montgomery, A. & Sheridan, P. J. (1991). Allelic association of the D_2 dopamine receptor gene with receptor-binding characteristics in alcoholism. *Archives of General Psychiatry, 48*(7), 648-54.

Nurnberger, J. I., Jr., Foroud, T., Flury, L., Su, J., Meyer, E. T., Hu, K., et al. (2001). Evidence for a locus on chromosome 1 that influences vulnerability to alcoholism and affective disorder. *American Journal of Psychiatry, 158*(5), 718-24.

O'Brien, C. P. (2001). Drug addiction and drug abuse. In J. G. Hardman, L. E. Limbird & A. G. Gilman, eds. *Goodman & Gilman's: The Pharmacological Basis of Therapeutics* (10th ed., pp. 621-41). New York: McGraw-Hill.

Office of National Drug Control Policy. (2001). *National Drug Control Strategy: 2000 Annual Report.* Bethesda, MD: National Drug Clearinghouse.

Olds, J. (1956). Pleasure centers in the brain. *Scientific American, 195*(4), 105-16.

Olds, J. & Milner, P. (1954). Positive reinforcement produced by electrical stimulation of septal area and other regions of rat brain. *Journal of Comparative and Physiological Psychology, 47*(6), 419-27.

O'Malley, S. & Volpicelli, J. (1995). Slip vs. relapse (in-house study). *Haight Ashbury Files.*

Peele, S. & Brodsky, A. (1991). *The Truth About Addiction and Recovery.* New York: Simon & Schuster.

Petry, N. M. (2005). *Pathological Gambling: Etiology, Comorbidity, and Treatment.* Washington, DC: American Psychological Association.

Pliszka, S. R. (2003). *Neuroscience for the Mental Health Clinician.* New York: The Guilford Press.

Pollard, K. S., Salama, S. R., Lambert, N., Lambot, M. A., Coppens, S., Pedersen, J. S., et al. (2006). An RNA gene expressed during cortical development evolved rapidly in humans. *Nature, 443*(7108), 167-72.

Potenza, M. N. (2001). The neurobiology of pathological gambling. *Seminars in Clinical Neuropsychiatry, 6*(3), 217-26.

Pothos, E. N. (2001). The effects of extreme nutritional conditions on the neurochemistry of reward and addiction. *Acta Astronautica, 49*(3-10), 391-97.

Purves, D., Augustine, G. J., Fitzpatrick, D., Katz, L. C., LaMantia, A. & McNamara, J. O. (1997). *Neuroscience.* Sunderland, MA: Sinauer Associates, Inc.

Reuter, M., Netter, P., Roqausch, A., Sander, P., Kaltschmidt, M., Dorr, A., et al. (2002). The role of cortisol suppression on craving for and satisfaction from nicotine in high and low impulsive subjects. *Human Psychopharmacology, 17*(5), 213-24.

Robbins, S. J., Ehrman, R. N., Childress, A. R., Cornish, J. W. & O'Brien, C. P. (2000). Mood state and recent cocaine use are not associated with levels of cocaine cue reactivity. *Drug and Alcohol Dependence, 59*(1), 33-42.

Scherrer, J. F., Xian, H., Kapp, J. M., Waterman, B., Shah, K. R., Volberg, R., et al. (2007). Association between exposure to childhood and lifetime traumatic events and lifetime pathological gambling in a twin cohort. *Journal of Nervous and Mental Disease, 195*(1), 72-78.

Schroeder, B. E., Holahan, M. R., Landry, C. F. & Kelley, A. E. (2000). Morphine-associated environmental cues elicit conditioned gene expression. *Synapse, 37*(2), 146-58.

Schoenbaum, G., Roesch, M. R. & Stalnaker, T. A. (2006). Orbitofrontal cortex, decision-making, and drug addiction. *Trends in Neuroscience, 29*(2), 116-24.

Schuckit, M. A. (1986). Genetic and clinical implications of alcoholism and affective disorder. *American Journal of Psychiatry, 143*(2), 140-47.

Schuckit, M. A. (2000A). Genetics of the risk for alcoholism. *American Journal of Addiction, 9*(2), 103-112.

Schuckit, M. A. (2000B). *Drug and Alcohol Abuse.* New York: Kluwer Academic/Plenum Publishers.

Schuckit, M. A. & Smith, T. L. (2001). The clinical course of alcohol dependence associated with a low level of response to alcohol. *Addiction, 96*(6), 903-10.

Shaffer, H. (February 28, 1998). Lecture to casino executives, Las Vegas gaming convention. *Medford Mail Tribune.*

Smith, D. E. & Seymour, R. B. (2001). *Clinician's Guide to Substance Abuse.* New York: McGraw-Hill.

Snyder, S. H. (1996). *Drugs and the Brain.* New York: Scientific American Library.

Sowell, E. R., Thompson, P. M., Holmes, C. J., Jerrigan, T. L. & Toga, A. W. (1999). In vivo evidence for post-adolescent brain maturation in frontal and striatal regions. *Natural Neuroscience, 2*(10), 859-61.

Spragg, S. D. S. (1940). Morphine addiction in chimpanzees. *Comparative Psychology Monograph, 15*(7), 1-132.

Stahl, S. M. (2000). *Essential Psychopharmacology.* Cambridge, England: Cambridge University Press.

Suzuki, D., producer. (1994). *The Brain: Our Universe Within.* Maryland: Discovery Channel.

Swaim, R. C., Oetting, E. R., Edwards, R. W. & Beauvais, F. (1989). Links from emotional distress to adolescent drug use: A path model. *Journal of Consulting and Clinical Psychology, 57*(2), 227-31.

Thompson, P. M., Giedd, J. N., Woods, R. P., MacDonald, D., Evans, A. C. & Toga, A. W. (2000). Growth patterns in the developing brain detected by using continuum mechanical tensor maps. *Nature, 404*(6774), 190-93.

Trauth, J. A., Seidler, F. J., Ali, S. F. & Slotkin, T. A. (2001). Adolescent nicotine exposure produces immediate and long-term changes in CNS noradrenergic and dopaminergic function. *Brain Research, 892*(2), 269-80.

True, W. R., Xian, H., Scherrer, J. F., Madden, P. A., Bucholz, K. K., Heath, A. C., et al. (1999). Common genetic vulnerability for nicotine and alcohol dependence in men. *Archives of General Psychiatry, 56*(7), 655-61.

Tsai, G., Gastfriend, D. R. & Coyle, J. T. (1995). The glutamatergic basis of human alcoholism. *American Journal of Psychiatry, 152*(3), 332-40.

Vergano, D. (August 7, 2006). Study: Ask with care: Emotions rule brain's decisions. *USA Today,* p. 6D.

Volkow, N. D., Chang, L., Wang, G. J., Fowler, J. S., Ding, Y. S., Sedler, M., et al. (2001). Low level of brain dopamine D_2 receptors in methamphetamine abusers: association with metabolism in the orbitofrontal cortex. *American Journal of Psychiatry, 158*(12), 2015-21.

Volkow, N. D., Fowler, J. S. & Wang, G. J. (2004). The addicted human brain viewed in the light of imaging studies: Brain circuits and treatment strategies. *Neuropharmacology, 47*(suppl. 1), 3-13.

Volkow, N. D., Fowler, J. S., Wang, G. J., Hitzemann, T., Logan, J., Schlyer, D. J., et al. (1993). Decreased dopamine D_2 receptor availability is associated with reduced frontal metabolism in cocaine abusers. *Synapse, 14*(2), 169-77.

Volkow, N. D., Wang, G. J., Begleiter, H., Porjesz, B., Fowler, J. S., Telang, F., et al. (2006). High levels of dopamine D_2 receptors in unaffected members of alcoholic families: Possible protective factors. *Archives of General Psychiatry, 63*(9), 999-1008.

Wang, G. J., Volkow, N. D., Logan, J., Pappas, N. R., Wong, C. T., Zhu, W., et al. (2001). Brain dopamine and obesity. *Lancet, 357*(9253), 354-57.

Wickelgren, I. (1998). Teaching the brain to take drugs. *Science, 280*(5372), 2045-46.

Wilkinson, G. R. (2001). Pharmacokinetics. In J. G. Hardman, L. E. Limbird & A. G. Gilman, eds. *Goodman & Gilman's: The Pharmacological Basis of Therapeutics* (10th ed., pp. 3-29). New York: McGraw-Hill.

Zhang, J., Walsh, R. R. & Xu, M. (2000). Probing the role of the dopamine D_1 receptor in psychostimulant addiction. *Annals of the New York Academy of Sciences, 914,* 13-21.

Zinberg, N. (1984). *Drugs, Set and Setting.* New Haven: Yale University Press.

Uppers

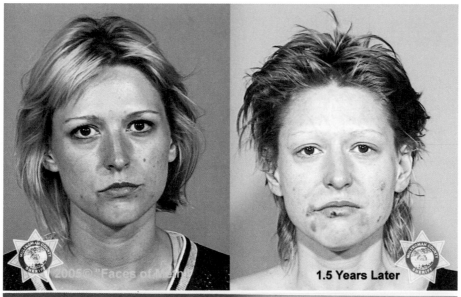

2005© "Faces of Meth"

1.5 Years Later

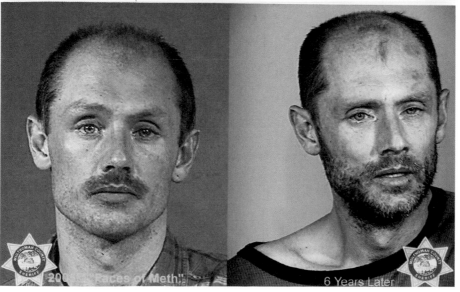

2005© "Faces of Meth"

6 Years Later

Normally you can't see the effects of meth on the faces of users but in some heavy users their faces really tell the story. The visible effects include weight loss, tooth and gum damage, pasty complexion, sores on the skin from scratching, and malnutrition. These pictures from the Multnomah County Sheriff's Office in Oregon are part of its Faces of Meth™ project to educate and scare the public about the damage that methamphetamine abuse can wreak. The pictures were taken each time a meth abuser was booked at the Multnomah County Detention Center.

- **General Classification.** Uppers include very strong stimulants (e.g., cocaine and amphetamines), moderate stimulants (e.g., diet pills and Ritalin®), milder plant stimulants (e.g., khat, betel nut, and ephedra), and legal mild stimulants (e.g., caffeine, energy drinks, and nicotine).

- **General Effects.** Stimulants force the release of the body's own energy chemicals and stimulate the brain's reward/reinforcement center. They also constrict blood vessels, increase heart rate, and raise blood pressure. Prolonged use of the stronger stimulants depletes energy resources, induces paranoia, and triggers intense craving.

- **Cocaine.** Usually injected, snorted, or smoked, cocaine, an extract of the coca leaf, causes the most rapid stimulation and subsequent severe comedown of all the stimulants.

- **Smokable Cocaine (crack, freebase).** The basic effects of smoking cocaine are almost the same as snorting or injecting it. Smoking crack is the most rapid-acting method of use and creates the greatest compulsion.

- **Amphetamines.** Longer lasting and usually cheaper than cocaine, these synthetic stimulants, including methamphetamine ("meth," "crank," "crystal," and "ice"), saw an increase of use in the 1990s and 2000s. Amphetamine analogues (especially ecstasy, a psycho-stimulant) witnessed explosive increased use and abuse by the 2000s.

- **Amphetamine Congeners.** Methylphenidate (Ritalin®) is used to treat attention-deficit/hyperactivity disorder (ADHD) in children and adults. Diet pills are used to control weight gain.

- **Look-Alike & Over-the-Counter (OTC) Stimulants.** Counterfeit stimulants, often containing caffeine or other mild stimulants, are falsely advertised as amphetamines, cocaine, or even MDMA (ecstasy). Legal mild OTC stimulants when used to excess can have toxic cardiovascular effects.

- **Miscellaneous Plant Stimulants.** Extracts of plants, such as khat, yohimbe, betel nuts, and ephedra, are used worldwide in addition to coffee, tea, and colas. Synthetic versions of plant extracts (e.g., methcathinone and pseudoephedrine) have many of the effects of methamphetamine.

- **Caffeine.** Coffee, tea, chocolate, and most soft drinks contain the alkaloid caffeine and can be mildly addicting. Many OTC medications contain caffeine. A recent phenomenon is the popularity of energy drinks such as Red Bull,® which rely mainly on caffeine for their kick.

- **Nicotine.** Nicotine is a toxic alkaloid found in tobacco. When tobacco is smoked or chewed, it first stimulates, then relaxes. Hundreds of other by-products and additives in tobacco, such as tar and nitrosamines, can cause respiratory or cardiovascular diseases as well as cancer.

- **Conclusions.** Though stimulants initially boost energy and drive, they have a number of side effects, toxic consequences, and addiction problems when overused.

GENERAL CLASSIFICATION

"Meth addicts fill up 'detox.'"

(*Mail Tribune*, 2005)

"Potent Mexican meth floods in as states cut domestic variety."

(*New York Times*, 2006)

"4 arrested in meth lab explosion case." (*Chicago Sun-Times*, 2006)

"Congress OKs landmark restrictions to fight meth." (*Oregonian*, 2006)

"No decline in meth arrests."

(*Honolulu Advertiser*, 2006)

"New health curriculum to address meth use." (*USA Today*, 2006)

"Research shows how meth use erodes brain." (*Seattle Times*, 2005)

Although a good many of the U.S. drug headlines in 2005 and 2006 were about methamphetamine, the majority of strong stimulant users still preferred cocaine.

Last year:

◇ **5.6 million Americans used cocaine, including crack, while 1.4 million shot, snorted, ate, or smoked methamphetamines for nonmedical reasons.**

Americans' love affair with stimulants was not confined to illegal substances. Last year in the United States:

◇ 83 million smoked cigarettes, puffed cigars, or chewed tobacco;

◇ 166 million drank coffee, most on a daily basis;

◇ 56 gallons of soft drinks per person (many of them caffeinated) were drunk.

In the past year worldwide, the use of stimulants was even more prevalent:

◇ 200 million people used **betel nut** the way others use coffee.

◇ Thailand and a number of Southeast Asia countries had a severe problem with **yaa baa**, an increasingly popular form of methamphetamine.

◇ In Ethiopia, Somalia, and Yemen, the majority of the male population and much of the female population used **khat**, a stimulant leaf used for many social occasions.

◇ More than 1.3 billion people worldwide smoked **cigarettes**.

◇ Colombia continued to grow almost all of the world's **coca leaf** as its local addict population continued to expand.

◇ The average daily **caffeine** consumption worldwide was 70 milligrams (mg) (about one cup of coffee), though in some countries it was as high as 400 to 500 mg per day.

(AMonline.com, 2005; Food and Agriculture Organization of the United Nations, 2006; Substance Abuse and Mental Health Services Administration [SAMHSA], 2006)

In the restless world of the twenty-first century, dominated by intense business activity, workers holding two or three jobs, high stress levels, grinding poverty, and millions of dreamers dashing after the brass ring, it seems appropriate that stimulants are so plentiful. **Some stimulants are found in plants**: the coca shrub (cocaine), the tobacco plant (nicotine), the khat bush (cathinone), the ephedra bush (ephedrine), the betel nut (arecoline), and the coffee plant (caffeine). **Other stimulants are synthesized** in legal or "street" laboratories. Methamphetamines, diet pills, methylphenidate

TABLE 3–1 UPPERS (stimulants)

Drug Name	Some Trade Names	Street or Slang Names
COCAINE (from coca leaf)		
Cocaine HCL (hydrochloride) (Schedule II)	None but it is manufactured and sold legally for medical purposes (topical anesthetic)	Coke, blow, toot, snow, flake, girl, lady, nose candy, big C, la dama blanca
Cocaine freebase (Schedule II but extra legal penalties)	None	Crack, base, rock, basay, boulya, pasta, paste, hubba, basuco, pestillos, primo
AMPHETAMINES (synthetic)		
d,l amphetamine (Schedule II)	Adderall,® Biphetamine®	Crosstops, whites, speed, black beauties, bennies, cartwheels, pep pills, addies
Benzphetamine (Schedule III)	Didrex®	
Dextroamphetamine sulfate (Schedule II)	Dexedrine®	Dexies, Christmas trees, beans
Dextromethamphetamine (dextro isomer methamphetamine)	None	Crystal meth, ice, yaa baa, glass, batu, shabu, yellow rock, Nazi speed
Freebase methamphetamine (Schedule II)	None	Snot, peanut butter
Levo amphetamine (no schedule)	Vicks® Vapor Inhaler®	
Methamphetamine HCL (Schedule II)	Desoxyn®	Crank, meth, crystal, peanut butter speed, pervitin (overseas)
Methyldioxymethamphetamine (MDMA) & other amphetamine analogues (MDA, MMDA, and MDE)	*see Chapter 6*	Ecstasy
AMPHETAMINE CONGENERS		
Dexfenfluramine (Schedule IV)	Redux® (no longer sold in the United States)	The combination of dexfenfluramine and fenfluramine with phentermine HCL or phentermine resin was called "fen-phen"
Diethylpropion (Schedule IV)	Tenuate®	
Fenfluramine (Schedule IV)	Pondimin®	Fen-phen (in combination)
Methylphenidate (Schedule II)	Ritalin,® Concerta,® Metadate CD,® Methylin,® Day Trana Patch®	Pellets
Phendimetrazine (Schedule III)	Bontril,® Prelu-2®	Pink hearts
Pemoline (Schedule II) (and street methyl pemoline)	Cylert®	Popcorn coke U4EUH, euphoria
Phentermine HCL (Schedule IV)	Adipex-P,® Banobese,® Obenix,® Zantryl®	Robin's eggs, black-and-whites, fen-phen (in combination)
Phentermine resin complex (Schedule IV)	Ionamin®	Part of fen-phen
OTHER DIET PILLS & ATYPICAL STIMULANTS		
Modafinil	Provigil®	
Sibutramine (Schedule IV)	Meridia®	
Atomoxetine	Straterra®	
LOOK-ALIKE & OVER-THE-COUNTER STIMULANTS		
Can contain caffeine, ephedrine, phenylephrine, phenylpropanolamine (taken off the market), and/or pseudoephedrine	Look-alikes: Super Toot® OTCs: Dexatrim,® Acutrim,® Sudafed®	Legal speed, robin's eggs, black beauties
Herbal caffeine, herbal ephedra	Herbal Ecstasy,® Herbal Nexus,® Cloud Nine,® Nirvana®	Herbal X

continued

TABLE 3–1   (continued)

Drug Name	Some Trade Names	Street or Slang Names
MISCELLANEOUS PLANT STIMULANTS		
Arecoline (betel nut)	None	Areca, supai, pan parag, marg, maag, pinang
Cathinone, cathine (khat bush) (*Catha edulis*) (methcathinone is the synthetic version)	None	Cat, qat, chat, miraa, Arabian tea, catha, goob, ikwa, ischott, khat kaad, kafta, la salade, liss, bathtub speed, wild cat
Ephedrine (ephedra bush)	Many commercial products	Ma huang, marwath
Yohimbine (yohimbe tree)	Yohimbi 8,® Manpower®	
CAFFEINE (xanthines)		
Chocolate (cocoa beans)	Hershey,® Nestlé®	
Coffee	Colombian, French, espresso	Java, joe, mud, roast, latte
Colas (from cola nut)	Coca-Cola,® Pepsi®	Coke
Over-the-counter stimulants	NoDoz,® Alert,® Vivarin®	
Tea	Lipton,® Stash®	Cha, chai
Guarana, maté, yoco	Various	
Energy drinks	Red Bull,® Blast,® Rockstar®	
NICOTINE		
Chewing tobacco	Day's Work,® Beechnut,® Levi-Garrett,® Redman®	Chew, chaw
Cigarettes, cigars	Marlboro,® Kent,® Pall Mall,® American Spirit®	Cancer stick, smoke, butts, toke, coffin nails
Pipe tobacco	Sir Walter Raleigh®	
Snuff	Copenhagen,® Skoal®	Dip

(Ritalin®), methcathinone, and look-alike stimulants are the most common.

There is also a whole class of designer drugs that are variations of the amphetamine molecule (amphetamine analogues). **Drugs such as MDMA (ecstasy), MDA, MMDA, and MDE are classified as psycho-stimulants** and are covered extensively in Chapter 6. It is important to remember that in addition to their psychedelic effects, the drugs still cause methamphetamine-like physical and mental effects.

GENERAL EFFECTS

Though there is a great difference in strength, **all stimulants increase the chemical and electrical activity in the central and peripheral nervous systems**. In low doses, stimulants boost energy, raise the heart rate and the blood pressure, increase respiration, reduce appetite, and subdue thirst. They also make the user more alert, active, confident, anxious, restless, and ag-gressive. Those effects allow some stimulants to be:

◊ **used clinically to treat narcolepsy, obesity, and attention-deficit/hyperactivity disorder (ADHD);**

◊ **used illegally to keep the user awake and energized, increase confidence, reduce weight, and induce euphoria.**

The major effects of stimulants occur because of the way they manipulate energy chemicals and trigger the reward/reinforcement circuitry of the brain.

BORROWED ENERGY

The biochemical process that increases energy involves at least two adrenaline neurotransmitters:

◊ **epinephrine (E), which has greater effects on physical energy;** and

◊ **norepinephrine (NE), which has greater effects on confidence, mo-**tivation, and feelings of well-being.

◊ **Two other neurotransmitters—serotonin (5-HT) and dopamine (DA)—also affect energy but to a lesser extent.**

Most E and NE neurons arise in a small area in the brainstem called the *locus coeruleus*. This area contain some 3,000 E/NE neurons that extend to almost every part of the brain, transmitting messages across synaptic gaps that affect one-third to one-half of all the cells in the brain (King & Ellinwood, 2005; Snyder, 1996). Remember that a single neuron can have thousands of dendrites and terminals. As expected, more of these energy chemicals are released while we are awake than when we are asleep, but the average 24-hour output is fairly constant. In time they are reabsorbed and rereleased when needed, or they are metabolized and depleted, signaling the nerve cells to synthesize fresh neurotransmitters.

Sometimes the body needs extra energy or a shot of confidence, such as when a person exercises, is scared and needs to flee, is making love, or is in a fight. At these moments **the nervous system automatically and naturally releases extra epinephrine, norepinephrine, and other chemicals**. Remember that initial burst of energy the body experiences when you start to exercise? Eventually, the extra energy chemicals are reabsorbed or metabolized, allowing the body to calm down and return to normal.

"The closest thing I've had to a natural high was the rock climb, and I was terrified. The adrenaline is just pumping through your system, and you're just so high off of that your heart is pumping and you sit down. We sat up there about five minutes after the climb, and I never felt so good and alone with myself other than when I was using drugs."
18-year-old recovering cocaine abuser

In contrast to the natural release of energy chemicals, **stimulants *force* the release of energy chemicals and infuse the body with large amounts of extra energy before the body needs it**. The extra energy is manifested through physical activity, talking, and hypervigilance. The effect is multiplied with strong stimulants (cocaine and amphetamines) because they keep the neurotransmitters circulating by blocking their reabsorption and/or by blocking their metabolism.

"I did it for the adrenaline. I did it to stay awake. I did it 'cause I enjoy life a lot and wanted to get the most out of life. I stayed awake and did it, and did it, and did it."
19-year-old recovering stimulant addict

Crash & Withdrawal

If strong stimulants are taken only occasionally, the body has time to recover. But if they are taken in large quantities or continuously over a long period of time, the **energy supplies become depleted and the body is left without reserves**. It is squeezed dry—exhausted. With stronger stimulants this crash and its subsequent withdrawal symptoms and **severe depression can last for days or weeks or occasionally months** (McGregor, Srisurapanont, Jittiwutikarn, et al., 2005). Even a mild stimulant like coffee can lower energy supplies as the user builds a tolerance. Six or eight cups a day will not keep the user as awake and alert as they did in the beginning.

"There is only so much you can do, and after awhile you don't get high anymore, no matter how much more you do. You just need to crash, and the depression is terrible: the fatigue, not even being able to walk, not being able to get out of bed, and just being desperate to sleep. The depression lasts up to 8 days, but it is intensely acute for 3 or 4 days in my case."
36-year-old female recovering methamphetamine addict

It is important to remember that **the energy and the confidence received from stimulants are not a gift**; they are a loan from the rest of the body and must be repaid by giving the body time to recover.

REWARD/REINFORCEMENT PATHWAY

Besides the physical stimulation, cocaine, amphetamines, and other strong stimulants disrupt the reward/reinforcement pathway, as explained in Chapter 2. Even the milder stimulants have some effect on this system. Normally, **this center, which exists in all mammals, is a survival mechanism that gives a surge of pleasure when a physiological or psychological need is being satisfied** (e.g., hunger, thirst, or sexual desire) (Goldstein, 2001; Meyer & Quenzer, 2005). The **stronger stimulants artificially overstimulate this pathway** and signal the brain that hunger is being satisfied although no food is being eaten, that thirst is being satisfied although no liquid is being drunk, and that sexual desire is being satisfied although there has been no sexual activity. This stimulation is perceived as an overall high (feelings of pleasure and well-being). Stronger stimulants, especially when smoked or injected, start with an intense rush, especially early on in use. As the drug is used more and more, the intensity of this rush and stimulation diminishes, but the emotional memories linger on. **Dopamine is the neurotransmitter most often involved in triggering these feelings.**

HEY, CARMEN! LOOKY WHAT I GOT!

A MEGA-KHAOS-FULL THROTTLE-RED BULL-MONSTER-RELOAD-CRUNK-DIESEL-VAULT-SURGE ENERGY DRINK!!!

GREAT! JUST WHAT RITALIN NATION NEEDS...

"The drug starts working on your brain. Pretty soon your brain is telling you, 'You want that drug, you like that drug, you like what you are doing.'"
32-year-old female recovering meth abuser

National Institute on Drug Abuse (NIDA) researchers have imaged the limbic (emotional) system of the brain during cocaine craving, using a positron emission tomography (PET) scan. They found that cocaine craving activates this circuitry to an exceptionally high level—especially the amygdala, the brain's emotional switchboard (Childress, McElgin, Mozley, et al., 1996; Childress, Mozley, McElgin, et al., 1999; Garavan, Pankiewicz, Bloom, et al., 2000; Schmidt, Anderson, Famous, et al., 2005). These effects on the brain are also true for methamphetamine.

WEIGHT LOSS

Normally, the hypothalamus mediates hunger; but because stimulants fool the body into thinking that its basic needs have been satisfied, the user can become malnourished and dehydrated. In fact, many long-term users of stimulants develop vitamin and mineral deficiencies that can damage teeth and cause other health problems (King & Ellinwood, 2005).

The fact that stimulants fool the body into thinking it has satisfied hunger without eating and thereby cause weight loss is one of the main reasons for their use. Even tobacco can decrease appetite because of this effect. The fear of gaining weight causes many cocaine, amphetamine, nicotine, and even caffeine users to maintain their habit.

"I was fat from about the age of 8. My doctor put me on amphetamines when I was 16. Unfortunately, they made my heart race, so I gave them up. In my senior year, I took up smoking, and that kept the weight off 'cause when I gave them up 10 years later I gained about 30 pounds. In college I started drinking coffee to study for exams. Unfortunately, I figure all these stimulants have screwed up my

appestat [appetite regulator] or whatever controls appetite 'cause I've kept gaining weight ever since."
64-year-old male recovering compulsive overeater

CARDIOVASCULAR SIDE EFFECTS

Many stimulants, including nicotine and caffeine, **induce spasms and constrict blood vessels**, thus decreasing blood flow to tissues and organs, including the skin. (Notice the pale, pasty complexion of heavy smokers and meth addicts.) Because blood flow is decreased, tissue repair and healing are slowed. In addition, **heart rate is increased** and, with the stronger stimulants, various heart arrhythmias, including tachycardia, can occur. At the same time, **blood pressure increases**, so a ruptured vessel (a stroke if it's in the brain) is possible though unusual during early use. The **chronic use of these drugs weakens blood vessels**, however, it increases the risk of stroke (Gold & Jacobs, 2005).

Polydrug use of a stimulant with a depressant can cause additional, unexpected, and possibly life-threatening cardiovascular effects. Alcohol and cocaine metabolize to cocaethylene, a potent metabolite that can have more serious cardiovascular effects (higher rate of heart attacks the day after a cocaine/alcohol binge) than only one of the drugs.

EMOTIONAL/MENTAL SIDE EFFECTS

Initial release of extra neurotransmitters by the stronger stimulants tends to **increase confidence and induce euphoria**.

"It was just a form of taking a vacation, like I was on a launching pad. I'd smoke it or snort it, then I'd just feel myself taking off like I was in a spaceship orbit for a few days. I thought it was normal."
43-year-old recovering meth abuser

But as use continues, the imbalance of dopamine, serotonin, epinephrine, norepinephrine, and other neurotrans-

mitters often transforms those feelings into **talkativeness, restlessness, irritability, insomnia, and, eventually, paranoia, aggression, and violence**. During a two-month period in Japan, 30 of the 60 murder cases that occurred were related to amphetamine/methamphetamine abuse (Schuckit, 2000). Excess use of even milder stimulants, including caffeine, khat, and ephedra, can cause restlessness, talkativeness, insomnia, and irritability.

"It's almost like there's a veneer over the nerves and it takes off that veneer, that coating, and you are just like a live wire. You'll be on a crowded bus and you might go into a rage very spontaneously, without any real cause."
25-year-old meth abuser

High-dose or prolonged methamphetamine/cocaine use can cause **drug-induced paranoia and psychosis** by increasing the level of dopamine in the central nervous system (CNS). Even high-dose methylphenidate use can sometimes induce paranoia and psychosis. The drug-induced psychosis is hard to distinguish from a real psychosis, such as schizophrenia.

"I used to drive around and hear my motorcycle talking to me, and I would see faces come out of the trees and I'd see all kinds of crazy stuff. After 10 days of no sleep, it's like living in a dream 'cause I couldn't distinguish reality from what the drug was doing to me. I was that far gone."
22-year-old meth addict living in a therapeutic community

TOLERANCE & ADDICTION LIABILITY

As stimulants force the release of extra neurotransmitters, the central nervous system loses some of its ability to synthesize these chemicals thus contributing to the **rapid development of tolerance**. This causes other physiological changes in the user's neurochemistry that promote the rapid development of physical and psychological dependence. The continued use of strong stimulants causes a decrease in the number of serotonin and dopamine receptor sites in the nucleus accumbens and other areas, a process called *down-regulation*. This decrease causes the CNS to crave even more of the drug to overstimulate the small number of remaining receptors (Repetto & Gold, 2005). While the physical dependence of extended cocaine and methamphetamine use isn't quite as severe as with heroin, the psychological dependence is just as powerful and causes severe craving during the crash and subsequent withdrawal.

Tolerance and dependence can also develop with methamphetamine congeners, caffeine, nicotine, and other milder stimulants. In fact, the strongest dependence, both physical and mental, develops with tobacco.

COCAINE

Besides the occasional headline about the latest movie or sports star to get busted for cocaine use, the publicity and the notoriety surrounding this drug have diminished drastically since the crack epidemic of the 1980s and 1990s. This is partly due to the media interest in methamphetamines and ecstasy as well as the cyclical nature of drug epidemics.

Cocaine epidemics seem to occur every few generations. The first was at the end of the nineteenth century; the next in the 1920s and 1930s. Then it wasn't until the 1970s and 1980s that use exploded with the popularization of smokable cocaine (crack). Since then experimentation and casual use have declined somewhat, but **hardcore use of cocaine has remained strong into the 2000s.** The average age of those coming into treatment has gone up while the younger generation has turned to MDMA (ecstasy) as the psychoactive stimulant drug of choice for recreational use.

As with any newly discovered drug, cocaine spawned many myths and advocates when it first became popular. In 1886 **Robert Louis Stevenson wrote *The Strange Case of Dr. Jekyll and Mr. Hyde* in just six days**

under the influence of cocaine, which he was taking to treat tuberculosis.

"I have more than once observed that in my second character, my faculties seemed sharpened to a point and my spirits more tensely elastic; thus it came about that, where Jekyll perhaps might have succumbed, Hyde rose to the importance of the moment. My drugs were in one of the presses of my cabinet; how was I to reach them?"

Robert Louis Stevenson, *Dr. Jekyll and Mr. Hyde*, 1886

The novel's theme concerns the dramatic transformation of Dr. Jekyll when he takes an experimental medication and the consequences of this experimentation. The mania of his alter ego, Mr. Hyde, can be likened to some of the effects of intense use of cocaine, particularly if drug-induced psychosis, paranoia, and anger are manifest. This idea of opposites, of ups and downs, of dramatic personality transformations is always present when the effects of cocaine are examined.

The Erythroxylum coca plant.
Courtesy of the Fitz Hugh Ludlow Memorial Library

BOTANY, CROP YIELDS & REFINEMENT

The coca shrub dates back millions of years. One writer half-jokingly speculated that eating the plant caused the extinction of the dinosaurs because of its toxicity. The coca bush, which contains the alkaloid cocaine, **grows mainly on the slopes of the Andes Mountains in South America** (Peru, Bolivia, Ecuador, and mainly Colombia). Lesser amounts are grown in certain parts of the Amazon jungle and on the island of Java in Indonesia. The South American cultivation of the *Erythroxylum coca* and *Erythroxylum novogranatense* plants accounts for 97% of the world's crop. The green-yellow shrubs, which grow best at altitudes between 1,500 and 5,000 feet, are 6 to 8 feet tall. **The leaves of the coca bush contain 0.5% to 1.5% by weight of the alkaloid cocaine.** One acre of coca bushes will yield 1.5 to 2 kg of cocaine (Grinspoon & Bakalar, 1985).

The **cocaine refinement technique is a 4- or 5-step process** depending on the chemicals used (Karch, 2001): (1) Soak the leaves in an alkali and water, (2) add gasoline, kerosene, or acetone, (3) discard the waste leaves and add acid, (4) mix in lime and ammonia, and (5) separate the cocaine hydrochloride from the paste.

SMUGGLING & THE STREET TRADE

"Five years and $3 billion into the most aggressive counter-narcotics operation ever here, American and Colombian officials say they have eradicated a record-breaking million acres of coca plants, yet cocaine remains as available as ever on American streets, perhaps more so."

Joel Brinkley, *New York Times*, April 27, 2005

Besides cocaine's being readily available, as noted in the *New York Times,* the White House's Office of National Drug Control Policy says that the **prices on the street have remained stable while the purity has improved**. Part of the problem is that the coca bush will yield three to four crops per year, so even if the fields are

This Bolivian farm worker is sorting coca leaves. It takes 250 kg of leaves to make 1 kg of cocaine. Refinement often involves toxic substances like gasoline, kerosene, and sulfuric acid. If the refining is not done carefully, the resulting cocaine can contain many of these toxic chemicals.

© 1990 Alain Labrousse

• • • • • • • • • • • • • • • • •

caine were produced in the Andean region in 2005 (DEA, 2006B; Lichtblau & Schrader, 1999; United Nations Office on Drugs and Crime [UNODC], 2006).

The amount of money in the cocaine trade is staggering, even when the drug first became popular. Back in 1884, because the interest in cocaine was so intense, the price of a gram rose to $7.50—about four times what it is today, figuring for inflation. Cocaine production increased from three-fourths of a pound in 1883 to 158,352 lbs. in 1886 (Karch, 2005). Currently, the money involved in the trade is just as remarkable:

◊ Americans spent an estimated $36.1 billion (retail) on cocaine in 2004.

◊ At the wholesale level, cocaine prices varied from $12,000 to $35,000 per kilogram ($23,000 average) of refined cocaine with an average purity of 84%.

◊ At the street level, prices varied from $50 to $200 per gram (gm) ($90/gm average) in the United States (and worldwide) with an average purity of 57%.

◊ "Rocks" of crack cocaine, varying in size from one-tenth to one-half of a gram, sell for $10 to $20 each.

◊ The average hardcore cocaine user spends about $186 per week, about half of what was spent by users 10 years ago.

(DEA, 2001; DEA, 2006A&B; UNODC, 2006)

Estimates of the number of casual cocaine users and hardcore users vary widely, depending on the survey and the definition of hardcore users. Is someone who binges once a month a hardcore user? For example, in 2004 the National Household Survey on Drug Abuse (NHSDA) estimated 445,000 hardcore cocaine users and 2,155,000 occasional users in the United States. The **Drug Use Forecasting (DUF) program**, however, which questions arrestees in city jails about their drug use and backs up the questions with urinalysis, **estimates 3,103,000 hardcore users**. The DUF data seems closer to the truth because it represents the very population most likely to be involved in hardcore use.

sprayed, the farmer will still have two or three crops that year. Because coca leaves are difficult to grow outside of South America and the extraction process is fairly complex, highly organized crime cartels (Medellin and Cali) developed in Colombia in the 1980s to operate the cocaine trade. When international efforts shut down cocaine cultivation in Peru and Bolivia during the 1990s, Colombian production boomed. In addition, Caqueta, an area in the Amazon basin in southern Colombia controlled by the Marxist FARC (Revolutionary Armed Forces of Colombia), became a major coca grower and cocaine paste producer. (The FARC takes 30% of all transactions to finance its activities.) Although in recent years the Colombian army has driven the FARC and the coca fields deeper into the Amazon basin (Villalon, 2004), it is estimated that the FARC still controls half of the world's cocaine trade. In 2006 the United States indicted 50 of these rebel leaders on drug

charges, but only three are in custody (Forero, 2006).

About **two-thirds of the actual smuggling into the United States in recent years has been handled by drug gangs and cartels centered in Mexico.** Caribbean groups are also involved. All of these groups prefer sea routes due to increased surveillance of airspace and greater scrutiny of the southern U.S. border due to the September 11, 2001, terrorist attacks. The Colombian trafficking groups in the United States are based on close-knit criminal cells operating within a given geographic area; and because there is minimal contact between cells, the organization is hard to break up (Drug Enforcement Administration [DEA], 2006A).

North America consumes 40% to 50% of the world's cocaine. The federal government seized more than 130 metric tons of cocaine in 2005, yet an estimated 100 to 200 metric tons still got through to U.S. markets. It was estimated that about 780 metric tons of co-

What both methods have in common is a consistency of survey methods from year to year, so many surveys are more valuable to judge trends in use rather than absolute numbers (Office of National Drug Control Policy [ONDCP], 2003).

HISTORY OF USE

Many landmarks in the history of coca and cocaine use have to do with the changing methods of use and the purity of the substance. The methods include chewing the leaf or chopping it with ash and placing it on the gums; drinking the refined cocaine alkaloid in wine; injecting a solution of the drug in a vein; snorting cocaine hydrochloride; and smoking freebase or crack crystals.

The effects of cocaine are directly related to the blood levels of the drug. The more cocaine that reaches the brain, the more intense the high, the greater the craving, and the more quickly tolerance, abuse, and addiction occur.

Chewing the Leaf

Native cultures in South America have chewed coca leaves for thousands of years for social and religious occasions and to lessen hunger, fight off fatigue, and increase endurance. **The Incas usually chewed the leaf for the juice, adding some lime or ash (from ground shells) to increase absorption by the mucosal tissue in the cheeks and gums, which takes three to five minutes.** If the chewer swallows the coca juice, not only does the digestive system break down most of the drug but it takes longer (20 to 30 minutes) to reach the brain. A habitual user might chew 12 to 15 gm of leaves three or four times a day, but even so the maximum amount of cocaine available for absorption would be just 690 mg. The chopped leaves mixed with ash can also be spooned under the tongue for absorption.

The Incas in Peru integrated the use of the coca leaf in every part of their lives much as coffee or tea are part of an American's everyday life. Use was originally confined to priests and the nobility, but when the Conquistadors subjugated the Inca Empire in the sixteenth century, they greatly increased the cultivation and the availability of the leaf. **They grew it for personal profit, to generate government taxes, and to enable the Incas to work more efficiently at high altitudes,** digging in the silver mines (Karch, 2005; Monardes, 1577).

Even to this day, up to 90% of the Indians living in coca-growing regions chew the leaf. In many native homes in Bolivia, visitors are ceremoniously offered pieces of leaves to chew even before refreshments are served. The cocaine blood levels for a coca leaf chewer are about one-fourth those of smokers and one-seventh those of IV users (Karch, 2001). In addition to the stimulation and hunger control, about 4 oz. of chewed leaves provide the recommended dose of all vitamins and minerals (Rätsch, 2005). The cultivation, trade, and chewing or brewing of coca leaves is legal in Bolivia, Peru, and northwestern Argentina. *Coca y bica* (coca leaves and bicarbonate of soda or other alkaline substance) are sold at markets, newsstands, and other small shops.

"Bolivian president-elect Evo Morales, a former coca farmer and former political leader of the cocaleros (coca growers) who had campaigned on the promise of agrarian reform and decriminalization of all cultivation of coca, was sworn in today at the presidential palace in La Paz. He pledged to fight drug trafficking while finding other markets for coca-based products such as tea. 'Cocaine is not part of the Andean culture,' Morales said. 'We must finish with drugs.'"
Los Angeles Times, January 26, 2006

This seemingly contradictory statement merely emphasizes the historic impact of refining and concentrating the active ingredients of a psychoactive drug (e.g., opium to heroin, 1% THC in marijuana to 12% THC in sinsemilla-grown plants).

Carrying on a centuries-old tradition, this Colombian coca chewer carries his leaves in a pouch hung on his shoulder. The poporo (gourd) in his right hand contains powdered lime (llipta) that he mixes in his mouth with the coca to increase absorption of the coca juice.
Courtesy of the Fitz Hugh Ludlow Memorial Library

In 1859 Albert Niemann, a graduate student in Gottingen, Germany, isolated cocaine from the other chemicals in the coca leaf. This powerful alkaloid, **cocaine hydrochloride, was 200 times more powerful by weight than the coca leaf**, thus setting the stage for the widespread use and abuse of the drug. It took 20 years, however, before word about the drug spread, due in part to the physician Karl Koller, who discovered its anesthetic properties, and to **Sigmund Freud**, who promoted the medical and psychiatric uses of refined cocaine hydrochloride in his book *Über Coca*. The drug was recommended for a variety of ailments, including depression, tuberculosis, gastric disorders, asthma, and morphine or alcohol addiction. Its use as a local anesthetic or even as an aphrodisiac was also suggested (Guttmacher, 1885). It was the stimulating and mood-enhancing qualities that most interested Freud; but because cocaine was a new drug that hadn't been studied over time, he made a number of errors of judgment.

"Coca is a far more potent and far less harmful stimulant than alcohol and its widespread utilization is hindered at present only by its high cost.... I have already stressed the fact that there is no state of depression when the effects of coca have worn off."
Sigmund Freud, (Freud, 1884)

The overly optimistic judgments of Freud and others were made early in the experimental process before cocaine dependence and addiction were recognized problems. When the drug was made more widely available and some people became chronic users, the true nature and liabilities of refined cocaine became obvious even to Freud and his colleagues.

Drinking Cocaine

The fact that the newly refined cocaine hydrochloride could be dissolved in water or alcohol made other routes of use possible, namely drinking, injecting, and contact absorption. **Beginning in the late 1860s, cocaine wines became popular** in France and Italy; but it wasn't until a clever manufacturer and salesman, Angelo Mariani, concocted Vin Mariani and promoted its use through the first celebrity endorsements (e.g., Thomas Edison, Robert Louis Stevenson, and Pope Leo XIII) that the first cocaine epidemic began. Although the wine contained only a modest amount of cocaine (two glasses of wine contained the equivalent of one line of cocaine), its effect was more than modest because it was used with alcohol (Karch, 2005). **It takes 15 to 30 minutes for the metabolites of cocaine to reach the brain after oral ingestion.**

Suddenly, in the 1880s and 1890s, patent medicines laced with cocaine, opium, morphine, heroin, *Cannabis,* and alcohol became the rage. They were touted as cure-alls for ailments ranging from asthma and hay fever to fatigue, depression, and anxiety and dozens of other illnesses.

Because these patent medications controlled pain and induced a certain euphoria, the perception that they cured illness rather than just controlled the symptoms was perpetuated. **In the late 1800s, the prolonged use of cocaine and other prescription medications created a large group of dependent users and addicts, the majority being women** (Aldrich, 1994).

Injecting Cocaine

The **invention of the hypodermic needle in 1853** had a more immediate effect on the use of morphine than on cocaine for two reasons. First, the refinement of morphine from opium occurred 50 years earlier than the refinement of cocaine, and, second, the use of an opiate painkiller such as morphine had a natural outlet in the Crimean War and the U.S. Civil War as well as in the civilian population as a remedy for pain, anxiety, and diarrhea.

Medically, the subcutaneous injection or application on moist tissues of cocaine caused topical anesthesia, useful for minor surgery. Unfortunately, when physicians first began using cocaine medicinally, many were unaware of the overdose potential, even from topical use, and a number of deaths occurred.

Injecting cocaine intravenously results in an intense rush within 30 seconds and gives the highest blood cocaine level. The rush is more intense than chewing the leaf, drinking cocaine wine, or snorting cocaine hydrochloride, so the alteration in brain chemistry and in the reward/reinforcement pathway is more rapid. Because cocaine is rapidly metabolized by the body, intravenous (IV) use means that the rush and the subsequent crash will be equally intense. If cocaine is injected **subcutaneously or intramuscularly, the high is delayed three to five minutes** and is not quite as intense.

Snorting Cocaine

The early 1900s gave rise to a popular new form of cocaine use: snorting the powder into the nostrils. Called "tooting," "blowing," or "horning," **this method gets the drug to the nasal mucosa and into the brain in three to five minutes**. Peak effects take a few more minutes to occur.

"What snorting I have done burns the nose terribly and is very uncomfortable. It's much delayed, where shooting is quicker. In fact, after 20 minutes [with snorting] I was still getting higher to the point where I did not want to be."
26-year-old recovering cocaine addict

Snorting cocaine is a self-limiting method of use: the drug constricts the capillaries that absorb the drug, so the more that is snorted, the slower the absorption. The blood level of cocaine is much lower than with IV use. As the constricting effect of cocaine wears off, **the nasal tissues swell, causing the runny, sniffling nose** characteristic of cocaine snorters. Chronic use can kill nasal tissues and in a few cases perforate the nasal septum that divides the nostrils (Smith & Seymour, 2001). The first case of a perforated nasal septum was described in medical literature in 1910 (Karch, 2005).

Mucosal & Contact Absorption

Besides absorption through mucosa in the nose, gums, and cheeks, cocaine can be **absorbed through mucosal tissue in the rectum and the**

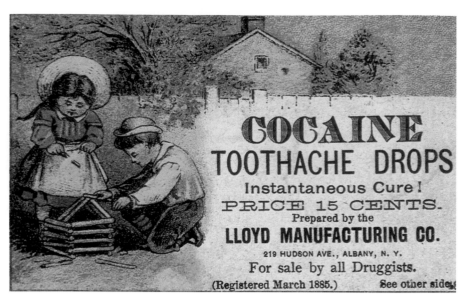

The anesthetic effects of cocaine made the drug a favorite among dentists long before Novocain® (procaine hydrochloride) was synthesized.

Courtesy of the National Library of Medicine, Bethesda, MD

• •

vagina and act as a topical anesthetic. Rectal application is used in parts of the gay male community (Karch, 2001). Cocaine can also be absorbed through the outer skin (epidermis) but not at levels high enough to cause effects, merely to be detectable in the bloodstream (and cause problems in drug testing). Cocaine has to be injected under the skin to numb the skin itself.

Smoking Cocaine

Although there is some evidence that coca leaves were burned and the smoke inhaled by Peruvian shamans to alter their state of consciousness and help commune with their gods, it wasn't until cocaine was refined that experimenters looked for ways to inhale the more concentrated smoke. In 1914 Parke-Davis Pharmaceuticals introduced cigarettes that contained refined cocaine, but the high temperature (195°C, or 383°F) needed to convert cocaine hydrochloride to smoke resulted in the destruction of many of its psychoactive properties. Thus chewing, drinking, injecting, and snorting cocaine remained the principal routes of administration until the mid-1970s, when street chemists **converted cocaine hydrochloride to freebase cocaine. This process lowered the vaporization point to 98°C and made the drug smokable.** Unlike the cocaine hydrochloride cigarettes introduced in 1914, freebase cocaine could be smoked without destroying most of its psychoactive properties. In the early and mid-1980s, an easier method of making freebase cocaine (called "dirty basing") was developed, setting the stage for another cocaine epidemic. This new form of smokable cocaine was called "crack."

When absorbed through the lungs, cocaine reaches the brain in only 5 to 8 seconds compared with the 15 to 30 seconds it takes when injected through the veins. The smokable cocaine reaches the brain so quickly that it causes more-dramatic effects before it is swiftly metabolized. This rapid up-and-down roller-coaster effect results in intense craving and an **extreme binge pattern of use**.

"The first time I smoked crack cocaine, when I put the glass pipe up to my lips, it made my lips burn, it made them numb, and the smell of smoking rock cocaine or crack is gross; it is the smell that you'll never forget. I felt glazed over and I felt like I escaped and I could just float."

27-year-old female recovering crack smoker

PHYSICAL & MENTAL EFFECTS

Metabolism

Because **cocaine is metabolized very quickly, effects dissipate faster than with amphetamines** and amphetamine congeners. Cocaine is metabolized to ecgonine methyl ester, benzoylecgonine, and, if alcohol is present, cocaethylene. The half-life of cocaine is 30 to 90 minutes. This means that half the drug is metabolized to pharmacologically inactive metabolites in that period of time. Even after the drug has almost disappeared from the blood, however, effects continue to occur. **Cocaine use is usually detectable in the urine for up to 36 hours.**

Medical Use

As the **only naturally occurring topical anesthetic with powerful vasoconstriction effects**, cocaine is used in aerosol form to numb the nasal passages when inserting breathing tubes in a patient, to numb the eye or throat during surgery, and to deaden the pain of chronic sores. (This topical anesthetic effect also numbs the nasal passages when the drug is snorted.) Cocaine receptors are also found on the bronchi and the smooth muscles of the lungs, so **stimulation causes dilation of the bronchi**. Because of this effect, cocaine was once used to treat asthma. Synthetic topical anesthetics, particularly procaine and lidocaine, that mimic the effects of cocaine are used nowadays for eye surgery, dental procedures, and other minor surgeries because they are much less stimulating to the brain. None of the synthetic anesthetics constricts blood vessels, so they are combined with epinephrine, a vasoconstrictor, to prevent excess bleeding.

Neurochemistry & the Central Nervous System

Most of cocaine's effects are the result of its influence on serotonin and two catecholamine neurotransmitters—**norepinephrine and dopamine. Cocaine primarily prevents the reabsorption of these neurotransmitters thus increasing their concentration in the synapse and intensifying the effects** (Meyer & Quenzer, 2005). In an experiment with cocaine users at NIDA's Regional Neuroimaging Center, Dr. Nora Volkow used PET scans to show that **cocaine blocked 60% to 77% of the dopamine reuptake sites**. At least 47% of the sites had to be blocked for users to feel a drug-induced high (Volkow, Fowler, Wang, et al., 1997; Volkow, Fowler, Wang, et al., 2005).

The Crash.   By blocking the reuptake ports, cocaine leaves those neurotransmitters vulnerable to metabolism by enzymes that circulate among the brain cells, resulting in their depletion (Smith & Seymour, 2001). Because cocaine is metabolized so quickly, the initial euphoria, the feeling of confidence, the sense of omnipotence, the surge of energy, and the satisfied feelings disappear as suddenly as they appeared, so **the crash after using cocaine can be intensely depressing**. This depression can last a few hours, several days, or even weeks.

"Initially, I remember the mood swings, but then the swings became farther and farther apart and the depression got deeper and deeper and deeper and of course eventually it led me to my attempt at suicide. I really did want to die, and that I remember as being way out of proportion to the actual events of my life."
44-year-old recovering cocaine addict

The biological mechanisms of cocaine are quite complex. For example, in an experiment at Massachusetts General Hospital, **brain scans of 10 cocaine addicts just after injection of the drug showed 90 distinct areas of brain activation**, especially the amygdala and nucleus accumbens (Breiter, Gollub, Weisskoss, et al., 1997). Unfortunately, the intense stimulation has a price. It's like putting 230 volts into a 115-volt light bulb. The bulb burns more brightly, but the strain on the filament can eventually burn it out. For example:

◇ **Dopamine** coordinates fine motor skills, signals the reward/reinforcement pathway, and regulates thoughts, but it can also **overstimulate the brain's fright center,**

causing the paranoia experienced by many cocaine abusers. The fright center is a survival mechanism to warn us of danger, but overstimulation causes overreaction or paranoia. A shadow, sudden movement, or loud voice may seem unbearably threatening.

"There were these little nail holes in the door, and he swore up and down that someone was looking at us through them. I put my feet down on the bed, and he would slap the shit out of me, 'Bitch, who you signaling?' He would get on his knees and look under the bed."
34-year-old recovering crack abuser

◇ **Catecholamines (epinephrine and norepinephrine)** increase confidence and energy and cause a euphoric rush that seems extremely pleasurable. Eventual depletion of the catecholamines causes exhaustion, lethargy, anhedonia (the inability to feel pleasure), and low blood pressure.
◇ **Serotonin** initially causes elation, facilitates sleep, raises self-esteem, and increases sexual activity, but with excessive use it becomes insomnia, agitation, and severe emotional depression (Sora, Hall, Andrews, et al., 2000).
◇ **Acetylcholine** increases reflexes, alertness, memory, learning, and aggression, but that can turn into muscle tremors, memory lapses, mental confusion, and even hallucinations.

Sexual Effects

"It makes you feel like, you know, you're really sexy and, you know, makes you feel like you're the best man in the whole world."
36-year-old recovering cocaine addict

"The first time I did it, I felt all bubbly and like orgasmic and touch was very sensual, but that went away very quickly."
28-year-old female recovering cocaine addict

Cocaine and amphetamines have similar sexual effects. Cocaine at **low doses enhances sexual desire, delays ejaculation**, and is considered an aphrodisiac by many users. In some cases it causes spontaneous ejaculation. **With higher doses and chronic use, sexual dysfunction becomes more common** (e.g., the inability to achieve an erection and disinterest in sex at all).

"After awhile when you keep doing it, it's just like you're impotent and you can't . . . it doesn't have no effect. The opposite sex can do anything they want to you and you won't react. Your body doesn't react to it, to any kind of touch or emotion, you know."
36-year-old recovering cocaine addict

In addition, the need to raise money plus the disinhibiting effects of cocaine lead to **high-risk sexual behavior** and unusual sexual practices (Smith & Wesson, 1985).

Aggression, Violence & Cocaethylene

Cocaine use is associated with increased aggression and violence, especially in those prone to violence. The disruption of neurotransmitter levels is heavily implicated in these emotions. When

◇ **inhibitory functions are suppressed** in the anterior cingulate gyrus and temporal lobes,
◇ **emotional triggers are overstimulated** in the amygdala,
◇ **the fright center is hyperactivated** in the limbic system, and
◇ the normal function of the **temporal lobes is disrupted,**

aggression and occasionally violence are often just a glance away (Amen, Yantis, Trudeau, et al., 1997).

"I found that using cocaine, mainlining it straight to the nervous system, it's like I want to kill people. It is a very unhealthy state of mind. . . . It is like spinning out of control and all the thoughts are centered around

Operation Trifecta, run by the federal Drug Enforcement Administration (DEA), the Federal Bureau of Investigation, the Internal Revenue Service, and several other U.S. agencies, resulted in the arrests in 2006 of more than 240 individuals involved in the Zambada-Garcia drug organization in Mexico. The investigation was triggered by the interdiction of The Macel, a ship trying to smuggle 9,291 kg of cocaine into the United States.
Courtesy of the Drug Enforcement Administration

• •

'Where should I hit them first?' Damn, I want to hurt people, you know. It is just psychotic thinking."
32-year-old recovering cocaine abuser

In a small study of domestic violence, researchers found that 67% of the perpetrators had used cocaine the day of the incident and virtually all of those had also used alcohol. Interviews and research seem to indicate that **cocaethylene (an active metabolite when cocaine and alcohol are taken together) induces greater agitation, euphoria, and violence** than cocaine alone (Brookoff, O'Brien, Cook, et al., 1997; Landry, 1992).

"My mate hallucinated from smoking too much, thinking I was trying to do his brothers, and I got my face damaged badly because of the hallucinations. He slammed my face into concrete."
28-year-old female recovering crack abuser

The cocaethylene reaches the brain as easily as the cocaine and has almost identical effects but is somewhat more toxic. **Cocaethylene also seems more likely to induce cardiac conduction abnormalities** compared with cocaine and therefore is more likely to induce a heart attack. Because the average half-life of cocaethylene is more than three times that of cocaine by itself (two hours vs. 38 minutes), its effects, including high blood pressure, last longer (Karch, 2001; Repetto & Gold, 2005). Many cocaine abusers are aware of this extended half-life effect, so they "front load" with alcohol to prolong the effects of the more expensive cocaine. It is theorized, however, that the extended anxiety and panic attacks common with cocaine abusers, even after they quit, could be attributed to the slow elimination of cocaethylene (Pennings, Leccese & Wolfe, 2002; Randall, 1992).

The paranoia and dysfunctional lifestyle involved with cocaine use engenders excess violence. Autopsies showed that 31% of all homicide vic-

tims in New York in the early 1990s had cocaine in their bodies (1,332 out of 4,298 victims). Two-thirds of those who tested positive were 15 to 34 years old, 86% were male, and 87% were African American or Latino (Tardiff, Marzuk, Leon, et al., 1994).

Cardiovascular Effects

"There was a heavy beating, tachycardia, a sense of not being able to get my breath, the sensation of everything moving very quickly and very intensely."
34-year-old female recovering cocaine abuser

Physiologically, it is the cardiovascular system that is most affected by long-term cocaine use. Cocaine affects the circulatory system by direct contact (due to receptors directly on the heart and blood vessels) and by its effect on the sympathetic part of the autonomic nervous system in the brain. When injected, **cocaine raises the heart rate and constricts blood vessels, causing a 20- to 30-unit rise in blood pressure,** sometimes more (Tuncel, Wang, Arbique, et al., 2002). This means that while more blood is available for central blood vessels to energize muscles and increase blood flow to the heart, less is available for the smaller vessels to heal damaged tissues, aid digestion, and infuse other peripheral systems with sufficient oxygen. This leads to cellular changes, including **damage to heart muscles, coronary arteries, and other blood vessels.**

The raised blood pressure can also **weaken the walls of the blood vessels and cause a stroke,** usually within three hours of use. The effects of chronic cocaine use are similar to those of chronic stress. The hearts of chronic abusers are often slightly enlarged, and coronary arterial blood flow is sluggish. Chronic cocaine use also causes disorganization in the usual formation of heart muscles and the scarring of these muscles known as *constriction bands.* This makes chronic users more likely to suffer a cocaine-induced heart attack (Gold & Jacobs, 2005; Karch, 2001).

Dr. Shenghan Lai and his colleagues at Johns Hopkins University found that cocaine abuse builds up cal-

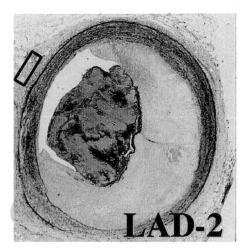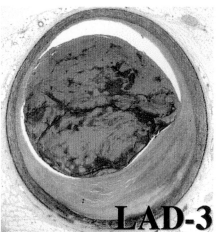

These cross sections of the left anterior descending (LAD) coronary artery are from a 36-year-old long-term IV cocaine user who died from acute myocardial infarction. The clot that caused the heart attack can be seen in both cross sections of the lumen (interior) of the LAD. It overlays the fatty plaque that built up over the years on the walls of the coronary artery, probably due to the cocaine use.

Courtesy of Dr. Rene Virmani, chair, Department of Cardiovascular Pathology, Armed Forces Institute of Pathology

●●

cium and fat deposits on the inner walls of blood vessels. They detected this problem in relatively young cocaine users at a much higher rate than in nonusing young adults. They also found that if the cocaine user also had HIV, the rate of calcification was even greater (Lai, Lima, Lai, et al., 2005).

Neonatal Effects

"Three of my children have been taken directly from me in the hospital, like directly out of my arms to the nursery, found out they were positive for cocaine and, you know, back to the nursery, and I wasn't allowed to, like, see them."

30-year-old recovering crack user

When a pregnant woman uses cocaine, her **baby is exposed to the drug** within seconds. Because of the stimulatory effects on the cardiovascular system, the chances of **miscarriage, stroke, placental separation, and sudden infant death syndrome** (SIDS) due to raised blood pressure and blood vessel malformations are increased (Gold & Jacobs, 2005).

In one study of 717 cocaine-exposed infants, at birth the babies were about 1.2 weeks younger, weighed 536 g less, measured 2.6 centimeters (cm) shorter, and had a head circumference 1.5 cm smaller than nonexposed infants (Bauer, Langer, Shankaran, et al., 2005). Another analysis of 36 studies of physical growth, cognition, language skills, motor skills, and behavior in cocaine-exposed children up to the age of six, however, showed minimal effects, suggesting that many children can outgrow some of the effects or develop alternate methods of learning (Frank, 2001).

In a Toronto inner-city hospital, 12% to 20% of all newborns had been exposed to cocaine (Foreman, Klein, Barks, et al., 1994). Infants born cocaine-affected have been called "jittery babies" because they are agitated, have higher blood pressure, and are more irritable.

"The first two or three weeks out of the hospital, the babies are pretty normal and then all of a sudden the chemical that they were born with is out of the system. They go through a couple of weeks of severe withdrawal, where they have seizures, tremors, vomiting, and diarrhea, screaming 16 to 20 hours a day. After about two weeks of that, the brain releases some of that cocaine [actually, a metabolite of cocaine] back into the system, then we have a couple of weeks of reprieve, and then that whole process starts over again."*

Foster mother who cares for drug-affected babies

Many of the abnormalities in the newborns of drug users have more to do with the mother's lifestyle than the drug itself. For example, amphetamine and cocaine abusers are generally malnourished, so the fetus suffers from malnutrition. The mothers are more likely to smoke tobacco and to have a venereal or IV drug-induced disease, such as hepatitis or AIDS, so the fetus is infected, too. A drug-dependent mother is more likely to be indifferent to the daily demands of an infant than a nonusing mother, so neglect, bonding problems, and emotional deprivation are more likely. For example, in a study of 218 cocaine-exposed babies of high-risk, low-socioeconomic-status mothers, the mental retardation rate was five times that of the general population but only twice the rate for non-cocaine-exposed children of the same socioeconomic group. **The rate of mild or greater mental delays was also double that of the nonexposed children** (Singer, Arendt, Minnes, et al., 2002).

Despite the severe problems of cocaine toxicity and withdrawal noted in cocaine-exposed fetuses and babies, there is hope. Demonstration projects like those of the Haight Ashbury Free Clinics' Moving Addicted Mothers Ahead (MAMA) and Ujima House Centers have shown that **good prenatal and postnatal care of these infants**, along with continued excellent pediatric and parenting resources, **results in toddlers who catch up in their emotional and physical development** to non-cocaine-exposed children by their eighth to tenth birthdays.

Tolerance

Tolerance to the euphoric effects can develop after the first injection or smoking session. Binge or chronic users have escalated their doses from one-eighth of a gram to 3 gm per day within only a few days or weeks while chasing the rush of the initial high.

Tolerance is related to the adaptation of the brain to a reduction in the amount of dopamine in the nucleus accumbens, which in turn **diminishes the rewarding effects of the drug** (Ahmed & Koob, 1998; Ahmed, Lin, Koob, et al., 2003). Tolerance does not occur with all effects of the drug, however; paranoia continues to increase, and cardiovascular tolerance develops more slowly (Repetto & Gold, 2005).

Withdrawal, Craving & Relapse

Contrary to notions held by many researchers until the 1980s, **there are true withdrawal symptoms** when cocaine use ceases. Although similar to the crash, withdrawal effects can last months, even years, depending on dosage, frequency, length of use, and any pre-existing mental problems. The major symptoms are:

◊ **anhedonia** (the lack of ability to feel pleasure),

◊ **anergia** (a total lack of energy),

◊ **emotional depression,**

◊ **loss of motivation** or initiative,

◊ **anxiety,**

◊ vivid and unpleasant dreams,

◊ insomnia,

◊ increased appetite,

◊ psychomotor agitation,

◊ and an **intense craving** for the drug.

(American Psychiatric Association [APA], 2000; Gorelick & Cornish, 2003)

"I got shot in the leg. I have a bullet in my leg now. I was bleeding to death, and the only thing I wanted to do was smoke [cocaine]. I told my buddy, 'Come on give me a hit, give me a hit.' I am smoking the pipe, the pipe is full of blood. I am smoking, trying to get high, and here I am about to bleed to death."
65-year-old recovering crack addict

These symptoms are also common in amphetamine withdrawal. It is these symptoms, particularly craving, that generally cause the recovering compulsive user to relapse again and again. The time frame for a **typical cycle of compulsive cocaine (or amphetamine) use is** as follows:

◊ Immediately after a binge, usually lasting several days, **the user crashes,** sleeps all day long trying to regain energy, and then swears off the drug forever.

◊ A few days later, **the user usually feels much better** and may leave or drop out of treatment at this time. This temporary return to normal feelings is called *euthymia.*

◊ About a week or 10 days after quitting, however, the **craving starts to build,** the energy level drops, and the user feels very little pleasure from any surroundings, activities, or friends. Emotional depression increases.

◊ So, two to four weeks after vowing to abstain, users feel the **craving and depression build to a fever pitch** and, unless they are in intensive treatment, they will often relapse.

Overdose

Cocaine was involved in 41% of the emergency department visits in major cities in 2004, with 25% of those attributable to crack (Drug Abuse Warning Network [DAWN], 2006). A cocaine overdose can be caused by as little as one-fiftieth of a gram or as much as 1.2 gm. The "caine reaction" is very intense and is generally short in duration. **Most often an overdose is not fatal.** It only feels like impending death.

"I almost did too much and I felt after I did it, I felt my knees buckle and I fell on the toilet stool, you know. And I was just shaking, like in a convulsion, you know. And if my buddy wasn't there to grab me and put me in the shower, I don't know what would've happened."
36-year-old cocaine addict

In 2,000 to 3,000 U.S. cases every year, however, death occurs within 40 minutes to five hours after exposure (occasionally the next morning). Death usually results from either the initial stimulatory phase of toxicity (seizures, hypertension, hyperthermia, stroke, and tachycardia) or the later depression phase terminating in extreme respiratory depression and coma (Karch,

2005). Heart seizures and death occasionally occur the morning after heavy use due to cocaethylene that lasts in the blood and the brain after the cocaine and the alcohol have been metabolized (Landry, 1992).

"I have seen a friend go through overdose. His skin was gray-green. His eyes rolled back, his heart stopped, and there was a gurgling sound that is right at death; and I had to bring him back and that's enough to put the fear of God in anybody."
Intravenous cocaine user

First-time users and even those who have used cocaine before can get an exaggerated reaction far beyond what might normally occur or beyond what they have experienced in the past. This is partially due to the phenomenon known as **inverse tolerance,** or "kindling." This means that as people use cocaine, they get more sensitive to its toxic effects rather than less sensitive as one would expect.

Miscellaneous Effects

Formication. A side effect of long-term or high-dose cocaine and amphetamine use is an imbalance in sensory neurons that causes **sensations in the skin that feel like hundreds of tiny bugs** ("coke bugs," "meth bugs," or "snow bugs") crawling under one's skin. Users on coke or "speed runs" have been known to scratch themselves bloody trying to get at the imaginary bugs.

Dental Erosions. These frequently occur as a result of **malnutrition, poor dental hygiene, the erosive effects of acidic cocaine** that has trickled down from the sinuses to the upper front teeth, repetitive and compulsive overbrushing of the teeth while intoxicated, or a combination of these effects. Recent research has shown that both cocaine and amphetamines **cause intense oral dehydration that also promotes dental erosion,** resulting in the condition being called "meth mouth" (Palmer, 2005).

Seizure. This effect is caused by overdose, stroke, or hemorrhage and occurs in 2% to 10% of regular co-caine users (Karch, 2001). Three times as many women as men have seizures from cocaine overdoses.

Gastrointestinal Complications. Though more unusual than cardiovascular effects, problems such as gastric ulcerations, retroperitoneal fibrosis, visceral infarction, intestinal ischemia, gastrointestinal tract perforation, and colonic ischemia have been observed in heavy cocaine users (Lindner, Monke-muller, Raijman, et al., 2000).

"Crack or Meth Dancing" (choreo-athetoid movements).   Another side effect of long-term or high-dose use is the occurrence of involuntary writhing, flailing, jerky, and sinuous movement mostly of the hands and arms but also of the legs. It is believed to be a result of dopamine changes in the cerebellum that result from cocaine or amphetamine toxicity (Darras, Koppel & Atas-Radzion, 1994).

Cocaine Psychosis & Other Mental Problems

Schizophrenia is usually caused by hereditary imbalances of brain dopamine in the mesolimbic dopamine pathway. It can also be caused by diseases or drugs that increase dopamine. **Because cocaine increases dopamine, repeated use can trigger stimulant-induced paranoid psychosis/schizophrenia** (Stahl, 2000). This cocaine psychosis was first documented in the late 1880s when intensive cocaine experimentation and abuse began. In the 1970s the progression from euphoria to dysphoria and ultimately to psychosis was observed to be mostly dose related, but the setting in which the drug is taken can also affect the quality of the symptoms (Post & Kopanda, 1976). Excessive methamphetamine use is more likely than cocaine to cause a stimulant psychosis because meth lasts much longer in the system than cocaine, which is rapidly metabolized and therefore becomes quite expensive to keep using.

Symptoms of cocaine psychosis include prominent auditory, visual, or tactile hallucinations and paranoid delusions (APA, 2000). **It is difficult for**

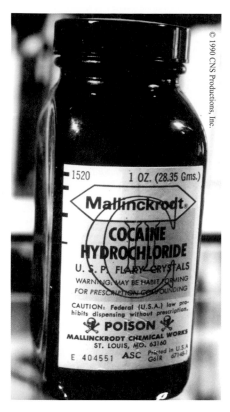

In 2006, 1 oz. of cocaine when sold legally in the United States for medicinal purposes cost about $150. When sold illegally, 1 oz. of cocaine costs up to $2,000.
© 1990 CNS Productions, Inc.

● ●

clinicians to tell the difference between a pre-existing psychosis and cocaine/methamphetamine-induced psychosis. A thorough psychological and drug history and a drug test are necessary to determine the cause. One of the sure signs is that the **symptoms disappear after a period of abstinence from the stimulant**, which may range from a few hours to a few days or occasionally even months (Ziedonis, Steinberg, Smelson, et al., 2003). Repeated use of cocaine can sensitize the user, so smaller and smaller doses will induce the psychotic symptoms. Milder symptoms of transient paranoia appear in 33% to 50% of chronic cocaine users (Satel & Lieberman, 1991).

OTHER PROBLEMS WITH COCAINE USE

Polydrug Use

Cocaine's stimulating effects can be so intense that the user needs a

downer to take the edge off or to get to sleep. The most common drugs used for this purpose are alcohol, heroin, and a sedative-hypnotic, although any downer will do in a pinch. The combination of cocaine or methamphetamine with heroin or another downer is known as a "speedball." Sometimes the second drug can be more of a problem than the cocaine itself. Nicotine is also frequently combined with cocaine. For reasons yet to be defined, a person who smokes cigarettes is 22 times more likely to use cocaine than a nonsmoker (Schmitz & DeLaune, 2005).

Adulteration & Contamination

Even with the increased supplies coming into the country, the increased purity, and the lower prices, **cocaine at the street level is almost always adulterated**. The street dealer will add an adulterant to lower the purity from 80% to 90% down to approximately 60%, often to pay for his or her own habit or just to make a few extra dollars. Adulteration of cocaine involves dilution with such diverse products as baby laxatives, lactose, vitamin B, aspirin, Mannitol,® sugar, Tetracaine® or Procaine® (topical anesthetics), and even talcum powder (Marnell, 2006).

"I have had lots of problems like veins I've missed and gotten it underneath the skin, causing abscesses, hematoma. My veins in certain spots have turned rock hard... my arm apparently has some level of vein infection, which I am now on antibiotics for."
27-year-old recovering cocaine abuser

When the drug is used intravenously, not only are **diluents put into the bloodstream but so are bacteria and viruses** from contaminated drugs or needles that can transmit diseases, including blood and heart infections, AIDS, hepatitis B, and especially hepatitis C. The use of other contaminated paraphernalia, such as snorting straws, can also transmit infection. **The hepatitis C infection rate for IV drug users is 50% to 90%** in most studies. The use of cocaine seems to aggravate various

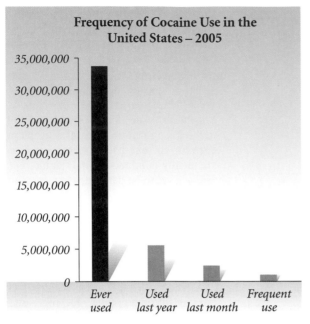

Frequency of Cocaine Use in the United States – 2005

Figure 3-1 •
Of the estimated 34 million Americans who have experimented with cocaine, 5.5 million used it in the past year, 2.4 million used it in the past month, and about 1.5 million reported cocaine dependence or abuse over the past year. Of these figures about one-fourth smoked the drug (crack).
(SAMHSA, 2006)

that it is not so much a want of sleep or the absence of food, as the want of coca that puts an end to the lengthened debauch."
Von Tschudi, 1854 (Karch, 2001)

SMOKABLE COCAINE (CRACK, FREEBASE)

"I couldn't bear to be sober. I needed to smoke crack cocaine because smoking crack cocaine takes away all your thoughts. You don't think about reality. You don't think about your bills, 'Oh, I have to pay this tomorrow.' You don't think about yourself. You don't think about nobody around you but crack cocaine."
43-year-old female recovering crack, heroin, and meth addict

conditions, especially AIDS, increasing viral loads and lowering CD$_4$ counts (Roth, Tashkin, Choi, et al., 2002).

COMPULSION

Considering all the problems with cocaine—the expense, the adulteration, the illegality, the possibility of overdose, and the physical and psychological dangers—two questions come to mind: *Why do people use cocaine?* and *Why do they use it so compulsively?*

"At first it was maybe every hour because the feeling would only last that long, and the more I did it, the feeling didn't even last that long, and I would eventually get up to about maybe 10 minutes, and maybe every five minutes. I would try to pace myself and make however much I had last as long as I could, but it was usually out of control, you know."
26-year-old recovering crack abuser

There are a number of reasons for the compulsive use of cocaine:

◇ Users want to **recapture the initial rush** (the energy surge and the stimulation of the reward/reinforcement pathway), which is extremely intense.

◇ They want to **avoid the crash** that is inevitable after the intense high. In many cases a user will shoot up or smoke every 20 minutes or even every 10 minutes in a binge episode. In fact, **all available cocaine is used in a binge pattern**.

◇ Users want to continuously **avoid life's problems**, such as loneliness, difficult relationships, traumatic events, a hated job, or a lack of confidence and self-esteem.

◇ They want to **control the symptoms of a mental illness**, especially depression.

◇ People use in response to their **hereditary predisposition to use**.

◇ Cocaine, in and of itself, **changes the brain's neurochemical balance and creates an intense craving** that will cause users to keep shooting, snorting, or smoking (bingeing) until every last microgram is gone, until they pass out, until an overdose occurs, or until they land in jail. Even coca leaf chewing is often done in a binge pattern as noted by Johan von Tschudi, an early explorer of the Amazon Basin, in his book *Travels in Peru.*

"They give themselves up for days together to the passionate enjoyment of the leaves . . . it, however, appears

Even though smokable cocaine had been around since the mid-1970s in the form of freebase cocaine, **the smokable-cocaine epidemic didn't start until around 1981**, when a glut of the powder from the Bahamas, the major transshipment point from Colombia, caused the price to drop by 80%. **Dealers made a shrewd marketing decision to convert the powder to crack.** This way they could sell small chunks, or "rocks," for prices as low as $2.50 a hit. Immigrants to Florida taught the process to young people in Miami, and southern Florida became the hub of conversion laboratories (DEA, 2006B).

The use of crack spread to the rest of the United States, supported at first by after-hours cocaine clubs, then by freebase parlors, then by crack houses (1984), and finally by curbside distribution and use (Hamid, 1992). Initially, in the New York City area three-fourths of the new users were young white professionals or middle-class youths from Long Island, New Jersey, or Westchester County (mostly freebase users). Because of the low per-unit price of crack, however, the use of this form of freebase soon spread to less affluent neighborhoods. It was estimated in the late 1980s that 10,000 gang members were dealing cocaine (and other drugs) in some 50 cities across the United States.

Some attributed the spread of crack to the office, factory, schoolyard, ghetto, and barrio to media attention. Others thought that the basic properties of smokable cocaine were the cause of the epidemic. The fact that the use of **crack remains a severe problem despite vastly curtailed media coverage speaks to the addictive nature of smokable cocaine** rather than to the influence of the media.

By 1986 the crack epidemic crossed all social and economic barriers. By the 1990s it had become ingrained in the American psyche as one of the main causes of society's ills: gang violence, AIDS, crime, and addiction. Then the epidemic began to wane. At the beginning of the twenty-first century, an older, smaller core of crack abusers had become entrenched in society, many in lower-income groups. In one study about half of the women seeking treatment in 2004 were 35 or older, and 42% had been using for 11

The crack cocaine in these close-ups is off-white, but the color can vary widely depending on diluents or the substance used to alter the cocaine hydrochloride to freebase cocaine.

Courtesy of the Drug Enforcement Administration

• •

years or more (Treatment Episode Data Sets, 2005). Although three or four times as many cocaine abusers snort or shoot the drug rather than smoke it, **72% of all those admitted for cocaine treatment were crack smokers** due to the intense compulsive nature of the drug.

PHARMACOLOGY OF SMOKABLE COCAINE

In the early 1970s, South American **cocaine refinery workers realized that cocaine paste**, an intermediate step in cocaine refinement, **could be smoked without destroying its euphoric and stimulating effects**. Chemically, cocaine paste is cocaine freebase. The doughy off-white substance also contains such chemicals as kerosene, sulfuric acid, and sodium carbonate. It is usually smoked with tobacco or marijuana by the middle- and lower-income classes. When smoked in a marijuana joint, it is called "bazooka," "basuco," or "pasta." In a study of 158 "pasta" smokers in Lima, Peru, the effects were reported to be similar to snorted cocaine but more intense and immediate (Jeri, Sanchez, Del Pozo, et al., 1992).

"After a few minutes of intense enjoyment, they developed anxiety and vehement wishes to continue smoking, leading to repeated or chain smoking. When they run out of 'paste,' they try to obtain or buy more in a state of compulsive anxiety. The user does not sleep, has no appetite, and his/her only wish is to continue smoking. Some patients from the very first puffs experience perceptual disturbances (visual hallucinations)."

(Jeri, Sanchez, Del Pozo, et al., 1992)

Making cocaine suitable for smoking (freebasing, "basing," or "baseballing") involves dissolving cocaine hydrochloride in an alkali solution and heating it to create crystals of freebase cocaine. This **leaves behind pure cocaine freebase crystals**.

"Cheap basing" or **"dirty basing"** involves dissolving the cocaine in a solution of baking soda and water and

heating it until crystals precipitate out. **This method does not remove as many impurities** or residues as freebasing, so contaminants like baking soda remain. The chunks of smokable cocaine made by this method are called "crack" because of the crackling sound that occurs when it is smoked or "rock" because the product looks like little rocks.

The converted freebase cocaine, made by either the "basing" method or the crack method, has four chemical properties sought by users:

◇ **It has a lower melting point than the powdered form** (98°C vs. 195°C), so it can be heated easily in a glass pipe and vaporized to form smoke at a lower temperature. Too high a temperature destroys most of the psychoactive properties of the drug.

◇ Smokable cocaine **reaches the brain faster** because it enters the system directly through the lungs.

◇ Freebase cocaine is **more readily absorbed by fat cells of the brain**, causing a more intense reaction.

◇ Users are also able to **get a much higher dose of cocaine in their systems over a short period of time** because of the very large surface area in the lungs (about the size of a football field).

Besides the names "crack," "rock," and "freebase," smokable cocaine has also been called "paste," "base," "basay," "hubba," "gravel," "Roxanne," "girl," "fry," and "boulya." There is a frequent misperception that crack and freebase are different drugs than cocaine. They aren't. **Crack and freebase are just a different chemical form of cocaine that makes them smokable. Crack seems to be more addicting**, according to users, because the overwhelming craving it produces is much more powerful, blocks the ability to function normally, and causes a much more rapid downslide.

"It tastes like more because that is all you want . . . more. Not like if you smoke a joint, you high. You ain't looking for no more, but this, this is a trip because this little bitty thing that

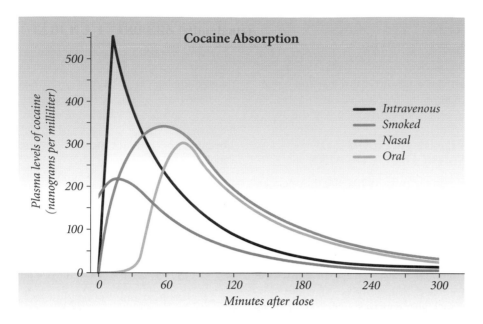

Figure 3-2 •

This graph shows the plasma levels of cocaine after equivalent doses were taken through different methods. Whereas smoking gets cocaine to the brain slightly more rapidly than IV use, injection puts a larger amount into the system at one time. When coca leaves are chewed, peak blood plasma levels are about one-fourth to one-eighth the levels obtained by smoking.

NIDA Research Monograph 99, Research Findings on Smoking of Abused Substances

costs $20 is gone in three minutes, maybe five."

36-year-old female recovering crack user

EFFECTS & SIDE EFFECTS

The effects of smoking crack are almost the same as snorting or injecting cocaine; but because cocaine that is smoked reaches the brain more quickly, the **effects and the side effects seem more intense.** Unfortunately for the crack smoker, much of the cocaine is lost to the air—about 50% when smoked in a cigarette and about 75% when smoked in a glass pipe (Siegel, 1992). For this reason much **more cocaine has to be smoked than injected to achieve the same effects.** Smoking and IV use can produce similar blood levels of cocaine; but because cocaine is so short acting (15 to 20 minutes), one has to keep using to keep the brain reacting. It is much easier and less painful to do this by smoking than by injecting.

Smoking crack gives a rush that lasts as little as five to 10 seconds and a subsequent euphoria, excitation, and arousal that lasts for several minutes more. After five to 20 min-

utes, these feelings are replaced by irritability, dysphoria (a general feeling of unease), and anxiety. These feelings lead the user to smoke again to try to recapture the high. Thus **crack is almost always used in a binge pattern** particularly when smoked.

The **physical side effects of smokable cocaine include thirst, coughing, tremors, dry skin, slurred speech, and blurred vision.** As use becomes chronic, chest pains, sore throat, black or bloody sputum, hypertension, weight loss, insomnia, tremors, and heart damage can occur.

Some of the other, more unusual physical side effects include:

◇ **crack keratitis,** or abrasions of the eye due to the anesthetic effects of cocaine that make the user unaware of damage caused by rubbing the eye too much;

◇ **crack thumb** and **crack hands,** caused by repetitive use of butane lighters to heat up crack pipes; a callus builds up on the thumb, and the hand has multiple burns;

◇ superficial **crack burns** to the face and hands due to the use of small

torches to melt freebase in a short glass pipe; more-severe body burns result when the ether explodes during the freebase process.

Unwanted psychological effects of chronic use include paranoia, intense craving, asocial behavior, attention problems, irritability, drug dreams, hyperexcitability, visual and auditory hallucinations, depression, cocaine psychosis, and certain social problems such as high-risk sexual activity (Castilla, Barrio, Belza, et al., 1999; Siegel, 1992).

Respiratory Effects

Because a user inhales an extremely harsh substance, smoking cocaine can also cause **chest pains, pneumonia, coughs, crack lung, and other respiratory complications,** including hemorrhage, respiratory failure, and death due to the drug's effect on the medullary centers (respiratory control) of the brain. Crack lung, a relatively new syndrome, is defined by the pain, breathing problems, and fever that resemble pneumonia (Repetto & Gold, 2005). Crack reduces the ability of the lungs to diffuse carbon dioxide. Many crack users smoke the tarlike black residue in crack pipes and overload their lungs with this sticky substance, making it difficult for the normal clearance mechanisms of the lungs to function, resulting in black or dark brown sputum (Greenbaum, 1993). **All of the respiratory problems are further aggravated because the majority of users also smoke cigarettes.** Irritation, destruction of mucous membranes, and lung cancer are often consequences of this combination.

Polydrug Abuse

As with snorted and injected cocaine, the intensive stimulation caused by smokable cocaine increases the potential for the abuse of depressants, especially alcohol.

"Crack was my drug of choice. I would have a drink to mellow myself out. If the drink wouldn't do it, I would go get me some heroin and snort it. It would make me come down, but it would be a whole different high and it would

make me sick because I don't do heroin!"

36-year-old female recovering crack user

Some smokers combine **freebase and marijuana in a combination called "champagne," "caviar,"** "gremmies," "fry daddies," "cocoa puff," "hubba," or "woolies." Users are even mixing crack with PCP (phencyclidine) or ketamine in a nasty mixture called "space basing," "whack," or "tragic magic." Further, there is the addition of freebase cocaine to smokable tar heroin to make a **smokable speedball called "hot rocks"** or "Belushi rocks." Finally, crack or cocaine hydrochloride is being used with wine coolers for an oral speedball known as "crack coolers."

Overdose

The most frequent symptoms of overdose that people experience when smoking cocaine are on the mild side— **very rapid heartbeat and hyperventilation**—but these reactions are often accompanied by a feeling of impending death. Although most people survive and only get very sweaty and clammy and feel that they are going to die, several thousand are in fact killed by cocaine overdose every year. There were more than 4,500 deaths in 2004 due to the direct and indirect effects of cocaine use (DAWN, 2006). The **deaths resulted from cardiac arrest, seizure, stroke, respiratory failure, and even severe hyperthermia** (extra high body temperature).

"A friend was freebasing heavily, and he started going into convulsions and throwing up blood. It was real awful. I was really scared and I thought he was going to die. Me and my other friend, we just kept freebasing . . . and then when he came out of it, he started freebasing again."

16-year-old female recovering crack user

OTHER CONSEQUENCES OF CRACK USE

Economic Consequences

The crack trade expanded rapidly in the late 1980s because the dealers used the best sales strategies of a free-enterprise system: reduce the price to increase sales; increase the size of the sales force to cover the territory more efficiently; encourage free trade to avoid tariffs and impounding; and **create appealing packaging to make the product attractive to a wider segment of the population** (Wesson, Smith & Steffens, 1992).

Crack is not cheaper than cocaine hydrochloride; it is just sold in smaller units. One gram of cocaine hydrochloride is the standard street sale amount, going for $50 to $100. Now one-tenth of a gram that has been converted to crack or "rock" can be bought for $10 to $20, a manageable sum for teenagers and incidentally about twice the price of cocaine hydrochloride when figured on a per-gram basis (ONDCP, 2003). The economics of crack cocaine created more dealers and increased the availability of the drug. **There is also an addiction to the money and the lifestyle that comes with dealing** (Cross, Johnson, Rees Davis, et al., 2001).

"I know it's jive. I know it's negative. I'm trapped in something here. But I'm used to the money. What else can I do? You gonna send me to McDonald's? After I'm generating this kind of money every day, I can't go back to McDonald's for $6.50—what is it?—$6.75 an hour today, which is still insulting."

16-year-old crack dealer/user

Though a few young dealers buy new cars and show off their wealth, **the majority of small-time dealers make just enough to support their own habit** or get by. Drug gang homicides are common as local gangs, along with gangs from other countries, vie to control the crack trade. The gangs include the Bloods and the Crips, along with Dominicans, Puerto Ricans, Mexicans, Jamaicans, and especially Colombians. A number of these gangs have also expanded the trade to smaller cities.

Social Consequences

"It seems like every time I would hit the pipe, my daughter would say,

'Mommy.' And so I would say, 'Why are you bothering me?' It really made me crazy. I mean, my son, he would just pick on things and make noise or something just to bother me because he knew that I was doing this."

Recovering crack user

Because of the compulsive nature of crack, **addictive use of the drug is having devastating social ramifications** in the United States that include **high rates of neglect, abandonment, and abuse of children** by single- and even no-parent families and the increasing number of burned-out grandmothers who are caring for their crack-addicted daughters' children. It has also brought about the **formation of an underclass of women who trade sex for crack** at whatever price they can get.

"It's two types of women using cocaine. One's a 'tossup' [a woman who trades sex for crack]. They're the ones who are down there. They done lost everything they have. They have no self-respect. Me and my sister, we'd work a brother in a minute to get his dope. Once we got his dope—'Go on, get outta' my house.' Me and my sister, we paid our rent, we paid our utilities, we fed our children, we kept clothes on their backs, we kept the house clean. We had not lost our self-esteem. We had not hit rock bottom yet."

24-year-old female recovering crack user

In an earlier study of 283 women who exchanged sex for money or crack, 30% were infected with HIV (Edlin, Irwin & Faruque, 1994). For many men (particularly in some inner-city communities), a major impact on their families and on society has occurred because of the **high rate of crime associated with crack use**. There have been high rates of imprisonment, violent deaths, and child abandonment by addicts. In fact, about **53% of all inmates in prisons come from a home without a father whereas 70% of incarcerated juveniles come from single-parent homes** (U.S. Department of Justice, 2002). The disruptive family environment coupled with cocaine use leads to economic and social chaos.

COCAINE VS. AMPHETAMINES

Although all of the **physical and mental effects of cocaine and amphetamines are very similar**, there are differences.

Price. A heavy user of cocaine spends $100 to $300 per day, whereas a heavy user of amphetamine spends about $50 to $100 a day. If the amphetamine user has developed a very high tolerance, however, the costs are comparable.

Quality of the Rush or the High. When either cocaine or an amphetamine is smoked or injected intravenously, it produces an intense rush followed by a high or euphoria. When either drug is snorted, the intense rush usually doesn't occur, only the euphoria. When cocaine or an amphetamine is drunk, again, there is usually no rush, only the euphoria. Although it is hard to demonstrate experimentally, the majority of users claim that **the rush and the high from cocaine is greater than that from amphetamines but amphetamines release greater amounts of prolonged energy**.

"Cocaine is more euphoric and not as intense as speed. Speed is very intense, and you're going, going, going. The coke is shorter lasting, but the cravings are much worse. When I wanted to do speed, it was mainly because I wanted to get things done. I felt speed helped me perform. And the cocaine, I felt like I had absolutely no choice. Cocaine took me down real fast and real hard."
Crack cocaine smoker

Duration of Action. Cocaine's major effects last about 40 minutes; amphetamine's last four to six hours.

Manufacture. Cocaine is plant derived; amphetamines are synthetic.

Methods of Use. The most popular ways of using cocaine are snorting, smoking, and shooting. Methamphetamines are also smoked, snorted, and injected, but they are also ingested orally.

Addiction Rate. A survey of clients at one treatment center showed that methamphetamine users fell into addiction more quickly than cocaine users and came into treatment sooner (Gonzalez Castro, Barrington, Walton, et al., 2000). When smoking crack is involved, the slide to compulsive use is much quicker than from snorting cocaine hydrochloride.

AMPHETAMINES

CLASSIFICATION

Amphetamines are known as *sympathomimetic agents* because they stimulate the release of neurotransmitters in the brain that activate our sympathetic nervous system, which in turn controls our fight-or-flight response. They also stimulate the reward/reinforcement pathway. These amphetamines are known on the street as meth, "uppers," "speed," "crank," "crystal," "ice," "shabu," and "glass." They are a class of **powerful synthetic stimulants with effects that are similar to cocaine but that last much longer and are somewhat cheaper to use**. Amphetamines are most often snorted, injected, or taken orally. Recently, smoking methamphetamine has increased in popularity, especially with the more readily available methamphetamine called "ice," "crystal," or "glass."

There are several different types of amphetamines: amphetamine, methamphetamine, dextroamphetamine, and dextro isomer methamphetamine (the most common). The effects of each type are similar, the major differences being strength and method of manufacture. There is also a difference in the dominance of psychological effects versus physical effects.

HISTORY OF USE

The growth of amphetamine abuse rose to so-called epidemic proportions during the early 2000s. It was reported that **worldwide more than 33 million people used amphetamines and methamphetamines** in 2003, con-

In the past, traditional types of amphetamines were small tablets of amphetamine ("crosstops"), Biphetamine® ("black beauties"), Dexedrine® ("dexys" or "beans"), Benzedrine® ("bennies"), and Methedrine.® In the past 10 years, the most common methamphetamine has been crystal meth, which is stronger than the traditional methamphetamine. It is quite pure, with just a trace of residual chemicals as seen in these DEA macrophotographs of the crystallized dextro isomer methamphetamine (crystal meth). Recently, the amphetamine Adderal® has been widely used to treat attention-deficit/ hyperactivity disorder.
Courtesy of the Drug Enforcement Administration

trasted with 15 million cocaine, 10 million heroin, and 160 million marijuana users (UNODC, 2006). In the United States, however, cocaine is more popular, but methamphetamine is catching up (2.4 million vs. 1 million). As with cocaine, methamphetamine has gone through several popularity cycles. The first wave began in the 1930s, the second in the 1960s, and the third in the 1990s.

Discovery

German chemist L. Edeleano **first synthesized amphetamine in 1887** in a systematic effort to find a substitute for ephedrine, a natural extract of the ephedra bush, that had been used for centuries to treat asthma. **Methamphetamine, a variation of the amphetamine molecule, was synthesized in Japan in 1919.** The drugs' stimulant qualities and medical applications weren't utilized until the 1930s, however, when Methedrine® (methamphetamine) and Benzedrine® (dextroamphetamine) inhalers were marketed as bronchodilators to help asthmatics breathe. These drugs were also recognized as stimulants that could **energize the user, counter low blood pressure, reduce the need for sleep, and suppress appetite.** The drugs were also used to treat minimal brain dysfunction (MBD), a condition known today as attention-deficit/hyperactivity disorder. As word of the nonrecommended use of the drugs spread (they could be bought without a prescription), different methods of use arose: pulling the drug-soaked cottons from the inhalers and soaking them in a drinkable liquid or chewing the cotton wicks and absorbing the solution on the gums or swallowing it. (The inhalers were sold over-the-counter until 1959; prescription Methedrine® wasn't taken off the market until 1968.)

Amphetamines were widely used in pill form during World War II by Allied, German, and Japanese forces to keep pilots alert for extended missions and to keep ground troops awake and more aggressive in battle. The Germans dispensed 35 million doses of Pervitin,® a methamphetamine, to energize their troops. Toward the end of the war, they experimented with a pill that contained a combination of cocaine and an opiate painkiller in addition to Pervitin® to try to create a supersoldier. On the U.S. side, an estimated 200 million Benzedrine® tablets were legally dispensed to American GIs during World War II and another 225 million during the Vietnam conflict between 1966 and 1969 (Grinspoon & Hedblom, 1975; Miller & Kozel, 1995).

Amphetamines were also used to **treat narcolepsy (falling-asleep sickness), epilepsy (a subtype), and depression.** At the same time, amphetamines came to be abused by students cramming for exams, truckers on long hauls, and workers laboring long hours.

Japanese Epidemic

Abuse of amphetamines in Japan continued after World War II, when large stocks of the drug were looted from military supplies and sold on the black market. Although the enactment of Japan's Stimulant Drug Program in 1951 brought the problem under some control (Fukui, Wada & Iyo, 1991), amphetamine abuse continues. There are still 1 million to 2 million amphetamine users in Japan and 15,000 to 25,000 arrests for dealing and using each year. The Japanese crime syndicates (Yakuza) smuggle the drugs from China (e.g., the Fujian Province), Thailand, Myanmar, or the Philippines and control the sales. One bust alone seized 500 kg of the substance worth more than $200 million in retail sales.

Diet Pills

Recognizing the appetite-suppressing properties of amphetamines, U.S. pharmaceutical companies in the 1950s and 1960s promoted the use of diet pills to a growing segment of society that wanted to lose weight. Their advertising led to huge quantities of amphetamines and methamphetamines, including Dietamine,® Nobese,® Obetrol,® Bar-Dex,® Dexedrine,® and Dexamyl,® flooding the prescription drug market. Worldwide legal production in 1970 was estimated to be 10 billion tablets (Karch, 2001). **In 1970 an estimated 6% to 8% of the American population was using prescription amphetamines, mostly for weight loss** (Ellinwood, 1973). The fact that amphetamines also induced euphoria and elation did not hurt the appeal of the drugs. As early as 1943, more than half of Smith, Kline & French Pharmaceuticals' Benzedrine® sales were prescribed for people who wanted to lose weight or counteract depression. It was in fact one of the first antidepressants available to physicians (Grinspoon & Hedblom, 1975).

Street Speed

The 1960s were the peak of the speed craze that was supplied by both diverted and illegally manufactured amphetamines. The power for the "Summer of Love," one of the turning points of the hippie movement, was fueled by the energy chemicals released by amphetamines.

"If you're going to San Francisco, be sure to wear some flowers in your hair.
If you come to San Francisco, Summertime will be a love-in there."
John Phillips, "San Francisco," 1967

Thousands of young people flocked to the Haight Ashbury neighborhood in San Francisco to be a part of the "hippie experience," which included LSD, marijuana, STP, MDA, and particularly amphetamines. In fact, the Haight Ashbury Free Clinics came into existence in 1967 to treat an influx of users who had severe physical and mental reactions to the unfamiliar drugs.

In response to the speed (amphetamine) epidemic, the **Comprehensive Drug Abuse Prevention and Control Act of 1970 classified amphetamines as Schedule II drugs** and made it hard to buy them legally in the United States. In addition, prescription use of the drugs was more tightly regulated. The street market expanded to fill the need, so instead of buying legally manufactured amphetamines that had been diverted, people bought speed and "crank" that had been manufactured illegally. The purity rose from an average of 30% in the early 1970s to 60% by 1983 despite the fact that the act also controlled most of the then known immediate precursors to make methamphetamine (King & Ellinwood, 2005).

The most popular form of street speed was the "crosstop." Also called "cartwheels" and "white crosses," these were diverted or smuggled into the United States from Mexico. In the early 1970s, they cost $5 to $10 per 100 tablets. In the 1990s the price was $1 to $5 per tablet if they could be found. As of the 2000s, what are most often available are bogus (look-alike) "crosstops" that contain either caffeine or ephedrine instead of amphetamine.

The late 1980s and 1990s saw a resurgence in the availability and the abuse of illicit methamphetamines, particularly **"crank" (methamphetamine sulfate)** and **"crystal" (methamphetamine hydrochloride)**. Once stymied by the tight control of chemicals needed to produce illegal amphetamines, clever street chemists of this era learned to produce speed by altering commonly available chemicals meant to treat colds and asthma. Some of the street methamphetamines, even in the 1980s, however, were actually look-alike drugs that combined phenylpropanolamine (a decongestant), ephedrine, pseudoephedrine, or simply caffeine tablets disguised to look like amphetamine products.

"Ice"

As the 1990s began, a highly potent and **smokable form of methamphetamine**, dextro isomer methamphetamine ("ice," "glass," "batu," or "shabu"), had emerged as a major new drug abuse trend. By the mid-2000s, this type of methamphetamine in its hydrochloride salt form had become the predominant street speed, widely abused across the United States. Besides its smokability, greater strength, and longer duration of effects, "ice" had the appeal of a new fad. As with the spread of smokable crack cocaine, "ice" was initially being marketed as a "newer, better amphetamine." It cost two to three times as much as other street methamphetamines, which is surprising because it can be made from methamphetamine hydrochloride with a very simple and safe crystallization process.

The nickname "ice" was common only to some Asian nations, Hawaii, and a few places on the West Coast. By the mid-1990s, virtually all U.S. street samples of methamphetamine seized by the federal Drug Enforcement Administration consisted of this new form of the drug (DEA, 2006A), but it was called a wide variety of other street names, including "crystal," "crystal meth," "tina," "peanut butter," "dead head," "chalk," "tweak," "yellow rock," "glass," and "rose quartz speed."

Many Asian countries also developed severe abuse problems with this drug by the mid-2000s. It is known as "shabu" or "kakuseizai" in Japan, "bato" in the Philippines, "batu" in Malaysia, "philopon" in South Korea, "yaotouwan" (head-shaking pill) in China, and "yaa baa" or "yaa maa" in Thailand, Myanmar, Laos, and Cambodia. By the mid-2000s, explosive growth in the abuse of dextro isomer methamphetamine had also been seen in Vietnam and South Korea. Of the 10,304 drug offenders arrested in South Korea in 2000, 69% were methamphetamine abusers (Burnet Institute, 2002).

Current Use

Licit Use. Currently, amphetamines and methamphetamines are used to **treat attention-deficit/hyperactivity disorder, narcolepsy**, and occasionally **weight control**.

Illicit Use. Historically, **stimulant epidemics last 10 to 15 years** and go in waves from one coast of the United States to the other. **Due to the intensity of the high and the severity of the side effects, amphetamine abuse eventually becomes self-limiting** and the rapid growth of use levels out. The current epidemic hasn't yet run its course. **From 1993 to 2003, the number of people admitted for amphetamine addiction more than quadrupled**, due in part to:

◇ the aging of that population,
◇ the extended periods of chronic use, and
◇ the spread of use to other states (DASIS Report, 2006).

The resurgence, particularly in the use of illicit methamphetamines (predominantly "crank" and "crystal meth"), was evident by the dramatic increase in the number of methamphetamine labs raided by the authorities, particularly in California, Oregon, Washington, Texas, and, more recently, the Midwest. Recently, the number of raided labs has decreased slightly. Although methamphetamine use in 2005 was less than half the high level of the early 1980s, the current growth is troublesome (SAMHSA, 2006). An additional worry is that the age of first use has dropped: some 10- to 13-year-olds are smoking, eating, and snorting "crystal." **Some of the reasons for this upsurge are lower prices and increased availability.**

While the use of methamphetamine had dropped a bit in the West by 2005, it has increased in the northeast region of the country. Hawaii also continues to have a severe problem; about 60% of those admitted for drug treatment listed methamphetamine as their primary drug (National Drug Intelligence Center [NDIC], 2005; National Institute on Drug Abuse [NIDA], 2005). By the same token, however, Lt. Governor James "Duke" Aiona of Hawaii warned that anti-drug forces are too focused on "ice" and not enough on the gateway drugs: alcohol and marijuana. This doesn't minimize the severity of compulsive meth use or the secondary repercussions, particularly crime.

"I started shooting speed and I couldn't keep getting $20 bucks from my mom, you know. I had to either start selling it or start stealing stuff 'cause I had a big habit. So I was stealing cars and I was jacking stereos and I would rip anybody off who gave me money just to get myself high. Incidentally, stealing the car was also a high."

17-year-old recovering IV meth user

The profile of the typical user is a white male between the ages of 19 and 40. In younger users (eighth- and tenth-graders), however, and in some parts of the West, especially in Hawaii, an almost equal number of methamphetamine abusers are women. Further, the great majority of the known users in Hawaii are of Asian and Pacific Islander decent. Recently, meth abuse in the Black and Latino communities has increased.

Meth use has been particularly rampant in the gay community. A study of 2,335 gay and bisexual men in the New York area found that 10.4% had used meth in the past three months, a rate 10 to 15 times that of the overall population. After alcohol and marijuana, "crystal meth" is the drug of choice in the gay community. Meth is used more often in the younger gay community, often in gay bars, bathhouses, and sex clubs or at "circuit par-

This typical makeshift methamphetamine laboratory is just one of 12,484 labs busted in the United States in 2005. Chemicals such as benzene, sulfuric acid, red phosphorous, anhydrous ammonia, and battery acid are often dumped at the scene or just left to pollute the environment, with cleanup costs running into thousands of dollars per site.
Courtesy of the Drug Enforcement Administration

ties," which are highly organized events that emphasize sex and drugs (Cabaj, 2005; SAMHSA, 2005; Sanello, 2005). Unfortunately, the **incidence of HIV/ AIDS in the gay community is also extremely high and due mostly to the disinhibiting effects of meth and to IV use.** Because of homophobia, fear of coming out, and fear of being oneself, emotional problems are generally more prevalent in the gay community, increasing the tendency to use drugs to self-medicate.

"As long as I was high, and dancing, or having sex, whatever, I didn't have to think. I didn't have to deal with my depression. I didn't have to cringe whenever my mom or dad called and asked how I was doing."
25-year-old gay male recovering meth abuser

Methamphetamine Manufacturing

In the past **much of the street manufacturing and dealing of methamphetamines was by biker gangs** (Hell's Angels and Gypsy Jokers) because of the money involved and the partiality of bikers to the drug. But there has been an **ever-increasing involvement of Mexican gangs and drug cartels** in its manufacture and distribution.

Some of the reasons for the increase in the supply of methamphetamine has been **new, somewhat safer, cheaper, and almost odor-free manufacturing techniques. Illicit methamphetamine manufacturing used to be an extremely risky business.** The fumes were toxic, and explosions could and did occur if the chemicals were handled improperly. The foul odors that

emanated from the "cookers" were of great help to law enforcement agencies in locating meth labs. Now meth can even be made on a stovetop using pseudoephedrine, a semi-synthetic version of ephedrine, a stimulant that is extracted and refined from the ephedra bush or synthesized. The DEA estimates that **there are now more than 300 ways to manufacture methamphetamine using pseudoephedrine** (Uncle Fester, 1998). At a local hardware store, a street chemist can get rock salt, battery acid, red phosphorus road flares, iodine, anhydrous ammonia, pool acid, mason jars, coffee filters, and plastic tubing to help in the manufacturing (Keefe, 2001). This coupled with wide-open spaces to dissipate the smell led to a proliferation of labs in rural areas (Lee, 2006).

The pseudoephedrine was being purchased in large quantities and diverted to illegal channels or being bought in small quantities in any store that sold certain cold medications. **Ephedrine and pseudoephedrine are manufactured in 8 plants throughout the world (5 in India, 2 in China, and 1 in Germany). Much of the precursor destined for U.S. markets has been diverted to illicit channels in Mexico.** In the past most of the laboratories were small enterprises capable of producing only a pound or so of methamphetamine a day, but those run by Mexican gangs (26% of the total number of labs and mostly in the West) can cook 10 to 150 lbs. in just two days. The DEA estimates that the Mexican-run labs manufacture three-fourths of the methamphetamine consumed in the United States (DEA, 2006A).

In response to the proliferation of mom and pop labs, first Oklahoma in April 2004 and then many other states enacted laws requiring pharmacies to limit the amount of pseudoephedrine-containing cold tablets that could be purchased at any single time and to keep such products behind the counter to prevent easy access and shoplifting. By mid-August 2005, Oregon became the first state to classify as Schedule III controlled substances all cold, allergy, and asthma products containing ephedrine, pseudoephedrine, and phenylpropanolamine, requiring prescriptions for purchase.

To control the larger labs, a federal

bill attached to the USA Patriot Act was signed on March 9, 2006, by President George W. Bush. The Combat Meth Act of 2005 (H.R.314 and S.103) federally restricted access to pseudoephedrine and allowed the federal government to track sales of the methamphetamine precursor (Barnett, 2006).

New efforts to limit the importation of precursor chemicals, especially pseudoephedrine, have caused a decrease in purity from 72% in 1994 to 35% today. Special efforts of the Mexican government along with the international controls on precursors have also decreased the importation of pseudoephedrine into Mexico from 224 tons in 2004 to just 76 tons in 2006. Agencies have estimated that 70 tons would fulfill Mexico's need for cold medicine. The other 150 tons were being diverted to illegal manufacturers.

The price of meth varies radically from location to location. The DEA reported that the price for 1 lb. of dextro isomer methamphetamine on the street in 2003 ranged all the way from $1,600 to $45,000, 1 oz. from $270 to $5,000, and 1 gm from $20 to $300 (NDIC, 2005).

A recent development has been the expansion **of meth trafficking to Canada.** Asian gangs of Indian and Chinese descent have begun operating megalabs using bulk ephedrine from India and China. The threat is particularly serious to the U.S. Pacific Northwest. These same organizations have also displaced Europe as the main supplier to the United States of the club drug ecstasy. Much of the seized ecstasy contains some amount of crystal meth.

Another problem with the illegal synthesis of methamphetamine is the **environmental danger of the chemicals used in the manufacturing process** even with the newer manufacturing methods. Labs have been found in apartments, rented hotel rooms, trunks of cars—even tents on public land. When done making the meth, the "cooks" simply abandon the property. Toxins and cancer-causing agents such as acetone, red phosphorus, hydrochloric acid, benzene, and lead acetate are left behind or secretly dumped into streams and landfills. It costs thousands of dollars to clean up each raided laboratory; there are 5 to 7 pounds of toxic waste for each pound of methamphetamine.

In 2005 in the United States, **12,484 methamphetamine laboratories, dumpsites, and such were seized by the DEA and state law enforcement agencies.** This is down significantly from the previous year, but most of the busts have been the mom-and-pop labs and not the megalabs.

One of the more **recent developments internationally is the use of "ya ba,"** also called "yaa maa," "yaa baa," and "Nazi speed." Manufactured in Thailand, Laos, and particularly Myanmar, the little brightly colored pills are being smuggled into the United States in ever-increasing amounts. "Ya ba" is taken orally or crushed and smoked on a piece of foil. This methamphetamine is abused mainly in Thailand and other Asian countries, where it sells for $2 to $3 per pill (Chouvy & Meissonnier, 2004; Leinwand, 2002A). It is estimated that 1 billion pills were made last year in dozens of secret laboratories on the Myanmar border. It used to be the drug of poor men—taxi and long-distance drivers—to stay awake and keep working, but recently, as with other countries, use spread to discotheques and schools. About 700 patients are being treated at the main drug detoxification hospital in Bangkok.

EFFECTS

Routes of Administration

Snorting methamphetamine causes irritation and pain to the nasal mucosa especially when used to excess.

Intravenous use puts large quantities of the drug directly into the bloodstream and causes a more intense high than snorting or swallowing; however, it often causes pain in the blood vessels. Also, with IV use there is the attendant risk of contaminated needles. One study in Los Angeles found the rate of HIV infection among meth users to be three times higher than among nonusers (Jacobs, 2006).

Oral ingestion used to be more popular, but it takes longer to reach the brain. Because of the extremely bitter taste of methamphetamines, they are often put into a gelatin capsule or in a piece of paper when taken orally.

Smoking "crystal meth" or "ice" is similar to smoking freebase cocaine (in a pipe).

No matter how the drug is taken, **amphetamines last four to six hours compared with only 10 to 90 minutes for cocaine.** Some of the effects of "ice" are alleged to last at least eight hours, some say up to 24, after it is smoked.

Neurochemistry

The use of amphetamines increases the levels of catecholamine neurotransmitters (**norepinephrine, epinephrine,** and **dopamine**) in three ways:

◇ First, amphetamines **force the release of these neurotransmitters from the vesicles in the nerve terminals**.

◇ Then tiny pumps called **transporters that normally reabsorb neurotransmitters reverse their direction and expel neurotransmitters back into the synaptic gap**, creating an excess.

◇ Finally, **amphetamines block the enzymes that metabolize the excess neurotransmitters**, allowing the chemicals to accumulate and cause continued overstimulation.

This last effect means that when methamphetamine is used, the excess catecholamines stay in the synapse for a much longer time than with cocaine. This is the main reason why the amphetamine high lasts so much longer than the cocaine high.

Continued use of amphetamines causes long-term and even permanent alterations in the body's ability to produce these vital neurotransmitters. In animal studies norepinephrine levels were still depressed three to six months after cessation of heavy use (King & Ellinwood, 2005). Dopamine levels also remained depressed after cessation of use. Another study comparing former methamphetamine abusers with a nonusing control group showed a 24% decrease in dopamine transporters, thus causing a disruption in movement control and feelings of pleasure (Volkow, Chang, Wang, et al., 2001). This means that users come to rely on artificial stimulants to keep their dopamine and norepinephrine activities functioning so they can feel normal, but not high. In other words **prolonged amphetamine use,**

in and of itself, alters brain chemistry in a way that increases craving. This process also occurs with cocaine.

Research demonstrates that in addition to depleting neurotransmitters, high-dose methamphetamine use causes definitive degeneration of serotonin fibers in the brain within hours after use (Ernst, Chang, Leonido-Yee, et al., 2000; Zhou & Bledsoe, 1996).

More disturbing findings occurred in a study of 22 heavy users of methamphetamine which found that their **brains had an average loss of 11.3% of their limbic gray matter, particularly the hippocampus**, cingulate gyrus, and paralimbic cortices—areas associated with craving, emotions, mood, and memory.

"My memory, oh my God, I have none. I couldn't even tell you what I did five years ago, and that's sad. My youngest kid is going to be 15 this year, and I can't tell you anything about his life other than little glimpses of it, little pieces of it."

32-year-old female recovering meth abuser

Surprisingly, the study also found that, overall, the users' brains were on average about 10% larger than normal brains due to an increase in white matter, possibly due to methamphetamine-caused inflammation (Thompson, Hayashi, Simon, et al., 2004). Many of the methamphetamine-caused structural changes such as hippocampal shrinkage will disappear, but it can take months or even years in some cases (Wang, Volkow, Chang, et al., 2004). Because of these abnormalities, abstinence-induced depression and anxiety have to be dealt with in recovery (London, Simon, Berman, et al., 2004).

"A lot of times I have trouble with concentration. When I read a book, sometimes the words on the page look like they're dancing around, and I know that's a direct result of the meth use. I know there's damage there. It's something that I'm learning to live with."

43-year-old male recovering meth abuser

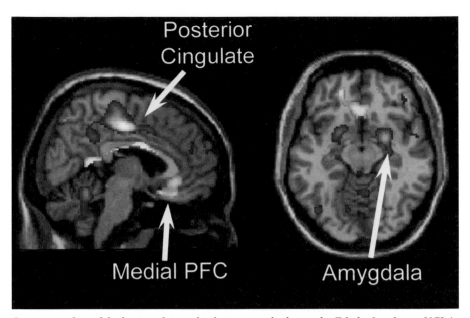

Imaging studies of the brains of recently abstinent meth abusers by Edythe London at UCLA have shown neurochemical changes that help explain the relapse potential of methamphetamine users. Specifically, the amygdala, the emotional center of the brain, is highly activated (red area) in recently abstinent meth abusers while the prefrontal cortex, the thinking area of the brain that helps control the amygdala, exhibits very low activity (blue area). This means that when craving is triggered in the amygdala, the newly abstinent meth abuser's ability to control that craving is impaired.

Recent MRI studies at the University of California at San Diego have dramatically expanded on the studies of Doctors Volkow, London, and others to recognize patterns in the brains of recovering methamphetamine users that signal a risk of relapse. They found that users with a strong tendency to relapse had subdued activity in five different regions of the brain when trying to solve two decision-making tasks (Paulus, Tapers & Schuckit, 2005). This implies that **those with a tendency to relapse have an impaired decision-making ability and find it hard to refuse a craving**. The five areas are the right insula, right inferior parietal lobule, right middle temporal gyrus, left caudate putamen, and left cingulate gyrus.

Physical Effects & Side Effects

As with cocaine, the initial physiological effects of small-to-moderate doses of amphetamines include **extra energy, increased heart rate, raised body temperature, rapid respiration, higher blood pressure, dilation of bronchial vessels, and appetite suppression.**

"I would inject some speed and, right after doing it, get an incredible rush, which some people compare with sexual feelings. And your heart pounds and I've seen people actually pass out from having too much speed. My heart would pound, and I would sweat, and the rush would pass, and then I would just be very high energy."

19-year-old recovering meth user

The high energy and the confidence are two of the reasons why amphetamines are used by athletes looking for an edge. In addition, the anorectic (weight-loss) effects are sought by wrestlers, gymnasts, and other athletes who need to meet certain weight requirements.

As with cocaine abusers, **methamphetamine abusers go on binges, or "runs," staying up for 3, 4, or even 10 days at a time,** putting a severe strain on their bodies, particularly the cardiovascular and nervous systems. During these runs people will try to use their excess energy in any way they can—

dancing, exercising, disassembling a car, or painting the house.

"I liked to do little intricate drawings. I would draw for hours, anything small with a lot of detail. I would clean my apartment from top to bottom, even doing my floor with Brillo® pads—my wooden floor—vacuuming my ceiling. If I ran out of stuff to do, I would dump out everything in the vacuum cleaner and vacuum it back up. I didn't like to be outside because I would get paranoid."
38-year-old recovering amphetamine user

Tolerance to amphetamines is pronounced. Whereas 15 to 30 mg per day is the usual prescribed dose, a long-term user might use 5,000 mg or 5 gm over a 24-hour period during a "speed run." This means that extended use (or the use of large quantities) will lead to extreme depression and lethargy because it depletes the energy neurotransmitters.

Long-term use can cause sleep deprivation, heart and blood vessel toxicity, and severe malnutrition. The blood vessel toxicity can cause extensive damage to cerebral vasculature, resulting in multiple aneurysms (the ballooning out of arterial and occasionally venous weak spots) and strokes. With long-term use and hypertensive episodes, the user can experience heart arrhythmias, possibly caused by heart muscle lesions (King & Ellinwood, 2005). Malnutrition, cravings for sweet foods, poor dental hygiene, severe oral dehydration, plus the calcium-leaching effects of **amphetamine overuse often result in bad gums and rotted teeth, known as "meth mouth."** In fact, one of the confirming signs of amphetamine abuse is a unique pattern of poor dental health (Palmer, 2005).

Finally, if the user has not built up a tolerance, is unusually sensitive, or takes a very large amount, an **overdose can occur**, resulting in convulsions, hyperthermia, stroke, cardiovascular overexcitation, and collapse.

"I shot some speed once and immediately had a seizure. Apparently, my heart stopped beating and the person I was with was pounding on my chest. I was real sore and black and blue the next day, but I didn't stop using."
38-year-old meth user

Neonatal Effects

Almost half of all methamphetamine abusers are women in the United States, more so in Hawaii, Oregon, and parts of California. Its ability to kill appetite along with its positive reward/reinforcement effects may help explain why **methamphetamine abuse is so prevalent in women than men, unlike the gender distribution seen with other drugs of abuse**. Most women who abuse methamphetamine are in their childbearing years. Methamphetamine use during pregnancy poses significant risks to both mother and fetus and considerable consequences to the baby's physical and mental development after birth. The damage can stem from the direct effects of the drug as well as from the lifestyle consequences of meth addiction, such as malnutrition and IV drug use with contaminated needles or drugs. Intrauterine and neonatal risks include:

◇ **irritable baby syndrome**, including neonatal intolerance to light and touch, tremors, muscle coordination problems, abnormal reflexes, sucking and swallowing problems, and disturbed sleep;
◇ **premature delivery** and congenital deformities (club foot and limb abnormalities);
◇ increased risk of gastroschises (an opening in the stomach with some of the small and large intestines poking through);
◇ **risk of placental separation** and hemorrhage in the mother, potentially lethal to both mother and fetus;
◇ intrauterine brain hemorrhage and stroke;
◇ **increased risk for HIV and hepatitis B and C infection**.

Developmental risks of methamphetamine-exposed infants include:

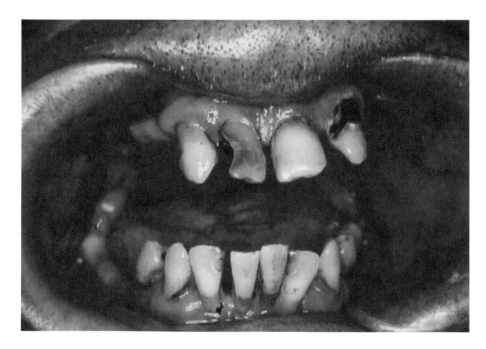

This is the mouth of a long-term methamphetamine abuser. Dentists who work in areas where meth use is rampant see dozens of cases of meth mouth and can recognize it easily. Symptoms include bad breath, tooth loss, malnutrition/bone loss, shrunken vessels that supply blood to oral tissues, receding gums, bleeding and infected gums, and heart problems.
Courtesy of the Advantage Dental Plan

◇ **growth and developmental delays;**
◇ **learning disabilities;**
◇ **increased incidence of ADHD;**
◇ increased risks for rage disorder;
◇ greater incidence of SIDS.
(Lester et al., 2005)

A recent study of 406 children born to 153 methamphetamine-abusing women found a reported disability rate of 33% (Brecht, 2005).

Mental & Emotional Effects

Amphetamines initially **produce a mild-to-intense euphoria, alertness, sexual feelings, and a sense of well-being and confidence. But with prolonged use, irritability, paranoia, anxiety, aggression, mental confusion, poor judgment, impaired memory, and even hallucinations** can be induced by the unbalanced neurotransmitters.

Amphetamines release neurotransmitters that mimic sexual gratification. Thus they are sometimes used to augment sexual activity (as in the gay community) and by those prone toward multiple partners and/or prolonged sexual interactions. But, again, because of the rapid development of tolerance and the depletion of neurotransmitters, there is often an eventual decrease of sex drive and performance. For many users **the rush from shooting or smoking methamphetamine becomes a substitute for sexual activity.**

"I didn't really go out with anybody when I was using. I chose the drugs over any girl, anytime. If I asked a girl out and she told me to meet her somewhere, and my dealer told me to meet him at the same time, I'd go with my dealer and try to score more drugs than go with her. The girls were always last on my list."
19-year-old recovering meth abuser

Aggression caused by excessive methamphetamine use depends on the dose, the setting, and the user's preexisting susceptibility to violence. **The increased suspiciousness, paranoia, and overconfidence lead to misinter-** pretations of others' actions and hence to violent reactions. Taken to extremes, prolonged use can result in violent, suicidal, and even homicidal thoughts.

"I could just go off on my girlfriend when I was high. I would get superparanoid. I hit her so hard I bruised my hand."
36-year-old recovering meth abuser

This tendency toward aggression translates into increased levels of child abuse and neglect. In Oregon, where 1,850 meth labs were busted in 2004, fully 80% of child abuse/neglect cases were tied to meth use (Sud, 2005).

Amphetamines and other stimulants also cause an increase in the brain's serotonin activity. This effect has recently been projected to explain their **effectiveness in treating ADHD** (Gainetdinov, Wetwel, Jones, et al., 1999). The most widely used ADHD drug is Adderall,® which is a mixture of four different amphetamine salts. The other amphetamine used is Dexedrine,® or dextroamphetamine sulfate (one of the four salts in Adderall®).

Excessive methamphetamine use can cause amphetamine psychosis just as excessive cocaine use can cause cocaine psychosis. And just as with cocaine, **symptoms include hallucinations, loss of contact with reality, and pressed speech that is almost indistinguishable from true schizophrenia or paranoid psychosis.** The ability of methamphetamines to release excess dopamine accounts for most of the symptoms. Conversely, the drugs that control the symptoms limit or block dopamine release. The amount of amphetamines necessary to precipitate a psychosis has been the subject of several investigations. Early studies reported cases in which a mere 55 mg precipitated a psychosis and others in which it took 2,000 to 5,000 mg. Half of the users in one study experienced psychotic episodes within two years of beginning use, and others took 10 years to react so severely (Grinspoon & Hedblom, 1975).

"I just got so sick of it, you know, just being high for so long. It just messes up your mind. I once stayed up for 23 days with no sleep—not one hour of sleep, not one wink of sleep. When you stay up for that long, you're just like a pile of mush. Your brain's just nothing, you know. You can't even talk. And it just doesn't even feel good. I don't want that feeling anymore."
17-year-old recovering meth abuser

The first amphetamine psychoses were noted in the late 1930s shortly after the drug came into common usage. Many more cases were noted during World War II and in the 1950s and 1960s, when amphetamines became the drug of choice. Amphetamine psychosis from excessive use and the severe depression that often accompanies withdrawal of high-dose intravenous use or heavy smoking of "ice" are usually not permanent.

The disturbed user will usually return to some semblance of normalcy after the brain chemistry has been rebalanced, usually within a few days or weeks, though some experience cravings and a lack of energy along with depression and psychosis for much longer (Zhou & Bledsoe, 1996). If there was a pre-existing mental condition, recovery can take even longer. Because extended use can also damage nerve cells, a number of the changes in long-term users can last a lifetime (even without pre-existing mental problems) (Richards, Baggot, Sabol, et al., 1999).

Dextromethamphetamine ("ice," or "crystal meth") stimulates the brain to a greater degree than the other amphetamines and methamphetamines but stimulates the heart, blood vessels, and lungs to a lesser degree. The decrease in cardiovascular effects (up to 25% less than that of regular "crank") encourages users to smoke more "ice" to continue and intensify the high. This results in more overdoses and a quicker disruption of neurotransmitters. The disruption also means **more "tweaking," or severe paranoid, hallucinatory, and hypervigilant thinking, along with greater suicidal depression and addictive use.** The experience of a number of detoxification clinics over the years has shown that detoxification from the mental and psychotic symptoms of excessive "ice" use usually takes several days longer than detoxifying from regular methamphetamine abuse.

Right-Handed & Left-Handed Molecules

When a molecule is created, **nature often adds a mirror image of that structure, called an** *optical isomer* (Figure 3-3), so you have a right-handed (dextro) isomer and a left-handed (levo) isomer. In the case of amphetamines, this translates into l-amphetamine and d-amphetamine as well as l-methamphetamine and d-methamphetamine. "Ice" is only the d-methamphetamine, or dextromethamphetamine form of the drug.

The amazing aspect of this fact is that the two individual isomers often have very different effects on the body. **Dextromethamphetamine is three to four times stronger in stimulating the brain than levomethamphetamine** (Logan, 2002). The levo isomer, however, is two to four times stronger in stimulating the heart, blood vessels, and nasal sinuses than the dextro isomer. For this reason levomethamphetamine has been used in nasal-congestion products. By the late 1980s, street chemists learned that pure left-handed pseudoephedrine could be used to make pure right-handed or dextro isomer methamphetamine ("ice"), which is stronger, longer lasting, and more smokable than regular "crank."

AMPHETAMINE CONGENERS

When the prescription use of amphetamines was severely limited because of federal legislation, physicians turned to amphetamine congeners to treat certain problems (mainly ADHD and obesity) that had previously been treated with amphetamines. **Amphetamine congeners are stimulant drugs that are chemically dissimilar but pharmacologically related to amphetamines and that produce many of the same effects (but are purportedly not as strong).** Concerns regarding potential stimulant drug abuse in patients treated with these congeners have been tempered by several studies that found no or very minimal abuse but only when used under appropriate medical supervision and dosage (Wilens, Farone, Biederman, et al., 2003). As with many drugs, it's the excess, inappropriate, or diverted use that causes problems.

ATTENTION-DEFICIT/ HYPERACTIVITY DISORDER (ADHD) & METHYLPHENIDATE (Ritalin®)

Methylphenidate (Ritalin®) is the most widely used amphetamine congener. Although it is prescribed as both a mood elevator and a treatment for narcolepsy (a sleep disorder), it is most often prescribed for attention-deficit/ hyperactivity disorder (APA, 2000). Amphetamines such as Adderall® and Dexedrine® are also widely prescribed for ADHD. From 2000 to 2005, use of ADHD drugs in children and adolescents rose 57% (Cuffe, Moore & McKeown, 2005; MEDCO Health Solutions, 2006).

Diagnosis of ADHD

Tests for ADHD often rely on diagnostic interview methods; and because **there is still no explicit diagnostic test, controversy surrounding the extent and the severity of this disorder continues** (Furman, 2005; National Institutes of Health, 1998). Diagnosis is particularly difficult in early childhood because other conditions can cause many of the same symptoms. For example, inattention often occurs among children with a low IQ as well as those with high intelligence who are placed in understimulating environments.

To attain more-precise diagnoses, Dr. Daniel Amen, an ADHD specialist, and others have used various brain imaging techniques, especially SPECT scans (single photon emission computerized tomography), to pinpoint brain activity that signifies ADHD. His clinic also scans the brains of suspected ADHD clients before and after using methylphenidate, to help with the diagnosis (Amen, 2006A, B).

In one imaging study, part of the corpus callosum in children with ADHD was smaller than in a control group, suggesting dysfunction in self-regulation and attention (Semrud-Clikeman, Filipek, Biederman, et al., 1994). Recent magnetic resonance imaging (MRI) studies of 152 children with ADHD found that their cerebrums were 3.2% smaller compared with a control group, while the underlying white matter was 6% smaller. The smaller brain did not signify lower intelligence (Castellanos, Lee, Sharp, et al., 2002; Krain & Castellanos, 2006). One of the main deficits was in the executive control part of the brain; patients were inefficient in allocating their attentional resources (Gualtieri & Johnson, 2006). It will take many years of additional research to be able to accurately diagnose ADHD, and then the questions of treatment come to the fore. For this reason **the use of medications to treat ADHD remains controversial**.

Classification. This disease is classified under the *International Classifica-*

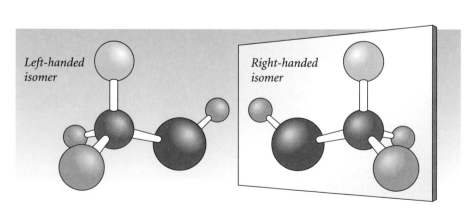

Figure 3-3 •

In this example of right- and left-handed molecules, notice that you need four nonidentical bonds of the same atoms.

© 2000 CNS Productions, Inc.

Within the figure: *Left-handed isomer*   *Right-handed isomer*

tion of Diseases (ICD-10) of the World Health Organization (WHO) into three subtypes:

1. hyperkinetic disorder,
2. disturbance of activity and attention, and
3. hyperkinetic conduct disorder (which includes 1 and 2) (World Health Organization [WHO], 1998).

In the United States, the three subtypes of ADHD according to the *DSM-IV-TR Diagnostic Manual of the American Psychiatric Association* are:

1. ADHD, combined type
2. ADHD, predominantly inattentive type
3. ADHD, predominantly hyperactive-impulsive type

The person with **ADHD, predominantly inattentive type** (attention-deficit disorder, or ADD) has six or more of the following symptoms.

Inattention

a. Displays **inattention to details** that causes careless mistakes in school or at work.
b. Has **difficulty sustaining attention** at work or play.
c. **Doesn't seem to listen** when spoken to directly.
d. **Doesn't follow through** on schoolwork, chores, or duties.
e. Has **difficulty organizing** tasks or activities.
f. **Avoids tasks that require sustained mental effort**.
g. Often loses things necessary for tasks or activities.
h. Is often easily distracted by extraneous stimuli.
i. Is often forgetful in daily activities.

The person with **ADHD, predominantly hyperactive-impulsive type** (hyperactivity disorder, or HD) has six or more of the following symptoms.

Impulsivity

a. Often **fidgets** with hands or feet or squirms in seat.
b. Often **leaves seat**.

c. Often **runs about or climbs excessively** in inappropriate situations.
d. Has **difficulty playing or engaging in leisure activities quietly**.
e. Is often on the go or often **acts as if driven**.
f. Often **talks excessively**.

Hyperactivity

a. Often **blurts out answers** before questions are completed.
b. Often has **difficulty awaiting turn**.
c. **Often interrupts** or intrudes on others.

In diagnosing any type of ADHD:

a. some **symptoms must be present before the age of 7**;
b. symptoms should manifest themselves in at least **two different settings**;
c. there must be evidence of **impairment of social functioning**;
d. symptoms are **not better accounted for by other mental disorders (or simply childhood rambuctiousness)**.
(APA, 2000)

The person with the **combined type of ADHD** meets the criteria for both other types: he or she has six or more symptoms of the inattention type plus six or more symptoms of the hyperactive-impulsive type.

Epidemiology

Because diagnostic judgments are necessarily subjective, estimates of the prevalence of ADHD vary widely.

◇ **Between 3% and 7.4% of all school-age children in the United States have ADHD** compared with a **worldwide rate of 2% to 9.5%** (APA, 2000; Cuffe, Moore & McKeown, 2005; Strine, Lesesne, Okoro, et al., 2006).
◇ A study of North American vs. European/African/Australian children found similar rates of ADHD except that North American girls had a significantly higher proportion with the disorder. In both populations **most patients had a positive family history of ADHD and**

previous stimulant treatment (Buitelaar, Barton, Danckaerts, et al., 2006; Waldman & Gizer, 2006). Another study of 183 youth found that if parents had a substance-use disorder and or ADHD, the chance of the children having ADHD rose. If the parents had both disorders, the odds rose to 50-50 (Wilens, Hahesy, Biederman, et al., 2005).

◇ ADHD is at least **two to three times as prevalent in boys** as in girls (Barkley, 1998). Mood changes, social withdrawal, and fear are more common in girls than the aggressiveness and impulsivity found in boys.
◇ If one examines children receiving psychiatric treatment, 40% to 70% of inpatients and 30% to 50% of outpatients could be diagnosed with ADHD (Biederman, Faraone, Spencer, et al., 1993; Cantwell, 1996; Pliszka, 1998).
◇ Anywhere **from 2.9% to 16.4% of adults could be diagnosed with ADHD**, depending on whether a narrow or a broad definition is used (Faraone & Biederman, 2005).
◇ In addition, **10% to 50% of children with ADHD will continue to have symptoms in adulthood** (Mannuzza, Klein, Bonagura, et al., 1991).

Pharmacotherapy for ADHD

It seems a contradiction that in small doses many stimulants have the ability to focus attention and control hyperactivity. It is theorized that **dopamine depletion is one of the main causes of ADHD**, and amphetamines or amphetamine congeners force the release of dopamine and prevent its reuptake and metabolism. **Amphetamines are prescribed for this condition.** In addition, stimulants increase the activity of serotonin in the brain, and this has been looked at as an explanation of their seemingly calming effect on those with ADHD (Gainetdinov, Wetwel, Jones, et al., 1999). Recent research has shown that methylphenidate works in the same brain areas and affects the same brain neurotransmitters as cocaine and amphetamine (Volkow, Fowler, Wang, et al, 2002).

It is estimated that 750,000 to 1 million schoolchildren and a number of adults are receiving more than

The concerns about giving kids too many drugs are not limited to Ritalin® and Adderall.® People are also concerned about overuse of antidepressants and other psychiatric medications.

20 million prescriptions per year for ADHD stimulants, and the figure is growing (RXList, 2006). These drugs, such as

◇ **methylphenidate (Ritalin® and Concerta®)** (10 million prescriptions per year);
◇ **d-amphetamine (Adderall®)** (7.7 million prescriptions per year; also called "rails," "amps," "a-bombs," "addies," "jollies," and "smurphs");
◇ **atomoxetine (Strattera®)** (5.8 million prescriptions per year); and
◇ **pemoline (Cylert®)**

seem to work for about 75% of ADHD children. Pemoline use is decreasing because of the need to monitor liver function. A drug that has seen some success is modafinil (Provigil®), a new stimulant. Other drugs that have been tried with varying degrees of success are bupropion (Wellbutrin®) and clonidine (Catapres®).

Recently, different formulations of methylphenidate have been accepted for the ADHD market, including Metadate CD,® Methylin,® DayTrana® (a transdermal patch), and, the most widely used, Concerta,® a time-release formulation of the drug. Atomoxetine (Strattera®), a specific norepinephrine reuptake inhibitor approved for the treatment of ADHD in 2002, was re-

quired by the Food and Drug Administration (FDA) in December 2004 to warn of possible liver damage. Thus the search for less stimulating or abusable and less toxic ADHD medications continues, with current interest in serotonin reuptake inhibitors like sertraline (Zoloft®) and paroxetine (Paxil®), which have demonstrated some effectiveness and fewer side effects than the stimulant medications.

In addition to drug therapy, other **adjunctive, or separate, therapies include education, exercise, lifestyle changes, behavior modification, psychotherapy, parenting classes, parent support groups, avoiding excess TV and computer games, and especially dietary changes** (Pary, Lewis, Arnp, et al., 2002; Szabo, 2006). Dietary changes and nutritional supplements are the most common alternative therapies tried by parents (Sinha & Efron, 2005).

Research by the National Institutes of Health studied the effectiveness of methylphenidate by itself, methylphenidate in conjunction with behavior management therapy, behavior management therapy alone, and standard therapy available in the community. Working at six separate sites, the researchers found that **for those with ADHD alone, methylphenidate by itself was as effective as methylpheni-

date and therapy and was more effective than therapy alone**. On the other hand, 70% of the children studied also had other problems, such as depression and anxiety. In those cases behavior therapy provided significant benefits especially when used in combination with methylphenidate (MTA Cooperative Group, 1999).

Concerns Regarding ADHD Pharmacotherapy

At the beginning of 2006, an FDA advisory committee was trying to determine the risk of psychosis or mania due to ADHD drugs in regard to labeling and warnings. The committee had received several hundred reports of psychosis or mania, especially hallucinations among patients (mostly adolescents) who used the drugs and who had no other risk factors. In addition, although methylphenidate and other amphetamine congeners seem to be used appropriately in medical settings, their **diversion to nonmedical use had led to a growing abuse of these substances** by the mid-2000s (Rubin, 2006). In 2005 the annual nonmedical use of methylphenidate was 2.4% of eighth-graders, 3.4% of tenth-graders, and 4.4% of twelfth-graders in the United States (Monitoring the Future, 2006). This report also documented that **more high school students were using the drug nonmedically than those being treated with it**. Methylphenidate has been sold on the street and used as a party drug. A few teenagers even appropriate their younger brother's or sister's supply to party with or to sell. When sold on the streets, methylphenidate tablets (called "pellets," "vitamin R," and "rids") sell for $3 to $10 each.

"At college my roommate would go to the health service and get a prescription for Ritalin® and then sell it to other students on a per-pill basis. He made a lot of money. He even got them to switch him to Adderall® and made even more money with that."
21-year-old male college student

Because of concerns about ADHD therapy, the **U.S. military decided to** bar anyone who had used methyl-phenidate in childhood (after the age of 12) from military service. The military services are exempt from the Americans with Disabilities Act of 1990, so they can bar potential enlistees because of ADHD. The irony of this stance is the fact that most governments, including the United States, have made amphetamines readily available to soldiers in combat.

Methylphenidate is a Schedule II drug (as are amphetamines), which means it has strong addiction liability. Users who abuse methylphenidate will develop a tolerance quickly and continue to increase dosage. Occasionally, they will even snort or inject the drug to try to recapture the original effects.

There are also **grave questions about the long-term effects of giving strong stimulants to children** in general and whether it leads to dependence on these kinds of drugs. Interestingly, studies have shown an **increased risk of alcohol and drug abuse among adults with untreated ADHD**, but the reasons for this relationship are hard to pinpoint (Biederman, Wilens, Mick, et al., 1999). Finally, in a group of adolescents in treatment for substance-abuse disorders, about half also had diagnosable ADHD (Horner & Scheibe, 1997). Most studies, however, don't show that adolescents who receive appropriate treatment are more likely to have problems with drugs and alcohol in adulthood (Wilens, Farone, Biederman, et al., 2003).

The high occurrence of ADHD in drug abusers might have several explanations:

◇ Their drug use could be an attempt at **self-medication**.
◇ It could be that **ADHD leads to social alienation and problems with self-esteem**, both of which are predictors of problems with alcohol and other drugs.
◇ There could be a **pre-existing mental condition** making one more inclined toward compulsive behavior.
◇ It could be that psychoactive stimulants make one more susceptible to drug use because of neurotransmitter disruption or increased **acceptance of the idea of taking drugs to alleviate mental problems**.

◇ Finally, there could be **genetic factors common to both ADHD and substance-abuse disorders**. One study found that the chance of an identical twin's having the disorder if his brother has it is 11 to 18 times greater than that of a nontwin sibling (Barkley, 1998). Another study at the University of Oslo found that heritability factors accounted for 80% of the differences between those with the disorder and those without it. Other researchers found a strong genetic link between ADHD and other addictions or impulse-control disorders, including gambling, compulsive overeating, heavy alcohol and drug use, and even Tourette's syndrome (Blum, Braverman, Holder, et al., 2000; Comings, Wu, Chiu, et al., 1996; Miller & Blum, 1996; Waldman & Gizer, 2006).

Nearly half of these children with ADHD have oppositional defiant disorder, a condition with which they are stubborn or act defiant, overreact to slights, and can have outbursts of temper. If left untreated, these can progress to more-serious conduct disorders, including stealing, vandalism, and arson (National Institute of Mental Health, 1999).

On the positive side, a Harvard Medical School study showed that boys (six to 17 years old) with ADHD who are treated with stimulants, including Ritalin,® are 84% less likely to abuse drugs and alcohol when they get older compared with those who are not treated (Wilens, Farone, Biederman, et al., 2003).

Over the past few years, attention has focused on the continued presence of ADHD in large numbers of adults. Though earlier research had shown a reduction in the continuation of ADHD symptoms once puberty was reached, the **new research indicates the need to treat some ADHD patients with drugs like methylphenidate throughout their lives**. The growth of stimulant use for adult ADHD in the 22-to-44 age group increased 164% for males over the past five years (MEDCO Health Solutions, 2006).

DIET PILLS

In 2001 it was estimated that 300 million people worldwide were obese and 750 million were overweight; of those about 150 million were in the United States. By 2006 the Centers for Disease Control and Prevention estimated that a whopping 65% of the U.S.

population was either overweight or obese. Surgeon General Richard H. Carmona has estimated that obesity contributes to 300,000 U.S. deaths every year and costs our economy about $120 billion annually.

At any given time, 24% of men and 38% of women in the United States are trying to lose weight at a cost of more than $33 billion for supplements, pills, and equipment (Kruger, Galuska, Serdula, et al., 2004). The market for people who want to lose weight is vast, and historically pharmaceutical companies have aggressively pursued this population segment with a wide variety of prescription and over-the-counter medications. Although only 2% to 3% currently use diet pills, that still amounts to nearly 3 million people. Unfortunately, **each wave of diet-drug use seemed to create problems**. In the fifties, sixties, and seventies, amphetamines and methamphetamines saturated the market but were found to cause heart problems, malnutrition, and dependence. Amphetamine congeners were the next wave; and makers of those diet pills, with names like Adipex® and Obetrol,® again saturated the market, saying they were safer than amphetamines and methamphetamines. It should also be noted that when taken alone without other weight-control activities, stimulants resulted in only a temporary weight loss that was undermined by regaining the weight as tolerance to the drugs developed.

On September 30, 1999, as the defendant in a class-action lawsuit in federal court, American Home Products agreed to pay $3.75 billion to $4.8 billion to everyone who had used two amphetamine congener diet pills—fenfluramine (Pondimin®) and dexfenfluramine (Redux®)—and suffered or may suffer heart-valve damage. Prescription records show that approximately 5 million Americans had been prescribed Pondimin® or Redux.® The other amphetamine congener implicated in these cases of heart-valve damage was phentermine (Ionamin® and Fastin®). **The combination of phentermine and fenfluramine or dexfenfluramine became known as "fenphen"**; and like other diet pill fads, a severe price was paid for a pharmaco-

logical shortcut to weight loss. The lawsuit was supported by a 1997 a report by the Mayo Clinic that said its doctors had found 24 cases of heart-valve damage in "fen-phen" users (all women) (Connolly, Crary, McGoon, et al., 1997). In September 1997 the FDA announced the withdrawal of fenfluramine and dexfenfluramine from the U.S. market. The desire to lose weight is so great that many dieters continued to take the medications and avoided having their hearts checked even after the negative reports were released (Blanck, Khan & Serdula, 2004).

Other popular amphetamine congeners used as diet pills include pemoline (Cylert®) and diethylpropion (Tenuate® and Tepanil®). The stimulation, mood elevation, and loss of appetite induced by amphetamine congener diet pills are weaker but similar to the effects of amphetamines, with some of the same side effects: excitability, nervousness, and increased respiration, blood pressure, and heart rate. If used to excess, convulsions, heart irregularities, and (rarely) even stroke, coma, and death can occur.

Pemoline and atomoxetine can also cause liver damage. Despite their widespread use to control appetite and shed weight—there is significant weight loss in the first four to six months—users usually regain and even surpass their starting weights.

In general, **diet pills (amphetamines and amphetamine congeners) are recommended only for short-term use**, so careful monitoring by physicians is very important. Long-term and high-dose use of diet pills has been associated with the development of abuse and addiction.

LOOK-ALIKE & OVER-THE-COUNTER (OTC) STIMULANTS

LOOK-ALIKES

The look-alike phenomenon of the 1980s contributed to the abuse of stimulants. By taking advantage of the interest in stimulant drugs, a few legitimate manufacturers began making

legal OTC products that looked identical to prescription stimulants. Their various products **contained ephedrine and occasionally pseudoephedrine (anti-asthmatics), phenylpropanolamine (PPA, a decongestant and mild appetite suppressant), and caffeine (a stimulant)**. These look-alikes were being combined, packaged, and sold as "legal stimulants" in a deliberate attempt to misrepresent them as controlled drugs (Morgan, Wesson, Puder, et al., 1987). The same chemicals were also showing up as illicit amphetamine look-alikes, such as "street speed," "cartwheels," and "crank," and as cocaine look-alikes, such as Supercaine,® Supertoot,® and Snow.® The cocaine look-alikes often added benzocaine or procaine to mimic the numbing effects of the actual drug. Now there is even an energy drink called Cocaine® that contains caffeine, some herbs, and a few vitamins.

The problem with the look-alike products was their toxicity when overused, particularly when two or more of the drugs were combined. Also, an amphetamine-like drug dependence developed in users who chronically abused them (Tinsley & Wadkins, 1998). The physical ramifications, especially **cardiovascular problems, could be particularly severe because large amounts were required to get a speed- or cocaine-like high**. For these reasons, in the early 1980s the FDA banned the OTC sale of products containing two or more of these ingredients. Since that time the sale of look-alikes persists with individual OTC stimulants being packaged to resemble controlled prescription stimulants. Some manufacturers circumvented the combination ban by combining herbs that contain ephedrine, caffeine, or PPA rather than using the drugs themselves. (*See Herbal Ecstasy® and Herbal Nexus® later in this chapter.*) In 2000 the FDA issued a warning about using PPA, especially for young women. It recommended using products with pseudoephedrine instead. In August 2005 Oregon reclassified ephedrine, pseudoephedrine, and phenylpropanolamine to Schedule III status because of diversion to methamphetamine manufacturing. Several other states and a federal bill also made this change. How this will affect the look-alike stimulant and diet-drug market remains to be seen, but many providers have already shifted to caffeine as the active ingredient and the Internet as their primary marketing outlet. Part of that drug market has been taken over by energy drinks as examined in the caffeine section of this chapter.

OTHER OVER-THE-COUNTER STIMULANTS

Pseudoephedrine and phenylpropanolamine, which have **decongestant, mild anorexic, and stimulant effects**, used to be found in hundreds of allergy and cold medications (often in combination with antihistamines, such as Benadryl®) and in OTC diet pills like Dexadiet® and Dexatrim.® Individuals who ingested these drugs and drank coffee or other caffeinated beverages often experienced anxiety attacks and rapid heartbeats. With the restrictions on pseudoephedrine and the warning on phenylpropanolamine, drug manufacturers have turned to other drugs, such as phenylephrine, that couldn't be made into amphetamines and that have fewer stimulant or other unwanted side effects.

Caffeine has been sold as an OTC stimulant for years in tablets with trade names such as NoDoz® and Vivarin.® The FDA is continuing to examine all of these products, issuing warnings, and sometimes banning them outright. The debate continues.

MISCELLANEOUS PLANT STIMULANTS

Caffeine from the coffee bush and cocaine from the coca bush are often thought of by Americans as the principal plant stimulants, but worldwide dozens of plants or their extracts with stimulant properties have been used for centuries by hundreds of millions of people, often in the Middle East, Far East, and Africa. These plants include the **khat bush, the betel nut, the yohimbe tree, and the ephedra bush.**

Khat is used socially in many countries in eastern Africa, southern Arabia, and the Middle East. Notice the piles of khat leaves on the dining table at this wedding in Yemen. The inset shows khat plants wrapped in banana leaves, which were intercepted by a number of law enforcement agencies during Operation Somalia Express, an investigation that led to the indictments of 44 members of an international khat trafficking ring responsible for smuggling more than 25 tons of the leaf from Africa to the United States.

© 1990 Alain Labrousse. Inset courtesy of the Drug Enforcement Administration

KHAT & METHCATHINONE
Khat ("qat," "shat," and "miraa")

January 1, 2005: Customs agents in Baltimore seize 2,400 lbs. of plant matter suspected to be khat.

March 24, 2006: 170 lbs. of khat were seized during a routine traffic stop on the Ohio Turnpike.

U.S. Customs seizures of khat leaves, a plant stimulant, increased dramatically from about 1,760 lbs. in 1992 to 30 metric tons in just the first six months of 2002. This hardly compares with the 1.5 million lbs. of marijuana seized in the same year (and the 12 million to 25 million lbs. that got through), but it indicates that khat abuse is a growing problem. Most of the leaves were destined for East African and Middle Eastern immigrants, who have large enclaves in Dallas, Los Angeles, New York, and Washington, DC. In those cities khat branches with leaves are sold in bundles in certain stores and restaurants (Leinwand, 2002B). **Cathinone, the key stimulant in the plant, evaporates from the leaves within 48 hours** after harvesting, making access to freshly cut bundles a must in the use of this substance (Crenshaw, 2004). There is, however, a growing group of **teens and young adults who use cathinone's stronger synthetic version, methcathinone, as a stimulant** and exchange relevant information about the drug via the Internet. Methcathinone, know on the street as "cat" or "qat," is synthesized by street chemists from ephedrine and pseudoephedrine, the same precursors used to manufacture methamphetamine (DEA, 2002).

Back in 1992 when the United States sent troops to Somalia, the soldiers were surprised to find a large percentage of the population chewing the leaves, twigs, and shoots of the khat shrub (*Catha edulis*) to get stimulant sensations somewhere between those of coffee and methamphetamine. In Yemen, another country on the Arabian peninsula, more than half of the population uses khat, and it is not unusual for people to spend more than one-third of their family income on the drug. **It is the driving economic force in Somalia, Yemen, and a few other countries in eastern Africa, southern Arabia, and the Middle East.** Such drug use is not a new development in those countries. References to khat can be found in Arab journals from the thirteenth century. The leaves were used by some physicians as a treatment for depression, but **mostly khat was and is used in social settings.** Many homes in some Middle Eastern countries have a room dedicated to khat chewing, similar to British homes that have a tearoom or parlor. Khat-chewing gatherings in these rooms are called "*majlis* parties." Khat is used mostly by men in the countries in which it is cultivated.

The khat shrub is 10 to 20 ft. tall. Because the main active ingredients can lose potency unless handled quickly, the leaves and sprouts are harvested early in the morning, kept moist, and speedily transported to market, where they are sold by noon. **The fresh leaves and tender stems are chewed, and the juice is swallowed.** Dried leaves and twigs, which are not as potent as the fresh leaves, can be **crushed for tea or made into a chewable paste** (Crenshaw, 2004; Kalix, 1994; U.S. Department of Justice, 2002).

The **main psychoactive ingredient, cathinone**, has a half-life in the body of only about 90 minutes, so the leaf must be chewed continuously to sustain a high. Cathinone is a naturally occurring amphetamine-like substance that produces a similar **mild euphoric effect, along with exhilaration, talkativeness, hyperactivity, wakefulness, aggressiveness, enhanced self-esteem, and loss of appetite** (Dhaifalah & Santavy, 2004). Side effects of excess use include anorexia, tachycardia, hypertension, dependence, chronic insomnia, and gastric disorders (Al-Habori, 2005). People who use too much can also become irritable, angry, and possibly violent.

Chronic khat abuse can result in physical exhaustion and suicidal depression upon withdrawal, symptoms similar to those seen with amphetamine withdrawal. There are also rare reports of paranoid hallucinations and even overdose deaths. In experiments with monkeys, where the animals were allowed to self-administer the drug to see if it was addictive, cathinone was shown to have a powerful reinforcing effect. The binge pattern of use found with cocaine and amphetamines was repeated in experiments with monkeys and cathinone (Goudie & Newton, 1985).

Hundreds of millions of dollars are spent on the drug worldwide, even in poor countries. The stimulation and the subsequent crash caused by khat has had an economic impact in numerous countries, including reduced work hours, decreased production, income loss, and malnutrition (Giannini, Burge, Shaheen, et al., 1986).

Methcathinone

In the early 1990s in the United States, manufacture of **methcathinone, a synthetic version of cathinone**, was begun in illegal laboratories in the Midwest; it was sold on the street as a powerful alternative to methamphetamine. It is **usually snorted** but can also be taken intravenously, mixed in a liquid and swallowed, or smoked in a cigarette, joint, or crack pipe. It is cheap to manufacture, and 1 gm of the drug sells for $40 to $120 compared with methamphetamine, which sells for $40 to $200 (DEA, 2002).

Methcathinone (also known as ephedrone) was originally synthesized by Parke-Davis Pharmaceuticals in 1957 in the United States, but it was rejected for production due to side effects. The formula became widely known in Russia, and by the early 1980s methcathinone manufacturing and illicit use were widespread. It has been estimated that **20% of illicit-drug abusers in the Russian Republic use methcathinone** (Calkins, Aktan & Hussain, 1995).

Using methcathinone instead of khat is similar to using cocaine instead of the coca leaf. **Methcathinone is much more intense than khat**, so its addictive properties and side effects can be more intense (and **quite similar to the effects of methamphetamines**). Side effects include nervousness, labored respiration, and lack of coordination. PET scans of long-term methcathinone users show lasting reductions in dopamine production that can lead to nervous system and muscular problems, such as Parkinsonism (a dopamine-deficiency disease) (Ricaurte et al., 1997).

BETEL NUTS

Although some evidence has been found in Thailand that people have chewed betel nuts for 12,000 years, specific references to the betel nut (**seeds of the betel palm**, *Areca catechu*) date back about 23 centuries (Rätsch, 2005). Its use as a stimulant was first described by Herodotus in 340 B.C. Marco Polo brought betel nuts back to Europe in 1300.

The nut has been **widely used in India, Pakistan, the Arab world, Taiwan, Malaysia, the Philippines, New Guinea, Polynesia, southern China, and some countries in Africa**. Today anywhere **from 200 million to 450 million people worldwide use betel nuts** not only as a recreational drug but also as a medication. In Taiwan alone 17% of men and 1% of women—an estimated 2 million people—chew the nut on a regular basis.

The betel palm is widely cultivated, usually on large plantations, in a number of countries with a tropical climate. Each palm produces about 250 seeds per year. The main active ingredient, arecoline, increases levels of epinephrine and norepinephrine. The effects of these CNS stimulants are similar to those of nicotine or strong coffee and include a **mild euphoria, excitation, and a decrease in fatigue**. Maximum effects occur six to eight minutes after chewing begins. Some users claim that betel chewing lowers tension, reduces appetite, and induces a feeling of well-being (Bibra, 1995). Betel nut abusers chew from morning until night, whereas other users do so only in social situations. Some liken the practice to gum chewing or cola drinking in the West. Unfortunately, this drug can produce psychological dependence (Chu, 2001). A certain physical dependence also develops because there is a prominent and identifiable set of withdrawal symptoms similar to those experienced during withdrawal from caffeine.

The betel nut (husk and/or meat) is generally chewed in combination with another plant leaf (such as peppermint or mustard) and some slaked lime to make it more palatable and to increase absorption. The juice of this mixture **stains the teeth and the mouth dark red** over time. In high doses arecoline can be toxic. Another substance in betel nuts, muscarine, is epidemiologically linked to esophageal cancer. Up to 7% of regular users have cancer of the mouth and the esophagus. **The most common danger has to do with tissue damage to mucosal linings of the mouth and the esophagus** (Warnakula-suriva, Trivedy & Peters, 2002).

In the 1990s a product called *gutka* **gained popularity and was heavily marketed in India.** Gutka is a sweetened mixture of tobacco, betel nut, and betel leaves. It was sold at price affordable even to children (about 40¢ to 50¢) and packaged to attract their attention. The sale of these products has already exceeded $1 billion due to the habituating nature of the substances. Children as young as 12 were diagnosed with precancerous lesions in their mouths due to gutkha use when the product had been available in India for only a few years. Continuing attempts by various citizen and governmental groups to ban the substance or at least one of the additives, magnesium carbonate, have had only limited success.

By 2003, 18% of Taiwanese youth 12 to 18 years old admitted to betel nut chewing, and 7.3% were regular users. This in part resulted from the expanded marketing of the substance a few years earlier. "Betel Quids," a mixture of betel nut, betel peppermint leaves (piper betel), and lime (calcium oxide), were prepared by scantly clad young women and sold out of glass-walled road kiosks (Parsell, 2005). These women were called "Binlang Girls," "Betel Nut Beauties," or "Betel Nut Girls." The concerned Taiwan government passed laws in 2002 requiring the Betel Nut Beauties to cover their exposed breasts, bellies, and buttocks. This seems to have decreased consumption somewhat by the mid-2000s (*Taipei Times*, 2003).

While coffee shops and kiosks are in vogue in the United States, "betel nut beauties" are all the rage in Taiwan and a few other countries. They have betel kiosks or bicycles with rolling carts from which they sell the mild stimulant. Their scanty outfits have compelled some local authorities to insist that the young ladies cover up in the interest of public morals.

Courtesy of the *Shanghai Star* (China Daily)

YOHIMBE

Yohimbine, a bitter spicy extract from the African **yohimbe tree** (*Corynanthe* and *Pausinystalia yohimbe,* a member of the coffee family), can be brewed into a stimulating tea or used as a medicine. **It is reported to be a mild aphrodisiac.** The active ingredient is an alpha-2 adrenergic antagonist that seems to increase the activity of the neurotransmitter norepinephrine. This results in more penile blood inflow, which has led to the use of yohimbine as a treatment for erectile dysfunction in men as well as for inducing sexual arousal in women, though its effectiveness is debatable (Morales, 2000). The drug also increases blood pressure and heart rate and has local-anesthetic effects.

The yohimbe tree contains several alkaloids; yohimbine constitutes 0.6% to 0.9% of the bark. The yohimbine in the bark can be extracted and formulated into either tablets or a tincture for oral ingestion (Zanolari, Ndjoko, Isoset, et al., 2003). Yohimbine was isolated from the bark of the tree in 1896.

Yohimbine has been reported to **produce a mild euphoria and occasional hallucinations; in larger doses it can be toxic** and even cause death by respiratory paralysis (Marnell, 2006). The bark can be bought at some herbalists' shops along with a whole series of yohimbine medications for increasing potency, with names like Male Performance,® Yohimbe Power,® Manpower,® and Aphrodyne® (prescription only).

EPHEDRA (ephedrine)

The **ephedra bush** (*Ephedra equisetina*), found in deserts throughout the world, contains the drug ephedrine. This drug is **a mild-to-moderate stimulant used medicinally to treat asthma, narcolepsy, other allergies, and low blood pressure**. Many use it to make tea; the Mormons brew it as a substitute for coffee (which is forbidden by their religion). Ephedrine, also known as "marwath" and "**ma huang**," has been mentioned as a stimulant tonic and a medication in China for more than 5,000 years and is still sold in herbalists' shops. Ephedrine was isolated and synthesized in 1885, but it was then forgotten for almost 50 years before a scientific paper recommended it for asthma. Its popularity increased dramatically because until then epinephrine, which could only be injected, was the sole effective medication used to treat asthma.

Although ephedrine has more-peripheral effects, such as bronchodilation, and fewer CNS effects than amphetamines (e.g., euphoria), one of the common side effects of excessive ephedrine use is drug-induced psychosis (Karch, 2001). Extract of ephedrine has been **used by athletes for an extra boost, but overuse can lead to heart and blood vessel problems**. The cardiovascular dangers moved the National Football League to ban ephedrine use by players. A weightlifter's death in Ohio led to the sales ban of the extract in that state. Many other states have followed suit and banned the sale of all ephedrine-based products. A number of look-alike and OTC products that advertise themselves as MDMA, amphetamine substitutes, or other stimulants (e.g., Cloud 9® and Nirvana®) contain ephedrine as the active ingredient.

Natural ephedra, synthetic ephedrine, and pseudoephedrine are also the main ingredients in the synthesis of methamphetamine and methcathinone; and because of the demand for them, a large illegal trade has sprung up along with extensive smuggling from China and Germany. Restriction of these chemicals and phenylpropanolamine to prescription and Schedule III controlled substances in Oregon and other states has made it difficult for street chemists, but it will also make it more difficult for those with legitimate asthma and cold symptoms to gain access to medications that were over-the-counter drugs until 2004.

Herbal Ecstasy® & Herbal Nexus®

In an attempt to cater to some people's desire for abusable stimulants and psychedelics, entrepreneurs have introduced stimulant herbal products. These capsules and tablets combine the **herbal form of ephedrine (ephedra) and an herbal extract of caffeine (possibly from the kola nut)** with other herbs and vitamins; they are advertised as Herbal Ecstasy,® Herbal Nexus,® and other catchy names. The use of herbal substances is an attempt to get around the FDA ban on some combinations of these products and to cash in on the interest in certain psychoactive drugs, including MDMA (ecstasy), nexus (CBR), and other psycho-stimulants. Some of these herbal products also contain vitamins and are touted as buffers for the toxic effects of the real ecstasy and nexus. The resulting problems, even with herbal ephedra, have caused several states to go beyond merely limiting the amount that can be bought to placing outright bans on products with any form of ephedra or ephedrine.

CAFFEINE

"Coffee is a great power in my life; I have observed its effects on an epic scale. Many people claim coffee inspires them, but, as everybody knows, coffee only makes boring people more boring."
Honoré de Balzac, *On Modern Stimulants,* 1839

Caffeine is not only the most popular stimulant in the world but also the world's most popular mood-altering and habit-forming drug (Reid, 2005). Caffeine is found in coffee, tea, chocolate, soft drinks, energy drinks, 60 different plants, and hundreds of over-the-counter and prescription medications. It has become ingrained in so many cultures that efforts at any kind of prohibition or reduction of use are doomed to failure. **In America 85% of the population consumes substantial amounts of caffeine every day** (Weinberg & Bealer, 2001). There is the morning coffee, the latte on the way to work, the coffee breaks at work, coffee and colas at meetings and conferences, the tablet of NoDoz® to stay awake on the drive home, and even the steaming cup of decaf after dinner to keep the ritual going. As with many psychoactive drugs, the ritual surrounding the use of coffee or tea is often as important as the stimulation. Some of the rituals include selecting the coffee and grinding the beans; finding a favorite drive-thru coffee kiosk; collecting dozens of cups, demitasses, or mugs; reading the newspaper; and finding the right pastry or scones to go with the morning brew or the afternoon tea.

HISTORY OF USE

Tea

Tea is the most widely consumed beverage in the world besides water. It was thought to have been **present in China as early as 2700 B.C.,** but the first written record dates back only to 221 B.C., when the Chinese emperor Tsching-schi-huang-ti placed a tax on tea. The Buddhist Monk Saichô brought the tea plant to Japan in A.D. 801, but the green tea didn't become an important part of Japanese culture until the fifteenth century. **A tea ceremony became an important ritual in Japanese homes and castles.** Its purpose is to enter a mental state in which one's true self can be discovered. Tea was introduced into Europe around the end of the sixteenth century and immediately became quite popular, particularly in England and subsequently English colonies such as America (Harler, 1984).

"The power and effect of this drink is that it dispels immoderate sleep; but afterward those in particular feel very good who have overburdened their stomachs with food and have loaded the brain with strong beverages."
Johan Neuhof, 1655

The Boston Tea Party in 1774, when irate Bostonians threw tea into Boston Harbor to protest a tax on tea, reflected the importance of this psychoactive substance in colonial life. Today the **primary exporters of tea are India (2 billion lbs. per year), China, and Sri Lanka**, although other regions are becoming major players (e.g., Kenya, southern Brazil, and Australia). The primary importers are the United Kingdom, the United States, and Pakistan. About 75% of the world's tea is black tea and 22% is green tea.

Coffee

Coffee was first cultivated in Ethiopia around A.D. 650. Legend says that the stimulant properties of coffee were discovered when Kaldi, an Arab goatherd, noticed the friskiness of his goats when they ate red berries from the coffee bush. Later on Arabs learned how to prepare a hot drink from the berries rather than just chewing them. Use spread to Arabia in the thirteenth century and finally to Europe. The drink was so stimulating that **many cultures banned it as an intoxicating drug**. In colonial America it was suggested that the use of tea and coffee led to the use of tobacco, alcohol, opium, and other drugs (Juliano & Griffiths, 2005). **Coffee and tea were also great sources of revenue**, and the pressure against prohibition, from both the government and the general public, was immense.

The use of caffeinated beverages continued to expand. Today in the United States alone, each coffee drinker consumes about 20 lbs. of coffee per year. There has been an incredible growth in the number of specialty coffeehouses in the United States. Every parking lot and gas station seems to have a coffee kiosk, and many discount department stores and grocery chain stores have coffee bars. The number of coffee beverage retailers has grown from 200 in 1989 to more than 21,400 in 2005, and the numbers are accelerating, leading to an outcry from neighbors. Starbucks,® the largest of the retailers, was estimated to have more than 11,000 stores at the beginning of 2006 worldwide, with net revenues of $7.2 billion. Starbuck's goal is to have 40,000 coffee stores worldwide (Mintel Group, 2006; Starbucks, 2006; Allison, 2006). Even McDonald's and Burger King have upgraded their coffees to premium roasts because of the increased competition.

Cocoa

Residue in ancient Mayan pots found in Belize in Central America, dating back to 600 B.C., showed traces of a cocoa beverage (Hurst, Tarka, Powis, et al., 2002). Cocoa from the roasted and ground beans of the **cacao tree** (*Theobroma cacao*) was **first used in the New World by Mayan and later Aztec royalty** not only as an unsweetened drink or as a spice but also as a food, a stimulant, and even a currency. It was brought to Europe by Hernando Cortez in 1528. Initial preparations in Europe were promoted as love drinks. Widespread use of other preparations didn't occur until the nineteenth century, when the first chocolate bars appeared on the market. **There is a relatively small amount of caffeine in chocolate, but the other active ingredient, theobromine, also has stimulatory effects.**

Caffeinated Soft Drinks (colas)

The average American drank the equivalent of 828 eight-ounce glasses of soft drinks in 2005, most of those caffeinated. This figure is down slightly from the previous year. Part of the reason for this decline seems to be the increased concerns about obesity and the fact that a giant 44 oz. nondiet drink contains more than 400 calories. A recent study of children's eating habits found that simply avoiding sugared soft drinks led to modest weight loss.

Energy drinks and energy packets have become particularly popular among adolescents and young people. Caffeine is the main ingredient, but vitamin B_6, guarana, taurine, sugar, minerals, and ginseng are also included. As with any stimulant, excess use and long-term heavy use cause cardiovascular and other problems.

© 2007 CNS Productions

Caffeinated soft drinks (colas) are carbonated beverages that sometimes contain a caffeine extract of the kola nut from the **African kola tree** (*Cola nitida* or *Cola acuminata*), but **mostly they use caffeine extracted from the process of decaffeinating coffee**. The caffeine of the kola nut is released by cracking it into small pieces and then chewing it. The kola nut has been used in some East African countries for centuries. The use of the nut for chewing and as a syrup (made from powdered nut) spread to Europe in the mid-1800s. By the late 1800s, cola drinks made with carbonated or phosphated liquids, such as Coca Cola,® became popular in the United States (Kuhar, 1995). It is important to note that caffeine is added to other soft drinks and not just colas. Mountain Dew,® orange soda, and even some lemon-lime soft drinks now contain this drug.

Energy Drinks Phenomenon

Austrian entrepreneur Dietrich Mateschitz created Red Bull® in 1987. With 80 mg of **caffeine**, Red Bull® has more than twice the amount of a 12 oz.

Coca Cola® (35 mg) but still less than half that of 8 oz. of brewed coffee (135 mg) (Reid, 2005). In addition to caffeine, **it also contains taurine, ginseng, guarana, glucose or glucuronolactone, B-complex vitamins, minerals, and carbohydrates** to provide a quick energy boost. The marketing of Red Bull as an energy-providing beverage led to its immediate worldwide popularity. Now a plethora of so-called energy drinks dominates shelves at minimarts, dance clubs, bars, gyms, and university shops, with trade names like Rockstar,® Lift Off Orange,® Lo-Carb Monster Energy,® Red Rave,® Blast,® Zoom,® Wired X-3000,® Bliss,® SoBe Adrenaline Rush,® Killer Buzz,® and even Cocaine.® More than 200 new drinks came on the market in 2006.

Despite their tremendous popularity and huge profits, whether they actually increase energy, awareness, and performance remains controversial, with some studies demonstrating positive results (Kennedy & Scholey, 2004) and others finding no benefits (Smit, Cotton, Hughes, et al., 2004). The latest fad with energy drinks is the combined ingestion of them with alcohol in a sort of new age speedball. This is most often done by mixing vodka or other liquor with an energy drink. This cocktail is **believed to prevent getting too drunk or having a hangover**. Research findings regarding the effectiveness of this practice, even by the same research team, are also mixed (Ferreiri, de Mello, Rossi, et al., 2004).

By 2004 growing concern about the health consequences of energy drinks led to a **ban of Red Bull® sales in France, Denmark, and Canada**. Concern focused on increased heart rate and blood pressure, with palpitations and dehydration. Consequences of ingesting it while pregnant included miscarriage, low birth weight, and difficult delivery. Sweden documented several deaths after Red Bull® ingestion (British Broadcasting Corporation, 2001); and an 18-year-old male in Ireland who drank four cans of the energy drink before a basketball game collapsed and died. Concern regarding energy drink cocktails has grown as well, especially in various university media; such cocktails are presumed to increase dehydration, mask the toxic effects of both the alcohol and the energy drink, and promote the false impression of being sober when one is really drunk and impaired.

Other Plants Containing Caffeine

Other plants containing caffeine include guarana (*Paullinia cupana*), maté (*Ilex paraguarenis*), and yoco (*Paullinia yoco*)—all found in South America (Weinberg & Bealer, 2001). **Guarana is the national drink of Brazil.** Made from the guarana shrub, it has more caffeine (3% to 4%) than coffee beans (1% to 2%) and is made into sweet carbonated beverages with 30 mg of caffeine per 12 oz. (Coca Cola has 35 mg/12 oz.) (Barone & Roberts, 1996). Guarana beans are sold in health-food stores under names like Zing and advertised as a folk cure although the main ingredient is simply a hearty dose of caffeine. **Maté is the most popular caffeinated drink in Argentina; and, after the tea plant, coffee bean, and cacao tree, maté is the largest source of caffeine in the world** (3% of the world's caffeine). It is a hot, tealike drink made from the leaves of a certain holly plant

and is often used as a vehicle for other herbal medications. It is thought to strengthen the stomach, treat rheumatism, and help heal sores when used as a plaster. Maté leaves can be bought in a number of health-food stores. Maté should not be confused with mate de coca,® which contains coca leaves instead of tea leaves. Maté is about 0.7% caffeine, whereas yoco is about 2.7% (Rätsch, 2005; Weil & Rosen, 2004; Weinberg & Bealer 2001).

PHARMACOLOGY

Caffeine is an alkaloid of the chemical class called *xanthines*. It is found in more than 60 plant species, including *Coffea Arabica* (coffee), *Thea sinensis* (tea), *Theobroma cacao* (chocolate), and *Cola nitida* (cola drinks). The white, bitter-tasting crystalline powder ($C_8H_{10}N_4O_2$) was isolated from coffee by Friedlieb Ferdinand Runge in 1819 and from tea eight years later. Tea leaves contain a higher percentage of caffeine than coffee, but less tea is used for the average cup. Caffeine can be used orally, intravenously, intramuscularly, or rectally, though most consumption is by mouth. The **half-life of caffeine in the body is 3 to 7 hours**, so it takes 15 to 35 hours for 95% of the caffeine to be excreted. School-age children eliminate caffeine twice as fast as adults (Silverman & Griffiths, 1995A).

In the **United States, per-capita consumption of caffeine is 211 mg per day** (about two cups of regular coffee plus a cola); in Sweden, 425 mg (85% from coffee); and in the United Kingdom, 445 mg (72% from tea).

◇ About 17% of the per-capita daily consumption of caffeine in the United States is from tea, 16% from soft drinks, and 60% from coffee (American Beverage Association, 2006; Silverman & Griffiths, 1995B).

◇ About half of all Americans drink 3.3 cups of coffee on any given day, and most of that is regular coffee (not the lattes and espressos found in specialty coffees that have exploded in popularity in recent years) (Coffee Science Source, 1998).

◇ 20% of U.S. adults consume more than 350 mg of caffeine per day, and 3% consume more than 650 mg.

◇ There are about 450 different soft drinks available in the United States, of which 65% contain caffeine.

"I start in the morning with a double latte. That's 300 to 400 mg of caffeine. I'll have two Cokes for lunch; that's another 100 mg. Then a couple of cups of regular coffee in the afternoon— another 200 mg. That's 700 mg minimum. I know plenty of people at work who will have at least 10 cups of coffee besides the lattes and chocolate bars. They're up to 2,000 mg a day. Their tolerance is incredible. They'll drink a cup and fall asleep."
36-year-old caffeinated businessman

PHYSICAL & MENTAL EFFECTS

As with any drug, an individual's reaction to caffeine varies widely. Differences in caffeine metabolism; a high level of tolerance; an illness that exaggerates the effects; or the use of other substances, including alcohol, tobacco, or other stimulant—all can alter the reactions to caffeine and make it difficult to predict specific effects for any given person (Weinberg & Bealer, 2001). **Medically, caffeine is used as a bronchodilator** in asthma patients. It has been used as an adjunct to pain medication and to counteract a sudden drop in blood pressure. **It is found in a number of OTC preparations: decongestants, diuretics, analgesics, alertness aids, appetite suppressants, and menstrual pain controllers.** Caffeine constricts blood vessels in the brain, making it valuable as a **treatment for headaches, especially migraine headaches**. A recent study found that drinking several cups of coffee every day may counteract the liver damage from alcohol and greatly lower the damage cause by cirrhosis (Klatsky, Morton, Udaltsova, et al., 2006).

Nonmedically, caffeine is most widely known and used as a mild stimulant. In low doses (100 to 200 mg), **caffeine can increase alertness, dissipate drowsiness or fatigue, and facilitate thinking**. Even at doses above 200 mg, there can be increased alert-

TABLE 3–2   CAFFEINE CONTENT IN VARIOUS SUBSTANCES

Amount of Beverage or Food	Caffeine	Amount of Beverage or Food	Caffeine
Coffee (1 cup)		**Energy Drinks**	
demitasse espresso (4 oz.)	200 mg	Red Bull® (8.3 oz.)	80 mg
brewed coffee (8 oz.)	135 mg	SoBe Adrenaline Rush® (8.3 oz.)	80 mg
instant coffee (8 oz.)	95 mg	Starbucks 2X Shot® (6.5 oz.)	105 mg
decaf coffee (8 oz.)	7 mg	**Other Plants**	
Tea (8 oz.)		Guarana tea (8 oz.)	100–200 mg
1-minute brew	25 mg	Guarana soft drink (8 oz.)	20 mg
3-minute brew	40 mg	Maté (8 oz.)	35–130 mg
5-minute brew	60 mg	Yoco (8 oz.)	100–200 mg
green tea	30 mg	**Energy Packets**	
Commercial Iced Teas (16 oz.)		Ultimate Energizer® (1 capsule)	140 mg
Arizona, various flavors	23 mg	Stacker® (1 capsule)	250 mg
Nestea Pure Lemon	22 mg	**Medications**	
Snapple, all flavors	42 mg	Dexatrim® (1 capsule)	200 mg
Soft Drinks (12 oz.)		NoDoz® Max. (1 tablet)	200 mg
Jolt Cola®	70 mg	Vivarin® (1 tablet)	200 mg
Mountain Dew®	54 mg	Excedrin® (1 tablet)	65 mg
Coca-Cola®	35 mg	Midol® (1 tablet)	32 mg
Pepsi Cola®	38 mg	Percodan®	32 mg
Sunkist Orange	42 mg		
Barqs Root Beer	23 mg	(Barone & Roberts, 1996)	
Chocolate			
hot chocolate (8 oz.)	5 mg		
chocolate milk (6 oz.)	4 mg		
milk chocolate (4 oz.)	24 mg		
dark chocolate (4 oz.)	80 mg		
baking chocolate (4 oz.)	140 mg		
M&M's® (1.75 oz.)	15 mg		
Häagen Dazs® coffee ice cream (1/2 cup)	32 mg		

ness and performance. Six hundred mg of caffeine is approximately the equivalent of taking 20 mg of amphetamine.

The stimulation is caused by caffeine's inhibiting effect on adenosine, a neuromodulator that normally depresses mood, induces sleep, has anticonvulsant properties, and causes low blood pressure, a slow heart rate, and the dilation of blood vessels. When caffeine blocks adenosine, the result is wakefulness, raised mood, high blood pressure, fast heart rate, and vasoconstriction (Weinberg & Bealer, 2001). Because caffeine users' reactions to the drug often depend on heredity, the rise in blood pressure is more pronounced in those prone to high blood pressure (Rachima-Maoz, Peleg & Rosenthal, 1998).

At doses of more than 350 mg per day (three or four cups of coffee), again depending on the user's susceptibility and tolerance, **anxiety, insomnia, gastric irritation, high blood pressure, nervousness, and flushed face can occur**. In one study, at doses of 500 mg, stress hormones were elevated about 32% above normal and persisted hours after use. Coffee drinkers also felt more stressed than on the days they didn't use caffeine (Lane, Pieper & Phillips-Bute, 2002). At doses above 1,000 mg taken over a short period of time, increased heart rate, palpitations, muscle twitching, rambling thoughts, jumbled speech, sleep difficulties, motor disturbances, ringing in the ears, and even vomiting and convulsions can occur. **Caffeine is lethal at about 10 grams** (100 cups of coffee). Because excessive caffeine use can trigger nervousness, **people who are prone to panic attacks should avoid caffeine** (Juliano & Griffiths, 2005). Physicians and psychiatrists of patients with symptoms of anxiety should ask about their caffeine consumption. In fact, physicians rarely consider caffeine consumption in patients with cardiovascular, sleep, gastric, and other problems.

"When I was 14, a friend of mine and I got a couple of boxes of NoDoz® and downed the whole two boxes of 'em between us. We got way sick, very sick, way more sick than I've ever gotten off of alcohol. The room was spinning,

●●●

and spinning, and spinning. Caffeine overdose: not fun."
Caffeine abuser

Consuming 350 mg or more of caffeine can lower fertility rates in women and affect fetuses in the womb (e.g., higher blood pressure). A retrospective study at the University of Utah of 2,500 pregnant women found that **six or more cups of coffee per day almost doubled the risk of miscarriage** compared with women who either didn't drink coffee or drank only one or two cups per day (Klebanoff, Levine, DeSimonian, et al., 1999). It is also thought by a number of researchers that some susceptible women develop benign lumps in their breasts from drinking too much coffee. Some researchers also feel that caffeine use makes it harder to lose weight. This difficulty happens because **caffeine stimulates the release of insulin**. Insulin metabolizes sugar thus reducing the level of sugar in the blood and triggering hunger in the user.

Coronary heart disease, ischemic heart disease, heart attacks, intestinal ulcers, diabetes, and some liver problems have been seen in long-term, high-dose caffeine users, more often in countries with very high per-capita caffeine consumption. On the other hand, a re-cent study of 110,000 Japanese found that daily coffee drinkers had half the liver cancer risk of coffee abstainers (Kurozawa, Ogimoto, Shibata, et al., 2005).

TOLERANCE, WITHDRAWAL & ADDICTION

Tolerance to the effects of caffeine does occur, although there is a wide variation among the ways different people react to several cups of coffee or tea. Coffee drinkers might eventually need three cups to wake up instead of the usual single cup with lots of cream and sugar. For those with a high tolerance, a cup of coffee can even encourage sleep. PET scans of habitual coffee drinkers showed that they needed to drink coffee to activate their brains but only to the level of someone who rarely drinks coffee (Reid, 2005).

Continuous caffeine use increases the number of adenosine receptor sites, so it takes more caffeine to block them; this is one of the main mechanisms for the development of tolerance (James, 1991). Withdrawal symptoms do occur after cessation of long-term high-dose use and can occur after levels of use as low as 100 mg per day, which is one strong cup of coffee or two colas. These symptoms appear in 12 to 24 hours, peak in 24 to 48 hours, and last two days to a week. **The most prominent withdrawal symptom is a throbbing headache** that is worsened by exercise but of course relieved by a cup of coffee. Other symptoms include **sleepiness, fatigue, lethargy, depression, decreased alertness, sleep problems, irritability, and even flulike symptoms of nausea, vomiting, and muscle pain or stiffness**. The subjects in one extensive experiment had withdrawal symptoms when ceasing an average intake of 235 mg per day, or two to three cups of coffee (Juliano & Griffiths, 2005).

Withdrawal symptoms are observed in newborns whose mothers have been drinking 200 to 1,800 mg per day. Irritability, jitteriness, and vomiting occurred an average of 20 hours after delivery, then disappeared (McGowan, Altman & Kanto, 1988).

Dependence can occur with daily intake levels of 500 mg (about 5 cups of coffee, 10 cola drinks, or 8 cups of tea) (Weinberg & Bealer, 2001). Coffee creates a milder dependency than is found with amphetamines and cocaine. It interferes less with daily functioning and is not as expensive as the stronger stimulants, although a $4 latte three times a day is pushing the limits. Two-thirds of those treated for excessive caffeine use (caffeinism) relapse after treatment.

Because 65% of the soft drinks sold in the United States contain caffeine, a question comes to mind: Why is it put in drinks? It's not for the flavor: one study found that **only 8% of soda drinkers could taste the presence of caffeine**; so it seems that colas, like coca wine, are popular because they stimulate the mind and the body (Griffiths & Vernotica, 2000). The concerns about soft drinks loaded not only with caffeine but also with large amounts of sugar led a number of school districts, particularly the Los Angeles School District, to restrict soda sales (Severson, 2002).

NICOTINE

"One of the sounds I remember from growing up in the forties and fifties was the sound of my dad's cigarette cough. It started deep in the lungs and ended in an explosion of air.

I could tell he was approaching from a block away. I just accepted it as a fact of life. He later became advertising director for American Tobacco just when the first Surgeon General's Report on Health and Tobacco was released in 1964. He gave up smoking in 1976 after retiring but died of throat cancer 17 years later, caused by his years of smoking [according to his oncologist]. Talk about mixed feelings . . . tobacco supported our family then took his life and those of millions of others."

William E. Cohen, co-author of *Uppers, Downers, All Arounders*

Nicotine is found in the leaves and other parts of a plant species belonging to the genus *Nicotiana,* a member of the deadly nightshade family that also includes tomatoes, belladonna, henbane, and petunias. There are 64 *Nicotiana* species, but **most commercial tobacco comes from the milder broad-leafed *Nicotiana tabacum* plant** and a number of its variants. Though tobacco is available in cigarettes, cigars, pipe tobacco, snuff, and chewing tobacco, **cigarettes account for 90% of all tobacco use in America.** In a country such as **India, chewing tobacco is more popular (85% of all men).** Whether it is smoked, chewed, absorbed through the gums, or even used as an enema, this stimulant ultimately affects many of the same areas of the brain as cocaine and amphetamines though not so intensely.

HISTORY

American Indians & Tobacco

Tobacco was venerated as a plant of the gods and used in spiritual and health rituals in ancient Mesoamerica (Mexico and parts of Central America), South America, and some Caribbean Islands. Civilizations such as the Maya (2500 B.C.), Zapotec (1700 B.C.), Aztecs (A.D. 1300), Incas (A.D. 1300), Arawaks (A.D. 1400), and a dozen others—all cultivated and hybridized various species of *Nicotiana.* **The use of tobacco didn't reach Europe and Asia until the late 1400s.**

The explorers of the New World—Christopher Columbus, Amerigo Vespucci, and a number of other French, Portuguese, and Spanish adventurers—noticed that the American Indians "drank the smoke" of certain dried leaves and seemed to receive both stimulatory and sedative effects from the process (Heimann, 1960; O'Brien, Cohen, Evans, et al., 1992; Rätsch, 2005). Explorers, writers, and diplomats, such as Jean Nicot de Villemain, Ramon Pane, and Fernando Cortez, **introduced tobacco to Europe, where it was used for recreation and as a medicine.** It was listed as a cure for almost every known illness, including ulcerated abscesses, fistulas, and sores. (In this century it is listed as the *cause* of just as many diseases.) Use spread via sailors, who carried the leaves and the methods of use to Europe, Russia, Japan, Africa, and China in the 1600s and later to virtually every country in the world. **Originally, smoking tobacco in a pipe several times a day was the most common form of use, but in the eighteenth century chewing tobacco and using**

This lithograph by F. W. Fairholt is titled Les Fumeurs et les Priseurs, *or* Smokers and Snuff Users. *He did this woodcut and others for his 1859 book* Tobacco: Its History and Associations.

snuff became popular in Europe and America. Smokeless tobacco remained the preferred method of use until the end of World War I (Benowitz & Fredericks, 1995).

Growth of Cigarette Smoking

As with most other psychoactive drugs, technical and social developments greatly increased the use of tobacco and allowed the accumulation of the active psychoactive ingredients (particularly nicotine) in users:

◇ **improved cigarette-manufacturing technology (cigarette rolling machine),**

◇ **a milder type of tobacco** that allowed for deeper inhalation and more-continuous use,

◇ **lower prices** due to mass production,

◇ **increased and more-skillful advertising,** and

◇ **more aggressive marketing techniques.**

For example, new marketing concepts during World Wars I and II initiated millions of GIs into smoking cigarettes. **Cigarette companies supplied free or cheap cigarettes to soldiers** in an effort to expand their markets. England even stockpiled cigarettes during World War II in case of invasion or an interruption in the supply. Interestingly, some of the reasons for the switch to cigarettes were worries about the health risks of smokeless tobacco, including the fear that chewing caused tuberculosis. In the nineteenth and early twentieth centuries, dread of tuberculosis was the equivalent of our present-day fear of cancer (O'Brien, Cohen, Evans, et al., 1992; Slade, 1992).

If a user smoked 40 cigarettes per year in the late 1800s, nicotine and tars were not the health problems they are today, when the **consumption of an average heavy smoker is 20 to 40 cigarettes per day, or more than 10,000 per year**. This new popularity of tobacco increased not only the number of smokers but also governmental income from excise taxes. Gross sales of tobacco products in the United States in 2005 were approximately $89 billion (U.S. Census Bureau, 2007). Although the

number of U.S. smokers has declined steadily since 2000, in 2004:

◇ **60.5 million Americans age 12 or older (24.9% of that population) smoked cigarettes in the past month,**

◇ 51 million (20.9% of adults) smoked cigarettes every day,

◇ 13.6 million smoked cigars,

◇ 2.2 million smoked tobacco in pipes, and

◇ 7.7 million used smokeless tobacco. (SAMHSA, 2006)

Smokeless Tobacco

The three types of smokeless tobacco (also referred to as "spitting tobacco") are moist snuff, powder snuff, and loose-leaf.

Moist snuff is finely chopped tobacco that is stuck in the mouth next to the gums, where the nicotine is absorbed into the capillaries. Popular brands are Copenhagen® and Skoal.® Moist snuff is the most popular form of smokeless tobacco in America. **Gutka is a form of moist snuff that is extremely popular in India.** It consists of betel nuts, betel leaves, tobacco paste, clove oil, glycerin, spearmint, menthol, and camphor. Gutka may have an even higher rate of health and cancer

problems associated with its use than American moist snuff.

Powder snuff (dry snuff) is a fine powder that is most often sniffed into the nose or rubbed on the gums. Stems and leaves of the tobacco plant are fermented, dried, and then ground into powder. Dry snuff is available as plain, toast (very dry), medicated (flavored with menthol, camphor, or eucalyptus), and scented, as well as a German variety called *schmalzler.* American snuff is more coarsely ground and is meant to be "dipped," or applied to the gums for absorption. Today sniffing snuff is not nearly as popular as smoking or chewing tobacco. This method of use is irritating to mucosal tissues and deadens the sense of smell.

With loose-leaf chewing tobacco, larger sections of leaf are stuffed into the mouth and chewed to allow the nicotine-laden juice to be absorbed. It comes in three forms; twist, plug, and scrap. Brands include Beech-Nut® and Red Man.® There were approximately 7.7 million regular smokeless-tobacco users in the United States in 2005, with sales of more than $1 billion (SAMHSA, 2006). Chewing tobacco and snuff are used by some professional and amateur male athletes in America for both the stimulation and the calming effect.

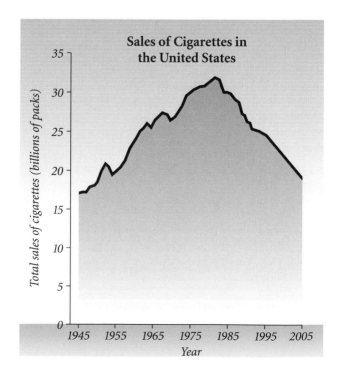

Figure 3-4 •
Sales of cigarettes have climbed from 18 billion packs per year in 1945 to a peak of 32 billion packs per year in 1985. By 2006 U.S. sales had dropped to 18.9 billion packs.

Three forms of smokeless tobacco are powder snuff on the left, loose-leaf chewing tobacco in the middle, and moist snuff on the right. More than 120 million lbs. of chewing tobacco and snuff were sold in the United States last year—20 lbs. per user.

© 2007 CNS Productions, Inc.

●●●

PHARMACOLOGY

Nicotine

Nicotine is the crucial ingredient in tobacco in terms of cardiovascular and psychoactive effects. The average tobacco leaf (*Nicotiana tabacum*) contains 2% to 5% nicotine, a bitter, smelly, colorless, and highly poisonous alkaloid that, when mixed in water, is a powerful insecticide. Smoking and inhaling a cigarette delivers nicotine to the brain in 5 to 8 seconds. Chewing tobacco or placing snuff on the gums delivers the nicotine in 3 to 8 minutes.

◇ **The average cigarette contains 10 mg of nicotine but delivers only 1 to 3 mg of that to the lungs** when burned and inhaled. Chain smokers might get up to 6 mg in their lungs before rapid distribution and metabolism put a damper on high blood-nicotine levels. About 70 mg ingested at one time is fatal.

◇ In comparison **one chew of tobacco will deliver approximately 4.5 mg of nicotine, and one pinch of snuff has about 3.6 mg**.

◇ The actual blood-nicotine level of one cigarette is measured as approximately 25 micrograms per liter of blood (25 µg/L). The average smoker will maintain a nicotine level of 5 to 40 µg/L, depending on the time of day (Schmitz & DeLaune, 2005).

◇ **The nicotine in the first cigarette of the day raises the heart rate by an average of 10 to 20 beats per minute and the blood pressure by 5 to 10 units.**

The effects of nicotine are the main reason for the widespread use of tobacco. **Nicotine, a central nervous system stimulant, disrupts the balance of neurotransmitters (endorphins, epinephrine, dopamine, and particularly acetylcholine). Acetylcholine** affects heart rate, blood pressure, memory, learning, reflexes, aggression, sleep, sexual activity, and mental acuity. Nicotine mimics acetylcholine by slotting into nicotinic acetylcholine receptor sites, so those cholinergic effects are exaggerated. The release of dopamine makes a smoker feel satisfied and calm, so **a cigarette both stimulates and tranquilizes**.

"Cigarettes calm me down, although they don't give me a rush or high like coke or even marijuana. I think what they do is satisfy my nicotine need; and since I can't smoke in the house anymore, it gets me away from the kids. Also, it's something I can do by myself."
39-year-old female pack-a-day smoker

Reasons for Continued Use

Besides the mildly pleasurable effects that smokers receive from tobacco, some of the reasons for continuing to smoke include the:

◇ **social context** (the ubiquitous smoke break at work, after meals, or after sex),
◇ **ritual aspects** of lighting up and smoking,
◇ perception of smoking as an **adult activity**,
◇ **desire to manipulate mood**,
◇ desire to **be rebellious**, and
◇ perception that smoking is **sexually attractive**.

The two most important reasons why people continue to smoke, however, have to do with weight loss and, above all, craving.

Weight Loss.   Nicotine suppresses appetite and increases metabolism. On average, smokers weigh 6 to 9 lbs. less than nonsmokers (Klesges, Meyers, Klesges, et al., 1989; Schmitz & DeLaune, 2005). Because withdrawal from smoking is often accompanied by weight gain, the **fear of putting on pounds can keep smokers from quitting** or cause relapse when they do quit. A hypothesis about weight gain is that nicotine raises the metabolic rate to burn more calories and lowers the inherited weight setpoint (Chen, Hansen, Jones, et al., 2006; Perkins, 1993).

Research also finds smoking to be a way to self-medicate depression. Major depression occurs two times as often in smokers than in nonsmokers

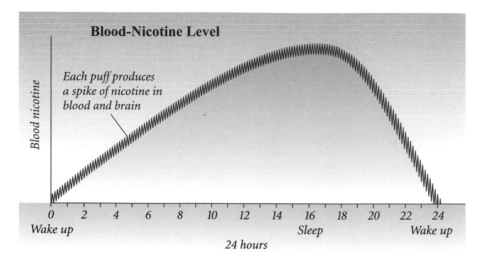

Blood-Nicotine Level

Each puff produces a spike of nicotine in blood and brain

Blood nicotine

0   2   4   6   8   10   12   14   16   18   20   22   24
Wake up   Sleep   Wake up

24 hours

Figure 3-5 •

This chart shows the change in blood-nicotine levels in a heavy smoker for a 24-hour period. Notice how the overnight drop in the blood level might lead to that intense craving for a cigarette and a cup of coffee first thing in the morning.

(6.6% to 2.7%). Smokers who have had at least one episode of major depression are less likely to succeed in tobacco cessation than those who haven't (14% to 28%) (Schmitz & DeLaune, 2005).

Craving.   An intense desire to maintain a certain nicotine level in the blood and the brain to avoid withdrawal symptoms is the biggest reason why people continue to smoke. In addition, the authors believe that **the very act of relieving withdrawal symptoms can activate the nucleus accumbens, inducing a certain sense of reward.** This same effect has been postulated for a certain rush that comes from reversing heroin/opioid withdrawal by using (Goldstein, 2001).

"It calms me down. Now I think I'm not sure if it's mostly the calm or just the fact of getting rid of the stress of having a nicotine fit . . . keeping the nicotine levels up to a point where I don't stress out, or freak out, or bitch at anybody, or yell, or scratch their eyes out."

20-year smoker

Continued use of a drug to avoid negative effects of withdrawal is known as *negative drug reinforcement.*

TOLERANCE, WITHDRAWAL & ADDICTION

Tolerance

Physiological adaptation to the initial effects of nicotine develops quite rapidly, some say even faster than with heroin or cocaine. A few hours of smoking are sufficient for the body to begin learning how to handle these new toxins, probably through neural adaptation. As with users of other drugs, **smokers say that the first hit in the morning is the best as they raise their nicotine level back up.** Smokers who have quit and then start again initially feel the dizziness and nausea of a novice user.

"The first time I smoked, it was to impress a girl. I got dizzy and high and had to sit down. A year later my thirtieth cigarette of the day gave me only a mild stimulation, a fit of coughing, and then a calm. Now all I have left is the cough, withdrawal relief, and a bunch of smoking rituals, and it costs five bucks a pack."

Two-pack-a-day smoker

Once smokers adapt to the initial effects of tobacco, they find a level of

smoking that they can maintain over time, so the **tolerance does not continue to build as it does with amphetamines or benzodiazepines**. One study showed that regular smokers who increased their average intake by only 50% experienced dizziness, nausea, vomiting, headache, and dysphoria (Collins, 1990).

Withdrawal

Withdrawal from a one-pack- or two-pack-a-day habit after prolonged use can cause **headaches, nervousness, fatigue, hunger, severe irritability, poor concentration, depression, increased appetite, sleep disturbances, and intense nicotine craving.** The severity of these symptoms is the main cause of relapse during smoking cessation (Xian, Scherrer & Madden, 2005). A true physiological dependence has developed through rapid tissue and chemical alterations in the brain. One causal process is the creation of more acetylcholine receptors, particularly the nicotinic receptors; so when a smoker stops using tobacco, the activity of acetylcholine is greatly exaggerated by all these extra activated receptors, making the user restless, irritable, and discontent (Stein, Pankiewicz, Harsch, et al., 1998). Soon **the smoker comes to depend on smoking to stay normal**, that is, to avoid these withdrawal effects. Research has demonstrated that abrupt withdrawal from nicotine results in a significant dampening of the brain's reward function, an effect that lasts for days (Epping-Jordan, Watkins, Koob, et al., 1998). The resultant lack of a reward function drives a person to crave nicotine when use is discontinued.

The sense of relaxation and well-being that most smokers receive from a cigarette is, in fact, the sensation of the withdrawal symptoms' being subdued. For this reason smokers try to maintain a constant level of nicotine in the bloodstream and the brain. Even when smokers switch to a low-tar and low-nicotine brand, they often increase the number of cigarettes they smoke to maintain their target nicotine levels. In fact, nicotine craving may last a lifetime.

Addiction

"I cannot refrain from a few words of protest against the astounding fashion lately introduced from America, a sort of smoke-tippling, which enslaves its victims more completely than any other form of intoxication, old or new. These madmen will swallow and inhale with incredible eagerness, the smoke of a plant they call 'herba Nicotiana,' or tobacco."

German ambassador to The Hague, 1627

The use of tobacco is a pure example of the addictive process. The pleasure received from the direct effects of smoking is not as intense as the initial pleasure derived from alcohol, cocaine, or almost any other psychoactive drug. For almost all novice smokers, the negative feelings from early tobacco use outweigh any perceived pleasurable ones. Nicotine addicts rarely identify their very first use of tobacco as pleasurable.

"When I counsel recovering cocaine or heroin addicts, they can describe the high they got early on in their drug-using history; they can go on and on describing the rush and the euphoria. But when I ask them to describe their tobacco high, they hem and haw and say that after they got used to the coughing, dizziness, headache, and even nausea, they got a mild stimulation or calming effect. And yet nicotine is considered to be just as addicting as heroin."

Darryl Inaba, Pharm.D., co-author of Uppers, Downers, All Arounders

The cost of a two-pack-a-day habit can run $2,920 per year at $4 a pack or, in New York City, $5,475 at $7.50 a pack. The health problems and the premature deaths that result from smoking are too numerous to mention, and yet people continue to smoke. In fact, 80% of smokers believe that cigarette smoking causes cancer, yet they still smoke (Harris Poll, 1999).

One of the strongest indications of the addictive potential of tobacco can be seen when you look at the percentage of casual U.S. tobacco users who become compulsive users vs. the percentage of casual U.S. users of other psychoactive drugs who become compulsive users of those drugs:

◇ 23 million people have tried cocaine; about 600,000 are weekly users (2.6%), but only a tiny fraction of cocaine users do it on a daily basis.

◇ 72 million people have tried marijuana, but only 6.8 million use it weekly (9.4%), and only a fraction on a daily basis.

◇ 198 million people have tried alcohol, yet fewer than 48 million drink on a weekly basis (27%), and only 20 million drink on a daily basis (11%).

◇ 162 million people have smoked cigarettes; 60 million have smoked in the past month (37%), and 37 million smoke on a daily basis (22.7%).

(SAMHSA, 2006)

These figures mean that **almost one-fourth of those who ever tried a cigarette became daily habitual users compared with one-tenth of alcohol experimenters who become daily abusers.** And yet people continue to experiment with cigarettes.

Granted you might say that people want to keep using cigarettes because smoking is really pleasurable and that the choice is theirs; however, according to one survey, **80% of smokers interviewed say they want to quit, and another 10% say they want to limit the amount they smoke**. That means that 9 out of 10 smokers are unhappy with their smoking yet they continue to smoke. Only in the past few years have tobacco companies started to admit that nicotine is indeed addicting. In fact, in the past 10 years, the percentage of nicotine in cigarettes has actually increased.

In many countries the rate of daily use is even higher than in the United States: 50% in China, 40% in England, and 50% in Japan (WHO, 1997). In a British study, 90% of the teenagers who had smoked just three or four cigarettes at the time of the survey were found to be compulsive smokers years later. This statistic means that even the most casual use of tobacco usually leads to compulsive use. And yet people continue to smoke. Globally, 12% of women and 47% of men smoke.

It is worth noting that nicotine craving is much subtler and less noticeable to the user than cocaine, heroin, or alcohol craving, but the craving is nevertheless extremely powerful and may be associated with what is called a "self-determined nicotine state of consciousness" or "state dependence."

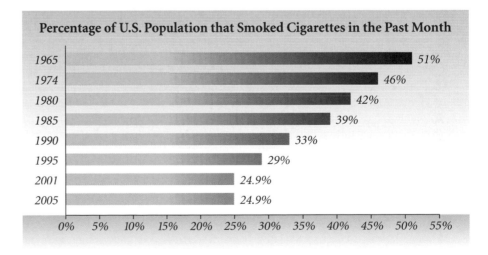

Percentage of U.S. Population that Smoked Cigarettes in the Past Month

Year	Percentage
1965	51%
1974	46%
1980	42%
1985	39%
1990	33%
1995	29%
2001	24.9%
2005	24.9%

Figure 3-6 •

Smoking rates in most other countries are higher than in the United States.

(National Household Survey on Drug Abuse, 2006)

State dependence means that people will try to achieve a certain mental and physical state that may be neither pleasurable nor objectionable but it is a state with which they are familiar and one that they, and not others, have determined.

Recent research indicates that **there may be a genetic predisposition to nicotine addiction** that makes tobacco use harder to stop for some than for others (Xian, Scherrer & Madden, 2005). One of the suspect genes is the same reward pathway gene—$DRD_2 A_1$ allele—implicated in predisposition to alcoholism and other drug addictions (Spitz, 1998). This discovery may also help explain why smoking cigarettes is so closely connected to the abuse of other drugs. Teen surveys have found that an adolescent smoker is 3 times more likely to also abuse alcohol, 8 times more likely to abuse marijuana, and a staggering 22 times more likely to abuse cocaine than nonsmoking teens (Schmitz & DeLaune, 2005). Scientists have also located one of the key proteins in the nicotine receptor (the acetylcholine receptor beta 2 subunit) that seems to be responsible for the positive-reinforcement properties of nicotine. When the scientists developed a strain of mice without the key protein (one of the 10 proteins that form the nicotinic receptor), the mice had no desire to self-administer nicotine on a regular basis. Even when injected with nicotine, the level of the calming/reinforcing neurotransmitter dopamine did not increase (NIDA, 2000; Zickler, 2005).

EPIDEMIOLOGY

One interesting note, in 1994 only 5% of Black high school seniors said they smoked on a daily basis compared with 10.6% for Hispanics and 23% for Whites. In focus groups children said such things as "Smoking hurts stamina for sports," "Boys don't like girls who smoke," and "We believed the media about the dangers of cigarettes." But a 2000 survey found that the rate for Black teenagers had risen to 8%; for Hispanics, 15.7%; and for Whites, 25.7% (Monitoring the Future, 2002).

Smokeless-tobacco use in the past month among twelfth-graders dropped from 12.2% in 1995 to 7.6% in 2005;

TABLE 3–4 CIGARETTE USE IN THE UNITED STATES—2005

Age	Ever Used	Used Past Year	Used Past Month
12-17	6.8 million	4.4 million	2.7 million
18-25	21.9 million	15.3 million	12.7 million
26 and older	133.2 million	51.1 million	45.1 million
Totals	**161.9 million**	**70.8 million**	**60.5 million**

National Survey on Drug Use and Health 2005 (SAMHSA, 2006)

TABLE 3–5 SMOKELESS TOBACCO USE IN THE UNITED STATES—2005

Gender	Ever Used	Used Past Year	Used Past Month
Male	38.1 million	9.5 million	7.2 million
Female	6.7 million	0.9 million	0.5 million
Totals	**44.8 million**	**10.4 million**	**7.7 million**

National Survey on Drug Use and Health 2005 (SAMHSA, 2006)

for tenth-graders those figures decreased from 9.7% to 5.6% (Monitoring the Future, 2006).

SIDE EFFECTS

The process of smoking exposes one to many toxic substances, not just nicotine. **Tobacco contains some 4,000 to 4,800 chemicals; 400 are toxins, and 69 are known cancer-causing substances** (e.g. cadmium, hydrogen cyanide, vinyl chloride, toluene, benzene, and arsenic) (Hoffmann, Hoffmann & El-Bayoumy, 2001). When tobacco is burned in a cigarette or cigar, the smoke consists of fine particles and droplets of tar (a blackish substance that has direct effects on the respiratory system) and nitrosamines (some of which are carcinogenic) (Glantz, 1992; Hecht, 2001). It is inevitable that some of these toxins will have adverse effects on the body. The large body of research regarding the health effects of smoking is second only to that on the health effects of alcohol.

Worldwide **in 2000 tobacco smoking was estimated to cause 5 million premature deaths** (Ezzati & Lopez, 2004). This figure will increase to 8.4 million annually by 2020. In China alone about 3 million smokers (mostly men) will die prematurely each year by the middle of this century (WHO, 2002).

It is estimated that in the United States 392,000 smokers die prematurely (264,000 men, 178,000 women). Most of these deaths are from lung cancer, heart disease, and lung disease. **Another 50,000 nonsmokers die from secondhand smoke.** (U.S. Surgeon General, 2004; Centers for Disease Control and Prevention [CDC], 2006).

About 8.6 million U.S. residents have at least one serious illness caused by smoking, meaning that for every smoking-related death, 20 more live a lower quality of life due to cigarettes.

The main reason for the extremely high figures is that it often takes 20, 30, or even 40 years for tobacco's most dangerous effects to become lethal. Most people who die from smoking have been using for more than 20 years, so the immediate warning signs of overdose—heart palpitations, blackouts, hangovers, rage, paranoia, and nausea—common with other psychoactive drugs are missing. Except for the coughing, dizziness, initial nausea, bad breath, green mucous, lowered lung capacity, and lowered energy levels, there are no immediate flashing warning signs. **Recognizing the warning signs of cocaine, heroin, or alcohol** use is a very visceral, very immediate process. Those of tobacco are very subtle and slow. The dangerous side effects weigh directly against the pleasure received. With tobacco that craving can be countered only by an intellectual appreciation of the long-term dangers. In most cases, the craving and the fear of withdrawal win out over common sense.

In 2004 Surgeon General Richard Carmona reported that **smoking costs the United States about $157 billion each year in health-related economic losses** (U.S. Surgeon General, 2004). This works out to more than $7.18 for each pack sold, or $3,391 per smoker per year.

Longevity

"It might be shortening my life, and I don't breath as well. I love to hike and that's difficult. I get short of breath too easily. Get dizzy. I want to be around when my kids get older, my future grandchild. I'd like to be around, and these don't seem to be conducive to that."

Female 20-year smoker

The exceptional healthy 75-year-old smoker should not be seen as confirmation that smoking won't shorten life or impair health. One has to look at the overall statistics. On average, adult male smokers lose 13.2 years of life; adult female smokers lose 14.5 years of life (CDC, 2006; U.S. Surgeon General, 2004). **Internationally and in the United States, the average life span loss to those smokers who die in middle age (before the age of 70) will be 22 years** (WHO, 2002). In the most extensive study of smoking mortality, British researchers who had followed a group of 35,000 doctors found that, on average, smokers lost 10 years of their lives (Doll, Peto, Boreham, et al., 2004).

Almost as important as these premature-death statistics is the issue of quality of life. Because of breathing difficulties, poor circulation, and a dozen other imbalances caused by tobacco, a smoker will be less able to participate in physical activity and will be unable to live life to the fullest.

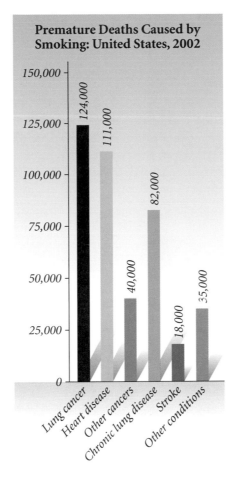

Premature Deaths Caused by Smoking: United States, 2002

Figure 3-7 •

Total estimated premature deaths caused by smoking is 442,000. (25,000 additional misceellaneous deaths)

(CDC, 2006)

Cardiovascular Effects

Smoking accelerates the process of plaque formation and hardening of the arteries (atherosclerosis), the major cause of heart attacks, by increasing low-density fats, increasing blood coagulability, and triggering cardiac arrhythmias (irregular heartbeat). The inhaled carbon monoxide created by tobacco combustion also accelerates the process of atherosclerosis. In addition, because nicotine constricts blood vessels, it restricts blood flow and raises blood pressure, increasing the risk of a stroke (ruptured/blocked blood vessel in the brain). The combination of nicotine and carbon monoxide also increases the risk of angina attacks (heart pain).

In 2005 in the United States, **one-third of the deaths from smoking-**related illnesses were due to cardiovascular disease; 35,000 of those cardiovascular deaths were from secondhand smoke (American Heart Association, 2006). Worldwide 11% of all cardiovascular deaths are due to smoking (Ezzati, Henley, Thun, et al., 2005).

"Probably 30% to 40% of my patients have a significant smoking history. The main problem is atherosclerosis, or hardening of the arteries; . . . even a few cigarettes a day will insult the linings of the arteries. The more smoking, the more blockage. People think that only a few cigarettes a day won't hurt, but the opposite is true. One of the reasons is that artery blockage does not progress little by little up to a blocked artery, resulting in a heart attack. <u>The truth is usually that 80% of heart attacks start as only a 20% blockage in the morning, but the plaque on the wall of the artery ruptures, causing this debris to block the artery completely.</u> Because coronary arteries are so small, they are often the first to be blocked, but atherosclerosis forms in carotid arteries, renal arteries, and femoral arteries. Even a few cigarettes a day raises the risk of death or heart attack more than 400%. Incidentally, the other biggest risk factor is diabetes, most often caused by overeating. No smoking, good nutrition, and a little exercise and my patient load drops drastically."

Kent W. Dauterman, M.D., FACC, chief of cardiology, Rogue Valley Medical Center, Medford, OR

Respiratory Effects

Cigarette smokers have a much higher rate of bronchopulmonary disease, such as **emphysema, chronic bronchitis, and chronic obstructive pulmonary disease (COPD)**. Children who live with smokers have a much higher incidence of asthma, colds, and bronchitis from inhaling secondhand smoke. Finally, environmental pollu-

(a)

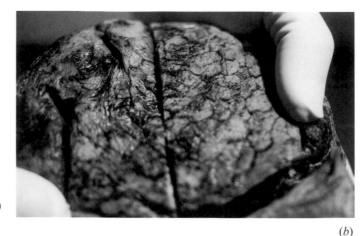

(b)

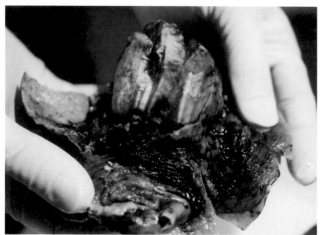

(c)

A normal lung (a) is pink and spongy. It is protected by the rib cage from external damage. Smoking deposits tar, other chemicals, and irritants in the alveoli (air sacs) and destroys the cilia (fine hairs lining the membranes) that help remove foreign particles. The smoker's lung (b) is blackened by these deposits. Many of the chemicals in tobacco, particularly the tar, cause cancer (c). More than 100,000 people die prematurely from tobacco-induced lung cancer every year.

Courtesy of Leslie Parr, Ph.D.

tants, such as asbestos and volatile chemicals, greatly increase the rates of respiratory illness and cancer in smokers above the levels due to exposure from just smoking alone or just breathing dirty air. **Approximately 80% to 90% of COPD deaths (from emphysema and chronic bronchitis) are due to smoking** (American Lung Association, 2006). Worldwide, 650,000 deaths from COPD are attributable to smoking (Ezzati & Lopez, 2004).

Cancer

The increase in lung cancer since the 1930s, when the use of cigarettes started to accelerate, is startling. The rate has gone up ninefold in women and 15-fold in men. Figure 3-8 juxtaposes the per-capita smoking rate from 1930 with the present alongside the per-capita death rate from lung cancer. In 1988 lung cancer deaths in women surpassed deaths from breast cancer for the first time in history. According to the American Cancer Society:

◇ **Men who smoke are 22 times more likely to develop lung cancer than men who don't.**

◇ **Women who smoke are 12 times more likely to develop lung cancer than women who don't.**

◇ **About 85% of men with lung cancer and 75% of women with lung cancer smoke.**

◇ In 1979 in the United States, women composed 26% of lung cancer deaths; by 2002 that number had grown to 42.8%.

(American Cancer Society 2006; American Lung Association, 2006).

An estimated 1.42 million cancer deaths (1.18 million men and 0.24 million women) occurred worldwide, and 21% of these were caused by smoking (Ezzati, Henley, Lopez, et al., 2005).

The most likely **culprits are the tars and other byproducts of combustion that the smoker inhales**. Studies at the University of California at Los Angeles show that precancerous alterations in

bronchial epithelium can occur not only from habitual cigarette smoking but also from habitual smoking of crack cocaine and marijuana, particularly if cigarettes are also being used (Barsky, Roth, Kleerup, et al., 1998; Tashkin, 2005). Pipe and cigar smokers are less likely than cigarette smokers to get lung cancer but are more likely than nonsmokers to get not only lung cancer but also cancers of the larynx, mouth, and esophagus.

Fetal Effects

When mothers smoke during pregnancy, the newborns have the same nicotine level as grown-up smokers. About 15% of pregnant women smoke during the nine-month gestation period, so when they give birth their babies go through withdrawal. The carbon monoxide and nicotine in tobacco smoke reduces the oxygen-carrying capacity of a pregnant mother's blood, so **less oxygen gets to the baby, contributing to a somewhat lower birth weight and a higher incidence of crib**

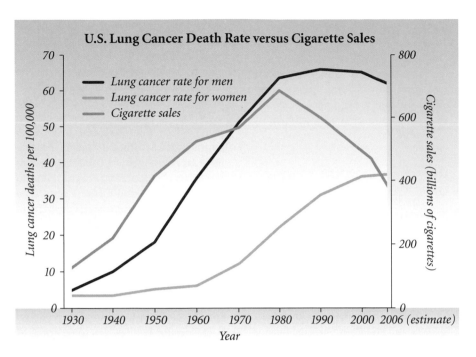

U.S. Lung Cancer Death Rate versus Cigarette Sales

— Lung cancer rate for men
— Lung cancer rate for women
— Cigarette sales

Figure 3-8 •

Because it takes 10 to 40 years for lung cancer to develop, there is a delay in decreasing rates of lung cancer even though cigarette sales among men have been declining for a number of years.

death (SIDS). Research indicates that women who smoke heavily during pregnancy are **twice as likely to miscarry and have spontaneous abortions as nonsmokers**. In one study the offspring of mothers who smoked during pregnancy were four times more likely to have ADHD (Milberger, Biederman, Faraone, et al., 1998). There was also an increased risk of early-onset conduct disorder and even drug dependence (Weissman, Warner, Wickramaratne, et al., 1999). An extensive Russian study found that prenatal smoking increased asthma, chronic bronchitis, and chronic respiratory symptoms in later life. The effect of secondhand smoke when the child was older was not as great (Jaakkola, Kosheleva, Katsnelson, et al., 2006).

The 2004 Surgeon General's report concluded that evidence is sufficient to infer a causal relationship between sudden infant death syndrome, fetal growth restriction, low birth weight, premature rupture of membranes, placenta previa, placental abruption, preterm delivery, and shortened gestation with maternal active smoking during and after pregnancy. Smoking was also found to reduce fertility in women (U.S. Surgeon General, 2004).

Smokeless-Tobacco Effects

Tobacco is as addicting in its smokeless form as in its smoked form even though the nicotine takes three to five minutes to affect the central nervous system when chewed or pouched in the cheek compared with the seven to 10 seconds it takes when inhaled from a cigarette. But more nicotine reaches the bloodstream and the brain with smokeless tobacco (4 mg or more) than by smoking a cigarette (1 to 3 mg), and the rush is somewhat more intense because **many smokeless-tobacco products have more nicotine, and more tobacco is used when chewing or dipping**. Smokeless tobaccos are also formulated with a higher pH that promotes passage into the capillaries, and they have a greater concentration of freebase nicotine to pass into the brain. Dipping snuff eight to 10 times per day has been found to put as much nicotine in the body as smoking 30 to 40 cigarettes (Mayo Clinic, 2001). The **effects of chewing are almost identical to the effects of smoking**, including a slight increase in energy, alertness, blood pressure, and heart rate.

The main advantage of smokeless

tobacco over cigarettes is the protection it gives the lungs because no smoke is inhaled. Lung cancer rates and other respiratory problems drop dramatically. There are, however, other problems just as severe with smokeless tobacco.

"I can't think of a more disgusting habit than chewing tobacco. I broke up with my boyfriend because he was always dripping tobacco juice, spitting, and had those awful brown stains on his clothing. Ugh."
17-year-old high school student

Smokeless tobacco is irritating to the tissues of the mouth and the digestive tract. Many users experience leukoplakia, a thickening, whitening, and hardening of the tissues in the mouth. **Their gums can become inflamed, causing more dental problems**; and although the risk of lung cancer is reduced compared with smoking, **the risks of oral, pharyngeal, and esophageal cancers are increased**. In addition, because blood vessels are constricted by nicotine whether chewing or smoking, circulatory and cardiovascular problems are just as grave with smokeless tobacco. One study found that dry snuff has a higher oral cancer risk than wet snuff or chewing tobacco (Rodu & Cole, 2002). Data presented by the American Cancer Society indicates that **chronic snuff users are up to 50 times more at risk to develop cheek and gum cancer** than nonusers. It is estimated that 27,260 new cases of oral cancers were diagnosed in the United States during 2004 (American Cancer Society, 2006).

BENEFITS FROM QUITTING

A surprising number of beneficial physiological changes occur upon quitting smoking:

◇ Within 20 minutes of quitting, blood pressure and pulse rate drop to normal as does the temperature of the hands and feet.

◇ Within 8 hours carbon monoxide level drops and oxygen levels increase, both to normal.

◇ Within 24 hours the risk of a sudden heart attack decreases.

◇ Within 48 hours nerve endings adjust to the absence of nicotine, and the senses of smell and taste begin to return.

◇ Within 1 week the risk of heart attack drops, breathing improves, and constricted blood vessels begin to relax.

◇ Within 2 to 12 weeks, **circulation improves, lung function increases up to 30%, and the complexion looks healthy again**.

◇ Within 1 to 9 months, fatigue, coughing, sinus congestion, and shortness of breath decrease, and the lungs increase their ability to handle mucus, thereby reducing the chance of infection.

◇ Within 1 year the risk of coronary heart disease is half that of someone who is still smoking.

◇ Within 5 years the heart disease death rate returns to that for a nonsmoker, the lung cancer death rate decreases 50% compared with a pack-a-day smoker, and risk of mouth cancer is half that of a tobacco user.

◇ Within 10 years the lung cancer death rate drops almost to that for a nonsmoker, precancerous cells are replaced, and the incidence of other cancers decreases. Risk of stroke is lowered to that of someone who never smoked.

◇ **Within 10 to 15 years, the risk of all major diseases caused by smoking decreases to nearly that of someone who never smoked.**

(Glantz, 1992; Mets, Gregersen & Malhotra, 2004).

The potential benefits to the lungs of quitting may not be as great for someone who started smoking as a teenager. Studies have shown that smoking in teenagers caused permanent genetic DNA damage to their lung cells, leaving them forever at increased risk for lung cancer even if they quit; if they stop, however, that risk still drops. Such damage was less likely among users who started smoking in their twenties (Wiencke, Thurston, Kelsey, et al., 1999).

Mentally there are other beneficial changes:

◇ Initially, there is anxiety, anger, difficulty concentrating, increased appetite, and craving due to withdrawal.

◇ After two weeks most of these side effects disappear with the exception of craving and appetite control. Unfortunately, even years later, the nicotine addict is still extremely vulnerable to relapse.

THE TOBACCO INDUSTRY & TOBACCO ADVERTISING

The Business of Tobacco

In 2005 U.S. cigarette sales were at their lowest point in 55 years, about 18.9 billion packs. **Recognizing the decline in American sales over the past 30 years, tobacco companies have tried to increase sales overseas.** Cigarette and smokeless-tobacco use is growing 3% per year in developing countries, raising the number of people who use tobacco worldwide to 1.3 billion. U.S. exports of cigarettes rose to 250 billion by 1996 and have remained high ever since (Maxwell Report, 2004; U.S. Surgeon General, 2004).

In the United States, just a handful of companies control the tobacco market. Philip Morris (Marlboro,® Virginia Slims,® and Basic®), R.J. Reynolds/Nabisco® (Winston,® Camel,® and Salem®), Lorillard (Newport®), American Brands (Carlton,® Lucky Strike,® and Pall Mall®), British American Tobacco (Kool®), and U.S. Tobacco (Copenhagen® and Skoal®) account for more than 95% of sales.

Because of the ever-increasing cost of a pack of cigarettes, in the 1980s many manufacturers came out with generic brands that were cheaper (e.g., Basic® by Philip Morris). To win back some of that market, the big manufacturers also lowered the prices on name brands. In addition, in 2006 the tobacco companies came out with smokeless-tobacco products, for example Camel Snus® or Philip Morris's Taboka,® which contain 12 or so tobacco pouches that nicotine users stick in their cheeks to absorb the nicotine. Cynics say it is a way to keep the nicotine craving alive in those who are afraid of the health risks of smoking and inhaling carcinogens.

Another attempt to expand the market has taken the form of **hand-rolled bidi cigarettes**. These innocuous-looking cigarettes are made in India but are also sold in the United States. They are made of tobacco wrapped in a tendu or temburni leaf (plants native to Asia). The colorful packages seem aimed at children, mainly teenagers, and even come in flavors: grape, chocolate, and root beer to name a few. **The dark Indian tobacco contains three times as much nicotine as American-grown tobacco.** In one NIDA test, *bidi* smokers were found to have a higher blood-nicotine level than conventional smokers. Even carbon monoxide levels were higher in some of the *bidi* smokers. The *bidis* are sold for $1.50 to $3.50 for a pack of 20, often in "head shops" and health-food stores. **In India *bidis* account for about 70% of the tobacco that is smoked.** The Centers for Disease Control and Prevention (CDC) estimates that 2% to 5% of U.S. teens have tried *bidis*.

Kreteks (clove cigarettes), from Indonesia, contain a mixture of tobacco, cloves, and other additives. Like *bidis* they deliver more nicotine, carbon monoxide, and tar than conventional cigarettes (CDC, 2005).

Advertising

Advertising by the tobacco industry exceeds $13 billion per year including giveaways, premiums, promotional allowances to retailers, and other expenditures. Advertising works. As a result of the Joe Camel® advertising campaign, sales of Camel® cigarettes to teenage smokers ages 12 to 18 more than tripled over a five-year period while sales to adult Camel® smokers remained the same. The Joe Camel® campaign was finally dropped in July 1997 due to political and social pressure.

While the media focused on Joe Camel,® however, the most popular cigarette among teenagers has been Marlboro.® In 2004 sales of Marlboro® were greater than the next five leading brands combined. In national surveys it is the cigarette of choice for 50% of 12- to-17-year-old smokers, 53% of smokers 18 to 25, and 37% of smokers 26 and older. In 2004 the top cigarette markets shares were 39% for Marlboro,® 8% for Newport,® 6% for Camel,® 5% for Doral,® 4% for Winston,® and 4% for Basic® (Maxwell Report, 2004).

Ethnically, the differences in brand

Tobacco advertising has come a long way since this ad from the 1940s.

●●●●●●●●●●●●●●●●●

◇ *In your ads, create a situation taken from the day-to-day life of the young smoker but in an elegant manner have this situation touch on the basic symbols of the growing-up, maturity process.*

◇ *To the best of your ability (considering some legal constraints), relate the cigarette to 'pot,' wine, beer, sex, etc.*

◇ *Don't [their emphasis] communicate health or health-related points."*

In the early 1970s, the U.S. tobacco industry voluntarily agreed to a partial advertising ban rather than face a total ban or a requirement to surrender $1 for every $3 spent on advertising that the government would use to create antismoking advertisements. When done well, antismoking advertising is extremely effective. In the 1990s antitobacco ads in Arizona, California, Massachusetts, and Oregon reduced tobacco sales by 43%—about twice the national average. In Massachusetts $70 million spent on a prime-time TV antitobacco campaign resulted in a 20% drop in cigarette sales compared with a national-average drop of 3% (Soldz, Clark, Stewart, et al., 2002). Lung and bronchial cancer rates in California fell three times faster than the national average. The adult smoking rate has dropped from 23% to 16%; high school rates dropped from 22% to 13%. California spent $75 million on anti-tobacco advertising in 2005. **The tobacco industry spends $35 million per day on marketing nationwide. Part of that campaign has been an anti-smoking Web site by Philip Morris. Cynics suggest that the purpose of the site is to forestall even more effective antitobacco campaigns by state and federal governments.**

preferences are dramatic among 12- to 17-year-olds:

◇ **42.2% of Whites preferred Marlboro**® while only 16.5% preferred Newport®;

◇ **59.7% of Hispanics preferred Marlboro**® while only 18.6% preferred Newport®; and

◇ **43.9% of Blacks preferred Newport**® while only 8.1% preferred Marlboro.®
(SAMHSA, 2001)

Another target of cigarette advertising has been women. The tobacco companies did extensive research, and subsequent advertising directed at women emphasized longer, slimmer, and "healthier" cigarettes. Worldwide smoking rates for women are expected to increase 20% by 2025 even though rates for men have been falling.

Studies have shown that starting to smoke in the teen years is more addictive to the user than starting during adulthood. Smokers who begin young are also less likely to break the habit than adult-onset smokers, making the

teen market extremely attractive to cigarette manufacturers (Wiencke, Thurston, Kelsey, et al., 1999). **The CDC found that approximately 80% of adult smokers started smoking before the age of 18** (CDC, 2006). The significance of this statistic cannot be overemphasized in terms of prevention and addiction. Proof of this fact can be seen by the tobacco companies' emphasis on appealing to new, young smokers. For example, in a confidential memo a number of years ago one tobacco company advised its advertising department as follows:

"Thus, an attempt to reach young smokers, starters, should be based, among others, on the following major parameters:

◇ *Present the cigarette as one of a few initiations into the adult world.*

◇ *Present the cigarette as part of the illicit pleasure category of products and activities.*

Comprehensive bans that prohibit all tobacco advertising have had a significant effect on reducing tobacco consumption. Four countries that enacted such advertising bans on tobacco—Finland, France, New Zealand, and Norway—experienced a per-capita cigarette consumption drop of 14% to

37% (Luk, 2000). More and more countries are increasing limitations on where one can smoke. Even Cuba, well known for its cigars, banned smoking in public places in 2005.

Lawsuits & Laws

In 2004 the U.S. government filed a $280 billion racketeering case against the tobacco industry for allegedly misleading and defrauding the U.S. public for 50 years regarding the health consequences of cigarette smoking (Kaufman, 2004). A federal appeals court later ruled that the government cannot force the tobacco companies to turn over $280 billion in profits. The government was then expected to reduce the figure to $130 billion but instead, by 2006, reduced the amount to $10 billion over the objections of a number of health advocates and congressional representatives. The $10 billion was considered grossly inadequate for a national quit-smoking program it was supposed to finance over a 25-year period.

In 2006 the Oregon Supreme Court affirmed a $79.5 million award against Philip Morris brought by a smoker's widow. Philip Morris vowed to appeal the award again. **Lawsuits on behalf of dead or living smokers with cancer**

have been expanding and are being won (although all judgments are appealed). In 2005 the Canadian Supreme Court ruled that tobacco firms can be sued for health costs.

Because of the coughing and tearing caused by secondhand smoke, as well as actual documented health problems, numerous laws and statutes have been passed at the local, state, and federal levels prohibiting the use of tobacco products in a variety of spaces and buildings (e.g., sections of restaurants, airplanes, some businesses, and state and federal buildings).

From indifference to other peoples' habits in the early 1980s, to a powerful crusade in the 1990s, to a growing tide of legislation in the 2000s, public opinion toward smoking has changed. **Unfortunately, tobacco has long been exempt from laws protecting the health of Americans.** The principal law that has been superseded is the one stating that "no substance that causes cancer may be sold for human consumption." Congress exempted tobacco from this law. Tobacco companies have long been heavy contributors to federal and state legislators in hopes of stalling or delaying laws that would limit their profits (White, 1999). Given the addictive nature of tobacco, some think that such

contributions are the equivalent of marijuana or coca growers giving money to politicians to promote drug legalization.

By 1995 the FDA and the Clinton administration were ready for a full-scale assault on the tobacco industry. The administration said its goal was to cut teenage smoking in half by sharply curtailing "the deadly temptations of tobacco and its skillful marketing" by the industry. **The industry said the real aim of the antismoking forces and the new legislation was to outlaw smoking altogether.**

The biggest assault on tobacco companies has come from a number of lawsuits by state governments. Some suits are for the extra cost of health care due to smoking; others accuse the industry of manipulating nicotine levels to keep smokers addicted. Brown and Williamson, the nation's fifth-largest manufacturer (Chesterfield® and Eve®), settled a lawsuit in 1996 by agreeing to pay 5% of its pretax profits ($50 million per year) toward programs that help people stop smoking.

To resolve two major lawsuits and hopefully forestall further litigation, **the major tobacco companies agreed to $40 billion and $206 billion settlements** to help pay for the medical costs of tobacco-induced illnesses, to finance smoking-prevention campaigns (particularly aimed at teenagers), and to support other state programs. The money is to be paid over 25 years. Unfortunately, due to reduced state tax income in the early 2000s, **many state governments have redirected the money away from antismoking campaigns** and into general funds. In desperation several states decided to borrow against future moneys thus receiving only a percentage of the settlement. In 2001 each state received an average of $164 million from the settlement, but they distributed only 6% to tobacco-control programs instead of the 20% to 25% suggested by the CDC. States with the highest smoking rates tended to spend the least on these prevention efforts (Gross, 2002). In 2006 the tobacco companies withheld some of the funds because they said their sales were down.

Internationally, the European Union Health Ministers recently passed a ban on tobacco advertising on the radio, in print, and on the Internet. Tobacco ad-

vertising had already been banned on television. England and Germany objected to this new ban.

Secondhand Smoke

Besides the issue of the addictive nature of tobacco and nicotine, a key battle over secondhand smoke (the smoke that is inhaled by nonusers in a room with smokers) was begun in the 1990s. It is estimated that **one person dies from secondhand smoke (mostly from cardiovascular disease) for every eight smoker deaths, which works out to 40,000 to 50,000 death each year**. When the issue was first raised in the early 1980s, evidence was scant; but since that time the U.S. Surgeon General's office, the National Research Council, the Occupational Safety and Health Administration, and the International Agency for Research on Cancer have concluded that secondhand smoke does cause lung cancer, cardiovascular disease, and stroke. Other studies have connected secondhand smoke to other illnesses, including asthma and bronchitis in the children of smokers (SCOTH, 2004).

One of the reasons for the danger from secondhand smoke is that the sidestream smoke, mostly from a smoldering cigarette when the user is not inhaling, has higher concentrations of the substances, such as tar, that cause respiratory problems. So while secondhand smoke has small amounts of nicotine, it has up to 40 times the amount of carcinogens found in mainstream (inhaled) smoke (Schick & Glantz, 2005). Experience with bars and restaurants that banned smoking seems to bear out the health problems with secondhand smoke. In Ireland a study of bar and restaurant employees one year after a smoking ban took effect showed a 17% decline in respiratory ailments. In Northern Ireland, where there was no smoking ban, there was no drop in respiratory problems (Szabo, 2005).

In 1996 California; Utah; Vermont; Flagstaff, Arizona; New York City; and Boulder, Colorado, had banned smoking in all bars and restaurants despite warnings from the owners that business would drop. The results of a study showed that, in fact, revenues increased in four localities and stayed the same in

It is interesting to compare the warnings found on American cigarette packages and Canadian cigarette packages. The Canadians are willing to tell the complete truth about tobacco.

© 2002 CNS Productions, Inc.

four localities; in only one did the rate of increase slow down but not decrease (Glantz & Charlesworth, 1999). By 2005 only 18 of the 50 states had not enacted some form of workplace or public smoking ban (Smoke Free World, 2005).

THE 2004 SURGEON GENERAL'S REPORT ON HEALTH CONSEQUENCES OF SMOKING

The most recent Surgeon General's report on smoking acknowledges the effectiveness of efforts since the first report was released in 1964 to reverse the epidemic of lung cancer deaths in men. The overall proportion of adults who are current smokers has been reduced by half since 1965, but the rate of decline has slowed in recent years. The report quickly acknowledges, however, that **smoking remains the leading preventable cause of disease and death in the United States**. It documents that the number of diseases recognized to be caused by smoking continues to increase and concludes that **smoking is shown to harm nearly every organ of the body** and, in general, greatly diminishes any smoker's health. The Surgeon General goes on to

state that while the knowledge that smoking can adversely affect health has become widespread among the general public, the grave extent of those health risks remains poorly understood.

The 2004 report also reviewed current strategies to reduce tobacco use and agreed that the lack of progress in tobacco control is attributable more to the failure to implement proven strategies than to a lack of knowledge about what to do. Here are some of the strategies outlined in the 2000 Surgeon General's report:

◇ Educational strategies, conducted in conjunction with community and media-based activities, can postpone or prevent smoking onset in 20% to 40% of adolescents.

◇ Pharmacological treatment of nicotine addiction combined with behavioral support will enable 20% to 25% of users to remain abstinent at one year post treatment. Even less intense measures, such as physicians' advising their patients to quit smoking, can produce cessation proportions of 5% to 10%.

◇ Regulation of advertising and promotion, particularly that directed at young persons, is very likely to reduce both the onset and the overall prevalence of smoking.

◇ Clean-air regulations and restriction of minors' access to tobacco products contribute to a changing social norm with regard to smoking and may influence prevalence directly.

(U.S. Surgeon General, 2000)

CONCLUSIONS

Stimulants seem like all-American drugs because initially they mimic virtues that are highly prized in our culture: alertness, confidence, aggression, mental acuity, and the ability to work hard and stay up late. Americans want a cup of coffee or a cigarette to wake up; more coffee at work to get going; a cola or energy drink in the afternoon to carry on; an OTC product or prescription diet pill to suppress the appetite; a snort of methamphetamine to make the work less boring; a daily dose of Ritalin® to keep the kids in line; and a "rock" of crack to bring out the party animal. Instant energy, confidence, and gratification are sought.

Compare the use of stimulants to gain energy and confidence with natural methods, where energy supplies are replenished through sleep, naps, relaxation, light morning exercise, good nutrition, and, in general, a healthy lifestyle. The natural methods create the energy supplies before they are used and allow them to be replenished. The chemical methods drain the body of its energy supplies, so it has to shut down to recover. The natural methods work time after time. The chemical methods cause tolerance and psychological dependence to develop, so the resulting excess use damages neurochemistry and most body systems.

CHAPTER SUMMARY

General Classification

1. Uppers are central nervous system (CNS) stimulants.

2. The seven principal stimulants are cocaine (including crack), amphetamines, amphetamine congeners (e.g., Ritalin® and diet pills), look-alike and over-the-counter stimulants, miscellaneous plant stimulants, caffeine, and nicotine.

General Effects

3. By increasing chemical and electrical activity in the central nervous system, stimulants increase energy and raise heart rate, blood pressure, and respiration; they make the user less hungry and more alert, active, confident, anxious, restless, and aggressive.

4. The stronger stimulants are used clinically to treat narcolepsy, obesity, and attention-deficit/hyperactivity disorder (ADHD).

5. Uppers cause many of their effects by forcing the release of energy chemicals (particularly norepinephrine and epinephrine). Serotonin and dopamine also affect energy and feelings.

6. Most problems with stimulants occur when the body isn't given time to recover and its energy supply becomes depleted. The user can fall into a severe depression.

7. Another set of problems with the stronger stimulants comes when the overstimulated reward/reinforcement pathway does not signal the need for food, drink, or sexual stimulation, resulting in malnutrition, dehydration, or a reduced sex drive.

8. Because stimulants reduce appetite, almost all of them are used to lose weight. Excess use can cause various health problems.

9. Cardiovascular side effects can include high blood pressure, weakened blood vessels, heart arrhythmias, constricted blood vessels, and heart disease.

10. Though stimulants initially increase confidence and induce a certain euphoria, excessive use of the stronger stimulants can cause mental imbalances. A user can become paranoid, aggressive, and even psychotic.

11. A major problem with overuse of all stimulants is their ability to rapidly induce tolerance and eventually abuse and addiction.

Cocaine

12. Cocaine epidemics occur every few generations.

13. The coca leaf, grown mostly on the Andes Mountains in South America, is chewed and the stimulating juice is absorbed through the buccal mucosa in three to five minutes. The cocaine constitutes only 0.5% to 1.5% of the leaf.

14. Colombian cartels and the FARC (Revolutionary Armed Forces of Columbia) grow and control most of the cocaine in the world, although most of the smuggling into the United States (and 70% of the world's cocaine supply) is through Mexican gangs. There are 3 million hardcore cocaine abusers in the United States.

15. The refined cocaine hydrochloride, popularized by Sigmund Freud, can be snorted (2 to 5 minutes), injected (15 to 30 seconds), drunk (15 to 30 minutes), or absorbed through mucosal tissues. Cocaine freebase (crack, or "rock") is smoked. Smoking is the fastest route to the brain: 7 to 10 seconds.

16. Cocaine is noted for the speed with which it is metabolized in the body. Medically, it is the only naturally occurring topical anesthetic (e.g., for eye surgery or skin lesions); it constricts blood vessels,

and it causes dilation of bronchi to treat asthma.

17. Cocaine mimics and intensifies natural body functions and highs by forcing the release and blocking the reuptake of norepinephrine, dopamine, and serotonin.

18. The comedown is equally intense, so the user keeps taking the drug to stay up, eventually depleting neurotransmitters. Following the high and intense energy come insomnia, agitation, and emotional and physical depression.

19. Cocaine as well as amphetamines initially delay orgasm and so are taken to try to enhance sexual activity; prolonged use eventually causes sexual dysfunction, including a decrease in orgasm.

20. Cocaine, especially when used in combination with alcohol (creating cocaethylene), can precipitate violence, often domestic violence.

21. Cocaine can also cause heart damage and weaken blood vessels, increasing the risk of a stroke.

22. A fetus exposed to the mother's cocaine has an increased chance of miscarriage, stroke, and placental separation. The mother's lifestyle has a great influence on the fetus.

23. Tolerance develops rapidly, causing severe psychological dependence. Withdrawal symptoms are more severe than the crash and include anhedonia (inability to feel pleasure), anergia (total lack of energy), and intense craving, which usually leads to a relapse.

24. A cocaine overdose can result from as little as one-fiftieth of a gram or as much as 1.2 gm. Most overdose reactions are not fatal, but death can come from cardiac arrest, respiratory depression, and seizures.

25. Overuse of cocaine can cause extreme itching, dental problems, and twitching.

26. Cocaine is often used in conjunction with other drugs either to come down or to enhance the effect. Street cocaine is often adulterated, although the concentration is fairly high. Diseases such as AIDS and hepatitis C are common among IV cocaine users.

27. The compulsion to use cocaine (usually in a binge pattern) is due to hereditary liabilities, altered brain chemistry, and a desire to recapture the initial rush, avoid the crash, avoid solving personal problems, and self-medicate.

Smokable Cocaine (crack, freebase)

28. The smokable-cocaine epidemic started in the late 1970s and early 1980s.

29. Freebase cocaine and crack are smokable forms of cocaine. Crack has more impurities than freebase.

30. Smoking freebase cocaine is more intense than snorting cocaine because it has a lower melting point, reaches the brain more quickly, is more fat-soluble, and can be absorbed over a large area (the lungs).

31. The effects of smoking are similar to snorting and shooting. Unique effects are eye abrasions from the smoke, burns on the hands from the pipe, chest pains, pneumonia, coughs, and crack lung. Smoking cigarettes multiplies the effects. Overdose results from cardiac arrest, seizure, stroke, respiratory failure, and even severe hyperthermia.

32. Crack cocaine causes many problems because of the economics of the drug. Despite its being sold in smaller units, the compulsivity quickly accelerates binge use to a $100- to $300-per-day habit.

33. The compulsivity of crack leads to the dissolution of families and to parentless children.

34. The compulsivity also leads to high-risk sexual activity and a high crime rate.

Amphetamines

35. Amphetamines are very similar to cocaine, the main difference being that they are synthetic, longer acting, and cheaper to buy.

36. Amphetamines were originally prescribed to fight exhaustion, low blood pressure, depression, narcolepsy, asthma, some forms of epilepsy, and obesity but were often taken for their mood-elevating and euphoric effects.

37. Their use to control weight led to widespread abuse in the 1960s until the Comprehensive Drug Abuse Prevention and Control Act of 1970 restricted their use.

38. Amphetamines can be shot, snorted, eaten, and, more recently, smoked. The most popular form is smokable dextromethamphetamine, popularly known as "crystal" or "ice." It can also be snorted, shot, or eaten. In Asia the drug is called "yaa baa," "shabu," and a dozen other names.

39. Amphetamines are used to treat ADHD and narcolepsy and for weight control.

40. Meth use is widespread in the gay community.

41. Manufacturing has become simpler, using ephedrine and pseudoephedrine as the raw materials. Many laboratories have been raided, and the areas around them have had to be decontaminated.

42. Amphetamines last four to six hours. They force the release of certain neurotransmitters, expel them into the synapse, and prevent their reabsorption as well as their metabolism.

43. They alter the brain chemistry to increase craving. They also deplete neurotransmitters and shrink the gray matter, especially the hippocampus.

44. They increase energy, speed the heart rate, raise body temperature, speed respiration, raise blood pressure, and suppress appetite.

45. Prolonged use of amphetamines can induce paranoia, heart and blood vessel problems, twitching, increased body temperature, dehydration, malnutrition, and rotted teeth known as "meth mouth."

46. Tolerance develops rapidly with amphetamines. Amphetamine and cocaine withdrawal causes physical and emotional depression, extreme irritability, nervousness, anergia, anhedonia, and craving.

47. Amphetamines damage a fetus and can cause miscarriages, premature delivery, irritable baby syndrome, learning disabilities, growth and developmental delays, and increased risk for ADHD, AIDS, and hepatitis B and C.

48. Mentally and emotionally, amphetamines produce euphoria, sexual feelings, confidence, and alertness; but with prolonged use come irritability, paranoia, anxiety, mental confusion, poor judgment, impaired memory, aggression, excess violence, and even hallucinations. Paranoid psychosis is mimicked by overuse.

49. "Crystal" causes more mental stress but slightly less physical stress than other forms of methamphetamines, so "tweaking," paranoia, hallucinations, and other mental problems are more common.

Amphetamine Congeners

50. Many diet pills and mood elevators (amphetamine congeners) mimic the actions of amphetamines but are not quite as strong.

51. Congeners like methylphenidate (Ritalin® and Concerta®) and pemoline (Cylert®) are used in the treatment of ADHD. Amphetamines (e.g., Adderall® and Dexedrine®) are also used. There is growing abuse of these drugs through diversion of legitimate prescriptions. Methylphenidate has a strong addiction liability.

52. There are three subtypes of ADHD: ADHD, combined type; ADHA, predominantly inattentive type; and ADHD, predominantly hyperactive-impulsive type. Between 3% and 7.4% of all school-age children in the United States have ADHD.

53. Non-drug therapies such as diet and behavior management therapy are also used to treat ADHD.

54. Untreated adolescents with ADHD have a greater chance of abusing street drugs later in life.

55. Diet pills are recommended only for short-term use because they lose their effectiveness after a few months. They can still cause many of the problems seen with amphetamines and can be addicting. The diet pill combination of phentermine and fenfluramine or dexfenfluramine, called "fen-phen," was found to cause heart damage and was taken off the market.

Look-Alike & Over-the-Counter (OTC) Stimulants

56. Look-alike drugs were popularized to take advantage of the desire for cocaine and amphetamines. They are composed of OTC stimulants. Heavy use can cause heart and blood vessel problems as well as dependence.

Miscellaneous Plant Stimulants

57. Other plant stimulants, such as khat, betel nut, yohimbe, and ephedra, have been used by hundreds of millions of people, particularly in the Middle East and Africa, since ancient times. They are still used today.

58. A synthetic form of khat, methcathinone, is widely used in Russia and is being made in the United States.

59. Betel nuts and their extracts are used by up to 450 million people worldwide. The active ingredient causes a mild stimulation especially when mixed with tobacco in a form called gutka, popular in India.

60. Yohimbine from the African yohimbe tree is often used as an aphrodisiac by itself or in herbal and even prescription medications.

61. Ephedra from the ephedra bush is a mild-to-moderate stimulant used medicinally to treat asthma, narcolepsy, other allergies, and low blood pressure. It has also been abused by athletes looking for a stimulant edge. Its sale has recently been severely restricted.

Caffeine

62. Caffeine, particularly coffee, is the most popular stimulant in the world. Besides coffee, caffeine is found in tea, chocolate (cocoa), soft drinks, energy drinks and packets, 60 different plants, and a number of OTC products.

63. Tea was supposedly first used 4,000 to 5,000 years ago, coca more than 2,600 years ago, and coffee about 1,500 years ago. Most soft drinks contain caffeine as do the latest phenomenon, energy drinks such as Red Bull® and Blast.® Energy drinks also contain other herbal stimulants, vitamins, minerals, and sugar. There are also energy packets containing the same ingredients as energy drinks that sell for a dollar or so for a few pills.

64. Other beverages with caffeine, mostly in South America, are guarana, maté, and yoco.

65. A brewed cup of coffee contains about 135 mg of caffeine, a soft drink about 35 mg, and an energy drink, 80 mg.

66. Medically, caffeine is a bronchodilator for asthma patients; it is also a decongestant, a diuretic, an appetite suppressant, and a treatment for migraine headaches.

67. Tolerance can develop with caffeine. Withdrawal symptoms such as headaches, depression, sleep problems, and irritability do occur, particularly if ceasing consumption of more than five cups of coffee a day.

Nicotine

68. Tobacco, originally grown in Central and South America, was brought to the rest of the world by Christopher Columbus and other explorers and seamen.

69. Nicotine use spread because of technology, a milder tobacco leaf, lower prices, and intensive advertising/marketing.

70. Nicotine (tobacco) is the most addicting psychoactive drug. In the United States, at least 37 million people smoke every day.

71. Smokeless tobacco comes in moist snuff, powder (dry) snuff, and loose-leaf chewing tobacco.

72. Nicotine is the crucial ingredient in tobacco in terms of cardiovascular and psychoactive effects as well as addiction.

73. One of the main reasons for tobacco's addictive nature, besides

the slight stimulation it gives, is the need for the smoker's body to maintain a certain level of nicotine in the blood to avoid severe withdrawal symptoms, such as headache, nervousness, fatigue, hunger, irritability, and intense craving. Most who tried tobacco became addicted.

74. Up to 4,800 chemicals, 69 of them known carcinogens, are in tobacco smoke, causing 392,000 deaths per year, mostly from heart disease and lung cancer. Many respiratory diseases are caused by smoking. Smoking shortens the average life span by more than 10 years.

Millions more suffer from dozens of tobacco-caused diseases.

75. Smokeless tobacco is as addicting and as damaging as tobacco that is smoked, with the exception of lung damage. Oral diseases are more common.

76. By quitting smoking, a user's life span is increased and the chance of disease can come close to normal after 10 to 15 years.

77. About 18.9 billion packs of cigarettes were sold in 2005 to the 1.3 billion people worldwide who smoke. Tobacco companies spend more than $13 billion per year in advertising and marketing.

78. Lawsuits brought by local, state, and federal governments in the United States, as well as individual and class-action suits, are being won against tobacco companies for increasing the addictive nature of their products and for the health damage caused by smoking and the secondhand effects of smoking.

Conclusions

79. Though stimulants initially boost many of the qualities we admire, they have a full share of side effects that cause damage when the substance is abused.

REFERENCES

Ahmed, S. H. & Koob, G. F. (1998). Transition from moderate to excessive drug intake change in hedonic set point. *Science, 282*(5387), 298-300.

Ahmed, S. H., Lin, D., Koob, G. F. & Parsons, L. H. (2003). Escalation of cocaine self-administration does not depend on altered cocaine-induced nucleus accumbens dopamine levels. *Journal of Neurochemistry, 86*(1), 102-13.

Aldrich, M. R. (1994). Historical notes on women addicts. *Journal of Psychoactive Drugs, 26* (1), 61-64.

Al-Habori, M. (2005). The potential adverse effects of habitual use of catha edulis (khat). *Expert Opinion on Drug Safety, 4*(6), 1145-54.

Allison, M. (2006, October 6). Caffeinating the world. *Seattle Times*, C1, 6.

Amen, D. G. (2006A). *Images of Attention Deficit Disorder*. http://www.amenclinic.com/bp/atlas/ch12.php (accessed February 1, 2007).

Amen, D. G. (2006B). *Brain Pollution and the Real Reason You Shouldn't Use Drugs*. http://www.amenclinic.com/bp/atlas/ch15.php (accessed August 10, 2006).

Amen, D. G., Yantis, S., Trudeau, J., Stubblefield, M. S. & Halverstadt, J. S. (1997). Visualizing the firestorms in the brain using brain SPECT imaging. *Journal of Psychoactive Drugs, 29*(4), 307-20.

American Beverage Association. (2006). *Beverage Industry Basics*. http://www.ameribev.org/index.aspx (accessed January 25, 2006).

American Cancer Society. (2006). *Cancer Facts and Figures*. http://www.cancer.

org/docroot/stt/stt_0.asp (accessed January 25, 2007).

American Heart Association. (2006). *Heart Disease and Stroke Statistics, 2006 Update*. http://www.americanheart.org/downloadable/heart/1136308648540Statupdate2006.pdf (accessed August January 9, 2007).

American Lung Association. (2006). *Lung Disease Data: 2006*. http://www.lungusa.org (accessed February 1, 2007).

American Psychiatric Association [APA]. (2000). *Diagnostic and Statistical Manual of Mental Disorders* (4th rev, ed. [DSM-IV-TR]). Washington, DC: Author.

AMonline.com. (2005). *Survey Indicates U.S. Coffee Consumption Rebounding*. http://www.amonline.com/article/article.jsp?siteSection=1&id=14261 (accessed November 1, 2006).

Barkley, R. A. (September 10, 1998). Attention-deficit/hyperactivity disorder. *Scientific American*, pp. 18-23.

Barnett, J. (March 10, 2006). Bush signs bill to fight spread of meth. *Oregonian*, p. 1.

Barone, J. J. & Roberts, H. R. (1996). Caffeine Consumption. *Food Chemistry and Toxicology, 34*, 119-29.

Barsky, S. H., Roth, M. D., Kleerup, E. C., Simmons, M. & Tashkin, D. P. (1998). Histopathologic and molecular alterations in bronchial epithelium in habitual smokers of marijuana, cocaine, and/or tobacco. *Journal of the National Cancer Institute, 90*(16), 1198-1205.

Bauer, C. R., Langer, J. S., Shankaran, S., Bada, H. S., Lester, B., Wright, L. I., et al. (2005). Acute neonatal effects of cocaine exposure during birth. *Archives of Pediatric Adolescent Medicine, 159*(9), 824-34.

Benowitz, N. L. & Fredericks, A. (1995). History of tobacco use. In J. H. Jaffe, ed. *Encyclopedia of Drugs and Alcohol* (Vol. III, pp. 1032-36). New York: Simon & Schuster Macmillan.

Bibra, E. F. (1995). *Plant Intoxicants: Betel and Related Substances*. Rochester, VT: Healing Arts Press.

Biederman, J., Faraone, S. V., Spencer, T., Wilens, T., Norman, D., Lapey, K. A., et al. (1993). Patterns of psychiatric comorbidity, cognition and psychosocial functioning in adults with AD/HD. *American Journal of Psychiatry, 150*, 1792-98.

Biederman, J., Wilens, T., Mick, E., Spencer, T. & Faraone, S. V. (1999). Pharmacotherapy of AD/HD reduces risk for substance use disorder. *Pediatrics, 104*(2).

Blanck, H. M., Khan, L. K. & Serdula, M. K. (2004). Prescription weight loss pill use among Americans. *Prevention Medicine, 39*(6), 1243-48.

Blum, K., Braverman, E. R., Holder, J. M., Lubar, J. F., Monastra, V. J., Miller, D., et al. (2000). Reward deficiency syndrome (RDS). *Journal of Psychoactive Drugs, 32*(suppl.).

Brecht, M. L. (2005). *Epidemiological Trends in Drug Abuse*, 39-40 (NIDA/CEWG). http://www.drugabuse.gov/PDF/CEWG/AdvReport_Vol1_105.pdf (accessed January 10, 2007).

Breiter, H., Gollub, R., Weisskoss, R., Kennedy, D. N., Makris, N., Berk, J. D., et al. (1997). Acute effects of cocaine on human brain activity and emotion. *Neuron, 19,* 591-611.

British Broadcasting Corporation. (July 12, 2001). Red Bull in suspected link to death. BBC News.

Brookoff, D., O'Brien, K. K., Cook, C. S., Thompson, T. D. & Williams, C. (1997). Characteristics of participants in domestic violence: Assessment at the scene of domestic assault. *JAMA, 277*(17), 1369-72.

Buitelaar, J. K., Barton, J., Danckaerts, M., Friedrichs, E., Gillberg, C., Hazell, P. L., et al. (2006). A comparison of North American versus non-North American ADHD study populations. *European Child Adolescent Psychiatry.* Prepublication.

Burnet Institute. (2002). *Revisiting the Hidden Epidemic: A Situation Assessment of Drug Use in Asia in the Context of HIV/AIDS.* http://www.chr.asn.au/publications/10214 (accessed January 25, 2007).

Cabaj, R. P. (2005). Gays, lesbians, and bisexuals. In J. H. Lowinson, P. Ruiz, R. B. Millman & J. G. Langrod, eds. *Substance Abuse: A Comprehensive Textbook* (4th ed., pp. 1129-41). Baltimore: Williams & Wilkins.

Calkins, R. F., Aktan, G. B. & Hussain, K. L. (1995). Methcathinone: The next illicit stimulant epidemic? *Journal of Psychoactive Drugs, 27*(3), 277-85.

Cantwell, D. P. (1996). Attention-deficit disorder: A review of the past 10 years. *Journal of the American Academy of Child and Adolescent Psychiatry, 35.*

Castellanos, F. X., Lee, P. L., Sharp, W., et al. (2002). Developmental trajectories of brain volume abnormalities in children and adolescents with ADHD. *JAMA, 288,* 1740-48.

Castilla, J., Barrio, G., Belza, M. & de la Fuente, L. (1999). Drug and alcohol consumption and sexual risk behavior among young adults: Results from a national survey. *Drug and Alcohol Dependence, 56,* 47-53.

Centers for Disease Control and Prevention [CDC]. (2005). *BIDIS and Kreteks Fact Sheet.* Tobacco Information and Prevention Source (TIPS). http://www.cdc.gov/tobacco/factsheets/bidisandkreteks.htm (accessed December 30, 2006).

Centers for Disease Control and Prevention. (2006). *Health effects of cigarette smoking.* Tobacco Information and Prevention Source (TIPS). http://www.cdc.gov/tobacco/research_data/mmwr.htm (accessed February 4, 2007).

Chen, H., Hansen, M. J., Jones, J. E., Vlahos, R., Bozinovski, S., Anderson, G. P., et al. (March 10, 2006). Cigarette smoke exposure reprograms the hypothalamic neuropeptide Y axis to promote weight loss. *American Journal of Respiratory Critical Care Medicine.* Prepublication.

Childress, A. R., McElgin, W., Mozley, D., Reivich, M. & O'Brien, G. (1996). Brain correlates of cue-induced cocaine and opiate craving. *Society for Neuroscience Abstracts, 22:365.5.*

Childress, A. R., Mozley, P. D., McElgin, W., Fitzgerald, J., Reivich, M. & O'Brien, C. P. (1999). Limbic activation during cue-induced cocaine craving. *American Journal of Psychiatry, 156*(1), 11-18.

Chouvy, P. & Meissonnier, J. (2004). *Yaa Baa: Production, Traffic, and Consumption of Methamphetamine in Mainland Southeast Asia.* Singapore: IRASEC.

Chu, N. S. (2001). Effects of betel nut chewing on the central and autonomic nervous system. *Journal of Biomedical Science, 8*(3), 229-36.

Coffee Science Source. (1998). *Coffee Facts and Figures.* http://www.coffee-science.org/media (accessed February 25, 2007).

Collins, A. C. (1990). An analysis of the addiction liability of nicotine. In C. K. Erikson, M. A. Javors & W. W. Morgan, eds. *Addiction Potential of Abused Drugs and Drug Classes.* New York: The Haworth Press.

Comings, D. E., Wu, S., Chiu, C., Ring, R. H., Gade, R., Ahn, C., et al. (1996). Polygenic inheritance of Tourette's syndrome, stuttering, AD/HD, conduct, and oppositional defiant disorder: The additive and subtractive effect of the three dopaminergic genes-DRD_2, D beta H, and DAT_1. *American Journal of Medical Genetics, 6*(3), 264-88.

Connolly, H. M., Crary, J. L., McGoon, M. D., Hensrud, D. D., Edwards, B. S., Edwards, W. E., et al. (1997). Valvular heart disease associated with fenfluramine-phentermine. *New England Journal of Medicine, 337*(9).

Crenshaw, M. J. (2004). Khat: A potential concern for law enforcement. *FBI Law Enforcement Bulletin.* http://www.cancer.org/docroot/stt/stt_0.asp (accessed December 20, 2006).

Cross, J. C., Johnson, B. D., Rees Davis, W. & Liberty, J. J. (2001). Supporting the habit: Income generation activities of frequent crack users compared with frequent users of other hard drugs. *Drug and Alcohol Dependence, 64,* 191-201.

Cuffe, S. E., Moore, C. G. & McKeown, R. E. (2005). Prevalence and correlates of ADHD symptoms in the National Health Interview Survey. *Journal of Attention Disorders, 9*(2), 392-401.

Darras, M., Koppel, B. S. & Atas-Radzion, E. (1994). Cocaine induced choreoathetoid movements ("crack dancing"). *Neurology, 44*(4), 751-52.

DASIS Report. (2006). *Trends in Methamphetamine/Amphetamine Admissions to Treatment, 1993-2003.* http://www.oas.samhsa.gov/2k6/methTx/methTX.cfm (accessed January 25, 2007).

Dhaifalah, I. & Santavy, J. (2004). Khat habit and its health effect: A natural amphetamine. *Biomedical Papers, 148*(1), 11-15.

Doll, R., Peto, R., Boreham, J. & Sutherland, I. (2004). Mortality in relation to smoking: 50 years' observations on male British doctors. *British Medical Journal, 328*(1519).

Drug Abuse Warning Network [DAWN]. (2006). *Emergency Department Trends from DAWN, 2004.* https://dawninfo.samhsa.gov/default.asp (accessed January 5, 2007).

Drug Enforcement Administration [DEA]. (2001). Congressional testimony by Errol J. Chavez, Special Agent in Charge, DEA. April 13, 2001. http://www.usdoj.gov/dea/pubs/cngrtest/ct041301.htm (accessed January 25, 2007).

Drug Enforcement Administration. (2002). *Khat.* http://www.usdoj.gov/dea/concern/khat.html (accessed January 25, 2007).

Drug Enforcement Administration. (2006A). *National Drug Threat Assessment, 2007.* http://www.usdoj.gov/dea/concern/18862/ (accessed January 25, 2007).

Drug Enforcement Administration. (2006B). *Cocaine.* http://www.dea.gov/concern/18862/cocaine.htm#Strategic (accessed August 10, 2006).

Edlin, B. R., Irwin, K. L. & Faruque, S. (1994). Intersecting epidemics: Crack cocaine use and HIV infection among inner-city young adults. *New England Journal of Medicine, 331,* 1422-27.

Ellinwood, E. H. (1973). Amphetamine and stimulant drugs. *Drug Use in America: Problem in Perspective. Second report. Marijuana and Drug Abuse Commission,* 140-57.

Epping-Jordan, M. P., Watkins, S. S., Koob, G. F. & Markou, A. (1998). Dramatic decreases in brain reward function during nicotine withdrawal. *Nature, 393*(6680), 76-79.

Ernst, T., Chang, L., Leonido-Yee, M. & Speck, O. (2000). Evidence for long-term neurotoxicity associated with methamphetamine abuse. *Neurology, 54*, 1344-49.

Ezzati, M. & Lopez, A. D. (2004). Disease specific patterns of smoking-attributable mortality in 2000. *Tobacco Control, 13*(4), 388-95.

Ezzati, M., Henley, S. J., Lopez, A. D. & Thun, M. J. (2005). Role of smoking in global and regional cancer epidemiology, mortality. *International Journal of Cancer, 116*(6), 963-71.

Ezzati, M., Henley, S. J., Thun, M. J. & Lopez, A. D. (2005). Role of smoking in global and regional cardiovascular mortality. *Circulation, 112*(4), 489-97.

Faraone, S. V. & Biederman, J. (2005). What is the prevalence of adult ADHD? Results of a population screen of 966 adults. *Journal of Attention Disorders, 9*(2), 384-91.

Ferreiri, S. E., de Mello, N, T., Rossi, M. V. & Souza-Formigoni, M. L. (2004). Does an energy drink modify the effects of alcohol in a maximal effort test? *Alcohol Clinical Experimental Research, 28*(9), 1408-12.

Food and Agriculture Organization of the United Nations. (2006). *Higher World Tobacco Use Expected by 2010.* http://www.fao.org/english/newsroom/news/2003/26919-en.html (accessed January 25, 2007).

Foreman, R., Klein, J., Barks, J., et al. (1994). Prevalence of fetal exposure to cocaine in Toronto, 1990-1991. *Clinical Investment Medicine, 17*(3), 206-11.

Forero, J. (March 23, 2006). U.S. indicts 50 leaders of Colombian rebels in cocaine trafficking. *New York Times,* p. A3.

Frank, D. A. (2001). Cocaine called no more teratogenic than other drugs. *JAMA, 285*, 1613-27.

Freud, S. (1884). *Über Coca.* In R. Byck, ed. (1974). *The Cocaine Papers of Sigmund Freud.* New York: Stonehill.

Fukui, S., Wada, K. & Iyo, M. (1991). History and current use of methamphetamine in Japan. In S. Fukui et al., eds. *Cocaine and Methamphetamine: Behavioral Toxicology, Clinical Pharmacology and Epidemiology.* Tokyo: Drug Abuse Prevention Center.

Furman, L. (2005). What is ADHD? *Journal of Child Neurology, 20*(12), 994-1002.

Gainetdinov, R. R., Wetwel, W. C., Jones, S. R., Levin, E. D., Jaber, M. & Caron, M. G. (1999). Role of serotonin in the paradoxical calming effect of psychostimulants on hyperactivity. *Science, 283*(5400), 397-401.

Garavan, H., Pankiewicz, J., Bloom, A., Cho, J. K., Sperry, L., Ross, T. J., et al. (2000). Cue-induced cocaine craving: Neuroanatomical specificity for drug users and drug stimuli. *American Journal of Psychiatry, 157*(11), 1789-98.

Giannini, A. J., Burge, H., Shaheen, J. M. & Price, W. A. (1986). Khat: Another drug of abuse. *Journal of Psychoactive Drugs, 18*(2), 155-58.

Glantz, S. A. (1992). *Tobacco: Biology & Politics.* Waco, TX: Health Edco.

Glantz, S. A. & Charlesworth, A. (1999). Tourism and hotel revenues before and after passage of smoke-free restaurant ordinances. *JAMA, 281*, 1911-8.

Gold, M. S. & Jacobs, W. S. (2005). Cocaine and crack: Clinical aspects. In J. H. Lowinson, P. Ruiz, R. B. Millman & J. G. Langrod, eds. *Substance Abuse: A Comprehensive Textbook* (4th ed., pp. 403-20). Baltimore: Williams & Wilkins.

Goldstein, A. (2001). *Addiction: From Biology to Drug Policy* (2nd ed.). New York: Oxford University Press.

Gonzalez Castro, F., Barrington, E. H., Walton, M. A. & Rawson, R. A. (2000). Cocaine and methamphetamine: Differential addiction rates. *Psychology of Addiction Behavior, 14*(4), 390-96.

Gorelick, D. A. & Cornish, J. L. (2003). The pharmacology of cocaine, amphetamines, and other stimulants. In A. W. Graham, T. K. Schultz, M. F. Mayo-Smith, R. K. Ries & B. B. Wilford, eds. *Principles of Addiction Medicine* (3rd ed., pp. 157-90). Chevy Chase, MD: American Society of Addiction Medicine, Inc.

Goudie, A. & Newton, T. (1985). The puzzle of drug-induced taste aversion: Comparative studies with cathinone and amphetamine. *Psychopharmacology, 87*, 328-33.

Greenbaum, E. (1993). Blackened bronchoalveolar lavage fluid in crack smokers, a preliminary study. *American Journal of Clinical Pathology, 100*, 481-87.

Griffiths, R. R. & Vernotica, E. M. (2000). Is caffeine a flavoring agent in cola soft drinks? *Archives of Family Medicine, 9*(8).

Grinspoon, L. & Bakalar, J. B. (1985). *Cocaine: A Drug and Its Social Evolution.* New York: Basic Books, Inc.

Grinspoon, L. & Hedblom, P. (1975). *The Speed Culture: Amphetamine Use and Abuse in America.* Cambridge, MA: Harvard University Press.

Gross, C. P. (2002). U.S. states not using tobacco dollars wisely. *New England Journal of Medicine, 347,* 1080-88, 1106-8.

Gualtieri, C. T. & Johnson, L. G. (2006). Efficient allocation of attentional resources in patients with ADHD. *Journal of Attention Disorders, 9*(3), 534-42.

Guttmacher, H. (1885). New medications and therapeutic techniques concerning the different cocaine preparations and their effects. In R. Byck, ed. (1974). *The Cocaine Papers of Sigmund Freud.* New York: Stonehill.

Hamid, A. (1992). The developmental cycle of a drug epidemic: The cocaine smoking epidemic of 1981-1991. *Journal of Psychoactive Drugs, 24*(4), 337-48.

Harler, C. R. (1984). Tea production. *Encyclopaedia Britannica* (Vol. 18, pp. 16-19). Chicago: Encyclopaedia Britannica.

Harris Poll. (1999). Relapse of smokers. *USA Today.*

Hecht, S. S. (2001). Tobacco smoke carcinogens and lung cancer. *Journal of the National Cancer Institute, 91*(14), 1194-1210.

Heimann, R. K. (1960). *Tobacco & Americans.* New York: McGraw-Hill Book Company, Inc.

Hoffmann, D., Hoffmann, I. & El-Bayoumy, K. (2001). *Chemical Research in Toxicology, 14*(7), 767-90.

Horner, B. R. & Scheibe, K. E. (1997). Prevalence and implications of AD/HD among adolescents in treatment for substance abuse. *Journal of the American Academy of Child and Adolescent Psychiatry. 36*(1), 30-36.

Hurst, W. J., Tarka, S. M., Powis, T. G., Valdez, F. & Hester, T. R. (2002). Cacao usage by the earliest Mayan civilizations. *Nature, 418*, 289-90.

Jaakkola, J. J., Kosheleva, A. A., Katsnelson, B. A., Kuzmin, S. V., Privalova, L. I. & Spengler, J. D. (2006). Prenatal and postnatal tobacco smoke exposure and respiratory health in Russian children. *Respiratory Research, 7*(1).

Jacobs, A. (February 21, 2006). Battling HIV: Counselors reach out at the junction of sex and crystal meth. *New York Times,* p. C12.

James, J. E. (1991). *Caffeine and Health.* London: Harcourt Brace Jovanovich.

Jeri, F. R., Sanchez, C., Del Pozo, T. & Fernandez, M. (1992). The syndrome of coca paste. *Journal of Psychoactive Drugs, 24*(2), 173-82.

Juliano, L. M. & Griffiths, R. R. (2005). Caffeine. In J. H. Lowinson, P. Ruiz, R. B. Millman & J. G. Langrod, eds. *Substance Abuse: A Comprehensive Textbook* (4th ed., pp. 403-20). Baltimore: Williams & Wilkins.

Kalix, P. (1994). Khat, an amphetamine-like stimulant. *Journal of Psychoactive Drugs, 26*(1), 69-73.

Karch, S. B. (2001). *The Pathology of Drug Abuse.* Boca Raton, FL: CRC Press.

Karch, S. B. (2005). *A Brief History of Cocaine* (2nd ed.). Boca Raton, FL: CRC Press.

Kaufman, M. (September 20, 2004). Tobacco lawsuit is finally heading for court. *Washington Post.*

Keefe, J. D. (2001). *Clandestine methamphetamine laboratories.* DEA congressional testimony by Joseph D. Keefe, Chief of Operations, DEA. July 12, 2001. http://www.usdoj.gov/dea/pubs/cngrtest/ct071201.htm (accessed November 1, 2006).

Kennedy, D. O. & Scholey, A. B. (2004). A glucose-caffeine energy drink ameliorates subjective and performance deficits. *Appetite, 42*(3), 331-33.

King, G. R. & Ellinwood, E. H. (2005). Amphetamines and other stimulants. In J. H. Lowinson, P. Ruiz, R. B. Millman & J. G. Langrod, eds. *Substance Abuse: A Comprehensive Textbook* (4th ed., pp. 277-301). Baltimore: Williams & Wilkins.

Klatsky, A. L., Morton, C., Udaltsova, N. & Friedman, G. D. (2006). Coffee, cirrhosis, and transaminase enzymes. *Archives of Internal Medicine, 166*(11), 1190-95.

Klebanoff, M. A., Levine, R. J., DeSimonian, R., Clemens, J. D. & Wilkins, D. G. (1999). Maternal serum paraxanthine, a caffeine metabolite, and the risk of spontaneous abortion. *New England Journal of Medicine, 341*(22), 1639-44.

Klesges, R. C., Meyers, A. W., Klesges, L. M. & LaVasque, M. E. (1989). Smoking, body weight, and their effects on smoking behavior: A comprehensive review of the literature. *Psychological Bulletin, 106,* 204-30.

Krain, A. L. & Castellanos, F. X. (February 8, 2006). Brain development and ADHD. *Clinical Psychology Revue.* Prepublication.

Kruger, J., Galuska, D. A., Serdula, M. K. & Jones, D. A. (2004). Attempting to lose weight: Specific practices among U.S. adults. *American Journal of Prevention Medicine, 26*(5), 402-6.

Kuhar, M. J. (1995). Cola/cola drinks. In J. H. Jaffe, ed. *Encyclopedia of Drugs and Alcohol* (Vol. I, pp. 251-52). New York: Simon & Schuster Macmillan.

Kurozawa, I., Ogimoto, I., Shibata, A., Nose, T., Yoshimura, T., Suzuki, H., et al. (2005). Coffee and risk of death from hepatocellular carcinoma in a large cohort study in Japan. *British Journal of Cancer, 93*(5), 607-10.

Lai, S., Lima, J. A., Lai, H., Vlahov, D., Celentano, D., Tong, W., et al. (2005). Human immunodeficiency virus infections, cocaine, and coronary calcification. *Archives of Internal Medicine, 165*(6), 690-5.

Landry, M. (1992). An overview of cocaethylene. *Journal of Psychoactive Drugs, 24*(3), 273-76.

Lane, J. D., Pieper, C. F., Phillips-Bute, B. G., Bryant, J. E. & Kuhn, C. M. (2002). Caffeine affects cardiovascular and neuroendocrine activation at work and home. *Psychosomatic Medicine, 64,* 595-603.

Lee, S. J. (2006). Overcoming Crystal Meth Addiction. New York: Marlowe $ Company.

Leinwand, D. (August 21, 2002A). 10 held in smuggling of "Nazi speed." *USA Today,* p. 1.

Leinwand, D. (August 23, 2002B). U.S. seizures of narcotic shrub on the rise. *USA Today,* p. 1.

Lester, et al. (2005). *Epidemiological Trends in Drug Abuse,* 40-43 (NIDA/CEWG).http://www.drugabuse.gov/PDF/CEWG/AdvReport_Vol1_105.pdf (accessed August 10, 2006).

Lichtblau, E. & Schrader, E. (December 1, 1999). U.S. fears it badly underestimated cocaine production in Colombia. *Los Angeles Times.*

Lindner, J. D., Monkemuller, K. E., Raijman, I., Johnson, L., Lazenby, A. J. & Wilcox, M. (2000). Cocaine-associated ischemic colitis. *Southern Medical Journal, 93*(9), 909-13.

Logan, B. K. (2002). *Methamphetamine: Effects on Human Performance and Behavior* (pp. 153). Seattle, WA: Central Police University Press.

London, E. D., Simon, S. L., Berman, S. M., Mandelkern, M. A., Lichtman, A. M., Bramen, J., et al. (2004). Mood disturbances and regional cerebral metabolic abnormalities in recently abstinent methamphetamine abusers. *Archives of General Psychiatry, 61*(1), 73-84.

Luk, J. (2000). The effectiveness of banning advertising for tobacco products. International Union Against Cancer, 11th World Conference on Tobacco and Health.

Mannuzza, S., Klein, R. G., Bonagura, N., Malloy, P. & Giampino, T. L. (1991). Hyperactive boys almost grown up. *Archives of General Psychiatry, 48,* 565-76.

Marnell, T., ed. (2006). *Drug Identification Bible.* Denver: Drug Identification Bible.

Maxwell Report. (2004). *Tobacco Brand Preference Fact Sheet.* Tobacco Information and Prevention Source (TIPS). http://www.cdc.gov/tobacco/factsheets/Tobacco_Brand_Preferences_Factsheet.htm (accessed December 5, 2006).

Mayo Clinic. (2001). *Mayo Clinic Report: Spit Tobacco: Does Smokeless Mean Harmless?*

McGowan, J. D., Altman, R. E. & Kanto, W. P. Jr. (1988). Neonatal withdrawal symptoms after chronic ingestion of caffeine. *Southern Medical Journal, 81*(9), 1092-94.

McGregor, C., Srisurapanont, M., Jittiwutikarn, J., Laobhripatr, S., Wongtan, T. & White, J. M. (2005). The nature, time course and severity of methamphetamine withdrawal. *Addiction, 100*(9), 1320-29.

MEDCO Health Solutions. (2006). *News.* http://www.medco.com (accessed November 1, 2006).

Mets, C. N., Gregersen, P. K. & Malhotra, A. K. (2004). Metabolism and biochemical effects of nicotine for primary care providers. *Medical Clinics of North America, 88*(6), 1399-413.

Meyer, J. S. & Quenzer, L. F. (2005). *Psychopharmacology: Drugs, the Brain, and Behavior.* Sunderland, MA: Sinauer Associates, Inc.

Milberger, S., Biederman, J., Faraone, S. V. & Jones, J. (1998). Further evidence of an association between maternal smoking during pregnancy and ADHD. *Journal of Clinical Child Psychology, 27,* 352-58.

Miller, D. & Blum, K. (1996). *Overload: Attention-Deficit Disorder and the Addictive Brain.* Kansas City: Andrews and McMeel.

Miller, M. & Kozel, N. (1995). Amphetamine epidemics. In J. H. Jaffee, ed. *Encyclopedia of Drugs and Alcohol* (Vol. I, pp. 110-17). New York: Simon & Schuster Macmillan.

Mintel Group. (2006). *Coffeehouses and Donut Shops.* http://reports.mintel.com/sinatra/reports/display/id=165823 (accessed August 10, 2006).

Monardes, N. (1577). *Joyfull Newes Out of the Newe Founde Worlde.* Translated by Frampton, J. Reprinted in 1967. New York: AMS Press, Inc.

Monitoring the Future. (2002). *Cigarette Brands Smoked by American Teens.* http://www.umich.edu/~newsinfor/ (accessed OOO, XX, 200X).

Monitoring the Future. (2006). *National Results on Adolescent Drug Use.* http://monitoringthefuture.org/pubs/monographs/overview2005.pdf (accessed August 10, 2006).

Morales, A. (2000). Yohimbine in erectile dysfunction: The facts. *International Journal of Impotence Research, 12*(suppl. S), 70-74.

Morgan, J. P., Wesson, D. R., Puder, K. S. & Smith, D. E. (1987). Duplicitous drugs: The history and recent status of looka-like drugs. *Journal of Psychoactive Drugs, 19*(1), 21-31.

MTA Cooperative Group. (1999). A 14-month randomized clinical trial of treatment strategies for AD/HD. *Archives of General Psychiatry, 56*(12), 1073-86.

National Drug Intelligence Center [NDIC]. (2005). *National Drug Threat Assessment, 2005.* http://www.usdoj.gov/ndic/pubs11/12620/meth.htm#Top (accessed August 10, 2006).

National Institute of Mental Health. (1999). Attention-Deficit/Hyperactivity Disorder. *NIH Publication No. 96-357.2.*

National Institute on Drug Abuse [NIDA]. (2000). Nicotine and dopamine. *NIDA Notes, 15*(2).

National Institute on Drug Abuse. (2005). *NIDA InfoFacts: Methamphetamine.* http://www.nida.nih.gov/Infofacts/methamphetamine.html (accessed August 10, 2006).

National Institutes of Health. (1998). Diagnosis and treatment of ADHD. http://consensus.nih.gov/1998/1998AttentionDeficitHyperactivityDisorder110html.htm (accessed August 10, 2006).

O'Brien, R., Cohen, S., Evans, G. & Fine, J. (1992). *The Encyclopedia of Drug Abuse* (2nd ed.). New York: Facts On File.

Office of National Drug Control Policy [ONDCP]. (2003). *Cocaine.* http://www.whitehousedrugpolicy.gov/publications/factsht/cocaine/ (accessed March 15, 2006).

Palmer, C. (August 18, 2005). Meth mouth tells devastating story. *American Dental Association News.*

Parsell, D. (2005). Palm-nut problem: Asian chewing habit linked to oral cancer. *Science News, 167*(3).

Pary, R., Lewis, S., Arnp, C. S., Matuschka, P. R. & Lippmann, S. (2002). AD/HD: An update. *Southern Medical Journal, 95*(7), 743-49.

Paulus, M. P., Tapers, S. F. & Schuckit, M. A. (2005). Neural activation patterns of methamphetamine dependent subjects during decision making predict relapse. *Archives of General Psychiatry, 62*(7), 761-68.

Pennings, E. J., Leccese, A. P. & Wolfe, F. A. (2002). Effects of concurrent use of alcohol and cocaine. *Addiction, 97*(7), 773-83.

Perkins, K. A. (1993). Weight gain following smoking cessation. *Journal of Consulting Clinical Psychology, 61,* 768-77.

Pliszka, S. R. (1998). Comorbidity of AD/HD in children. *Journal of Clinical Psychiatry, 59* (suppl. 7), 50-58.

Post, R. M. & Kopanda, R. T. (1976). Cocaine, kindling, and psychosis. *American Journal of Psychiatry, 133,* 627-34.

Rachima-Maoz, C., Peleg, E. & Rosenthal, T. (1998). The effect of caffeine on ambulatory blood pressure in hypertensive patients. *American Journal of Hypertension, 11,* 1426-32.

Randall, T. (1992). Cocaine, alcohol mix in body to form even longer lasting, more lethal drugs. *JAMA, 267,* 1043-44.

Rätsch, C. (2005). *The Encyclopedia of Psychoactive Plants.* Rochester, VT: Park Street Press.

Reid, T. R. (January 2005). Caffeine. *National Geographic Magazine.*

Repetto, M. & Gold, M. S. (2005). Cocaine and crack: Neurobiology. In J. H. Lowinson, P. Ruiz, R. B. Millman & J. G. Langrod, eds. *Substance Abuse: A Comprehensive Textbook* (4th ed., pp. 195-217). Baltimore: Williams & Wilkins.

Ricaurte, B., et al. (1997). Reductions in brain dopamine and serotonin transporters detected in humans previously exposed to repeated high doses of methcathinone using PET. *Society for Neuroscience Abstracts, 22,* 1915. Also in *NIDA Notes, 11*(5).

Richards, J. B., Baggot, M. J., Sabol, K. E. & Seiden, L. S. (1999). A high-dose methamphetamine regimen results in long-lasting deficits on performance. *Journal of Psychoactive Drugs, 31*(4).

Rodu, B. & Cole, P. (2002). Smokeless tobacco use and cancer of the upper respiratory tract. *Journal of Oral Surgery, Oral Medicine, Oral Pathology, Oral Radiology, and Endodontics, 93*(5), 511-15.

Roth, M. D., Tashkin, D. P., Choi, R., Jamieson, B. D., Zack, J. A. (2002). Cocaine enhances human immunodeficiency virus replication in a model of severe combined immune deficient mice implanted with human peripheral blood leukocytes. *Journal of Infectious Diseases, 185*(5), 1-5.

Rubin, R. (March 22, 2006). Re: Labeling ADHD drugs as psychosis/mania risk. *USA Today,* p. D8.

RXList. (2006). *The Top 300 Prescriptions for 2005.* http://www.rxlist.com/top200.htm (accessed August 10, 2006).

Sanello, F. (2005). *Tweakers: How Crystal Meth Is Ravaging Gay America.* Los Angeles: Alyson Books.

Satel, J. A. & Lieberman, J. A. (1991). Schizophrenia and substance abuse.

Psychiatric Clinics of North America, 16(2), 401-12.

Schick, S. & Glantz, S. (2005). Philip Morris toxicological experiments with fresh sidestream smoke: More toxic than mainstream smoke. *Tobacco Control, 14*(6).

Schmidt, H. D., Anderson, S. M., Famous, K. R., Kumaresan, V. & Pierce, R. C. (2005). Anatomy and pharmacology of cocaine priming-induced reinstatement of drug seeking. *European Journal of Pharmacology, 526*(1-3), 65-76.

Schmitz, J. M. & DeLaune, K. A. (2005). Nicotine. In J. H. Lowinson, P. Ruiz, R. B. Millman & J. G. Langrod, eds. *Substance Abuse: A Comprehensive Textbook* (4th ed., pp. 387-402). Baltimore, MD: Williams & Wilkins.

Schuckit, M. (2000). *Drug and Alcohol Abuse* (5th ed.). New York: Kluwer Academic/Plenum Publishers.

SCOTH. (2004). Secondhand smoke: Review of evidence since 1998. *Scientific Committee on Tobacco.* Department of Health.

Semrud-Clikeman, M., Filipek, P. A., Biederman, J., Steingard, R., Kennedy, D., Renshaw, P. & Bekkin, K. (1994). Attention-deficit/hyperactivity disorder: Magnet resonance imaging morphometric analysis of the corpus callosum. *Journal of the American Academy of Child Adolescent Psychiatry, 33*(6), 875-81.

Severson, K. (September 29, 2002). L.A. school district officials vote to restrict soda sales. *San Francisco Chronicle,* p. A3.

Siegel, R. K. (1992). Cocaine freebase use: A new smoking disorder. *Journal of Psychoactive Drugs, 24*(2), 183-209.

Silverman, K. & Griffiths, R. R. (1995A). Coffee. In J. H. Jaffee, ed. *Encyclopedia of Drugs and Alcohol* (Vol. I, pp. 250-51). New York: Simon & Schuster Macmillan.

Silverman, K. & Griffiths, R. R. (1995B). Tea. In J. H. Jaffee, ed. *Encyclopedia of Drugs and Alcohol* (Vol. III, pp. 1018-19). New York: Simon & Schuster Macmillan.

Singer, K, T., Arendt, R., Minnes, S., Farkas, K., Salvator, A., Kirchner, H. L. & Kliegman, R. (2002). Cognitive and motor outcomes of cocaine-exposed infants. *JAMA, 287,* 1952-60.

Sinha, R. & Efron, D. (2005). Complementary and alternative medicine use in children with attention deficit hyperactivity disorder. *Journal of Pediatric Child Health, 41*(1-2), 23-26.

Slade, J. (1992). The tobacco epidemic: Lessons from history. *Journal of Psychoactive Drugs, 24*(2), 99-110.

Smit, H. J., Cotton, S. C., Hughes, J. R. & Rogers, P. J. (2004). Mood and cognitive performance effects of energy drink constituents. *Nutritional Neuroscience, 7*(3), 127-39.

Smith, D. E. & Seymour, R. B. (2001). *Clinician's Guide to Substance Abuse.* New York: McGraw-Hill.

Smith, D. E. & Wesson, D. R. (1985). *Treating the Cocaine Abuser.* Center City, MN: Hazelden.

Smoke Free World. (2005). *Smoke Free U.S.A.* http://www.smokefreeworld.com/usa.shtml (accessed August 10, 2006).

Snyder, S. H. (1996). *Drugs and the Brain.* New York: W. H. Freeman and Sons.

Soldz, S., Clark, T. W., Stewart, E., Celebucki, C. & Klein, W. D. (2002). Decreased youth tobacco use in Massachusetts 1996 to 1999: Evidence of tobacco control effectiveness. *Tobacco Control* (suppl. 2), II14-II19.

Sora, L., Hall, F. S., Andrews, A. M., Itokawa, M., Li, X. F., Wei, H. B., et al. (2000). Molecular mechanisms of cocaine reward combined dopamine and serotonin transporter knockouts eliminate cocaine place preference. *Proceedings of the National Academy of Sciences, 98*(9), 5300-5305.

Spitz, M. (March 5, 1998). Gene can help smokers kick the habit. *San Francisco Chronicle,* p. A4.

Stahl, S. M. (2000). *Essential Psychopharmacology.* Cambridge, England: Cambridge University Press.

Starbucks. (2006). *Starbucks press release.* http://www.starbucks.com/aboutus/pressdesc.asp?id=640 (accessed August 10, 2006).

Stein, E. A., Pankiewicz, J., Harsch, H. H., Cho, J., Fuller, S. A., Hoffmann, R. G., et al. (1998). Nicotine-induced limbic cortical activation in the human brain: A functional MRI study. *American Journal of Psychiatry, 155*(8), 1009-15.

Strine, T. W., Lesesne, C. A., Okoro, C. A., McGuire, L. C., Chapman, D. P., Balluz, L. A., et al. (2006). Emotional and behavioral difficulties and impairments in everyday functioning among children with a history of ADHD. *Preventing Chronic Disease, 3*(2).

Substance Abuse and Mental Health Services Administration [SAMHSA]. (2001). *Tobacco Use in America: Findings from the 1999 National Household Survey on Drug Abuse.* Rockville, MD: SAMHSA, Office of Applied Studies.

Substance Abuse and Mental Health Services Administration. (2006). *2005 National Survey on Drug Use and Health: National Findings.* http://www.oas.samhsa.gov/NSDUH/2k5NSD

UH/tabs/Sect2peTabs1to57.htm#Tab2.2 1A (accessed January 25, 2007).

Sud, S. (June 22, 2005). New cold pills signal end for meth labs. *Oregonian,* p. 1.

Szabo, L. (October 18, 2005). Ireland's smoking ban reaps benefits. *USA Today,* p. 7D.

Szabo, L. (March 27, 2006). ADHD treatment is getting a workout. *USA Today,* p. 6D.

Taipei Times. (August 25, 2003). Binlang girls. *Taipei Times.*

Tardiff, K., Marzuk, P. M., Leon, A. C., Hirsch, C. S., Stajic, M., Portera, L. & Hartwell, N. (1994). Homicide in New York City: Cocaine use and firearms. *JAMA, 272,* 43-46.

Tashkin, D. P. (2005). Smoked marijuana as a cause of lung injury. *Monaldi Archives of Chest Diseases, 63*(2), 93-100.

Thompson, P. M., Hayashi, K. M., Simon, S. L., Geaga, J. A., Hong, M. S., Sui, Y., et al. (2004). Structural abnormalities in the brain of human subjects who use methamphetamine. *Journal of Neuroscience, 24*(26), 6028-36.

Tinsley, J. A. & Wadkins, D. D. (1998). Over-the-counter stimulants: Abuse and addiction. *Mayo Clinic Proceedings, 73*(10), 77-982.

Treatment Episode Data Sets. (2005). *Treatment Episode Data Sets: 1994-2004.* http://wwwdasis.samhsa.gov/tedso4/tedsad2k4web.pd (accessed January 3, 2007).

Tuncel, M., Wang, Z., Arbique, D., Fadel, P. J., Victor, R. G. & Vongpatanasin, W. (2002). *Circulation, 105*(9), 1054-59.

Uncle Fester. (1998). *Advanced Techniques of Clandestine Psychedelic & Amphetamine Manufacture.* Port Townsend, WA: Loompanics Unlimited.

United Nations Office on Drugs and Crime [UNODC]. (2006). *2006 World Drug Report.* http://www.unodc.org/pdf/WDR_2005/volume_1_web.pdf (accessed January 15, 2007).

U.S. Census Bureau. (2007). *2007 Statistical Abstract. Tobacco Products -Summary: 1990 to 2005.* http://www.census.gov/compendia/statab/manufactures/nondurable_goods_industries/ (accessed, January 25, 2007).

U.S. Department of Justice. (2002). *Responsible fatherhood and the role of the family.* http://www.ojp.usdoj.gov/reentry/responsible.html (accessed March 8, 2006).

U.S. Surgeon General. (2000). *Reducing tobacco use: A report to the Surgeon General.* http://www.cdc.gov/tobacco/sgr/sgr_2000/sgr_tobacco_aag.htm (accessed August 10, 2006).

U.S. Surgeon General. (2004). *Health*

Consequences of Smoking: A Report of the Surgeon General. http://www.hhs.gov/surgeongeneral/library/smokingconsequences (accessed August 10, 2006).

Villalon, C. (July 2004). Cocaine Country. *National Geographic,* pp. 34-55.

Volkow, N. D., Chang, L., Wang, G. J., Fowler, J. S., Leonido-Yee M., Franceschi, D., et al. (2001). Association of dopamine transporter reduction with psychomotor impairment in methamphetamine abusers. *American Journal of Psychiatry, 158*(3), 383-89.

Volkow, N. D., Fowler, J. S., Wang, G., Ding, Y. & Gatley, S. J. (2002). Mechanism of action of methylphenidate: Insights from PET imaging studies. *Journal of Attention Disorders, 6*(1), 431-43.

Volkow, N. D., Fowler, J. S., Wang, G., Learned-Coughin, S., Yang, J., Logan, J., et al. (2005). The slow and long-lasting blockade of dopamine transporters in human brain induced by the new antidepressant drug radafaxine predict poor reinforcing effects. *Biological Psychiatry, 57*(6), 640-46.

Volkow, N. D., Fowler, J. S., Wang, G. J., Logan, J., Gatley, S. J. & Hitzemann, R. (1997). Relationship between subjective effects of cocaine and dopamine transporter occupancy. *Nature, 386,* 827-30.

Waldman, I. D. & Gizer, I. R. (February 27, 2006). *Clinical Psychology Revue.* Prepublication.

Wang, G. J., Volkow, N. D., Chang, L., Miller, E., Sedler, M. & Hitzemann, R. (2004). Partial recovery of brain metabolism in methamphetamine abusers after protracted abstinence. *American Journal of Psychiatry, 161*(2), 242-48.

Warnakulasuriva, S., Trivedy, C. & Peters, T. J. (2002). Editorial: Areca nut use: An independent risk for oral cancer. *British Medical Journal, 324.*

Weil, A. & Rosen, W. (2004). *From Chocolate to Morphine.* Boston: Houghton Mifflin Company.

Weinberg, B. A. & Bealer, B. K. (2001). *The World of Caffeine.* New York: Rutledge.

Weissman, M. M., Warner, V., Wickramaratne, P. J. & Kandel, D. B. (1999). Maternal smoking during pregnancy and psychopathology in offspring followed to adulthood. *Journal of the American Academy of Child and Adolescent Psychiatry, 38,* 892-99.

Wesson, D. R., Smith, D. E. & Steffens, S. C. (1992). *Crack and Ice: Treating Smokable Stimulant Abuse.* Center City, MN: Hazelden.

White, B. (January 11, 1999). Soft money donations soared despite ongoing investigations. *Washington Post,* p. A17.

Wiencke, J. K., Thurston, S. W., Kelsey, K. T., Varkonyi, A. & Wain, J. C. (1999). Early age at smoking initiation and tobacco carcinogen DNA damage in the lung. *Journal of the National Cancer Institute, 91*(7), 614-19.

Wilens, T. E., Farone, S. V., Biederman, J. & Gunawardena, S. (2003). Does stimulant therapy of ADHD beget later substance abuse? A meta analytic review of the literature. *Pediatrics, 111,* 174-85.

Wilens, T. E., Hahesy, A. L., Biederman, J., Bredin, E., Tanquay, S., Kwon, S., et al. (2005). Influence of parental SUD and ADHD on ADHD in their offspring. *American Journal of Addiction, 14*(2), 179-87.

World Health Organization [WHO]. (1997). The smoking epidemic: A fire in the global village. http://www.who.int/archives/inf-pr-1997/en/pr97-61.html (accessed May 22, 2007).

World Health Organization. (1998). International Classification of Diseases (ICD-10). Author.

World Health Organization. (2002). *Tobacco Epidemic: Health Dimensions.* WHO fact sheet. http://www5.who.int/tobacco/page.cfm?sid=47 (accessed August 10, 2006).

Xian, H., Scherrer, P. A. & Madden, P. A. (2005). Latent class typology of nicotine withdrawal. *Psychological Medicine, 35*(3), 409-19.

Zanolari, B., Ndjoko, K., Isoset, J. R., Marston, A. & Hoslettmen, K. (2003). Qualitative and quantitative determination of yohimbine. *Phytochemical Analysis, 14*(4), 193-201.

Zhou, F. C. & Bledsoe, S. (1996). Methamphetamine causes rapid varicosis, perforation and definitive degeneration of serotonin fibers. *Neuroscience Net,* Vol. 1, Article #00009.

Zickler, P. (2005). Site on Brain Cells Appears Crucial to Nicotine Addiction. *NIDA Notes, 20*(2), 1, 6. http://www.drugabuse.gov/NIDA_notes/NNvol20N2/Site.html (accessed August 10, 2006).

Ziedonis, D., Steinberg, M. A., Smelson, D. & Wyatt, D. O. (2003). Psychotic disorders. In A. W. Graham, T. K. Schultz, M. F. Mayo-Smith, R. K. Ries & B. B. Wilford, eds. *Principles of Addiction Medicine* (3rd ed., pp. 1297–320). Chevy Chase, MD: American Society of Addiction Medicine, Inc.

Downers:
Opiates/Opioids &
Sedative-Hypnotics

Because many patent medicines and cure-alls contained opium, sedatives, and other psychoactive drugs, patients often became addicted. This 1882 lithograph by Friedrich Graetz imagined a future where the drugstore replaced the pub as a gathering place for those who wanted to socialize and get high. Drugstores could have been the focus of Prohibition instead of alcohol.

Courtesy of the National Library of Medicine, Bethesda, MD

GENERAL CLASSIFICATION

- **Major Depressants.** The three major classes of downers (depressants) are opiates/opioids, sedative-hypnotics, and alcohol (*see Chapter 5*).
- **Minor Depressants.** The four minor downers are skeletal muscle relaxants, antihistamines, over-the-counter depressants, and look-alike depressants.

OPIATES/OPIOIDS

- **Classification.** Opiates are natural or semisynthetic derivatives of the opium poppy (e.g., morphine and heroin). Opioids are synthetic versions of opiates (e.g., fentanyl and methadone).
- **History of Use (*see Chapter 1*).** New refinement methods and the development of different routes of administration have helped increase the intensity of effects and consequently the abuse potential.
- **Effects of Opioids.** Most opiates and opioids, such as morphine and OxyContin,® control pain and often induce euphoria (an intense feeling of elation or well-being). The drugs also suppress coughs and control diarrhea. Opiates' and opioids' mimicking and manipulation of naturally occurring neurotransmitters cause most of these effects.
- **Side Effects of Opioids.** These drugs create problems, e.g., depressed respiration and heart rate, constipation, and slurred speech; these side effects worsen as use and dosage increase due to the development of tolerance, tissue dependence, and withdrawal symptoms.
- **Additional Problems with Heroin & Other Opioids.** Dangerous fetal effects, overdose, drug contamination, dirty needles, high cost, sexually transmitted diseases, abscesses, polydrug use problems, and especially addiction often occur with these drugs.
- **Morphine & Other Opioids.** Morphine is the standard drug used for pain relief; heroin causes the most social and health problems. Codeine, hydrocodone (Vicodin®), oxycodone (OxyContin®), methadone, meperidine (Demerol®), and other opioid analgesics (painkillers) are widely used and also abused.

SEDATIVE-HYPNOTICS

- **Classification.** Benzodiazepines, e.g., alprazolam (Xanax®) and clonazepam (Klonopin®), are the most frequently prescribed sedative-hypnotics. Sedatives are calming drugs, whereas hypnotics are sleep-inducing drugs.
- **History.** Calming and sleep-inducing drugs have always been desired. Sedative-hypnotics have ranged from bromides and chloral hydrate to barbiturates and benzodiazepines.
- **Use, Misuse, Abuse & Addiction.** Society's attitudes toward sedative-hypnotics swing between avid acceptance and wariness of addictive potential. Misuse and abuse of sedative-hypnotics occur due to a variety of reasons.
- **Benzodiazepines.** These sedative-hypnotics were developed as safe alternatives to barbiturates, but tolerance, addiction, withdrawal symptoms, and overdose still occur. These drugs can impair memory, and some have been used as a date-rape drug.
- **Barbiturates.** Since 1900 more than 2,500 barbiturate compounds have been developed (e.g., Seconal,® phenobarbital); they were often abused and widely used (until the introduction of benzodiazepines).
- **Other Sedative-Hypnotics.** These drugs, e.g., Ambien,® Lunesta,® Rozerem,® and GHB, prescribed for anxiety and other problems, were also abused for their psychic effects. GHB has been abused at rave and dance parties.

OTHER PROBLEMS WITH DEPRESSANTS

- **Drug Interactions.** Using two or more downers at one time (especially alcohol with a benzodiazepine) can lead to overdose, especially respiratory depression. Cross-tolerance and cross-dependence also develop.
- **Misuse & Diversion.** Two hundred million doses of prescription drugs are diverted to illicit channels each year in the United States. Besides diversion there are such problems as polydrug use and drug synergism.
- **Prescription Drugs & the Pharmaceutical Industry.** Worldwide expenditures on prescription drugs will be $665 billion to $685 billion in 2007. U.S. expenditures will be slightly more than one-third of the total. Of the over 3 billion prescriptions written each year in the United States, approximately 250 million were for psychoactive drugs, mostly downers. In addition Americans spend $15 billion to $20 billion each year on over-the-counter medications. Some of the most common are antihistamines, sleep aids, nondepressant analgesics, and anti-inflammatories (IMS Health, 2007).

Raids target gang ring behind deadly heroin

Chicago police officer among dozens arrested in 3 states

Sleeping pill competition heats up

Sleeping pill prescriptions grew "I don't think it is a deal break- ried," said David Woodburn, an er," said Dr. Timothy Komoto, a analyst at Prudential Equity Group LLC.

Methadone: GOOD DRUG, BAD DRUG

Mike Roberts is shown with his children, from left, Christopher, 9, Caitlin, 9, and Shay-Lynn, 7.
Photo courtesy Lisa Taylor

Prescription reactions sicken 700,000

Soma Addiction Among APAs a Growing Concern

By STEVEN TANAMACHI
Nichi Bei Times
A drug known as "soma" is

"For parents, it's hard watching

At least that many

Multiple medications can add to health risks

Professionals warn patients about taking improper combinations
By BILL KETTI

Man charged with forging prescriptions

Suspect in 100-plus instances of drug tampering is a technician at RVMC

Afghan opium production spikes

Lucrative trade puts more pressure on

Final figures, and an estimate um accounted for 92 perce of opium resin from Afghanistan's gross dom

Study: More teens pilfer legal drugs to get their buzz

Docs say many suffer needlessly from pain

Date-rape drug gains popularity

GHB, able to induce coma or death, is becoming more common on the scene
CROMBIE
ONIAN

Latest trend in drug abuse: Youths risk death for cough-remedy high

Hospitals, schools report

Drugs to warn of sleep dangers

Pain-pill abuse grows

Drug Facts in serious conse

DEA to change rules on addictive prescriptions

Overall, fewer teens drank alcohol, By PAUL RE the Associated

Deadly abuse of methadone tops other prescription drugs

Only cocaine kills

Mexico's drug war death toll tops 2,000

Survey: Chronic pain often goes untreated

One in five

Dulling the pain

Study: OTC drugs, prescriptions send more to ER than cocaine

Stolen, counterfeit drug problems rise

Survey: More teens using Oxycontin

Marijuana, other drug usage declines, but 'huffing' of inhalants rebounding

Pharmaceutical abuse rises
In 2004, 1.3 million people visited emergen rooms for ailments involving the abuse or misuse of drugs:
Illicit drugs such as Pharmaceuticals

By Donna Leinwand
USA TODAY
Abuse of prescription and over-the-counter drugs is sending more people to emergency rooms than cocaine, according to new

Study: USA ranks first worldwide in incidents
By Julie Appleby
USA TODAY
Counterfeiting, theft and diver-

the motive. "America has become the go-to market for counterfeiters because we pay the highest prices of anyone in the world," says Katherine Eban, author of Dangerous Doses: How Counterfeiters are Contaminating America's Drug Supply.

Teens and drugs: Good news and bad

4.0% 4.5% 5.0%
2002 2003 2004

GENERAL CLASSIFICATION

"Heroin is my doctor. Any pain that I had, be it physical or mental or whatever, that's what it's there for, for my—depression, whatever. It's just like medicine pretty much. And I don't know, after a while it became more like life itself. Like I needed it just to exist."

20-year-old male heroin addict

In the 2000s:

◇ a deadly mixture of heroin and fentanyl, a powerful opioid, made in a clandestine lab in Mexico, was said to be responsible for hundreds of deaths and hundreds of visits to emergency rooms in the United States, particularly in the Chicago area (Coen & Maxwell, 2006);

◇ the National Institute on Drug Abuse (NIDA) and the Drug Enforcement Administration (DEA) continued to issue warnings and papers about the **increase in prescription drug abuse**, reminiscent of the overprescription and overuse of opiates and stimulants in patent medicines at the end of the nineteenth century (National Institute on Drug Abuse [NIDA], 2005);

◇ the synthetic opioid painkillers (depressants) **hydrocodone (Vicodin,® Lortab,® and Norco®) and**

OxyContin® continued to be **abused** by a large segment of the opiate-using population;

◇ **"pharm parties,"** where teenagers would bring sedatives and opioid pills from their parents' medicine cabinets or from street dealers, became widespread (Leinwand, 2006);

◇ the United Nations antidrug chief announced that in 2006 **Afghanistan's opium harvest reached the highest levels ever recorded** (Drug Upsurge, 2006); and

◇ **alcohol (see Chapter 5) continues to be most ingrained in most of the word's cultures** along with caffeine and tobacco; it also causes the most social problems.

In general, **downers (depressants) depress the overall functioning of the central nervous system** (CNS) to induce sedation, muscle relaxation, drowsiness, and even coma (if used to excess). Some downers also induce a rush/high and often cause disinhibition of impulses and emotions. Unlike uppers that release and enhance the body's natural stimulatory neurochemicals, depressants produce their effects through a wide range of biochemical processes at different sites in the brain, spinal cord, and other organs such as the heart.

Some depressants mimic the body's natural sedating or inhibiting neurotransmitters (e.g., endorphins, enkephalins, or GABA [gamma amino butyric acid]), whereas others directly suppress the stimulation centers of the brain. Still others work in ways scientists haven't yet fully understood. Because of these variations, the depressants are grouped into a number of subclasses based on their chemistry, medical use, and legal classification.

◇ The three major classes of depressants are **opiates/opioids, sedative-hypnotics, and alcohol**.

◇ The four minor classes of depressants are **skeletal muscle relaxants, antihistamines, over-the-counter (OTC) downers, and look-alike downers**.

MAJOR DEPRESSANTS

OPIATES/OPIOIDS

Refinements and synthetic versions of the opium poppy's active ingredients, such as opium, morphine, codeine, hydrocodone (Vicodin®), oxycodone (OxyContin®), methadone, and even heroin, were **developed for the treatment of acute pain**, diarrhea, coughs, and a number of other illnesses. Most illicit users take these opiate/opioid drugs to experience euphoric effects, to avoid emotional and physical pain, and to suppress withdrawal symptoms.

SEDATIVE-HYPNOTICS

Sedative-hypnotics represent **a wide range of synthetic chemical substances developed to treat anxiety and insomnia**. The first, barbituric acid, was created in 1864 by Dr. Adolph Von Bayer. Other barbiturates (phenobarbital and Seconal®) followed until more than 2,500 had been created. Bromides, paraldehyde, and chloral hydrate were also widely used until the late 1940s. Since 1950 dozens of different sedative-hypnotics, such as meprobamate (Miltown®), Doriden,® methaqualone (Quaalude®—available only overseas), flunitrazepam (Rohypnol®—available overseas), GHB, and especially benzodiazepines (e.g., Valium® and Xanax®), have been created. All have toxic side effects when misused and can cause tissue dependence. Benzodiazepines are the most widely used prescription drugs, although psychiatric drugs, especially antidepressants such as Prozac,® have taken over a substantial share of the market.

ALCOHOL

Alcohol, the natural by-product of fermented plant sugars or starches, is the oldest psychoactive drug in the world. It has been widely used over the centuries for social, cultural, spiritual, and religious occasions. It is used for a number of medical remedies from sterilizing wounds to lessening the risk of heart attacks. Abuse also makes alcohol the world's second most destructive drug in terms of health consequences (after tobacco) and social consequences.

MINOR DEPRESSANTS

SKELETAL MUSCLE RELAXANTS

Centrally acting skeletal muscle relaxants include carisoprodol (Soma®), chlorzoxazone (Parafon Forte®), cyclobenzaprine (Flexeril®), baclofen (Lioresal®), and methocarbamol (Robaxin®). **They are synthetically developed CNS depressants aimed at areas of the brain responsible for muscle coordination and activity.** They are used to treat muscle spasms and pain. Although abuse of these products has been rare, their overall depressant effects on all parts of the central nervous system produce reactions similar to those caused by other abused depressants.

Recently, **carisoprodol (Soma®)** has shown up in drug-screening urine tests of a number of addicts, often in combination with other drugs, particularly benzodiazepines. In San Francisco it is used as a recreational drug of abuse among young Asians. It seems that carisoprodol (an unscheduled drug) is metabolized to meprobamate (a Controlled Substance Schedule IV sedative-hypnotic) that has anxiolytic, anticonvulsant, and muscle-relaxing properties. Because of the drug's abuse potential, some states (Alabama, Arizona, Arkansas, Florida, Georgia, and Idaho) have rescheduled carisoprodol to Schedule IV. Besides the Asian youth, users are typically White men or women (in equal numbers) in their early 40s (Bailey & Briggs, 2002). Abuse of carisoprodol caused more than 17,000 visits to emergency rooms in 2004, up from 10,000 in 2002 (Drug Abuse Warning Network [DAWN], 2007).

ANTIHISTAMINES

Antihistamines, **found in hundreds of prescription and OTC cold and allergy medicines** (including Benadryl,® Actifed,® and Tylenol P.M. Extra®), are synthetic drugs that were developed during the 1930s and 1940s for treatment of allergic reactions, prevention of ulcers, shock, rashes, motion sickness, and even symptoms of Parkinson's disease (Physicians' Desk Reference [PDR], 2007). In addition to blocking the release of histamine, these drugs cross the blood-brain barrier to induce the common and oftentimes potent side effect of depression of the central nervous system, resulting in drowsiness. Even antihistamines are occasionally abused for their depressant effects.

OVER-THE-COUNTER DOWNERS

Depressants, such as Nytol,® Sleep-Eze,® and Sominex,® are sold legally in stores without the need for a prescription. Depressants that were used in the 1880s became marketed as **sleep aids or sedatives** in the twentieth century. Scopolamine in low doses, antihistamines, bromide derivatives, and even alcohol constitute the active sedating components in many of these products. As with other depressant drugs, these products are occasionally abused for their sedating effects.

LOOK-ALIKE DOWNERS

Look-alike depressants were advertised along with look-alike stimulants in the early 1980s. The great commercial success of the look-alike stimulants encouraged exploitative drug manufacturers to sell **products that looked like prescription downers**. These companies took legally available antihistamines and packaged them in tablets and capsules that resembled restricted depressants, such as Quaalude,® Valium,® and Seconal.® As with the other antihistamines, look-alike downers cause drowsiness as a side effect thereby mimicking some of the effects of more-potent downers. They are rarely found nowadays except in a few magazine ads.

OPIATES/OPIOIDS

In the 2000s most of the headlines concerning opiates/opioids have involved:

◇ the lethal use of fentanyl-tainted heroin,

◇ the diversion of OxyContin,®

◇ the continuing abuse of hydrocodone (Vicodin®), and

◇ the expanded opium harvest from fields in Afghanistan.

To a lesser extent, media attention has focused on the treatment of pain in a clinical setting and the need to use sufficient opiates/opioids to give patients relief without fear of addicting them. In terms of treatment for opioid dependence, attention has focused on making therapeutic drugs such as **buprenorphine available through physicians' offices** and not just in drug treatment clinics.

Opiates/opioids, some of the **oldest and best-documented groups of drugs**, not only have been the principal drugs used to treat pain (analgesic), diarrhea, and coughs but have also been the source of continual and occasionally explosive worldwide problems, e.g., nineteenth-century Opium Wars, the rise of drug crime cartels, and the spread of AIDS and hepatitis C from shared infected needles. Heroin receives the most publicity, but other opiates/opioids also create problems and can be used compulsively. The actual incidence of hydrocodone (Vicodin®) and oxycodone (OxyContin®) abuse in the United States is greater than that of heroin during the 2000s.

Since the 1970s **the discovery of the body's own natural painkillers— endorphins and enkephalins— significantly changed our understanding of opiates/opioids** as well as the whole field of addictionology, biochemical research, and pain management (Goldstein, 2001).

CLASSIFICATION

OPIUM, OPIATES & OPIOIDS

Opioids are fully synthetic versions of opiates. Opium is processed from the milky fluid of the unripe seedpod of the opium poppy plant (*Papaver somniferum*). The white, opaque, milky sap coagulates and turns brown or black when exposed to air. This gummy sap is scraped from the poppy with a blunt iron blade. It will secrete the fluid for several days, and it may be tapped up to six times. Smaller amounts of opium can also be extracted from the rest of the plant (called "poppy straw"). There are other poppy plants, but only the *Papaver somniferum,* which is 1 to 5 ft. tall, produces opium in any quantity. (*Papaver bracteatum* produces a small amount of opium.) There are more than 25 known alkaloids in opium, but the two most prevalent, called *opiates,* are **morphine (10% to 20% of the milky fluid) and codeine (0.7% to 2.5%)** (Karch, 1996; Marnell, 1997). Although a small amount of opium is used to make antidiarrheal preparations (e.g., tincture of opium and paregoric), virtually all the opium coming into this country is refined into morphine, codeine, and the baine. The main reason for the decline in the popularity of opium is the availability of semisynthetic and synthetic prescription opioids.

◇ **Opium poppy extracts** include morphine, codeine, and thebaine.

◇ **Semisynthetic opiates**, e.g., heroin, hydrocodone (Vicodin®), oxycodone (OxyContin® and Percodan®), and hydromorphone (Dilaudid®), are made from the three opium poppy extracts (alkaloids).

◇ **Fully synthetic opiatelike drugs** include meperidine (Demerol®), methadone, and propoxyphene (Darvon®).

◇ **Synthetic opioid antagonists** (naloxone and naltrexone) block the effects of opiates and opioids.

In general, **opium extracts and semisynthetic opium preparations are referred to as** *opiates.* **Synthetic opiates are referred to as** *opioids.* ***Opioid* is also used as a generic term for all drugs in this category.**

HISTORY OF USE

It used to be thought that the cultivation of opium poppies was first common in ancient Mesopotamia, Egypt, and Greece around 3400 B.C. and spread eastward to Asia. The remains of cultivated poppy seeds and pods from 4000 B.C. have been found in Neolithic villages in Switzerland, however, suggesting that opium was culti-

Afghan militiamen tend their fields of opium poppies in 1990. They still do the same almost 20 years later. Many militias around the world fund their insurgencies with money from growing and trafficking drugs. Currently, Afghanistan grows more than 90% of the world's opium in spite of the overthrow of the Taliban and the presence of NATO military forces.
© 1990 Alain Labrousse

of Melos wrote, "It is better to suffer pain than to become dependent on opium." Erasistratus of Ceos said, "Opium should be completely avoided [due to addiction]."

Over the centuries,

◊ experimentation with **different methods of use**,
◊ development of **new refinements of the drug**,
◊ **synthesis of molecules** that act like the natural opiates, and
◊ **time-release versions** of the drugs

have slowly increased not only the benefits of these substances but also their potential for abuse.

ORAL INGESTION

Opium, from the Greek word *opòs*, meaning "juice" or "sap," was originally **chewed, eaten, or blended in various liquids and drunk**. Although the seeds can be pressed to yield vegetable oil and the residual can be used

vated in eastern Europe and spread from there (Booth, 1999).

The ancient Sumerians and Egyptians recorded the paradoxical nature of opium in their medical texts, listing it as a **cure for all illnesses, a pleasure-inducing substance, and a poison**. When Socrates was ordered to commit suicide, he drank from a cup that contained not only poisonous hemlock but also opium to dull the pain of dying. Ironically, modern-day euthanasia or assisted-suicide formulas often include morphine or other opioids. Greek writings told of the gods' use of opium for mystical or mythical purposes; Greek heroes, such as Jason, used opium to sedate monsters. Demeter, the Greek goddess of agriculture, took opium to sleep and forget the death of her daughter, Persephone. Hippocrates, the "father of medicine," was more practical about its use. He prescribed it for sleep, diarrhea, pain, female ills, and epidemics (Booth, 1999; Hoffman, 1990; Latimer & Goldberg, 1981).

The addictive liability of opium was recognized early on. Around 500 B.C., the Greek philosopher Diagoras

In the nineteenth century, patent medicines laced with morphine, opium, cocaine, and Cannabis could be bought anywhere. Physicians prescribed opiates as freely as aspirin and, as a result, physician-induced addiction (iatrogenic addiction) became common, especially among women.
Courtesy of the National Library of Medicine, Bethesda, MD

TABLE 4–1   OPIATES/OPIOIDS

Generic Drug Name	Trade Names	Street Names
OPIATES (opium poppy extracts)		
Opium (Schedule II)	Pantopon,® Laudanum®	"O," op, poppy
Diluted opium (Schedule III)	Paregoric®	
Morphine (Schedule II)	Infumorph,® Kadian,® Avinza,® Roxanol,® MS Contin,® Kadian®	Murphy, morph, "M," Miss Emma
Codeine (Schedule III) (also called "methylmorphine") (usually w/aspirin or Tylenol®)	Empirin® w/codeine Tylenol® w/codeine Doriden® w/codeine Robitussin A-C	Number 4s (1 grain), Number 3s (1/2 grain) Loads, sets, 4s, and doors
Thebaine (Schedule II)	None	None
SEMISYNTHETIC OPIATES		
Diacetylmorphine (Schedule I)	Heroin	Smack, junk, tar (chiva, puro, goma, puta, chapapote), Mexican brown, cheese, China white, Harry, skag, shit, Rufus, Perze, "H," horse, dava, boy
Hydrocodone (Schedule III)	Vicodin,® Hycodan,® Lortab,® Lorcet,® Zydone,® Norco,® Tussend®	Vike, Vic, Watson 387
Hydromorphone (Schedule II)	Dilaudid,® Hydal,® Sophidone,® Hydrostat®	Dillies, drugstore heroin
Oxycodone (Schedule II)	OxyContin,® Percodan,® Tylox,® Combunox,® Endocodone,® Oxydose,® OxyFAST,® Percolone®	Percs, hillbilly heroin, ocs, oxy, oxy-80s. oxycotton, o'coffin
SYNTHETIC OPIATES (OPIOIDS)		
Buprenorphine (Schedule V)	Buprenex,® Subotex,® Zyban® Suboxone® (w/naloxone)	Bupe, sub
Butorphanol (Schedule IV)	Stadol®	
Fentanyl (Schedule II) Sufentanil	Sublimaze,® Duragesic,® Actiq,® Sufenta®	Street derivatives are misrepresented as China white
Levomethadyl acetate (Schedule II) (long-acting methadone)	LAAM®	Lam
Levorphanol (Schedule II)	Levo-Dromoran®	
Meperidine (Schedule II)	Demerol,® Mepergan,® Pethidine®	Dummies
Methadone (Schedule II)	Dolophine®	Juice
Oxymorphone (Schedule II)	Numorphan®	
Pentazocine (Schedule IV)	Talwin®	Part of Ts and blues
Propoxyphene (Schedule IV)	Darvon,® Darvocet-N,® Dolene,® Wygesic,® Propacet®	Pink ladies, pumpkin seeds
Tramadol	Ultram,® Ultracet®	
OPIOID ANTAGONISTS		
Naloxone	Narcan,® Nalone,® Narconti®	
Naltrexone	Revia,® Trexan,® Depade® time release-Naltrel,® Vivitrol®	

as fodder for cattle, it is the medicinal properties that make it so valuable. Though in past eras, the drug was used extensively, the abuse potential of opium was relatively low because it had a **bitter taste and a low concentration of active ingredients, and the supplies were limited**. When taken orally the drug must go through the digestive sys-

tem before it enters the bloodstream and makes its way to the brain 20 or 30 minutes later.

In ancient writings opium is listed as an ingredient in more than 700 remedies. The use of opium in medications and potions continued through the Middle Ages and into the Renaissance (in the early 1500s), when it was repop-

ularized by the **Swiss alchemist Paracelsus, who concocted laudanum**, a tincture of opium (powdered opium in alcohol) that he prescribed for dysentery, pain, diarrhea, and coughs (O'Brien, Cohen, Evans, et al., 1992). Over the next three centuries, other opium mixtures were developed, especially **paregoric (opium in alcohol plus cam-**

phor), for the treatment of diarrhea. Paregoric is still available as a prescription drug.

SMOKING

In the sixteenth century, opium smoking via the **introduction of the pipe from North America to Europe and Asia** by Portuguese traders **set the stage for the widespread nonmedical use of opium.** Smoking puts more of the active ingredients of the drug into the bloodstream by way of the lungs; the vaporized opium reaches the brain in seven to 10 seconds. The higher concentration of the opiate produces a stronger sense of euphoria, relaxation, and well-being than when the drug is ingested, thereby encouraging abuse.

Although opium smoking was initially limited to the middle and upper classes in China (because of the high cost of the drug), it caused so many social and health problems that it was banned in 1729. Because the opium trade had become extremely lucrative, however, stopping it was incredibly difficult. In the early 1800s, when prohibition was again tried, the powerful trading companies of the West (e.g., the East India Company of England) along with their governments forced the Chinese government, through the **Opium Wars,** to continue the trade and to cede Hong Kong to the British (Hanes & Sanello, 2002; Latimer & Goldberg, 1981).

As the supplies became more plentiful, use increased. **Opium smoking was introduced to the United States by some of the 70,000 Chinese workers who were brought over to build the railroads and to mine gold, copper, and mercury.** The bigoted reaction to these Asian immigrants produced headlines that screamed "yellow fiends" and "seducers of white women," resulting in a spate of prohibitory laws that often focused on opium smoking.

In the twentieth century, heroin smoking gained in popularity especially as higher grades became available. One of the current methods of smoking heroin is to heat some on tin foil and inhale the fumes through a straw. This method is called "chasing the dragon." The abuse potential of this method of use is extremely high.

"I had a very close friend who I was associated with who was smoking a pretty vast quantity every day . . . a half a gram to a gram every day, and he used to really get on me and tell me that I was a junkie because I was putting a needle in my arm. And I would tell him, 'Hey, okay, my method is different, but you're a junkie, too. You have a habit.'"

34-year-old recovering heroin addict

REFINEMENT OF MORPHINE, CODEINE & HEROIN

In 1805 German pharmacist **Frederick W. Serturner isolated morphine from opium**. He found it to be **10 times as strong as opium** and therefore a much better pain reliever. For the first time, exact measured doses of an opiate anodyne (painkiller) were possible. (The strength and the purity of opium varied widely.) Morphine eased the pain of wounded soldiers beginning with the Crimean War. In America during the U.S. Civil War, poppies were cultivated in Virginia, Tennessee, South Carolina, and Georgia. Unfortunately, the greater strength of morphine and the intensity of intravenous (IV) use increased the potential for opiate addiction or morphinism. Opium was still widely used during the war to treat diarrhea and malaria. Morphine was eventually also prescribed for anemia, asthma, cholera, nervous dyspepsia, insanity, neuralgia, and vomiting.

In 1832 codeine, the other major component of opium, was isolated. It got its name from the Greek word *kodeia,* which means "poppyhead." Because it was only **twice as strong as opium**, it was often used in cough syrups and patent medicines.

In 1874 British chemist **C. R. Alder Wright refined heroin (diacetylmorphine) from morphine** in an attempt to find a more effective painkiller that didn't have addictive properties. This powerful opiate (five to eight times more powerful than morphine) stayed on the shelf until 1898, when Heinrich Dreser, working at Bayer and Company in Germany, thought it should be pro-

moted for coughs, chest pain, tuberculosis, pneumonia, and even as a cure for morphinism (Trebach, 1981). **Heroin crossed the blood/brain barrier much more rapidly than morphine. The rush and the subsequent euphoria came on more quickly and were more intense** (Karch, 1996). The new drug created a subculture of compulsive heroin users. It was estimated that there were between 250,000 and 1 million opium, morphine, and heroin abusers in the United States shortly after the turn of the century.

INJECTION USE

Another major development of the nineteenth century regarding opiate use was **the development of the hypodermic needle in 1853**, credited to Dr. Alexander Wood of Edinburgh and Dr. Charles Hunter of St. Georges Hospital in London. Initially, drugs were injected only subcutaneously, but users found that intravenous use could **inject high concentrations of the drug directly into the bloodstream** through the veins. Because the early glass syringes and needles were so expensive, many early morphine addicts were from the middle and upper classes.

It takes 15 to 30 seconds for an injected opiate or opioid to affect the central nervous system. If the drug is injected just under the skin or in a muscle ("skin popping" or "muscling"), the effects are delayed by five to eight minutes. Until the development of the hypodermic needle, oral use of morphine and smoking of opium induced a certain euphoria and relief from physical and emotional pain, but **with intravenous use an intense rush also occurred**. The intensity of the user's first rush from IV heroin injection made compulsive drug-seeking behavior more likely. Many IV heroin users spend their whole drug-using careers trying to reexperience that rush of euphoria.

PATENT MEDICINES

During the 1800s opiates became so popular that **hundreds of tonics and medications,** such as Mrs. Winslow's Soothing Syrup, Dover's Powder, McMunn's Elixir of Opium, and Godfrey's Cordial came on the market to treat everything from tired blood and colicky babies to coughs, diarrhea, and toothaches (Armstrong & Armstrong, 1991). The working classes often put their babies under the care of baby minders who kept their dozen charges half-loaded with Godfrey's Cordial or other opiate-laced syrup, and then the mothers who came home from 14 hours of work would give them some more so they could get some sleep and be ready for the next day's work. The working-class parents also used opium-laced mixtures to ease their pain.

The use of opioids for pleasure (recreational use) by the middle and upper classes also came into vogue as the number of opium parlors and the availability of newly concocted opiate mixtures increased. In addition, physicians were not fully aware of or simply ignored the addictive potential of opiate drugs, so **iatrogenic (physician-induced) addiction** was a common problem. In fact, four to eight times as many opiate prescriptions per capita were written at the start of the twentieth century compared with the present day. Surveys in the 1880s showed that **between 56% and 71% of opium addicts were women** (Hoffman, 1990). Some of the more famous female opiate users were the pioneering social worker Jane Addams, the well-known actress Sarah Bernhardt, and the writers Elizabeth Barrett Browning, Charlotte Brontë, and Louisa May Alcott. Male writers and poets were not immune to the drug. Samuel Coleridge, Charles Baudelaire, Lord Byron, John Keats, Edgar Allan Poe, and Algernon Swinburne used laudanum and other opiates (Aldrich, 1994; Zackon, 1992).

"I arrived on the stage in a semiconscious state, yet delighted with the applause I received."
Sarah Bernhardt, 1890 (Palmer & Horowitz, 1982)

SNORTING

In addition to drinking, eating, smoking, and injecting opiates, new immigrants from Europe introduced the habit of sniffing or snorting heroin (also called "insufflation" and "intranasal use"). It takes five to eight minutes for the drug to enter the nasal capillaries and reach the central nervous system. From the turn of the century until the 1920s, heroin addicts were split evenly between sniffers and shooters (Karch, 1996). Because more of the drug is needed when snorted to get the same high as when injected, low prices of heroin encouraged insufflation especially for those who were afraid of the needle. This route was popular with heroin-using GIs in Vietnam because of the easy availability and high purity of the drug. **More than half of all heroin addicts entering treatment began their heroin use by insufflation** (Casriel, Rockwell & Stepherson, 1988; Treatment Episode Data Sets [TEDS], 2007). A recent trend has been to dissolve heroin in water and use it as a nasal spray; this method is called "shabanging."

TWENTIETH CENTURY

Rising concern over the problems caused by use and abuse of opium, morphine, and especially heroin spurred various governments to action. Casual **nonmedical use of opiates was declared illegal at the beginning of the twentieth century** by the international community through the Hague Resolutions and by the United States through **the Pure Food and Drug Act in 1906 and the Harrison Narcotics Act in 1914.** By 1924 production of heroin in the United States was prohibited. The gradual proliferation of laws also increased the jail population. Commitments to federal prisons for violations of the narcotics law rose from 63 in 1915 to 2,529 in 1928 (about one-third of all federal prisoners) (Musto, 1973). In 2004 the number of federal prisoners held for drug offenses was 155,900, which represented about 86.5% of the 180,328 federal prisoners that year (U.S. Department of Justice, 2006).

In the first two decades of the twentieth century, opioid addiction was considered a medical problem and was treated by physicians. Even though alcoholism was considered more debilitating and certainly more expensive than opioid addiction, a number of heroin treatment centers were opened. The federal government opened two facilities, one in Lexington, Kentucky (1935 to 1974) and the other in Fort Worth, Texas (1935 to 1972).

The Kentucky facility housed approximately 1,400 "narcotics addicts."

The availability or prohibition of different opiates/opioids shifted methods of use. When the importation of smokable opium was banned in 1909, it produced a shift to heroin (Zule, Vogtsberger & Desmond, 1997). Because these restrictions limited supplies and made opium and heroin valuable commodities, **growing, processing, and distributing opiates/opioids, especially heroin, became major sources of revenue for criminal organizations worldwide**. These groups have included the Chinese Triads, the Mafia and the French Connection, Mexican *narcoficantes,* African traffickers, the Russian Mafia, and, more recently, the Colombian Cartels.

In addition, **diversion of legal prescription opiates/opioids,** such as oxycodone (OxyContin®), hydrocodone (Vicodin®), and cough syrups, through theft, bogus purchases, forged prescriptions, and especially through easy Internet accessibility created an expanding illegal market of prescription opioids.

"I went to different physicians. I would rip off prescription pads, and since I worked in the medical field, writing my own prescriptions was no problem except that I committed a felony every time I did it, which was once a week. I never got caught, but I always lived in mortal fear that they would get me."
Recovering Darvon® (propoxyphene) abuser

Currently, an estimated **4.6 million Americans use prescription opiates/opioids illicitly every month** compared with 136,000 to 800,000 heroin abusers. (The estimates of heroin users vary radically. For example, New York City alone is estimated to have 200,000 heroin addicts.) Approximately 3.5 million Americans have tried heroin (Substance Abuse and Mental Health Services Administration [SAMHSA], 2006). In 2004 approximately one-third of heroin treatment admissions inhaled the drug and almost two-thirds injected it (DASIS, 2004; TEDS, 2007). Recently, smoking and snorting heroin have increased in popularity in the United States due to an influx of white heroin from Colombia, the Golden Triangle, and Afghanistan and tar heroin from Mexico. Larger percentages of "sniffers" and smokers are more likely to be found in the eastern half of the United States. Some of the "snorters" mix tar heroin with water and snort it out of a Visine® spray bottle. The latest wrinkle (popular in the Dallas, Texas schools) is a heroin-laced powder called *cheese*. This drug is a mixture of a little bit of heroin (maybe 10%) mixed with Tylenol PM®; a quarter gram sells for five dollars.

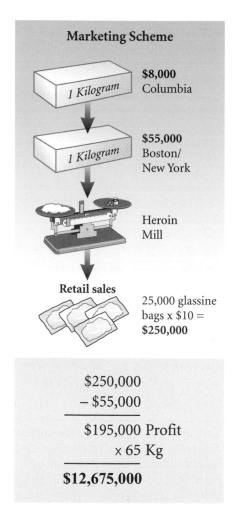

Marketing Scheme

$8,000 Columbia — 1 Kilogram

$55,000 Boston/New York — 1 Kilogram

Heroin Mill

Retail sales

25,000 glassine bags x $10 = **$250,000**

$250,000
– $55,000
———————
$195,000 Profit
x 65 Kg
———————
$12,675,000

Figure 4-1 •

The raw opium sells for a few hundred dollars per kilogram (kg) in Colombia. When refined to heroin, the price goes up to $8,000. On the East Coast of the United States, the price rises to $55,000. After it is adulterated and divided into 25,000 glassine bags that sell for $10 each ("dime bags"), with 40 to 50 milligrams (mg) in each bag, the money grows to $250,000.

(Drug Enforcement Administration [DEA], 2006)

A DEA agent and a Thai soldier stand at an illegal opium jungle laboratory in Thailand that has just been raided. The 55-gallon barrel is filled with cooked opium ready to be transformed into 20 kg of morphine and then into an equal weight of heroin. A small jungle lab such as this can process 60 kg of heroin every four days.

Courtesy of George Skaggard

. . . .

HEROIN: A WORLD VIEW

Since 1992 there has been a steady increase in heroin use worldwide due mostly to increased supply and decreased cost. There are **5 million to 10 million regular heroin users worldwide**, and a dozen countries are battling the growth, use, smuggling, and exportation of heroin on their own soil. Since 1986 worldwide production of illicit opium, the raw ingredient to make heroin, has more than doubled. Even with the increase in supply, **the United States consumes only 3% (10 to 15 metric tons) of the world's heroin supply**.

The major illicit opium grower is Afghanistan, part of what used to be called the Golden Crescent (Afghanistan and Pakistan). **Afghanistan grew more than 6,100 metric tons of opium (the equivalent of 600 tons of heroin) in 2006, 92% of the world's supply; most Afghani heroin is used in Europe and Asia.** This was an all-time record for opium growing in spite of the U.S. drug czar's claim that we

were reducing opium poppy cultivation in Afghanistan. Opium is supporting a good part of the Taliban counterinsurgency in Afghanistan.

The Golden Triangle (Myanmar [Burma], Thailand, and Laos) is the only other significant grower of illicit opium (386 metric tons of opium, or 38 metric tons of heroin) (United Nations, 2006). Other countries grow heroin, but their markets are smaller and more regional. Several ex-Soviet republics, especially Tajikistan and Turkmenistan, qualify as "narco-states."

In the United States, most heroin comes from Mexico (8 metric tons) and Colombia (3.5 metric tons) (Chronicle News Service, 2006; United Nations, 2006). **The amount coming from Colombia has dropped significantly** (about 75% less) in the past five years, whereas the amount coming from Mexico has been fairly constant. India is the largest grower of opium, but it is all legal and the trade is highly regulated; the vast majority of the crop is used for medical purposes.

The events of September 11, 2001, and the subsequent overthrow of the Taliban government in Afghanistan have confused the opium control efforts of the United Nations and the United States. The **increased drug trade has been used to finance the renewed insurgency by supporters of the Taliban.** This is part of the reason why insurgents increased their activity four-fold in 2006 (Insurgents, 2006). It is likely that opium will continue to come out of Afghanistan for many generations to come.

Southwest Asian heroin from Iran, Turkey, and Lebanon is often known as smokable "Persian brown" or "Perze," which can be more than 90% pure. Many of the countries that grow opium now also have exploding addict populations. There are an estimated 1.9 million opioid users in Pakistan alone. Thailand and Myanmar have 0.5 million addicts each.

Since the 1940s Mexico has been a major supplier of heroin to the United States. Perhaps the 2,000-mile-long U.S.-Mexico border is more porous than other routes. Mexico became the number one supplier when the Turkish opium fields dried up in the early 1970s. Most of the heroin was light or dark brown powder and not as pure as Golden Triangle white heroin. Many of the present-day gangs, based mostly in the Mexican states of Durango, Michoacán, Nuevo Leon, and Sinaloa, have been in operation for more than 20 years. Violent battles and even beheadings have become common in those states, particularly in Michoacán.

In the 1980s a relatively new form of **Mexican heroin, known as "tar" or "black tar,"** took over a large part of the market in the western United States. Tar heroin is potent, 40% to 80% pure, but it also has more plant impurities than the Asian or Colombian refinement of the drug. A small chunk (black or brown) the size of a match head, which is enough for two to five doses, costs $20 to $25. Tar heroin, also called "chapapote," "puta," "goma," "chiva," and "puro," is unique in that it's sold as a gummy, pasty substance rather than in the usual powder form. Tar heroin dissolves easily in water and is also more likely to be smoked than other types of heroin.

"I came from the Midwest, where we mostly get China white, and that to me is a whole lot cleaner than tar. I'd never seen an abscess or anything like that. People on the West Coast have abscesses all the time because here it is black tar. The stuff I see when I break it down—there's so much crap in it. It's like, yuck, I can't believe I put that shit in my veins, but I do it anyway."
27-year-old female heroin addict

In addition to countries that grow, refine, and sell the drug, several countries **have major refining facilities or act as transshipment points** for heroin. These transshipment countries include the Netherlands, Canada, Italy (especially Sicily), France, and Nigeria (the latter also produces its own heroin). Also many ex-Soviet republics and satellites (e.g., Armenia, Uzbekistan, Kazakhstan, and Turkmenistan) are involved in transshipment as well as production of heroin (DEA, 2006; National Drug Intelligence Center, 2007).

In the early 1990s, a number of **Colombian cocaine cartels diversified and started to grow and distribute opium/heroin** (in addition to their fields of coca shrubs) in an effort to cash in on the growing heroin market. Their existing cocaine distribution channels enabled them to expand rapidly. They also sold purer and cheaper heroin to compete with the China white imported by the Mafia and Asian gangs. The Colombian cartels distribute mostly on the U.S. East Coast in New York, Newark, Boston, and Philadelphia (DEA, 2006). With the decline in Colombian heroin production, however, Afghani and Golden Triangle heroin might start flowing more freely to the East Coast. According to the DEA, it is unlikely that Mexican tar heroin will expand to fill this need.

***NOTE:* For the rest of this chapter, we use the generic term *opioids* to denote both natural and semisynthetic *opiates* and synthetic *opioids*.**

EFFECTS OF OPIOIDS

Medically, physicians most often prescribe opioids to:

◇ **deaden pain**,
◇ **control coughing**, and
◇ **stop diarrhea**.

The seized kilogram of tar heroin, the most common type of heroin on the U.S. West Coast, is broken down into small 50 mg packets by the time it reaches the streets.
Courtesy of the U.S. Drug Enforcement Administration

Nonmedically, users self-prescribe opioids to:

◇ **drown out emotional pain,**
◇ **get a rush,**
◇ **induce euphoria,** and
◇ **prevent withdrawal symptoms.**

But to truly comprehend opioids, it is important to understand how pain and pleasure are connected to the nervous system.

PAIN

Pain is a warning signal that tells us whether we are being damaged. A physical injury sends a message to the spinal cord and on to the brainstem and the medial portion of the thalamus in our brain, which in turn tells the body to protect itself from further damage (Knapp, Ciraulo & Jaffe, 2005). **The pain message is transmitted from nerve cell to nerve cell by a neurotransmitter called *substance P.*** This neuropeptide, first discovered in 1931, signals the intensity of painful stimuli.

If the pain is too intense, the body tries to protect itself by softening the pain signals. It does this by flooding the brain and the spinal cord with endorphins and enkephalins. These neurotransmitters, which are released by secondary terminals, attach themselves principally to opioid mu, kappa, and delta receptor sites.

Receptors in the spinal cord are crucial in pain control. These sites can be on the sending neuron or receiving neuron. On the sending neuron, they inhibit the release of substance P as well as slow the firing rate. On the receiving neuron, they also decrease the firing rate of substance P (Figure 4-2) (DeVane, 2001; Meyer & Quenzer, 2005). Many pain signals, however, still get through.

If the pain remains unbearable, opioid medications can be used to relieve the agony. **Opioid drugs are effective because they act like the body's endogenous (naturally occurring) painkillers (endorphins and enkephalins).** Opioid medications (exogenous or external opioids) not only limit the release of substance P but also help block what little does get

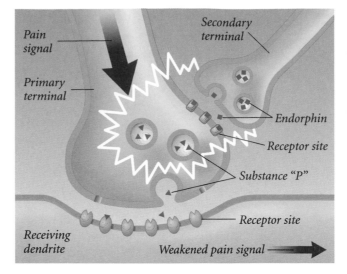

Figure 4-2 •
This diagram of a synapse shows that when pain signals are being transmitted through the nervous system, a secondary terminal releases endorphins that then slot into receptor sites on the primary terminal and limit the release of the pain neurotransmitter substance P.
© 2003 CNS Productions, Inc.

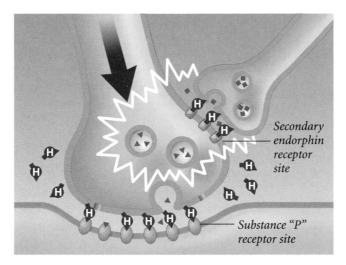

Figure 4-3 •
Heroin (or any opioid) slots into the secondary endorphin receptor sites, limiting the release of substance P. It also blocks most of the substance P that gets through by slotting into the primary substance P receptor sites on the receiving dendrite of the next neuron.
© 2003 CNS Productions, Inc.

through to the receiving neurons (Figure 4-3).

Pain control is not limited only to physical pain. Decreased anxiety, a sense of detachment, drowsiness, and a deadening of unwanted emotions are often experienced by opioid users. This is due to the drug's inhibiting effect on the locus coeruleus on top of the brainstem and its influence on the dopaminergic reward/reinforcement pathway. Experiments have shown that **severe stress alone can activate natural endorphins to mitigate emotional pain** (Goldstein, 2001). In one animal experiment, the greater the stress relief, the more the use of morphine was remembered, thus imprinting and reinforcing the concept

that emotional agitation can be relieved by drugs (Will, Watkins & Maier, 1998). This negative reinforcement uses many of the same brain mechanisms that cause positive reinforcement of drug-seeking behavior.

"When you are loaded on heroin, you can watch your best friend get hit by a car, all your friends could be dying, your dog could come down with rabies, and you could get AIDS, herpes, and cancer all at once and you don't care. You're separated from it and blocked off from your emotions."

18-year-old female heroin addict

Even though all opioids relieve pain, small alterations in the molecular structure of the various opioids can produce dramatic differences in the strength of the drug, how long it will last, and what the side effects will be. For example, heroin, codeine, and Darvon® will relieve pain for four to six hours, whereas fentanyl will barely last one hour but is strong enough to be used as an anesthetic during surgery.

PLEASURE

The other major effect of opioids involves endorphins and dopamine and their effect on the mesolimbic dopaminergic reward/reinforcement pathway, which includes the nucleus accumbens. As described in Chapter 2, this system, through a variety of mechanisms, **positively reinforces actions that are good for the body's survival**. The normal activation of this system **gives a surge of pleasure that encourages repetition of an action**, such as eating or having sex. Animal research suggests that in addition to giving a surge of positive reinforcement, **dopamine release in this pathway helps the brain remember (unconsciously) what was done** so it can be done again in the future (Wickelgren, 1998).

"The last shot is never good enough. You're always looking for a certain shot. You're looking for the same shot you had when you first did the drug, which you'll never get again."
22-year-old recovering heroin addict

Searching for a high (or relief from pain, which can both feel the same), some people try opioids because the drugs activate this reward/reinforcement pathway. Opioids affect this pathway by:

◇ **slotting into the receptor sites meant for endorphins/enkephalins;**

◇ **inhibiting the action of GABA,** resulting in increased activation of the pathway;

◇ **triggering glutamate receptors** that enhance responsiveness of dopamine neurons, resulting in activation of the pathway; and

◇ **increasing the release and enhancing the effect of dopamine** (Carlezon, Boundy, Haile, et al., 1997).

Of the various opioids, **heroin has the strongest effect on the reward/ reinforcement pathway**.

"It's like putting all your troubles in one bag and you have a solution for it and that's heroin. Your one problem is to worry about getting your heroin every day."
72-year-old recovering heroin addict

When the natural (endogenous) endorphins and enkephalins give a surge of pleasure (positive reinforcement), various cells in the brain monitor the action and **when the need is filled, the cutoff signal goes out: "you can stop now," "mission accomplished," "that's enough."** Powerful psychoactive drugs, including **heroin, can disrupt this cutoff switch** in a variety of ways and reinforce the desire to continue the behavior. Genetically, some people are more susceptible to disruption of the switch. In others, excessive drug use is the more powerful factor. The more frequently this circuit is overloaded by heroin or other powerful opioids, the greater the malfunction of the satiation switch (Hyman, 1998).

FROM PLEASURE TO PAIN

As we've seen, people use an opioid to either

◇ alleviate emotional/mental/physical pain or
◇ induce a good feeling/rush/high.

What is interesting is that **the area of the brain that signals pleasure/ reward is the same area that signals alleviation of pain** (Goldstein, 2001), **so relief from the pain of withdrawal symptoms is also a powerful motivator for continued use**. In an experiment at the University of Cambridge in England, researchers found in animal experiments that **the relief of withdrawal symptoms functioned as a much more effective incentive for self-administration of the drug than simply a desire for the rush, and the**

longer the heroin was used, the greater the incentive to use during withdrawal (Hutcheson, Everitt, Robbins, et al., 2001).

Because one of the functions of the reward/reinforcement pathway is to encourage a person to repeat whatever activated it, the rush or the pain alleviation is interpreted as something that is good for the body. People who have become **drug abusers will keep using past the point of pain relief, searching for an emotional high, whereas nonabusers stop at pain relief**. Nonusers often think that chronic heroin users don't get a rush or high after chronic use and that their body merely returns to a nonwithdrawal or almost normal state when they shoot up, snort, or smoke. They often don't understand the power of opioid-induced pain relief in the addict. Sometimes even the addict doesn't recognize the incentive and the euphoria of immediate pain relief.

"Heroin lasts, like the part where you're getting high, lasts for maybe a couple of months tops, and then I don't remember exactly but it seems it was like all of a sudden like a maintenance kind of thing."
26-year-old heroin addict

RECEPTOR SITES

There are actually **multiple natural opioid receptor sites** for the body's own opioids (endorphins, enkephalins, and dynorphins). **The main receptors, μ (mu), κ (kappa), and σ (sigma)**, are found in the brain, the spinal cord, the gastrointestinal track, the autonomic nervous system, on white blood cells, and on a variety of other organs. **Opioids slot into these same receptor sites** but cause more-intense reactions than the body's own (endogenous) opioids. Each opioid drug has a unique affinity for each site. At one synapse the drug might act like an agonist and trigger effects; at another it might act as an antagonist, blocking changes; at a third it might work as a combination agonist and antagonist. For example:

◇ mu and sigma receptors trigger the reward/reinforcement pathway, block pain transmission, alter mood, cause pupil contraction, and depress the autonomic nervous system, including respiration and blood pressure;

◇ kappa receptors seem to induce dysphoria and endocrine changes as well as mediate (control) pain at the spinal cord level (Borg & Kreek, 2003; Knapp, Ciraulo & Jaffe, 2005; Simon, 2005).

So one drug, such as fentanyl, will subdue pain more than heroin, whereas heroin has a greater influence on the rush and the high.

COUGH SUPPRESSION & DIARRHEA CONTROL

Besides pain control and pleasure, opioids are used to suppress coughs and control diarrhea. They suppress coughs by **controlling activation of the cough center in the brainstem** that signals the body to cough when the respiratory tract is irritated. Opiates work by desensitizing the cough centers to the irritation signals that are being sent to the brain. Codeine- and hydrocodone-based cough medications are still widely prescribed (e.g., Robitussin A-C® and Hycodan Syrup®). One problem with Robitussin® is that people can abuse either the codeine for the opioidlike high or the dextromethorphan (cough suppressant) for the psychedelic effects. Unfortunately, tolerance to the codeine doesn't translate into tolerance for the dextromethorphan and vice versa, so reactions like respiratory suppression, nausea, and vomiting are common. In one study of coroners' reports, when opioids in cough suppressants were involved in overdose deaths, it was most often in combination with other drugs, particularly alcohol, benzodiazepines, and antidepressants (Schifano, Zamparutti, Zambello, et al., 2006).

Diarrhea is also controlled because opioids affect areas in the brainstem that **inhibit gastric secretions and depress activity of intestinal muscles.** Constipation can be a severe problem in surgical patients or in those with intractable pain who use opioids over a long period. Severe constipation is also seen in opioid addicts who are able to maintain their dependence without having to go through withdrawal.

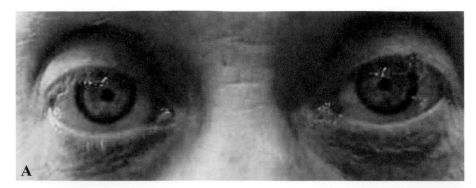

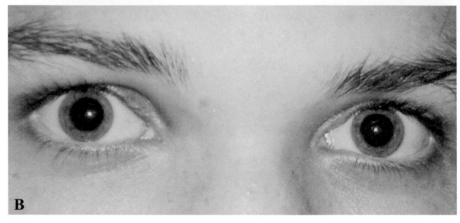

Law enforcement as well as treatment personnel can get a strong indication of drug use from the size of pupils.
A. Opioids, especially heroin, constrict pupils.
B. Methamphetamine, ecstasy, and cocaine (stimulants) dilate pupils.
Courtesy of the California Highway Patrol.

SIDE EFFECTS OF OPIOIDS

PHYSICAL SIDE EFFECTS

Opioids, particularly heroin, **affect many organs and tissues in every part of the body** particularly when used to excess. The heart, lungs, brain, eyes, voice box (larynx), muscles, cough and nausea centers, reproductive system, digestive system, excretory system, and immune system are all compromised. Some of the major physical side effects of heroin are:

◇ **insensitivity to pain,** which can keep a user from treating a damaging ailment such as an abscess;
◇ **lowered blood pressure;**
◇ **lowered pulse and respiration rate;** and
◇ **confusion**.

Some of the **side effects of the stronger opioids are quite identifiable** in the heavier user, particularly with heroin:

◇ **eyelids droop and the head nods forward;**
◇ **speech becomes slurred, slowed, and raspy or hoarse;**
◇ **the walking gait and coordination are slowed;**
◇ **pupils become pinpoint** and do not react to light; and
◇ skin dries out and **itching increases** due to histamine release.

Some of the desired medicinal effects can also become problems:

◇ suppression of the cough center in the brain can **hinder clearance of phlegm** in those users with respiratory ailments such as emphysema, pneumonia, and tuberculosis;

◊ opioids can **trigger the nausea center**; some heroin addicts know a batch of heroin is good if it makes them vomit;

"It hit from the feet going up to the head. I was yelling at him to take the needle out, and I was on the toilet seat. I mean I hugged that toilet bowl for hours, vomiting."
23-year-old heroin user

◊ opioids are used to treat diarrhea, but they **cause severe constipation** with chronic use;

"I'd go to the bathroom maybe about once a week, but it didn't bother me because I was on painkillers, so it wasn't really an issue."
28-year-old recovering heroin abuser

◊ and finally opioids affect the hormonal system; a **woman's period is delayed** and a man produces less testosterone; **sexual desire is dulled** often to the point of indifference.

"When I'm on heroin, I can't have an orgasm. It's just one of those things. I can have sex for hours and it starts to get painful. Heroin makes my whole body numb; I don't want to move around and I don't want to have sex when I'm high."
24-year-old dealer/heroin addict

TOLERANCE, TISSUE DEPENDENCE & WITHDRAWAL

The desire for relief from pain and the experiencing of pleasure combined with **tolerance, tissue dependence, and withdrawal are the main reasons for the addictive nature of opioids.**

"Since the first day I started using heroin, I was using it every day. I thought it was a joke that people wouldn't get addicted the first time, but I went ahead and did it anyway. After about two weeks of use, I ran out of money and I found out how bad I

could get sick. I wish I wasn't sick any of the time, but it's kind of like a requirement. Once you're a junkie, you've got to be sick."
27-year-old female heroin addict

Tolerance

Tolerance **occurs when the body tries to neutralize the heroin** (or any other psychoactive drug) by a variety of methods. It may:

◊ **speed up the metabolism**, particularly in the liver;
◊ **desensitize the nerve cells** to the drug's effects;
◊ **excrete the drug more rapidly** out of the body through urine, feces, and sweat; and
◊ **alter the brain and body chemistry** to compensate for the effects of the drug.

The body's adjustment requires the user to increase dosage if the same effects are desired. Because tolerance occurs rapidly with opioids, users might need 10 times as much drug (e.g., morphine) in as little as 10 days (O'Brien, 2001). **There is almost no limit to the development of opioid tolerance.** After a year of opioid use, one terminal cancer patient was using five fentanyl patches, 20 Demerol® tablets, and continuous morphine suppositories. This limitless tolerance compares to a drug such as nicotine, where three packs a day are usually the limit.

"After a while they [#4 codeine tablets] didn't really have any effect on me and the pain was taking over with the drug, so I started taking more codeine. And I took more and more and finally I was going through like two bottles of codeine a week."
Recovering codeine abuser

Tolerance develops at different rates for different body systems. Tolerance will develop more rapidly for pain relief, respiratory depression, vomiting, and euphoria and more slowly for constriction of pupils or for constipation (Knapp, Ciraulo & Jaffe, 2005).

Tissue Dependence

The adaptation of the body to the effects of **a strong opioid will temporarily and sometimes permanently alter brain chemistry.** An animal study by Dr. Eric Nestler and colleagues at Yale University showed that chronic administration of morphine to rats actually reduced the size of dopamine-producing cells (in the ventral tegmental area) by one-fourth (Nestler & Aghajanian, 1997; Sklair-Tavron, Shi, Lane, et al., 1996). This means that **when chronic morphine (or heroin) use is stopped, the body has less ability to produce its own dopamine and therefore less ability to feel elated or even normal. This depletion intensifies the desire to use the drug again.**

This and many other changes in body chemistry result in tissue or physical dependence because **the body relies on the drug to stay normal.** Researchers also found that tissue dependence developed more rapidly in animals that became physically dependent, then were withdrawn, and then were readministered the drug. **Tolerance and physical dependence can extend to other opioids.** That is, if users build a tolerance to and a physical dependence on heroin, they will also have a tissue dependence on and a tolerance to morphine, codeine, and other opioids (cross-dependence).

"My tolerance to Demerol,® morphine, and things like that was tremendous. I had to have tons of the stuff. I went to have a local surgery and they were like, 'Okay, how's that?' and I was like, 'Is this just a test or what?'"
35-year-old recovering opioid addict

This **cross-dependence** is the basis for methadone maintenance treatment in which one opioid (heroin) is replaced by another (methadone) less-damaging one. Tolerance and physical dependence appear to be receptor specific, however, so an opioid, such as heroin, that works at the mu receptors will not create as much tolerance as one that works at kappa receptors (Knapp, Ciraulo & Jaffe, 2005). This is known as **"select tolerance."**

Withdrawal

For powerful opioids there are three withdrawal phases:

◇ acute withdrawal (detoxification),
◇ post-acute withdrawal, and
◇ protracted withdrawal.

Acute withdrawal occurs when tissue dependence has developed after chronic use and the person suddenly stops using. The physiology has changed enough to trigger this rebound effect as **the body tries to return to normal too quickly**.

"Your muscles are like wrenching, your entire digestive tract is going crazy. Stomach cramps—but not just stomach cramps, also diarrhea. Everything that can go wrong with your intestinal tract happens. Your legs, you kick constantly; that's why I think they call it 'kicking.' Your legs will jerk and kick uncontrollably. You have insomnia. You vomit, have sweats, and what else, oh yeah, the craziness, delirium."
27-year-old female heroin user

Post-acute withdrawal is the persistence of subtle emotional and physical symptoms (e.g., mood swings and sleep problems) for three to six months although some say it can last up to 18 months after discontinuing drug use. The homeostasis (balance) of brain chemistry has been so disrupted by use that it will take the brain many months to regain its normal functioning (*see Chapter 9*).

Protracted withdrawal (extended withdrawal symptoms) lasts for months after abstinence has begun. Mostly, it is a part of post-acute withdrawal. Initially, symptoms such as mild increases in blood pressure, body temperature, respiration, and pupil size occur from week 4 up to week 10. A later phase that can last 30 weeks or more also shows a decrease in blood pressure, body temperature, and respiration along with a general unease. The discomfort and other psychological factors play a significant role in long-term relapse (Schuckit, 2000). These, like most post-acute withdrawal symptoms,

fluctuate but improve incrementally with continued abstinence. Protracted withdrawal is **also the occasional recurrence of withdrawal symptoms brought about by an environmental trigger** (sight, odor, neighborhood, or the like) that stimulates an addict's past memory of using or getting high. Known also as "environmentally cued" or "triggered" craving, this phenomenon can persist for several decades after stopping use.

In general:

◇ **short-acting opioids (2 to 3 hours), like heroin, morphine, and hydromorphone (Dilaudid®), result in more-acute withdrawal symptoms that begin 8 to 12 hours** after cessation of chronic use, reach peak intensity within 48 hours, and then subside over a period of 5-7 days;

◇ **long-acting opioids, such as methadone and LAAM,® will delay the withdrawal symptoms from 36 to 72 hours,** reach peak intensity in 4 to 6 days, and persist for 14 days or more (Knapp, Ciraulo & Jaffe, 2005; Schuckit, 2000);

◇ other opioids, such as codeine, oxycodone (OxyContin® and Percodan®), and propoxyphene (Darvon®), have withdrawal phenomena somewhere between those two extremes.

One reason why the hyperactivity of withdrawal occurs is the sudden release of excess norepinephrine that has been produced but not released during use of the opioid because the drug inhibits the release of these neurotransmitters in the locus coeruleus (Borg & Kreek, 2003).

It is important to remember that although acute heroin withdrawal feels like an incredibly bad case of the flu, **it is almost never life threatening** as is acute withdrawal from alcohol or sedative-hypnotics. Unfortunately, because acute opioid withdrawal symptoms can be painful and seem so frightening or create so much anxiety, **the fear of withdrawal becomes a greater trigger for continued use** than even the desire to repeat the rush.

"I have at times wished I was dead. That's how severe it would be. I've seen

TABLE 4–2	OPIOID WITHDRAWAL SYMPTIONS

Bone, joint, and muscular pain

Insomnia, anxiety

Sweating, runny nose

Stomach cramps, vomiting

Diarrhea, anorexia

High blood pressure

Rapid pulse, tachycardia

Coughing, excessive yawning

Dilated pupils, teary eyes

Hyper reflexes, muscle cramps

Fever, chills, goose flesh

people in jail try to hang themselves. I've seen people in jail shoot their own urine to try and get the heroin out of the urine that's left in there."
72-year-old recovering heroin addict

ADDITIONAL PROBLEMS WITH HEROIN & OTHER OPIOIDS

NEONATAL EFFECTS

Most opioids, especially heroin and morphine, quickly **cross the placental barrier** between the fetus and the mother thereby sending large doses of the drug to the developing infant. Pregnant heroin users have a greater risk of miscarriage, placental separation, premature labor, breech birth, stillbirth, and eclampsia (increased blood pressure and convulsions). **When born to an addicted mother, the baby is also addicted**; and because babies are much smaller than adults, the tissue dependence and the withdrawal symptoms are more severe. These neonatal withdrawal symptoms include low birth weight, a high-pitched cry, irritability, tremors, exaggerated reflexes, diarrhea, rapid breathing, sweating, and vomiting along with sneezing, yawning, and hiccupping (Finnegan & Kandall, 2005). These symptoms can last five to eight weeks; and, unlike adults, **babies in opioid withdrawal can die**.

"The two infants that I had that were heroin affected... heroin addicted at birth... were managed on morphine for 3 months and then continued to do withdrawal for another 3 to 6 months before the chemicals were out of their bodies. While they're going through withdrawal, they are not developing. They are not rolling over, they are not sitting, they are not playing with toys."
36-year-old foster mother of children born to drug-using mothers

The use of methadone to stabilize the fetal environment in an opioid-dependent pregnant woman has been used successfully; however, the fetus is still born physically dependent on the drug and subject to withdrawal symptoms. With intensive medical management, some pregnant users have used naltrexone to help with detoxification and to temper any return to opioid use. **Infants born addicted often have to be medically managed.** The opiate paregoric seems to decrease seizure activity, increase sucking coordination, and decrease the incidence of explosive stools. Phenobarbital is also used. In addition to using drugs for detoxification, a restful comforting environment is soothing to the withdrawing infant (Kandall, 1993). **The amount of prenatal care received by the pregnant opioid addict is crucial in the health of the fetus and the neonate**; the more care they receive, the fewer neonatal health problems and the less morbidity.

OVERDOSE

"I've seen her go out like twice and I had to revive her once and that was the most terrifying moment of my entire life, like seeing her on the bed, pretty much dead, and having to shake her, and beat her, and pick her up, and drop her until she like came to 'cause I didn't know CPR [cardiopulmonary

resuscitation]. And she didn't remember anything of it. When she woke up, she said, 'Why the hell are you screaming? You're going to freak out our parents.' She had no idea."
26-year-old heroin addict

Of 1.5 million drug-related emergency department (ED) visits in 2005 (out of 108 million total ED visits), there were about 164,572 that involved heroin compared with 448,481 for cocaine, 138,950 for amphetamine and methamphetamine, and 492,654 that involved alcohol alone or in combination with another drug (DAWN, 2007). In addition there were more than 100,000 cases involving opioid prescription drugs such as OxyContin,® Vicodin,® and methadone. It is estimated that each year 4,000 to 5,000 people actually die from opioid overdoses alone or in combination with other depressants, especially alcohol. **Severe respiratory depression is the major cause of overdose deaths with opioids.** The user passes out and unless quickly revived will slip into a coma, stop breathing, and die.

Generally, about half of all heroin users will experience a clinically significant overdose (McGregor, Darke, Ali, et al., 1998). In one study 57% of the **overdoses were accidental while 43% were deliberate**. The accidental overdoses were due to unexpectedly pure heroin, to the synergistic effect of alcohol, to relapse after abstinence, or to sudden resumption of use upon release from jail (Pfab, Eyer, Jetzinger, et al., 2006). Studies have found that most users do not have sufficient knowledge of the dangers of overdose after a period of abstinence or when using alcohol or another depressant. To counter this problem, San Francisco initiated a lifesavers program for heroin addicts to help revive their using partners who had overdosed. They learn CPR, the use of naloxone, and other lifesaving techniques and are provided with vials of naloxone and disposable syringes (Costello, 2005).

In an overdose, blood pressure drops, the heart beats too weakly to circulate blood, and lungs labor and fill with fluid. The victim often has blue

lips and a pale or blue body, pinpoint pupils, fresh needle marks, gasping or rattling respirations, cardiac arrhythmia, and convulsions.

"You know, people who do heroin aren't worried about dying because like if three people die from a new batch of heroin, everybody wants to know where they are getting that heroin so they can go get some because it's the best and they figure they will just do a little less."
41-year-old recovering heroin addict

When aiding a heroin overdose victim, after establishing an airway, checking heartbeat, and preventing aspiration, the overdose can be counteracted by a shot of an **opioid antagonist—naloxone (Narcan®)—to block and reverse the life-threatening effects** of too much drug (Schuckit, 2000). The Narcan® also obliterates the high and will cause severe withdrawal effects if the overdose victim is an addict.

DIRTY & SHARED NEEDLES

Of the quarter million treatment admissions for heroin use, 58% were injection drug users (IDUs). The opioid users had been using for an average of 14 years before coming in for treatment (TEDS, 2007). This excessive use of the injection method for opioids is important because the most dangerous problem with heroin, the one that causes the most illness and death, is dirty or shared needles. Even in China half of AIDS patients are IDUs (Tang, Zhao, Zhao, et al., 2006). Needles put a large amount of the drug into the bloodstream at one time, but **users can also unknowingly inject adulterants**. **Infectious bacteria and viruses can also be transmitted**, including those that cause hepatitis B or C, endocarditis, malaria, syphilis, flesh-eating bacteria, gangrene, and the HIV virus that causes AIDS. **Injection as a method of use is more common with heroin** than with any other psychoactive drug.

Hepatitis C & HIV

Various studies have shown that **50% to 90% of all needle-using**

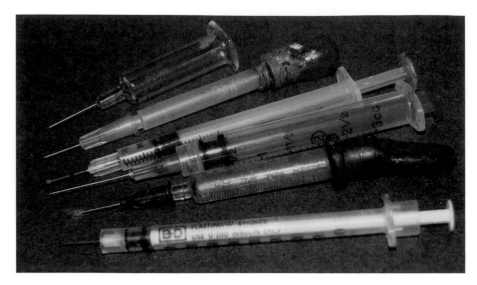

Addicts will use diabetic syringes, eyedroppers, veterinary needles, and anything else that's handy to inject their heroin or other opioids.

© 1983 CNS Productions, Inc.

• •

heroin addicts carry hepatitis C. Even those with less than one year of IV drug use had a positive rate of 71.4%. Once infected 20% to 40% will develop liver disease and 4% to 16% will develop liver cancer (Payte, Zweben & Martin, 2003). Since the hepatitis C virus (HCV) was identified in 1988 and a test devised for it, the number of cases of HCV caused by transfusion has dropped dramatically, but IV drug use transmission remains high. IV users have created a well of infection to be spread to their partners or co-users.

"I watched somebody who refused to wash the syringe out after I had it and I told him I had AIDS, I'm positive, I have the disease. And he said, 'I really don't care.' Didn't wash it out and you could see when he pulled back and the outfit was clear and it had blood in it and he shot it up. I mean I hope the man's alive."
29-year-old recovering heroin addict with AIDS

The transmission of HIV by IV drug use is also substantial. More than half of IV drug users carry the HIV virus, although the percentages vary radically from city to city. It is estimated that:

◇ about 25% of all U.S. HIV/AIDS cases (190,000 of 758,675) were transmitted to an IV drug user by a contaminated needle (about three-fourths are male);

◇ 7% to 10% were transmitted to heterosexual or homosexual partners of IV drug users through sexual contact; and

◇ 70% of children infected with HIV had mothers who were IV drug users or had sexual contact with IV drug users (Centers for Disease Control, 2005).

Since the epidemic began in the 1980s though 2006, about 560,000 Americans have died from AIDS. Internationally, the figures are worse. In Myanmar the World Health Organization has estimated that between 74% and 91% of the country's IV heroin addicts are HIV positive. In China the IV use of opioids accounts for 51% of the cases (Tang, Zhao, Zhao, et al., 2006). To counter this statistic, Mainland China is promoting needle-exchange programs and have cut the number of junkies who share needles from 62.8% in 2004 to 13.7% in 2006. It is estimated by the United Nations that worldwide, in 2006, 40 million people are HIV/AIDS positive (from all causes), half of them women. About 60% of those infected are from sub-Saharan Africa (UNAIDS, 2006). Worldwide 25 million people have died from AIDS.

Abscesses & Other Infections

Excess needle use continually traumatizes the blood vessels, often causing them to collapse. This is why injection drug users are forced to switch to locations other than the antecubital fossa opposite the elbow. Injection sites include the wrist, between the toes, in the neck, or even in the dorsal vein of the penis.

Septic abscesses and ulcerations caused by soft-tissue infections are common among IV drug users because most heroin abusers will shoot up four to six times a day often with a contaminated needle. The most common infectious organisms are *staphylococcus aureus* and *beta-hemolytic streptococci* (Orangio, Pitlick, Della Latta, et al., 1984). The immunosuppressive effects of the drugs themselves add to the severity of these infections (Brown & Ebright, 2002). Other signs of IV drug use are lesions or "tracks," which are scars on the skin often caused by constant inflammation at the injection site and hyperpigmentation. Sterile abscesses can be caused by irritation. Cellulitis (deep inflammation of soft or connective tissue) can be caused by bacteria or by irritation from repeated use or adulterants.

"They can be life threatening if you let them go to a point . . . but I've also lost all my veins. I've hit nerves; I've hit arteries. If you should shoot into an artery, it's extremely painful. Having to wear long-sleeved shirts to work is like an inconvenient thing about shooting up."
40-year-old recovering heroin addict

One of the worst infections is necrotizing fasciitis, an infection that destroys fascia and subcutaneous tissue but is not immediately visible on the surface. Bacteria like *clostridium perfinges* and variant strains of *streptococcus* and *staphylococcus* cause this condition, known as "flesh-eating disease." Large amounts of infected tissue have to be cut away.

Endocarditis, an infection of heart valves, is found more often in IV drug users. Research points to a variety of organisms (including those involved in abscesses) that are dislodged from the injection site and settle in heart valves.

"With endocarditis, infection gets to the heart valves. If antibiotics don't work, they try surgery. In my daughter's case, they repaired one heart valve and replaced one with a pig valve. A week later they had to go back in and put in a pacemaker. My daughter started using heroin when she was 24; she got sick when she was 25 and died when she was 27."

38-year-old mother of an IV heroin user

Cotton fever, caused by endotoxins (which thrive in cotton), is another illness found more frequently in IV drug users. The term *cotton fever* is also used by addicts to describe any short-term bacterial infection or pyrogen reaction resulting in fever, chills, tremors, aches, and pains.

DILUTION & ADULTERATION

One of the reasons why an overdose occurs is that **street drugs can vary radically in purity**. Street heroin varies from 0% to 99% pure, so if a user is expecting 3% heroin and gets 30%, the results could be fatal. Dilution of an expensive item like heroin with a cheap substitute such as starch, sugar (dextrose or lactose), aspirin, Ajax,® quinine, caffeine, or talcum powder is extremely common. According to the DEA, heroin purity for retail-level sale is 10% to 70% compared with 1% to 10% just 20 years ago. **Part of the reason for the increased purity is the influx of large amounts of unadulterated Southeast Asian and South American heroin and more recently some Afghani heroin** (DEA, 2006). Because of increased production and a proliferation of street chemists, it is also much easier to come across synthetic high-potency opioids. The recent series of deaths in the United States from fentanyl-laced heroin emphasizes the unreliability of street heroin.

COST

Contrary to popular belief promoted by television and movies that show heroin addicts as derelicts, criminals, and people who have a mental illness, **a majority of heroin users (79%) are gainfully employed** (Camilleri, Carise & McLellan, 2006). Because of the buildup of tolerance and the high cost of heroin, however, a great many users must turn to illegal methods to pay for their habits. **The cost of a heroin habit can range from $20 to $200 a day**, depending on the level of use. It is estimated that Americans spend about $12 billion a year on heroin (compared with $42 billion on cocaine).

"When we were really strung out, we were spending $150 to $200 a day to feel normal. It's one thing to spend that kind of money and get loaded, but when you're spending that kind of money to just function as a human being, it's irritating."

32-year-old recovering heroin addict

The overwhelming need to support an opioid habit makes antisocial behaviors, such as robbery, and eventual involvement with the legal system almost inevitable. It is estimated that **60% of the cost of supporting a habit is gotten through consensual crime, including prostitution and drug dealing**, and supplemented by welfare payments or occasional work. Most of the remaining 40% comes from shoplifting and burglary.

The other costs are the healthcare expenses associated with addiction. The lifetime cost of treating an HIV-positive IV drug user is about $600,000. This is close to the lifetime cost for heart disease and a few other chronic conditions (Schackman, Gebo, Walensky, et al., 2006).

POLYDRUG USE

Multiple Drug Use. A heroin user might start with heroin in the morning to stop withdrawal symptoms and calm down. Later he might take some speed to get energetic and in the evening use marijuana to relax.

Mixing. A common polydrug combination is cocaine or amphetamine with heroin. This **upper/downer combination, called a "speedball,"** can enhance the euphoric and painkilling ef-

The abdomen and the arm of this recovering IV drug user became infected with necrotizing fasciitis (flesh-eating bacteria) from a contaminated needle. The infected flesh has to be cut away immediately to prevent its spread to the rest of the body. The client is presently on methadone maintenance treatment, although she did shoot up for a short while after the surgery.
© 2005 CNS Productions, Inc.

fects of both drugs (Karch, 1996). It can also be dangerous because the user doesn't know which drug will kick in. An increasing polydrug problem is methadone. Many methadone users take clonazepam (Klonopin®) to enhance their methadone because the combination feels somewhat like a heroin high. OxyContin® is often mixed with other drugs to simulate a heroinlike high. Some dealers are spiking poor-quality marijuana with heroin to give it an extra kick and sell it as high-quality pot. Opioids can have additive and synergistic effects when used with most depressant drugs, especially alcohol and benzodiazepines. **These opioid/downer combinations increase the potential for respiratory depression**, lethargy, possible overdose, and even death.

"I'd be waiting and waiting and during the time that I was waiting I'd be getting drunk. By the time I got around to doing my shot, I was already drunk. I'd hit up and boom, I'd be on the floor."
36-year-old male heroin user in treatment

Morphing. To counter the depressant effects of heroin, addicts might use uppers to change their mood. They then might get so wired from the cocaine or methamphetamine that they will use alcohol or heroin again to come down.

Cycling. Heroin addicts often stop using it for several weeks and switch to a cheaper high to give the body a chance to lower its tolerance and tissue dependence. This is done to reduce the cost of their addiction because they can use less heroin to get the same high after their tolerance has decreased. They might switch to alcohol, benzodiazepines, or marijuana in the interim and then cycle on and off heroin for the next few months.

Sequentialing. This is a long-term consequence of using drugs. Someone might use heroin for several years and then switch to alcohol because they can't stand the IV drug user lifestyle. After a few years of alcohol and a bloated liver, they might then switch to marijuana only to switch back to heroin once again a few years later.

FROM EXPERIMENTATION TO ADDICTION

The number of people admitted for heroin treatment has gone up in the past 10 years. **The majority (58%) of the 265,000 entering treatment had been injecting heroin.** First-time admissions, however, involved more smokers, snorters, and sniffers than injectors (TEDS, 2007).

Experimentation with alcohol, marijuana, and tobacco begins much earlier than experimentation with heroin. The mean age of first heroin use was about 22.2 years of age in 2005 compared with 17.4 for first marijuana use, 17.3 for tobacco, and 16.4 for alcohol (SAMHSA, 2006). **It takes an average of one year of sporadic heroin use for someone to develop a daily habit**, although some users with a predisposition to opioid addiction might jump to daily use within 15 days.

"I'd wake up in the morning and before I'd go to work (when I was working), I'd have to do a hit of dope just to function. I'd have to do a hit of dope just to get out of bed. I'd have to do a hit of dope to go to the bathroom. It wasn't a matter of getting high anymore; it was a matter of getting functional."
38-year-old male recovering heroin abuser

After a while the pain of withdrawal often becomes greater than the pain the user might have been trying to avoid, so the motivation to continue use is reinforced. Also, the emotional and physical pain relief offered by the heroin becomes greater than the pleasure. It's as if users unconsciously learn that the numbing effect that heroin creates is the rush or relief they get from using. It's not really pleasure per se but the pleasure of relief of emotional pain and suffering that is motivation for continued use.

"After a while you're not just killing your pain, you start to kill your feelings, any feelings you might have regardless of whether you're having pain. It's not the pain that you're killing. It's never really the pain."
36-year-old recovering heroin abuser

If an opioid user has passed from experimentation to abuse or addiction, **treatment becomes a physiological as well as a psychological process. Physically, the addict has to be detoxified from the heroin** or other opioid, often with the use of medications such as Darvon® (a milder opioid than heroin), methadone (a long-lasting opioid), LAAM® (a very long-lasting opioid but not readily available in the United States), or buprenorphine (a powerful opiate agonist at low doses and an antagonist at high doses). In addition, cravings have to be controlled to maintain abstinence. Psychologically, the addict has to learn a new way of living because emotional and environmental cues often lead to relapse (*see Chapter 9*).

A comprehensive long-term study of 582 heroin-addicted criminal offenders over a period of 33 years showed that their lives were characterized by repeated cycles of drug abuse and abstinence interspersed with health and social problems. More than half had died (overdose, accidental poisoning, homicide, suicide, accident, liver disease, and other) and of the remaining 242 still living, 40% had used heroin in the past year. Their **death rate was 50 to 100 times the rate among the general population of men in the same age range** (Hser, Hoffman, Grella, et al., 2001).

The Vietnam Experience

The road from experimentation to addiction can be better understood by looking at the use of heroin in Vietnam by U.S. soldiers from 1967 to the end of the war in 1973. Dr. Lee N. Robins, a psychiatrist at Harvard, and others tested several groups of GIs, first while still stationed in Vietnam and then after they had returned to the United States. Almost half the GIs had experimented with opium or heroin; 20% had been addicted at one time and reported withdrawal symptoms. Because heroin was so readily available, experimentation was easy even for those who were too young to drink. So the usual progression from alcohol, cigarettes, and marijuana to heroin or cocaine was re-

versed. According to Robins, the most startling part of the study was that **only 5% of those who had become addicted in Vietnam relapsed within 10 months after they returned to the United States** and only 12% relapsed even briefly within three years. Most of the returning GIs didn't even go through treatment (Robins & Slobodyan, 2003). This seems to suggest that even though tissue dependence caused by use of drugs can be powerful, other factors, especially pre-existing sensitivity determined by heredity and environment, have a greater influence.

MORPHINE & OTHER OPIOIDS

MORPHINE

When Frederick Serturner isolated morphine in 1805, physicians embraced this truly effective painkiller and its sales soared in the mid- to late 1800s. Profits from this revolutionary new medicine established a number of drug companies. It wasn't until 1952 that researchers were able to fully synthesize morphine. It remains **the standard by which effective pain relief is measured**. Morphine is processed from opium into white crystal hypodermic **tablets, capsules, suppositories, oral solutions, and injectable solutions**. This analgesic may be drunk, eaten, absorbed under the tongue, absorbed rectally by suppository, or injected into a vein, a muscle, or under the skin. Different routes of administration have different effects. For example, **three to six times more morphine must be taken orally to achieve the same effects as injecting**.

The liver is the principal site of metabolism and, along with other tissues, converts the morphine into metabolites that more readily cross the blood/brain barrier and are possibly more potent than the morphine itself (Karch, 1996). Some of the morphine is excreted quickly in the urine, while some remains in measurable amounts in the plasma for four to six hours and can be detectable in the urine for several days.

Therapeutic Pain Control

An estimated 50 million Americans have chronic pain, from arthritis, back injury, and chronic illness to cancer, burns, and severe tissue or nerve damage. In some community clinics, 37.5% of appointments involved patients with chronic pain complaints (Upshur, Luckmann & Savageau, 2006). In one survey about 72% of chronic pain sufferers had pain for more than three years and 34% for more than 10 years (Rubin, 2004). About half of those with chronic pain take a prescription drug, although many are afraid of becoming dependent on an opioid, a muscle relaxant, or a sedative-hypnotic.

"My nurse told me, 'You don't need extra pain medication. I've been through this a hundred times before, and I know you're not in pain.'"
Patient in burn treatment unit

Pain is certainly a subjective judgment by the patient, so it can be difficult to know what a patient feels. Physicians and nurses ask patients to self-rate their pain on a scale of 1 to 10 with 10 being the worst. The prescribing of morphine, different opioids, or other painkillers is based partly on this rating. In addition, several other concerns affect the amount of medication prescribed:

◇ **fear that tissue dependence and addiction might develop;**

◇ concern that the opioid will **mask clues to a serious disease;** and

◇ concern that the **patient may be faking symptoms** to get drugs to supply a habit (purposive withdrawal).

These three concerns might keep some physicians from prescribing sufficient pain medication even when appropriate. A recent survey of primary care physicians found that the majority of physicians were comfortable prescribing opioids to terminal cancer patients but less comfortable prescribing opioids to patients with low-back pain and those with a history of drug or alcohol abuse (Bhamb, Brown, Hariharan, et al., 2006). The fear of government action for overprescribing is also a factor in the undertreatment of pain when in fact in 2003 there were only 47 arrests from among 963,385 doctors registered with the DEA (Jung & Reidenberg, 2006). The current problems with OxyContin,® hydrocodone, and methadone and past problems with drugs such as codeine, Percodan,® and Dilaudid® have made adherence to medically sound prescribing practices difficult. To help establish a better policy to guide the physician, the State Federation of Medical Boards, the American Society of Addiction Medicine (ASAM), and others have adopted guidelines for the use of controlled substances in treating pain.

For example, a **Pain Patient's Bill of Rights** was enacted into law in California. It states that:

◇ inadequate treatment of acute and chronic pain is a significant health problem;

◇ a physician should prescribe in conformance with the provisions of the California Intractable Pain Treatment Act; and

◇ the physician may refuse to prescribe opiate medication for a patient who requests the treatment for severe chronic intractable pain; however, that physician shall inform the patient that there are physicians who specialize in treating that kind of pain with methods that include the use of opioids.

ASAM guidelines, first issued in 1997, recommend that the physicians use more of their own judgment in prescribing and that they should not be held responsible if the patient cons them into prescribing unneeded opioids. They also suggest, however, that continuing overprescription practices as well as underprescribing that keeps a legitimate patient in pain should both be remedied by education first rather than sanctions that might interfere with the practice of good medicine (California Society of Addiction Medicine, 1997, 2004).

In general, iatrogenic (physician-induced) addiction is unusual nowadays unlike at the turn of the twentieth century, when physicians were not as knowledgeable about the risks of long-term opioid use. Most of the problems with moderate-strength prescription opioids (e.g., hydrocodone and codeine) come from long-term use. It seems that by relying on the drug to relieve the pain, **the patient becomes more sensitive to pain because the body produces fewer of its own painkillers** and down-regulates its own opioid receptors.

"I had been masking the pain for so long that I didn't know how much pain I had or didn't have, and when I didn't really have pain, per se, that was pathological. I couldn't deal with the slightest little thing."
37-year-old recovering prescription opioid addict

Because some level of tissue adaptation occurs with even the initial dose of an opioid, some care does need to be taken in prescribing. **The physician needs to learn about risk factors for addiction** such as:

◇ physical health, e.g., kidney and liver function;

◇ drug-abuse history, medical drug use history, and mental health history; and

◇ possible hereditary factors that make the patient more susceptible.

In addition, the physician has to:

◇ develop a working diagnosis and treatment plan;

◇ discuss risks vs. benefits and compliance with the patient;

◇ keep up-to-date on recent trials of medications or consult with someone familiar with the drugs;

◇ get constant feedback from the patient as to effects, efficacy, and side effects;

◇ be willing to modify the type of medication and dosages; and

◇ keep accurate records concerning effects and patient reaction

(American Pain Society, 2006; Verhaag & Ikeda, 1991).

CODEINE

"For me codeine is just weak heroin. It doesn't do much for me. Codeine just stops the pain and stops your nose from running. It just gets you able to function enough in order to go get you some heroin."
42-year-old male recovering heroin user

Codeine is extracted directly from opium or refined from morphine. Also known as methylmorphine, it is about one-fifth as strong as morphine and is generally used for the relief of moderate pain. The most common drugs mixed with codeine are aspirin or acetaminophen because of synergistic analgesia (the drugs compliment each other's strength). Codeine is also **commonly used to control severe coughs** (Robitussin A-C® and Cheracol®). It is a Schedule V drug in cough syrups and is even sold over the counter in some states. It is a Schedule II drug by itself and a Schedule III drug when mixed with other drugs and used for analgesia. **Codeine used to be the most widely prescribed and abused prescription opioid** in the United States and other countries, but hydrocodone (Vicodin®) has taken over that dubious honor. Some addicts drink large amounts of codeine-based cough syrup to relieve heroin withdrawal symptoms. One of the problems with codeine, as with many opioids, is that it triggers nausea. Many physicians switched to hydrocodone for moderate pain relief because it is more effective. The half-life of codeine is about three hours, and the drug is detectable in the blood for up to 24 hours and in the urine for up to three days. If physical dependence develops, withdrawal symptoms can begin within a few hours and peak within 36 to 72 hours.

HYDROCODONE (Vicodin,® Hycodan,® Tussend,® Norco®)

The expansion of drug Web sites that offer "no prescription Vicodin® and its generic version hydrocodone" or other opioids has exploded over the past few years. More than 300 such sites were identified in a 2006 survey (Forman, Woody, McLellan, et al., 2006). A number of headlines concerning opioids refer to movie, television, or sports stars who developed a dependence on the Schedule III opioid hydrocodone (Vicodin®). It often followed prolonged prescriptive use for chronic pain, especially back pain and pinched nerves. **More than 120 million prescriptions were written for hydrocodone in 2006, the most of any drug being prescribed** (Berenson, 2006; IMS Health, 2007; Pharmacy Times, 2006). One survey of a group of prescription opioid addicts showed that most began their use through legitimate prescriptions for real ailments, but when the dependency escalated, most bought their drugs through street dealers who had access to legitimate supplies (Passik, Hays, Eisner, et al., 2006). Radio talk-show host Rush Limbaugh supposedly bought more than $30,000 worth of pharmaceuticals, mostly hydrocodone, through an associate (CNN.com, 2006).

This **most widely prescribed opioid** (semisynthetic) has many of the same actions as codeine but produces less nausea. Compared with codeine doctors write four times as many hydrocodone prescriptions for analgesia. Hydrocodone is also used in cough preparations, called antitussives (e.g., Hycomine Syrup®). As with other opioids, respiratory depression and masking of illness can be dangerous especially when other depressants are used at the same time. There have been reports that abuse of hydrocodone (more than 20 pills a day for at least two months) can precipitate a sudden hearing loss. The House Ear Institute in Los Angeles and several other medical centers have identified at least 48 patients with this condition (Marsa, 2001). Further research of this serious side effect is needed.

About 600 deaths are reported each year due to hydrocodone overdose, although more occur when it is used with other depressants (DAWN, 2007).

"I injured myself and I was on hydrocodone, you know. I'd take one, next hour and a half I'd be real sleepy and lightheaded . . . be dizzy. It's like being drunk. I developed a small addiction to it, you know. It was an easy escape; pop a pill, drink some water, drown my fears away, drown the pain away—feel good for a while."
24-year-old weightlifter

METHADONE (Dolophine®)

When the United States and its allies embargoed morphine to Germany during World War II, German laboratories developed methadone, a synthetic opioid, weaker than heroin but longer lasting, to supplement their limited supply of painkillers. Demerol® and Darvon® were also developed at about this time (O'Brien, Cohen, Evans, et al., 1992). Methadone made its way to the United States in 1947. It is a **legally authorized opioid used to treat heroin addiction** through a program known as "methadone maintenance" (*see Chapter 9*). Under this harm reduction program started in New York in 1965, methadone is dispensed to addicts to lower their craving for heroin (Payte, 1997). The addict comes into the clinic every day to receive a dose (usually mixed with fruit juice). On a few occasions (e.g., when the methadone user has to go out of town), a take-home dose is given in tablet form. There are **approximately 228,000 heroin addicts involved in methadone treatment in more than 1,292 methadone treatment programs nationwide** (N-SSATS, 2006). About 47 other countries have methadone maintenance programs, with an enrollment of more than 500,000 addicts. Methadone can also be used to detoxify a heroin abuser who has become tissue or physically dependent.

Because this long-acting synthetic opioid **reduces drug craving and blocks withdrawal symptoms for 24 to 72 hours**, it diminishes the abuse

of heroin, which has a shorter duration of action, causes more-intense highs and lows than the methadone, and is illegal. The disappearance of the intense need to use heroin and come up with increasing amounts of money has led to a dramatic decrease in crime among those in methadone maintenance (Bell, Mattick, Hay, et al., 1997). A recent study seemed to show that within two months of beginning treatment cognitive performance improved with such skills as verbal learning and memory, visuospatial memory, and psychomotor speed (Gruber, Tzilos, Silveri, et al., 2006). Like any opioid, methadone also has painkilling and depressant effects that can be used in clinical situations. The analgesic effects last only four to six hours.

Like heroin, **methadone is addicting and must be monitored closely to prevent diversion** into illegal channels. Despite heavy regulation of methadone clinics and tight controls of the supply, methadone is still sold on the street, abused, and responsible for a number of overdose deaths every year (Breslin & Malone, 2006). Addicts will combine methadone with other drugs, such as clonazepam (Klonopin®), clonidine (Catapres®), carisoprodol (Soma®), and alprazolam (Xanax®), to intensify the high and make it resemble the feeling they get from heroin. Physicians' increasing prescription use of methadone strictly as a pain reliever has increased in recent years. This increased availability has expanded the street supply of the drug.

There has also been a subsequent increase in inadvertent overdoses as there is with any strong opioid. **In 2004 there were 3,800 deaths from methadone overdose** compared with 780 in 1999, 70% of those in people who were not on methadone maintenance. Out of 2 million ED visits for drug-related problems in 2004, about 32,000 involved methadone (DAWN, 2007). Some reports suggest that the mortality rate due to methadone may be greater than that due to heroin, whereas others suggest not. Because the actual cause of death can be an unknown, these figures are not exact; however, the number of overdose deaths from heroin addiction in those who have left methadone maintenance treatment is about four

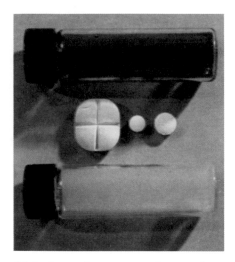

Methadone, a bitter-tasting white powder, can be mixed with orange juice for use at a methadone maintenance clinic, or it can be dispensed in tablets for take-home doses. It also comes in injectable form for pain management.

Courtesy of the U.S. Drug Enforcement Administration

••••••••••••••••••••••••••••

times that of those who stay in treatment (Latowsky, 2006).

There is some concern about the cardiovascular effects of methadone particularly in novice users. One common condition is called *torsade de pointes,* which means a disruption of the electrical heart mechanism. A number of heart arrhythmias due to methadone and or methadone combined with other drug use have been found (Latowsky, 2006). Swiss researchers say they can reformulate methadone to reduce the risk of irregular heartbeats on a small percentage of users (NZZ Online, 2007). There is also concern that **a pregnant addict in methadone maintenance will give birth to a baby who must go through opioid withdrawal**. The preferred protocol is to wean the pregnant mother in the third trimester; but if the woman's recovery is shaky, many treatment professionals feel that controlling the baby's withdrawal symptoms is preferable to the risks of needle infection, overdose, and placental separation in an active heroin addict (Toler, 2006).

There have been proposals, research, and trials by the U.S. Department of Health and Human Services, among others, to make methadone treatment more convenient and bring it into the mainstream of healthcare. Rather than have recovering addicts get their methadone only from methadone clinics, the drug would also be available through certified physicians and nonmethadone drug clinics. So far the increased incidence of problems just from the increased prescribing by mainstream physicians of methadone for pain has soured regulators on allowing a wider availability of methadone. There is also still much controversy in the treatment community about the overall efficacy of methadone maintenance and other drug replacement (harm reduction) therapies.

HYDROMORPHONE (Dilaudid®)

Hydromorphone, a short-acting semisynthetic opioid, can be taken orally or injected. Hydromorphone is refined from morphine through a process that makes it **seven to 10 times more potent gram-for-gram than morphine**. Hydromorphone is used as an alternative to morphine for the treatment of moderate-to-severe pain. Because it is more potent than morphine, it has a higher abuse potential. Illegally diverted Dilaudid® became increasingly attractive to cocaine users for the drug combination known as a "speedball" (hydromorphone and cocaine or methamphetamine). A 4 mg tablet of Dilaudid® sold on the street ranges from $30 to $70. Though it is quite potent, just a few deaths from overdose are reported each year.

OXYCODONE (OxyContin,® Percodan®)

In 2005 **Purdue Pharma's sales of OxyContin®** were about $1 billion, down from $1.5 billion in 2001. The decrease in sales was due more to the introduction of generic versions of the drug rather than a decreased demand (Smith, 2007). In addition, hundreds of on-line pharmacies offer the drug without a prescription. Users run the risk of getting bogus or counterfeit OxyContin® that does not contain any oxycodone.

This semisynthetic derivative of codeine is used for the relief of moderate-to-severe pain. Oxycodone in standard form (Percodan®) is usually taken orally, often in combination with aspirin or acetaminophen. By this route it usually takes about 30 minutes for the effects to appear, which then last four to six hours. Its pain-relieving effect is **much stronger than that of codeine but weaker than that of morphine or Dilaudid.**®

Since OxyContin® was released in 1995, abuse of the time-release version of oxycodone has increased; more than 7 million prescriptions were written for this analgesic in 2005. Purdue Pharma introduced the long-acting formulation in 1995 for the treatment of severe chronic pain. What some people have been doing **with OxyContin® is chewing, crushing, and injecting, or crushing and sniffing the time-release formulation** that holds the oxycodone. **This destroys the time-release effect**, so a much larger blood level of oxycodone is achieved. Heroin and other **opioid abusers describe the high as somewhat similar to heroin**, so they try to get the drug prescribed to them or they divert legal supplies. According to the DEA, the abuse of OxyContin® has caused more than 400 deaths, although Purdue Pharma called the DEA report flawed (National Council on Alcohol and Drug Dependence, 2002). A number of the deaths involved more than one drug, particularly alcohol.

The introduction of this powerful time-release analgesic occurred at the same time that the medical community was increasing its emphasis on the proper treatment of postoperative pain and moderate-to-severe chronic pain. Because of this new emphasis, long-acting medications gained favor due to better compliance rates, better long-term control of pain, and fewer side effects when compared with short-acting narcotics (when used as directed).

A year after its introduction, reports of increased illicit use started coming in. The drug, which was also called "ocs," "oxy," "o'cotton," and "hillbilly heroin," originally came in 10 mg, 20 mg, 40 mg, 80 mg, and 160 mg tablets. The large tablets were known as "blue bombers" and "o'coffins" due to a high rate of overdose. Shipments of the 160 mg tablets were suspended by the manufacturer. Street prices have av-

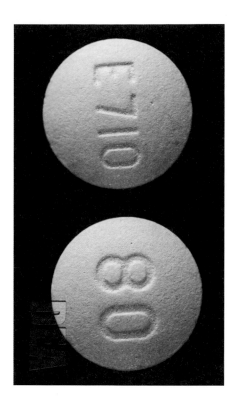

These 80 mg tablets of OxyContin® are presently the largest dose available. A pill this size could go for $40 to $80 on the street vs. $6 at a pharmacy.
Courtesy of the U.S. Drug Enforcement Administration

• •

eraged about $1 per milligram or $10 for the smallest-dose tablets.

As with other desired opioids that were available in pharmacies, drugstore robberies and diversion of legitimate supplies increased.

◇ Some legitimate prescribers wanting to treat pain more humanely were easily duped into writing prescriptions.

◇ Some physicians and pharmacists tried to make money by writing prescriptions for bogus patients (100 of the 40 mg tablets could bring in $4,000).

◇ Legitimate patients sold their supplies to others.

In addition, overblown media coverage not only increased general knowledge of the drug but also caused legitimate prescribers to limit treatment of real chronic pain.

MEPERIDINE (Demerol,® Pethidine,® Mepergan®)

A synthetic phenylpiperidine derivative, this short-acting opioid is **one of the most widely used analgesics** for moderate-to-severe pain though it is only one-sixth the strength of morphine. It is most often injected but can also be taken orally. This drug can be neurotoxic in large doses. Demerol's affect on the brain **causes as much sedation and euphoria as morphine but less constipation and cough suppression**. Because it is eliminated by the kidneys, patients with impaired kidneys should avoid the drug. Though less potent by weight than morphine, it is often the opioid most often abused by medical professionals.

PENTAZOCINE (Talwin® NX)

Talwin® NX, prescribed for chronic or acute pain, comes in tablets (combined with naloxone) or as an injectable liquid. It has a fraction of the potency of morphine and **acts as a weak opioid antagonist as well as an opioid agonist**. This drug was frequently combined and injected with pyrabenzamine, an antihistamine drug ("Ts and blues") for the heroinlike high. Increased vigilance and reformulation of Talwin® (including the addition of naloxone, a more powerful opioid antagonist) by its manufacturer have almost put a stop to these problems, although some people still abuse Talwin® NX orally by itself. There are no current ED reports of pentazocine overdoses perhaps because of its reformulation.

PROPOXYPHENE (Darvon,® Darvocet,® Propacet,® Wygesic®)

Used for the **relief of mild-to-moderate pain**, this odorless white crystalline powder is often prescribed by dentists. More than 23 million prescriptions were written for propoxyphene in 2005 (Drug Topics, 2007). It is taken orally for moderate pain, and the effects last four to six hours. Propoxyphene is occasionally used as an alternative to methadone maintenance and **for heroin detoxification**, especially for younger addicts, because it has only one-half to two-thirds the potency of codeine. Although it has abuse potential, Darvon® (and especially Darvon-N,® napsylate salt) continues to be used successfully in the detoxification of heroin addicts. The older the user, the slower the metabolism, so the drug is more potent in seniors. Misuse of this drug makes someone susceptible to overdose or addiction. Only about 4% of opioid fatalities involve propoxyphene (usually in combination with alcohol).

"After seven years of doing Darvon,® I started having withdrawals after three to four hours from the last pill that I had taken, so I was addicted to my watch. Then it got to where it was like two hours, so I needed like 14 or 16 Darvons to get through the day."
43-year-old female recovering Darvon® abuser

FENTANYL (Sublimaze®)

Even in its milder therapeutic formulation, fentanyl, introduced in 1968, is **the most powerful of the opioids**-50 to 100 times as strong as morphine on a weight-for-weight basis. It is used intravenously during and after surgery for severe pain. Structurally, this synthetic phenylpiperidine derivative is related to meperidine (Demerol®). It is also available in a skin patch to give steady pain relief for patients with intractable pain. A fentanyl lollipop was introduced in 1994 to be used for postoperative pain in children. Recently, an oral-transmucosal version (Actiq®) was developed to be dissolved slowly in the mouth. Unfortunately, fentanyl is favored as a drug of abuse by some surgical assistants and anesthesiologists due to its strength and availability.

The drug is diverted from normal channels in pill form, liquid suspension, or in a patch. In Florida in 2004, 115 people died from fentanyl (about four times as many abusers died from heroin and methadone overdoses). Many of those used the fentanyl patch and took a three-day supply of the powerful drug at one time.

In September 2002 Chechen rebels took over a theatre in Russia, holding 500 patrons hostage and threatening to kill them if their demands were not met. Russian troops used a gas to knock out the rebels and, unfortunately, also the hostages. The gas used was based on fentanyl, so those inside the theater were essentially knocked out by the equivalent of an opioid overdose; and because no one knew how potent the drug would be, 119 hostages died, along with 50 rebels. Most died of respiratory depression and heart failure.

There are street versions of fentanyl (alpha, 3-methyl) and meperidine (MPPP) manufactured in illegal laboratories. They are **extremely potent**, often more than the drugs they are imitating. Sold as "China white," these drugs bear witness to a growing sophistication of street chemists who now can bypass the traditional smuggling and trafficking routes of heroin. Because these designer drugs are made without controls on purity or dosage, they represent a tremendous health threat to the opioid-abusing community. There have been numerous outbreaks of overdose deaths due to ultrapotent fentanyl being sold as normal-potency heroin.

"When I first got out here on the West Coast, I found out that it [China white] wasn't white dope at all—it was fentanyl. And it wasn't even pharmaceutical fentanyl; it was bathtub fentanyl, and people were dying on it."
Dealer/heroin user

If improperly made, street **Demerol**® (MPPP) can contain the chemical MPTP, which **destroys dopamine-producing brain cells** that control voluntary muscular movement. The subsequent loss of control mimics the degenerative nerve condition known as Parkinson's disease. This degeneration causes a condition known as the "frozen addict" in which the addict loses the ability to move for the rest of his or her life.

LAAM® (levomethadyl acetate)

LAAM® is another **long-acting opioid that is used for heroin replacement therapy** similar to methadone maintenance. It prevents withdrawal symptoms and lasts 2 to 3 days compared with methadone's duration of action of 1 to 2 days. This reduces clinic visits for the drug to every other day or 3 days a week. It also reduces the need for take-home doses, thereby reducing the potential of street trade with the drug. The half-life of LAAM® is 48 hours, and the half-life of its active metabolites is 96 hours. Though the drug was developed in the late 1940s as a possible substitute for morphine, the slow onset and the long duration of action made it **unsuitable for pain management**. It has been studied since the mid-1960s as a treatment for opioid-dependent individuals, but it wasn't until 1993 that the federal Food and Drug Administration (FDA) made LAAM® available for clinical use. In one study at Johns Hopkins Medical School, the effectiveness of LAAM,® methadone, and buprenorphine were compared. All three seemed to be equally effective in the treatment of heroin abuse (Longshore, Annon, Anglin, et al., 2005). In another comparison of LAAM® and methadone at the University of California at Los Angeles, LAAM® was somewhat more effective in preventing heroin use during treatment (Marsch, Stephens, Mudric, et al., 2005).

The main detriment to the use of LAAM,® according to a survey of LAAM® clinics, seems to be the complicated paperwork and regulatory hurdles involved with use, along with staff attitude toward the drug (Rawson, Hasson, Huber, et al., 1998). The drug itself seems to work as well as methadone. As a result, only a small percentage of clinics that utilize opioid replacement therapy use LAAM.®

By the early 2000s, a number of cardiac arrhythmias were documented in patients treated with LAAM.® In response Roxanne Pharmaceuticals voluntarily ceased production of the medication in 2003. LAAM® is no longer available in the United States despite the fact that it remains an FDA-approved treatment for opioid replacement therapy.

NALOXONE (Narcan®) & NALTREXONE (Revia,® Vivitrol®)

Naloxone and naltrexone are **opioid antagonists**. They block the effects of heroin, hydrocodone, and other exogenous opioids as well as blocking endorphins and enkephalins, the body's own endogenous opioids.

Naloxone (Narcan®) is effective in treating heroin or opioid drug overdose. When a heroin overdose victim is injected with the drug, opioid effects (e.g., respiratory depression, low blood pressure, and sedation) are immediately halted or reversed and the person snaps back to consciousness within a matter of seconds up to two minutes (Physicians' Desk Reference [PDR], 2007). Naloxone is short acting, however, and when it wears off, the patient can fall back into a coma because the heroin is still in the system and its dangerous toxic effects can resume. Often naloxone must be injected repeatedly until the heroin is completely metabolized from the body. Naloxone itself will not cause significant effects when the heroin has left the body except in those who are physically addicted to opiates. Then it will cause major withdrawal symptoms.

"I just remember finding a vein finally and then waking up with a plastic tube in my nose, getting hit in the chest by a paramedic. Then everything went from black to light and they're standing over me and I was really pissed off at them for killing my buzz. And they're like, 'We just saved your life,' and I said, 'Maybe I didn't want you to. You just wasted $20.'"
20-year-old male recovering heroin addict

Naltrexone (Revia®) is used to prevent relapse and to help break the cycle of addiction to opioids. Taking naltrexone daily effectively **blocks the effects of heroin and any other opioid**. Its blocking mechanism will last up to 72 hours. Some clients take it daily for three months or longer, whereas others use it only when the cravings get too strong. Naltrexone is also being used to **reduce cravings for alcohol and cocaine** in support of detoxification and abstinence (Burattini, Burbassi, Aicardi, et al., 2007; Pettinati, O'Brien, Rabinowitz, et al., 2006). There are time-release injectable versions of the drug (e.g., Vivitrol®) for alcohol craving, and there are even injectable implants and depo products (time-release injections) in development for opioid addiction treatment. These injectable products are being developed to increase medication compliance and help prevent relapse (Colquhoun, Tan & Hull, 2005). Although naltrexone is not addicting in itself, if someone is using opioids for pain relief, the naltrexone will block the effects of the opioid. If people who are physically (tissue) dependent on opioids take naltrexone, they will suffer severe withdrawal symptoms. Side effects are usually minimal but can include nausea, irritability, headache, fatigue, and dizziness (Volpicelli, Pettinati, McLellan, et al., 2001). Naltrexone has also been proven effective in smoking-cessation programs particularly among female smokers (Gold, Jacobs, McGhee, et al., 2002).

BUPRENORPHINE (Buprenex,® Subutex,® Suboxone®)

Buprenorphine is **a powerful opioid agonist at low doses and an opiate antagonist at high doses**. In low doses it is used as an analgesic alternative to morphine, being 50 times stronger than heroin. At high doses it blocks the opioid receptors by hyperpolarizing or overactivating it. This is called an *inverse agonistic effect*. Buprenorphine continues to block the effects of morphine and heroin for about 30 hours after use (Strain, Walsh, Preston, et al., 1997). It has been approved as **an alternative to methadone for detoxification, buprenorphine maintenance, and transition away from methadone maintenance**. It is somewhat more attractive to treatment professionals because it has a high degree of safety, a long duration of action, flexible dosing, and milder withdrawal effects. It can also be prescribed by an approved physician rather than only being available daily at specialized treatment clinics.

The exact dosage for detoxification from heroin and other opioids varies, with the average term of use lasting three to 21 days. There is even a one-day detoxification protocol. **For detoxification it is used at low doses as an opioid agonist**, replacing the riskier drug of addiction such as heroin. If it is used for longer-term maintenance, it is dispensed in low doses, much like methadone. If the goal is to wean the addict from all use of opioids, the dose is gradually increased until it becomes an antagonist and begins to block the opioid effects of itself and any other opioid the addict might try.

There is abuse potential when the drug is used in low doses as an agonist, so its manufacturer (Reckitt Benckiser, a British pharmaceutical company) has combined buprenorphine with naloxone to diminish the opiate agonist effects of the drug if the tablet is crushed and injected (Strain, Stoller, Walsh, et al., 2000). In Europe, Nepal, and India, abuse of buprenorphine is widespread.

Two drugs, **Subutex® and Suboxone,® were approved in 2002 for treatment of patients with opioid dependence.** Subutex® contains only buprenorphine, whereas Suboxone® combines buprenorphine and naloxone. The important part of the FDA approval is that buprenorphine may now be prescribed by qualified physicians in their offices rather than only at a drug treatment clinic. The theory is that many addicts do not have access to methadone clinics or other treatment facilities, so making this milder drug more widely available will increase treament options for the heroin addict. It is still required that addicts receiving buprenorphine treatment be simultaneously enrolled in counseling and clinical treatment services for their addiction.

With a number of years of experience to draw from, the view of buprenorphine is mixed particularly from the addicts' perspective. **Buprenorphine doesn't cover all the withdrawal symptoms**, so clients have slightly unrealistic expectations about the effectiveness of the drug. Other medications are often used for those symptoms not handled by buprenorphine And, like methadone, it seems to be more appreciated and used as a replacement therapy than simply as a detoxification drug.

CLONIDINE (Catapres®)

This nonopioid, originally prescribed for the treatment of hypertension, is often **used to diminish opioid withdrawal symptoms** such as nausea, anxiety, and diarrhea. It also seems to alleviate opioid craving. Because it acts

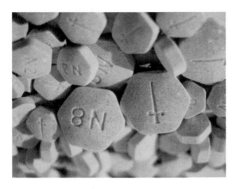

Suboxone® comes in 2 mg tablets and 8 mg tablets manufactured by Reckitt Benckiser.®

Courtesy of the National Advocates for Buprenorphine Treatment

on norepinephrine receptors to control their overactivity, one of the main causes of severe opioid withdrawal symptoms, it shortens withdrawal time from almost a month down to a couple of weeks in some cases. When used in combination with naltrexone, it shortens severe withdrawal symptoms to about five days in a process called *rapid opioid detoxification.*

BUTORPHANOL (Stadol®) & TRAMADOL (Ultram®)

These newer synthetic opioid analgesics were **developed with the intent of being less abusable and addictive than the older opioids**. Unfortunately, butorphanol was quickly found to be abused like opioids and is a Schedule IV drug. Since its release in a nasal spray form, abuse and overdose deaths have increased. As of 2007 tramadol is not a controlled substance but is becoming more abused and has an opioidlike overdose liability. Though both tramadol and butorphanol have less addiction and overdose potential than the more powerful opioids like meperidine and morphine, they are capable of producing the same type of addiction as seen with other opioids. Both drugs are also in evaluation as potential treatments for other addictions.

ULTRARAPID OPIOID DETOXIFICATION

In this medically supervised process, the patient is given naltrexone orally or intravenously while heavily sedated or even under general anesthesia to **avoid the pain of acute withdrawal symptoms** precipitated by the opioid antagonist. There is much controversy about this process along with fatal complications if mistakes are made. Some say that even if the physical withdrawal is treated, the psychological addiction will continue and eventually cause a relapse (Smith & Seymour, 2001) (*see Chapter 9*).

SEDATIVE-HYPNOTICS

The market for sedative-hypnotics is in the billions of dollars. Advertising used to be directed at those with prescriptive authority, but recently prescription drug advertisements in print and on television have directed their message at the consumer so they will suggest a certain drug to their doctor.

tens of thousands of patients in the United States and Europe became dependent on a variety of psychoactive drugs overprescribed by their doctors (**iatrogenic addiction**). The ingredients were more likely to be cocaine, opium, morphine, heroin, or marijuana because the modern era of drug development and synthesis was just beginning. As newer compounds were discovered and as pharmaceutical companies developed sophisticated manufacturing and marketing systems, the use and occasionally the abuse spread.

America has gone through several periods of sedative-hypnotic abuse as each new drug or family of drugs is released. Stories have abounded through the decades of barbiturate abuse in the 1930s and 1940s, Miltown® abuse in the 1950s, benzodiazepine abuse in the 1970s through the present, and abuse to one degree or another of almost any sedative-hypnotic drug in spite of continued assurances that "this one is not addictive." Currently, prescription drug abuse, particularly among younger users, is again increasing. Though prescription opioids are the most abused in this regard, abuse of prescription sedative-hypnotics is also on the rise.

"The late Supreme Court Chief Justice William Rehnquist took a powerful sedative (Placidyl®) during his first decade on the high court and grew so dependent on it that he became delusional and tried to escape from a hospital in his pajamas when he stopped taking the drug in 1981, according to newly released FBI files. Rehnquist began taking the drug for insomnia after back surgery in 1971, the year before he joined the court. By 1981 he apparently was taking 1,500 mg a day, three times the usual starting dose. It is not usually prescribed for more than a week at a time."

Seattle Times, January 5, 2007

Prescription drugs have been called the middle and upper classes' abusable drugs of choice. While a large amount of the abused prescriptions are for pain pills and secondarily for sedative-hypnotics, any psychoactive prescription drug can create dependency in people who inadvertently or deliberately overuse it. They eventually learn how to divert legitimate prescriptions and find street dealers and online Web sites that will sustain their dependency.

In the late 1800s and early 1900s,

CLASSIFICATION

Americans spent $274.9 billion on prescription drugs in 2006, an increase of almost $125 billion from just four years earlier. Driven by the Medicare Part D prescription benefit, more generic drugs, and an aging population, pharmacies filled more than 3.5 billion prescriptions, an average of $60 to $70 per prescription, in 2006. More than **60 million of those prescriptions were for sedative-hypnotics** (mostly benzodiazepines). Their use in other coun-

Name	Trade Name	Street Name
BENZODIAZEPINES	**Various**	**Benzos, tranx, BDZs, downers**
Very-Long-Acting		
Flurazepam	Dalmane®	
Halazepam	Paxipam®	
Prazepam	Centrax®	
Quazepam	Doral®	
Intermediate-Acting		
Chlordiazepoxide	Librium,® Libritabs,® Limbitrol®	Libs
Clonazepam	Klonopin®	Klonnies, klons, Klondike bars
Clorazepate	Tranxene®	
Diazepam	Valium®	Vals, valley girl
Short-Acting		
Alprazolam	Xanax®	Xannies, bars, x-boxes, coffins
Lorazepam	Ativan®	
Midazolam	Versed®	
Oxazepam	Serax®	
Temazepam	Restoril®	Mazzies, eggs
Very-Short-Acting		
Estazolam	Pro-Som®	
Triazolam	Halcion®	
Banned in the United States		
Flunitrazepam	Rohypnol®	Ruffies, roofies, roachies
BARBITURATES	**Various**	**Barbs, downers, barbies**
Long-Acting		
Phenobarbital	Luminal®	Phenos
Mephobarbital	Mebaral®	
Intermediate-Acting		
Amobarbital	Amytal®	Blue heaven, blues
Aprobarbital	Alurate®	
Butabarbital	Barbased,® Butisol®	
Talbutal	Lotusate®	
Equal parts secobarbital and amobarbital	Tuinal®	Rainbows, tuies, double trouble
Short-Acting		
Butalbital	Esgic,® Fiorinal®	
Hexobarbital	Sombulex®	
Pentobarbital	Nembutal®	Yellows, yellow jackets, nebbies
Secobarbital	Seconal®	Reds, red devils, F-40s
Very-Short-Acting		
Methohexital	Brevital®	
Thiamylal sodium	Surital®	
Thiopental sodium	Pentothal®	Truth serum
NONBENZODIAZEPINE, NONBARBITURATE SEDATIVE-HYPNOTICS		
Bromides		
Buspirone	BuSpar®	
Chloral hydrate	Noctec,® Somnos®	Jelly beans, Mickeys, knockout drops
Eszopiclone	Lunesta®	
Ethchlorvynol	Placidyl®	Green weenies
GHB (gammahydroxybutyrate)	Xyrem®	Grievous bodily harm, liquid E, fantasy, Georgia homeboy
GBL (gamma butyl lactone)	Blue Nitro,® Revivarant,® Insom-X,® Revivarant G,® Gamma G,® GH Revitalizer,® Remforce®	(GBL is a chemical and biologic precursor to GHB)
Glutethimide (obsolete)	Doriden®	Goofballs, goofers
Glutethimide and codeine	Doriden® and codeine	Loads, sets, setups, hits, C&C, fours and doors
Meprobamate	Equinil,® Miltown,® Meprotabs,® Deprol®	Mother's little helper
Methaprylon	Noludar®	Noodlelars
Methaqualone (only illegal forms)	Quaalude,® Soper,® Somnafac,® Parest,® Optimil®	Ludes, sopes, sopers, Q
Paraldehyde	Paral®	
Pregabalin	Lyrica®	
Ramelteon	Rozerem®	
Zaleplon	Sonata®	
Zolpidem	Ambien®	

tries is also widespread (IMS Health, 2007). Many more prescriptions used to be written for sedative-hypnotics in the 1960s, 1970s, and 1980s, but the use of **psychiatric medications for depression has taken over a significant part of the sedative-hypnotics market share**, with tricyclic antidepressants and the newer selective serotonin reuptake inhibitor (SSRI) antidepressants, such as Prozac® (fluoxetine), Paxil® (paroxetine), and Zoloft® (sertraline). At least 98 million prescriptions were written in 2001 for psychiatric medications, 45 million for antidepressants alone (Drug Benefit Trends, 2001, 2002).

Almost all sedative-hypnotics are available as pills, capsules, or tablets, though some, such as diazepam (Valium®) and lorazepam (Ativan®), are used intravenously for more-immediate treatment of seizures and panic attacks. **The two main groups of sedative-hypnotics are benzodiazepines and barbiturates.** There are also a number of nonbenzodiazepine, nonbarbiturate sedative-hypnotics.

The **effects of sedative-hypnotics are generally similar to the effects of alcohol** (e.g., lowered inhibitions, physical depression, sedation, and muscular relaxation); and like alcohol, sedative-hypnotic drugs can cause memory loss, tolerance, tissue dependence, withdrawal symptoms, and addiction. The obvious basic difference between the two depressants is their potency. On a gram-by-gram basis, sedative-hypnotics are much more potent than alcohol.

Sedatives are calming drugs, e.g., alprazolam (Xanax®), diazepam (Valium®), and meprobamate (Miltown®). They are also called "minor tranquilizers." A number of benzodiazepines act on the neurotransmitters GABA, serotonin, and dopamine to help control anxiety and restlessness. Sedatives are also capable of causing muscular relaxation, body heat loss, lowered inhibitions, reduced intensity of physical sensations, and reduced muscular coordination in speech, movement, and manual dexterity. They are also used to help with alcohol or heroin detoxification and to control seizures.

Hypnotics are sleep inducers, i.e., short-acting barbiturates and benzodi-

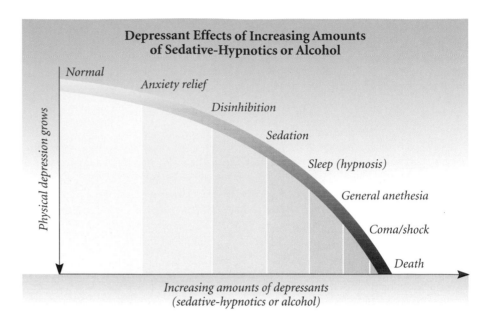

Figure 4-4 •

As this chart shows, increasing the dose of a sedative-hypnotic can be used simply to calm or to anesthetize for surgery. When users self-medicate with sedative-hypnotics and/or alcohol, they often lose track of where they will end up on the scale.

azepines such as Halcion® that work on the brainstem. They also depress most body functions, including breathing and muscular coordination. Some sedatives are used as hypnotics and some hypnotics are used as sedatives, so it is sometimes difficult to separate the two.

HISTORY

Calming and sleep-inducing drugs have been around for millennia. The ones used in ancient cultures were natural plant-derived substances (especially opium) or products of fermentation processes that were probably first discovered by accident or through experimentation. In the past 150 years, with the increasing sophistication of chemical processes, virtually all of the sedative-hypnotics have been developed in the laboratory.

At the turn of the century, bromides, chloral hydrate, and paraldehyde were commonly used. Though chemically quite different, they all depress the central nervous system.

◇ **Bromides**, used as sedatives or anticonvulsants, were first introduced

in the 1850s and often sold over the counter; they had a long half-life, however, so prolonged or nonsupervised use could build up toxic doses in the body.

◇ **Chloral hydrate** could be purchased at many drugstores in 1869; it was used as both a sedative and a hypnotic. It relieved tension and pain and helped treat alcoholics' insomnia. It was often prescribed for women to treat delirium tremens and to help pregnant women cope (Kandall, 1993). When slipped into a drink, it was the original "Mickey Finn" used to knock out and shanghai sailors. It is still sometimes used because it has a higher margin of safety than barbiturates when used to treat sleep problems.

◇ **Paraldehyde**, developed in 1882, was used to control the symptoms of alcohol withdrawal. Despite its offensive odor and tendency to become addictive, it is still occasionally used to treat alcohol withdrawal (Hollister, 1983).

◇ **Barbiturates** were first developed at the end of the nineteenth century and slowly grew in popularity; they peaked in the 1930s and 1940s.

Phenobarbital, secobarbital, and pentobarbital were among the hundreds of compounds synthesized from barbituric acid. Appreciation of the toxic potential of barbiturates due to a low margin of safety, a low degree of selectivity, and a high dependence and addictive potential instilled an apprehension of use and encouraged researchers to look for new classes of sedative-hypnotics.

◇ **Meprobamate (Miltown®)** was developed in the late 1940s and 1950s. Known as "mother's little helper," this long-acting sedative replaced many long-acting barbiturates, including phenobarbital. Its popularity peaked from 1955 to 1961, when benzodiazepines took center stage.

◇ **Glutethimide (Doriden®)** was tried as a barbiturate substitute, but it seemed to have many of the same disadvantages without enough advantages. It was also weaker than phenobarbital and subject to abuse, especially when it was abused in combination with codeine ("loads," "sets," and "setups") to potentiate the effects of both drugs. It is no longer manufactured in the United States.

◇ **Benzodiazepines** were first discovered in 1954 (Librium®) and then rediscovered in 1957 at Hoffman-La Roche Laboratories in a deliberate search for a safer class of sedative-hypnotics. When Librium® (chlordiazepoxide) and Valium® (diazepam) were synthesized and marketed in 1960 and 1963, respectively, they quickly became immensely popular because they were less toxic than barbiturates, meprobamate, and glutethimide, although many of the sites of action in the central nervous system were similar to those of barbiturates. Over the years more than 3,000 compounds were developed, but only 20 or so were marketed and released (Sternbach, 1983). To this day benzodiazepines dominate the market for sedative-hypnotics. Though they are less toxic than other sedatives, benzodiazepines can be very addictive and have dangerous withdrawal symptoms.

◇ **Other sedative-hypnotics** are being developed in an attempt to improve this class of drugs while tempering their addictive properties. Drugs such as **Lunesta,® BuSpar,® Rozerem,® Ambien,® and Lyrica®** are being advertised as safer and less addictive. The only two that rigorous research seems to validate as nondependence producing are BuSpar® and Rozerem.®

USE, MISUSE, ABUSE & ADDICTION

In 1993 the average number of prescriptions per person was seven; in 2006 it was more than 12. In fact, almost half of all Americans use at least one prescription drug on a daily basis (Critser, 2005). In the twentieth and twenty-first centuries, society's attitude toward the use of sedative-hypnotics and psychiatric medications has swung like a pendulum. The liberal use of barbiturates in the 1930s and 1940s, along with the vision of a drug-controlled society as written about in Aldous Huxley's futuristic novel *Brave New World,* led to a search for nonaddictive alternatives. But the widespread use of Miltown® in the fifties, which eventually led to an attitude of "better living through chemistry" in the sixties, seemed to confirm Huxley's fears. Subsequently, **benzodiazepines were hailed as miracle drugs and prescribed in huge amounts** (100 million prescriptions per year in the United States by 1975), and again fear of becoming a drug-dependent society came to the fore (90 million prescriptions in 2005) (Drug Topics, 2007). More recently, the increase in psychiatric medications has somewhat diminished the appeal of sedative-hypnotics, but they are still widely prescribed.

To complicate matters, a turf war has developed that pits some of those in the medical and treatment communities who want the freedom to prescribe benzodiazepines and other sedative-hypnotics as they see fit against others who feel that overuse of prescription drugs needs to be brought under control. Even within some drug compa-

nies, there is a conflict between the research/development departments that want to develop drugs with very targeted effects and the marketing departments that would like to have their drugs approved for as many conditions as possible and used for extended periods of time (Critser, 2005).

When used properly, sedative-hypnotics can be beneficial therapeutic adjuncts for treatment of a variety of psychological and physical conditions. When misused they can cause undesirable side effects, dependence, abuse, addiction, and even death.

"You don't think that a pill is going to make you go after more and more and more pills like a fix of heroin. And then it becomes a habit. It becomes as hideous as any illicit drug habit. It can become more dangerous actually. I've had a more dangerous time with the taking care of my [pill] habit."
43-year-old recovering benzodiazepine abuser

Sedative-hypnotic (as well as opioid) misuse or abuse can occur when patients:

◇ **overuse the drug** prescribed by the physician;

◇ **use them in combination with other psychoactive drugs** to potentiate or counteract effects;

◇ **borrow the drugs from a friend** to self-medicate;

◇ **steal drugs** from their parents' or friends' medicine cabinets; or

◇ **divert the drugs from legal sources** through forged prescriptions, buying on the black market, or stealing to get high or medicate emotional pain
(DEA, 2000).

Over the years in popular and scientific literature and movies, **sedative-hypnotics have been associated with both accidental and intentional drug overdoses**. Many movies use the image of an empty prescription vial to indicate a suicide attempt or the need for stomach pumps.

In the *Annual Emergency Room Data Survey,* physicians list which

TABLE 4–4   MENTIONS OF DRUG PROBLEMS IN U.S. EMERGENCY ROOMS, 2005

(More than one drug is found in many incoming patients.)

Drugs	Number of Drug Mentions
Alcohol alone (21 and older only)	98,430
Alcohol in combination with other drugs	394,224
Cocaine	448,481
Heroin	164,572
Marijuana	242,200
Benzodiazepines (Xanax,® Klonopin®)	172,388
Aspirin, acetaminophen, ibuprofen, non-steroidal anti-inflammatory drugs (NSAIDs), and other OTC pain relievers	103,000
Narcotic analgesics (morphine, (hydrocodone, OxyContin,®)	196,225
Antidepressants (Zoloft,® Trazadone®)	61,023
Amphetamines and methamphetamine	138,950
Other sedative-hypnotics and anxiolytics (Ambien®)	31,553 (12,765)
Antipsychotics	37,327
Barbiturates	11,013
Ketamine and PCP	7,810
GHB	1,861
Rohypnol	596
MDMA	10,752
LSD	1,864
Other hallucinogens	3,792
Inhalants	4,312
Illicit drug abuse only	**816,696**
Total drug misuse and abuse mentions	**1,449,154**

(DAWN, 2007)

drugs cause medical problems severe enough to make people seek medical attention. Table 4-4 shows which drugs are reported most often. Overall there are about 1.5 million visits to EDs for drug misuse and abuse problems such as overdose, dependence, withdrawal syndrome, and drug interactions. About half of those are for illicit drugs.

Studies of sedative-hypnotic drug misuse and overdose conducted by the National Institute on Drug Abuse reveal some other factors that contribute to misuse, abuse, or overdose with these drugs.

◇ Because sedatives impair memory, awareness, and judgment, **individuals forget how many sedatives they have ingested** to help them get

to sleep or to relieve stress. Rather than waiting long enough for the full dose of the drug to affect them, they continue to take more of the drug and accidentally reach a toxic state. This effect has been called *drug automatism.*

◇ **Ignorance of additive and synergistic effects** resulting from combining these drugs with alcohol or other sedatives is widespread.

◇ **Selective tolerance to some effects of the drug** but not to its toxic effects results in a narrowing window of safety, where the amount needed to produce a high comes closer to the lethal dose of the drug.

◇ **Adolescent attitudes of invulnerability** promote risk-taking behav-

ior with respect to the amount of drug ingested when used illicitly.
(NIDA, 2005)

BENZODIAZEPINES

Benzodiazepines are by far **the most widely used sedative-hypnotics in the United States**. This class of drugs was developed in the 1950s as an alternative to barbiturates. Because benzodiazepines have a fairly large margin of safety, many healthcare professionals initially overlooked their peculiarities: the length of time they last in body tissues, their ability to induce tissue dependence at low levels of use, and the severity of withdrawal from the drug. For these reasons almost all recommendations for benzodiazepine use today emphasize that **they should be used short term and for specific conditions, not as long-term medications**.

The most widely used benzodiazepines are **alprazolam (Xanax®**—34 million prescriptions in 2005), **lorazepam (Ativan®**—19 million), **clonazepam (Klonopin®**—16.7 million), **diazepam (Valium®**—12 million), and **temazepam (Restoril®**—7.6 million).

MEDICAL USE OF BENZODIAZEPINES

Medically, benzodiazepines are used to:

◇ provide short-term treatment for the symptoms of **anxiety and panic disorders**;

◇ control anxiety and **apprehension** in surgical patients and diminish traumatic memories of the procedure;

◇ treat **sleep problems**;

◇ control **skeletal muscular spasms**;

◇ elevate the seizure threshold (anticonvulsant) and control **seizures**; and

◇ control **acute alcohol withdrawal symptoms** (e.g., severe agitation, tremors, impending acute delirium tremens, and hallucinosis).

"The enclosed space of the MRI machine they were going to slip me

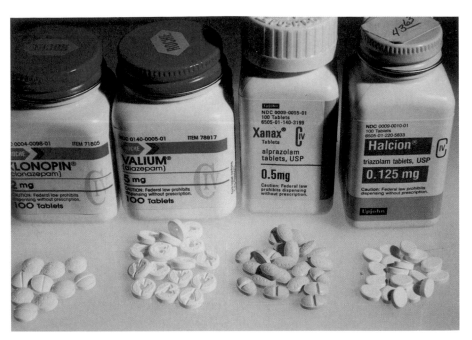

Most benzodiazepines have come off patent, so the vast majority of prescriptions are for the generic versions of the drug. The most prescribed benzodiazepines by number of prescriptions are, first, alprazolam (Xanax®), then lorazepam (Ativan®), clonazepam (Klonopin®), diazepam (Valium®), temazepam (Restoril®) and triazolam (Halcion®).
© 2007 CNS Productions, Inc.

● ●

into really triggered one of my claustrophobic panic attacks, so we couldn't finish. I was yelling, 'Get me outta here,' along with some nasty threats to do them bodily harm. The next time they gave me some Valium,® and though I still felt nervous, it did calm me enough so I could have the scan done. It seemed like a dream."
50-year-old female with no drug problem

NONMEDICAL USE OF BENZODIAZEPINES

Because the desirable **emotional and physical effects of benzodiazepines are very similar to those of alcohol,** they are sometimes used for the same reasons a person drinks. A double-blind study on non-drug addicts compared the effects of low-dose diazepam injections and alcohol injections. The subjects found the highs from each of the drugs to be extremely similar; however, higher-dose diazepam produced more physical impairment (Schuckit, Greenblatt, Gold, et al., 1991).

Benzodiazepines alone can be abused but they are **most often abused in conjunction with other drugs**. Methamphetamine and cocaine abusers often take a benzodiazepine to come down from excess stimulation. This combination is connected with spasms of the coronary arteries that can damage the heart (Starcevic & Sicaja, 2007). Heroin addicts frequently take a benzodiazepine when they can't get their drug of choice, and alcoholics use them or are prescribed them to prevent convulsions and other life-threatening withdrawal symptoms. For example, depending on the study, 20% to 40% of alcoholics and 25% to 50% of heroin or methadone-maintained addicts abused benzodiazepines (Miller & Gold, 1990). In another treatment center study, 10% of polydrug clients abused benzodiazepines. In one older study, almost 100% of benzodiazepine addicts reported dependence on or addiction to other drugs (Busto, Sellers, Naranjo, et al., 1986). **Benzodiazepine abusers are more likely to be older than 30 years of age, White, well educated, and female.**

"If I threw down 10 Valium,® I didn't really feel that much. It wasn't

like taking Nembutal® or other barbiturates where you get a real rush. I would have to take an awful lot to feel anything. It relieved certain anxieties; it alleviated depression. You tell the doctor, 'I'm anxious or depressed.' 'Okay, take some Valium.®'"
48-year-old female recovering benzodiazepine abuser

NEUROCHEMISTRY & GABA

Benzodiazepines have been shown to exert their sedative effects in the brain by potentiating (increasing the effects of) a naturally occurring neurotransmitter called *GABA* (gamma amino butyric acid) in the cerebellum, cerebral cortex, and limbic system (Potokar & Nutt, 1994). **GABA is recognized as the most important inhibitory neurotransmitter**, so when a drug, like alprazolam (Xanax®), greatly increases the actions of GABA, it subsequently inhibits anxiety-producing thoughts and overstimulating neural messages (Stahl, 2000). Other neurotransmitters, such as serotonin and dopamine, are also increased.

Most benzodiazepines are prodrugs. This means that the liver converts a certain percentage of a drug, like diazepam (Valium®), to a psychoactive metabolite (e.g., nordiazepam). **The metabolites can be as active or even more active than the original drug itself.** Nordiazepam can be further converted to temazepam and oxazepam (Jenkins & Cone, 1998). (These last two active metabolites are also manufactured separately by pharmaceutical companies as Restoril® and Serax.®) The metabolites, along with the original drug, are very fat-soluble (lipophilic) and therefore stay in the body for a long time.

Specific benzodiazepines have been developed to treat specific conditions. For example:

◇ short-term alprazolam (Xanax®) is used for immediate relief of the symptoms of generalized anxiety disorder, panic disorder, and depression resulting from anxiety (many patients are prescribed alprazolam just for depression);

◊ triazolam (Halcion®) is used for short-term (seven to 10 days) treatment of insomnia;

◊ diazepam (Valium®) is used to treat anxiety, to gain relief from skeletal muscle spasms caused by inflammation of the muscles and joints, and to control seizures such as those that occur during severe alcohol or barbiturate withdrawal; and

◊ intravenous Valium® is used as a sedative just before surgery.

TOLERANCE, TISSUE DEPENDENCE & WITHDRAWAL

Tolerance

Tolerance to benzodiazepines develops as **the liver becomes more efficient in processing the drug.** Age-dependent reverse tolerance also occurs with these drugs, however, meaning that **a younger person can tolerate higher doses of benzodiazepines than can someone older.** The effect of a dose on a 50-year-old first-time user can be two to four times stronger than the same dose on a 20-year-old. Many diagnoses of dementia are actually due to overuse of benzodiazepines and other drug interactions.

"I was unhappy and I wanted the easy way out. I will go back to the same psychiatrist and get a prescription of Xanax.® It starts out at 25 mg, and I ended up doing between 800 to 1,000 mg a day."
43-year-old recovering benzodiazepine abuser

Tissue Dependence

Physical addiction to a benzodiazepine can develop if the patient takes 10 to 20 times the normal dose daily for a couple of months or longer or takes a normal dose for a year or more. Because many benzodiazepines are de-activated over a period of several days, **even low-dose use can lead to tissue dependence and addiction** when these drugs are taken daily over a number of years. In addition, the pleasant mental effects and reinforcing aspects of the drugs can result in a psychological dependence.

Withdrawal

After high-dose continuous use for about one to three months or lower-dose use for at least one to two years, **withdrawal symptoms can be severe**. It can take a dependent benzodiazepine user **several months to taper off from the drug** and allow the body to return to normal. If tapering isn't carefully monitored, withdrawal seizures can occur, sometimes with fatal results.

"Benzo detox in the morning is very frightening because your mind is just telling your body that 'we are not connected.' It took maybe 10 days before the manic depressive state of the detox finally started to show some light at the end of the tunnel."
34-year-old recovering benzodiazepine abuser

Withdrawal symptoms can include:

◊ recurrence of the original symptoms that were being treated with the benzodiazepine;

◊ magnification of the symptoms that were being treated;

◊ pseudowithdrawal in which the user exaggerates the recurrence of symptoms; and

◊ true withdrawal in a patient who has become physically dependent, often caused by low GABA and excess epinephrine and norepinephrine.

The drug is long lasting, so **with true withdrawal the onset of symptoms is delayed**—about 1 day for short-acting and up to 5 days for long-acting benzodiazepines. **The symptoms can last 7 to 20 days for short-acting and up to 28 days for long-acting benzodiazepines** (Dickinson, Mayo-Smith & Eickelberg, 2003).

Because many of the symptoms of true withdrawal are similar to those of an anxiety or depressive disorder, it can be **hard to judge the level of dependence.** First a craving for the drug occurs. This is the tissue-dependent brain's attempt to avoid the onset of withdrawal symptoms. Drug craving is followed by headaches, tremors, muscle twitches, nausea and vomiting, anx-

iety, restlessness, yawning, tachycardia, cramping, hypertension, inability to focus, sleep disturbances, and dizziness. Some people even experience a temporary loss of vision, hearing, or smell and other sensory impairments while in withdrawal; occasionally, they have hallucinations (Dickenson, Mayo-Smith & Eickelberg, 2003; Miller & Gold, 1990). The symptoms continue and peak in the first through third weeks. These symptoms occasionally include multiple seizures and convulsions that can be fatal.

"I stopped taking them, and on the third day I remember I was sweating. I changed the sheets on the bed. I took a shower. I was fairly relaxed and I went into a convulsion. I don't remember what happened. All I can remember is waking up and all my front teeth were knocked out. I ended up going through about 80 convulsions."
Recovering Valium® abuser

The persistence of benzodiazepines (Figure 4-5) in the body from low- or regular-dose use taken over a long period of time results not only in prolonged withdrawal symptoms but in **symptoms that erratically come and go in cycles separated by two to 10 days.** These symptoms are sometimes bizarre, sometimes life threatening, and all are complicated by the cyclical nature of benzodiazepine withdrawal. Short-acting barbiturates, on the other hand, follow a fairly predictable course, where the symptoms come and then go and do not return. Called **protracted withdrawal,** the symptoms of benzodiazepine withdrawal may persist for several months after the drug has been terminated.

More than 170,000 ED visits were due to problems with benzodiazepines (DAWN, 2007). The reason why actual overdoses and suicides have decreased with the increased use of benzodiazepines and the decreased use of barbiturates is that the benzodiazepines have a much greater *therapeutic index* (the lethal dose of a drug divided by its therapeutic effective dose). The therapeutic

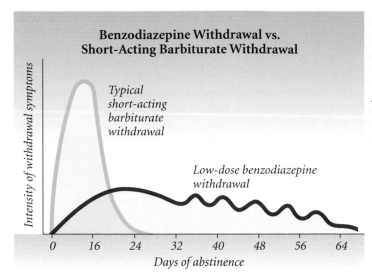

Benzodiazepine Withdrawal vs. Short-Acting Barbiturate Withdrawal

Typical short-acting barbiturate withdrawal

Low-dose benzodiazepine withdrawal

Intensity of withdrawal symptoms

0 16 24 32 40 48 56 64
Days of abstinence

Figure 4-5 • The delay in the occurrence of withdrawal symptoms can be dangerous to benzodiazepine abusers who abruptly stop using.

index of barbiturates is 10 to 1, whereas the therapeutic index of benzodiazepines is 700 to 1. With barbiturates it means that 10 times a therapeutic dose in an individual who has not developed tolerance can be fatal. For benzodiazepines 700 times the therapeutic dose can be fatal. **This margin of safety is tremendously diminished when benzodiazepines are taken in combination with alcohol**, other benzodiazepines, phenothiazines, MAO inhibitors, barbiturates, opioids, antidepressants and other depressant drugs (PDR, 2007).

Symptoms of overdose include drowsiness, loss of consciousness, depressed breathing, coma, and death if left untreated; however, it might take 50 to 100 pills to cause a serious overdose. Street versions of the drug, often misrepresented and sold as Quaaludes,® are so strong that only 5 or 10 pills can cause severe reactions.

MEMORY IMPAIRMENT

Benzodiazepines impair the ability to learn new information. They disrupt the transfer of information from short- to long-term memory. They also slow the ability to shift one's attention from one job to another (American Psychiatric Association, 1990; Boucart, Waucquier, Michael, et al., 2007; Juergens & Cowley, 2003). The amnestic effect of benzodiazepines (medically known as either **retrograde or anterograde amnesia**), also commonly called a drug "blackout" or "brownout," helps patients forget trau-

matic surgical and other medical procedures. This effect has unfortunately been **used by a few sexual predators** to cause victims to forget they were sexually assaulted.

"They took advantage when I passed out at a party and I was sleeping on a couch and I woke up and they were doing stuff to me that they shouldn't have. And I remember running into the bathroom and throwing up and then sleeping on the floor that night. I'm careful now about my surroundings. If it's a safe place where I know I can have a few beers and have fun with my friends, I'll do it; but I'm a little bit wary of where I drink or whatever just because of that experience."
20-year-old woman

The drug most associated with date rape in the past was the benzodiazepine Rohypnol® (flunitrazepam). Like other benzodiazepines, Rohypnol® also causes relaxation and sedation. Rohypnol® (or another very-short-acting benzodiazepine) is slipped into an alcoholic beverage, which, when drunk, **incapacitates the person, lowers inhibitions, and disrupts the memory**. This illicit use began in Europe in the 1970s but didn't occur in the United States until the 1990s. The manufacturer,

Roche Pharmaceuticals, recently added a blue dye to the tablet to make it more detectable when put into a drink. More recently, another date rape drug, GHB, has become popular for this purpose.

Rohypnol® is 10 times more potent by weight than Valium® and is short acting (two to three hours), but it has a long half-life (15 to 35 hours) and its frequent use will cause a buildup of the drug in the body's tissues. When it's taken with alcohol, the safety margin is greatly reduced. It used to be possible to fill a Rohypnol® prescription in Mexico (25¢ to 30¢ per pill) and then bring it into the United States for street sale ($1 to $5 per pill). **But in 1996 the FDA banned all imports of the drug** even for personal use. New laws adding 20 more years to the sentence of anyone convicted of using Rohypnol,® GHB, or any drug to sexually assault someone or commit violence were enacted in 1996 (*see GHB in this chapter*).

BARBITURATES

Though **barbituric acid was first synthesized in 1863**, it remained a medical curiosity until 1903, when the molecule was modified to create **barbital (Veronal®)**. The chemical modification made it possible for the drug to enter the nervous system and induce sedation. It was originally believed to be free of the addictive propensities of opiates and opioids. Phenobarbital came next in 1913, and since then about 50 of the **2,000 other barbiturates** that have been created have been marketed. By the time there had been extensive clinical experience with these drugs, many dangers such as overdose, severe withdrawal symptoms, dependence, and addiction had become apparent (Lukas, 1995). Since the peak of their use in the 1940s and 1950s and their abuse in the 1950s, 1960s, and 1970s, their **licit and illicit use has declined dramatically, due primarily to increased scrutiny of their production and prescribing practices**.

EFFECTS

◇ The **long-acting barbiturates**, such as phenobarbital, last 12 to 24 hours and are used mostly as **day-**

time sedatives or to control epileptic seizures.

◊ The **intermediate-acting** barbiturates, such as butabarbital (Butisol®), are used as **longer-acting sedatives** and last 6 to 12 hours.

◊ The **short-acting** compounds, including butalbital and, in the past, Seconal® ("reds") and Nembutal® ("yellows"), last 3 to 6 hours and are used to **induce sleep**. They can cause pleasant feelings along with the sedation (at least initially), so they are more likely to be abused.

◊ The **very short-acting** barbiturates, such as Pentothal,® are used mostly for **anesthesia** and can cause immediate unconsciousness. The high potency of these barbiturates makes them extremely dangerous if abused.

As with benzodiazepines, barbiturates affect GABA, therefore acting as a brake on inhibitions, anxiety, and restlessness. Because they can **induce a feeling of disinhibitory euphoria**, barbiturates seem to have an initial stimulatory effect but eventually become sedating. To an even greater extent than with benzodiazepines, the effects of barbiturates are very similar to those of alcohol. Excessive or long-term use can lead to changes in personality and emotional stability, including mood swings, depression, irritability, and boisterous behavior (Lukas, 1995).

The effects of barbiturates often depend on the mood of the user and the setting where taken. An agitated barbiturate user might become combative, whereas a tired barbiturate user in a quiet setting might go to sleep.

TOLERANCE, TISSUE DEPENDENCE & WITHDRAWAL

Tolerance to barbiturates develops in a variety of ways. The most dramatic tolerance, dispositional tolerance (metabolic tolerance), results from the physiologic **conversion of liver cells to more-efficient cells that metabolize or destroy barbiturates more quickly**. The other process, pharmacodynamic tolerance, **causes affected nerve cells and tissues to become less sensitive.**

Tissue dependence to barbiturates occurs when eight to 10 times the normal dose is taken daily for 30 days or more.

Within six to eight hours after stopping use of short-acting barbiturates, users will begin to experience **withdrawal symptoms such as anxiety, agitation, loss of appetite, nausea, vomiting, increased heart rate, excessive sweating, abdominal cramps, and tremulousness**. The symptoms tend to peak on the second or third day. The more intense the use, the more severe the symptoms. Withdrawal symptoms resulting from heavy tissue dependence are **very dangerous and can result in convulsions within 12 hours to one week from the last dose**.

OTHER SEDATIVE-HYPNOTICS

BUSPIRONE (BuSpar®)

Buspirone is a sedative-hypnotic medication that is not pharmacologically or chemically related to the other drugs in this category. It is most **used as an anxiolytic or anti-anxiety medication but is also used in combination with SSRI antidepressant medications to treat depression**. Exactly how buspirone works to reduce anxiety and augment the effects of SSRI drugs is unknown. Research has shown it to have a high affinity for serotonin receptors and a moderate affinity for dopamine D_2 receptors in the brain. Unlike the other sedative-hypnotics, buspirone does not appear to have any direct effects on the GABA neurotransmitter system, and it **lacks the ability to produce abuse, addiction, or withdrawal symptoms** (Lader, 1987). It is therefore more appropriate to use buspirone for anxiety treatment when there is a concern about patient risk of addiction or relapse. It will not suppress withdrawal seizures and should not be used to detoxify alcohol or sedative-hypnotic dependence unless another antiseizure medication is used with it. Buspirone and ramelteon (Rozerem®) are the only two medications in this class that have not been demonstrated to produce an addiction liability. Their

use is less than what would be expected given this benefit probably because **most people (and especially addicts) have come to expect a high or buzz from a sleeping pill or an anti-anxiety medication**. So although buspirone has been demonstrated to effectively reduce panic and anxiety, whereas ramelteon demonstrates an ability to induce sleep, many feel that the drugs are ineffective because they don't experience the typical downer buzz when they take them.

ESZOPICLONE (Lunesta®)

This drug is a **hypnotic agent prescribed for insomnia**. As with other insomnia treatments, it seems to affect GABA and the benzodiazepine receptor complex that augments the effects of GABA. For some people Lunesta® can cause a severe allergic reaction. When used longer than a few weeks at a high dose, it can cause dependence. There is an additive effect when it is taken with other sedatives or opioids. Though stated to be less severe than benzodiazepines and barbiturates, significant withdrawal symptoms can result if dependence has developed; symptoms include stomach and muscle cramps, vomiting, sweating, and shakiness. Relative to other sedative-hypnotics, eszopiclone has been found to be less abusable than diazepam but more so than oxazepam. It was found to be as toxic in overdose as other benzodiazepines (Griffiths & Johnson, 2005).

ETHCHLORVYNOL (Placidyl®) and CHLORAL HYDRATE (Noctec,® Somnos,® Aquachloral®)

Two of the older sedative-hypnotics in continuous use are Placidyl® (called "green weenies" on the street) and chloral hydrate. Both are volatile liquids at room temperature that have been enclosed in a suppository or gelatin capsule for ease of administration. **Ethchlorvynol is actually a chemical ether**, and ether was one of the first hypnotic drugs discovered. **Chloral hydrate has the same effects and liabilities as alcohol and is actually three molecules of ethanol that have been fused together.** It also has the potential for adverse reactions if taken with

Antabuse.® Both are controlled substances that are often ignored because they are abused less frequently than the newer sedative drugs. Noctec® was reported to be one of the 15 medications found in the autopsy of celebrity Anna Nicole Smith, who died from an accidental drug overdose in 2007. Ativan,® Klonopin,® methadone, Robaxin,® Soma,® Topamax,® Valium,® and Benadryl® were the other psychoactive drugs identified during the autopsy (Goodnough, 2007). **Ethchlorvynol and chloral hydrate are used to induce sleep, and both have a long history of toxic overdoses and patterns of addictive use.**

GHB (gamma hydroxybutyrate)

GHB is a strong, rapidly acting CNS depressant. The drug was initially available in health-food stores or by mail order and was described as a nutrient rather than a sedative. It is a metabolite of GABA and is found in all mammalian brains. Most brain scientists believe that GHB is also a neurotransmitter as its molecular structure is closely related to that of GABA and glutamic acid but a specific receptor site for GHB has yet to be discovered. GHB was used as a **sleep inducer** in the 1960s and 1970s. By the nineties this slightly salty-tasting white powder, which is taken orally, had also become popular among bodybuilders because it changed the ratio of muscle to fat and was **thought to increase the body's levels of human growth hormone (HGH). It also induces effects similar to alcohol (sedation and disinhibition), ecstasy (empathy and sensory enhancement), and even heroin intoxication (euphoria)**, so in recent years it has become popular as a club drug, along with LSD, ecstasy, ketamine, and Rohypnol.® Ecstasy and alcohol are the two drugs that are most often taken with GHB. Both enhance the euphoric feelings experienced from GHB while their own effects are enhanced as well.

GHB has been called "liquid ecstasy," "scoop," "Georgia home boy," "easy lay," and "grievous bodily harm" (NIDA, 2006). Because of the wide availability of GHB analogs and precursors, along with the large number of manufacturing kits and recipes available on the Internet, adulteration or misrepresentation does not seem to be a problem with knowledgeable buyers. When it's bought on the street, however, dosage and purity are major concerns. By the 1990s the FDA decided that there were enough health risks to take GHB off the market. Congress added it to the Controlled Substances Act of 1970 in the year 2000. Street chemists have since rushed in to fill the void.

"I remember like for the first hour I just felt really woozy and then all of a sudden I like—it started to build and about an hour later like I couldn't move. Like I felt like my head was gonna detach from my body and I just couldn't move my arms and I just stayed that way for about four hours I think it was, maybe longer."

19-year-old club drug user

Despite its abuse GHB was researched and found to be safe and effective for the treatment of narcolepsy (involuntary sleep episode) and cataplexy (transient sudden loss of voluntary muscle control), leading to its being approved as the prescription drug Xyrem® in 2002.

GHB is usually dissolved in water or alcohol by the capful or teaspoonful or as a premixed solution. It is most often dissolved into commercial mineral waters so it can be brought into rave events or music festivals without being detected. A dose costs $5 to $10, and **the effects last three to six hours**.

◊ With 1 gram (gm) there is a feeling of relaxation.

◊ With 2 gm the relaxation increases while heart rate and respiration fall. Balance, coordination, and circulation are disrupted (2.5 gm or a level teaspoon is the preferred amount).

◊ With 2 to 4 gm, coordination and speech become impaired.

◊ Despite a very steep dose-response curve, the rapid development of tolerance has enabled some individuals to take as much as 30 gm in one day. High doses result in a longer duration of action.

Depending on the susceptibility of the user, side effects include nausea, vomiting (which are signs of an impending overdose), depression, delusions, hallucinations, seizures, amnesia, respiratory depression, and coma with a greatly reduced heart rate (Nicholson & Balster, 2001; Office of National Drug Control Policy, 2007). GHB is thought to lower dopamine levels in the brain by inhibiting its release. This can induce a deep sleep in a GHB user, who will then awaken very aroused and active. This may be due to the drug's capacity to cause an accumulation and then a sudden release of the dopamine.

In 2005 the number of ED visits for GHB had fallen sharply from just a few years earlier down to 1,861 compared with 10,752 for ecstasy (DAWN, 2007). Most of the problems seem to occur with naive users who become anxious that the first dose isn't working and keep using until they feel something, but by then they've taken too much.

Because GHB causes a mild euphoria and lowers inhibitions, **it has been used by sexual predators to lower the defenses of women**. These effects, along with its ability to induce coma and amnesia, caused its name to be added to the list of date-rape drugs (ElSohly & Salamone, 1999). GHB's use spurred the passage of the Drug-Induced Rape Prevention and Punishment Act of 1996, which increased federal penalties for use of any controlled substance to aid in sexual assault or violence.

Case histories of GHB abuse indicate that it can be addicting because of the significant degree of tolerance that occurs with its use. Cessation of daily prolonged use results in severe and difficult-to-treat sedative-like drug withdrawal symptoms that may even include dangerous seizures (Sivilotti, Burns, Aaron, et al., 2001).

GBL (gamma butyrolactone or 2[3H]-furanone dihydro) & BD (1,3 butanediol)

Increased legal scrutiny of GHB has resulted in the abuse of GBL and BD. **GBL and BD are prodrugs (they are metabolized to GHB in the body).** They are also ingredients in liquid paint strippers and are available through chemical suppliers in the United States and on the Internet. GBL and BD were quickly formulated into mint-flavored elixirs for the rave club scene. These elixirs are sold under the trade names Blue Nitro,® Revivarant,® Gamma G,® Remforce,® and Insom-X.® Some abusers have even drunk diluted paint stripper or "huffed" the hardware store products containing GBL. Many states are now urging the FDA to take regulatory action against GBL.

METHAQUALONE (Quaalude,® Mandrax®)

Methaqualone was developed in India in 1955 as a safe **barbiturate substitute** and originally marketed in Japan and Europe. In 1965 it was the most commonly prescribed sedative-hypnotic in England. The reasons for the popularity of methaqualone were its overall sedative effect and the prolonged period of mild euphoria caused by the suppression of inhibitions. **This disinhibitory effect is similar to that caused by alcohol and can last 60 to 90 minutes; the sedating effects last six to 10 hours.** Larger doses can bring about depression, irrational behavior, poor reflexes, slurred speech, and reduced respiration and heart rate. Tolerance to methaqualone develops quickly.

Although Quaalude® was widely used at one time as a sleep aid, the heavy nonmedical abuse led to the withdrawal of this product from the legitimate U.S. market. **In 1984 it was made a Schedule I drug.** This change led to a tremendous increase in the illicit production of Quaalude® (known as bootleg "ludes" that look identical to the original prescription drug). The active chemical in Quaalude,® methaqualone, is manufactured by street chemists or smuggled in from Europe, South Africa, or Colombia. In the 1970s and 1980s in Europe and other countries, Mandrax® (methaqualone and an antihistamine) had great popularity. The antihistamine exaggerated the effect of the methaqualone.

Today South Africa still has many Mandrax® abusers. There is no guarantee that the street versions of Quaalude® contain actual methaqualone; even when they do, the dosage may vary dramatically, making an overdose more likely.

PREGABALIN (Lyrica®)

Pregabalin is FDA approved to treat nerve pain from shingles or diabetes as well as to help treat seizures. It seems to work by modulating calcium ion influx in hyperexcited neurons, which results in decreased release of neurotransmitters. In 2007 **the FDA was considering approving Lyrica® for the treatment of anxiety and sleep or mood disorders** because it is already actively used for these conditions and is approved for such uses in Europe. Like other sedatives, its use can cause dizziness, drowsiness, lethargy, and memory problems that are exaggerated when taken with narcotics, sedatives, or alcohol. Euphoria has also been associated with its use, and it does have a **mild potential for abuse and dependence**. Pregabalin is classed as a Schedule V drug.

RAMELTEON (Rozerem®)

This medication is a **new approach in the treatment of insomnia**. Ramelteon's mechanism of action is its ability to directly activate the brain's melatonin receptors. Melatonin is the natural neurotransmitter that helps maintain the body's circadian rhythm responsible for normal sleep/wake cycles. It is usually recommended for short-term treatment of sleep problems—one or two days up to one or two weeks. Adverse effects include dizziness and excessive sleepiness, but abuse and dependence have not been associated with its use, and it is not a controlled substance. **Ramelteon and alcohol have additive toxic effects** and should not be used in combination with each other (Johnson, Suess & Griffiths, 2006).

ZALEPLON (Sonata®), ZOPICLONE (Imovane®) & ZOLPIDEM (Ambien®)

Zaleplon (Sonata®), zopiclone (Imovane®), and zolpidem (Ambien®) are **known as the Z-hypnotics because they have similar actions and their chemical names all began with the letter Z**. Eszopiclone (Lunesta®) is also considered a Z-hypnotic because it has the same mechanism of action and effects as the others even though its chemical name actually starts with *E*.

The Z-hypnotics are short-acting, with one- to four-hour half-lives and are thought to have a lower risk of addiction than most benzodiazepines though **they all work by activating the benzodiazepine receptor to enhance the effect of GABA in the brain**. Excess use can cause nausea, diarrhea, headaches, dizziness, and drowsiness the following day. As with benzodiazepines **the Z-hypnotics can cause memory, performance, and learning impairment**. In 2007 the FDA began requiring Ambien,® Rozerem,® Lunesta,® and 10 other sleep aids to carry warnings about the small risk of "complex behavior impairments such as driving, preparing food, or even gambling in almost a hypnotic or sleepwalking state." The other drugs include Calmane,® Doral,® Halcion,® Placidyl,® ProSom,® Restoril,® Seconal,® Sonata,® and Carbrital® (Rubin, 2007).

The Z-hypnotics have a high therapeutic index and **rarely cause overdose deaths except when taken in combination with other depressants**. The liability for abuse and addiction of Z-hypnotics is found to be less than that of diazepam (Valium®) and about the same as flurazepam (Dalmane®) or Oxazepam (Serax®) (Griffiths & Johnson, 2005). Tissue dependence and withdrawal have also been reported with the use of Z-hypnotics. Withdrawal effects peak within 24 to 36 hours and include tremors, cramps, insomnia, anxiety, confusion, rigidity of limbs, and possible hallucinations and seizures.

OTHER PROBLEMS WITH DEPRESSANTS

DRUG INTERACTIONS

Pharmacologic research has found that **more than 150 prescription and OTC medications interact negatively with alcohol**. This doesn't include those that interact negatively with each other. Drug interactions are a large problem because one in six Americans takes three or more prescription drugs per day. This is a particular problem with those over 65: they make up just 12% of the U.S. population but consume more than 25% of all prescription medications, often seven or more per day. They are also more sensitive to the effects of drugs because of changes in the efficiency of organs, particularly the liver.

SYNERGISM

If more than one depressant drug is used, **the polydrug combination can cause a much greater reaction than simply the sum of the effects**. One of the reasons for this synergistic effect (unintentional drug interaction) lies in the chemistry of the liver.

For example, if alcohol and alprazolam (Xanax®) are taken together, **the liver becomes busy metabolizing the alcohol**, so the sedative-hypnotic passes through the body at full strength. Alcohol also dissolves the alprazolam more readily than stomach fluid, allowing more alprazolam to be absorbed rapidly into the body. Alprazolam exerts its depressant effects on different parts of the brain from those affected by alcohol. Thus when combined alcohol and alprazolam cause more problems than if they were taken at different times. **Exaggerated respiratory depression is the biggest danger** with the use of alcohol and another depressant. This combination also causes more blackouts (a period of amnesia or loss of memory while intoxicated).

"I took my little medication with me one night, drinking in the bar. I played some pool and that's all I remember. This was on a Sunday. When I woke up, it was Wednesday."
Recovering polydrug abuser

According to the Centers for Disease Control, synergistic effects cause about **19,000 deaths per year**. In addition almost **275,000 people are treated in EDs** because of adverse reactions to nonmedical use of multiple drugs.

CROSS-TOLERANCE & CROSS-DEPENDENCE

Cross-tolerance is the development of tolerance to other drugs by the continued exposure and development of tolerance to the initial drug. For example, a barbiturate addict who develops a tolerance to a high dose of Seconal® is also tolerant to and can withstand high doses of Nembutal,® phenobarbital, anesthetics, opiates, alcohol, Valium,® and even blood-thinning medication. One explanation of cross-tolerance is that many drugs are metabolized, or broken down, by the same body enzymes. As one continues to take barbiturates, the liver creates more enzymes to rid the body of these toxins. The unusually high levels of these enzymes result in tolerance to all barbiturates as well as to other drugs also metabolized by those same enzymes.

Cross-dependence occurs when an individual becomes addicted or tissue dependent on one drug, resulting in biochemical and cellular changes that support an addiction to other drugs. A heroin addict, for example, has altered body chemistry, so he or she is also likely to be addicted to another opiate/opioid, e.g., hydrocodone, oxycodone, meperidine, morphine, codeine, methadone, or propoxyphene (Darvon®). As in this example, cross-dependence most often occurs with different drugs in the same chemical family. A diazepam (Valium®) addict is also tissue dependent on alprazolam, lorazepam, and other benzodiazepines. A heavy butalbital user is also tissue dependent on phenobarbital. Cross-dependence has also been documented to some extent with opiates/opioids and alcohol, cocaine and alcohol, and benzodiazepines and alcohol.

MISUSE & DIVERSION

"'In the United States, the abuse of painkillers, stimulants, tranquilizers, and other prescription medications has gone beyond "practically all illicit drugs," with the exception of Cannabis,' the U.N.-affiliated International Narcotics Control Board said in its annual report. Outside the United States, prescription drug abuse has already outstripped traditional illegal drugs such as heroin and cocaine. The number of Americans who have abused prescription drugs nearly doubled from 7.8 million in 1992 to 15.1 million in 2003 and even more today [6.4 million are addicted to prescription drugs]."
San Francisco Chronicle, March 1, 2007

As a class, sedative-hypnotic drugs and prescription opioids are frequently misused and **diverted to abuse from legitimate prescribing practices**. This abuse of legitimate prescriptions has seen an especially large increase among teenagers since 2001 even though their abuse of illicit drugs has gone down 23%. The medicine cabinet of most homes is a likely target for young and old prescription drug users and abusers.

"When I got the word there would be a BYO pharm party, I'd check our medicine chest. Mom always had a supply of hydrocodone for her many so-called aches. She doesn't get as much Xanax® or whatever the generic name is [alprazolam] as she used to, but I can get up to five bucks for a 0.25 mg one of those."
16-year-old prescription drug abuser

Another main supplier of prescription drugs for drug abusers is physicians. One pattern of illicit use results when a patient is treated for multiple medical complaints by many **different physicians and each prescribes a different sedative or opioid** that is then dispensed by different pharmacies. For example, Dalmane® will be prescribed for sleep, Serax® for anxiety, Xanax® for depression, Valium® for muscle spasms, and Librax® for stomach problems. Each prescription, in and of itself, may be at a nonaddictive level, but all of the prescriptions together result in a large enough dose of benzodiazepines to create tissue dependence. Unfortunately, unscrupulous, addicted, or naive medical professionals also participate in unethical, criminal, or inappropriate prescribing practices.

"This doctor and I parted paths when I found another doctor who was in the business of prescribing whatever medication you wanted. You know, you pay him, and he will take care of your pharmaceutical needs, so to speak."
38-year-old recovering sedative-hypnotic abuser

Because of their widespread use for a variety of medical indications, sedative-hypnotics and opioids are also subject to **forged prescriptions or prescription manipulations** (photocopying or changing dosage, amount, or number of refills) that provide an abuser with enough drugs for diversion to illicit street sales or to feed an addiction. To combat this problem, many states have mandated triplicate prescriptions for benzodiazepines and added other stringent mechanisms to prevent diversion, much as they have done for opioids. Many physicians and psychiatrists see triplicate prescriptions for benzodiazepines as an intrusion into their practice of medicine as well as an unnecessary obstacle for those with legitimate medical needs.

Another form of diversion is **smuggling drugs and drug precursors that are legal outside the United States**. Rohypnol,® which is banned in the United States, is smuggled in from Europe or Mexico. Ephedrine is smuggled through Canada or Mexico to make methamphetamine.

Misuse and diversion of drugs cause toxic effects, adverse drug reactions, and various drug problems. These troubles also occur with legally prescribed medications and nonprescription drugs as well. A study led by Dr. Bruce Pomeranz at the University of Toronto estimated that **each year between 76,000 and 137,000 Americans die and an additional 1.6 million to 2.6 million are injured due to bad reactions from legally prescribed drugs and OTC medications**. The figures do not include drug abuse or prescribing errors. While some disagree with the magnitude of the numbers, they do agree that the problem is very real and widespread.

Some of the actions that could help control prescription drug abuse as described by Drs. Peter Lurie and Philip R. Lee at the University of California Medical Center in San Francisco are:

◇ better education of physicians regarding pharmacotherapy and the effects of drugs;

◇ better education and research regarding pain control and the use of opioids;

◇ more-accurate information regarding drugs rather than just inserts or overdone *Physicians' Desk Reference* information;

◇ limited interaction between drug company detailers (salesman) and medical personnel;

◇ increased role for the pharmacist in identifying drug interactions and inappropriate prescribing;

◇ more-careful prescribing in hospitals and nursing homes;

◇ greater patient participation in deciding which drug to use;

◇ more attention to patient feedback to judge the effectiveness of drugs;

◇ more testing in geriatric populations to make sure prescribed drugs are not debilitating;

◇ restricting to specialists the prescribing of certain powerful drugs;

◇ limited prescribing of psychoactive drugs (e.g., duplicate and triplicate prescriptions for scheduled drugs);

◇ less drug advertising in medical journals; and

◇ more peer scrutiny of prescribing practices of fellow physicians
(Lurie & Lee, 1991).

PRESCRIPTION DRUGS & THE PHARMACEUTICAL INDUSTRY

In 2006 Americans spent about **$274.9 billion, or 9% of their total medical expenditures of approximately $2.1 trillion, on prescription medications.** This was almost half of the world's total expenditures for prescription drugs (IMS Health, 2007). It was also twice as much as was spent just four years before in the United States. Healthcare expenditures are supposed to double in 10 years to $4 trillion, so one must assume that prescription drug expenditures will top $0.5 trillion by then (Centers for Medicare and Medicaid Services, 2007). **Legal psychoactive drugs, including psychiatric medications, account for approximately 10% to 12% of prescriptions written in the United States.** The other prescriptions include cardiovascular medications, antibiotics, menopause medications, hormones, birth-control pills, ulcer medications, diabetes-control medications, antihistamines, thyroid drugs, and bronchodilators.

Americans also spent more than $25 billion on OTC drugs such as aspirin, laxatives, and vitamins.

There has also been a **significant increase in the use of prescription medications for children**. Antidepressants and drugs for attention-deficit/hyperactivity disorder (ADHD), along with increasingly more therapeutic medication, are mostly responsible for this change.

From the industry perspective, the high cost of prescription drugs is justified. The **cost of developing a new medication is enormous**, often in the hundreds of millions of dollars, even billions; $55.2 billion was spend on research and development in 2006, according to the industry's association (PhRMA, 2007). **Drug patents are good for only 17 years (including testing time)**, so the companies have to recoup their research-and-development and start-up production costs in a short period of time. The proliferation of generic versions of the drug as soon as the patent runs out also makes drug companies want to protect their investments. The industry has tried a number of tactics over the years to preserve its profits. Generics were kept off the market for many years because the FDA didn't have a streamlined approval process for these drugs (lobbyists fought these changes, but the approval process became much simpler for generics). The industry tried to extend the life of the patent past 17 years. That effort failed. What the industry does do is manufacture its own generics, use legal challenges to delay the introduction of generics, and make slight changes in formulation or simply bring out a time-release version of popular drugs to keep people buying the name brands.

In addition, the industry is trying to limit to purchase of drugs online whether it's a local dealer or a foreign source, asserting that there is no guarantee of quality or even if it is the same drug. Consumers claim that they are being denied access to cheaper versions of the drugs they need.

Greg Critser in his book *Generation Rx* worries that **we are becoming a prescription drug-dependant society**. He thinks the increase in prescription drug use comes from more-sophisticated marketing by the drug companies. Advertising spending aimed at consumers for pharmaceuticals has gone from $2 million in 1980 to $1.85 billion in 1999, to $4.35 billion in 2004, while overall promotional spending was four to five times that amount (Critser, 2005). Patients ask their doctor why they can't have that pill that's advertised on TV. According to the National Institute for Health Care Management's Research and Educational Foundation, sales of the 50 most heavily advertised drugs in 2000 were responsible for almost one-half (47.8%) of the $20.8 billion increase in retail spending on prescription drugs over the past year.

In contrast to the $274.9 billion spent on prescription drugs, about:

◇ $70 billion to $75 billion was spent on illegal drugs,

◇ $70 billion to $80 billion was spent on tobacco, and

◇ $150 billion to $160 billion was spent on alcohol.

These figures do not include the financial consequences of using psychoactive drugs. If our healthcare costs are more than $2 trillion, the medical consequences of that abuse could easily approach $1 trillion. Focusing on lifestyle changes and effective prevention programs is a much more cost-effective method for reducing overall medical costs. The problem is that **when free enterprise is at odds with public policy, inaction and delaying tactics are often the result, usually to the detriment of the general public**.

CHAPTER SUMMARY

GENERAL CLASSIFICATION

1. In the 2000s there has been an increase in prescription drug abuse, particularly opioids such as hydrocodone (Vicodin,® Lortab,® and Norco®) and oxycodone (OxyContin®).

2. Downers are central nervous system (CNS) depressants.

Major Depressants

3. The three major downers are opiates/opioids (treat pain), sedative-hypnotics (treat anxiety and insomnia), and alcohol.

Minor Depressants

4. The four minor downers are skeletal muscle relaxants, antihistamines, over-the-counter (OTC) depressants, and look-alike depressants. The abuse of carisoprodol (Soma®) has been increasing in recent years.

OPIATES/OPIOIDS

Classification

5. Opium comes from the milky fluid of the opium poppy and contains morphine and codeine.

6. Opiates (from the opium poppy and semisynthetic versions) and opioids (fully synthetic versions of opiates) were developed for the treatment of acute pain, to control diarrhea, and to suppress coughs.

7. Opiates include opium, morphine, codeine, heroin, hydrocodone (Vicodin® and Lortab®), hydromorphone (Dilaudid®), and oxycodone (OxyContin®). Opioids include methadone, propoxyphene (Darvon®), meperidine (Demerol®), and fentanyl. Opioid antagonists used in treatment include naloxone (Narcan®) and naltrexone (Revia®).

History of Use

8. The change in routes of administration (from ingesting, to smoking, to injecting, to snorting), along with refinement and synthesis of stronger opioids (from opium, to morphine, to codeine, to heroin, to fentanyl), new compounds, and time-release versions of the opioids have increased the effectiveness as well as the addiction liability of opioids.

9. The Opium Wars were fought so that England and other countries could continue to sell opium in China.

10. Opium and morphine were very popular in hundreds of patent medicines, in prescription medicines, and as recreational drugs. Women addicts outnumbered male addicts in the late 1800s and early 1900s.

11. More than half of all heroin addicts entering treatment began their heroin use by snorting the drug.

12. Early in the twentieth century, opioid addiction was considered a medical problem and treated by a physician, but drug laws and regu-

lations in the twentieth century limited the supplies and created a criminal subculture that used, grew, processed, and distributed heroin and other drugs worldwide.

13. Diverted prescription opiates are used by 4.6 million Americans for nonmedical purposes each month.

14. There are 5 million to 10 million regular heroin users worldwide. The United States only uses 3% of the world's supply.

15. Afghanistan grows more than 90% of the world's supply of opium (6,100 metric tons). The major opium-growing areas are the Golden Crescent (Afghanistan and Pakistan) and the Golden Triangle (Myanmar [Burma], Thailand, and Laos). The increased drug trade helps support the Taliban in Afghanistan.

16. Most heroin sold in the United States comes from Mexico (black tar heroin and brown heroin), from Colombia (black tar heroin and white heroin), and more recently from Afghanistan.

Effects of Opioids

17. Medically, opioids are used to deaden pain, control coughing, and stop diarrhea; nonmedically, it's used to deaden emotional pain, get a rush, induce euphoria, and prevent withdrawal symptoms.

18. Pain is normally a warning signal of physical or mental damage. The body's own natural painkillers—endorphins and enkephalins—are mimicked by opioids. These analgesic drugs block the transmission of pain messages to the brain by substance P.

19. Opioids can also cause pleasure and euphoria by stimulating the dopaminergic reward/reinforcement pathway.

20. The satiation, or on/off switch, can be disrupted by opioids.

21. The alleviation of pain activates the same area of the brain that causes euphoria.

22. The relief of withdrawal symptoms is a powerful incentive for continued use of the drug.

23. These drugs control activation of the cough center and stop diarrhea by inhibiting gastric secretions and intestinal muscles.

Side Effects of Opioids

24. Opioids mask pain signals, lower blood pressure, depress heart rate, slow respiration, depress muscular coordination, increase nausea, induce pinpoint pupils, cause itching, delay a woman's period, and create mental confusion.

25. A physical tolerance to opioids develops rapidly, increasing the rate at which the body tissues become physically dependent on the drug.

26. Acute withdrawal from opioids is like an extreme case of the flu (e.g., stomach cramps, diarrhea, chills, muscle aches, and twitching), but it is rarely life threatening.

27. Protracted withdrawal can last for months, even years, causing relapses.

28. Short-acting opioids like heroin result in more-acute withdrawal symptoms.

Additional Problems with Heroin & Other Opioids

29. Opioids cross the placental barrier and affect fetuses. Babies can be born addicted and can die from opioid withdrawal. Prenatal care is crucial in avoiding drug-affected babies.

30. Overdose kills 4,000 to 5,000 heroin users each year mostly through extreme respiratory depression. It can be counteracted by the opioid antagonist naloxone (Narcan®).

31. Contaminated needles transmit hepatitis C and HIV. A majority of drug users carry one or both of these viruses. Injecting heroin also causes abscesses (skin infections), endocarditis, cotton fever, and flesh-eating disease.

32. About 40 million people worldwide are HIV/AIDS positive; 25 million have died from it.

33. Adulteration of drugs, the high cost of an addiction (up to $200 a day), increased crime, and the dangers of polydrug use (e.g., speedballs) are part of the complications of heroin addiction.

34. The progression from experimentation to physical dependence can occur in a month, in a year, or longer, depending on the user's susceptibility, amount used, and frequency of use. Pain relief can create the desire to continue use.

35. Treatment is a physiological and psychological process. The addict has to be detoxified from the drug.

36. Most returning Vietnam veterans who had developed physical dependence on heroin while in Vietnam did not continue use after returning home, showing that addiction results from many factors.

Morphine & Other Opioids

37. Morphine, the standard drug used for severe pain relief, can be taken by mouth, by injection, or by suppository.

38. The therapeutic use of opioids for pain is subject to much controversy. Some doctors underprescribe due to fear of patient addiction and other reasons.

39. Codeine, which is refined directly from opium, used to be the most widely used and abused prescription opioid for moderate pain and cough control.

40. Hydrocodone (Vicodin®), a stronger synthetic version of codeine, has become the most widely used and abused prescription opioid. More than 120 million prescriptions were written for hydrocodone in 2006.

41. Methadone is a long-lasting opioid that heroin addicts use (methadone maintenance) to avoid withdrawal and the craving to return to heroin abuse.

42. A number of synthetic and semi-synthetic opioids—such as hydromorphone (Dilaudid®), oxycodone (Percodan® and OxyContin®), meperidine (Demerol®), propoxyphene (Darvon®), and fentanyl—have made their way to the illicit market. In recent years OxyContin,® a time-release version of oxycodone,

has been widely abused, most often by crushing the pills and injecting or snorting the drug.

43. Highly potent synthetic heroin designer drugs (fentanyl and Demerol® derivatives) have appeared on the street, increasing the danger of overdose and other toxic problems.

44. Other drugs used to treat opioid addiction are LAAM® (a long-acting opioid), naloxone and naltrexone (opioid antagonists), buprenorphine (Subutex® and Suboxone®), propoxyphene (Darvon®), and clonidine. Buprenorphine may be prescribed through a physician's office, not just through a drug treatment facility.

SEDATIVE-HYPNOTICS

Classification

45. Sixty million prescriptions were written for sedative-hypnotics, although psychiatric medications (e.g., antidepressants) have taken over a large share of this prescription drug market.

46. The two main groups of sedative-hypnotics are benzodiazepines and barbiturates, although recently new formulations such as Lunesta,® Rozerem,® and Ambien® have become popular.

47. The effects of sedative-hypnotics are similar to those of alcohol.

48. Sedatives (minor tranquilizers or anxiolytics) are calming drugs used mostly to treat anxiety. Hypnotics are used mainly to induce sleep.

History

49. Early civilizations used opioids as calming drugs, but over the past 150 years sedative-hypnotics have included bromides, chloral hydrate, paraldehyde, barbiturates, carbamates (Miltown®), benzodiazepines, and a new group of sleep aids and minor tranquilizers.

Use, Misuse, Abuse & Addiction

50. Societal acceptance of sedative-hypnotics has varied from decade to decade from avid acceptance to fear of overuse. They are usually prescribed to control anxiety, induce sleep, relax muscles, and act as mild tranquilizers, but many physicians fear their potential for overdose, physical dependence, and addiction.

51. Misuse can occur from overuse, using with other drugs, and borrowing or stealing drugs.

52. Emergency department visits are high for sedative-hypnotics especially when used with alcohol and other drugs. The reasons vary from forgetting how much has been taken, to ignorance of the additive effects of polydrug use, to suicide attempts.

Benzodiazepines

53. Benzodiazepines, the most widely used sedative-hypnotic, include alprazolam (Xanax®), lorazepam (Ativan®), clonazepam (Klonopin®), diazepam (Valium®), and temazepam (Restoril®).

54. Benzodiazepines are usually used medically to manage anxiety, treat sleep problems, control muscular spasms and seizures, and subdue the symptoms of alcohol withdrawal. They are used nonmedically to relieve agitation, induce a mild euphoria, and lower inhibitions. They are often used in conjunction with other drugs.

55. Benzodiazepines work on the inhibitory transmitter GABA as well as on serotonin and dopamine.

56. Benzodiazepines can stay in the body for days and even weeks. When tolerance and tissue dependence have developed, withdrawal symptoms can occur for several days and even weeks after ceasing use.

57. It can take several months to taper off of benzodiazepines.

58. More than 170,000 ED visits involved benzodiazepines even though it has a high margin of safety (therapeutic index).

59. Although it is most often abused as a recreational drug, Rohypnol® and GHB are also used as date-rape drugs because they can cause amnesia.

Barbiturates

60. More than 2,000 barbiturates have been developed over the past 100 years, but only 50 have been marketed.

61. Barbiturates include butalbital, Nembutal® ("yellows"), Tuinal® ("rainbows"), and phenobarbital.

62. These drugs are mostly used to control seizures, induce sleep, and lessen anxiety, but benzodiazepines and other psychiatric drugs have replaced their use over the past 40 years.

63. Tolerance, tissue dependence, and withdrawal liability develop swiftly with barbiturates.

Other Sedative-Hypnotics

64. GHB, a strong depressant, has become popular in the party scene. Effects include sedation and euphoria. GBL is also used in the same way as GHB. These drugs, like Rohypnol,® have been used by sexual predators.

65. Other nonbarbiturate sedative-hypnotics include street methaqualone (Quaalude®), meprobamate (Equanil®), buspirone (BuSpar®), chloral hydrate (Noctec®), pregabalin (Lyrica®), ramelteon (Rozerem®), etchlorvynol (Placidyl®) and the so-called Z-hypnotics: Zaleplon (Sonata®), zopiclone (Imovane®), zolpidem (Ambien®), and eszopiclone (Lunesta®). Most of the newer sleep aids, with a few exceptions, have dependence liability.

OTHER PROBLEMS WITH DEPRESSANTS

Drug Interactions

66. Alcohol and sedative-hypnotics used together can be especially life threatening. They cause a synergistic (exaggerated) effect that can suppress respiration and heart functions.

67. Cross-tolerance and cross-dependence occur within the sedative-hypnotic class of drugs, within the opioid class of drugs, and to a lesser extent among sedative-hypnotics, opioids, and alcohol.

Misuse & Diversion

68. Hundreds of millions of doses and prescriptions of sedative-hypnotics and prescription opioids are diverted to illicit channels each year through smuggling, conning of physicians, forgery, and theft.

Prescription Drugs & the Pharmaceutical Industry

69. Americans spent more than $274.9 billion on prescription drugs. Of the 3.5 billion prescriptions written each year, more than 350 million were for psychoactive drugs, particularly opioids, sedative-hypnotics, skeletal muscle relaxants, and psychiatric drugs (antidepressants and antipsychotics).

70. The cost of developing new drugs is enormous, and the expense is passed on to the consumer. Increased advertising has increased our use and dependence on prescription drugs.

REFERENCES

Aldrich, M. R. (1994). Historical notes on women addicts. *Journal of Psychoactive Drugs, 26*(1), 61-64.

American Pain Society. (2006). *The Use of Opioids for the Treatment of Chronic Pain.* http://www.ampainsoc.org/advocacy/opioids.htm (accessed April 13, 2007).

American Psychiatric Association. (1990). *Task Force Report on Benzodiazepines.* Washington, DC: American Psychiatric Association Press.

Armstrong, D. & Armstrong, E.M. (1991). *The Great American Medicine Show.* New York: Prentice Hall.

Bailey, D. N. & Briggs, J. R. (2002). Carisoprodol: An unrecognized drug of abuse. *American Journal of Clinical Pathology, 117*(3), 396-400.

Bell, J., Mattick, R., Hay, A., Chan, J. & Hall, W. (1997). Methadone maintenance and drug-related crime. *Journal of Substance Abuse, 9,* 15-25.

Berenson, A. (November 14, 2006). Big drug makers see sales decline with their image. *New York Times,* p. C1.

Bhamb, B., Brown, D., Hariharan, J., Anderson, J., Balousek, S. & Fleming, M. F. (2006). Survey of select practice behaviors by primary care physicians on the use of opioids for chronic pain. *Current Medical Research and Opinion. 22*(9), 1859-65.

Booth, M. (1999). *Opium: A History.* New York: St. Martin's Griffin.

Borg, L. & Kreek, M. J. (2003). The pharmacology of opioids. In A. W. Graham, T. K. Schultz, M. F. Mayo-Smith, R. K. Ries & B. B. Wilford, eds. *Principles of Addiction Medicine* (3rd ed., pp. 141-53). Chevy Chase, MD: American Society of Addiction Medicine, Inc.

Boucart, M., Waucquier, N., Michael, G. A. & Libersa, C. (2007). Diazepam impairs temporal dynamics of visual attention. *Experimental and Clinical Psychopharmacology, 15*(1), 115-22.

Breslin, K. T. & Malone, S. (2006). Maintaining the viability and safety of the methadone maintenance treatment program. *Journal of Psychoactive Drugs, 38*(2), 157-60.

Brown, P. D. & Ebright, J. R. (2002). Skin and soft tissue infections in injection drug users. *Current Infectious Disease Reports, 4*(5), 415-19.

Burattini, C., Burbassi, S., Aicardi, G. & Cervo, L. (2007). Effects of naltrexone on cocaine- and sucrose-seeking behavior in response to associated stimuli in rats. *International Journal of Neuropsychopharmacology.* Prepublication.

Busto, U., Sellers, E. M., Naranjo, C. A., Cappell, H., Sanchez-Craig, M. & Sykora, K. (1986). Withdrawal reaction after long-term therapeutic use of benzodiazepines. *New England Journal of Medicine, 315*(14), 854-59.

California Society of Addiction Medicine. (1997, 2004). *CSAM Newsletter, 24*(2), *29*(2).

Camilleri, A., Carise, D. & McLellan, A. T. (2006). *Are Prescription Opiate Users Different from Heroin Users?* http://www.tresearch.org/resources/presentations/CamilleriCPDD.ppt#1 (accessed April 13, 2007).

Carlezon, W. A. Jr., Boundy, V. A., Haile, C. N., Lane, S. B., Kalb, R. G., Neve, R. L., et al. (1997). Sensitization to morphine induced by viral-mediated gene transfer. *Science, 277*(5327), 812-14.

Casriel, C., Rockwell, R. & Stepherson, B. (1988). Heroin sniffers: Between two worlds. *Journal of Psychoactive Drugs, 20*(4), 437-40.

Centers for Disease Control. (2005). *HIV/AIDS Surveillance Report, 2005.* http://www.cdc.gov/hiv/topics/surveillance/resources/reports/2005report/pdf/2005SurveillanceReport.pdf (accessed April 14, 2007).

Centers for Medicare and Medicaid Services. (2007). *National Health Expenditure Projections 2006-2016.* http://www.cms.hhs.gov/NationalHealthExpendData/downloads/proj2006.pdf (accessed April 13, 2007).

Chronicle News Service. (September 3, 2006). Drug upsurge feared as Afghan poppy crop soars. *San Francisco Chronicle,* p. A3.

CNN.com. (April 29, 2006). Rehab, $30,000 to keep Limbaugh out of court. http://www.cnn.com/2006/LAW/04/28/limbaugh.booked (accessed April 7, 2007).

Coen, J. & Maxwell, T. (June 6, 2006). Illegal lab may have lethally tainted street drugs. *Wenatchee* (Washington) *World,* p. A7.

Colquhoun, R., Tan, D. Y. & Hull, S. (2005). A comparison of oral and implant naltrexone outcomes at 12 months. *Journal of Opioid Management, 1*(5), 249-56.

Costello, D. (October 31, 2005). Addicts learn to save others from death. *Los Angeles Times,* p. B1.

Critser, G. (2005). *Generation Rx.* Boston: Houghton Mifflin Company.

DASIS Report. (2004). *Characteristics of Primary Heroin Injection and Inhalation Admissions: 2002.* http://oas.samhsa.gov/2k4/heroin/heroin.htm (accessed April 13, 2007).

DeVane, C. L. (2001). Substance P: A new era, a new role. *Pharmacotherapy, 21*(9), 1061-69.

Dickinson, W. E., Mayo-Smith, M. F. & Eickelberg, S. J. (2003). Management of sedative-hypnotic intoxication and withdrawal. In A. W. Graham, T. K. Schultz, M. F. Mayo-Smith, R. K. Ries & B. B. Wilford, eds. *Principles of Addiction Medicine* (3rd ed., pp. 633-50). Chevy Chase, MD: American Society of Addiction Medicine, Inc.

Drug Abuse Warning Network [DAWN]. (2007). *Drug Abuse Warning Network 2005.* https://dawninfo.samhsa.gov/files/DAWN-ED-2005-Web.pdf (accessed April 14, 2007).

Drug Benefit Trends. (2001). Drugs take bigger slice of total health care expenditures. *Drug Benefit Trends, 13*(8).

Drug Benefit Trends. (2002). Advertised prescription drugs are the hot sellers. *Drug Benefit Trends, 14*(4).

Drug Enforcement Administration [DEA]. (2000). *A Pharmacist's Guide to Prescription Fraud.* http://www.deadiversion.usdoj.gov/pubs/brochures/pharmguide.htm (accessed April 13, 2007).

Drug Enforcement Administration. (2006). *National Drug Threat Assessment.* http://www.dea.gov/concern/18862/index (accessed March 15, 2007).

Drug Topics. (2007). *Drug topics: Pharmacy facts and figures.* http://www.drugtopics.com (accessed April 13, 2007).

Drug Upsurge. (September 3, 2006). Drug upsurge feared as Afghan poppy crop soars. *San Francisco Chronicle,* p. A3.

ElSohly, M. A. & Salamone, S. J. (1999). Prevalence of drugs used in cases of alleged sexual assault. *Journal of Analytical Toxicology, 23*(3), 141-46.

Finnegan, L. P. & Kandall, S. R. (2005). Maternal and neonatal effects of alcohol and drugs. In J. H. Lowinson, P. Ruiz, R. B. Millman & J. G. Langrod, eds. *Substance Abuse: A Comprehensive Textbook* (4th ed., pp. 805-39). Baltimore: Williams & Wilkins.

Forman, R. F., Woody, G. E., McLellan, T. & Lynch, K. G. (2006). The availability of Web sites offering to sell opioid medications without prescriptions. *American Journal of Psychiatry, 163*(7), 1233-38.

Gold, M. S., Jacobs, W. S., McGhee, D. L., McGraw, D. C., Grost-Pineda, K. & Croop, R. (April 25, 2002). Naltrexone augments the effects of nicotine replacement therapy in female smokers. Paper presented at the 33rd Annual Meeting of the American Society of Addiction Medicine, Inc., Atlanta, GA.

Goldstein, A. (2001). *Addiction: From Biology to Drug Policy.* New York: W. H. Freeman and Company.

Goodnough, A. (March 27, 2007). Anna Nicole Smith died from drug overdose. *San Francisco Chronicle,* p. A2.

Griffiths, R. R. & Johnson, M. W. (2005). Relative abuse liability of hypnotic drugs: A conceptual framework and algorithm for differentiating among compounds. *Journal of Clinical Psychiatry, 66*(suppl. 9), 31-41.

Gruber, S. A., Tzilos, G. K., Silveri, M. M., Pollack, M., Renshaw, P. F., Kaufman, M. J., et al. (2006). Methadone maintenance improves cognitive performance after two months of treatment. *Psychopharmacology, 14*(2), 157-64.

Hanes, W. T. & Sanello, F. (2002). *The Opium Wars.* Naperville, IL: Sourcebook Inc.

Hoffman, J. P. (1990). The historical shift in the perception of opiates: From medicine to social medicine. *Journal of Psychoactive Drugs, 22*(1), 53-62.

Hollister, L. E. (1983). The pre-benzodiazepine era. *Journal of Psychoactive Drugs, 15*(1-2), 9-13.

Hser, Y. I., Hoffman, V., Grella, C. E. & Anglin, M. D. (2001). A 33-year follow-up of narcotics addicts. *Archives of General Psychiatry, 58*(5), 503-508.

Hutcheson, D. M., Everitt, B. J., Robbins, T. W. & Dickinson, A. (2001). The role of withdrawal in heroin addiction: Enhances reward or promotes avoidance? *Nature Neuroscience, 4*(9), 943-47.

Hyman, S. E. (March 30, 1998). *An interview with Steven Hyman, M.D., Close to Home.* http://www.pbs.org/wnet/closetohome/science/html/hyman.html (accessed April 14, 2007).

IMS Health. (2007). *IMS Health Reports U.S. Prescription Sales Jump 8.3 Percent in 2006, to $274.9 Billion.* http://www.imshealth.com/ims/portal/front/articleC/0,2777,6599_3665_80415465,00.html (accessed April 13, 2007).

Insurgents. (November 12, 2006). Insurgent activity rising in Afghanistan. *New York Times,* p. A1.

Jenkins, A. J. & Cone, E. J. (1998). Pharmacokinetics: Drug absorption, distribution, and elimination. In S. B. Karch, ed. *Drug Abuse Handbook* (pp. 181-84). Boca Raton, FL: CRC Press.

Johnson, M. W., Suess, P. E. & Griffiths, R. R. (2006). Ramelteon: A novel hypnotic lacking abuse liability and sedative adverse effects. *Archives of General Psychiatry, 63*(10), 1149-57.

Juergens, S. M. & Cowley, D. R. (2003). The pharmacology of benzodiazepines and sedative-hypnotics. In A. W. Graham, T. K. Schultz, M. F. Mayo-Smith, R. K. Ries & B. B. Wilford, eds. *Principles of Addiction Medicine* (3rd ed., pp. 119-38). Chevy Chase, MD: American Society of Addiction Medicine, Inc.

Jung, B. & Reidenberg, M. M. (2006). The risk of action by the Drug Enforcement Administration against physicians prescribing opioids for pain. *Pain Medicine, 7*(4), 353-57.

Kandall, S. R. (1993). *Improving Treatment for Drug Exposed Infants.* U.S. Department of Health and Human Services Administration: *DHHS Publication no. (SMA) 93-2011.*

Karch, S. B. (1996). *The Pathology of Drug Abuse.* Boca Raton, FL: CRC Press.

Knapp, C. M., Ciraulo, D. A. & Jaffe, J. H. (2005). Opiates: Clinical aspects. In J. H. Lowinson, P. Ruiz, R. B. Millman & J. G. Langrod, eds. *Substance Abuse: A Comprehensive Textbook* (4th ed., pp. 180-94). Baltimore: Williams & Wilkins.

Lader, M. (1987). M. Assessing the potential for buspirone dependence or abuse and effects of its withdrawal. *American Journal of Medicine, 82*(5A), 20-26.

Latimer, D. & Goldberg, J. (1981). *Flowers in the Blood: The Story of Opium.* New York: Franklin Watts.

Latowsky, M. (2006). Methadone death, dosage and torsade de pointes: Risk-benefit policy implications. *Journal of Psychoactive Drugs, 38*(4), 513-19.

Leinwand, D. (June 13, 2006). Prescription drugs find place in teen culture. *USA Today,* p. A1.

Longshore, D., Annon, J., Anglin, M. D. & Rawson, R. A. (2005). Levo-alpha-acetylmethadol (LAAM) versus methadone: treatment retention and opiate use. *Addiction, 100*(8), 1131-39.

Lukas, S. E. (1995). Barbiturates. In J. H. Jaffe, ed. *Encyclopedia of Drugs and Alcohol* (Vol. I, pp. 141-46). New York: Simon & Schuster Macmillan.

Lurie, P. & Lee, P. R. (1991). Fifteen solutions to the problems of prescription drug abuse. *Journal of Psychoactive Drugs, 23*(4), 349-57.

Marnell, T., ed. (1997). *Drug Identification Bible.* Denver: Drug Identification Bible.

Marsa, L. (September 10, 2001). Misuse of pain drug linked to hearing loss. *Los Angeles Times.*

Marsch, L. A., Stephens, M. A., Mudric, T., Strain, E. C., Bigelow, G. E. & Johnson, R. E. (2005). Predictors of outcome in LAAM, buprenorphine, and methadone treatment for opioid dependence. *Experimental Clinical Psychopharmacology, 13*(4), 293-302.

McGregor, C., Darke, S., Ali, R. & Christie, P. (1998). Experience of non-fatal overdose among heroin users in Adelaide, Australia: Circumstances and risk perceptions. *Addiction, 93*(5), 701-11.

Meyer, J. S. & Quenzer, L. F. (2005). *Psychopharmacology: Drugs, the Brain, and Behavior.* Sunderland, MA: Sinauer Associates, Inc.

Miller, N. S. & Gold, M. S. (1990). Benzodiazepines: Tolerance, dependence, abuse, and addiction. *Journal of Psychoactive Drugs, 22*(1), 23-22.

Musto, D. F. (1973). *The American Disease: Origins of Narcotic Control.* New Haven, CT: Yale University Press.

National Council on Alcohol and Drug Dependence. (April 16, 2002). OxyContin deaths higher than expected. *Reuters.*

National Drug Intelligence Center. (2007). National Drug Threat Assessment. http://www.usdoj.gov/ndic/pubs21/21137/21137p.pdf (accessed April 13, 2007).

National Institute on Drug Abuse [NIDA]. (2005). *Prescription Drugs: Abuse and Addiction. Research Report Series.* http://www.nida.nih.gov/ResearchReports/Prescription/Prescription.html (accessed November 1, 2006).

National Institute on Drug Abuse. (2006). *Rohypnol and GHB. NIDA InfoFacts.* http://www.drugabuse.gov/infofacts/RohypnolGHB.html (accessed March 15, 2007).

Nestler, E. J. & Aghajanian, G. K. (1997). Molecular and cellular basis of addiction. *Science, 278*(5335), 58-63.

Nicholson, K. L. & Balster, R. L. (2001). GHB: A new and novel drug of abuse. *Drug and Alcohol Dependence, 63*(1), 1-22.

N-SSATS. (2006). *National Survey of Substance Abuse Treatment Services (N-SSATS): 2005.* http://www.dasis.samhsa.gov/05nssats/nssats2k5web.pdf (accessed January 8, 2007).

NZZ Online. (2007). Scientists get a fix on methadone risks. http://www.nzz.ch/2007/03/06/eng/article7589443.html (accessed April 13, 2007).

O'Brien, C. P. (2001). Drug addiction and drug abuse. In J. G. Hardman & L. E. Limbird, eds. *Goodman & Gilman's The Pharmacological Basis of Therapeutics* (10th ed., pp. 621-41). New York: McGraw-Hill.

O'Brien, R., Cohen, S., Evans, G. & Fine, J. (1992). *The Encyclopedia of Drug Abuse* (2nd ed.). New York: Facts On File.

Office of National Drug Control Policy. (2007). *Drug Facts: Club Drugs.* http://www.whitehousedrugpolicy.gov/drugfact/club/index.html (accessed April 14, 2007).

Orangio, G. R., Pitlick, S. D., Della Latta, P., Marino, C., Guarneri, J. J., Giron, J. A., et al. (1984). Soft tissue infections in parenteral drug abusers. *Annals of Surgery, 199*(1), 97-100.

Palmer, C. & Horowitz, M., eds. (1982). *Shaman Woman, Mainline Lady: Women's Writings on the Drug Experience.* New York: Quill, Inc.

Passik, S. D., Hays, L., Eisner, N. & Kirsh, K. L. (2006). Psychiatric and pain characteristics of prescription drug abusers entering drug rehabilitation. *Journal of Pain and Palliative Care Pharmacotherapy, 20*(2), 5-13.

Payte, J. T. (1997). Methadone maintenance treatment: The first thirty years. *Journal of Psychoactive Drugs, 29*(2), 149-53.

Payte, J. T., Zweben, J. E. & Martin, J. (2003). Opioid maintenance therapies. In A. W. Graham, T. K. Schultz, M. F. Mayo-Smith, R. K. Ries & B. B. Wilford, eds. *Principles of Addiction Medicine* (3rd ed., pp. 751-66). Chevy Chase, MD: American Society of Addiction Medicine, Inc.

Pettinati, H. M., O'Brien, C. P., Rabinowitz, A. R., Wortman, S. P., Oslin, D. W., Kampman, K. M., et al. (2006). The status of naltrexone in the treatment of alcohol dependence: Specific effects on heavy drinking. *Journal of Clinical Psychopharmacology, 26*(6), 610-25.

Pfab, R., Eyer, F., Jetzinger, E. & Zilker, T. (2006). Cause and motivation in cases of non-fatal drug overdoses in opiate addicts. *Clinical Toxicology, 44*(3), 255-59.

Pharmacy Times. (2006). *Top 200 Prescription Drugs of 2005.* http://www.pharmacytimes.com/article.cfm?ID=3468 (accessed April 13, 2007).

Physicians' Desk Reference [PDR]. (2007). *Physicians' Desk Reference* (61st ed.). Montvale, NJ: Medical Economics Company.

PhRMA. (2007). Industry Profile, 2005. PhRMA (Pharmaceutical Research and Manufacturers of America Publications) http://www.phrma.org (accessed March 7, 2007).

Potokar, J. & Nutt, D. J. (1994). Anxiolytic potential of benzodiazepine receptor partial agonists. *CNS Drugs, 1,* 305-315.

Rawson, R. A., Hasson, A. L., Huber, A. M., McCann, M. J. & Ling, W. (1998). A 3-year progress report on the implementation of LAAM in the United States. *Addiction, 93*(4), 533-40.

Robins, L. N. & Slobodyan, S. (2003). Post-Vietnam heroin use and injection by returning U.S. veterans: Clues to preventing injection today. *Addiction, 98*(8), 1053-60.

Rubin, R. (August 12, 2004). Pain experts, DEA seek consensus on abuse. *USA Today,* p. 7D.

Rubin, R. (March 15, 2007). Drugs to warn of sleep dangers. *USA Today,* p. 9D.

Schackman, B. R., Gebo, K. A., Walensky, R. P., Losina, E. Muccio, T., Sax, P. E., et al. (2006). The lifetime cost of current human immunodeficiency virus care in the United States. *Medical Care, 44*(11), 990-97.

Schifano, F., Zamparutti, G., Zambello, F., Oyefeso, A., Deluca, P., Balestrieri, M., et al. (2006). Review of deaths related to analgesic- and cough suppressant-opioids; England and Wales 1996-2002. *Pharmacopsychiatry, 39*(5), 185-91.

Schuckit, M. A. (2000). *Drug and Alcohol Abuse.* New York: Kluwer Academic/Plenum Publishers.

Schuckit, M. A., Greenblatt, D., Gold, E. & Irwin, M. (1991). Reactions to ethanol and diazepam in healthy young men. *Journal of Studies on Alcohol, 52*(2), 180-87.

Simon, E. J. (2005). Opiates: Neurobiology. In J. H. Lowinson, P. Ruiz, R. B. Millman, & J. G. Langrod (Eds.), *Substance Abuse: A Comprehensive Textbook* (4th ed., pp. 164-179). Baltimore: Williams & Wilkins.

Sivilotti, M. L., Burns, M. J., Aaron, C. K. & Greenberg M. J. (2001). Pentobarbital for severe gamma-butyrolactone withdrawal. *Annals of Emergency Medicine, 38*(6), 660-65.

Sklair-Tavron, L., Shi, W. X., Lane, S. B., Harris, H. W., Bunney, B. S. & Nestler, E. J. (1996). Chronic morphine induces visible changes in the morphology of mesolimbic dopamine neurons. *Proceedings of the National Academy of Sciences, 93*(20), 11202-207.

Smith, A. (January 27, 2007). *Abuse-resistant OxyContin faces hurdles.* CNN.com. http://money.cnn.com/2007/01/19/news/companies/durect/index.htm (accessed April 13, 2007).

Smith, D. E. & Seymour, R. B. (2001). *Clinician's Guide to Substance Abuse.* New York: McGraw-Hill.

Stahl, S. M. (2000). *Essential Psychopharmacology.* Cambridge, England: Cambridge University Press.

Sternbach, L. H. (1983). The benzodiazepine story. *Journal of Psychoactive Drugs, 15*(1-2), 15-17.

Strain, E. C., Stoller, K., Walsh, S. L. & Bigelow, G. E. (2000). Effects of buprenorphine versus buprenorphine/naloxone tablets in non-dependent opioid abusers. *Psychopharmacology, 148*(4), 374-83.

Strain, E. C., Walsh, S. L., Preston, K. L., Liebson, I. A. & Bigelow, G. E. (1997). The effects of buprenorphine in buprenorphine-maintained volunteers. *Psychopharmacology, 129*(4), 329-38.

Starcevic, B. & Sicaja, M. (2007). Dual intoxication with diazepam and amphetamine: This drug interaction probably potentiates myocardial ischemia. *Medical Hypotheses.* Prepublication.

Substance Abuse and Mental Health Services Administration [SAMHSA]. (2006). *National Household Survey on Drug Abuse, 2005.* Rockville, MD: SAMHSA, Office of Applied Studies.

Tang, Y. L., Zhao, D., Zhao, C. & Cubells, J. F. (2006). Opiate addiction in China: Current situation and treatments. *Addiction, 101*(5), 657-65.

Toler, T. (October 27, 2006). Babies born dependent. *Bluefield* (West Virginia) *Daily Telegraph,* p. A2.

Trebach, A. (1981). *The Heroin Solution.* New Haven, CT: Yale University Press.

Treatment Episode Data Sets [TEDS]. (2007). *Treatment Episode Data Sets (TEDS)-2005.* http://wwwdasis.samhsa.

gov/teds05/tedshi2k5_web.pdf (accessed April 15, 2007).

UNAIDS. (2006). *UNAIDS home page.* http://www.unaids.org/en/ (accessed November 24, 2006).

United Nations. (2006). *2006 World Drug Report.* United Nations Office of Drugs and Crime. http://www.unodc.org/unodc/en/world_drug_report.html (accessed April 13, 2007).

Upshur, C. C., Luckmann, R. S. & Savageau, J. A. (2006). Primary care provider concerns about management of chronic pain in community clinic populations. *Journal of General Internal Medicine, 21*(6), 652-55.

U.S. Department of Justice. (2006). Criminal offenders statistics. http://www.ojp.usdoj.gov/bjs/crimoff.htm#feds (accessed April 13, 2007).

Verhaag, D. A. & Ikeda, R. M. (1991). Prescribing for chronic pain. *Journal of Psychoactive Drugs, 23*(4), 433-44.

Volpicelli, J., Pettinati, H., McLellan, A. T. & O'Brien, C. (2001). *Combining Medication and Psychosocial Treatments for Addictions.* New York: Guilford Publications.

Wickelgren, I. (1998). Teaching the brain to take drugs. *Science, 280*(5372), 2045-46.

Will, M. J., Watkins, L. R. & Maier, S. F. (1998). Uncontrollable stress potentiates morphine's rewarding properties. *Pharmacology, Biochemistry, and Behavior, 60*(3), 655-64.

Zackon, F. (1992). *The Encyclopedia of Psychoactive Drugs: Heroin, the Street Narcotic.* New York: Chelsea House Publishers.

Zule, W. A., Vogtsberger, K. N. & Desmond, D. P. (1997). The intravenous injection of illicit drugs and needle sharing: An historical perspective. *Journal of Psychoactive Drugs, 29*(2), 199-204.

Downers:
Alcohol

Caricature of the etiquette of alcohol drinking. Etching by Louis Léopold Boilly, c.1826.
Courtesy of the National Library of Medicine, Bethesda, MD

- **Overview.** Alcohol is the oldest and most widely used psychoactive drug; it is legal in most countries. About 119 million Americans drank alcohol last month, and 16 million are considered heavy users. Around 10,000 years ago, grain was cultivated for bread and alcohol. Mead (fermented honey), beer (fermented barley), wine (fermented grapes and fruit), and finally distilled spirits (usually made from grain) were discovered by succeeding generations. Throughout history societies' laws and morals regarding alcohol have wavered from prohibition and temperance to unrestricted drinking.

- **Alcoholic Beverages.** Alcohol is fermented from the sugar or carbohydrates in grapes and other fruits, vegetables, and grains. Ethyl alcohol (ethanol) is the main psychoactive component in all alcoholic beverages. Beer is 5% to 9% alcohol, wine is 12% to 14%, and distilled liquor is 40% to 50%.

- **Absorption, Distribution & Metabolism.** Though alcohol is absorbed by the body at different rates depending on weight, gender, age, and a dozen other factors, it is metabolized at a steady rate, mostly by the liver, and subsequently excreted through urine, sweat, and breath. The higher the blood alcohol concentration (BAC), the more severe the effects. A BAC of 0.08 signifies legal intoxication in the United States.

- **Desired Effects, Side Effects & Health Consequences:**
  - ◇ **Levels of Use.** Alcohol use, like other drugs, ranges from abstinence, experimentation, and social/recreational drinking to habitual use, abuse, and addiction (dependence or alcoholism).
  - ◇ **Low-to-Moderate-Dose Episodes.** If a person is not at risk (e.g., pregnant, genetically susceptible, in recovery), there are some documented health benefits from light alcohol use. In general, sedation, muscle relaxation, some heart benefits, and lowered inhibitions accompany low-dose use. The disinhibitory neurotransmitter GABA and the mood transmitter serotonin are most affected by alcohol.
  - ◇ **High-Dose Episodes.** A range of effects occurs, from decreased alertness and exaggerated emotions to shock, coma, and death. Effects are directly related to the amount, frequency, and duration of use. They also depend on the user's tolerance to alcohol. Blackouts (retrograde amnesia) are common among alcoholics.
  - ◇ **Chronic High-Dose Use.** Depending on a drinker's habits and susceptibility, organ damage (particularly liver damage), cardiovascular problems, nervous system damage, gastrointestinal damage, reproductive disruption, cancer, and impaired mental and emotional processes are common.
  - ◇ **Mortality.** Chronic high-dose drinkers are likely to die 10 to 22 years earlier than the general population.

- **Addiction (alcohol dependence or alcoholism).** Historically, there have been many attempts to classify alcoholism (alcohol dependence) as a disease. Heredity and environment, along with the use of alcohol and other psychoactive drugs, help determine a person's susceptibility to abuse and addiction. The development of tolerance and the onset of withdrawal symptoms advance a user from experimentation to abuse and alcohol dependence (alcoholism). Much of the current research in the field of alcohol dependence involves identifying the precise biological mechanisms involved in the development of addiction.

- **Other Problems with Alcohol.** Polydrug abuse, mental problems, fetal damage during pregnancy, excess aggression and violence, and driving-related accidents can happen at many levels of alcohol use.

- **Epidemiology.** The culture of the drinker (e.g., wet cultures vs. dry cultures), ethnic background, gender, age, and socioeconomic factors help determine how a person drinks.

- **Conclusions.** Because alcoholism can take anywhere from three months to 30 years to develop, it is important for drinkers to assess their current level of use and their susceptibility to compulsive use.

Alcohol abuse claims 75,000 Men with high blood pressure may benefit from alcohol

Study finds 1 or 2

Beer, hard liquor take ugly toll on lower digestive system

Drink a day helps reduce risk of death

Nine-year study also underscores benefits of moderate use of alcohol

Only red wine drinkers

Colleges are reaching their limit on alcohol

Domestic Abuse Linked To Alcohol, Job Stability

Study: 1 in 5 have binged on alcohol recently

New Studies Strongly Link Alcohol and Breast Cancer

14.6M have used pot in past month

Crash suspect had 3 DUI convictions

S.F. man faces charges in deaths of cabbie, student

Alcohol Warning for Pain Drugs

Young Drinkers More Likely to Turn Alcoholic

Male et a factor, **Booze and babies: How much danger?**

Lawsuits target alcohol industry

Alcohol, sex in a memorable relationship

Injected drug, plus counseling, may help men reduce drinking

Even aspirin called unsafe with drinks

By Marlene Cimons
Los Angeles Times

Washington

The younger children or teenagers are when they start to drink, the more likely they are to become alcoholics, government researchers said yesterday.

OVERVIEW

INTRODUCTION

Whether it is *bojalwwa,* a home-brewed beer-like drink from Botswana; *mosto,* a grape wine from Argentina; *arrack,* a traditional drink distilled from fermented molasses in India; or *pontikka,* distilled spirits from Finland, alcohol consumption is a worldwide phenomenon.

"Russia is a drinking culture. Refusing to drink is unacceptable unless you give a plausible excuse, such as explaining that health or religious reasons prevent you from imbibing."

Sergei Ivanchuk on the Russian business culture Web site Executive Planet, 2006

"A pragmatic race, the Japanese appear to have decided long ago that the only reason for drinking alcohol is to become intoxicated and therefore drink only when they wish to be drunk."

William Gibson, Tokyo Pastoral, 1982

"To drink in the French style, moderately and with meals, being

afraid for one's health, is to limit too much the favors of Bacchus, that god. In any case, getting drunk is almost the only pleasure revealed to us by the passing of the years."

Anonymous, 1991

"Everyone thinks that Australians drink just beer and during the day that's pretty much true; when you go out in the afternoon, you have a beer. But at night, like nightclub hours, you drink hard alcohol, that's it."

Australian bartender, 2002

Worldwide:

◊ **the majority of people in most countries, except Islamic countries, drink alcoholic beverages;**

◊ China's alcohol consumption has doubled;

◊ India's alcohol consumption has increased 50%;

◊ 23% of English boys and 27% of English girls 15 to 16 years old were drunk three times or more in the past month; and

◊ Russian men consume the equivalent of six to seven bottles of vodka per capita per year.

Unfortunately:

◊ 75,000 alcoholics were homeless in Japan (there are about 100,000 homeless in Japan);

◊ **more than 2 million people died due to alcohol;** and

◊ **approximately 10% of all diseases and injuries were a direct result of alcohol abuse.**

In the United States:

◊ **last month about 126 million Americans (52% of those 12 or older) had at least 1 beer, 1 glass of wine, or 1 cocktail; 16 million of this group are considered heavy drinkers** (5 or more drinks in one sitting at least five times in the past month);

◊ more than two-thirds of the 11 million college students (at four-year colleges) had 1 drink, and more than two-thirds of those drinkers had 5 or more drinks on at least one occasion;

◊ about 6.2% of eighth-grade students, 18.5% of tenth-grade students, and 30.0% of twelfth-grade students had been drunk;

◊ yesterday about $250 million was spent at bars, restaurants, and liquor stores for alcoholic drinks; and

◊ champagne toasts were made to 7,500 brides and grooms.

Unfortunately:

◇ **25% to 30% of hospital admissions were due to direct or indirect medical complications from alcohol;**

◇ **about half of the murder victims and half of the murderers were drinking alcohol at the time of the crime;**

◇ more than half of the rapes that occurred involved alcohol;

◇ about half of American adults have a close family member who has or has had alcoholism;

◇ some 2.7 million crime victims reported that the offender had been drinking alcohol prior to committing the crime; and

◇ every year alcohol abuse and addiction cost businesses, the judicial system, medical facilities, and the United States more than $184 billion, or $638 for every man, woman, and child.

(Bellandi, 2003; Dawson & Grant, 1998; Harwood et al., 2000; Internal Revenue Service, 2006; Johnston, O'Malley, Bachman, et al., 2006A&B; National Institute on Alcohol Abuse and Alcoholism [NIAAA], 2000; Nelson, Naimi, Brewer, et al., 2005; Substance Abuse and Mental Health Services Administration [SAMHSA], 2005 & 2006; U.S. Department of Justice, 1998; World Health Organization [WHO], 2005)

HISTORY

A few years ago, archeologists uncovered evidence of the use of a fermented rice, honey, and fruit alcoholic beverage in Jiahu, China, dating back to 7000 B.C. (McGovern, Zhang, Tang, et al., 2004). Other excavators have also found a recipe for beer along with alcohol residues in clay pots in Mesopotamia and Iran dating from 5400 to 3500 B.C. **Alcohol is the oldest known and at present the most widely used psychoactive drug in the world.** It has presumably been present since airborne yeast spores started fermenting plants into alcohol about 1.5 billion years ago.

Our ancient ancestors' discovery of **this first psychoactive drug probably occurred by accident** when a bunch of grapes or a batch of plums was left standing in the sun, allowing the fruit sugar to ferment into alcohol. Perhaps some wild honey that had fermented was found, diluted with water, and sampled. This early alcoholic beverage would later be called *mead.* People were most likely drawn to the taste and the mood-altering effects. Curiosity was followed by experimentation as thirsty farmers discovered that the starch in potatoes, rice, corn, fruit, and grains could also be fermented into alcohol (beer or wine). Further experimentation found the value of alcohol as a medicine and as a solvent for other therapeutic substances.

The desire for ready access to the pleasurable effects as well as the health benefits of beer and wine led humans to search out and grow the raw ingredients for alcohol. Some historians believe that about 10,000 years ago **the first civilized settlements were created to ensure a regular supply of grain for food and beer, grapes for wine, and poppies for opium** (Keller, 1984).

The use of alcohol is documented in almost all civilized societies throughout history, in myths, religions, rituals, stories, songs, hieroglyphs, sacred writings, and commercial sales records written on clay tablets. The Babylonian *Epic of Gilgamesh* says that wine grapes were given to the earth as a memorial to fallen gods. The Bible contains more than 150 references to wine, some positive, some negative.

"God give you of the dew of the sky, of the fatness of the earth, and plenty of grain and new wine."
Genesis 27:28

"And don't get drunk with wine, which leads to reckless actions, but be filled with the Spirit: speaking to one another in psalms, hymns, and spiritual songs, singing and making music to the Lord in your heart."
Ephesians 5:18-19

THE LEGAL DRUG

Historically, the acceptability of alcohol has been intertwined with cultural, social, and financial imperatives. It has been used as a **reward** for pyramid workers, as a **food** (grain-rich beer) for peasants, as a solvent for opium in the eighteenth-century **cure-all** known as *laudanum,* as a **sacrament** for Jewish and Christian religious ceremonies, as a **water substitute** for contaminated wells, as a **social lubricant** for all classes, as a **tranquilizer** for the anxious, and as a **source of taxes** for the ruling class.

Because beer, wine, and liquor were so widely available and legal in most societies (except in Muslim-governed countries) and because they were promoted by custom and advertising, many people did not think of alcohol as a drug (though that attitude has almost disappeared over the past few decades). Whether it's been used for those desirable reasons or as the focus of prohibition forces, alcohol will continue to be the object of both desire and vilification, depending on moral attitude, social acceptability, and the politics of the prevailing government.

Almost every country has had periods in its history in which alcohol use was restricted or even banned completely. Those prohibitions were usually rescinded (Langton, 1995).

◇ The *Chinese Canon of History,* written about 650 B.C., recognized that complete prohibition was almost impossible because men loved their beer (Keller, 1984).

◇ Many Buddhist sects in India prohibited alcohol starting in 500 B.C. and continuing to this day.

◇ In sub-Saharan Africa, the idea of banning alcohol was usually avoided because home-brewed beers had great nutritional value.

◇ The **Gin Epidemic in England** in the 1700s emphasized that poverty, unrestricted use, and industrial despair coupled with the higher concentration of distilled alcohol soon led to abuse and, for many, addiction. The unrestricted sale of gin (20 million gallons per year in England) and the resulting problems of illness, public inebriation, absenteeism from work, and death led to increased taxes and severe restrictions on its manufacture just a few decades after its use was promoted by the government (O'Brien & Chafetz, 1991).

◊ **In colonial America alcohol was a part of everyday life.** The Pilgrims on the *Mayflower* regarded it as an "essential victual"; the founding fathers realized that the cultivation, manufacture, sale, and taxation of whiskey and rum could finance the American Revolution (and the slave trade).

◊ There were attempts at temperance and treatment by such groups as the Washington Temperance Society in the 1840s, the Oxford Group in the 1920s, and Alcoholics Anonymous in the 1930s, the latter of which believed in the **concept of recovering from alcohol abuse and addiction through personal spiritual change** (Alcoholics Anonymous, 1934, 1976; Miller et al., 1998; Nace, 2005).

◊ Official prohibition of alcohol by the U.S. government started in 1920, but widespread flouting of the law, criminalization of the manufacturing and distribution system, and **pressure by those who wanted to drink, including the Wet Party, led to the repeal of Prohibition** 13 years later.

One reason why many restrictions, and even Prohibition, have been overturned is the value of alcohol as **a major source of excise taxes as well as a commodity**. Currently, the federal government collects $13.50 per proof gallon that's shipped from distilleries while state governments collect up to $6.50 per gallon.

Because alcohol has played a central economic and social role since colonial times in America (and even farther back in other countries' cultures), contemporary society's view of the heavy drinker is more forgiving than its view of a cocaine, heroin, LSD, or even marijuana user.

ALCOHOLIC BEVERAGES

THE CHEMISTRY OF ALCOHOL

There are **hundreds of different alcohols.** Some are made naturally through fermentation while most that are used industrially are synthesized. Some of the more familiar alcohols include:

◊ **ethyl alcohol (ethanol, grain alcohol), the main psychoactive component in all alcoholic beverages;**
◊ methyl alcohol (methanol or wood alcohol), a toxic industrial solvent;
◊ isopropyl alcohol (propanol or rubbing alcohol), used in shaving lotion, shellac, antifreeze, antiseptics, and lacquer; and
◊ butyl alcohol (butanol), used in many industrial processes.

Ethyl alcohol is the least toxic of the alcohols. Few people drink pure ethyl alcohol because it is too strong and fiery tasting. By convention any beverage with an alcohol content greater than 2% is considered an alcoholic beverage.

Alcoholic beverages also include trace amounts of other alcohols, such as amyl, butyl, and propyl alcohol, that result from the production process and storage (e.g., in wooden barrels). Other components produced during fermentation, known as *congeners,* **contribute to the distinctive tastes, aromas, and colors of the various alcoholic beverages.** Congeners include acids, aldehydes, esters, ketones, phenols, and tannins. Beer and vodka have a relatively low concentration of congeners while aged whiskeys and brandy have a relatively high concentration. It is thought that congeners may contribute to the severity of hangovers and other toxic problems of drinking, though the main culprit is the ethyl alcohol.

When airborne **yeast feeds on the sugars** in honey or any watery mishmash of overripe fruit, berries, vegetables, or grain, **the resulting fermentation process results in ethyl alcohol and carbon dioxide** (Figure 5-1). Elephants, bears, deer, birds, and insects have been observed in a state of intoxication, exhibiting unsteady and erratic behavior after eating fermented plant matter.

TYPES OF ALCOHOLIC BEVERAGES

The principal categories of alcoholic beverages are beer, wine, and distilled spirits.

Alcohol is a legal drug in most countries. The preference for beer, wine, or distilled liquors depends on the country's culture, on the availability of certain kinds of beverages, and on the specific occasion. These soccer fans are consoling themselves after their team's defeat. They would probably be doing the same drinking if their team had won.
© 1996 CNS Productions, Inc.

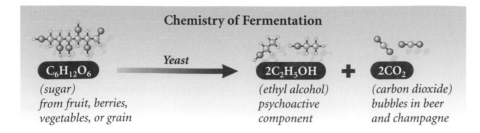

Chemistry of Fermentation

$C_6H_{12}O_6$
(sugar)
from fruit, berries,
vegetables, or grain

→ *Yeast*

$2C_2H_5OH$
(ethyl alcohol)
psychoactive
component

+ $2CO_2$
(carbon dioxide)
bubbles in beer
and champagne

Figure 5-1 •
Yeast feeds on sugar and excretes alcohol and carbon dioxide.

◊ **Beer** is produced when **grain** ferments.
◊ **Wine** is produced when **fruit** ferments.
◊ **Distilled spirits** with different concentrations of alcohol are made from **fermented grains, tubers (e.g., potatoes), vegetables, and other plants**. They can also be **distilled from wine or other fermented beverages**.

Some examples of fermented plant matter are Mexican *pulque* made from cactus, Russian *kvass* made from cereal or bread, Asian *kumiss* made from mare's milk, and even California garlic wine.

The actual consumption of beer vs. wine vs. distilled alcohol depends very much on the culture of a country. For example, Germans drink six times as much beer per capita as they do wine; the French drink eight times more wine per capita than do Americans.

Beer

Beer brewing and bread making were probably started about 8000 B.C. in neolithic times. The raw ingredients (usually grain) were produced in cultivated fields. Some of the first written records concerning beer were found in Mesopotamian ruins dating back to 5400 to 3500 B.C. It seems the Mesopotamians taught the Greeks how to brew beer, and the Europeans in turn learned it from the Greeks.

Beer is produced by first allowing cereal grains, usually barley, to sprout in water, where an enzyme called *amylase* is released. After the barley malt is crushed, the amylase helps convert the starches into sugar. This crushed malt

is boiled into a liquid mash, which is then filtered, mixed with hops (an aromatic herb first used around A.D. 1000-1500) and yeast, and allowed to ferment. **Beer includes ale, stout, porter, malt liquor, lager, and bock beer.** The differences among beers have to do with the type of grain used, the fermentation time, and whether they are top-fermenting beers (those that rise in the vat) or bottom-fermenting beers. Top-fermenting beers are more flavorful and include ales, stouts, porters, and wheat beers. Bottom-fermenting beers include the most popular pale lager beers (e.g., Budweiser® and Coors®). Traditional home-brewed

beers are dark and full of sediment, minerals, vitamins (especially B vitamins), and amino acids and thus have appreciable food value, unlike modern commercial beers that are highly filtered.

The **alcohol content of most lager beers is 4% to 5%**; ales, 5% to 6%; ice beers, 5% to 7%; malt liquors, 6% to 9%; while light beers are only 3.4% to 4.2% alcohol.

Wine

In some early cultures, **beer was the alcoholic beverage of the common people and wine was the drink of the priests and nobles** possibly because vineyards were more difficult to establish and cultivate. In Egypt, however, pharaohs did have beer entombed with them in their pyramids to sustain them on their afterlife journeys and to offer a gift to the gods. Ancient Greek and Roman cultures seem to have preferred wine; the ruling classes kept the best vintages for themselves. These cultures also cultivated vineyards in many of their colonies. After the fall of the Roman Empire, many monasteries in Germany, France, Austria, and Italy

Virtually every country makes beer as either a national enterprise or a local business. These beers and ales come from Italy, Germany, the United States, China, Peru, Thailand, Japan, and Vietnam.

© 2000 CNS Productions, Inc.

TABLE 5-1 CONSUMPTION OF BEER & WINE IN EUROPE & THE UNITED STATES		
	Liters per Capita	
	Beer	**Wine**
Germany	131	22
England	103	13
United States	95	20
France	40	60
Italy	103	59
(Eurocare, 2005)		

carried on the cultivation of grapes and even hybridized new species.

Wines are usually made from grapes, though some are made from berries, other fruits (e.g., peaches and plums), and even starchy grains (e.g., Japanese saké rice wine). Generally, grapes with a high sugar content are preferred. A disease-resistant hybrid of *Vitas vinifera* grafted onto several American species was heavily planted worldwide particularly in the temperate climates of France, Italy, Spain, Argentina, California, and New York. Wine had a short shelf life until the 1860s, when Louis Pasteur showed that heating it would halt microbial activity and keep the wine from turning into vinegar (pasteurization).

Grapes are crushed to extract their juices. Either the grapes contain their own yeast, or yeast is added and fermentation begins. The kind of wine produced depends on the variety and the ripeness of the grapes, the quality of the soil, the climate, the weather, and the balance between acidity and sugar. White wines typically are aged from six to 12 months, red wines from two to four years.

European wines contain 8% to 12% alcohol, whereas **U.S. wines have a 12% to 14% alcohol content**. Wines with an alcohol content higher than 14% are called *fortified wines* because they have had pure alcohol or brandy added during or after fermentation; their final alcohol content is 17% to 21%. Wine coolers, which are usually diluted with juice, contain an average of 6% alcohol.

Distilled Spirits (liquor)

The alcoholic content of naturally fermented wine is limited to about 14% by volume. Recently, new fermentation techniques and more-resistant yeasts have allowed alcohol concentrations to reach 16% and even slightly higher. At higher levels the concentration of alcohol becomes too toxic and kills off the fermenting yeast, thus halting the conversion of sugar into alcohol. Outside of Asia, drinks with greater than 14% alcohol weren't available until about **A.D. 800, when the Arabs discovered distillation**. Distillation is the process of liquid separation by evaporation and condensation. A liquid can be separated from solid particles or from another liquid with a different boiling point. This eventually led to the production of distilled spirits such as brandies, whiskeys, vodka, and gin.

Brandy is distilled from wine, rum from sugar cane or molasses, whiskey and gin from grains, and vodka from potatoes. Distilled spirits can be produced from many other plants, including figs and dates in the Middle East and agave plants in Mexico (to make mescal and tequila).

One result of the invention of distilled beverages was that eventually it became much easier to get drunk. Initially, distilled alcohol was used more for medical reasons. **Alcoholism eventually exploded in Europe and other countries due to the increased manufacture of distilled spirits and the desire for excise tax revenues.** Similarly, alcoholism became a major social problem in colonial America with the manufacture of increasing amounts of corn whiskey and rum that was easier and more profitable to transport and market than bushels of corn. Grains and other sugar-producing commodities could be reduced in volume into more potent, portable, and higher-priced commodities. Rum was so popular that the second publicly funded building in New Amsterdam (New York) was a rum distillery on Staten Island.

Distillatio by Philip Galle. Distillation in this sixteenth-century Dutch laboratory supplies alcohol for making medicines and for drinking. In distillation a liquid is boiled and the vapors are drawn off, cooled, and condensed into a clear, colorless, almost 100% pure grain alcohol distillate.

Courtesy of the National Library of Medicine, Bethesda, MD

TABLE 5–2 PERCENTAGE OF ALCOHOL BY VOLUME

WINE

Unfortified (red, white)	12-14%
Fortified (sherry, port)	17-21%
Champagne	12%
Vermouth	18%
Wine cooler	6%

BEER

Regular beer	4-5%
Light beer	3.4-4.2%
Malt liquor	6-9%
Ale	5-6%
Ice beer	5-6%
Low-alcohol beer	1.5%
Nonalcoholic beer	0.5%

MALT BEVERAGES

Hard lemonade, Bacardi Silver,® Smirnoff Ice®	5-6%

LIQUORS & WHISKEYS

Bourbon, whiskey, Scotch, vodka, gin, brandy, rum	40-50%
Overproof rum	75%
Tequila, cognac, Drambui®	40%
Amaretto,® Kahlúa®	26%
Everclear®	95%

Note: To calculate the proof of a product, double the alcohol content (e.g., 40% alcohol = 80 proof; 100% alcohol = 200 proof).

ABSORPTION, DISTRIBUTION & METABOLISM

ABSORPTION & DISTRIBUTION

When beer, wine, or other alcoholic beverage is drunk, it is partially metabolized by digestive juices in the mouth and the stomach. Because alcohol is readily soluble in water and doesn't need to be digested, it immediately begins absorption and distribution. **Absorption of alcohol into the bloodstream takes place at various sites along the gastrointestinal tract, including the stomach, the small intestines, and the colon.** In men 10% to 20% of the alcohol is absorbed by the stomach; in women there is very little absorption there. **Most of the alcohol enters the capillaries in the walls of the small intestines** through passive diffusion (movement from an area of higher concentration of alcohol to an area of lower concentration without an energy expenditure).

Given the same body weight, women and men differ in their processing of alcohol. **Women have higher blood alcohol concentrations than men do from the same amount of alcohol.** A woman who weighs the same as a man and drinks the same number of drinks as a man absorbs about 30% more alcohol into the bloodstream and feels its psychoactive effects faster and more intensely (NIAAA, 1999).

This difference between women's and men's reactions to alcohol results from three possible explanations:

◇ Women have a lower percentage of body water than men of comparable size, so there is less water to dilute the alcohol.

◇ Women have less alcohol dehydrogenase enzyme in the stomach to break down alcohol, so less alcohol is metabolized before getting into the blood.

◇ Finally, changes in gonadal hormone levels during menstruation affect the rate of alcohol metabolism. Women absorb more alcohol during the premenstrual period than at other times (NIAAA, 1997; Register, Cline & Shively, 2002).

Thus chronic **alcohol use causes greater physical damage to women than to men**—female alcoholics have death rates 50% to 100% higher than male alcoholics (Blume & Zilberman, 2005; NIAAA, 2000).

The alcohol is absorbed into the bloodstream and partially metabolized by the liver (first-pass metabolism) and then quickly distributed throughout the body. Because alcohol molecules are small, water- and lipid-soluble, and move easily through capillary walls by passive diffusion, they can enter any organ or tissue. If the drinker is pregnant, the alcohol will cross the placental barrier into the fetal circulatory system. Once alcohol passes through the blood/brain barrier, psychoactive effects begin to occur.

The highest levels of blood alcohol concentration occur 30 to 90 minutes after drinking. How quickly the effects are felt is determined by the rate of absorption. Absorption is influenced by an individual's weight and body fat, body chemistry, and such factors as emotional state (e.g., fear, stress, fatigue, or anger), health status, and even environmental temperature.

Other **factors that speed absorption** in both men and women are:

◇ increasing the amount drunk or the drinking rate;

◇ drinking on an empty stomach;

◇ using high alcohol concentrations in drinks, up to a maximum of 95% with Everclear®;

◇ drinking carbonated drinks, such as champagne, sparkling wines, soft drinks, and tonic mixers; and

◇ warming the alcohol (e.g., hot toddies, hot saké).

Factors that slow absorption are:

◇ eating before or while drinking (especially eating meat, milk, cheese, and fatty foods)

◇ diluting drinks with ice, water, or juice.

METABOLISM

Because the body treats alcohol as a toxin or poison, elimination begins as soon as it is ingested. Approximately 2% to 10% of the alcohol is eliminated directly without being metabolized (a small amount is exhaled while additional amounts are excreted through sweat, saliva, and urine). The remaining **90% to 98% of alcohol is neutralized through metabolism (mainly oxidation) by the liver and then by excretion through the kidneys and the lungs** (Jones & Pounder, 1998).

Alcohol is metabolized in the liver, first by alcohol dehydrogenase (ADH) into acetaldehyde, which is very toxic to the body and especially the liver, and then by acetaldehyde dehydrogenase (ALDH) into acetic acid, which is finally oxidized into carbon dioxide (CO_2) and water (H_2O) (Figure 5-2).

Metabolism of Alcohol

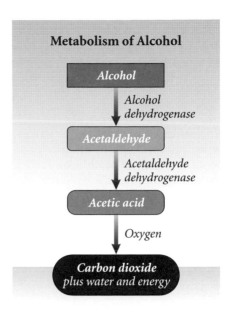

Figure 5-2 •

Metabolism is accomplished in several stages involving oxidation. First the enzyme alcohol dehydrogenase (ADH), found in the stomach and the liver, acts on the ethyl alcohol (C_2H_5OH) to form acetaldehyde (CH_3CHO), a highly toxic substance. Acetaldehyde is then quickly altered by a second enzyme, acetaldehyde dehydrogenase (ALDH), that oxidizes it into acetic acid (CH_3COOH). Acetic acid is then further oxidized to carbon dioxide (CO_2) and water (H_2O).

The varying availability and the metabolic efficiency of ADH and ALDH, due in part to hereditary factors, account for some of the variation in people's reactions to alcohol (Bosron, Ehrig & Li, 1993; Lin & Anthenelli, 2005; Prescott, 2002).

For example, it is suspected that the high rate of alcoholism and the high rate of cirrhosis of the liver in American Indians are due to disruptions in the ALDH and ADH systems as well as a tradition of binge-drinking patterns (Foulks, 2005). Besides ALDH irregularities, drugs such as aspirin also inhibit metabolism of alcohol and lead to higher blood alcohol concentration in both men and women (Schuckit, Edenberg, Kalmijn, et al., 2001).

"We get drunk and we have fun. We have a good time. That's what we're about. And I'm healthy. I'm in better shape than any of you guys, well maybe not on the inside. My stomach's kind of messed up a little bit. I can't drink liquor that good. I did take blood tests. I get my results on Friday . . . I forgot."

25-year-old male alcohol abuser

Blood Alcohol Concentration (BAC)

Though absorption of alcohol is quite variable, **metabolism occurs at a relatively defined continuous rate**. About 1 oz. of pure alcohol (1.5 drinks) is eliminated from the body every three hours. Thus we can estimate the amount of alcohol that will be circulating through the body and the brain and how long it will take that amount to be metabolized and eliminated. Due to heredity, however, each person's biochemical makeup can have a strong effect on metabolism and elimination.

The actual reaction and level of impairment can vary widely, depending on a person's drinking history, behavioral tolerance, mood, and a dozen other factors. Physical impairment is greater in a rising BAC. From the moment of ingestion, it takes 15 to 20 minutes for alcohol to reach the brain via the intestines and begin to cause impairment. **It takes 30 to 90 minutes after ingestion to reach maximum blood alcohol concentration** (NIAAA, 1997).

This **BAC table** (Table 5-3) measures the concentration of alcohol in an average drinker's blood. (Other versions of BAC tables give slightly lower levels than this one; the differences are minimal.) In all 50 states as of August 2005, **legal intoxication is defined as 0.08 whether or not the driver can function.** Some think it should be 0.05 for safety. For truck drivers the legal limit is 0.04; for pilots it is 0.02. The unit of measurement for BAC is weight

TABLE 5–3 APPROXIMATE BLOOD ALCOHOL CONCENTRATION FOR DIFFERENT BODY WEIGHTS

No. of Drinks	1	2	3	4	5	6	7	8	9	10
Male										
100 lbs.	0.043	0.087	0.130	0.174	0.217	0.261	0.304	0.348	0.391	0.435
125 lbs.	0.034	0.069	0.103	0.139	0.173	0.209	0.242	0.287	0.312	0.346
150 lbs.	0.029	0.058	0.087	0.116	0.145	0.174	0.203	0.232	0.261	0.290
175 lbs.	0.025	0.050	0.075	0.100	0.125	0.150	0.175	0.200	0.225	0.250
200 lbs.	0.022	0.043	0.065	0.087	0.108	0.130	0.152	0.174	0.195	0.217
225 lbs.	0.019	0.039	0.058	0.078	0.097	0.117	0.136	0.156	0.175	0.195
250 lbs.	0.017	0.035	0.052	0.070	0.087	0.105	0.122	0.139	0.156	0.173
Female										
100 lbs.	0.050	0.101	0.152	0.203	0.253	0.304	0.355	0.406	0.456	0.507
125 lbs.	0.040	0.080	0.120	0.162	0.202	0.244	0.282	0.324	0.364	0.404
150 lbs.	0.034	0.068	0.101	0.135	0.169	0.203	0.237	0.271	0.304	0.338
175 lbs.	0.029	0.058	0.087	0.117	0.146	0.175	0.204	0.233	0.262	0.292
200 lbs.	0.026	0.050	0.076	0.101	0.126	0.152	0.177	0.203	0.227	0.253

If a person drinks over a period of time, the alcohol is metabolized at a rate of 0.015 per hour. Use the following table to factor in the time since the first drink.

TIMETABLE FACTORS

Hours since first drink	1	2	3	4	5
Subtract from BAC	0.015	0.030	0.045	0.060	0.075

(O'Brien & Chafetz, 1991)

Drink Equivalency

| 1½ oz. brandy | 1½ oz. liquor with mixer | 1½ oz. liquor straight | 12 oz. beer | 7 oz. malt liquor | 5 oz. wine | 10 oz. wine cooler |

Figure 5-3 •
One drink is defined as 1.5 oz. brandy, 1.5 oz. liquor (with or without mixer), 12 oz. lager beer, 7 oz. malt liquor, 5 oz. wine, or 10 oz. wine cooler. There is slightly more than 0.5 oz. of pure alcohol in the average alcoholic beverage.
© 1995 CNS Productions, Inc.

by volume (e.g., milligrams per deciliter), but it can also be expressed as a percentage (e.g., 10% alcohol by volume). In Europe most countries set the limit at just 0.025. England allows .04, Norway just 0.10, and Australia 0.05.

For example, if a 200 lb. male has 5 drinks in 2 hours, his blood alcohol would be 0.108 minus the timetable factor of 0.030, so his BAC would be about 0.078 and he would be legally sober enough to drive. If his 200 lb. female companion has 5 drinks in 2 hours, her blood alcohol level would be 0.126 minus the timetable factor of 0.030, so her BAC would be 0.096; not only would she be quite a bit more intoxicated than her companion even though they weighed the same and drank the same amount over the same period of time but she would also be legally impaired in all states.

DESIRED EFFECTS, SIDE EFFECTS & HEALTH CONSEQUENCES

"Little by little alcohol became my friend. It would give me confidence and it would give me that buzz, and I would get that euphoric feeling that you feel when you've got alcohol."
43-year-old man

"Escape, absolutely escape. It's all about running away, numbing your feelings because you can't, I can't, accept life on life's terms."
35-year-old woman

LEVELS OF USE

The effects of any drug depend on the dosage. The same substance can be a poison, a powerful prescription medication, or an over-the-counter medicine, depending on the dose and the frequency of use. Alcohol is no exception and, as with other psychoactive drugs, there are **escalating patterns of use**.

Abstention (nonuse)

"My brother experimented with Puerto Rican rum on New Year's Eve when he was 15. He threw up on me on the way to the toilet. That took care of his drinking for five years and mine forever."
54-year-old nondrinker

Experimentation (use for curiosity with no subsequent drug-seeking behavior)

"When you're a little boy, your dad says, 'Go get me a beer.' You pop it open for him, and he lets you take a sip every once in a while as long as Mom's

not looking. It tasted good. When you're 10 or 12, you don't really know what alcohol is, you just experience it every once in awhile."
33-year-old drinker

Social/Recreational Use (sporadic infrequent drug-seeking behavior with no established pattern)

"We know which dorm has the drinkers, so when we feel like a bit of a party and a few drinks, that's where we go. They're more serious about their drinking; they like forties [40 oz. malt liquor bottles or cans], but I can take it or leave it."
20-year-old college sophomore

Habituation (established pattern of use with no major negative consequences)

"I think the pleasure left. This was the only way I knew how to have fun. This was the only way I knew how to feel better. But it didn't work, and it took me a while to realize that it had become a habit."
36-year-old recovering alcoholic

Abuse (continued use despite negative consequences)

"I always got Bs, and then my grades dropped down to Ds, and then I started failing my classes, and I skipped school, and I got suspended all the time for that when I got caught. I'd skip school and I'd go get high, or we'd just skip it because we were always high."
15-year-old high school dropout in treatment

Addiction (compulsion to use, inability to stop use, major life dysfunction with continued use)

"I would have the shakes, just really sick. I mean my body could not take alcohol at all. I would be sick in the morning like for days. It was hard to

go to work and hard to take care of my children, hard to do my daily chores. It took me a long time to get well in the morning until I realized there was a magical cure. I could start drinking Bloody Marys."
33-year-old recovering alcoholic

The effects of alcohol depend on the amount used, the frequency of use, and the duration of use:

◊ **low-to-moderate-dose use** (up to one drink a day for women and two drinks a day for men) can occur with experimentation, social/recreational use, and even habituation;

◊ **high-dose use** can occur at any level of drinking; and

◊ **chronic high-dose use** occurs with abuse and addiction (alcoholism).

LOW-TO-MODERATE-DOSE EPISODES

Most studies show that:

◊ **small amounts of alcohol and even infrequent mild intoxication episodes generally do not have negative health consequences for men**, even over extended periods of time;

◊ however, **low-level alcohol use is generally not safe for** people who are **pregnant**;

◊ have certain **pre-existing physical or mental health problems** that are aggravated by alcohol;

◊ are **allergic to alcohol, nitrosamines, or other congeners and additives**;

◊ have a high **genetic/environmental susceptibility** to addiction;

◊ have a **history of abuse and addiction problems** with alcohol or other drugs; and

◊ are **at risk for breast cancer**.

Each person has a different definition of *moderate drinking*. We define it as *drinking that doesn't cause problems for the drinker or for those around him or her*. Drinkers begin to have pathological consequences from alcohol, however, when they have more than

two drinks per day in men and one drink per day in women. Severe effects, especially long-term health and social consequences, usually result from high-dose use episodes and frequent high-dose (chronic) use.

Low-to-Moderate-Dose Use: Physical Effects

Therapeutic Uses. Alcohol is used as a solvent for other medications because it is water- and lipid-soluble. It is used as a **topical disinfectant, as a body rub to reduce fever** because it evaporates so quickly, and as a **pain reliever** for certain nerve-related pain; it is occasionally used to prevent premature labor (Woodward, 2003). Systemically, ethanol is used to treat methanol and ethylene glycol poisoning.

Desired Effects. Some people who drink alcoholic beverages think that they **taste good, quench the thirst, and relax muscle tension**. Consumed in low doses before meals, alcoholic beverages activate gastric juices, improve stomach motility, and **stimulate the appetite**. They produce a feeling of warmth because vessels dilate and increase blood flow to subcutaneous tissues (Woodward, 2003). Red wines made from muscadine grapes and others high in antioxidants have an anti-inflammatory effect on the circulatory system (Greenspan, Bauer, Pollock, et al., 2005). In general, light-to-moderate use of alcohol (1 to 2 drinks per day for men and 1 or less for women [Puddey & Beilin, 2006]) has been shown to **reduce the incidence of heart disease and plaque** formation whether the cause is:

◊ the anti-inflammatory effect;

◊ an increase in high-density lipoproteins, particularly HDL_3;

◊ a different interaction with lipoproteins; or

◊ simply the decrease in tension that a drink can induce.

The doses must be low enough to not cause liver damage, induce other adverse health effects, or trigger heavier drinking (Mukamal, Conigrave, Mittleman, et al., 2003; NIAAA, 2000). This is especially true in women who are more susceptible to the adverse effects of al-

cohol than men. Of course any beneficial effects may also be obtained through exercise, low-fat diet, stress-reduction techniques, and an aspirin a day. (Upon autopsy many end-stage alcoholics have clean blood vessels, but they also have cirrhotic livers, flabby hearts, and damaged brains.)

One or two drinks decrease the chance of gallstones in men and women. In postmenopausal women alcohol seems to slow bone loss because of its effect on estrogen. Women who drink in moderation seem to have a higher bone mass than women who don't drink (Turner & Sibonga, 2001).

Researchers at Columbia University found in a study of 677 stroke victims that those who have one or two drinks per day have a **lower risk of stroke** because alcohol keeps blood platelets from clumping (Sacco, Elkind, Boden-Albala, et al., 1999). But, again, because heavy drinking actually increases the risk of stroke, and even moderate drinking has unwanted side effects, and because no benefit is shown in recommending moderate drinking to abstainers, using alcohol as a stroke-preventive measure should be done only in consultation with a physician.

Sleep. Alcohol is often used by people **to get to sleep**, particularly if anxiety is causing insomnia. In fact, alcohol does decrease the time it takes to fall asleep, but it also seems to disturb the second half of the sleep period especially if consumed within an hour of bedtime (Landolt et al., 1996; Vitiello, 1997). It interferes with rapid eye movement (REM) and dreaming—both essential to feeling fully rested. Disturbances in sleep patterns can also decrease daytime alertness and impair performance (Roehrs & Roth, 2001). Chronic drinking also puts one at a higher risk for experiencing obstructive sleep apnea, a disorder whereby the upper breathing passage (pharynx) narrows or closes during sleep, causing the person to wake up, often a number of times during a sleep period, thus leading to severe fatigue as well as neurological and cardiac problems. Alcoholics not only have an increased risk of sleep apnea but they seem to aggravate their disease by drinking (Brower, 2001; Dawson, Bigby, Poceta, et al., 1993; Miller et al., 1988).

Low-to-Moderate-Dose Use: Psychological Effects

The mental and emotional effects depend more on the environment (setting) in which the drug is used, along with the mood and the general psychological makeup of the user (set).

In general, alcohol affects people psychologically by **lowering inhibitions, increasing self-confidence, and promoting sociability.** It calms, relaxes, sedates, and reduces tension.

"I started out drinking when I was about 15 out of peer pressure, but it made me forget about everything. It felt like a whole new way of life. I was happy, I was gregarious, I was outgoing—more extroverted I guess. I love dancing, and I thought I was Ginger Rogers in that I thought I could do anything."
42-year-old recovering alcoholic

Unfortunately, for someone who is lonely, depressed, angry, or suicidal, **the depressant and disinhibiting effects of alcohol can deepen negative emotions,** including verbal or physical aggressiveness and even violence. Low-to-moderate doses in both men and women can also result in **vehicular crashes and legal conflicts.** Disinhibition can also promote **high-risk sexual activity** leading to unwanted pregnancies and sexually transmitted diseases (STDs).

"When I used, my behavior was really dangerous. I'd do things that normal people wouldn't do. I was very promiscuous; I had a lot of unsafe sex. I contracted hepatitis C. I don't know if I'm HIV. I get tested periodically but I'm, like, very high risk. I've also had numerous STDs."
37-year-old female recovering alcoholic

Neurotransmitters Affected by Alcohol

The psychological effects of alcohol are caused by its alteration of neurochemistry in the higher centers of **the cortex that control reasoning and judgment and the lower centers of the limbic system that rule mood and emotion.** Most psychoactive drugs affect just a few types of receptors or neurotransmitters (e.g., anandamide for marijuana; norepinephrine, epinephrine, and dopamine for cocaine). Alcohol, on the other hand, interacts with receptors, neurotransmitters, cell membranes, intracellular signaling enzymes, and even genes.

◇ Alcohol initially elevates mood by causing the release of **serotonin** (a key mood neurotransmitter), then depletes it with excess use; serotonin scarcity causes depression.

◇ **Dopamine** release at multiple levels of alcohol use gives a surge of pleasure in the mesolimbic dopaminergic reward pathway as does **norepinephrine** release. Dopamine D1, D2, and most recently D3 receptors are involved (Heidbreder, Andreoli, Marcon, et al., 2004).

◇ **Met-enkephalin** release by drinking reduces pain.

◇ **Glutamate** release causes a certain pleasurable stimulation thus reinforcing the drinking.

◇ The alcohol-induced release of **endorphins** and **anandamides** also enhances the reinforcing effect (Colombo, Serra, Vacca, et al., 2005).

◇ In addition, alcohol reduces excitatory neurotransmission at the **NMDA receptors** (a subtype of glutamate receptors), inhibiting their reactions and affecting memory and movement (Stahl, 2000).

◇ **Most important, alcohol causes GABA (the major inhibitory neurotransmitter in the brain)** to enhance neurotransmission at the GABA-A receptor thus lowering psychological inhibitions and eventually slowing down all of the brain processes (Boehm, Valenzuela & Harris, 2005; Koob, 2004).

"I always had to use alcohol to be able to socialize. If I go to the party and I'm not drinking, I wouldn't be able to function. I felt like I couldn't dance right or everybody was looking at me, just really uncomfortable. One or two
drinks, that'd loosen me up and then I'd keep going 'til I got to a level that I wanted to be at. Where I thought that I was acceptable."*
43-year-old recovering alcoholic

Low-to-Moderate-Dose Use: Sexual Effects

Alcohol's physical effects on sexual functioning are closely related to blood alcohol levels. **In low doses alcohol usually increases desire in males and females, often heightening the intensity of orgasm in females while slightly decreasing erectile ability and delaying ejaculation in males** (Blume & Zilberman, 2005).

"It's no mystery why guys in college fraternities, many of whom don't have all that much money, still come up with plenty of money to have outrageous amounts of alcohol and let any woman in for free. The whole point is they're setting up an environment whereby people are going to get more drunk. Women's inhibitions and a guy's inhibitions are going to get lowered."
23-year-old college peer counselor

More than any other psychoactive drug, alcohol has insinuated itself into the lore, culture, and mythology of sexual and romantic behavior: a singles' bar to look for a date, a glass of wine before sex, or champagne to celebrate an anniversary. Almost **half of a group of 90,000 college students at a number of two- and four-year institutions believed that alcohol facilitates sexual opportunities** (Presley, 1997). Whether it does so because of actual psychological and physiological changes or because of heightened expectations is still open to question.

The acceptability of using alcohol in sexual situations extends to high school students. A survey done for the U.S. Surgeon General found that 18% of high school females and 39% of high school males say it is acceptable for a boy to force sex if the girl is stoned or drunk (U.S. Surgeon General, 1992).

MISTER BOFFO

by Joe Martin

PEOPLE UNCLEAR ON THE CONCEPT

JUST ONCE! JUST ONCE I'D LIKE TO TAKE THIS TEST SOBER! I'D SHOW 'EM!!

© 1995 Joe Martin, Inc. Distributed by Neatly Chiseled Features.

HIGH-DOSE EPISODES

High-Dose Use: Physical Effects of Intoxication

For many the purpose of drinking is to get intoxicated, often with a disregard for physical consequences. In fact, **intoxication is a combination of psychological mood, expectation, mental/physical tolerance, and past drinking experience** as well as the physiological changes caused by elevated blood alcohol levels. Up to a certain point, some of the effects of intoxication can be partially masked by experienced drinkers (behavioral tolerance).

In surveys and research, *binge drinking* **is defined as consuming five or more drinks at one sitting for males and four or more for females.** About 44% of college students say they are binge drinkers, and 21% (of the total) say they binge frequently (Wechsler, Lee, Kuo, et al., 2002). Adults between 21 and 25 went on drinking binges an average of 18 times in the past year, while those between 18 and 20 did it 15 times (Bellandi, 2003). Underage binge drinking has increased almost 50% since 1993. Many who are defined as "bingers" say that five drinks won't get them drunk but will raise their BAC over 0.08 and make them liable for a DUI (driving under the influence) arrest.

Heavy drinking **is defined as five or more drinks in one sitting at least**

five times a month. Any person who binge drinks (whether sporadically or frequently) is more likely to have hangovers, experience injuries, aggravate medical conditions, damage property, and have trouble with authorities.

After enough drinks are consumed, the depressant effects of the alcohol take over. Expectation, setting, and the mood of the drinker cease to have a strong influence. Blood pressure is lowered, motor reflexes are slowed, digestion and absorption of nutrients become poor, body heat is lost as blood vessels dilate, and sexual performance is diminished. In fact, every system in the body is strongly affected. Slurred speech, staggering, loss of balance, and lowered alertness are all physical signs of an increased state of intoxication (Figure 5-4).

High-Dose Use: Mental & Emotional Effects

"When a man drinks wine he begins to be better pleased with himself, and the more he drinks the more he is filled full of brave hopes, and conceit of his power, and at last the string of his tongue is loosened, and fancying himself wise, he is brimming over with lawlessness, and has no more fear or respect, and is ready to do or say anything."

Athenian Stranger in *The Laws by Plato,* 360 B.C.

Level of Impairment vs. Blood Alcohol Concentration

.00 Blood Alcohol Concentration

Lowered inhibitions, relaxation
Some loss of muscular coordination
Decreased alertness
Reduced social inhibitions
Impaired ability to drive
Further loss of coordination
Slowed reaction time
Clumsiness, exaggerated emotions
Unsteadiness standing or walking
Hostile behavior
Exaggerated emotions
Slurred speech
Severe intoxication
Inability to walk without help
Confused speech
Incapacitation, loss of feeling
Difficulty in rousing
Life-threatening unconsciousness
Coma
Death from lung and heart failure

.50 Blood Alcohol Concentration

Figure 5-4 •

As consumption increases, the amount of alcohol absorbed increases and therefore the effects increase but at different rates depending on the physical and mental makeup of the drinker.

High-dose alcohol use depresses other functions of the central and peripheral nervous systems. Initial relaxation and lowered inhibitions at low doses often become **mental confusion, mood swings, loss of judgment, and emotional turbulence at higher doses**. At a BAC above 0.12, a drinker may demonstrate **slurred speech** and, beyond that level, **progressive mental confusion** and **loss of emotional control**. Heavy alcohol consumption before sleep, as with light-to-moderate consumption, may also **interfere with the REM, or dreaming sleep**, essential to feeling fully rested. Chronic alcoholics may suffer from fatigue during the day and insomnia at night as well as nightmares, bed wetting, and snoring.

High-Dose Use: Alcohol Poisoning (overdose)

If truly large amounts of alcohol are drunk too quickly, severe alcohol poisoning occurs, with **depression of the central nervous system (CNS) possibly leading to respiratory and cardiac failure, then to unconsciousness (passing out), coma, and death**. Some clinicians use a BAC level of 0.40 as the threshold for alcohol poisoning, although lower levels can be deadly to novice drinkers. When other depressants, including sedative-hypnotics or opiates, are used, the danger is greatly increased because metabolism of alcohol takes precedence over metabolism of other substances thus delaying neutralization and elimination of those other drugs.

Blood alcohol concentration levels of 0.20 or greater, especially in individuals who have low tolerance, can result in severely depressed respiration and vomiting while semiconscious. The vomit can be aspirated or swallowed, blocking air passages to the lungs, resulting in asphyxiation and death. This can also cause infections in the lungs.

"A freshman died from alcohol poisoning during a pledge incident, and we have had two other students die in the past going through their rite of passage of 21 drinks on their twenty-first birthday. I think there's a myth with this age group

that alcohol is so accepted that it is not harmful and that you may get a hangover but you'll wake up in the morning, but that's not always the case."

Shauna Quinn, drug and alcohol counselor, California State University, Chico

High-Dose Use: Blackouts

About one-third of all drinkers report experiencing at least one blackout; the percentage more than doubles for alcohol-dependent individuals (Schuckit, 2000). **During blackouts a person seems to be acting normally and is awake and conscious but afterward cannot recall anything that was said or done.** Sometimes even a small amount of alcohol may trigger a blackout, which is caused by an alcohol-induced electrochemical disruption of the brain. Blackouts are often early indications of alcoholism. They are different from passing out or losing consciousness during a drinking episode. **A drinker can also have only partial recall of events, which is known as a *brownout*.**

A possible indicator of susceptibility to blackouts and brownouts and therefore a marker for alcoholism can be seen on an electroencephalogram (EEG). The marker is a dampening of the P3 or P300 brain wave that affects cognition, decision-making, and processing of short-term memory. **This dampening is found in alcoholics and their young sons** but generally not in individuals without a drinking problem (Begleiter, 1980; Blum, Braverman, Holder, et al., 2000). Other researchers found that auditory-cued P300 amplitude waves are also reduced in alcoholics, particularly in those with anxiety disorders (Enoch, White, Harris, et al., 2001).

"With alcohol I was out of control because I would drink to the point where I didn't know what I was doing, which made it easier for the man to do whatever he wanted and my not realizing it until the next day or the next morning when I woke up and didn't have any recollection of what had happened."

32-year-old female recovering binge drinker

High-Dose Use: Hangovers

The causes of hangovers are not clearly understood. Additives (congeners) in alcoholic beverages are thought to be partly responsible although even pure alcohol can cause a hangover. Irritation of the stomach lining by alcohol may contribute to intestinal symptoms. Low blood sugar, dehydration, and tissue degradation may also play their parts. Symptoms vary according to individuals, but it is evident that the greater the quantity of alcohol consumed, the more severe the aftereffects (Swift & Davidson, 1998).

The effects of **a hangover can be most severe many hours after alcohol has been completely eliminated** from the system. Typical effects include nausea, occasional vomiting, headache, thirst, dizziness, mood disturbances, abbreviated sleep, sensitivity to light and noise, dry mouth, inability to concentrate, and a general depressed feeling (Finnegan, Schulze, Smallwood, et al., 2005). Hangovers can occur with any stage of drinking, from experimentation to addiction. More-severe **withdrawal symptoms usually occur with chronic high-dose users**.

Some research shows that those with a high genetic susceptibility to alcoholism suffer more-severe hangover and withdrawal symptoms and often continue drinking to find relief (NIAAA, 1998; Piasecki, Sher, Slutske, et al., 2005; Span & Earleywine, 1999).

High-Dose Use: Sobering Up

A person can control the amount of alcohol in the blood by controlling the amount drunk and the rate at which it is drunk. But the elimination of alcohol from the system is a constant. The body metabolizes alcohol at the rate of 0.25 oz. to 0.33 oz. of pure alcohol per hour. Until the alcohol has been eliminated and until hormones, enzymes, body fluids, and bodily systems come into equilibrium, hangover symptoms will persist. An analgesic may lessen the headache pain, and fruit juice can help hydrate the body and correct low blood sugar, but neither coffee, nor exercise, nor a cold shower cures a hangover. Feeling better comes only with rest and sufficient recovery time. One danger of using too much acetaminophen (e.g., Tylenol®) to relieve a hangover-induced headache while alcohol is still in the system is the chance of liver damage.

CHRONIC HIGH-DOSE USE

The effects of long-term alcohol abuse not only on physical health but also on neurochemistry and cellular function are more wide-ranging and profound than for most other psychoactive drugs.

"In the past year due to my alcoholism and drug addiction, I have had two overdoses. I have been in 2 North—that is the mental ward of the hospital. I have set myself on fire, passed out with a cigarette in my hand, and have fallen down all over the place, receiving various broken bones. The last time my husband saw me, I was near death."

43-year-old recovering alcoholic

Digestive System & Liver Disease

The main impact of alcohol on the digestive system is caused by its direct effects on organs and tissues. Because roughly 80% of the alcohol drunk passes through the liver and must be metabolized, high-dose and chronic drinking inevitably compromise this crucial organ. When the liver becomes damaged due to **fatty liver, hepatitis, or cirrhosis,** its ability to metabolize alcohol decreases, allowing the alcohol to travel to other organs in its original toxic form. Even persistent moderate drinking can damage the liver. For example, **fatty liver—the accumulation of fatty acids in the liver—can occur after just a few days** of heavy drinking. Abstention will eliminate much of the accumulated fat. About 20% of alcoholics and heavy drinkers develop fatty liver (Mann, Smart, Govoni, et al., 2003).

Unfortunately, as the heavy drinking continues, the problems become more severe. In the United States, approximately **10% to 35% of heavy drinkers develop alcoholic hepatitis and 10% to 15% develop cirrhosis** (Mann, Smart & Govoni, 2003).

"Until I am clean and sober long enough for them to do more testing on me and to do another liver panel, I do not know how much damage has been done."

34-year-old female practicing alcoholic

Alcoholic hepatitis causes inflammation of the liver, areas of fibrosis (formation of scarlike tissue), necrosis (cell death), and damaged membranes. Although alcoholic hepatitis often follows a prolonged bout of heavy drinking, it usually takes months or years of heavy drinking to develop this condition, which is manifested by jaundice, liver enlargement, tenderness, and pain. It is a serious condition that can be arrested only by abstinence from alcohol, and even then the scarring of the liver and the collateral damage remains (Saitz & O'Malley, 1997). (It is important to remember that alcoholic hepatitis is not directly related to hepatitis A, B, or C.) Continued heavy drinking by those with alcoholic hepatitis will lead to cirrhosis in 50% to 80% of the cases (Kinney, 2005).

Cirrhosis occurs when alcohol kills too many liver cells and causes scarring. It is the most advanced form of liver disease caused by drinking and is the leading cause of death among alcoholics. Approximately 12,000 Americans die each year from cirrhosis due to alcohol consumption (Centers for Disease Control & Prevention [CDC], 2006). The damaging effects of alcohol to tissues occur not only because alcohol itself is toxic but also because the metabolic process produces metabolites, such as free radicals and acetaldehyde, that are even more toxic than the alcohol itself (Haber, 2003; Kurose, Higuchi, Kato, et al., 1996). Cirrhosis is even less amenable to treatment and cannot be reversed, although abstinence, diet, and medications can often arrest the progression of the disease.

"I was sick to my stomach and I threw up and little did I know because it was dark that it was blood and I turned on the light and I had a little garbage can there by the bed and the

TABLE 5-4   RATES OF CIRRHOSIS OF THE LIVER IN THE UNITED STATES

Year	Rate of Cirrhosis per 100,000
1911	17.0
1932	8.0 (end of Prohibition)
1973	14.9
2004	9.0 (26,549 deaths)

(Grant, 1985; National Center for Health Statistics, 2005; Saadatmand, Stinson, Grant, et al., 2000)

damn thing filled up. There was an artery in my liver that had just exploded I guess, and they said when that happens it's a gusher. And so after they put me out, they said, 'You've got cirrhosis very bad.' Well they put me on the transplant list. I didn't know it at the time but you have to be sober for a year before they'll even consider transplanting your liver."

65-year-old recovering alcoholic

Over the years liver cirrhosis rates have gone up and down with the rise and fall of alcohol consumption. With the dramatic increase in hepatitis C, however, many more nonalcohol-related cases of cirrhosis will be altering the statistics.

It is estimated that alcoholic cirrhosis is a major contributing factor in about 80% of all cases of cirrhosis in the United States (Nidus Information Services, 2002). The prevalence of cirrhosis in the United States also varies by age, gender, and ethnic group. For example, in one study by the National Institute on Alcohol Abuse and Alcoholism (NIAAA), Hispanic men showed the highest cirrhosis mortality rates followed by Black men, White men, Hispanic women, Black

TABLE 5–5   WORLDWIDE PER-CAPITA USE OF ALCOHOL VS. INCIDENCE OF CHRONIC LIVER DISEASE

| | Alcohol in Liters of Pure Ethanol | | | Cirrhosis Rate per 100,000 | | |
	Total	Beer	Spirits	Wine	Overall Rate	Men	Women
Germany	13.77	8.01	2.50	3.26	15.4	22.6	9.0
France	14.37	2.45	3.01	8.91	12.1	17.8	7.2
Greece	12.54	2.43	4.23	5.88	3.4	5.4	1.6
Spain	11.06	3.86	2.86	4.34	12.2	19.1	6.2
Italy	10.21	1.41	1.06	7.74	13.9	19.6	9.0
Australia	10.57	6.07	1.72	2.78	4.6	7.0	2.4
United Kingdom	10.00	6.34	1.72	1.94	6.4	8.3	4.7
United States	8.91	5.36	2.43	1.12	7.7	10.9	4.8
Japan	5.97	3.21	2.62	0.14	7.2	11.2	3.5
Kazakhstan	7.72	0.47	7.09	0.16	23.9	33.2	16.8
Israel	1.75	0.81	0.42	0.52	4.9	7.3	2.9

(WHO, 2005)

women, and White women. A majority of the Hispanic men were of Mexican ancestry (Singh & Hoyert, 2000). About 2.5 times more men than women of all races die from cirrhosis (mostly because more men drink than women).

The drinking habits of various cultures worldwide have a strong effect on the incidence of cirrhosis. **Heavy-drinking countries such as France and Germany have rates of cirrhosis two to three times higher than the United States** (Table 5-5).

A problem with estimates about drinking rates is that in many countries, particularly poorer ones, large amounts of alcohol production and consumption go unreported. The World Health Organization (WHO) reports that in a country such as Kenya about 80% of alcohol consumption is not officially reported. In the Russian Federation, one-half to four-fifths of the consumption goes unreported, while in Slovenia 50% is unreported (WHO, 2005). In comparing the increase in drinking, the WHO report found that the largest increases in consumption were among developing countries and those in transition, such as former Soviet bloc countries.

Other Digestive Organs

While lower doses of alcohol can aid digestion, moderate-to-higher doses stimulate the production of stomach acid and delay the emptying time of the stomach. **Excessive amounts of alcohol can cause acid stomach and diarrhea.**

"So I was, oh, six hours into my drinking; I was in the bathroom by the toilet all night long. I couldn't leave. Every minute I was throwing up; and when I couldn't throw up, I was dry heaving. And at the end when I wasn't throwing up anymore, I wanted to drink again."

43-year-old female recovering alcoholic

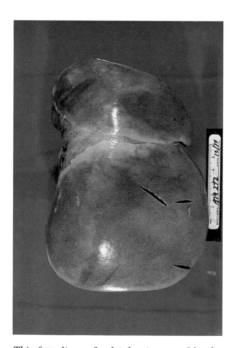

This fatty liver of a drinker is caused by the accumulation of fatty acids. When drinking stops, the fat deposits usually disappear.
Courtesy of Boris Ruebner, M.D.

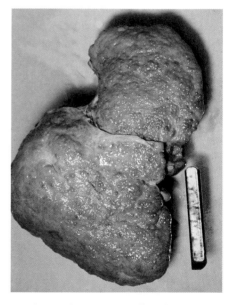

Cirrhosis of the liver usually takes 10 or more years of steady drinking. The toxic effects of alcohol cause scar tissue to replace healthy tissue. This condition remains permanent even when drinking stops.
Courtesy of Boris Ruebner, M.D.

Gastritis (stomach inflammation) is common among heavy drinkers as are inflammation and irritation of the esophagus, small intestine, and pancreas (**pancreatitis**). Inflammation of the pancreas is often caused by blockage of pancreatic ducts and overproduction of digestive enzymes. Other serious disorders, including **ulcers, stomach hemorrhage, gastrointestinal bleeding, and the risk of cancer,** are also linked to heavy drinking.

Pure alcohol contains calories (about 150 per drink) but almost no vitamins, minerals, or proteins. Heavy drinkers receive half their energy but little nutritional value from their drinking. As a result, **alcoholics may suffer from primary malnutrition,** including vitamin B$_1$ deficiency leading to beriberi, heart disease, peripheral nerve degeneration, pellagra, scurvy, and anemia (caused by iron deficiency). In addition, because heavy drinking irritates and inflames the stomach and the intestines, alcoholics may suffer from secondary malnutrition (especially from distilled alcohol drinks) as a result of faulty digestion and absorption of nutrients even if they eat a well-balanced diet.

Another problem with alcohol is its effect on the body's sugar supply. **Alcohol can cause hypoglycemia (too little sugar [glucose]) in drinkers who are not getting sufficient nutrition** and have depleted their own stores of glucose. The liver is kept busy metabolizing the alcohol, so it cannot use other nutrients to manufacture more glucose. Blood sugar levels can drop precipitously, causing symptoms of weakness, tremor, sweating, nervousness, and hunger. If the levels drop too low, coma is possible, particularly for those with liver damage or for diabetics who are insulin dependent. **If there is sufficient nutrition, alcohol use can cause the opposite effect—hyperglycemia (too much sugar)**—in susceptible individuals. This condition is of particular danger to diabetics who have problems controlling their blood sugar in the first place (Kinney, 2005).

Cardiovascular Disease

Though many headlines tout the positive cardiovascular effect of light-

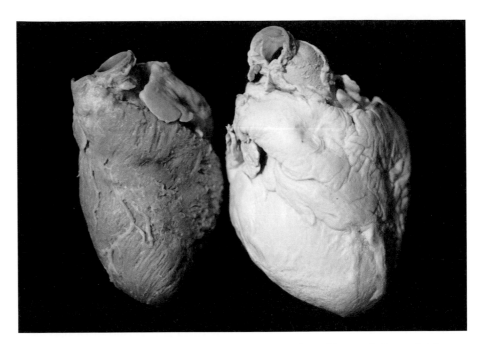

On the left is a normal heart. On the right is a fatty and enlarged heart of a heavy drinker.
© 2000 CNS Productions, Inc.

to-moderate drinking, **chronic heavy drinking is related to a variety of heart diseases, including hypertension (high blood pressure) and cardiac arrhythmias** (abnormal irregular heart rhythms). Heavy drinking increases the risk of hypertension by a factor of 2 or 3 (He, 2001). Coronary diseases occur in alcohol-dependent people at a rate up to six times normal (Schuckit, 2000). One form of irregular heart rhythm is called *holiday heart syndrome* because it appears in patients from Sundays through Tuesdays or around holidays after a large amount of alcohol has been consumed.

Because acetaldehyde, a metabolite of alcohol, damages striated heart muscles directly, **cardiomyopathy—an enlarged, flabby, and inefficient heart**—is found in some chronic heavy drinkers. The heart of a heavy drinker can be twice the size of a normal heart. This condition is also known as *alcoholic heart muscle disease* (*AHMD*). Full-blown AHMD is found in only a small percentage (2%) of heavy drinkers, but the great majority (80%) have some heart muscle abnormalities.

Heavy drinking **increases the risk of stroke** and other intracranial bleeding within 24 hours of a drinking binge

(Brust, 2003). The exact mechanism for many of the cardiovascular problems is not definitely known, but the connection is clear.

Nervous System

Physiologically, alcohol limits the brain's ability to use glucose and oxygen thus killing brain cells as well as inhibiting message transmission. Low-to-moderate use does not seem to cause permanent functional loss, whereas **chronic high-dose use causes direct damage to nerve cells** that can have far-reaching consequences in susceptible individuals. Alcohol-induced malnutrition, not just the direct toxic effects, can also injure brain cells and disrupt brain chemistry.

Both physical brain damage and impaired mental abilities have been linked to advanced alcoholism. Brain atrophy (loss of brain tissue) has been documented in 50% to 100% of alcoholics at autopsy. Breathing and heart rate irregularities caused by damage to the brain's autonomic nervous system have also been traced to brain atrophy. **Dementia (deterioration of intellectual ability, faulty memory, disorientation, and diminished**

problem-solving ability) is a further consequence of prolonged heavy drinking. Abnormalities in the corpus callosum are much greater in older long-term drinkers, aggravating the effects of the alcohol abuse (Pfefferbaum, Adalsteinsson & Sullivan, 2005).

One of the more serious diseases due to brain damage caused by chronic alcoholism and thiamine (vitamin B_1) deficiency is **Wernicke's encephalopathy**, whose symptoms include delirium, imbalance, visual problems, and impaired ability to coordinate movements particularly in the lower extremities (ataxia). The other serious condition that involves thiamine deficiency is **Korsakoff's psychosis**. Its symptoms include disorientation, memory failure, and repetition of false memories (confabulation). Most alcoholics suffering from Wernicke's encephalopathy develop Korsakoff's psychosis (Johnson & Ait-Daoud, 2005; Martin, Singleton & Hiller-Sturmhofel, 2003).

"Exactly what I have is called atrophy of the cerebellum, which is the back part of the brain that goes into your spinal cord that has to do with coordination and balance. My drinking for probably 20 years has caused it to shrink."
Ex-drinker with Wernicke's encephalopathy

Hippocrates wrote about the association between alcohol and seizures/epilepsy more than 2,000 years ago. The prevalence of epilepsy is up to 10 times greater in those with alcoholism (Devantag, Mandich, Zaiotti, et al., 1983). Although the seizures could be caused by head trauma due to drunkenness or other causes, the direct damage to neurological systems as well as the adrenaline storm caused by withdrawal is strongly implicated.

Sexual Desire & the Reproductive System

Female.   Although light drinking lowers inhibitions, prolonged use **decreases desire and the intensity of orgasm**. In one study of female chronic alcoholics, 36% said they had orgasms less than 5% of the time. Chronic alco-

hol abuse can inhibit ovulation, decrease the gonadal mass, delay menstruation, and cause sexual dysfunction (Blume & Zilberman, 2005). Heavy drinking also raises the chances of infertility and spontaneous abortion (Emanuele, Wezeman & Emanuele, 2002).

Male.   Though low-to-moderate levels of alcohol can lower inhibitions and enhance the psychological aspects of sexual activity, the depressant effects soon take over. Chronic use causes effects beyond a temporary inability to perform. Researchers in one study of 66 alcoholics found an erectile dysfunction rate of 71% vs. just 7% for abstainers (Muthusami & Chinnaswamy, 2005). Long-term alcohol abuse **impairs gonadal functions and causes a decrease in testosterone** (male hormone) levels. Decreased testosterone causes an increase in estrogen (a female hormone) that can lead to male breast enlargement, testicular atrophy, low sperm count, loss of body hair, and loss of sexual desire. When resuming sexual activity, a recovering alcoholic may experience excessive anxiety; dysfunction can be intensified by one or two bad performances.

One of the most long-lasting effects of alcohol abuse is an inability to experience normal sexual relationships because, before recovery, romance usually occurred in bars or at parties where alcohol was readily available.

"I don't really remember making love with a woman when I was sober. It was usually when I had a couple of drinks in me or if I was that far gone, then I would probably go with the woman or bring the woman home, and I would go to bed with her, and I would probably fall asleep."
43-year-old recovering alcoholic

Cancer

Breast Cancer.   The association between heavier drinking (three or more drinks per day) and breast cancer is clear. The evidence concerning the correlation between drinking small amounts of alcohol and the incidence of breast cancer is less compelling. In

one study of 1,200 women with breast cancer, there was an association between moderate alcohol use and breast cancer (even amounts as low as one drink per day increased the risk by 50%. In fact, 25% of all breast cancer was associated with even brief use of alcohol (Bowlin, 1997). Other studies, however, have found only small increases in the incidence of breast cancer (Ellison, Zhang, McLennan, et al., 2001; Terry, Zhang, Kabat, et al., 2005; Zhang, Lee, Manson, et al., 2007).

Other Cancers.   The risk of mouth, throat, larynx, and esophageal cancer are 6 times greater for heavy alcohol users, 7 times greater for smokers, and an astonishing **38 times greater for those who smoke and drink alcohol** (Blot, 1992). Liver cancer is also a risk in those with longstanding cirrhosis. Some studies give different rates of cancer in heavy drinkers, but the increase is there in all cases (Bagnardi, Blangiardo, Vecchia, et al., 2001).

Systemic Problems

Musculoskeletal System.   Alcohol leeches minerals from the body, causing a **much greater risk of a fracture** of the femur, wrist, vertebrae, and ribs. The unbalancing of electrolytes by chronic or acute use, along with direct toxic effects, can cause myopathy (painful swollen muscles).

Dermatologic Complications.   The reddish complexion and other skin conditions of chronic alcoholics is caused by a number of factors: the **dilation of blood vessels near the skin**, malnutrition, jaundice, thinning of the skin, and liver problems all add to the alcoholic's appearance. Other infections and conditions potentiated by the toxic effects of alcohol include **acne rosacea, psoriasis, eczema, and facial edema**.

Immune System.   Heavy drinking may disrupt white blood cells and in other ways weaken the immune system, resulting in **greater susceptibility to infections**. Excessive drinking has been linked to cancer as well as such infectious diseases as respiratory infections, tuberculosis, and pneumonia.

Chronic High-Dose Use: Mental/Emotional Effects

With chronic high-dose use, almost **any mental, emotional, or psychiatric symptom is a possibility**, including memory problems, hallucinations, paranoia, severe depression, insomnia, and intense anxiety. These symptoms, particularly amnesia and blackouts, become more common as alcohol abuse progresses. The inability to learn problem-solving techniques that help one cope with life is a long-lasting effect of alcoholism (and most addictions).

"It's like I'm a 30-year-old woman stuck with these 12-year-old issues and I don't know what to do with them, not because I'm not willing or not because I don't have my intellectual mind but it's what is going on inside of my heart and my feelings, not knowing what to do with my feelings and then just pushing it all down."
30-year-old female recovering alcoholic

Alcohol and memory problems go hand-in-hand. Alcohol damages activity in the frontal lobes and the hippocampus, making it difficult to concentrate and get information into the brain. Alcohol also damages the memory centers, so heavy drinkers have trouble retaining information not just getting it into the brain.

MORTALITY

Heavy drinking shortens the alcoholic's life span (e.g., 4 years from alcohol-induced cancer, 4 years from heart disease, and 9 to 22 years from liver disease (NIAAA, 2000; Vaillant, 1995). Overall, **if people continue heavy drinking, they are likely to die 15 years earlier than the general population** (Moos, Brennan & Mertens, 1994).

ADDICTION (alcohol dependence, or alcoholism)

◇ **10% to 12% of the 140 million adult drinkers in the United States have developed alcoholism.**
◇ The incidence of **alcoholism in men is approximately two to three times greater than in women** (14% of male drinkers vs. 6% of female drinkers).
◇ The onset of alcoholism usually occurs at a younger age in men than in women.
◇ In terms of consumption, **20% of drinkers consume 80% of all alcohol** (Greenfield & Rogers, 1999).

CLASSIFICATION

Early Classifications

Over the years there have been many attempts to classify different types of alcoholism. **The purpose of classification is to develop a framework by which an illness or a condition can be studied systematically** rather than relying strictly on experience (Hasin, 2003).

One of the earliest attempts at imposing scientific reasoning on drinking patterns was attempted by **Dr. Benjamin Rush**, physician, medical educator, patriot, reformer, and the first U.S. Surgeon General. He published the first American treatise on alcoholism in 1804—*An Inquiry into the Effects of Ardent Spirits on the Human Body and Mind.* It was a compendium of current attitudes toward alcohol abuse.

At about the same time, **Dr. Thomas Trotter** in *An Essay, Medical, Philosophical and Chemical, on Drunkenness and Its Effects on the Human Body* expounded, in scientific terms, his thesis that drunkenness was a disease produced by a remote cause that disrupts health.

According to scientific literature from the nineteenth and early-twentieth centuries, researchers developed dozens of classifications of alcoholics (e.g., acute, periodic, and chronic oenomania; habitual inebriate; continuous and explosive inebriate; and dipsomaniac, among others).

It wasn't until the 1930s that scientific progress on the study of alcoholism really accelerated with the experiences of the newly created **Alcoholics**

TABLE 5–6   SOME ALCOHOL-RELATED CAUSES OF DEATH

Diseases *(directly caused by alcohol)*	Diseases *(indirectly caused by alcohol)*	Injuries/Adverse Effects *(indirectly caused by alcohol)*
Alcoholic psychoses	Tuberculosis	Boating accidents
Alcoholism (dependence)	Cancer of the lips, mouth, and pharynx	Motor vehicle, bicycle, other road accidents
Alcohol abuse	Cancer of the larynx, esophagus,	Airplane accidents
Nerve degeneration	stomach, and liver	Falls
Heart disease	Diabetes	Fire accidents
Alcoholic gastritis	Hypertension	Drowning
Fatty liver	Stroke	Suicides, self-inflicted injuries
Hepatitis	Pancreatitis	Homicides or shootings
Cirrhosis	Diseases of stomach, esophagus,	Choking on food
Other liver damage	and duodenum	Domestic violence
Alcohol poisoning	Cirrhosis of bile tract	Rapes or date rapes
Seizure activity		

Anonymous and the founding of **Yale's Laboratory of Applied Psychology** (Trice, 1995). Researchers Yandell Henderson, Howard Haggard, Leon Greenberg, and later E. M. Jellinek made the study of alcoholism scientifically respectable, aided by their founding of the *Quarterly Journal of Studies on Alcoholism* and the Yale Center of Alcohol Studies.

E. M. Jellinek

In 1941 psychiatrist Karl Bowman and biometrist E. M. Jellinek presented an integration of 24 classifications of alcoholism that had appeared over the years in scientific literature, reducing alcoholics into four types:

◇ primary or true alcoholics: immediate liking for alcohol and rapid development of an uncontrollable need;

◇ steady endogenous symptomatic drinkers: alcoholism is secondary to a major psychiatric disorder;

◇ intermittent endogenous symptomatic drinkers: periodic binge drinking, again often with a psychiatric disorder; and

◇ stammtisch drinkers: drinkers in whom alcoholism is precipitated by outside causes, often start as social drinkers.

Twenty years later Jellinek, in his landmark book *The Disease Concept of Alcoholism*, proposed five types of alcoholism: alpha, beta, gamma, delta, and epsilon. Gamma and delta alcoholics were considered true alcoholics (Jellinek, 1961).

◇ **Gamma alcoholics** have a high psychological vulnerability but also a high physiological vulnerability; they develop tissue tolerance rapidly, they lose control quickly, and their progression to uncontrolled use is marked.

◇ **Delta alcoholics** have strong sociocultural and economic influences along with a high physiological vulnerability; they also acquire tissue dependence rapidly, and it's hard for them to abstain. Their progression to alcoholism is much slower than that of gamma alcoholics.

(Babor, 1996; Jellinek, 1961)

Modern Classifications

As valuable as Jellinek's classification was, the scientific basis for alcoholism wasn't as clear-cut as with other illnesses and conditions. Four developments starting in the 1950s led to a deeper understanding of alcoholism as a biological phenomenon.

◇ First was the **discovery of the nucleus accumbens**, the area of the brain that gives a surge of pleasure and a desire to repeat the action when stimulated by an experience, by electricity, or by psychoactive drugs (Olds, 1956; Olds & Milner, 1954).

◇ Next was the **discovery of endogenous neurotransmitters**, starting in the 1970s, that showed that drugs worked by influencing existing neurological pathways and receptor sites in the central nervous system, including the reward pathway that researchers had hinted at in the 1950s and 1960s (Goldstein, 2001).

◇ In the 1980s and 1990s, **genetic research tools** developed insights into hereditary influences on addiction; in 1990 the first gene (DRD_2A_1 allele) that seemed to have an influence on vulnerability to alcoholism was discovered (Blum, Braverman, Holder, et al., 2000; Noble, Blum, Montgomery, et al., 1991).

◇ In the 1990s and 2000s, **imaging techniques** visualized the actual reaction of the brain to drugs (Gatley, Volkow, Wang, et al., 2005; Volkow, Wang & Doria, 1995).

These developments moved the classification of alcoholism and addiction away from qualitative classification toward a more quantifiable and empirical basis.

Type I & Type II Alcoholics. These studies were based on an extensive study of Swedish adoptees and their biological or adoptive parents by Dr. C. Robert Cloninger and colleagues. *Type I alcoholism* (also called *milieu-limited*) was defined as a later-onset syndrome that can affect both men and women. It requires the presence of a genetic and environmental predisposition, it can be moderate or severe, and it takes years of drinking to trigger it

(much like Jellinek's delta alcoholic). *Type II alcoholism* (also called *male-limited*) mostly affects sons of male alcoholics, is moderately severe, is primarily genetic, and is only mildly influenced by environmental factors (Bohman, Sigvardson & Cloninger, 1981; Cloninger, Bohman & Sigvardson, 1996).

Type A & Type B Alcoholics. Dr. T. F. Babor and his research colleagues at the University of Connecticut School of Medicine introduced the A/B typologies in 1992. They are similar to Dr. C. Robert Cloninger's type I/II typologies. *Type A*, like type I, is a later onset of alcoholism with less family history of alcoholism and less severe dependence. *Type B*, like type II, refers to a more severe alcoholism with an earlier onset, more-impulsive behavior and conduct problems or disorders, more co-occurring mental disorders, and more-severe dependence (Babor, Dolinsky, Meyer, et al., 1992).

The Disease Concept of Alcoholism

Much of the current research in the treatment of alcoholism is based on the disease concept. The idea of alcoholism as a disease goes back thousands of years but only recently has the concept become widely accepted.

◇ In 1972 the National Council on Alcoholism developed *Criteria for the Diagnosis of Alcoholism, Signs and Symptoms* and defined it as a "chronic progressive disease, incurable but treatable."

◇ In 1980 the American Psychiatric Association (APA) made Substance Use Disorders a separate major diagnostic category in its *Diagnostic and Statistical Manual of Mental Disorders,* also known as *DSM.*

◇ *The Natural History of Alcoholism* published in 1983 by Dr. George Vaillant, professor of psychiatry at Harvard Medical School, was based mostly on a long-term study of two groups of men (college students vs. inner-city young men). His major conclusions were that poverty and pre-existing psychological problems were not predictors of the development of alcoholism. The predictors of alcoholism were much more likely to be a family history of alcoholism and/or an environment with a high rate of alcoholism.

◇ In 1994 remission and substance-induced conditions were defined in *DSM-IV.*

◇ The latest edition of the APA manual, *DSM-IV-TR,* lists *alcohol dependence* and *alcohol abuse* under Alcohol Use Disorders. Under Alcohol-Induced Disorders it lists *alcohol intoxication, alcohol withdrawal, delirium,* and 10 other conditions (American Psychiatric Association, 2000).

Both the World Health Organization and the American Medical Association view alcoholism as a specific disease entity. In 1992 a medical panel from the American Society of Addiction Medicine and the National Council on Alcoholism and Drug Dependence defined alcoholism as follows:

"Alcoholism is a primary chronic disease with genetic, psychosocial, and environmental factors influencing its development and manifestation. The disease is often progressive and fatal. It is characterized by impaired control over drinking, preoccupation with the drug (alcohol), use of alcohol despite adverse consequences, and distortions in thinking, most notably denial. Each of these symptoms may be continuous or periodic." (Morse, Flavin, et al., 1992)

"I don't consider myself an alcoholic. I have five drinks a day—and that's an average. It's always three and sometimes it's a lot more but it's never interfered with my work. I haven't been to the doctor for 15 years. But since it's never interfered with my work, I see nothing wrong with sitting down and having a drink."
47-year-old avowed habitual drinker

HEREDITY, ENVIRONMENT & PSYCHOACTIVE DRUGS

Instead of focusing on typologies, it is useful to look at alcoholism and addiction as continuums of severity that depend, to varying degrees, on genetic predisposition, environmental influences (family, workplace), and the actual use of alcohol and other psychoactive drugs themselves, which can alter the body's neurochemistry and instill an intense vulnerability to craving (*see Chapter 2*).

Heredity

"Women who drink wine excessively give birth to children who drink excessively of wine."
Aristotle, 350 B.C.

As early as the fourth century B.C., the philosopher Aristotle wrote about the tendency of alcohol abuse to run in families, but not until the past 40 years has the scientific basis for this belief been explored.

"I think that there are genes that impact a variety of different characteristics that increase or decrease your risk for alcoholism. We already know the genes related to the alcohol-metabolizing enzymes; some very good laboratories are closing in on some of the genes likely to contribute to disinhibition. Other laboratories are certainly actively searching for genes that might indirectly increase your risk for alcoholism through psychiatric disorders, such as schizophrenia and bipolar disorder. And our group and others are searching for the genes that are contributing to the low response to alcohol, which indirectly increases your risk for alcoholism in a heavy drinking society (Schuckit, Edenberg, Kalmijn, et al., 2001). Obviously there are going to be a whole slew of genes that contribute to the alcoholism risk but altogether they're explaining a very important part of the picture, probably 60% of the risk."
Marc Schuckit, M.D., professor of psychiatry,
University of California Medical School, San Diego, CA

Family studies, twin studies, animal studies, and adoption studies show strong genetic influences particularly in severe alcoholism (Anthenelli & Schuckit, 2003; Blum, Braverman, Holder, et al., 2000; Knop, Goodwin, Teasdale, et al., 1984; Li, Lumeng, McBride, et al., 1986; Lin & Anthenelli, 2005; Woodward, 2003). A study that assessed alcohol-related disorders among 3,516 twins in Virginia concluded that the genetic influence was 48% to 58% of the various influences, a rate much higher than postulated in the past (Prescott & Kendler, 1999).

It is widely theorized that **several genes have an influence on one's susceptibility to alcoholism and other drug addictions**. A person could have one, several, or all of the genes that make someone susceptible to addiction not just a single gene such as the dopamine DRD_2 A_1 allele receptor gene (Blum, Braverman, Holder, et al., 2000) (*see Chapter 2*). The drinker could have a defective $ALDH_2$ gene that encodes aldehyde dehydrogenase, a key liver enzyme that helps metabolize alcohol. The defective gene is more prevalent in Asians. Because the defective gene means less enzyme to rid the body of alcohol, its presence acts as a preventive to alcoholism because the person becomes uncomfortable or ill after even a few drinks. In addition about half of all Japanese, along with some other Asian populations (e.g., Chinese), are born with a more efficient ADH (alcohol dehydrogenase), called *atypical ADH,* and a less efficient form of $ALDH_2$, known as *KM $ALDH_1$.* Thus, when they drink even small amounts of alcohol, the toxic acetaldehyde builds up (up to 10 times the normal amount) and causes a flushing reaction due to vasodilation. Tachycardia and headaches also occur. At higher doses edema (water retention), hypotension, and vomiting ensue (Goedde, Harada & Agarwal, 1979; Teng, 1981; Woodward, 2003; Yokoyama, Yokoyama, Yokoyama, et al., 2005). Though Asians have a higher rate of abstention and a lower rate of alcoholism, Asian Americans' rate of alcoholism is higher, showing that environmental and cultural influences can overcome some biological propensities (Lee, 1987). Other genes being studied include the HT-TLPR, which alters the function of serotonin transporters and seems to affect the stress response, anxiety, and dysphoria—factors that can lead to relapse (Oroszi & Goldman, 2004).

Other markers for a strong genetic influence are a tendency to have blackouts, a greater initial tolerance to alcohol, an impaired decision-making area of the brain, a major shift in personality while drinking, an impaired ability to learn from mistakes, retrograde amnesia, and a low level of response (LR) to alcohol. LR is one of the stronger markers. One study of adolescents (average age 12.9 years) showed that a low level of response correlated with a higher level of drinking even at an early age (Schuckit, Smith, Beltran, et al., 2005).

"When I was younger, I was always surrounded by alcohol and drugs. My mom became an alcoholic, my sister used, and so did my two stepbrothers and stepsister. My stepdad also used to grow [marijuana]. So I was kind of around it a lot."
19-year-old recovering alcoholic

There also seems to be a hereditary link to the physical consequences of alcoholism, especially cirrhosis and alcoholic psychosis (Reed, Pagte, Viken, et al., 1996).

Environment

For other people the environmental factors are the overwhelming influences: child abuse; alcohol- or other drug-abusing parents, friends, and/or relatives; chaotic familial relations; peer pressure; and extreme stress. Easy access to alcohol, a permissive societal view of drinking, unsafe living conditions, poor nutrition, and limited access to healthcare and drug recovery programs are also influential.

"I remember holidays, it being pretty disgusting; my father would be pretty intoxicated. And I remember the Tooth Fairy, the Easter Bunny, and Santa Claus all smelling the same way."
23-year-old recovering alcoholic

Sexual, physical, and emotional abuse at a young age are the most

powerful environmental factors in raising a person's susceptibility to alcohol/drug abuse. In one study of 275 women and 556 men receiving detoxification services, 20% of the men and 50% of the women said that they had been subject to physical or sexual abuse (Brems, Johnson, Neal, et al., 2004). Abuse is also a powerful factor in the development of behavioral addictions.

Alcohol & Other Drugs

Once the genetic and environmental factors have determined susceptibility, the toxic effects of alcohol and other drugs that change neurochemistry come into play.

"After a while it got to the point where I didn't care what it tasted like. I just wanted that buzz to keep going. The brain was craving alcohol. It was the hard liquor and the higher volume of alcohol involved with it, I think. To this day I still like the taste of Jack Daniel's® and I watch myself real close."
32-year-old recovering alcoholic

Often, long after the reasons for seeking the rush or escape have faded, the craving remains. In the end what is important varies with the point of view of the person involved.

◇ To a researcher or scientist, classification and a systematic view of alcoholism are important.

◇ To a psychiatrist, counselor, or social worker, the environmental factors and the neurochemical effects of addiction are important because they lead to strategies to counteract craving and regain control.

◇ To the problem drinker or alcoholic, any help, knowledge, or techniques that will keep them sober up and lessen the craving are important.

"Most alcohol-dependent people or drug-dependent people, when terrible crises occur, they can stop. Their trouble, however, is staying stopped. So when they go back to use, whether

it's the first or the thirtieth time they use, you can bet money that one of those times they won't be able to stop and problems are going to develop dramatically."
Marc Schuckit, M.D., professor of psychiatry, University of California Medical School, San Diego, CA

TOLERANCE, TISSUE DEPENDENCE & WITHDRAWAL

"Exposure of the brain to alcohol initiates a process of adaptation that works to counteract the altered brain function resulting from initial exposure to alcohol. This adaptation or change in brain function is responsible for the processes called 'alcohol tolerance,' 'alcohol dependence,' and 'alcohol withdrawal syndrome.'"
Tenth Special Report to Congress on Alcohol and Alcoholism (NIAAA, 2000)

Tolerance

Tolerance is a process through which the brain defends itself against the effects of alcohol. Dispositional (metabolic) tolerance, pharmacodynamic tolerance, behavioral tolerance, and acute tolerance are four ways the body tries to adapt to the effects of alcohol. The result of tolerance is that the chronic drinker is able to handle larger and larger amounts of alcohol. It also indicates the body's growing dependence (tissue dependence) as it attempts to maintain its normal physiological balance in the face of alcohol's toxic effects. The rate at which tolerance develops varies widely among drinkers.

"Well, I started drinking one beer and then I went on to two. A week later I went on to a six-pack, and then through the years I went on to two six-packs, and then I ended up drinking tequila. I used to drink a fifth of tequila two years after I got addicted to the alcohol."
38-year-old female recovering alcoholic

Dispositional (metabolic) tolerance means the body changes so that it me-

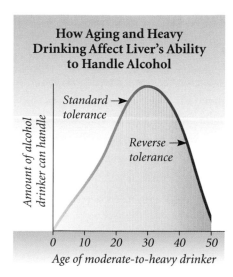

How Aging and Heavy Drinking Affect Liver's Ability to Handle Alcohol

Standard tolerance →

Reverse → tolerance

Amount of alcohol drinker can handle

0 10 20 30 40 50

Age of moderate-to-heavy drinker

Figure 5-5 •
This graph shows the decrease in liver capacity to process alcohol as a person ages. As the liver is taxed and poisoned by the alcohol, its capacity is diminished to the point where an older chronic drinker can get tipsy on just one drink.

tabolizes alcohol more efficiently. As a person drinks over a period of time, the liver adapts to create more enzymes to process the alcohol and its metabolite acetaldehyde (Tabakoff, Cornell & Hoffman, 1992; Woodward, 2003). This accelerated process eliminates alcohol more quickly from the body. It also accelerates the elimination of other prescription drugs, lessening their effectiveness. In addition, because liver cells are being destroyed by drinking and by the natural aging process, **the liver eventually becomes less able to metabolize the alcohol, a process called** *reverse tolerance*. A heavy drinker who could handle a fifth of whiskey at the age of 30 can become totally incapacitated by a two glasses of wine or less at the age of 50.

Pharmacodynamic tolerance means brain neurons and other **cells become more resistant to the effects of alcohol** by increasing the number of receptor sites needed to produce an effect or by creating other cellular changes that make tissues less responsive to alcohol (e.g., GABA becomes less sensitive to ethanol) (Boehm, Valenzuela, Harris, et al., 2005).

Behavioral tolerance means drinkers learn how to "handle their

liquor" by modifying their behavior or by trying to act in such a way that they hope others won't notice they are inebriated. (Vogel-Sprott, Rawana & Webster, 1984).

Acute tolerance also develops from high-dose alcohol use. **This rapid tolerance starts to develop with the first drink** and is the body's method of providing instant protection from the poisonous effects of ethanol.

Select tolerance means that **tolerance does not develop equally to all the effects of alcohol**, so while a person may learn how to walk steadily with a 0.14 BAC, he might have trouble threading a needle.

Withdrawal

"Your body is going through so many changes, you can hardly breathe; you're shaking. A hangover, yeah, you might be sick for a couple of hours. That's different than withdrawals; but with withdrawals, it will kill you."

32-year-old female recovering alcoholic

As mentioned, **hangovers can occur with any level of drinking from experimentation to addiction. More severe withdrawal symptoms occur with chronic high-dose use**.

"I hurt so much when I sobered up that I said, 'the heck with this.' I said, 'If that's going to kill the pain, I'll go back to drinking,' and I really thought about it several times, and it was a war within myself whether to drink or not drink."

65-year-old recovering alcoholic

Although a majority of patients develop significant symptoms of withdrawal when they come in for detoxification and treatment for their alcoholism (Saitz & O'Malley, 1997), **85% to 95% of those experiencing withdrawal will have only the more minor symptoms**, not the life-threatening ones (Schuckit, 1996). The presence of true withdrawal symptoms is one important indication that the drinker has developed a dependence on alcohol.

Night/Morning by Robert Seymour, etched by Shortshanks, c. 1835. Drinkers generally don't distinguish between a hangover and true withdrawal symptoms.
Courtesy of the National Library of Medicine, Bethesda, MD

The alcoholic coming into treatment will often try to explain away what he or she is feeling as a hangover instead of accepting it as true withdrawal.

Various classic experiments have shown that **minor withdrawal symptoms will develop for people who drink heavily for 7 to 34 days whereas major withdrawal symptoms will probably develop after 48 to 87 consecutive days of heavy drinking** (Isbell, Fraser, Wikler, et al., 1955). Many withdrawal symptoms involve the autonomic nervous system.

Minor symptoms of withdrawal include rapid pulse, sweating, increased body temperature, hand tremors, anxiety, depression, insomnia, and nausea or vomiting.

Major symptoms of withdrawal include tachycardia; transient visual, tactile, or auditory hallucinations and illusions; psychomotor agitation; grand mal seizures; and delirium tremens.

"I was very sick—very nauseous, pains in my stomach, headaches, shaking, filled with sheer terror. I've never known fear like that in my life. This has been the hardest thing I've had to do, but the alternative is worse."
34-year-old recovering alcoholic

Because the main symptoms of severe withdrawal can combine with complications, such as malnutrition or liver problems, **medical care for a chronic alcohol abuser must be considered in any course of treatment.**

In less than 1% of serious cases of alcohol withdrawal, full-blown **delirium tremens, called "the DTs,"** occurs. The DTs usually begins 48 to 96 hours after the last drink in a long period of heavy drinking and can last for 3 to 5 sometimes up to 10 days, although some cases have lasted up to 50 days (Mayo-Smith, 2003). The dramatic symptoms can include trembling over the whole body, grand mal seizures, disorientation, insomnia, and delirium, and severe auditory, visual, and tactile hallucinations. The DTs are **a serious condition requiring hospitalization.** Untreated, the mortality rate ranges from 10% to 20%.

Neurotransmitters & Withdrawal.
At first, alcohol increases the effectiveness of GABA, blocking the actions of the brain's energy chemicals and thus making the person drowsy and depressing other body functions. Over time **the brain compensates by creating an excess of energy chemicals and decreasing (down regulating) the number of GABA receptors, resulting in hyperarousal.** During withdrawal the rebound excess of energy chemicals causes anxiety, increased muscular activity, tachycardia, hypertension, and occasionally seizures. The brain becomes less able to control the hyperactivity (Blum & Payne, 1991). Current research also explores the role of serotonin in the alcohol withdrawal process. A 30% reduction in the availability of brainstem serotonin transporters was found in chronic alcoholics, which correlates with their self-reported ratings of depression and anxiety during withdrawal (Gorwood, Lanfumey & Hamon, 2004; Heinz, Ragan, Jones, et al., 1998).

Kindling. With many long-term heavy drinkers, a process called *kindling* occurs: **repeated bouts of drinking and withdrawal actually intensify subsequent withdrawal symptoms and can cause seizures.** The theory is that the repeated presence of alcohol actually alters brain chemistry, impairing the body's natural defenses against damage from alcohol (Becker, 1998). Kindling is also known as *inverse tolerance.*

DIRECTIONS IN RESEARCH

As it becomes more evident that the cause of alcoholism is a combination of heredity, environment, and the toxic effects of alcohol, research has divided itself along those lines.

Research into heredity has focused on identifying the genes that make a user more susceptible to addiction (e.g., DRD_2A_1 allele, $ALDH_2$).

"If you are going to have a way to intervene therapeutically, what you want to know is which are the most important genes and which are the most important proteins and enzymes that are carrying out the mission of those genes because those are the ideal targets for new medications. I can imagine a day in the future when we will be able to sort out the different kinds of alcoholic subjects, and we'll learn that some of them have problems with one transmitter system, others have a problem with a different transmitter system, but the treatment designed for those patients will be designed to meet their specific needs."
Ivan Diamond, M.D., director, Ernest Gallo Clinic and Research Center

Research into environmental causes of alcoholism has focused on **identifying which changes in the addict's surroundings will decrease the use of alcohol and other drugs.** Studies on raising the drinking age, reducing child abuse in the home, limiting sale of alcohol, and lowering stress in everyday life are reported every month in dozens of professional medical and sociological journals worldwide.

Research into drug-caused physiological and psychological changes that occur with chronic and high-dose use also keeps many researchers occupied. Studying the impacts on the immune system, on the development of dispositional and pharmacodynamic tolerance, on the beneficial cardiovascular effects, and on the learning disabilities in drug-affected infants all show promise in developing treatment for alcoholism.

In addition, research into various drugs that could reduce the craving for alcohol is intense. The CB1 receptors, which are sensitive to cannabinoids, have been found to help modulate the reinforcing effects of alcohol and other abused drugs (Thanos, Dimitrakakis, Rice, et al., 2005).

OTHER PROBLEMS WITH ALCOHOL

These issues with alcohol—polydrug abuse, mental problems, alcohol use during pregnancy, aggression and violence, and drunk driving and associated injuries and suicide—can occur at almost any level of use although high-dose chronic use and alcoholism are involved most often.

POLYDRUG ABUSE

Most illicit-drug users also drink alcohol, and most alcohol abusers use other drugs. In one European study of 600 adolescent drug users, 80% used both marijuana and alcohol (Redzic, Licanin & Krosnjar, 2003). In the United States, the figure for alcohol and illicit-drug use among a group in treatment is 96%. Among all heavy drinkers, 32.2% were also current illicit-drug users (SAMHSA, 2006). Some 80% to 95% of alcoholics smoke cigarettes, while 70% are heavy smokers (NIAAA, 1998). The reasons for using alcohol and another drug vary:

◇ Alcohol and tobacco are widely used to facilitate social situations.

◇ Alcohol and marijuana can be used together to rapidly increase relaxation.

◇ Alcohol taken before using cocaine will prolong and intensify the cocaine's effects by creating the metabolite cocaethylene, which also seems to intensify a predisposition to violence.

◇ Alcohol can be used to come down off a three-day methamphetamine run.

◇ Sedative-hypnotics or opioids can be used to get loaded if alcohol is unavailable.

◇ Compulsive gamblers drink while gambling or gamble while drinking.

"I used downers just to come down off the alcohol because I was so shaky. And then I would try using amphetamines just to lift me up so I wouldn't drink so much. But what I would do was stay awake longer and drink more, so that didn't work."

40-year-old recovering polydrug abuser

Polydrug abuse has become so common that treatment centers often have to treat simultaneous addictions. Although the emotional roots of addiction are similar no matter what drug is used, the physiological and psychological changes that each drug causes, particularly during withdrawal, often have to be treated differently. For example, if a client has a serious alcohol and benzodiazepine problem, the clinic has to be extremely careful detoxifying the client because it can't use a benzodiazepine to try to control alcohol withdrawal symptoms.

Although **70% of alcoholics are heavy smokers** (more than one pack a day) compared with 25% of the general population, the converse is not as dramatic: smokers are only slightly more likely to drink alcohol compared with nonsmokers (SAMHSA, 2006). But there is a strong link between alcohol and early use of tobacco. Adolescents who smoke are three times more likely to begin using alcohol (Shiffman & Balabanis, 1995).

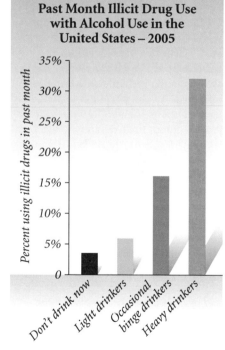

Past Month Illicit Drug Use with Alcohol Use in the United States – 2005

Figure 5-7 •

This chart shows that excessive drinking is associated with the use of other illicit drugs. Whether it's the association with other people who drink and use drugs, the lowering of inhibitions that makes other drug use acceptable, or the desire for stronger and more-intense experiences, the association is quite clear. In terms of percentages, 83% of the illicit-drug use is marijuana and 17% is cocaine.

(SAMHSA, 2006)

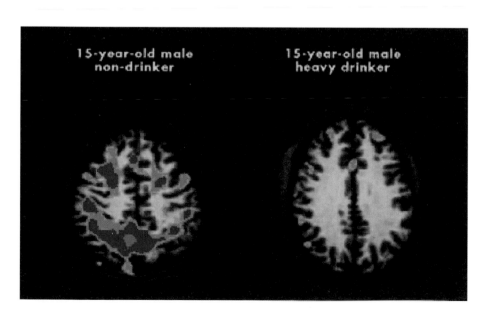

Figure 5-6 •

The brain images show the differences between the brain of a young male nondrinker and that of a heavy drinker. The red and pink show brain activity during a memory task. Brain activity in the young heavy drinker is greatly suppressed, leading to problems in later life. According to one study, 47% of those who begin drinking alcohol before the age of 14 become alcohol dependent at some time in their lives compared with 9% of those who wait until age 21.

Courtesy of Susan Tapert, Ph.D., University of California, San Diego.

ALCOHOL & MENTAL PROBLEMS

Alcohol is most often used to change one's mood or mental state. The mood could be mild anxiety, confusion, boredom, or sadness. The mental state could be symptoms of a pre-existing mental illness such as major depression or a personality disorder (Petrakis, Gonzalez, Rosenheck, et al., 2002). For example, a study of adults with panic disorder showed that the subjects reported significantly less anxiety and fewer panic attacks when drinking. Unfortunately, the use of alcohol to control the symptoms resulted in a higher rate of alcohol-use disorders among those with panic disorder (Kushner, Abrams, Thuras, et al., 2005).

An association has been found between drinking and certain mental illnesses. In a study of alcohol-dependent men and women, 4% also had an independent bipolar disorder-four times the rate for the general public (Schuckit, Tipp, Bucholz, et al., 1997). Whether the relationship is causal or associative, it is the subject of much debate among professionals in the mental health community and those in the chemical dependency treatment community. In the two major studies about dual diagnosis, the **incidence of major depression among those diagnosed with alcohol dependence was about 28% and the incidence of anxiety was 37%,** which is much, much higher than for the general population (5.3% and 16.4%, respectively) (Kessler, Nelson & McGonagle, 1996; Regier, Farmer, Rae, et al., 1990).

"I would pick up some beer to put me out of it. I didn't like the effect that regular psychiatric drugs, such as antidepressants, had on my brain and I'd rather just put myself out with the booze."

Patient with major depression and an alcohol problem

On the other hand, if alcohol is used to excess, **drinking or withdrawal can induce symptoms of mental illness.** For example, a person who uses alcohol to escape sadness might advance to depression though chronic drinking (Miller, Klamen, Hoffman, et al., 1995). In one study de-pressed subjects with a history of alcoholism showed higher lifetime aggression and impulsivity and were more likely to report a history of childhood abuse, suicide attempts, and tobacco smoking (Oquendo, Galfalvy, Grunebaum, et al., 2005). Some of the reasons for mental problems are that heavy drinking disrupts opioid peptides, dopamine, serotonin, and GABA, neurotransmitters that trigger feelings of well-being in the mesolimbic/dopaminergic reward pathway. In addition, **heavy drinking raises the levels of neurochemicals that cause tension and depression** (Koob, 1999). The brain tries to compensate for the depletion of neurotransmitters by releasing corticotropin-releasing factor, a stress chemical that unfortunately can induce depression. Alcohol-induced mental problems, particularly if they are adult onset, will abate as the brain chemistry rebalances itself (Dammann, Wiesbeck & Klapp, 2005).

"The problems did get worse when I was drinking. That was one reason why I never figured out I was a manic-depressive. I figured I was depressed because I was drunk all the time."

Alcoholic with bipolar illness

Any psychiatric diagnosis must always take into account the possibility of drug-induced symptoms, so the professional must often wait weeks or months for the user's brain chemistry and cognition to stabilize before making an accurate diagnosis (Shivani, Goldsmith & Anthenelli, 2002). **The majority of alcoholics who came into the Haight Ashbury Detox Clinic for treatment were initially diagnosed as suffering from depression,** but after treatment and abstinence began (often taking a month or more), the percentage of depressed clients dropped dramatically (from approximately 70% to 30%).

At the other end of the spectrum, a hasty diagnosis of alcohol dependence can attribute all of the erratic behavior to the effects of the drug and miss the psychiatric diagnosis. **The client with co-occurring disorders keeps relapsing because the more serious psychiatric problems have not been ad-dressed.** Experience has shown that if indeed there is a true dual diagnosis, both conditions must be treated to achieve an effective recovery. Some research of bipolar patients with alcoholism found it important to discover which illness came first because those who exhibited the bipolar illness first were slower to recover (Strakowski, DelBello, Fleck, et al., 2005).

These problems are especially confusing with psychiatric diagnoses of antisocial personality disorder (ASPD) and borderline personality disorder (BPD). The symptoms of these two illnesses are very common in those who seek treatment.

The symptoms of high impulsivity, no remorse for causing harm to others, and an inability to learn from mistakes are found in ASPD and among drug abusers (Dom, Hulstijn & Sabbe, 2005). BPD is characterized by intense negative emotions such as depression, self-hatred, anger, and hopelessness, and these individuals often use impulsive maladaptive behaviors such as suicidal actions and substance abuse to deal with their feelings.

To diagnosis borderline personality disorder or antisocial personality disorder, the symptoms should exist outside of the drug-seeking/using behavior and should have existed prior to the drug use. **There is much debate as to the actual incidence of these diseases, particularly BPD,** because its symptoms often shift from moment to moment and can be drug induced. Some treatment personnel refer to the diagnosis of BPD as a "catchall diagnosis" when the real problems aren't clear. Patients who actually have these problems are difficult to treat and consume a disproportionate amount of the staff's time.

One evaluation of public and private inpatient alcohol-abuse programs measured the incidence of ASPD at 15% for male alcoholics and 5% for female alcoholics. Conversely, **80% of those with ASPD develop substance dependence** (Schuckit, 2000; Schuckit, Tipp, Bucholz, et al., 1997). In one older study of alcohol treatment admissions, the incidence of BPD was 13% (Nace, Saxon & Shore, 1983). Among admissions for any drug abuse, the incidence of BPD was 17% (Nace, Saxon, Davis, et al., 1991).

ALCOHOL & PREGNANCY

Maternal Drinking

"When I was pregnant with my daughter Casey, I was drinking between three and four liters of wine daily until I was about eight months and got into the recovery network. And consequently she was born with fetal alcohol effects. She also had a hole in her heart, her digestive system was all messed up, she had projectile vomiting, and she didn't gain any weight for about a month."

24-year-old recovering alcoholic

Alcohol use during pregnancy is the **leading cause of mental retardation in the United States** (May & Gossage, 2001; West & Blake, 2005). Excess drinking during pregnancy also increases the number of miscarriages and infant deaths, causes more problem pregnancies, and gives rise to smaller and weaker newborns (NIAAA, 2000).

A survey of pregnant women in the United States found that:

◇ **12.4% drank some alcohol during several months of pregnancy**;
◇ 4% used in a binge pattern;
◇ 0.7% were heavy drinkers;
◇ 18% smoked cigarettes; and
◇ 4.3% used illicit drugs at least once (SAMHSA, 2005).

"I had been using for years before I got pregnant; and when I got pregnant, I tried to stop but I just couldn't do it. I wanted the drug more than I wanted the baby."

27-year-old recovering alcoholic

Dr. Sarajini Budden, an expert on pregnancy and alcohol at Legacy Emmanuel Children's Hospital in Portland, Oregon, did a survey of the mothers of 293 infants born with fetal alcohol syndrome (FAS) or alcohol-related neurodevelopmental disorder (ARND), both caused by heavy drinking. **During their pregnancies about 89% of the women were using alcohol with at least two other drugs**, and 49% were

The rate of alcoholism in Russia is extremely high as is the incidence of fetal alcohol syndrome. These two children at an orphanage outside of Yelisovo in Kamchatka, Russia, have FAS, identified by the facial anomalies. In a few areas of Russia, the rate of fetal alcohol syndrome disorder (FASD), which includes fetal alcohol syndrome and other less severe alcohol-induced disorders, is more than 50% of all births—an incredibly high percentage.
Courtesy of Douglas G. Smith, O.D., optometric physician, Medford, OR

using just two drugs, usually alcohol and cocaine. Interestingly, all of them were smoking, so nicotine was included as one of the toxins. Most were single moms, most were school dropouts, most had been or were being physically or sexually abused, and often there was a history of alcohol or drug abuse in the family. There is also a suspicion that a number of the mothers had learning problems in school and possibly were alcohol or drug affected themselves.

Through the University of Washington in Seattle, two groups of children with FAS were studied. By the time the first group was five years old, 38% of the biological mothers had died as a direct result of their alcoholism. By the time the second group was in early adolescence, 69% of the biological mothers died as a direct result of their alcoholism.

Fetal Alcohol Syndrome (FAS), Alcohol-Related Neurodevelopmental Disorder (ARND) & Alcohol-Related Birth Defects (ARBD)

"He was very inconsolable. He would take 10 cc of feed; he wouldn't sleep. He

slept for maybe 15, 20 minutes at a time, 24 hours a day. That's what we went through, and it was like that for a couple of years. He was a very hard baby to parent, but we loved him."

Foster mother of child with FAS

Certain specific toxic effects of alcohol on a developing fetus are known as **fetal alcohol syndrome (FAS)**, a term coined in 1973 although the diagnosis was first written about in France in 1968 (Jones & Smith, 1973). Initially, it was thought that the defects were the result of malnutrition, but the **toxicity of alcohol was eventually recognized as the cause**. The symptoms can range from obvious gross physical defects to mental deficits to behavioral problems (Sood, Delaney-Black, Covington, et al., 2001). Not all women who drink heavily during pregnancy bear children with FAS.

In 1996 the Institute of Medicine of the National Academy of Sciences reclassified the effects of prenatal alcohol exposure into five categories. Three categories refer to the facial features and two categories are for alcohol-affected infants without the specific facial features. The last two categories are **alcohol-related neurodevelopmental disorder (ARND)**, marked by CNS abnormalities, and **alcohol-related birth defects (ARBD)**, marked by any number of physical anomalies (Stratton, Howe & Battaglia, 1996). ARND and ARBD used to be referred to as *FAE* (fetal alcohol effects) or *PFAE* (possible fetal alcohol effects), but the complexity of the diagnosis made it necessary to expand the definitions. Because of the wide range of symptoms, the term **fetal alcohol spectrum disorder (FASD)** is used to refer to this whole range of effects caused by prenatal exposure to alcohol.

There is as yet no definitive test for confirming FAS at birth, and only the most severe cases are diagnosable at that time. The minimal standards for a diagnosis of FAS are:

◇ **retarded growth** before and after birth, including height, weight, head circumference, brain growth, and brain size;

◇ **facial deformities**, including shortened eye openings, thin upper lip, flattened midface, and missing groove (filtrum) in the upper lip;

◇ occasional **problems with the heart and the limbs**; and

◇ **central nervous system involvement**, such as delayed intellectual development, neurological abnormalities, behavioral problems, visual problems, hearing loss, and balance or gait problems (Sokol & Clarren, 1989).

In tests of 178 individuals with **FAS, IQ test scores ranged from 20 to 120 with a mean of 79**; in 295 individuals who were FAE, PFAE, or ARND, IQ scores ranged from 49 to 142 with a mean score of 90 (Streissguth, Barr, Kogn, et al., 1996). (Mental retardation is defined as an IQ of less than 70.)

Alcohol kills cells and changes the wiring of the fetus's brain. Huge gaps during brain development destroy natural connections that can never be regained. For example, SPECT scans in a Finnish study found smaller brain volume in a group of FAS and FAE children as well as abnormalities in serotonin and dopamine functioning (Riikonen, Nokelainen, Valkonen, et al., 2005).

Other specific problems associated with FAS as well as ARND in terms of a neurocognitive profile include:

◇ **difficulty with short-term memory,**

◇ **problems storing and retrieving information,**

◇ impaired ability to form links and make associations,

◇ difficulty making good judgments and forming relationships,

◇ problems controlling temper and aggression,

◇ oversensitivity to such stimuli as a bright light, loud sound, sharp smell, or certain kinds of textures or tastes.

"Our other son has some of the characteristics like the filtrum, but from every other aspect of it he looks normal. But his IQ is low, yet he comes across as being very smart. He has severe behavioral issues."
Mother of adopted children with FAS or FAE

These cognitive/behavioral deficits are not unique to alcohol exposure. Many other substances and physiological problems can cause similar conditions in children. For that reason a diagnosis of FASD is often missed in the absence of those unique facial features. Many of the symptoms are not obvious until several years after birth.

"What you're seeing at birth is a disorder of the brain's ability to regulate itself and its emotions; later on, especially in the toddler and preschool years, what you're seeing are problems with sleep and behavior; they're sitting and playing and they're pretty happy and then suddenly out of the blue they become aggressive. They throw temper tantrums, and you really don't know what's going on. But that's the up-and-down emotional instability that these children demonstrate."
Sarajini Budden, M.D., FAS specialist, Legacy Emmanuel Children's Hospital, Portland, OR

Recently, researchers have found that early diagnosis of FASD in newborns plus a supportive environment can give the children a chance at a better, functional life (Streissguth, Bookstein, Barr, et al., 2004).

Worldwide studies estimate that **FAS births occur in anywhere from 0.33 to 2.9 cases per 1,000 live births**. The incidence can vary greatly (e.g., the rate in one survey in South Africa where alcoholism is rampant was 40 cases per 1,000). The worldwide incidence of ARBD and ARND (which are difficult to diagnose) is probably five to 10 times greater than the incidence of FAS and FAE (Hans, 1998; May, 1996; Pagliaro & Pagliaro, 2003).

In the United States, FAS rates of 0.2 to 1.5 per 1,000 are the accepted figures. African Americans have about 6 FAS births per 1,000; Asians, Hispanics, and Whites have 1 to 2; and American Indians have about 30, although rates from 10 to 120 per 1,000 have been reported in various specific American Indian and Canadian Indian communities (May, Brooke, Gossage, et al., 2000). In the United States, the incidence of ARND and ARBD is three times the incidence of FAS (CDC, 2004).

Critical Period. Because the brain is among the first organs to develop and the last to finish, it appears to be vulnerable throughout pregnancy, although **weeks 3 through 8, at the onset of embryogenesis (formation of the embryo), are crucial**. For example, the corpus callosum, a crucial structure that connects the cerebral hemispheres, is extremely vulnerable to alcohol use during the sixth to eighth gestational weeks; damage to the basal ganglia affects fine motor coordination and cognitive ability (Rosenberg, 1996). Generally:

◇ during the first trimester, alcohol interferes with the migration and the organization of brain cells;

◇ in the second trimester, especially the tenth to twentieth weeks, facial features are greatly affected;

◇ during the third trimester, the hippocampus is strongly affected, which leads to difficulties encoding visual and auditory information

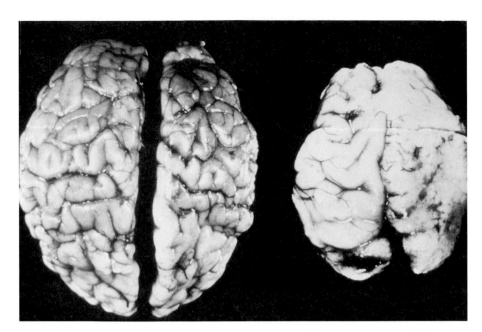

The greatest danger of alcohol use by a pregnant woman is fetal brain damage. The larger brain on the left is the normal brain of a human newborn (who died in an accident). The smaller brain on the right is of a child born with FAS. The FAS brain is obviously small and malformed. Further, more subtle damage can be missed on a brain scan, however, particularly if behavioral and physical manifestations of the damage are not obvious.
Courtesy of Sterling K. Clarren, M.D., Children's Hospital, Seattle, WA

(Coles, 1994; Goodlett & Johnson, 1999; Miller, 1995; Streissguth, 1997).

Critical Dose.   Animal models suggest that peak blood alcohol concentration rather than the total amount of alcohol drunk determines the critical level above which adverse effects are seen. A pattern of rapid drinking and the resulting high BAC seems to be the most dangerous style of drinking.

How many drinks are safe during pregnancy? One study concludes that **seven standard drinks per week by pregnant mothers are a threshold level below which most neurobehavioral effects are not seen.** This might lead some healthcare professionals to feel that they need not recommend total abstinence. Seven drinks per week are an average, however, and if a pregnant woman consumes a large number of those drinks in one sitting, the fetus may be much more at risk.

"I think the message really is that if you know you're pregnant, don't drink because you don't know whether an ounce is going to cause a problem or whether 12 ounces is going to cause a problem because it may have a different effect on people."
Sarajini Budden, M.D., FAS specialist, Legacy Emmanuel Children's Hospital, Portland, OR

A recent study in rats showed that when the developing brain is creating neurons and neuronal connections at a furious pace, even one high-dose use episode of drinking will also kill brain cells at a furious pace. The experiment showed that normally 1.5% of brain cells die during a certain period in a rat's growth; but in rats exposed to alcohol during that critical period, 5% to 30% of neurons died. When extrapolating these results to humans, the blood alcohol concentration would be 0.20, about twice the legal allowable limit for drivers, and the crucial period would be six months into the pregnancy until the baby is born. During the brain growth spurt, **a single prolonged contact with alcohol lasting four hours or more is enough to kill vast numbers of brain cells** (Ikonomidou, Bittigau, Ishimaru, et al., 2000).

The U.S. Surgeon General advises that women should not drink at all while pregnant because **there is no way to determine which babies might be at risk from even very low levels of alcohol exposure** (Hans, 1998; Maier & West, 2001; NIAAA, 1997).

"I think like anybody who has a child with FAS or FAE, we have a tendency to take a closer look at people who are not acting quite right. The behaviors are a little bit different, and you start to wonder if there isn't some alcohol in their past."
Foster father of 13-year-old with FAS

Paternal Drinking

"For children whose fathers have chanced to beget them in drunkenness are wont to be fond of wine, and to be given to excessive drinking."
Plutarch, Moralia: The Education of Children, A.D. 110

As noted in Chapter 2, genetic transmission of alcoholism by fathers is strongly suspected. There is now evidence that some of the **detrimental effects of alcohol on the fetus may also be transmitted by paternal alcohol consumption.** Researchers are unable to say definitively whether paternal exposure to alcohol results in FAS or in some other damage. In laboratory tests alcoholic-sired rats of nonalcohol-using mothers produced male offspring with disturbed hormonal functions and spatial learning impairments. Adolescent male rats subjected to high alcohol intake produced both male and female offspring suffering from abnormal development, including decreased body weight (Bielawski, Zaher, Svinarich, et al., 2002).

Observations of male children of alcoholic fathers indicate no gross physical deficits but do show an association with intellectual and functional deficits in these offspring. In addition to the deficits in verbal, thinking, and planning skills, sons of male alcoholics exhibit further deficiencies in visual/spatial skills, motor skills, memory, and learning (NIAAA, 2000).

Some explanations of the causes of these abnormalities suggest that alcohol may mutate genes in sperm, kill off certain kinds of sperm, or biochemically and nutritionally alter semen and influence sperm (Little & Sing, 1986).

AGGRESSION & VIOLENCE

In a situation involving violence, there are usually **three people involved: the victim, the perpetrator, and one or more bystanders.** The victim can be the recipient of physical or sexual assault (by a spouse or parent). The perpetrator can be of any age; the common denominator being anger often with alcohol thrown into the mix. Most often the bystanders are children who witness violence in their homes or neighborhoods.

"I've always just been an angry child, growing up with a lot of anger that's been stuffed. And then it's like on the fifth drink I'm a party girl, but on the seventh drink I'd kick in your car door, you know. I'd just totally change to that Dr. Jekyll and Mr. Hyde syndrome. There's no end to my anger when I drink. Mine comes from a lot of past abuse as a kid and it comes from just not fitting in."
28-year-old female recovering alcoholic

Most research suggests that a tendency to violence already resides in some people and is due to a combination of factors (heredity, environment, and alcohol or other drugs) working together to biochemically and emotionally put them at risk (Hines & Saudino, 2005; Koenen, 2005; Stoff & Cairns, 2005).

"He was a pretty mean guy when he wasn't drunk when I think about it, so it is really hard for me to tell. But I know that when people are addicted and are alcoholics, they can be dry drunks, which makes them just as mean when they're not using as when they are."
38-year-old victim of domestic violence

Among many neurochemical effects, alcohol has been shown to increase aggression by **interfering with GABA (the main inhibitory neurotransmitter) in ways that provoke intoxicated people with pre-existing aggressive tendencies**. In addition, alcohol decreases the action and the levels of serotonin thus lowering impulse control (Javors, Tiouririne & Prihoda, 2000; Miczek, Fish, Almeida, et al., 2004). Lowered impulse control can cause drinkers to act out their aggressive impulses but also makes them less able to stop drinking once they have started (Gustafson, 1994).

"On a typical Friday night, at least 50% of our calls will be some kind of alcohol and drug violent behavior situation whether it be a shooting, a stabbing, or a beating. A lot of those involve significant others, a spouse, or cohabitants."
Emergency medical technician, San Francisco Fire Department

Even the expectation that alcohol will make one braver can lead people to be more aggressive—even if they are drinking a nonalcoholic beverage that they believe contains alcohol (Bushman, 1997; Higley, 2001). Drinking can impair information processing, leading a drinker to misjudge social cues, thereby overreacting to a neutral, "Hello, how are you?" from the opposite sex. Misjudging intentions can also cause a person to perceive a threat where none exists, leading to a violent overreaction (Miczek, Fish, de Almeida, et al., 2004).

Based on victim reports, 15% of robberies, 26% of aggravated assaults, and 50% of all homicides involved alcohol use. **About 30% of the victims of violent crime reported that the offender had been drinking alcohol at the time of the offense.** Not only had the offenders been drinking but their blood alcohol concentrations were two or three times the drunk-driving threshold: levels of 0.18 for probationers, 0.20 for local jail inmates, and an incredible 0.28 for state prisoners at the time of their offenses. In domestic-violence situations, the association is particularly important—alcohol is involved at least three-fourths of the time

(Bureau of Justice Statistics, 1998 & 2006; NIAAA, 2000; Roizen, 1997).

In a study in Memphis, Tennessee, that examined police calls for domestic violence in that city, 92% of the perpetrators had used alcohol and 67% had used cocaine on the day of the assault. Almost half of the perpetrators had been loaded on alcohol and/or cocaine often during the past 30 days. Other studies (Figure 5-7) showed similar results.

"The use of alcohol would really bring out the hit man in me. I mean, I could talk to my partner or whoever fairly good if I was sober, but after I started drinking the deep emotions really would come out."
28-year-old male in an anger management class

Alcohol encourages the release of pent-up anger, hatred, and desires discouraged by society, especially in people prone to violence. Alcohol can also undermine moral judgment and reasoning; so when someone drinks, the common sense that would keep that person out of trouble is often suppressed (Collins & Messerschmidt, 1993).

"Seems like alcohol is always referred to as this 'liquid courage,' you know? And I guess it depends where you're at: courage to do what? Courage to ask a girl on a date that you hadn't had the courage to do before, or courage to dance like a fool on the floor, or is it courage to beat your wife or beat your girlfriend 'cause you didn't have the guts to do it before?"
College peer counselor

There are three major kinds of interpersonal violence, and one can escalate into another: **emotional violence, physical violence, and sexual violence**. The most common form of violence as well as the most underreported is emotional violence, which includes verbal abuse often caused by alcohol's freeing effect on the tongue.

"If you talk about someone being emotionally violated, who goes to jail

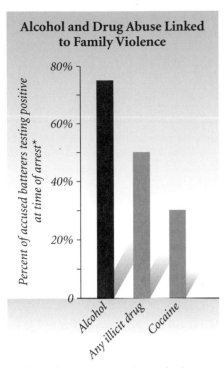

Alcohol and Drug Abuse Linked to Family Violence

Percent of accused batterers testing positive at time of arrest*

*Figures do not total 100% since many abusers take more than one substance.

Figure 5-8 •
Three out of four of those arrested for family violence tested positive for alcohol. Half had used some illicit drug, and more than one in four tested positive for cocaine.
The National Research Council

for that? You don't have any bruises that you can see, but there are scars there."
36-year-old ex-wife of an alcoholic

Any type of violence can cause permanent biochemical changes in the victim that can make them more susceptible to drug abuse and other emotional problems. Magnetic resonance imaging (MRI) studies in 1997 at Yale and Harvard Universities showed that severely abused children had permanent changes to the brain. These changes often led to more behavioral problems, including hyperactivity, impulsive behavior, increased aggression, exaggerated fears and nightmares, trouble keeping a job, and difficulty with relationships. The studies showed that the changes could also be caused by severe emotional abuse.

"It doesn't matter if alcohol was involved in the situation. He raped me. There's more attention paid to the fact that there was alcohol involved than the fact that a woman was assaulted and that her life changed and that all of these things happened as a result of that. Alcohol's involved in almost every social situation, but it doesn't mean that we recognize it or validate it."
22-year-old female college senior (rape victim)

Depending on the study, **34% to 74% of sexual-assault perpetrators had been drinking as had 30% to 79% of the victims**. In most cases the perpetrator and the victim are drinking simultaneously; rarely is the victim drinking alone (Abbey, Zawacki, Buck, et al., 2001).

DRIVING UNDER THE INFLUENCE

"An officer can pull up to a traffic light, and the person is staring straight ahead and their face is up against the windshield of the car. Those are all indicators that the person might be under the influence of intoxicants. The people whom we arrest try to stall as much as they can. They'll ask for a lawyer, they'll ask all kinds of questions, they'll try to let enough time go by. But it's been our experience that it doesn't help. The alcohol's gonna be in their system."
Lt. Rich Walsh, Ashland, OR, Police Department

Approximately 40% of motor vehicle fatalities (16,885) in 2005 involved alcohol use. About 90% of those involved had a BAC of 0.08 or higher (legally drunk). Another 275,000 persons were injured in crashes where alcohol was present. Over the past 10 years, however, there has actually been an 18% drop in the rate of fatalities. In addition, of the 3 million traffic-related accidents, 1 million were alcohol related (Hingson & Winter, 2003; National

Highway Traffic Safety Administration [NHTSA], 2005 & 2006). According to the National Highway Traffic Safety Administration (NHTSA):

◇ more than 1 in 4 drivers gets behind the wheel within two hours of drinking;

◇ on any weekday night between 10 p.m. and 1 a.m., 1 in 13 drivers is legally drunk; on weekend mornings between 1 and 6 a.m., 1 in 7 drivers is drunk (Miller, Lestina & Spicer, 1996);

◇ **of those convicted of DUI, 61% drank beer only**, 2% drank wine only, 18% drank liquor only, and 20% drank more than one type of alcoholic beverage; and

◇ **alcohol-related crashes cost an estimated $148 billion in the United States every year** (NHTSA, 2005, NIAAA, 2000).

Because alcohol is a depressant, susceptibility to traffic accidents and fatalities is usually directly related to the blood alcohol level: coordination is decreased, and judgment is impaired. **Some skills are impaired at even a 0.02 BAC,** such as the ability to divide attention between two or more visual inputs. At a 0.05 BAC, eye movement, glare resistance, visual perception, and reaction time are affected (Moskowitz, Burns, Fiorentino, et al., 2000; Moskowitz & Fiorentino, 2000). Impairment for other forms of transportation also begins at relatively low BAC levels. Flight simulators show impaired pilot performance at 0.04 BAC and for up to 14 hours after reaching BACs between 0.10 and 0.12 (Yesavage & Leirer, 1986).

"A number of years ago, I did a test in which I brought a number of individuals down to the police department; I had them drink various amounts of alcohol and then drive a short obstacle course. Some were social drinkers and some didn't drink at all except on very rare occasions. What I found was this:

◇ *One of the social drinkers felt he did the driving test fairly well and that he felt 'absolutely fine to*

TABLE 5–7	BAC VS. CHANCES OF BEING KILLED IN A SINGLE-VEHICLE CRASH	
Blood Alcohol Concentration	**Chances of Being Killed**	
0.02-0.04	1.4 times normal	
0.05-0.09	11.0 times normal	
0.10-0.14	48.0 times normal	
0.15 and above	380.0 times normal	

(Zador, 1991)

TABLE 5–8	PERMISSIBLE BAC LIMITS IN OTHER COUNTRIES
Country	**Permissible BAC**
United States	0.08
CAustria, Canada, Germany, Switzerland, United Kingdom	0.08
Australia	0.05-0.08
Belgium, Finland, France, Israel, Netherlands	0.05
Japan	0.03
Poland, Sweden	0.02

drive.' I told him I would have arrested him for driving under the influence. When I put him on the Breathalyzer machine, his was the highest blood alcohol of everybody there. This overconfidence in drinkers is fairly common.

◇ *The people who didn't drink very often and actually had much less to drink than this individual were saying when they took the driving test, 'There's no way in the world that I'd drive.' Their Breathalyzer results were way under the limit."*

Traffic Safety Officer, Ashland, OR, Police Department

The laws in the United States do not make exceptions. **When the BAC is over the legal limit of 0.08, the officer does not have to prove that the person is impaired; the driver is guilty per se.** Usually, though, an officer will first observe the driver for telltale signs; the officer will then pull the driver over and test coordination and physical abilities for physical or mental impairment before requiring a breath or blood test. One of the most effective tests given on the spot is the eye nystagmus test.

"For some reason alcohol affects the eyeballs, and the eyeball will start jerking if it tries to follow a moving finger or object. It's amazing: you can watch people's eyes just twitching away when they're under the

influence. They can't follow the finger to the side; they're turning their whole head back and forth."

Lt. Rich Walsh, Ashland, OR, Police Department

Among those arrested for DUI, two-thirds have never been arrested before, so laws and programs have to be aimed at all segments of the population. In fact, a majority of drivers in fatal alcohol-related crashes did not have a DUI conviction on their record, and many did not have a history of problem drinking (Baker, Braver, Chen, et al., 2002; NHTSA, 2006). More important, **only one driver is arrested for every 300 to 1,000 drunk-driving trips,** so effective enforcement can be a daunting task (Voas, Wells, Lestina, et al., 1997).

Quite a few **prevention strategies** have reduced the number of alcohol-related traffic fatalities and injuries over the years:

◇ lowering the BAC limit from 0.10 to 0.08;

◇ imposing administrative license revocation in which a police officer or other official can immediately confiscate the license of a driver whose BAC exceeds the legal limit;

◇ increasing the minimum legal drinking age to 21 years;

◇ having zero-tolerance laws for drivers under 21 (i.e., prohibiting driving with any alcohol or a minimum of alcohol in the system [0.01 or 0.02 BAC for drivers under 21]); these laws have reduced alcohol-related crashes involving youth by 17% to 50%;

◇ impounding or towing vehicles of drunk drivers;

◇ requiring mandatory treatment for DUI arrestees; and

◇ training alcohol servers and mandating sanctions and liability; legally servers have to stop serving drinkers who seem intoxicated.

There is no single prevention strategy that is most effective. The best results seem to occur with communitywide efforts when a combination of the above suggestions, along with media campaigns, police training, high school and college prevention programs, and better control of liquor sales, are implemented.

Injuries & Suicide

"I was medicating myself, covering it up. I would take a sports bottle of wine with me to work in the morning, and I was operating heavy machinery. I would go home for lunch, refill it, and come back and drive a forklift and operate this thing with spinning blades—and it's just insanity."

40-year-old female recovering alcoholic

Medical examiner reports indicate that alcohol dramatically increases the risk of injury:

◇ Emergency room studies confirm that **15% to 25% of emergency patients tested positive for alcohol** or reported alcohol use, with relatively high rates among those involved in fights, assaults, and falls.

◇ Alcoholics are 16 times more likely to die in falls and 10 times more likely to become burn or fire victims.

◇ The U.S. Coast Guard reported that **31% of boating fatalities had a BAC of 0.10 or more.**

◇ In the workplace up to **40% of industrial fatalities** and 47% of injuries involved alcohol.

(Bernstein & Mahoney, 1989; National Clearinghouse on Alcohol and Drug Information [NCADI], 2006; SAMHSA, 2005)

"Putting a guy in the ground did nothing for our feeling indestructible, you know, kids that we were. That age of, 'God, we're young and strong and there's nothing we can't do. There are no consequences to this behavior.' And even seeing it, going to the funeral, watching the hearse drive by, it was like, 'Duh, didn't make the connection.'"

40-year-old recovering alcoholic, concerning a friend who died while driving drunk

Among adult alcoholics, suicide rates are twice as high as for the general population and even greater than the non-mentally ill population; rates also increase with age. One reason for the increase in suicide with age is that the longer the alcoholism, the greater the social, health, and interpersonal problems. The alcoholic suicide victim is typically White, middle-aged, male, and unmarried with a long history of drinking. Additional risk factors for suicide include depression, loss of job, living alone, poor social support, and other illnesses.

"I just didn't want to live. I mean, my family and people that I love so much, I feel like they hated to see me coming, and it's something that I wouldn't wish on anybody to go through. I was drinking on a day-to-day basis, just drinking—and then I wound up at the hospital. I had tried to commit suicide, and they put me in the psych ward."

38-year-old female recovering alcoholic

EPIDEMIOLOGY

PATTERNS OF ALCOHOL CONSUMPTION

It is difficult to get accurate, comparable, and consistent alcohol use data in other countries, but as Table 5-5 (earlier in this chapter) points out, most European countries have higher per-capita alcohol consumption rates than the United States while most Asian countries have lower per-capita consumption. These differences result from a combination of physiological, cultural, social, religious, and legal factors.

Culture is one of the main determinants of how a person drinks (Health-EU, 2006). Different drinking patterns are found in the so-called *wet* and *dry* drinking cultures in Europe and North America (although some recent research suggests that the distinctions aren't as clear-cut as they were once thought to be).

Wet drinking cultures (e.g., Austria, Belgium, France, Italy, and Switzerland) sanction daily or almost daily use and **integrate social drinking into everyday life**. In France children are served watered-down wine at the dinner table (Vaillant, 1995). Wet cultures consume more wine and beer— five times the amount of wine drunk in dry cultures.

Dry drinking cultures (e.g., Denmark, Finland, Norway, and Sweden) **restrict the availability of alcohol** and tax it more heavily. Dry cultures consume more distilled spirits— almost 1.5 times the amount in wet cultures—and are characterized by binge-style drinking, particularly by males on weekends.

Canada, England, Germany, Ireland, the United States, and Wales exhibit combinations of both wet and dry cultures. In such **mixed drinking cultures**, patterns such as binge drinking in social situations are common. A relatively higher incidence of violence against women is found in mixed drinking cultures than in dry or wet cultures, probably because binge drinking often occurs in social situations.

Chinese families generally don't drink much, often because of cultural pressures. In Japan and South Korea,

however, social pressures to drink are very strong. **In Japan most of the men and half of the women drink**, yet their alcoholism rate is half of that in the United States.

In Russia vodka is traditionally drunk in large quantities between meals. Vodka is the preferred drink because 500 years previously Czar Ivan the Terrible forcibly replaced the sale of beer and mead with state-controlled vodka, served in state-run taverns. Alcoholism became so rampant in Russia over the centuries that in 1985 Premier Mikhail Gorbachev severely restricted the availability of alcohol almost to the point of prohibition. The number of illegal stills and the consumption of anything with alcohol in it, such as shoe polish and insecticides, soared. In one year, despite prohibition, 11,000 Russians died of alcohol and alcohol-related poisonings. When many of the restrictions were lifted, the number of alcohol-poisoning deaths is reported to have soared to 40,000. When the restrictions had been in place, Russian male life expectancy started to increase. Once the restrictions were lifted, male life expectancy dropped six years. Drinking on the job is one of the major consequences of the easy availability of alcohol and a culture that has few recovery programs (Badkhen, 2003; Bobak, 1999; Courtwright, 2001; Davis, 1994; Segal, 1990).

In England recently about half the country's 60,000 pubs curbed the promotion of happy hours and removed the 11 p.m. closing hour, which had encouraged binge drinking and expelled thousands of drunks onto the streets at one time. These are strong changes for a country with a tradition of warm beer and darts at the local pub. About **70% of Britons drink regularly**, with two-thirds of the alcohol consumption in beer. In a recent campaign to stem alcoholism, Britons were urged to reduce their average daily consumption to just three drinks a day.

In the United States, much drinking is done in social settings away from lunch and dinner tables. In a land of many different cultures and lifestyles, there is a wide variety of culturally influenced drinking customs. The 18-to-25 age group is the most likely to binge drink (SAMHSA, 2006).

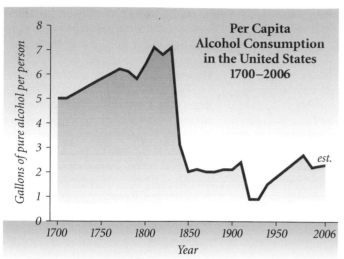

Figure 5-9 •
In the United States, the per-capita consumption of pure alcohol at present is 2.2 gallons, but, as this chart shows, the rate has varied wildly with the rise and fall of prohibition movements, health concerns, and availability of a good water supply.
Adapted from David F. Musto's "Alcohol in American History," *Scientific American,* April 1996 (SAMHSA, 2006)

POPULATION SUBGROUPS

Men

In all age groups, **men drink more per drinking episode than women** do, regardless of the culture. Much of this difference has to do with the cultural acceptability of male drinking and the disapproval of female drinking. The other reason for the difference reflects men's ability to more efficiently metabolize higher amounts of alcohol. As expected, **men also have more adverse social and legal consequences** and develop problems with alcohol abuse or alcohol dependence at a higher rate than women.

Women

Women's alcohol problems become greater in their thirties, not in their twenties as for men (Blume & Zilberman, 2005). Alcohol-dependent women as a group drink about one-third less alcohol than alcohol-dependent men (Center for Science in the Public Interest, 2006).

The magnitude of the genetic influence in women from one or two alcoholic parents hasn't been as widely examined as in men, but a survey of research seems to indicate a similar genetic susceptibility between men and women (Prescott, 2002). In fact, the **rate of alcoholism in relatives of females diagnosed with alcoholism is somewhat higher than in relatives of male alcoholics**.

Several studies demonstrate that even low levels of drinking in women

with a certain genetic susceptibility can result in major health consequences such as an increase in breast cancer (Thun, Peto, Lopez, et al., 1997; Zhang, Lee, Manson, et al., 2007). **Proportionally more women than men die from cirrhosis of the liver, circulatory disorders, sui-**

cide, and accidents. As mentioned, female alcoholics have a 50% to 100% higher death rate than male alcoholics. But just as health problems develop after sustained heavy drinking, some health disorders, especially depression, may precede heavy drinking and even contribute to it. Also, because women get higher BACs than men from the same amount of alcohol drunk, negative health consequences develop faster for women than for men (Maher, 1997; NIAAA, 1997; Register, Cline & Shively, 2002).

Because **society more readily accepts the alcoholic male but disdains the alcoholic female**, women are less likely to seek treatment for alcoholism but are quicker to utilize mental health services when, in fact, their primary problem is alcohol or other drugs. Women are also more likely to enter treatment when their physical or mental health is suffering, whereas men are more likely to seek treatment when they have problems with their employment or with the law (Gomberg, 1991; Kinney, 2005; Ross, 1989).

TABLE 5–9   ALCOHOL ABUSE OR DEPENDENCE WITHIN THE PAST MONTH

	Males	Females	
Any alcohol use	58.19%	45.9%	
Binge drinkers	30.5%	15.2%	(5 or more drinks on the same occasion at least once in the past 30 days)
Heavy drinkers	10.3%	3.1%	(5 or more drinks per day at least 5 or more days in the past 30 days)

(SAMSHA, 2006)

TABLE 5–10   WOMEN & ALCOHOL PROBLEMS

More Likely to Have Drinking Problems	Less Likely to Have Drinking Problems
Younger women	Older women (60+)
Loss of role (mother, job)	Multiple roles (married, stable, work outside the home)
Never married	Married
Divorced, separated	Widowed
Unmarried and living with a partner	Children in the home
White women	Black women
Using other drugs	Hispanic women
Experiencing sexual dysfunction	Nondrinking spouse
Victim of childhood sexual abuse	

(National Institute on Drug Abuse, 1994)

Adolescents

Adolescence is often a time when one feels invulnerable or at the very least does not give full credence to the cautions of others. Drinking alcohol and smoking tobacco are the two most obvious activities. All research seems to indicate that **the younger one starts smoking or drinking, the more likely he or she will have a problem with tobacco or alcohol later in life**. Almost one-third of all teenagers report having their first drink before they were 13 years old, most often due to peer encouragement.

"I was a city kid, and it was pretty much a standard rite of passage when you're 12, 13, 14 to, you know, one way or another get your hands on a six-pack for a Saturday night—and that's how drinking started for all of us in my neighborhood."
22-year-old recovering alcoholic

In a major survey of students, Monitoring the Future, the **percentage of teenagers who had been drunk in the past month:**

eighth grade	6.2%
tenth grade	18.8%
twelfth grade	30.0%

Interestingly, the percentages that reported daily use were only 0.5%, 1.3%, and 3.1%, respectively, emphasizing the binge nature of teenage drinking (Johnston, O'Malley, Bachman, et al., 2006C).

Adolescent binge drinkers were also 17 times more likely to smoke than non-binge drinkers, a combination that can aggravate one's health with gastrointestinal, respiratory, or other problems.

The three most popular locations for adolescent drinking were in someone's home, outdoors, and in a moving car or truck. The latter two choices often lead to driving under the influence (Windle, 2003).

Because adolescence is a time of intense emotional growth, the disinhibiting effects of alcohol can **encourage unsafe sexual practices**, which lead to higher rates of unplanned pregnancies, sexual aggression, and sexually transmitted diseases.

Adolescents' heavy involvement in alcohol (and other drugs) tends to **limit emotional growth**; so, when they stop using, they often have remained emotionally the same age as when they started. Recovery is therefore not just a matter of stopping use but also learning what they failed to grasp during their use.

College Students & Learning

"We drank quite a bit in my dorm and, generally, when somebody came into my dorm room on a weekend night, you had to take a bong—a beer bong. And we'd have the funnel that held like two and a half beers, and it was just the rule. We kinda pressured people to keep up, like you had to stay with the crowd."
College student in his junior year

It used to be that only college students, away from the control of their parents, began heavy drinking. But in the 1990s and 2000s, the age of first use and heavy use dropped to where many students had "done it all" by the time they finished their senior year in high school. Studies have shown that the majority of students (as high as 86%) kept the same pattern of drinking from high school to college (Reifman & Watson, 2003). In college many of them refined those habits or cut back. The problem is that because so much development takes place during high school and college years, **drinking usually has negative effects on learning and maturation**.

"Often it's the style of drinking, not experimentation, that gets college students in trouble. Many think the name of the game is to get drunk. They drink too fast, they drink without eating, they play drinking games or contests, or they binge drink. But because they drink heavily only once or twice a week, they think that there is no problem. But there usually is a problem: lower grades, disciplinary action, or behavior they regret, which usually means sexual behavior."
Shauna Quinn, drug and alcohol counselor, California State University, Chico

Forty-four percent of college students admit to binge drinking at least

Doonesbury   BY GARRY TRUDEAU

TABLE 5–11 AVERAGE NUMBER OF DRINKS PER WEEK, BY GRADE AVERAGE

Grade Average	Drinks Per Week		
	Males	Females	Overall
A	5.4	2.3	3.3
B	7.4	3.4	5.0
C	9.2	4.1	6.6
D or F	14.6	5.2	10.1

(College Core Study of 56 four-year and 22 two-year colleges by Southern Illinois University, Carbondale, 1993)

once every two weeks (Wechsler, Lee, Kuo, et al., 2002). *Binge drinking* (many students, particularly males, object to the term) is defined as having five or more drinks at one sitting for males, four for females. About half of the students in one study who admitted to binge drinking also admitted that their grades fell into the C-to-F range. Many binge drinkers missed classes on a regular basis (O'Malley & Johnston, 2002). In a national study, there was a direct correlation between the number of drinks consumed per week and the grade-point average (Table 5-11).

Notice that women's grades start to deteriorate at slightly less than half the drinking level it takes for men's grades to go down. The *National Household Survey on Drug Abuse* (Figure 5-10) indicates that the higher the level of educational attainment, the more likely was the current use (not necessarily abuse) of alcohol. This seems a contradiction with the statistics about grade performance; however, the rate of heavy alcohol use in the 18-to-34 age group among those who had not completed high school was twice that of those who had completed college. In general, college students learn to moderate their drinking before they graduate.

"Secondhand drinking is a large problem on a college campus, and it is a problem on our campus. We have a lot of students complain about their roommate or their boyfriend or girlfriend you know, being drunk,

violence occurring, vandalism occurring, being unable to study, having to stay up all night with that person who may have had too much to drink and they need to stay with them to make sure they make it through the night and they don't die from alcohol poisoning."
Shauna Quinn, drug and alcohol counselor, California State University, Chico

"I guess studying on the weekends was a lot more difficult because a lot of people tend to party and drink a lot more. People banging on the walls and coming into your room, trying to get you to come out and party with them. On a Friday or Saturday night, you had to take your studies elsewhere."
College senior, Southern Oregon University

In general:

◇ **male students binge somewhat more than female students (48.6% to 40.9%);**
◇ white students (50.2%) are more likely to binge than Hispanic (34.4%), Asian/Pacific Islander (26.2%), or Black (21.7%) students; and
◇ fraternity members (75.4%) drink more than dormitory residents (45.3%), off-campus residents (54.5%), or married residents (26.5%) (Wechsler, Lee, Kuo, et al., 2002).

Unfortunately, the tendency to **binge drink in college leads to about 1,700 deaths per year, 696,000 physical assaults, 599,000 injuries, and 97,000 sexual assaults** (Hingson, Heeren, Winter, et al., 2005).

Older Americans

"I visited my granddad in the retirement center/nursing home when he was 93 years old. He showed me the medicine cabinet. It was a small closet that, when opened by a nurse, revealed dozens of bottles of alcohol—whiskey,

rum, scotch, vodka, and a variety of wines—each one with the name of one of the elderly residents. Depending on the health of the patient, they could have one or two drinks a day for their health. He was still healthy at 96 when a fall killed him."
42-year-old grandson

People who are 65 years or older constitute the fastest-growing segment of the U.S. population. From 6% to 21% of elderly hospital patients, 20% of elderly psychiatric patients, and 14% of elderly emergency room patients exhibit symptoms of alcoholism (American Medical Association, 1996). One study indicates that approximately **2.5 million older adults have alcohol-related problems** (NIAAA, 2004).

Research indicates that **patterns of drinking persist into old age** and that the amount and the frequency of drinking are a result of general trends in society rather than the aging process. Hip

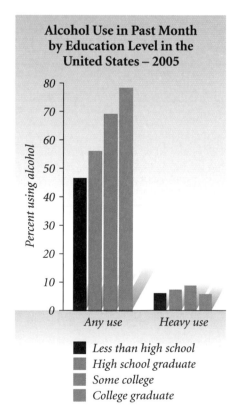

Alcohol Use in Past Month by Education Level in the United States – 2005

Figure 5-10 •
This chart compares the use and abuse of alcohol with the level of education.
(SAMHSA, 2006)

fractures, one of the most debilitating injuries that occurs to the elderly, increase with alcohol consumption mainly due to **decreases in bone density caused by the deleterious effects of alcohol** (Adams, Yuan, Barboriak, et al., 1993; Blow, 2003). In nursing homes as many as 49% of the patients have drinking problems, although some nursing homes are used to hospitalize problem drinkers, so the rate may seem higher than the general population (Joseph, 1997). Another problem is that the average American over 65 years old takes two to seven prescription medications daily, so **alcohol/prescription drug interactions among older people are quite common** (Korrapati & Vestal, 1995). Pharmacologic research has found more than 150 prescription and over-the-counter medications that interact negatively with alcohol (NIAAA, 2003).

About one-third of elderly alcohol abusers are of the late-onset variety (Rigler, 2000). Some older people may increase their drinking because of isolation, retirement, more leisure time, financial pressures, depression over health, loss of friends or a spouse, lack of a day-to-day structure, or simply the access to and availability of alcohol in the home or at friends' homes. The elderly alcohol abuser is less likely to be in contact with a workplace, the criminal justice system, or drug-abuse treatment providers. Thus it may be **more difficult to identify elderly abusers and get them help**. This is also because of a more tolerant attitude toward drinking by the elderly. The common reaction is *So what, if they are heavy drinkers? At their age, they deserve it. They've contributed to society and what harm could it do now anyway?*

"Give strong drink unto him that is ready to perish, and wine unto those that be of heavy hearts."
Proverbs 31:6

Diagnosis of drug or alcohol problems in the elderly is often difficult because of the **coexistence of other physical or mental problems** that become much more prevalent due to the aging process. Dementia, depression, hypertension, arrhythmia, psychosis, and panic disorder are just some of the conditions whose symptoms are mimicked by either the use of or the withdrawal from alcohol and other drugs (Gambert, 2005). **It is often up to the physicians seeing these patients for medical conditions to recognize alcohol problems and do brief interventions to get them help.**

Even with all the reasons and the pressures to drink, however, **people 65 and older have the lowest prevalence of problem drinking and alcoholism.** There are several reasons for the lower rates:

◇ People who become alcohol abusers or alcoholics usually do so before the age of 65, suggesting a high degree of self-correction or spontaneous remission with age.
◇ Cutting down on drinking or giving up drinking may be related to the relatively high cost of alcohol for those on a fixed income.
◇ The body is less able to handle alcohol because liver function declines with age. The general aging process also decreases tolerance and slows metabolism, so the older drinker often has to limit intake.
◇ Side effects are increased if someone is ill or is taking medications thus encouraging temperance.

"For certainly, old age has a great sense of calm and freedom; when the passions relax their hold, then, as Sophocles says we are freed from the grasp not of one mad master only, but of many."
Plato, The Republic, 30 B.C.E. (translated by Benjamin Jowett)

Homeless

San Francisco spent $11.6 million in one 18-month period in 2004 and 2005 just to send ambulances 3,869 times to pick up 362 homeless alcoholics. For these severe alcoholics, that worked out to 10 emergency calls each. The study involved those who were picked up more than four times. The top 10 alcoholics were picked up an average of 70 times. The 11.6 million is only a portion of the cost to a municipality (e.g., healthcare, jail time, and welfare) (Lelchuk, 2005). The city is trying to implement a number of legal, social, and treatment solutions. The fact that each dollar spent in treatment saves $7 to $20 in other costs is also applicable for the homeless.

It is hard to estimate the total number of people affected by homelessness each year in the United States. A recent survey by the Department of Housing and Urban Development put the number at 754,000 (DHUD, 2007). A number of homeless advocates disagreed with that number saying that **1.5 million is a truer figure** (Knight, 2007). **The average length of homelessness is six months**. The breakdown of the homeless population is:

◇ **41% are single males, 14% are single women;**
◇ **40% are families with children, 25% are children;**
◇ 17% are employed, 10% are veterans; and
◇ some ethnic groups are overrepresented: **49% are African American**, 13% are Hispanic, 35% are White, 2% are American Indians, and 1% are Asian.

Finally, it is estimated that:

◇ 8% have HIV or AIDS,
◇ **23% could be considered mentally ill,**
◇ and **30% have serious substance-abuse problems** (this figure has dropped from 46% over the past 10 years)

(Blow, 2003; U.S. Conference of Mayors, 2005; U.S. Department of Health and Human Services, 2005).

Street young adult: "We wake up and we drink."
Street teenager #1: "Drink a beer."
Street teenager #2: "And we go to sleep right after we're done drinking at night. But we drink all day long, every day, all the time, constantly."
Street teenager #3: "Except for right now 'cause we don't have enough money for a beer."

Counselor: "How long have you been doing that?"

Street young adult: "All my life, pretty much since I was a teenager."

Counselor: "How old are you now?"

Street young adult: "Twenty-eight. And I've been living like this since I was 13. I take breaks. I'll get a job and shit, but I still drink then too. Don't get me wrong. I have money for beer even if I have to pawn stuff."

Interview with street people by a counselor from the Haight Ashbury Free Clinics Youth Outreach Program

The reasons for homelessness vary widely. There are:

◊ the **situationally homeless**, who, because of **poverty, job loss, spousal abuse, a shortage of af-**

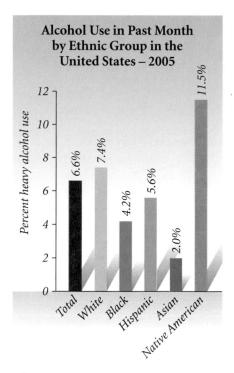

Figure 5-11 •

In the United States during 2005, Whites continued to have a high rate of heavy alcohol use (five or more drinks five or more times in the past month) at 7.4%. The rate for Hispanics was 5.6%; for African Americans, 4.2%; for Asians, 2.0%; and for American Indians, 11.5%. (SAMHSA, 2006)

fordable rental housing, or eviction, find themselves on the street;

◊ the **street people**, who have made the streets their home and have adjusted to living outside;

◊ the **chronic mentally ill**, who have been squeezed out of inpatient mental facilities over the past three decades in favor of less costly outpatient health facilities; and

◊ the **homeless substance abusers**, particularly alcohol abusers, whose lives center around their addiction, which has made them incapable of living within the boundaries of normal society.

The last two groups include the mentally ill person who has begun to use drugs (often to self-medicate) and the drug abuser who has developed mental/emotional problems as a result of drug use. One of the common denominators among all of these groups is their **lack of affiliation with any kind of support system**. Services that identify and treat substance abuse and mental health problems are hard to come by or, if available, are shunned by the homeless person (Joseph & Langrod, 2005).

A comprehensive program to alleviate drug and mental problems among the homeless usually involves outreach that will provide some basic services and which encourages clients to enter treatment facilities. Many cities try to locate services at shelters and gathering places for the homeless, but because numerous services are needed to meet the wide variety of problems, budget constraints often become the deciding factor (U.S. Conference of Mayors, 2005).

UNDERREPRESENTED POPULATIONS

Biological and neurochemical differences between different ethnic groups account for some of the different patterns of alcohol and drug use in different communities. **Diverse cultural traditions seem to make a greater contribution to alcohol use and abuse patterns**, however, as does the degree of assimilation into the drinking patterns of the dominant culture. Sensitivity to ethnic traditions and degrees of assimilation can help us understand how alcohol use affects the

TABLE 5–12 HISTORY OF ALCOHOLISM IN FAMILIES IN THE UNITED STATES	
American Indians and Alaskan natives	48%
Whites	23%
African Americans	22%
Hispanics	25%

(NCADI, 2006)

health, family life, and social interactions of various cultures and in turn can contribute to more-effective treatment and prevention (Galvin & Caetano, 2003).

African Americans

Contrary to popular belief, the African American community is actually a diverse multicultural society with at least three subgroups:

◊ African Americans who were born in the United States but who are descendants of African slaves;

◊ descendants of African slaves of the Caribbean who migrated to the United States; and

◊ those who were born in Africa and migrated to the United States and who represent a number of cultures and countries.

Research that takes this diversity into account is limited, however, so the information is not as specific as it could be (Madray, Brown & Primm, 2005).

In the 2005 *National Household Survey on Drug Abuse,* **heavy use of alcohol was lower among African Americans (4.2%) than among Whites (7.4%) and Hispanics (5.6%)** as in previous years. Use on a monthly basis by Black men (40.8%) is also less than that by White men (56.5%) (SAMHSA, 2006). On the other hand, even though more Black women abstain than White women, there is greater heavy drinking among those Black women who do drink. **Peak drinking for Blacks occurred after the age of 30,** whereas drinking among Whites peaked at a younger age. Two reasons for the higher rate of abstention and the lower rate of heavy drinking among

African Americans is their long history of spirituality along with a strong matriarchal family structure, both of which look down on heavy drinking (James & Johnson, 1996). Both these factors also have an impact on recovery.

"Subliminally, there was a return back to our youth, back to the time when we were attending churches under the guidance many times and most times of our grandmothers. There are a significant number of clients who began their recovery [from alcoholism] with a vision of a dead grandmother telling them things like, 'You know, I did not teach you and grow you up and love you and give you what I gave you in order to be an addict.'"

Rafiq Bilel, former director, Black Extended Family Program, Glide Memorial Church, San Francisco, CA

One disturbing fact is that **medical problems brought on by heavy drinking among African Americans are more severe** (Caetano & Clark, 1998). This is probably due to less access to healthcare facilities, insurance programs, and prevention programs as well as a delayed entrance into treatment for alcoholism when compared with Whites (Madray, Brown & Primm, 2005). In many instances unemployment and racism are also strong factors that aggravate this higher vulnerability.

Hispanics

In 2004 there were **41.3 million Hispanics in the United States, or about 14.1% of the total population** (U.S. Bureau of the Census, 2006). That figure is expected to grow to 102 million by 2050. One of the problems with examining Hispanic alcohol or drug use is the diversity of cultures involved: Mexican American, Cuban American, Puerto Rican, Colombian American, and individuals from dozens of other Spanish-speaking countries. In addition, a single culture consists of anywhere from first- to tenth-generation immigrant Americans. **About 60% of all Hispanics in the United States are of Mexican origin**, 9.5% of the total are of Puerto Rican origin, and 3.2%

are of Cuban origin (U.S. Bureau of the Census, 2005). In a survey done in the early 1980s, heavy alcohol use was highest in the Mexican-American community, somewhat lower in the Puerto Rican community, and very low among Cuban Americans. Alcohol use in Hispanic communities in 2005 was: past-month use, 46.7%; binge use, 25.8%; heavy drinking, 8.1%; and those reporting dependence in the past year, 6.2% (SAMHSA, 2006).

Unlike the general population, drinking in the Hispanic community increases with both sexes as education and income increase. One of the problems with alcohol abuse and addiction in the Hispanic community is a **lack of culturally relevant treatment facilities and personnel**. The problem is exacerbated by the disruption of the family unit and the degree of assimilation.

"I think the cultural differences are crucial. To give you an example: I was in detox once and this woman came in, a Hispanic woman, and she was being interviewed by another counselor, and she was in an abusive relationship, and the other counselor told her that she would have to leave her relationship if she wanted to stay clean. And I thought, 'This woman's going to bolt. She's not going to leave her family.' And I had to intervene in a delicate way because otherwise I felt we were going to lose her."

35-year-old Hispanic female drug counselor

The rate of alcohol use among female Hispanics has grown over the past 20 years possibly due to the different attitude toward women's rights, more female heads of household, or different cultural traditions. Generally, Hispanic women still drink considerably less than Hispanic men. In treatment, strong family involvement is necessary plus an appreciation of the values of *dignidad, respeto, y cariño* (dignity, respect, and love) (Ruiz & Langrod, 2005).

Asians & Pacific Islanders (APIs)

Asians and Pacific Islanders (APIs) are the **fastest-growing ethnic**

group in the United States, though currently they constitute only about 4% of the total population, approximately 11 million people. Because the label *API* encompasses dozens of distinct ethnicities throughout the Pacific Basin, including Japanese, Chinese, Filipino, Korean, Vietnamese, Thai, Indonesian, Burmese, and Pacific Islanders, making generalized statements about APIs can lead to inaccuracies regarding the extent of their drug use and the reasons for it; however, a few generalizations can be made.

Asians and Pacific Islanders are reported to have the **lowest rate of drinking and drug problems in the United States**. As APIs became more highly acculturated (more generations in America and increased ease with English), however, drinking increased (Sue, 1987; Zane & Kim, 1994). There are genetic factors that may help deter heavy drinking among APIs. The other major influence seems to be cultural (i.e., heavy drinking is strongly disapproved of in most API cultures). Surveys confirm that there are significant differences in drinking patterns among different national API groups (Johnson & Nagoshi, 1990). Note that there are sometimes large differences between Asian and Asian-American drinking patterns for the same country—foreign-born vs. American-born Asians of the same ethnic origin and even among the same generation of Asian Americans with identical ethnicities (Tsuang, 2005).

In one study in Los Angeles (Table 5-13), **Filipino Americans and Japanese Americans were twice as likely to be heavy drinkers as Chinese Americans**. Korean Americans have the highest number of abstainers. In general, educated, middle-class Asian-American males under 45 are most likely to drink, but there is relatively little problem drinking even among this group, although as they become more culturally acclimated, the drinking increases (Makimoto, 1998).

As with other ethnic groups, treatment is much more effective when it is culturally relevant. For example, in San Francisco at the Haight Ashbury Detox Clinic, relatively few APIs came in for treatment because of the **stigma involved in admitting that there was a problem**. Researchers studying the

TABLE 5–13   DRINKING PATTERNS OF 1,100 LOS ANGELES ASIAN AMERICANS

Group Drinking	Heavy Drinking	Moderate Drinking	Abstaining Drinking
Japanese Americans	25%	42%	33%
Chinese Americans	11%	48%	41%
Korean Americans	14%	24%	62%
Filipino Americans	20%	29%	51%

(NIAAA, 1991)

drug use patterns of the API communities in San Francisco found that **when more API counselors were hired, and when a specific treatment facility for Asian Americans was created, the API population in treatment vastly increased.**

American Indians & Alaskan Natives

There are approximately 2.7 million American Indians and Alaskan Natives in the United States. The average age is 22.9 years compared to 31.1 for Whites (U.S. Bureau of the Census, 2006). They represent **more than 300 tribal or language groups. In general, drinking patterns vary widely among these tribes,** who make up about 1% of the population of the United States. About 70% live in rural areas (Foulks, 2005). Some tribes are mostly abstinent; some drink moderately with few problems; and some have high rates of heavy drinking and alcoholism. Stereotypes and old western movies seem to have influenced much of the thinking about American Indians and drinking. The picture of the "Indian who can't hold his liquor" has been perpetuated for generations. One explanation is that although the rate of abstinence is quite high in many tribes, it is the pattern of heavy binge drinking among males in various tribes, especially on reservations, that accounts for the highly visible American Indian alcoholic. (In a survey of Sioux tribes, however, the women drank as much as the men.) The fact that many surveys are done on reservations where only one-third of the total American Indian population lives, coupled with the grinding poverty on many of those reservations, may explain the rates of heavy drinking reported for this population (Beauvais, 1998; Foulks, 2005).

Historically, American Indians drank only weak beers or other fermented beverages and usually just for ceremonial purposes. When distilled alcoholic beverages were introduced, most American Indian cultures did not have time to develop ethical, legal, and social customs to handle the stronger drinks.

A study of a group of American Indians (Mission Indians) looked at the inherited sensitivity to alcohol and found that they were not more sensitive to the effects of alcohol. Rather they were less sensitive and so had to drink more to get drunk (a sign of susceptibility to developing alcoholism) (Garcia-Andrade, Wall & Ehlers, 1997).

Generally, the abuse of alcohol accounts for five of the 10 leading causes of death in most American Indian tribes. Alcohol-related motor vehicle deaths are 5.5 times higher than for the rest of the U.S. population. Cirrhosis of the liver is 4.5 times higher; alcoholism, 3.8 times higher; homicide, 2.8 times higher; and suicide, 2.3 times higher. Although American Indian women drink less than men, they are especially vulnerable to cirrhosis and account for almost half of the deaths from cirrhosis (Manson, Shore, Baron, et al., 1992).

One study in Oklahoma found that alcohol-related causes of death varied from less than 1% to 24% among the 11 tribes surveyed compared with 2% for Blacks and 3% for Whites (Manson, Shore, Baron, et al., 1992).

CONCLUSIONS

Because alcohol causes many serious health and societal problems, its use has often been restricted or banned by almost every country. Most restrictions are ultimately overturned, however, because of demand and the lure of tax revenues by governments.

The road to alcoholism can take three months or 30 years—or it may never occur. One has to recognize that alcohol is a psychoactive drug that can cause irreversible physiological changes that make one more susceptible to alcoholism with continued use.

CHAPTER SUMMARY

Overview

1. Except for Islamic countries and a few others, drinking alcoholic beverages is a worldwide phenomenon.

2. Last month 126 million Americans drank some alcoholic beverages.

3. 25% to 30% of all U.S. hospital admissions were due to alcohol.

4. Two million people worldwide died last year due to alcohol.

5. Because the process of fermentation occurs naturally, alcohol was initially discovered by accident and then purposefully cultivated and manufactured.

6. Over the centuries alcohol, a central nervous system (CNS) depressant, has been used as a reward, as food, as a medicine, as a sacrament, as a water substitute, as a social lubricant, as a source of taxes,

and as a tranquilizer (to cover emotional and mental problems).

7. Because alcohol (a legal drug) also causes most of the world's health and societal problems, its use has often been restricted or banned by almost every country in the world; but because of consumer demand and governmental desire for tax revenues, most severe restrictions were eventually overturned.

Alcoholic Beverages

8. Though there are hundreds of different alcohols, ethyl alcohol (ethanol) is the main psychoactive ingredient in all alcoholic beverages, along with nonpsychoactive fermentation products called congeners that add tastes, colors, and aromas.

9. When yeast is added to certain fruits, vegetables, or grains, they ferment into alcoholic beverages.

10. When fruits (particularly grapes) ferment, wine is the result. When grains ferment, beer is the result (e.g., ale, stout, lager, malt beverages). More highly concentrated spirits are distilled from the original fermentation of grains or vegetables such as potatoes (vodka) and from wine.

11. Most wines are 12% to 14% alcohol; most beers are 4% to 7% alcohol; and most liquors and whiskeys are 35% to 45% alcohol. Higher-proof alcoholic beverages increase the incidence of alcoholism.

Absorption, Distribution & Metabolism

12. When alcohol is drunk, it is absorbed (mostly through the capillaries in the small intestine), metabolized (mostly in the liver), and then excreted.

13. The rate of absorption depends on body weight, gender, health, and a dozen other factors, including the additives in the drink. The effects on women of a given amount of alcohol are generally more damaging than for men.

14. Alcohol dehydrogenase (ADH) and acetaldehyde (ALDH) are cen-

tral to the liver's metabolism of alcohol.

15. From 2% to 10% of alcohol is excreted directly through the urine and the lungs. The rest is metabolized by the liver and then excreted as carbon dioxide and water through the kidneys and the lungs.

16. Alcohol is metabolized at a defined continuous rate, so it is possible to roughly approximate what level of drinking will produce a certain blood alcohol concentration (BAC). A BAC of 0.08 defines legal intoxication in all 50 states, although behavioral reactions vary widely. It takes 30 to 40 minutes to reach maximum alcohol concentration after taking a drink.

DESIRED EFFECTS, SIDE EFFECTS & HEALTH CONSEQUENCES

Levels of Use

17. The six levels of alcohol use are abstention, experimentation, social/recreational use, habituation, abuse, and addiction (alcohol dependence, or alcoholism).

Low-to-Moderate-Dose Episodes

18. People who are pregnant and have pre-existing physical or mental health problems, allergies to alcoholic beverages, high genetic/environmental susceptibility to addiction, pre-existing abuse problems, or a high risk for breast cancer should avoid any use of alcohol.

19. Small amounts of alcohol or occasional episodes of intoxication are usually not harmful and have some positive benefits (e.g., topical anesthetic, pain reliever, thirst quencher, appetite stimulant, lowered risk of heart disease and stroke, sleep inducer, lowered inhibitions, and sociability).

20. The negative side effects of low-to-moderate drinking include a deepening of negative emotions, leading to relationship problems, accidents, legal problems, and high-risk sexual behavior.

21. Alcohol's influence on the brain's neurotransmitters (serotonin,

dopamine, met-enkephalin, glutamate, and especially GABA, the main inhibitory neurotransmitter) cause the effects.

22. In low doses alcohol often increases sexual desire but eventually decreases sexual performance.

High-Dose Episodes

23. Intoxication is a combination of blood alcohol concentration, psychological mood, expectation, and drinking history.

24. Binge drinking (five or more drinks for men at one sitting and four or more for women) and heavy drinking (bingeing five or more times a month) cause the most problems.

25. As the BAC rises, depressant effects go from lowered inhibitions and relaxation, to clumsiness, decreased alertness, mental confusion, loss of judgment, sleep disturbances, and emotional turbulence, to slurred speech and inability to walk, and finally to alcohol poisoning that can result in unconsciousness and death (respiratory and cardiac failure).

26. Blackouts are caused by heavy drinking in susceptible individuals and are marked by memory loss even though the drinker is awake and conscious. Partial blackouts are known as brownouts.

27. Hangovers usually disappear within hours on their own whereas withdrawal symptoms that occur with chronic high-dose use can last for days.

28. Alcohol is eliminated from the system at a constant rate, so hangover cures such as coffee or exercise don't work. Time and rest are the best cures.

Chronic High-Dose Use

29. The liver is the organ most severely affected. Problems include a fatty liver, alcoholic hepatitis, and cirrhosis (a scarring of the liver that is often eventually fatal). Usually the higher a country's drinking rate, the higher the cirrhosis rate.

30. Digestive effects of chronic drinking include gastritis, ulcers, pancreatitis, malnutrition, and internal bleeding. Low blood sugar and high blood sugar often result from chronic drinking.

31. Though beneficial to the cardiovascular system at low doses, chronic high-dose drinking leads to an enlarged heart, high blood pressure, intracranial bleeding, and stroke.

32. Heavy drinking kills nerve cells because alcohol is toxic to all cells. Alcohol-caused vitamin B_1 deficiency can cause brain damage and dementia (e.g., Wernicke's encephalopathy and Korsakoff's psychosis).

33. With chronic use, alcohol can decrease desire and orgasm in females and impair gonadal functions and decrease testosterone in males. Studies find a high rate of erectile dysfunction in male alcoholics.

34. In moderate-to-heavy drinkers, the risk of breast cancer in women as well as the chance of mouth, throat, and esophageal cancer in both men and women increases, especially if they also smoke.

35. Mental and emotional problems, particularly depression and anxiety, increase with chronic use. Chronic use also impairs concentration and memory.

Mortality

36. The average life span of the chronic heavy drinker is shortened by 15 years.

Addiction (alcohol dependence, or alcoholism)

37. Between 10% and 12% of drinkers in the United States progress to frequent, high-dose use (alcoholism); two to three times more men than women have a major problem with alcohol.

38. Just 20% of drinkers consume 80% of all alcohol.

39. There have been numerous attempts to classify alcoholism so that the condition can be studied more systematically and strategies for treatment can be more effective.

40. Classifications have progressed from E. M. Jellinek's gamma and delta alcoholics, to type I and II alcoholics, to type A and B alcoholics, and finally to the concept of alcoholism as a disease.

41. Most current concepts look at addiction as a progressive disease that is caused by a combination of hereditary and environmental influences that are triggered and aggravated by the use of alcohol or other drugs.

42. Tolerance and tissue dependence occur as the body, especially the liver, attempts to adapt to the increasing levels of drinking and the cumulative toxic effects of alcohol.

43. Withdrawal after cessation of frequent high-dose use can be painful and even life threatening. Symptoms (e.g., tremors, anxiety, and rapid pulse, breathing, and heart rate) will occur after cessation of 7 to 34 days of heavy drinking. More-serious symptoms develop after 48 to 87 consecutive days. Delirium tremens (DTs) are a life-threatening form of severe withdrawal that includes hallucinations and convulsions.

44. Research is focusing on: identifying marker genes that make one more susceptible to alcoholism; learning which environmental changes will lessen risk; and studying specific physical and mental changes caused by chronic use.

Other Problems with Alcohol

45. Most drug abuse involves more than one substance, one of them usually being alcohol. The problems of polydrug abuse can be synergistic not just additive. Simultaneous addictions must be treated simultaneously. Approximately 70% of alcoholics are heavy smokers.

46. Drinkers can have pre-existing mental health problems and may try to self-medicate symptoms; or the alcohol and other drugs can induce symptoms of mental illness, particularly depression, and lead to misdiagnosis of mental problems.

47. Personality disorders, especially antisocial and borderline personality disorders (BPDs), seem overrepresented among alcoholics and addicts.

48. Heavy drinking during pregnancy—the leading cause of mental retardation in the United States—can cause birth defects, most notably fetal alcohol syndrome (FAS), that involve abnormal growth and mental problems. It is not known what level of drinking and drug use, if any, is safe during pregnancy. Mental deficits, particularly memory problems, without facial abnormalities (ARND), are more likely to affect the infant. Drinking during weeks 3 through 8 of pregnancy is the most dangerous to the fetus. Paternal drinking can also affect the fetus.

49. Alcohol is heavily involved in emotional/physical/sexual violence, mostly from the lowering of inhibitions in people with a predisposition to violence. Alcohol and violence affect the victim, the perpetrator, and one or more bystanders. The mood of the drinkers and the setting also affect violence. From 34% to 74% of sexual assault perpetrators had been drinking, about the same percentages as for victims.

50. Approximately 40% of motor vehicle fatalities involve alcohol. A 0.08 BAC means legal guilt even though the level of impairment can vary greatly. An intoxicated driver is arrested for every 300 to 1,000 drunk-driving trips.

51. Between 15% and 25% of emergency room patients tested positive for alcohol. Large percentages of homicides, suicides, and accidents involve alcohol.

Epidemiology

52. Culture is one of the main determinants of how a person drinks. Wet cultures (e.g., France) integrate social drinking into everyday life whereas dry cultures (e.g., Denmark) place numerous limita-

tions on the use of alcohol. The United States has a mixed drinking culture and does much social drinking away from lunch and dinner tables.

53. Men drink more per episode than women and have a higher level of addiction and of sociolegal consequences whereas women suffer more health consequences. This is because of a combination of hereditary, social expectations, and physiological and psychological differences.

54. The younger one starts smoking or drinking, the more likely he or she will have a problem with tobacco or alcohol later in life. At an emotionally chaotic age, heavy drinking can encourage unsafe sexual practices and limit emotional growth.

55. The style of drinking causes problems for college students. About 44% of college students have five or more drinks at one sitting. The greater the amount of alcohol used, the lower the grade-point average. Secondhand drinking causes prob-

lems for those who choose to study rather than party.

56. About 2.5 million older Americans have alcohol-related problems even though, as a group, they have the lowest rate. As the drinker ages, the liver is less able to handle alcohol. Interactions with prescribed medications is a problem with the elderly, who use more than the general population. It's more difficult to diagnose alcoholism abuse in the elderly, and physicians are the main line of intervention.

57. About 30% of the 2 to 3 million homeless have serious substance-abuse problems, and 23% have a mental illness. Treatment must be brought to the homeless, rather than expecting them to come to an agency for treatment.

58. Each ethnic group in the United States has unique drinking patterns and problems due to physiological and cultural variances.

59. Heavy drinking is lower in the African-American community than in the White and Hispanic

communities, although medical problems from drinking are more severe among Blacks. The Hispanic community is also extremely diverse, so the need for culturally relevant treatment is crucial. The Asian and Pacific Islander (AIP) community has so many components that it is hard to make generalizations, although generally the rate of heavy drinking is lower. There is also a wide variation in the American Indian communities, although in some tribes five of the 10 leading causes of death are due to alcohol. In all groups a lack of culturally relevant treatment facilities is a major barrier to recovery.

Conclusions

60. The road to alcoholism can take three months or 30 years—or it may never occur. One has to recognize that alcohol is a psychoactive drug that can cause irreversible physiological changes that make one more susceptible to alcoholism with continued use.

REFERENCES

Abbey, A., Zawacki, M. A., Buck, M. A., Clinton, A. M. & Auslan, P. (2001). Alcohol and sexual assault. *Alcohol Research & Health, 25*(1), 43-51.

Adams, W. L., Yuan, Z., Barboriak, J. J. & Rimm, A. A. (1993). Alcohol-related hospitalizations of elderly people. *JAMA, 270*(10), 1222-25.

Alcoholics Anonymous. (1934, 1976). *Alcoholics Anonymous.* New York: Alcoholics Anonymous World Services, Inc.

American Medical Association. (1996). Alcoholism in the elderly. AMA Council on Scientific Affairs. *JAMA, 275*(10), 797-801.

American Psychiatric Association. (2000). *Diagnostic and Statistical Manual of Mental Disorders* (4th ed., text revision [DSM-IV-TR]). Washington, DC.

Anthenelli, R. M. & Schuckit, M. A. (2003). Genetic influences in addiction. In A. W. Graham, T. K. Schultz, M. F. Mayo-Smith, R. K. Ries & B. B. Wilford, eds. *Principles of Addiction Medicine* (3rd ed., pp. 41-51). Chevy

Chase, MD: American Society of Addiction Medicine, Inc.

Babor, T. F. (1996). The classification of alcoholics. *Alcohol Health & Research World, 20*(1), 6-18.

Babor, T. F., Dolinsky, Z. S., Meyer, R. E., Brock, M., Hofmann, M. & Tennen, H. (1992). Types of alcoholics: Concurrent and predictive validity of some common classification schemes. *British Journal of Addiction, 87,* 1415-31.

Badkhen, A. (September 5, 2003). 500 years later, a czar's command is Russia's curse—vodka. *San Francisco Chronicle,* p. A8.

Bagnardi, V., Blangiardo, M., La Vecchia, C. & Corrao, G. (2001). Alcohol consumption and the risk of cancer. *Alcohol Research & Health 25*(4), 264-70.

Baker, S. P., Braver, E. R., Chen, L. H., Li, G. & Williams, A. F. (2002). Drinking histories of fatally injured drivers. *Injury Prevention, 8,* 221-26.

Beauvais, F. (1998). American Indians and alcohol. *Alcohol Health & Research World, 22*(4), 253-59.

Becker, H. C. (1998). Kindling in alcohol withdrawal. *Alcohol Health & Research World, 22*(1), 25-33.

Begleiter, H. (1980). *Biological Effects of Alcohol.* New York: Plenum Press.

Bellandi, D. (January 1, 2003). Underage binge drinking climbs by 56 percent. *Medford Mail Tribune,* p. 1.

Bernstein, M. & Mahoney, J. J. (1989). Management perspectives on alcoholism: The employer's stake in alcoholism treatment. *Occupational Medicine, 4*(2), 223-32.

Bielawski, D. M., Zaher, F. M., Svinarich, D. M. & Abel, E. L. (2002). Paternal alcohol exposure affects sperm cytosine methyltransferase messenger RNA levels. *Alcoholism: Clinical and Experimental Research, 26,* 347-51.

Blot, W. J. (1992). Alcohol and cancer. *Cancer Research Supplement, 52,* 2119s-2121s.

Blow, F. C. (2003). Special issues in treatment: Older adults. In A. W. Graham, T. K. Schultz, M. F. Mayo-Smith, R. K. Ries & B. B. Wilford, eds. *Principles of*

Addiction Medicine (3rd ed., pp. 581-607). Chevy Chase, MD: American Society of Addiction Medicine, Inc.

Blum, K., Braverman, E. R., Holder, J. M., Lubar, J. F., Monastra, V. J., Miller, D., et al. (2000). Reward deficiency syndrome: A biogenetic model for the diagnosis and treatment of impulsive, addictive, and compulsive behaviors. *Journal of Psychoactive Drugs, 32*(suppl.), 1-112.

Blum, K. & Payne, J. E. (1991). *Alcohol and the Addicted Brain* (p. 165). New York: The Free Press.

Blume, S. & Zilberman, M. L. (2005). Alcohol and women. In J. H. Lowinson, P. Ruiz, R. B. Millman & J. G. Langrod, eds. *Substance Abuse: A Comprehensive Textbook* (4th ed., pp. 1049-63). Baltimore: Williams & Wilkins.

Bobak, M. (1999). Alcohol consumption in a national sample of the Russian population. *Addiction, 94*(6), 857-66.

Boehm II, S. L., Valenzuela, C. F. & Harris, R. A. (2005). Alcohol: Neurobiology. In J. H. Lowinson, P. Ruiz, R. B. Millman & J. G. Langrod, eds. *Substance Abuse: A Comprehensive Textbook* (4th ed., pp. 121-51). Baltimore: Williams & Wilkins.

Bohman, M., Sigvardson, S. & Cloninger, C. G. (1981). Maternal inheritance of alcohol abuse: Cross-fostering analysis of adopted women. *Archives of General Psychiatry, 38,* 965-69.

Bosron, W. F., Ehrig, T. & Li, T. K. (1993). Genetic factors in alcohol metabolism and alcoholism. *Seminars in Liver Disease, 13*(2), 126-35.

Bowlin, S. J. (1997). Alcohol intake and breast cancer. *International Journal of Epidemiology, 26,* 915-23.

Brems, C., Johnson, M. E., Neal, D. & Freemon, M. (2004). Childhood abuse history and substance use among men and women receiving detoxification services. *American Journal of Drug and Alcohol Abuse, 30*(4), 799-821.

Brower, K. J. (2001). Alcohol's effects on sleep in alcoholics. *Alcohol: Research & Health, 25*(2), 110-25.

Brust, C. M. (2003). Neurologic disorders related to alcohol and other drug use. In A. W. Graham, T. K. Schultz, M. F. Mayo-Smith, R. K. Ries & B. B. Wilford, eds. *Principles of Addiction Medicine* (3rd ed., pp. 1147-56). Chevy Chase, MD: American Society of Addiction Medicine, Inc.

Bureau of Justice Statistics. (1998). *Alcohol and Crime.* http:www.ojp.usdoj.gov/bjs/pub/pdf/ac.pdf (accessed February 5, 2007).

Bureau of Justice Statistics. (2006). *Crime Characteristics.* http://www.ojp.usdoj.

gov/bjs/cvict_c.htm (accessed February 5, 2007).

Bushman, B. J. (1997). Effects of alcohol on human aggression. In M. Galanter, ed. *Recent Developments in Alcoholism* (Vol. 13, pp. 227-43). New York: Plenum Press.

Caetano, R. & Clark, C. L. (1998). Trends in alcohol-related problems among Whites, African Americans, and Hispanics: 1984-1995. *Alcoholism: Clinical and Experimental Research, 22*(2), 534-38.

Center for Science in the Public Interest. (2006). Alcohol Policies Project Fact Sheet: Women and Alcohol. http://www.cspinet.org/booze/women.htm (February 5, 2007).

Centers for Disease Control and Prevention (CDC). (2004). *FAS Fast Facts.* http://www.cdc.gov/ncbddd/fas/fasask.htm#how (accessed February 5, 2007).

Centers for Disease Control and Prevention. (2006). *Health, United States, 2005.* http://www.cdc.gov/nchs/data/hus/hus05.pdf (accessed February 5, 2007).

Cloninger, C. R., Bohman, M. & Sigvardson, S. (1996). Type I and type II alcoholism: An update. *Alcohol Health & Research World, 20*(1), 18-23.

Coles, C. (1994). Critical periods for prenatal alcohol exposure: Evidence from animal and human studies. *Alcohol Health & Research World, 18,* 22-29.

Collins, J. J. & Messerschmidt, P. M. (1993). Epidemiology of alcohol-related violence. *Alcohol Health & Research World, 17*(2), 93-100.

Colombo, G., Serra, S., Vacca, G., Carai, M. A. & Gessa, G. L. (2005). Endocannabinoid system and alcohol addiction: Pharmacological studies. *Pharmacology of Biochemical Behavior, 81*(2), 369-80.

Courtwright, D. T. (2001). *Forces of Habit.* Cambridge, MA: Harvard University Press.

Dammann, W. M., Wiesbeck, G. A. & Klapp, B. F. (2005). Psychosocial stress and alcohol consumption. *Neurological Psychiatry, 73*(9), 517-25.

Davis, R. (1994). Drug and alcohol use in the former Soviet Union: Selected factors and future considerations. *International Journal of Addictions, 29*(3), 88-89.

Dawson, A., Bigby, B. G., Poceta, J. S. & Mitler, M. M. (1993). Effect of bedtime ethanol on total inspiratory resistance and respiratory drive in normal nonsnoring men. *Alcoholism: Clinical and Experimental Research,* 17(2), 256-62.

Dawson, D. A. & Grant, B. F. (1998). Family history of alcoholism and gen-

der. *Journal of Studies on Alcohol, 59*(1), 97-106.

Department of Housing and Urban Development (DHUD). (2007). *Annual Homeless Assessment Report.* http://www.hud.gov/offices/cpd/homeless/ahar.cfm (accessed February 4, 2007).

Devantag, F., Mandich, G., Zaiotti, G. & Toffolo, G. G. (1983). Alcoholic epilepsy: Review of a series and proposed classification and etiopathogenesis. *Harvard Journal of Neurologic Science, 4,* 275-84.

Dom G., Hulstijn, W. & Sabbe, B. (2006). Differences in impulsivity and sensation seeking between early- and late-onset alcoholics. *Addictive Behaviors, 31*(2), 298-308.

Ellison, R. C., Zhang, Y., McLennan, C. E. & Rothman, K. J. (2001). Exploring the relation of alcohol consumption to risk of breast cancer. *American Journal of Epidemiology, 154,* 740-47.

Emanuele, M. A., Wezeman, F. & Emanuele, N. V. (2002). Alcohol's effects on female reproductive function. *Alcohol Research & Health, 26*(4), 274-81.

Enoch, M., White, K. V., Harris, C. R., Rohrbaugh, J. W. & Goldman, D. (2001). Alcohol use disorders and anxiety disorders: Relation to the P300 event-related potential. *Alcohol Clinical Experimental Research, 25*(9), 1293-1300.

Finnegan, F., Schulze, D., Smallwood, J. & Helander, A. (2005). The effects of self-administered alcohol-induced "hangover" in a naturalistic setting on psychomotor and cognitive performance and subjective state. *Addiction 100*(11), 1680-89.

Foulks, E. E. (2005). Alcohol use among American Indians and Alaskan Natives. In J. H. Lowinson, P. Ruiz, R. B. Millman & J. G. Langrod, eds. *Substance Abuse: A Comprehensive Textbook* (4th ed., pp. 1119-27). Baltimore: Williams & Wilkins.

Galvin, F. H. & Caetano, R. (2003). Alcohol use and related problems among ethnic minorities in the United States. *Alcohol Research & Health, 27*(1), 87-94.

Gambert, S. R. (2005). The elderly. In J. H. Lowinson, P. Ruiz, R. B. Millman & J. G. Langrod, eds. *Substance Abuse: A Comprehensive Textbook* (4th ed., pp. 1038-48). Baltimore: Williams & Wilkins.

Garcia-Andrade, C., Wall, T. L. & Ehlers, C. L. (1997). The firewater myth and response to alcohol in Mission Indians. *American Journal of Psychiatry, 154,* 983-88.

Gatley, S. J., Volkow, N. D., Wang, G. J., Fowler, J. S. Logan, J., Ding, Y. S. &

Gerasimov, M. (2005). PET imaging in clinical drug abuse research. *Current Pharmaceutical Design, 11*(25), 3203-19.

Goedde, H. W., Harada, S. & Agarwal, D. P. (1979). Racial differences in alcohol sensitivity: A new hypothesis. *Human Genetics, 51,* 331-34.

Goldstein, A. (2001). *Addiction: From Biology to Drug Policy* (2nd ed.). New York: W. H. Freeman and Company.

Gomberg, E. A. L. (1991). Alcoholic women in treatment: New research. *Substance Abuse, 12*(1), 6-12.

Goodlett, C. R. & Johnson, T. B. (1999). Temporal windows of vulnerability to alcohol during the third trimester equivalent. In J. H. Hannigan, L. P. Spear, N. E. Spear & C. R. Goodlett, eds. *Alcohol and Alcoholism: Effects on Brain and Development* (pp. 59-91). Hillsdale, NJ: Lawrence Erlbaum Associates.

Gorwood, P., Lanfumey, L. & Hamon, M. (2004). Alcohol dependence and polymorphisms of serotonin-related genes. *Medical Science (Paris), 20*(12), 1132-38.

Grant, B. F. (1985). Liver cirrhosis mortality in the United States. *Alcohol Epidemiologic Data Reference Manual* (2nd ed., Vol. 2). Washington, DC: Department of Health and Human Services. http://www.cdc.gov/mmwr/preview/mmwrhtml/00000821.htm (accessed November 1, 2006).

Greenfield, L. A. (1998). *Alcohol and crime.* Report prepared for National Symposium on Alcohol Abuse and Crime. Washington, DC: U.S. Department of Justice. http://www.ojp.gov/bjs/abstract/ac.htm (accessed February 5, 2007).

Greenfield, T. K. & Rogers, J. D. (1999). Who drinks most of the alcohol in the U.S.? The policy implications. *Journal of Studies on Alcohol,* 60(1), 78-89.

Greenspan, P., Bauer, J. D., Pollock, S. H., Gangemi, J. D., Mayer, E. P., Ghaffar, A., et al. (2005). Antiinflammatory properties of the muscadine grape. *Journal of Agriculture and Food Chemistry, 53*(22), 8481-84.

Gustafson, R. (1994). Alcohol and aggression. *Juvenile Offender Rehabilitation, 21*(3/4), 41-80.

Haber, P. S. (2003). Liver disorders related to alcohol and other drug use. In A. W. Graham, T. K. Schultz, M. F. Mayo-Smith, R. K. Ries & B. B. Wilford, eds. *Principles of Addiction Medicine* (3rd ed., pp. 1077-98). Chevy Chase, MD: American Society of Addiction Medicine, Inc.

Hans, S. L. (1998). Developmental outcomes of prenatal exposure to alcohol and other drugs. In A. W. Graham & T. K. Schultz, eds. *Principles of Addiction Medicine* (2nd ed., pp. 1223-37). Chevy Chase, MD: American Society of Addiction Medicine, Inc.

Harwood, H., et al. (2000). *Updating Estimates of the Economic Costs of Alcohol Abuse in the United States.* Report prepared by the Lexin Group for the National Institute on Alcohol Abuse and Alcoholism. http://pubs.niaaa.nih.gov/publications/economic-2000 (accessed February 5, 2007).

Hasin, D. (2003). Classification of alcohol use disorders. *Alcohol Research & Health, 27*(1), 5-17.

He, J. (2001). Alcohol reduction advised for heavy drinkers with hypertension. *Hypertension, 38,* 1112-17.

Health-EU. (2006). *Report: Alcohol in Europe.* http://ec.europa.eu/health-eu/news_alcoholineurope_en.htm (accessed February 5, 2007).

Heidbreder, C. A., Andreoli, M., Marcon, C., Thanos, P. K., Ashby, C. R. Jr. & Gardner, E. L. (2004). Role of dopamine D3 receptors in the addictive properties of ethanol. *Drugs Today 40*(4), 355-65.

Heinz, A., Ragan, P., Jones, D. W., Hommer, D., Williams, W., Knable, M. B., et al. (1998). Reduced central serotonin transporters in alcoholism. *American Journal of Psychiatry, 155*(11), 1544-49.

Higley, J. D. (2001). Individual differences in alcohol-induced aggression. *Alcohol Research & Health, 25*(1), 12-19.

Hines, D. A. & Saudino, K. J. (2005). Genetic and environmental influences on intimate partner aggression: A preliminary study. *Violence and Victims, 19*(6), 701-18.

Hingson, R., Heeren, T., Winter, M., & Wechsler, H. (2005). Magnitude of alcohol-related mortality and morbidity among U.S. college students ages 18-24: Changes from 1998 to 2001. *Annual Review of Public Health, 26,* 259-79.

Hingson, R. & Winter, M. (2003). Epidemiology and consequences of drinking and driving. *Alcohol Research & Health, 27*(1), 63-78.

Ikonomidou, C., Bittigau, P., Ishimaru, M. J., Wozniak, D. F., Koch, C., Genz K., et al. (2000). Ethanol-induced apoptotic neurodegeneration and fetal alcohol syndrome. *Science, 287*(5455), 1056-60.

Internal Revenue Service. (2006). *Federal excise taxes.* http://www.irs.gov/pub/irs-soi/histab21.xls (accessed July 21, 2006).

Isbell, H., Fraser, H. F., Wikler, A., Belleville, R. E. & Eisenman, A. J. (1955). An experimental study of the etiology of rum fits and delirium tremens. *Quarterly Journal of Studies on Alcohol, 16*(1), 1-33.

James, W. H. & Johnson, S. L. (1996). *Doin' Drugs: Patterns of African American Addiction.* Austin, TX: University of Texas Press.

Javors, M., Tiouririne, M. & Prihoda, T. (2000). Platelet serotonin uptake is higher in early-onset than in late-onset alcoholics. *Alcohol and Alcoholism, 35,* 390-93.

Jellinek, E. M. (1961). *The Disease Concept of Alcoholism.* New Haven, CT: College & University Press.

Johnson, R. A. & Ait-Daoud, N. (2005). Alcohol: Clinical aspects. In J. H. Lowinson, P. Ruiz, R. B. Millman & J. G. Langrod, eds. *Substance Abuse: A Comprehensive Textbook* (4th ed., pp. 151-63). Baltimore: Williams & Wilkins.

Johnson, R. C. & Nagoshi, C. T. (1990). Asians, Asian Americans and alcohol. *Journal of Psychoactive Drugs, 22*(1), 45-52.

Johnston, L. D., O'Malley, P. M., Bachman, J. G. & Schulenberg, J. E. (2006A). *Monitoring the Future: National Survey Results on Drug Use, 1975-2005. Vol. I: Secondary School Students* (NIH Publication No. 05-5883). Bethesda, MD: National Institute on Drug Abuse.

Johnston, L. D., O'Malley, P. M., Bachman, J. G. & Schulenberg, J. E. (2006B). *Monitoring the Future: National Survey Results on Drug Use, 1975-2005. Vol. II: College Students and Adults Ages 19-45* (NIH Publication No. 04-5884). Bethesda, MD: National Institute on Drug Abuse.

Johnston, L. D., O'Malley, P. M., Bachman, J. G. & Schulenberg, J. E. (2006C). *Monitoring the Future: National Survey Results on Drug Use, 2006.* http://www.monitoringthefuture.org/data/06data.html#2006data-drugs (accessed February 5, 2007).

Jones, A. W. & Pounder, D. J. (1998). Measuring blood alcohol concentration for clinical and forensic purposes. In S. B. Karch, ed. *Drug Abuse Handbook* (pp. 327-55). Boca Raton, FL: CRC Press.

Jones, K. L. & Smith, D. W. (1973). Recognition of the fetal alcohol syndrome in early infancy. *Lancet, 2,* 999-1001.

Joseph, C. L. (1997). Misuse of alcohol and drugs in the nursing home. In A. M. Gumack, ed. *Older Adults' Misuse of Alcohol, Medicines, and Other Drugs: Research and Practice Issues.* New York: Springer Science.

Joseph, H. & Langrod, D. (2005). The homeless. In J. H. Lowinson, P. Ruiz, R. B. Millman & J. G. Langrod, eds. *Substance Abuse: A Comprehensive*

Textbook (4th ed., pp. 1141-68). Baltimore: Williams & Wilkins.

Keller, M. (1984). Alcohol consumption. *Encyclopaedia Britannica* (Vol. 1, pp. 437-50). Chicago: Encyclopaedia Britannica.

Kessler, R. C., Nelson, C. B. & McGonagle, K. A. (1996). Epidemiology of co-occurring addictive and mental disorders: Implications for prevention and service utilization. *American Journal of Orthopsychiatry, 66*(1), 17-31.

Kinney, J. (2005). *Loosening the Grip* (8th ed.). Boston: McGraw-Hill.

Knight, H. (2007, March 1). Unique national homeless count found 754,000 in 2005. *San Francisco Chronicle*, A9.

Knop, J., Goodwin, D. W., Teasdale, T. W., Mikkelsen, U. & Schulsinger, F. A. (1984). A Danish prospective study of young males at high risk for alcoholism. In D. W. Goodwin, K. Van Dusen & S. A. Mednick, eds. *Longitudinal Research in Alcoholism*. Boston: Kluwer-Nijhoff.

Koenen, K. C. (2005). Genetically informative designs contribute to understanding the effects of trauma and interpersonal violence. *Journal of Interpersonal Violence, 20*(4), 507-12.

Koob, G. (2004). A role for GABA mechanisms in the motivational effects of alcohol. *Biochemical Pharmacology, 68*(8), 1515-25.

Koob, G. (August 23, 1999). Alcohol stimulates release of stress chemicals. Speech presented at a meeting of the American Chemical Society, New Orleans, LA.

Korrapati, M. R. & Vestal, R. E. (1995). Alcohol and medications in the elderly: Complex interactions. In T. Beresford & E. Gomberg, eds. *Alcohol and Aging* (pp. 42-55). New York: Oxford University Press.

Kurose, I., Higuchi, H., Kato, S., Miura, S. & Ishii, H. (1996). Ethanol-induced oxidative stress in the liver. *Alcoholism: Clinical and Experimental Research, 20*(1), 77A-85A.

Kushner, M. G., Abrams, K., Thuras, P., Hanson, K. L., Brekke, M. & Sletten, S. (2005). Follow-up study of anxiety disorder and alcohol dependence in comorbid alcoholism treatment patients. *Alcohol Clinical Experimental Research, 29*(8), 1432-43.

Landolt, H. P., et al. (1996). Late-afternoon ethanol intake affects nocturnal sleep and the sleep EEG in middle-aged men. *Journal of Clinical Psychopharmacology, 16*(6), 428-36.

Langton, P. A. (1995). Temperance movement. *Encyclopedia of Drugs and Alcohol* (Vol. 3, pp. 1019-23). New York: Simon & Schuster Macmillan.

Lee, J. A. (1987). Chinese, alcohol and flushing: Sociohistorical and biobehavioral considerations. *Journal of Psychoactive Drugs, 19*(4), 319-27.

Lelchuk, R. (May 5, 2005). S.F. tries to aid homeless alcoholics. *San Francisco Chronicle*, pp. A1, A14.

Li, T. K., Lumeng, L., McBride, W. J., Waller, M. B. & Murphy, J. M. (1986). Studies on an animal model of alcoholism. In M. C. Braude & J. M. Chao, eds. *Genetic and Biological Markers in Drug Abuse and Alcoholism. NIDA Research Monograph 66*. Rockville, MD: Department of Health and Human Services.

Lin, S. W. & Anthenelli, R. M. (2005). Determinants of substance abuse and dependence. In J. H. Lowinson, P. Ruiz, R. B. Millman & J. G. Langrod, eds. *Substance Abuse: A Comprehensive Textbook* (4th ed., pp. 33-47). Baltimore: Williams & Wilkins.

Little, R. E. & Sing, C. F. (1986). Association of father's drinking and infant's birth weight. *New England Journal of Medicine, 314*, 1644-45.

Madray, C., Brown, L. S. & Primm, D. J. (2005). African Americans: Epidemiology, prevention, and treatment issues. In J. H. Lowinson, P. Ruiz, R. B. Millman & J. G. Langrod, eds. *Substance Abuse: A Comprehensive Textbook* (4th ed., pp. 1093-1102). Baltimore: Williams & Wilkins.

Maher, J. (1997). Exploring alcohol's effects on liver function. *Alcohol Health & Research World, 21*(1), 10.

Maier, S. E. & West, J. R. (2001). Drinking patterns and alcohol-related birth defects. *Alcohol Research & Health, 25*(3), 168-74.

Makimoto, K. (1998). Drinking patterns and drinking problems among Asian Americans and Pacific Islanders. *Alcohol Health & Research World, 22*(4), 265-69.

Mann, R. E., Smart, R. G. & Govoni, R. (2003). The epidemiology of alcoholic liver disease. *Alcohol Research & Health 27*(3), 209-20.

Manson, S. M., Shore, J. H. & Baron, A. E. (1992). Alcohol abuse and dependence among American Indians. In J. E. Helzer & G. J. Canino, eds. *Alcoholism in North America, Europe, and Asia* (pp. 113-30). New York: Oxford University Press.

Martin, P. R., Singleton, C. K. & Hiller-Sturmhofel, S. (2003). The role of thiamine deficiency in alcoholic brain disease. *Alcohol Research & Health 27*(2), 134-43.

May, P. A. (1996). Research issues in the prevention of fetal alcohol syndrome

and alcohol-related birth defects. *Research Monograph 32, Women and Alcohol: Issues for Prevention Research*. Bethesda, MD: National Institute on Alcohol Abuse and Alcoholism.

May, P. A., Brooke, L., Gossage, J. P., Croxford, J., Adnams, C., Jones, K. L., et al. (2000). Epidemiology of FAS in a South African community. *American Journal of Public Health, 90*(12), 1905-12.

May, P. A. & Gossage, J. P. (2001). Estimating the prevalence of fetal alcohol syndrome. A summary. *Alcohol Research & Health, 25,* 159-67.

Mayo-Smith, M. (2003). Management of alcohol intoxication and withdrawal. In A. W. Graham, T. K. Schultz, M. F. Mayo-Smith, R. K. Ries & B. B. Wilford, eds. *Principles of Addiction Medicine* (3rd ed., pp. 621-632. Chevy Chase, MD: American Society of Addiction Medicine, Inc.

McGovern, P., Zhang, J., Tang, J., Zhang, Z., Hall, G. R., Moreau, R. A., et al. (2004). Fermented beverages of pre- and proto-historic China. *Proceedings of the National Academy of Sciences, 101,* 17593-98.

Miczek, K. A., Fish, E. W., de Almeida, R. M., Faccidomo, S. & Debold, J. F. (2004). Role of alcohol consumption to violence. *Annals of the New York Academy of Sciences, 1036,* 278-89.

Miller, M. M. (1995). Effect of pre- or postnatal exposure to ethanol: Cell proliferation and neuronal death. *Alcohol Clinical Experimental Research, 19*(5), 1359-63.

Miller, M. M. (1998). Traditional approaches to the treatment of addiction. In A. W. Graham & T. K. Schultz, eds. *Principles of Addiction Medicine* (2nd ed., pp. 315-26). Chevy Chase, MD: American Society of Addiction Medicine, Inc.

Miller, M. M., et al. (1988). Bedtime ethanol increases resistance of upper airways and produces sleep apneas in asymptomatic snorers. *Alcohol Clinical Experimental Research, 12*(6), 801-5.

Miller, N. S., Klamen, D., Hoffman, N. G. & Flaherty, J. A. (1995). Prevalence of depression and alcohol and other drug dependence in addictions treatment populations. *Journal of Psychoactive Drugs, 28*(2), 11-124.

Miller, T. R., Lestina, D. C. & Spicer, R. S. (1996). Highway crash costs in the United States by driver age, blood alcohol level, victim age, and restraint use. In *40th Annual Proceedings of the Association for the Advancement of Automotive Medicine* (pp. 495-517).

Moos, R. H., Brennan, P. L. & Mertens, J. R. (1994). Mortality rates and predictors of mortality among late, middle-aged and older substance abuse patients. *Alcoholism: Clinical and Experimental Research, 18,* 187-95.

Morse, R. M., Flavin, D. K., et al. (1992). The definition of alcoholism. *JAMA, 268,* 1012-14.

Moskowitz, H., Burns, M., Fiorentino, D., Smiley, A., and Zador, P. (2000). *Driver Characteristics and Impairment at Various BACs.* Washington, DC: National Highway Traffic Safety Administration.

Moskowitz, H. & Fiorentino, D. (2000). *A Review of the Literature on the Effects of Low Doses of Alcohol on Driving-Related Skills.* Washington, DC: National Highway Traffic Safety Administration.

Mukamal, K. J., Conigrave, K. M., Mittleman, M. A., Camargo, C. A., Jr., Stampfer, M. J., Willett, W. C., et al. (2003) Roles of drinking pattern and type of alcohol consumed in coronary heart disease in men. *New England Journal of Medicine, 348*(2), 109-18.

Muthusami, K. R. & Chinnaswamy, P. (2005). Effect of chronic alcoholism on male fertility hormones and semen quality. *Fertility and Sterility, 84*(4), 919-24.

Nace, E. P. (2005). Alcoholics Anonymous. In J. H. Lowinson, P. Ruiz, R. B. Millman & J. G. Langrod, eds. *Substance Abuse: A Comprehensive Textbook* (4th ed., pp. 587-98). Baltimore: Williams & Wilkins.

Nace, E. P., Saxon, J. J., Davis, C. W. & Gaspari, J. P. (1991). Axis II comorbidity in substance abusers. *American Journal of Psychiatry, 148,* 118-20.

Nace, E. P., Saxon, J. J. & Shore, N. (1983). A comparison of borderline and nonborderline alcoholic patients. *Archives of General Psychiatry, 40,* 56-58.

National Center for Health Statistics. (2005). *Fast stats.* http://www.cdc.gov/nchs/fastats/liverdis.htm (accessed July 21, 2006).

National Clearinghouse on Alcohol and Drug Information [NCADI]. (2006). *Alcohol.* http://ncadistore.samhsa.gov/catalog/facts.aspx?topic=3&h=Publications (accessed February 5, 2007).

National Highway Traffic Safety Administration [NHTSA]. (2006). *Alcohol-Related Fatalities in 2005.* http://www.nrd.nhtsa.dot.gov/pdf/nrd-30/NCSA/RNotes/2006/810686.pdf (accessed February 5, 2007).

National Highway Traffic Safety Administration. (2005). *Traffic Safety Facts, 2004.* http://www.nrd.nhtsa.dot.gov/pdf/nrd-30/NCSA/TSFAnn/

TSF2004EE.pdf (accessed November 1, 2006).

National Institute on Alcohol Abuse and Alcoholism [NIAAA]. (1991). Alcohol & Asian Americans. *Alcohol Health & Research World, 2*(2), 41. Rockville, MD: U.S. Department of Health and Human Services.

National Institute on Alcohol Abuse and Alcoholism. (1997). Alcohol metabolism. *Alcohol Alert No. 35.* Rockville, MD: U.S. Department of Health and Human Services.

National Institute on Alcohol Abuse and Alcoholism. (1998). Alcohol and tobacco. *Alcohol Alert No. 39.* Rockville, MD: U.S. Department of Health and Human Services.

National Institute on Alcohol Abuse and Alcoholism. (1999). Are women more vulnerable to alcohol effects? *Alcohol Alert No. 46.* Rockville, MD: U.S. Department of Health and Human Services.

National Institute on Alcohol Abuse and Alcoholism. (2000). *Tenth Special Report to U.S. Congress on Alcohol and Health.* Bethesda, MD: U.S. Department of Health and Human Services.

National Institute on Alcohol Abuse and Alcoholism. (2003). *Helping People with Alcohol Problems: A Health Practitioner's Guide.* National Institutes of Health Pub. No. 03-3769. Bethesda, MD: U.S. Department of Health and Human Services.

National Institute on Alcohol Abuse and Alcoholism. (2004). *National Epidemiologic Survey on Alcohol and Related Conditions.* http://niaaa.census.gov (accessed July 21, 2006).

National Institute on Drug Abuse. (1994). *Women and drug abuse: You and your community can help.* Bethesda, MD: Substance Abuse and Mental Health Services Administration.

Nelson, T. F., Naimi, T. S., Brewer, R. D. & Wechsler, H. (2005). The state sets the rate: The relationship of college binge drinking to state binge drinking rates and selected state alcohol control policies. *American Journal of Public Health, 95*(3), 441-46.

Nidus Information Services. (2002). *What is cirrhosis?* http://www.reutershealth.com/wellconnected/doc75.html (accessed February 2, 2007).

Noble, E. P., Blum, K., Montgomery, A. & Sheridan, P. J. (1991). Allelic association of the D2 dopamine receptor gene with receptor-binding characteristics in alcoholism. *Archives of General Psychiatry, 48,* 648-54.

O'Brien, R. & Chafetz, M. (1991). *The Encyclopedia of Alcoholism* (2nd ed.). New York: Facts on File.

Olds, J. (1956). Pleasure centers in the brain. *Scientific American, 195*(4), 105-16.

Olds, J. & Milner, P. (1954). Positive reinforcement produced by electrical stimulation of septal area and other regions of rat brain. *Journal of Comprehensive Physiology and Psychology, 47,* 419-27.

O'Malley, P. M. & Johnston, L. D. (2002). Epidemiology of alcohol and other drug use among American college students. *Journal of Studies on Alcohol Supplement, 14,* 23-39.

Oquendo, S. L., Galfalvy, H. C., Grunebaum, M. F., Burke, A. K., Zalsman, G. & Mann, J. J. (2005). The relationship of aggression to suicidal behavior in depressed patients with a history of alcoholism. *Addictive Behavior 30*(6), 1144-53.

Oroszi, G. & Goldman, D. (2004). Alcoholism: Genes and mechanisms. *Pharmacogenomics 5*(8), 1037-48.

Pagliaro, A. M. & Pagliaro, L. A. (2003). Alcohol and other drug use during pregnancy: Effects on Developing fetus, neonate, and infant. In A. W. Graham, T. K. Schultz, M. F. Mayo-Smith, R. K. Ries & B. B. Wilford, eds. *Principles of Addiction Medicine* (3rd ed., pp. 1247-1258) Chevy Chase, MD: American Society of Addiction Medicine, Inc.

Petrakis, I. L., Gonzalez, G., Rosenheck, R. & Krystal, J. H. (2002). Comorbidity of alcoholism and psychiatric disorders: An overview. *Alcohol Research & Health, 26*(2), 81-89.

Pfefferbaum, A., Adalsteinsson, E. & Sullivan, E. V. (June 15, 2005). Dysmorphology and microstructural degradation of the corpus callosum: Interaction of age and alcoholism. *Neurobiology of Aging.* Prepublication.

Piasecki, I. M., Sher, K. J., Slutske, W. S. & Jackson, K. M. (2005). Hangover frequency and risk for alcohol use disorders: Evidence from a longitudinal high-risk study. *Journal of Abnormal Psychology, 114*(2), 223-34.

Plato. (360 B.C.) The Symposium, The Republic, The Laws. In L. R. Loomis, ed. *Plato, Five Great Dialogues.* New York: Gramercy Books.

Prescott, C. A. (2002). Sex differences in the genetic risk for alcoholism. *Alcohol Research & Health, 26*(4), 264-73.

Prescott, C. A. & Kendler, K. S. (1999). Genetic and environmental contributions to alcohol abuse and dependence in a population-based sample of male twins. *The American Journal of Psychiatry, 156,* 34-40.

Presley, C. A. (1997). *Alcohol and Drugs on American College Campuses: Issues of Violence and Harassment.*

Carbondale: Southern Illinois University at Carbondale.

Puddey, I. B. & Beilin, L. J. (2006). Alcohol is bad for blood pressure. *Clinical and Experimental Pharmacology and Physiology, 33*(9), 847-52.

Redzic, A., Licanin, I. & Krosnjar, S. (2003). Simultaneous abuse of different psychoactive substances among adolescents. *Bosnian Journal of Basic Medical Science 3*(1), 44-48.

Reed, T., Pagte, W. F., Viken, R. J. & Christian, J. C. (1996). Genetic predisposition to organ-specific endpoints of alcoholism. *Alcohol Clinical Experimental Research, 20*(9), 1528-33.

Regier, D. A., Farmer, M. E., Rae, D. S., Locke, B. Z., Keith, S. J., Judd, L. L., et al. (1990). Comorbidity of mental disorders with alcohol and other drug abuse. Results from the Epidemiologic Catchment Area (RCA) study. *JAMA, 264*(19), 2511-18.

Register, T. C., Cline, J. & Shively, C. A. (2002). Health issues in postmenopausal women who drink. *Alcohol Research & Health, 26,* 299-307.

Reifman, A. & Watson, W. K. (2003). Binge drinking during the first semester of college: Continuation and desistance from high school patterns. *Journal of American College Health, 52*(2), 73-81.

Rigler, S. K. (2000). Alcoholism in the elderly. *American Family Physician 61*(6), 1710-16.

Riikonen, R. S., Nokelainen, P., Valkonen, K., Kolemainen, A. I., Kumpulainen, K. I., Kononen, M., et al. (2005). Deep serotonergic and dopaminergic structures in fetal alcohol syndrome. *Biological Psychiatry 57*(12), 1565-72.

Roehrs, T. & Roth, T. (2001). Sleep, sleepiness, and alcohol use. *Alcohol: Research & Health, 25*(2), 101-9.

Roizen, J. (1997). Epidemiological issues in alcohol-related violence. In M. Galanter, ed., *Recent Developments in Alcoholism* (Vol. 13). New York: Plenum Press.

Rosenberg, A. (1996). Brain damage caused by prenatal alcohol exposure. *Science & Medicine, 3*(4), 43-51.

Ross, H. E. (1989). Alcohol and drug abuse in treated alcoholics: A comparison of men and women. *Alcohol Clinical & Experimental Research, 13,* 810-16.

Ruiz, P. & Langrod, J. G. (2005). Hispanic Americans. In J. H. Lowinson, P. Ruiz, R. B. Millman & J. G. Langrod, eds. *Substance Abuse: A Comprehensive Textbook* (4th ed., pp. 1103-12). Baltimore: Williams & Wilkins.

Saadatmand, F., Stinson, F. S., Grant, B. F. & Dufour, M. C. (2000). *Surveillance Report #54. Liver Cirrhosis Mortality in the United States, 1970-1997.* Bethesda,

MD: National Institute on Alcohol Abuse and Alcoholism.

Sacco, R. L., Elkind, M., Boden-Albala, B., Lin, I. F., Kargman, D. E., Hauser, W. A., et al. (1999). The protective effect of moderate alcohol consumption on ischemic stroke. *JAMA, 281*(1), 53-60.

Saitz, R. & O'Malley, S. S. (1997). Pharmacotherapies for alcohol abuse. Withdrawal and treatment. *Medical Clinics of North America, 81,* 881.

Schuckit, M. A. (1996). Hangovers: A rarely studied but important phenomenon. *Vista Hill Foundation Drug Abuse & Alcoholism Newsletter, 23*(1).

Schuckit, M. A. (2000). *Drug and Alcohol Abuse* (5th ed.). New York: Kluwer Academic/Plenum Publishers.

Schuckit, M. A., Edenberg, H. J., Kalmijn, J., Flury, L., Smith, T. L., Reich, T., et al. (2001). A genome-wide search for genes that relate to a low level of response to alcohol. *Alcohol Clinical and Experimental Research, 25*(3), 323-29.

Schuckit, M. A., Smith, T. L., Beltran, I., Waylen, A., Horwood, J., Davis, J. M., et al. (2005). Performance of a self-report measure of the level of response to alcohol in 12- to 13-year-old adolescents. *Journal of Studies on Alcohol 66*(4), 452-58.

Schuckit, M. A., Tipp, J. E., Bucholz, K. K., Nurnberger, J. I., Jr., Hesselbrock, V. M., Crowe, R. R., et al. (1997). The life-time rates of three major mood disorders and four major anxiety disorders in alcoholics and controls. *Addiction, 92*(10), 1289-304.

Segal, B. (1990). *The Drunken Society: Alcohol Abuse and Alcoholism in the Soviet Union.* New York: Hippocrene Books.

Shiffman, S. & Balabanis, M. (1995). Associations between alcohol and tobacco. In J. B. Fertig & J. P. Allen, eds. *Alcohol and Tobacco: From Basic Science to Clinical Practice, NIAAA Research Monograph No. 30* (pp. 17-36). Washington, DC: U.S. Government Printing Office.

Shivani, R., Goldsmith, J. & Anthenelli, R. M. (2002). Alcoholism and psychiatric disorders. *Alcohol Research & Health, 26*(2), 90-98.

Singh, G. K. & Hoyert, D. L. (2000). Social epidemiology of chronic liver disease and cirrhosis mortality in the United States, 1935-1997. *Human Biology, 72,* 801-20.

Sokol, R. J. & Clarren, S. K. (1989). Guidelines for use of terminology describing the impact of prenatal alcohol on the offspring. *Alcoholism: Clinical and Experimental Research, 13*(4), 597-09.

Sood, B., Delaney-Black, V., Covington, C., Nordstrom-Klee, B., Ager, J., Templin, T., et al. (2001). Prenatal alcohol exposure and childhood behavior at age 6 to 7 years. Dose response effect. *Pediatrics, 108*(2), E34.

Span, S. A. & Earleywine, M. (1999). Familial risk for alcoholism and hangover symptoms. *Addictive Behaviors, 24*(1), 121-25.

Stahl, S. M. (2000). *Essential Psychopharmacology* (pp. 522-23). Cambridge, England: Cambridge University Press.

Stoff, D. M. & Cairns, R. B., eds. (2005). *Aggression and Violence: Genetic, Neurobiological, and Biosocial Perspectives.* Mahwah, NJ: Lawrence Erlbaum Associates.

Strakowski, S. M., DelBello, M. P., Fleck, D. E., Adler, C. M., Anthenelli, R. M., Keck, P. E., Jr., et al. (2005). Effects of co-occurring alcohol abuse on the course of bipolar disorder following a first hospitalization for mania. *Archives of General Psychiatry 62*(8), 851-58.

Stratton, K., Howe, C. & Battaglia, F., eds. (1996). *Fetal Alcohol Syndrome: Diagnosis, Epidemiology, Prevention, and Treatment.* Washington, DC: National Academy Press.

Streissguth, A. P. (1997). *Fetal Alcohol Syndrome.* Baltimore: Paul H. Brookes Publishing Co.

Streissguth, A. P., Barr, H. M., Kogn, J. & Bookstein, F. L. (1996). *Understanding the occurrence of secondary disabilities in clients with FAS and FAE* (Tech. Rep. No. 96-106). Atlanta, GA: Centers for Disease Control and Prevention.

Streissguth, A. P., Bookstein, F. L., Barr, H. M., Sampson, P. D., O'Malley, K. & Young J. K. (2004). Risk factors for adverse life outcomes in fetal alcohol syndrome and fetal alcohol effects. *Journal of Developmental and Behavioral Pediatrics, 25*(4), 228-38.

Substance Abuse and Mental Health Services Administration [SAMHSA]. (2006). *Overview of Findings from the 2005 National Survey on Drug Use and Health.* http://www.oas.samhsa.gov/NSDUH/2k5NSDUH/tabs/Sect2peTabs1to57.htm#Tab2.1A (accessed February 5, 2007).

Substance Abuse and Mental Health Services Administration. (2005). *Substance Use During Pregnancy. The NSDUH Report.* http://www.oas.samhsa.gov/2K5/pregnancy/pregnancy.cfm (accessed January 4, 2007).

Sue, D. (1987). Use and abuse of alcohol by Asian Americans. *Journal of Psychoactive Drugs, 19*(1), 57-66.

Swift, R. & Davidson, D. (1998). Alcohol hangover: Mechanisms and mediators.

Alcohol Health & Research World, 22(1), 54-60.

Tabakoff, B., Cornell, N. & Hoffman, P. L. (1992). Alcohol tolerance. *Annals of Emergency Medicine, 15*(9), 1005-12.

Teng, Y. S. (1981). Human liver aldehyde dehydrogenase in Chinese and Asiatic Indians: Gene deletion and its possible implications in alcohol metabolism. *Biochemical Genetics, 19*, 107-14.

Terry, M. B., Zhang, F. F., Kabat, G., Britton, J. A., Teitelbaum, S. L., Neugut, A. I., et al. (2005). Lifetime alcohol intake and breast cancer risk. *Annals of Epidemiology, 16*(3), 230-40.

Thanos, P. K., Dimitrakakis, E. S., Rice, O., Giffore, A. & Volkow, N. D. (2005). Ethanol self-administration and ethanol conditioned place preference are reduced in mice lacking cannabinoid CB1 receptors. *Behavioral Brain Research, 164*(2), 206-13.

Thun, M. J., Peto, R., Lopez, A. D., Monaco, J. H., Henley, S. J., Heath, C. W. & Doll, R. (1997). Alcohol consumption and mortality among middle-aged and elderly U.S. adults. *New England Journal of Medicine, 337*(24), 1711.

Trice, H. M. (1995). Alcohol: History. In D. B. Heath, ed., *Encyclopedia of Drugs and Alcohol* (Vol. 1, pp. 85-92). New York: Simon & Schuster Macmillan.

Tsuang, J. W. (2005). Asian Americans and Pacific Islanders. In J. H. Lowinson, P. Ruiz, R. B. Millman & J. G. Langrod, eds. *Substance Abuse: A Comprehensive Textbook* (4th ed., pp. 1113-18). Baltimore: Williams & Wilkins.

Turner, R. T. & Sibonga, J. D. (2001). Effects of alcohol use and estrogen on bone. *Alcohol Research & Health*, *25*(4), 276-81.

U.S. Bureau of the Census. (2005). *Hispanic Population Passes 40 Million, Census Bureau Reports.* http://www. census.gov/Press-Release/www/ releases/archives/population/005164. html (accessed February 5, 2007).

U.S. Bureau of the Census. (2006). *The American Indian and Alaska Native Population: 2000.* http://www.census. gov/prod/2002pubs/c2kbr01-15.pdf (accessed February 2, 2007).

U.S. Conference of Mayors. (2005). *A Status Report on Hunger and Homelessness in America's Cities, 2004.* http://www.usmayors.org/uscm/hunger-survey/2004/onlinereport/HungerAndHomelessnessReport2004.pdf (accessed February 2, 2007).

U.S. Department of Health and Human Services. (2005). *National Resource and Training Center on Homelessness and Mental Illness. Get the Facts.* http://www.nrchmi.samhsa.gov/facts/facts_ question_1.asp (accessed February 2, 2007).

U.S. Department of Justice. (1998). *Alcohol and crime: An analysis of national data on the prevalence of alcohol involvement in crime.* http://www.ojp.gov/bjs/ pub/pdf/ac.pdf (accessed January 2, 2007).

U.S. Surgeon General. (1992). *Youth and Alcohol: Dangerous and Deadly Consequences: Report to the Surgeon General.* Bethesda, MD: Substance Abuse and Mental Health Services Administration.

Vaillant, G. E. (1995). *The Natural History of Alcoholism Revisited.* Cambridge, MA: Harvard University Press.

Vitiello, M. V. (1997). Sleep, alcohol, and alcohol abuse. *Addiction Biology, 2*, 151-58.

Voas, R. B., Wells, J. K., Lestina, D. C., Williams, A. F. & Greene, M. A. (1997). *Drinking and Driving in the U.S.: The 1996 National Roadside Survey.* NHTSA Traffic Task No. 152. Arlington, VA: Insurance Institute for Highway Safety.

Vogel-Sprott, M., Rawana, E. & Webster, R. (1984). Mental rehearsal of a task under ethanol facilitates tolerance. *Pharmacology, Biochemistry & Behavior, 21*(3), 329-31.

Volkow, N., Wang, G. J. & Doria, J. J. (1995). Monitoring the brain's response to alcohol with positron emission tomography. *Alcohol World: Health and Research: Imaging in Alcohol Research, 19*(4), 296-299.

Wechsler, H., Lee, J. E., Kuo, M., Seibring, M., Nelson, T. F. & Lee, H. (2002). Trends in college binge drinking during a period of increased prevention efforts. *Journal of American College Health, 50*(5), 203-17.

West J. R. & Blake C. A. (2005). Fetal alcohol syndrome: An assessment of the field. *Experimental Biological Medicine, 230*(6), 354-56.

Windle, M. (2003). Alcohol use among adolescents and young adults. *Alcohol Research & Health, 27*(1), 79-86.

Woodward, J. J. (2003). The pharmacology of alcohol. In A. W. Graham, T. K. Schultz, M. F. Mayo-smith, R. K. Ries & B. B. Wilford, eds. *Principles of Addiction Medicine* (3rd ed., 101-18). Chevy Chase, MD: American Society of Addiction Medicine, Inc.

World Health Organization. (2005). *Alcohol consumption.* http://www.who.int/sub stance_abuse/PDFfiles/global_alco hol_status_report/4Alcoholconsumptio n.pdf (accessed November 11, 2006).

Yesavage, J. A. & Leirer, V. O. (1986). Hangover effects on aircraft pilots 14 hours after alcohol ingestion. *American Journal of Psychiatry, 143*(12), 1546-50.

Yokoyama, M., Yokoyama, A., Yokoyama, T., Funazu, K., Hamana, G., Kondo, S., et al. (2005). Hangover susceptibility in relation to aldehyde dehydrogenase-2 genotype, alcohol flushing, and mean corpuscular volume in Japanese workers. *Alcohol Clinical Experimental Research, 29*(7), 1165-71.

Zador, P. L. (1991). Alcohol-related relative risk of fatal driver injuries in relation to driver age and sex. *Journal of Studies of Alcohol, 52*(4), 302-10.

Zane, N. W. & Kim, J. C. (1994). In N. W. Zane, D. T. Takeuchi & K. N. J. Young, eds. *Confronting Critical Health Issues of Asian and Pacific Islander Americans* (pp. 316-46). Thousand Oaks, CA: Sage Publications.

Zhang, S. M., Lee, I. M., Manson, J. E., Cook, N. R., Willett, W. C. & Buring, J. E. (2007). Alcohol consumption and breast cancer risk in the Women's Health Study. *American Journal of Epidemiology.* (Prepublication).

All Arounders

The Vapor Room in San Francisco, a medical marijuana club, uses a vaporizer to aerosolize the drug for its clients who have a medical marijuana card. This method of marijuana use avoids the carcinogens and hot gases that occur when it is smoked. As of 2006 there were 32 medical marijuana clubs in San Francisco.

©2006, CNS Productions, Inc.

- **Introduction & History.** Psychedelics alter a user's perception of the world. For this reason human beings have used such *all arounders* for tens of thousands of years to cope with their fears and environment. They used them for religious, social, ceremonial, and medical purposes. Psychedelics were originally found in some of the 4,000 plants and fungi that have psychoactive effects. In the past century many psychedelics have been synthesized.

- **Classification.** LSD, MDMA, ketamine, psilocybin mushrooms, DMT, PCP, peyote, and especially marijuana are the most commonly used all arounders (also called *hallucinogens* and occasionally *entactogens* or *empathogens*).

- **General Effects.** Effects often depend on the user's mind-set and the physical setting in which the drug is used. Psychedelics cause intensified sensations, crossed sensations (*synesthesia,* e.g., visual input becomes sound), illusions (mistaken perceptions of real stimuli), delusions (a mistaken belief that is not swayed by reason), and hallucinations (a completely imaginary sensory experience). Physical stimulation, impaired judgment, and distorted reasoning are also common.

- **LSD, Psilocybin Mushrooms & Other Indole Psychedelics.** Indole psychedelics exert many of their effects through serotonin receptors. LSD, an ergot fungus toxin (which can be synthesized), is very potent. It causes stimulation, mood changes, loss of judgment, sensory distortions, hallucinations, and illusions. Bad emotional reactions ("bum trips") can result. It was initially popularized by Dr. Timothy Leary and writer Ken Kesey in the 1960s. Psilocybin mushrooms cause nausea and induce hallucinations. Three other indole psychedelics, ibogaine, DMT, and ayahuasca (yage), are much less common.

- **Peyote, MDMA & Other Phenylalkylamine Psychedelics.** Phenylalkylamines are chemically related to adrenaline and amphetamine. Mescaline (peyote cacti), used in sacred rituals and ceremonies, causes more hallucinations than LSD. Effects last about 12 hours. Psycho-stimulants like MDMA (ecstasy), MDA, and 2C-B or CBR cause feelings of well-being, empathy, and calming along with their stimulatory effects. They cause excess release of serotonin. MDMA is one of the club drugs (e.g., ketamine, nitrous oxide, GHB, and dextromethorphan).

- **Belladonna & Other Anticholinergic Psychedelics.** Plants such as belladonna, jimsonweed, and henbane have been used in the rituals of ancient cultures for more than 3,000 years mostly to induce visions. Their active ingredients are hyoscyamine, atropine, and scopolamine. These drugs speed up the heart, raise body temperature, and cause a separation from reality.

- **Ketamine, PCP & Other Psychedelics.** Ketamine is an anesthetic used on animals and humans. It causes mind/body separation, a sensory-deprived state, and hallucinations. PCP is similar to ketamine and produces many of the same effects. It predates ketamine in street popularity. PCP and ketamine are also known as *dissociative anesthetics. Amanita* mushrooms, nutmeg, and mace are also psychedelics but are rarely used in Europe and the United States. *Salvia divinorum* (diviner's sage) has become somewhat popular in the 2000s. Dextromethorphan is a nonprescription cough suppressant that can cause psychedelic effects (and health liabilities) when used to excess.

- **Marijuana & The Cannabinoids.** Marijuana (e.g., *Cannabis sativa, Cannabis indica*) is the most popular illicit psychoactive drug, used by 160 million people worldwide. It magnifies the existing personality traits of users. Effects often depend on the mind-set of the user and the setting in which it is used. Marijuana can cause relaxation, sedation, increased appetite, heightened sense of novelty, giddiness, bloodshot eyes, short-term memory impairment, impaired tracking ability, and mental confusion. Hemp, a fibrous version of the Cannabis plant, is used to make ropes, sails, and clothing. There have been intense social and legal battles over the use of marijuana for medical purposes. A recent U.S. Supreme Court ruling permits federal anti-marijuana laws to supersede state medical marijuana laws.

Ecstasy to be tested on cancer patients

FDA OKS RESEARCH

patients come to terms with the ... Psychedelic Studies. The Saraso-... ta, Fla.-based nonprofit has orga-

VENETA — Drug agents raided an unusual mushroom-growing farm near Veneta, seizing 500 pounds of hallucinogenic mushrooms with an estimated street value of $800,000

Peyote Church's Holy Sacrament
American Indians defend use of hallucinogen

Court rejects medical pot laws

Medicinal pot loss

The ruling The U.S. Supreme Court ruled that federal may prosecute individuals who grow or use marijuana for m purposes.

place California's medical marijuana law allows smoke or obtain marijuana for medical needs with a mendation. Ten other states, including Oregon, have

reasoning Justice John Paul Stevens, writing y, said federal drug laws clearly cover marijuana

'Date rape' drug GHB making inroads in nation's club scene
As its popularity grows,
mal people don't say, 'I'm looking forward to my next coma.'

Rave parties pose problem in France

Events are drawing

Love Parade, which drew at least 800,000 last month, and Zurich's Lake Parade, which drew 750,000. I

Bid to sue over LSD rejected

Jimson weed users chase high all the way to hospital
By Donna Leinwand

Agents arrest 4 in hallucinogenic-mushroom raid

By KATHLEEN MONJE
Correspondent, The Oregonian

"They're complicated and difficult to put together ... so you don't just see them very often."

Narcotics agents had been investigating the case for nearly six months before the arrests, said Capt. Tim Birr, spokesman for the Eugene Public Safety Department.

The men were arraigned Tuesday

lived in nearby Eugene.
The owner of the farm, John David Seleen, 33, was arrested at his Eugene home. Investigators seized records and a small amount of mushrooms at Seleen's residence. A third search warrant is to be executed at an undisclosed location and more arrests may follow, Siel said.

three others that police had seized over the last several years.
The Veneta operation consisted of several steps in four different buildings. Purified barley had to be heated in a kiln on the property to develop spores for the mind-altering mushrooms, Siel said.
The spores then were transferred

CLUB SCENE GROWS UP
By Carolyne Zinko | CHRONICLE STAFF WRITER

Jersey Poison Information and Education System in Newark. New Jer-

"Hot as a hare, blind as a bat, dry as a bone, red as a beet, mad as a hatter." Such patients are "hallucinating up a

► CLUBS: Page A20

INTRODUCTION & HISTORY

"When I got up and walked about, I could do so quite normally. Space was still there but it had lost its predominance. The mind was primarily concerned not with measures and locations but with being and meaning. And along with indifference to space there went an even more complete indifference to time."

Aldous Huxley after experimenting with peyote in The Doors of Perception, 1954

Uppers stimulate the body and downers depress it. All arounders (psychedelics) usually act as stimulants and occasionally as depressants but mostly **psychedelics dramatically alter a user's perception and create a world in which reason takes a back seat to intensified sensations by creating illusions, delusions, and hallucinations**.

Psychedelic plants and fungi have been around for 250 million years and have probably been used

Some anthropologists are partial to the *Cannabis*–dinosaur extinction theory.

L S STURGEON

by **human beings since they've walked the earth** (Schultes & Hofmann, 1992). Plants and fungi mutated and developed chemical defenses against animals, insects, and disease. Often those defenses were bitter alkaloids such as cocaine and nicotine that could induce psychoactive and sometimes psychedelic effects. **More than 4,000 plants have psychedelic (hallucinogenic) or psychoactive properties** but only a few hundred have continued to be used over the ages. Primitive people most likely tried these plants and fungi as food but had hallucinogenic and psychoactive experiences that frightened yet intrigued them (Siegel, 1985).

Neanderthals and eventually shamans, brujas, witches, and healers experimented with different methods of ingestion: boiling and drinking, smoking, eating, or absorbing (through the nasal passages, the gums, or the skin). Even after the hypodermic needle was invented more than 150 years ago, hallucinogens were rarely injected because the **object of using them was to alter one's consciousness and perception of reality rather than to induce an immediate rush** (Escohotado, 1999).

"When the mushrooms took effect on them, then they danced, then they wept. But some, while still in command of their senses, entered and sat there by the house; they danced no more, but only sat there nodding. . . . And when the effects of the mushrooms had left them, they consulted among themselves and told one another what they had seen in vision."

Bernardo de Sahagun, Spanish missionary and archeologist specializing in Aztecs, 1542 (Sahagun, 1985)

Over the past four millennia, *Amanita* mushrooms were eaten in India, belladonna was drunk in ancient Greece, marijuana was inhaled in ancient China, and poisonous ergot, found in rye mold (a natural form of LSD), was accidentally consumed in renaissance Europe. No matter where explorers and anthropologists ventured, they found that every culture had dis-

covered and was using a psychoactive/psychedelic substance (Goldstein, 2001).

The majority of psychedelics are grown and used in the Americas, Europe, and Africa (the major exception is marijuana, grown and used in most countries). Hundreds of tribes in the Americas, such as the Aztecs and the Toltecs in the past and the Kiowas and Huichols in the present, have used peyote, psilocybin mushrooms, yage, marijuana, and morning glory seeds **for religious, social, ceremonial, and medical purposes** (Diaz, 1979; Efferink, 1988). Over the past 100 years, the development of synthetic drugs has expanded the psychedelic alphabet: DMT, MDA, MDMA, LSD, and PCP.

There was an upsurge of interest in psychedelics in the mid- to late 1990s among U.S. college, high school, and even middle school students, and then a decline in the early 2000s (except marijuana). Here's a snapshot of use by high school seniors over the past five years:

◇ MDMA—2.3% in 2000 down to 1.3% in 2006;
◇ LSD—4.0% in 1995 down to 0.6% in 2006;
◇ Marijuana—37.4% in 1979, 11.9% in 1992, 23.9% in 1999, and 18.3% in 2006.

(Monitoring the Future, 2006)

Other than marijuana, **psychedelics, like in the 1960s and 1970s, are still most popular among young White users**, then Hispanics, and, finally, the lowest per-capita use, the Black community (Substance Abuse and Mental Health Services Administration [SAMHSA], 2006).

Over the centuries, the legality of psychedelics has varied widely and often; as one substance is made illegal, others pop up. Classification of these substances is more complex than with stimulants, opioids, or benzodiazepines.

CLASSIFICATION

From alphabet soup psychedelics (MDMA, LSD, PMA) to naturally occurring plants used socially, therapeutically, or in religious/spiritual ceremonies (marijuana, peyote, mush-

rooms, belladonna), all arounders represent a diverse group of substances.

There are five main chemical classifications of psychedelics:

◇ the *indoles* (e.g., **LSD, psilocybin mushrooms**);
◇ the *phenylalkylamines* (e.g., **peyote, MDMA [ecstasy]**);
◇ the *anticholinergics* (e.g., **belladonna, datura**);
◇ those in a class by themselves (e.g., **ketamine, PCP, *Salvia divinorum*, dextromethorphan [DXM]**); and
◇ the cannabinoids found in **marijuana (*Cannabis*) plants.**

GENERAL EFFECTS

ASSESSING THE EFFECTS

Despite the fact that many psychedelics predate more-modern stimulants and depressants such as methamphetamine and benzodiazepines, the research has been minimal because most psychedelics are grown illegally or manufactured by street chemists. For this reason **much of the information about the effects of psychedelics has been anecdotal rather than the result of extended scientific testing.** In addition **most plant-based psychedelics contain more than one active ingredient**, so it is hard to say which chemical is causing which effect. Many drugs that are sold as one psychedelic may actually be another, cheaper psychedelic, so even the anecdotal information can be incorrect. Some common examples of misrepresentation are ketamine sold as THC (the active ingredient in marijuana) or regular mushrooms dosed with LSD and sold as psilocybin mushrooms (Rosen & Weil, 2004).

Besides the toxicity, the effects of many psychedelics are dependent on the amount of drug ingested. A drug like LSD is thousands of times more powerful by weight than a similar amount of peyote.

Besides the toxicity of the psychedelic and the amount used, the effects depend on

◇ **experience with the drug,**
◇ **the basic emotional makeup of the user,**

TABLE 6–1 ALL AROUNDERS (PSYCHEDELICS)

Common Names	Active Ingredients	Street Names
INDOLE PSYCHEDELICS		
LSD (LSD-25 & -49) (Schedule I)	Lysergic acid diethylamide	Acid, sugar cube, windowpane, blotter, illusion, boomers, yellow sunshine
Mushrooms (Schedule I)	Psilocybin	'Shrooms, magic mushrooms
Tabernanthe iboga (Schedule I)	Ibogaine	African LSD
Morning glory seeds or Hawaiian woodrose	Lysergic acid amide	Heavenly blue, pearly gates, wedding bells, ololiuqui
DMT (synthetic or from yopo beans, epena, or Sonoran Desert toad) (Schedule I)	Dimethyltryptamine	Businessman's special, cohoba snuff
Ayahuasca (*hoasca*), yage, caapi, daime	Harmaline (also mixed with DMT)	Visionary vine, vine of the soul, vine of death, mihi, kahi
Foxy	5-Me-DIPT	Foxy
AMT	Alphamethyltryptamine, IT-290	Foxy methoxy, Amtrak
PHENYLALKYLAMINE PSYCHEDELICS		
Peyote cactus (Schedule I)	Mescaline	Mesc, peyote, buttons
Designer psychedelics, e.g., MDA, MDMA (MDM), MMDA, MDE (Schedule I)	Variations of methylenedioxy-amphetamines	Ecstasy, rave, love drug, XTC, Adam, Eve, thizz, stunna
Bromo-benzodifuranyl-isopropylamine		Bromo-Dragon Fly, ABDF
2C-B or CBR (Schedule I)	4-bromo-2,5-dimethoxy-phenethylamine	Nexus
2C-T-2 (Schedule I)	2,5-dimethoxy-4-ethyl-thiophenethylamine	
2C-T-7 (Schedule I)	2,5-dimethoxy-4-propyl-thiophenethylamine	Blue Mystic®, tripstacy
STP (DOM) (synthetic) (Schedule I)	4 methyl 2,5 dimethoxy-amphetamine	Serenity, tranquility, peace pill
STP-LSD combo	Dimethoxy-amphetamine with LSD	Wedge series, orange and pink wedges, Harvey wallbanger
PMA (Schedule I)	Paramethoxyamphetamine	Death, Mitsubishi double-stack
U4Euh (Schedule I)	4-methylpemoline	Euphoria
ANTICHOLINERGICS		
Belladonna, mandrake, henbane, datura (jimson weed, thornapple), wolfbane (Schedule I)	Atropine, scopolamine, hyoscyamine	Deadly nightshade, dwale, divale, devil's herb, black cherry, stinkweed
Artane® Trihexyphenidyl		
Cogentin®	Benztropine	
Asmador® cigarettes	Belladonna alkaloids	
OTHER PSYCHEDELICS		
Ketamine (Schedule III)	Ketajet,® Ketalar®	Special K, K, vitamin K, super-K
PCP (Schedule II)	Phencyclidine ozone, Sherms,® Shermans®	Angel dust, hog, peace pill, krystal joint,
Nutmeg and mace	Myristicin	
Amanita mushrooms (fly agaric)	Ibotenic acid, muscimole	Soma
Salvia divinorum	Salvinorin A	Diviner's sage, sage, Sally-D
DM in Romilar,® Coricidin®	Dextromethorphan	DXM, robo, red devils, skittles, dex
CANNABINOIDS		
Marijuana (Schedule I) (Marinol,® Cesamet,® and Sativex are legal prescription THCs)	Δ-9-tetrahydro-cannabinol (THC)	Grass, pot, weed, Mary Jane, joint, reefer, dank, dubie, mota, blunt, bhang, ditch weed, Colombian, BC bud, honey blunt, chronic, sens, stink weed, herb, charas, ganja, grifa, the kind, 420
Sinsemilla (Schedule I)	High-potency THC	Sens, skunk weed, ganja
Hashish, hash oil (Schedule I)	High-potency THC	Hash

◇ **the mood and the mental state at the time of use,**

◇ **any preexisting mental illnesses,**

◇ **and the surroundings in which the drug is taken**

are also crucial to the type, duration, and intensity of the effects. For instance, a first- or second-time psychedelic user may become nauseated, anxious, depressed, or totally disoriented whereas an experienced user may experience only euphoric feelings or some mild illusions. A user with schizophrenia or major depression could get a severe reaction from LSD because it might trigger a mental instability.

PHYSICAL & MENTAL EFFECTS

LSD, ecstasy, and most other **hallucinogens stimulate the sympathetic nervous system.** This stimulation results in a rise in pulse rate and blood pressure. Many psychedelics also cause sweating, palpitations, or nausea. Generally, psychedelics interfere with neurotransmitters such as dopamine, norepinephrine, acetylcholine, anandamide, glutamate, alpha psychosin, and especially serotonin. *Serotonin* affects sensory perception and a number of other functions; and because serotonin neurons are amply represented in the limbic system (the emotional center of the brain), most psychedelics greatly affect mood.

The stimulation of the brainstem, and specifically the reticular formation, can **overload the sensory pathways, making the user acutely aware of all sensation.** Disruption of visual and auditory centers can confuse perception. An auditory stimulation such as music might jump to a visual pathway, causing the music to be "seen" as shifting light patterns; visual impulses might shift to auditory neurons, resulting in strange sounds. **This crossover or mixing of the senses is known as** *synesthesia.* Some practitioners of certain forms of religion or mysticism say that many psychedelic experiences are similar to the transcendental state of mind achieved through deep meditation. Recent research at Yale suggests that LSD increases glutamate, which in turn affects synapses not directly in the

pathway activated by the electrical stimulus. Such spillover is posited to induce certain cognitive, affective, and sensory abnormalities, including synesthesia (Lambe & Aghajanian, 2005).

Illusions, Delusions & Hallucinations

It is important to note the differences among an illusion, a delusion, and a hallucination.

An *illusion* **is a mistaken perception of an external stimulus.** For example, a rope can be misinterpreted as a snake. A bush can be misperceived as a threatening animal.

"I've had illusions, not hallucinations, but just where different colors stand out, things move, different objects, just little things you never really think twice about. It's just part of your high, I guess, but as you become more immune to it, not too much like that happens."
19-year-old male marijuana smoker

A *delusion* **is a mistaken idea or belief that is not swayed by reason or other contradictory evidence.** An example is someone who thinks he can fly or thinks he has become deformed or ugly.

"I have strange thoughts. I have a tunnel vision effect. I feel unified. I feel very asexual, like sex would be beside the point because I feel unified with everything."
38-year-old psychedelic user

A *hallucination* **is a sensory experience that doesn't come from external stimuli,** such as seeing a creature or hearing a sound that doesn't exist.

"You go to places that you could never reach before to where you were never coming back and then out of a dream and you step up back into your body and come back to your senses and come back to reality."
16-year-old psychedelic user

With LSD and most psychedelics, illusions and delusions are the primary

experiences. With mescaline, psilocybin, and PCP, hallucinations are more commonly experienced.

LSD, PSILOCYBIN MUSHROOMS & OTHER INDOLE PSYCHEDELICS

Indole psychedelics are also known as *serotonin-like* psychedelics because they seem to **exert many of their effects through interactions with serotonin receptors, particularly those designated** $5HT_2A$. The strength of most psychedelics is directly related to their influence on the $5HT_2A$ receptors. **Besides affecting mood, sleep, and anxiety, serotonin influences areas of the brain that are most likely involved in generating hallucinations and illusions** (the medial prefrontal cortex and the anterior cingulate cortex) (Gresch, Strickland & Sanders-Bush, 2002). Interestingly, the down-regulation of $5HT_2A$ receptors is believed to be responsible for the rapid development of tolerance in those who overuse LSD and other indole psychedelics (Aghajanian & Marek, 1999; Meyer & Quenzer, 2005).

LYSERGIC ACID DIETHYLAMIDE (LSD)

"LSD was very colorful, a super rush, magical, trippy, giggly, sometimes scary. I was called the 'King of Acid' because I always had a very good trip unlike some friends who took it every day. I waited at least three or four days in between trips because your body needs some time to recover. My friends who used it daily, they got pretty burnt out with insomnia, grinding teeth, and exhaustion because of the total nerve action."
48-year-old accountant, former "Deadhead" (fan of the band the Grateful Dead)

History

"Sacrament," "acid," "blotter," "barrels," "orange sunshine," "illusion," and "windowpanes" are just some of the street names for **LSD (lysergic acid diethylamide), a semisynthetic form of an ergot fungus toxin that infects rye and other cereal grasses**. The brownish purple fungus, *Claviceps purpurea,* was responsible for many outbreaks of ergot poisoning (*ergotism*) and thousands of deaths over the centuries when farmers and town folk accidentally ate the infected grain (mostly rye), particularly in areas of France, Belgium, eastern Europe, and Russia. There are two types of ergotism: gangrenous and convulsive. **Gangrenous ergotism, also known as "Saint Anthony's Fire," is marked by feverish hallucinations and a rotting away of gangrenous extremities** of the body. The gangrene is caused by the extreme vasoconstriction of small blood vessels that causes the unnourished tissues to die. **Convulsive ergotism is marked by visual and auditory hallucinations**, painful muscular contractions, vomiting, diarrhea, headaches, disturbances in sensation, mania, psychosis, delirium, and convulsions (Siegel, 1985).

LSD was first extracted in 1938 by Dr. Albert Hoffman at the Sandoz pharmaceutical company when he and Dr. Arthur Stoll were investigating the alkaloids of *Claviceps purpurea,* looking for a circulatory stimulant (*analeptic*). LSD (technically LSD-25) was the twenty-fifth derivative the doctors tried. Five years later Dr. Hoffman discovered the hallucinogenic properties of the new drug when he accidentally ingested a dose of LSD while developing a new method to chemically synthesize it.

"I suddenly became strangely inebriated. The external world became changed as in a dream. Objects appeared to gain in relief, they assumed unusual dimensions and colors, became more glowing. Even self-perception and the sense of time were changed. [Another time] I lost all control of time; space and time became more and more disorganized, and I was overcome with fears that I was going crazy."

Dr. Albert Hoffman in 1943, describing one of his experiences with LSD (Stafford, 1992)

SCIENTIFIC INTELLIGENCE MEMORANDUM

POTENTIAL NEW AGENT FOR UNCONVENTIONAL WARFARE

Lysergic Acid Diethylamide (LSD)
(N, .N-Diethyllysergamide).

CIA/SI 101-54
5 August 1954

CENTRAL INTELLIGENCE AGENCY

OFFICE OF SCIENTIFIC INTELLIGENCE

This CIA memorandum referred to LSD as a potential truth drug. The U.S. Army considered it as an airborne agent that could confuse enemy troops.

LSD was investigated as a therapy for mental illnesses and alcoholism and as a key to investigating thought processes (Marnell, 2005). In the 1950s it was sold as Delysid® (the trade name for LSD) and prescribed to enhance psychological insight in psychotherapy. In the early 1950s, the CIA conducted a number of experiments with LSD as a potential truth drug or mind-control drug in a program codenamed MK-ULTRA. The drug did not live up to expectations, and by the mid-1960s the program was discontinued (Stafford, 1985).

"Back in the fifties we had gallon jars of LSD in our lab. My experiments with primates related to eye movements, but the big picture was they were trying to figure out how to use it on the battlefield and aerosolize it or get the wind to disperse it to disorient troops. My supervisor kept trying to get me to take it but I never did."

Excerpt from an interview with a researcher in U.S. Army LSD experiments in 1952

LSD-25 was popularized by Harvard psychologists Drs. Timothy Leary and Richard Alpert (among others), who did psilocybin and LSD research in the 1960s as a way to explore consciousness and feelings. Dr. Leary's first experience with a large amount of LSD kept him "unable to speak for five days." He wrote that he never recovered from that mind-shattering experience. He even started a religion called the "League for Spiritual Discovery" (Stafford, 1992). Dr. Leary's slogan **"Turn on, tune in, and drop out"** was used in endless newspaper articles and TV news shows as the rallying cry for the youth of the 1960s and 1970s. It led to the suspicion that the media was as much responsible for the rise and fall of LSD as was its identification and subsequent vilification as the drug of the hippie generation.

Ken Kesey, who wrote *One Flew Over the Cuckoo's Nest,* was a subject of early LSD experiments. He went on to become one of the founders of the Merry Pranksters, a group of counterculture advocates who popularized psychedelics, particularly LSD, through a series of happenings, often involving the Grateful Dead. They traveled cross-country in a converted school bus and held happenings called the "Kool-Aid Acid Test," where diluted vats of LSD were distributed freely to all partygoers (Wolfe, 1968).

LSD was made illegal on February 1, 1966, under provisions of the Federal Drug Abuse Control Amendments. It was classified as a Schedule I drug in 1970, and in 1974 the National Institute of Mental Health concluded that LSD had no therapeutic use (Lee, 1985; Henderson & Glass, 1994). Scientific research virtually ceased in the early seventies, and it wasn't until recently that any research on LSD or psychedelics in general was renewed. LSD use continued to decline in the 1980s, but in the 1990s there was a resurgence. Over the past few years, use among junior high, high school, and college students as well as the general public has once again dropped dramatically (Monitoring the Future, 2006).

Manufacture of LSD

"We had Palo Alto Owsley stuff— Augustus Stanley Owsley. He ran the sound for the Grateful Dead for years. Supposedly, he made pure LSD with no additives or bad chemistry. I started with 200 mics, then up to 400. The best dose was 100 to 150. If we were out of doors, we would only take 50 so we'd still be able to navigate. Back in 1969 and the early '70s, it cost about $1 to $3 a hit."

52-year-old former LSD user

Over the years, **the majority of LSD was manufactured in northern California**, mostly in the San Francisco Bay Area, although LSD street chemists have been operating in the Pacific Northwest and more recently in the Midwest (Drug Enforcement Administration [DEA], 2006A). The labs are hard to find because the quantities of raw material needed to make the drug are very small. Indeed the entire U.S. supply for one year could be carried by a single person. For example, 60 lbs. of ergotamine tartrate, the basic synthetic raw ingredient for LSD, could produce 11 lbs. of LSD, the nation's annual consumption (Marnell, 2005). LSD can also be synthesized from morning glory plants that contain lysergic acid amide. The production of LSD is tedious and involves volatile and dangerous chemicals. The end product of the initial synthesis, **crystalline LSD, is dissolved in alcohol; drops of the solution are put on blotter paper and chewed or swal-**

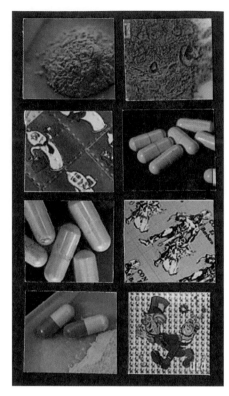

The hallucinogen LSD is manufactured as a liquid and then converted to a number of forms for ingestion: pills, powders, and, most common, blotter paper. The blotter paper, divided into small squares, contains dozens of doses, usually 25 to 200 micrograms of LSD per square. The squares are swallowed.

Courtesy of the Drug Enforcement Administration

• •

lowed. It has also been put into microdots or tiny squares of gelatin and eaten or dropped onto a moist body tissue and absorbed (National Institute on Drug Abuse [NIDA], 2001). Each dose on the blotter is 1 centimeter (cm) square and has been impregnated with 10 to 50 µg (micrograms, or "mics") of liquid LSD. To reach the younger group of potential users, illegal manufacturers have even printed images of Mickey Mouse, Donald Duck, a teddy bear, Felix the Cat, Beavis and Butt-Head, and other characters on the blotter paper.

Epidemiology

Younger and younger Americans were using LSD in the early 1990s, but, for a number of reasons, those numbers dropped by the early 2000s. First was the increasing popularity of the psycho-stimulant ecstasy. Then federal efforts to restrict the manufacture of LSD have, according to the Drug Enforcement Administration (DEA), reduced the supply in the United States by 95%. In particular, a bust in rural Kansas uncovered the largest LSD laboratory ever found, along with 91 pounds of LSD and precursor chemicals (Grim, 2004). Because the demand remained steady but the supply dropped drastically, the price jumped from $1 to $5 for a single hit to $20 or more. In the past you could buy a sheet of 100 blotter stamps (hits) for $50 to $350 whereas now you might find a block of only 10 or 12 hits for a lot more money.

In the 1960s "acidheads" were usually in their early twenties and, besides the usual reasons for using (experimentation, peer pressure, availability, and curiosity), many were searching for a quasi-religious experience. In the 1990s and 2000s, most younger teenagers said they just wanted to get high or augment the effects of ecstasy, GHB, or ketamine at "rave" clubs, desert "raves," or parties. Another reason for the brief resurgence in use was that **standard drug testing usually does not test for LSD**; and even when tested for, the effective dose is so small that it is extremely difficult to detect.

Pharmacology

LSD ($C_{20}H_{25}N_3O$) is remarkable for its potency. Doses as low as 25 µg, or **25 millionths of a gram, can cause stimulatory effects along with mental changes** (spaciness, decreased perception of time, and mild euphoria). **Effects appear 15 to 60 minutes after ingestion, peak at 2 to 4 hours, and last 6 to 8 hours overall. The user returns to the predrug state 10 to 12 hours after ingestion** (Pechnick & Ungerleider, 2005). The usual psychedelic dose of LSD is 150 to 300 µg. The DEA reports that the current strength of LSD street samples ranges from 20 to 80 µg. In the late 1960s and 1970s, samples ranged from 100 to 200 µg or more (DEA, 2006A).

Tolerance develops very rapidly to the psychedelic effects of LSD. Within a few days of daily use, a person can tolerate a 300 µg dose without experiencing any major psychedelic effects. The tolerance is lost rapidly after cessation of use—usually within a few days. Some cross-tolerance can also develop to the effects of mescaline and psilocybin, but there is little cross-tolerance between LSD and DMT, another indole psychedelic (Pechnick & Ungerleider, 2005). **Withdrawal after LSD use is usually more mental and emotional than physical—a psychedelic hangover.**

"Withdrawal was like the next day; the Germans call it 'Katzenjammer,' which is like a chemical depletion of mind and body, similar to a really bad hangover. You're still psychedelically spaced the next day and you're dealing with all the revelations. Dependence was more of a social urge to do it rather than a private urge."

24-year-old male former LSD user

Physical Effects

LSD can cause a **rise in heart rate and blood pressure, a higher body temperature, dizziness, dilated pupils, and some sweating**, much like amphetamines. Users see many light trails, like after-images in cheap televisions; this effect is known as the "trailing phenomena."

Mental Effects

"In a real strong acid, you'll see the walls melting like candles and water running down the wall. That kind of distortion is not a complete hallucination or anything real solid, like, there's a bottle where you wonder whether it's there or not. The thing that got me really crazy was hearing a dog or an airplane or a passenger car miles away and you didn't know whether that was real or an illusion."

Recovering 38-year-old LSD and marijuana user

LSD overloads the brainstem, the sensory switchboard for the mind, causing **sensory distortions (seeing sounds, feeling smells, or hearing colors [synesthesia]), dreaminess, deper-**sonalization, altered mood, and impaired concentration and motivation**. The locus coeruleus is activated to release extra amounts of norepinephrine, which greatly enhances alertness. This heightened awareness of the senses is an explanation for the introspection and awareness of the inner self that is common with LSD users (Snyder, 1996).

It becomes difficult to express oneself verbally while on LSD. Single-word answers and seemingly unassociated comments (non sequiturs) are common. A user might experience intense sensations and emotions but find it difficult to tell others what he or she is feeling.

"It is fake, ersatz. Instant mysticism. . . . There's no wisdom there. I solved the secret of the universe last night, but this morning I forgot what it was."

Arthur Koestler, writer, LSD user

One of the **greatest dangers of LSD is the impaired reasoning and loss of judgment**. This, coupled with slowed reaction time and visual distortions, can make driving a car recipe for disaster.

"I stuck my hand in this flame and then I went, 'Uh-oh, my hand is in the flame,' and I pulled it out and I thought it didn't burn, but later that night my hand started blistering, and I'm going, 'Oh no, I got burned.'"

43-year-old male former LSD user

Bad Trips (acute anxiety reactions)

"One thing they don't talk about with LSD is the tremendous anxiety you feel even if you are an experienced user. Feelings of impending doom, extreme worry, fidgeting, feeling like you got to move. It's not the paranoia a speed freak feels; all the nerves are tingling."

33-year-old male LSD user

Because LSD affects the emotional center in the brain and distorts reality, some users, particularly **first-time users who take it without supportive experienced users around them, are** subject to the extremes of euphoria and panic**. Depersonalization and lack of a stable environment can trigger acute anxiety, paranoia, fear over loss of control, and delusions of persecution or feelings of grandeur, leading to dangerous behaviors. One survivor of a jump from the Golden Gate Bridge claimed he was jumping through the "golden hoop". *(See Chapter 9 concerning treatment for bad trips.)*

Mental Illness & LSD

Much of the research, as well as the enthusiasm for LSD as an adjunct to psychotherapy, has decreased over the years. Proponents of psychotherapeutic use claim that **drug-stimulated insights afford some users a shortcut through the extended process of psychotherapy** in which uncovering traumas and conflicts from the subconscious helps the patient heal. Others emphasized that self-experimentation by mental health professionals could give them an understanding of the schizophrenic mind and help them provide more-effective therapy (Grof, 2001). Opponents of this kind of therapy say that the dangerous side effects of LSD more than outweigh any perceived benefits.

The popular scenario of someone using LSD just once and becoming permanently psychotic or schizophrenic is misleading. It is a very unusual occurrence. What usually happens is that **users with a pre-existing mental illness or instability can aggravate those conditions with LSD into more-severe mental disturbances**. Use can also cause some people to experience their mental illness at an earlier age, or it may provoke a relapse in someone who has previously suffered a psychotic disorder or a major depression.

"The whole thing started with my schizophrenia. That always plays a part. And anytime I get too involved in the music scene, the acid starts to trigger the schizophrenia, like flashbacks, and sometimes it makes me want to use. But I'm drawn to it like a moth to a light."

Recovering LSD user with schizophrenia, former Deadhead

Also some otherwise normal users can be thrown into a temporary but prolonged psychotic reaction or severe depression that requires extended treatment. Prolonged trips (extended LSD effects) devoid of other psychiatric symptoms have also occurred. Though very rare, these reactions can be emotionally crippling and may last for years (NIDA, 2001).

Hallucinogen Persisting Perception Disorder (HPPD). A number of users experience mental flashbacks of sensations or of a bad trip they had while under the influence of LSD even when they have not used any drugs in several months or even years. The flashbacks, which can be triggered by stress, the use of another psychoactive drug, or even exercise, re-create the original experience. This sensation can also cause anxiety and even panic because it is unexpected and the user seems to have little control over its recurrence. Most flashbacks are provoked by some sensory stimulus: sight, sound, odor, or touch. Seeing trails of moving objects also seems fairly common (American Psychiatric Association, 2000). It is thought that HPPD has a strong hereditary component.

Though the flashback/post-traumatic stress disorder type of HPPD is most associated with psychedelic abuse, a second type more accurately describes this disorder. This is the **long-term intermittent or continuous experience of LSD-like visual and perceptual disturbances that occur on a chronic basis.** For those affected this creates stress, social impairment, occupational problems, and difficulty with other areas of functioning. This type of HPPD may resolve within five years or may persist indefinitely. Some of the common symptoms associated with HPPD include difficulty reading, memory problems, color confusion, halos around objects, visual after-images (trails), intensified colors, illusions of movement, geometric pseudo-hallucinations, flashes of color, imagined images, objects appearing abnormally large (*macropsia*) or small (*micropsia*), static vision, and visualization of "floaters" (small bacteria-like objects) (Lerner, Gelkopf, Skladman, et al., 2002).

A number of psychedelics have the capacity to cause HPPD (e.g., LSD, MDMA, MDA, mescaline, DMT, PCP, marijuana, and psilocybin), though it is most common with LSD. It has been estimated that flashbacks (of widely varying intensities) occur in 23% to 64% of regular LSD users (Hollister, 1984; Jaffe, 1989; Carroll & Comer, 1998; Snow, 2003). Although the **LSD flashback appears to be similar to a post-traumatic stress disorder**, recent case reports suggest that medications like sertraline, clonidine, and naltrexone may be useful in treating this problem (Lerner, Oyffe, Issacs, et al., 1997; Young, 1997; Lerner, Gelkopf, Oyffe, et al., 2000; Wilkins & Gorelick, 2003). A number of other medications have been tried on HPPD with limited success.

Dependence

Because LSD does not generally produce compulsive drug-seeking behavior, it is not considered addictive though some use it frequently. The 500 or more LSD trips reported by a number of users are probably due to **a psychological dependence rather than a physical dependence** even though tolerance does develop rapidly. Frequent and repeated use of low-dose LSD for

its stimulant not its psychedelic effects is an example of this psychological dependence.

"MAGIC MUSHROOMS" (psilocybin & psilocin)

Psilocybin and psilocin are the active ingredients in a number of psychedelic mushrooms found in Mexico, the United States, South America, Southeast Asia, and Europe. These mushrooms, originally called *Teonanacatl* (divine flesh) by the Aztecs, were especially important to Indian cultures in Mexico and in the pre-Columbian Americas; they were **used in ceremonies dating as far back as 1000 B.C.** More than 200 stone sculptures of mushrooms have been found in El Salvador, Guatemala, and parts of Mexico (Furst, 1976). Evidence of a mushroom cult that flourished from 100 B.C. to A.D. 400 has been found in northwestern Mexico (Schultes & Hofmann, 1992). They are still used today, although persecution by the **Spaniards, who conquered much of Central and South America in the sixteenth and seventeenth centuries, drove the ceremonial use of mushrooms underground for hundreds of years.** It

These are one type of the 75 species of mushrooms containing psilocybin or psilocin. The "shrooms" can be used fresh or dried, although fresh psilocybin mushrooms are more potent than dried ones.

wasn't until the 1950s that much was known about the ceremonies conducted by Mazatec, Chol, and Lacandon Mayan shamans, or *curanderas* (medicine women or men). The ceremonies include eating or drinking the extracted psychedelic substances to get intoxicated, along with hours of chanting—all to **induce visions that will help treat illnesses, solve problems, or contact the spirit world**.

The famous Mazatec shaman María Sabina wrote:

"The sacred mushroom takes me by the hand and brings me to the world where everything is known. It is they, the sacred mushrooms, that speak in a way I can understand. When I return from the trip that I have taken with them, I tell what they have told me and what they have shown me."

María Sabina (Schultes & Hofmann, 1992)

In 1957, when mushroom researcher R. Gorden Wasson's article "Seeking the Magic Mushroom" appeared in *Life* magazine, millions of Americans were introduced to the concept of psychedelic fungi; over the next 10 years, experimentation began (Stamets, 1996).

Pharmacology

In 1956 the active psychedelic ingredients psilocybin and psilocin were isolated by mycologist (mushroom expert) Roger Heim and researcher Dr. Albert Hoffman, the same scientist at Sandoz who had discovered LSD-25. **The chemical structure of psilocybin is similar to that of LSD.**

Psilocybin and psilocin are found in about 75 different species of mushroom from four genera: *Psilocybe, Panaeolus, Stropharia,* and *Conocybe* (Stamets, 1996). Fifteen species have been identified in the U.S. Pacific Northwest.

Both wild and cultivated **mushrooms vary greatly in strength, so a single potent mushroom might have as much psilocybin as 10 weak ones.** When the caps and the stems are ingested, either fresh or dried, the psilocybin is converted to psilocin, although psilocybin is more plentiful and is almost twice as potent as psilocin. It also crosses the blood/brain barrier more readily. Psychic effects are obtained from doses of 10 to 60 milligrams (mg) and generally **last three to six hours**.

Effects

"We were living in an Indian village in the mountains of central Mexico where the hongos [mushrooms] grow. One night when it rained, the locals were shouting, 'Hongos mañana,' and they were right. We got some and it made all the colors seem softer and more pastel. My body felt like there was a river running through it, and all sorts of visceral feelings were let loose."

Former psychedelic user

Most mushrooms containing psilocybin cause nausea and other physical symptoms before the psychedelic effects take over. The psychedelic effects include **visceral sensations; changes in sight, hearing, taste, and touch; and altered states of consciousness**. There seems to be less disassociation and panic than with LSD, and prolonged psychotic reactions are rare. These effects are not consistent with every user, however, and depend on the setting in which the drug is taken. As with LSD and other indole psychedelics, many of the effects are caused by disruption of the neurotransmitters serotonin and dopamine along with the sudden release of norepinephrine, a stimulatory neurotransmitter that oversensitizes the senses (Pechnick & Ungerleider, 2005).

There is a small market for mail-order kits containing spores for growing mushrooms in a closet or basement. Some users also tramp the countryside, looking for a certain species. **The major danger in "'shroom" harvesting is mistaking poisonous mushrooms for those containing psilocybin.** Some poisonous mushrooms (e.g., *Amanita phalloides*) can cause death or permanent liver damage within hours of ingestion. Further, grocery store mushrooms are sometimes laced with LSD or PCP and sold to those seeking the "magic mushroom" experience.

OTHER INDOLE PSYCHEDELICS

Ibogaine

Produced by the African *Tabernanthe iboga* shrub and some other plants, **ibogaine in low doses acts as a stimulant; in higher doses it produces long-acting psychedelic effects** and a self-determined catatonic reaction that can be maintained for up to two days. It is rarely found in the United States, although it has been synthesized in laboratories. Its use is generally limited to native cultures in western and central Africa, such as the Bwiti tribe of Gabon, who use it to stay alert and motionless while hunting. They also claim to experience ancestral visions while under the influence (O'Brien, Cohen, Evans, et al., 1992).

There has been **research into the use of ibogaine to treat heroin, alcohol, and cocaine addiction**. One animal study found that a synthetic derivative of ibogaine reduced withdrawal symptoms and self-administration of morphine (Panchal, Taraschenko, Maisonneuve, et al., 2005). Anecdotal reports as well as some limited studies claim that just a few treatments eliminated withdrawal symptoms and craving for opioids, although several deaths have been associated with ibogaine administration. Animal studies indicate that cerebellum neurotoxicity can result from ibogaine use. These concerns have effectively limited further research into ibogaine as a medical treatment for heroin dependence (Wilkins & Gorelick, 2003).

Morning Glory Seeds (ololiuqui)

Seeds from the morning glory plant (*Ipomoea tricolor*) or the Hawaiian woodrose (*Argyreia nervosa*) **contain several LSD-like substances, particularly lysergic acid amide, which is about one-tenth as potent as LSD**. The lysergic acid amide can be used to make lysergic acid diethylamide (LSD). Indians in Mexico used the drug before the Spanish arrived. Because several hundred seeds have to be taken to get high, the drug's nauseating properties are magnified. In sufficient quantities the seeds cause LSD-like effects, but they are not particularly popular among those who use psychedelics. Along with sensory disturbances and mood changes come nausea, vomiting, drowsiness, headache, and chills. Effects last up to six hours and LSD-like flashbacks are somewhat common. **Morning glory seeds are sold commercially**; but to prevent misuse, many are dipped in a toxin that induces vomiting (O'Brien, Cohen, Evans, et al., 1992). The seeds have street names such as "heavenly blue," flying saucers," and "pearly gates."

DMT (dimethyltryptamine)

First synthesized in 1931, dimethyltryptamine (DMT) is found naturally in South American trees, vines, shrubs, and mushrooms (e.g., yopo beans) and is also synthesized by street chemists. DMT is a psychedelic substance similar in structure to psilocin. Because digestive juices destroy the active ingredients, the drug isn't eaten; instead the white, yellow, or brown powder is usually smoked, but it can also be snorted or injected. DMT is often used with a monoamine oxidase inhibitor (MAOI) such as harmaline (an indole alkaloid found in several other psychedelic plants, such as the Syrian rue, an herb from China) in an ayahuasca brew. South American tribes have used it for at least 400 years. They **prepare it from several different plants as a snuff** called "yopo," "cohoba," "vilca," "cebil," or "epena." They blow it into each other's nose through a hollow reed and then dance, hallucinate, and sing. The synthetic form can be made in basement laboratories (Schultes & Hofmann, 1992).

DMT causes intoxication, intense visual rather than auditory hallucinations, and often a loss of awareness of surroundings lasting 30 to 60 minutes or less (and as little as 10 minutes when inhaled rather than eaten). The **short duration of action** gave rise to the nickname "businessman's special" because the white-collar worker can get high and then almost sober again during lunch.

Newspaper reports have sensationalized a variant of DMT called 5-MeO-DMT, the venom of the Sonoran Desert toad. Contrary to anecdotes about people licking the toad to get high, the substance is milked onto cigarettes, dried,

and then smoked (Chilton, Bigwood & Jensen, 1979; Lyttle, Goldstein & Gartz, 1996).

Foxy (5-methoxy-N, N-diisopropyltryptamine [5-Me-DIPT]) & AMT (alphamethyltryptamine)

These two psychedelic tryptamines appeared in the early 2000s, before they were listed as scheduled drugs under the Comprehensive Drug Abuse Prevention and Control Act of 1970 (the Controlled Substances Act), yet they have been prosecuted under the federal drug analogue statute. Law enforcement agencies have seized samples in a number of states, but the drugs have been used only occasionally at raves in Arizona, California, Florida, and New York (DEA, 2002).

Effects include hallucinations, euphoria, empathy, visual and auditory disturbances (illusions), formication (intense itching), paranoia, and emotional distress (Wilson, McGeorge, Smolinske, et al., 2005). They also can cause nausea, vomiting, and diarrhea. The effects from 20 mg of either of the drugs can last 12 to 24 hours whereas smaller doses will last only 3 to 6 hours. The powder is prepared in capsules or tablets in a variety of colors.

Ayahuasca (yage)

Ayahuasca, also called yage, is a psychedelic drink made from the leaves, bark, and vines of *Banisteriopsis caapi* and *Banisteriopsis inebrians,* Amazon Jungle vines. Drinking this preparation **causes intense vomiting, diarrhea, and then a dreamlike condition that lasts up to 10 hours**. The Chama, Tukanoan, and Zaparo Indians of Peru, Brazil, and Ecuador use it for prophecy, divination, sorcery, and medical purposes. They believe that yage frees the soul to wander and return at will and to communicate with ancestors. Users believe that it will also induce trance states for prophecy, cure mental illness, and facilitate social interaction (Schultes & Hofmann, 1992; Dobkin de Rios & Grob, 2005).

The active ingredient is the indole alkaloid harmaline. Native cultures often mix yage with DMT plant extracts to intensify the effects. It has been recently discovered that harma-

line protects the DMT from being deactivated by gastric enzymes, thus allowing DMT to be effective when taken orally.

Over the past few years, cults using ayahuasca as the focus of their beliefs have sprung up in Brazil. Uniao do Vegetal (UDV) (with 9,000 members) and Santo Daime, among others, are recognized by the Brazilian government. The UDV, for example, uses it only in religious ceremonies twice a month for four hours at a time. The ayahuasca tea is drunk by adults and adolescents. They believe it is psychologically beneficial to the youth of their congregation (Doering-Silveira, Lopez, Grob, et al., 2005). The use has spread to the United States and other countries.

PEYOTE, MDMA & OTHER PHENYL-ALKYLAMINE PSYCHEDELICS

This class of psychedelics is **chemically related to adrenaline and amphetamine**, although many of the effects are quite different. Whereas the effects of amphetamines will peak within half an hour (and much sooner if smoked), many of the **phenylalkylamines take several hours to reach their peak**.

PEYOTE (mescaline)

The search for connections to the inner self and the outer spiritual worlds led many cultures to experiment with hallucinogenic plants. In the late-nineteenth and early-twentieth centuries, the interest in the inner workings of the mind, as delineated in the writings of Drs. Sigmund Freud, Alfred Adler, and Carl Jung, among others, led many to search for the philosopher's stone (plant) that would chemically help them understand themselves. Aldous Huxley, one of the earliest writers/philosophers of the twentieth century to examine this connection, used mescaline from the peyote cactus for his exploration.

A mature peyote cactus (Lophophora williamsii) is ripe for harvesting. Each button (the top of the cactus) contains about 50 mg of mescaline. It can take two to 10 buttons to get high.
© 1983 CNS Productions, Inc.

* * *

"The urge to transcend self-conscious selfhood is, as I have said, a principal appetite of the soul. When, for whatever reason, men and women fail to transcend themselves by means of worship, good works, and spiritual exercises, they are apt to resort to religion's chemical surrogates— alcohol and 'goof pills' in the modern West, alcohol and opium in the East, hashish in the Mohammedan world, alcohol and marijuana in Central America, alcohol and coca in the Andes."

Aldous Huxley, The Doors of Perception, 1954

Mescaline is the active component of the peyote cactus (*Lophophora williamsii*) and the San Pedro cactus (*Trichocereus pachanoi*). San Pedro cacti have been depicted in 3,000-year-old Chavin art from coastal Peru. The use of the peyote cacti stretches back to at least 3700 B.C. (Meyer & Quenzer, 2005). Over the centuries the Aztecs, Toltecs, Chichimecas, and several Meso-American cultures included it in their rituals. When they invaded the New World, the Spanish conquistadores regarded peyote as evil and the hallucinations as an invitation from the devil. They tried to abolish it but never succeeded. In the 1800s its use spread north to the United States, where close to 50 North American tribes were still taking it through the early 1900s (Furst, 1976).

Many challenges have been made concerning the legality of using a psychedelic substance for a religious ceremony. **In 1996 the U.S. Supreme Court ruled that the use of peyote during religious ceremonies by Native Americans is protected by the Constitution and that individual states cannot ban its use. Peyote is used by the Native American Church of North America**, with a claimed membership of 250,000, as part of its ceremonies; its stated reason for using peyote is to build spirituality and community. In the 1950s and 1960s, peyote cacti (called "buttons") were available by mail order. They are still available by mail, but one has to file documentation of membership in the Native American Church. About 2 million buttons are harvested in Texas each year. Heavy users might consume up to 1,000 buttons a year. There are nine licensed distributors of peyote in the United States (Marnell, 2005; DEA, 2006A).

Peyote cacti are still eaten in spiritual ceremonies by the tribes in northern Mexico (Huichol, Tarahumara, and Cora Indians) and by the Southwest Plains Indian tribes (Comanche, Kiowa, and Ute).

Effects

The gray-green crowns of the peyote cactus are cut at ground level or uprooted and can be **used fresh or dried**. The bitter, nauseating substance is either eaten (seven to eight buttons is an average dose) or boiled and drunk as a tea. It can also be ground and eaten as a powder (Schultes & Hofmann, 1992). Mescaline was extracted and isolated in 1896 and synthesized in 1919. The synthetic form consists of thin, needlelike crystals that are sold in capsules. **The effects of mescaline last approximately 12 hours and are very similar to LSD with an emphasis on colorful visions and hallucinations.** Although users term it the "mellow LSD," actual hallucinations are more common with mescaline than with LSD. Each use of peyote is usually accompanied by a severe episode of nausea and vomiting, although some users develop a tolerance to these side effects. As with most psychedelics, tolerance to the mental effects can also develop rapidly (La Barre & Weston, 1979).

A peyote ceremony might consist of ingesting the peyote buttons, then singing, drumming, chanting hymns, and trying to understand the psychedelic visions to have spiritual experiences. Many participants also have hallucinatory visions of a deity or spiritual leader with whom they are able to converse for guidance and understanding (Furst, 1976).

"When you get fresh buttons, they go down easier. No doubt about it, peyote is the worst taste I've ever experienced. Whenever I took it, I got into projectile vomiting. It would happen as I was coming on to it. My reaction was intensely visual, but it was different than LSD in that I could have a conversation despite the hallucinations."

52-year-old male former psychedelic user

Because the reaction to many psychedelics depends on the mind-set and the setting almost as much as on the actual properties of the drug, **use of a mind-altering substance in a structured ceremonial setting can induce more spiritual feelings than use at a rock concert**. Peyote's connection to spiritual matters limits abuse. For example, a study of long-term peyote users (61 Navaho Native American Church members) found no significant psychological or cognitive deficits when it was used in a religious setting (Halpern, Sherwood, Hudson, et al., 2005).

PSYCHO-STIMULANTS (MDA, MDMA, 2C-B, PMA, 2C-T-7, 2C-T-2, et al.) & CLUB DRUGS

"There is a wealth of information built into us . . . tucked away in the genetic material in every one of our cells. Without some means of access, there is no way even to begin to guess at the extent and quality of what is there. The psychedelic drugs allow exploration of this interior world and insights into its nature."

Dr. Alexander Shulgin, psychopharmacologist and chemist

One of the first groups of synthetic drugs used for mental exploration and later for so-called recreational purposes was designer psychedelics or psychostimulants, chemically defined as **phenylethylamine derivatives similar to mescaline**. Phenylethylamines are naturally occurring compounds found in the human brain (Shulgin & Shulgin, 2000).

The first of these **laboratory variations of the amphetamine molecule** was synthesized in 1910 (methylenedioxyamphetamine, or MDA), although the psychic effects weren't examined until a generation later. These drugs can **cause feelings of well-being and euphoria, some psychedelic and stimulatory effects**, as well as side effects and toxicity similar to amphetamines. The differences among the more than 150 compounds of these psycho-stimulants in current limited use have to do with duration of action; extent of delusional, illusional, or hallucinogenic

effects; and degree of euphoria. Hundreds of other compounds have been created but strictly for experimental purposes.

MDA was the first of these compounds to be widely used and abused (in the late 1960s, 1970s, and early 1980s), often on college campuses. Though it was originally designed as a medication to stop bleeding, when the psychic effects were discovered it became the "love drug," touted to increase libido. With research showing some damage to serotonin-producing neurons in the brain, a few overdose deaths, and increased legal scrutiny, however, its popularity waned, and by the mid-1980s **MDMA had taken over as the psycho-stimulant of choice**.

MDMA (ecstasy)

The psycho-stimulant **MDMA, chemical name 3,4-methylenedioxymethamphetamine**, is shorter acting than MDA (4 to 6 hours vs. 10 to 12). It has numerous street names including "ecstasy," "XTC," "X," "Adam," and "E." MDMA can be swallowed, snorted, or injected, much like methamphetamine, though it is **usually sold as a capsule, tablet, or powder**. MDMA is often taken at parties, raves, and music clubs because users claim it creates a strong desire to move about, dance, and interact with other people (Grob & Poland, 2005).

"We'd have 'E' parties; a bunch of people would take 'E' and, like, it's really like a friendly drug. You take it and then you feel happy, so you talk to your friends a lot, you talk to strangers, and you find things in common, and everyone is like your best friend; but when you come down off the drug, it's like a totally different experience—it's like a downer."

17-year-old ecstasy user

History. German pharmaceutical company Merck first discovered MDMA in 1914 as an intermediate chemical step in its synthesis of MDA. It didn't surface again until 1953, when the U.S. Army carried out psychological warfare/brainwashing experiments on

animals and humans with a number of psychedelic compounds, including MDPEA, MDA, BDB, DMA, TMA, and MDMA. Because of the death of a male test subject due to MDA, and the subsequent uproar, it was another 16 years before the **first published human study of MDMA appeared, written by Dr. Alexander Shulgin** (a chemist and psychopharmacologist) and his colleague Dave Nichols (Grob & Poland, 2005). They described the insight that the drug seemed to give and **recommended its use to a number of therapists to help their patients tap their emotions and repressed memories**. Dr. Ann Shulgin, a psychotherapist (who, along with her husband, Alexander, developed more than 150 amphetamine analogues, many for the DEA), estimated that as many as 4,000 therapists were introduced to MDMA in the late 1970s and 1980s (Shulgin & Shulgin, 2000; Pentney, 2001). Part of its value was to give the therapists themselves empathy for the feelings and the fears of their clients (Holland, 2001). In recent years a few therapists continue to experiment with MDMA as a treatment for psychological disorders such as post-traumatic stress disorder (Doblin, 2002).

As with any drug that develops a reputation, entrepreneurs started making it available (legally) for recreational use. After a series of hearings, starting in 1985 and continuing for several years, MDMA was ultimately **banned as a Schedule I drug in 1988 in the United States**, making it impossible to legally continue psychotherapeutic experimentation. Of course all the publicity made the drug more desirable among experimenters. The name "ecstasy" was supposedly chosen by a street chemist as a marketing tool possibly because the name "empathy," which is closer to the true initial effects of the drug, wasn't sexy enough for the young club crowd.

"I had no inhibitions. I mean it was like whatever sexual compromise or, you know, touching or conversation that I would have normally had boundaries for, I didn't when I took ecstasy."

28-year-old ecstasy user

When ecstasy was legal, the main manufacturer sold up to 50,000 tablets a week. In 2006 a single Dutch trafficker was sentenced to 20 years in prison for importing 1.7 million ecstasy tablets into the United States. It was a sign that trafficking in this psycho-stimulant is continuing but not quite at the rate of a few years ago. Most of the MDMA used in the United States has been smuggled in by western European, Russian, and Israeli drug trafficking syndicates (DEA, 2001). Recently, however, a significant amount of "E" tabs have been manufactured by clandestine laboratories in Canada and across the United States; these illegal labs use a variety of safrole compounds extracted from sassafras oil to synthesize MDMA (DEA, 2006A). Asian gangs, particularly in Vietnam and China, have increased their smuggling, often through Canada.

In 2006 about **6.5% of high school seniors had used MDMA, but only 1.3% used on a monthly basis**; this is somewhat more than those who had tried LSD but a lot less than the peak year of 2000, when 3.6% used MDMA on a monthly basis (Monitoring the Future, 2006). By comparison, 18.3% used marijuana on a monthly basis, 21.6% smoked cigarettes, and 45.3% drank alcohol. Recent reports indicate that the use of ecstasy has leveled off. The use by the 18- to 25-year-olds (the second most common MDMA users) is almost one-third lower than high school seniors and has also dropped in the past few years as well.

Use & Cost. Ecstasy use is often called "rolling," the Generation X term derived from the practice of concealing an "E" tablet in a Tootsie Roll® that is then rewrapped. Vicks® inhalants and other pungent substances that are said to be pleasingly enhanced by the use of "E" are also found at rave clubs, along with Tiger Balm® and certain oils used while massaging the muscle tightness that occurs with the onset of MDMA effects. Glow or light sticks are waved in front of someone who is rolling to produce mesmerizing effects.

A capsule, a tablet, or an equivalent powder packet (75 to 125 mg) costs anywhere from $10 to $40 (even as high as $70). The cost of producing each tablet ranges from 50¢ to $2, so the profit margin is huge. Wholesale prices in the United States for large quantities range from $8 to $12 per pill (DanceSafe, 2006). Tablets come in almost every color, with off-white to a light tan being the most common. They are also stamped with a variety of designs, including the Mitsubishi® logo, a butterfly, and various heart renditions.

A DEA report found that **30% to 50% of the tablets sold as MDMA at raves actually contain no MDMA** but rather other illicit drugs such as PCP, methamphetamine, PMA, or MDA. Of those with MDMA, only 24% had only MDMA and no other psychoactive drug. In addition, 57% of "rolling ravers" were knowingly under the influence of other illicit drugs besides "E" (DEA, 2001; DEA; 2006A).

"The first time I did 'E,' I chewed the bottom of my lip open because there was so much speed in it. I woke up the next morning and my stomach was like completely hollow. I felt like there was nothing in my stomach at all. My legs were going, I was bouncing my legs and they were vibrating; they were going so fast. It was so weird. My eyes were popping out of their sockets."
17-year-old ecstasy user

At a number of raves and concerts, a private organization called DanceSafe® tests ecstasy samples so that people who buy pills can find out if they are actually MDMA. The main problem is that the tests are rudimentary and cannot determine what else is actually in the pills. Some users can get a false sense of security and take the drug anyway. The testing group does give out information about ecstasy and other drugs, so it does have a harm reduction effect that minimizes some of the damage that "rollers" can do to themselves (DanceSafe, 2006).

Physical Effects. MDMA has many stimulant effects similar to amphetamines, such as increased heart rate and respiration, excess energy, fainting, sweating, chills, and hyperactivity. The more that is used, the greater the physical effects. The effects of "E" appear about 30 minutes after ingestion (the usual route of administration). **The onset usually consists of tightness in muscles with generalized spasms, trismus (jaw muscle spasm), and bruxism (clenching of the teeth) just before most of the psychic effects begin to appear.** Because of the clenched jaw and other effects, a variety of paraphernalia is associated with MDMA, including baby pacifiers and lollipops to avoid tooth damage. Though some report more-heightened sexual sensations, prolonged use decreases orgasm in men and arousal in women (DuPont, 2000; Gable, 2004). Because MDMA releases less adrenaline than most methamphetamines, a user doesn't receive quite as much sympathetic nervous system stimulation of heart rate and blood pressure. **For occasional users of low or moderate amounts, most of the physical effects are relatively benign;** however, **tolerance to its mental effects develops rapidly, so users increase doses, often causing greater physical liability**.

The more serious MDMA effects include:

◇ water toxicity and electrolyte imbalances as well as dehydration;

◇ pupil dilatation, blurred vision, and eyelid twitching;

◇ headaches, agitation, nausea, and anorexia;

◇ serotonergic axon apoptosis (cell death caused by dopamine uptake in serotonergic cells and the subsequent production of hydrogen peroxide), resulting in thought and memory impairment (Hrometz, Brown, Nichols, et al., 2004);

◇ rapid and potentially dangerous heart rhythm problems;

◇ seizure activity, stroke, cardiovascular failure, and coma; and

◇ malignant hyperthermia (**high body temperature**) that can also result in rhabdomyolysis (muscle damage) and renal (kidney) failure; the extreme heat can even coagulate the blood.

"At raves ecstasy causes the natural thermostat in your body to go haywire, so there's a lot of heat because people

are very active. It's a stimulant, so people are dancing, forget to drink water, forget to hydrate; and these places are mostly hot, and we've seen people with extended body temperatures. So those are the things to spot, cool down, and then in the extreme states, medicate and transport."

Glen Razwick, director, Rock Medicine Program, Haight Ashbury Free Clinics

Very high-dose use can result in high blood pressure and seizure activity much like that seen in amphetamine overdose. In experiments with rats and monkeys, researchers found that MDMA damaged serotonin-producing neurons in the brain similar to the way that MDA was proven to do in humans. Much of the damage in animals remained even 12 to 18 months after MDMA use. In human assays of party and rave attendees, methamphetamine was often found in the blood along with MDMA, thus amplifying the serotonin damage (Fischer, Hatzidimitriou, Wlos, et al., 1995; Irvine, Keane, Felgate, et al., 2006).

Mental/Emotional Effects. Twenty minutes to 1 hour after ingestion and continuing for 3 to 4 more hours, MDMA induces feelings of happiness, clarity, peace, pleasure, and altered sensory perceptions without causing any depersonalization or detachment of the users from the realities of their environment. Users also say that they experience increased **nonsexual empathy for others, more self-awareness, and heightened self-esteem, open mindedness, acceptance, and intimacy** in their interactions. For these reasons it is also called a "hug drug" rather than a "love drug" like MDA.

Many of the psychic effects are probably due to serotonergic activity, though it doesn't give the visual illusions most often associated with psychedelics (Snyder, 1996). For the first few hours of use, **ecstasy continues to overwhelm the vesicles and forces them to discharge their reservoirs of serotonin** into the synaptic gap, thus continuing to dramatically amplify the brain's response to its internal and external environment.

After about three hours, ecstasy is still trying to force the vesicles to release more serotonin, but the supplies have been depleted. More ecstasy is usually taken at this point, but it results in lesser effects. Because of this reaction, ecstasy is often combined with other drugs like LSD and amphetamines to prolong the feelings. **It can take up to a week or more to produce a sufficient amount of serotonin to re-experience similar feelings.**

Due to this excessive stimulation, serotonin receptors also retreat into the cell membrane to avoid damage. This process, called "down regulation," leads to more long-lasting mood changes because there are now fewer receptors to respond to the serotonin.

"The next day you wake up and it's what you call 'E-tarded.' You feel retarded but you're coming off of 'E' so you're 'E-tarded' and you're just, you know, totally tired and just, you know, just, 'Duh, what's going on?' You are really slow in your thinking."

17-year-old ecstasy user

Following an ecstasy experience, some users have also been known to become extremely depressed and suicidal. **High-dose use can result in an acute anxiety reaction** and even flashbacks after cessation of use (Grob & Poland, 2005).

Physical dependency is generally not a problem, but, as with amphetamines and cocaine, psychological dependence can cause compulsive use. If used daily, tolerance develops rather quickly, as with amphetamines (Mendelsohn, 2003).

MDMA Polydrug Combinations. Ecstasy is currently being ingested simultaneously with a number of other prescription and illicit drugs.

◇ **LSD with ecstasy**, known as "candy flipping," "flip flopping," "X & Ls," and "candy snaps," is said to intensify the effects of both drugs and increase the duration of action of MDMA.

◇ **Hydrocodone/OxyContin®/codeine/heroin with ecstasy** is a Generation X **speedball combination** that can enhance the euphoric feelings of both drugs.

◇ **GHB with ecstasy** is another type of modern-day speedball.

◇ **Nitrous oxide with ecstasy** is used to intensify the inhalant rush, sometimes resulting in traumatic injuries from passing out.

◇ **Prozac®** (fluoxetine) with ecstasy is thought to protect serotonin brain cells from the neurotoxic effects of ecstasy. Recent animal studies indicate that Prozac® may actually neutralize all effects of MDMA when both are taken together. Users therefore take the Prozac after the effects of ecstasy have worn off.

◇ **MDMA with Viagra®** when used to enhance sexuality is called "sextacy."

"I smoked a 'blunt' that had about a gram of coke in it and five pills of ecstasy. And the ecstasy, I had gotten, I had about a thousand pills, I was doing it a lot. It was bad, it was a bad dose. And it put me in the hospital for about a month; attacked my heart. The doctors suggested that I'm going to need a heart transplant before I am 25-years-old."

22-year-old recovering addict

Parties, Festivals, Raves & Music Clubs

The term *rave* was coined in England in the late 1960s by those of Caribbean descent to describe a dance party. The more popular recent terms for rave include *clubbing, party, festival,* and *electronic dance club.*

Raves evolved into gatherings where very loud computer-generated **techno or electronic trance beat music was played, light shows and laser light effects performed, and, at many, both club drugs and drug paraphernalia were condoned.** They were convened in actual dance clubs (usually with no alcoholic drinks for sale), at rented warehouses and abandoned buildings, and even at desolate outdoor locations (outlaw or underground raves and desert raves). Today some of the clubs are legal and some are nomadic.

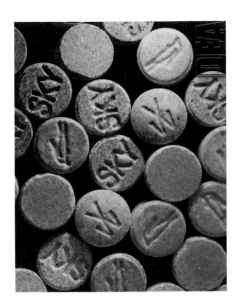

These are some MDMA (ecstasy) tablets confiscated by the DEA. Seizures by the U.S. Customs Service soared from 400,000 pills in 1997 to 7.2 million in 2001. By 2003 the seizures had dropped significantly to less than 1 million, partly due to the manufacture of more and more ecstasy in Canada instead of Europe. There are still a significant number of clandestine MDMA labs in the United States (DEA, 2006A).

Courtesy of the Drug Enforcement Administration

● ●

When a party/festival/club show is going to occur, flyers are handed out during the week for a party that weekend; the exact time and date are available on the Internet only a few hours before the party to avoid police involvement. These gatherings are so popular that they have become a big business enterprise, often charging as much as $20 to $50 admission. The drugs that have become popular at these gatherings are **primarily ecstasy, nitrous oxide ("laughing gas"), GHB or GBL, and occasionally dextromethorphan, ketamine, PCP, and nexus (2C-B). The more traditional street drugs are also available**, especially methamphetamine and marijuana and, to a lesser extent, cocaine, LSD, and psilocybin mushrooms (Parks & Kennedy, 2004). Alcohol is always available (often on a bring-your-own basis) along with various prescription sedative-hypnotics (e.g., Rohypnol®) and prescription stimulants (Ritalin® and Adderall®).

"I did a lot of ecstasy when I went to raves, and 'special K' and coke, and even meth every now and then. It intensifies it. When you're on ecstasy like you take a hit of nitrous, you don't even need like a balloon, you just need like a whippet can and you're, like it intensifies it like a hundred times more for just those 30 seconds and I remember doing that like all the time but, um, I never thought of whip cream cans as a drug."

17-year-old ecstasy "roller"

Most attendees at these gatherings do not suffer adverse effects and simply enjoy the music, dancing, and socialization; but as with any large gathering, problems do occur, including **harmful physical reactions to drugs, overheating, falling injuries, passing out, bad psychedelic experiences, and mental destabilization**. Most of the trips to emergency rooms are due (in order of frequency) to alcohol, then methamphetamines, LSD, GHB, MDMA, and ketamine abuse (Drug Abuse Warning Network [DAWN], 2005).

By 2006 use of "E" and other club drugs spread to singles bars, dorm rooms, rock concerts, and especially the San Francisco Bay Area Asian-American home or "house" party settings with an advocacy for "PLUR" = peace, love, unity, and respect (Hunt, Evens, Wu, et al., 2006). "E" also moved heavily by 2006 into the African-American youth hip-hop/rap music scene and the "sideshow" auto-dragging scene, where the drug is known as "thizz" or "stunnas" and being under the influence is called "thizzin," "zoning," and "stuntin or bustin your head." Wild dancing while under the influence of "thizz" in this community is called "getting hyphy" if you are from northern California or "goin' crunk" if you are from the South (Swan, 2006).

2C-T-7 & 2C-T-2

Two other phenethylamines, originally developed by Dr. Alexander Shulgin in his 1991 book *PiHKAL: A Chemical Love Story,* have also found their way into the recent psychedelic drug-taking subculture. The common effects of these two phenethylamine psycho-stimulant drugs are their ability to **induce delirium, heighten sensitivity, and increase awareness** in the user (Shulgin & Shulgin, 2000). They can also cause dangerous cardiovascular effects and even death when taken in high doses.

Known by its Netherlands trade name Blue Mystic,® 2C-T-7 (2,5 dimethoxy-4-propylthiophenethyamine) was first synthesized in January 1986. By 2000 "smart shops" were selling the psycho-stimulant under the brand names "Tripstacy," "7th Heaven," "7-Up," "Lucky 7," and "Beautiful" (Erowid, 2001). These shops, the current equivalent of "head shops," are boutiques that promote and sell New Age psychedelic substances, paraphernalia, literature, and fashion accessories that promote drug use. There are more than 200 of such shops in Holland, and most sell fresh and dried varieties of magic mushrooms, herbal ecstasy (sold with trade names like Cloud 9, Ultimate Xphoria, or Herbal Ecstasy containing caffeine and/or ephedrine). They also sell guarana, other herbal stimulants, psychoactive herbs, *Cannabis* seeds, and grow kits.

The abuse of a similar drug, 2C-T-2, spread through "smart shops" in the Netherlands, Sweden, Germany, and even Japan led to its being banned in the Netherlands on April 12, 1999. The high, according to some users, comes with somewhat more-unpleasant physical effects (nausea, vomiting, and muscle tension) and not as good mental effects as 2C-T-7 (Erowid, 2006).

Nexus (2C-B [CBR] or 4-bromo-2,5-dimethoxy phenylethylamine)

"I found only mild visual and emotional effects at the 20 mg dose, so I took the remaining 44 mg. I was propelled into something not of my choosing. Everything that was alive was completely fearsome. My gaze moved to the right and caught a bush growing outside the window and I was petrified. It was a life form I could not understand."

40-year-old physician (Shulgin & Shulgin, 2000)

This rarely used amphetamine-like chemical was synthesized by Dr. Alexander Shulgin. Like many of the psycho-stimulants, the effects of 2C-B are **very dependent on the amount taken: mild stimulation at low doses and intense psychedelic experiences at high doses**.

A number of users combine 2C-B and MDMA to intensify the experience. Experienced psychedelic users have generally learned to control their reactions to various substances and can report on the subtleties between one psycho-stimulant and another, but most experiment with whatever drug is available.

STP (DOM) (2,5-dimethoxy-4-methylamphetamine)

STP, also called the "serenity," "tranquility," or "peace" pill, is similar to MDA. It causes a 12-hour intoxication characterized by intense stimulation and several mild psychedelic reactions. It was used in the 1960s and 1970s but is rarely seen today because of the high incidence of bad trips.

PMA (4-MA or paramethoxyamphetamine)

Recently, PMA has been found in pills purporting to be ecstasy that were smuggled in from Europe. After an hour this short-acting drug causes a sudden rise in blood pressure, distinct after-images, and a pins-and-needles tingly feeling like a chill or hair standing on end.

This hallucinogen can negatively surprise the unaware user, causing severe sympathetic nervous system stimulation (seizures), hyperthermia, coagulation of blood, and muscle damage. PMA became popular because street lore said it was close to LSD in its effects (which was not really true).

BROMO-DRAGON FLY

Bromo-DragonFLY, also known as "B-Fly" or just "Fly", is a powerful hallucinogenic drug first synthisized in 1998. It has 1/3rd to 1/10th the potency of LSD based on weight, but has an extremely long duration of action, sometimes days. Hallucinations, delusions, and memory loss are some major effects.

BELLADONNA & OTHER ANTICHOLINERGIC PSYCHEDELICS

BELLADONNA, HENBANE, MANDRAKE & DATURA (jimson weed, thornapple)

From ancient Greek times through the Middle Ages and the Renaissance, **these plants, which contain hyoscyamine, atropine, and scopolamine, have been used in magic ceremonies, sorcery, witchcraft, and religious rituals**. They've also been used as a narcotic, a diuretic, a sedative, an antispasmodic, a poison, to mimic insanity, and even as a beauty aid by ancient Greek, Roman, and Egyptian women because they dilate pupils and make the eyes more striking (Ott, 1976). In fact *belladonna* in Latin means "beautiful woman." Belladonna, a short bush (2 to 4 feet) with green leaves, is widely distributed over central and southern Europe and Southwest Asia and is cultivated in England, France, and North America. Datura is more widely grown, and references to it are found in Chinese, Indian, Greek, and Aztec history.

One of the effects of these plants is to block acetylcholine receptors in the central nervous system. Acetylcholine helps regulate reflexes, aggression, sleep, blood pressure, heart rate, sexual behavior, mental acuity, and attention. This disruptive effect can cause a form of delirium and make it hard to focus vision. It can also **speed up the heart, cause intense thirst, and raise the body temperature to dangerous levels. Anticholinergics also create some hallucinations, a separation from reality, and a deep sleep for up to 48 hours** (Schultes & Hofmann, 1980). They are still used today by some native tribes in Mexico and Africa. Synthetic anticholinergic prescription drugs like Cogentin® and Artane® that are used to treat the side effects of antipsychotic drugs and Parkinson's disease symptoms are diverted from legal sources and abused for their psychedelic effects. Further, even belladonna cigarettes (Asmador®) used to treat asthma have been abused in the past by youth in search of a cheap high (Smith, 1981).

Jimson weed, also known as "thornapple," "angel's trumpet," "Jamestown weed," "mad apple," "moonflower," and "stinkweed," is a bristly-looking plant with coarse green leaves and white flowers found growing naturally in many parts of the United States. Users eat the seeds, drink jimson tea, and smoke cigarettes made from the leaves. The drug induces jerky movements, tachycardia, hypotension, and especially severe hallucinations such as imaginary snakes, spiders, and lizards. Not too many users try the drug twice because it is often described as a horrible experience that can last for days. More than 975 jimson weed poisonings were reported in the United States in 2005 (American Association of Poison Control Centers, 2005). Many emergency room visits are also due to impaired judgment and coordination, which lead to risk-taking activities. ER personnel describe jimson weed users as "Hot as a hare, blind as a bat, dry as a bone, red as a beet, mad as a hatter" (Leinwand, 2006).

KETAMINE, PCP & OTHER PSYCHEDELICS

There are other lesser-known psychedelics whose popularity comes and goes as **each generation seems to forget the problems that these drugs caused societies in the past**. For example, PCP was somewhat popular in the early and mid-1970s. It caused problems for police, for parents, and in schools because of the violence it engendered. By 2005 and 2006, a new generation of users started taking their "fry" or "fry daddies" **(marijuana dipped in embalming fluid) and adding PCP**. ("Fry" and "fry daddies" were once street names for marijuana mixed with crack cocaine.) This combination, also called "dipstick" or "wet," has been reported mostly in the eastern United States. To the generally younger users, it was a novelty; but like the use of PCP in previous decades, the unexpected effects of disassociation, anger, and insensitivity to pain has caused a number of injuries and arrests.

KETAMINE

The effects of ketamine, a dissociative general anesthetic used in

This etching on leather by Adrien Hubertus from medieval Europe gives the artist's impression of hallucinations caused by the hexing herbs, along with visions of sexual activity and death.

EMB Service for Publishers. Reprinted by permission.

human and veterinary medical procedures, are very similar to those of PCP, its close chemical relative and predecessor. Both share the same receptor sites in the brain although each has a different duration of action—PCP lasts longer than ketamine. *Dissociative* means that users are less connected to themselves and the world around them. Ketamine (first synthesized in 1962) was the most used anesthetic in the Vietnam War. It continued to be widely used on humans until reports of its side effect—unwanted visions—changed its target patients to animals rather than humans. Because it doesn't suppress breathing as much as most other anesthetics, it is still frequently used as a human anesthetic. It is also used as a co-analgesic, often with an opioid. It wasn't rated as a scheduled substance (depressant—Schedule III) until 1999.

As an abused club drug, the IV solution of ketamine is diverted from medical and dental supplies to be crystallized by a microwave-oven heating process. **The crystals are then smoked in a crack pipe or snorted**, the most common method of use. Occasionally, the drug is taken orally or injected. Ketamine is sold under the trade names Ketanest,® Detaset,® and Ketalar® and is known on the streets as "special K," "vitamin K," and "kit kat."

In 2002 raids in the United States, Mexico, and Panama by the DEA and local authorities dismantled North America's largest illegal producer and distributor of ketamine. The group allegedly handled 60% to 70% of the illegal ketamine sold in the United States. About 200,000 vials of the drug were confiscated in a veterinary office in Tijuana, Mexico (Fox, 2002). A number of

veterinary offices in the United States have been burglarized for ketamine.

"K-heads" (ketamine abusers) often use a micro-spoon, about 20 mg of powder piled up as a "line" on a mirror, or a "bump" from a plastic snorting device called a "bullet," snorted up each nostril two to five times until the desired effects are achieved. **A "K-land" dose of 100 to 200 mg** results in a mild dreamlike intoxication, a sensation of a mind/body separation, dizziness, initial free-floating giddiness, slurred speech, and impaired muscular coordination (Jansen, 2001).

"You don't care about anything whatsoever. You are a distance from whatever it is. Whether someone is talking to you, whether there is an argument going on right next to you,

you don't know it. You are in your own little place. Nothing around you is connected to you."

43-year-old recovering psychedelic user

A 300 to 500 mg dose of ketamine is usually needed to produce the full psychedelic experience known as **"being in a K-hole," described as an out-of-body near-death encounter with depersonalization, hallucinations, delirium, and occasionally bizarre or mystical experiences.** Users are also anesthetized against pain, including injuries sustained by rough activities such as fighting or dancing in a "mosh pit" at a rock concert, where people bang against each other.

"I walked into a cactus garden during a party. I just walked right through, walked right out. The next day my feet were all bloody and I was pulling stickers out and stuff but at the time there wasn't anything to it."

43-year-old recovering psychedelic user

Ketamine's toxic side effects from a K-hole dose or an overdose include respiratory depression, increased heart rate and blood pressure, combative or belligerent behavior, convulsions, and, in a few cases, coma.

The wholesale price of ketamine for veterinarians is about $7 per vial. Midlevel street dealers pay $30 to $45 per vial, and users may pay $100 to $200 per vial, or $20 to $25 per dose. A vial contains about 1 gram of liquified ketamine (five to 10 doses) (DEA, 2003).

Several researchers have used ketamine to treat alcoholism in a technique known as *ketamine-assisted psychotherapy.* The ketamine is injected intramuscularly, supposedly to make the brain more accessible to emotions and dialogue. The researchers reported that about two-thirds of their clients treated this way stayed abstinent for more than a year compared with one-fourth of a control group who tried conventional treatment (Krupitsky & Grinenko, 1997).

Rapid and dramatic development of tolerance, along with a profound psychic dependence, occurs with regu-

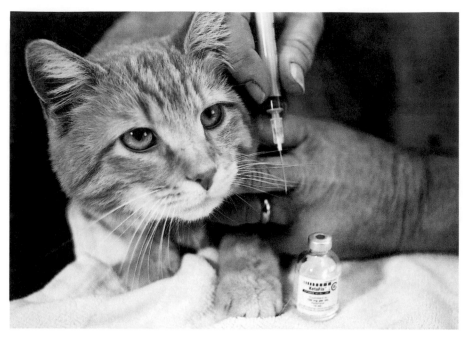

Ketamine is most often used as an animal tranquilizer.
© 2003 CNS Productions, Inc.

lar daily use of ketamine (Jansen & Darracot-Cankovic, 2001). **Major ketamine effects last for only about an hour or less whereas PCP effects last for several hours.** Coordination, judgment, and sensory perceptions, however, may be affected for 18 to 24 hours after ketamine use.

PCP

PCP (phencyclidine hydrochloride) was originally created during the 1950s by Parke-Davis Pharmaceuticals under the trade name Sernyl® as a new type of dissociative general anesthetic for humans. The frequency and the severity of toxic and hallucinogenic effects, however, soon limited its use to veterinary medicine starting in 1965 (Petersen, 1980; Zukin, Sloboda & Javitt, 2005). Eventually, use of PCP was completely discontinued. **Now the only supplies are illegal ones.** The drug is fairly easy to manufacture in a home laboratory, although the pungent odor is easily detectable.

Also called "angel dust," "peep," "KJ," "Shermans," or "ozone," PCP is **often misrepresented as THC, mescaline, or psilocybin.** It comes in liquid, crystal, tablet, or powdered form. It is often smoked in a Nat Sherman® ciga-

rette or sprinkled onto marijuana in a joint. **PCP can be smoked, snorted, swallowed, or injected.**

As with ketamine, PCP appears to disconnect sensory messages being sent to the central nervous system, dissolving inhibitions, deadening pain, and resulting in the same mind/body separation as ketamine. In one study almost three-fourths of the users reported forgetfulness, difficulty concentrating, aggressive and violent behavior, depersonalization, and/or estrangement whereas **a smaller percentage (about 40%) reported hallucinations (tactile, visual, or auditory)** (Siegel, 1989). The most problematic effects of PCP—self-inflicted injuries and violent run-ins with authorities—occur because PCP's dissociative effects prod users to overstress muscles, sinews, and flesh and numb them from experiencing pain. This leads to a number of newspaper stories reporting apparent feats of incredible strength along with movies, such as *The Terminator* and *Death Wish II,* where characters fight like robots and feel no pain.

"When I smoke PCP, I feel just like on top of the world, you know. You don't feel pain. You don't think about your

past. It's a good drug if you want to cover up your feelings, you know? You feel like Superman. It's like acid without the mind trip. A couple of times I got scared on it though 'cause I smoked too much."
Recovering PCP user

Because PCP is so strong, particularly for first-time users, the range between a dose that produces a pleasant sensory-deprivation effect and one that induces catatonia, coma, or convulsions is very small. Low dosages (2 to 5 mg) produce mild depression then stimulation. Moderate doses (10 to 15 mg) can produce a more intense sensory-deprived state. Dosages just a little higher (above 20 mg) can cause catatonia, coma, and convulsions. Large PCP doses have also produced seizures, respiratory depression, rigidity of muscles, cardiovascular instability, and even kidney failure (Jaffe, 1989).

"I've had seizures before on it and banged my head really hard—continually on hard objects—and got lots of bumps and everything and felt them the next few days but never realized I was doing it and never felt hurt from it."
Recovering PCP user

A low dose of PCP will last 1 to 2 hours, a moderate dose 4 to 6 hours, but the effects of a large dose can last up to 48 hours, much longer than the effects produced by a comparable dose of LSD. PCP is not widely taken by the general drug-using population because **there is a high frequency of bad trips associated with it.** When the psychedelic effects kick in, first-time or surprised users can have a bad trip and often do not even remember it. This type of amnesia is called *anterograde amnesia.* There is also some loss of memory of events that occurred shortly before the drug was taken; this type is called *retrograde amnesia.* Both types of memory loss are frequently seen with date-rape drugs like Rohypnol® or GHB and with alcohol (blackouts). Surprisingly, a number of long-term users have figured

a personal dose for these drugs that doesn't result in radical side effects.

SALVIA DIVINORUM (salvinorin A)

"Me and my friends, when we did it, there wasn't very much communication. We were just pretty much all trapped in our little trip. We weren't very talkative. It's not a party drug at all.
18-year-old psychedelic user

In the past few years *Salvia divinorum* ("sage," "diviner's sage," "Sally-D"), **a plant whose unique psychic effects have been likened to taking a combination of various psychedelic drugs,** has started showing up more frequently in some high schools and colleges. At different dosages and in different settings, some have described it to be LSD-like, DMT-like, ketamine-like, and PCP-like—but not exactly the same effects as these substances. *Salvia divino-*

Salvia divinorum, a member of the sage family, is cultivated in many parts of the United States.

rum has been used for centuries by Mazatec shamans and *curanderas* (medicine men and women) in the Sierra Madre in northeastern Mexico. It is used to induce a trancelike state to search for the cause of the patient's illness.

Dried leaves and live cuttings of this member of the mint family can be chewed and absorbed through the buccal membranes or smoked and absorbed through the lungs, **causing dreamlike hallucinations, occasional delirium, and out-of-body sensations**. When it is smoked, **the major effects last for only a few minutes, taper off after 7 to 10 minutes**, and disappear within 30 minutes, much like DMT. As with most psychedelics, the experience is quite dependent on the user's mind-set and surroundings. An ounce of Salvinorin A can be extracted from 100 to 200 leaves, enough for four to 12 doses, although the strength of the plant and the susceptibility of the user vary widely. **Salvorin is thought to be the key psychoactive chemical** responsible for *Salvia divinorum*'s major psychoactive effects. When smoked, doses of 200 to 500 μg of salvinorin A are said to produce similar yet more-intense psychedelic effects than 100 to 200 μg of LSD (Bucheler, Gleiter, Schwoerer, et al., 2005).

"And then there's the extract of Salvia, which is a whole other ballgame. It's similar to a DMT experience but without such a hard-edge thing going on. You definitely get removed from whatever situation you are in at the moment."

24-year-old Salvia divinorum user

It takes 3 lbs. of leaves to make 1 oz. of extract. Using salvinorin A extract can also produce hallucinations, delirium, and out-of-body sensations, along with an inability to function physically or even communicate. It is not yet understood how the extract works in the brain, and no receptor sites have been identified as its site of action. As of 2007 **Salvia divinorum was legal**, although it is illegal to sell it for human consumption. Live cuttings of the plant can even be obtained on the Internet. There are some indications that the authorities are reviewing the substance for scheduling as a controlled substance. It is currently illegal in Australia, Denmark, Italy, Norway, and South Korea.

AMANITA MUSHROOMS

On the Internet one can buy 25 grams (g) of minced *Amanita* mushrooms for about $25. The *Amanita* mushroom is one of the few psychedelics that **can be sold legally in the United States** and a number of other countries. It is illegal to sell the mushroom for human consumption, however. Although many members of this family of mushrooms are deadly, the *Amanita muscaria* (fly agaric) and the *Amanita pantherina* (panther mushroom) have been used as psychedelics for centuries. The *Amanita* mushroom is mentioned in sacred writings (the four *Vedas*) in India dating back to 1500 B.C., where a drinkable preparation of it is referred to as the god Soma.

Amanita has also been used by na-tive tribes in Siberia, but its use in the modern age is limited because of the unpredictability of its effects and because many even more deadly mush-rooms can be mistaken for it. The use of *Amanita muscaria* in ancient ritual cer-emonies is still practiced today by some Ojibway Indians in Michigan (Ott, 1976).

Come thou to our libations, drink of Soma; Soma-drinker thou! The rich One's rapture giveth kine. So may we be acquainted with thine innermost benevolence: Neglect us not, come hitherward.

Rig-Veda, Hymn IV, Indra (Internet Sacred Text Archive, 2006)

The *Amanita muscaria* is a large mushroom with an orange, tan, red, or yellow cap with white spots. It **can cause dreamy intoxication, hallucina-tions, delirious excitement, and deadly physical toxic effects as well**. The effects start a half hour after inges-tion and can last four to eight hours (Schultes & Hofmann, 1992). The active in-gredients are ibotenic acid and the al-kaloid muscimole, substances that re-semble the inhibitory neurotransmitter GABA. The *Amanita pantherina* con-tains more of the active ingredients, and taking too much of the mushroom can make the user sick for up to 12 hours (Rosen & Weil, 2004).

DEXTROMETHORPHAN (Robitussin DM,® Romilar® & other cough syrups)

In low doses dextromethorphan (DM) is sold in **nonprescription cough suppressants, though it's chemically similar to morphine**. DM is more anti-cough, however, and has less of the opioid side effects. It has been available in many cold and cough medications, such as Coricidin,® Romilar,® Robitussin DM,® and more than 140 other liquids, tablets, and cap-sules since the 1960s. Early on, users found that the high concentrations of dextromethorphan in some cough preparations would cause psychoactive effects. It was withdrawn from the mar-ket and eventually reintroduced in lower concentrations. In many states **even the weaker preparations are**

kept behind the pharmacy counter and require an ID for purchase. Users discovered that 10 to 15 times the pre-scribed dose of the weaker preparation would cause such psychoactive effects as **euphoria, mind/body separation, auditory and visual hallucinations, and a loss of coordination.** The princi-pal molecular target of dextrometh-orphan is probably the NMDA receptor.

One drug Web site, the Vaults of Erowid, describes four levels of experi-ence based on how much is taken. The first level is mildly stimulating with a small buzz, similar to MDA. The sec-ond is described as being drunk and stoned simultaneously. The third level is similar to the dissociative effects of a low dose of ketamine. The fourth is similar to a fully dissociative effect caused by a high dose of ketamine (Erowid, 2006). Because alcohol is found in many of these cough medications, the effects can be similar to those of some-one who is both drunk and delirious.

"I only took a capful and it was kind of a bluish tint. It kinda' reminded me of acid sort of, where like wherever I'd walk, I'd feel like the world was kinda' rushing toward me. Wherever I looked, it was just like the visuals, almost like tracers, coming at me. I smoked a lot of weed with those."

Recovering club drug user

Occasional reports of dextrometh-orphan abuse have persisted since the early 1960s, resulting in the evolution of many street names for the drug, such as "orange crush," "CCC," "robo," "dex," "DXM," and even "red devils" (also an old street name for Seconal® in the 1960s).

A normal therapeutic dose is 10 to 50 mg or up to 120 mg in a 24-hour pe-riod. **A strong dose by a drug abuser who wants the psychedelic effects is 300 to 600 mg, and the effects will last 6 to 8 hours.** Some will take a heavy dose (600 to 1,500 mg) in the search for more mental effects. Those who get totally carried away might use 2,500 to 20,000 mg, and at that level death can occur, particularly if used in conjunction with alcohol.

The drug can also dilate pupils, decrease orgasm, upset the stomach, and induce nausea. Additional negative reactions include itching, rashes, fever, and tachycardia; and these toxic side effects can cause acute anxiety and panic reactions. Tolerance to dextromethorphan does develop, and when used in excess it can be mildly addicting. Because DXM is an opioid, an overdose can result in coma and respiratory depression that is somewhat treatable with naloxone, an opioid antagonist (Elora, 2001). Dextromethorphan has also been studied as a treatment for heroin and opioid addiction both by addicts themselves and by researchers (*see Chapter 9*).

NUTMEG & MACE

At the low end of the psychedelic drug spectrum, nutmeg and mace— both from the nutmeg tree (*myristica fragrans*)—**can cause varied effects from a mild floating sensation to a full-blown delirium**. So much has to be consumed (about 20 g) that the user is left with a bad hangover and a severely upset stomach. The active chemicals in nutmeg and mace are variants of MDA (Marnell, 2005). Because this dose exposes a user to the nauseating and toxic effects of other chemicals in nutmeg, its **abuse is extremely rare**

outside of prisons, where convicts use it because they have limited access to other psychedelics.

MARIJUANA & THE CANNABINOIDS

"More than 250 marijuana plants were found at a home that caught fire this morning in San Francisco, according to San Francisco police officer Maria Oropeza. Police were called to the scene around 4:20 a.m. after firefighters put the one-alarm blaze out."
San Francisco Chronicle, *February 5, 2006*

"With at least tacit support from several local elected officials, operators of a San Francisco medical cannabis dispensary raided by U.S. drug agents last month thumbed their nose at federal authorities and handed out bags of pot-laced confections and marijuana cigarettes in Civic Center Plaza outside City Hall on Wednesday."
San Francisco Chronicle, January 10, 2006

"Braided rope made from 100% hemp is an item right out of antiquity. This incredibly strong natural rope is handmade in Romania. The manufacturing of this hemp rope uses the same techniques practiced for hundreds of years. This is the same type of rope used in the old sailing ships."
Ad from the Hemp Traders Web site, which sells products made from hemp

The *Cannabis,* or hemp, plant, also called *marijuana,* produces fibers, grows edible seeds (*akenes*), has an oil that is used as a fuel and a lubricant, contains a number of medicinal ingredients, produces psychedelic resin that can alter consciousness, and is illegal in most countries.

"A divided U.S. Supreme Court [6 to 3] on Monday said federal law enforcement can disregard state medical marijuana laws and seize plants and make arrests."
Portland Oregonian, June 7, 2005

HISTORY OF USE

A relationship between *Cannabis* and *Homo sapiens* has existed for at least 10,000 years. From its probable origin in China or central Asia, **hemp cultivation has spread to almost every country in the world**. There is a variety of species; **some *Cannabis* plants are better for fiber, some for food, some for medications, and some for inducing psychedelic effects.**

The plant was probably first used for nutrition because primitive people were always searching for new sources of food. Our ancient ancestors undoubtedly experienced some psychedelic effects when the plant was eaten. Next *Cannabis* was most likely utilized as a fiber for rope and nets. After that various medicine men, especially the semi-legendary Chinese emperor Shen Nung (c. 2700 B.C.), experimented with *Cannabis* for its medicinal benefits. Finally, experimenters searched for different ways to extract and consume the plant's psychedelic components.

Around 1500 B.C. the Indian *Vedas* (which also praised *Amanita* mushrooms) described *Cannabis* as a divine nectar that could deter evil, bring luck, and cleanse man of sin. It was listed as one of the five sacred plants to bring about freedom from stress (Booth, 2004).

"We speak to the five kingdoms of the plants with soma the most excellent among them. The darbha-grass, hemp, and mighty barley: they shall deliver us from calamity!"
Atharva Veda, VI 43

Indian writings also described *Cannabis*'s medicinal use to relieve headaches, control mania, counteract insomnia, treat venereal disease, cure whooping cough, and even arrest tuberculosis (Touw, 1981). Over succeeding millennia *Cannabis* continued to be used in all its forms. Galen, the "father of modern Western medicine," wrote in A.D. 200 that it was sometimes customary to give *Cannabis* to guests to induce enjoyment and mirth. In third-century Rome, ropes and sails for ships' riggings were made from hemp fiber (Brunner, 1977). Medieval physicians cultivated hemp for the treatment

In India ganja, the more potent leaves and flowering tops of the Cannabis plant, are smoked in chillums, hollow cone-shaped pipes. The smoker cups his hands over the opening at the bottom of the pipe and draws the smoke in through his hands.
© 2000 CNS Productions, Inc.

of jaundice or coughs and recommended weedy hemp to treat cancer.

Because ***Cannabis* was not specifically banned in the Koran by the Prophet Mohammed**, Islamic cultures spread its use to Africa and Europe. Hashish, the concentrated form of marijuana, was written about in certain ancient texts, some of them originating about A.D. 1000.

"When he had earned his daily wage, he would spend a little of it on food and the rest on a sufficiency of that hilarious herb. He took his hashish three times a day: once in the morning on an empty stomach, once at noon, and once at sundown. Thus he was never lacking in extravagant gaiety."
"A Tale of Two Hashish Eaters" from <u>A Thousand and One Arabian Nights</u>

In later centuries the use of hashish and marijuana was discouraged then condemned in Islamic countries. In Africa beginning about 600 years ago, marijuana was used in social/religious rituals and in medicinal preparations to treat dysentery, fevers, asthma, and even the pain of childbirth (DuToit, 1980).

As the Age of Exploration increased the need for rope, sails, and paper, many newly established colonies were encouraged to grow the more fibrous variants of *Cannabis* and export the hemp to the mother country. Even George Washington had large fields of *Cannabis* growing on his plantation. ***Cannabis* was widely cultivated in the Americas until the nineteenth century, when the end of slavery made it less profitable to harvest and process the plant.** The importation of *Cannabis* into the Americas for the psychoactive effects of smoking are thought to have originated with African slaves kidnapped from Angola and brought to plantations in northeastern Brazil. From there it eventually spread north to the Caribbean Islands and Mexico (Courtwright, 2001).

After World War I, **migrant laborers who worked in the United States introduced the habit of smoking marijuana for its psychoactive effects**. Initially, its use was confined to poor and minority groups, but in the 1920s the use of *Cannabis* as a substitute for prohibited alcohol spread in popularity. Marijuana "tea pads," similar to opium dens, became popular. It is estimated that there were more than

500 "tea pads" in New York by the beginning of the 1930s. Many of the "tea pads" were simply apartments where tenants and their smoking friends would get together to smoke pot. Some of these gatherings soon evolved into "rent parties," where tenants charged daily admission fees to help make their rent payments (O'Brien, Cohen, Evans, et al., 1992; Booth, 2004).

This expanded use of marijuana alarmed prohibitionists, who were left without a cause when the Eighteenth Amendment was repealed. Added to this prohibitionist atmosphere was a series of crusading articles against the drug by the Hearst newspapers. They popularized the word *marijuana* in their campaign. As a result, the **use of Cannabis (except for sterilized bird seed) was banned by the Marijuana Tax Act of 1937**. Although medical use was still permitted, any prescribing of the substance was actively discouraged. Pharmaceutical manufacturers removed *Cannabis* from a list of 28 medications that were being widely prescribed at the time (Walton, 1938).

Movies such as Reefer Madness (1936) and Devil's Harvest (1942) exploited the sensationalism that surrounded psychoactive drugs in the 1930s. With the passage of the Marijuana Tax Act of 1937, drug exploitation films fell out of favor until the early 1950s.

With the advent of World War II, the fear of an interruption in the importation of hemp fiber to America generated government support for locally grown hemp fields and plants that could turn it into ropes and fibers for the war effort. In addition, the Office of Strategic Services (OSS, later the Central Intelligence Agency) started a secret program to develop a speech-inducing drug to unseal the lips of spies during interrogations. One of the drugs they came up with was a potent extract of *Cannabis* that was odorless, tasteless, and colorless, code-named "TD," or truth drug. Remember that this was in the early 1940s, only a few years after marijuana had been banned as "the killer weed."

Since the end of World War II, the use of marijuana has been illegal in the United States and most other countries, although the level of enforcement varies widely from country to country. Currently, however, **several countries are cultivating a fibrous variant of the Cannabis plant to supply pulp and fiber** to make paper, textiles, and rope. France, Italy, Yugoslavia, and to a lesser extent England and Canada now permit the growing of hemp. The Netherlands permits personal use of marijuana in so-called coffee shops mainly in Amsterdam. In spite of restrictions, **marijuana is still used in some form by 160 million people worldwide**.

EPIDEMIOLOGY

"Before I tried marijuana myself, I thought that it smelled like musk because everyone in the sixties and seventies used musk perfume to hide the real marijuana smell from the cops."

30-year-old marijuana smoker

In 1960 only 2% of people in the United States (3.4 million) had tried any illegal drug. By the late 1960s, the growth of the counterculture, fueled by the Baby Boom, greatly increased the use of marijuana and other illicit drugs. By 1979, 68 million people in the United States had tried marijuana and 23 million were using it on a monthly basis. Its popularity led 10 states to decriminalize possession of small

amounts of the drug for personal use, but by the 1990s the resurgence of the concept of complete prohibition had recriminalized the use of "pot" in most states. It also greatly increased the number of people in prison for marijuana possession and use. By 1992 the monthly rate of use had dropped to one-third of its 1979 peak level, but recently those levels have begun to climb, particularly among teenagers.

By 2005 more than 14.6 million Americans (about 6% of the U.S. population 12 and older) were using marijuana on a monthly basis, an average of 18.7 joints, whereas 3.2 million used on a daily basis (SAMHSA, 2006).

◇ According to the Drug Abuse Warning Network, more than **80,000 visits to emergency rooms listed marijuana as a contributing factor**.

◇ The National Institute of Justice's Arrestee Drug Abuse Monitoring Program found that **44% of adult male arrestees and 32% of adult female arrestees tested positive for marijuana, as did 57% of juvenile male arrestees and 32% of juvenile female arrestees**.

(DAWN, 2004 & 2005; Arrestee Drug Abuse Monitoring Program, 2005; United Nations Office on Drugs and Crime, 2005)

"You want to use it all the time. You want to be high, you want to hang out with the kids that are high so you get the same feeling or you're at the same level as them. You just want to hang out with them, just be cool."

18-year-old marijuana smoker

BOTANY

"Most of the marijuana in the late sixties was 'brown Mexican,' but we also had access to 'Colombian gold,' 'Panama red,' 'Acapulco gold,' and 'Thai sticks,' so we had plenty of high-concentration THC. We also had connections for Vietnamese pot. They didn't check the GIs' duffel bags. A lot of pot nowadays just makes you

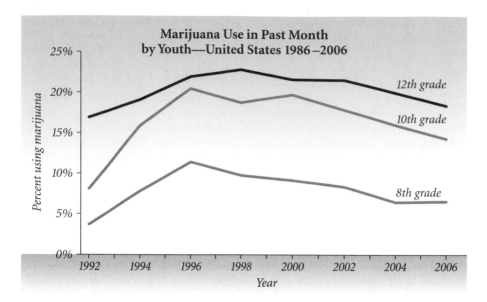

Marijuana Use in Past Month by Youth—United States 1986–2006

Figure 6-1 •

In 1978, 37% of high school seniors used marijuana at least once a month. By 1992 that percentage had dropped to 12%; but after peaking in 1999, it was still 18.3% in 2006. Daily use for high school seniors rose from 1.9% in 1992 to 5% in 2006. This rise in monthly and daily use since 1992 is also apparent in the eighth and tenth grades (Monitoring the Future, 2006).

incapacitated or you munch and go to sleep or have just a 20-minute mystery trip or rush, then you munch, then crash out."

48-year-old former marijuana smoker

There is much confusion over the various terms used to describe the *Cannabis* plant. Terms such as *vulgaris, pedemontana, lupulus, Mexicana,* and *sinensis* have been used in the past hundred years, but there is a growing consensus about some of the terminology. *Cannabis* is the botanical genus of all these plants. **Hemp is generally used to describe *Cannabis* plants that are high in fiber content. *Marijuana* is used to describe *Cannabis* plants that are high in psychoactive resins** (Booth, 2004).

Species

Over the years marijuana has had many street names: "pot," "muggles," "420," "Mary Jane," "grifa," "bud," "herb," "chronic," "dank," "da kind," "grass," "leaf," "ganja," "charas," "sens," "weed," and "dope." There are also hundreds of strains that sound like geographic brand names: "African black," "Panama red," "Acapulco gold," "Maui wowie," "Humboldt green," "BC [British Columbia] bud," and "Buddha Thai." Constant experimentation by growers has resulted in variations in the plant size, concentration of psychoactive resin, and even the shape of the leaf. Some botanists say that *Cannabis sativa* is the only true species; others think that there are three distinct species, but all agree that there are hundreds of unique variants of the plant (Emboden, 1981). Unfortunately, intensive hybridization and cultivation has made them hard to identify. In this book we designate three species: *Cannabis sativa, Cannabis indica,* and *Cannabis ruderalis.*

The most common species is *Cannabis sativa*, grown in tropical, subtropical, and temperate regions throughout the world. Variations of *Cannabis sativa* have sufficient quantities of active resins to cause psychedelic phenomena while other variations have a high concentration of fiber and are used for hemp. The average plant will grow from 5 to 12 ft. tall but can grow up to 20 ft. There are generally five thin serrated leaves on each stem plus two smaller vestigial leaves at the ends of the leaf clusters. Some variants have even more leaves. A typical plant will produce 1 to 5 lbs. of buds and smokable leaves, both of which contain high concentrations of the psychedelic resin called *THC (tetrahydrocannabinol).* It can grow in a variety of conditions.

The second species, ***Cannabis indica,* sometimes called "Indian hemp," is a shorter, bushier plant** with fatter leaves and is generally not used for its fibers. It is especially plentiful in India, Afghanistan, Pakistan, and the Himalayas. It didn't make it to Europe until the mid-1800s, when its geographical area of cultivation expanded. ***Cannabis indica* is the source of most of the world's hashish.** Modifications of the plant have resulted in a stronger, smellier variety, earning it the nickname "skunk weed" (Rätch, 2005). **Many illegal growers have come to prefer *Cannabis indica*** as the base plant on which to use the sinsemilla growing technique in the mistaken belief that *Cannabis indica* is legal because the law as written prohibits only *Cannabis sativa.* Legal challenges have resulted in the interpretation that it is marijuana that's illegal regardless of the specific species.

The third species, ***Cannabis ruderalis* (weedy hemp), a small thin plant, has a small amount of THC** and is especially plentiful in Siberia and western Asia. It is most likely the species that the historian Herodotus described the ancient Scythians using thousands of years ago in the Middle East.

Sinsemilla & Other Forms of Marijuana

The sinsemilla growing technique increases the potency of the marijuana plant and is used with both *Cannabis indica* and *Cannabis sativa.* The sinsemilla technique involves separating female plants from male plants before pollination. Female plants produce much more psychoactive resin than male plants especially when they are unpollinated and therefore bear no seeds. *Sinsemilla* means "without seeds" in Spanish. The term *commercial grade* refers to marijuana that is not grown by the sinsemilla technique.

The female flowering top of Cannabis sativa has relatively long, slender leaf projections.
Courtesy of Michael Aldrich

Immature Cannabis indica has shorter, stout leaves.
Courtesy of Michael Aldrich

Cannabis ruderalis from southern Siberia has relatively little THC content.
Courtesy of Michael Aldrich

Dried marijuana buds, leaves, and flowers **can be crushed and rolled into "joints." They can also be smoked in pipes.** In India and some other countries, marijuana in its various forms is smoked in *chillums,* which are cone-shaped pipes made out of clay, stone, or wood. Marijuana can also be taken in food and drinks, or the leaves can be chewed. In India and several other countries, marijuana is divided into three different strengths, each one coming from a different part of the plant.

◇ **Bhang** is made from the stem and the leaves and has the lowest potency. In central Asia and India, it is often prepared as a drink, often with honey, sugar, molasses, and even yogurt.

◇ **Ganja** is made from the stronger leaves and the flowering tops. It is smoked alone or sometimes mixed with other herbs.

◇ **Charas** is the concentrated resin from the plant and is the most potent. It can be mixed with foods and eaten or smoked either alone or with other herbs (Rätch, 2005).

Marijuana buds grown by the sinsemilla technique are saturated with THC.
© 2006 CNS Productions, Inc.

When the sticky resin is pressed into cakes, it is called "hashish"; the resin contains most of the psychoactive ingredients. This concentrated form of *Cannabis* is usually smoked in water pipes called "bongs" or "hookahs," or it can be added to a marijuana cigarette to enhance the potency of the weaker leaves. Bongs can also be used to smoke the less-concentrated parts of the marijuana plant. In India, Nepal, and other countries in the region, hashish use has been widespread. An early writer in the nineteenth century described five or six methods for collecting the resin and another dozen methods of preparing it for use, including pressed cakes, small pills, candies, or simply tiny balls of the dark brown resin (Bibra, 1855/1995).

Hash oil can be extracted from the plant (using solvents) and added to foods. Most often it is smeared onto rolling paper or dripped onto crushed marijuana leaves and smoked to enhance the psychoactive effects. The THC concentration of hash oil has been measured as high as 70%.

Growers

In 2006 federal agents discovered a 6-by-12-foot tunnel, 2,400 ft. long, under the U.S.-Mexico border in Tijuana. In the tunnel were 2 tons of marijuana, ready to be smuggled into the United States. Since 9/11, 20 tunnels (most of them smaller) have been found along this border. These discoveries emphasize the fact that **the majority of the marijuana used in the United States comes from Mexico and Colombia**. A disturbing recent change has been noted in California, where three-fourths of the marijuana seized in the state during the fall of 2002 was grown by Mexican cartels running growing operations in the richer soils of remote U.S. forests. The plantings contained anywhere from 2,000 to 10,000 plants (Meyers, 2006). The Campaign Against Marijuana Planting (CAMP) in California seized more than a million plants in 2005. A single bust in Oregon in 2006 netted 10,000 plants worth $50 million; another just north of San Francisco at Point Reyes National Seashore netted almost 23,000 plants. The federal

Office of National Drug Control (ONDCP) policy estimates that growing 1 acre of marijuana damages 10 acres of land through runoff, excess fertilizer, deadly pesticides, and damage to trees and other foliage (Squatriglia, 2006). **In the United States, 10% to 50% of the available marijuana is homegrown.** Because of stiffer penalties and greater surveillance by law enforcement agencies, more growers have moved their operations indoors. The latest wrinkle is occurring in the suburbs, where drug traffickers buy ordinary-looking suburban homes and refit them with grow lights, plant beds, and bootlegged electricity as indoor growing operations. Thousands of plants were seized from a single four-bedroom colonial home in New Hampshire (Ritter, 2007).

The indoor growing of marijuana has led to very high-potency plants grown all over the world. Some marijuana is even grown *hydroponically* (in water). Other major growing countries in the Western Hemisphere besides Canada, Colombia, Mexico, and the

United States are Belize, Brazil, Guatemala, Jamaica, Trinidad, and Tobago. In the Far East, Cambodia, Laos, Thailand, and the Philippines are big growers. The African and Middle Eastern countries Lebanon (greatly reduced in recent years), Morocco, Nigeria, and South Africa produce mostly *Cannabis indica*. In southwest and central Asia, Afghanistan and Pakistan are the big producers (DEA, 2006A).

The average street price of marijuana in the United States rose steadily from 1981 to a peak in 1991. Retail prices fell over the next decade but began to level off in the late 1990s to the present. Because the common unit of sale for marijuana is 1 oz. (called a "lid"), the average street price in the United States ranges from $100 to $400 per "lid," although the high price has led to sales of smaller and smaller amounts. A gram (28.3 g equals 1 oz.) averages $10, while one-eighth of an ounce (about 3 to 4 g), the most common measure, goes for $50 to $60 (Marijuana Seeds, 2006; Office of National Drug Control Policy, 2006). The average mari-

Drug Enforcement Administration agents and Immigration and Customs Enforcement personnel uncovered a massive cross-border drug tunnel between the United States and Tijuana, Mexico. The 2,400 foot long tunnel had electricity, ventilation, and more than two tons of marijuana ready for smuggling.

Courtesy of the Drug Enforcement Administration

juana joint uses 0.5 to 1 g of the substance. Prices for commercial-grade marijuana when bought in larger quantities have remained relatively stable (High Times, 2006). Prices for 1 lb. range widely:

◊ $50 to $100 in Mexico,
◊ $200 to $1,000 on the U.S.-Mexico border,
◊ $700 to $2,000 in the Midwest and the Northeast,
◊ $2,000 to $6,000 in northern California, and
◊ $900 to $6,000 in British Columbia.

The profits can be enormous: 500 lbs. of marijuana bought in Mexico for $50,000 can bring $400,000 in St. Louis.

PHARMACOLOGY

To date, researchers have discovered **more than 420 chemicals in a single *Cannabis* plant.** Interestingly, some teenagers use the number 420 as their phone-beeper code to signal the availability of marijuana. At least 30 of these chemicals, called *cannabinoids,* have been studied for their psychoactive effects. **The most potent psychoactive chemical by far is called Δ-9-tetrahydrocannabinol, or "THC,"** discovered in 1964 by two Israeli researchers. Cannabinol and cannabidiol are two other prominent cannabinoids, but they are not thought to have psychoactive properties. When smoked or ingested, these potent psychoactive chemicals are converted by the liver into more than 60 other metabolites, some of which are also psychoactive. When smoked, only about 20% of the THC in the joint is absorbed; however, the longer a lungful of smoke is held, the greater the amount of THC absorbed and the stronger the high.

The widespread use of the sinsemilla growing technique has increased the average concentration of THC from 1% to 3% in the 1960s to 4% to 15% and occasionally 25% since then (Rätch, 2005; DEA, 2006A). **High-concentration THC marijuana has been around for many years—it just hasn't been so readily available.** This means a user would have to smoke 3 to 5 of the weak joints from the 1960s and 1970s to equal just 1 of the stronger

joints available today. Many of the early studies on marijuana—and many of the attitudes of the counterculture about the effects of the drug were based on the weaker plants. Today the greater strength of marijuana is an accepted fact by the using population. An accelerating level of research with higher percentages of THC has given some crucial insights into the psychoactive mechanisms of the drug.

Marijuana Receptors & Neurotransmitters

In 1988 and 1990, researchers detected receptor sites in the brain that were specifically reactive to THC (Howlett, Evans & Houston, 1992). This discovery implied that the brain had its own natural neurotransmitters that fit into these receptor sites and that they affected the same areas of the brain as marijuana. These brain chemicals were called *endogenous cannabinoid neurotransmitters* or *endocannabinoids.*

Two years later researchers at the National Institute on Drug Abuse announced the **discovery of anandamide, an endocannabinoid that fits into the cannabinoid receptor sites** (Devane, Hanus, Breuer, et al., 1992). A few years later, another endocannabinoid called 2-arachidonyl glycerol (2AG) was discovered. 2AG is more abundant but not as active as anandamide in the brain though it may be more active on other body receptors. There is evidence of other endocannabinoids that have yet to be discovered.

Receptors for anandamide were initially found in several areas of the limbic system, including the reward/reinforcement pathway. In succeeding years **the two major receptors discovered were designated the CB_1 and CB_2 receptors.** CB_2 receptors seem to be limited to the immune system and a few other sites in the lower body whereas CB_1 receptors are found mostly in the brain, in particular the hippocampus, amygdala, basal ganglia (including the nucleus accumbens), and cerebellum (Welch, 2005). These parts of the brain regulate the **integration of sensory experiences with emotions as well as those controlling functions of learning, memory, a sense of novelty, motor**

coordination, and some automatic bodily functions. The presence of CB_1 anandamide receptors means that these areas of the brain are also quite affected by marijuana.

It is important to note that there are fewer anandamide receptors in the brainstem for marijuana, compared with endorphin receptors for opioids and norepinephrine receptors for cocaine, because this area of the brain controls heart rate, respiration, and other bodily functions. This is why dangerous overdoses can occur with cocaine and opioids, like respiratory depression or cardiac overstimulation, and why it is so **difficult to physically overdose with marijuana** (Smith, Compton, Welch, et al., 1994; Huestis, Gorelick, Heishman, et al., 2001). On the other hand, there are 10 times as many anandamides in the body as there are endorphins. They're involved in a vast range of physical and mental functions, most of which involve **increasing or decreasing the sensitivity of our mind to certain sensory inputs.**

SHORT-TERM EFFECTS

Physical Effects

The immediate physical effects of marijuana often include **physical relaxation or sedation, some pain control, bloodshot eyes, coughing from lung irritation, an increase in appetite, and a small to moderate loss in muscular coordination.** Other physical effects include a moderately increased heart rate, decreased blood pressure, decreased eye pressure (Marinol® capsules or marijuana joints are used as a treatment for glaucoma), **increased blood flow through the mucous membranes of the eye resulting in conjunctivitis or red eye**, and decreased nausea (capsules and joints are also used for cancer patients undergoing chemotherapy).

Marijuana impairs tracking ability (the ability to follow a moving object, such as a baseball) and causes a trailing phenomenon where one sees an afterimage of a moving object. Impaired tracking ability, the trailing phenomenon, and sedating effects make it more difficult to perform tasks that require depth perception and good hand/eye coordination, such as flying an airplane or catching a football.

Marijuana can act as a stimulant as well as a depressant, depending on the variety and the amount of chemical that is absorbed in the brain, the setting in which it is used, and the personality of the user.

"Marijuana is not a downer for me, it's a speed thing. I have plenty of friends who smoke marijuana and become quiet. They can't speak. They become immobile. They're total veggies, you know, sitting around and cannot move whereas I become more active."
48-year-old marijuana smoker

Marijuana also causes a small, temporary disruption of the secretion of the male hormone testosterone. That might be important to a user with a hormonal imbalance or somebody in the throes of puberty and sexual maturation. The testosterone effect also results in a slight decrease in both sperm count and sperm motility in chronic "pot" users (Joy, Watson & Benson, 1999; Wilkins, Mellott, Markvitsa, et al., 2003; Marnell, 2005). **Marijuana increases hunger**, often called "the munchies." Normally, the endocannabinoid system controls food intake through both central and peripheral mechanisms, particularly the CB_1 receptors in the hypothalamus. By flooding the receptors with THC, appetite is greatly increased. When marijuana is smoked, it doesn't seem to sharpen one's sense of taste; in fact, tests have shown that marijuana use does not change the perception of sourness, sweetness, saltiness, and bitterness nor does there appear to be an impairment of the satiation mechanisms. The **enhancement of the sensory appeal of foods, especially in a friendly environment, does seem to increase**, however. Once a person starts eating a food, the sense of novelty caused by marijuana (as described later in this section) makes the smoker pay attention to tastes and sensations.

"When I was I high, I got hungry and then I started eating and I couldn't stop and I'd keep going until I couldn't move. It tastes a lot better than normally. The taste seemed like it was

more intense. Even stuff I hadn't really liked that much before . . . it didn't make a difference. Before we smoked we made sure we had enough munchies on hand."*
18-year-old recovering marijuana user

Discovering the effects of cannabinoids on hunger has led to experiments with cannabinoid CB_1 antagonists (SR141716A and AM251) that block normal activity, thus leading to significant decreases in appetite (McLaughlin, Winston, Swezey, et al., 2003). SR141716A, marketed as Acomplia® (rimonabant), has been the subject of numerous clinical trials. It has been shown to reduce hunger by blocking the CB_1 receptors.

Mental Effects

Within a few minutes of smoking marijuana, the user becomes a bit confused and **mentally separated from the environment**. Marijuana produces a feeling of déjà vu, where everything seems familiar but really isn't. Additional effects include **drowsiness, an aloof feeling, and difficulty concentrating**.

"It's kind of like life without a coherent thought. It's kind of like an escape. It's like when you go to sleep, you forget about things. It's like everything's dreamlike and there are no restraints on anything. You can have freedom to say what you want to say."
16-year-old marijuana smoker

Stronger varieties of marijuana can produce giddiness, increased alertness, and major distortions of time, color, and sound. Very strong doses can even produce a sensation of movement under one's feet, visual illusions, and sometimes hallucinations.

"I have had illusions, not hallucinations, on marijuana but just where different colors stand out, things, different objects move, just little things that you never think twice about. It's just part of your high, I guess."
19-year-old marijuana user

Two of the most frequently mentioned psychological problems with smoking marijuana are paranoia and a depersonification (detachment from one's sense of self).

"You can't be there for people when you're not inside yourself. And when you get loaded, you're not inside yourself. It's like you remove yourself from yourself and then you're another person."
35-year-old marijuana user

Marijuana acts somewhat as a mild hypnotic. Charles Baudelaire, the nineteenth-century French poet, referred to it as "the mirror that magnifies." **It exaggerates mood and personality and makes smokers more empathetic to others' feelings** but also makes them more suggestible.

The **effects of THC on the amygdala, the emotional center of the brain, are key** to understanding many of the effects. The amygdala helps regulate appetite, pain, anxiety, fear, the suppression of painful memories, and, most important, the sense of novelty.

Novelty

Part of the **amygdala's function is judging the emotional significance of objects and ideas** that people encounter in their environment. For example, if a person encounters an unknown object, the amygdala is activated by the release of anandamides that alert his brain to beware of possible dangers or benefits, so the object is of greater interest. When a person uses marijuana, the **THC artificially stimulates the amygdala, making even mundane objects interesting**. Some users describe it as "virtual novelty" (drug-induced novelty). **The senses themselves aren't sharpened, just the way the brain processes the information** (Cermak, 2004).

"When I smoked, I loved colors, shapes, smells, sounds, my spouse. I don't think I actually heard or saw or smelled better, I just paid more attention. Even the fifth rerun of Gilligan's Island episode #29 was interesting."
38-year-old recovering marijuana user

As the amygdala is continually bombarded with THC, the CB$_1$ receptors respond with delight. But soon, particularly with excess use, these **cells react to the overstimulation by retracting into the cell membrane and becoming inactive (down regulation)** (*see Chapter 2*). If marijuana is used chronically, these receptors are even dismantled and their numbers can be reduced by up to 70% (Breivogel, Scates, Beletskaya, et al., 2003; Sim-Selley, 2003). This means that to a person who becomes down regulated and then stops smoking and has just a normal amount of anandamide but way fewer receptor sites, **even things that are truly novel may not have that freshness and everything becomes very boring.** So to regain that sense, one has to continue to use (Cermak, 2004).

If a marijuana smoker isn't really interested in working, isn't really interested in studying, isn't really interested in a relationship, when he smokes his primitive brain takes over and says, "Forget it, let's not do this." Once CB$_1$ receptor sites are down regulated, it takes approximately two weeks for them to recover. But for really heavy smokers, it might take four to six weeks or longer.

Memory & Learning

The hippocampus is the part of the brain most involved in short-term memory. Normally, the hippocampus stores current input for immediate use. Eventually, the short-term information is shifted to long-term memory. The body's own anandamide determines how much of the hippocampus is available, depending on the complexity of the activity. For a straightforward sport like baseball, the hippocampus input is limited so only a small portion of it is made available. Cramming for an exam requires greater capacity, so more of the hippocampus is made available. When an external cannabinoid like **THC is taken into the body, it severely limits the available amount of hippocampal short-term memory.**

"If you go home and have homework to do that night and you say, 'Okay, I'm going to get stoned before I do my homework,' you're never going to get your homework done."
High school student

Similar problems can occur on the job when there are a lot of details that have to be manipulated.

"I'd be doing the job and all of a sudden I'd look up and freeze and not know what to do. I would have a handful of checks in my hand and just look at the machine for a while and think to myself, 'What is this? What do I do with it?' So I just stand there and think to myself, 'Okay, it's going to come. It's going to come.' And eventually it would."
36-year-old male recovering marijuana smoker

· As use is discontinued, the short-term memory is almost restored, but if previous experiences and facts were never processed through short-term memory, they will never be remembered. The more regular the use, the larger the chunks of one's life that are forgotten.

"I don't remember the years that I did smoke. I remember the most important things, but the little details I couldn't tell you. I don't remember what I ate a little bit ago."
20-year old male marijuana smoker

Although marijuana slows learning and disrupts concentration by its influence on short-term memory, it has a much smaller effect on long-term memory. This explains why some students have been able to maintain good grades while using marijuana on a regular basis while others end up flunking out. A recent study of 150 heavy marijuana users in treatment found that not only memory but also attention span and cognitive functioning were impaired and, as expected, the heavier the use, the greater the impairment (Solowij, Stephens, Roffman, et al., 2002). Overall in one study, those who averaged a D in school were four times more likely to have used marijuana than those who got A's (SAMHSA, 2005).

"School was boring to a point before I started weed, but once I started smoking it more and more, it just got even more boring. I didn't want to go, I didn't want to interact at school. I went there and skipped a lot of classes. Actually I skipped more than half the year."
18-year-old recovering marijuana abuser

With marijuana many thoughts and feelings are internalized. Long-term marijuana smokers feel that they're learning, thinking, feeling, and communicating better.

"When I got high I thought I was the smartest person in the world. I knew I had the answer to everything, and one day I sat down with the tape recorder and I started rattling off all this brilliance that I had; the next day when I woke up in the morning and I played it back, it was almost like I wasn't even speaking English."
38-year-old recovering compulsive marijuana smoker

Marijuana affects the juvenile brain more severely than an adult brain. This is because in a juvenile's frontal lobes, around the age of 12, there is an explosion in the number of connections and synapses among the nerve cells. Over the succeeding 10 to 12 years, there is a gradual pruning process as these connections are strengthened or weakened. So when a person is experiencing a new idea or sensory input, the connections will be strengthened. Unused connections will be weakened and then break. Cannabinoid receptors are more dense here than in any other part of the cortex, so excess marijuana use can cause somewhat distorted thinking. For example, **the ability to hone in on things that are important and ignore things that are not is reduced over time.** This deficit can impair a person's ability to judge that which is dangerous and which situation has to be handled first.

The use of ecstasy and marijuana in combination is relatively popular among young people. Research has found that this combination has a synergistic negative effect on memory (Young, McGregor & Mallet, 2005).

Time

The **distortion of a sense of time (temporal disintegration)** is responsible for several of the perceived effects of marijuana. Dull repetitive jobs seem to go by faster. In Jamaica some cane field workers smoke "ganja" to make their hard, monotonous work pass by more quickly. On the other hand, students who smoke marijuana while studying (a more complex activity) get easily bored and often abandon their books.

The effects of distortion of the passage of time, impaired judgment, and short-term memory loss result in a user's inability to perform multiple and interactive tasks, like installing a computer program, while under the influence (Stafford, 1992; Joy, Watson & Benson, 1999; Wilkins, Mellott, Markvitsa, et al., 2003; Marnell, 2005). A study of current and former marijuana users tested the smokers at 1, 7, and 28 days after stopping various levels of use. Significant impairment was found at days 1 and 7 for heavy users, but by day 28 the difference in impairment had mostly disappeared (Pope, Gruber, Hudson, et al., 2001).

LONG-TERM EFFECTS

Respiratory Problems

Although the main psychoactive substances are different (THC vs. nicotine), the **smoke of both marijuana and nicotine contains a mixture of toxic gases and particulate matter**. As smoking becomes chronic, so does irritation to the breathing passages. Because marijuana is grown under a wide variety of conditions and is unrefined, the joints made from the buds and/or leaves are harsh, unfiltered, irregular in quality, and composed of many different chemicals. Therefore, when it is inhaled and held in the lungs, smoking four to five joints gives the same exposure to the lungs and mucous membranes as smoking a full pack of cigarettes, according to studies by Dr. Donald Tashkin at UCLA (Tashkin, Simmons & Clark, 1988; Joy, Watson & Benson, 1999; Tashkin, 2005). For these and other reasons, a major concern of health pro-

fessionals is the damaging effect that marijuana smoking has on the respiratory system. **Marijuana smoking on a regular basis leads to symptoms of increased coughing with acute and chronic bronchitis.** In microscopic studies of these mucous membranes, Dr. Tashkin has found that **most damage occurs in the lungs of those who smoke both cigarettes and marijuana.** This is significant because approximately 75% of marijuana smokers also smoke cigarettes (Richter, Kaur, Reznicow, et al., 2005).

In the series of slides (Figure 6-2), the normal ciliated surface epithelial cells in the mucous membranes of a nonsmoker of either cigarettes or marijuana (6-2a) show healthy, densely packed cilia that clear the breathing passages of mucous, dust, and debris. The breathing passage of a chronic marijuana smoker (6-2b) shows increased numbers of mucous-secreting surface epithelial cells that do not have cilia, so **phlegm production is increased but is not cleared as readily from the breathing passages.**

Finally, the breathing passage of a chronic smoker of both marijuana and cigarettes (6-2c) shows that the normal surface cells have been completely replaced by nonciliated cells resembling skin, so the **smoker has to cough to clear any mucous from the lungs because the ciliated cells are gone.**

"I'm sure I've done some damage to my lungs. I mean, you can't put that kind of tar down in your system, heated tar going into your system constantly for 23 years, and sit here and say there's nothing wrong and nothing has happened. Surely something has happened."

48-year-old marijuana smoker

Although marijuana smoking damages lung tissue, whether it causes cancer is unclear. Some of the changes involving the cell nucleus suggested to researchers that malignancy may be a consequence of regular marijuana

(a)

(b)

(c)

Figure 6-2 •

(a) Healthy mucous membrane of nonsmoker.

(b) Mucous membrane of a marijuana smoker.

(c) Mucous membrane of a marijuana and cigarette smoker.

Courtesy of Dr. Donald Tashkin, Pulmonary Research Department, UCLA Medical Center, Los Angeles, CA

smoking because the changes observed are precursors of cancer. In 2006, however, Dr. Tashkin and other researchers at UCLA released a study funded by the National Institute on Drug Abuse of 1,200 people with lung, neck, or head cancer and another 1,000 controls and found **no link between marijuana smoking and lung cancer**, even among heavy marijuana smokers. Cigarette smokers were found to have a 20-fold increased risk for cancer if they smoked two packs or more per day. As an explanation for this lowered cancer risk in marijuana smokers, some researchers postulate that the THC in marijuana might kill aging cells that could become cancerous (Tashkin, 2006).

Immune System

Epidemiologic studies have **identified marijuana as a cofactor in the progression of HIV infection**. Animal studies at UCLA found that the administration of marijuana increased the replication of the immunodeficiency virus and measurably suppressed immune function (Roth, Tashkin, Whittaker, et al., 2005). Another animal study found that **THC can lead to enhanced growth of tumors due to suppression of the anti-tumor immune response, including breast cancer** (McKallip, Nagarkatti & Nagarkatti, 2005).

Some evidence suggests that heavy marijuana use can also make users more susceptible to a cold, the flu, and other viral infections. If such were the case, it could be somewhat counterproductive for people who are already immune depressed to smoke marijuana for therapeutic purposes. In addition, the user is further exposing the lungs to pathogens, such as fungi and bacteria, found in marijuana smoke. The total health impact of marijuana on the immune system remains unclear.

Acute Mental Effects

There is still much debate about whether marijuana will cause a psychosis or serious mental illness rather than just increasing paranoia, acute anxiety, or depression. One reason is because it is **hard to separate other factors, especially pre-existing mental problems, from the precipitating influence of marijuana**. Often the use of marijuana (particularly that with high levels of THC) will tip the mental balance of someone just holding on. In a number of studies of patients in treatment, thorough investigation found the vast preponderance of psychoses and mental problems to be pre-existing (Os, Bak, Hanssen, et al., 2002; Grinspoon, Bakalar & Russo, 2005).

Some users believe that they have lost control of their mental state. Besides paranoia there is often a belief that they have severely damaged themselves or that their underlying insecurities are insurmountable. These acute problems are usually treatable, but it is problematic when the symptoms persist. Recovery counselors have seen a number of cases of people who, after experiencing a bad trip, don't come all the way back and may have problems going on with their lives. They experience continued confusion, difficulty concentrating, and memory problems and feel as though their mind is in a fog.

"I once worked with a 13-year-old client who had no premorbid symptoms that could be identified prior to his thirteenth birthday, when his friends turned him on to a 'honey blunt,' which is a cigar packed with marijuana soaked in honey and dried. It happened to be very strong sinsemilla, and he experienced an acute anxiety reaction followed by a hallucinogen persisting perceptual disorder, including a profound depression and an inability to concentrate. We don't know how long these problems will last."
Counselor, Genesis Recovery Center

Even veteran smokers who've been smoking some low-grade "pot" and then get some strong "BC bud" sinsemilla may feel that somebody has slipped them a psychedelic like PCP or LSD. They experience anxiety and paranoia that then creates even more anxiety.

There is also an increase in the practice of mixing marijuana with other drugs like cocaine, amphetamine, and PCP that can cause exaggerated reactions. Some users even smoke joints that have been soaked in formaldehyde and embalming fluid ("clickems" or "fry") for a bigger kick. "Clickems" give a PCP-like effect when smoked.

TOLERANCE, WITHDRAWAL & ADDICTION

Tolerance

Tolerance to marijuana occurs fairly rapidly, even though initially smokers become more sensitive, not less, to desired effects (inverse tolerance). Although high-dose chronic users can recognize the effects of low levels of THC in their systems, they are able to tolerate much higher levels without some of the more severe emotional and psychic effects experienced by first-time users. Current research suggests that *pharmacodynamic tolerance* (reduction of nerve cell sensitivity to marijuana) is the mechanism rather than reduced *bioavailability* (speeding up the breakdown of the drug known as drug *dispositional tolerance*).

"Originally, when we first got it, we could smoke, say, two bong loads and be just totally stoned whereas now we have to keep continuously smoking just to keep the high going, even with the higher-potency stuff."
24-year-old recovering marijuana user

One great concern is that **marijuana persists in the body of a chronic user for up to three months**, though the major effects last only four to six hours after smoking. These residual amounts in the body can disrupt some physiological, mental, and emotional functions.

Withdrawal

Because there is not the rapid onset of withdrawal from marijuana as with alcohol or heroin, many people deny that withdrawal occurs. The withdrawal from marijuana is more drawn out because much of the THC has been retained in the brain and **only after a relatively long period of abstinence will the withdrawal effects appear**.

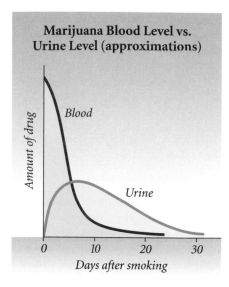

Marijuana Blood Level vs. Urine Level (approximations)

Figure 6-3 •
This chart shows the blood and urine levels of marijuana over time. The marijuana persists in the urine longer. The majority of drug testing measures only marijuana in the urine.

"Sometimes people who've been smoking for five years decide to quit. They stop 1, 2, 3 days, even a week, and they (especially those who think marijuana is benign), say, 'Wow, I feel great. Marijuana's no problem. I have no withdrawal. It's nothing at all.' Then they start up again. They never experience withdrawal. We see that withdrawal symptoms to marijuana are delayed sometimes for several weeks to a month after a person stops."
Darryl Inaba, Genesis Recovery Center

The discovery by French scientists in 1994 of an antagonist that instantly blocks the effects of marijuana enabled researchers to search for true signs of tolerance, tissue dependence, and withdrawal symptoms in long-term users. Experiments demonstrated that cessation of marijuana use could cause true physical withdrawal symptoms. Dr. Billy Martin of the Medical College of Virginia gave the THC antagonist SR14176A to rats that had been exposed to marijuana four days in a row. The antagonist negated the influence of the marijuana. Within

10 minutes the rats exhibited immediate physical withdrawal behaviors that included "wet dog shakes" and facial rubbing, which is the rat equivalent of withdrawal. These experiments indicated that **marijuana dependence occurs more rapidly than previously suspected** (Rinaldi-Carmona, Barth, Heauline, et al., 1994; Tsou, Patrick & Walker, 1995; Aceto, Scates & Martin, 2001).

Withdrawal effects of marijuana include:

◊ **anger**, irritability, anxiety, and/or aggression;
◊ **aches**, pains, chills;
◊ **depression**;
◊ **inability to concentrate**;
◊ slight tremors;
◊ sleep disturbances;
◊ decreased appetite and stomach pain;
◊ **sweating**; and
◊ **craving**.

Not everyone will experience all of these effects, but **everyone will experience some of them, especially craving**. Recent human research demonstrated that irritability, anxiety, aggression, and even stomach pain caused by marijuana withdrawal occurred within three to seven days of abstinence (Haney, Ward, Comer, et al., 1999; Kouri, Pope & Lukas, 1999; Budney, Hughes, Moore, et al., 2001; Zickler, 2002).

"I would break into a sweat in the shower. I could not maintain my concentration for the first month or two. To really treasure my sobriety, it took me about three or four months before I really came out of the fog and really started getting a grasp of what was going on around me."
38-year-old recovering marijuana addict

Addiction

Just as the refinement of coca leaves into cocaine and opium into heroin led to greater abuse of those drugs, so have better sinsemilla cultivation techniques leading to **higher THC concentrations increased the compulsive liability of marijuana** use.

Unlike opiates, sedative-hypnotics, alcohol, and some stimulants, psychological addiction is more of a factor than physical addiction.

"I thought I could control it because when I woke up in the morning, I didn't get high for the first hour and a half. I figured an hour and a half, that proves that I'm not hooked on this stuff because I don't really need it."
Recovering user in Marijuana Anonymous, a 12-step program

The research of the 1990s and 2000s has provided a different view of the addiction potential of this substance. **Today many people smoke the drug in a chronic, compulsive way and have difficulty discontinuing their use.** Like cocaine, heroin, alcohol, nicotine, and other addictive drugs, marijuana does have the ability to induce compulsive use in spite of the negative consequences it may be causing in the user's life.

"Today's potent form of marijuana is causing a lot more problems than we saw in the 1960s. I never treated a single marijuana self-admitted addict in the clinic throughout the sixties nor the seventies and pretty much through the eighties. But by the late eighties, we started seeing people coming in. Every one of them came in on their own volition, saying, 'Help me. I want to stop smoking pot. It is causing me these problems, causing me to have memory problems, causing me to be too spaced out. I have withdrawal symptoms. I want to stop and I can't.' At our program in San Francisco, we have about 100 patients who are in treatment at any given time specifically for marijuana addiction."
Darryl Inaba, Pharm.D., former CEO and president, Haight Ashbury Free Clinic Foundation

Although the dependence liability of marijuana is supposedly lower than with other drugs, the bottom line, as with any addiction, is the consequences.

"What are the consequences? Is something costing you more money than you should be spending? Is it jeopardizing your job? Is it jeopardizing your relationship with your spouse or your lover or your children? Are you alienated because of that? Those are the consequences."

36-year-old recovering marijuana abuser

"Why am I doing this? What's wrong with me? Why do I have to keep doing this? And I did this for a good eight to 10 years. I started buying dime bags, figuring it would cost a lot more and then eventually I'd get the point. It didn't work. I just kept on buying."

38-year-old recovering marijuana abuser

Is Marijuana a Gateway Drug?

In antidrug movies from the 1930s like *Reefer Madness* and *Marijuana, Assassin of Youth,* the claim was that marijuana physically and mentally changed users, so they started using heroin and cocaine and became helpless addicts. The exaggeration of this idea undermined drug education because people who smoked marijuana didn't become raving lunatics or depraved dope fiends. The experimenters who had tried marijuana said, "I tried marijuana and that didn't happen, so I guess they're lying about all the drugs."

This exaggeration and resultant ridicule of propagandistic or scare films and books probably caused more drug abuse than it prevented. It also obscured an important idea: the real role that marijuana use plays in future drug use and abuse.

"I've been in a 12-step program [Narcotics Anonymous] for a little over six years, and I'm not going to say, like, one and one equal two, but just about everybody I meet in the 12-step program started out with either marijuana or alcohol."

Recovering marijuana addict

Marijuana is a gateway drug in the sense that **if people smoke it, they will probably hang around others who smoke it or use other drugs, so the opportunities to experiment with other drugs are greater**. Viewed from this perspective, it is not surprising that **most users of other illicit drugs have used marijuana first but only after they began using alcohol and/or nicotine** (Kandel, Yamaguchi & Chen, 1992; Kandel & Yamaguchi, 1993; Joy, Watson & Benson, 1999).

No two people will have the exact same reaction to marijuana, but what has been observed is that those who continue to use it regularly establish a pattern of use and begin to find opportunities where drugs other than marijuana are available. There is also growing evidence that the use of any addictive drug at an early age changes vulnerable young brain functions that makes a person more likely to develop addiction.

"The majority of people that I know, that I hang around with, if they ain't smoking weed, they're smoking crack or drinking. I'm not saying that they are bad people, but that's just how it is."

30-year-old polydrug user who started smoking marijuana at the age of 13

A study of 311 young adults in Australia who were identical or fraternal twins found that **those who smoked *Cannabis* by age 17 had a 2.1 to 5.2 times higher chance of other drug use, alcohol dependence, and drug abuse/dependence** than those who didn't smoke it. There was no significant difference in drug/alcohol use or dependence between fraternal or identical twins, emphasizing the direct effect of marijuana and of environmental influences (Lynskey, Heath, Bucholz, et al., 2003). A Dutch study of twins found that early *Cannabis* use in one twin increased that individual's later illicit drug use but did not increase future drug use in the twin who did not use marijuana while young (Lynskey, Vink & Boomsma, 2006).

MARIJUANA (*Cannabis*) & THE LAW

Marijuana has never been out of favor over the past 40 years in the United States and is still popular at the start of the twenty-first century. Internationally, marijuana is the most widely used illicit drug in countries such as Australia, Canada, Costa Rica, El Salvador, Mexico, Panama, and South Africa (DEA, 2006B). Penalties vary widely from country to country.

In the United States, the **penalties for marijuana use or possession vary from federal laws to state laws and from state to state**. Federal laws focus more on heavy trafficking, although there are penalties for simple possession and personal use. For example, sale of 200 to 2,000 pounds will result in federal penalties of 5 to 40 years and up to a $2 million fine. State penalties are for possession or sale. Possession of up to 1 lb. will bring sentences of 180 days to 2 years in Texas and up to 4 years in New York (National Organization for the Reform of Marijuana Laws, 2006). In 2004, 44.2% of the 1,745,712 arrests for drug abuse violations were for marijuana, more than 90% for possession alone (Drug War Facts, 2006). Marijuana arrests went from 401,982 in 1980 to 771,605 in 2004.

◇ Austria, Belgium, Germany, Greece, Ireland, Italy, and Spain don't prosecute for possession of small amounts for personal use.

◇ In England *Cannabis* is designated as a "class B" drug by the Misuse of Drugs Act of 1971. Possession could lead to a five-year prison term, though most sentences handed down are minimal.

◇ In the Netherlands use is kept within the so-called coffee shop system, and sales outside of this system are illegal.

◇ In Japan people can go to jail for possessing less than 1 g of marijuana. Smugglers with a few hundred grams, up to a few kilograms, are routinely sent to prison for three to four years. Foreigners caught with marijuana are deported after serving their sentence, often with up to a lifetime ban (e.g., Paul McCartney).

◇ Countries with a death penalty for drug dealing (usually hard drugs) and in some cases possession are Algeria, Indonesia, Iran, Malaysia, Singapore, Thailand, and Turkey.

◇ In India you can get up to 10 years for smoking *Cannabis*.

◇ In Venezuela drug carriers face minimum 10-year prison sentences.
(TheSite.org, 2006)

Worldwide **the push for the medical use of marijuana has caused a reassessment of many of the legal penalties for use and even sale (e.g., medical marijuana clubs)**. In the United States, approval by a number of states of the medical use of marijuana has come in conflict with the 2005 Supreme Court ruling that allowed federal law to supercede state-enacted marijuana laws. (There is more on medical marijuana later in this chapter.)

Marijuana, Driving & Drug Testing

In more and more arrests for reckless driving or in investigations at the scene of an accident, the driver is tested for marijuana and other drugs. There are four problems associated with marijuana testing:

◇ the drug persists for a number of days in the body and can sometimes still be detected weeks after use;

◇ the elimination rate varies radically compared with alcohol, which has a defined rate of metabolism;

◇ there is a scarcity of good data about the level of marijuana in the blood vs. the level of impairment;

◇ and, most important, usually there is another drug besides marijuana in the system, especially alcohol.

So even if marijuana has a relatively small effect, it is magnified by polydrug use and abuse. Added to the fact that 65% of heavy drinkers also use marijuana, it's no wonder that **positive polydrug test results are the rule and not the exception in drivers arrested for driving while under the influence** (Gieringer, 1988; SAMHSA, 2005).

When it comes to driving a car, **tests showed lower levels of impairment after smoking a small amount of marijuana compared with drinking a small amount of alcohol.** As the dosages increased, impairment for the marijuana smokers increased but not as fast as it did for drinkers. Interestingly,

the smokers *thought* they did worse than they actually did while the drinkers *thought* they did better. **Drinking boosts overconfidence whereas marijuana makes the drivers overly wary and even paranoid** (Mathias, 1996).

"At first I wouldn't drive when I was stoned, but after it became more of a habit and it didn't do as much to me. I was more conscientious of my driving. I would drive the speed limit. I didn't want to get pulled over."

19-year-old male marijuana user

One study found that 60% of marijuana smokers failed a field sobriety test 2.5 hours after smoking moderate amounts; other tests have shown some impairment 3 to 7 hours after smoking. Some tests even showed minimal impairment up to 8 hours later (Reeve, Robertson, Grant, et al., 1983; Hollister, 1986; Smiley, 1986).

The problem is that repetitive tasks such as normal, uneventful driving are not huge problems when smoking marijuana, but **if a complicated driving situation arises that requires decision-making and swift reaction time, the chances of error when marijuana is in the system are significantly increased**. In a number of U.S. studies, 4% to 14% of drivers who were injured or killed in accidents tested positive for marijuana or marijuana and another drug (Ramaekers, Berghaus, van Laar, et al., 2004). On the other hand, though 2.5% of fatal crashes in a French study involved marijuana, 11 times that amount (28.6%) involved alcohol. As a side note, a further survey of 6,766 French drivers considered at fault in accidents found that 681 were positive for marijuana (Laumon, Gadegbeku, Martin, et al., 2005).

Testing machines can measure minute amounts of the THC metabolite but are generally calibrated to start registering at 50 nanograms per milliliter (ng/mL) in urine samples. The 50 ng level doesn't necessarily measure impairment but only the fact that marijuana was used. Generally, for long-term smokers it would take about 3 weeks before they wouldn't register

on a test with a 50 ng/mL cutoff and another 3 weeks to be completely negative. In a few instances, it has taken 10 weeks for the drug to clear completely. Someone who smoked a joint at a party but is not a longtime user usually tests negative 24 to 48 hours after use. **The Olympic Committee uses just 15 ng as its cutoff level.**

Medical Use of Marijuana

After the Ninth U.S. Circuit Court of Appeals in San Francisco ruled that Congress did not have the constitutional authority to regulate the noncommercial cultivation and use of marijuana that does not cross state lines, the **U.S. Supreme Court, in a 6-to-3 decision, ruled that the federal government had the right to supercede state laws that permitted the medical use of marijuana** and that Congress had acted within its mandate to control interstate trade (Egelko, 2005). This was but the latest skirmish in the battle to legalize marijuana at the very least for medical purposes and at the most for unrestricted use.

Over the past 150 years or so, the medical profession has attempted to clinically and scientifically examine the use of *Cannabis* and its extracts for medicinal purposes. Because there were a limited number of all-purpose medications available over the millennia (e.g., opium, theriac, willow bark), substances that had real therapeutic effects were prized. Dr. William O'Shaughnesy spurred curiosity about the drug in Europe in the 1830s. In 1860 in a report to the Ohio State Medical Society, *Cannabis* researcher and physician Dr. R. R. McMeens said he was convinced of its immense value because of the immediate action of the drug in appeasing the appetite for chloral hydrate or opium and restoring the ability to appreciate food. He also recommended it as a treatment for disordered bowels, as a diuretic, and as a sleeping tonic (McMeens, 1860).

As in the present day, there were also warnings about the drug's dangers. For example, in 1890, in writing about his 30 years of experience using *Cannabis* medicinally, Dr. J. Russel Reynolds said that the problems included a wide variation in the strength of any

Cannabis indica preparation, that people vary widely in their reaction to the same dose, and that if high concentrations are taken, severe reactions are quite possible (Reynolds, 1890). By 1900 a number of prominent drug companies marketed *Cannabis* extracts and patent medicines as cures for a variety of illnesses.

Historically marijuana has been used:

◇ as a **muscle relaxant**;
◇ as a **painkiller** (analgesic);
◇ as an **appetite stimulant**;
◇ to control spasms and convulsions;
◇ to calm anxiety;
◇ to treat asthma;
◇ to treat jaundice, beriberi, and ague;
◇ to stimulate childbirth;
◇ to relieve coughs (anti-tussive);
◇ to treat withdrawal from opiates and alcohol; and
◇ as an antibiotic.

Passage of the Marijuana Tax Act of 1937 discouraged research for many years until the 1980s. By 1996 a number of states had passed laws permitting medicinal use of the drug. The resumption of research has explored and in some cases **recommended *Cannabis* for some types of glaucoma, nausea and pain control, to subdue uncontrolled movements (e.g., multiple sclerosis), and to stimulate weight gain for wasting illnesses such as cancer and AIDS** (Mikuriya, 1973; Aldrich, 1997; Gurley, Aranow & Katz, 1998; Earlywine, 2002; Booth, 2004; Grinspoon, Bakalar & Russo, 2005; Rätsch, 2005; Pertwee, 2006). A recent study of AIDS patients at San Francisco General Hospital found substantial pain relief from smoking marijuana. The most pain relief occurred on the first day of use (Russel, 2007).

There is evidence that marijuana does reduce intraocular pressure in glaucoma patients, does calm nausea, does reduce some pain, and does encourage people to eat, though there are other drugs that are also effective or in some cases better. The fact that there are other medications as or more effective than those under examination, however, has never been a bar to the de-

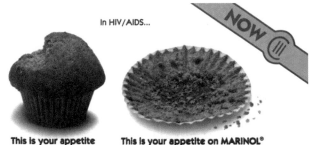

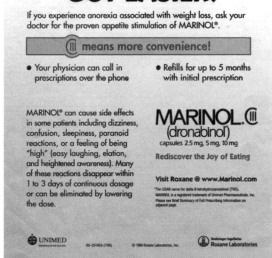

This is your appetite   **This is your appetite on MARINOL®**

Unimed,® a subsidiary of Roxane Laboratories,® is the only manufacturer of dronabinol (Marinol®), which contains synthetic Δ-9 THC. It is mostly recommended for wasting diseases with which the patient becomes malnourished, often due to chemotherapy. The advertisement cautions the user about side effects, including paranoia and a feeling of being high.

velopment and prescribing of less effective ones (e.g., pain killers, sedative-hypnotics, and antidepressants). **The medicinal use of psychoactive substances that have therapeutic value has always created conflict** between those who minimize or simply accept the dependency and collateral health liabilities and those who don't. The over- and under-prescription of opiates is a prime example of this kind of conflict.

A recent report by the U.S. General Accounting Office found that in Alaska, Hawaii, and Oregon and where prescribing *Cannabis* is legal, **the average medical marijuana user is male (70%) and in his 40s (70%)** (Medical Marijuana, 2002). In the states where it is legal to prescribe, there are marijuana buyers' clubs and growers who supply marijuana for those who have a medical marijuana card, prescription, or license. **There has been abuse of the system in several states due to over-prescription of the medical marijuana cards**, sometimes to people who just don't

want to be hassled by law-enforcement for their recreational use of the drug. A somewhat similar problem has existed for years with opiates, sedative-hypnotics, and even ADHD stimulant medications such as Ritalin® in the United States and abroad. Some states allow growing by authorized users of medical marijuana or by their registered suppliers. In almost all states, however, growing by unauthorized users is illegal even if they are supplying their drug to medical marijuana buyers' clubs (Egelko, 2002).

Synthetic THC called dronabinol (**Marinol®**) is theoretically available for treatment of these health problems but in practice is rarely prescribed. People say they prefer marijuana in its smokable form because it works faster than Marinol.® If they smoke, they can smoke as much or as little as they need to relieve symptoms, whereas if they take a premeasured Marinol® capsule, it may be too much or not enough for their condition. In 2006 a second synthetic marijuana drug was reintroduced into the United States—**Cesamet®**—which has been used in Canada since 1981. Cesamet® or Marinol® can cost $30 per day. In 2004 a third product—**Sativex®**—was developed and conditionally approved to be used in spray form in an inhaler. Sativex® was approved in 2005 in Canada to treat multiple sclerosis. It is being directed at many of the 110,000 multiple sclerosis sufferers in the United Kingdom. Worldwide an estimated 2.5 million people have MS; 400,000 in the United States (Willing, 2004).

A major obstacle with smoking or ingesting marijuana for medical purposes is the great variation in the amount of active ingredients in any given marijuana plant. Variations in Δ-9-THC potency, the relative concentration of other active cannabinoids, and the inconsistency of botanical factors make it difficult to rely on this substance to treat medical problems. For example, some forms of marijuana have been shown to increase intraocular pressure, making someone's glaucoma worse, although normally most forms of marijuana will lower intraocular pressure.

Beyond the physiological effects, there are the mental effects of marijuana. Like opium cure-alls, such as theriac and laudanum, and even prescription opiates or sedative-hypnotics, **it is often the mental effects of calming, anxiety relief, or mild euphoria that make people feel good and think they are getting better even if the drug isn't helping the illness as much as it's supposed to**.

There is, however, reluctance in the medical community to prescribe or even approve of marijuana for medical use for several reasons, including those already stated.

◇ Marijuana smoke contains a number of irritants, carcinogens, pathogens, fungi, insecticides, and other chemicals, most of which have not been studied. If marijuana is baked in brownies or otherwise eaten, the respiratory problems are avoided but the 420 or more compounds contained in marijuana remain, along with all their side effects.

◇ Marijuana is a psychoactive drug with dependency potential, which is **particularly problematic for those who are recovering from abuse or addiction**. It can cause its own dependency or relapse to other dependencies.

Medical research about marijuana continues in many countries. Since the 1970s more than 14,000 scientific studies have been conducted, yet results remain conflicting, making it difficult to substantiate appropriate medical use of marijuana.

1999 REPORT FROM THE INSTITUTE OF MEDICINE TO THE ONDCP

In 1996 the federal Office of National Drug Control Policy commissioned a study by the Institute of Medicine of the National Academy of Sciences to review the scientific evidence and do field research concerning the health benefits and risks of marijuana. When the ensuing report, entitled *Marijuana and Medicine: Assessing the Science Base,* was released in 1999, both sides of the argument (pro- and anti-marijuana forces) went in front of the media and translated the report, colored by what they thought it said. The result was that unless one read the original report, it was extremely difficult to know what was actually written.

Some Conclusions of the Report

◇ Cannabinoids likely have a natural role in pain modulation, control of movement, and memory.

◇ Scientific data indicate the potential therapeutic value of cannabinoid drugs, primarily THC, for pain relief, for control of nausea and vomiting, and as an appetite stimulation; smoked marijuana, however, is a crude THC delivery system that also delivers harmful substances.

◇ The psychological effects of cannabinoids, such as anxiety reduction, sedation, and euphoria, can influence the potential therapeutic value.

◇ Numerous studies suggest that marijuana smoke is an important risk factor in the development of respiratory disease.

Some Recommendations of the Report

◇ **Research should continue into the physiological effects of synthetic and plant-derived cannabinoids and the natural function of cannabinoids in the body.**

◇ **Clinical trials of cannabinoid drugs for symptom management should be conducted with the goal of developing safe, reliable, and rapid-onset delivery systems.**

◇ Psychological effects of cannabinoids such as anxiety reduction and sedation, which can influence medical benefits, should be evaluated in clinical trials.

(Joy, Watson & Benson, 1999; the full report is available online at http://newton.nap.edu/catalog/6376.html)

In April 2006 the Food and Drug Administration declared that "no sound scientific studies" support the medical use of smoked marijuana. The statement seems to ignore two of the main conclusions of the report, which emphasize the importance of finding a less damaging delivery system but does accept studies about the efficacy of marijuana for pain, nausea, and wasting diseases. As with so many pronouncements about marijuana, **political considerations are in a constant battle with scientific information** as well as with those who would simply like marijuana to be legalized (Harris, 2006).

CHAPTER SUMMARY

Introduction & History

1. Psychedelics cause reason to take a back seat to intensified and distorted sensations (illusions, delusions, and hallucinations).

2. All arounders, also known as psychedelics, hallucinogens, and psycho-stimulants, have been around since before the origin of man. Virtually all of the early psychedelics were derived from some of the more than 4,000 plants and fungi known to have psychoactive properties. Now, besides marijuana, chemists produce most psychedelic drugs.

3. Instead of a rush or high, psychedelics were most often used to alter one's reality and consciousness for religious, social, ceremonial, and medical reasons.

4. Recently, the most popular psychedelics besides marijuana (e.g., LSD, MDMA) have been synthetics, mostly used among young White users.

Classification

5. The most commonly used psychedelics are marijuana, LSD, MDMA (or other variations of the amphetamine molecule), psilocybin ("magic mushrooms"), peyote, ketamine, and PCP. The chemical classifications are indoles, phenylalkylamines, anticholinergics, atypical psychedelics, and cannabinoids.

General Effects

6. The effects of all arounders are particularly dependent on the size of the dose, the emotional makeup of the user, the mood, the surroundings, previous psychedelic experiences, and pre-existing mental illnesses.

7. A major physical effect of some psychedelics (e.g., LSD, psilocybin, peyote, MDMA) is stimulation.

8. Psychedelics overload the sensory pathways, making the user acutely aware of all sensations.

9. The most frequent mental effects of psychedelics are mixed-up sensations (synesthesia), along with illusions (mistaken perceptions of stimuli), delusions (mistaken belief), and hallucinations (sensing nonexistent objects, smells, and sounds).

LSD, Psilocybin Mushrooms & Other Indole Psychedelics

10. Indole psychedelics exert many of their effects through serotonin and the $5HT_2A$ receptors (mainly mood, anxiety, and sleep).

11. LSD (derived from an ergot fungus) is extremely potent. Doses as low as 25 μg (25 millionths of a gram) can cause stimulant effects and some psychic effects.

12. LSD has been tried as a therapy for mental illnesses, as a truth/mind control drug (by the CIA), and as a mind-expanding experience (Timothy Leary, Ken Kesey, et al.). It was made illegal in 1966 and classified as a Schedule I drug in 1970.

13. In the 1990s many younger students experimented with LSD, but in the late 1990s and early 2000s the number shrank, possibly due to the popularity of MDMA (ecstasy) and to the arrest of a major manufacturing ring.

14. Blotter acid is the most popular dosage form of LSD. Effective dosages range from 25 to 200 μg ("mikes").

15. LSD also acts like a stimulant and, like many other psychedelics, overloads the reticular formation in the brainstem—the sensory switchboard for the mind—and creates illusions, delusions, and hallucinations that can last six to eight hours.

16. Sensory distortions, dreaminess, depersonalization, altered mood, and impaired concentration are common.

17. A first-time user or someone with a pre-existing mental condition is more likely to have a bad trip and later experience hallucinogen persisting perception disorder (flashbacks or prolonged effects).

18. Most often a mental problem is aggravated rather than caused by a psychedelic.

19. Psilocybin and psilocin (chemically similar to LSD) are the active ingredients in more than 75 species of "magic mushrooms."

20. Psychedelic mushrooms have been used for spiritual rites and healing for 3,000 years by many Native American and Mexican Indian tribes.

21. After initial nausea or vomiting, the most common effects of mushrooms are visceral sensations, visual illusions, other sensory distortions, and a certain altered state of consciousness lasting three to six hours.

22. Many mushrooms are poisonous, and store-bought mushrooms spiked with LSD or other psychedelics are often misrepresented as psilocybin mushrooms.

23. Other indole psychedelics include ibogaine, which is also a stimulant; morning glory seeds (ololiuqui); DMT, a naturally occurring short-acting psychedelic snuff that can be extracted from several plants or synthesized; ayahuasca (yage) a longer-acting psychedelic that induces a dreamlike condition; and Foxy, 5-Me-DIPT, and AMT.

Peyote, MDMA & Other Phenylalkylamine Psychedelics

24. These drugs, chemically related to adrenaline and amphetamines, take several hours to reach their peak effects and continue for 10 hours more.

25. Peyote, legal for the Native American Church of North America, is used in spiritual ceremonies.

26. Mescaline is the active ingredient of the peyote and San Pedro cacti.

27. Eating peyote buttons or drinking them in a prepared tea causes vi-

sual distortions and vivid hallucinations after an initial nausea and physical stimulation.

28. Designer psychedelics, variations of the amphetamine molecule, include psycho-stimulants such as MDMA, MDA, 2C-B, and PMA. Their chemical structures are similar to mescaline.

29. MDMA, usually sold as a capsule or tablet for anywhere from $10 to $40, came to public attention in 1978 and was used widely by therapists to help patients see into their emotions and repressed memories.

30. MDMA (ecstasy) causes feelings of empathy for others, more self-awareness, heightened self-esteem, open mindedness, acceptance, and intimacy mostly by its excess release of serotonin.

31. Physically, MDMA stimulates heart and respiration, tightens muscles, and causes teeth clenching and a dangerous rise in body temperature.

32. Ecstasy use, called "rolling," is popular at rave and other music parties, along with techno, rap, or electronic trance beat music and other psychedelics, inhalants, stimulants, and depressants (e.g., nitrous oxide, LSD, cocaine, methamphetamine, GHB, and alcohol).

33. Other phenylalkylamines include phenylethylamines such as 2C-T-7, 2C-T-2, nexus, STP, and PMA.

Belladonna & Other Anticholinergic Psychedelics

34. Belladonna and other nightshade plants, such as henbane, mandrake, and datura, contain scopolamine, hyoscyamine, and atropine and have been used in magic ceremonies, sorcery, witchcraft, and religious rituals.

35. In low doses these substances can speed up the heart, create an intense thirst, and dangerously raise body temperature; mentally they can cause a mild stupor, but as the dose increases, delirium, hallucinations, and a separation from reality are common.

Ketamine, PCP & Other Psychedelics

36. Ketamine and PCP ("angel dust") are anesthetics that deaden physical sensations. Mentally they disassociate users from their surroundings and senses. A psychotic psychedelic experience from high doses is described as "being in a K-hole."

37. Effects of the drugs include amnesia, extremely high blood pressure, and combativeness. Higher doses can produce tremors, seizures, catatonia, coma, and even kidney failure.

38. PCP is often used to adulterate a marijuana joint; it is also misrepresented and sold as THC in a capsule.

39. Ketamine ("special-K"), which lasts about an hour, has become a popular drug in the rave club scene.

40. *Salvia divinorum* ("designer sage") has become popular as a legal, short-acting psychedelic.

41. DXM (dextromethorphan), in many cough or cold preparations, continues to be abused because it acts as a psychedelic when ingested in high doses. Sales are more tightly controlled now because of this abuse.

Marijuana & the Cannabinoids

42. Historically, the *Cannabis* plant has been grown to produce fibers for rope and cloth, seeds for food, various chemicals for medicinal effects, and a psychoactive resin for psychedelic effects.

43. The use of *Cannabis* was banned in the United States in 1937 except during World War II, when hemp growing for the fiber was encouraged. Many other countries still grow hemp for fiber.

44. Marijuana is used by about 6% of the 12-and-older population in the United States (about 14 million people); 160 million people worldwide use marijuana on a monthly basis.

45. The two most widely used marijuana species are *Cannabis sativa* and *Cannabis indica*. *Cannabis sativa* can be used for hemp or psychedelic effects. *Cannabis indica* is used only for its psychedelic effects. *Cannabis ruderalis* is not nearly as potent or widespread.

46. The sinsemilla technique of growing *Cannabis sativa* or *Cannabis indica* greatly increases the concentration of Δ-9-THC, the main psychoactive ingredient in marijuana. There are at least 420 other ingredients.

47. The most potent cannabinoid in marijuana is Δ-9 THC.

48. Street marijuana that is readily available in the 2000s is five to 14 times stronger than the marijuana of the 1960s and 1970s.

49. Much of the marijuana comes from Colombia and Mexico, although there is a large homegrown market. Much growing is done indoors to avoid detection. This has led to even more-potent plants.

50. Discoveries in the 1990s of a marijuana receptor site, a neurotransmitter (anandamide) that fits into that receptor site, and a marijuana antagonist (that precipitates withdrawal) have accelerated research into the effects of marijuana.

51. Endocannabinoids (anandamide and 2AG) are found inside the body whereas exocannabinoids (*Cannabis*) come from marijuana plants.

52. The two major receptors for cannabinoids are CB_1 and CB_2 receptors. CB_1 receptors, found mostly in the brain, are responsible for the integration of sensory experiences with emotion, memory, a sense of novelty, motor coordination, and some automatic bodily functions.

53. Physical short-term effects of smoking marijuana include physical relaxation, some pain control, bloodshot eyes, coughing, increased appetite, and some loss of muscular coordination. It also impairs tracking ability and causes a trailing phenomenon.

54. Mentally, effects include a separation from one's environment, an aloof feeling, drowsiness, and difficulty concentrating. Stronger va-

rieties can produce giddiness, increased alertness, and major distortions of time, color, and sound. It also exaggerates mood and personality.

55. By stimulating the amygdala, the brain's emotional center, marijuana exaggerates the novelty of sensory input and makes even mundane things interesting. For long-term users, when they aren't using, even fresh things become boring.

56. The hippocampus, involved in short-term memory, is affected by marijuana. This memory impairment can affect learning, but long-term memory is not affected.

57. Marijuana affects the juvenile brain more severely than an adult brain.

58. The sense of time passing is distorted by the drug.

59. Respiratory effects include a decrease in the cilia lining the breathing passages, which makes the smoker more susceptible to coughs, chronic bronchitis, and emphysema. Smokers of both marijuana and cigarettes do much more damage to their air passages and lungs than a smoker of only marijuana or only cigarettes. Marijuana smoking doesn't seem to cause lung cancer, however.

60. Marijuana can hinder the immune system to a small degree and make one more susceptible to catching colds and viral infections and of accelerating the progression of HIV/AIDS.

61. Acute mental effects include anxiety, temporary psychotic reactions, and paranoia. It can also precipitate pre-existing mental illnesses.

62. Tolerance develops fairly rapidly with chronic marijuana use. It can persist in the body for weeks and even months.

63. When stopping chronic marijuana use, a person can suffer delayed withdrawal symptoms that include anxiety, depression, irritability, aggression, sleep disturbances, decreased appetite, and continued craving for the drug.

64. As the THC concentration in marijuana increases, the compulsive liability increases. Dependency is more common in the 2000s.

65. Cigarettes, alcohol, and marijuana are usually the first drugs that teenagers use. One who uses marijuana is more likely to hang around people who use other drugs and so is more likely to experiment.

66. Legal penalties for marijuana possession and intent to sell vary widely from state to state and country to country, from turning a blind eye up to the death penalty.

67. Most of those arrested for driving under the influence usually have several drugs in their system. Marijuana use impairs decision-making and reaction time in complex situations.

68. The medical use of marijuana is the controversial new battleground. Proponents say it should be available as a medicine (for glaucoma, nausea, pain, uncontrolled movements, and wasting diseases) whereas opponents say there are better medicines that are more reliable, don't aggravate the lungs, and don't have all the other chemicals with unresearched side effects. Several states have passed laws allowing the medical use of marijuana, but a recent U.S. Supreme Court ruling permits federal anti-marijuana laws to supercede state medical marijuana laws.

69. *Marijuana and Medicine: Assessing the Science Base,* a 1999 report by the Institute of Medicine of the National Academy of Sciences, accepts the value of marijuana for pain, nausea, and wasting diseases but recommends a better delivery system to reduce respiratory and other problems.

REFERENCES

Accto, M. D., Scates, S. M. & Martin, B. B. (2001). Spontaneous and precipitated withdrawal with a synthetic cannabinoid. *European Journal of Pharmacology, 416*(1-2), 75-81.

Aghajanian, G. K. & Marek, G. J. (1999). Serotonin and hallucinogens. *Neuropsychopharmacology, 21*, 165-235.

Aldrich, M. R. (1997). History of therapeutic *Cannabis*. In M. L. Mathre, ed. Cannabis *in Medical Practice*. Jefferson, NC: McFarland & Company, Inc.

American Association of Poison Control Centers. (2005). *Poison Center Survey Results*. http://www.aapcc.org (accessed February 20, 2007).

American Psychiatric Association. (2000). *Diagnostic and Statistical Manual of Mental Disorders* (4th ed., text revisions [DSM-IV-TR]). Washington, DC: Author.

Arrestee Drug Abuse Monitoring Program [ADAM]. (2005). *Drug and Alcohol Use and Related Matters Among Arrestees, 2003*. National Institute of Justice. http://www.ncjrs.gov/nij/adam/ADAM2003.pdf (accessed October 5, 2006).

Bibra, B. E. (1855/1995). *Plant Intoxicants*. Rochester, VT: Healing Arts Press.

Booth, M. (2004). *Cannabis: A History*. New York: Thomas Dunne Books, St. Martin's Press.

Breivogel, C. S., Scates, S. M., Beletskaya, I. O., Lowery, O. B. & Martin, B. R. (2003). The effects of Δ 9-tetrahydrocannabinol physical dependence on brain cannabinoid receptors. *European Journal of Pharmacology, 459*(2-3), 139-50.

Brunner, T. F. (1977). Marijuana in ancient Greece and Rome? The literary evidence. *Journal of Psychoactive Drugs, 9*(3).

Bucheler, R., Gleiter, C. H., Schwoerer, P. & Gaertner, I. (2005). Use of nonprohibited hallucinogenic plants: Increasing relevance for public health? A case report and literature review of the consumption of *Salvia divinorum* (Diviner's sage). *Pharmacopsychiatry, 38*(1), 1-5.

Budney, A. J., Hughes, J. R., Moore, B. A. & Novy, P. L. (2001). Marijuana abstinence effects in marijuana smokers maintained in their home environment. *Archives of General Psychiatry, 58*(10), 917-24.

Carroll, M. & Comer, S. (1998). The pharmacology of phencyclidine and the hallucinogens. In A. W. Graham & T. K. Schultz, eds. *Principles of Addiction Medicine* (2nd ed., pp. 153-62). Chevy Chase, MD: American Society of Addiction Medicine, Inc.

Cermak, T. L. (2004). Update on marijuana: Why it works and why it doesn't. *San Francisco Medicine, May 2004.* http://www.sfms.org/AM/Template.cfm?Section=Home&template=/CM/HTMLDisplay.cfm&ContentID=1555 (accessed October 5, 2006).

Chilton, W. S., Bigwood, J. & Jensen, R. E. (1979). Psilocin, bufotenine and serotonin: Historical and biosynthetic observations. *Journal of Psychoactive Drugs, 11*(1-2), 61-69.

Courtwright, D. T. (2001). *Forces of Habit.* Cambridge, MA: Harvard University Press.

DanceSafe. (2006). Party drug Web site. http://www.dancesafe.org/about.html (accessed October 5, 2006).

Devane, W. A., Hanus, L., Breuer, A., Pertwee, R. G., Stevenson, L. A., Griffin, G., et al. (1992). Isolation and structure of a brain constituent that bonds to the cannabinoid receptor. *Science, 258*(5090), 1882-84, 1946-49.

Diaz, J. L. (1979). Ethnopharmacology and taxonomy of Mexican psychodysleptic plants. *Journal of Psychoactive Drugs, 11*(1-2), 71-101.

Dobkin de Rios, M. & Grob, C. S. (2005). Ayahuasca use in cross-cultural perspective. *Journal of Psychoactive Drugs, 37*(2), 119-22.

Doblin, R. (2002). A clinical plan for MDMA (ecstasy) in the treatment of posttraumatic stress disorder (PTSD). *Journal of Psychoactive Drugs, 34*(2), 312-19.

Doering-Silveira, E., Lopez, E., Grob, C. S., de Rios, M. D., Alonso, L., Tacla, C., et al. (2005). Ayahuasca in adolescence: A neuropsychological assessment. *Journal of Psychoactive Drugs, 37*(2), 123-28.

Drug Abuse Warning Network [DAWN]. (2004). *Club Drugs, 2002 Update.* http://www.oas.samhsa.gov/2k4/clubDrugs/clubDrugs.pdf (accessed October 5, 2006).

Drug Abuse Warning Network. (2005). *DAWN 2003: Interim National Estimates of Drug-Related Emergency Department Visits.* http://dawninfo.samhsa.gov/files/DAWN_ED_Interim2003.pdf (accessed October 5, 2006).

Drug Enforcement Administration [DEA]. (2001). *Ecstasy: Rolling Across Europe.* http://www.usdoj.gov/dea/pubs/intel/01008/index.html (accessed December 5, 2005).

Drug Enforcement Administration. (2002). *Trippin' on Tryptamines. The Emergence of Foxy and AMT As Drugs of Abuse.* http://www.usdoj.gov/dea/programs/forensicsci/microgram/mg0503/mg0503.html (accessed February 26, 2006).

Drug Enforcement Administration. (2003). *Ketamine.* http://www.usdoj.gov/dea/concern/ketamine.html (accessed October 5, 2006).

Drug Enforcement Administration. (2006A). *Drug Trafficking in the United States.* http://www.usdoj.gov/dea/concern/drug_trafficking.html (accessed February 25, 2006).

Drug Enforcement Administration. (2006B). *Federal Trafficking Penalties.* http://www.usdoj.gov/dea/agency/penalties.htm (accessed October 5, 2006).

Drug War Facts. (2006). *Drug War Facts: Marijuana.* http://www.drugwarfacts.org/marijuan.htm (accessed October 5, 2006).

DuPont, R. L. (2000). *The Selfish Brain.* Washington, DC: American Psychiatric Press, Inc.

DuToit, B. M. (1980). *Cannabis in Africa.* Rotterdam: Balkema.

Earlywine, M. (2002). *Understanding Marijuana.* New York: Oxford University Press.

Efferink, J. G. R. (1988). Some little-known hallucinogenic plants of the Aztecs. *Journal of Psychoactive Drugs, 20*(4), 427-34.

Egelko, B. (October 15, 2002). Court affirms medical pot law limits. *San Francisco Chronicle,* p. 1.

Egelko, B. (June 7, 2005). Medical pot users say they won't stop. *San Francisco Chronicle,* p. 1.

Elora, H. (2001). Adolescent dextromethorphan abuse. *Toxalert, 18*(1), 1-3.

Emboden, W. A. (1981). The genus *Cannabis* and the correct use of taxonomic categories. *Journal of Psychoactive Drugs, 13*(1), 15-22.

Erowid. (2006). *The Vaults of Erowid: DXM.* http://www.erowid.org/chemicals/dxm/dxm.shtml (accessed October 5, 2006).

Erowid. (2001). *The Vaults of Erowid: Sulfurous Samadhi: An Investigation of 2C-T-2 & 2C-T-7.* http://www.erowid.org/chemicals/2ct7/article1/article1.shtml (accessed October 5, 2006).

Escohotado, A. (1999). *A Brief History of Drugs.* Rochester, VT: Park Street Press.

Fischer, C., Hatzidimitriou, G., Wlos, J., Katz, J. & Ricaurte, G. (1995). Reorganization of ascending 5-HT axon projections in animals previously exposed to recreational drug 3,4-methelene-dioxymethamphetamine (MDMA, ecstasy). *Journal of Neuroscience, 15,* 5476-85.

Fox, B. (October 3, 2002). Authorities break up big club-drug ring. *Medford Mail Tribune,* p. 11.

Furst, P. T. (1976). *Hallucinogens and Culture.* San Francisco: Chandler & Sharp Publishers, Inc.

Gable, R. S. (2004). Acute toxic effects of club drugs. *Journal of Psychoactive Drugs, 36*(3), 303-14.

Gieringer, D. H. (1988). Marijuana, driving, and accident safety. *Journal of Psychoactive Drugs, 20*(1), 93-100.

Goldstein, A. (2001). *Addiction: From Biology to Drug Policy* (2nd ed.). New York: W. H. Freeman and Company.

Gresch, P. J., Strickland, L. V. & Sanders-Bush, E. (2002). Lysergic acid diethylamide-induced Fos expression in rat brain: Role of serotonin-2A receptors. *Neuroscience, 114,* 707-13.

Grim, R. (April 1, 2004). *Who's Got the Acid?* MSN News. http://www.slate.com/id/2098109 (accessed October 5, 2006).

Grinspoon, L., Bakalar, J. B. & Russo, E. (2005). Marijuana: Clinical aspects. In J. H. Lowinson, P. Ruiz, R. B. Millman & J. G. Langrod, eds. *Substance Abuse: A Comprehensive Textbook* (4th ed., pp. 263-76). Baltimore: Williams & Wilkins.

Grob, C. S. & Poland, R. E. (2005). MDMA. In J. H. Lowinson, P. Ruiz, R. B. Millman & J. G. Langrod, eds. *Substance Abuse: A Comprehensive Textbook* (4th ed., pp. 374-86). Baltimore: Williams & Wilkins.

Grof, S. (2001). *LSD Psychotherapy.* Sarasota, FL: MAPS.

Gurley, R. J., Aranow, R. & Katz, M. (1998). Medicinal marijuana: A comprehensive review. *Journal of Psychoactive Drugs, 30*(2), 137-48.

Halpern, J. H., Sherwood, A. R., Hudson, J. I., Yurgelun-Todd, D. & Pope, J. G. Jr. (2005). Psychological and cognitive effects of long-term peyote use among Native Americans. *Biological Psychiatry, 15*(8), 624-31.

Haney, M., Ward, A. S., Comer, S. D., Foltin, R. W. & Fischman, M. W. (1999). Abstinence symptoms following smoked marijuana in humans. *Psychopharmacology, 141,* 395-404.

Harris, G. (April 21, 2006). FDA's missive against medical pot. *New York Times,* p. A1.

Henderson, L. & Glass, W., eds. (1994). *LSD Report.* Lexington, MA: Lexington Books.

High Times. (2006). http://www.hight-imes.com/ht/home (accessed October 5, 2006).

Holland, J. (2001). *Ecstasy: The Complete Guide.* Rochester, VT: Park Street Press.

Hollister, L. E. (1984). Effects of hallucinogens in humans. In B. L. Jacobs, ed. *Hallucinogens: Neurochemical, Behavioral, and Clinical Perspectives* (pp. 19-34). New York: The Raven Press.

Hollister, L. E. (1986). Health aspects of cannabis. *Pharmacological Revues, 38*(1), 1-20.

Howlett, A. C., Evans, D. M. & Houston, D. B. (1992). The cannabinoid receptor. In L. Murphy & A. Bartke, eds. *Marijuana/Cannabinoids: Neurobiology and Neurophysiology* (pp. 35-72). Boca Raton, FL: CRC Press.

Hrometz, S. L., Brown, A. W., Nichols, D. E. & Sprague, J. E. (2004). MDMA-mediated production of hydrogen peroxide. *Neuroscience, 367*(1), 56-59.

Huestis, M. A., Gorelick, D. A., Heishman, S. J., Preston, K., Nelson, R. A., Mookhan, E. T., et al. (2001). Blockade of effects of smoked marijuana by the CBI-selective cannabinoid receptor antagonist SR141716. *Archives of General Psychiatry, 58*(4), 322-28.

Hunt, G., Evens, K., Wu, E., Reyes, A. (2006). Asian American youth: The dance scene and club drugs. *Journal of Drug Issues, 35*(4), 695-731.

Internet Sacred Text Archive. (2006). *The Vedas, Rig Veda, Hymn IV.* http://www.sacred-texts.com/hin/rigveda/rv01004.htm (accessed October 5, 2006).

Irvine, R. J., Keane, M., Felgate, P., McCann, U. D., Callaghan, P. D. & White, J. M. (2006). Plasma drug concentrations and physiological measures in "dance party" participants. *Neuropsychopharmacology, 31*(2), 424-30.

Jaffe, J. H. (1989). Psychoactive substance abuse disorder. In H. Kaplan & B. J. Sadock, eds. *Comprehensive Textbook of Psychiatry* (5th ed., pp. 642-86). Baltimore: Williams & Wilkins.

Jansen, K. (2001). *Ketamine: Dreams and Realities.* Sarasota, FL: MAPS.

Jansen, K. L. R. & Darracot-Cankovic, R. (2001). The nonmedical use of ketamine, Part Two: A review of problem use and dependence. *Journal of Psychoactive Drugs, 33*(2), 151-58.

Joy, J. E., Watson, S. J., Jr. & Benson, J. A., eds. (1999). *Marijuana and Medicine: Assessing the Science Base.* Washington, DC: National Academy Press. http://newton.nap.edu/catalog/6376.htm (accessed October 5, 2006).

Kandel, D. B. & Yamaguchi, K. (1993). From beer to crack: Developmental patterns of drug involvement. *American Journal of Public Health, 83,* 851-55.

Kandel, D. B., Yamaguchi, K. & Chen, K. (1992). Stages of progression in drug involvement from adolescence to adulthood: Further evidence for the gateway theory. *Journal of Alcohol Studies, 53,* 447-57.

Kouri, E. M., Pope, H. G. & Lukas, S. E. (1999). Changes in aggressive behavior during withdrawal from long-term marijuana use. *Psychopharmacology, 143,* 302-308.

Krupitsky, E. M. & Grinenko, A. Y. (1997). Ketamine psychedelic therapy (KPT). A review of the results of ten years of research. *Journal of Psychoactive Drugs, 29*(2), 165-83.

La Barre, J. & Weston, D. (1979). Peyote and mescaline. *Journal of Psychoactive Drugs, 11*(1-2), 33-39.

Lambe, E. K. & Aghajanian, G. K. (2005). Hallucinogen-induced UP states in the brain slice of rat prefrontal cortex: Role of glutamate spillover and NR2B-NMDA receptors. *Neuropsychopharmacology, 31*(8):1682-89.

Laumon, B., Gadegbeku, B., Martin, J. L., Biecheler, M. B. & SAM Group. (2005). Cannabis intoxication and fatal road crashes in France: Population based case-control study. *British Medical Journal, 331*(7529): 1371.

Lee, M. A. & Shlain, B. (1985). *Acid Dreams: The Complete Social History of LSD.* New York: Grove Weidenfeld.

Leinwand, D. (November 2, 2006). Jimson weed users chase high all the way to hospital. *USA Today,* p. 2A.

Lerner, A. G., Gelkopf, M., Oyffe, I., Finkel, B., Katz, S., Sigal, M. & Weizman, A. (2000). LSD-induced hallucinogen persisting perception disorder treatment with clonidine: An open pilot study. *International Clinical Psychopharmacology, 15*(1), 35-37.

Lerner, A. G., Gelkopf, M., Skladman, L., Oyffe, I., Finkel, B., Sigal, M., et al. (2002). Flashback and hallucinogenic persisting perceptual disorder: Clinical aspects and pharmacological treatment approach. *Israel Journal of Psychiatry and Related Sciences, 39*(2), 92-99.

Lerner, A. G., Oyffe, I., Isaacs, G. & Sigal, M. (1997). Naltrexone treatment of hallucinogen persisting perception disorder. *American Journal of Psychiatry, 154*(3), 437.

Lynskey, M. T., Heath, A. C., Bucholz, K. K., Slutske, W. S., Madden, P. A., Nelson, E. C., et al. (2003). Escalation of drug use in early-onset *Cannabis* users vs. co-twin controls. *Journal of the American Medical Association, 289*(4), 427-33.

Lynskey, M. T., Vink, J. M. & Boomsma, D. I. (2006). Early onset *Cannabis* use and progression to other drug use in a sample of Dutch twins. *Behavioral Genetics 36*(2): 195-200.

Lyttle, T., Goldstein, D. & Gartz, J. (1996). Bufo toads and bufotenine: Fact and fiction surrounding an alleged psychedelic. *Journal of Psychoactive Drugs, 28*(3), 267-70.

Marijuana Seeds. (2006). *Marijuana Seeds.* http://www.marijuana-seeds.net/The-Rising-Prices-of-Marijuana.html (accessed October 5, 2006).

Marnell, T., ed. (2005). *Drug Identification Bible* (3rd ed.). Denver: Drug Identification Bible.

Mathias, R. (1996). Marijuana Impairs Driving-related Skills and Workplace Performance. *NIDA Notes, 11*(1). http://www.drugabuse.gov/NIDA_Notes/NNVol11N1/Marijuana.html (accessed October 5, 2006).

McKallip, R. J., Nagarkatti, M. & Nagarkatti, P. S. (2005). Delta-9-tetrahydrocannabinol enhances breast cancer growth and metastasis by suppression of the antitumor immune response. *Journal of Immunology, 174*(6), 3281-89.

McLaughlin, P. J., Winston, K., Swezey, L., Wisniecki, A., Aberman, J., Tardif, D. J., et al. (2003). The cannabinoid CB$_1$ antagonists SR 141716A and AM 251 suppress food intake and food-reinforced behavior in a variety of tasks in rats. *Behavioral Pharmacology, 14*(8), 583-88.

McMeens, R. R. (1860). Report to the Ohio State Medical Committee on *Cannabis indica.* In T. H. Mikuriya, cd. *Marijuana: Medical Papers 1839-1972.* Oakland, CA: Medi-Comp Press.

Medical marijuana users are male, 40ish. (December 2, 2002). *Medford Mail Tribune,* p. 6A.

Mendelsohn, J. (2003). MDMA (Ecstasy): Clinical aspects. In A. W. Graham, T. K. Schultz, M. F. Mayo-Smith, R. K. Ries & B. B. Wilford, eds. *Principles of Addiction Medicine* (3rd ed., pp. 191-92). Chevy Chase, MD: American Society of Addiction Medicine, Inc.

Meyer, J. S. & Quenzer, L. F. (2005). *Psychopharmacology: Drugs, the Brain, and Behavior.* Sunderland, MA: Sinauer Associates, Inc.

Meyers, H. (2006). *Organized Crime in Oregon.* http://www.doj.state.or.us/hot_topics/pdf/oc_report_final.pdf (accessed October 5, 2006).

Mikuriya, T. H., ed. (1973). *Marijuana: Medical Papers 1839-1972.* Oakland, CA: Medi-Comp Press.

Monitoring the Future (2006). *2006 Data from In-school Surveys of 8th-, 10th-, and 12th-Grade Students.* http://www.monitoringthefuture.org/data/06data.html#2006data-drugs (accessed February 20, 2007).

National Institute on Drug Abuse [NIDA]. (2001). *Research Report Series: Hallucinogens and Dissociative Drugs.* http://www.drugabuse.gov/ResearchReports/Hallucinogens/Hallucinogens.html (accessed October 5, 2006).

National Organization for the Reform of Marijuana Laws. (2006). *NORML State by State Laws.* http://www.norml.org/index.cfm?Group_ID=4516 (accessed October 5, 2006).

O'Brien, R., Cohen, S., Evans, G. & Fine, J. (1992). *The Encyclopedia of Drug Abuse* (2nd ed.). New York: Facts On File.

Office of National Drug Control Policy. (2006). *National Drug Control Strategy, 2006.* Bethesda, MD: National Drug Clearinghouse.

Os, J., Bak, M., Hanssen, R. V., Bijl, R. V., Graaf, R. & Verdous, H. (2002). *Cannabis* use and psychosis: A longitudinal population-based study. *American Journal of Epidemiology, 156,* 319-27.

Ott, J. (1976). *Hallucinogenic Plants of North America.* Berkeley, CA: Wingbow Press.

Panchal, V., Taraschenko, O. D., Maisonneuve, I. M. & Glick, S. D. (2005). *European Journal of Pharmacology, 525*(1-3): 98-104.

Parks, K. A. & Kennedy, C. L. (2004). Club drugs: Reasons for and consequences of use. *Journal of Psychoactive Drugs, 36*(3), 295-302.

Pechnick, R. N. & Ungerleider, J. T. (2005). Hallucinogens. In J. H. Lowinson, P. Ruiz, R. B. Millman & J. G. Langrod, eds. *Substance Abuse: A Comprehensive Textbook* (4th ed., pp. 313-33). Baltimore: Williams & Wilkins.

Pentney, A. R. (2001). An exploration of the history and controversies surrounding MDMA and MDA. *Journal of Psychoactive Drugs, 33*(3), 213-21.

Pertwee, R. G. (2006). Cannabinoid pharmacology: The first 66 years. *British Journal of Pharmacology, 147* (suppl. 1): S163-71.

Petersen, R. C. (1980). *Phencyclidine: A Review* (NIDA Publication No. 1980-0-341-166/614). Washington, DC: U.S. Government Printing Office.

Pope, H. G., Gruber, A. J., Hudson, J. I., Huestis, M. A. & Yurgelun-Todd, D. (2001). Neuropsychological performance in long-term *Cannabis* users. *Archives of General Psychiatry, 58*(10): 909-15.

Ramaekers, J. G., Berghaus, G., van Laar, M. & Drummer, O. H. (2004). Dose re-

lated risk of motor vehicle crashes after *Cannabis* use. *Drug and Alcohol Dependency 73*(2), 109-19.

Rätch, C. (2005). *The Encyclopedia of Psychoactive Plants.* Rochester, VT: Park Street Press.

Reeve, V. C., Robertson, W. B., Grant, J., Soares, J. R., Gillespie, H. K., et al. (1983). Hemolyzed blood and serum levels of delta-9-THC: Effects on the performance of roadside sobriety tests. *Journal of Forensic Sciences, 28*(4), 963-71.

Reynolds, J. R. (1890). Therapeutical uses and toxic effects of *Cannabis indica.* *Lancet, 1,* 637-38. In T. H. Mikuriya, ed. *Marijuana: Medical Papers 1839-1972.* Oakland, CA: Medi-Comp Press.

Richter, K. P., Kaur, H., Reznicow, K., Nazir, N., Mosier, M. C. & Ahluwalia, J. S. (2005). Cigarette smoking among marijuana users in the United States. *Substance Abuse, 25*(2), 35-43.

Rinaldi-Carmona, M., Barth, M., Heauline, M., Shire, D., Calandra, B., et al. (1994). SR141716, a potent and selective antagonist of the brain cannabinoid receptor. *Federation of European Biochemical Sciences Letters, 350*(2-3), 240-44.

Ritter, J. (February 7, 2007). Pot growing moves to suburbs. *USA Today,* p. A3.

Rosen, W. & Weil, A. (2004). *From Chocolate to Morphine.* Boston: Houghton Mifflin Company.

Russel, S. (February 13, 2007). Medical pot cuts pain study finds. *San Francisco Chronicle,* p. B1.

Roth, M. D., Tashkin, B. P., Whittaker, K. M., Choi, R. & Baldwin. G. C. (2005). Tetrahydrocannabinol suppresses immune function and enhances HIV replication in the huPBL-SCID mouse. *Life Sciences, 77*(14), 1711-22.

Sahagun, B. (1985). *The Florentine Codex: General History of the Things of New Spain.* Santa Fe, NM: The School of American Research.

Schultes, R. E. & Hofmann, A. (1980). *The Botany and Chemistry of Hallucinogens.* Springfield, IL: Charles C. Thomas.

Schultes, R. E. & Hofmann, A. (1992). *Plants of the Gods.* Rochester, VT: Healing Arts Press.

Shulgin, A. & Shulgin, A. (2000). *PiHKAL: A Chemical Love Story.* Berkeley, CA: Transform Press.

Siegel, R. K. (1985). LSD hallucinations: From ergot to electric Kool-Aid. *Journal of Psychoactive Drugs, 17*(4), 247-56.

Siegel, R. K. (1989). *Life in Pursuit of Artificial Paradise.* New York: E. P. Hutton Publishing.

Sim-Selley, L. J. (2003). Regulation of cannabinoid CB$_1$ receptors in the central nervous system by chronic cannabi-

noids. *Critical Review of Neurobiology, 15*(2), 91-119.

Smiley, A. (1986). Marijuana: On-road and driving simulator studies. *Alcohol, Drugs, and Driving: Abstracts and Reviews, 2*(3-4), 121-34.

Smith, M. V. (1981). *Psychedelic Chemistry.* Port Townsend, WA: Loompanics Unlimited.

Smith, P. B., Compton, D. R., Welch, S. P., Razdan, R. K., Mechoulam, R. & Martin, B. R. (1994). The pharmacological activity of anandamide, a putative endogenous cannabinoid, in mice. *Journal of Pharmacology and Experimental Therapeutics, 270*(1): 219-27.

Snow, O. (2003). *LSD.* New York: Thoth Press.

Snyder, S. (1996). *Drugs and the Brain.* New York: W. H. Freeman and Company.

Solowij, N., Stephens, R. S., Roffman, R. A., Babor, T., Kadden, R., Miller, M., et al. (2002). Cognitive functioning of long-term heavy *Cannabis* users seeking treatment. *Journal of the American Medical Association, 287*(9): 1123-31.

Squatriglia, C. (September 6, 2006). Pot farms ravaging park land. *San Francisco Chronicle,* p. A1.

Stafford, P. (1985). Recreational uses of LSD. *Journal of Psychoactive Drugs, 17*(4), 219-28.

Stafford, P. (1992). *Psychedelics Encyclopedia* (Vol. 1, p. 157). Berkeley, CA: Ronin Publishing.

Stamets, P. (1996). *Psilocybin Mushrooms of the World.* Berkeley, CA: Ten Speed Press.

Substance Abuse and Mental Health Services Administration [SAMHSA]. (2005). *Summary of Findings from the 2004 National Household Survey on Drug Abuse.* Rockville, MD: SAMHSA, Office of Applied Studies.

Substance Abuse and Mental Health Services Administration. (2006). *Summary of Findings from the 2005 National Household Survey on Drug Abuse.* Rockville, MD: SAMHSA, Office of Applied Studies.

Swan, R. (March 15, 2006). Feelin' their thizzle: How the culture of ecstasy has changed. *East Bay Express,* pp. 15-25.

Tashkin, D. P. (2005). Smoked marijuana as a cause of lung injury. *Monaldi Archives for Chest Disease, 63*(2), 93-100.

Tashkin, D. P. (May 23, 2006). Cancer and smoking marijuana. Paper presented at the American Thoracic Society 102nd International Conference, San Diego, CA.

Tashkin, D. P., Simmons, M. & Clark, V. (1988). Acute and chronic effects of marijuana smoking compared with tobacco smoking on blood carboxyhemoglobin levels. *Journal of Psychoactive Drugs, 20*(1), 27-32.

TheSite.org. (2006). *Drug Laws Abroad.* http://www.thesite.org/travelandfree time/travel/beingthere/druglawsabroad (accessed October 5, 2006).

Touw, M. (1981). The religious and medicinal uses of *Cannabis* in China, India, and Tibet. *Journal of Psychoactive Drugs, 13*(1), 23-33.

Tsou, K., Patrick, S. L. & Walker, J. M. (1995). Physical withdrawal in rats tolerant to delta 9-tetrahydrocannabinol precipitated by a cannabinoid receptor antagonist. *European Journal of Pharmacology, 280*(3): R13-R15.

United Nations Office on Drugs and Crime. (2005). 2005 World Drug Report. http://www.unodc.org/pdf/WDR_2005/ volume_1_web.pdf (accessed October 5, 2006).

Walton, R. P. (1938). *Marijuana: America's New Drug Problem.* Philadelphia: Lippincott.

Welch, S. P. (2005). The neurobiology of marijuana. In J. H. Lowinson, P. Ruiz, R. B. Millman & J. G. Langrod, eds. *Substance Abuse: A Comprehensive Textbook* (4th ed., pp. 252-63). Baltimore: Williams & Wilkins.

Wilkins, J. N., Mellott, K. G., Markvitsa, R. & Gorelick, D. A. (2003). Management of stimulant, hallucinogen, marijuana, and phencyclidine intoxication and withdrawal. In A. W. Graham, T. K. Schultz, M. F. Mayo-Smith, R. K. Ries & B. B. Wilford, eds. *Principles of Addiction Medicine* (3rd ed., pp. 671-95). Chevy Chase, MD: American Society of Addiction Medicine, Inc.

Wilkins, J. N. & Gorelick, D. A. (2003). Pharmacological therapies for other drug and multiple drug addiction. In A. W. Graham, T. K. Schultz, M. F. Mayo-Smith, R. K. Ries & B. B. Wilford, eds. *Principles of Addiction Medicine* (3rd ed., pp. 815-22). Chevy Chase, MD: American Society of Addiction Medicine, Inc.

Willing, R. (February 16, 2004). British test inhaler that dispenses medical marijuana. *USA Today*, p. 4A.

Wilson, J. M., McGeorge, F., Smolinske, S. & Meatherall, R. (2005). A foxy intoxication. *Forensic Science International, 148*(1), 31-36.

Wolfe, T. (1968). *The Electric Kool-Aid Acid Test.* New York: Bantam Books.

Young, C. R. (1997). Sertraline treatment of hallucinogen persisting perception disorder. *Journal of Clinical Psychiatry, 58*(2): 85.

Young, J. M., McGregor, I. S. & Mallet, P. E. (2005). Co-administration of THC and MDMA (ecstasy) synergistically disrupts memory in rats. *Neuropsychopharmacology, 30*(8), 1475-82.

Zickler, P. (2002). Study demonstrates that marijuana smokers experience significant withdrawal. *NIDA Notes, 17*(3). http://www.drugabuse.gov/NIDA_notes /NNVol17N3/Demonstrates.html (accessed October 5, 2006).

Zukin, S. R., Sloboda, Z. & Javitt, D. C. (2005). Phencyclidine (PCP). In J. H. Lowinson, P. Ruiz, R. B. Millman & J. G. Langrod, eds. *Substance Abuse: A Comprehensive Textbook* (4th ed., pp. 324-35). Baltimore: Williams & Wilkins.

CHAPTER 7

Other Drugs, Other Addictions

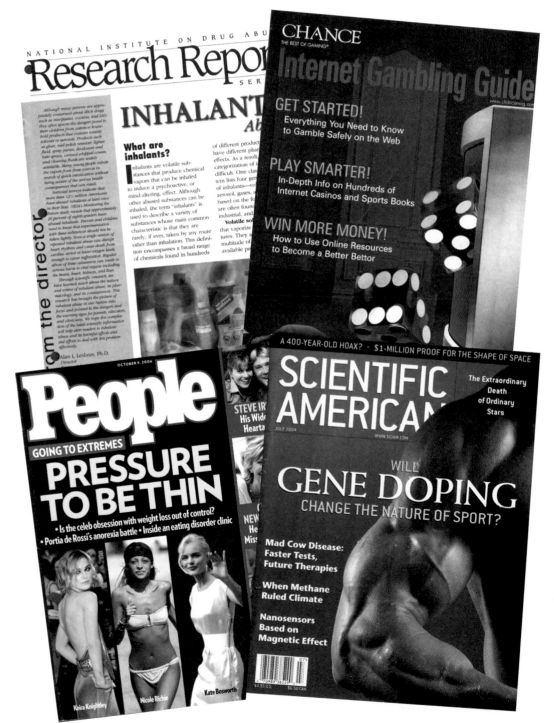

As the numbers of inhalant abusers, steroid-using athletes, pathological gamblers, and those with eating disorders grow, researchers, the media, and the general public have come to realize that addiction isn't limited to street drugs and alcohol.

- **Introduction.** It is rare than an addict is limited to one compulsion, and this includes compulsive behaviors as well as drug addictions.

OTHER DRUGS

- **Inhalants.** The major inhalants (volatile solvents, volatile nitrites, and anesthetics [e.g., nitrous oxide]) can cause mood elevation, central nervous system depression, disorientation, inebriation, and delirium. Dangerous effects include nerve damage, memory impairment, lack of coordination, and hypoxia (lack of oxygen leading to passing out or occasionally death).
- **Sports & Drugs.** Athletes have used therapeutic drugs, performance-enhancing drugs (especially steroids), and recreational/mood-altering drugs (legal and illegal). Steroids can build muscles and increase weight, but they can also cause aggression, physical problems, abuse, and addiction. Performance-enhancing stimulants (e.g., ephedra and methamphetamine) and some other drugs (e.g., human growth hormone and erythropoietin) are almost as widely used in some sports as steroids to increase training efficiency and improve performance.
- **Miscellaneous Drugs.** Gasoline, toad secretions, embalming fluid, kava, and even cough medicine have been used to get high. In attempts to change mood and improve health, herbal medicines and supplements, so-called smart drugs, amino acids, vitamins, and nutrients have been taken.

OTHER ADDICTIONS

- **Compulsive Behaviors.** People use compulsive behaviors to change their mood, get a rush, or self-medicate much as they do with psychoactive drugs. Compulsive behaviors include compulsive gambling, compulsive shopping and hoarding, eating disorders, sexual addiction, Internet addiction, compulsive TV viewing, and even excessive cell phone use.
- **Heredity, Environment & Compulsive Behaviors.** As with drug addictions, these three factors can change brain chemistry and make someone more susceptible to a behavioral addiction.
- **Compulsive Gambling.** Gambling has grown dramatically over the past 30 years, particularly in the United States. Almost 9 million U.S. adults are problem or pathological gamblers, and another 15 million are at risk. Internet gambling had shown the largest growth spurt in recent years until the Congress blocked U.S. banks and credit card companies from transferring money.
- **Compulsive Shopping & Hoarding.** In an era of easy credit and shopping networks, the debt load of the average American has exploded; many of those debtors are compulsive shoppers.
- **Eating Disorders.** There are three basic eating disorders:
  ◊ **Anorexia Nervosa.** Starving oneself by extreme measures to look thin and feel in control of one's life.
  ◊ **Bulimia Nervosa.** Uncontrolled overeating followed by risky behaviors, such as vomiting, excessive exercise, and taking laxatives to avoid weight gain.
  ◊ **Binge-Eating Disorder (including compulsive overeating).** Uncontrolled eating, often involving large weight gains—usually a lifetime problem.
  All three eating disorders combine behavior and a substance (food) to create the addictions.
- **Sexual Addiction.** Sexual compulsivity, particularly pornography and masturbation, is often used to cope with personal problems and childhood traumas or stress.
- **Internet Addiction.** There are several Internet compulsions involving online services, such as chat rooms, list servers, and even e-mail.
  ◊ **Cybersexual Addiction.** This includes online pornography and X-rated chat rooms.
  ◊ **Computer Relationship Addiction.** This involves having relationships online in an obsessive manner.
  ◊ **Internet Compulsions.** These consist of online gambling, game playing, shopping, auctions, stock day trading, and other Internet activities.
  ◊ **Information Addiction.** Endless surfing of the Internet for information and data is part of this compulsion.
  ◊ **Computer Games Addiction.** Online games, e.g., World of Warcraft, along with handhelds such as Nintendo DS® and Sony PlayStation® games, have become as popular and as addictive as any drug.
- **Television Addiction.** This involves excessive TV viewing to the exclusion of many activities in a user's life (e.g., family, friends, and work).
- **Cell Phone Addiction.** Research on this newest compulsion is still in its infancy. It will take time for the cultural and addictive ramifications to become clear.
- **Conclusions.** Although the roots of many compulsions are similar, one still has to be aware of differences, for example, abstinence is necessary for recovery from some addictions whereas a return to normal levels of activity is necessary with others (e.g., eating disorders).

INTRODUCTION

"Addiction is a state of mind. I was thinking of what addictions I have or have had. Well, eating—that's my addiction. Well, no, I gamble—I got that. I watch TV too much—four hours a day. Smoking, I smoked for 10 years—three packs a day. Drinking—I was drunk for six straight months in the Air Force and on a binge basis after that. It's not the substance. It's not the gambling. It's not the specific thing I do. It's all these behaviors. Instead of solving a problem to change how I feel in the long term, I take something or do something to change how I feel right now."

65-year-old male in recovery

It is rare that an addict is limited to one compulsion. Most marijuana smokers also puff cigarettes; many co-caine abusers have an alcohol problem. And addictions aren't limited to psychoactive drugs. Behavioral addictions (e.g., compulsive gambling, eating disorders, and sexual addiction) are also common among substance abusers. For example, more than half of all compulsive gamblers are alcoholics. It is important to examine all substances and behaviors when studying the roots of compulsivity.

OTHER DRUGS

In addition to stimulants, depressants, and psychedelics, three classes of drugs that are used for the way they alter the mental and physical balance of users are:

◊ **inhalants**, volatile liquids or aerosol sprays that have many of the same psychoactive effects as street drugs;

◊ **sports drugs**, a variety of natural and synthetic substances that are used to heal injuries, increase performance, or alter the athlete's state of consciousness; and

◊ hard-to-classify drugs, such as **animal extracts, herbal preparations, smart drugs/drinks, and nootropics**, some of which have been used for their psychoactive effects and others which are purported to improve one's physical and mental health.

INHALANTS

"'Huffing'? I 'huffed' gas when I was 9 years old. And then when I was 11 or 12, I 'huffed' for a year. I'd inhale 12 cans of air freshener a day. My mom would buy the big packs at Costco® — she didn't know I was 'huffing' them 'cause I'd throw them away, and then

Solvent causes numb feeling

The Associated Press

ATLANTA — Repeated exposure to a chemical found in some car maintenance products

Youth trying to get high dies sniffing ScotchGard

14-year-old friend arrested on charge of manslaughter

System in Sacramento. "We are not talking about smoking and then dying 40 years down the road. We are talking about you are 14 — and then you ...

breathe. He fell down and friend struggled to help.

Paramedics ...

Swedes Say Laughing Gas Can Be Trouble

Reuters

Stockholm

Millions of U.S. kids have tried huffing

dangerous for regular users as well ... who've never tried

First-time inhalant users

to 17 who reported an av grade of D in school were times more likely ...

Newest dangerous high: embalming fluid abuse

Many h shoe p 12, and

By Kathleen Fa USA TODAY

By JOANN LOVIGLIO
The Associated Press

PHILADELPHIA — Embalming fluid is becoming an increasingly popular drug for users looking for a new and different high — one that often comes with violent and psychotic side effects.

Users — mainly teenagers and people in their 20s — are buying tobacco or marijuana cigarettes that have been soaked in the fluid, then dried. They cost about $20 apiece and are called by nearly a dozen names nationwide, including "wet," "fry" and "illy."

"The idea of embalming fluid appeals

to people's morbid curiosity about death," said Dr. Julie Holland of New York University School of Medicine.

Formaldehyde can be bought in drug stores and beauty supply stores. It is also available in many school science labs. In addition, there have been reports of embalming fluid thefts from funeral homes in Louisiana and New York.

Although there are no national statistics on usage, many drug experts say it appears to have spread from the inner cities to well-to-do neighborhoods and college campuses.

"Whether they live in a million-dollar

house or a $5,000 house, kids who are smoking pot or crack and are looking for a different type of high are turning to wet," said Julie Kirlin, a juvenile probation officer in Reading, about 50 miles from Philadelphia.

Embalming fluid is a compound of formaldehyde, methanol, ethanol and other solvents.

The high depends on what the user is really getting: Often the drug PCP is mixed in.

Twenty Houston-area users interviewed for a 1998 study by the Texas Commission on Drug Abuse said the effects

include visual and auditory hallucinations, euphoria, a feeling of invincibility, increased pain tolerance, anger, forgetfulness and paranoia.

Stranger symptoms reported include an overwhelming desire to disrobe and a strong distaste for meat.

Other symptoms may include coma, seizures, kidney failure and stroke. The high lasts from six hours to three days.

"Fry users are described like those who do a lot of inhalants — they're just spaced-out, dissociative," said Jane Maxwell of the National Institute on Drug Abuse's Community Epidemiology

Work Group. When they've taken PCP, "they come into the emergency room and are just wild. They have to be strapped down in their beds or they destroy the room."

In the Philadelphia suburb of Morrisville, a 14-year-old boy fatally stabbed a 33-year-old neighbor more than 70 times last year after smoking wet.

The boy, who said he took wet to quiet the voices in his head, is serving a seven-year sentence.

"This is a violent drug, and it will turn into a big fire if it's not watched very closely," Kirlin said

when she found out, I had to stop. I'm surprised I'm not dead from it because I did it for a long time. I'd just sit there and use until I passed out."
17-year-old recovering inhalant and alcohol abuser

Inhalants, sometimes classified as deliriants, comprise a wide variety of substances: volatile liquids that give off fumes, gases that come in pressurized tanks or bottles, and aerosol cans that are sprayed. The volatile substances are often present in a wide variety of commercial products, such as paints, solvents, and anesthetics.

Inhalants are used for their stupefying, intoxicating, and occasionally psychedelic effects. Inhalants, which are inhaled through the nose and/or mouth and occasionally sprayed directly in the mouth or nose, are classified differently from substances like tobacco, crack, and heroin, which are heated or burned and then smoked. They are also different from powders like cocaine hydrochloride or crystal meth, which are snorted.

There are three main groups of inhalants and dozens of subgroups (Table 7-1).

◇ **Volatile solvents (and aerosols).** Most of these substances are **synthesized from petroleum and combined with other chemicals.** Volatile solvents (hydrocarbons) are found in glues, gasoline, and nail polish remover, among others. Some aerosols, which can be sprayed to produce a foggy mist, are inhaled for their gaseous propellants rather than for their primary contents. Besides volatile hydrocarbons, some other volatile organic compounds that can be abused are esters, ketones (e.g., acetone), alcohols, and glycols.

◇ **Volatile nitrites.** These drugs, including amyl and butyl nitrite, are used clinically as blood vessel dilators (vasodilators) for heart problems and in the past as over-the-counter room fresheners (butyl and isopropyl). They are also used recreationally, often at a party and in sexual situations.

◇ **Anesthetics.** These were developed to block pain or induce uncon-

The three groups of inhalants are anesthetics such as nitrous oxide in little canisters (on the front left), volatile solvents and aerosols (in the middle and the back), and volatile nitrites (on the front right).
© 2007 CNS Productions, Inc.

sciousness during surgical or other medical procedures; their recreational use was exploited at the same time. Nitrous oxide (N_2O), also known as "laughing gas," is still used as an anesthetic (usually in dentistry) but is better known as a party drug that induces giddiness and a certain euphoria.

The most widely abused inhalants are nitrous oxide, nitrites, gasoline (and its additives), glue, spray paint, aerosol spray, lacquer thinner, and correction fluid.

Inhalants have some distinct differences from other psychoactive drugs.

◇ They are **quick acting and have intense effects**. They are absorbed through the lungs and into the bloodstream, which carries them rapidly to the brain. Their intoxicating effects occur within 7 to 10 seconds and last no more than 30 to 60 minutes after exposure; some last only a few minutes.

◇ They are **cheap, readily available, and widespread**. More than 1,500 chemical products can be inhaled for their psychoactive effects.

◇ Because psychoactive gases and liquids are present in the home, garage, and workplace, they are **readily accessible to children and adolescents**.

◇ They have **more-direct toxic effects on body tissues** than most other psychoactive drugs.

◇ They get inadequate attention from parents, educators, the media, and law enforcement personnel because of the **lack of awareness of inhalant abuse as a drug problem**. Dismissive and derogatory attitudes toward solvent abusers compound the difficulty of establishing effective prevention and treatment programs.

"At 15 maybe 16 I started doing, like, nitrous and I only did it at raves, like people would be walking around with a whole bunch of sagging balloons, laughing, and, like, they were a dollar each and you would just go up to people and say, 'Can I buy balloon?' and you just inhale them."
18-year-old inhalant abuser

TABLE 7–1   INHALANTS

Product	Chemicals
Volatile Solvents & Aerosols	
Gasoline and gasoline additives	Gasoline and high-octane fuel additives (e.g., STP®)
Airplane glue	Toluene, ethyl acetate
Rubber cement and other glues	Toluene, hexane, methyl chloride, acetone, methyl ethyl ketone, methyl butyl ketone
PVC cement	Trichloroethylene, tetrachlorethylene
Paint sprays (especially gold and silver metallic paints)	Toluene, butane, propane, fluorocarbons
Hairsprays and deodorants	Butane, propane, chlorofluorocarbons (CFCs)
Lighter fluid	Butane, isopropane
Fuel gas	Butane, isopropane
Dry-cleaning fluid, spot removers, correction fluid, degreasers	Tetrachloroethylene, trichloroethane, trichloroethylene, xylene, petroleum distillates, chlorohydrocarbons
Nail polish remover	Acetone, toluene, ethyl acetate
Paint remover/thinners	Toluene, methylene chloride, methanol, acetone, ethyl acetate, esters
Analgesic/asthma sprays	Chlorohydrofluorocarbons
Air dusters (End Dust,® Dust Off®)	Difluorethene, propane, isobutane, tetrafluoroethene
Volatile Nitrites	
Room odorizers ("poppers") (Locker Room,® Rush,® Liquid Gold,® Ram,® Rock Hard,® Stag,® Stud,® Thrust,® TNT®)	(Iso)amyl nitrite, (iso)butyl nitrite, isopropyl nitrite, cyclohexyl nitrite
Heart medication ("poppers, snappers")	Amylnitrite (prescription inhalant)
Anesthetics	
Nitrous oxide whipped cream propellant ("whippets," laughing gas, "blue nun," nitrous)	Nitrous oxide
Chloroform	Chloroform
Ether	Ether
Halothane, enflurane (liquid)	Bromo chloro trifluoro ethane, chloro trifluoro ether
Local anesthetic	Ethyl chloride

(Adapted from Sharp & Rosenberg, 2005)

HISTORY

The practice of inhaling gaseous substances to get high goes back to ancient times. For example, beginning around 1400 B.C., the Greek Oracle at Delphi was said to breathe in vapors from the earth (naturally occurring carbon dioxide by some accounts, ethylene gas or ethene by others) before uttering her prophecies (Brecher, 1972; Giannini, 1991). Ethene is produced naturally by decaying fruits and vegetables. In the Judaic world, spices, gums, herbs, and incense were burned and inhaled during religious ceremonies, a practice shared by other Mediterranean, African, and American Indian peoples (Swan, 1995).

In 1275 a Spanish chemist discovered **ether**, called it "sweet vitriol," and used it to treat a variety of illness and even as a substitute for alcohol. It took another 570 years before it was used as an anesthetic in 1842 in an English hospital to remove two tumors. **The discovery of nitrous oxide (laughing gas) and chloroform in the late 1700s and the rediscovery of ether ushered in the modern era of inhalant abuse** because experimenters and medical professionals found that inhalants could also be used to get high (Weil & Rosen, 2004). Nitrous oxide and the other anesthetics became popular in the United States, France, and the United Kingdom at parties, at "gas frolics," in bordellos, and in other places where the gases were available (Smith, 1974). There were public exhibitions in the 1800s where an upper-middle-class audience could inhale nitrous oxide and get high.

Later, at the beginning of the twentieth century when petroleum refining created a whole new set of products—solvents, thinners, and glues to name a few—many more substances were being inhaled for their intoxicating or euphoric effects. In the 1930s sniffing carbon dioxide (used to make seltzer bubbles) had a brief fling with popularity as did sniffing gasoline (Giannini, 1991). **After World War II, the abuse of glue and metallic paints rose dramatically** particularly in the midwestern United States and Japan. The practice persists as a drug abuse problem into the twenty-first century; **inhalants are responsible for 700 to 1,200 deaths each year in the United States** (Drug Abuse Warning Network, 2003). The actual number of deaths is thought to be underreported because medical examiners sometimes mistake death from inhalant abuse as suicide, suffocation, or an accident unrelated to inhalant abuse.

EPIDEMIOLOGY

Inhalant abuse often has an episodic pattern with brief outbreaks in particular schools or regions. **Abuse is most prevalent among adolescents.** Adults, however, also abuse inhalants, including painters, chemical company workers, healthcare professionals (especially in dentistry and anesthesiology), and others who have access to inhalants at work. The use among transients is particularly high—four to five times that of the general adult population.

Inhalant abuse remains a worldwide problem according to a World Health Organization (WHO) report. **Internationally, it afflicts primarily the young, the poor, street children, recent migrants to cities, indigenous peoples, and children exposed to chemicals daily**, such as children of cleaners or shoemakers. **The inhalant of choice in many countries is gasoline** because of its wide availability (World Health Organization [WHO], 1998).

Use by Gender & Age

Generally, more young people than adults abuse inhalants (Table 7-2); and among 12- to 17-year-olds, more young men than young women abuse, although overall in the United States females use slightly more than males. In adult populations the number of abusers declines by two-thirds or more after the age of 25 (Office of National Drug Control Policy, 2006). Adult inhalant abusers tend to start their inhalant use in adulthood. In addition they use less frequently, use fewer inhalants, and are not as likely to engage in criminal activities (Wu & Ringwalt, 2006). Inhalant use in eighth-, tenth-, and twelfth-graders has generally gone down since 1995 (University of Michigan, 2006).

Ethnically, **use is highest among American Indians and Whites** and lowest among Asians and Blacks (SAMHSA, 2006). In terms of treatment, however, 67% of adolescents admitted for inhalant abuse were White, 20% were Hispanic, 7% were American Indian/ Alaska Native, and 3% were Black (National Inhalant Prevention Coalition [NIPC], 2006). This last statistic says more about the availability of treatment in some communities rather than reflecting actual use.

METHODS OF INHALATION

Although there have been reports of people spraying aerosols onto bread and eating the bread or inserting small bottles of inhalants, such as correction fluid, into the nostrils, there are about seven common forms of inhalation.

1. **"Sniffing"** is breathing in the inhalant through the nose directly from the container. "Sniffing" puts the vapor into the lungs in contrast with "snorting," which puts solids, like cocaine, in contact with the mucosal lining of the nasal passages.

2. **"Huffing"** is putting a solvent-soaked rag, sock, or other material over or in one's mouth or nose and inhaling. ("Huffer" is also a term for any inhalant abuser no matter which route is used.)

3. **"Bagging"** means placing the inhalant or inhalant-soaked material in a plastic bag and inhaling by nose, mouth, or both. Rebreathing the exhaled air intensifies the effect.

4. **"Spraying"** means spraying the inhalant directly into the nose or mouth.

5. **"Balloons and crackers"** is the use of a pin or other "cracking" device to puncture a can of nitrous oxide or other inhalant while a balloon is placed over the end of the can. The gas in the balloon is then inhaled.

6. Spraying an aerosol into a bag, putting the bag over one's head, and inhaling is another form of use.

7. Pouring or spraying inhalants onto cuffs, sleeves, or collars and then sniffing over a period of time is occasionally used.

Some users heat the solvent to make it more volatile, a particularly dangerous practice that has resulted in explosions, burns, and deaths. Directly breathing and spraying pressurized inhalants into the mouth or nose are particularly toxic methods. These techniques expose an abuser's fragile membranes to the caustic effects of these substances. They also **put a dangerous amount of pressure into the lungs and can freeze tissue** as the substances quickly vaporize, taking heat from everything around them. The choices of inhalant and method of inhalation allow great control over the intensity and the duration of the effects.

"A Woodland boy died after he tried to get high by sniffing a common water repellent, Scotchguard,® and a 14-year-old friend who also was inhaling the aerosol was arrested on suspicion of involuntary manslaughter. The boys

---

TABLE 7–2 PERCENTAGE OF AMERICANS WHO HAVE USED ANY INHALANT—2005

Age	Ever Used	Last Year	Last Month
12–17	10.5%	4.5%	1.2%
18–25	13.3%	2.1%	0.5%
26 & up	8.5%	0.2%	0.1%
Total users 12 & up	**22,745,000**	**2,187,000**	**611,000**

Source: National Household Survey on Drug Abuse (Substance Abuse and Mental Health Services Administration [SAMHSA], 2006)

TABLE 7–3 INHALANT LIFETIME USE BY TYPE AND AGE

	12–17 Years	18–25 Years
Glue, shoe polish, or toluene	4.3%	2.0%
Gasoline or lighter fluid	3.6%	2.1%
Spray paints	3.0%	1.2%
Correction fluid, degreaser, or cleaning fluids	2.2%	1.5%
Other aerosol sprays	2.2%	2.1%
Amyl/butyl/cyclohexyl nitrites	1.6%	2.3%
Lighter gases (butane, propane)	1.2%	0.7%
Nitrous oxide	1.6%	9.2%

(Note that as "huffers" grow older, their preferences change, e.g., much more nitrous oxide and nitrites.)

Source: National Household Survey on Drug Abuse (SAMHSA, 2006)

LIVING MADE EASY.

PRESCRIPTION FOR SCOLDING WIVES.

This 1830 print from England with its caption "Living Made Easy" depicts a "gas frolic." Many lectures on chemistry were illustrated by offering "laughing gas" to members of the audience.

Courtesy of the National Library of Medicine, Bethesda, MD

used a plastic bag to inhale the chemicals. They passed the bag back and forth. Suddenly the boy couldn't breathe."

Scripps-McClatchy News Service, September 17, 1998

VOLATILE SOLVENTS

These are mostly **carbon- and hydrocarbon-based compounds that are volatile (turn to gas) at room temperature**. They include such common materials as gasoline and gasoline additives, kerosene, paints (especially metallic paints), air dusters, paint thinners, lacquers, nail polish remover, spot removers, glues and plastic cements, lighter fluid, and a variety of aerosols.

These volatile solvents are quick acting because they are **absorbed into the blood almost immediately after inhalation and they then move to the heart, brain (within 7 to 10 seconds), liver, and other tissues**. Solvents are exhaled by the lungs (in which case a telltale odor remains on the breath) and excreted by the kidneys (NIPC, 2006).

Short-Term Effects

Inhaling these substances produces a **temporary stimulation, an elevated mood, and reduced inhibitions**. A sol-

vent like toluene affects the reward/reinforcement pathway just as cocaine and other psychoactive drugs do (Gerasimov, Ferrieri, Schiffer, et al., 2002). Impulsiveness, excitement, and irritability also occur. Soon the depressive effects begin including **dizziness, slurred speech, unsteady gait, and drowsiness**. These symptoms along with impaired judgment as well as falling or fainting increase the danger of an accident or injury.

High dosage or individual susceptibility results in major central nervous system (CNS) effects—**illusions, hallucinations, and delusions may develop**. The abuser might experience a dreamy stupor culminating in a short period of sleep. The **effects resemble alcohol or sedative intoxication** (inhalant abuse has been called a "quick drunk"). The intoxicated state may last from minutes to an hour or more, depending on the kind, quantity, and length of exposure to the solvent inhaled. Headaches and nausea may follow as part of an inhalant hangover.

"I came to the conclusion that the headaches my son had been complaining about were due to 'huffing.' We found empty spray cans out in the woods near

the house. Of course when I confronted him, he said, 'No way. Headaches must be from not having enough caffeine today.' He was doing bug spray, air freshener, Arid® deodorant, and whipped cream [the propellant]. When he was coming down, he would be real angry and violent. When loaded, he did stupid things."

Mother of a 14-year-old "huffer"

After prolonged inhalation, **delirium with confusion, psychomotor clumsiness, emotional instability, impaired thinking, and coma** have been reported. These neurological effects from both low-level, chronic, and high-level (acute) exposure to volatile solvents are usually reversible, although dangerous and even fatal consequences can result from initial and high dose inhalation.

◇ Heart and vascular problems. **Arrhythmias and myocarditis** are common with volatile solvents and can even induce cardiac arrest. When cardiac arrest occurs from inhalation, resuscitation is extremely difficult. This condition is known as "sudden sniffing death syndrome," which is caused by certain inhalants' effects on the heart's wiring. This condition can be caused by the freons in halogenated hydrocarbons, by gasoline, and by nitrites, among others.

◇ Lung problems. Solvents can cause **pulmonary hypertension, respiratory distress**, and lowered breathing capacity. Carried to extremes, asphyxia and respiratory arrest due to occlusion are possible.

◇ Liver problems. Chronic exposure to many solvents will cause some **liver toxicity** and subsequent damage, which is often mostly reversible. Unfortunately, concurrent heavy drinking greatly increases hepatoxicity due to solvent inhalation.

◇ Blood problems. A solvent like methylene chloride increases carboxyhemoglobin in the circulatory system, causing brain damage.

◇ Neonatal problems. It is rare that a "huffer" uses only inhalants, so oftentimes fetal damage could also be attributed to the alcohol or other substances that are abused. Toluene has been shown to cause growth retardation, some odd facial features, and tremors, in newborns (Balster, 2003; Sharp & Rosenberg, 2005).

Long-Term Effects

Chronic abuse is characterized by a lack of coordination, an inability to concentrate, weakness, disorientation, and weight loss. Because solvents have been shown to affect the hippocampus (a memory center), long-term use will impair memory (National Institute on Drug Abuse [NIDA], 2000B). Chronic abuse can involve extremely high concentrations of fumes, sometimes thousands of times higher than industrial exposure, so **some mental and neurological effects can be irreversible though not progressive after abuse ceases**. Magnetic resonance imaging (MRI) scans of the brains of abusers of toluene and other volatile solvents showed abnormalities in several areas of the brain that translated to **low levels of general intellectual functioning, particularly those involving working memory and executive cognitive functions**, which include the inability to focus attention, plan, solve problems, and control one's behavior (Rosenberg, Grigsby, Dreisbach, et al., 2002). Chronic abuse of toluene can result in dementia, spastic movements, and other CNS dysfunction, whereas occupational exposure to toluene has not produced these effects probably due to the use of protective equipment.

Complications may result from the effect of the solvent or other toxic ingredients, such as lead in gasoline. **Injuries to the brain, liver, kidneys, bone marrow, and particularly the lungs** may result either from heavy exposure or because of individual hypersensitivity. Blood irregularities and chromosome damage can result. Chronic abuse of some of these solvents can produce ulcers around the nose and mouth as well as cancerous growths (Sharp & Rosenberg, 2005).

"I have a friend that does the spray cans and his brother overdosed on it. His mom found his older brother in his room with a plastic bag over his mouth from inhaling and he had all the gold paint all over his mouth and his nose and that's what he looks like now; he just looks totally like a bum, you know, kinda stupid, and his eyes are halfway shut all the time. He's just out of it. He's still my friend but I hate to see a person like that, you know."

19-year-old recovering drug user

Psychiatric Effects

Although chronic use is rarely associated with psychiatric disorders, antisocial personality disorders are common among abusers. Hallucinations are more common among susceptible users than in "huffers" in general. Because inhalant abusers are more likely to abuse other drugs, it can be hard to determine which substance was responsible for what behavior. In addition, a study of emergency room admissions showed that inhalant abusers were more likely to engage in self-destructive, suicidal, and homicidal behavior (Korman, Trimboli & Semler, 1980). A more recent study found a twofold increase in conduct disorders among recovering inhalant abusers although they were not worse than the nonusing controls in terms of crime (Sakai, Mikulich-Gilbertson & Crowley, 2006).

Toluene (methyl benzene)

The most abused solvent is toluene because it is found in so many substances: glues, drying agents, solvents, thinners, paints, inks, and cleaning agents. Several studies have suggested that toluene has an extremely high abuse potential (Sharp, Beauvais & Spence, 1992). Chronic abuse can affect balance, hearing, and eyesight and, most often, cause problems with neurological functions and cognitive abilities. In one study **65% of chronic abusers of toluene in spray paint had neurological damage** (Hormes, Filley & Rosenberg, 1986; Sharp & Rosenberg, 2005). That damage translated to cognitive dysfunction. Heavy abuse can result in deafness, trembling, and dementia. Other severe abnormalities include midrange hearing loss and changes to the white matter of the CNS. "Texas shoeshine," spray paint containing toluene, is widely abused often among painters. Kidney disorders sometimes result from toluene abuse (O'Brien, 2001).

Trichloroethylene (TCE)

This common organic solvent is used in correction fluids, paints, metal degreasers, and spot removers and in extracting oils and fats from vegetable products. Occupationally, more than 3.5 million people are exposed to TCE. Like two other volatile solvents—toluene and acetone—trichloroethylene (TCE) **causes overall depression effects and moderate hallucinations**. The toxic effects of TCE have been known for 50 years and are similar to those of toluene. It was once even used as an anesthetic despite dangerous side effects. The effects of low-to-moderate doses of TCE are generally reversible, but at higher doses various neuropathies (any disorder affecting the CNS) occur (Sharp & Rosenberg, 2005). Some of these neuropathies can be permanent.

N-Hexane & Methyl Butyl Ketone (MBK)

Used as a solvent for glues and adhesives, as a diluent for plastics and rubber, and in the production of laminated products, n-hexane has caused neurological damage. Similarly, methyl butyl ketone (MBK), used as a paint thinner and a solvent for dyes, causes some of the same damage. There are **numerous reports of brain damage from occupational exposure as well as from deliberate recreational use**. Recovery in severe cases can take as long as three years.

Alkanes

The smaller molecules of **this class of hydrocarbons are gases at room temperature**. The most common alkanes include methane, ethane, butane, and propane. They are inhaled for their effects but unfortunately can also cause cardiac arrhythmias and sudden death (Siegel & Wason, 1990). The larger molecules of this class include hexane and pentane and are very neurotoxic (NIDA, 2000B).

Gasoline

Gasoline sniffing, especially common among solvent abusers on American Indian reservations, introduces into the system various components and additives of gasoline, including solvents, metals, and chemicals. **Effects include insomnia, tremors, anorexia, and sometimes paralysis** (Beauvais, Oetting & Edwards, 1985). When leaded gas is inhaled, symptoms can also include hallucinations, convulsions, and the chronic **irreversible effects of lead poisoning** (brain, liver, kidney, bone marrow, and lung damage). The major effects last only 3 to 5 minutes, but residual effects and intoxication can last 5 to 6 hours. Almost half of all inhalant deaths are due to gasoline (TESS, 2007). Internationally, gasoline is the substance of choice because even in remote areas it is not under scrutiny and is cheap to acquire (especially if siphoned from a vehicle) (WHO, 1998).

"I was at this party once and all my friends were soaking these rags with gasoline and putting it in their nose and just sniffin' it. They told me try it, you know? They said it was really cool and really fun. Well, I was sitting down when I was doing it, but when I stopped I got up and I felt like I had drank like a couple bottles of tequila."

24-year-old ex-"huffer"

Alcohols

Ethanol, methanol, and isopropanol are the most commonly abused alcohol solvents. Remember the feeling when inhaling deeply from a brandy snifter? When inhaled too deeply and for too long a period of time, rather than drunk, alcohols can cause a mild high along with nausea, vertigo, weakness, vomiting, headaches, and abdominal cramping. Isopropanol, found in paints, rubbing alcohol, formaldehyde, and perfumes, can induce severe CNS depression (Giannini, 1991).

Warning Signs of Solvent Abuse

Though solvent abuse can be difficult to spot, there are still various warning signs:

◊ headaches;

◊ **chemical odor** on the body and clothes or in the room;

◊ **red, glassy, or watery eyes and dilated pupils;**

◊ **inflamed nose, nosebleeds, and rashes** around the nose and mouth;

◊ **slow, thick, or slurred speech;**

◊ **staggering gait, disorientation, and a lack of coordination;**

◊ pains in the chest and stomach;

◊ fatigue;

◊ nausea;

◊ shortness of breath;

◊ loss of appetite;

◊ intoxication;

◊ irritability and aggression;

◊ seizure; and

◊ coma.

"I felt like really stupid. I couldn't, like, focus on anything, you know? When I'd be in school, I mean, I got an F in Spanish class and I'm Mexican, you know? I know Spanish very well, but that stuff just really got me very stupid. But now it's like I feel much better, you know? I can, I can focus on everything."

17-year-old inhalant abuser

VOLATILE NITRITES

The first of the nitrites, amyl nitrite, was discovered in 1857. It was used to relieve angina (heart pains). The substances known as "aliphatic nitrites" or "alkyl nitrites" could be made with any convenient organic chemical, so the family of nitrites expanded to include **isoamyl, butyl, isobutyl, isopropyl, and most recently cyclohexyl nitrites**. Restrictions exist on all but cyclohexyl nitrite.

These inhalants dilate blood vessels, so the heart and the brain (as well as other tissues) receive more blood. Effects start in 7 to 10 seconds and last for 30 to 60 seconds. Blood pressure reaches its lowest point in 30 seconds and returns to normal at around 90 seconds. Nitrites are sometimes called "poppers" because amyl nitrite used to come in glass capsules wrapped in cotton that were broken open (with an audible pop) and sniffed (Weil & Rosen, 2004). Besides angina, amyl nitrite can be used to treat cyanide poisoning.

"Amyl nitrite, you crack 'em, inhale 'em, and you are off to the races; your head, your whole body is just enveloped. I don't know how to describe it better. My whole body, my vision, everything would be blurred around the edges. Sounds are muffled. I would use them with partners, with girlfriends in intimate moments, and it would heighten the experience in some aspects."

42-year-old recovering "huffer" and psychedelic abuser

On inhalation there is a **feeling of fullness in the head, a rush, mild euphoria, dizziness, and giddiness**. (First-time abusers have reported feeling panic attacks.) As the effects wear off, the user might experience a headache, nausea, vomiting, and a chill (because of dilation of blood vessels near the skin) (Wood, 1994). **Excessive abuse can cause oxygen deprivation, fainting or passing out, and temporary asphyxiation.** An intense increase in heart rate and palpitations can make nitrite inhalation extremely unpleasant. First aid for the headaches includes abstinence. Overdose treatment requires removing the abuser from exposure and ensuring that respiration and blood flow are maintained. Occasionally, cardiopulmonary resuscitation (CPR) is used. Chronic abuse causes methemoglobinemia, a condition that reduces the blood's ability to carry oxygen.

Nitrites, thought to enhance sexual activity, are sought after especially by some gay males for their euphoric and physiological effects, which include relaxation of smooth muscles such as the sphincter muscle. Repeated abuse may alter blood cells and impair the immune system, increasing susceptibility to HIV infection. There is some evidence that nitrites inhibit the functioning of the white blood cells. Nitrites are also converted to nitrosamines in the body, which are potent cancer-causing chemicals (Tran, Brazeau, Nickerson, et al., 2006).

Warnings have been issued about using poppers, Viagra,™ and methamphetamine in combination (particularly at rave clubs and gay bathhouses) because the first two substances lower blood pressure and the combination of all three drugs can cause fainting or even death ("Viagra, poppers," 1999). Tolerance develops rapidly to the effects of nitrites.

"Heart would race—just boom, boom, boom, boom in your chest. It feels like all the blood was rushing to your head. I've seen myself in the mirror after doing it—bright red. I don't imagine that that is a good sign."

42-year-old nitrite abuser

Nitrites, amyl nitrite in particular, have a sweet odor when fresh but a wet-dog or spoiled-banana smell when stale. Amyl nitrite is available only by prescription; and although butyl and propyl nitrites were banned in the United States, variants of these formulations are still sold as room deodorizers, tape head cleaners, and even sneaker cleaners (see Table 7-1). Street supplies of the drug also come from diverted legal sources or are smuggled in from other countries (DrugScope, 2003). **Two-thirds of nitrite abusers use at least three other inhalants, one-third abuse alcohol, and one-third abuse another drug other than inhalants** (Wu, Schlenger & Ringwalt, 2005). Nitrites have been popular in England for quite a while among teenagers. One study found that 20% of 16-year-olds in northwest England had used nitrites.

ANESTHETICS

At the end of the eighteenth century, newly discovered volatile substances were found to have anesthetic as well as euphoric effects. Experimentation began in both directions with such substances as chloroform, ether, oxygen, and nitrous oxide. Abuse of nitrous oxide (inhaling and drinking) was reported among Harvard medical students starting in the nineteenth century.

Abuse continues today by young experimenters, particularly at rave and dance parties as well as among middle-class and professional groups, particu-larly dentists, doctors, anesthesiologists, hospital workers, and healthcare professionals. They abuse nitrous oxide, halothane, and other anesthetics such as ether, ethylene, ethyl chloride, and cyclopropane (Luck & Hedrick, 2004).

Nitrous Oxide (N$_2$O)

The rave and party scene that began in the 1990s brought back an interest in nitrous oxide (N$_2$O), also known as "laughing gas," principally because of its dramatic **rapid onset and equally rapid dissolution of desired effects**. In addition, N$_2$0 is said to enhance the effects of ecstasy, the most well-known club drug.

Nitrous oxide, discovered by Dr. Joseph Priestly in 1776, was popularized by the physician Sir Humphrey Davy for both its anesthetic/analgesic and euphoric effects. Davy talked about a "pleasurable thrilling in the chest and extremities along with auditory and visual distortions." He also wrote about his recreational use of the gas. In 1869 the gas was commercially used to effervesce or aerate drinks (Lynn, Walter, Harris, et al., 1972). Medically, nitrous is used most often by dentists; and because the pain-numbing effects are short acting, the gas has to be delivered continuously during oral surgery or other dental procedures.

The most commonly abused form of N$_2$0 is **sold in small, pressurized metal or plastic canisters** intended for home use to charge whipping-cream bottles. These Whip-It!® or EZ Whip® cartridges are sold in boxes of 10, 12, or 24 for about 50 cents per canister. **Large commercial tanks are also diverted from medical or dental suppliers** for abuse (they are painted blue and are thus called "blue nuns"). Both contain N$_2$0 under great pressure, and the **rapid vaporization of the gas will cause freezing to oral, nasal, or lung tissues if inhaled directly** from the source container. Most often a source container is used to **inflate a balloon, and users then inhale the nitrous from the inflated balloon**. Large tanks come with valves and fittings that can be adapted to fill balloons, but the smaller Whip-It!® containers must be opened with a metal device called a "cracker" that is sold for about $10.

Nitrous oxide is abused for its mood-altering effects. Within 8 to 10 seconds of inhaling from a balloon, the gas produces:

◇ **dizziness, giddiness, and disorientation**, often accompanied by **silly laughter**;
◇ a throbbing or pulsating **buzzing in the ears**; and
◇ occasional **visual hallucinations**.

"I did nitrous, the silver caps: you put it in balloons and then you put it up to your mouth and you breathe in three times. And as soon as you let go, man, you feel like your head is gonna pop and again the wha-wha sound and it felt like my head was in a bell that just rang. I was shaking laughing, and my face was pale again and my lips were blue and I did that so much that night I ended throwing up."

16-year-old "huffer"

N$_2$0 can also cause:

◇ **confusion and headache**;
◇ **a sense that one is about to collapse or pass out**; and
◇ **impaired motor skills and fainting** that can result in traumatic injuries such as a broken nose or arm.

"People who fall normally have injuries on their knees and their hands because it's a natural reaction to break your fall. These people [nitrous users] would literally hit the ground face first, and for a person who's 6 feet tall, that's a long fall. We have a number of broken noses and broken teeth, and we would always say to them, 'Have you been doing nitrous oxide?' 'Oh, no, no, no, no, no.'"

Glen Razwyck, former director, Haight Ashbury Rock Medicine

These feelings quickly cease when the gas leaves the body. **The maximum effect lasts only two or three minutes**, though experienced users seem to feel physical effects somewhat longer than novice users; this is possibly a form of reverse tolerance, where less and less gas is needed to produce the same effects. **Cognitive functioning is diminished during the peak of the high but returns to normal within five minutes.** If used more extensively, the impaired thinking can last longer.

"I'd go to school and my head just wouldn't be there and it wouldn't be there for weeks on end. It would be gone; it would be in a daze the whole time; you wouldn't be able to concentrate. You had to shake it off or something; it just didn't go away."
22-year-old "huffer"

Long-term exposure can cause central and peripheral nerve cell and brain cell damage due to a lack of sufficient oxygen because N_2O replaces oxygen in the blood. For this reason, when dentists use N_2O on their patients they co-administer oxygen; and when they stop the N_2O, they continue the oxygen for a few minutes to completely clear the gas from the blood. Symptoms of long-term exposure to N_2O include loss of balance and dexterity, overall weakness, and numbness in the arms and legs.

"Me and my friend went on a nitrous binge that went on for like about three weeks. We had spent easy 80 bucks each on just nitrous, doin' like 100 canisters a day and did that for about three weeks and ever since then I've had, I have balance problems still from that."
18-year-old nitrous abuser

Most of the nerve damage is seen in users who employ dental gas masks or some other inhalation devices that expose them to the gas continuously over long periods of time, depriving their nerve cells of sufficient oxygen. There is also a **significant potential of seizures, cardiac arrhythmias, and asphyxia leading to central or peripheral nerve damage and even death**. The nerve damage has been shown to occur even when there is suf-

ficient oxygen. Further, N_2O abuse can lead to physical dependence in some users and has been a **major addiction problem for dentists and anesthesiologists** over the past few decades.

Although N_2O is not classified as a controlled substance, possession with intent to use the gas for other than medical, dental, or commercial purposes is a misdemeanor in most states.

Halothane

Halothane, first synthesized in 1951, is a prescription surgical anesthetic gas sold under the trade name Fluothane.® In the West it has mostly been replaced with sevoflurane and desflurane and is more widely used in third world countries and in veterinary procedures because of its lower cost. Its effects are extremely rapid and powerful enough to induce a coma for surgery. Because of its limited availability, it has been most often abused by anesthesiologists and hospital personnel.

DEPENDENCE

The *Diagnostic and Statistical Manual of Mental Disorders* (*DSM-IV-TR*) classifies inhalant disorders as "inhalant dependence and abuse, intoxication, induced delirium, dementia, psychotic disorder, mood disorder, and anxiety disorder." These are based on abuse of volatile solvents (hydrocarbon or other volatile compounds). *DSM-IV-TR* classifies abuse of nitrites and anesthetics as "psychoactive substance dependence not otherwise specified" (American Psychiatric Association [APA], 2000).

Though tolerance to volatile solvents will develop, the **liability for physical and psychological dependence and addiction to these inhalants is less than that for other depressants**; younger children get into long-term abuse of inhalants more often than adults perhaps because of the availability and the low cost.

Breaking the habit or treating the compulsion can be difficult because most users are young and immature and because **continued use can cause cognitive impairments that hinder comprehension and recovery**. There have been isolated reports of withdrawal symptoms after cessation of long-term

use (hallucinations, chills, cramps, and occasionally delirium tremens). A cross-tolerance to other depressants, including alcohol, will develop with long-term use. Interestingly, among drug addicts **inhalant abuse is looked down upon as low class and inferior to other highs**.

PREVENTION

The dangers of inhalant abuse have not been publicized as widely as the dangers of alcohol, tobacco, and other drugs. Parents and young people may not be aware of the risk of sudden death or brain damage from inhaling volatile substances. **Law enforcement officers, healthcare workers, teachers, and parents need to be trained to recognize signs and symptoms of inhalant abuse** and to spot which youths are particularly at risk. Further, it is necessary to be aware of or monitor the potentially abusable substances that are used in common household or business products.

SPORTS & DRUGS

INTRODUCTION

In August 2006 U.S. sprinter Justin Gatlin gave up his world record in the 100-meter event as part of an agreement with the U.S. Anti-Doping Agency when he tested positive for testosterone and other steroids. As testing procedures become more sophisticated, the number of sports that have to change their regulations and penalties has increased. The most severely affected sport has been baseball.

"I have never knowingly used steroids."
Barry Bonds, left fielder for the San Francisco Giants

Having set the single-season home run record of 73 in 2001, Barry Bonds, one of the greatest power hitters in the history of baseball, passed Babe Ruth's lifetime home run record of 714 on May 28, 2006. The celebrations were muted because suspicions that Bond's successes were aided by the use of illegal substances. *Game of Shadows: Barry Bonds, BALCO, and the Steroids Scandal That Rocked Professional*

Drugs have often been a part of professional and amateur athletics, some legally and some not. There are three main categories of drugs used in sports:

◊ **therapeutic drugs** (e.g., analgesics, muscle relaxants, anti-inflammatories, and asthma medications) used for specific medical problems and administered with proper medical supervision;

◊ **performance-enhancing drugs (ergogenic drugs)**, such as steroids, growth hormones, blood-doping drugs, and stimulants, some legal and some not (most are banned from competition); and

◊ **recreational and mood-altering drugs**, both legal and illegal (e.g., cocaine, marijuana, alcohol, and tobacco), used to induce euphoria, reduce pain or anxiety, lower inhibitions, escape boredom, reproduce the rush of an on-field performance, or simply to enhance the senses.

It is the performance-enhancing drugs that cause the most problems, although many athletes will try a wide variety of legal drugs to enhance their strength, stamina, and lap times. A study by the International Olympic Committee (IOC) of more than 2,000 athletes at the 2000 Olympic Summer Games in Sydney, Australia, discovered that each competitor had taken between six and seven legal medications in the previous three days. The medications included vitamins, cold tablets, anti-inflammatories, and food supplements. One athlete used as many as 29 different medications and supplements.

Some athletes perceive drugs, often illicit ones, as the quick way to put on pounds and muscle, to increase stamina, to get up for a game, to relieve pain, or to keep up with other athletes who use drugs. Because many drugs used in sports create feelings of confidence and excitement,

Sports, a book by two reporters for the *San Francisco Chronicle*, claimed that according to secret grand jury testimony, Bonds had indeed used steroids (the most controversial being tetrahydrogestrinone [THG], an undetectable steroid developed at BALCO [Bay Area Laboratory Cooperative] by its founder Victor Conte). Whether or not it was true, the specter of steroids has continued to haunt baseball especially since Ken Caminiti talked about his use of performance-enhancing drugs (particularly during his MVP season in 1996 at third base with the San Diego Padres) and said he saw nothing wrong with it.

"It's no secret what's going on in baseball. At least half the guys are using steroids. They talk about it. They joke about it with each other."

Ken Caminiti, former Major League Baseball player and 1996 MVP

With that statement and other comments in the June 3, 2002, issue of *Sports Illustrated*, Caminiti reignited the controversy about drug use in baseball (Sports Illustrated, 2002B). He died in 2005 at the age of 46 from a heart attack due to a drug overdose.

The real bombshell was a 2005 book by Jose Canseco titled *Juiced*. A power hitter in the 1980s and 1990s with the Oakland Athletics and several other teams, Canseco admitted using steroids, starting in the 1980s, and named other players whom he claimed did the same, including Mark McGuire and Sammy Sosa (Canseco, 2005). Canseco said he wrote the book because he was tired of people thinking he was the only one who used the drugs. During that era power hitting surged as did the renewed popularity of America's pastime (mostly due to the McGuire/Sosa home run race); and even though baseball had an antisteroid policy, most ignored it. **In March 2005 a number of players were called before a U.S. House Government Reform Committee hearing, where they denied the use of steroids** or avoided the questions, but later events, including an admission of steroid use by Yankee outfielder Jason Giambi and a positive drug test by Baltimore Oriole slugger Rafael Palmeiro, seemed to confirm many of Canseco's claims.

"The challenge is not to find a top player who has used steroids. The challenge is to find a top player who hasn't. No one who reads this book from cover to cover will have any doubt

This poster for the 1912 Olympic Games was designed by Olle Hjortzberg. The only controversy in these Olympics was the disqualification (due to a question about his amateur status) of the great American athlete Jim Thorpe, who had won the pentathlon and the decathlon with ease. The medals were restored 70 years later.

• •

drugs themselves can motivate athletes to abuse them.

HISTORY

The use of drugs in sports is nothing new. Greek Olympic athletes in the third century B.C. ate large amounts of mushrooms or meat to improve their performance. About the same time, athletes in Macedonia prepared for their events by drinking ground donkey hooves boiled in oil and garnished with rose petals. Roman gladiators took stimulants (betel nuts or ephedra) to give them endurance (Hanley, 1983). Aztec Indians found a stimulant in a native cactus, which they used for running; the drug lasted up to three days. By the 1800s cyclists, swimmers, and other **athletes used opium, morphine, cocaine, caffeine, nitroglycerin, sugar cubes soaked in ether** (Dutch canal swimmers), **and even low doses of strychnine** (marathoners). Around 1875 race walkers in England chewed coca leaves to improve their performance. **Boxers drank water laced with cocaine** between rounds. Long-distance

runners were followed on bicycles by doctors who gave them a mixture of brandy and strychnine (Wooley, 1992).

Amphetamines, which were developed in the 1930s, increased alertness and energy for competition. In World War II, amphetamines were administered to troops of various countries to delay fatigue and increase endurance. When veterans returned home to the playing fields, some continued to rely on the drugs to give themselves a competitive edge or increase their athletic endurance.

International Politics

The male hormone testosterone had been isolated in the 1930s and was used in its pure form or in compounds to help injury victims heal and survivors of World War II concentration camps gain weight. During the Cold War era, **the Soviet weightlifting team used steroids in the 1952 Olympics to garner medals**. When this information was revealed in 1954 to the U.S. weightlifting coach, the argument was soon made that the U.S. team should also have access to steroids if they wanted a chance of staying ahead of the Soviets and the rest of the Communist bloc (Todd, 1987). **The use of performance-enhancing drugs was thought to be the only way that Americans could maintain their competitive edge in international athletics.** At the 1956 Olympics, the Soviets and many of the Communist bloc countries, especially East Germany, were rumored to be using anabolic steroids not only in weightlifting and strength sports but also in swimming. Use of performance-enhancing drugs continued in subsequent Olympic Games.

"The [East German] athletes themselves came out and told that these coaches and scientists forced these drugs on them. And then they found the records of that. I've seen their health problems afterwards. They would have medical problems that they, of course, wouldn't openly say but many of them suffered from that a lot."
Suha Tukman, coach and former 1972 Olympic swimmer for Turkey

By 1958 steroids were available and abuse by athletes had become widespread even in the face of growing evidence of negative side effects. At first they were abused by bodybuilders and weightlifters who wanted to increase weight and strength and later by many athletes to accelerate their training and development. Typical dosages have been greatly increased from 30 to 40 milligrams (mg) per day in the 1970s to 10 times that amount in the 1990s. In the 1994 World Championships, winning swimmers from the Peoples Republic of China were accused of using performance-enhancing drugs and subsequently a number of them tested positive.

Over the past 50 years, cyclists have used a wide variety of substances and techniques to increase their endurance and strength: nitroglycerin, caffeine, various amphetamines, strychnine, cocaine, heroin, and most recently erythropoietin (EPO) and blood doping. In 2006 the largest scandal to hit the sport ended in forcing nearly a dozen riders, including two of the favorites, Jan Ullrich and Ivan Basso, to withdraw from the Tour de France when they were implicated in a Spanish probe of doping. The winner, **American Floyd Landis, tested positive for excess testosterone and was sharply criticized although he still claims his innocence and continues to fight the charges**.

Suspicion of drug-enhanced performances continues to plague the sport of cycling. Lance Armstrong, the 35-year-old cycling phenom who won the coveted Tour de France title for seven straight years (1999–2005), was accused many times and is still the target of many accusations. Critics went back to one positive test in 1999 for proof of their suspicions, but a thorough investigation by the International Cycling Federation completely cleared him.

The most important development in regard to drug use in sports was the creation in 1999 of the World Anti-Drug Agency (WADA) and the World Anti-Doping Code as a respected testing and regulatory agency with a strong antidrug policy. The mission of the international independent organization is to "promote, coordinate, and monitor the fight against doping in sport in all its forms." WADA works toward "a vision of the world that values and fosters doping-free sport" (World Anti-Doping Agency, 2006). The code covers such topics as anti-doping rules violations, proof of doping, a list of prohibited drugs, testing standards, results management, sanctions, appeals, and education (Pound, 2006).

The 2004 Olympics recorded 24 doping violations out of more than 3,000 tests. It is hard to say whether the number of drug users is increasing or if the increased testing is simply catching more violators. The 2006 Winter Olympics had stricter and more-sophisticated testing policies and techniques than ever before, and this seemed to limit the use of banned substances and the number of violations.

Commercialization of Sports

Beginning in the 1970s, the excellence of an athlete's performance mattered less and less. With televised sporting events, the explosive growth of professional sports, larger and larger salaries, and big money for commercial endorsements of products, the public's attitude changed from respect for athletic excellence to envy of athletes' salaries and an expectation that for that kind of money they had better be win-

ners. **Many coaches echoed this attitude of winning at any cost.**

"Winning is not the most important thing, it's the only thing."
Vince Lombardi, coach, Green Bay Packers, 1956–1964

Over the past 30 years, **the social and financial pressures to win have encouraged athletes to try drugs as a way to gain an advantage**. "Do what you have to but just win, baby, win" became our society's most common advice to athletes. Many athletes earn more from endorsements than from playing sports, making winning even more crucial in their minds.

Extent of Abuse

At the beginning of the twenty-first century, some athletes continue to use and abuse substances that cover a wide and diverse range of drugs and chemicals, many of which are not psychoactive but are being misused in the context that they are taken. The actual extent of the problem is hard to judge as **athletes are reluctant to admit use because that would get them suspended or expelled from sports, make them an undesirable spokesperson for a product, or force them to surrender a world record**.

In the past, when many performance-enhancing drugs were legal, use was

extremely high. In the 1970s a large percentage of National Football League (NFL) players admitted to using amphetamines regularly. A 15-year study published in 1985 reported that 20% of college athletes said they had used anabolic steroids compared with 1% of nonathlete students, though anecdotal evidence in football and other strength sports suggests that the numbers were much higher. The number of people using performance-enhancing substances has dropped because of increased drug testing (National Collegiate Athletic Association [NCAA], 2003A&B).

"There is a misconception that athletes use drugs [other than steroids] more than the rest of the college student body and that's not true. The studies show that student-athlete use of drugs is actually at a level less than the rest of the student body."
Frank Uryasz, former director, NCAA Sports Sciences

In 2006 it was estimated that at least 200,000 junior high and high school students had tried steroids (University of Michigan, 2006); this figure shows a 50% drop from just four years earlier. Another report indicates that as collegiate testing for steroids becomes more stringent, **young athletes are encouraged to bulk up on them during**

TABLE 7–4   NATIONAL COLLEGIATE ATHLETIC ASSOCIATION (NCAA) SURVEY OF DRUG USE BY STUDENT-ATHLETES

| | ERGOGENIC DRUG USE | | | | | | | |
| | Amphetamines | | | Anabolic Steroids | | | Ephedrine | |
Men's Sports	**1985**	**1993**	**2001**	**1985**	**1993**	**2001**	**1997**	**2001**
Baseball	8.1%	1.7%	2.7%	3.5%	0.7%	2.3%	3.3%	3.3%
Basketball	4.4%	0.7%	1.4%	3.6%	2.6%	1.4%	1.4%	3.0%
Football	10.1%	2.9%	4.2%	8.4%	5.0%	3.0%	5.3%	3.4%
Tennis	10.7%	0.0%	2.2%	3.6%	0.0%	0.6%	2.9%	3.8%
Track/field	3.5%	1.1%	1.4%	4.7%	0.0%	1.2%	2.4%	2.8%
Women's Sports								
Basketball	10.8%	1.0%	2.0%	0.8%	0.4%	0.7%	1.8%	5.6%
Softball	10.9%	4.7%	3.9%	0.8%	0.4%	0.8%	1.1%	2.5%
Swimming	7.8%	4.7%	3.3%	1.0%	0.8%	1.3%	0.5%	3.4%
Tennis	11.3%	2.5%	2.7%	0.0%	0.3%	0.0%	1.9%	2.6%
Track/field	4.9%	2.1%	1.6%	1.2%	0.6%	0.6%	0.9%	1.8%

(NCAA, 2003A&B)

high school and then go clean when they get to college. This is particularly disturbing because anabolic steroids stunt bone development and disrupt hormonal function in adolescents.

To understand the physical, mental, legal, and moral consequences of drug use in sports, it is necessary to examine the drugs themselves. Although there are literally hundreds of drugs and techniques that are used in connection with sports, we have focused on the most used and abused. The three categories of drugs used in sports (therapeutic, performance-enhancing, and recreational or mood-altering) are based on athletes' motives and the context in which use occurs more than the pharmacological properties of the substances.

THERAPEUTIC DRUGS

These are **drugs used for specific medical problems**, usually in accordance with standards of good medical practice, and they fall into four main groups:

◊ analgesics (painkillers) and anesthetics,

◊ muscle relaxants,

◊ anti-inflammatories, and

◊ asthma medications.

Analgesics (painkillers) & Anesthetics

These drugs are normally used to deaden pain. They include both **topical anesthetics** that desensitize nerve endings on the skin (alcohol and menthol or local anesthetics, such as procaine and lidocaine) and **systemic analgesics**, such as aspirin, ibuprofen, and acetaminophen (Tylenol®) for mild-to-moderate pain or narcotic (opioid) analgesics for moderate-to-severe pain. The most common opioids used in sports are **hydrocodone (Vicodin,® the most prescribed)**, meperidine (Demerol®), morphine, codeine, and propoxyphene (Darvon®). These drugs are either ingested or injected. Besides the pain-killing effects, opioids can cause sedation, drowsiness, dulling of the senses, mood changes, nausea, and euphoria.

"Pain is something you can play with. Everybody experiences pain at one time

When injured, athletes who continue to compete by masking the pain with drugs can aggravate the injury.
© 2003 CNS Productions, Inc.

· ·

in their life or another, and your body's just telling you something. Injury is a totally different situation. You don't participate when you're injured."
Bob Visgar, strength coach, California State University, Sacramento

For athletes, **the biggest danger from these drugs results from their ability to block pain without repairing the damage**. Normally, pain is the body's warning signal that some muscle, organ, or tissue is damaged and that it should be protected. If those signals are constantly short-circuited, the user becomes confused about what the body is saying. In addition, because tolerance develops so rapidly with opioids, increasing amounts become necessary to achieve pain relief. The problem is that **tissue dependence can develop**, along with the analgesic effects, making it easier for the user to slip into compulsive use.

Muscle Relaxants

Muscle relaxants are drugs that depress neural activity within skeletal muscles. They are used to treat muscle strains, ligament sprains, and the resultant severe spasms and to control tremors or shaking. Some athletes also use them to control performance anxiety. This class of drugs includes skeletal muscle relaxants, such as carisoprodol (Soma® and Vanadom®) and methocarbamol (Robaxin®), and benzodiazepines, such as diazepam (Valium®) or clonazepam (Klonopin®) (Arnheim & Prentice, 1993; Brukner & Khan, 2002).

As with analgesics, the performance enhancement of these drugs is minimal because the drugs are depressants and can also cause sedation, blurred vision, decreased concentration, impaired memory, respiratory depression, and mild euphoria especially if overused. Skeletal muscle relaxants are **occasionally abused for their mental effects, particularly carisoprodol. It is used to enhance the effects of other drugs and when taken in large doses it causes giddiness, drowsiness, and relaxation. There have been a number of overdoses and deaths from overuse** (McCutcheon, 2005). Benzodiazepines have a higher dependence liability because accelerating use causes tolerance and tissue dependence. The benzodiazepines also stay in the body for a long period of time, causing prolonged and even undesired effects.

Anti-Inflammatory Drugs

These drugs control inflammation and lessen pain. Anti-inflammatory drugs come in two classes. One class is **nonsteroidal anti-inflammatory drugs (NSAIDs)**, typically aspirin, ibuprofen (Motrin® and Advil®), indomethacin (Indocin®), phenylbutazone (Butazoliden®), sulindac (Clinoril®), rofecoxib (Vioxx® [no longer available]), and celecoxib (Celebrex®). Even these drugs can cause problems. Aspirin and ibuprofen can cause ulcers and renal problems, whereas Vioxx® has been withdrawn from the market because of cardiovascular problems. Celebrex® is recommended only for arthritis and osteoarthritis, not sports injuries, and is required to have a black-box warning about potential heart and gastrointestinal problems.

The other class of anti-inflammatories is **corticosteroids, such as cortisone and Prednisone®** (corticosteroids are different than androgenic-anabolic steroids, described below) (Physicians' Desk Reference [PDR], 2006). **With corticosteroids, side effects are a significant consideration.** Prolonged use can cause water retention, bone thinning, muscle and tendon weakness, skin problems such as delayed wound healing, vertigo, headaches, and glaucoma. Psychoactive effects are minimal at low doses, but severe psychosis results from excessive high-dose use.

As with analgesics and skeletal muscle relaxants, athletes using anti-inflammatory drugs must be carefully examined to ensure that the injury is not serious and that practice or play can continue without risk of aggravating the injury. Anti-inflammatories should not be used solely to enable the athlete to resume activity but **should be part of the overall healing process.** Ice, elevation, rest, physical therapy, and other treatment measures must accompany pharmacological relief of pain and inflammation.

Asthma Medications (beta$_2$ agonists)

At the 2004 Summer Olympics in Athens, 4.2% of the 10,653 athletes who competed received permission to use a beta$_2$ agonist for asthma. This is down from 5.7% of the athletes at the 2000 Summer Olympics at Sydney (Anderson, Sue-Chu, Perry, et al., 2006). Perhaps the stricter rules about drug use made a difference.

Asthma affects 10% of the general population and is aggravated by heavy exercise in sports that require continuous exertion (e.g., cycling, rowing, and middle- to long-distance running). It is also aggravated by the excess stress that comes from preperformance anxiety. A lesser condition, exercise-induced asthma (EIA), has been identified. **The incidence of EIA is 11% to 23% in athletes** (Rupp, Brudno & Guill, 1993; Fuentes & DiMeo, 1996). Because asthma is so widespread in ath-

letics, permission to use certain asthma medications is granted. Other beta$_2$ agonists used to control asthma include clenbuterol (banned in sports) and albuterol (limited use in sports). Beta$_2$ stimulation also increases muscle energy and growth but to a lesser extent than steroids. Asthma medications like ephedrine are stimulants and are therefore banned in sports. These drugs can slightly increase oxygen intake by bronchodilation that is helpful to the asthmatic. Other asthma medications such as theophylline and cromolyn are allowed by both the IOC and the National Collegiate Athletic Association (NCAA) (Rosenberg, Fuentes, Wooley, et al., 1996).

ANABOLIC STEROIDS & OTHER PERFORMANCE-ENHANCING (ergogenic) DRUGS

"If steroids didn't work, athletes wouldn't use them."

Don Catlin, M.D., director, UCLA Olympic Laboratory (on Costas Now, HBO)

Most performance-enhancing drugs, substances, and techniques are banned by the various sports-governing bodies especially the International Olympic Committee and the National Collegiate Athletic Association. These ergogenic and energy-producing drugs, substances, and techniques are used to build muscles, increase stamina, enhance self-image, and boost confidence and aggression.

Anabolic-Androgenic Steroids (AAS or "roids")

"It's a performance-enhancing drug. I mean, that's what it did: it enhanced my performance. There were a few side effects, but for the most part I had pretty good results from them as far as gaining strength and power."

21-year-old college weightlifter

The most abused performance-enhancing drugs today, **anabolic-androgenic steroids (AASs), are derived from the male hormone testosterone** or synthesized. *Anabolic*

means "muscle building," *androgenic* means "producing masculine characteristics," and *steroid* is the chemical classification of the natural and synthetic compounds resembling hormones like testosterone and cortisone. AASs are used clinically to treat testosterone insufficiency, delayed puberty, wasting diseases, osteoporosis, certain types of anemia, some breast cancers, endometriosis, and a few other conditions (Lukas, 2003).

For the athlete these drugs have marked benefits that include **increased body weight, lean muscle mass, muscular strength, and, to a lesser extent, stamina. Psychologically, increases in aggressiveness and confidence** are of value in sports like football and baseball. First isolated in 1935, testosterone and some early derivatives were given to German troops to increase their combat effectiveness. Ironically, it was also given to concentration camp survivors to help them regain weight and muscles on their emaciated bodies (Kochakian, 1990).

Many students use AASs strictly to enhance personal appearance. A much higher level of dissatisfaction with body image (e.g., feeling too small or weak looking) is often found in AAS users, especially body builders and those who developed a dependence on the drugs. Many females also exhibit dissatisfaction with their body image. As with any drug that's misused, less desirable side effects occur. So far no pharmacological process has been able to separate the desirable muscle-building properties of AASs from their undesirable or dangerous hormonal side effects.

"The men I knew who used steroids, most were 5 feet 8 inches and under, and they talked about how they were the runts of the class and the 98-pound weakling at the beach. Steroid use is one way they felt they could overcome that."

Ex-weightlifter

Patterns of Use. AAS users may take 20 to 200 times the clinically prescribed daily dosage. Instead of 75 to 100 mg per week, weightlifters, bodybuilders, wrestlers, and other illicit users have taken 1,000 to 2,100 mg

Meyer's Take by Tom Meyer

YOU WANT SOME HUMAN GROWTH HORMONE?

NEW BASEBALL DRUG POLICY

WHAP WHAP WHAP

per week (Yesalis, Herrick, Buckley, et al., 1988; Mottram, 2002). Some athletes practice **steroid stacking** by using three or more kinds of oral or injectable steroids and by alternating between cycles of use and nonuse.

"Basically, I go on about 10 weeks, then I'll go off for a little while. So I would kind of cycle it to where it would peak me out at a certain time in the season."
24-year-old weightlifter

Cycling steroids means taking the drugs for a four- to 18-week period during intensive training, then stopping the drugs for several weeks or months to give the body a pharmacological rest, and then beginning another cycle. Some athletes cycle to escape detection. Studies have reported that **82% of athletes using "roids" during a training cycle combined three or more different anabolic steroids** in that time, and 30% used seven or more.

Physical Side Effects.   In men the initial masculinization effect includes

an increase in muscle mass and muscle tone. Many physicians believe that this increase causes a much **higher incidence of ruptured tendons and damaged ligaments**. Most users also report an initial bloated appearance. Long-term use results in **suppression of the body's own natural production of testosterone**. As a consequence **long-term male steroid users develop more-feminine characteristics** (e.g., swelling breasts [gynecomastia], nipple changes, decreased size of sexual organs, and an impairment of sexual functioning) (Pope & Katz, 1994). In the *Sports Illustrated* interview, Ken Caminiti said he used steroids so heavily that his testicles shrank and retracted and his body stopped producing its own testosterone. It took four months after stopping for his testicles to drop on their own (Sports Illustrated, 2002B).

In females similar gains in muscular development may be considered beautiful by some, but **long-term use by women results in masculinizing effects**, increased facial hair, decreased breast size, lowered voice, and clitoral enlargement. **Many of these masculin-**

ization effects in women are largely irreversible.

"With women, I've seen a change in the facial jaw line—their voices too. There are definitely things that, as a woman, are not in your favor. And the lasting results too are something that I often wonder why a person chooses to go that route."
Female bodybuilder

In both men and women, **severe cystic acne is common** (about half of users in several studies). It is also believed that more-rapid balding is a consequence of steroid abuse.

Although **AASs can be taken orally, by adhesive patch, as a topical gel, or via an implant, of special concern is the fact that up to 99% of "roid" users have injected the drug**; most increase their dosage during the course of their training, making them susceptible to blood-borne infections, including AIDS and hepatitis B and C.

Cardiovascular changes in steroid abusers are also of great concern. For example, changes in serum lipids (fats in the blood) are reflected by increases in the levels of LDLs (bad lipids), decreases in the levels of HDL (cardioprotective lipids), and increases in the cholesterol-to-HDL ratio (Eisenberg & Galloway, 2005). There have also been a great number of cases of unexpected cardiovascular problems, including hypertension, thrombosis, and cardiomyopathy. The higher blood pressure caused by AASs could be aggravated by fluid retention that results in a need for diuretics.

The role of AASs in causing cancer has been demonstrated in a number of studies particularly because one of the effects of testosterone is to encourage cell growth.

Mental & Emotional Effects. Anabolic-androgenic steroids do make users feel more confident and aggressive, but as use continues **emotional balance starts to swing from confidence to aggressiveness, to emotional instability, to rage, to hypomania, to depression, to psychotic symptoms, and to paranoia**. This condition is known as **"roid rage"** and often progresses to irrational behavior (Pope & Katz, 1994).

"After a dinner date, this one guy attacked me in my apartment. He was in the middle of a 'roid' cycle. I put up a great fight, and he gave up, but if he was determined, there was no way I could have overpowered him. I don't know if it was the drugs or he was just crazy."
Female college student

"Roid rage" is more likely to occur in people who already have a tendency toward anger or who take excessive amounts of steroids. One study of 12 steroid-using bodybuilders compared with a control group found much higher tendencies toward paranoid, schizoid, antisocial, borderline, histrionic, and passive-aggressive personality profiles due to use. Before steroid use the two groups were about equal in regard to abnormal personality traits (Cooper, Noakes, Dunne, et al., 1996). Violent behavior does occur in some users with no prior violent behavior or other risk factors; however, even in those with a previous history of violence, **when not using, the aggression usually disappears.**

Compulsive Use & Addiction. Unlike most psychoactive drugs, **AASs are not generally used for their immediate psychoactive effect but rather for longer-term gains.** About one-third of users, however, do experience a sense of euphoria or well-being (at least initially) that contributes to their continued and compulsive abuse of steroids.

Various surveys of weightlifters found complaints of **distinct withdrawal symptoms indicative of dependence and abuse.** Withdrawal symptoms include craving, fatigue, dissatisfaction with body image, depression, restlessness, insomnia, headaches, no desire to eat, and a lack of sexual desire (NIDA, 2000B). Even between training cycles, users will continue with low doses to avoid withdrawal. As with other drug use, compulsive use of steroids makes the user more likely to use other psychoac-

tive drugs to enhance performance, as a reward, or in social situations.

"It was addicting, mentally addicting. I just didn't feel strong unless I was taking something. When I retired, I kept taking the stuff. I couldn't stand the thought of being weak."
Lyle Alzado, former NFL star (deceased)

Researchers have tried to determine whether the compulsive use of steroids is due to the mental effects of increased confidence or if a biochemical dependence develops. In animal experiments where confidence was a moot point, researchers found that dependence did develop and that dopamine blockers in the nucleus accumbens did negate that craving (Wood, 2004).

Do Steroids Work? In 1984 the American College of Sports Medicine stated that **steroids can increase muscle mass and strength when combined with diet and exercise.** A 1996 double-blind study by Dr. Shalender Bhasin of Charles R. Drew University in Los Angeles involving 43 male volunteers showed large measurable increases in strength and weight due to steroids. When steroid use was combined with exercise, the gains in muscle size and strength were significantly greater (Bhasin, Storer, Berman, et al., 1996). What the study didn't cover was the use of multiple steroids and of excessive amounts of steroids over long periods of time.

"I took steroids from 1976 to 1983. In the middle of 1979, my body began turning a yellowish color. I was very aggressive and combative, had high blood pressure and testicular atrophy. I was hospitalized twice with near kidney failure, liver tumors, and severe personality disorders. During my second hospital stay, the doctors found I had become sterile. Two years after I quit using and started training without drugs, I set six new world records in power lifting, something I

thought was impossible without the steroids."
Richard L. Sandlin, former assistant coach, University of Alabama (U.S. Congress, 1990)

Supply & Cost. Athletes obtain steroids in different ways: on the black market (through gyms, friends, mailorder companies or over the Internet) or illicitly from doctors, veterinarians, or pharmacists. **Serious users spend $200 to $400 per week** on anabolic steroids and other strength drugs, so a single cycle can cost thousands of dollars. Some professional athletes spend $20,000 to $30,000 per year. At a conservative estimate, the black market for steroids grosses $300 million to $500 million per year (NIDA, 2000A). Most of the product comes from underground laboratories in the United States and foreign countries.

"We all knew who was using. We exchanged information on any new drugs that were on the market. We got our steroids through the gym owner. In fact, he would inject them for us in the rear."
28-year-old weightlifter

Evaluation & Testing. Several signs of AAS abuse are visible: **overdeveloped muscles, bloating, changes in facial appearance, needle tracks in muscles, severe acne, overdeveloped breasts, excess hair in women, unexplained aggression, unusual injuries** (muscles, ligaments, or tendons), thin abdominal skin folds, tight hamstrings, excess sweating, overconfidence, and euphoria. **Blood and urine testing** and occasionally hair and saliva analyses are becoming increasingly more sophisticated as abusers try to outwit the testing agencies. Besides testing for specific substances, laboratories can **test for changes in body chemistry** (e.g., hemoglobin, cholesterol, and lutenizing hormone) that will indicate abuse of AAS drugs.

Major League Baseball owners and players finally agreed on a new drug policy that includes a 50-game suspension for a first positive steroid test, a 100-game suspension for second positive test, and a lifetime ban

TABLE 7–5   ANABOLIC-ANDROGENIC STEROIDS

Chemical Name (DEA schedule)	Trade Name
U.S. Approved	
Adanazol (no schedule)	Danocrin® (tablet or capsule)
Boldenone undecylenate (Schedule III)	Equipoise® (injection)
Fluoxymesterone (Schedule III)	Halotestin® (tablet or capsule)
Methyltestosterone (Schedule III)	Android,® Metandren,® Testred,® Virilon® (tablet or capsule)
Nandrolone phenpropionate (Schedule III)	Durabolin® (injection)
Nandrolone decanoate (Schedule III)	Deca-Durabolin® (injection)
Oxandrolone (Schedule III)	Oxandrin® (tablet or capsule)
Oxymetholon (Schedule III)	Anadrol-50® (tablet or capsule)
Stanozolol (Schedule III)	Winstrol® (tablet or capsule)
Testolactone (Schedule III)	Teslac®
Testosterone cypionate (Schedule III)	Depo-Testosterone,® Virilon IM® (tablet or capsule)
Testosterone enanthate (Schedule III)	Delatestryl® (injection)
Testosterone propionate (Schedule III)	Testex,® Oreton Propionate®
Tetrahydrogestrinone (illicit)	"THG"
Veterinary	
Boldenone (Schedule III)	Equipoise®
Mibolerone (Schedule III)	Cheque Drops®
Stanozolol (Schedule III)	Winstrol-V®
Trenbolone (Schedule III)	Finaplix Gold®
Zeranol (Schedule IV)	Ralgro®
Not U.S. Approved	
Bolasterone	Finiject 30®
Ethylestrenol	Maxibolan®
Gestrinone	Dimetrose®
Mesterolone	
Methandrostenolone	Dianabol® (tablet or capsule)
Methenolone	Primobolan®
Methenolone enanthate	Primobolan Depot®
Norethandrolone	Nilexor®
Oxandrolone	Anavar®
Oxymesterone	Oranabol®

Other anabolic steroids or agents on the IOC and NCAA lists of banned substances include clostebol, metandienone, metenolone, -19-norandrostenediol, -19-norandrostenedione, clenbuterol, dromostanolone, dehydrochlormethyltestosterone, and dehydroepiandrosterone (DHEA). (Adapted from Eisenberg & Galloway, 2005)

for a third positive test. By contrast this new drug policy stipulates that the first positive *stimulant* test calls for additional testing, the second for a 25-game suspension, the third for an 80-game suspension, and the fourth is at the commissioner's discretion. **Until 2005 there was no testing for amphetamine use in Major League Baseball.**

The National Football League enforced penalties for steroid and illegal drug use long before the most recent Major League Baseball agreement. However even then players who were intent on chemically improving their performances developed strategies to avoid detection.

"As soon as they found out that something could be tested for, I stopped taking it. I didn't want that embarrassment but I pushed that envelope ethically and morally because if I could take something that would help me perform better and it wasn't on the list, I was going to take it."

Bill Romanowski, NFL linebacker (49ers, Eagles, Broncos, Raiders), 1988–2003

Even the sport of competitive bicycling has problems with steroids. The 2006 Tour de France champion, American Floyd Landis, tested positive for testosterone and synthetic testosterone and was sharply criticized by the Tour de France governing body.

STIMULANTS

In some sports such as football, the use of stimulants is more widespread than the use of steroids. **Central nervous system stimulants often start out as performance boosters, but the basic pharmacology of most stimulants often makes use self-defeating.** The IOC and all other sports organizations have banned the use of any kind of amphetamine and most other strong stimulants in competition. Stimulants used in sports include methamphetamines, diet pills, methylphenidate, ephedrine, caffeine, nicotine, occasionally cocaine, and some herbal or dietary supplements.

Amphetamines (amphetamine & methamphetamine)

"As a pitcher, I won't ever object to a sleepy-eyed middle infielder 'beaning up' [using amphetamines] to help me win. That may not be the politically correct spin on the practice, but I really couldn't care less."

David Wells, Major League pitcher

Amphetamines are referred to as *sympathomimetics* because they mimic the stimulation of the sympathetic nervous system, that part of the nervous system that controls involuntary body functions, including blood circulation, respiration, and digestion. Some athletes use amphetamines (meth, Adderall,® and "crank") as a way of getting up for competition. Initially, many users feel energetic and alert. Athletes also take amphetamines to make them more aggressive and confident. Some take them after an event to sustain the competitive high. Studies have shown that amphetamines will increase strength by 3% to 4% and endurance by 1.5% in low doses (Rosenberg, Fuentes, Wooley, et al., 1996). Other studies have shown that **much of the** increase in performance comes from the focusing effects of amphetamines and the increase in aggressiveness rather than specific muscular changes as seen with anabolic steroids. Improvement seems to be in complex tasks that require concentration.

Tolerance to amphetamines develops quite rapidly, and the beneficial effects of the drug diminish as tolerance develops. Negative effects include anxiety, restlessness, and impaired judgment. In some cases amphetamine users (e.g., football players) can overreact to plays and literally overrun the action. The increased aggressiveness caused by amphetamines can get out of hand, causing injury to the users and their opponents. Physically, **heavy use can bring on heart and blood pressure problems, exhaustion, and malnutrition**. There have also been reports of fatal heat stroke among athletes because these strong stimulants redistribute blood away from the skin, thereby impairing the body's cooling system (Mottram, 2002). Mentally, high-dose use can bring on paranoia and even amphetamine psychosis.

Amphetamines can be detected up to four days after use by the gas chromatography/mass spectrometry testing procedure. A newer procedure that can test for a number of amphetamine-like compounds is liquid chromatography/mass spectrometry (Deventer, Van Eenoo & Delbeke, 2006).

Caffeine

This mild stimulant is found in coffee, tea, cola-flavored beverages, and cocoa. It also comes in tablet form and can be very toxic in high doses. It increases wakefulness and mental alertness at blood levels of 10 milligrams per milliliter (mg/mL) by stimulating the cerebral cortex and medullar centers. It also **increases endurance slightly during extended exercise** and increases muscle contraction (Spriet, 1995). The increased endurance supposedly comes from its ability to increase the body's fat- and sugar-burning efficiency and reduce the sense of fatigue. Various studies have demonstrated this increased endurance. Unfortunately, side effects such as increased digestive

secretions (that can cause stomach discomfort) or increased urination (and possibly dehydration) can also occur and limit performance (Weinberg & Bealer, 2001).

The IOC puts a limit on caffeine of 12 mg/mL—about three strong cups of coffee—just before competition (International Olympic Committee [IOC], 2006). Some athletes had been using a combination of caffeine, ephedrine or ephedra (sales have been restricted), and aspirin to try to increase endurance even though the cardiovascular effects can be risky.

Ephedra (ma huang) & Ephedrine

Ephedra (ma huang), a mild stimulant, is a traditional Chinese herb that **comes from the ephedra bush. The active ingredients are ephedrine (a bronchodilator) and, to a lesser extent, pseudoephedrine (a nasal decongestant)**, substances that can also be synthesized in laboratories. Ephedra contains about 6% ephedrine. **Ephedra and ephedrine used to be found in hundreds of legal over-the-counter cold and asthma medications. They were also used in some herbal teas, energy drinks, energy bars, energy pills, and especially diet medications.** Ephedra and ephedrine have been used both by themselves and in combination with other mild stimulants (e.g., kola nut and guarana, both of which contain caffeine) to supposedly increase strength and endurance and/or promote weight loss.

Ephedra and ephedrine are used to treat asthma and upper respiratory infections because they ease bronchial spasms and relieve swelling in mucous membranes. For dieters they suppress appetite and stimulate the thyroid gland. When taken in excess or by susceptible individuals, they **can cause jitteriness, anxiety, headaches, high blood pressure, cardiac arrhythmia, poor digestion, and overheating** (Hespel, Maughan & Greenhaff, 2006).

A sharp increase in the use of ephedrine in sports coupled with the publicity over the recent deaths of a few athletes forced the Food and Drug Administration (FDA) to warn 24 manufacturers of ephedra products to stop

their various marketing campaigns aimed at athletes. The FDA also proposed labels warning that ephedra can cause heart attacks and strokes and even kill. Two years later the FDA banned ephedra in dietary supplements. In 2005 a court reversed the ban, but the FDA continued to stand by its own ruling (Thiessen, 2005). In an analysis of reports to the American Association of Poison Control Centers, ephedra and ephedrine accounted for 64% of herb-related adverse reactions in 2001, a figure that is startling because only 1% of herbal products sold back then contained ephedra (Bent, Tiedt, Odden, et al., 2003).

Ephedrine is banned by the NFL, the IOC, and the NCAA, but so far not by the National Basketball Association, the National Hockey League, or Major League Baseball. As a result of the deaths of some athletes, however, ephedra and ephedrine were banned in the minor leagues and players will be tested for the drug. In addition, the players' union sent a warning notice to its members about use of the drug. The NFL Players Association says that football players need dietary supplements and unfortunately many that have been used contained ephedrine (Wood, 2002). In urine testing for ephedrine and methylephedrine, the limit is 10 micrograms per milliliter (g/mL); for pseudoephedrine and phenylpropanolamine, the limits are 25 g/mL (IOC, 2006).

Tobacco

The nicotine in cigarettes is a **mild stimulant, but it does little for performance except perhaps increase alertness**. Like other stimulants, nicotine constricts blood vessels thus raising blood pressure. After the mild stimulation, it often acts as a relaxant. Unfortunately, smoking reduces lung capacity thus hindering performance and endurance.

Smokeless tobacco (spit tobacco) has many of the same effects as cigarettes except for the reduction in lung capacity. **Chewing tobacco was a mainstay of baseball** dugouts, and the image of the baseball player with a large wad of 'chew' in his cheek, spitting in the dugout, was common. Fortunately, it has become less popular partly due to an increasing number of players who speak out about their health problems over the years due to the habit (e.g., Brett Butler, the ex-Dodger leadoff man, who underwent surgery for throat cancer that he feels was caused by chewing tobacco). Babe Ruth, who used smokeless tobacco extensively (as well as alcohol, which is a cofactor), died at the age of 51 of an oropharyngeal cancerous tumor in the back of his throat.

"You know the first time you try chewing tobacco, it is absolutely disgusting. You get dizzy because of all the nicotine rushing into your bloodstream. I saw some baseball player from the fifties—he had to have a big old chew in his mouth, so now, like half of his face is gone."
28-year-old weightlifter

In 1994 the NCAA banned the use of all tobacco products during NCAA-sanctioned events. You rarely see smokeless tobacco at Major League games—just chewing gum, sunflower seeds, and beef jerky.

HUMAN GROWTH HORMONE (HGH)

In 2006, 38-year-old Arizona Diamondback pitcher Jason Grimsley was suspended for 50 games for using human growth hormone (HGH). He was also let go from the Diamondbacks after he admitted using HGH and amphetamines to enhance his performance. Federal agents had raided his home during an investigation into performance-enhancing drugs.

Human growth hormone is a polypeptide hormone produced by the pituitary gland that **stimulates growth in children**. It is prescribed medically to correct short statures in children who have an HGH deficiency and for those with a wasting disease such as AIDS to help build their strength. HGH is used illegally by athletes to increase muscle strength and growth because it was thought that its side effects were less damaging than those of steroids. Studies have found that HGH reduces fat by altering lipolytic effects; it also

increases muscle mass, skin thickness, and connective tissues in muscles (Schnirring, 2000). Some studies have found that it has little effect on muscle development in those with normal HGH production. Gigantism and acromegaly (abnormal bone growth) along with **metabolic and endocrine disorders have been widely reported. Abuse is also associated with cardiovascular disease, goiter, menstrual disorders, decreased sexual desire, and impotence** while decreasing life span by up to 20 years (Jacobson, 1990). HGH was once harvested from human cadavers, but techniques for synthesis were developed in 1986. Cadaver HGH usually contains contaminants, unlike synthetic HGH, which is pure. Both the U.S. Olympic Committee (USOC) and the NCAA ban HGH, although it is difficult to detect because it is found naturally in the body. Testing for HGH is done through blood samples and is very expensive.

OTHER PERFORMANCE-ENHANCING DRUGS & TECHNIQUES

Androstenedione & Dehydroepiandrosterone (DHEA)

In a 1998 interview with Mark McGwire, a reporter asked about a bottle of medication on his locker shelf. The first baseman for the St. Louis Cardinals, on his way to smashing the 37-year-old home run record, identified it as androstenedione, **a natural hormone that is a direct precursor in the biosynthesis of testosterone**, the basic male hormone. At the time the so-called dietary supplement was legal in Major League Baseball but banned by the IOC, the NFL, the NCAA, and professional tennis. McGwire said that the supplement merely helped him train longer by energizing muscles but that the real work was the thousands of hours he spent training (Patrick, 1998). In response to his capacity as a role model, in 1999 McGwire announced that he had stopped using the supplement. He still hit 65 home runs in 1999. Unfortunately, six years later his silence about steroid use before the congressional committee greatly damaged his credibility.

Androstenedione is produced in all mammals by the gonads and the adre-

nal glands and is metabolized in the liver into testosterone. In an eight-week study of 20 healthy men with normal testosterone levels, half of the 20 subjects used androstenedione and half used a placebo, but they all did resistance training for the eight weeks. The researchers found no difference in strength between the two groups and no change in testosterone levels; there was, however, a higher level of estradiol, a female hormone, in the group that used the drug as well as an increase in high-density cholesterol (King, Sharp, Vukovich, et al., 1999). The logical conclusion would be that **in people with low testosterone, the substance would increase levels of the male hormone and increase endurance and muscle size, but in those with normal levels, it probably would not**.

DHEA, a somewhat similar hormone, has been tried in an attempt to increase gonadal and peripheral testosterone as well as estrogen production because it is a precursor of those hormones. Over-the-counter sales were banned in 1985. Studies have found little effect from the substance, but it has shown some unwanted side effects such as reduced natural testosterone production and liver damage (Earnest, 2001).

Beta Blockers (propranolol [Inderol®] & atenolol [Tenormin®])

Beta blockers are normally prescribed by physicians to lower blood pressure, decrease heart rate, prevent arrhythmias, and reduce eye pressure. They work by blocking nerve cell activity at the brain, heart, kidney, and blood vessels. They keep adrenaline from binding onto beta receptors on the heart. **Their ability to block nerve cell activity in the brain calms and steadies the body** (Gordon & Duncan, 1991). Beta blockers are also used to control the symptoms of a panic attack or stage fright. Because of their ability to calm the brain and tremors, they are sought by some athletes involved in riflery, archery, diving, ski jumping, biathlon, and pentathlon (Fuentes, Rosenberg & Davis, 1996). Beta blockers are also banned by the IOC and most athletic organizations for specific events.

Meyer's Take by Tom Meyer

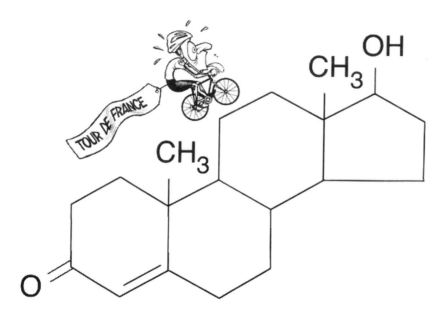

Beta blockers can cause fatigue, lethargy, dangerously low blood pressure, gastritis, occasional nausea, vomiting, and temporary impotence (Provencher, Herve, Jais, et al., 2006). A great danger in the use of these drugs is their potential to intensify some forms of asthma and heart problems that can be fatal to the user.

Erythropoietin (EPO)

Even though American cyclist Lance Armstrong was completely exonerated of using illegal substances like EPO (erythropoietin) after his phenomenal run of seven Tour de France wins, mean-spirited critics still tried to sow suspicion. This most widely used drug in competitive cycling, **EPO is a blood oxygen booster that mimics the human peptide hormone that stimulates bone marrow to produce more red blood cells that carry oxygen to muscles.** It takes two to three weeks after beginning injections for full manifestation of the effects. Drug-testing researchers have developed methods to test blood and urine for use of recombinant protein (rhEPO) as well as EPO analogues (Pascual, Belalcazar, de Bolos, et al., 2004); but experimenters are even now trying to develop artificial red cells and other substances that will increase the oxygen-carrying capability of the circulatory system (Schumacher & Ashenden, 2004).

The dangers from unsupervised EPO administration result from the thickening of the blood that can lead to clots that might cause stroke or heart attack. Sweating, edema, and the accompanying increase in blood viscosity magnify this **potential danger of blood clots.** A number of deaths among European cyclists from blood manipulation have been reported over the past 15 years. EPO is banned by the NCAA, the USOC, and most every other sport agency.

Blood Doping

While not involving a drug, blood doping **does increase endurance by transfusing extra blood to boost the number of red blood cells available to carry oxygen.** Normally about two units of the athlete's own blood or someone else's with the same blood type are withdrawn, frozen to minimize deterioration, and then reinfused five or six weeks later (about one to seven days before competition) after the athlete's blood volume has returned to normal. **Blood doping is used in endurance sports,** usually cycling, long-distance running, and cross-country skiing. Tests have shown that blood doping lowers performance times for a 5-mile race by an average of 45 seconds and a 3-mile run by about 24 seconds (Williams, Wesseldine, Somma, et al., 1981; Goforth, Campbell, Hodgdon, et al., 1982).

Because doping involves blood transfusion, dangers include poor storage, viral or bacterial infections, and even fatal reactions due to mislabeling. Several tests do exist to detect blood doping, but they are expensive and difficult to confirm.

Herbal Medicines

Athletes have used **herbs, animal extracts, vitamins, minerals,** proteins, and any other substance they think will improve their competitive edge; but because of increased scrutiny and more-intense testing, they have had to be extremely careful about which substances they use. **Often some of the ingredients are not listed on the label and could trigger a positive test for banned substances.** Some tests showed that androstenedione is in many supplements but not listed on the label and that minimal exposure caused a positive test (Van der Merwe & Grobbelaar, 2005). Generally, the governing agencies list banned herbal substances. The NFL went further and set up a certification system to make sure that banned substances are not used. Unfortunately, because of the complexity and the cost of the rules, only one company had complied (Weisman, 2005).

In a study of 11 U.S. poison control centers, their hot lines received more than 2,300 calls about dietary supplements. About 500 of the callers had mild-to-severe symptoms that were believed to be caused by the supplements; there were probably many more problems that were never reported. The symptoms reported ranged from seizure, arrhythmias, and liver dysfunction. Four deaths were thought to be supplement related (Palmer, Haller, McKinney, et al., 2003).

One of the most popular supplements used is **creatine, an amino acid that is a nutritional supplement created naturally in the body and also**

found in fish and meat. It is used by athletes to delay muscle fatigue, store energy that can be used in short bursts, extend workout time, and help muscles recover faster. Three pounds of meat contain 5 grams (gm) of creatine. Sales have exploded in recent years. The use of creatine in muscle energy metabolism has been researched for the past 100 years (Rosenberg, Fuentes, Wooley, et al., 1996). Creatine supplementation also **seems to benefit sprint disciplines, such as running, swimming, cycling, and many power sports**. A study in which athletes were given 20 gm of creatine suggests that the supplement helps the body store energy and helps muscles recover faster. The creatine was coupled with six weeks of resistance training, while the control group did only resistance training. In another trial, cyclists increased their endurance from 30 minutes to 37 minutes. The substance is very effective during very intense workouts (Becque, Lochmann & Melrose, 2000; Okudan & Gokbel, 2005).

"It gives you energy so your muscles don't get tired and just takes away some of the soreness that enables you to work out longer and harder."
College football player

The overuse of creatine by athletes has been shown to produce some dehydration, stomach cramps with nausea and diarrhea, as well as muscle pulls, strains, and damage, although a recent study downplayed the actual damage (Watson, Casa, Fiala, et al., 2006). Also there is an increasing concern that creatine causes undue stress on the kidneys.

"The greatest danger that I see with nutritional supplements is that there's the tendency of athletes to try to overuse them to compensate for other things. For example, if a certain supplement supposedly works at one dosage, a lot of times an athlete will take two or three times that because they think that will give them more of an effect."
Lawrence Magee, M.D., director of sports medicine, University of Kansas

Because it is classified as a nutritional supplement, **creatine is sold over the counter and is not yet banned by any sports agency**.

Gamma-hydroxybutyrate (GHB)

This supplement was sold in the 1980s and the early 1990s as **a fat burner, an anabolic agent, a sleep aid, a muscle definer, a plant-growth supplement, and a psychedelic**. It was touted as an amino acid that acts like a diuretic to reduce anabolic steroid water-weight gain and raised levels of HGH as well. Abuse at raves and other parties has become more widespread, accounting for a number of visits to emergency rooms because of excess use that can cause respiratory depression, amnesia, occasionally coma, and a dramatic slowing of the heart rate. GHB has also been used by sexual predators as a date-rape drug. It is now a Schedule III drug (Xyrem®) for treatment of muscle weakness (*see Chapter 4*).

Soda Doping

Some athletes believe that ingesting alkaline salts (sodium bicarbonate) about 30 minutes prior to exercise **delays fatigue by decreasing the development of acidosis**. It seems somewhat effective for shorter events (30 seconds to 10 minutes) rather than for endurance activities (Rosenberg, Fuentes, Wooley, et al., 1996). Its use can cause diarrhea, while the 5 gm of salt in an ergogenic dose (10 times the daily requirement) can cause excess water retention.

Weight Loss

Attaining a specific weight is necessary or strongly desired in a number of sports, especially wrestling, gymnastics, and horse racing (jockeys usually weigh less than 125 lbs.). Athletes trying to make their weight will **use diuretics, laxatives, exercise, fasting, self-induced vomiting, and excess sweating** in a sauna. This is done in spite of the evidence that dehydration significantly diminishes performance. Some athletes will lose 3% to 5% of their total body weight in a couple of days.

"We can definitely see that gymnasts are worried about their weight. I mean

we walk around in leotards and we still say we're fat and there's probably not an ounce of fat on any of our bodies."
19-year-old college female gymnast

Besides dieting and exercise, **stimulants are used to control weight**, e.g., diet pills (prescription and over-the-counter), illegal amphetamines, tobacco, and caffeine. After a few months of continuous use, most diet pills and amphetamines don't work as well, and the rising tolerance and the development of tissue dependence can trigger abuse and addiction. Many amphetamine addicts started using the drug to lose weight. **Bulimia (eating and purging) and anorexia (starvation eating) can also result from the desire to stay thin or make a weight.** The NCAA recently changed training rules for wrestlers as a result of an increasing number of injuries and deaths due to dehydration and excessive weight loss. Wrestlers are not allowed to use any mechanism for shedding weight during training. The NCAA also allowed greater flexibility in weight, permitting up to a 7 lb. variance in the listed weight categories.

The flip side of anorexia is a newly defined disorder called *muscle dysmorphia*, a preoccupation with body development: no matter how sculpted his body is, the athlete looks in a mirror and still sees himself as a 98 lb. weakling, so he continues to lift weights and often take supplements and steroids.

Diuretics (e.g., furosemide [Lasix®], ethracrynic acid, and toresemide) are also extensively used to lose weight. These drugs increase the rate of urine formation thus speeding the elimination of water from the body. Athletes use these drugs:

◇ **to lose weight rapidly**, which is important in those sports where people compete in certain weight classes;

◇ **to limit the bloating caused by steroids;**

◇ **to avoid detection of illegal drugs** during testing by increasing urination; and

◇ **to lose weight to look thinne**r.

The main danger from diuretics is dehydration, which when coupled with exercise can lead to heat stroke and organ damage.

"I was given a diuretic a week before I was to compete, with instructions not to drink more than a half cup of water per day. I probably lost 12 lbs. of water that week. I left the dorm the morning of my competition, and my neighbor across the hall didn't recognize me because my face was so drawn. I wouldn't have placed second if the gym owner hadn't given me the diuretic."

Competitive wrestler

Miscellaneous Performance-Enhancing Drugs

◊ **Adrenaline and amyl or isobutyl nitrite.** This combination is taken by weightlifters just prior to competing to increase strength. The downside includes dizziness (a dangerous side effect with a 400 lb. barbell over one's head), rapid heartbeat, and hypertension.

◊ **Bee pollen.** This supplement is sold in pellets that consist of plant pollens, nectar, and bee saliva that contain 30% protein, 55% carbohydrates, some fat, and minerals. The anecdotal reports claim that it increases energy levels and performance, boosts immunity, relieves stress, and improves digestion. Most scientific studies, however, do not show any performance or energy benefits. Bee pollen it is not banned by the IOC or the NCAA (IOC, 2006).

◊ **Calcium pangamate.** This nonvitamin (its deficiency is not linked to any disease), also called "vitamin B_{15}" or "pengamic acid," supposedly keeps muscle tissue better oxygenated, but this desired effect is supported by testimonials rather than scientific research. It is reportedly a carcinogen.

◊ **Cyproheptadine (Periactin®).** Used for colds and allergic reactions, this antihistamine (serotonin and histamine antagonist) is believed to cause weight gain and increase strength. Some users believe that this prescription drug acts like steroids, but in fact the increase in muscle size comes from excess caloric intake caused by serotonin's effect on appetite. Side effects include decreased performance, sweating, and sedation.

◊ **Darbepoetin (Aranesp®).** Designed to treat chronic anemia, this drug boosts the amount of oxygen in the blood. By the 2002 Winter Olympics, a test was developed to detect this drug in urine. One Spanish and two Russian cross-country skiers tested positive, forcing forfeiture of their medals.

◊ **Human chorionic gonadotropin (HCG).** HCG, clomiphene, or tamoxifen is occasionally used after anabolic steroid treatment to try to restart the body's own testosterone production. Clomiphene and tamoxifen also block the effects of estrogen in men (e.g., gynecomastia) after anabolic steroid use. Toxic effects on the liver and reproductive system have been reported.

◊ **Modafinil (Provigil®).** This prescription drug, used to treat narcolepsy, acts as a stimulant. People who used THG (tetrahydroges Trinone), a banned steroid, thought that modafinil would mask the use of that drug.

◊ **Ornithine and arginine.** These amino acids are taken to try to increase muscle mass because they supposedly cause the release of growth hormone. High doses can lead to kidney damage.

◊ **Primagen.** This drug increases steroid production in the body and is mainly used by European athletes.

◊ **Vitamin B_{12}.** This vitamin is injected supposedly to ward off illness and provide extra energy. It's also used to mitigate the effects of heavy drinking.

Athletes, like many people, enjoy the excitement of playing and winning and want to recreate that high off the field. Some use alcohol, meth, and other psychoactive drugs to get that feeling.

RECREATIONAL/MOOD-ALTERING USE OF DRUGS BY ATHLETES

Many of the more common psychoactive drugs, legal and illegal, are used to enhance performance as well as **to adjust moods, help the user fit into social situations, comply with peer pressure, imitate the behavior of older role models, or conform to one's image of an athlete**. Athletes may also turn to drugs to help **cope with the demands of a heavy schedule** (practice, travel time, course work), to reduce stress, to compensate for loneliness, or to fill up time on long road trips.

"I don't think you could find too many college programs—basketball programs, football, track, any sport— that their athletes don't drink. And I'm sure that there are a lot of people who smoke weed too."
21-year-old college basketball player

Stimulants

Many stimulants, such as amphetamines, caffeine, and tobacco, are used not only to enhance performance but also for recreation. The **advantages and the problems with these drugs are the same as with use by nonathletes** (*see Chapter 3*).

Cocaine, one of the strongest stimulants, isn't often used as a performance enhancer for two reasons. First, it is short acting (30 to 60 minutes), so one would have to reuse during the game for a consistent effect; second, the rapid rebound depression is too intense and will impair performance unless the cocaine can be used every 30 minutes or so.

"When you have played before 70,000 people and come off the field, you're back down to normal, so to speak. You want to get back up there with cocaine. It replaces that high with an artificial stimulation. But the comedown from cocaine is very, very draining, emotionally, physically, and nutritionally. It's totally different than coming down from the natural high."
Delvin Williams, former NFL rushing back, recovering cocaine user

Sedative-Hypnotics

Some athletes use drugs such as alprazolam (Xanax®), barbiturates, and even opioids as self-rewards for enduring the stress of performing before so many people. They also use these drugs as a tranquilizer **to unwind after the excitement of competition** or to counteract the effects of stimulants used to enhance performance. Depressants are counterproductive as a performance enhancer, although their painkilling effects can keep athletes performing even while injured.

Alcohol

"We were 16 and 17 years old, and our club coach told us, 'If you can go get hammered the night before the game and still come out and play awesome and play to your maximum performance, go ahead. But if you can't, and you know your body, and you know you won't be able to play well enough if you get drunk the night before, don't do it.'"
20-year-old college soccer player

In general, **alcohol can negatively affect reaction time, coordination, and balance**, although studies suggest that low-dose alcohol consumption does not produce impaired performance in all people. The NFL drug policy states that alcohol is "without question the most abused drug in our sport." The problem is how to alert athletes to the health and performance consequences of a drug that has general social, legal, and moral acceptance in society.

"When [athletes] have a problem with alcohol or marijuana, things of that nature, you'll see a decline in their academics. You'll see a decline in athletics. You just see a decline in everything. And we see it as coaches,
and the players see it, so we try to address it right away."*
Patti Phillips, college women's soccer coach

The NCAA specifically bans alcohol for riflery competition. The USOC does not ban it, however, because it does not generally enhance performance. The problems with alcohol in sports are its **excess use as a reward for performance, its use as a way to unwind, and its use as a consolation prize**. Excess use causes the same problems in athletes as are found in the general population. A survey by the NCAA found similar levels of drinking among student-athletes as among the general populace, but one study found a five-times-greater incidence of acquaintance rape involving athletes; alcohol was involved in most of the cases (Bausell, Bausell & Siegel, 1994).

"Women are more vulnerable sexually when they've had too much to drink. They're more likely to be raped, date-raped, or otherwise. Study after study has shown that. Male athletes, when they've had too much to drink, tend to become extraordinarily aggressive."
Judith Davidson, Ph.D., athletic director, California State University, Sacramento

Alcohol is generally not tested for unless the athlete exhibits abuse and addiction problems. Unfortunately, student-athletes are less likely than other college students to seek help for substance abuse problems, especially alcohol, from treatment professionals in their university community.

Marijuana

Marijuana can either stimulate or depresses the user depending on the strength of the drug and the mood of the smoker. The most consistent effect of marijuana use is an increase in pulse rate of about 20% during exercise (Arnheim & Prentice, 1993). **In general, marijuana hinders, not helps, performance.** Marijuana:

◇ lowers blood pressure, which has caused fainting spells in football linemen who have to go quickly from a down position to a standing one many times during a game;

◊ inhibits sweating, which has caused heat prostration and strokes in athletes;

◊ impairs the ability of users to follow a moving object like a ball in play (decreased tracking ability);

◊ hinders the ability to do complex tasks, such as hitting a golf ball;

◊ diminishes hand/eye coordination;

◊ decreases oxygen intake because the drug is smoked;

◊ is a banned substance that will result in a one-year suspension from any NCAA sport; and

◊ is illegal and can destroy an athlete's career.

Because marijuana is extremely fat-soluble and lasts so long in the body, **impairment can persist for a day or two after casual use and longer after cessation of chronic use**.

In a study at a major university, athletes who admitted using marijuana thought they were doing well and performing well; but in an objective study of their performance, those who smoked marijuana did much worse—they dropped more passes, committed more errors, and suffered more injuries during their college careers.

Currently, the NCAA bans all marijuana use more for ethical and moral reasons than for performance reasons. The IOC also bans marijuana use. Its testing cutoff level is 15 nanograms per milliliter (ng/mL) compared with a higher cutoff level (25 to 50 ng/mL) for job or treatment testing

TESTING

In an effort to reduce the use of illicit drugs in sports, various **drug-testing programs have been instituted by sports organizations and even individual colleges**. The NCAA has two drug-testing programs. The first, started in 1986, tests at all NCAA championships and at postseason football bowl games. The second is a year-round anabolic steroid testing program that started in 1990. Banned drugs—including anabolic steroids, diuretics, beta blockers, alcohol, methamphetamines, most street drugs, and even high

levels of caffeine—can be therapeutic, performance enhancing, and recreational. The first positive test causes the student to lose eligibility for one year, and a second positive test means a permanent loss of college eligibility. In a survey of NCAA schools, only 56% of the respondents had an alcohol/drug education program for student-athletes. Three-fourths of the respondents said they refer student-athletes with problems to community agencies (NCAA, 2003A&B).

Testing for the Olympics over the years has generated much controversy. In 1999 the IOC reached agreement on the creation of the World Antidoping Agency to coordinate drug-testing programs, intensify research, create educational programs, and publish an annual list of banned substances (Pound, 2006).

As street chemists become more knowledgeable, they develop ergogenic drugs (such as THG) faster than they can be detected. **THG** is a banned steroid (made famous by the baseball drug scandals) that had been tweaked by chemists from BALCO to make it undetectable by normal dope tests. Now that there is a test, some sports agencies are testing older samples from previous Olympics and world championships that had been preserved.

ETHICAL ISSUES

Using illegal drugs and using drugs illegally to improve athletic performance is, by definition, against the rules in all sports and is illegal in most states. **Drugs undermine the assumption of fair competition on which all sports rest**, and they violate the very nature of sport, which since the time of the ancient Greeks was a measure of personal excellence, the result of a sound mind in a healthy body. The public wants the outcome of athletic contests to be determined by discipline, training, and effort.

There is a real threat today that **the public will turn away from sports if they perceive that winning is based on access to the latest pharmacology** and schemes to evade drug testing. This is already happening in baseball, where reports of steroid, HGH, and stimulant use abound. Many baseball fans want asterisks on any records that occurred between 1987 and 2005.

Drugs can also rob the athlete of feelings of self-accomplishment and tarnish the pride of winning. Because our society treats sports figures as heroes and role models, drug-abusing athletes diminish all of us.

"If I could take a drug and set the world record out of reach for everybody and the tradeoff would be I would be dead in five years, I definitely wouldn't do it. I mean because to me, why is it so important? I want to have a chance to grow old and play with my grandkids and my great-grandkids."
Allen Johnson, 1996 Olympic gold medalist, 110-meter hurdle

MISCELLANEOUS DRUGS

UNUSUAL SUBSTANCES

It's amazing what substances and methods some people will use to get high. They include smoking aspirin; chewing dandelion root; drinking gasoline, rubbing alcohol, or hydrogen peroxide; putting Ambesol® (topical anesthetic) in the eye; and smoking toad secretions.

Other psychoactive substances are provided by street chemists, who either synthesize drugs that were once legally available, such as Quaaludes® and phencyclidine (PCP), or produce illegal drugs, including MDMA, MDE, and methcathinone (synthetic khat). The danger is that street drugs have not been tested and are not made under any kind of control. Irregular doses, incomplete chemical reactions, or contaminants in the manufacturing process can have disastrous effects on an unsuspecting user.

Gasoline

A few people have been known to mix gasoline with orange juice and drink it in spite of the toxicity of leaded or unleaded gasoline. Users call it "Montana gin," a particularly lethal beverage. Most often gasoline fumes are inhaled for their effects.

Embalming Fluid (formaldehyde)

Mortuaries have been broken into and robbed of their embalming fluid. It can be either directly abused **(inhaled for its depressant and psychedelic effects)** or used in the manufacture of other illicit drugs. Some abusers soak marijuana joints or cigarettes in the fluid and smoke them. Called "clickers," "clickems," "fry," "wet," or "illy," the mixture gives a PCP-like effect. PCP is sometimes mixed in with the fluid in the joint. Effects include visual and auditory hallucinations, a feeling of invincibility, pain tolerance, anger, paranoia, and memory problems. The effects last from six hours to three days (Loviglio, 2001; Klein & Kramer, 2004). Formaldehyde, a known carcinogen, also contains methanol, ethanol, and other solvents. It has also been used in the illicit manufacture of methamphetamine.

Raid,® Hairspray & Lysol®

Abusers puncture the aerosol cans, draining out the liquid that they swallow mainly for its alcohol content. These items are rarely abused in the general population but find more use in rural, isolated areas where access to alcohol is limited. Recently, inner-city youths have been spraying Raid® onto marijuana and rolling it into a joint. It is said to intensify the effects of marijuana; this combination is called "canaid."

Kava

Kava is made from the roots of the *Piper methysticin* plant, which is found on the islands of the South Pacific (Oceana) and in South America. The roots are chewed or crushed into a soapy liquid and drunk. This milky exudate of the root contains at least six chemicals, such as alpha-pyrones, that **produce a drunken state, similar to that of alcohol, when used in large quantities.** Users claim that the effects of smaller quantities are more pleasurable and relaxing than the effects of alcohol, without the hangover. Kava is used as an antianxiety drug much as a drink of alcohol is used in rest homes to relax the elderly clients. In fact, one of the sites of action in the brain is the same one affected by benzodiazepines.

Antianxiety effects are found at the 70 mg level, whereas 125 to 250 mg induces sleep and 500 mg or more can induce drunkenness and stupor.

Kava is also sold as an herbal supplement to relieve anxiety, stress, and insomnia. In 2000 kava in pill form became popular, bringing in about $30 million in sales. There have been a few reports of liver damage, especially in those with preexisting liver problems. One theory is that the use of the root in commercial preparations, not in traditional preparations, added a more toxic substance to the mix.

In the Fiji Islands, kava is served in coconut shells as a welcome libation for visitors. The cup is passed around, and no business is discussed until the relaxing effects of the drink make everyone amenable to reason. Visitors unfamiliar with the drink find the taste somewhat unpleasant and numbing to the lips and tongue. In addition, because human saliva is an important ingredient in the preparation of this drug, its use has not found popularity in other cultures.

Camel Dung

Some Arab countries produce hashish by force-feeding ripe marijuana plants to camels. Their four-chambered stomachs convert the marijuana into hashish camel dung.

Toad Secretions (bufotenine)

The *Bufo* genus of toads (Colorado River, Sonoran Desert, Cane, and others) secretes a psychedelic substance from pores located on the back of the neck. This substance, bufotenine, is milked and smeared onto cigarettes that are then smoked to induce a psychedelic experience.

HERBAL PREPARATIONS & SMART DRUGS/DRINKS

Herbal Preparations

For thousands of years, herbal preparations and other natural "cures" were the only medicines available. Their effectiveness was real and highly valued, but some of those curative effects came from the spiritual power given the substances by healers, medicine men, *curanderas, brujas,* and

the power of faith. As the science of pharmacology advanced along with the science of testing (clinical studies to see if the drugs or herbs worked), some of the mystique and "placebo power" of these substances diminished. Unfortunately, some of this loss of faith in traditional herbal medicines was replaced with an overreverence for the scientific approach even though many modern medications are based on herbal preparations (e.g., aspirin from the bark of the willow and digitalis from the foxglove plant). In addition, a number of modern medications turned out to have severe side effects that became evident only after a long period of time or that were downplayed by the manufacturer. Fortunately, good herbal medicine is making a strong comeback in the West, with many medical schools and clinics integrating herbal medicine and acupuncture into their standard curriculum.

One problem with substances that have not been rigorously tested is that **some marketing and sales departments overpromote the healing properties of their products** much to the dismay of the research department. In recent years rigorous testing of many herbal supplements has shown that a number of the advertising promises outstripped actual benefits. Preparations such as Saint-John's-wort, echinea, saw palmetto, glucosamine chondroitin, and even vitamins ($4.1 billion in annual sales) are not the panaceas they were touted to be (Caruso, 2002; Torassa, 2002; Helmich, 2006; Marchione, 2006).

Another point of concern is that some herbal preparations have been found to contain prescription drugs such as Valium® or indomethacin (Indocin®), nonlabeled fillers that can have deleterious effects, and, in a few cases, known carcinogens. In addition, Internet sites have expanded the public's access to these substances with very little quality control. Preliminary warnings are becoming more common as more and more substances call themselves "food additives" rather than "herbal medications" to avoid regulation. The FDA seized 20 different products from an importing company that made false health claims about its dietary supplements (U.S. Food and Drug Administration, 2003). In 2003 the FDA proposed standards for labeling so that at the very least the user is getting the substances that arc listed on the bottle and nothing else.

Smart Drugs/Drinks & Nootropics

"Smart drugs" are the drugs, nutrients, drinks, vitamins, extracts, and herbal potions (e.g., ginseng, gingko biloba, and caffeine) that manufacturers, distributors, and proponents think will boost intelligence, improve memory, sharpen attention, increase concentration, detoxify the body (especially after alcohol or other drug abuse), and energize the user. **They are also promoted as natural, healthy, and legal substitutes for club drugs or other illegal substances.** Popular smart drugs have included Cloud 9,® Brain Tonix,® Brain Booster,® Nirvana,® SAMe® (S-adenosyl-L-methionine), Helicon,® and Sention,® among others. Proponents range from AIDS activists to health faddists, New Agers, anti-aging seekers, and members of the technoculture who feel they are on the edge of a new field of mental development.

A number of smart drinks are non-alcoholic mixtures of vitamins, powdered nutrients, and amino acids in a fruit drink, purchased in a "smart bar" for $4 to $6. More recently, smart drugs and drinks have contained combinations of medications usually prescribed for Parkinsonism, Alzheimer's disease, or dementia. It is believed that these drugs more effectively rebalance the brain after abusing drugs. **It is also claimed that they will slow or reverse the aging process.** The consumers are typically young (age 17 to 25) urban students or professionals looking for an intellectual edge or more stamina to work or party harder.

Critics of these products attribute their success to either a placebo effect (only the expectation and not the product produces the effect) or to the caffeine, ephedra (ma huang), and sugar that are among the ingredients. Especially when taken in high doses, smart drugs containing stimulants could lead to problems for someone with high blood pressure or a heart condition or in those prone to stroke.

Investigation of New Age smart drugs such as hydergine, selegiline, vasopressin, 5HT, modafinil, piracetam, and oxiracetam has led to the proposal for a **new classification of these drugs as *nootropics*.** Substances in this new psychotropic drug class would be those that **improve learning, memory consolidation, and memory retrieval** without other CNS effects and with low toxicity, even at extremely high doses (Dean & Morgenthaler, 1991; Buccafusco, 2004). The theory is that nootropics work by increasing the brain's supply of certain neurotransmitters such as acetylcholine, increase the brain's supply of oxygen, or stimulate nerve growth (Wikipedia, 2006). One main proposed mechanism of nootropics and other smart drugs is that they enhance the conversion of short-term memories to long-term memories (Rubin, 2004).

Americans import nootropic drugs from Europe, where many can be purchased that are not yet approved by the FDA for sale in the United States. Critics of these and other prescription drugs, including researchers, doctors, and the FDA, point out that, at the very least, claims of the drugs' efficacy have not been substantiated. Advocates argue that these and other smart drugs improve mental ability for people suffering from debilitating mental disorders and that they can enhance mental capacity in normal people too. Nootropic drugs include those prescribed for some mental or medical disorders (but not FDA approved for the nootropic uses that are advocated) (Erowid, 2006).

OTHER ADDICTIONS

COMPULSIVE BEHAVIORS

"If you're a drug addict, or a food addict, or an alcoholic, or a sex addict, it's not about the addiction, it's about all the other things in your life that you're doing."

36-year-old recovering compulsive overeater

Compulsive gambling, overeating, shopping, sexual behavior, Internet use, and TV watching, along with pathological lying, shoplifting, hair pulling, and fire setting—all offer opportunities for **repetitive compulsive behaviors.** Some of these disorders are classified as impulse-control disorders (e.g., compulsive gambling and hair pulling) whereas others have their own classification (e.g., eating disorders). Some people confuse impulse-control disorders with obsessive-compulsive disorders.

The hallmark of **impulse-control disorders** as listed in the *DSM-IV-TR* diagnostic manual is a **failure to resist an impulse that is harmful to the individual or others but often starts out as pleasurable.** The other major hallmark is an increasing sense of tension or arousal before actually committing the act, often followed by gratification, pleasure, relief, and then remorse and guilt over the consequences of that act (McElroy, Soutullo, Goldsmith, et al., 2003).

The hallmark of **obsessive-compulsive disorders**, including hand washing, checking things, ordering, counting, and praying, is **repetitive activities whose goal is to reduce anxiety or distress caused by obsessive thoughts, not to provide pleasure or gratification though they can relieve stress** (APA, 2000).

Addictive behaviors alter brain chemistry in much the same ways as psychoactive drugs do.

"Every thought we have, every single thought we have, every action we do has an impact on the brain. I mean the brain in some ways causes it, but then the thought or the behavior actually loops back and impacts the brain, so you can actually get a high from a

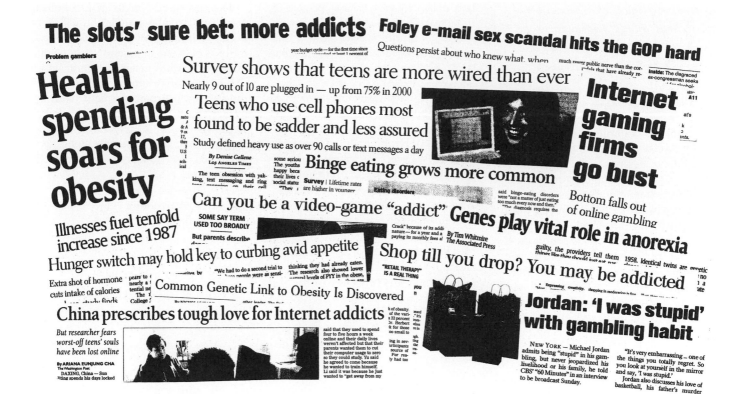

The slots' sure bet: more addicts

Foley e-mail sex scandal hits the GOP hard

Questions persist about who knew what, when

Health spending soars for obesity

Survey shows that teens are more wired than ever

Nearly 9 out of 10 are plugged in — up from 75% in 2000

Teens who use cell phones most found to be sadder and less assured

Study defined heavy use as over 90 calls or text messages a day

Internet gaming firms go bust

Illnesses fuel tenfold increase since 1987

Binge eating grows more common

Bottom falls out of online gambling

Can you be a video-game "addict"　**Genes play vital role in anorexia**

Hunger switch may hold key to curbing avid appetite

Shop till you drop? You may be addicted

Common Genetic Link to Obesity Is Discovered

Jordan: 'I was stupid' with gambling habit

China prescribes tough love for Internet addicts

---

sexual act, you can get a high from the excitement that comes from stealing things, you can get a high from being in a gambling environment, which is likely related to dopamine, and people then start to chase the high."

Daniel Amen, M.D., director, Amen Clinic for Behavioral Medicine

The reasons why people engage in compulsive behavior are the same reasons why they engage in compulsive drug use: to get an instant rush, to forget problems, to control anxiety, to oblige friends, to self-medicate, and so forth. Above all, they desire to change their mood—to alter their state of consciousness.

At the Department of Radiology at Massachusetts General Hospital, functional MRI scans of the brain showed that the same areas of the brain activated by abusing drugs were also activated while gambling or anticipating a desired food. The same regions of the brain (i.e., nucleus accumbens, extended amygdala, and orbitofrontal cortex) that responded to the prospects of winning and losing money while

gambling responded to the use of cocaine in cocaine addicts (Breiter, Aharon, Kahneman, et al., 2001).

It is instructive to **compare the major hallmarks of drug addiction with those of compulsive behavioral addiction**.

Drug users:

◇ use and think about using most of the time (**compulsion**);

◇ need greater amounts of the drug with continued use (**tolerance**);

◇ experience symptoms when abstinence begins (**withdrawal**);

◇ continue to use despite adverse medical, social, family, and legal consequences (**abuse**);

◇ do not accept that they have a problem (**denial**); and

◇ have a strong tendency to use again after quitting (**relapse**).

If one takes these elements of drug addiction and replaces the word *using* with the words *eating, gambling, surfing the Internet, shopping, watching TV,* or *having sex,* it is easier to see that compulsion isn't limited to psychoactive substances.

Compulsive gamblers:

◇ are always playing a poker machine, buying lottery tickets, trying to raise money, or thinking about where they are going to gamble (**compulsion**);

◇ feel the need to increase the bet amount whether it's at a slot machine or a poker table (**tolerance**);

◇ feel intensely restless and discontent when not gambling (**withdrawal**) (Rosenthal & Lesieur, 1992);

◇ continue gambling though they lose most of their paycheck each month to slot/poker machines, lotteries, or table games (**abuse**);

◇ think they can control their gambling and that their only real problem is cash flow (**denial**); and

◇ will gamble again, even after weeks of abstinence, particularly if they have money in their pockets (**relapse**).

"Food does for me what alcohol and drugs and other things do for other people. If I'm feeling angry and I eat, it takes the anger away. If I'm feeling

lonely or sad and I eat, it takes care of the feelings. If I feel inadequate or empty, I fill myself with food, or I used to. I don't do it anymore. It's just a drug to me."
36-year-old recovering compulsive overeater

Another example of the relationship between compulsive drug use and compulsive behaviors is that 12-step groups such as Gamblers Anonymous and Overeaters Anonymous use concepts and literature taken directly from Alcoholics Anonymous. Even the structure of the meetings is similar as is the philosophy that tries to get people to understand that **addiction involves lack of control over the behavior and tries to make them see the necessity of changing their lifestyle and beliefs** (Nakken, 1996).

"I have to work on my behavior. How do I act with my husband? How do I act with my children? How do I act in relationships? My addiction carries over to all that—carries over to my whole life. So I had to change the way I treat people, the way I treat myself."
36-year-old recovering compulsive overeater

HEREDITY, ENVIRONMENT & COMPULSIVE BEHAVIORS

Like substance abuse, **compulsive behaviors can be triggered by genetic predisposition, by environmental stresses, and by the repetitive behavior itself.** Increased dopamine levels in compulsive gamblers, overeaters, and shoppers suggest a common biochemical thread.

HEREDITY

Studies of twins have already identified a genetic connection to alcoholism and drug addiction. **Other twin studies and nuclear family studies have also shown a connection between heredity and compulsive behaviors that don't involve psychoac-**tive drugs (Hudson, Lalonde, Berry, et al., 2006; Rankinen & Bouchard, 2006). For example, recent discoveries show a relationship between 5HT serotonin function and binge-eating disorder (Monteleone, Tortorella, Castaldo, et al., 2006).

In fact, compulsive overeating was the first addiction shown to be partly hereditary. A study by the National Institutes of Health of 400 twins over a period of 43 years found that **"cumulative genetic effects explain most of the tracking in obesity over time."** This means that a much higher-than-normal percentage of twins born to obese parents but subsequently raised in totally different households ended up obese. The researchers also found that **"shared environmental pressures were not significant"** in affecting the twins' weight gain (Bouchard, 1994). Five studies of adopted children bolstered this finding by discovering that the family environment—such as the size and the frequency of meals, the amount of food in the house, and the level of exercise of the family—plays very little or no role in determining the obesity of children. They found that **only dramatic environmental differences could mitigate the influence of a genetic profile that made one susceptible to obesity.** Twin studies of risk takers have also found a genetic component that resulted in a higher percentage of children of risk takers being risk takers themselves.

By the mid-1990s genetic connections between alcohol abuse, compulsive drug use, and other compulsive behaviors were being confirmed by research efforts. Kenneth Blum, Eric Braverman, David Comings, John Cull, (researchers at various universities), and others have postulated a genetic basis not only for alcoholism but for people with other addictive, compulsive, and impulsive disorders, such as compulsive overeating, pathological gambling, attention-deficit disorder, and Tourette's syndrome (compulsive verbal outbursts or strong muscular tics). They call this genetic predisposition the "reward deficiency syndrome" (Blum, Cull, Braverman, et al., 1996; Blum, Braverman, Cull, et al., 2000).

Specifically, their studies indicate that **a marker gene associated with** the most severe forms of alcoholism also has a strong association with several addictive compulsive behaviors. This is only one of several yet-to-be discovered marker genes that indicate an imbalance of certain neurotransmitters in the reward/reinforcement pathway. They found that, whereas this marker gene (DRD$_2$ A$_1$ allele gene) appears in only 19% to 21% of nonalcoholic, nonaddicted, and noncompulsive subjects, it exists in:

◇ 69% of alcoholic subjects with severe alcoholism;
◇ 45% of compulsive overeaters;
◇ 48% of smokers;
◇ 52% of cocaine addicts;
◇ 51% of pathological gamblers;
◇ 76% of pathological gamblers with drug problems; and
◇ 45% of people with Tourette's syndrome.

In addition, a study of children with attention-deficit disorder found that 49% had the marker gene compared with only 27% of the control group (Blum, Braverman, Cull, et al., 2000).

These findings suggest that a biochemical difference or anomaly draws some people to compulsive behaviors. The researchers postulate that **carriers of this A$_1$ allele gene have a deficiency of dopamine receptors in the reward/reinforcement pathway.** This dopamine receptor site deficiency means that activities that normally give people a surge of satisfaction, pleasure, and satiation by releasing dopamine do not give that same level of satisfaction to people who lack receptor sites. Such people are more likely to seek out substances and activities that release additional dopamine (e.g., alcohol, drugs, or repetitive compulsive behaviors). **The release of extra dopamine caused by repetitive compulsive behaviors stimulates the reward/reinforcement pathway to a greater degree than normal.** People with this lack of receptors suddenly feel pleasure that they normally don't experience.

It is important to note that **there isn't just one marker gene for compulsive drug use and compulsive behaviors.** This is because there are several neurotransmitters involved that can alter the reward/reinforcement sites in the brain (*see Chapter 2*). For example, in the urine and spinal fluid of pathological gamblers, researchers have discovered higher-than-normal levels of norepinephrine, the neurotransmitter that produces stimulation, alertness, and confidence. Scientists funded by the National Institute of Mental Health discovered abnormal functioning in serotonin and norepinephrine in acutely ill bulimic and anorexic patients, further suggesting a link between these disorders at the level of neurotransmitters and their brain receptors (Health, 2003).

ENVIRONMENT

It is fairly easy to understand how environment could intensify most compulsive behaviors.

◊ Compulsive gambling is triggered by **an abundance of state lotteries, slot and poker machines, Internet betting, legal off-track betting, and American Indian gambling casinos, along with the growth of gambling** in New Jersey and Nevada.

◊ Compulsive overeating and other eating disorders are aggravated by **plentiful fast-food restaurants, a lack of daily physical activity**, an abundance of fats and sugars in food that can induce craving, parents who overfeed their children, and chaotic childhoods that make people search for ways to calm themselves or overcome depression.

◊ Compulsive sexual activity is made easier by **copious sexual situations in the media**, an abundance of latchkey kids without supervision or close emotional family connections, and an overabundance of easily accessible erotic material and pornography on the Internet.

◊ Internet addiction is fueled by **a rapidly expanding network of games, gambling, and chat rooms** that make compulsive use as easy as turning on the computer. A recent explosive development in this form of compulsive behavior is known as "massively multiplayer

online role-playing game" (MMORPG). These are online video games where a large number of subscription and non-subscription participants can interact with each other (e.g., World of WarCraft® or WOW, and Lord of the Rings Online®). Some 15 million global participants brought in over $1 billion in Western revenues during 2006. Dedicated players will play on-line for 8 hours or more a day, similar to any addiction.

◊ Compulsive shopping has been spawned by **the ease of obtaining credit, a materialistic view of life, the endless barrage of advertisements** and catalogs, 24-hour TV shopping networks urging people to buy, and accessibility to Internet shopping and auction sites.

A history of physical, emotional, and sexual abuse in the lives of many who practice these compulsive behaviors also suggests the importance of environmental conditioning and reinforcement.

PRACTICING COMPULSIVE BEHAVIORS

It is also easy to understand how **engaging in the activity itself can lead to compulsive behavior.**

◊ **Having a big win while gambling** imprints the brain in much the same way as a potent dose of heroin or cocaine does early in one's drug-using career (Shaffer, 1998).

◊ The compulsive eater strains the digestive system with excess food, particularly fats and sugars, and changes the body's chemistry, so **the person eats to change mood rather than sustain life** (Gold & Star, 2005).

◊ The compulsive shopper or collector walking through the mall and spotting an item she/he has to have, phoning the Home Shopping Network® for a piece of Joan River's jewelry, or bidding on a one-of-a-kind doll on eBay, imprints the brain with **anticipation of ownership of a coveted item,**

thereby kindling a surge of pleasure with no regard for financial responsibility or even the need for such an item (Ditmar, Beattie & Friese, 1996).

◊ The sexual compulsive's repeated use of pornography, masturbation, and participation in other **compulsive sexual behaviors can make him or her avoid normal sexual or emotional relationships**.

COMPULSIVE GAMBLING

In 2006 the World Series of Poker in Las Vegas consisted of 45 tournaments involving 30,000 players and more than $100 million in prize money. The main event had more than 8,000 players, 32 hours of live broadcasting, and a grand prize of $12 million (DiMeglio, 2006). The explosive growth of poker (e.g., Texas Holdem, Omaha, and seven-card stud) is just a reflection of the nationwide growth in gambling. Casino gambling revenue climbed to $55 billion in 2005 ($23 billion of that from American Indian casinos), a 49% increase since 2000. Lotteries added $16 billion to state budgets. **U.S. gambling revenues will top $75 billion by 2010, while worldwide revenues from gambling will top $125 billion.**

Gamblers Anonymous (GA), a 12-step recovery program, has a rigorous definition of gambling. GA literature states, "**any betting or wagering, for self or others, whether for money or not, no matter how slight or insignificant, where the outcome is uncertain or depends upon chance or skill constitutes gambling**" (Gamblers Anonymous [GA], 1998). Gambling includes:

◊ poker, blackjack, craps, roulette, and pai gow;

◊ standard slot machines and video poker machines;

◊ horse and dog races;

◊ jai alai;

◊ bingo and raffles;

◊ state-run lotteries and keno games;

◊ sports betting, both legal and illegal;

In Japan a form of pinball called pachinko is extremely popular. Japanese men and women spend endless hours on these machines to win a variety of prizes. Pachinko parlors are as popular in Japan as casinos and slot machines are in the United States.
© 2002 Darryl Inaba

◇ Super Bowl office pools and bets on the golf course;

◇ schoolyard games (e.g., lag pennies, flip coins);

◇ bar games (e.g., liar's dice);

◇ stock speculation such as day trading, commodities, and options; and

◇ Internet gambling.

There are more opportunities for gambling today than ever before, and the sheer availability of all these outlets, mostly legal now, are triggering problem and pathological gambling in greater and greater numbers. **The problems that result from pathological and problem gambling are as severe as any drug-based addiction.**

"You go over it and over it and over it in your mind and say, 'How could you be this stupid? How could you not have any inkling of what was happening to you? How could you be so bright in academia and so stupid in your everyday life?'"
53-year-old recovering poker player

HISTORY

Gambling in Ancient Civilizations

The record of **gambling by Homo sapiens predates recorded history**. Archeologists have unearthed prehistoric gambling bones from 40,000 B.C. called *astragali*, four-sided rolling bones from the ankles of small animals. They were used to make decisions on matters believed to be in the gods' hands (e.g., rain or drought). Six-sided dice made from pottery, wood, or ivory were used as early as 3000 B.C. in Mesopotamia. The ancient Greeks played dice around the time of the Trojan War (1200 B.C.), using bone and ivory dice that resemble today's dice. Dice rollers appealed to Tyche, the goddess of fortune, to improve their luck. Other gaming artifacts, such as throwing sticks, have been found in ancient Britain and Rome and in Mayan ruins in pre-Columbian America (Schwartz, 2006). The casting of lots is recorded in the Bible as a means of ending disputes or distributing property. It also records that **Roman soldiers cast lots for the robes that Jesus wore at the Crucifixion** (Herman, 1984). Even knights of the Crusade gambled at dice in an early version of backgammon that they learned from the Arabs, who had learned it from the Persians.

Along with the desire to gamble came prohibitions against it. An early Indian *Veda* (tale) of gambling woes, *The Gambler's Lament*, written in Sanskrit about 1000 B.C., told of a king who gambled away all his wealth and his wife due to his obsession (Grinols, 2004).

"The dice goad like hooks and sting like whips; they enslave, deceive, and torment. They give presents as children do, striking back at the winners. They are coated with honey—an irresistible power over the gambler."
The Gambler's Lament, 1000 B.C.

Over the centuries many of the upper classes kept gambling from the lower classes; Roman emperors, for example, kept "dicing" to themselves. In later centuries churchmen sermonized against gambling in the Middle Ages, and Louis IX of France made dice illegal in 1255. Henry VIII made public gaming houses unlawful in England because he thought they distracted young men from the art of war. At the beginning of the twentieth century, gambling was considered the leading vice in England.

Thou knowest, Lord, the fell disease.
Has smitten myriads, rich and poor;
The workman's hour, the wealth of ease
Are squandered for the gambler's store.
Palace and cottage, works and mart
Are suffering from the fatal bane;
Prison, asylum, refuge, home,
Are peopled with the victims slain.
"A Leprosy Is o'er the Land," winner of the National Anti-Gambling League's hymn-writing competition, 1905 (Flavin, 2003)

The earliest playing cards date from the eleventh century in Chinese Turkestan. It was the French, in the fourteenth century, who first introduced the cards (ace through king) and suits (club, diamonds, hearts, and spades) that we use today. Other forms of gambling arose, often reflecting the culture of a country.

In Japan *hana fuda* uses cards with pictures of chrysanthemums, storks, and other national symbols. The most common form of gambling in Japan is pachinko, a vertical pinball game with the same popularity as slot machines in the United States. In India betting on cricket matches is big business along with traditional games introduced by the British when India was a colony.

The first slot machines were invented in San Francisco in 1905 by Charles Fey. The symbols started as hearts, spades, and diamonds, changed into the familiar fruits (e.g., cherries and oranges), and now have hundreds of symbols and even the faces of celebrities (Schwartz, 2006).

Gambling in America

Three waves of gambling have swept the United States. The first was from the settling of the United States until the mid-1800s. Lotteries, popular for centuries in both Asia and Europe, were imported in the 1700s to the American colonies, where their proceeds were used to build roads, schools (e.g., Harvard and Yale), hospitals, and other public works (Dunstan, 1999). Betting on horse races, cockfights, and dogfights was popular among gentry and farmers alike. Gambling even financed some of the Revolutionary War, though certain antigambling laws were later passed by a number of the original 13 colonies as corruption and scandal brought lotteries to an end (Clotfelter, Cook, Edell, et al., 1999).

The second wave began at the end of the Civil War in 1865 with the expansion of the western frontier. Riverboat gambling on the Mississippi, saloon card games, roulette wheels, and dice games became part of the lore of the Wild West. But, again, scandals and Victorian morality caused their demise around 1910 (Fleming, 1992).

The third wave began in the 1930s with the legalization of gambling in Nevada and the opening of racetracks in 21 states. New Hampshire rediscovered the state lottery in 1964, but it wasn't until the late 1970s that gambling really took off with the opening of casinos in Atlantic City, the expansion of lotteries to 38 states, off-track betting, riverboat casinos, and finally the legalization of gambling casinos on American Indian lands.

For much of the nineteenth and twentieth centuries, gambling remained popular, though it was considered immoral and preyed on human weakness. Gamblers have also been considered decadent, irresponsible, or insane. But in the past 40 years, **gambling has become a legal, respectable pastime.** By the mid-1990s all states except Hawaii and Utah had established some kind of gambling. In addition, the Indian Gaming Regulatory Act, approved in 1988, had spurred a construction explosion of American Indian-run casinos. By 2005 **more than 220 of the 554 American Indian tribes in the United States collectively had 387 gambling facilities in 28 states.** Gaming revenues from 1988 to 2005 went from $220 million to $25.1 billion, the total being more than that of Las Vegas and Atlantic City combined (National Indian Gaming Commission, 2007).

State-supported lotteries were established through the 1980s and 1990s to supplement tax dollars and generate jobs. From 1974 to 2004, the public increased its wagers on legal gambling from $17 billion to more than $500 billion per year, generating profits in 2004 of more than $65 billion. The revenue is so large that just nine months after Hurricane Katrina devastated the Gulf Coast and destroyed 12 floating casinos in August 2005, three were back in business with more on the way. Some argue that legalized gambling imposes a very regressive tax on low-income gamblers. The poor devote 2.5 times more of their income on gambling than does the middle class (National Research Council, 1999).

"I could be behind on bills for my electric, my rent, whatever . . . telephone, and I'll be, like, 'Well, I don't have the money,' but if I get the urge to go gamble, I'll find a way that day to come up with a couple of hundred dollars. Amazing what you can do."
23-year-old compulsive sports gambler

The growth in gambling has been explosive worldwide. Besides the unfettered expansion of online gambling, many countries and travel destinations are expanding their gambling facilities. Macau on the South China coast recently overtook Las Vegas as the number one gambling market in the world, with 2006 revenues of $6.9 billion. It draws most of its visitors from Mainland China, especially since Portugal ceded the territory back to China in 1999 (Wiseman, 2007). Even in Kazakhstan, a former Soviet republic, casinos are being built to take advantage of the increasing income in developing countries. In cities like Kapchagai and Shchuchinsk in this oil-rich republic, there are at least 132 casinos and 2,000 smaller gaming parlors (Greenberg, 2007). In tandem with the desire to expand revenue from gambling is the concern of citizens that this growth in casinos and gambling will also bring more crime, corrupt the morals of the youth, and inflate housing costs.

Politics of Gambling

Earl Grinols in his fine book *Gambling in America: Costs and Benefits* (Grinols, 2004) dispels many of the myths regarding the economic benefits of gambling to a community and to a state. Gambling interests emphasize the money that will come into a community from outside visitors, the jobs that will be created, and the tax revenues that will be generated. Initially, the construction of the casino does bring in outside revenue, but soon the net flow of money reverses. In a study of Illinois casinos, about 75% of casino visitors came from within 35 miles of the casino and only a few percent from more than 100 miles away. **Each dollar spent at the casino or buying state lottery tickets, playing state-owned slot machines, or betting on keno numbers is a dollar that is only partly recycled into the local community.** Grinols refers to this money as "cannibalized dollars," not fresh infusions of money into the community.

As for state income, Oregon is a good example. The state collects about $380 million from its various gambling enterprises, about 7% of the state budget. Gamblers have to lose three times that amount, however, for the state to get its percentage. As a result, the social and economic costs of the gambling (i.e., embezzlement, lost working hours, unemployment, and state support) add up to $361 million. Despite this, politicians seem addicted to gambling money because they don't have to appear to raise taxes to bring in extra state income. Unfortunately, other tax revenues decline, so the overall benefit to the state is less than advertised. Contributions to political campaigns in most states from gambling interests are as large as are contributions from the tobacco and alcohol industries.

Online Gambling

With the increasing accessibility of the Internet in the 1990s and 2000s, **online gambling exploded**. Revenues from a variety of games, including poker, roulette, dice, and even online slot machines, went from $445 million in 1997 to almost $15 billion worldwide in 2006, half of that from the United States (Wardell, 2006). **In October 2006, Congress passed a law criminalizing the processing of online wagers by U.S. banks and credit card companies.**

"I would wait until my wife was asleep, about one or two in the morning, and I would go into the dining room where the computer was, and I would go to the thumbnail porno pictures or play Texas Holdem online. I'd play for a couple of hours, lose a few hundred dollars, try to go back to bed, and wake up tired for the office. It wasn't until I blew $1,700 at online poker and I got a lousy job evaluation that I tried to get help. Unfortunately, only Gamblers Anonymous was available, but I just celebrated my third GA birthday clean."

28-year-old compulsive gambler/Internet addict

Problem & Pathological Gambling

In classifying compulsive gamblers, the designations *problem gambler* and *pathological gambler* are used.

◊ **Problem gambling** is defined as gambling behavior that causes problems in any department of one's life—psychological, physical, sociological, or vocational.

◊ **Pathological gambling** adds the element of persistence, that is, continual and significant disruption of most departments of one's life.

Another common classification system divides gambling activity into four levels: level 0 are those who have never gambled, level 1 are social or recreational gamblers, level 2 are problem gamblers, and level 3 are pathological gamblers (Petry, 2005).

In reality, because compulsive gambling is a progressive disease, **the only differences between problem and pathological gambling are time and money.** According to estimates, the average problem gambler spends $3,000 per year whereas the pathological gambler loses $11,000 per year (Grinols, 2004). Even when gamblers could be classified as having a gambling problem, however, they often suffer years of losses before seeking help. The average indebtedness of gamblers entering Gamblers Anonymous is $60,000 for women and $100,000 for men. Most have lost track of their lifetime losses, which are often in the hundreds of thousands of dollars.

Losses are relative depending on the gambler's income and resources. Former drug czar William Bennett admits to losing $8 million; golfer John Daly admits to losing more than $50 million in the 1990s; superstar Michael Jordan talks about the millions he lost while still playing basketball; and Larry Flynt, publisher of *Hustler* magazine, plays blackjack for $25,000 or more per hand—but they still have large amounts of money to live on. The lower-income compulsive gambler who loses his paycheck, however, can't pay his rent, put food on the table, or buy gas to get to work.

"I never, 'til I got into desperate trouble at the end, felt that I was a gambler. Never! Never once heard the word compulsive gambling! I'm sure I heard it. Never has that registered yet in my mind. Never heard the

words Gambler's Anonymous. Never! I wasn't a gambler!"

42-year-old male pathological gambler

In the early 2000s, most states had not adequately studied compulsive gambling nor had they established prevention or treatment programs. Only Louisiana, Minnesota, Oregon, and Washington had funded treatment programs. Because of the proliferation of gambling outlets, 17 states now fund some kind of gambling treatment. This is only right because so many **governments encourage gambling and legitimize it.** The gambling industry often sees excess concern over compulsive gambling as an impediment to its growth because **the majority of states' and casinos' gambling income derives from problem and especially pathological gamblers.** One study by Henry Lesieur, a pioneer in the field, found that problem and pathological gamblers lose 10 to 20 times a much as nonproblem gamblers (Lesieur, 2002). In a study in Connecticut, 47% of casino patrons were pathological or problem gamblers even though they comprise less than 5% of the overall population (Bettor Choices. (2007). In Minnesota 2% of the gamblers generated 63% of the state's revenue (Tice, 1993). A study of seven states found that more than half of their revenue came from problem or pathological gamblers, who represented only 1% to 5% of the public at large (Lesieur, 1998).

"Let me tell you the things that I know for sure. I've spent my daughter's college money. I've spent my daughter's future. You want a money amount to it? I know my husband has personally written checks, cashed checks for over $100,000 in the 13 years he's been with me. I know that personally I have gone through . . . I couldn't begin to tell you how much."

35-year-old female recovering gambler

The media directly or indirectly supports gambling by publishing odds, sports scores, players' injury reports, winning lottery numbers, stories of big winners, and ads for gambling excursions. CNN Headline News offers a sports ticker listing running scores across the bottom of the screen. There is also simultaneous picture-in-picture coverage of multiple games.

Fear of betting scandals in the 2006 World Cup soccer championships led members of its governing body, the Fédération Internationale de Football Association, to sign pledges that neither they nor their immediate families would wager on the tournament. The referees who are so crucial to the game's outcome were essentially sequestered for the duration of the tournament.

EPIDEMIOLOGY

There is controversy over estimates of how many compulsive gamblers there are. The confounding factor is that **the sheer availability of gambling outlets has a dramatic effect on the number of pathological and problem gamblers**. In a state like Oregon, the percentage of compulsive and problem gamblers jumped dramatically as 11,000 poker machines, thousands of keno games, scratch-offs in every convenience store, and nine American Indian casinos delivered a chance to place a bet around every corner.

An earlier meta-analysis study at Harvard Medical School estimated that **125 million U.S. adults gamble and, of those, 2.2 million are pathological gamblers and 5.3 million are problem gamblers** (Shaffer, Hall & Vander Bilt, 1999). In addition, there are about 1.1 million adolescent pathological gamblers (National Research Council, 1999; Blume & Tavares, 2005). Another study, by the University of Chicago, estimated the total number of adult gamblers at 148 million, pathological gamblers at 2.5 million, problem gamblers at 3 million, and those **at risk for problem gambling at 15 million** (NORC, 1999). Those numbers have increased since the survey because the number of gambling outlets has grown along with the total amount of money bet. **Male compulsive gamblers outnumber female compulsive gamblers 2 or 3 to 1, although that ratio is changing due to the proliferation of slot machines** (Cunningham-Williams & Cottler, 2001). Women more than men seem to use gambling as a means of escape from depression, traumas, or relationship problems. In Las Vegas almost half the members of Gamblers Anonymous are now women. In addition, minorities seem to have a higher rate of pathological and problem gambling than Whites in the United States (Petry, 2005).

The similarity of gambling to substance addictions is emphasized by the **high rate of other addictions among pathological gamblers** whether they are male or female; other behavioral and substance addictions occur in 25% to 63% of pathological gamblers (NORC, 1999).

"I didn't see that one was just making the other worse. The more drugs and alcohol I did, it seemed that I wanted to gamble more. The more I gambled, if I lost especially, then I wanted to do more drugs."
24-year-old recovering compulsive gambler

A recent major study of co-occurring disorders found that among pathological gamblers 73% had an alcohol problem, 38% had a drug problem, 60% smoked, 50% had a mood disorder, 41% had an anxiety disorder, and 60% had a personality disorder (Petry, Stinson & Grant, 2005). One confounding factor about co-occurring drug and gambling addictions is that gambling often becomes a problem when the person abstains from his or her other addiction.

"In our Gamblers Anonymous groups, many members have eight, 10, or more years of sobriety from alcohol but they replaced their drinking with heavy gambling. A smaller percentage practiced both addictions simultaneously. I know I wanted to stay sober when gambling, so I'd drink tons of coffee."
45-year-old pathological gambler in recovery

A recent trend has been the **increase in older gamblers**. The greatest growth in gambling in the past 20 years has been among those over 65 years old (Gerstein, Murphy & Toce, 1999). One survey of residential and assisted-care facilities found that 16% of their seniors go to casinos at least once a month on

The busiest day at casinos is usually senior day. Casinos often provide free or inexpensive transportation to bring seniors. They know that retirement, the problems of aging, or the empty-nest syndrome tend to draw many seniors to casinos, even those with limited incomes.
Courtesy of the Washington State Council on Problem Gambling

facility-sponsored trips, while the casinos themselves offer day trips to two-thirds of the facilities (McNeilly & Burke, 2001). Senior day is most often the busiest time at casinos.

"The greatest thing that compelled me toward gambling was the fact that I had lost all structure in my life. I just felt like life has come to an end. I am no longer important. I am no longer needed. I have retired. The world is running on just fine without me."
67-year-old recovering female compulsive gambler

College students have a higher rate of pathological/problem gambling than the general population. In a major study, 42% of 10,765 students in 119 different colleges said they had gambled in the past year, but only 2.6% said they gambled weekly or even more frequently (LaBrie, Shaffer, LaPlante, et al., 2003). In contrast, a study in Connecticut, a state with more gambling outlets than most other states, 4% of female students and 18% of male students said gambling led to at least three negative life consequences (e.g., gambled more than intended, couldn't pay bills). Problem-gambling students were more likely to be smokers, heavy drinkers, and marijuana users (Engwall, Hunter & Steinberg, 2004). Among college students, pathological gamblers were absent more often and got lower grades than other students. Even high school students can get caught up in gambling. A Canadian study of grades 7 through 13 found that 5.8% of students met the criteria for past-year problem gambling and an additional 7.5% met the criteria for at-risk gambling (Adlaf & Ialomiteanu, 2001).

CHARACTERISTICS

Besides pathological and problem gamblers, there are several other types.

◊ **Recreational/social gamblers.** These players are able to separate gambling from the rest of their lives; they are the majority of gamblers.
◊ **Professional gamblers.** These gamblers are able to take losses as part of the game. It's a business for

them, and they are able to make a living at it. Professionals used to be few and far between, but with increasing TV coverage, a dramatically larger pool of money, exponentially more tournaments, and lucrative sponsorships, this number is increasing.
◊ **Antisocial gamblers.** These individuals will steal to gamble and have no conscience; they can be compulsive gamblers as well.

There are two subtypes of pathological or problem gamblers: the action-seeker and the escape-seeker (although even action gamblers seek escape). The **action-seeking gambler** is the stereotype: frenetic, excited, and always in action although also wanting to escape.

"More than anything, I just wanted to be a big shot. I didn't care if I was winning or losing or if you saw me go back to the same place day after day after day. Somebody was going to think, 'God, this kid is a high roller or something because he's here every single day.'"
23-year-old recovering action-seeking pathological gambler

The other type that is growing in number, the **escape-seeking gamblers, are often drawn to slot machines**, especially poker machines (they are also called machine gamblers). Unlike a good many action gamblers, these machine players were often responsible people with good jobs who for a variety of reasons (e.g., child leaves home, divorce, retires from job) begin gambling to escape their emotions or just to escape boredom. Many experience the equivalent of a blackout while gambling, where hours pass without conscious awareness.

"There were no feelings. That's why I played it. There were no feelings; blocked all the feelings; blocked all the stress; blocked all the anxiety. There were no feelings."
42-year-old recovering escape-seeking compulsive slot machine player

Like other addictions, pathological gambling is a progressive disorder requiring more gambling episodes and larger bets to engender excitement and relieve anxiety.

Symptoms of persistent recurrent pathological gambling (positive diagnosis with five or more of the following) are:

◊ **preoccupation with gambling** (reliving past gambling experiences, planning future ones);
◊ **gambling with ever-increasing amounts of money**;
◊ **repeated unsuccessful efforts to control, cut back, or stop gambling**;
◊ restlessness and irritability when attempting to control, cut back, or stop;
◊ using gambling as an escape;
◊ attempts to recoup previous losses (chasing);
◊ lying to others to conceal gambling;
◊ illegal acts to finance gambling;
◊ jeopardizing or losing job, relationship, or educational or career opportunity; and
◊ reliance on others to get bailed out of pressing debts (APA, 2000).

A male pathological gambler often begins gambling as an early adolescent. Female pathological gamblers typically begin later in life. Both are more likely than the general population to have a parent who was a problem gambler. One study found that the risk of heavy or compulsive gambling was 65% if the father gambled, 30% if the mother gambled, and 40% if a sibling gambled (Lesieur, Blume & Zoppa, 1986).

Dr. Robert Custer, a clinician at the Brecksville, Ohio, VA hospital treatment unit, the first unit for compulsive gamblers, described three phases of gambling: winning phase, losing phase, and desperation phase. To these three, researchers Henry Lesieur and Robert Rosenthal added a fourth: a giving-up phase.

Winning Phase

Initially, gambling is recreational and pleasurable for the action-seeking gambler. Bets are small and consequences are negligible. The feelings that come from playing and winning or breaking even seem to satisfy the gambler.

"For me it was a rush, you know— nothing like alcohol, nothing like anything I've ever experienced. It was nervousness yet excitement; and if you won, you know, the excitement turned into happiness. If you lost, you didn't feel too good unless there was another race to bet on and you had more money."

23-year-old recovering sports gambler

Skills improve and the gambler becomes more confident and even overconfident in his or her abilities. The winning phase can last one year or 10 years. A winning phase doesn't really exist for escape gamblers (such as poker machine, slot machine, keno, bingo, and lottery players) if they play on a regular basis. They will have days where they win, but overall they will lose. For them a good day is breaking even while staying in action for hours at a time. **The key to escape for all gamblers is to stay in action as long as possible—winning is secondary.**

Early on, for 70% to 80% of both action and escape gamblers, **there was a big win that fueled the craving to gamble.** The amount could have been anywhere from a few hundred to tens of thousands of dollars; it's all relative. The big win to the gambler is like the first intense rush to the cocaine or heroin user—never forgotten and forever chased.

"I had a winning phase that lasted me for probably 12 to 15 years, and I actually lived on my gambling. I thought I was a semiprofessional but I still did it in the closet."

42-year-old male recovering compulsive gambler

A gambler with a susceptibility to compulsion **begins to devote more time and wager more money.** Stakes increase from nickel-and-dime poker, to $5 or $10, to table-stake games, while blackjack goes from $2 a hand to $20 on two different hands; sports bets escalate from $5 on the Super Bowl to $100 on 10 different football games on the weekend. A $2 bet on the favorite at the racetrack ends up with $20 on the trifecta and $100 on every other race. Day traders start by depositing $500 to cover their trades and soon up it to tens of thousands of dollars if they have a run of luck, good or bad. The player comes to rely more and more on the high to deal with undesired moods and relationships or other problems.

"The longer you could stay in action, for me anyways, the more I could escape from the reality of what my life really had become."

43-year-old recovering action-seeking gambler

They begin to believe in luck and magic to solve their problems. **They remember their wins and minimize their losses.** Their self-esteem is boosted by their gambling ability and, for action gamblers, the camaraderie of other gamblers. Gambling increases heart rate significantly, and it remains elevated during gambling; cortisol (the stress hormone) also increases (Meyer, Hauffa, Schedlowski, et al., 2000).

Losing Phase

"I would talk less and less to the people around me. I would play for hours and hours and hours till I was practically in a stupor. We don't stop to eat; we don't stop to drink anything; we don't stop to go to the bathroom; we don't leave the machine for an instant."

63-year-old female recovering pathological gambler

A losing phase for both action and escape gamblers often starts with **a losing streak that is inevitable due simply to the laws of chance**; but if the gambler's tolerance has increased and he is betting large sums, the suddenness of heavy indebtedness can be startling. **They try to recoup their losses, and they begin chasing their money.** A sports gambler may listen to three or four games simultaneously, while a compulsive stock or commodities speculator may call for quotes frequently or be glued to a quote screen. Poker ma-

chine players will stay with specific machines and spend hundreds of dollars because they "just know the machine is ready to pay off." Again, the point is to stay in action. Social, job, and family tensions multiply. Gamblers may deny that there is a problem or may lie to conceal the amount of money involved or the frequency of their gambling. Now emotional satisfaction, ego, self-esteem, and money are involved. The magic is gone and, for the action gambler, the emotional anguish of appearing to be a loser can be overwhelming. Chasing brings other changes in the gambler: depression, lying, isolation, and irritability. **But even when losing, gamblers still rely on gambling for their emotional satisfaction.**

"My mind told me, 'Yes, you're going to lose'; but your mind also tells you, 'But if you do this, you don't have to feel either.' As long as you don't have to feel the price you're paying, whether it be weight gain or whether it be for the money, it is almost worth it at that point."

44-year-old recovering compulsive gambler

As losses multiply, the gambler tries to recover financially by gambling more, tries unsuccessfully to cut back, swears he or she will never gamble again (but always does), and often seeks a bailout to get out of trouble.

Desperation Phase

In the end stages, which could take decades to develop or may take just a year, especially with machine players, **pathological gamblers often lose jobs, max out credit cards, borrow from friends and family, and even turn to illegal activities like theft, embezzlement, and drug dealing.** Their desperation causes them to play badly because they lose patience and common sense. They play too many hands in poker, they get mad at the slot machines and swear they won't let a machine beat them, and their sense of being lucky turns into a lament that they are the unluckiest people in the world.

DILBERT *Scott Adams*

> I PLAN TO OPEN A GAMBLING CASINO FOR PEOPLE WHO HAVE EXTRAORDINARILY BAD LUCK.

> HOW CAN YOU TELL WHO HAS EXTRAORDINARILY BAD LUCK?

> THEY WOULD BE THE ONES THAT GO TO MY CASINO.

"After 15 years it got really bad in dollars—hundreds of thousands of dollars lost—loss of my marriage, my self-esteem, my vehicles, my homes. At one other point in time, I lost my mother's home. I don't even know how I got them [my parents] to sign on the dotted line."

43-year-old recovering gambler

Gamblers often bankrupt their families and suffer divorce or separation because of deteriorating family relationships, long absences from home, arguments over money, and indifference to the welfare of family members and others.

Giving-Up Phase

At this stage pathological gamblers **stop thinking they will win it all back and just want to stay in action so they don't have to think**. Gamblers can experience elated moods when they win and **mania, depression, panic attacks, insomnia, health problems, and suicidal thoughts or actual attempts when they lose**. One study of GA members found severe depression in 72% of those who say they have hit bottom; **suicide attempts occurred in 17% to 24% of them** (Linden, Pope & Jonas, 1986).

"Every time I get out from the casino, I want to kill myself. Then it's going to be over. Then it's going to end. I tried to

kill myself twice. I took my car to the mountains. I just wanted to—I decided I didn't want the pain anymore."

38-year-old recovering compulsive gambler

Often the problems become so overwhelming that they can precipitate the final crisis that hopefully leads the pathological gambler into treatment rather than to suicide.

UNDERSTANDING THE COMPULSIVE GAMBLER

It is hard for social gamblers or nongamblers to understand the compulsive gambler. One phrase that helps explain the difference is ***"It's not about the money."*** This means that **compulsive gamblers want the rush from a large win or the zoning out while gambling more than they want to achieve some financial goal**. Even when there is a win, its only value is that it allows the gambler to continue gambling.

"I would get a bigger rush from starting out the evening being down $1,000 and then fighting my way back to being only stuck $100 than I would from getting ahead a few hundred dollars and ending the evening ahead about the same amount. People don't get that."

38-year-old Texas Holdem player

Gambling is a binge activity, meaning that gamblers will keep gambling until they have no more access to money and have run out of people from whom to borrow.

"Toward the end of my card-playing career, I used to lose deliberately so I could leave the Holdem poker table. As long as I had money, I couldn't leave, literally. I just had to keep going. At least when I drank, I would pass out before I did too much damage."

55-year-old male recovering pathological gambler

In terms of recovery, more than one-third of all compulsive gamblers recover on their own, often due to a devastating financial loss. For the others the options range from pharmacotherapy adjuncts such as antidepressants and anticraving drugs to gambling groups such as Gamblers Awareness in Oregon, which treats upward of 2,000 gamblers each year, to **Gamblers Anonymous, which has chapters in all 50 states plus 45 countries worldwide.**

GAMBLERS ANONYMOUS

Gamblers Anonymous was formed in 1957 on the model of Alcoholics Anonymous. **Its basic concept is to let problem/compulsive/pathological gamblers help themselves by developing spirituality and ultimately changing the way they live so they**

can stop gambling. At present it is almost the only stopgap and hope between pathological gamblers and their addiction.

GA lists several characteristics of the compulsive gambler, including immaturity, emotional insecurity, and an inability and unwillingness to accept reality. These traits draw the problem gambler into a dream world that can lead to destruction.

"A compulsive gambler finds he or she is emotionally comfortable only when 'in action.' It is not uncommon to hear a Gamblers Anonymous member say, 'The only time I felt like I belonged was when I was gambling. Then I felt secure and comfortable. No great demands were made upon me. I knew I was destroying myself, yet at the same time I had a certain sense of security.'"

Gamblers Anonymous Combo Book (GA, 1998)

The above statement is often read as part of a meeting. Members also read the 12 steps and answer the 20 questions in the yellow meeting booklet that reminds gamblers of the havoc their addiction has had on themselves and their families. It is also a good self-test for those who are not sure if they are problem or pathological gamblers.

(See Chapter 9 for information about treatment for pathological gambling.)

COMPULSIVE SHOPPING & HOARDING

Total consumer credit debt in the United States is more than $1.7 trillion. That works out to about $5,700 for every man, woman, and child (and it doesn't include the $8.4 trillion government debt that is owed by the citizens). **Problems handling money in a responsible manner is the hallmark of almost any addict.** To the addict, money is a means to buy drugs, keep gambling, sit at a bar longer, buy as much binge food as needed, or purchase things that stimulate, sedate, or alter one's mood. The craving can overwhelm common sense. The addict does what feels good at the time for immediate gratification or immediate relief from anxiety and pain. For this reason, budgets, layaway shopping, and avoiding debt or loans are generally not in the addict's vocabulary; compulsive shopping is.

Compulsive shopping (oniomania) is often a manifestation of the personality factors that are present in most addicts. The *DSM-IV-TR* diagnostic manual puts compulsive shopping under "impulse-control disorders not otherwise specified." This category also includes sexual addictions and even repetitive self-mutilation (APA, 2000). **Compulsive shoppers have described the relief from depression and the subsequent high when buying as being similar to the high from cocaine. Both result in a subsequent crash accompanied by more depression and guilt than was felt before buying** (McElroy, Satlin, Pope, et al., 1991; Black, 2001). As a result, **the highest level of excitement for compulsive shoppers comes just before they tell the sales clerk, "I'll buy it!" rather than after the actual act of spending the money.**

"To save money, I would push the cart around and fill it up with whatever I wanted till the cart was full. Then I would just abandon the cart in one of the aisles. I almost felt like a bulimic who eats everything in sight and then throws up. Now I just avoid going to stores completely."

39-year-old recovering compulsive shopper

Studies in the United States, Germany, Canada, and the United Kingdom put the number of compulsive

---

TABLE 7–5   THE 20 QUESTIONS OF GAMBLERS ANONYMOUS

1. Did you ever lose time from work or school due to gambling?
2. Has gambling ever made your home life unhappy?
3. Did gambling affect your reputation?
4. Have you ever felt remorse after gambling?
5. Did you ever gamble to get money with which to pay debts or otherwise solve financial difficulties?
6. Did gambling cause a decrease in your ambition or efficiency?
7. After losing did you feel you must return as soon as possible and win back your losses?
8. After a win did you have a strong urge to return and win more?
9. Did you often gamble until your last dollar was gone?
10. Did you ever borrow to finance your gambling?
11. Have you ever sold anything to finance gambling?
12. Were you reluctant to use "gambling money" for normal expenditures?
13. Did gambling make you careless of the welfare of yourself and your family?
14. Did you ever gamble longer than you had planned?
15. Have you ever gambled to escape worry or trouble?
16. Have you ever committed, or considered committing, an illegal act to finance gambling?
17. Did gambling cause you to have difficulty sleeping?
18. Do arguments, disappointments, or frustrations create within you an urge to gamble?
19. Did you ever have an urge to celebrate any good fortune by a few hours of gambling?
20. Have you ever considered self-destruction or suicide as a result of your gambling?

Most compulsive gamblers will answer yes to at least seven of these questions (GA, 1998).

shoppers somewhere between 2% and 10% (University of Sussex, 1997). Some put the number of Americans who are extreme impulse or compulsive buyers at 5% to 10% of the population—people whose debts are measured in the tens of thousands or even hundreds of thousands of dollars (Koran, Chuong, Bullock, et al., 2003). Clearly, citizens of poor countries do not have this problem except in the middle or wealthy classes.

The roots of compulsive shopping are similar to many aspects of pathological gambling. Pathological gamblers feel their worth and self-esteem come from gambling because they believe they have control—the house brings them free drinks at casinos, and if they lose a lot, they are treated like kings and queens. Casinos and clubs issue membership cards to frequent gamblers, who are treated, if not with respect, at least with acceptance.

Compulsive shoppers, if they have money, are treated well; and if they can spend a lot, they are graciously waited on with enthusiasm. That's just good business. For most shoppers, shopping is a pleasant outing, a chance to buy needed or desired items; but **to some, a store is one of the few places they can get respect or get lost in fantasy, much like action-seeking and escape-seeking gamblers. All they need is a charge card or some checks.**

A study of 25 compulsive shoppers found a number of commonalties. Buying urges occur from a few times a week to once a week; and though they try to fight the urges, they give in 74% of the time. When they enter the shopping area or mall, however, they **often don't know what they want to buy and frequently purchase on impulse.** About 50% of household income goes toward paying debts (Christenson, Faber, de Zwaan, et al., 1994).

In preliminary studies by the Economic and Social Research Council in the United Kingdom, researchers found a large discrepancy between the way shopping addicts see themselves (their actual self) and the way they wish to be (their ideal self). **They believe that buying and acquiring things will bring them closer to their ideal self.** Others with the same problem might turn to drugs or compulsive eating. Women tend to buy things that enhance

their uniqueness, including jewelry, clothes, and cosmetics, whereas men prefer high-tech, electronic, and sports equipment (Dittmar, Beattie & Friese, 1996). **Debt counseling is only a stopgap measure because the roots of the condition have not been addressed**, much like a temporary bailout for a pathological gambler.

Wintertime is when consumers incur 40% of their actual debt, often because the holidays can bring up old resentments and magnify feelings of loneliness and depression (Mellan, 1995). **Depression seems a major part of compulsive shopping.** In one study 10 of 13 compulsive shoppers who received antidepressants reported a complete, or at least partial, reduction in their compulsive buying behavior (McElroy, Soutullo, Goldsmith, et al., 2003). Dr. Eric Hollander of the Compulsive, Impulsive, and Anxiety Disorders Program at Mount Sinai School of Medicine in New York believes that low serotonin levels (which cause depression) lead women more to compulsive shopping and eating disorders while it leads men to risk taking and violence (Koran, Chuone, Bullock, et al., 2003).

Recent studies using cognitive behavioral therapy to treat compulsive buying showed marked improvement and fewer buying episodes after six months (Mitchell, Burgard, Faber, et al., 2006). Weekly therapy that helps interrupt the cycle of compulsive buying, making out a budget and sticking to it, plus working on the inner issues regarding self-image and self-esteem are steps toward recovery. As with other addictions, attending a self-help group for support is an alternative to going shopping. **There are more than 400 Debtors Anonymous groups in the United States.**

Collecting, accumulating, and hoarding are offshoots of compulsive shopping; that is, one's worth and self-esteem come from objects and one's ability to get them. There are numerous articles and case studies of people whose desire to accumulate things affects every aspect of their life to the detriment of their everyday existence. The objects can vary from antiques and other objects of true value and beauty to more-current products that have been made desirable through publicity

and fads (e.g., Beanie Babies,® baseball cards, fabric, stamps, Barbie® dolls, and thousands of other objects that can be found on eBay).

"I'm into baseball cards. I'm bidding for these boxes of cards on eBay for $50 and above and hoping the more valuable cards will be in the boxes. So my plan was to buy and sell these and make some money, but I have yet to sell any. I just buy them and have tens of thousands of cards. It's almost like being in action at a slot machine or poker table when I'm in the bidding process."
28-year-old recovering collector

There is an **increasing number of cases of hoarding of relatively valueless objects**: daily newspapers and monthly magazines, stuffed animals, live animals such as cats or, in a recent case in San Francisco, thousands of rats (Fimrite, 2006), and, in extreme cases, even Styrofoam boxes from McDonald's.® Often the objects collected have some association with memories of enjoyable childhood experiences and feelings. There is a need to re-create those feelings, almost like a heroin addict chasing that high. The estimates of the number of hoarders pegs the total at more than a million—a lot more than commonly thought. There are probably many more who are borderline hoarders, but unless it makes the news it remains a hidden disease, often among the elderly.

EATING DISORDERS

"China is supersizing its children as fast as its economy, prompting fears of an American-style obesity crisis here. Over 8% of Chinese boys 10 to 12 years old in 2005 were considered obese, and an additional 15% were overweight."
USA Today, February 4, 2007

As the standard of living rises all over the world, the rate of obesity increases. In England the current obesity

Meyer's Take by Tom Meyer

rate is 22%, 13% in Spain, 9% in France, and 9% in Italy. In **2005, 33% of American adults were considered obese compared with just 15% in 1980.** If you include Americans who are overweight, that percentage climbs to 66%. In addition to simply overeating, eating disorders include anorexia, bulimia, and binge eating.

"I went to this eating disorder clinic for my bulimia. There were also anorexics and overeaters there. At the meal table, the staff kept an eye on everyone. They made sure the anorexics ate something and didn't give it to the overeaters or bulimics, or go to the bathroom immediately after to throw up, or start exercising to incredible excess. They also checked under the table for thrown-away food. We bulimics, they just had to keep us away from the bathroom, so everyone had to stay in the meal room for at least a half hour after eating. A year after I stopped throwing up because of

health reasons, I ballooned up to 360 lbs. Now I'm just a plain old compulsive overeater or, as they call it now, 'binge-eating disorder.'"
35-year-old male recovering bulimic, former college wrestler

Since ancient times the concept of beauty has changed from generation to generation and from culture to culture. **Thinness used to be a sign of poverty and lower-class status, while plumpness was a sign of wealth and upper-class membership.** In the United States at the beginning of the twentieth century, the ideal of the buxom, upper-class, bustle-supported, full-figured grand dame of the Victorian era gave way to the svelte fun-loving flappers of the twenties. Following the Depression and World War II, the "voluptuous female" that had become popular, typified in the forties and fifties by Jane Russell and Marilyn Monroe, gave way in the sixties to the very boyish figures of Audrey Hepburn and British model Twiggy. That ideal was reinforced by fashion magazines, television ads featuring painfully thin models, and films

showcasing slender stars with large bosoms.

The paradox of body image in modern society is that while the ideal splashed in the media is thinness, youth, and beauty, the advertisements promote soda, cookies, and candy bars. As a further contradiction, supermarket shelves are loaded with high-calorie foods side-by-side with fat-free versions and diet aids to further imprint the emaciated ideal. Being greatly overweight may also subject a person to social isolation, job discrimination, and ridicule that foster feelings of inferiority and guilt. A common compliment in our society is "You've lost weight—you look good." People are given mixed messages—look thin, stay slim, but eat up.

The average height and weight of women in the United States is 5 ft. 4 in. and 164 lbs. The average height and weight of fashion models is 5 ft. 9 in. and 110 lbs. (Wolf, 1992; National Center for Health Statistics, 2004). The diet and exercise industries capitalize on this disparity and still persistently urge us to achieve a slim look. Americans spend more than $50 billion per year on diet programs and products. The fact that a number of chronic eating disorders have sprung from these conflicting messages is no great surprise (Helmich, 2003).

Obesity is a problem not just in the United States and not just with adults. The WHO estimates that **300 million people worldwide are obese and 750 million are overweight**. In addition, in a number of countries the average rate of obesity for 10-year-olds is 25%, and in the United States it's 27%. This leads to increasing numbers of illnesses in children, such as diabetes, sleep apnea, and, to a lesser extent, asthma and gallbladder disease (Barlow, Dietz, Klish, et al., 2002). Even small children in the United States, ages two to five, have an overweight rate of 10% (Centers for Disease Control [CDC], 2005).

The three main eating disorders as defined by the *DSM-IV-TR* are anorexia nervosa, bulimia nervosa, and binge-eating disorder.

◇ **Anorexia nervosa** is an addiction to weight loss, fasting, and minimization of body size.

◇ **Bulimia nervosa** is an addiction to binge-eating large amounts of food often followed by purges using self-induced vomiting, fasting, or excessive exercise. Body weight, although on the lighter side, is within normal limits.

◇ **Binge-eating disorder** is basically defined as "bulimia without vomiting, laxatives, or other compensatory activities."

There is a much **larger group of individuals who are described simply as compulsive overeaters** but who are not considered to have an illness as defined by the *DSM-IV-TR* criteria. These individuals make up the bulk of membership in Overeaters Anonymous, Weight Watchers, and other self-help groups.

Like other addictions, **eating disorders involve a sense of powerlessness when dealing with food** even though it is often a desire for control over something in one's life that leads to eating disorders.

"My mom had schizophrenia, my dad drank, and I felt I couldn't help or change anything in my life. One of the only things I could control was and still is what I eat. I could choose anything in that icebox. I can go to a restaurant and order anything. Nobody can tell me what to eat. The irony of course is that eating is the thing I have the least control over."

43-year-old male compulsive overeater

Eating disorders involve obsession with thoughts of food, use of food to escape undesirable feelings (e.g., depression or boredom), secretive behavior, guilt, denial, and continued overeating or fasting regardless of the harm done.

Some regard eating disorders as learned behaviors that can be unlearned with treatment. Others believe they are physiological and psychological addictions. Many believe that the causes of these behaviors arise during infancy and early childhood, one of the key factors being abuse (sexual, physical, or emotional) (Ackard & Neumark-Sztainer, 2003).

Evidence suggests that eating disorders are a combination of genetic, neurochemical, psychological development, and sociocultural factors (Becker, Grinspoon, Klibanski, et al., 1999; Gold & Star, 2005).

Neurochemistry of Eating. One of the main mechanisms that controls appetite involves the hormone grehlin. An empty stomach releases this hormone, which then affects the hypothalamus, the area of the brain that controls metabolism and appetite. The hypothalamus triggers the release of dopamine, which stimulates the nucleus accumbens and striatum, encouraging the conscious brain to search for food. Norepinephrine is also involved in this mechanism (Meyer & Quenzer, 2005). The sight, smell, and taste of food also encourage the person to eat by releasing endorphins from the orbito-frontal cortex and by stimulating the amygdala, the emotional center. Eventually, the hormone leptin, released by fat cells, counteracts the grehlin and tells the hypothalamus to stop the dopamine release, resulting in decreased appetite (Forbes, 2005). Another natural appetite suppressant, GLP-1, was recently discovered at the Royal Postgraduate Medical School in London. It is postulated to have a similar function to leptin in humans. Another mechanism involved in hunger includes the endocannabinoid CB_1 receptor, the same one that is stimulated when marijuana is smoked, causing the munchies; and scientists are even finding that high-sugar foods, particularly refined sugars, actually change the normal neurochemistry of appetite.

The high-energy concentration in pure sugar or high-fructose corn syrup, a common ingredient in many foods, overwhelms the dietary mechanism and reduces the body's metabolic efficiency. This resets the body's natural appetite (Levine, Kotz & Gosnell, 2003). Food manufactures know that a sweet taste appeals to the human palate.

Consider how the concentration of drugs through refinement and synthesis increased their addiction liability over the centuries and then compare that with how the concentration of high-calorie foods, particularly refined carbohydrates, increased compulsive overeating.

Genetic Factors. There is a very strong genetic component to compulsive overeating and, to a lesser extent, to anorexia and bulimia. **The genes that seem to have the greatest impact are those that affect hunger, satiety, and food intake rather than metabolic rates.** Metabolism seems to be more affected by food intake rather than the reverse, implying that obesity is primarily a neurobehavioral disease (O'Rahilly & Farooqi, 2006). One of the genes that signals a tendency to alcohol and drug addiction also signals a susceptibility to compulsive overeating. The DRD_2 A_1 allele gene, found in 70% of alcoholics but only 30% of social drinkers, is often found in compulsive overeaters. This gene signals a lack of dopamine receptors in the nucleus accumbens in the reward/reinforcement pathway, encouraging attempts at overeating to obtain satiation (Blum, Braverman, Cull, et al., 2000). Other genes that affect obesity are those that affect leptin and melanocortin, the hormones that control hunger (Clement, 2006; Clement & Sorensen, 2007). Still another recently discovered gene that has an effect on obesity controls fatty acid and cholesterol synthesis (Herbert, Gerry, McQueen et al., 2006).

Environmental Factors. Nutritional biologist Hans-Rudolf Berthoud suggests that **in a restrictive food environment where feast and famine are cyclical, the body's homeostatic control system regulates body weight quite well.** In other words, when food is scarce, the body alters its metabolism to get the maximum nutrition and energy out of limited supplies. It also stores fat to be released when famine takes its turn. **In a society where rich food is readily available,** however, and where the need to do extended physical activity most of the day is no longer necessary, obesity does occur and **the natural subconscious control of the appetite and metabolism becomes ineffective.** It is necessary to take cognitive control of one's eating habits—to intellectually control one's intake rather than judge by appetite and craving. This loss of control occurs to an excessive degree in those who are already genetically predisposed to retaining every morsel that's put into their body

(Berthoud, 2003, 2004A&B). In any other situation, **this ability to alter metabolism to maximize one's intake is a survival trait**. In a modern wealthy society, it is often injurious to individual and societal health.

Diabetes. A good example of loss of appetite control, known as *appetitive dysfunction*, is diabetes, which has become epidemic in the United States over the past two or three generations and which is spreading to other countries as they strive to emulate our standard of living. Excess intake of high-carbohydrate food coupled with a sedentary lifestyle damages the body's ability to produce insulin, which metabolizes sugar and other carbohydrates. Often the body becomes insulin resistant. The National Health and Nutrition Examination survey found that **9.3% (19.3 million) of U.S. adults had diabetes and another 26% (54 million) were at risk for the disease** (Cowie, Rust, Byrd-Holt, et al., 2006). That amounts to almost one-third of the U.S. adult population that is at risk for a disease caused by food abuse and addiction, mostly due to excessive refined carbohydrates and fats. Worldwide the number of cases is growing as access to increasing amounts of unhealthy food spreads to other countries. **The onset of obesity predicts the onset of diabetes**; the sooner an overeater becomes obese, the sooner Type II adult-onset diabetes is likely to occur (Hillier & Pedula, 2001). There is also a strong racial and nationality component to diabetes in much the same way as to alcoholism. The highest rates of actual diabetes are seen in American Indians (15.5%), Blacks (10%), Mexican Americans (6.5%), and Whites (5.6%). The highest rates are in those age 65 and older (15.8%) (American Diabetes Association, 2006).

Co-Occurring Disorders. There is also a high incidence of depression, anxiety, substance abuse, and personality disorders among people with eating disorders (Herzog, Nussbaum & Marmor, 1996). From 12% to 18% of those with anorexia and between 30% and 70% of those with bulimia abuse tobacco, alcohol, amphetamines, prescription drugs, or over-the-counter substances.

Recent research on genetic and biochemical factors has been particularly suggestive. **The brain does not seem to differentiate between the euphoric feelings generated by bingeing and those generated by fasting** (Gold & Star, 2005). Some bulimics, for instance, report feeling a rush while purging and peacefulness afterward. Anorexic women describe feelings of powerfulness, blissfulness, and even a floating sensation because starving oneself releases endorphins that in turn release dopamine in the reward/reinforcement pathway, similar to an endorphin or opioid high (Kaye, Pickar, Naber, et al., 1982). Overeaters say that when they load up on carbohydrates, they feel like they're loaded on alcohol. **High levels of sugar have been found to reduce the levels of corticosteroids, the body's stress hormones** (Bell, Bhargava, Soriano, et al., 2002).

Brookhaven National Laboratory used positron emission tomography (PET) scans to measure changes in dopamine in the subjects' brains during food and neutral stimulations. Just looking at, smelling, and tasting their favorite foods but not actually eating them caused an increase in dopamine in the dorsal striatum (Volkow, 2002). In associated research at Brookhaven, 20% fewer dopamine D_2 receptors were found in compulsive overeaters, implying that much greater-than-normal amounts of food are needed to stimulate their reward/reinforcement pathway to raise their mood and make them feel satisfied (Wang, Volkow, Logan, et al., 2001).

EPIDEMIOLOGY

Most eating disorders begin in adolescence, are chronic, and affect women disproportionately (Herzog, Dorer, Keel, et al., 1999). About 3% of young women have one of the three main *DSM-IV-TR* eating disorders: anorexia nervosa, bulimia nervosa, and binge-eating disorder (Becker, Grinspoon, Klibanski, et al., 1999; National Institute of Mental Health, 2001). In high school the rate is much higher: nearly 33% of girls and 16% of boys show symptoms of an eating disorder (Forman-Hoffman, 2004). With a national obesity rate exceeding 33%, the number of women and men

who are compulsive overeaters, a diagnosis not listed in the *DSM-IV-TR,* is high. A recent study through the Columbia University Medical Center of 2,900 men and women found that 0.6% of them had anorexia, 1% had bulimia, and 2.8% had a binge-eating disorder (Binge eating, 2007).

Anorexia and bulimia are overwhelmingly female disorders especially when compared with compulsive overeating. An estimated 90% to 95% of anorexics and bulimics are women (Pritts & Susman, 2003). **Women have been socialized to regard their self-worth as closely tied to their physical appearance**, especially their size and weight. Girls in high school in particular have a distorted perception of how they look; 36% of twelfth-graders think they are overweight while in reality only 6.3% are. The same distorted thinking is found in the ninth, tenth, and eleventh grades as well (CDC, 2002). Second, both bulimia and anorexia involve collateral elements of depression, secrecy, and low self-esteem. The illness is often triggered by a stressful event like the breakup of a relationship, a social rejection, or going off to college.

Today anorexia and bulimia seem **more common in developed nations with an abundance of food** and media promotion of thin-body beauty ideals for women. But recent studies of schoolgirls in Cairo, Egypt, found rates for anorexia and bulimia about the same as those in England. At the Hospital for Anorexia and Bulimia in Buenos Aires, Argentina, hundreds of emaciated teenage girls are patients. More than 70 new ones arrive each week. Almost 1 in 10 Argentinean teenage girls suffers from clinical anorexia or bulimia ("Argentina Struggles," 1997). The globalization of pop culture seems to have helped spread these disorders.

Certainly in the United States, cases of anorexia and bulimia are quickly increasing. From the mid-1950s to the mid-1970s, cases of anorexia grew by 300% (Fairburn & Beglin, 1990; NOAH, 1996). According to a recent survey by the National Eating Disorders Association, **approximately 20% of college women have an eating disorder** (NEDA, 2006).

Anorexia nervosa is most frequent in young women from 14 to 18

years old. It afflicts an estimated 0.5% to 1% of women in their late teens and early adulthood. Women over 40 seldom develop anorexia (APA, 2000). The illnesses can, however, strike all age groups from children to the elderly. A high incidence of anorexia in males is found in high school and college wrestlers who must maintain a certain weight to stay in a category. There is also a high incidence among rowers.

"It was our coach who taught us how to throw up to maintain our weight in high school on the wrestling team. We'd go to smorgasbords, eat a bunch, throw up in the bathroom, eat again, throw up again. Most of the team did it. Of course we weren't supposed to tell anybody, but about a year and a half later word got out and he was fired."
College wrestler

Females involved in sports who are at risk for eating disorders include gymnasts, runners, swimmers, dancers, cheerleaders, and figure skaters, many of whom are prodded or compelled by teachers, coaches, and trainers to maintain a certain weight no matter what.

A complex of disorders afflicting women athletes has been called the "female athlete triad." It consists of:

◇ an eating disorder such as anorexia or bulimia but also includes elimination of certain food groups and abuse of weight-control methods such as dieting, fasting, and the use of diet aids and laxatives;

◇ irregular menstruation (i.e., missing more than one period); and

◇ osteoporosis or irreversible loss of bone density, which can result in pain and fractures (Beals & Manore, 2002).

It is not clear whether eating disorders precede or follow women's participation in sports. Any extreme method of weight loss has physiological and psychological consequences. Even moderate dieting increases the risk of eating disorders in adolescent girls (Daee, Robinson, Lawson, et al., 2002).

ANOREXIA NERVOSA

In recent years the **age of onset of anorexia nervosa has dropped from as low as 13 years old to just nine**. Children starve themselves, overexercise, use diuretics and laxatives, and throw up to stay thin. It is a growing obsession in modern society (Tyre, 2005).

Historically, anorexia existed in the Middle Ages as the "holy anorexia," when monks and nuns piously starved themselves to achieve an ideal of holiness and control over the desires of the flesh. It was first described in 1689 by British physician Richard Morton and designated "nervous consumption caused by sadness." Over the past three centuries, there have been numerous descriptions of anorexia that are quite similar to the modern-day definition (Morton, 1694; Bell, 1985). In the Victorian era around the end of the nineteenth century, eating and all that was associated with it—defecation, breaking wind, and even food preparation—were considered beneath the values of a prim young woman, so careful, abstemious eating was considered proper and the way to not become ugly or lose a spouse, feelings that exist in the present day (Brumberg, 2000).

Definition

Although *anorexia* means "without appetite," the condition has less to do with loss of appetite than with what one expert calls **"weight phobia."** Some anorexics, the so-called anorexia restrictors, will **keep losing weight by limiting their food intake through dieting, fasting, the use of amphetamines and other diet pills, and excessive exercise**. Binge-eating/purging types promote weight loss by purging through the use of diuretics, laxatives, enemas, or self-induced vomiting (APA, 2000). Some people even stimulate weight loss through liposuction (surgical removal of fat) or gastric bypass surgery (where part of the stomach or small intestine is clamped off).

Sometimes the line between anorexia and bulimia becomes blurred. **Bulimic symptoms appear in 30% to 80% of all anorexics.** The major difference is that bulimics usually eat huge amounts of food and then purge to maintain a low weight whereas anorex-

ics usually starve themselves though they may occasionally binge. Thus anorexics are severely underweight and bulimics are not. Bulimics are also less likely to suffer menstrual irregularities and more likely to admit to having an eating disorder.

People afflicted with anorexia nervosa are afraid of weight gain and eventually may lose from 15% to 60% of their weight. They will not maintain a normal body weight, and **they have a distorted perception of their body's shape and size**, often feeling, even when emaciated, that their body or parts of it are overweight. Their emotional state is tied to their weight. They let the scale dictate how they feel about themselves. Often there is ignorance or denial of the seriousness of low body weight. Peer approval may aggravate the condition by praising the anorexic and encouraging "the look," which confers high status among adolescents not just in the United States but in other industrialized nations (Aronson, 1993; Rukavina & Pokrajac-Bulian, 2006).

Causes

Some psychologists see anorexia as a compensatory behavior for people who are too concerned with following directions and pleasing others. Young females may be model students, good athletes, and academically talented and **may have a tendency to perfectionism but they lack self-esteem and a sense of self.** A refusal to eat gives them a measure of control in their lives, and continuous weight loss can be an index of their discipline, achievement, self-esteem, and status among their peers.

"I didn't have a sense of myself or my body growing up, but I tried to be so perfect. But whenever I do anything, I feel I'm going to be criticized for it, especially by my mother. I mean, even when she's not around, I still hear her. And she's not a bad person. So the only thing I could control was my eating. And the more they tried to get me to eat, the more I could say no. I thought that if I could control my eating, I could control the rest of my life."
19-year-old recovering anorexic

Additional **characteristics of anorexia include delusions and compulsions**. Anorexic *delusions* are persistent unshakable ideas that one is unattractive or overweight; *compulsions* are rigid, self-imposed rituals, such as weighing food, dividing it into small pieces, or eating in a prescribed order.

Family studies, including twin studies, indicate a higher prevalence of anorexia if one has an immediate relative who is anorexic (Treasure & Campbell, 1994; Bellodi, Cavallini, Bertelli, et al., 2001; Rybakowski, Slopien, Dmitrzak-Weglarz, et al., 2006). Research at the University of Pennsylvania identified a susceptibility to anorexia on chromosome one (Grice, Halmi, Fichter, et al., 2002). One theory suggests that **what initially may begin as a strict diet in about three months begins to change brain chemistry**, so more of the body's natural opiates (endorphins) are produced and the person becomes addicted to those brain chemicals (Marazzi & Luby, 1989). The act of eating something precipitates withdrawal symptoms similar to heroin withdrawal, thus encouraging further abstinence.

Effects

Semistarvation strains all of the body's systems, especially the heart, liver, and brain. Dehydration from vomiting depletes electrolytes, a dangerous condition that can lead to arrhythmias and even cardiac arrest. In addition, mild anemia, swollen joints, constipation, and lightheadedness can also occur. Females can decrease their estrogen levels; males can deplete their testosterone levels. Amenorrhea (absence or abnormal cessation of menstruation) often occurs in women with anorexia. It can take several months of treatment before a normal menstrual cycle is reestablished. Other disturbances include stomach cramps, dry skin, and lanugo (a downy body hair that develops on the trunk). There is also a growing belief that the early use of amphetamines and other strong stimulants to control weight will disrupt normal weight-control mechanisms.

With anorexia nervosa additional dangers are osteoporosis, sterility, miscarriage, and birth defects. **Death rates** among anorexic patients have been **estimated at 4% to 20%** over the life of the disease, with risks increasing as weight loss approaches 60% of normal. The most frequent causes of death are heart disease, especially congestive heart failure, and suicide (APA, 2000). Studies suggest that gray matter volume deficits remain even after the patient has received sufficient nutrition for a period of time (Tamburrino & McGinnis, 2002).

BULIMIA NERVOSA

Definition

Although *bulimia* means "ox hunger" ("I'm so hungry I could eat an ox"), the term generally is used to designate the eating disorder **characterized by eating large amounts of food in one sitting [bingeing] followed by inappropriate methods of ridding oneself of the food**. These methods include self-induced vomiting (used by 80% to 90% of those with this disorder), use of diuretics or laxatives, fasting, and excessive exercise. These methods of eliminating food are used primarily to keep from gaining weight (APA, 2000).

"It was like depression, you know. I'd just keep eating all day and so I got to the point where I was gaining weight too fast. I spoke with a friend about it, and she said, 'Do like I do—throw it up.' I went into this mad trip of eating everything I could shove down my throat and then if I felt bad about it or if I felt any guilt at all, I could throw it back up and all the guilt would go away."

28-year-old recovering bulimic

People with bulimia often are ashamed of their behavior, eat secretly, and consume food rapidly. Although a slightly overweight condition may precede bulimia, those suffering from the disorder often are within a few pounds of normal weight. People with bulimia may feel loss of control during binges and guilt after them. Bulimia was first described in 1979 (Russell, 1979).

Generally, a *binge* is "an abnormally large amount of food on the order of a holiday meal, eaten in two hours or less but definitely more than other people would eat in the same time span." Continuous snacking during the day does not constitute a binge. Diagnosis of bulimia requires that bingeing and purging occur at least twice a week for three months. Although many binge eaters prefer sweet, high-calorie foods like ice cream, soft drinks, and cookies, bulimia has more to do with the amount of food than the types of food. During binge episodes there may be **a feeling of frenzy and of not being in control and a sense of being disconnected from one's surroundings**. Between binges low-calorie foods and drinks are often consumed to control weight.

Causes

As with anorexia, there are multiple causes of bulimia. Because the disease spans different races and classes, it is clear that environmental pressures to be slim are extremely influential. For example, when television was widely introduced in 1995 in the Pacific Island nation of Fiji, only 3% of girls reported they vomited to control their weight. Three years later the number had grown to 15%. In addition, the study found that 74% of the Fijian girls reported feeling "too big or fat," while almost two-thirds reported dieting in the past month. In the past, before the slender bodies of TV stars such as those on *Melrose Place* and *Ally McBeal* were on television, extreme thinness was a sign of illness. About 84% of Fijian women were what insurance charts consider overweight, but there was a cultural acceptance of that look (Becker, Grinspoon, Klibanski, et al., 1999).

Some claim that the socialization of women to an ideal of excessive thinness begins with the Barbie® dolls young girls receive—dolls that if extrapolated into an adult female's measurements would produce a woman with a 36 in. bust, an emaciated 18 in. waist, and 33 in. hips. The average model's measurements are 36–23–33. The contemporary "starved" look popularized by the 92 lb., 5 ft. 6 in. Twiggy has given way to the "heroin chic" ultrathin look of current actresses such as Lara

Flynn Boyle and Kate Moss. One study found that **between 1979 and 1988, the weights of models and beauty pageant contestants averaged 13% to 19% below the average weights of women in relevant age groups** (Wiseman, 1992).

The **biochemical changes involved with bulimia can make the disorder self-perpetuating.** There is evidence that metabolism adapts to the bulimic cycle and slows down, so more weight is gained with the same intake of food. This increased weight gain is then seen as even more reason to continue to binge and purge. There is also evidence that purging through vomiting or laxatives produces higher levels of natural opioids (endorphins), so people suffering from bulimia become addicted to the body's own natural drugs (Gold & Star, 2005).

Effects

Effects and health consequences are less severe with bulimia if it does not progress into anorexia. Problems include **dental complications and a greater liability for alcohol and drug abuse,** even among those suffering from anorexia. Dependency on laxatives for normal bowel movements can occur along with a **high rate of depression and a greater risk of suicide.**

Because of the frequency of vomiting, bulimia puts people at risk for **stomach acid burns to the esophagus and throat,** resulting in chronic sore throat and greater risk of cancer. When vomiting is practiced with either bulimia or anorexia, the **tooth enamel can be permanently eaten away by acid.** There is also a high incidence of cavities, and front teeth can appear ragged, chipped, and mottled. **Dental professionals are often the first to spot bulimic activities.** The back of the fingers and hands can become scarred from abrading the skin on the teeth while pushing the hand down the throat to induce vomiting.

"Bingeing and purging is the choice of my best friend, and it's easy to see the signs: the skin on a finger eaten away and yellow from the acids in the vomit."

Part of the blame for the great numbers of obese people is placed at the doors of fast-food restaurants. High fat, high refined carbohydrates, oversized portions, and easy availability have added to America's waistlines and health problems.
© 2007 CNS Productions, Inc.

You feel guilt for eating even a salad with no dressing. If you eat only once a day, your mind screams at you to not eat, to say no. The guilt of eating anything almost consumes you. I used to do it, too."
19-year-old female college student

As with anorexia, **heart problems, such as arrhythmias, can develop as can electrolyte imbalances** and irregular menstrual periods or no periods at all. Additional problems are caused by the abuse of ipecac syrup. This medication, usually taken to induce vomiting in cases of accidental poisonings, is often used on a regular basis by bulimics and can cause heart problems, tears in the esophagus or stomach lining, vomiting of blood, seizures, and even death.

Psychological effects include loneliness and self-imposed isolation, difficulty dealing with any activities involving food, irritability, mood changes, and depression.

BINGE-EATING DISORDER (including compulsive overeating)

"During your life, my child, see what suits your constitution,
*   do not give it what you find disagrees with it;*
for not everything is good for everybody,
*   nor does everybody like everything.*
Do not be insatiable for any delicacy,
*   do not be greedy for food;*
for overeating leads to illness,
*   and excess leads to liver attacks.*
Many people have died from overeating;
*   control yourself, and so prolong your life."*
Sirach 37:27-31

Internationally, **for the first time in history, there are as many people overweight as underweight,** about 1.1 billion of each in a worldwide population of 6 billion. In North America, overweight people outnumber those who are underweight by a ratio of 12 to

1; in Europe, 9 to 1; and in Latin America, 5 to 1. In Africa they are about equal, and in Southeast Asia there are five times as many underfed as overfed people (Gardner & Halweil, 2000). In the United States, one major study found that **obesity (more than 30 lbs. overweight) increased from 15% of the population in 1980 to 33% in 2005.** That figure is expected to rise to 38% by 2008 (Helmich, 2003). The greatest increase was found in 18- to 29-year-olds, in those with some college education, those of Hispanic ethnicity, and those from the south Atlantic states.

"Eating has become a recreational sport here in America and in more and more countries throughout the world. Most people eat so they can live their lives. I live my life so I can eat. For me every activity can be punctuated by eating. Any reward I give myself usually involves food. All social things I do revolve around food."
28-year-old 290 lb. compulsive overeater

Definition

There is much debate on how to define *obesity.* For example:

◇ Is obesity a specific syndrome or is it a symptom of a number of conditions such as metabolic disorders, psychological disorders, or simply situational factors (there are too many fast-food restaurants and people don't get enough exercise)?

◇ Is obesity an outcome of the metabolic changes wrought by excessive eating and overuse of refined carbohydrates?

◇ Is obesity the result of childhood traumas and damaged self-image that occurred in infancy?

◇ Is obesity genetically determined as was suggested when scientists created fat mice simply by genetic manipulation?

The current *DSM-IV-TR* says that binge-eating disorder affects 4.6% of the community at large and 28.7% of those in a weight-loss program (Spitzer,

Yanovski, Wadden, et al., 1993). **Binge-eating disorder is marked by recurrent episodes of binge eating without use of vomiting, laxatives, or other compensatory activities.** A pattern of frequent eating and snacking over a period of several hours is a symptom of this condition.

"Why do I always empty the plate no matter what I eat? After I finish a normal meal, I am hungrier . . . no that's not true . . . I just want to eat more, binge more. It's as if the food primes my appetite . . . it doesn't lessen it . . . so it can't be true hunger. I just want the mild high I get from eating, particularly my comfort foods. Unfortunately, the fat comes with the high."
51-year-old 281 lb. male compulsive overeater, always in recovery

Certain foods and excessive intake activate the mesolimbic dopaminergic reward circuit during ingestion of food and not only give pleasure but block out unwanted emotions (Blum, Braverman, Holder, et al., 2000). This section uses the term *compulsive overeater* and acknowledges that there are several causes of obesity but that the main ones are remarkably similar. With compulsive overeating and binge-eating disorder, **people eat in response to emotional states rather than to true hunger signals.** Symptoms of compulsive overeating and binge-eating disorder include:

◇ frequent episodes of eating what other people consider large quantities;

◇ feeling a lack of control while overeating or bingeing;

◇ eating rapidly and swallowing food without chewing;

◇ eating when uncomfortably full;

◇ eating large amounts when not feeling physically hungry;

◇ eating alone because of embarrassment about how much one is eating;

◇ feeling disgusted and distressed when one is overeating; and

◇ having a preference for refined carbohydrates, including high-sugar junk food as well as high-fat foods (APA, 2000).

"Eating at 3 o'clock in the morning; sneaking food when my husband was asleep and my kids were in bed; hiding food so my kids wouldn't know I had it because I didn't want to share it with them; and it would be junk, it would be cakes and cookies and sweet stuff, sugars. That was probably the height of it and feeling so lousy about myself because of the weight."
Recovering binge eater

People with a binge-eating disorder feel that **they cannot control the amount eaten, the pace of eating, and the kind of food eaten. They will stop only when it becomes painfully uncomfortable.** Most people with this disorder are obese, but those of normal weight can suffer from this disorder as well.

Causes

Food is used to modify emotions, especially anxiety, solitude, stress, and depression. Eating controls anxiety because **food has a calming and sedating effect.** Dieting may trigger binge-eating disorder in some cases, but one study found that nearly 50% of all cases had the disorder before starting to diet. Two different studies of adolescents found that **depressed mood more than doubled the risk of obesity and increased the risk of bulimia and anorexia as well** (Goodman & Whitaker, 2002; Johnson, Cohen, Kotler, et al., 2002). Unfortunately, weight gain may increase stress, guilt, and depression thus perpetuating the overeating cycle.

"I was molested, sexually abused, at 12, and I remember feeling really uncomfortable about my body after that and using food to just feel comfortable and maybe as a layer of protection to keep people away; not wanting to look good because then I might have to interact with the

opposite sex and maybe have some kind of altercation. I was just afraid of men after that."

36-year-old female recovering compulsive overeater

Effects

People who compulsively overeat are generally overweight and may suffer from medical conditions associated with obesity, including:

◊ **high blood pressure, high cholesterol, circulatory problems, and heart disease**;
◊ **Type II diabetes**;
◊ **sleep apnea**;
◊ gall bladder disease, gout, and arthritis; and, according to some studies,
◊ a 15% to 60% greater risk of cancer, including breast cancer in women (Calle, Rodriguez, Walker-Thurmond, et al., 2003).

Other psychological problems often develop. People who binge-eat:

◊ **exhibit higher rates of depression** than in the population at large;
◊ **become distressed, develop a negative body image**, and avoid going out in public or gathering socially; and
◊ **allow their self-esteem to suffer badly** because of the way they look or think they look.

Scientists at the University of Pennsylvania identified a fat-cell hormone they call *resistin* that blocks the effectiveness of insulin, accelerating the onset of diabetes. If the same hormone is a factor in human weight gain once a person has put on too much weight in the form of fat, this could explain the **high incidence of adult-onset diabetes in 15 million Americans** (Steppan, Bailey, Bhat, et al., 2001).

SUPPORT GROUPS

There are a number of support groups to help people with eating disorders. They range from commercial ventures like TOPS® (Take Off Pounds Sensibly), Weight Watchers,® and Jenny Craig,® to self-help 12-step

TABLE 7–6   COMPULSIVE OVEREATING SELF-DIAGNOSTIC TEST

The following questions are used by Overeaters Anonymous to help someone determine whether he or she is involved in compulsive overeating.

1. Do you eat when you're not hungry?
2. Do you go on eating binges for no apparent reason?
3. Do you have feelings of guilt and remorse after overeating?
4. Do you give too much time and thought to food?
5. Do you look forward with pleasure and anticipation to the time when you can eat alone?
6. Do you plan these secret binges ahead of time?
7. Do you eat sensibly before others and make up for it when alone?
8. Is your weight affecting the way you live your life?
9. Have you tried to diet for a week (or longer) only to fall short of your goal?
10. Do you resent others telling you to "use a little willpower" to stop overeating?
11. Despite evidence to the contrary, have you continued to assert that you can diet on your own whenever you wish?
12. Do you crave to eat at a definite time, day or night, other than mealtimes?
13. Do you eat to escape from worries or troubles?
14. Have you ever been treated for obesity or a food-related condition?
15. Does your eating behavior make you or others unhappy?

If people answer yes to three or more of these questions, it is probable that they are well on their way to having a compulsive overeating problem.

groups like Overeaters Anonymous, Food Addicts Anonymous, and GreySheeters Anonymous. Like all other addictions, compulsive eating is a lifetime problem and the most effective treatment is membership in some kind of support group.

SEXUAL ADDICTION

As of 2007 **there were more than 4 million pornographic sites on the Internet visited regularly by 40 million Americans**. About 70% of the visits are during working hours. Although most people visit the sites recreationally, 10% of cybersexual surfers are addicted and spend up to eight hours a day watching pornography online. In modern society the number of outlets for sexual activity and the willingness to exhibit or engage in such pursuits are vast. From softcore porn on pay TV to sexually explicit videos or DVDs, most limits have been breached in the United States and other industrialized nations. **The online porn industry is estimated by one organization to take in**

$57 billion per year worldwide, $12 billion of that in the United States (Internet Filter Review, 2007).

DEFINITION

The most accurate definitions of *sexual addiction* come from sex addicts themselves and from the 12-step recovery group Sexaholics Anonymous (SA).

"Early on we came to feel disconnected from parents, from peers, from ourselves. We tuned out with fantasy and masturbation. We plugged in by drinking in the pictures, the images, and pursuing the objects of our fantasies. We lusted and wanted to be lusted after. We became true addicts: sex with self, promiscuity, adultery, dependency relationships, and more fantasy. We got it through the eyes, we bought it, we sold it, we traded it, we gave it away. We were addicted to the intrigue, the tease, the forbidden. The only way we knew to be free of it was to do it."

Sexaholics Anonymous, 1989

Sexual addiction is marked by sexual behavior over which the addict has little control and little choice. Compulsive sexual behavior is practiced by males and females, young and old, gay and straight. **Sexual addiction can include masturbation and pornography (the most frequent behaviors) along with serial affairs, phone sex, and visits to topless bars and strip shows.** Some sexual activity that can be compulsive has legal penalties: prostitution, sexual harassment, sexual abuse, exhibitionism or flashing, child molestation, rape, and incest (Goodman, 2005).

The incidence of sexual addiction in some studies is 3% to 6% of the population (Coleman, 1992; Carnes & Schneider, 2000). About 80% of sex addicts are males, with the behaviors generally starting in the teen years, peaking at ages 20 to 40, and then gradually declining. There is also a high incidence among sex addicts of drug addiction and addictive behaviors, including gambling and compulsive shopping.

The *DSM-IV-TR* lists some separate sexual disorders under the heading of "paraphilias," including exhibitionism, fetishism, frotteurism (clandestine rubbing against another person), pedophilia, sexual masochism, sexual sadism, transvestic fetishism, and voyeurism. These are different from sexual addiction but may be part of a sex addict's activities. **Collateral addictions include love addictions** (romance addiction, the compulsion to fall in love and be in love) **and relationship addiction** (either a compulsive relationship with one person or multiple relationships).

"Once I got married, the first time, I wanted it all the time. And I masturbated quite a bit, you know. I mean, we had sex all the time but that wasn't enough. And it got to the point where I masturbated four, five, six times a day and wanted to go home and have sex with my wife."
34-year-old recovering sex addict

Aviel Goodman, M.D., director of the Minnesota Institute of Psychiatry, defines these activities as sexual addiction rather than as an impulse-control disorder or an obsessive-compulsive disorder (OCD). With all three definitions, the activities are often damaging both to the participant and to others. With impulse-control disorder, however, the impulsivity is aimed at receiving pleasure no matter what the cost. With OCD the object is to relieve anxiety, tension, or emotional pain through the activity. **With sexual addiction the object can be a pursuit of the pleasure and/or a desire to subdue pain or anxiety. Most significantly, there is a lack of control over the behavior, a continuation of the behavior despite adverse consequences, and a continuing obsession with doing, planning to do, or simply thinking about the behavior** (Goodman, 2005). Interestingly, some brain lesions or damage to such areas as the medial basal-frontal, diencephalic, or septal region can cause some hypersexual or paraphilic behavior.

EFFECTS & SIDE EFFECTS

Whether it's for the high or as **a way to cope with depression, anxiety, stress, solitude, or low self-worth**, compulsive sexual behavior conditions the body to the release of pleasure-giving neurotransmitters, especially dopamine, enkephalins, and endorphins (Bancroft & Vukadinovic, 2004). Tolerance develops to the behavior as it does with any psychoactive drug. More and more time must be spent in the sexual activity to gain any emotional benefit. Damage is done to careers, relationships, self-image, and peace of mind, but the activity continues despite all negative consequences.

With sexual addiction, sex becomes the person's most important all-consuming activity, and the pursuit of the addiction has been described as trancelike. Part of the elevated mood generated by the activity may involve risk. In addition, a routine or pattern may be followed that increases the excitement. **Usually, there is a culminating sexual event (e.g., exposure, rape, or molestation), usually involving orgasm, over which the addict has virtually no control.** It is often followed by remorse, guilt, fear of discovery, and resolutions to stop the behavior. Throughout, the sexual behavior is pursued with a sense of desperation, and the addict is demoralized and may suffer from low self-image, self-loathing, and despair over the time and the money wasted or the inherent danger of injury or disease. Sexaholics Anonymous, Sex and Love Addicts Anonymous, and other affiliated groups see compulsive sex as a progressive disease that can be treated.

"I think it was compulsive sexuality because I used to love just a man being with me. I liked the money, for one. I liked the money that men would give me for sex. So I think that anytime I would see someone that I knew personally, not as a prostitute, I would always have that temptation that I wanted to have sex with this person and I would always do it. I would always have sex with men who would be friends of mine or so-called friends."
38-year-old female recovering polydrug abuser and sex addict

Many drugs that influence sexual functioning can:

◇ release dopamine (stimulate the reward/reinforcement pathway);

◇ release norepinephrine and epinephrine to stimulate body functions and increase excitement (e.g., cocaine, methamphetamine, Viagra®);

◇ block acetylcholine and interfere with erection and orgasm (many downers); or

◇ release serotonin (which can inhibit sexual activity as with a selective serotonin reuptake inhibitor [SSRI]). Researchers feel that **drugs that act to stimulate serotonergic activity can possibly be used to treat sexual addiction** (Meston & Gorzalka, 1992; Goodman, 2005) while drugs that block serotonin seem to increase sexual activity. There are many reports of how SSRIs such as fluoxetine (Prozac®) decrease sexual craving.

The other influence of drugs on sexuality has to do with the **lowering of inhibitions, which can lead to high-**

TABLE 7–7   SEXAHOLICS ANONYMOUS SELF-TEST

The following self-test is for those who may not be sure they have a problem with compulsive sexuality or love addiction.

1. Have you ever thought you needed help for your sexual thinking or behavior?
2. Have you ever though that you'd be better off if you didn't keep "giving in"?
3. Have you ever felt that sex or stimuli are controlling you?
4. Have you ever tried to stop or limit doing what you felt was wrong in your sexual behavior?
5. Do you resort to sex to escape or to relieve anxiety or because you can't cope?
6. Do you feel guilt, remorse, or depression afterward?
7. Has your pursuit of sex become more compulsive?
8. Does it interfere with relations with your spouse?
9. Do you have to resort to images or memories during sex?
10. Does an irresistible impulse arise when the other party makes the overtures or sex is offered?
11. Do you keep going from one "relationship" or lover to another?
12. Do you feel the "right relationship" would help you stop lusting, masturbating, or being so promiscuous?
13. Do you have a destructive need-a desperate sexual or emotional need for someone?
14. Does pursuit of sex make you careless for yourself or the welfare of your family or others?
15. Has your effectiveness or concentration decreased as sex has become more compulsive?
16. Do you lose time from work for it?
17. Do you turn to a lower environment when pursuing sex?
18. Do you want to get away from the sex partner as soon as possible after the act?
19. Although your spouse is sexually compatible, do you still masturbate or have sex with others?
20. Have you ever been arrested for a sex-related offense?

© 1997–2003 Sexaholics Anonymous, Inc.

Five or more positive responses indicate a strong likelihood of sexual addiction.

risk sexual behavior. Activities that most people only think of can be acted out when drunk or high on methamphetamine.

INTERNET ADDICTION

"I tried to combine playing the Net with a home life, so I moved the computer into the family room. My wife said she got to know the back of my head very well, maybe five hours a night. I would be hunched over the computer, occasionally throwing out some miscellaneous fact I had Googled in between playing solitaire, Minesweeper,® or Sudoku.®"

54-year-old computer addict and information junkie

The growth of the Internet along with abuse by younger generations has not just been in the United States and Europe.

"The Chinese government in recent months has joined South Korea, Thailand, and Vietnam in taking measures to try to limit the time teens spend online. It has passed regulations banning youths from Internet cafés and has implemented control programs that kick teens off networked games after five hours."

(Cha, 2007)

DESCRIPTION

The predecessor to the Internet was the Advanced Research Projects Agency Network, a military network started in 1969 that was eventually opened to defense researchers at universities and other companies. In the late 1980s, most universities and many companies had come online. **In 1989 a British-born computer scientist, Tim Berners-Lee, proposed the World Wide Web project** with help from Robert Cailliau and others at CERN, now the European Particle Physics Laboratory. When commercial providers were allowed to sell online connections to individuals in 1991, the explosion of the Internet began. **As of 2006 more than 1 billion people worldwide were connected to the Internet**; 15% to 20% of that number use high-speed connections (Internet World Stats, 2006; Organisation for Economic Co-operation and Development, 2006). The highest rate is in North America; more than two-thirds of U.S. and Canadian citizens are connected.

The electronic media, like any business, offered services that users wanted. Of course what many wanted were games, erotic material, and, more recently, gambling—all pleasurable activities to many but which also had the potential for compulsive use. In addition, the ease and the anonymity of the Internet enabled people to start relationships and do things that they might have otherwise avoided. As the Internet has grown in size and sophistication in the 2000s, some studies show that the number of compulsive users is also growing not just in North America but worldwide. China, India, Korea, and Russia are just a few of the countries that report high levels of compulsive Internet use and that have established treatment centers specifically for addicts.

The qualities of the Internet that make it a valuable tool are the same ones that can lead to compulsive use. **Besides ease of use and anonymity, the Internet is inexpensive, always available, controllable by the Net surfer, validating (it doesn't criti-**

cize), rewarding, convenient, and escapist (Taintor, 2005).

Also called "Internet compulsion disorder" and "Internet addiction disorder," cyberaddiction is marked by compulsive involvement in chat groups, game playing, stocks or commodities market watching, online gambling, sexual relationships, and other online activities. Ironically, America Online® (AOL) established a chat group called AOL-Anon for those suffering from cyberaddiction. Overall 6% to 10% of all Web users are thought to display signs of addiction (Kershaw, 2005).

Symptoms of Internet addiction include:

◊ logging on every chance there is at home, work, or school (40 hours per week is not unusual, compared with eight hours for nonaddicts);

◊ thinking about the Internet constantly;

◊ feeling irritable and anxious when not online;

◊ needing progressively more time online to get the same satisfaction;

◊ losing track of time while logged on (hours go by like minutes);

◊ neglecting responsibilities;

◊ allowing relationships with spouse, family, co-workers, and friends to deteriorate;

◊ posting more and more messages and downloading more and more data;

◊ eating in front of the monitor; and

◊ checking e-mail upon arising and before going to bed at night; and getting up in the middle of the night to check it just in case.

Some people experience a stimulant-like rush when online, whereas others describe being tranquilized by their quiet isolated online experience. The two different styles of Internet addiction are similar to the difference between action and escape gamblers: some use it to zone out, whereas others prefer frequent human interaction. Repetitive compulsive use of the Internet induces tolerance and changes in physical and mental states. Symptoms include blurred vision, lack of sleep, twitching mouse fingers, and relationship problems.

According to the Center for Online Addiction, there are a number of areas involving the Internet where problems occur. These include **cybersexual addiction, computer relationship addiction, Internet compulsions, information addiction, and computer games addiction**.

CYBERSEXUAL ADDICTION

The use of the Internet to view an incredible amount of free pornography along with development of anonymous sexual relationships, which can start out with the person masturbating while chatting online or viewing pornography and escalate into phone sex and even meetings in person, is often tied to sexual addiction. **Overall about 40 million people visit porn Web sites regularly.** The difference is that the sheer availability of the medium, along with the anonymity inherent to the Internet, feeds into traits found in many sex addicts. The availability also encourages the idea that the practiced is sanctioned by society.

Many of those with cybersexual addiction **use chat rooms and message boards to find sex partners**. Unfortunately, sexual predators are sometimes involved, preying mostly on children and women. The problem has led the Federal Bureau of Investigation and many police departments to create Internet crime units and operate stings to arrest online predators. Austrian authorities recently busted a major international child pornography ring involving more than 2,360 suspects from 77 countries who paid to view videos of young children being sexually abused (Oleksyn, 2007).

As the compulsion increases, cybersexual surfers will become more secretive, hiding their activities from their partners. They can now avoid expensive 900 sex phone lines, trips to X-rated bookstores, and visits to prostitutes. They often will exclude forms of normal sexual activity.

One survey found that **70% of all Internet pornography traffic occurs during workday hours**.

COMPUTER RELATIONSHIP ADDICTION

If the connections made on the Internet don't particularly aim toward

sexual activity but become compulsive, they could be called "cyber-relationships." The problems begin when the **online relationship draws the Net surfer from his or her real-life relationships**. Online friendships can lead to "cyberaffairs," often to the devastation of the neglected partner. As with so many behavioral addictions, when use increases, it squeezes out other parts of the user's life.

INTERNET COMPULSIONS

The biggest problem with Internet compulsions is that of accessibility. **There are hundreds of online casinos, trading companies, and auction houses.** People can lose fortunes or at least their mortgage payments from the comfort of their own home, day or night. While there isn't quite the excitement of going to a casino, the element of control is important: "I can do it when and where I want." Online traders don't have to rely on brokers to buy stocks. They don't need so-called experts (Psychcentral, 2006). The promise of large winnings and profits is a spur to activity. For some these elements of accessibility and control can lead to compulsive gambling as described earlier in this chapter. The online gambler or trader goes through the same stages as compulsive gamblers: winning, losing, desperation, and giving-up (*see* Compulsive Gambling).

INFORMATION ADDICTION

The ability to access thousands of Web sites that cover virtually every subject is attractive to a wide variety of Internet surfers, and the number of Web sites seems to be growing exponentially. The problem with surfing the Net is that it requires little direct human contact. **Web surfers who start young and find that cyber activity is less threatening than actual human interaction may be less likely to learn how to deal with people**, forcing them to rely increasingly on electronic communication. Like other addictions, only a small percentage of users will have a problem.

COMPUTER GAMES ADDICTION

Nintendo,® Sony PlayStation,® and other computer game systems are receiving stiff competition from all the games available online and as part of computer operating systems. The early game of choice was solitaire, played for hours at a time by new computer users. It is still popular, but dozens of other games, such as FreeCell and Minesweeper, have been added along with hundreds of online games that can be played for fun or money. **Game playing is more common among men, teenagers, and children.** Interestingly, about a third of all games carry warnings concerning sexual or violent content, a dramatic increase from a few years ago. Average game players spend 30 to 60 minutes playing games. Game addicts can spend five or six hours a day online.

TELEVISION ADDICTION

The average American watches four hours of television a day, adding up to nine years of one's life span. In Britain the amount is about two hours a day. **For a growing number of compulsive TV watchers here and abroad, six to eight hours a day is not uncommon.** Half the people surveyed said they watch too much (similar to 80% of smokers who want to quit tobacco and yet keep smoking). To fuel this craving, the average cable or satellite television service supplies upward of 200 channels 24 hours a day, while more than 60% of American homes have three or more sets. In many households the TV is on more often than the lights (Nielsen, 2006).

The promise of TV as an information and education medium has been fulfilled. There are learning channels, insightful documentaries, top-notch entertainment, and an abundance of how-to shows. There is also a huge stream of debris that includes infomercials, self-serving political shows, and a host of reality events ranging from talent searches to narcissistic aggrandizements of semi-talents searching for their 15 minutes of fame. But whatever the quality of the programming, it still doesn't answer the question: *Is excessive TV watching really an addiction?*

"Well, I take in my drug through my eyes and ears, directly to my central nervous system. My equivalent crack pipe is the remote. I continue to watch even when I have things that need doing around the house. I would rather watch any sports event on TV rather than play with my three-year-old son. I endlessly plan what shows I'm going to watch that day, but I'll watch anything rather than get up. I don't care if anyone else watches with me. If I'm troubled and don't want to deal with a problem, I flip up the leg rest on my recliner and become a cliché."

46-year-old "TV addict"

Some of the benchmarks of addiction do hold true for television:

◇ **Compulsive use.** *"There are days when I watch the TV 8, 10, 12 hours a day. I can't seem to get up from the chair. 'Couch potato' is an understatement."*

◇ **Using TV to change one's mood.** *"TV is my sedative. . . . When I'm anxious or angry, I plop down and watch anything that's on, especially a show I already am familiar with so I don't have to think too much."*

◇ **Craving.** *"I crave it differently than I crave a cigarette . . . not as strong . . . but I can go to outrageous lengths to make sure there is a TV in any room I have to spend time in."*

◇ **Loss of control.** *"Even when I have a house full of guests, I sneak up to the bedroom to watch my favorite show."*

◇ **Continued use despite adverse consequences.** *"I just sit there watching while the grass grows, while my kids find their own way home from school, while my wife and I forget how to talk except to check the TV guide listing, while I remain slow to react to any chaos in my life."*

◇ **Development of tolerance.** *"Each year adolescents spend 1,500 hours watching TV (900 hours attending school) and view 20,000 commercials. By the age of 18, they have witnessed 200,000 acts of violence and 8,000 murders. The implication in reference to tolerance is that the brain has learned to ignore the huge volume of this emotional overload just as drug addicts ignore most of their environment. Advertising does work, but the development of tolerance has made the advertisers and the networks increase the frequency of their messages, so today instead of seven commercial minutes per hour there are 14, and in news shows, about 18."*

Rutgers University psychologist Robert Kubey listed six dependency symptoms of heavy TV viewing: using TV as a sedative, indiscriminate viewing, feeling loss of control while viewing, feeling angry with oneself for watching too much, an inability to stop watching, and feeling miserable when kept from watching (Kubey & Csikszentmihalyi, 2004; Nielsen, 2006).

If indeed environment is one of the factors that determines the abuse of drugs and addictive behaviors:

◇ **the distorted view of people's lives presented on many TV shows makes it harder for a compulsive viewer to make good decisions;**

◇ **the portrayal and promotion of dysfunctional families and relationships as the norm** rather than the exception is confusing to adolescents and young adults alike;

◇ the huge number of ads for fast-food restaurants that have a reputation for high-fat, high-sugar, and oversized portions of food has contributed to an epidemic of obesity; and

◇ the fear engendered by excessive reporting of murders, wars, and violence makes a viewer more likely to react violently to a benign act that the viewer perceives as a threat.

And, like cigarettes, alcohol, and other drugs of abuse, the younger a person gets into excessive TV viewing, the more extensive are the problems later in life. For example, among the 4,000 studies examining the effect of TV on children is one from New Zealand which says that **kids five to 15 years of age who watched the most TV were the least likely to graduate from high school or** college. The results took into account basic intelligence and financial means (Hancox, Milne & Poulton, 2005). Of course there's the possibility that those who don't do well in school are more likely to watch TV and those who are more motivated in school are less likely to watch.

CELL PHONE ADDICTION

"I can text message without looking at the keypad. I do about 100 text messages a day and 40 or 50 calls. I've never figured out the time I spend, but it's probably a couple of hours or more a day. But I'm in touch with all my friends constantly."

16-year-old female high school student

From 385,000 cell phones in 1985 to 33.8 million in 1995, to **203 million in 2006, the growth of cell phones in the United States has been phenomenal. Worldwide the growth has been equally astonishing: 2 billion cell phones in 2006** (Leo, 2006). Along with this growth in the number of phones has been a similar increase in individ-

ual use, especially as the price per call or text message has dropped. It's hard for teenagers to imagine their lives without cell phones, messaging capabilities, and a constant obedient tool of communication at their hip or in their purse. Two of every five U.S. youths own a cell phone and spend an average of one hour per day calling and text messaging. For an increasing number of users, 90 or more calls and text messages per day are not unusual (Gellene, 2006). Several studies in Japan and Korea as well as in the United States have found that **increasing numbers of students measure their self-esteem by the activity on their cell phones** (Kamibeppu & Sugiura, 2005).

The jury is still out as to whether the advantages in communication are overwhelmed by the loss of privacy as the Nokia tune rings out in church or at a meeting of Alcoholics Anonymous. According to a survey by the advertising agency BBDO, 15% of cell phone owners have interrupted sex to answer a call. This could be classified as continued use despite adverse consequences.

Most of the complaints about cell phones refer to bad manners, the cost of extra minutes or messaging, the cost of new phones, and only then to com-

pulsive use of the medium. The ability to always be accessible to family and friends has certain advantages, but the truth is that the cell phone/Blackberry/Internet revolution is still in its infancy, and its continuing impact on social and cultural behaviors is evolving. That said, there are enough instances of dysfunctional cell phone use to put it on the "need more research" list.

CONCLUSIONS

As useful as seeing the similarities between substance abuse and other all-consuming behaviors can be, **the danger in generalizing the concept of addiction obscures the distinctive characteristics of a specific addiction that need to be addressed in treatment.** For example, in eating disorders and sexual addiction, returning to normal levels of behavior is the preferred option, unlike gambling, alcohol, and other drug abuse that stress abstinence. Fortunately psychotherapy, behavioral therapies, self-help groups, and psychiatric medications tailored to specific compulsive disorders offer hope for effective treatment and recovery.

CHAPTER SUMMARY

Introduction

1. It is rare for a person to have only one addiction, and this includes compulsive behaviors as well as psychoactive drug addictions.

OTHER DRUGS

Inhalants

2. Inhalants (deliriants) are used for their stupefying, intoxicating, and occasionally psychedelic effects.

3. The three main groups of inhalants used are volatile organic solvents and aerosols, volatile nitrites, and anesthetics.

4. Inhalants are popular because they are quick acting, cheap, and readily available at work and in the home, especially to children, ado-

lescents, and the poor. Problems due to their use are mostly ignored.

5. The three main anesthetics—ether, nitrous oxide, and chloroform—were popularized for recreational use in the mid-1800s. With the widespread use of petroleum products in the twentieth century, a whole new class of inhalants, such as solvents, thinners, and glues, became available.

6. Inhalants are responsible for more than 1,000 deaths per year in the United States alone and for many more overseas, particularly among the young, the poor, street children, recent migrants, and indigenous peoples. Gasoline is the most widespread inhalant.

7. Inhalants can be "sniffed," "huffed," "bagged," or "sprayed."

The pressure from gas tanks and the freezing temperatures can damage lungs and other tissues.

8. Organic solvents (and aerosols) consist of hydrocarbon gases and liquids refined from oil that turn to gas at room temperature; these include gasoline (especially in poor countries) and gasoline additives, kerosene, model glue, nail polish remover, lighter fluid, carbon tetrachloride, and even embalming fluid.

9. The most common ingredients in solvents include toluene (glues, cleaning agents), trichlorethylene (paints, spot removers), hexane (glues), ketone (paint thinner), alkanes (butane, methane gases), and gasoline. Alcohol-based volatile solvents (some paints and some perfumes) are also abused.

10. The effects of volatile solvents that reach the brain in seven to 10 seconds through absorption into the capillaries in the bronchi of the lungs include an initial stimulation, mood elevation, impulsiveness, excitement, irritability, and reduced inhibitions.

11. The initial reactions turn to mostly depressant effects, including dizziness, slurred speech, unsteady gait, drowsiness, and, in a number of cases, hallucinations.

12. Prolonged use of volatile solvents, especially leaded gasoline, can cause brain, liver, kidney, bone marrow, and especially lung damage. Death can occur from respiratory arrest, asphyxiation, or cardiac irregularities.

13. Long-term use of solvents causes lack of coordination, poor concentration, weakness, disorientation, poor working memory and cognition, and weight loss. Some of the effects are irreversible though not progressive.

14. Warning signs of solvent abuse include headaches, chemical odor on the body, bloodshot eyes, inflamed nose, slurred speech, and staggering gait.

15. Volatile nitrites include (iso)amyl, (iso)butyl, isopropyl, and cyclohexyl nitrites. Because the nitrites ("poppers") dilate blood vessels and send a rush of blood to the brain, the immediate major effects, which last 30 to 60 seconds, are muscle relaxation, increased heart rate, dizziness, giddiness, a rush, and mild euphoria. Too much can lead to oxygen deprivation, fainting, vomiting, shock, unconsciousness, and blood problems.

16. Because nitrites dilate smooth muscles, they are used to enhance sexual activity.

17. Because most nitrites are illegal as recreational drugs, some are camouflaged and sold as tape head cleaner, sneaker cleaner fluid, or room fresheners.

18. Nitrous oxide, a dental anesthetic, produces a temporary giddiness, buzzing in the ears, disorientation, uncontrolled laughter, and occasional hallucinations that last for just a few minutes. Confusion, headache, impaired motor skills, and passing out are common. Occasionally, seizures, cardiac arrhythmias, and asphyxia can cause central and peripheral nerve cell damage from lack of oxygen.

19. Nitrous oxide is often sold in small canisters used to charge whipping cream bottles as well as large blue tanks. Direct inhalation can cause frozen and exploded lung tissue. Nitrous oxide is usually transferred to balloons and then inhaled.

20. Continued use can cause cognitive impairments that hinder comprehension and recovery.

21. Physical and psychological dependence can occur with inhalants. Prevention often involves education and learning how to recognize signs and symptoms.

Sports & Drugs

22. Three classes of drugs available to athletes are therapeutic drugs, performance-enhancing drugs, and recreational drugs.

23. Athletes use drugs, particularly steroids, to build muscle mass, increase stamina, lessen pain, and improve performance.

24. Drug use among athletes dates from ancient Greece to the present. Over the past 50 years, use has been spurred by East-West competition through the Cold War and the Olympics. It continues because of increased availability and synthesis of new drugs, a win-at-any-cost attitude, increased financial incentives, and unbridled ambition.

25. The World Anti-Drug Agency (WADA) and its code of conduct were established to promote drug-free competition in world sports.

26. Although use of performance-enhancing drugs among collegiate and professional athletes is decreasing (possibly because of increased testing), use continues especially among high school athletes beefing up for college.

27. A danger of various therapeutic (analgesic) pain-killing drugs (e.g., hydrocodone) is that athletes will unknowingly aggravate injuries because there's no pain to warn them of an imminent injury.

28. Other side effects of analgesics include mood changes, nausea, and tissue dependence. Substance dependence and addiction are also a real danger with opioid painkillers and with benzodiazepines such as Xanax.®

29. Muscle relaxants (e.g., carisoprodol or Soma®) when used for their mental effects are also occasionally abused, causing giddiness, drowsiness, and overdoses.

30. The two kinds of anti-inflammatory drugs are nonsteroidal anti-inflammatories, such as aspirin and ibuprofen, and corticosteroids such as cortisone. The latter has more-serious side effects.

31. Though many athletes suffer from exercise-induced asthma, many asthma medications are banned because of their stimulant effects.

32. Most performance-enhancing substances are banned by athletic organizations.

33. Anabolic-androgenic steroids, synthetic or natural, mimic the male hormone testosterone. Athletes use them to increase weight, strength, muscle mass, and definition. Some use them to boost aggressiveness, confidence, or appearance. They do increase muscle mass and strength when combined with diet and exercise.

34. The side effects of anabolic steroid abuse (20 to 200 times normal dosages in patterns known as stacking or cycling) are acne, lowered sex drive, shrinking of testicles in men, breast reduction and masculinization in women, bloated appearance, and emotional instability, including anger, aggressiveness, and "roid rage."

35. With excessive use (at an average cost of $200 to $400 per week), higher incidence of ruptured tendons and damaged ligaments along with withdrawal symptoms, abuse, and dependence are common.

36. Amphetamine and methamphetamine initially boost the athlete's

confidence, energy, alertness, aggression, and reaction time. Tolerance develops quite rapidly. The negative effects include irritability, restlessness, anxiety, anger, malnutrition, and heart or blood pressure problems.

37. Other stimulants that are used to enhance performance are caffeine, tobacco, and ephedrine.

38. Abuse of human growth hormone (HGH, which increases muscle mass) has become widespread. Somewhat less common is blood doping, involving injecting extra blood to increase endurance by increasing the oxygen content of the blood.

39. Androstenedione and dehydroepiandrosterone (DHEA) are used to increase endurance and muscle size. Beta blockers are used to steady the body. Erythropoietin (EPO) is used to increase oxygen, creatine to delay muscle fatigue, infusing extra blood to increase oxygen, and diuretics to lose weight. The use of EPO is common in cycling.

40. Losing weight to participate in certain events is common in athletics. Bulimia and anorexia are the extremes of this desire to improve competitiveness. Diuretics are also used to achieve weight loss.

41. Recreational drugs are used to adjust moods, to reward or console the athlete, and to cope with a heavy schedule.

42. Cocaine is occasionally used by athletes for performance and as a recreational drug; methamphetamine is also used recreationally. Alcohol is the most common recreational drug, though like marijuana it can hinder performance. Impairment from marijuana lasts days after cessation of use.

43. Drug-testing programs have been instituted by all sporting organizations. The major entity is the World Anti-Doping Agency. Drug use imperils the notion of fair competition.

Miscellaneous Drugs

44. Other substances used to get high have included embalming fluid, gasoline, kava, nutmeg, Raid,® and even camel dung.

45. Herbal preparations and dietary supplements have many of the same benefits and dangers as prescription medications.

46. Smart drugs/drinks and over-the-counter medications are often a mixture of herbal medicines, vitamins, powdered nutrients, and amino acids. Some drugs prescribed to treat diseases of aging are also promoted as smart drugs.

OTHER ADDICTIONS

Compulsive Behaviors

47. Repetitive compulsive behaviors are practiced for the same reasons that compulsive drug use occurs.

48. Addictive behaviors alter brain chemistry in much the same ways as psychoactive drugs do.

49. Many of the symptoms of compulsive behaviors are the same as those of compulsive drug use, such as compulsion, tolerance, withdrawal, abuse, denial, and relapse.

Heredity, Environment & Compulsive Behaviors

50. Twin studies and other research have shown that heredity plays a role in compulsive behaviors, involving many of the same areas of the brain that are involved in drug abuse. Dopamine is often involved in heredity influences.

51. Besides emotional needs created by a chaotic childhood, some environmental influences that can make users more susceptible to compulsive behaviors include a glut of fast-food restaurants, state-sponsored lotteries, and easy-to-get credit cards.

52. Engaging in a compulsive behavior changes brain and body chemistry to make the person more susceptible to repeat the behavior and eventually progress into abuse and addiction.

Problem & Pathological Gambling

53. Gambling includes not only slot machines, poker, dice, blackjack, lotteries, sports betting, and keno but also stock and commodities trading (especially day trading), online gambling, bingo, raffles, and office pools.

54. Although often considered a vice, historically governments have used gambling to raise funds, such as for financing the American Revolution. This was the first of three waves of gambling in the United States. The current wave has 48 states with legalized gambling, especially state lotteries and more than 367 American Indian gaming casinos, mostly to supplement tax revenues.

55. Though estimates vary, about 2.2 million to 2.5 million Americans are pathological gamblers, 3 million to 5.3 million are problem gamblers, and 15 million are at risk for problem gambling.

56. Male pathological and problem gamblers outnumber female gamblers 2 to 1, but only a fraction of women, compared with men, seek help. Older pathological gamblers are growing in number as are college students who gamble.

57. The four kinds of gamblers are recreational/social, professional, antisocial, and pathological. The two main types of pathological gamblers are action-seeking gamblers and escape-seeking gamblers.

58. Some characteristics of both types include preoccupation with gambling, betting progressively larger amounts of money, risky or illegal attempts to recoup losses, restlessness and irritability when trying to stop, and jeopardizing family, relationships, and job. Usually, an early big win triggers the compulsion.

59. The four phases of gambling are winning, losing (including chasing losses), desperation, and giving up.

60. Pathological gamblers are more concerned with getting the rush of a hit or staying in action than they are about achieving some financial goal.

61. Pathological gambling is treatable through Gamblers Anonymous (GA, a spiritual program), individ-

ual therapy, and abstinence from all gambling.

Compulsive Shopping & Hoarding

62. The inability to handle money is a hallmark of almost any addict.

63. Compulsive shopping (buying) is an impulse-control disorder. This means that the behavior initially gives pleasure and later relieves depression and tension. The crash after shopping is like a cocaine crash.

64. The control that compulsive shoppers feel along with the respect they feel they are getting at the store counteracts low self-esteem.

65. Collecting, accumulating, and hoarding are offshoots of compulsive shopping; one's worth and self-esteem come from objects and one's ability to acquire them.

Eating Disorders

66. More than one-third of U.S. adults are considered obese, more than twice as many as in 1980.

67. Society's promotion of underweight models and other role models has set up a false ideal of how we should look.

68. The three main eating disorders are anorexia nervosa, bulimia nervosa, and binge-eating disorder. Eating disorders (bingeing or fasting) are often used to escape undesirable feelings.

69. There is a high incidence of comorbid disorders, especially depression, anxiety, substance abuse, and personality disorders.

70. Up to 95% of anorexics and bulimics are female. The rate of eating disorders in high schools and colleges is much higher than for adults.

71. Anorexia is similar to a weight phobia. Dieting, fasting, excessive exercising, and diet pills are used to stay thin. It occurs mostly in girls and young women with a distorted perception of their body. They have a tendency to perfec-

tionism and low self-esteem. Age of onset is dropping.

72. Anorexic individuals lose up to 60% of their normal body weight. The health risks are enormous, especially to the heart, liver, and brain, with a mortality rate of 4% to 20%.

73. Bulimics usually look normal, but they stay that way by bingeing and then purging (throwing up) the large amounts of food they eat. The also use excessive exercise, laxatives, and fasting to control their weight.

74. Low self-esteem, the pursuit of thinness, society's image of the ideal woman, and biochemical changes induced by constant dieting trigger and perpetuate bulimia.

75. Depression, acid burns to the esophagus and throat, heart problems, dental complications, and electrolyte imbalances are common.

76. Of the U.S. population, 33% are considered obese, and 65% are considered overweight. Worldwide there are as many people overweight as underweight (about 1.1 billion). Bingeing without purging is a characteristic of binge-eating disorder.

77. With compulsive overeating, the desire to eat is triggered more by emotional states (to calm, to satisfy, to control pain, and to combat depression) than by true hunger.

78. Health problems due to eating disorders include heart disease, stroke, gout, cancer, arthritis, and especially adult-onset diabetes. More than 15 million Americans have adult-onset (Type II) diabetes. Depression, negative body image, and poor self-esteem are also common.

79. Treatment includes psychotherapy, self-help groups such as Overeaters Anonymous, and behavioral therapy to change eating habits and lifestyle.

Sexual Addiction

80. Compulsive sexual behaviors, such as love addiction, pornography

(particularly online), masturbation, phone sex, voyeurism, and flashing, are practiced as a way to control anxiety, stress, solitude, and low self-esteem.

81. The behaviors are continued despite adverse consequences.

82. After a culminating event such as orgasm, the person often feels guilt, remorse, and fear of being caught and resolves to stop the behavior.

Internet Addiction

83. One billion people use the Internet worldwide. They like the anonymity, the low cost, and the sense of control it gives. Symptoms of Internet addiction are similar to those of a drug addiction.

84. Some people use the Internet obsessively for stimulation; others use it for sedation.

85. About 6% of all Internet users have a compulsive use problem, including cybersexual addiction, cyber-relationship addiction, Internet compulsions, information addiction, and computer games addiction.

86. Cyberaddiction often means using the Internet or the computer to the exclusion of a socially interactive lifestyle.

87. Easy access to online casinos, anonymous chat rooms, game playing, and an endless supply of online pornography leads to more isolation and excess stimulation that perpetuate Internet addiction.

Television Addiction

88. Some compulsive TV viewers spend six to eight hours a day watching television.

89. The reasons for compulsive viewing include watching to change one's mood, craving, loss of control, and continued viewing despite adverse consequences—the same as for other addictions.

90. The distorted view of people's lives makes it hard for many television watchers to make good decisions.

Cell Phone Addiction

91. Worldwide there are more than 2 billion cell phones. The extent of cell phone addiction will not be clear for a few more years.

Conclusions

92. Although the roots of drug and behavioral addictions are similar, the differences should be understood; for example, abstinence is the goal for drug addictions, but controlled use is necessary for many other behavioral addictions such as eating disorders and sexual relationships.

REFERENCES

Ackard, D. M. & Neumark-Sztainer, D. (2003). Multiple sexual victimization among adolescent boys and girls: Prevalence and associations with eating behaviors and psychological health. *Journal of Child Sexual Abuse, 12*(1), 17-37.

Adlaf, E. M. & Ialomiteanu, A. (2001). Prevalence of problem gambling in adolescents: Findings from the 1999 Ontario Student Drug Use Survey. *Canadian Journal of Psychiatry, 45*(8), 752-55.

American Diabetes Association. (2006). *National Diabetes Fact Sheet.* http://www.diabetes.org/uedocuments/NationalDiabetesFactSheetRev.pdf (accessed December 15, 2006).

American Psychiatric Association [APA]. (2000). *Diagnostic and Statistical Manual of Mental Disorders* (4th ed., text revision [*DSM-IV-TR*]). Washington, DC. Author.

Anderson, S. D., Sue-Chu, M., Perry, C. P., Gratziou, C., Kippelen, P., McKenzie, D. C., et al. (2006). Bronchial challenges in athletes applying to inhale a beta 2-agonist at the 2004 Summer Olympics. *Journal of Allergy and Clinical Immunology, 117*(4), 767-73.

Argentina struggles with record anorexia. (July 6, 1997). *Washington Post.*

Arnheim, D. D. & Prentice, W. E. (1993). *Principles of Athletic Training* (8th ed.). St. Louis, MO: Mosby Year Book, Inc.

Aronson, J. K. (1993). *Insights in the Dynamic Psychotherapy of Anorexia and Bulimia: An Introduction to the Literature.* Northvale, NJ: Jason Aronson, Inc.

Balster, R. L. (2003). The pharmacology of inhalants. In A. W. Graham, T. K. Schultz, M. F. Mayo-Smith, R. K. Ries & B. B. Wilford, eds., *Principles of Addiction Medicine* (3rd ed., pp. 295-304). Chevy Chase, MD: American Society of Addiction Medicine, Inc.

Bancroft, J. & Vukadinovic, Z. (2004). Sexual addiction, sexual compulsivity, sexual impulsivity, or what? Toward a theoretical model. *Journal of Sex Research, 41*(3), 225-34.

Barlow, S. E., Dietz, W. H., Klish, W. J. & Trowbridge, F. L. (2002). Medical evaluation of overweight children and adolescents: Reports from pediatricians, pediatric nurse practitioners, and registered dietitians. *Pediatrics, 110*(1 Pt 2), 222-28.

Bausell, R. B., Bausell, C. R. & Siegel, D. G. (1994). The links among alcohol, drugs and crime on American college campuses: A national follow-up study (Unpublished report). Towson, MD: Towson State University Campus Violence Prevention Center.

Beals, K. A. & Manore, M. M. (2002). Disorders of the female athlete triad among collegiate athletes. *International Journal of Sport Nutrition and Exercise Metabolism, 12*(3), 281-93.

Beauvais, F., Oetting, E. R. & Edwards, R. W. (1985). Trends in the use of inhalants among American Indian adolescents. *American Journal of Drug and Alcohol Abuse, 11*(3-4), 209-29.

Becker, A. E., Grinspoon, S. K., Klibanski, A. & Herzog, D. B. (1999). Eating disorders. *New England Journal of Medicine, 340*(14), 1092-98.

Becque, M. D., Lochmann, J. D. & Melrose, D. R. (2000). Effects of oral creatine supplementation on muscular strength and body composition. *Medicine and Science in Sports and Exercise, 32*(3), 654-58.

Bell, M. E., Bhargava, A., Soriano, L., Laugero, K., Akana, S. F. & Dallman, M. F. (2002). Sucrose intake and corticosterone interact with cold to modulate ingestive behaviour, energy balance, autonomic outflow and neuroendocrine responses during chronic stress. *Journal of Neuroendocrinology, 14*(4), 330-42.

Bell, R. M. (1985). *Holy Anorexia.* Chicago: University of Chicago Press.

Bellodi, L., Cavallini, M. C., Bertelli, S., Chiapparino, D., Riboldi, C. & Smeraldi, E. (2001). Morbidity risk for obsessive-compulsive spectrum disorders in first-degree relatives of patients with eating disorders. *American Journal of Psychiatry, 158*(4), 563-69.

Bent, S., Tiedt, T. N., Odden, M. C. & Shlipak, M. G. (2003). The relative safety of ephedra compared with other herbal products. *Annals of Internal Medicine, 138*(6), 468-71.

Berthoud, H. R. (2003). Neural systems controlling food intake and energy balance in a modern world. *Current Opinions in Clinical Nutrition and Metabolic Care, 6*(6), 615-20.

Berthoud, H. R. (2004A). Mind versus metabolism in the control of food intake and energy balance. *Physiology & Behavior, 81*(5), 781-93.

Berthoud, H. R. (2004B). Neural control of appetite: Cross-talk between homeostatic and non-homeostatic systems. *Appetite, 43*(3), 315-17.

Bettor Choices. (2007). About problem gambling (in Connecticut). http://www.dmhas.state.ct.us/statewideservices/bettorchoices.htm#about (accessed April 12, 2007).

Bhasin, S., Storer, T. W., Berman, N., Callegari, C., Clevenger, B., Phillips, J., et al. (1996). The effects of supraphysiologic doses of testosterone on muscle size and strength in normal men. *New England Journal of Medicine, 335*(1), 1-7.

Binge eating. (February 7, 2007). Binge eating grows more common. *Oregonian,* p. A2.

Black, D. W. (2001). Compulsive buying disorder: Definition, assessment, epidemiology, and clinical management. *CNS Drugs, 15*(1), 17-27.

Blum, K., Braverman, E. R., Holder, J. M., Lubar, J. F., Monastra, V. J., Miller, D., et al. (2000). Reward deficiency syndrome: A biogenetic model for the diagnosis and treatment of impulsive, addictive, and compulsive behaviors. *Journal of Psychoactive Drugs, 32*(suppl. i-iv), 1-112.

Blum, K., Cull, J. G., Braverman, E. R. & Comings, D. E. (1996). Reward deficiency syndrome. *American Scientist, 84,* 132-35.

Blume, S. B. & Tavares, H. (2005). Pathologic gambling. In J. H. Lowinson, P. Ruiz, R. B. Millman & J. G. Langrod, eds. *Substance Abuse: A Comprehensive Textbook* (4th ed., pp. 488-98). Baltimore: Williams & Wilkins.

Bouchard, C., ed. (1994). *Genetics of Obesity.* Boca Raton, FL: CRC Press.

Brecher, E. M. (1972). *Licit and Illicit Drugs. Consumers Union Reports.* Boston: Little, Brown and Company.

Breiter, H. C., Aharon, I., Kahneman, D., Dale, A. & Shizgal, P. (2001). Functional imaging of neural responses to expectancy and experience of monetary gains and losses. *Neuron, 30*(2), 619-39.

Brukner, P. & Khan, K. (2002). *Clinical Sports Medicine.* Boston: McGraw-Hill.

Brumberg, J. J. (2000). *Fasting Girls: The History of Anorexia Nervosa.* New York: Vintage.

Buccafusco, J. J., ed. (2004). *Cognitive Enhancing Drugs.* Basel, Switzerland: Birkhäuser Verlag.

Calle, E. E., Rodriguez, C., Walker-Thurmond, K. & Thun, M. J. (2003). Overweight, obesity, and mortality from cancer in a prospectively studied cohort of U.S. adults. *New England Journal of Medicine, 348*(17), 1625-38.

Canseco, J. (2005). *Juiced: Wild Times, Rampant 'Roids, Smash Hits, and How Baseball Got Big.* New York: Harper Collins.

Carnes, P. & Schneider, J. P. (2000). Recognition and management of addictive sexual disorders: Guide for the primary care clinician. *Lippencotts Primary Care Practice, 4*(3), 302-18.

Caruso, D. B. (December 17, 2002). Study finds echinacea of little help. *Medford Mail Tribune,* p. 1B.

Centers for Disease Control (CDC). (2002). Youth Risk Behavior Surveillance: United States, 2001. http://www.cdc.gov/mmwr/preview/mmwrhtml/ss5104a1.htm (accessed December 15, 2006).

Centers for Disease Control. (2005). Prevalence of Overweight and Obesity Among Adults: United States, 2003-2004. http://www.cdc.gov/nchs/products/pubs/pubd/hestats/obese03_04/overwght_adult_03.htm (accessed December 15, 2006).

Cha, A. E. (February 23, 2007). China prescribes tough love for Internet addicts. *Medford Mail Tribune,* p. 10A.

Christenson, G. A., Faber, R. J., de Zwaan, M., Raymond, N. C., Specker, S. M., Ekern, M. D., et al. (1994). Compulsive buying: Descriptive characteristics and psychiatric comorbidity. *Journal of Clinical Psychiatry, 55*(1), 5-11.

Clement, K. (2006). Genetics of human obesity. *Journal of Social Biology, 200*(1), 17-28.

Clement, K. & Sorensen, T. I. A. (2007). *Genetics of Obesity.* London: Informa Healthcare.

Clotfelter, C. T., Cook, P. J., Edell, J. A. & Moore, M. (1999). *State Lotteries at the Turn of the Century: Report to the National Gambling Impact Study Commission.* Chapel Hill, NC: Duke University.

Coleman, E. (1992). Is your patient suffering from compulsive sexual behavior? *Psychiatric Annual, 22,* 320-25.

Cooper, C. J., Noakes, T. D., Dunne, T., Lambert, M. I. & Rochford, K. (1996). A high prevalence of abnormal personality traits in chronic users of anabolic-androgenic steroids. *British Journal of Sports Medicine, 30*(3), 246-50.

Cowie, C. C., Rust, K. F., Byrd-Holt, D. D., Eberhardt, M. S., Flegal, K. M., Engelgau, M. M., et al. (2006). Prevalence of diabetes and impaired fasting glucose in adults in the U.S. population: National Health and Nutrition Examination Survey, 1999-2002. *Diabetes Care, 29*(6), 1263-68.

Cunningham-Williams, R. M. & Cottler, L. B. (2001). The epidemiology of pathological gambling. *Seminar in Clinical Neuropsychiatry, 6*(3), 155-66.

Daee, A., Robinson, P., Lawson, M., Turpin, J. A., Gregory, B. & Tobias, J. D. (2002). Psychologic and physiologic effects of dieting in adolescents. *Southern Medical Journal, 95*(9), 1032-41.

Dean, W. & Morgenthaler, J. (1991). *Smart Drugs & Nutrients.* Santa Cruz, CA: B&J Publications.

Deventer, K., Van Eenoo, P. & Delbeke, F. T. (2006). Screening for amphetamine and amphetamine-type drugs in doping analysis by liquid chromatography/mass spectrometry. *Rapid Communication Mass Spectrometry, 20*(5), 877-82.

DiMeglio, S. (June 26, 2006). World series of poker ups ante. *USA Today,* p. 3C.

Dittmar, H., Beattie, J. & Friese, S. (1996). Objects, decision considerations and self-image in men's and women's impulse purchases. *Acta Psychologica, 93*(1-3), 187-206.

Drug Abuse Warning Network. (2003). New Dawn. https://dawninfo.samhsa.gov/default.asp (accessed September 4, 2006).

DrugScope. (2003). *Nitrites.* http://www.drugscope.org.uk/druginfo/drugsearch/ds_results.asp?file=\wip\11\1\1\nitrites.html (accessed December 15, 2006).

Dunstan, R. (1999). *History of Gambling in the United States.* http://www.library.ca.gov/CRB/97/03/Chapt2.html (accessed December 15, 2006).

Earnest, C. P. (2001). *Dietary androgen "supplements": Separating substance from hype.* http://www.physsportsmed.com/issues/2001/05_01/earnest.htm (accessed December 15, 2006).

Eisenberg, E. R. & Galloway, P. G. (2005). Anabolic-androgenic steroids. In J. H. Lowinson, P. Ruiz, R. B. Millman & J. G. Langrod, eds., *Substance Abuse: A Comprehensive Textbook* (4th ed., pp. 421-58). Baltimore: Williams & Wilkins.

Engwall, D., Hunter, R. & Steinberg, M. (2004). Gambling and other risk behaviors on university campuses. *Journal of American College Health, 52*(6), 245-55.

Erowid. (2006). *The Vaults of Erowid: Nootropics: "Smart drugs."* http://www.erowid.org/smarts/smarts.shtml (accessed December 15, 2006).

Fairburn, C. G. & Beglin, S. J. (1990). Studies of the epidemiology of bulimia nervosa. *American Journal of Psychiatry, 147*(4), 401-8.

Fimrite, P. (June 24, 2006). Reclusive rat owner fit profile of hoarder. *San Francisco Chronicle,* p. A1.

Flavin, M. (2003). *Gambling in the Nineteenth-Century English Novel: "A Leprosy Is o'er the Land."* Brighton, UK: Sussex Academic Press.

Fleming, A. M. (1992). *Something for Nothing: A History of Gambling.* New York: Delacorte Press.

Forbes. (January 10, 2005). Food on the brain. *Forbes Magazine,* p. 63-67.

Forman-Hoffman, V. (2004). High prevalence of abnormal eating and weight control practices among U.S. high-school students. *Eating Behaviors, 5*(4), 325-36.

Fuentes, R. J. & DiMeo, M. (1996). Exercise-induced asthma and the athlete. In R. J. Fuentes, J. M. Rosenberg & A. Davis, eds., *Athletic Drug Reference '96* (pp. 217-34). Durham, NC: Clean Data, Inc.

Fuentes, R. J., Rosenberg, J. M. & Davis, A., eds. (1996). *Athletic Drug Reference '96.* Durham, NC: Clean Data, Inc.

Gamblers Anonymous [GA]. (1998). *Gamblers Anonymous Combo Book.* Los Angeles: Gamblers Anonymous.

Gambler's Lament, The. (1000 B.C.). Traditions of Poetry in India. http://www-personal.umich.edu/~pehook/250w97.gambler.html (accessed December 15, 2006).

Gardner, G. & Halweil, B. (2000). *Underfed and overfed: The global epidemic of malnutrition. Worldwatch Paper #150.* http://www.worldwatch.org/node/840 (accessed December 15, 2006).

Gellene, D. (May 24, 2006). Teenage angst may drive youths to heavy cell phone use. *Portland Oregonian,* p. B2.

Gerasimov, M. R., Ferrieri, R. A., Schiffer, W. K., Logan, J., Gatley, S. J., Gifford, A. N., et al. (2002). Study of brain uptake and biodistribution of [11C]toluene in non-human primates and mice. *Life Sciences, 70*(23), 2811-28.

Gerstein, D., Murphy, S., Toce, C., et al. (1999). *Gambling Impact and Behavior Study: Final Report to the National Gambling Impact Study Commission.* Chicago: National Opinion Research Center. http://www.norc.org/new/gamble.htm (accessed December 15, 2006).

Giannini, A. J. (1991). The volatile agents. In N. S. Miller, ed., *Comprehensive Handbook of Drug and Alcohol Addiction.* New York: Marcel Dekker, Inc.

Goforth, H. W. Jr., Campbell, N. L., Hodgdon, J. A. & Sucec, A. A. (1982). Hematological parameters of trained distance runners following induced erythrocythemia. *Medicine and Science in Sports and Exercise, 14,* 174.

Gold, M. S. & Star, J. (2005). Eating disorders. In J. H. Lowinson, P. Ruiz, R. B. Millman & J. G. Langrod, eds. *Substance Abuse: A Comprehensive Textbook* (4th ed., pp. 469-87). Baltimore: Williams & Wilkins.

Goodman, A. (2005). Sexual addiction. In J. H. Lowinson, P. Ruiz, R. B. Millman & J. G. Langrod, eds. *Substance Abuse: A Comprehensive Textbook* (4th ed., pp. 504-39). Baltimore: Williams & Wilkins.

Goodman, E. & Whitaker, R. C. (2002). A prospective study of the role of depression in the development and persistence of adolescent obesity. *Pediatrics, 110*(3), 497-504.

Gordon, N. F., & Duncan, J. J. (1991). Effect of beta-blockers on exercise physiology: Implication for exercise training. *Medical Science Sports Exercise, 23*(6), 668-76.

Greenberg, I. (January 23, 2007). A sleepy city on the Steppe fears hordes of high rollers. *New York Times,* p. B3.

Grice, D. E., Halmi, K. A., Fichter, M. M., Strober, M., Woodside, D. B., Treasure J. T., et al. (2002). Evidence for a susceptibility gene for anorexia nervosa on chromosome 1. *American Journal of Human Genetics, 70*(3), 787-92.

Grinols, E. L. (2004). *Gambling in America: Costs and Benefits.* New York: Cambridge University Press.

Hancox, R. J., Milne, B. J. & Poulton, R. (2005). Association of television viewing during childhood with poor educational achievement. *Archives of Pediatrics and Adolescent Medicine, 159*(7), 614-18.

Hanley, D. F. (1983). Drug and sex testing: Regulations for international competition. *Clinical Sports Medicine, 2*(1), 13-17.

Health. (2003). Anorexia and Bulimia. http://www.health.com/health/wynks/Anorexia_BulimiaWYNK2000-MAL/whatishappening.html (accessed December 15, 2006).

Helmich, N. (February 7, 2003). Obesity rate could reach nearly 40% in five years. *USA Today,* p. 4A.

Helmich, N. (May 18, 2006). Panel neutral on multivitamins. *USA Today,* p. 11D.

Herbert, A., Gerry, N. P., McQueen, M. B., Heid, I. M., Pfeufer, A., Illig, T., et al. (2006). A common genetic variant is associated with adult and childhood obesity. *Science, 312*(5771), 279-83.

Herman, R. D. (1984). Gambling. In *Encyclopaedia Britannica* (Vol. 7, pp. 866-67). Chicago: Encyclopaedia Britannica.

Herzog, D. B., Dorer, D. J., Keel, P. K., Selwyn, S. E., Ekeblad, E. R., Flores, A. T., et al. (1999). Recovery and relapse in anorexia and bulimia nervosa: A 7.5-year follow-up study. *Journal of the American Academy of Child and Adolescent Psychiatry, 38*(7), 829-37.

Herzog, D. B., Nussbaum, K. M. & Marmor, A. K. (1996). Comorbidity and outcome in eating disorders. *Psychiatric Clinics of North America, 19*(4), 843-59.

Hespel, P., Maughan, R. J. & Greenhaff, P. L. (2006). Dietary supplements for football. *Journal of Sports Science, 24*(7), 749-61.

Hillier, T. A. & Pedula, K. L. (2001). Characteristics of an adult population with newly diagnosed type 2 diabetes: The relation of obesity and age of onset. *Diabetes Care 24*(9), 1522-27.

Hormes, J. T., Filley, C. M. & Rosenberg, N. L. (1986). Neurologic sequelae of chronic solvent vapor abuse. *Neurology, 36*(5), 698-702.

Hudson, J. I., Lalonde, J. K., Berry, J. M., Pindyck, L. J., Bulik, C. M., Crow, S. J., et al. (2006). Binge-eating disorder as a distinct familial phenotype in obese individuals. *Archives of General Psychiatry, 63*(3), 313-19.

International Olympic Committee [IOC]. (2006). Prohibited Classes of Substances and Prohibited Methods, 2006. http://www.olympics.org.uk/documents/downloads/educationpack.pdf (accessed December 15, 2006).

Internet Filter Review. (2007). *Internet Pornography Statistics.* http://internet-filter-review.toptenreviews.com/internet-pornography-statistics.html (accessed April 8, 2007).

Internet World Stats (2006). Internet Usage Statistics: The Big Picture. http://www.internetworldstats.com/stats.htm (accessed December 15, 2006).

Jacobson, B. H. (1990). Effect of amino acids on growth hormone release. *Physical Sports Medicine, 18*(1), 63.

Johnson, J. G., Cohen, P., Kotler, L., Kasen, S. & Brook, J. S. (2002). Psychiatric disorders associated with risk for the development of eating disorders during adolescence and early adulthood. *Journal of Consulting Clinical Psychology, 70*(5), 1119-28.

Kamibeppu, K. & Sugiura, H. (2005). Impact of the mobile phone on junior high-school students' friendships in the Tokyo metropolitan area. *Cyberpsychological Behavior, 8*(2), 121-30.

Kaye, W. H., Pickar, D., Naber, D. & Ebert, M. H. (1982). Cerebrospinal fluid opioid activity in anorexia nervosa. *American Journal of Psychiatry, 139*(5), 643-45.

Kershaw, S. (December 1, 2005). Hooked on the Web: Help is on the way. *New York Times,* p. B1.

King, D. S., Sharp, R. L., Vukovich, M. D., Brown, G. A., Reifenrath, T. A., Uhl, N. L., et al. (1999). Effect of oral androstenedione on serum testosterone and adaptations to resistance training in young men: A randomized controlled trial. *JAMA, 281*(21), 2020-28.

Klein, M. & Kramer, F. (2004). Rave drugs: Pharmacological considerations. *American Association of Nurse Anesthetists Journal, 72*(1), 61-67.

Kochakian, C. D. (1990). History of anabolic-androgenic steroids. In G. Lin & L. Erinoff, eds., *Anabolic Steroid Abuse* (pp. 29-59). Rockville, MD: National Institute on Drug Abuse.

Koran, L. M., Chuong, H. W., Bullock, K. D. & Smith, S. C. (2003). Citalopram for compulsive shopping disorder: An open-label study followed by double-blind discontinuation. *Journal of Clinical Psychiatry, 64*(7), 793-98.

Korman, M., Trimboli, F. & Semler, I. (1980). A comparative evaluation of 162 inhalant users. *Addictive Behavior, 5*(2), 143-52.

Kubey, R. & Csikszentmihalyi, M. (2004). Television addiction is no mere metaphor. *Scientific American, 286*(2), 74-80.

LaBrie, R. A., Shaffer, H. J., LaPlante, D. A. & Wechsler, H. (2003). Correlates of college student gambling in the United States. *Journal of American College Health, 52*(2), 53-62.

Leo, P. (March 16, 2006). Cell phone statistics that may surprise you. *Pittsburgh Post-Gazette*, p. 1B.

Lesieur, H. R. (1998). Costs and treatment of pathological gambling. *Annals of the American Academy of Political and Social Science, 556,* 153-71.

Lesieur, H. R. (2002). Pathological and problem gambling: Costs and social policy. Testimony to Special House Committee to Study Gambling. http://www.rilin.state.ri.us/gen_assem bly/gaming/Lesieur%20testimony.ppt#2 (accessed December 15, 2006).

Lesieur, H. R., Blume, S. B. & Zoppa, R. M. (1986). Alcoholism, drug abuse and gambling. *Alcohol Clinical Experimental Research, 10*(1), 33-38.

Levine, A. S., Kotz, C. M. & Gosnell, B. A. (2003). Sugars: Hedonic aspects, neuroregulation, and energy balance. *American Journal of Clinical Nutrition, 78*(4), 834S-842S.

Linden, R. D., Pope, H. G. Jr. & Jonas, J. M. (1986). Pathological gambling and major affective disorder: Preliminary findings. *Journal of Clinical Psychiatry, 47*(4), 201-3.

Loviglio, J. (2001). Newest dangerous high: Embalming fluid abuse. *Medford Mail Tribune*, p. 3B.

Luck, S. & Hedrick, J. (2004). The alarming trend of substance abuse in anesthesia providers. *Journal of Perianesthesia Nursing, 19*(5), 308-11.

Lukas, S. E. (2003). The pharmacology of steroids. In A. W. Graham, T. K. Schultz, M. F. Mayo-Smith, R. K. Ries & B. B. Wilford, eds., *Principles of Addiction Medicine* (3rd ed., pp. 305-21). Chevy Chase, MD: American Society of Addiction Medicine, Inc.

Lynn, E. J., Walter, R. G., Harris, L. A., Dendy, R. & James, M. (1972). Nitrous oxide: It's a gas. *Journal of Psychedelic Drugs, 5*(1), 1-7.

Marazzi, M. A. & Luby, E. D. (1989). Anorexia nervosa as an auto-addiction. *Annual of the New York Academy of Science, 575,* 545-47.

Marchione, M. (June 29, 2006). Study finds no evidence that folate and B vitamins help fight dementia. *San Francisco Chronicle*, p. A8.

McCutcheon, C. (2005). *Abuse of Muscle Relaxant Prompts Regulatory Moves.* Newhouse News Service. http://www.newhousenews.com/archive/mccutcheon071305.html (accessed December 15, 2006).

McElroy, S. L., Satlin, A., Pope, H. G. Jr., Hudson, J. I. & Keck, P. E. Jr. (1991). Treatment of compulsive shopping and antidepressants: A report of three cases. *Annals of Clinical Psychiatry, 3,* 199-204.

McElroy, S. L., Soutullo, C. A., Goldsmith, R. J. & Brady, K. T. (2003). Co-occurring addictive and other impulse-control disorders. In A. W. Graham, T. K. Schultz, M. F. Mayo-Smith, R. K. Ries & B. B. Wilford, eds. *Principles of Addiction Medicine* (3rd ed., pp. 1347-58). Chevy Chase, MD: American Society of Addiction Medicine, Inc.

McNeilly, D. P. & Burke, W. J. (2001). Gambling as a social activity of older adults. *International Journal of Aging and Human Development, 52*(1), 19-28.

Mellan, O. (1995). *Overcoming Overspending.* New York: Walker and Company.

Meston, C. M. & Gorzalka, B. B. (1992). Psychoactive drugs and human sexual behavior: The role of serotonergic activity. *Journal of Psychoactive Drugs, 24*(1), 1-40.

Meyer, G., Hauffa, B. P., Schedlowski, M., Pawlak, C., Stadler, M. A. & Exton, M. S. (2000). Casino gambling increases heart rate and salivary cortisol in regular gamblers. *Biological Psychiatry, 48*(9), 948-53.

Meyer, J. S. & Quenzer, L. F. (2005). *Psychopharmacology: Drugs, the Brain, and Behavior.* Sunderland, MA: Sinauer Associates, Inc.

Mitchell, J. E., Burgard, M., Faber, R., Crosby, R. D. & De Zwaan, M. (2006). Cognitive behavioral therapy for compulsive buying disorder. *Behavioral Research & Therapy, 44*(12), 1859-65.

Monteleone, P., Tortorella, A., Castaldo, E. & Maj, M. (2006). Association of a functional serotonin transporter gene polymorphism with binge eating disorder. *American Journal of Medical Genetics B Neuropsychiatric Genetics, 141*(1), 7-9.

Morton, R. (1694). *Phthisological: Or a Treatise of Consumptions.* London: Smith and Walford.

Mottram, D. R., ed. (2002). *Drugs in Sport* (3rd ed.). London: Routledge Press.

Nakken, C. (1996). *The Addictive Personality.* Center City, MN: Hazelden.

National Center for Health Statistics. (2004). *Americans Slightly Taller, Much Heavier Than Four Decades Ago.* http://www.cdc.gov/nchs/pressroom/04news/americans.htm (accessed December 15, 2006).

National Collegiate Athletic Association [NCAA]. (2003A). *NCAA Drug-Testing Program.* http://www.ncaa.org/library/sports_sciences/drug_testing_program/2002-03/drugTestingProgram.pdf (accessed December 15, 2006).

National Collegiate Athletic Association. (2003B). *NCAA Study of Substance Use Habits of College Student-Athletes.* http://www.ncaa.org/library/research/substance_use_habits/2001/substance_use_habits.pdf (accessed December 15, 2006).

National Eating Disorder Association [NEDA]. (2006). NEDA college poll. http://www.edap.org/p.asp?WebPage_ID=337 (accessed April 12, 2007).

National Indian Gaming Commission. (2007). *Tribal Data Overview.* http://www.nigc.gov (accessed April 12, 2007).

National Inhalant Prevention Coalition [NIPC]. (2006). *About Inhalants.* http://www.inhalants.org/about.htm (accessed December 15, 2006).

National Institute of Mental Health. (2001). *Eating Disorders: Facts About Eating Disorders and the Search for Solutions.* http://www.nimh.nih.gov/publicat/eatingdisorders.cfm (accessed December 15, 2006).

National Institute on Drug Abuse [NIDA]. (2000A). *Anabolic Steroid Abuse. NIDA Research Report.* http://www.drugabuse.gov/ResearchReports/Steroids/AnabolicSteroids.html (accessed December 15, 2006).

National Institute on Drug Abuse. (2000B). *Inhalant Abuse. NIDA Research Report.* http://www.nida.nih.gov/ResearchReports/Inhalants/Inhalants.html (accessed December 15, 2006).

National Research Council. (1999). Pathological Gambling: A Critical Review. *Committee on the Social and Economic Impact of Pathological Gambling.* Washington, DC: National Academy Press.

Nielsen, A. C. (2006). *Television & Health.* http://www.csun.edu/science/health/docs/tv&health.html (accessed December 15, 2006).

NOAH. (1996). *Eating Disorders: Anorexia and Bulimia Nervosa.* http://www.noah-health.org/en/mental/disorders/eating/index.html (accessed December 15, 2006).

NORC (1999). *Gambling Impact and Behavior Study. Report to the National Gambling Impact Study Commission.* http://govinfo.library.unt.edu/ngisc/index.htm (accessed December 15, 2006).

O'Brien, C. P. (2001). Drug addiction and drug abuse. In J. G. Hardman & L. E. Limbird, eds., *Goodman's & Gilman's Pharmacological Basis of Therapeutics* (10th ed.). New York: McGraw-Hill.

Office of National Drug Control Policy. (2006). *Inhalants.* http://www.whitehousedrugpolicy.gov/drugfact/inhalants/index.html (accessed December 15, 2006).

Okudan, N. & Gokbel, H. (2005). The effects of creatine supplementation on performance during the repeated bouts of supramaximal exercise. *Journal of*

Sports Medicine and Physical Fitness, 45(4), 507-11.

Oleksyn, V. (February 8, 2007). Austrians break international child pornography operation. *San Francisco Chronicle,* p. A11.

O'Rahilly, S. & Farooqi, I. S. (2006). Genetics of obesity. *Philosophical Transactions of the Royal Society of London, Series B, Biological Sciences, 361*(1471), 1095-105.

Organisation for Economic Co-operation and Development. (2006). *OECD Broadband Statistics.* http://www. oecd.org/document/9/0,2340,en_2649_ 37441_37529673_1_1_1_37441,00.htm l (accessed April 12, 2007).

Palmer, M. E., Haller, C., McKinney, P. E., Klein-Schwartz, W., Tschirgi, A., Smolinske, S. C., et al. (2003). Adverse events associated with dietary supplements: An observational study. *Lancet, 361*(9352), 101-6.

Pascual, J. A., Belalcazar, V., de Bolos, C., Gutierrez, R., Llop, E. & Segura, J. (2004). Recombinant erythropoietin and analogues: A challenge for doping control. *Therapeutic Drug Monitoring, 26*(2), 175-79.

Patrick, D. (August 24, 1998). McGwire taking hits over use of power pill. *USA Today,* p. 1D.

Petry, M. M. (2005). *Pathological Gambling: Etiology, Comorbidity, and Treatment.* Washington, DC: American Psychological Association.

Petry, N. M., Stinson, F. S. & Grant, B. F. (2005). Comorbidity of DSM-IV pathological gambling and other psychiatric disorders: Results from the National Epidemiologic Survey on Alcohol and Related Conditions. *Journal of Clinical Psychiatry, 66*(5), 564-74.

Physicians' Desk Reference [PDR]. (2006). *Physicians' Desk Reference.* Montvale, NJ: Medical Economics Company.

Pope, H. J. Jr. & Katz, D. L. (1994). Psychiatric and medical effects of anabolic-androgenic steroid use. A controlled study of 160 athletes. *Archives of General Psychiatry, 51*(5), 375-82.

Pound, D. (2006). *Inside Dope.* Mississauga, Ontario: John Wiley & Sons Canada, Ltd.

Pritts, S. D. & Susman, J. (2003). Diagnosis of eating disorders in primary care. *American Family Physician, 67*(2), 297-304.

Provencher, Herve, P., Jais, X., Lebrec, D., Humbert, M., Simonneau, G., et al. (2006). Deleterious effects of beta-blockers on exercise capacity and hemodynamics in patients with portopulmonary hypertension. *Gastroenterology, 130*(1), 120-26.

PsychCentral. (2007). Internet Addiction Guide. http://psychcentral.com/netaddiction/ (accessed April 12, 2007).

Rankinen, T. & Bouchard, C. (2006). Genetics of food intake and eating behavior phenotypes in humans. *Annual Review of Nutrition, 26,* 413-34.

Rosenberg, N. L., Grigsby, J., Dreisbach, J., Busenbark, D. & Grigsby, P. (2002). Neuropsychologic impairment and MRI abnormalities associated with chronic solvent abuse. *Journal of Toxicology, Clinical Toxicology, 40*(1), 21-34.

Rosenberg, N. L., Fuentes, R. J., Wooley, B. H., Reese, T. & Podraza, J. (1996). Questions and answers: What athletes commonly ask. In R. J. Fuentes, J. M. Rosenberg & A. Davis, eds., *Athletic Drug Reference '96.* Durham, NC: Clean Data, Inc.

Rosenthal, R. J. & Lesieur, H. R. (1992). Self-reported withdrawal symptoms and pathological gambling. *American Journal of Addictions, 1,* 150-54.

Rubin, R. (July 8, 2004). Smart pills make headway. *USA Today,* p. 1D.

Rukavina T. & Pokrajac-Bulian, A. (2006). Thin-ideal internalization, body dissatisfaction and symptoms of eating disorders in Croatian adolescent girls. *Eating and Weight Disorders, 11*(1), 31-37.

Rupp, N. T., Brudno, D. S. & Guill, M. F. (1993). The value of screening for risk of exercise-induced asthma in high school athletes. *Annual Allergy, 70*(4). 339-42.

Russell, G. (1979). Bulimia nervosa: An ominous variant of anorexia nervosa. *Psychological Medicine 9*(3), 429-48.

Rybakowski, F., Slopien, A., Dmitrzak-Weglarz, M., Czerski, P., Rajewski, A. & Hauser, J. (2006). The 5-HT2A-1438 A/G and 5-HTTLPR polymorphisms and personality dimensions in adolescent anorexia nervosa: Association study. *Neuropsychobiology, 53*(1), 33-39.

Sakai, J. T., Mikulich-Gilbertson, S. K. & Crowley, T. J. (2006). Adolescent inhalant use among male patients in treatment for substance and behavior problems: two-year outcome. *American Journal of Drug & Alcohol Abuse, 32*(1), 29-40.

Schnirring, L. (2000). Growth hormone doping: The search for a test. *The Physician and Sportsmedicine, 28*(4), 16-18. http://www.physsportsmed. com/issues/2000/04_00/news.htm (accessed December 15, 2006).

Schumacher, Y. O. & Ashenden, M. (2004). Doping with artificial oxygen carriers: An update. *Sports Medicine, 34*(3), 141-50.

Schwartz, D. G. (2006). *Roll the Bones: The History of Gambling.* New York: Gotham Books.

Sexaholics Anonymous. (1989). *Sexaholics Anonymous.* New York: SA Literature.

Shaffer, H. (February 28, 1998). Lecture to casino executives, Las Vegas gaming convention. *Medford Mail Tribune.*

Shaffer, H. J., Hall, M. N. & Vander Bilt, J. (1999). Estimating the prevalence of disordered gambling behavior in the United States and Canada: A research synthesis. *American Journal of Public Health, 89*(9), 1369-76.

Sharp, C. W., Beauvais, F. & Spence, R. (1992). Inhalant Abuse: A Volatile Research Agenda. *NIDA Research Monograph Series No. 129, NIH Publication No. 93-3480.* Rockville, MD: National Institutes of Health.

Sharp, C. W. & Rosenberg, N. L. (2005). Inhalants. In J. H. Lowinson, P. Ruiz, R. B. Millman & J. G. Langrod, eds., *Substance Abuse: A Comprehensive Textbook* (4th ed., pp. 336-66). Baltimore: Williams & Wilkins.

Siegel, E. & Wason, S. (1990). Sudden death caused by inhalation of butane and propane. *New England Journal of Medicine, 323*(23), 1638.

Smith, G. (1974). *When the Cheering Stopped.* Toronto: MacLeod.

Spitzer, R. L., Yanovski, S., Wadden, T., Wing, R., Marcus, M. D., Stunkard, A., et al. (1993). Binge eating disorder: Its further validation in a multisite study. *International Journal of Eating Disorders, 13*(2), 137-53.

Sports Illustrated. (February 2, 2002A). Olympic cross-country skiing. *Sports Illustrated,* pp. 24-26.

Sports Illustrated. (June 3, 2002B). Steroids in baseball. *Sports Illustrated,* pp. 35-49.

Spriet, L. L. (1995). Caffeine and performance. *International Journal of Sports Nutrition, 5,* S84-S99.

Steppan, C. M., Bailey, S. T., Bhat, S., Brown, E. J., Banerjee, R. R., Wright, C. M., et al. (2001). The hormone resistin links obesity to diabetes. *Nature, 409*(6818), 307-12.

Substance Abuse and Mental Health Services Administration [SAMHSA]. (2006). *Summary of Findings from the 2005 National Household Survey on Drug Abuse.* Rockville, MD: Substance Abuse and Mental Health Services, Office of Applied Studies.

Swan, N. (1995). Inhalants. In J. H. Jaffe, ed., *Encyclopedia of Drugs and Alcohol* (Vol. II, pp. 590-600). New York: Simon & Schuster Macmillan.

Taintor, Z. (2005). Internet/computer addiction. In J. H. Lowinson, P. Ruiz, R. B. Millman & J. G. Langrod, eds. *Substance Abuse: A Comprehensive Textbook* (4th ed., pp. 540-48). Baltimore: Williams & Wilkins.

Tamburrino, M. B. & McGinnis, R. A. (2002). Anorexia nervosa: A review. *Panminerva Medicine, 44*(4) 301-11.

TESS. (2007). *2005 American Association of Poison Control Systems TESS Report.* http://www.aapcc.org/2005.htm (accessed April 8, 2007).

Thiessen, M. (April 14, 2005). Judge rules against FDA ban on ephedra. *Washington Post,* p. E5.

Tice, D. J. (February 1993). Big spenders. *Saint Paul Pioneer Press* (Special Reprint Section).

Todd, T. (1987). Anabolic steroids: The gremlins of sport. *Journal of Sports History, 14,* 87-107.

Torassa, U. (April 10, 2002). Herbal supplement weakens cancer drug, scientists say. *San Francisco Chronicle,* p. A2.

Tran, D. C., Brazeau, D. A., Nickerson, P. A. & Fung, H. L. (2006). Effects of repeated in vivo inhalant nitrite exposure on gene expression in mouse liver and lungs. *Nitric Oxide, 14*(4), 279-89.

Treasure, J. & Campbell, I. (1994). The case for biology in the aetiology of anorexia nervosa. *Psychological Medicine, 24*(1) 3-8.

Tyre, P. (December 5, 2005). Fighting anorexia. *Newsweek,* p. 50-60.

U.S. Congress. (March 22, 1990). *Abuse of Steroids in Amateur and Professional Athletics.* Hearing before the Subcommittee on Crime of the Committee on the Judiciary, House of Representatives.

U.S. Food and Drug Administration. (2003). *Dietary Supplements: Warnings and Safety Information.* http://www.cfsan.fda.gov/%7Edms/ds-warn.html (accessed December 15, 2006).

University of Michigan. (2006). *Monitoring the Future Study. 2006 Data from In-School Surveys of 8th-, 10th-, and 12th-Grade Students.* http://www.monitoringthefuture.org/data/06data.html#2006 data-drugs (accessed April 8, 2007).

University of Sussex. (1997). *Shopping Addicts Need Help.* Bulletin in the University of Sussex newsletter. http://www.sussex.ac.uk/press_office/bulletin/17jan97/item5.html (accessed December 15, 2006).

Van der Merwe, P. J. & Grobbelaar, E. (2005). Unintentional doping through the use of contaminated nutritional supplements. *South African Medical Journal, 95*(7), 510-11.

Viagra, poppers are a fatal combination. (June 22, 1999). *San Francisco Chronicle,* p. B1.

Volkow, N. (2002). Dopamine May Play Role in Cue-Induced Craving Distinct from its Role Regulating Reward Effects. *NIDA Newscan.* http://www.drugabuse.gov/Newsroom/02/NS-05.html (accessed December 15, 2006).

Wang, G. J., Volkow, N. D., Logan, J., Pappas, N. R., Wong, C. T., Zhu, W., et al. (2001). Brain dopamine and obesity. *Lancet, 357*(9253), 354-57.

Wardell, J. (October 14, 2006). Internet gaming firms go bust. *San Francisco Chronicle,* p. C1.

Watson, G., Casa, D. J., Fiala, K. A., Hile, A., Roti, M. W., Healey, J. C., et al. (2006). Creatine use and exercise heat tolerance in dehydrated men. *Journal of Athletic Training, 41*(1), 18-29.

Weil, A. & Rosen, W. (2004). *From Chocolate to Morphine.* Boston: Houghton Mifflin Company.

Weinberg, R. A. & Bealer, B. K. (2001). *The World of Caffeine.* New York: Routledge.

Weisman, L. (June 2, 2005). Strict rules restrain NFL supplements. *USA Today,* p. 1C.

Wikipedia. (2006). Nootropic. http://en.wikipedia.org/wiki/Nootropic (accessed December 15, 2006).

Williams, M. H., Wesseldine, S., Somma, T. & Schuster, R. (1981). The effect of induced erythrocythemia upon 5-mile treadmill run time. *Medicine and Science in Sports and Exercise, 13*(3), 169-75.

Wiseman, C. V. (1992). Cultural expectations of thinness in women: An update. *International Journal of Eating Disorders, 11*(1), 42-49.

Wiseman, P. (January 22, 2007). Casinos, hotels bet on Macau. *USA Today,* p. 1B.

Wolf, N. (1992). *The Beauty Myth: How Images of Beauty Are Used Against Women.* New York: Anchor Books/Doubleday.

Wood, R. I. (2004). Reinforcing aspects of androgens. *Physiology and Behavior, 83*(2), 279-89.

Wood, R. W. (1994). Inhalants. In J. H. Jaffe, ed., *Encyclopedia of Drugs and Alcohol* (Vol. II, pp. 590-95). New York: Simon & Schuster Macmillan.

Wood, S. (November 21, 2002). Upshaw defends dietary extras. *USA Today,* p. 1C.

Wooley, B. H. (1992). Drugs of abuse in sport. In R. Banks, Jr., ed., *Substance Abuse in Sport: The Realities* (2nd ed., pp. 3-12). Dubuque, IA: Kendall/Hunt Publishing Company.

World Anti-Doping Agency. (2006). http://www.wada-ama.org/en/dynamic.ch2?pageCategory.id=255 (accessed December 15, 2006).

World Health Organization [WHO]. (1998). *Volatile Solvent Use: A Global Overview,* WHO/HSC/SAB/99.7. http://www.who.int/substance_abuse/activities/volatilesolvent/en (accessed December 15, 2006).

Wu, L. T. & Ringwalt, C. L. (2006). Inhalant use and disorders among adults in the United States. *Drug and Alcohol Dependence, 85*(1), 1-11.

Wu, L. T., Schlenger, W. E. & Ringwalt, C. L. (2005). Use of nitrite inhalants ("poppers") among American youth. *Journal of Adolescent Health, 37*(1), 52-60.

Yesalis, C. E., Herrick, R. T., Buckley, W. E., et al. (1988). Self-reported use of anabolic-androgenic steroids by elite powerlifters. *Physiology of Sports Medicine, 16,* 91-100.

Drug Use & Prevention:
From Cradle to Grave

Drug abuse prevention is a lifetime project.
© 2006 CNS Productions, Inc.

- **Introduction.** Because drug use affects people from cradle to grave, many drug educators believe that prevention should be practiced from cradle to grave.

PREVENTION

- **Concepts of Prevention.** Historically, substance-abuse prevention has included a wide range of philosophies, from total prohibition, to temperance, to harm reduction. Scare tactics, drug information programs, skill-building programs, and resiliency programs are some of the methods used over the years.
- **Prevention Methods.** The three main prevention methods are supply reduction (enforce legal penalties and interdict drugs), demand reduction (reduce craving for drugs), and harm reduction (minimize harm without requiring abstinence).
- **Challenges to Prevention.** The impediments to prevention efforts include the abundance of legal drugs, the availability of street drugs, the relatively slow rate of success of prevention programs, the difficulty of properly evaluating these efforts, and the lack of adequate funding.

FROM CRADLE TO GRAVE

- **Patterns of Use.** A pattern of earlier age of first use and high levels of overall use are associated with future development of drug problems. Drug abuse is not restricted to any race, socioeconomic class, age, gender, or level of intelligence.
- **Pregnancy & Birth.** Drugs cross the placental barrier and affect the fetus more strongly than the mother. The infant can be born addicted and go through dangerous withdrawal. Drug effects continue after birth.
- **Youth & School.** Alcohol is still the number one problem in schools, tobacco is second, and marijuana is third. In addition, the abuse of prescription drugs and stimulants like methamphetamine and ecstasy has risen rapidly. Increased alcohol abuse is being countered by recognizing risk factors, demystifying perceived benefits, bolstering resiliency, and using normative assessment. Prevention efforts are effective when taught throughout all grades.
- **Love, Sex & Drugs.** Psychoactive drugs are used to lower inhibitions to enhance sexual activity. Initially, some drugs may increase sensation but with continued use can diminish sexual performance and pleasure. Sexual violence, such as date rape, is strongly associated with drug use. High-risk sexual practices, aggravated by lowered inhibitions and contaminated needles, spread sexually transmitted diseases (e.g., HIV/AIDS, hepatitis, and gonorrhea).
- **Drugs at Work.** Employee assistance programs (EAPs) help control substance abuse in the workplace, which costs businesses and society more than $160 billion per year in lost productivity, lost earnings, and increased healthcare costs.
- **Drugs in the Military.** In the 1970s the U.S. Armed Forces began a drug-abuse prevention program that has been extremely effective.
- **Drug Testing.** Pre-employment testing, testing of people in treatment, military testing, sports testing, and random testing of workers responsible for public safety (e.g., pilots and nuclear technicians) are the common areas where drug testing is most used.
- **Drugs & the Elderly.** The elderly are more susceptible to the pharmacological effects of drugs. Alcohol abuse and prescription drug abuse are the biggest problems.
- **Conclusions.** To be successful, a prevention program must be specific to age, ethnicity, and cultural group, and the message must be consistent. Prevention efforts should also be practiced throughout everyone's lifetime.

Anti-Drug Gains in Colombia Don't Reduce Flow to U.S.

By JOEL BRINKLEY

Employers grapple with medical marijuana use

Drug czar: 'We're winning'

N.J. moves to end ban on over-the-counter syringes

At schools, less tolerance for 'zero tolerance'

Positive workplace drug tests at 18-year low

Singapore executes Australian trafficker

Parents clueless about kids' vices,

Cigarette tax hike would fund health care for kids

Over-the-counter drugs, pregnancy: a bad mix?

More drug treatment, prevention necessary for youths, officials say

Summit encourages drug testing in schools

College drug use, binge drinking rise

Bans push smoke-free taverns

Routine circumcision could reduce STD rate

Drug convictions costing students their financial aid

By Donna Leinwand

Anti-drug advertising campaign a failure, GAO report says

Movement to ban school junk food gets a big boost

Young teens' drug abuse falls to 10%

Older but not wise to addiction

Hepatitis C: Year of drug treatment can cost $36,000

INTRODUCTION

"Federal drug control spending for prevention and prevention research was just $1.57 billion in 2006. This is less than 1% of the estimated cost of drug abuse to the United States. In addition, according to many physicians, more than half of all hospital admissions are directly or indirectly due to drug, cigarette, and alcohol abuse whether it's pneumonia aggravated by smoking, cirrhosis of the liver from binge drinking, a heart attack from methamphetamine, or hepatitis C from a dirty needle. These expenditures could add another $500 billion to the cost of drug abuse. Good prevention is a difficult process because moral and legal issues become involved with medical and recovery issues. We concentrate on issues such as the illegality, the meth lab raids, the interdiction strategies, and mandatory sentencing. And while it has been proven that good prevention works as does good treatment, we keep trying to win a drug war through supply reduction rather than demand reduction, especially prevention."

Darryl Inaba, Pharm.D., clinical director, Genesis Recovery Center

Psychoactive drugs and addictive behaviors affect people's lives from conception to death. For example:

◇ a fetus absorbs heroin through the umbilical cord and the placental barrier when an addicted mother injects the drug;

◇ a 14-year-old is offered MDMA at a party so he can get "rolling";

◇ a college student troubled by bulimia makes herself throw up five times a week;

◇ a young mother with three children hides in her room to smoke crack;

◇ while having sex, a 28-year-old intravenous (IV) methamphetamine user infects his girlfriend with HIV he got through a contaminated needle;

◇ an office worker takes clonazepam (Klonopin®) to cope with job stress and anxiety, while a co-worker with major depression is prescribed Zoloft,® an antidepressant, to help him function;

◇ a mother, whose children have grown, battles boredom and the empty-nest syndrome by compulsively playing poker machines;

◇ a 50-year-old salesperson on the road smokes and drinks to cope with loneliness; and

◇ a 74-year-old borrows hydrocodone (Vicodin®), a prescription painkiller, from a neighbor to relieve arthritic pain.

Because drug use and abuse affects all ages, **prevention and treatment programs should also be continued throughout people's lifetimes.** Some strategies include:

◇ encouraging pregnant mothers to attend prenatal care programs to teach them how drugs affect their fetuses;

◇ limiting the use of club drugs at parties through greater public scrutiny of such events;

◇ offering counseling on eating disorders in high schools and colleges;

◇ using outreach workers to encourage drug users to practice safe sex

and use clean needles to prevent HIV or hepatitis C infection while trying to convince them to enter treatment;

◇ doing an intervention to get a heavy-drinking sales representative into an employee assistance program (EAP); and

◇ holding seminars to enlighten senior citizens about drug cross-reactions.

If the basic premise of practicing prevention at every age is accepted, the questions that need to be answered are: *What are the different theories and methods of prevention? Which prevention methods work?* and *How should they be implemented throughout people's lives?*

PREVENTION

CONCEPTS OF PREVENTION

PREVENTION GOALS

Each **society has to decide exactly what it is trying to prevent**. And because drug users are at different levels of use, from abstention to addiction, and because there is such a diversity of cultural practices in the United States, that decision can be difficult. **Is the society trying to prevent any use of any psychoactive drug, trying to ban just illicit drugs, or simply trying to limit the damage caused by use, abuse, and addiction?** In the United States and most countries, a combination of prevention goals is needed. They are:

◇ preventing the disease of addiction from ever developing by teaching skills that will help the individual resist drug use, make wise decisions, and resolve inner pain and conflict—all aimed at instilling resiliency and creating alternatives to drug use (**primary prevention**);

◇ stopping inappropriate or potentially destructive use as soon as possible where it has begun (**secondary prevention**); and

◇ in more advanced stages of abuse and addiction, reversing the progression, restoring people to health, and helping them find alternate ways of thinking and living (**tertiary prevention**).

"I set out on a mission to rebuild myself. I said, 'Okay, now what would you do if you had to rebuild a car? Well, you would take everything apart and you'd start all over.' So what I had to do was shed all the negativity and step down naked so to speak and just build myself up all over again. And this time, not making mistakes and not making the bad choices that I made before."
48-year-old recovering addict

Traditionally, there have been three methods to achieve the above prevention goals:

1. **Reduce the supply** of illegal drugs available in society. This is usually done through interdiction of drugs supplies, legislation against use, and legal penalties for possession, distribution, and use.

2. **Reduce the demand** for all psychoactive drugs, legal and illegal. This is done through treatment of drug dependency and prevention through education, emotional development, moral growth, and individual or community activities.

3. **Reduce the harm** that drugs do to users, friends, and relatives of users, and society as a whole. This more controversial alternative is done through such methods as promoting temperance, instituting needle exchanges with outreach components, using drug substitution programs (e.g., methadone maintenance), providing resources to lessen the consequences of abuse (e.g., designated-driver and needle-

exchange programs), and decriminalizing drug use.

Historically, **supply reduction and harm reduction (temperance) have been the most widely used methods**. In the twentieth century, with the recognition of addiction as a disease, demand reduction has become a viable method of prevention. Only one-third of the projected $12.96 billion in federal funds requested for drug control in 2008 is allocated for demand reduction (Office of National Drug Control Policy [ONDCP], 2007). Note that the figures do not include the costs of incarceration and parole, which would almost double the budget.

"A common fault in drug policy has been anticipating or promising dramatic results within an unrealistically brief period. Reducing and stopping drug use requires fundamental changes in the attitudes of millions of Americans, and that shift in attitude is more gradual than we would wish. The National Drug Control Strategy promotes a steady pressure against drug use and underscores why drug control must be lifted out of partisan conflict."
Barry R. McCaffrey, former director, Office of National Drug Control Policy (ONDCP)

"We know that treatment works. But we also know that there are too many Americans who, for a variety of reasons, cannot access the treatment they need. By giving people a choice and

TABLE 8–1   NATIONAL DRUG CONTROL BUDGET, 1995–2008 (in millions)

FUNCTIONAL AREAS	1995	1999	2004 (est.)	2008 (est.)
Demand Reduction				
Drug-abuse treatment	$2,175.8	$2.230.8	$2,941.9	$3,042.7
Drug-abuse prevention with research	$1,104.1	$1,461.9	$1,496.3	$1,575.1
Prevention research	$ 178.6	$ 249.9	$ 411.8	(incl. above)
Treatment research	$ 262.0	$ 373.5	$ 611.0	(incl. above)
Total Demand Reduction	**$3,720.5**	**$4,316.1**	**$5,461.0**	**$4,617.8**
Supply Reduction				
Domestic law enforcement	$1,993.4	$2,542.2	$3,036.1	$3,852.5
International	$ 232.5	$ 746.3	$1,078.9	$1,399.1
Interdiction	$1,099.3	$2,155.6	$2,103.3	$3,292.1
Total Supply Reduction	**$3,325.2**	**$5,444.1**	**$6,218.3**	**$8,543.7**
TOTAL BUDGET	**$7,045.7**	**$9,760.2**	**$11,679.3**	**$13,161.5**

Over the years an additional $6 billion to $10 billion has been spent in the federal, state, and local criminal justice systems.

(ONDCP, 2007)

the means to help connect them with effective treatment, we will be able to more directly help drug users who have recognized their problem."

John P. Walters, director, Office of National Drug Control Policy

HISTORY

Temperance vs. Prohibition

"I am aware that the efforts of science and humanity, in applying their resources to the cure of a disease induced by a vice, will meet with a cold reception from many people."

Benjamin Rush (Rush, 1814)

Attempts to regulate drugs, particularly alcohol, have wavered between moderation of use (temperance) and outright prohibition. In the United States, eighteenth- and early-nineteenth-century attempts to regulate alcohol consumption initially focused on the ideal of temperance. The guiding assumptions of temperance were that heavy drinking and especially drunkenness were destructive, sinful, and immoral, but moderate use could improve health and mood. Initial efforts consisted of convincing drinkers to switch from distilled spirits (hard liquor) to beer, wine, and fermented cider (White, 1998).

By the 1850s the ideal of total abstinence had replaced that of temperance. This ideal eventually led to passage of the Eighteenth Amendment to the Constitution, forbidding the manufacture, sale, and transportation of alcohol.

This conflict between moderate use of alcohol/psychoactive drugs and moral/legal abhorrence of any use of any amount persists to the present day. Historically, with alcohol the concept of complete prohibition, or lately zero tolerance, seems to run on a 70-year cycle: 1780, 1850, 1920, and 1990. Over the past 20 years, all states raised their drinking age to 21 while decreasing the allowable blood alcohol concentration (BAC) from 0.10 to 0.08. In 1995 Louisiana became the first state to lower the drinking age back to 18 years. Currently, several states have enacted zero-tolerance laws that suspend driver's licenses of youths under 21 convicted of driving with a BAC of just 0.01, the equivalent of about half a beer.

Did Prohibition Really Fail?

Popular belief over the decades has been that **Prohibition, enacted into law in 1917 by the Eighteenth Amendment (enforced starting in 1920 and repealed in 1933)**, was ineffective. An examination of medical records concerning diseases caused by excess alcohol consumption as well as criminal justice system (CJS) records shows that **Prohibition did reduce health problems, domestic violence, crime, and consumption**.

◇ Admissions to mental hospitals for alcoholic psychosis in Massachusetts fell from 14.6 per 100,000 in 1910 to 6.4 in 1922 and 7.7 in 1929. In New York the rate fell from 11.5 in 1910 to 3.0 in 1920, and it rose again to 6.5 in 1931 (Aaron & Musto, 1981).

◇ Nationally, death rates from cirrhosis of the liver fell from 14.8 per 100,000 in 1907 to 7.1 in 1920; they stayed below 7.5 through the rest of the 1920s (Jaffe & Shopland, 1995).

◇ In addition there were decreased legal costs of jailing drunks, less domestic violence, and less crime in general.

◇ Per-capita alcohol consumption dropped by half and did not return to pre-Prohibition levels until 20 to 30 years after Prohibition was repealed.

◇ As bootlegging increased the supply of alcohol in the late 1920s, medical problems increased again but still stayed way below pre-Prohibition levels.

The end of prohibition in 1933 was greeted with joy by the anti-prohibition forces known as the "Wets" and disgust by the prohibitionists and supporters of temperance.

Reprinted with permission of the Wisconsin Historical Society.

• •

The myth that Prohibition created organized crime isn't really true. **Criminal organizations existed long before Prohibition, although organizational techniques were refined during that era** and prepared the mobs to step into smuggling and distribution of illicit drugs.

Even though Prohibition did reduce illness and crime, or possibly because it did, concern for and treatment of the alcoholic decreased. Prohibitionists thought that all they needed to do was ban alcohol and the problems would be solved (Lender & Martin, 1987). They also tried to criminalize drinking itself, even though Prohibition only banned the "manufacture, sale, and transportation of intoxicating liquors." There was continuing support for Prohibition from Herbert Hoover and most state governors in 1929; and if the Great Depression hadn't occurred in the 1930s, the Eighteenth Amendment might have lasted years longer. **The need for increased tax revenue, the activities of the anti-Prohibition forces called the**

"Wets," and the general public's desire to drink again caused its repeal.

Scare Tactics & Drug Information Programs

Concerted attempts to lessen substance abuse didn't begin in earnest until the 1960s, when recreational drugs came out of the ghettos and barrios and began to affect middle-class kids. A number of grassroots prevention movements began in the sixties and seventies as the percentage of Americans who had used any illicit drug went from 2% in 1962 to 31% in 1979 (Rusche, 1995; Substance Abuse and Mental Health Services Administration [SAMHSA], 2006).

These early prevention programs assumed that young people lacked knowledge about the dangerous effects of psychoactive drugs. **Knowledge-based programs were established to teach students about pharmacological effects, causes of addiction, health effects of drug use, and legal penal-**

ties. Providing factual information with a heavy dose of scare tactics was considered enough to reduce drug use. Often the scare tactics overwhelmed the information or made the truth suspect to students. Early scare tactics also presented nonfactual or distorted information about drugs, destroying the credibility of the message.

"In the early 1970s, the government asked a group of treatment professionals, including myself, to review 297 drug education films that were available. We found that we could barely recommend even one or two of the films because most of them had bad information, relied only on scare tactics, or were just poorly made."

Darryl Inaba, Pharm.D., clinical director, Genesis Recovery Center

Although factual information produced documentable increases in knowledge and changes in attitude and is still thought to persuade some young people into rational abstention, **there is little evidence that drug information alone causes changes in behavior**.

"I received only one drug education lesson in my ninth-grade health class. They talked a lot about all the different types of drugs and drug use. The class actually made me quite aware that I was missing out on a whole lot of drugs. By the time I ended up in therapeutic boarding school, I knew a lot about drug use and abuse but only because of the extensive drug history I had."

21-year-old college student in recovery

The role of knowledge in comprehensive prevention programs is still unknown. Some studies indicate that among certain adolescent audiences, factual information actually stimulates experimentation (Moskowitz, 1989). It has been suggested that adolescents' feelings of invulnerability, a limited view of the future, and an indifference to long-term health consequences all frustrate information-only approaches. School-centered knowledge-based programs may also miss students who skip school frequently and are most at risk for health and crime problems associated with drug abuse. Although **good prevention efforts greatly lessen drug problems at a fraction of the cost of supply reduction efforts**, these programs often suffer from underskilled teachers and trainers, are not appropriate to the developmental level of targeted students, or are too brief.

Skill-Building & Resiliency Programs

As the disease concept of alcoholism and drug addiction took hold, **prevention efforts expanded to address the psychological and developmental factors that might predispose individuals to turn to drugs** as well as the social skills that might protect them from experimentation and abuse. The more risk factors that youths have, the more likely they are to abuse drugs (Bry, McKeon & Pandina, 1982; Pumariega, Kilgus & Rodriguez, 2005). Increasing skills that effectively address these risks may result in a solid prevention strategy.

◇ **General competency building.** The aim is to teach people how to adjust to life through **training in self-esteem, in socially acceptable behavior, and in decision-making, self-assertion, problem-solving, and vocational skills.** Programs employing these prevention strategies continue to report positive results, but once training ceases the gains are soon lost. Periodic "booster shots" of training throughout a student's educational career improve the effectiveness of this kind of prevention education.

◇ **Coping (resistance) skills.** Specific coping skills, like parenting classes, anger management, and even breathing techniques, are taught to help people face stressful situations. Coping skills are seen as a way to **develop the self-reliance, confidence, and inner resources needed to resist drug use.** Other techniques include psychological inoculation that is learning appropriate and healthy replies to frequently faced situations such as peer or advertising pressures.

◇ **Reinforcing protective factors and resiliency.** These are ways to **build on natural strengths that people already have available.** The factors that seem to increase resiliency are optimism, empathy, insight, intellectual competence, self-esteem, direction or purpose in life, and determination (Kumpfer, 1994). These factors, along with supportive friends and family and opportunities to belong to meaningful groups in their own communities—all emphasize that coping resources are usually available to most people (Botvin & Griffin, 2005).

◇ **Address and reverse risk factors.** Early aggressive/oppositional behavior, poverty, lack of parental supervision, dysfunctional drug-abusing peers, and other **risk factors associated with future substance use disorders can be examined while practicing strategies to minimize their development** (Kitashima, 1997).

◇ **Support system development.** The purpose of this method is to **provide easy access to sympathetic resources such as telephone reassurance for the elderly** who are living alone or homework hotlines for students struggling with the stress of school. Stress reduction leads to decreased drug and alcohol abuse.

Changing the Environment

Gradually, prevention programs began to look beyond individuals to the social and environmental influences on drug use, such as family and peer group values and practices as well as media influences. Community organization was stressed as a way to ensure cultural sensitivity and to provide local control over prevention efforts, like billboard and advertising distribution controls. Some community programs focused on societal and organizational change, such as altering practices in schools, work situations, organizations, cultures, and society at large. **These community-based systems-oriented programs have been effective in getting entire neighborhoods to take responsibility for preventing substance abuse.**

THIS IS YOUR BRAIN

THIS IS YOUR BRAIN AFTER 400 ANTI-DRUG COMMERCIALS

EGG NOG

Teen

Teen

Typical community coalition activities include:

◇ **assessing the needs** of the community and the patterns of drug abuse;
◇ **coordinating existing services** to avoid costly redundancy and fill in the service gaps;
◇ **changing laws and public policy** to reduce availability of alcohol and tobacco;
◇ **increasing funding** for family, school, and community prevention services; and
◇ **community-wide training and planning**

(Kumpfer, Goplerud & Alvarado, 1998).

Public Health Model

As the complexity of prevention efforts increased, a model was needed to better understand the relationships among all elements in society. The result was the public health approach to prevention.

The public health model holds that addiction is a disease in a **genetically predisposed host** (the actual user) who lives in a **contributory environment** (the actual location and the social network of the host) in which an **agent** (the drug or drugs) **introduces the disease. Therefore prevention is designed to affect the relationships among these three factors to control addiction.**

For example, programs to regulate cigarette advertising are designed to limit the pervasiveness of the agent in the environment. Programs to raise the drinking age or to have drug-free zones around schools are designed to limit the host's access to the agent. National antismoking, drunk-driving, and HIV risk reduction campaigns, which constitute the bulk of the highly visible programs, seek to limit the influence of the environment on the host.

Other prevention activities aimed at the environment/host relationship are designed to reinforce the emotional strengths and the protective elements already existing in people's lives or to improve the economic and emotional environment of those most at risk.

Family Approach

"When I ask the kids at 'juvie hall' about finishing their sentences and going home, a majority of them don't want to go home because for them, that's where the problem is. Over half of these kids have one or more parents who are either incarcerated or on probation, often for drug crimes. A majority of their parents use."
Juvenile detention center officer, Medford, OR

For a number of years, a family-focused approach has been embraced by treatment and prevention specialists. The family approach makes sense because susceptibility to addiction often stems from family dynamics. **Family support, skills training, and therapy, along with parenting programs, seem to reduce the risk factors** that lead to drug abuse and addiction (Kumpfer, Goplerud & Alvarado, 1998). Certainly, any process that reduces abuse, decreases parental use of drugs, and helps family members improve their relationships with one another must be of benefit to a potential abuser. Unfortunately, much of the focus is on the potential addict rather than on the total environment and the relationships that have the greatest effect on susceptibility to addiction. Occasionally, separation from one's family and placement in foster care or with another family member is preferable to continued abuse and exposure to drug and alcohol use, not to mention the chance of physical, emotional, or sexual abuse.

Multisystemic Therapy

This incorporates aspects of all major prevention strategies. It is an intensive home-based intervention for familes of youth with problems.

PREVENTION METHODS

Whatever method or combination of methods is deemed the most effective, it is necessary to examine supply, demand, and harm reduction in more detail.

SUPPLY REDUCTION

"Drug czar: 'We're winning.' Methamphetamine production is down."
Portland Oregonian, July 21, 2006

"Anti-drug gains in Colombia don't reduce flow to U.S."
New York Times, April 27, 2007

"Colombian Navy captures 15 tons of cocaine, hidden in an estuary outside of Bogotá worth $250 million.
UPI, May 2, 2007

The United States has spent billions of dollars helping the Colombian, Afghan, and other governments fight the production and smuggling of cocaine, heroin, methamphetamine, and marijuana, yet the flow of drugs into the United States has not diminished. The newly released International Narcotics Control Strategy Report produced by the U.S. State Department states that cocaine and marijuana production remains steady while heroin and methamphetamine production are up (U.S. Department of State, 2007).

Supply reduction seeks to decrease drug abuse by reducing the availability of drugs through regulation, restriction, interdiction, and law enforcement. Supply reduction is the responsibility of:

◇ state and local police departments;
◇ the Department of Justice, including the Federal Bureau of Investigation (FBI), the Bureau of Prisons, the Immigration and Naturalization Service (INS), and the Drug Enforcement Administration (DEA);
◇ the Treasury Department, including the Bureau of Alcohol, Tobacco, and Firearms (ATF), the Internal Revenue Service (IRS), and the Customs Service;

◇ the Department of Transportation, including the U.S. Coast Guard and the Federal Aviation Administration (FAA); and

◇ the Department of Defense (DOD).

This complex network of agencies is coordinated by the Office of National Drug Control Policy.

Some of the supply reduction activities include:

◇ **interdicting drug smugglers** by air, sea, and highway;

◇ **increasing law enforcement activities at border crossings**;

◇ interdicting and **limiting the supply of precursor chemicals** used in the manufacture of illicit drugs (e.g., ephedrine, a precursor of methamphetamines);

◇ identifying, disrupting, and **dismantling criminal gangs and organized crime**;

◇ supporting and **passing more-severe laws** while trying to make sentencing policies fair;

◇ funding the addition of community police officers;

◇ **disrupting money-laundering activities and seizing assets** of drug dealers to limit the profits from illegal-drug activities;

◇ supporting local and state police in high-intensity drug-trafficking areas as well as coordinating intelligence information and activities;

◇ breaking up domestic and foreign sources of supply by supporting eradication and the antidrug efforts of countries like Afghanistan, Colombia, Pakistan, and Mexico; and

◇ enacting treaties and other international agreements to work conjointly toward supply reduction goals

(Drug Enforcement Administration [DEA], 2006B; ONDCP, 2006; U.S. Department of State, 2007).

Legislation & Legal Penalties

Historically, laws to control the use of opium and other drugs did not exist in the United States prior to the nine-

In spite of record drug busts like this U.S. Coast Guard seizure of 21 tons of cocaine aboard the Panamanian-flagged motor vessel Gatun off the coast of Panama, the supply of cocaine to the United States has not diminished.

Courtesy of the U.S. Drug Enforcement Administration

teenth century. It wasn't until 1860 that the first antimorphine law was passed and not until 1906 that the Pure Food and Drug Act was approved by Congress. In 1914 the Harrison Narcotics Act was approved, enacting the first major drug controls. Since then laws such as the **Comprehensive Drug Abuse Prevention and Control Act of 1970**, the Sentencing Reform Act of 1984, and the Anti-Drug Abuse Acts of 1986 and 1988 established federal guidelines for mandatory minimum sentences, including a minimum five-year sentence for possession of 5 grams of cocaine base (crack).

Many believe these latter acts to be discriminatory against African Americans and other minority groups because possession of crack (which is more popular in poorer communities) results in significantly more jail time than a similar quantity of powder cocaine (which is more expensive and more widely used in the White community).

Other legislation has included the federal Controlled Substance Analogue Act of 1986 (which controls designer

psycho-stimulants), the Omnibus Drug Act of 1988 (which prosecutes money laundering and the smuggling of drugs and precursor chemicals), various asset forfeiture laws, chemical precursor laws, and most recently the Illicit Drug Anti-Proliferation Act, enacted in 2003 to protect youth from club drugs such as ecstasy (DEA, 2003A).

To curtail drug availability, stiffer penalties that include **long prison terms and asset forfeiture** are given to suppliers (those who manufacture, smuggle, and distribute). On the other hand, in the past 15 years **increased jail time just for use has increased dramatically**. Legal penalties increase for each conviction for possession. In most states it's illegal to possess syringes, although such laws raise the likelihood that injection drug users will share needles and increase exposure to blood-borne viruses like HIV and hepatitis C.

Women have been prosecuted for using dangerous substances during pregnancy ("Hands Off," 1998). Such prosecution can be counterproductive, however, because pregnant drug abusers might be less likely to present themselves for prenatal treatment of drug abuse and even normal prenatal care if they fear that they will be jailed or lose custody of their babies. Lack of prenatal care seems to have greater long-term adverse effects on the baby than the use of cocaine (Klein & Goldenberg, 1990). Pilot programs in New York City and in Michigan have tied welfare payments to drug testing as a way of routing clients into treatment ("Plans to Link," 1999).

"I was thinking about going out, but then I thought, You're gonna have to take the UA [urine drug test], and then your UA's gonna come up dirty, and then there goes your son, there goes your daughter, and the baby that's in your stomach. You lose your house, hell that was just too much work. I decided not to get loaded."

32-year-old woman in recovery

The so-called three-strikes-and-you're-out law requires a life sentence for three convictions (originally to get habitual violent criminals off the street but later expanded to other crimes). As a result of this and other laws, **the prison population (federal, state, and local) has more than tripled between 1980 and 2006 to approximately 2.3 million. Nearly 55% of the inmates in federal prisons were sentenced for drug offenses in 2005**, down from 60% in 1998 (U.S. Department of Justice [DOJ], 2006). Today, although just 20% of inmates in local, state, and federal facilities are in for specific drug-related crimes, if you include crimes committed to feed a habit, crimes committed under the influence of drugs and alcohol, or acts of violence triggered by substance abuse, between 60% and 80% of those in all prisons are there because of drugs. In fact, more than **half of all inmates reported drug use while committing the offense** that put them in prison. The percentage for teenagers is even higher (DOJ, 2002; Mumola, 1998; ONDCP, 2000).

Sales to minors or sales near schools may earn a perpetrator up to twice the usual sentence. Supply reduc-

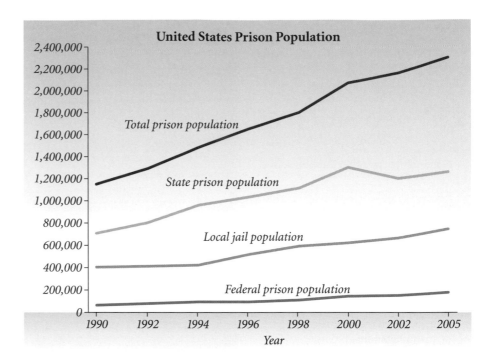

Figure 8-1 •
Nearly one in five inmates in state and local prisons and jails is incarcerated for violating a specific drug law. In federal prisons that figure is close to 50%.
(DOJ, 2006)

tion legislation sometimes extends to laws against products made from hemp and to advertising or sales of drug paraphernalia, the devices used to prepare or consume drugs, such as roach clips and water pipes sold in so-called head shops (DEA, 2006A). Governments also promulgate laws that regulate the sale of legal prescription drugs and the availability of alcohol and nicotine. Recent proposals target even precursor chemicals used to manufacture drugs illegally (e.g., ephedrine, ether, and sulfuric acid). In Oregon and an increasing number of other states, sales of products containing ephedrine and pseudoephedrine are restricted. This has led to a dramatic drop in mom-and-pop meth labs, although some of the void was immediately filled by an increased level of smuggling from Mexico and Canada.

Outcomes of Supply Reduction

The success of supply reduction approaches to the drug problem is debatable. Clearly, the estimated 10% to 15% of drugs that are kept off the mar-

ket means that a significant amount of illegal drugs never reach the streets (DEA, 2006B; ONDCP, 2006). The number of people imprisoned for drug crimes cuts down on the use and the distribution of drugs, and an unknown number of people are dissuaded from becoming involved with drugs by the threat of imprisonment. **Advocates of supply reduction say strict policies and strong penalties delay the impulse to use, get people into treatment, and keep people in treatment.**

Some, however, argue that increased law enforcement, court costs, and implementation of international drug-policing agreements make this an **extremely costly approach with a relatively minor impact on the supply**. In fact, despite a five-fold increase in federal expenditures for supply reduction efforts since 1986, cocaine is about 25% cheaper today than a decade ago (DEA, 2006B).

One of the bright spots in law enforcement is the **increased use of drug courts to avoid clogging the justice system with thousands of arrests for minor drug offenses** (Clay, 2006). First-time offenders are diverted to treatment, **shifting a supply reduction technique to a demand reduction strategy**. Further, treatment outcome studies suggest that mandated treatment of drug abuse by law enforcement results in better outcomes than those achieved through voluntary treatment (Anglin, Prendergast & Farabee, 1998; National Criminal Justice Reference System [NCJRS], 2007; Nurco, Hanlon, Bateman, et al., 1995).

DEMAND REDUCTION

Because supply reduction has been only marginally successful, demand reduction has become a more viable option among those who want to reduce drug abuse. Those pursuing demand reduction believe that the health, social, and crime problems associated with drug abuse could be greatly lessened at a fraction of the cost of supply reduction efforts if any of three conditions are met:

◇ if individuals never develop an interest in using psychoactive drugs **(primary prevention)**,

◇ if those using never progress to abuse or addiction **(secondary prevention)**, or

◇ if those who abuse or are addicted to drugs can get treatment and stop their continued use **(tertiary prevention)**.

The language of drug-abuse prevention changes often, but the principles remain the same. For example, some educators refer to primary, secondary, and tertiary prevention as *universal, selective,* and *indicated* prevention. In this textbook we will stay with *primary, secondary,* and *tertiary* (Eggert, 1996).

Primary Prevention

Primary prevention **tries to anticipate and prevent initial drug use**. It is intended mainly for young people who have little or no experience with alcohol, tobacco, or other drugs, especially those who are most at risk. Its goals are generally to:

◇ **promote nonuse or abstinence**;

◇ **help young people refuse drugs**;

◇ **delay the age of first use**, especially of the legal drugs alcohol and tobacco; and

◇ encourage healthy nondrug alternatives to achieving altered states of consciousness (e.g., sporting events or nonalcoholic, nondrug dances).

Primary prevention involves education about the harmful consequences of psychoactive substance use along with personal skill-building exercises designed to prevent or delay experimentation with abusable drugs. **It attempts to instill resistance by teaching skills in coping, handling peer pressure, decision making, conflict resolution**, and other abilities that help prevent young people from ever using psychoactive substances (Botvin & Griffin, 2005; Hazelden Foundation, 1993). It also undertakes to build self-esteem by examining the roots of susceptibility to addiction and helping children handle the confusion, anger, or pain of growing up. In a broad sense, primary prevention also includes nonpersonal strategies such as legislation, policy formulation, and school curriculum design meant to prevent or delay first use.

Though the importance of primary prevention is universally accepted, outcome evaluation of its effectiveness gives mixed reviews of program results. Controversy also exists over the best way to accomplish this important level of prevention.

The ONDCP designed a set of principles upon which prevention programming can be based (Table 8-2).

Because the lifetime cost of a drug addiction often runs into the hundreds of thousands of dollars, **primary prevention is the most important level of demand reduction**. Unfortunately, primary prevention is the level that **receives the least amount of federal, state, and local funding.**

TABLE 8–2 EVIDENCE-BASED PRINCIPLES FOR SUBSTANCE-ABUSE PREVENTION

A. **Address appropriate risk and protective factors** for substance abuse in a defined population.
   1. Define a population (e.g., by age, gender, race, neighborhood).
   2. Assess levels of risk, protection, and substance abuse for that population.
   3. Focus on all levels of risk, with special attention to those exposed to high risk and low protection.

B. **Use approaches that have been shown to be effective.**
   4. Reduce the availability of illicit drugs, alcohol, and tobacco for the underaged.
   5. Strengthen antidrug use attitudes and norms.
   6. Strengthen life skills and drug refusal techniques.
   7. Reduce risk and enhance protection in families by strengthening family skills.
   8. Strengthen social bonding and caring relationships.
   9. Ensure that interventions are appropriate for the populations being addressed.

C. **Intervene early at important stages and transitions.**
   10. Intervene at developmental stages and life transitions that predict later substance abuse.
   11. Reinforce interventions over time with repeated exposure to accurate and age-appropriate information.

D. **Intervene in appropriate settings and domains.**
   12. Intervene in appropriate settings that most affect risk, including homes, schools, and peer groups.

E. **Manage programs effectively.**
   13. Ensure consistency and coverage of programs and policies.
   14. Train staff and volunteers to communicate messages.
   15. Monitor and evaluate programs to verify that goals and objectives are being achieved.

(ONDCP, 2000)

Many studies over the past several years have demonstrated that the **age of first use is the strongest predictor of future drug or alcohol problems**. Youths who begin drug experimentation at age 10 to 12 are four to five times more likely to have future drug or alcohol problems than those who delay their first use to age 16 to 18. Others who delay their first use of drugs or alcohol until after the age of 25 rarely develop any drug problem (De Wit, Offord & Wong, 1997).

Secondary Prevention

Secondary prevention **seeks to halt drug use once it has begun**. It strives to keep experimental, social/ recreational, and habitual use, along with limited abuse, from turning into prolonged abuse and addiction by taking action when symptoms are first recognized. It educates people about specific health effects, legal consequences, and effects on a family. It can also provide counseling.

Secondary prevention **adds intervention strategies to education and skill building**. Once drug use is recognized, a number of different intervention techniques are employed to engage the user in educational and counseling processes that encourage abstinence and provide skills to avoid further use or abuse.

Drug diversion programs (e.g., drug courts) used at this level of prevention for first-time drug offenders **have proven to be useful and cost-effective**. Drug diversion programs route those arrested for possession or use to education and rehabilitation programs instead of jail.

Secondary prevention is somewhat handicapped by two actions typical of drug abusers and even casual users: concealment that makes use more difficult to detect and denial that prevents the user from acknowledging that there is a problem. On average it takes two years for parents to recognize drug use and abuse in their children.

Also complicating secondary prevention is the lag phase—the time between first use of a drug and the development of physical and emotional problems. The lag phase is particularly long for the physical con-

sequences of tobacco because it may take decades for severe health problems to develop after initial smoking begins. Because most drug users describe their initial use of drugs to be enjoyable and problem-free, denial and a sense of personal invulnerability to adverse consequences, along with the lag phase, make them less likely to believe that information about harmful effects applies to them.

"So for a long time it was a lot of fun. I don't regret any of it. It was fun. It was like the longest Mardi Gras from hell. You can't imagine. But I always had a good time."
38-year-old female practicing alcoholic

Tertiary Prevention

Tertiary prevention **seeks to stop further damage from habituation, abuse, and addiction to drugs and to restore drug abusers to health**. It joins drug-abuse treatment with strategies employed in primary and secondary prevention, such as intervention and drug diversion programs. Tertiary prevention seeks to end compulsive drug use with such relapse prevention strategies as:

◊ **group intervention** to engage a person in a treatment program focused on detoxification, abstinence, and recovery;

◊ **cue extinction therapy** that desensitizes clients to people, places, and things that trigger use;

◊ **family therapy** (especially for younger users), group psychotherapy, or residential treatment in therapeutic communities;

◊ **specific relapse prevention and life management skills** to maintain abstinence from substances or compulsive behaviors (an example of this is the processing of negative self-image with a counselor);

◊ **psychopharmacological strategies** like methadone maintenance and drugs that reduce craving;

◊ **promotion of a healthy lifestyle**; and

◊ **development of support and aftercare systems**, often 12-step programs.

Advocates of demand reduction, while admitting that interdiction decreases the availability of drugs, point out that young people reported that the current availability of drugs is similar to what it has been over the past 30 years (Monitoring the Future, 2007).

"Treatment on demand is the best and most effective tertiary treatment (and harm reduction) strategy possible. Although every treatment outcome study has shown treatment to be effective, only 1 out of every 20 adults and 1 of every 7 adolescents who need treatment for their drug problems can access it. These not only cost society hundreds of billions of dollars but it's an embarrassment to society that we cannot respond to this disease as we do to other illnesses."
Darryl Inaba, Pharm.D., clinical director, Genesis Recovery Center

Treatment of alcoholism and drug addiction has been extensively researched and has consistently been documented to be effective. **Treatment (tertiary prevention) results in abstinence or decreased drug use in 40% to 50% of cases, a great reduction in crime (74%), and a savings of $4 to $20 for every $1 spent by a community** (Gerstein, Johnson, Harwood, et al., 1994). Despite these results, funding for treatment programs consistently falls short of meeting the needs of those seeking treatment. Most publicly funded treatment programs consistently have hundreds of people on their waiting list every month. Only 20% to 30% of those on a waiting list stick around and come into treatment, possibly because they initially came for help at their most vulnerable and treatable moment. Approximately 15% of those who don't come back commit suicide. **Nationally, 7 million Americans are estimated to desire (not just need) treatment but only 1.4 million receive it** (ONDCP, 2007).

Drug courts have further increased treatment demand without providing more treatment resources. A drug court is a collaboration of the court, the prosecution, public defenders, probation officers, treatment providers, and the sheriff's department to coordinate treatment and facilitate processing of convicted drug offenders. As of 2006 there were 1,753 drug courts operating. Drug courts make sense because **incarceration costs between $20,000 and $40,000 a year per prisoner vs. $2,500 for a well-run drug court program** (Clay, 2006; NCJRS, 2007).

HARM REDUCTION

Harm reduction is a prevention strategy that recognizes the difficulty of getting and keeping people in recovery. **It focuses on techniques to minimize the personal and social problems associated with drug use rather than making abstinence the primary goal.**

One example of a harm reduction tactic is providing clean syringes to addicts. A recent study in Chicago found a long-term reduction in risky practices such as needle sharing (Huo & Ouellet, 2007). In an older study, a panel jointly convened by the National Research Council and the National Institute of Medicine found that **bleach distribution and needle-exchange efforts can reduce the spread of the AIDS virus without increasing illegal-drug use**. It is interesting to note that the study did not say "does reduce" or "has reduced" only that it "can reduce" the spread of AIDS (National Research Council, 1995). The controversy continues as to whether needle exchange itself actually works. By 2002 more than 131 needle-exchange programs provided more than 19 million syringes to IV drug users in the United States (Centers for Disease Control [CDC], 2005). In Australia, with a population one-tenth that of the United States, 10 million syringes are exchanged from 4,000 outlets. Less than 5% of Australian drug users are HIV-positive compared with an estimated 14% in the United States (Wodak & Lurie, 1997). The estimated smaller number of HIV infections in Australia saved about $220 million in drug-related expenses at a cost of $8 million for the 10 million needles and syringes (Feacham, 1995).

"The reason why we are so intent on needle use is because it's the route to the heterosexual population and to babies. If you can stop the needle from infecting heterosexual men [and women], you stop most of the cause of the spread of HIV to heterosexual women and to babies."

John Newmeyer, Ph.D., epidemiologist, Haight Ashbury Free Clinics

Another example of harm reduction involves **substituting a legal drug addiction for an illegal one as in methadone maintenance programs**. These programs have been shown to decrease crime and health problems in the user. About 228,000 patients were enrolled in 1,225 methadone maintenance programs and 250 methadone detoxification clinics, about 12% to 30% of all heroin addicts in the United States (depending on the survey) (N-SSATS, 2006). A study by the University of Pennsylvania found that comprehensive methadone treatment combined with intensive counseling reduced illicit-drug use by 79%. Clients were also five times less likely to get AIDS (Metzger, Woody, McLellan, et al., 1993). Additionally, criminal activity was reduced by 57% while full-time employment increased by 24% (Hubbard, Craddock, Anderson, 2003).

In the broad sense of reducing the harm of use without promoting abstinence, some harm reduction tactics for alcohol and tobacco are widespread. Examples include **designated-driver programs, encouraging eating when drinking**, and regulating alcohol and tobacco advertising.

These legal-drug prevention tactics receive some criticism because they may be misapplied. For example, one person gets even drunker when there is a designated driver, whereas another augments methadone with alcohol or another drug to try to get a rush. Besides needle exchange, **harm reduction practices and proposals that are very controversial include:**

◇ **responsible use education** that accepts some level of experimental or social use and seeks to inform people of ways of using drugs that minimize dangers;

◇ **decriminalization or even legalization** of all abused drugs;

◇ treatment of addicts merely to **reduce their habits to manageable levels**; and

◇ permitting addicts to totally design and manage their intervention and treatment processes.

Some harm reduction tactics also seem to be in conflict with federal drug policy based on zero tolerance (no use of illegal drugs). Changes in laws and policies will probably not be forthcoming soon because many elected officials are afraid of appearing soft on crime and drugs. "War on drugs" advocates fear that any attempt at decriminalization or legalization would introduce the kind of ambiguity about drugs that prevailed in the 1970s, creating confusion about whether drug use is undesirable. (*See Chapter 9 for further discussion of harm reduction.*)

"I had a parole officer who told me to leave those other drugs alone. Drinking is okay or smoking a little pot now and then, but I have come to believe that I can't take any mood-altering chemical into my body today and still remain in recovery. That is still what I stick to and believe in."

44-year-old recovering heroin addict

CHALLENGES TO PREVENTION

LEGAL DRUGS IN SOCIETY

In 1996 Seagram broke the liquor industry's self-imposed moratorium on television advertising that had been in effect for decades. By 2007 liquor advertising was common on the airwaves. The hypocrisy over hard-liquor advertising is surprising because beer advertising has never been banned. The pervasiveness of beer advertising and indignant attitudes toward liquor perpetuates the myth that beer drinking is safer than hard liquor. The fact is more cases of cirrhosis of the liver are due to beer drinking.

The social and health problems due to alcohol abuse, tobacco abuse, and, to a lesser extent, prescription

In Japan beer is available in vending machines. In other countries, especially the United States, this kind of environmental availability of alcohol is unheard of, but in Japan it is acceptable and not often abused by underage drinkers.

© 2002 Dr. Darryl Inaba

drug abuse are far greater than those due to illicit drugs. In recent years drug-abuse prevention and treatment efforts have recognized the fact that addiction is a disease and have increased the emphasis on prevention and treatment of alcohol and tobacco abuse and most recently on behavioral addictions such as gambling, eating disorders, and sexual addiction.

Legal drugs such as tobacco and alcohol are widely available and actively marketed by sophisticated advertising campaigns that attempt to show the fun to be found in psychoactive drugs and that try to establish brand recognition and loyalty at an early age. Joe Camel® and the Budweiser® frogs are examples of familiar cartoonlike characters that targeted young potential smokers and drinkers. Each year alcohol companies spend more than $5 billion and tobacco companies more than $13.1 billion on advertising and promoting their products through giveaways, coupons, premiums, and promotional allowances to retailers (Federal Trade Commission, 2006). This is not surprising because alcohol sales are over $150 billion per year and

tobacco sales exceed $50 billion per year.

There is something to be learned here. Because advertising is successful when targeting age- and culture-specific populations, prevention groups can do the same by customizing their messages. When Massachusetts spent money for prime-time antismoking messages, cigarette use dropped dramatically. Phillip Morris spends millions advertising its Web site, which talks about the dangers of smoking, but cynics say that this is a tactic to reduce the number of more powerful antismoking messages (e.g., a California spot that shows a nicotine addict smoking through a hole in her throat had a tremendous impact on Oregon and California smokers).

Billions are also spent advertising over-the-counter (OTC) and prescription drugs, thus promoting the concept that there is a chemical solution for any ailment or discomfort, particularly pain. This two-tiered approach—acceptable and unacceptable drugs—breeds cynicism and disbelief of prevention messages in adolescents and young adults. If pre-

vention messages aren't consistent and accurate, they are usually ineffective.

CONCLUSIONS

One of the realities of prevention is that there is no quick fix. If modern attempts to reduce smoking began with the first health warnings issued in the mid-1950s, the success of the **anti-smoking efforts have taken almost half a century** and are still developing. First knowledge must change, then attitudes, and finally practices. These changes can take a generation or more. When change comes it can be profound—no smoking in public buildings, restaurants, and offices was unheard of a few decades ago. In 2003 the state of New York passed a ban on smoking in virtually all businesses and indoor locations except in one's home or car, in cigar bars, and at American Indian casinos. California and Delaware also have stringent laws. Some local governments are trying to extend those prohibitions to outdoor locations. A few companies are offering treatment to their employees who smoke; and if they can't quit, they're fired.

A second reality of prevention is that the job is never complete. Each year there is a new group entering grammar school, middle school, high school, and college, who need to learn or at least be reminded of the potential dangers of smoking and drinking. The high level of adolescent smoking in the past decade is due in part to a diminished antismoking campaign compared with relatively strenuous efforts conducted in the late 1960s through the 1970s that included public service ads on TV, limitations on tobacco broadcast advertising, and increased cigarette taxes. (Taxing tobacco does work; an increase of taxes in Oregon reduced per-capita cigarette consumption 20% between 1997 and 1999 ["Tobacco Tax," 2000]).

Third, any prevention campaign becomes progressively more difficult. Prevention techniques succeed better with people ready to listen (those already predisposed to heed warnings. After initial successes it becomes harder to penetrate deeper into any particular generation to change attitudes and behaviors.

Another challenge to prevention is that **no single approach has been shown to work consistently**, probably because there are so many variables that contribute to substance abuse and addiction. There is no doubt that if and when prevention efforts become consistently and documentably successful, they will be cost-effective. The difficulty is finding undeniably effective prevention programs because it takes time before their effectiveness can be accurately measured.

A recent problem with legal drugs is the **increase in states that allow medical marijuana** or have reduced penalties for possession. As of May 2007 those included Alaska, California, Colorado, Hawaii, Maine, Montana, Nevada, New Mexico, Oregon, Rhode Island, Vermont, and Washington. Other states are considering legislation to allow medical marijuana. There is considerable conflict between the federal government and the individual states over this subject. There is also the problem of using medical marijuana on the job. Some employers allow it; others don't. Their reasoning is job safety and the zero-tolerance policies of the federal government (Chu, Block & Shell, 2007). Foreign governments are also grappling with this issue. Since 2001 in the Netherlands, pharmacies may fill prescriptions for marijuana with the cost being covered by insurance. Before, patients had to buy their own marijuana at one of the country's 800 so-called coffee shops.

It is important to remember that regardless of how individual states handle medical marijuana, possession and use of the substance still violates federal law.

FUNDING

As mentioned at the beginning of this chapter, **prevention is vastly underfunded when compared with the cost of alcohol and drug abuse and to the moneys committed to tobacco and alcohol advertising**. One problem is that prevention is not perceived as exciting because the basic message is very simple: don't smoke, don't drink to excess, and avoid drugs (and compulsive behaviors) that have long-term health and social consequences, especially if you are genetically and environmentally vulnerable to addiction. In a society that prizes free enterprise, it is hard to make large sums of money from prevention . . . only to save large sums.

In addition, the public generally does not support prevention activities through participation. Public information forums are often poorly attended, and smoking-cessation classes disappear for lack of participation. But more than that, unless there is a crisis or severe discomfort, people often feel they have more important things to do.

It is crucial that **prevention programs be available throughout a person's life** because each age has its own needs. Prevention programs should be:

◇ culturally specific,
◇ age specific,
◇ imaginative,
◇ non-judgmental or preachy,
◇ accurate and honest, and
◇ generously funded and supported.

FROM CRADLE TO GRAVE

PATTERNS OF USE

Because drug use affects us directly or indirectly from cradle to grave, examining the patterns of use of different age groups in our society makes it possible to design prevention programs that have a better chance of success.

USE BY RACE & CLASS

Addicts are often portrayed in the media as inner-city dwellers who are weak, bad, stupid, crazy, immoral, and poor or as the disenfranchised who have nothing else to turn to except drugs. When drug use is studied on a regional basis, the facts show that rural and small urban areas use as much and in some cases more drugs per capita than large urban areas (SAMHSA, 2006). And while one-third of the homeless are estimated to have a drug or alcohol problem, they represent only 5% of the addicted U.S. population overall. When ethnicity was used as a measure, the differences in overall drug use were minimal, although the use of some specific drugs is higher in certain ethnic, cultural, economic, or social communities (Joseph & Langrod, 2005).

Those least likely to have an alcohol problem were African Americans, while those of Hispanic origin were least likely to have an illicit-drug problem. Whites and African Americans were comparable in their use of illicit drugs (SAMHSA, 2006). The relatively high rate of African Americans in prisons suggests either this ethnic group tends to fall prey more readily to the negative aspects of addiction, including dealing, or that they are the target of greater law enforcement efforts. African Americans with drug problems tend to be incarcerated at a greater rate and receive treatment through the criminal justice system, whereas Whites are more likely to get probation and receive treatment from medical and social service programs. About 53% of those in prison for drug crimes are Black, although they represent just 12% of the population; just 26% of those in prison for drug crimes are White, although they represent more than 75% of the population (DOJ, 2007; U.S. Bureau of the Census, 2004).

"They come to Black neighborhoods to cop dope. It's like a pretty regular thing to see White people go slipping around through there at night. Now crack cocaine is not Black or White. Crack cocaine is dope. It doesn't care who it gets. I have sat down with people up here and I have sat down with people from down there, and when we do dope, it is all the same."
Recovering cocaine addict

Alcoholics and addicts include not only residents in the inner city but also the most skilled, talented, intelligent, and sensitive individuals in our society. For example, physicians are as likely to be as addicted as the general population, often due to accessibility to drugs. They are more likely to abuse prescription drugs rather than illicit substances (Anthony & Hetzer, 1991; Centrella, 1994; Weir, 2000). **Intelligence is not a guaranteed protection against addiction.** Members of MENSA, a high-IQ society, also have a relatively high rate of addiction as do gifted high school students. Members of the American clergy also have a higher-than-average rate of alcoholism. Even nuns have a problem with prescription drug abuse. If people use psychoactive substances, they are liable to addictive disease no matter what race, class, or region of the country they live in. Addiction is an equal opportunity disease.

USE BY AGE

Over the past 40 years, **one of the most important changes in drug abuse has been the gradual lowering of the age of drug users**. This is of particular concern because, as mentioned, one of the most reliable indicators of future addiction problems is early-onset drug use. A survey by the University of Michigan found that from 1991 to 2005, the use of marijuana by eighth- and tenth-graders rose 60% while the use by twelfth-graders went up 25% although use in the past three years has leveled off (Monitoring the Future, 2007). Another measure of increased use (and possible increased law enforcement) is that the percentage of male juvenile arrestees testing positive for any drug except alcohol went from 22% in 1990 to 48% to 65% in selected cities in 2005 (Arrestee Drug Abuse Monitoring [ADAM], 2003).

The number of Americans who used illicit drugs in the past month (19.7 million in a population of 243 million, 12 and older) may seem small; however, **they have an exaggerated effect on all levels of society** especially in regard to economic loss, accidents, assaults, suicides, crime, and domestic or other violence (SAMHSA, 2006).

© 1997 Dick Wright. Reprinted with permission.

TABLE 8–4   DRUG USE BY AGE GROUP, 2005

Age Group	Used Ever	Used Past Year	Used Past Month
12 to 17 (23 million)			
Any illicit drug	27.7%	19.9%	9.9%
Cigarettes	26.7%	17.3%	10.8%
Alcohol	40.6%	33.3%	16.5%
18 to 25 (29 million)			
Any illicit drug	59.2%	34.2%	20.1%
Cigarettes	67.3%	47.2%	39.0%
Alcohol	85.7%	77.9%	60.9%
26 & up (171 million)			
Any illicit drug	46.3%	10.2%	5.8%
Cigarettes	71.9%	27.6%	24.3%
Alcohol	88.2%	69.0%	55.1%
Total, 12 & up (223 million)			
Any illicit drug	46.1%	14.4%	8.1%
Cigarettes	66.6%	29.1%	24.9%
Alcohol	82.9%	66.5%	51.8%

(SAMHSA, 2006)

In the rest of this chapter, we examine the consequences of drug use during pregnancy, in school (K–12 and college), on the job (including a section on drug testing), and by the elderly. We also examine some of the most dangerous consequences of drug use—sexually transmitted diseases (STDs), hepatitis C, and AIDS. We also discuss some of the prevention and early intervention programs designed for those groups.

PREGNANCY & BIRTH

OVERVIEW

"Despite the overwhelming evidence that virtually all psychoactive drugs of abuse harm both mother and fetus during pregnancy, a number of people dispute these claims probably to try to shield pregnant drug-abusing women from the severe persecution and punishment that has become more common for the pregnant addict. Everybody has to keep in mind that the health of both the mother and the child should be the primary focus of drug abuse in pregnancy and that honest, non-judgmental information along with sufficient prenatal care and drug treatment programs are the most effective methods of preventing devastating health problems to both."

Darryl Inaba, Pharm.D., clinical director, Genesis Recovery Center

Drug abuse during pregnancy occurs in women of all ethnic and socio-economic backgrounds. According to the National Institute on Drug Abuse (NIDA), **18.6% of infants were exposed to alcohol** at some time during the nine months of gestation, 4.5% were exposed to cocaine, 17.4% to marijuana, and 17.6% to tobacco (May & Gossage, 2001; National Institute on Drug Abuse [NIDA], 1994). **Fetal alcohol syndrome (FAS) is the third most common birth defect and the leading cause of mental retardation in the United States.** Most psychoactive substances can be harmful to the developing fetus.

In the California Perinatal Substance Exposure Study (1991–1993), the California Department of Alcohol and Drug Programs tried to determine the prevalence of drug-exposed newborns (Table 8-5). While these rates are high, the actual exposure is probably even higher because most drugs are nondetectable three days after exposure. If one looks at drug use at various times during pregnancy, the use of alcohol is higher.

TABLE 8–5 PERCENTAGE OF INFANTS BORN EXPOSED TO DRUGS IN CALIFORNIA, 1991–1993

Substance	Asian & Pacific Islander	African American	Hispanic	White	Other	All
Alcohol	**5.07%**	**11.58%**	**6.87%**	**6.05%**	**4.03%**	**6.72%**
Tobacco	**1.73%**	**20.12%**	**3.29%**	**14.82%**	**4.81%**	**8.82%**
Prescription drugs	**1.49%**	**2.38%**	**1.26%**	**1.96%**	**1.31%**	**1.71%**
All illicit drugs	**0.39%**	**11.90%**	**1.51%**	**4.92%**	**1.57%**	**3.49%**
marijuana	0.21%	4.59%	0.61%	3.25%	1.21%	1.88%
cocaine	0.06%	7.79%	0.55%	0.60%	0.20%	1.11%
opioids	0.34%	2.54%	1.06%	1.59%	1.11%	1.47%
amphetamines (illicit and legal)	0.06%	0.19%	0.35%	1.32%	0.24%	0.66%
Total Positives (excluding tobacco)	**14.22%**	**24.02%**	**9.37%**	**12.28%**	**6.76%**	**11.35%**

Note: Some infants test positive for more than one drug.

California Perinatal Substance Exposure Study, 1993 (Noble, Vega, Kolody, et al., 1997)

Maternal Risks

"I used after my water broke and I was on my way to the hospital. I got high because I couldn't face bringing another child into domestic violence. And I figured if I got high, at that time, I thought they would take him from me so that he wouldn't have to come home to the violence."

26-year-old recovering addict

Historically, the effects of drugs and alcohol on pregnant women and their fetuses have been poorly researched and treated. Even when female opium and morphine addicts outnumbered male addicts at the turn of the twentieth century, most treatment facilities were aimed at men (Worth, 1991; Young, 1997). In fact, although damage to the fetus due to drinking has been recognized since ancient times, a specific clinical syndrome, FAS, was not identified until 1973 (Jones & Smith, 1973). Starting in the 1980s, interest and research on perinatal effects of drugs increased as did funding by the National Institute on Drug Abuse, the National Institutes of Health, and other government agencies.

When added to the normal stresses and medical complications of pregnancy,

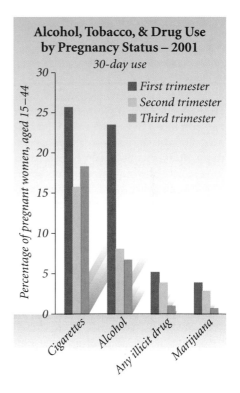

Alcohol, Tobacco, & Drug Use by Pregnancy Status – 2001

30-day use

- First trimester
- Second trimester
- Third trimester

Percentage of pregnant women, aged 15–44

Cigarettes · Alcohol · Any illicit drug · Marijuana

Figure 8-2 •

Notice that in the first and second trimesters, when the fetus is most vulnerable, drug use, particularly alcohol use, is much higher than during the third trimester.

National Household Survey on Drug Abuse, 1998 (SAMHSA, 1999A)

drug and alcohol abuse during this period puts women at even higher risk for medical and obstetrical complications. **Some conditions aggravated by drug use in a pregnant woman include anemia, sexually transmitted diseases, diabetes, high blood pressure, neurological damage, weakened immune system, and poor nutrition. In addition, hepatitis C, endocarditis, HIV/AIDS and other infections can be contracted from infected needles** (Finnegan & Kandall, 2005).

"When I used, my behavior was really dangerous. I'd do things that normal people wouldn't do. I was very promiscuous. I had a lot of unsafe sex. I contracted hepatitis C. I've had numerous STDs. You know, I'd use during all my pregnancies, so my children are affected. The aftereffects still physically affect them you know. It's something I have to live with."
29-year-old mother of four in recovery

Eighty percent of children with HIV in the United States were born to mothers who were IV drug abusers or sexual partners of IV drug abusers. That figure jumps to 90% worldwide in infants and children. The life expectancy of an infant born with HIV is less than two years. Surprisingly, in the United States, if AZT (an AIDS drug) therapy is used, only 8% of the newborns will be infected with the virus. If AZT is not used, there is a 25% infection rate (CDC, 1999; Harris, Thompson, Ball, et al, 2002). Newer medications lower the rate even more. In underdeveloped countries with less access to AZT and other drugs, that rate jumps to 35% to 40% (Amornwichet, Teeraratkul, Simonds, et al., 2002; CDC, 2006A; Quinn, 1996).

A pregnant addict often has had no prenatal care or medical intervention prior to delivery and often lives a chaotic lifestyle. Pregnant adolescents are at even greater risk. Even without the complicating factors of drug use, the infants of adolescent mothers are at higher risk than those born to women over 18 except for risk of Down's syndrome for pregnancies after the age of

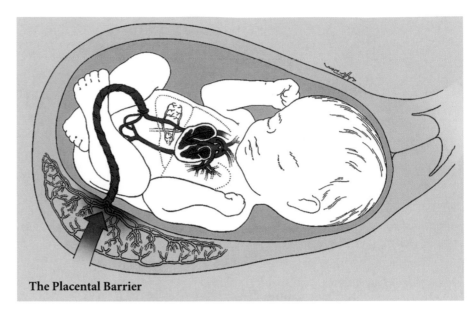

The Placental Barrier

Figure 8-3 •
The developing baby is protected by the placental barrier, which screens out substances that would affect the fetus. All psychoactive drugs breach this protective barrier and affect the baby, usually much more than the mother.
© 1998 CNS Productions, Inc.

30. All areas of functioning are affected because the adolescent herself has not yet developed physically, emotionally, or behaviorally (Finnegan & Kandall, 2005; Hechtman, 1989; Kaminer, 1994).

"Across from the hospital where I had my son, when I was supposed to be on my way there, I didn't make it past the park and the hospital was right across the street. I got stuck in the park, and I could literally see the windows of the NICU, know my son's there, but I ended up hangin' out at the park, getting drunk and getting loaded."
27-year-old recovering addict

Fetal & Neonatal Complications

If a woman is using psychoactive drugs, it is often **hard to separate the effects of her toxic environment on the fetus from the direct effects of the drug.** Poor nutrition, blood-borne infections, domestic violence, and STDs from high-risk behaviors can cause many of the side effects attributed to the drug itself. Sufficient research has been done to identify the direct effects

of various drugs. The overall epidemiology is somewhat harder to define.

Psychoactive drugs can easily cross the multiple cell layers of the placental barrier, the membrane separating the baby's and the mother's blood (Figure 8-3), so **a fetus is exposed to the same chemicals that a mother uses.** This placental barrier is more porous than the blood/brain barrier, although the blood/brain barrier is not fully developed in the fetus until several months or more after the baby is born. **After birth many drugs pass into a nursing mother's breast milk,** further exposing a nursing infant to dangerous chemicals.

Because of the fetus's and subsequently the infant's metabolic immaturity, each surge of effects caused by the psychoactive drug that the mother injects, ingests, snorts, or smokes may be prolonged in the fetus.

The period of maximum fetal vulnerability is the first 12 weeks. During this first trimester, development and differentiation of cells into fetal limbs and organs occur. This is when drugs pose the greatest risk to organ development. Because the central and peripheral nervous systems develop throughout the pregnancy, **the fetus is vulnerable to neurological damage no matter when a woman uses drugs**. The second trimester involves further maturation and continued vulnerability of the organs. Drug exposure at this stage creates a risk of abnormal bleeding or spontaneous abortion. The third trimester includes maturation of the fetus and preparation for birth. Powerful drugs such as heroin or cocaine can cause premature birth. Because drugs can have such a magnified effect on the fetus throughout pregnancy, it is crucial that a pregnant woman abstain from all unnecessary drug exposure.

"I was drinking between 3 and 4 liters of wine daily when I was pregnant with her until I was about eight months. And consequently she was born with fetal alcohol effects. She had a hole in her heart, her digestive system was all messed up, she had projectile vomiting, she didn't gain any weight for about a month. She had to stay in the hospital while I was released. But when she was three to five, she had to have speech therapy."
25-year-old recovering addict

The immaturity of the fetus's metabolic system also causes drugs to remain in the fetus for a longer period and in higher concentrations than in the mother. The problems of fetal drug exposure extend beyond the period of pregnancy. Many babies are born with compromised immune systems due to maternal drug use. **Definite syndromes of neonatal withdrawal, intoxication, and developmental or learning delays have been attributed to a variety of drugs, including alcohol** (Finnegan & Kandall, 2005). In a Florida study, the cost of newborn care of those affected by drugs was more than double the normal cost of care for newborns, $11,188 vs. $4,741 (Agency for Health Care Administration, 1999).

Long-Term Effects

"They're older now, and some of them have learning disabilities. My oldest son has ADD [attention-deficit disorder], my middle son has anger management problems, and because I raised these children in my addiction, you know, they suffer from depression, they have their antisocial skills. I passed the disease of addiction to my oldest son through my behavior and their father's behavior."
29-year-old mother of four in recovery

Research is still being done on the long-term effects in drug-exposed children when they enter school. Symptoms range from convulsive disorders in the most extreme cases, to poor muscular control and cognitive skills, hyperactivity, difficulty concentrating or remembering, violence, apathy, and lack of emotion. The good news is that recent research indicates that **the majority of drug-exposed babies who receive prenatal, perinatal, and postnatal care, along with continued pediatric services, manage to catch up developmentally to non-drug-exposed children after a slow start** (Frank, Augustyn, Knight, et al., 2001). Even without care, some of the effects are reversible. In a study in Ottawa, Canada, children of moderate-drinking mothers showed lower cognitive scores at 36 months but not at 48, 60, or 72 months (Fried, O'Connell & Watkinson, 1992). Other studies have found persistence of learning disabilities at age seven and beyond (Morrow, Culbertson, Accornero, et al., 2006).

SPECIFIC DRUG EFFECTS

Despite difficulties with scientific research on fetal effects of drug use during pregnancy, scientists have identified prenatal and postnatal symptoms and conditions due to specific psychoactive drugs.

Alcohol

Alcohol is the most widely researched drug in relation to its effect on the developing fetus during pregnancy. (*See Chapter 5 for complete coverage of alcohol's neonatal effects.*) A **number of conditions are grouped under the acronym FASD, or fetal alcohol spectrum disorders**. Imaging techniques have found a number of structural deformities in the heavy prenatal alcohol-exposed infant that include abnormalities in the corpus callosum, parietal lobe, cerebellar vermus, and caudate nucleus (Spadoni, McGee, Fryer, et al., 2007). **FAS, the best-known condition, is a definite pattern of physical, mental, and behavioral abnormalities in children born to mothers who drank heavily during pregnancy.** Symptoms include retarded growth (reduced height, weight, head circumference, brain growth, and brain size), facial deformities (shortened eyelids, thin upper lip, flattened midface, a shallow groove in the upper lip), occasional problems with heart and limbs, delayed intellectual development, neurological abnormalities, behavioral problems, visual problems, hearing loss, and balance or gait problems (Mattson, Schoenfeld & Riley, 2001; Sokol & Clarren, 1989; Streissguth, 1997).

There are **a number of other, less severe yet much more widespread conditions that mostly involve cognitive abilities**, such as alcohol-related neurodevelopmental disorder (ARND) and alcohol-related birth defects (ARBD), also known as "fetal alcohol effects."

Statistics show that **worldwide anywhere from 0.33 to 2.9 cases per 1,000 live births have FAS**, although individual countries, such as South Africa, can have a much higher incidence. **The incidence of ARND and ARBD is probably five to 10 times greater than FAS.** In the United States, 0.5 to 2.0 cases are the accepted number, but the rates of individual groups vary widely: African Americans have an incidence of 6 FAS births per 1,000; Asians, Hispanics, and Whites about 1 to 2; and American Indians about 10 to 30 (May, 1996; May & Gossage, 2001; Pagliaro & Pagliaro, 2003). A recent study examined the long-term effects of prenatal alcohol exposure and found that **growth problems with weight, height, and head circumference persisted into adolescence** (Lumeng, Cabral, Gannon, et al., 2007).

Dr. Sterling K. Clarren and his associates at Children's Hospital in Seattle located and interviewed 80 mothers of children with FAS. They asked them about 2,000 questions to get a profile of the patients.

"What we learned was really startling—100% of them had been severely physically and sexually abused, about 60% of it occurring before they were adults and the rest as adults. About 80% of them had major mental health diagnoses and not just one but many. The average patient had 6 distinct mental health diagnoses made through the DSM-IV system. Some of them had more than 10: schizophrenia, manic depression, phobias, posttraumatic stress disorder, and on and on."

Dr. Sterling K. Clarren (personal communication, 1999)

In addition to FAS and other abnormalities, the rate of sudden infant death syndrome (SIDS) is greatly increased when the mother drinks either while pregnant or when nursing. A study involving the Indian Health Service found that prevention efforts in the form of a visiting nurse who helped mothers with a drinking problem decreased the incidence of SIDS by 80%.

Cocaine & Amphetamines

In the past year, 558,000 women were considered dependent on cocaine and crack (and the number is growing yearly), with their average age in the early twenties, the most fertile childbearing years (SAMHSA, 2006). A percentage of these women use cocaine during pregnancy, although the rates vary widely from hospital to hospital and among different ethnic groups. In the 1980s, **when cocaine use was at its highest levels, it was estimated that about 4.5% of all U.S. infants were exposed to cocaine in utero** (Gomby & Shiono, 1991). Other studies from that era showed that from 15% to 25% of babies born in some inner-city hospitals were born cocaine affected (Bateman & Heagarty, 1989). The recent increase of methamphetamine abuse will certainly result in increased numbers of pregnancies affected by this stimulant.

"I was smoking crack cocaine and drinking alcohol, and he used to kick,

Often the physical effects of alcohol are not as obvious as on this child diagnosed with fetal alcohol syndrome.

Courtesy of Sterling K. Clarren, M.D., Children's Hospital, Seattle, WA

really, really bad. It was like he was having tremors or something inside of my stomach. Needless to say I had him six weeks early. And when he came out, he had to go to NICU, he had tubes coming out of everywhere, he could not breathe. My son was on a heart monitor. And two times out of that six months, his heart stopped beating."
24-year-old recovering crack user

The stimulants **cocaine and amphetamines increase heart rate and constrict blood vessels, causing dramatic elevations in blood pressure in both mother and fetus**. Constriction of blood vessels reduces the flow of

blood, nutrients, and oxygen to the placenta and the fetus, sometimes resulting in retarded fetal development, especially when the mother is a habitual user. Increased maternal and placental blood pressure can, in rare cases, cause the placenta to separate prematurely from the wall of the uterus (abruptio placentae), resulting in spontaneous abortion or premature delivery (Derlet & Albertson, 2002).

Acutely elevated blood pressure in the fetus can also cause a stroke in the fetus's brain. Fetal blood vessels in the brain are very fragile and may easily be damaged by exposure to cocaine and particularly amphetamines. **Third-trimester use of cocaine can induce sudden fetal activity, uterine contrac-**

tions, and premature labor within minutes after a mother has used (Plessinger & Woods, 1998).

Although there is no specific set of physical abnormalities connected to cocaine or amphetamine use during pregnancy, exposed babies can be growth retarded, with smaller heads, genito-urinary tract abnormalities, severe intestinal disease, and abnormal sleep and breathing patterns (Behnke, Eyler, Garvan, et al., 2001; Cherukuri, Minkoff, Feldman, et al., 1988; Smith, LaGasse, Derauf, et al., 2006).

Infants exposed to cocaine during pregnancy **often go through a withdrawal syndrome characterized by extreme agitation, increased respiratory rates, hyperactivity, and occasional seizures**. Because these babies are in withdrawal, intoxicated, or both, they are highly irritable, difficult to console, tremulous, and deficient in their ability to interact with their environment. Many of these initial effects disappear within a few weeks after birth, assuming the mother's breast milk is not contaminated with cocaine (Chasnoff, Anson, Hatcher, et al., 1998).

Infants exposed to cocaine, when studied at 3, 12, 18, and 24 months, seemed to require more stimulation to increase arousal and attention but were less able to control higher states of arousal than unexposed children (Lester, Tronick, LaGasse, et al., 2002; Mayes, Grillon, Granger, et al., 1998). A study of 150 cocaine-exposed infants also found that lower levels of alertness and attentiveness were directly related to the amount of cocaine used during pregnancy (Eyler, Behnke, Conlon, et al., 1998). Many of these infants showed some patterns of neurobehavioral disorganization, irritability, and poor language development. These infants may also have a slightly higher incidence of SIDS, although it is often hard to separate environmental and nutritional factors from the direct effects of drugs (Finnegan & Kandall, 2005).

Methamphetamine abuse during pregnancy is just beginning to be studied but is definitely having adverse effects on the developing fetus. A study of 406 children born to 153 meth-abusing women found a disability rate of 33%. This is a huge rate compared to non-drug abuse pregnancies (Brecht, 2005).

There is hope for parents, educators, and others involved with the education and care of these children. **Many abnormal neurobehavioral effects improve over the first three years of life.** Recent studies suggest that earlier predictions of severely impaired cocaine babies have been exaggerated (Frank, Augustyn, Knight, et al., 2001). Cocaine does harm the fetus, especially when the mother is a heavy user, but most children prenatally exposed to cocaine will have more-normal behavior by the age of three than was feared (Lumeng, Cabral, Gannon, et al., 2007). Reports of ADD and low frustration levels, however, are related by teachers and parents (Harvard University, 1998). It should also be noted that these studies were on children who had access to good neonatal and pediatric care. It is unclear whether cocaine-affected children will catch up to nonexposed children without that quality of care.

Opioids

With the increased use and abuse of prescription opioids, methadone, and buprenorphine, the focus of an assessment has to look beyond heroin when a drug test of a pregnant woman turns up positive for opioids. Physical dependence on opioids leads to more-continuous use, so the **effects on the fetus seem greater than with binge drugs such as cocaine**. People addicted to heroin, hydrocodone (Vicodin®), oxycodone (OcyContin®), and other opioids have a greater risk for fetal growth retardation, miscarriage, stillbirth, and abruptio placentae as well as **severe infections from intravenous use**.

For pregnant heroin users, the periods of daily withdrawal that alternate with the rushes following each drug snort or injection cause dramatic fluctuations in autonomic functions in the fetus believed to harm the fetus and contribute to maternal/fetal complications. Babies born to heroin-addicted mothers are **often premature, smaller, and weaker than normal** (Fulroth, Phillips & Durand, 1989; Zhu & Stadlin, 2000). Prenatal exposure to heroin has also been associated with abnormal neurobehavioral development. These in-

fants have abnormal sleep patterns and are at greater risk for SIDS. **A 600% increase in SIDS deaths was found in a study of 16,409 drug-exposed infants in New York City** (Kandall, Gaines, Habel, et al., 1993).

If a mother becomes truly addicted to opioids, so does the fetus. Depending on the mother's daily dose of shorter-acting opioids, such as heroin, **a majority (60% to 80%) of opioid-exposed infants exhibit the neonatal abstinence syndrome (withdrawal) 48 to 72 hours after birth** (Finnegan & Ehrlich, 1990). With longer-acting opioids, such as methadone, it can take one to two weeks. Symptoms include hyperactivity, irritability, incessant high-pitched crying, increased muscle tone, hyperactive reflexes, sweating, tremors, irregular sleep patterns, increased respiration, uncoordinated and ineffectual sucking and swallowing, sneezing, vomiting, and diarrhea. In severe cases failure to thrive, seizures, or even death may occur. These withdrawal effects may be mild or severe and may last from days to months (Weaver, 2005).

Because the onset of symptoms varies, close observation of the opioid-exposed neonate is necessary. Most cases of neonatal narcotic withdrawal can be treated with good nursing care, loose swaddling in a side-lying position, quiet and dimly lit surroundings, good nutrition, and normal maternal/infant bonding behaviors. Opioids have been found in breast milk in sufficient concentration to expose newborns. Only in severe cases is medication required for the infant, and then it should be a milder opioid such as paregoric (Kandall, 1993). **Opioid withdrawal in neonates can be fatal**, however, and should therefore be appropriately treated even before the baby is delivered (Oei & Lui, 2007).

The problems associated with a baby born addicted to an opiate are further complicated when methadone or buprenorphine are the treatment of choice. The outcomes are somewhat better even though the infant must be detoxified because the mother maintains her stability as well as avoids the problems associated with IV use of heroin. The mother is also more likely to participate in postnatal treatment

(Burns, Mattick, Lim, et al., 2007). Buprenorphine treatment presented some other problems. In one study 91% of the infants went through withdrawal while 57% needed morphine replacement therapy to detox. In addition, a number of sudden infant deaths occurred. The reasons for the SIDS wasn't clear (Kahila, Saisto, Kivitie-Kallio, et al., 2007).

Marijuana

Marijuana is used by 5% to 17% of pregnant women during their pregnancy (depending on the survey). Recent research has found high levels of anandamide in the uterus of mice and suggests that this neurotransmitter, mimicked by marijuana, helps regulate the early stages of pregnancy and perhaps control the pain of childbirth. This study found that high levels of anandamide inhibit the progression of the fertilized egg from blastocyst stage to embryo (Paria, Das & Dey, 1995; Paria, Zhao, Wang, et al., 1999; Schmid, Paria, Krebsbach, et al., 1997). These discoveries might give a better understanding of the process of gestation, but they also suggest that the use of marijuana might disrupt the birth process.

Most marijuana exposure in newborns goes undetected or is masked by the use of other drugs that can also cause problems. Some studies have reported reduced fetal weight gain, shorter gestations, and some congenital anomalies; however, most studies have found minimal developmental effects in regard to motor skills and mental functioning (Richardson, Day & Goldschmidt, 1995). Long-term development studies (Ottawa Prenatal Prospective Study) showed that intrauterine **exposure to marijuana led to poorer short-term memory and verbal reasoning at age 3** (Day, Richardson, Goldschmidt, et al., 1994; Richardson, 1998). Between the ages of 5 to 6 and 9 to 12 years, according to the Ottawa study, **marijuana-exposed children scored somewhat lower on verbal and memory performance tests, impulsive/hyperactive behavior, conduct problems, and distractibility**. They also scored lower on tasks associated with executive function—the individual's ability to plan ahead, anticipate, and suppress behaviors that are incompatible with a current goal (Fried,

O'Connell & Watkinson, 1992; Fried & Smith, 2001; Fried, Watkinson & Gray, 1998; Fried, Watkinson & Siegel, 1997).

Many of the problems with marijuana have to do with the delivery system. Marijuana is smoked and therefore limits oxygen to the body and the fetus, irritates alveoli and bronchii, and causes babies to weigh about 3.4 ounces less on average than nonexposed neonates (Fried, 1995; Zuckerman, Frank, Hingson, et al., 1989).

Because there are withdrawal symptoms after ceasing heavy or long-term use of marijuana and since the fetus is also exposed, it is logical to assume that neonates would exhibit withdrawal symptoms. Anecdotal reports relate that these **marijuana-exposed babies have abnormal responses to light and visual stimuli, increased tremulousness, "startles," and a high-pitched cry** associated with drug withdrawal (Fried & Smith, 2001). Unlike infants undergoing narcotic withdrawal, marijuana babies are not excessively irritable.

Prescription & OTC Drugs

The Food and Drug Administration developed a chart that categorizes and rates prescription drugs in terms of danger to a developing fetus:

◇ **Category A.** Controlled studies in humans have demonstrated no fetal risks. (Regular doses of vitamins are found here but not large doses of vitamins.)
◇ **Category B.** Animal studies indicate no fetal risks, but there are no human studies; or adverse effects have been demonstrated in animals but not in well-controlled human studies (Tylenol,® Motrin,® Pepcid).
◇ **Category C.** There are no adequate studies (animal or human) or there are adverse fetal effects in animal studies but no available human data. Many medications pregnant women use fall into this category (most drugs).
◇ **Category D.** There is evidence of fetal risk, but these drugs should only be used if the benefits are thought to clearly outweigh the risks (e.g., Dilantin,® benzodiazepines, and tetracycline).

◇ **Category X.** Proven fetal risks clearly outweigh any benefit. Accutane® would be an example.

Lactation risk guidelines for postpartum drug use have also been developed.

Over-the-counter and prescribed medications are the most common drugs used by pregnant women. About two-thirds of all pregnant women take at least one drug during pregnancy, usually vitamins or simple analgesics such as aspirin. In one study half of a group of newborns had non-steroidal anti-inflammatory drugs (NSAIDs) such as ibuprofen, naproxen, and particularly aspirin in their meconium (the baby's first intestinal discharge). In addition, the use of NSAIDs was often not reported to the obstetrician, and the incidence of pulmonary hypertension was high (Alano, Ngougmna, Ostrea, et al., 2001). Medications to treat maternal discomfort, anxiety, pain, or infection must be prescribed carefully because a variety of prescription drugs are harmful to the fetus. Sedative-hypnotics are among the most studied of these drugs.

Benzodiazepines accumulate in the fetal blood at more dangerous levels than in maternal blood at dosages normally safe for the mother alone. Besides high fetal drug concentrations, excretion is also slower. The drugs and their metabolites remain in fetal and newborn systems days or even weeks longer than in the mother, resulting in dangerously high concentrations of the drug, leading to fetal depression, abnormal heart patterns, or even death.

In the *Physician's Desk Reference* (*PDR*) under *alprazolam*, the warnings read:

"Because of experience with other members of the benzodiazepine class, Xanax® is assumed to be capable of causing an increased risk of congenital abnormalities when administered to a pregnant woman during the first trimester. Because use of these drugs is rarely a matter of urgency, their use during the first trimester should almost always be avoided."
(*Physicians' Desk Reference [PDR]*, 2007)

Studies have indicated an increased risk of cleft lip and/or cleft palate when diazepam was used in the first six months of pregnancy. A newborn addicted to benzodiazepines may exhibit a variety of neonatal complications. Infants may be floppy, have poor muscle tone, be lethargic, and have sucking difficulties. **A withdrawal syndrome, similar to narcotic withdrawal, may also result and may persist for weeks.** Because diazepam and its active metabolites are excreted into breast milk, it has been thought to cause lethargy, mental sedation/depression, and weight loss in nursing infants. Because diazepam and other benzodiazepines can accumulate in breast-fed babies, their use in lactating women is ill advised. Barbiturates are also to be avoided during pregnancy.

Withdrawal symptoms occur in infants born to mothers who receive barbiturates throughout the last trimester of pregnancy. Withdrawal symptoms include hyperactivity, disturbed sleep, tremors, and hyperreflexia. Prolonged withdrawal can be treated through tapering the infant with phenobarbital over a period of two weeks.

Anticonvulsants such as phenytoin (Dilantin®) increase a pregnant woman's chances of delivering a child with congenital defects such as cleft lip, cleft palate, and heart malformation. Consequently, the physician must carefully weigh the dangers of seizures vs. the chances of congenital defects in the neonate. Pregnancy also alters the absorption of the drug, so there is a chance of more-frequent seizures (PDR, 2007).

Even antibiotics such as tetracycline can cause a variety of adverse effects.

"The use of drugs of the tetracycline class during tooth development in the last half of pregnancy, infancy, and childhood to the age of eight years may cause permanent discoloration of the teeth (yellow-gray-brown)."
(PDR, 2007)

Many OTC medications contain stimulants, including caffeine or ephedrine, and their use should be carefully monitored by the pregnant woman and the physician.

Nicotine

In the overall population, the percentage of women who smoked in the past month steadily increased from 5% in the 1920s to 28.2% in 1997 but dropped to 22.5% in 2005. **About 17% of pregnant women smoked cigarettes** (SAMHSA, 2006). In an earlier study, the percentage of pregnant women who were using tobacco at the time they gave birth was 8.82%. The highest rates were among African Americans (20.12%) and Whites (14.2%) (Noble, Vega, Kolody, et al., 1997). After birth the rate of smoking returned to prepregnancy levels.

Smoking during pregnancy is particularly dangerous because tobacco smoke contains more than 2,000 different compounds, including nicotine and carbon monoxide. Both have been shown to cross the placental barrier and **reduce the fetal supply of oxygen**. In addition, smoking is a continuous activity—one, two, or three packs a day—so the impact on the fetus is constant.

The risk of preterm delivery is increased with smoking as well as with secondhand smoke (Fantuzzi, Aggazzotti, Righi, et al., 2007). Recent studies indicate that **women smokers with a heavy habit are about twice as likely to miscarry** or have spontaneous abortions as nonsmokers. Nicotine damages the placenta and has adverse effects on the developing fetus. Stillbirth rates are also higher among smoking mothers (Cook, Petersen & Moore, 1994).

As with many other psychoactive substances, smoking decreases newborn birth weights. Babies born to mothers who smoke heavily **weigh, on the average, 200 grams (7 oz.) less, are 1.4 centimeters shorter, and have a smaller head circumference** compared with babies of nonsmoking and non-drug-abusing mothers (Martin, 1992). Although the incidence of physical birth defects is very low in babies born to smoking mothers, there is still a significant increase in cleft palate and congenital heart defects. Smoking leads to potential minor brain and nerve defects that may be hard to detect. Because nicotine is toxic and creates lesions in that part of animal brains that controls breathing, it is given as one possible reason for the increase in SIDS in babies born to mothers who smoke heavily (Jaffe & Shopland, 1995).

Babies born to heavy smokers have been shown to have **increased nervous nursing (weaker sucking reflex)** and possibly a depressed immune system at birth, resulting in more pneumonia and bronchitis, sleep problems, and less alertness than other infants. Long-lasting effects of smoking exposure before birth can include **lower IQ and cognitive ability** along with lower verbal, reading, and math skills (Rush & Callahan, 1989). There is even some small association with smoking during pregnancy and the incidence of attention-deficit/hyperactivity disorder (Milberger, Biederman, Faraone, et al., 1998).

Smokeless tobacco also has an impact on the fetus. A study in India found that **pregnant women who used smokeless tobacco had a threefold increased risk of stillbirth and a two- to threefold increased risk of having a baby born with low-birth-weight**. Recently, several states in India have banned the sale and the manufacture of *gutka,* a combination of smokeless tobacco and betel nut, which has become very popular. One-third of tobacco consumption in India is smokeless (Gupta & Ray, 2003).

Caffeine

An early study of pregnant women found caffeine in 75% of infants at birth. In general, neonates, newborns, and infants have less tolerance for caffeine than adults (Weinberg & Bealer, 2001). In addition, pregnant women have decreased ability to metabolize methylxanthines, so the stimulatory effects of caffeine last longer in the fetus. No long-lasting fetal or neonatal effects have been conclusively proven, but **physicians recommend avoiding caffeine during pregnancy** (Browne, Bell, Druschel, et al., 2007). As big a problem as the effect of caffeine during pregnancy is the continued exposure of infants and small children to caffeine products, especially iced tea and colas.

PREVENTION

Because drugs can have such a magnified effect on a fetus throughout pregnancy, **it is crucial that a pregnant woman abstain from all**

This French prevention poster from the 1920s warns about the impact of parental alcohol use on infants.

Courtesy of the National Library of Medicine, Bethesda, MD

• •

unnecessary drug exposure. The challenge is identifying pregnant women who use alcohol and other drugs (AOD) and convincing them to enter not only a prenatal care program but also a drug treatment program if their use is problematic. Ideally, both should be available in a single facility. At the very least, especially if the mother's use is limited, she needs to be convinced that any AOD use can be damaging to her fetus. For these reasons **screening instruments and programs are important in identifying AOD use in the pregnant woman. Once AOD use is identified, treatment, brief intervention, and prevention services can be implemented.** Dr. Ira Chasnoff and his colleagues developed a screening program for pregnant mothers to identify AOD use (Chasnoff, McGourty, Bailey, et al., 2005). Their **4Ps Plus instrument** consists of five basic questions:

◇ **Parents.** Did either of your parents ever have a problem with alcohol or drugs?
◇ **Partner.** Does your partner have a problem with alcohol or drugs?
◇ **Past.** Have you ever drunk beer, wine, or liquor?
◇ **Pregnancy.** In the month before you knew you were pregnant, how many cigarettes did you smoke? In the month before you knew you were pregnant, how much beer, wine, or liquor did you drink?

Once identified, **women at risk can be more extensively screened and if necessary directed to treatment.** Extensive testing of this instrument has proven its effectiveness. Initially, it is also less threatening to the pregnant woman than many of the more complex questionnaires. This is important because in a number of states mothers have lost custody of their children or been convicted of drugging babies instead of being sent to treatment. Some experts fear that **such measures encourage pregnant addicts to avoid prenatal clinics and doctors and to give birth outside of hospitals to avoid imprisonment or loss of custody.** Other jurisdictions use a treatment alternative to jail. It has been suggested that if women do not have to give up their babies when they enter treatment, the treatment option will be more acceptable and successful. Combined prenatal care and substance-abuse treatment is very effective in reducing the damage to neonates (Armstrong, Gonzales Osejo, Lieberman, et al., 2003).

"These nurses would come in and take my child from me. That was a really painful experience, and it's painful now. It gets overwhelming, the feelings of wanting your child, knowing that this little person is very dependent on you, knowing that the meeting of their needs requires you to be clean and sober, requires you to be functional."
29-year-old pregnant addict in recovery

Some **experts call for more universal screening of pregnant women along with sufficient prenatal and drug treatment facilities** to stop the use and improve the overall health of the women (Chasnoff, Neuman, Thornton, et al., 2001). It is estimated that only 55% of women of childbearing age know about fetal alcohol syndrome, although as many as 375,000 children every year may be affected by their mothers' drinking and drug use. Reaching pregnant women with appropriate prevention messages through OB/GYN health professionals, prenatal and well-baby clinics, alcohol/drug warning labels, and public service messages is essential to reducing the effects of alcohol and drug use on babies (Hankin, 2002; NIDA, 1994).

Providing treatment to addicted pregnant women is vital. Many professionals know that if a drug-abusing pregnant woman can get off drugs in the third trimester, the baby will not be born addicted and will not have to go through detoxification. Most prevention professionals agree that because the effects of alcohol on a developing fetus are not yet fully known, clear multiple warnings to women not to drink or use drugs if they are pregnant or planning pregnancy should be given. Complete abstinence is the safest choice.

YOUTH & SCHOOL

"In high school we'd have 'keggers.' We found out whose parents wouldn't be home, have a keg delivered, and have the party there. In college the

drug scene was a little different. Besides the alcohol, you could get a better selection of drugs, but we were usually too poor in high school for those."

19-year-old college sophomore

In spite of all the headlines about crack, LSD, and methamphetamine use **among adolescents and college students, the most serious drug problem by far is still alcohol. Tobacco is a close second and marijuana third.** More recently, prescription drugs, especially opioids, have had a resurgence among youth, often at *pharm parties.* About 3.8% of twelfth-graders use prescription opioids on a monthly basis compared with 18.3% who use marijuana. Methamphetamine has also become popular, but in overall numbers the rate (3.7%) is still low compared with the legal drugs (Figure 8-4) (Monitoring the Future, 2007).

A problem with high school, college, and other drug surveys is that many users minimize or lie about their use of drugs even when assured that the survey is confidential. This is often part of the denial process. It has been found that **most figures on current or frequent use of illicit drugs in high schools and colleges are underreported** (Poteet-Johnson & Dias, 2003). In fact, underage drinkers account for nearly 20% of the alcohol consumed in the United States.

"We were supposed to put on a skit about drugs, and the minute we sat down we said, 'Now what do the parents want to hear about that?' That's the general attitude all my friends have in dealing with these programs: 'What do the parents want to hear from us?' And a lot of the people teaching these drug programs are also telling us what they think our parents want us to hear. It's all very stereotypical."

15-year-old high school student

The other drawback of doing surveys is that problematic use means different things for different people and for different drugs. For example, if a college freshman gets drunk only on Friday and Saturday nights, usually leading to a fight or unprotected sex, the student would probably swear that he or she doesn't have a drinking problem. But by the definition of abuse, that kind of drinking is problematic.

With cocaine, if a student goes on a three-day binge just once a month, spends all available money on the drug, and has nothing left for food or textbooks, that also could be defined as abuse. **The true value of youth surveys is that they show trends in drug use,** so it is possible to see changes from year to year and have a sense of where our society is headed. Surveys also give us a rough benchmark for measuring the effectiveness of the prevention efforts we as a society are expending. The difficult part is figuring out what to attribute an increase or decrease in drug use to: prevention spots, interdiction, the maturation process, school programs, a bad economy?

ADOLESCENTS & HIGH SCHOOL

How Serious Is the Problem?

"When I got to high school, a number of kids wanted me to try this and try that drug or 40-ouncer... and basically I told them, 'Been there, done that.' We were trying alcohol and marijuana, cigarettes, and even 'shrooms and occasionally meth starting in the sixth and seventh and eighth grades."

22-year-old female social drinker

Figure 8-5, which charts trends in drug use by high school seniors, shows that there has been a **decrease in high school alcohol consumption over the past 30 years, a similar decrease in cigarette smoking, and a smaller drop in marijuana use.** But even though there has been a slight downturn, the absolute numbers are still

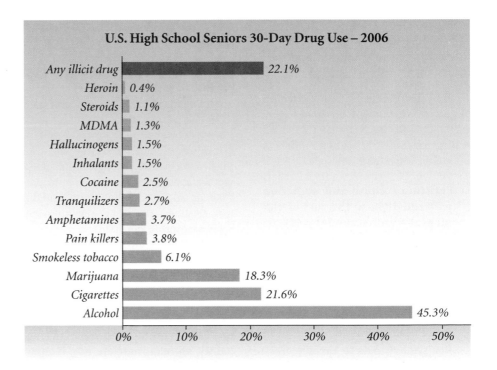

U.S. High School Seniors 30-Day Drug Use – 2006

Drug	Percentage
Any illicit drug	22.1%
Heroin	0.4%
Steroids	1.1%
MDMA	1.3%
Hallucinogens	1.5%
Inhalants	1.5%
Cocaine	2.5%
Tranquilizers	2.7%
Amphetamines	3.7%
Pain killers	3.8%
Smokeless tobacco	6.1%
Marijuana	18.3%
Cigarettes	21.6%
Alcohol	45.3%

Figure 8-4 •

Since 1992 decreased funding, greater availability of drugs, and a tolerance to drug use led to sharp increases in drug use among high school seniors as well as eighth- and tenth-graders. Recently, the levels of use have begun to drop.

(Monitoring the Future, 2007)

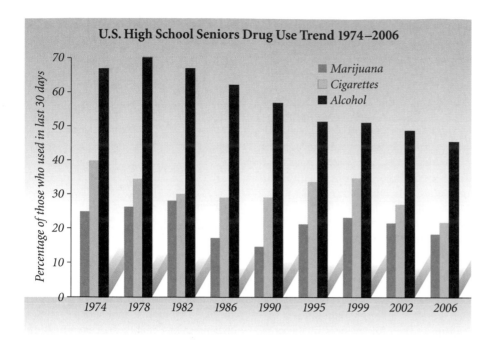

Figure 8-5 •

This graph compares the change in the 30-day use of alcohol, marijuana, and tobacco over the past 30 years by high school seniors.

(Monitoring the Future, 2007)

high. For example, smoking by seniors is half of what it was in 1974, but that still amounts to more than 1 million twelfth-graders.

In a 2001 report titled *Malignant Neglect: Substance Abuse and America's Schools,* the National Center on Addiction and Substance Abuse at Columbia University found that:

◇ **substance abuse and addiction will add 10% to the cost of elementary and secondary education** due to violence, special education, teacher turnover, truancy, property damage, injury, and counseling;

◇ the **school environment has the greatest influence on drug and alcohol use**; and

◇ **if a student gets to the age of 21 without smoking or using alcohol and other drugs, he or she probably never will**.

The report also found that experimentation is not benign. For example, of those students who have ever:

◇ tried cigarettes, 85.7% are still smoking in the twelfth grade;

◇ been drunk, 83.3% are still getting drunk; and

◇ tried marijuana, 76.4% are still smoking pot.

In addition, adolescents who use marijuana weekly reported that they were almost six times likelier to cut class or skip school than those who do not (National Center on Addiction and Substance Abuse [CASA], 2001).

Much of the alcohol and other drug use in high schools is experimental, social, or habitual with bouts of abuse. Most students haven't had enough time for addiction to occur. Unfortunately, they also **don't have much experience in their drinking and drug-taking habits, so inappropriate use, including intoxication, drunk driving, and unsafe sex, is more likely**. Another factor that can lead to inappropriate use occurs when young people drink or take drugs to control emotional turmoil, and they don't appreciate the collateral psychological effects of solving

problems with a substance. Part of the reason is society's semi-benign attitude toward legal psychoactive drugs.

Finally, because many **adolescents think of themselves as invulnerable to the consequences of use**, their level of concern is lower than that of older users. Whereas the majority of teenagers who experiment with drugs will not become addicted, some will, and for them the legal, academic, psychological, and physical effects of psychoactive drugs will be catastrophic:

◇ 70% of teen suicides involve alcohol or drugs;

◇ 50% of date rapes involve alcohol (victim and/or rapist); and

◇ 40% of drownings involve alcohol.

Psychological immaturity is another problem. Just three drinks in the younger user cause significantly more mental impairment than in an adult drinker (CASA, 2001).

Crime

The biggest effect of alcohol and drug use on adolescents is crime. In some cities the youth guidance centers or juvenile halls are clogged because of crimes related to drugs (using or being under the influence when committing the crime). Nationally, according to the Arrestee Drug Abuse Monitoring Program, **more than half of juvenile male arrestees tested positive for one or more illegal drugs**, with marijuana being by far the most frequent (ADAM, 2003). If the authorities had also tested for alcohol, the figures would be much higher. It has been estimated that the cost of youth alcohol abuse is more than $58 billion (e.g., $36 billion in violent crime, $18 billion in traffic accidents).

"I went to jail a lot for being drunk, being on drugs, for committing crimes, lots of assaults and weapons and things like that. I was a whole different person when I was using, you know, I wasn't giving a rat's ass about nobody or nothin'. I was just gang bangin' to the fullest, that was it."
17-year-old high school student

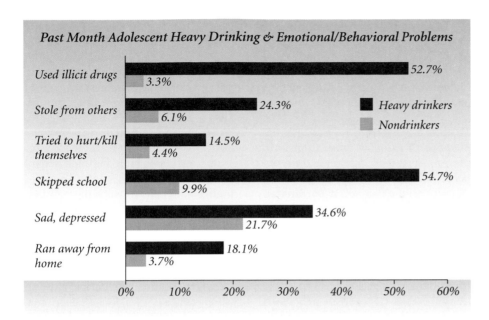

Past Month Adolescent Heavy Drinking & Emotional/Behavioral Problems

Used illicit drugs — 52.7% / 3.3%
Stole from others — 24.3% / 6.1%
Tried to hurt/kill themselves — 14.5% / 4.4%
Skipped school — 54.7% / 9.9%
Sad, depressed — 34.6% / 21.7%
Ran away from home — 18.1% / 3.7%

Heavy drinkers / Nondrinkers

0%   10%   20%   30%   40%   50%   60%

Figure 8-6 •

A survey of 12- to 17-year-olds showed that heavy drinkers were more likely to have emotional and behavioral problems. Some of the problems led to experimentation and eventually heavy use of alcohol, whereas others were caused by the heavy use itself.
(SAMHSA, 2000)

The Effects of Drugs on Maturation

A college newspaper did an unofficial survey to try to figure out how many years it takes to reach maturity in the United States. Their answer was **"To reach the emotional maturity of an average 18-year-old takes 25 years."** In a society where survival is comparatively easy, where one can delay entrance into the working world by living at home and not paying rent, and where, if you can afford it, you can stay in school until you're 25 or older, the need to reach adulthood is not as pressing. Being able to avoid handling and solving financial, emotional, and social problems delays maturation. **The difficulty with drugs is they help a person avoid these problems.**

"When you begin to use drugs around 12, 13, or 14, you never have rites of passage. You never get inducted into the adulthood of society. Many people that we talk to who come into treatment actually began using substances at that age, so their rites of passage haven't yet occurred when we see them at 30 or 35. And, essentially, we're talking to a 14- or 15-year-old in a 30- or 35-year-old body, and that's where we have to begin."

Jerry Clarke, counselor, Genesis Recovery Center

When drugs or alcohol are commonly used in adolescence to avoid stress, to drown out emotions, or as a shortcut to feeling good, **young people will not fully learn how to deal with life's conflicts without psychoactive substances.** They will not learn patience, they will not learn that emotional pain can be tolerated and even be used to grow, and they will not learn that being willing to do things you don't want to do is part of the maturation process.

Risk-Focused & Resiliency-Focused Prevention for Adolescents

Recent studies indicate that a number of conditions put some adolescents more at risk for substance abuse than others. These **risks include:**

◇ **being subject to physical, sexual, or emotional abuse;**
◇ **having emotional and mental disturbances;**
◇ **lacking self-esteem;**
◇ **being exposed to peer group tolerance or encouragement of drug use;**
◇ **being in a family that tolerates use, has no consistent rules,** lacks consistent discipline, and has absent and uninvolved parents or especially parents who use drugs;
◇ dropping out of school;
◇ getting caught in the juvenile justice system;
◇ getting pregnant;
◇ living in poverty;
◇ lacking alternative activities; and
◇ being in a school that has no policies, detection procedures, or referral services for users

(Juliana & Goodman, 2005, ONDCP, 2000).

"I believe both my parents were alcoholics. My brother's an addict and alcoholic. It runs in the family. So I basically followed in my father's footsteps—the drinking, the running around."

Recovering alcoholic

The challenge for prevention specialists is to develop programs that clearly identify the risks and teach adolescents to deal with them while enhancing the protective elements that promote healthy lifestyles and personal accomplishments. Researchers Steven Glenn, Ph.D. and Richard Jessor, Ph.D., present **four determinants that help children avoid drug use** (observable by age 12):

◇ **Strong sense of family participation and involvement.** Those children who feel that they are significant participants in and valued by their families seem to be less prone toward substance abuse in the future.

◇ **Established personal position about drugs, alcohol, and sex.** Children who have a position on these issues and who can articulate how they arrived at their position, how they would act on it, and what effect their position would have on their lives seem less likely to develop drug or alcohol problems.

◊ **Strong spiritual sense and community involvement.** Young people who feel that they matter, contribute to their community, and believe that they are individuals with a role and a purpose in society also seem less likely to develop significant drug or alcohol problems.

◊ **Attachment to a clean-and-sober adult role model.** Children who can list one or more non-drug-using adults (other than their parents) for whom they have esteem and to whom they can turn for information or advice seem less prone to develop drug-abuse problems. These positive role models, often persons like a coach, teacher, activities leader, minister, relative, neighbor, or family friend, play a critical role in the formative years of a child's development.

Primary, Secondary & Tertiary Prevention for Grades K Through 12

When prevention programs are planned, they need to keep the risk and resiliency factors in mind and **tailor programs not only for the specific age group but also for ethnicity, gender, culture**, and any other factors that will get the message across. Most good programs have:

◊ **structure**—program type, audience, and setting;

◊ **content**—information, skills development, methods, and services; and

◊ **a delivery system**—specific plans and facilities for implementation. **SAMHSA's National Registry of Evidence-Based Programs and Practices lists several model prevention programs** such as Dare to Be You (DTBY), Family Matter, Lion's Quest Skills for Adolescents, Multisystemic Therapy (MST), New Beginnings Program, Project Towards No Drug Abuse, Seeking Safety, and many others (NREPP, 2007).

Other popular programs include the Caring School Community program, Classroom-Centered and Family-School Partnership Intervention, Guiding Good Choices, AMPS, DARE, and LifeSkills Training (NIDA, 2003).

Primary Prevention. Because the purpose of primary prevention is to prevent or at least minimize drug experimentation and use, it needs to start as early as kindergarten. **Coordinated efforts among family members, teachers, and other school personnel are of great value.** Parent/teacher sessions and the incorporation of drug prevention lesson plans within the school's overall curriculum are the first steps. **School-based prevention programs can teach life skills, resistance education, and/or normative education** (Bates & Wigtil, 1994). Unfortunately, primary prevention can focus on only a few of the risk factors in an adolescent's or a teenager's life, which include personal, genetic, psychological, family, and social problems. One danger is to focus on punitive measures using drug testing and zero-tolerance policies rather than emphasizing personal development. For example, zero-tolerance policies that punish any use of alcohol or drugs are often used just to identify children for expulsion rather than to place them in appropriate treatment (CASA, 2001).

A **life skills program** being taught in grades 7 to 10, LifeSkills Training, focuses on **increasing social skills and reducing peer pressure to drink**. An evaluation of this program showed a decrease in the frequency of drinking and excessive drinking (Botvin & Griffin, 2005; LifeSkills Training, 2003).

One of the most widely used resistance education programs is **DARE (Drug Abuse Resistance Education)**, which consists of **16 or 17 weekly one-hour sessions conducted by uniformed police officers and presented to fifth- or sixth-graders.** The program teaches self-esteem, decision-making skills, and peer resistance training. Early studies found that the program had modest short-term (one year) effects on reducing drug use through improved self-assertiveness and increased knowledge about the dangers of alcohol and other drugs

(Ennet, Tobler, Ringwalt, et al., 1994). A study of students 10 years after they took the course found that its effects were not long lasting, however, and actual drug use was not reduced more than control groups (CASA, 2001; Lyman, Milich, Zimmerman, et al., 1999). In response to criticism and to update the courses, DARE revised its program. It has programs for junior high and high school students and involves students in more lifelike situations to teach them to better handle peer pressure. There is even a DARE program for parents to involve them in prevention.

Another resistance education program similar to DARE is **AMPS (Alcohol Misuse Prevention Study)**, which consists of a four-session curriculum for fifth- and sixth-graders. It educates as well as **develops peer resistance skills**. Studies of high-risk students who had taken the course found a 50% reduction in use after 26 months and through grade 12 (Dielman, 1995; Littlefield, 2003).

Normative education is a strategy that aims to correct erroneous beliefs about the prevalence and the acceptability of alcohol use and drug use among peers. This strategy was found to be a strong adjunct to resistance education, causing substantial drops in alcohol use among high school students (Hansen & Graham, 1991).

The most pertinent aspect of all of these programs is that primary prevention must be continual and not just limited to a one-year attempt at inoculating students against drug and alcohol use. Education and skills-training booster sessions need to continue through high school and into college. The most effective prevention programs seem to be those in which students are taught self-esteem and confidence and in which they learn not to be afraid of their feelings.

Because the roots of most addictions come from the family, **family-focused primary prevention is a necessary adjunct to any school-based program**. Programs such as parental skills training through the school, reduction in parental use of drugs or alcohol in front of the children, and greater positive participation of parents in their children's lives have a great influence on children's behavior. Results from a study by the Partnership for a Drug-Free America indicate that parents who have repeated discussions with their children about the risks of illicit drugs and who set clear rules do make a difference in adolescent drug use. About 45% of teenagers who heard nothing at home about drug risks used marijuana in the past year. That figure drops to 33% for those who learned a little at home and 26% for those who learned a lot (Parents' Resource Institute for Drug Education, 2002; Partnership for a Drug-Free America, 2005).

One evidence-based program for strengthening families is the **Iowa Strengthening Families Program (ISFP)**. The seven-session ISFP was designed to improve parents' family management practices and communication skills and childrens' personal skills, social skills, and ability to deal with peer pressure. Follow-up studies found that 48 months after the initial assessment, the proportion of new marijuana users among youths who didn't participate in the ISFP was 2.4 times greater than it was among youths who did participate. Furthermore, the divergence in drug use between youths who received the program in the sixth grade and those who didn't has widened in the four years since the study's pre-intervention assessment (Mathias, 2000).

Secondary Prevention. Once experimentation, social use, habituation, and occasional abuse have begun, usually starting in the sixth, seventh, and eighth grades (occasionally earlier), school-based prevention programs need to continue primary prevention but also need to add a number of secondary prevention programs and policies. **Junior high and high schools should include clear formulation and strict policies on substance use. Teachers and staff should be trained in recognizing drug use and how to deal with the consequences.** Training to enable parents to recognize problems due to drug use in their children, supporting their children, and seeking counseling should also be included. Additional services should include crisis intervention and referral. Other essential (but sometimes neglected) services are follow-up aftercare, support to make sure use does not reoccur, and care to ensure

that emotional, social, and physical problems leading to substance use are being corrected. Often these services are available through utilization of existing community services rather than hiring new and expensive staff.

At this level some other programs found to be effective in minimizing experimentation with drugs are peer educator programs, prevention curricula, positive role models, Students Against Drunk Driving, health fairs, and Friday Night Live alternative activities.

"When I was going through my wild stage, I think what changed my mind about drugs was seeing someone who went through their wild days and never stopped. So I think that there is a point when you cross over from experimentation and go on to abusing."
21-year-old college student

Tertiary Prevention. This level **(for students who have a problem with drugs)** uses student assistance programs that include counseling and social services, Alateen, and other 12-step anonymous meetings targeted for teenagers, and peer intervention teams aimed at getting drug abusers into early treatment. **The honesty of peers seems most effective in reaching students who are in trouble.**

The Positive Behavioral Interventions and Supports (PBIS) method under the U.S. Department of Education provides support for schools that want to establish or strengthen their prevention programs. The PBIS approach helps develop such programs as behavioral support for high-risk students, and includes:

◇ adjustments to the environment that reduce the likelihood of a problem;
◇ teaching replacement skills and building general competencies;
◇ implementing consequences to promote positive behaviors and deter problems; and
◇ a crisis management or relapse plan (if needed)
(PBIS, 2007).

A large part of secondary and tertiary prevention is recognizing the signs of drug use in teenagers. One CASA survey found that while only 12% of parents saw alcohol and drugs as a problem, 27% of teenagers ranked it their primary concern (CASA, 2006). An increasing number of public schools have implemented random drug testing. More than 350 secondary schools received testing money from the federal government in the 2005-2006 school year. Probably an equal number pay for their own testing. But this is still a fraction of the 28,000 schools nationwide (Leinwand, 2006). Home drug tests provide another way that parents monitor drug abuse. They use these drug tests when behavior suggests that family rules have been violated. Teenagers, however, may resent the tests as a breach of trust and an invasion of privacy.

Children of Alcoholics & Drug Abusers. It is estimated that one in four U.S. children under 18 years old are exposed to alcohol abuse or alcohol dependence in their family (Grant, 2000). So whether it's primary, secondary, or even tertiary prevention, teachers, counselors, and health professionals have to recognize that **children are affected by drugs and alcohol even when they don't use.** They have to be able to identify and deal with the different roles a child will take in an alcohol- or drug-using family because many of these roles will affect future drug use as well as their personalities. These roles include:

◇ **the hero (model child)**, a hard-working student who tries to bring pride to the family but is still affected by the intense stress of having an addict or alcoholic in the family; also known as the "chief enabler," this type of child often takes over the duties of dysfunctional parents;
◇ **the problem child** who experiences multiple personal problems, has a tendency to use drugs, and demands attention;
◇ **the lost child** who is extremely shy and deals with problems by avoiding family and social activities; and

◇ **the mascot (or family clown)** who tries to ease tension in a dysfunctional family by being funny or cute and has trouble maturing (Adger, 1998; Sher, 1997).

COLLEGE STUDENTS

Going to college, whether away or in one's hometown, is full of new experiences and pressures: living on one's own, developing autonomy and self-regulation, making a new set of friends, coping with peer pressure, rising to new academic demands, or simply being a small fish in a big brand-new pond. When trying fit in with the college culture, practicing one's autonomy, or handling the stresses of a new environment, alcohol and drug use becomes an option. Transitions from one culture to another are often times of high vulnerability.

Although illegal drugs, particularly marijuana, can be found on most college campuses, alcohol is still the drug that predominates. In a Carnegie Foundation survey, college presidents ranked alcohol abuse as the quality-of-campus-life issue that was their greatest concern. Drinking is embedded in college traditions and norms. College students are particular targets for advertising by the alcoholic beverage industry because a freshman who prefers a particular brand is expected to generate $20,000 to $50,000 in sales over his or her lifetime.

Prevalence

A new national college survey by the Center on Addiction and Substance Abuse at Columbia University found that **49% of full-time college students binge-drink and/or abuse prescription and legal drugs (3.8 million students)**. In addition, 1.8 million of those students meet the medical criteria for substance abuse and dependence. That figure is **two and a half times that found in the general population**. The figures also showed an increase in excessive binge drinking and prescription drug abuse. The use of prescription opioids tripled in the past two years, while the use of benzodiazepines (Xanax® and Valium®) went up fourfold (CASA, 2007). Other data showed that:

◇ rates of **daily smoking dropped from 15% in 1993 to 12% in 2005**, and daily heavy smoking dropped from 9% in 1993 to 7% in 2005;

◇ **fraternity and sorority members are likelier to drink than non-members (88% vs. 67%), binge-drink (64% vs. 37%)**, drink and drive (33% vs. 21%), use marijuana (21% vs. 16%), and smoke (26% vs. 21%);

◇ **only 6% of students who are deemed to be abusers or addicts seek help**; and

◇ close to **78% of college students who use illicit drugs have sex compared with 44% of those who never use drugs** (one of the main reasons students use drugs).

Consequences of drug and alcohol abuse on campuses included:

◇ 1,717 deaths from alcohol-related injuries;

◇ 97,000 victims of alcohol-related rape or sexual assaults; and

◇ 696 assaults by another student who had been binge drinking.

A change in federal law made people ineligible for student financial aid if they have a drug conviction on their record. In 2003 and 2004, of the 10,437,000 million who applied for federal financial aid for college, 41,000 were denied because of a conviction. An equal number who had a conviction on their record were eligible because they completed a drug treatment program or had another exemption (U.S. Department of Education, 2006). In 2007 the ACLU sued the federal government to repeal the financial aid restrictions, saying they constituted double jeopardy. The case will take some time to be adjudicated (Associated Press, 2007).

Secondhand Drinking

Many problems that occur on campuses are related to **secondhand drinking—the effect binge drinkers and heavy drinkers have on other students**. On campuses where more than 50% of students binge, 86% of non-binge-drinking students reported being victims of assault or unwanted sexual advances, having sleep and study time interrupted, suffering property damage, having to care for or clean up after a drunken student, or suffering from the general impairment of the quality of life on campus that drinking causes them (Wechsler, Kelley, Weitzman, et al., 2000).

Prevention in Colleges

College drinking games and songs date back to the Middle Ages as do attempts to control the damage students do to themselves and to one another. A sheriff still leads the commencement parade at Harvard graduation ceremonies, a centuries-old tradition to prevent drunken rowdy behavior. In England the recommended weekly upper limit for college students is 14 drinks for women and 21 for men (Polymeru, 2007). **One reason why the college drinking culture is hard to change is the view that sowing one's oats in college is a rite of passage to which students are entitled.** Drug experimentation is also considered part of this rite of passage.

Contemporary college prevention efforts date from the federal Anti-Drug Abuse Act of 1986 that set aside funds

for higher education and designated the **Fund for the Improvement of Post-Secondary Education** as the granting agency that reviewed prevention grant proposals and dispersed funds. Many current drug courses and campus prevention programs derive from that legislation. Newer programs include the counter-advertising campaigns of the National Association of State Universities and Land-Grant Colleges as well as programs by individual colleges.

Normative Assessment.   One prevention approach that has had success is **normative assessment**. This program **aims to change common misperceptions that drug and alcohol use among peers is higher than it really is**. It recognizes that if students think that heavy drinking or drug use is the normal thing to do, they will be more likely to do it themselves. If they recognize that heavy drinking or illicit-drug use is not normal, they are more likely not to use. At Hobart and William Smith Colleges in Geneva, New York, studies found that 68% of students believed that their peers found frequent intoxication acceptable when in fact only 14% found it acceptable (Perkins & Craig, 2002; Perkins, Meilman, Leichliter, et al., 1999). In the first 18 months of the program that disseminated the normative assessment information through a variety of media (including screen savers in university computers), there was a 16% reduction in drinking to get drunk, a 21% reduction in frequent heavy drinking, a 31% reduction in missed classes, a 36% reduction in property damage, and a 40% reduction in unprotected sex.

Instead of talking about drug and alcohol use, **normative assessment emphasizes that prevention efforts should talk about not using**. The key is to let students know what constitutes normal use on a particular campus rather than letting their perceptions be formed by sensational stories in the media or the exaggerations of their friends and classmates.

Other Programs.   The following list shows different **campus strategies directed at controlling alcohol use** and abuse:

◇ **regulate campus drinking** (25% of campuses ban beer, 32% prohibit liquor on campus, and 98% prohibit kegs in dorms) (Wechsler, Kelly, Weitzman, et al., 2000);

◇ **provide alcohol-, tobacco-, and drug-free dorms** (wellness halls) (two-thirds of campuses offer such dorms);

◇ **prohibit alcohol at campus events and fraternity/sorority parties**;

◇ announce and **enforce campus alcohol and other drug policies**;

◇ work with local communities to ensure that alcohol is not served to minors;

◇ strengthen academic requirements;

◇ schedule more classes on Friday;

◇ keep the library and recreational facilities open longer;

◇ restrict alcohol promotions on campus;

◇ notify parents when students run afoul of alcohol/drug laws and regulations;

◇ require that food and nonalcoholic beverages be served when alcohol is available;

◇ provide server training for bartenders at college-sponsored functions;

◇ ban or regulate alcoholic beverage advertising in campus newspapers (50% ban such advertising);

◇ integrate substance-abuse education into the curriculum;

◇ have a substance-abuse officer and a task force to deal with on-campus use and abuse;

◇ establish a higher-education prevention consortia in which several campuses pool their knowledge and efforts (about 90 such consortia exist);

◇ create programs to work with the neighborhood and the community; and

◇ initiate early detection, intervention, enforcement, and referral by residence hall assistants, peer counselors, and the health and counseling centers.

At the college level, primary prevention also includes well-publicized alcohol-free parties, weeklong "red ribbon" alcohol- and drug-free celebrations, and active outreach activities especially those promoting safe sex.

In an effective program, the three levels of drug-abuse prevention (primary, secondary, and tertiary) need to be tailored for 17- to 21-year-olds. One problem is that some educators forget the high level of sophistication of college students when it comes to knowledge about some aspects of drugs and alcohol. As a result, a good part of the message appears condescending to the average student. The lack of sophistication usually occurs regarding long-term health consequences. Strangely, students actually overexaggerate the dangers of risky behavior while at the same time overexaggerating the projected benefits even more, so often the risky behavior wins (Reyna & Farley, 2007). This has implications for drug education, which usually minimizes anything positive about a drug or alcohol.

If the benefits of drugs and alcohol were not underexaggerated and the side effects were not overexaggerated, perhaps that would provide a basis of knowledge that matched students' experiences and perhaps the messages of moderation and/or abstinence would be more believable.

Now whether students would actually translate ideas and beliefs into action is another question. Studies have shown that good drug education will encourage some experimentation but decrease abuse while bad drug education will often increase abuse. Fortunately, experience has shown that **as most college students mature, their alcohol and drug use becomes more sensible**.

"It's the freshmen that are the biggest pain—not all of them. They are free from their parents' supervision for the first time, they are in an exciting but lonely place, and they try out their wings. Those are the ones I try to keep an eye on and help, but if I'm too strict, they just drink off campus and come back and make noise and throw up. As dorm supervisor I turn a partial blind eye to the older students who have learned how to drink and close their

door and have a few beers or wine. I can't burst into their rooms and I don't want to lurk behind doors, but I do have to protect the other students. I do know that when the university instituted alcohol-free dorms, they were instantly popular."
Resident assistant at university dormitory

It is crucial to recruit peer counselors or dorm monitors who are themselves clean-and-sober and will model the kind of attitudes and behavior desirable in a prevention program.

LOVE, SEX & DRUGS

"The deepest human need is the need to overcome the prison of our aloneness."
Erich Fromm, The Art of Loving

Traditionally, alcohol has been the substance most associated with sexual activity, but **the advent of Viagra® (sildenafil citrate) in 1998, then Cialis® (tadalafil) in 2003, and finally Levitra® (vardenifil) in 2005 to treat erectile dysfunction has produced the biggest change in the use of drugs to enhance human sexuality.** They enhance nitric oxide that eventually relaxes smooth muscles in the corpus cavernosum erectile tissue, allowing greater blood flow. After years of searching, sex drugs that work have been discovered. The rush to find more medications to enhance sexuality continues. It is important to remember, however, that **these drugs have no effect in the absence of sexual stimulation** (PDR, 2007). The limited effect of these drugs emphasizes the complexity of human sexuality.

Our desire for friendship, affection, love, intimacy, and sex is a primary driving force in men and women, and drugs affect that primary force in many different and complicated ways. For example, some psychoactive drugs, such as alcohol, marijuana, and ecstasy, lower inhibitions. Others, including cocaine, amphetamines, marijuana, and some inhalants, are used to intensify

and otherwise alter the physical sensations of sexuality and to counter low self-esteem or shyness. Often psychoactive drugs **substitute a simple physical sensation, or the illusion of one, for more-complex (and often more rewarding) emotions**, such as desire for intimacy and comfort, love of children, or release from anxiety. Many psychoactive drugs manipulate natural biochemicals, thereby stimulating, counterfeiting, blocking, or mixing up physical sensations and emotions.

Drugs have an impact (both wanted and unwanted) on all phases of sexual behavior from puberty, through dating, to marital relations. The use of a glass or two of wine to get in the mood, the cigarette after sex, the popper to intensify an erection and orgasm, amphetamines to delay ejaculation, marijuana to enhance the newness of a situation, or ecstasy to increase empathy ensures that **drugs are desirable to a wide range of ages and cultures, particularly if shyness, lack of confidence, aging, or physical changes have diminished one's desire and abilities.**

The same drugs, when used long term or in large doses, can also cause the reverse effects: lack of interest, physical depression, and inability to achieve an erection or orgasm. Certain drugs can also trigger sexual aggression, sexual harassment, rape (including date rape), and child molestation, particularly if one is already prone to such behavior. **Drugs also encourage high-risk sexual behavior** like multiple partners, anonymous sex, unprotected sex, anal sex, and even prostitution to support one's habit—all of which can spread sexually transmitted diseases (e.g., syphilis, gonorrhea, hepatitis B and C, and HIV) (El-Bassel, Schilling, Gilbert, et al., 2000).

"I'm monogamous. I'm with just one boyfriend at a time. I've been with him for two months now. The one before, I was with for four months."
Teenage high school junior

The 1960s and 1970s signaled an increase in the use and the availability of marijuana, amphetamines, and several other psychoactive drugs—all of which affect sexual activity. **This eas-**

ier availability of drugs, coupled with less severe attitudes toward sexual activity, increased sexual contacts and drug experimentation. In addition, the onset of the cocaine and crack epidemic in the 1980s that continued into the 1990s and 2000s, as well as the increased use of methamphetamine, ecstasy, and other club drugs, encouraged high-risk sexual activity. The drugs' mood-altering effects, along with the need to make money to buy the drugs, added to the complexity of this interrelationship.

"These were women that otherwise I would never even have the nerve to approach. Once I've got crack, then I'm someone who's desirable and I can do with these women anything that I want to. And that's what got me involved with crack cocaine."
Crack user

GENERAL EFFECTS

The three main effects of psychoactive drugs on sexual behavior are on desire, excitation, and orgasm. Physically, psychoactive drugs affect hormonal release (testosterone, estrogen, and adrenaline), blood flow, blood pressure, nerve sensitivity, and muscle tension that in turn affect excitation (erectile ability) and orgasm. For example:

◇ heroin desensitizes penal and vaginal nerve endings;

◇ alcohol diminishes spinal reflexes, thus decreasing sensitivity and erectile ability;

◇ steroids increase testosterone that stimulates the fight center of the brain, making a user more sexually aggressive;

◇ cocaine and amphetamines release dopamine that stimulates the pleasure center in the limbic system, the same system stimulated during excitation and orgasm; and

◇ many psychoactive drugs affect the hypothalamus, which can trigger hormonal changes.

"It's a very euphoric satisfying kind of effect and it's similar to sex but

different. *If I have heroin, I don't want or need real sex."*
Heroin user

The actual effect of drugs in contrast with their expected effect can vary radically. Many addiction counselors observe that **regular drug users combined sex and drugs to lower their inhibitions, try to make themselves perform better, and increase their fantasies**.

"As a teenager I was sort of shy, and the meth made me feel I was supersmart, superpretty, a superperson. At that age I felt very awkward and uncomfortable without the drug."
Recovering meth user

Sex and love are such complicated processes and so tied to our mental state that **people use drugs not only to enhance their sexuality but also to shield themselves from their sexuality and even from emotional involvement**.

THE DRUGS

Drug-using behavior takes on a life of its own as tolerance, withdrawal, and side effects overwhelm the user's original intentions. **Most of the effects on sexuality are from the drugs' disruption of the neurotransmitters serotonin, dopamine, and norepinephrine.** Serotonin affects mood, aggression, and self-esteem; dopamine is believed to help regulate mood, emotional behavior, motor control, and orgasm; and norepinephrine stimulates heart rate and other body functions while increasing motivation and confidence (Peugh & Belenko, 2001).

Alcohol

"One drink of wine and you act like a monkey, two drinks and you strut like a peacock, three drinks and you roar like a lion, and four drinks, you behave like a pig."
Henry Vollam Morton, 1936

More than any other psychoactive drug, alcohol has insinuated itself into

the culture of romantic and sexual behavior—champagne to celebrate, cocktails before sex, or beer on a date. **Alcohol's physical effects on sexual functioning are closely related to blood alcohol levels. Its mental effects, however, are less strictly dose related and have more to do with the user's psychological makeup** and the setting in which it is used. Often there are pre-existing issues that are dealt with under the influence.

"It was making me feel better about myself. It was like I was a grown woman. I could take any man I wanted. It was like, 'Honey, let's go have a drink,' and there was always alcohol involved. And we would sit at a bar and then it was easy for them to invite me to a hotel for the night."
42-year-old recovering polydrug abuser

Women & Alcohol. In most societies more taboos and restrictions are placed on a woman's sexuality than on a man's. Many heavy drinkers seem to associate their identity as a woman with their sexual activity. Inevitably, **because alcohol diminishes sexual arousal, women can suffer lowered self-esteem and feelings of inadequacy**. Typically, the alcoholic denies that what is happening to her sexuality is related to what is happening with her progressive alcohol use.

"I was quite drunk. It was a 'kegger' party, and I remember sitting right next to the keg and just drinking constantly all night. I voluntarily went out to a car with a boy. I voluntarily had sex with that boy because I was quite drunk and I guess the thinking was that I wanted someone to hold me, and love me, and make me feel pretty."
24-year-old female heavy drinker

Even though many women report that alcohol use increases sexual pleasure, quantitative measures of physical sexual arousal and ability to have an orgasm decreased with a blood alcohol level increase (Peugh & Belenko, 2001). This seems to emphasize the powerful influence on emotions of lowered inhibitions in women. In men, however, the self-reported feelings and objective measures of physical arousal were more consistent.

In one study of chronic female alcoholics, 36% said they had orgasms less than 5% of the time. The study also found that sexual dysfunction was the best predictor of continued problems with alcohol abuse (Wilsnack, Klassen, Schur, et al., 1991). Heavy drinking produces increases in plasma testosterone. This seems to inhibit ovulation and can decrease fertility (Blume & Zilberman, 2005). Heavy drinking also causes menstrual disturbances, spontaneous abortions, miscarriages, and fetal alcohol spectrum disorders (Mello, Mendelson & Teoh, 1993).

In both women and men, **as the drinking progresses, alcoholic behavior is reinforced and it is difficult for the alcoholic to do anything but drink.** Sex is merely something to do while drinking.

Men & Alcohol. The familiar release of inhibitions both in word and deed is the key to alcohol's dual effect on a man's sexual activity (i.e., more desire/less performance). In men a blood alcohol concentration of 0.05 (about three beers in one hour) has a very measurable physical effect on erectile ability, and yet legal intoxication in most states is almost twice that amount. On the other hand, mentally, even one drink can loosen the tongue. **Physically alcohol diminishes spinal reflexes, thus decreasing sensitivity and erectile ability.** Even a few drinks lower testosterone levels. The long-term male drinker shows a greater decrease in testosterone, an increase in female sex steroids, such as estradiol, and abnormalities in sex steroid metabolism (Wright, Gavaler & Thiel, 1991; Zakhari, 1993).

Initially, however, alcohol gives men more confidence because **it acts on the area of the brain that regulates fight, fright, and fear, thereby promoting aggressiveness.** As alcoholism progresses many men feel less sexual (possibly due to decreased testosterone and preoccupation with alcohol) and tend to shy away from the bedroom and even become asexual. In one early study, impotence was reported in 60% of heavy alcohol abusers (Crowe & George, 1989).

"Sure I could have sex without alcohol. I've just never had occasion to do it."
43-year-old problem drinker

Cocaine & Amphetamines

Although cocaine and amphetamines are popular with heterosexuals, they are particularly popular with gay males because, for some, use **increases confidence, prolongs an erection, increases endurance, and intensifies an orgasm during initial low-dose use.** Crystal meth in particular has acquired a reputation for intensifying sexual feelings (Lee, 2006). Cocaine and amphetamines increase the supply of dopamine and norepinephrine in the nervous system, thus inducing a rush of pleasure by affecting centers in the brain involved with sexual activity mostly in the limbic system (Gold & Jacobs, 2005). The difference between the two drugs has most to do with the duration of action; **methamphetamine lasts hours longer than cocaine and thus prolongs the stimulation.** Men who used methamphetamine were able to sustain sexual functioning (erection and orgasm) longer than men who used cocaine (Werblin, 1998).

One difficulty with judging the effects of cocaine or amphetamines is the variability of the purity of the drug, the amount actually taken, and any drugs taken at the same time, particularly alcohol. The myth of stimulant effectiveness on sexual functioning often outweighs the reality, however, when controlled studies (which are limited) are conducted. One problem with the use of methamphetamine in particular is that the **initial feelings were so pleasurable that users came to depend on the drug to enjoy sex. Continued use can then start the cycle of dysfunction.** For example, the view is that crack cocaine enhances sexual pleasure but, in fact, particularly in women, it has been shown to induce a loss of sexual pleasure. People mistake desperately selling one's body for drugs with a desire for sex (Henderson, Boyd & Whitmarsh, 1995). Also, as with all drug use, **pre-existing sexual proclivi-ties are directly related to the effect and the effectiveness of a drug on sex.** For example, someone who is shy or sexually inhibited will often get a larger boost of confidence from cocaine or methamphetamines. Someone who has unusual sexual practices will be more likely to intensify those behaviors under the influence of these drugs.

"The kind of feeling you get when you inject it, it's sort of like the feeling when you're making love with your wife. After a while, when you keep doing it, you're impotent and it doesn't have any effect. The opposite sex can do anything they want to you and you won't react."
36-year-old male recovering cocaine addict

High-dose and prolonged use have quite the opposite effect on sexuality. In men **heavy or prolonged use often causes delayed ejaculation, a decrease in sexual desire, and difficulty achieving an erection** especially with cocaine. In women abuse can disrupt the menstrual cycle, cause difficulty in achieving orgasm, and decrease desire (Buffum, 1982; Smith, Wesson & Apter-Marsh, 1984).

Then too, in cocaine or amphetamine abusers, there is a higher incidence of antisocial and other personality disorders as well as a number of pre-existing social and emotional problems, so it is often difficult to measure just the effects of the stimulants.

"I was so loaded in the beginning that I would just blank my mind. I didn't want to think he was on top of me or anything because it would bring back [memories of] my stepfather. It would bring back what he was doing. He used his hands all over me."
42-year-old recovering crack abuser

Tobacco

From Humphrey Bogart's puffing on cigarette after cigarette in *Casablanca* to Brad Pitt's smoking in *Fight Club,* **the use of cigarettes in romantic and sexual situations has been portrayed by the movie indus-**

Past anti-tobacco advertising focused on demystifying the use of tobacco in sexual situations. The latest battlefield has been secondhand smoking.

© 2007 CNS Productions, Inc.

• •

try and encouraged **(often with financial incentives) by the tobacco industry**. The image of a cigarette after sexual activity was so common that now it is used satirically to denote sex. In 2007 the Motion Picture Association of America announced that smoking will be considered when rating movies and that "depictions that glamorize smoking or movies with pervasive smoking may receive a higher rating (Smoking, 2007).

Physically, nicotine can both stimulate and relax, depending on the set (mood and mental state) and the setting (location). In social situations it is a great distracter, something to do while figuring out what to do. One survey found that adolescents who smoke are more likely to participate in risky behaviors as they grow, including more sexual partners, than those who don't smoke (Camenga, Klein & Roy, 2006). Long-term tobacco use has been associated with lower testosterone and even erectile dysfunction in men and reduced fertility in women although not nearly to the degree caused by excessive cocaine or alcohol use (Augood, Duckitt & Templeton, 1998; CDC, 2006B; Rosen, 1991).

Opioids

Downers are often used to lower inhibitions, though **the physiological depressive effects often decrease performance and eventually desire**.

Some "nod off" when using; others feel "up." These differences can be explained by selective tolerance of different functions of the body to the effects of opioids. In a study at the Haight Ashbury Free Clinics in 1982 of men and women who had come in for heroin treatment, the majority of those who had some sexual dysfunction before using the drug reported an initial improvement in sexual functioning when they first began to use. Men reported an increased delay in ejaculation; women reported an increase in relaxation and lowered inhibitions. With continued use, however, some users became disinterested in sex, whereas others wanted to repeat the experience. **Long-term users reported impaired performance and a decrease in sexual drive.**

"You start to look more masculine. You feel out of your skin. You can't really feel yourself anymore. The same sort of people you really loved aren't attracted to you anymore."
Female heroin user

In the Haight Ashbury study, 60% of heroin addicts reported an overall decrease in desire. While they were high on heroin, that figure jumped to 90%. In another study 70% reported delayed ejaculation when using, which

is why some premature ejaculators self-medicate. Further, **the overall rate of impotence (inability to become aroused) in one study of male addicts was 39%**, jumping to 53% when they were actually high (Buffum, 1982; Shen & Sata, 1983). Reduced testosterone in men led to impotence in some, whereas long-term female users reported menstrual irregularities, reduced fertility, and frigidity (O'Brien, Cohen, Evans, et al., 1992). This is due to inhibition of gonadotropin-releasing hormone that regulates the testes or ovaries (Knapp, Ciraulo & Jaffe, 2005).

Sedative-Hypnotics

Many sedative-hypnotics, such as the benzodiazepines, barbiturates, and street Quaaludes,® have been called "alcohol in pill form" and touted as sexual enhancers. As with alcohol it is a case of **lowered inhibitions and relaxation vs. physical depression that lowers one's ability to perform or respond sexually**.

"Sexually and mentally, everything is so down. If I were a man, I couldn't have an erection. As a woman I don't have an orgasm. Your mind is just mush but you don't care. The last thing you worry about is sex."
37-year-old benzodiazepine addict

Along with the disinhibition, sedative-hypnotics also impair judgment, making the user more susceptible to sexual advances. As the dose increases, the sedative effects take over, making the user physically less able to ward off sexual aggressiveness. The user becomes lethargic and sleepy while experiencing extensive muscle relaxation. **With abuse comes sexual dysfunction and total apathy toward sexual stimulation** (Buffum, 1982).

Studies have not been done on the newer sleep medications such as Ambien,® Rozerem,® Sonata,® and Lyrica® and their effects on sexuality, but as depressants, the chances that they will diminish desire and orgasm as found in other sedative-hypnotics, should be considered.

Most of the short-acting sedative-hypnotics also cause amnesia (e.g., Rohypnol®). This has led sexual predators to use them to seduce and rape without concern that their victims will remember them.

Flunitrazepam (Rohypnol®). Flunitrazepam, dubbed the "date-rape drug," is marketed outside the United States as a sleeping pill. **It causes profound amnesia and lowered inhibitions as well as a decreased ability to resist a sexual assault.** Unfortunately, much of the publicity surrounding the drug educated some unscrupulous males in the predatory use of the drug for sex. Flunitrazepam also produces muscle relaxation and has an elimination half-life of 16 to 35 hours but can accumulate in the system. Though not as toxic as barbiturates, it can be dangerous when used with alcohol (NIDA, 1999; Smith, Wesson & Calhoun, 1995). This benzodiazepine, although legal in approximately 60 countries, is illegal in the United States. Also known as "roofies," "rophies," "ropes," and "roches," flunitrazepam is many times more powerful than Valium® and sells on the street for $5 to $10 per pill (Marnell, 1997). (*Also see Chapter 4.*)

GHB (gamma hydroxybutyrate). GHB is a sedative-hypnotic and a dopamine enhancer that was originally used as a sleep inducer but is now popular on the rave club scene. It has been touted as a drug that will **lower inhibi-**

tions and make sex more pleasurable. It was widely available in health-food stores in the 1980s and used by bodybuilders. The problem with GHB is that slight increases in the amount used can mean large differences in the effects. **Doubling the dose that induces a pleasant effect can disrupt coordination, cause sleep, and even induce coma** within 10 to 20 minutes (Morganthaler & Joy, 1994). It is often used with other drugs, causing synergistic effects that can add dangerous interactions, many of which disrupt sexual activity. The amnestic effects of the drug, which can be therapeutically valuable, lead to its exploitation as a date-rape predatory drug like Rohypnol.® GBL, another chemical, is converted to GHB in the body and is marketed as a sexual enhancer. It has been sold as Renewtrient,® Revivarant,® and Vitality® (Peugh & Belenko, 2001). GBL is also found in some paint thinners like Blue Nitro® which is diverted and abused.

Marijuana

Marijuana has been called the "mirror that magnifies" because many of its effects—sensory enhancement, novelty enhancement, seeming prolongation of time, increased affectionate bonding, disinhibition, diffusion of ego, and sexualized fantasy—suggest a preexisting desire for these sensations.

Most of the reported effects from marijuana are general comments, such as feelings of sexual pleasure, rather than specifics, like prolonged excitation or delayed orgasm. **Marijuana, more than any psychoactive drug, illustrates the difficulty in separating the actual effects from the influence of the mind-set and setting where the drug is used.** If the drug is shared in a social setting, at a party, or on a date, the expectation is that it will make people more relaxed, less inhibited, and more likely to do things they wouldn't normally do. In one of the few studies on drugs and sexual function, marijuana was associated with inhibited orgasm but not inhibited desire (Johnson, Phelps & Cottler, 2004).

A problem with excessive marijuana smoking is that **the user often forgets or never learns how to have sexual relations without being high**, so the cycle

of excess use is perpetuated. (The loss of sexual interest from hashish use is well known in other cultures.)

MDMA & MDA (ecstasy, rave)

In the past year, 0.8% of the general population and 4.1% of high school seniors used ecstasy (Monitoring the Future, 2007; SAMHSA, 2006). Users say that MDMA and MDA (at moderate doses), unlike methamphetamines, **calm them, give them warm feelings toward others, and induce a heightened sensual awareness**. The warm feelings supposedly make closer relations with those around them possible.

"I had no inhibitions. I mean it was like whatever sexual compromise or, you know, touching or conversation that I would normally have had boundaries for, I didn't when I took ecstasy."
22-year-old ecstasy user

Although the feelings of closeness and sensuality are enhanced, the ability to have an erection and an orgasm is more difficult to achieve (Holland, 2001). The neurological mechanism for some of **the effects of MDMA is the manipulation of serotonin**. Reportedly, it reverses the reuptake of this neurotransmitter, resulting in an excess in the synapse; thus it has a more calming effect than methamphetamine even though it is a psycho-stimulant. Supposedly, sexual excitement occurs more often when coming down from the drug than while under the influence, although only 25% to 50% of users reported any of these reactions. A survey of 100 MDMA users found that the drug induced pleasure in touching and physical intimacy rather than sexual experience (Beck & Rosenbaum, 1994). Most of the reports about the sexual effects of MDMA and MDA are anecdotal; and because polydrug use is quite widespread (especially involving amphetamine, marijuana, and alcohol) and an exciting set and setting can enhance the effects, accurate data is lacking. Possible dangers from excess use include high blood pressure, rapid heart rate, overheating, and prolonged **disruption of serotonergic activity in the**

MDMA is quite popular at raves because it heightens empathy. In addition, light sticks and other objects along with techno-music are used to intensify sensations.
Courtesy of the California Highway Patrol.

● ●

central nervous system. For some the emotional revelations brought on by the drug prove to be extremely upsetting.

PCP

PCP is generally not associated with sex, but because it is an anesthetic it has been **used to deaden the pain of some unusual sexual practices**, mostly in small segments of the gay and straight communities. And even though it is a dissociative anesthetic, making communication difficult when under the influence, low doses have been said to enhance sexual desire and performance in some, possibly from the lowering of inhibitions (Buffum, 1988; Peugh & Belenko, 2001).

LSD

The effects of a psychedelic like LSD are so confusing to the senses that it is **not considered a sexual enhancer** and as a result few controlled studies have been done. The same is true of psilocybin mushrooms and peyote.

Volatile Nitrites (amyl, butyl, and others)

Volatile nitrites are vasodilators and muscles relaxants. **If inhaled just prior to orgasm, they seemingly prolong and enhance the sensation.** Abused as orgasm intensifiers by both the gay and straight communities in the 1960s, they too gained the reputation of being yet another "love drug." They promote erection by dilating blood vessels in the penis. They are also used because they relax anal sphincter muscles. The side effects, however, of dizziness, weakness, sedation, fainting, and severe headaches often end up diminishing or occasionally counteracting the desired effects (O'Brien, Cohen, Evans, et al., 1992). Long-term continuous use can lead to an increase in methemoglobin levels that can be toxic and, on rare occasions, fatal (Sharp & Rosenberg, 2005).

Nitrous Oxide (laughing gas)

Nitrous oxide has become popular at music clubs and rave parties for the giddiness it produces. It is **not generally looked upon as a sexually enhancing** substance, although reports of sexual hallucinations, arousal, and orgasm have occurred in dentists' offices while under the influence for a procedure. One study of 15 dental personnel who abused the substance over a period of time found impotence in seven cases. The problem eventually was reversed when use of the gas was stopped (Jastak, 1991).

Psychiatric Drugs

Most patients who use psychiatric medications have pre-existing emotional problems that can impair sexual functioning. **By treating the mental condition, the psychotropic drugs can also affect the sexual functioning of the user.** For example, an antidepressant can make a patient more able to engage in intimate relations and sexual appreciation, capabilities that were impaired by the depression.

The neurotransmitter serotonin has been found to be involved with many aspects of sexual behavior. Depending on which serotonin receptor is involved, serotonin can either facilitate or inhibit sexual behavior.

Studies involving tricyclic antidepressants, such as desipramine (Norpramine®) and amitriptyline (Elavil®), **have linked them to decreased desire, problems with erection, and delayed orgasm**. Initially, however, in many cases the relief from depression makes the user more able to be sexually involved. Many of the newer antidepressants, known as selective serotonin reuptake inhibitors (SSRIs), such as **sertraline (Zoloft®), fluoxetine (Prozac®), and paroxetine (Paxil®), also cause delay or inhibition of orgasm and impaired erection ability** (Goldberg, 1998; Kline, 1989). Delayed orgasm often goes away with time. Prozac® has also been associated with a significant incidence of sexual disinterest where sex is possible but interest diminishes (Meston & Gorzalka, 1992; PDR, 2007).

Antipsychotics, such as thioridazine (Mellaril®), **inhibit erectile function and ejaculation**. Chlorpromazine (Thorazine®) and haloperidol (Haldol®) can inhibit desire, erectile function, and ejaculation. Impaired ejaculation appears to be the most common side effect of the major tranquilizers (antipsychotics).

With lithium (used for bipolar disorder), there are some reports of decreased desire and difficulty maintaining an erection as the dosage increases.

Even though there are numerous sexual side effects with many psychiatric drugs, patients are reluctant to discuss them with their physician, so the problem is often ignored (Rosenberg, Bleiberg, Koscis, et al., 2003).

Aphrodisiacs

The search for true aphrodisiacs is complicated by the complexity of the sexual response. Are people talking about affection, love, or lust when discussing drugs that enhance sexuality? Are they talking about drugs that change the mental or the physical aspects of sexuality? Is the drug expected to increase desire, prolong excitation, increase lubrication, delay orgasm, or improve its quality? Is a drug that lowers inhibitions an aphrodisiac? Heroin sometimes delays orgasm, cocaine sometimes increases desire or prolongs an erection, and alcohol lowers inhibitions thereby increasing desire.

As mentioned, **Viagra,® Cialis,® and Levitra® deal mostly with the ability to have an erection by enhancing blood flow,** but they are not actual aphrodisiacs. Some purported aphrodisiacs are discussed below.

◇ Spanish fly or ground rhinoceros horn work by irritating the urethra and the bladder, promoting a pseudosexual excitement. But Spanish fly (cantharidin derived from a beetle) is actually toxic.

◇ The scent of **pheromones— human hormones discovered in perspiration—has been shown to increase desire and sexual stimulation.** Interestingly, pheromones act as aphrodisiacs only if they come from people with differing immune systems.

◇ Yohimbine is an alkaloid obtained from several plant sources including the yohimbe tree in West Africa. This stimulant, which produces some hallucinations and mild euphoria, has been used in high doses as a treatment for impotence in men by increasing blood pressure and heart rate, thereby increasing penile blood flow. It can produce acute anxiety at low dosages (Morganthaler & Joy, 1994).

◇ L-dopa is a precursor to dopamine in the brain, and dopamine is the neurotransmitter involved in the mental experience of orgasm. It is used medically to treat Parkinson's disease and was touted as an aphrodisiac during the 1970s; however, effective treatment of lost muscle control caused by Parkinsonism may have been more responsible for this aphrodisiac claim.

One problem with purported sexual enhancers is that the body adapts to any drug, so its effectiveness decreases with time. Another problem with illegal substances is that controlled use is difficult and side effects start to overwhelm any benefits. Third, and perhaps most important, the psychological roots of most feelings are quite complex and generally more important to sexual functioning than mere enhancement of sensations. Drugs can distort, magnify, or eliminate feelings involved with erotic activities.

SUBSTANCE ABUSE & SEXUAL ASSAULT

"He definitely had been drinking. However, when I replay all the events of that night, I feel like he knew exactly what was going to happen or how he was going to attempt each move that led to me being assaulted [raped]. That included offering me and giving me alcohol. That's the thing I blame myself for. I don't think I was scared until I realized what was happening to me, until I realized that he was raping me. And at that point I started screaming although I did not hear myself screaming at all."
26-year-old woman

One in every three women in this country will be a victim of sexual violence in her lifetime. In one study of **sexual assaults, victims reported using drugs or alcohol in 51% of the cases; substance use by the assailants was found in about 44% of the cases** (Seifert, 1999). Another study found that approximately 60% of sexual offenders were drinking at the time of the offense (Roizen, 1997).

In most cases the male user already has tendencies toward improper or aggressive behavior, and the alcohol or other drug is the final trigger. The trigger can also be an emotion such as anger, hate, the need for control, or, in some cases, lust.

"In some men alcohol can disinhibit their aggressive tendencies and they become violent when they drink alcohol; but the violence was sitting in them and residing in their psyche way before they picked up that first drink."
Jackson Katz, executive director, MVP Strategies Inc. (Male Violence Prevention)

Some generalizations about the effects of psychoactive drugs on sexual behavior and violence can be made:

◇ **Alcohol lowers inhibitions and muddles rational thought**, making the user more likely to act out irrational or inappropriate desires.

◇ **Cocaine and amphetamines increase confidence and aggression**, making the male user more likely to assault his date.

◇ **Sedatives lower inhibitions**, making users more prone to sexual advances or making the woman less able to resist.

◇ **Marijuana makes users more suggestible** to sexual activity and more sensitive to touch.

◇ **PCP and heroin make users less sensitive or indifferent to pain** and therefore more liable to damage their partners or themselves.

◇ **Steroids can increase aggression** and irrational behavior.

"I've seen freshman girls drunk, so drunk that they couldn't even stand up, and guys totally grabbing on to them on the dance floor. And it saddens me because we should be able to have that privilege to go out and have fun, drink a few beers or whatever, and not have to worry about having someone taking advantage of us that night or waking up in a

strange room and not knowing where you are."

22-year-old female college student (rape victim)

With date rape the man may intend to just have sex, but when he is refused or doesn't get his way he becomes angry and takes what he feels is his right. In the final analysis, **rape is motivated by a need to overpower, humiliate, and dominate a victim not a desire to have sex**.

"Sexual abuse is very much a prevalent thing in domestic violence situations. We estimate through statistics that probably 50% of all women who are battered are raped by their intimate partners."

Karen Darling, director, Domestic Violence Education Center, Asante Health System

What also occurs with sexual abuse and domestic violence is that the emotional pain and trauma intensify the victim's need to block feelings, leading to their intensified use of drugs and alcohol.

"I remember being beat up physically and being emotionally abused and drinking a gallon of wine and feeling like I just wanted to be out of it. And for me that was the way to deal with the pain. And I think women tend to do those things—take drugs to be able to continue to have some kind of relationship."

38-year-old SUD counselor

SEXUALLY TRANSMITTED DISEASES

The Centers for Disease Control and Prevention estimate that 19 million new cases of sexually transmitted diseases occur each year in the United States (CDC, 2006C). Internationally, the World Health Organization (WHO) estimates that **333 million cases of STDs occur each year**. About 1% of those will eventually die from their STD. In contrast 39.5 million people are living with HIV/AIDS. Almost all of them will eventually die from HIV-

related diseases (World Health Organization [WHO], 2005).

Epidemiology

The dangers of sexually transmitted diseases, such as **chlamydia, gonorrhea, syphilis, and trichomonas (the four most common)** along with genital herpes, genital warts, and hepatitis B and C, are well known as are the mortal dangers of HIV disease. In spite of this knowledge and in spite of an increase in unwanted pregnancies, the practice of unsafe and unprotected sex by high school students, college students, and young adults in the United States continues. **About 85% of all STDs occur in people between the ages of 15 and 30.** Very often alcohol and other drugs are involved (CDC, 2006C).

A study by the National Center on Addiction and Substance Abuse at Columbia University that examined the habits of 34,000 teenagers from grades 7 to 12 found that students who drank and used drugs were five times more likely to be sexually active, starting sexual intercourse as early as middle school. They were also three times more likely to have had sex with four or more partners in the previous two years (CASA, 2002).

The use of crack cocaine, methamphetamine, and marijuana increases high-risk sexual activity due to intensified sensations, a lowering of inhibitions, and impaired judgment. In addition, the very nature of sexual activity clouds judgment, as do most drugs. Drugs also affect memory, so even if users do something dangerous while under the influence, they might not remember it or, if they do, they will see it in a more benign light. They most likely won't appreciate the risks they took, thus laying the groundwork for repetition of that behavior.

With this mix it is no wonder that **almost half of all teenagers who are very sexually active have had chlamydia**, the fastest-spreading STD. In fact, experts think that as many as 4 million Americans have caught the disease (often without knowing it), with 976,000 new cases in 2005 alone. Women outnumber men 3 to 1 when it comes to chlamydia. Perhaps 20% of all very sexually active men and

women have genital herpes. Even syphilis, which had diminished dramatically in the past 50 years, has started to climb again. Surprisingly, the number of people infected by the hepatitis C virus (about 4 million) outnumber the HIV-positive population 4 to 1. There were **41,755 new cases of AIDS in the United States in 2001** (CDC, 2006A).

"This woman was pregnant, she was living on the street, she was prostituting, was HIV-positive, and had a $250-a-day habit. I mean she's not a bad-looking woman, but she was definitely into her 'smack' and her cocaine. She told me she had to sleep with at least five guys a day, minimum, to support her habit. I wonder how many people she's given her diseases to."

27-year-old male AIDS patient

The **increased risk of STDs, including HIV disease, due to trading sex for drugs** is all too common among the drug-abusing population, who will often do anything to raise money to avoid a cocaine crash or a heroin withdrawal.

"I was selling dope and made $3,000 or $4,000 a week. I had women coming to me. I never 'tossed' a woman in my life. Those women were coming after me. I mean, you've got to look at both sides of it."

22-year-old recovering crack dealer/user

One thing to remember about STDs is that there is a **delayed incubation period before symptoms appear, so the disease can be unknowingly transmitted to others**. There are also some diseases where symptoms aren't evident but the illness is still transmittable.

NEEDLE-TRANSMITTED DISEASES

Many of the same illnesses that are transmitted sexually can also be transmitted through contaminated hypodermic needles when drugs are taken

TABLE 8–6   SEXUALLY TRANSMITTED DISEASES

Disease	First Symptoms	Typical Symptoms
Chlamydia or NGU	7 to 21 days	Discharge from genitals or rectum (nonspecific urethritis)
Pelvic inflammatory disease (PID)	Highly variable	Infection of uterus, fallopian tubes, and ovaries; a potential cause of infertility
Gonorrhea ("clap," "dose")	2 to 30 days	Discharge from genitals or rectum, pain when urinating, sometimes no symptoms
Herpes simplex I or II (cold sore, fever blister)	2 to 20 days	Painful blisters/sores on genitals or mouth, fever, malaise, swollen lymph glands
Venereal warts (genital warts)	30 to 90 days (even years)	Itch, irritation, and bumpy skin growths on genitals, anus, mouth, and throat
Syphilis ("syph," "bad blood," "lues")	10 to 90 days	Primary stage: chancre on genitals, mouth, and anus; secondary stage: diffuse rash, hair loss, malaise
Hepatitis B and C (serum hepatitis)	60 to 90 days	Yellow skin and eyes, dark urine, severe malaise, weight loss, abdominal pain
Trichomoniasis (trichomonas vaginalis parasite)	7 to 30 days	Women: vaginal discharge, itching, burning; men: usually no symptoms
Pubic lice ("crabs," "cooties")	21 to 30 days	Itching, tiny eggs (nits) on pubic hair
Scabies ("7-year itch")	14 to 45 days	Itching at night, bumps and burrows on skin
Monila (candidiasis, yeast)	Highly variable	Women: white thick vaginal discharge and itching; men: most often no symptoms
Bacterial vaginosis (gardnerella, nonspecific vaginitis, cervicitis)	Highly variable	Women: vaginal discharge, peculiar odor; men: most often no symptoms
HIV infection (leads to AIDS)	Many months (up to 5 years)	Weight loss, fever, swollen glands, diarrhea, fatigue, severe malaise, recurrent infections, sore throat, skin blotches

Courtesy of Venereal Disease Action Council of Portland, OR (CDC, 2006D)

intravenously, subcutaneously, and intramuscularly.

Needle kits containing syringes, cottons, rubber ties, a cooker, a lighter, and a razor blade are called "outfits," "fits," "rigs," "works," "points," and many other names. Intravenous drug use is also called "mainlining," "geezing," "slamming," and "hitting up." Problems with needle use come from several sources. Besides putting a large amount of the drug into the bloodstream in a short period of time, **needles also inject other substances, such as powered milk, procaine, or even Ajax,® that are often used to cut or dilute drugs. They can also inject dangerous bacteria and viruses that contaminate the drug** or which remain in the syringe, on the cotton, or on other contaminated elements of the needle kit.

Hepatitis A, B & C

Some of the most common diseases transmitted by needles are the various strains of hepatitis, viral infections of the liver. Hepatitis A is often transmitted by fecal matter and is associated more with unsafe sex and poor hygiene than with drug use. The two main types of hepatitis associated with drug use, specifically IV drug use, are hepatitis B and hepatitis C. Hepatitis B is marked by inflammation of the liver and general debilitation, but it is treatable with a convalescence of one to five months. **More than 75% of IV drug users test positive for hepatitis B.** Of those about 10% are chronic carriers, guaranteeing the continued spread of the disease (Gourivetch & Arnsten, 2005).

As discussed in Chapter 4, **the blood-borne hepatitis C virus (HCV) is more dangerous and can cause liver disease, including cancer.** Some people carry the disease for 10 to 20 years without symptoms, which include loss of appetite, jaundice, abdominal pain (right upper abdomen), low-grade fever, dark urine, nausea, vomiting, and a general malaise; the only way to be sure is to test for HCV antibodies. Chronic flare-ups can cause inflammation and scarring of the liver.

The positive rate of the hepatitis C virus in IV drug users is 50% to 90%. Of those who get infected with HCV, 20% to 40% will develop liver disease, and 4% to 16% will develop liver cancer (Cahoon-Young, 1997; CDC, 2006A; Novick, Reagan, Croxson, et al., 1997). The problem with HCV has become so severe that NIDA issued a special alert to increase counseling, treatment, and prevention.

◇ **About 4 million Americans are infected with HCV**, with a majority of those young adults ages 20 to 29, although chronic infections are highest among 30- to 39-year-olds.

◇ **Between 8,000 and 10,000 people die each year from the disease.**

◇ **Worldwide 170 million people are infected.**

◇ **Sharing needles is responsible for almost two-thirds of the infections.**

◇ New IV drug users acquire HCV at an alarming rate, with 50% to 80% becoming infected within six to 12 months. (The average incubation period is six to seven weeks.)

◇ The risk of sexual transmission of HCV is much lower than the risk of IV drug use transmission. About 20% of the cases are supposedly due to sexual activity particularly among those who have multiple partners. In long-term monogamous relationships, the rate is very low (0% to 4%).

◇ The risk of an infected mother passing the infection to her fetus is about 5% to 6%

(CDC, 2006C&D; NIDA, 2000).

Abscesses, Cotton Fever & Endocarditis

Needle use can also cause abscesses at an infected injection site, or it can inject bits of foreign matter in the bloodstream that can lodge in the spine, brain, lungs, or eyes and cause an embolism and other problems. Needle users can also contract cotton fever, a very common disease. The symptoms are similar to those of a very bad case

of the flu. Its cause is unknown, though some believe that it results from bits of cotton (used to filter the drug) that lodge in various tissues or from infections (viral or bacterial) carried into the body by cotton fibers injected into the blood. Starting in the mid- to late-1990s, more and more cases of necrotizing fasciitis (a flesh-eating bacteria and wound botulism or gangrene) have been reported.

"I started using drugs when I got together with my ex-boyfriend, but then I quit using them because I would get these big abscesses on my arms and stuff and my veins—like when I go to the doctor to get blood drawn now, they can't use my veins in my arms."
22-year-old recovering heroin user

Typically, veins of the arms, wrists, and hands are used first. As these **veins become hardened due to constant sticking**, the user will inject into the veins of the legs and then the neck. As it becomes difficult to locate usable veins, addicts will also shoot under the skin ("skin popping") or into a muscle in the buttocks, shoulder, or legs ("muscling"). If they become desperate as they run out of places to shoot themselves, they will inject into the foot, and males will even inject in the neck's

jugular vein or the dorsal vein in the penis.

"I'm addicted to needles. Like sticking any needle in my vein will pretty much alleviate my dope sickness even if it's like speed or even water. That would make it go away for a little while—just the part of my brain that would make me think that everything is all right."
17-year-old heroin addict

Another common problem is **endocarditis, a sometimes-fatal condition caused by certain bacteria that lodge and grow in the valves of the heart**. IV cocaine users seem to have a higher rate of endocarditis perhaps because the ups and downs of cocaine require many more injections than do heroin or methamphetamines (Saitz, 2003).

HIV Disease & AIDS

Human immunodeficiency virus (HIV) causes AIDS, which stands for *acquired immune deficiency syndrome*. AIDS is identified by the incidence of one or more of a group of serious illnesses, such as pneumocystis carinii pneumonia, Kaposi's sarcoma cancer, or tuberculosis, that develop when HIV has taken control of the patient's body and lowered its resistance. In 1993 a new qualifier to diagnose AIDS was added. AIDS is now also defined as "having a T-cell count below 200." T-cell counts measure the level of effectiveness of one's immune system.

AIDS is fatal because HIV destroys the immune system, making it impossible for the body to fight off serious illnesses. Usually, death occurs from a combination of many diseases and infections. Many needle users test positive for HIV/AIDS because they shared a needle used by someone already infected.

"I know I'm really lucky that I didn't get AIDS 'cause a lot of people that I knew used my needles and then they would put them back in my clean needles and I didn't know that they were using them. And I just thank

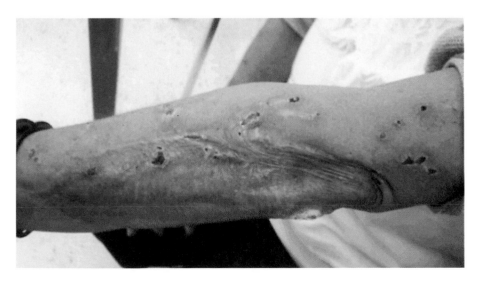

The arm of a typical IV drug user shows extensive scarring, multiple scabs, and a few open sores.
Courtesy of the California Highway Patrol. Used with permission.

God that I didn't get any diseases or I'm not dead right now."

22-year-old heroin user

It is impossible to overemphasize the danger of using infected needles because **IV use of a drug bypasses all the body's natural defenses, such as body hairs, mucous membranes, body acids, and enzymes**; and the virus itself destroys the body's last line of defense: the immune system. In fact, recent research shows that, in and of themselves, opioids and other drugs of abuse can weaken the immune system (Des Jarlais, Hagan & Friedman, 2005). This coupled with the malnutrition and unhealthy habits that compulsive drug use promotes makes the body unable to fight off any illness.

"I told this guy that was sharing some speed with me that I had AIDS and that he should clean the needle, but he was so strung out and anxious to shoot up that he pulled a knife on me and made me give him the needle."

Intravenous cocaine user

Worldwide there were 4.3 million new cases of HIV infection in 2006. Of the 39.5 million infected with HIV/AIDS, two-thirds are from sub-Saharan Africa. Most contract the infection by the age of 25 and die before their thirty-fifth birthday. By the end of 2006, 26 million people had died from AIDS (UNAIDS, 2006). The three main reasons for the worldwide spread are heterosexual sex, homosexual sex, and IV drug use. Infected drug users also spread the disease to non-drug users through unsafe sexual practices.

By comparison, approximately **1 million Americans are infected with HIV or have AIDS, while 550,000 have already died from the disease** since it first appeared on the scene in 1981 (CDC, 2006A). Since the beginning of the AIDS epidemic, more than one-third of all AIDS cases in the United States have involved IV drug use (26% from direct use and 10% from having sex with an IV drug user). Even in Russia and the Ukraine, the use of infected needles has more than doubled the rate of HIV infection. In 2006 about

940,000 Russians were living with HIV/AIDS (UNAIDS, 2007).

Intravenous drug use-associated AIDS accounts for a larger proportion of cases among adolescent and adult women than among men. Since the epidemic began, 57% of all AIDS cases among women have been attributed to IV drug use or sex with partners who inject drugs.

Racial and ethnic minority populations in the United States are the most heavily affected by AIDS especially in recent years. Almost 50% of new infections in 2001 were African Americans, though they are only 13% of the population. This compares with 19% of the new cases being Hispanic and 30% White.

Men who have sex with other men are still the greatest cause of AIDS cases in the United States. Among women 75% of the cases are from heterosexual contact. In 2001 Washington, DC, had the highest rate of new AIDS cases, whereas New York was second in rate but first in sheer numbers (Table 8-7).

PREVENTION OF DISEASE

It is important to remember that **communicable diseases start slowly**

but then rage through the most susceptible groups. In the case of HIV and AIDS in the United States, the gay community that practiced unsafe sex was the most vulnerable compared with other countries where heterosexual high-risk sexual activity spread the disease.

Once the most vulnerable have been infected, there is usually a lull in the spread of the disease. During such lulls a false sense of security, along with clouded judgment, builds up a new upwelling of infection. The majority of new cases of HIV in the United States (as in the rest of the world) will be in the heterosexual and drug-using communities. **Continuing public education and public health prevention activities are crucial to stem the spread of AIDS and, for that matter, all sexually transmitted diseases.**

"The only way the attitudes and practices toward AIDS would change is if everybody got these diseases, you hear what I'm saying? It doesn't really sink in unless it strikes close to you. Once the virus is in your own backyard, you become very serious.

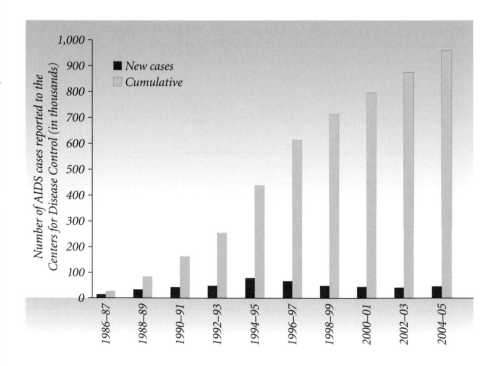

Figure 8-7 •

The Centers for Disease Control and Prevention keep track of all infectious diseases in the United States. The number of people living with HIV hovers around one million.

TABLE 8–7   NEW U.S. AIDS CASES—NUMBER & RATE, 2005

Selected States	Cases	Cumulative Cases
New York	6,299	172,377
Florida	4,960	100,809
California	4,088	139,017
Texas	3,113	67,227
Georgia	2,333	30,405
Illinois	1,922	32,595
Maryland	1,595	29,116
Pennsylvania	1,510	31,977
New Jersey	1,278	48,431
Puerto Rico	1,033	29,092
U.S. total new AIDS cases (2005)	**45,669**	**988,376**
Through 2005		
U.S. total HIV/AIDS living	**988,376**	
U.S. total AIDS deaths	**550,394**	
Through 2006		
World: newly infected with HIV, 2006	**4,300,000**	
World: total AIDS/HIV living	**39,500,000**	
World: total AIDS deaths	**26,000,000**	

(CDC, 2006A; WHO, 2007)

Kids wanna wear rubbers once they find out their father has it, you know what I mean? People are concerned once they find out their mother has it, or their brother has it, or they have it."
43-year-old recovering heroin addict with HIV

Numerous strategies exist to stop the spread of AIDS, particularly in the drug-using community:

◊ improved diagnosis and treatment of STDs;

◊ treatment on demand for drug addiction to encourage users to give up drugs;

◊ needle-exchange programs to control transmission of the disease;

◊ creation of outreach activities to get high-risk drug users into contact with the treatment community;

◊ education and counseling programs that teach about the dangers of AIDS and that teach the use of bleach to clean needles;

◊ availability of antiviral drugs such as AZT and other medications for HIV-positive pregnant women and anyone else exposed to the virus (Harris, Thompson, Ball, et al., 2002);

◊ vocational training to counteract poverty, a predisposing factor to drug use and HIV infection;

◊ education programs that teach about high-risk sexual activities;

◊ easy access to condoms at a reasonable price; and

◊ interdiction and law enforcement activities to limit the flow of drugs into the community (University of California at San Francisco, 2004).

In studies by the Centers for Disease Control and other agencies, **drug-abuse treatment along with education and needle-exchange programs that are tied to outreach components seem to be the most effective HIV disease or AIDS prevention strategies**.

Harm Reduction

In June 2003 **the health ministry of Canada approved North America's first legal safe injection site for illegal-drug users** in Vancouver, British Columbia. Addicts were able to shoot up under the supervision of a registered nurse. The purpose was to prevent overdoses and provide clean needles to reduce the spread of HIV, hepatitis, and other blood-borne diseases. Health Canada had put the center off limits to police. The Canadian experience was inconclusive as to the effectiveness of the strategy prompting the Federal Health Minister to be reluctant to renew the program (Health Canada, 2006). Similar programs have been tried in Switzerland, the Netherlands, and Australia. Results in those older programs have been mixed. Overdose deaths and the spread of diseases have declined somewhat, but addiction rates have not fallen. The director of the White House Office of National Drug Control Policy, John Walters, depicted the program as "state-sponsored personal suicide" (Boston Globe, 2003).

In San Francisco several HIV prevention groups have outreach programs meant to contact IV drug users who are not in treatment. **Outreach workers from these centers, armed with AIDS educational materials, free bottles of bleach, and free condoms, go out to the "shooting galleries," crack houses, "dope pads," and other areas to distribute these materials and provide treatment referrals if requested. Other groups distribute free needles.** It's an intervention into drug-related behavior without intervening into drug use. The drug use intervention part of the total policy is handled by the Community Behavioral Health Services of the county.

The problem with providing education only in addiction treatment settings is that it may miss the larger segment of IV drug users who are not ready for treatment (and therefore at highest risk for AIDS). Users alienated by the treatment community or in denial are hard to educate. To keep these people in treatment, some clinics instituted a more tolerant policy toward relapses and toward users who can't clean up during their first few tries. The idea is that at least the user is occasionally in contact with a facility that can intervene, present important information, and eventually get the client into treatment.

Education does work. In San Francisco in just a short period of time, drug users' awareness about the dangers of AIDS and the need to clean their needles jumped from a few percent to 85%. The HIV-positive segment of the IV drug-using population in San Francisco is 15% to 17% compared with 60% to 80% in New York. Part of this difference in the HIV infection rate between the two coasts seems to be due to the educational effort of the clinics, the San Francisco Health Department, and the gay community. Other differences seem to be the greater presence of "shooting galleries," the limited number of treatment facilities, the difficulty in obtaining clean needles, and language barriers in New York.

Many new drugs besides ziduvodine (AZT), one of the original AIDS drugs, have been developed and are showing promise in slowing or even halting the spread of HIV in the body. Antiretroviral drugs and protease inhibitors seemed more effective, but the complicated regimen of dozens of pills that have to be taken daily and the severe side effects have diminished some of the early promise. Recently, a group of top international scientists, supported by the Bill and Melinda Gates Foundation, called for the creation of a new global program to speed the discovery and the testing of new AIDS vaccines, a program that would be similar in scope to the $3 billion Human Genome Project (Russel, 2003). Barring the creation of a vaccine, they call for intense prevention and treatment programs.

In addition, **studies have shown that people who test positive for HIV who stay clean-and-sober and maintain a healthy lifestyle with plenty of rest, good food, and exercise will avoid full-blown AIDS for years longer (10 to 20 years in many cases)** (Fang, Chang, Hsu, et al., 2007). And those who have an AIDS diagnosis will live years longer. Improved treatment for opportunistic infections that can be so lethal to immune systems weakened by AIDS can also give years of life to infected individuals.

"As I've started going into recovery and learning that I'm worth something and learning that I can have a life even

though I'm HIV positive, yeah, it scares me to go back out there 'cause I know that when I use, I have unsafe sex, bottom line. And when I'm high, I'm not going to put on a condom. When I'm high, I will let people do things to me that I normally wouldn't let them do."
Recovering methamphetamine user with HIV

Unfortunately, many countries with the highest HIV/AIDS rates cannot readily afford the very expensive treatment called for in the HIV and AIDS antiretroviral therapies, so life expectancies there are dramatically reduced. They also cannot afford to fully treat the opportunistic infections that appear as a result of a weakened immune system.

DRUGS AT WORK

"About 10% of truckers heading south through the Salem area on Interstate 5 tested positive for controlled drugs during a three-day survey by police. Police said marijuana, meth, and opium-type drugs [prescription pain killers] were the most common."
Medford Mail Tribune, May 2, 2007

"I began to notice that because I was using marijuana on a day-to-day basis, my reactions were slower and my thought processes were certainly slower. In the electronics business, you really have to be thinking sharply."
33-year-old recovering marijuana abuser

"Drug use hits new low among U.S. workers in 2006 according to Quest Diagnostics' drug-testing index; lowest levels since 1988."
(Quest Diagnostics, 2007)

From a drug positivity rate of 13.6% in 1988 to a rate of 3.8% in 2006, drug use in companies that do drug testing has declined signifi-

cantly. Even the use of amphetamines has declined after five years of rising rates. In safety-sensitive industries, the positivity rate is half that of the general workforce (Quest Diagnostics, 2007). The concept of the drug-free workplace that includes pre-employment drug testing, employee assistance programs, and a greater understanding of the effects of drug abuse has led to this reduction in drug use and associated problems in the workplace. The other reason for the decline is that **drug users tend to avoid even applying at companies that do drug testing and have strict drug-free workplace programs.** This leaves a preponderance of drug users in jobs that generally don't do drug testing, such as some construction firms and food service industry establishments. **If you include all workers, 8.2% of those employed full-time were current illicit-drug users while 8.4% reported heavy alcohol use.**

Contrary to the popular picture of the unemployed drug or alcohol user,

◊ **74.8% of illicit-drug users age 18 or older work full- or part-time as did 80% of binge drinkers;**

◊ **62% of those actually diagnosed with a substance-abuse disorder were employed**; and

◊ about 1.6 million of these workers were both heavy alcohol and illicit-drug users

(U.S. Department of Labor [USDL], 2006).

The highest rates of illicit-drug use are in the construction and food preparation industries and among waiters, helpers, and laborers. The lowest rates are among police.

COSTS

Studies on the impact of alcohol and other drug abuse in the American workplace have resulted in estimates that substance abuse cost our industries about $200 billion (NIDA, 1998; ONDCP, 2000; SafeState, 2006).

Loss of Productivity

Compared with a non-drug-abusing employee, **a substance-abusing employee is:**

◊ **late 3 to 14 times more often;**

◊ **absent 5 to 7 times more often** and 3 to 4 times more likely to be absent for longer than eight consecutive days;

◊ involved in many more job mistakes;

◊ likely to have lower output, make a less-effective salesperson, experience work shrinkage (i.e., less productivity despite more hours put forth); and

◊ likely to appear in a greater number of grievance hearings

(SAMHSA, 1999B).

"If you're doing coke, you really don't like authority over you. You want to take your time to do what you have to do, and if a person has any kind of input, you have a tendency to rebel. I used to get in trouble a lot."
Recovering cocaine abuser

About 21% of workers report being injured, having to redo work or cover for a co-worker, needing to work harder, or being put in danger due to others' drinking; however, 60% of alcohol-related work performance problems can be attributed to occasional binge drinkers rather than alcoholics or alcohol-dependent employees (USDL, 1990).

Medical Cost Increases

Substance abusers as compared with non-drug-abusing employees:

◊ **experience 3 to 4 times more on-the-job accidents;**

◊ **use 3 times more sick leave;**

◊ **file 5 times more workers' compensation claims;**

◊ overutilize health insurance for themselves and their family members;

◊ increase premiums for the entire company for medical and psychological insurance; and

◊ endanger the health and well-being of co-workers

(USDL, 2007).

Legal Cost Increases

As tolerance and addiction develop, a drug-abusing employee often enters into some form of criminal activ-

ity. Crime in the workplace brought about by drug abuse results in:

◊ **direct and massive losses from embezzlement, pilferage, sales of corporate secrets, and property damaged during the commission of a crime;**

◊ **increased cost of improved company security**, more personnel, product monitoring, quality assurance, and intensified employee testing and screening;

◊ **more lawsuits**, both internal and external, expanded legal fees, court costs, and attorney expenses; and

◊ **negative publicity** and loss of customer goodwill from drug use and trafficking in the workplace, employee arrests, the perception that there are more substance abusers than just those arrested, and manipulation of corporate contracts or goods.

PREVENTION & EMPLOYEE ASSISTANCE PROGRAMS

"Really, what I've found now that I'm clean-and-sober is that it wasn't

those jobs that were intolerable, it was where I was with myself. I needed to look at myself and do some work on myself."
Recovering cocaine user

Workplace Drug Testing

Businesses attempt to control drug abuse in two ways: through drug testing and employee assistance programs. The cost of private-sector workplace drug testing has been estimated to range from $300 million to $1 billion per year (White, Nicholson, Duncan, et al., 2002). The various drug-testing programs used by industry have shown positive results. The most effective testing is pre-employment testing.

◊ Since 1988 the percentage of **positive drug tests among American workers dropped from 13.6% to 3.8%** in 2006.

◊ **The most common drug found in those testing positive is marijuana (48.8%)** compared with cocaine (16.4%), amphetamines (9.3%), opiates (6.7%), and benzodiazepines (5.4%). Generally,

---

TABLE 8–8 SUMMARY OF RECOMMENDATIONS FOR A DRUG-FREE WORKFORCE

To achieve a drug- and alcohol-free workforce, you must take a comprehensive approach. The approach should include:

◊ **A written policy.** Clear and definite guidelines should be written, explaining the reasons for a drug policy and actions that will be taken.

◊ **An employee assistance program.** Establish an EAP that provides counseling and referral programs to be operated either by your own staff or by a contractor.

◊ **Employee awareness and education.** Education about company policies along with drug education is necessary.

◊ **Supervisor training.** Offer supervisors substance-abuse training so that those closest to the problem can be coached on the signs, symptoms, behavior changes, performance problems, and intervention concepts attendant to drug and alcohol abuse.

◊ **Drug and alcohol testing.** Consider a drug- and/or alcohol-testing program to detect and deter drug and/or alcohol use or abuse. If testing is adopted, it should conform to proper procedures.

◊ **Sanctions.** Determine the consequences for those who violate the policy.

◊ **An appeals process.** Include an appeals process in the program and clearly define it in the policy.

◊ **Evaluation.** Monitor the success and the cost-effectiveness of the program.

(Adapted from Guidelines for a Drug-Free Workforce [DEA, 2003B])

employers do not test for alcohol without cause, although it is the most common drug used.

◇ In safety-sensitive industries such as transportation, the rate of positive drug tests is about half that of the general workforce.

◇ **About 26% of those tested for cause tested positive for an illicit drug.**

◇ The highest positive rates came from southern rural areas rather than from big cities like New York, Chicago, and Los Angeles

(Quest Diagnostics, 2003; SmithKline Beecham Clinical Laboratories, 1997; USDL, 2007).

Employee Assistance Programs

In response to the increased problem of drugs in the workplace and the resultant drain on profits and productivity, many employers have instituted an EAP. **Successful EAPs balance the needs of management to minimize the negative impact that drug abuse has on the business with a sincere concern for the better health of employees.** Once the benefits of EAPs were recognized, many companies initiated such programs. In 1980 there were 5,000 EAPs; in 1990 that number had grown to 20,000, and the number of covered employees grew from 12% to more than 35%. Today 45% of full-time employees are covered. In large companies with more than 500 employees, 70% are covered (Englehart & Barlow, 2005).

Designed as an employee benefit, these programs often encourage self-referral by the employee and/or a supervisor's referral as an alternative to more-stringent discipline for poor work performance. The successful EAP supports a broad-based strategy to address the full spectrum of substance-abuse prevention needs. The most successful EAPs share two overall design features:

◇ They frame the EAP drug-abuse services as part of a **full-spectrum prevention program** that minimizes employee attraction to drugs and helps those with problems get into treatment.

◇ They provide a **diverse range of services for a wide range of employee problems** (emotional, relationship, financial, and burnout).

These two design features lessen employees' apprehension about being labeled a drug abuser. They prevent drug problems before they start, and they identify drug problems for employees in denial who don't accept the fact that they have a problem and often first approach the EAP about another problem area. The EAP comprises six basic components:

◇ prevention/education/training;

◇ identification and confidential outreach;

◇ diagnosis and referral;

◇ treatment, counseling, and a good monitoring system (including drug testing);

◇ follow-up and focus toward aftercare (relapse prevention); and

◇ a confidential record system and effectiveness evaluation

(Employee Assistance Professionals Association, 1990; SAMHSA, 2007; USDL, 2007).

In a full-spectrum prevention program, the EAP provides primary, secondary, and tertiary prevention.

Primary Prevention. In the most effective EAPs, both corporate and individual denial are addressed with a systems-oriented approach to prevention. **Education and training about the impact of substance abuse are provided at all levels** in the corporation: to the administration, unions, and line staff. These segments agree on a single corporate policy on drug and alcohol abuse.

Secondary Prevention. Both education and training focus on **drug identification, major effects, and early intervention**, which are incorporated into the prevention curriculum. The corporation's legal, grievance, and escalating discipline policies are designed in light of EAP goals. Security measures (testing, staff review, and monitoring) are established in a manner that is legal and humane. These measures operate both as deterrents and as methods of identifying the abusers and getting them help.

Tertiary Prevention. The EAP formalizes its **intervention approach, al-** lowing for confidential self-referral, peer referral, and supervisor-initiated referral to the EAP. Many EAPs outsource the actual counseling and follow-up. A diagnostic process is established, along with a number of **appropriate treatment referrals.** Treatment is confidential, but the EAP monitors treatment to ensure proper follow-up aftercare and continued recovery efforts. The employment status of workers is evaluated on work performance and not on their participatory effort in the EAP.

Effectiveness of EAPs

Well-conceived successful programs have demonstrated great effectiveness and cost savings to businesses. **For every $1 spent on an EAP, employers save anywhere from $5 to $16.** The cost of providing EAP services ranges from $22 for outside programs and $28 for in-house programs per employee per year compared with $50,000 or more for finding and training a replacement (French, Zarkin, Bray, et al., 1999; USDL, 1990). Several studies in major corporations have documented a 60% to 85% decrease in absenteeism, a 40% to 65% decrease in sick time utilization and personal/family health insurance usage, and a 45% to 75% decrease in on-the-job accidents as well as other cost savings once the EAP system was put into operation.

◇ Northrup Corporation saw a 43% increase in productivity in its first 100 employees who entered an alcohol treatment program.

◇ Employees in the Philadelphia Police Department going through treatment reduced sick days by 38% and injury days by 62%.

◇ In Oldsmobile's Lansing, Michigan, plant, lost work hours declined by 49%, healthcare claims by 29%, sick leaves by 56%, grievances by 78%, disciplinary problems by 63%, and accidents by 82% (Campbell & Graham, 1988).

"I stopped using [marijuana] and I noticed a major difference in how I felt, the fact that I was able to get up okay in the morning. You know, I wouldn't

drive to work drowsy, and my thought processes were a lot clearer. I could even program my VCR."

38-year-old phone company worker

There are a number of different types of EAPs, often determined by financial considerations.

◇ **Internal/in-house programs.** These EAPs are usually found in large companies that can afford the expense. The staff is employed by the organization and counsels employees on-site.

◇ **Fixed-fee contracts.** The company contracts with an outside EAP provider for a number of services such as counseling and educational programs.

◇ **Fee-for-service contracts.** Outside EAP services are used and paid for only when employees use the service.

◇ **Consortia.** To save money, smaller employers pool their needs and contract with an outside EAP service provider.

◇ **Peer-based programs.** Peers and co-workers give education, training, assistance, and referrals to troubled workers. This type of program requires considerable education and training for employees (DEA, 2003B).

DRUGS IN THE MILITARY

One example of reducing the use of psychoactive drugs in the workplace is the experience of the U.S. military. In a survey of the military, the Research Triangle Institute in North Carolina found that **from 1980 to 1998, 30-day illicit-drug use dropped from 27.6% to just 2.7% of military personnel** (RTI International, 1999). **By 2005 that rate had dropped to just 1.11%.** The rate of heavy drinking showed a smaller drop, from 20.8% to 15.4%. Inhalants represent the third most commonly abused class of drugs in the military, but they are not tested for and often not screened for, and inhalant abuse is often misdiagnosed as fatigue or some other condition (Lacy & Ditzler, 2007).

The reasons for the drop in drug abuse are varied. Probably the strongest reason was an **intensified program of urine testing**, established in the early 1980s, with a positive result as grounds for referral to rehabilitation or, if that fails, discharge. The military does about 3 million drug tests each year. The message was zero tolerance. **In the past, drug users had been treated and kept in the military, but with zero tolerance they decided that there was no margin for having impaired people.** Discharge has become the preferred option.

A second reason for the drop in drug use was that drugs, in general, became less popular in society over that period of time. The drop in smoking from 51% to 33.8% over the same period was attributed to military smoking bans, an end to free cigarettes for GIs, and smoking-cessation programs as well as a general smoking decline in society as a whole (U.S. Medicine, 2004). The smoking rate has actually gone back up in the past few years.

Heavy drinking still occurs at a higher rate than in the general public: 17.1% in the military vs. 12% in society as a whole. The highest rate is in the Marine Corps and the lowest is in the Air Force. Part of the difficulty in reaching heavy drinkers who are mostly young enlistees is that there is a high turnover in the ranks and historically drinking has been acceptable. In a recent U.S. Navy study, the **prevalence of *DSM-IV* alcohol abuse was 28.2% of men and 15.1% of women.** Rates of frequent heavy drinking in the Navy were 13.7% for men and 8.9% for women (Ames, Cunradi, Moore, et al., 2007).

The military **has the advantage of being able to discharge almost anyone whom it defines as being dangerous to other military personnel** (Rhem, 2001). In addition, because it is the military, it **can conduct testing whenever and wherever it chooses**. Because the military attitude toward drugs other than alcohol is well known, applicants seeking to join the U.S. Armed Forces know that any drug use will be closely examined. Consequently, the rate of positive results for amphetamines, methamphetamines, and ecstasy was extremely low, about one-fifth of 1% (Klette, Kettle & Jamerson, 2006).

During the Vietnam War, drug use, particularly of heroin, was high. It was readily available, stress was intense, and the environment was strange and permissive (Robins, 1993). During the war in the Persian Gulf, drugs and alcohol were difficult to obtain, and as a result there were a lot fewer disciplinary problems among the troops (O'Brien, Cohen, Evans, et al., 1992).

Each branch of the service has created programs to help it control drug and alcohol use. The Air Force program is called the **Air Force Alcohol and Drug Abuse Prevention and Treatment (ADAPT) program**. The Army's is the **Army Substance Abuse Program (ASAP)**. The Navy's is the **Navy Alcohol and Drug Abuse Prevention (NADAP) program**. The Navy's policies include zero drinks for those under 21, those who are driving, and those on duty. For others, consumption should be limited to one drink per hour. All programs include prevention, education, treatment, and urinalysis. These policies have been in place for more than 20 years.

The ASAP along with the Army's Substance Abuse Rehabilitation Department provides individual counseling, family counseling, command consultation, outpatient counseling, arrangement for inpatient care, and coordination with self-help groups such as Alcoholics Anonymous. The Army also has an EAP for Department of the Army civilians.

Because of the wars in Afghanistan and Iraq, and the heavy use of the National Guard, several changes to Department of Defense policies were made:

◇ Institute minimum 100% random testing for active-duty, guard, reserve, and DOD agencies, including 100% random testing of troops deployed in Afghanistan (Reports of officially sanctioned amphetamine use in the Iraqi and Afghani wars still circulate).

◇ Require mandatory drug testing of all military applicants, to include testing within 72 hours of entering active duty.

◇ Institute policy to process military members who knowingly use a prohibited drug for separation from military service.

◇ Change the mandatory test panel to meet the new threats.

◇ Institute minimum 100% random DOD civilian testing and consolidated laboratory support.

DRUG TESTING

In a recent study of drug testing, changes in positive results over a 17-year period (1988–2004) at a major drug-testing facility were compared with changes in self-reported drug use in a national survey. Researchers found that **while drug testing had shown a 66% decrease in positives, self-reported drug use had increased by 30%** (Walsh, 2007). There are several reasons for this change. One is that many drug users avoid applying for work at businesses that require drug tests. Another factor is the number of methods for cheating on a drug test, such as diluting one's urine with water (although testers can use creatinine testing to check the validity of samples). Finally, there is an increased awareness of detection periods, so some users take their drug with sufficient time before a drug test so they avoid detection.

Increasingly, **drug testing has appeared in many areas, not just in business**. Drug testing has long been used to determine the blood, urine, or breath alcohol level of drivers suspected of drunk driving. Testing has been expanded to include:

◇ **pre-employment testing,**

◇ **for-cause testing,**

◇ **random testing,**

◇ **postaccident testing,**

◇ periodic testing,

◇ rehabilitation testing of ex-convicts or felons on probation or of others suspected of a crime,

◇ **testing for compliance in addicts who are in treatment,**

◇ testing by medical examiners to determine a cause of death, and

◇ testing of welfare recipients to get them into treatment (about 12 states allow this kind of testing).

The federal government issued **mandates in 1988 and 1998 for a drug-free workplace**. Although there is now a consensus that testing is effective, there have been a number of regulations and laws promulgated over the past 10 years that limit random testing.

At present **the most widespread use of drug testing is in the military, in the federal government, in pre-employment drug testing, in public-safety positions (mostly transportation), and in drug treatment facilities**. Most medium and large businesses routinely use pre-employment testing to keep drug users out (because once they are hired, the problems they engender can be very expensive). Because of the many challenges to random testing of those already employed, many businesses are leery of using it. **Random testing is still used in jobs involving public safety**, especially—jobs such as bus drivers, policemen, and pilots.

THE TESTS

Many different laboratory procedures are used to **test for drugs in the urine, blood, hair, saliva, sweat,** and even different tissues of the body. Each test possesses inherent differences in sensitivity, specificity, and accuracy along with other potential problems. The drugs most often tested for are **amphetamines, cannabinoids, cocaine, opioids, phencyclidine (PCP), and of course alcohol**. Other drugs commonly tested for are **barbiturates, benzodiazepines, methadone, propoxyphene (Darvon®), and methaqualone.** Those that can be tested for but usually are not include LSD, fentanyl, psilocybin, MDA, and designer drugs. It is important to remember that the metabolites of drugs are often the targets of the test, so heroin is tested for by looking for morphine.

Currently, some two dozen methods are used to analyze body samples for the presence of drugs. None is totally foolproof. The following are the most common methods (Vereby, Meenan & Buchan, 2005).

Thin Layer Chromatography (TLC)

TLC searches for a wide variety of drugs at the same time and is fairly sensitive to the presence of even minute amounts of chemicals. The major drawback is its inability to accurately differentiate among drugs that may have similar chemical properties. For example, ephedrine, a drug used legally in many OTC cold medicines in many states, may be misidentified as an illegal amphetamine.

Enzyme-Multiplied Immunoassay Techniques (EMIT), Radio Immunoassay (RIA), and Enzyme Immunoassay (EIA)

All immunoassays use antibodies to seek out specific drugs. **EMIT tests are extremely sensitive, very rapidly performed, and fairly easy to conduct**, although they cannot usually determine the concentration of the drug present. Also, a separate test must usually be run for each specific suspected drug. Immunoassay techniques are used for many home-testing kits. Some can test for several drugs at once (e.g., Ascend Multimmunoassay).

EMIT tests can also mistake nonabused chemicals for abused drugs (e.g., opioid alkaloids in the poppy seeds of baked goods for heroin or another opioid). One of the chemicals in Advil® or Motrin® may be mistaken for marijuana, and the form of methamphetamine in a Vicks Vapor Inhaler® is sometimes identified as "crank." This method can be so sensitive that breathing the air at most rock concerts will show a positive trace of marijuana even though the testee didn't smoke. Such mistakes are known as "false positives." This oversensitivity is corrected by raising the sensitivity level of the test so that only current users will test positive. But this correction may then miss detection of some users (false negatives).

Gas Chromatography/Mass Spectrometry Combined (GC/MS) & Gas Liquid Chromotography (GLC)

The GC/MS test is currently **the most accurate, sensitive, and reliable**

method of testing for drugs in the body. It uses gas chromatography separation and mass spectrometry fragmentation patterns to identify drugs. Being very sensitive, it can detect even trace amounts of drugs in the urine and therefore requires skilled interpreters to differentiate environmental exposure from actual use. It is very expensive, requires highly trained operators, and is a very lengthy and tedious process in comparison with other methods. The GLC test separates molecules by migration similar to TLC. This process is somewhat less accurate than GC/MS. Another variation is a liquid chromatography-tandem mass spectrometry (LC-MS-MS) method, which can test multiple urine samples at one time.

Hair Analysis

Hair analysis employs hair samples to detect drugs of abuse. Chemical traces of most psychoactive drugs are stored in human hair cells, so drugs can be detected as long as the hair stays intact—even years after a drug has been taken. This **gives a picture of the degree of drug use over a period of time** (to differentiate occasional use from chronic use) (Karacic, Skender, Brcic, et al., 2002; Kintz, 1996). Sections of the hair are identified and tested, so a single strand of hair might have three or four different tests. Radio immunoassay techniques are used for screening of hair samples, and GC/MS techniques are used for confirmation. More research needs to be done on the accuracy of hair testing, although a number of businesses, such as Nevada casinos, are using it in pre-employment drug testing. Because several tests are done on a single strand of hair, the cost can be rather high.

Saliva, Sweat & Breath

Less accurate tests look for traces of drugs in saliva, sweat, or exhaled air. These tests are less invasive, but they are much more prone to contamination by environmental traces of drugs. Saliva and breath tests can be useful in **on-the-spot testing of drivers involved in accidents or suspected of driving under the influence** (DUI). Confirmation tests are almost always mandatory because of the inaccuracy

of the tests and probable court challenges. For alcohol DUI situations, breathalyzers are valuable and admissible in court.

A study of the accuracy of saliva testing vs. urinalysis found increasing accuracy in the process, although the cutoff level that is used is crucial in determining drug use (Cone, Presley, Lehrer, et al., 2002). An on-site saliva-testing device with a high detection (cut-off) level was compared with saliva testing by a GC-MS. Of 66 drivers 18 tested positive for THC using the GC-MS but only one was detected with the on-site device (Kintz, Bernhard, Villain, et al., 2005). An on-site device using saliva (which is easy to do under close supervision) could be valuable in a DUI situation because the presence of THC in saliva is a better indication of recent use than urinalysis; so chances are if a driver tests positive, he is likely to be experiencing the pharmacological effects at that time.

DETECTION PERIOD

Many factors influence the length of time that a drug can be detected in someone's blood, urine, saliva, or other body tissues. These include an individual's drug absorption rate, metabolism, rate of distribution in the body, excretion rate, and the specific testing method employed. With a wide variation of these and other factors, **a predictable drug detection period would be, at best, an educated guess.** Despite this, the public interest requires that some specific estimates be adopted. For urine testing these estimates can be divided into three broad periods: **latency, detection period range, and redistribution**.

Latency

Drugs must be absorbed, circulated by the blood, and finally concentrated in the urine in sufficient quantity before they can be detected. This process, called **latency, generally takes about two to three hours for most drugs except alcohol, which takes about 30 minutes.** Thus someone tested just 30 minutes after using a drug would probably (but not always) test negative for that drug though they might already be under the influence. A chronic user,

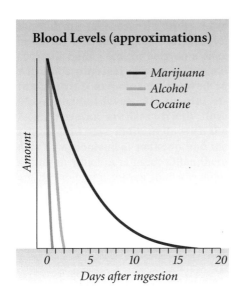

Blood Levels (approximations)

— *Marijuana*
— *Alcohol*
— *Cocaine*

Amount

Days after ingestion

Figure 8-8 •

This graph compares the length of time that cocaine, alcohol, and marijuana remain in the blood. For purposes of testing, there is a cutoff level for certain drugs, so even when some of the drug is still in a person's blood or urine, it will not be detected by the standard test.

however, should have enough chemicals already present to test positive even if tested within 30 minutes of use (Warner, 2003).

Detection Period Range

Once sufficient amounts of a drug enter the urine, **the drug can be detected for a certain length of time by urinalysis.** The rough time estimates for the more common drugs of abuse are shown in Table 8-9. Again, these are merely rough estimates with wide individual variations. Thus a person delaying a urine test for five days because of cocaine abuse will probably, but not definitely, test negative for cocaine.

Redistribution, Recirculation, Sequestration & Other Variables

Long-acting drugs like PCP and possibly marijuana can be distributed to certain body tissues or fluids, be concentrated and stored there, and then **be recirculated and concentrated back into the urine even weeks or months after stopping use.** Although not common, this can result in a posi-

TABLE 8–9   DETECTION PERIOD RANGE CHART FOR URINE TESTING

Alcohol	$^1/_2$ to 1 day*
Amphetamine	2 to 4 days
Methamphetamines	2 to 4 days
Barbiturates	
short-acting	24 hours
intermediate-acting (pentobarbital)	2 to 4 days
long-acting (phenobarbital)	16 to 30 days
Benzodiazepines	
short-acting (triazolam)	24 hours
intermediate-acting (clonazepam)	40 to 80 hours
long-acting (diazepam)	7 days or more (up to 30 days)
Cocaine	
cocaine (coke, crack)	6 to 8 hours
cocaine metabolite (benzoylecgonine)	2 to 3 days
Marijuana	
single use	1 to 3 days
casual use to 4 joints per week	4 to 7 days
daily use	10 to 15 days
chronic, heavy use	1 to 2 months
Nicotine	12 hours
Opioids	
buprenorphine	48 to 56 hours
buprenorphine conjugates	5 to 7 days
codeine	1 to 2 days
heroin (morphine is measured)	2 to 4 days
hydromorphone (Dilaudid®)	2 to 4 days
methadone (limited use)	2 to 3 days
methadone (maintenance)	7 to 9 days
morphine	2 to 4 days
oxycodone (OxyContin®)	2 to 4 days
propoxyphene (Darvon®)	6 to 48 hours
PCP	
casual use	2 to 8 days
chronic, heavy use	several months
Psychedelics & Psychostimulants	
LSD (& its metabolite ISU-LSD)	2 to 4 days
Ecstasy	30 to 48 hours

(Adapted from Erowid, 2007; Wolff, Farrell, Marsden, et al., 1999;)

*Testing for ethanol glucoronate, a specific metabolite of alcohol avoids false positives of urine fermentation and is detectable for 3 to 5 days after use.

tive test following negative tests and several months of abstinence.

ACCURACY OF DRUG TESTING

Despite many claims of confidence in the reliability of drug testing, independent blind testing of laboratory results continues to document high error rates for some testing programs. For this reason **many companies and agencies use a medical review officer (MRO) to review positive results and rule out any errors in procedure, environmental contamination, or alternative medical explanations**. The MRO usually interviews the testee, checks the chain of custody, and/or asks for retesting to search for explanations of a positive result because the consequences can greatly affect the person's future. In some cases the MRO will look at indeterminate results where manipulation of the specimens is suspected (e.g., when the urine sample is too dilute, suggesting tampering) (Macdonald, DuPont & Ferguson, 2003).

False-positive tests could result from the limitations of testing technology. For example, dextromethorphan, found in many cold products, has been misidentified as an opioid. Herbal teas have been implicated in producing a false cocaine-positive result. Poppy seeds in baked goods have been mistaken for an opiate.

Errors also can result from the mishandling of urine and other specimen samples. Tagging the specimen with the wrong label, mixing and preparing the testing solutions incorrectly, errors in calculations, mistakes in coding the samples and the solutions, reporting the wrong results, as well as exposure of samples to destructive conditions, other drugs in the laboratory, and even urine fermentation—all have resulted in inaccurate tests.

False-negative results, not false positives, constitute the bulk of urine-testing errors. These result from laboratories' being overly cautious in reporting positive results and from specimen manipulation by the testee. Many manipulations, some effective and some just folklore, have been used by drug abusers to prevent the detection of drugs in their urine. **Substitution methods include a concealed container, urine injection into the bladder, catheterization, urine from a clean donor, synthetic urine, and even dog urine.**

Attempts to manipulate urine tests have grown to such proportions that "clean pee" (drug-free urine) has become a profitable black market item. Substances such as aspirin, goldenseal tea, niacin, zinc sulfate, bleach, Klear,® water, ammonia, Drano,® hydrogen peroxide, lemon juice, liquid soap, vinegar, and even Visine® have been tried to mask drugs in urine. Most are ineffective. Further, drug testing companies now test for substances that are commonly used to mask drugs in the urine. Positive results for these substances are reported as possible suspected use of abused drugs even if no abused drug is detected. Many inaccuracies about beating drug tests are disseminated on the Internet. For example, even though there is no proof that it works, large doses of niacin (vitamin B_3) have been touted as being able to defeat a urine test. Unfortunately, excess niacin can occasionally merit a trip to the emergency room (MMWR, 2007). Further, recent designer drugs create a major problem in drug testing. Many

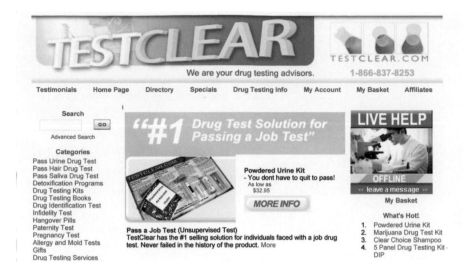

This is just one of hundreds of products that are advertised to help one pass a drug test. In small print it says, "You don't have to quit to pass."

state that they wished they had been tested and identified before their lives had been destroyed. Drug abusers in treatment often request increased urine testing to help them focus on abstinence and resist peer pressure. They can say, "Hey, I can't use. I have to be tested." **Treatment programs use testing to overcome denial and dishonesty in addicts during early treatment.** Recovering addicts in jobs that expose the public to high risk would not be acceptable without a reliable drug-testing program.

DRUGS & THE ELDERLY

"They never told me when I was young what indulgences of my youth I would have to pay for. My compulsive eating earned me two heart stents; my drinking gave me a liver that doesn't work as well now that I'm 66; and my smoking three packs a day in my teens and twenties hasn't got me yet, but my dad died of throat cancer from

have no standard to test against, and some are so potent (the effective dose so small) that they are almost impossible to identify in the body. Inaccurate tests also result from disease states, pregnancy, medical conditions, interference of prescribed drugs, and individual metabolic conditions.

With the technology available at this time, **the best chance for a reliable drug-testing program would include direct observation of the body specimen and a rigid chain of custody of the sample**. It would also include testing for a wide range of abused drugs and using the most accurate testing methods available (e.g., GC/MS), with a mandatory second confirmatory test via a different method. It would include the use of an MRO along with a detailed medical and social history with which to interpret the lab results.

Consequences of False Positives & Negatives

Concerns about false-positive test results are well publicized, debated, and feared. **People could lose their jobs, be denied employment, be disqualified from the Olympics, or even risk prison following an erroneous positive result.** Less publicized or feared but just as critical are the false-negative results that prevent the discovery of drug abuse and feed the already strong

denial process in the user. They permit the addict to become progressively more impaired and dysfunctional until a major life crisis occurs.

Nevertheless **drug testing is still an effective intervention, treatment, and monitoring tool** especially when used to intervene with heavy users and to discourage casual use. Addicts often

Isolation, ill health, and financial worries are some of the problems that can lead the elderly to drug abuse.
© 1996 CNS Productions, Inc.

TABLE 8–10 PAST-YEAR DRUG USE FOR SELECTED AGES

Substance	All Ages	21 yrs.	55 to 59 yrs.	60 to 64 yrs.	65 yrs. & up
Any illicit drug	14.4%	35.8%	5.6%	3.2%	1.7%
Pain relievers (illicit)	4.9%	13.1%	1.9%	1.1%	0.6%
Tobacco	34.9%	56.5%	27.7%	25.2%	15.2%
Alcohol	66.5%	84.2%	62.5%	60.2%	52.3%

(SAMHSA, 2006)

smoking even though he had quit 15 years earlier. My mother died of lung cancer at 73, and she was still smoking."

66-year-old male

SCOPE OF THE PROBLEM

Overall Drug Use

The number of elderly Americans has doubled since 1950. At present **13% of the U.S. population is 65 years or older**, and that figure will increase to 21% by 2030. By 2050, 85 million Americans will be over the age of 65 (U.S. Bureau of the Census, 2004). As the population grows, the problems with drug overuse, abuse, and addiction will grow as well.

From 363 million filled prescriptions in 1950 to more than 3.5 billion in 2006 ($274 billion), the increase in the use of prescribed medications has been fueled by a larger medical care system, a longer life span, and the discovery of hundreds of new compounds (IMS Health, 2007). This surfeit of available remedies for the illnesses and the problems of the aging process has also increased the chances of adverse reactions from medications along with the chances of abuse of drugs with psychoactive properties. In addition, use of OTC medications is most prevalent after the age of 65, and these too can have adverse reactions and interactions with other drugs. Because more than four out of five elderly suffer from some chronic disease **by age 65, 83% of them take at least one prescription drug per day; an astonishing 30% take eight or more.**

Chemical Dependency

Up to 17% of adults age 60 and older abuse alcohol and legal drugs (Hazelden Foundation, 2006). Besides drinking or using socially, some **elderly abuse these and other psychoactive drugs to deal with problems**: their feelings of loneliness, of being unwanted, of not being respected, and of being rejected by their families and the workplace. Events such as retirement, illness, the death of a spouse, loss of physical appearance, financial worries, and ageism can also increase drug use and abuse (Simoni-Wastila & Yang, 2006).

Although most older adults (87%) see physicians regularly, it is estimated that 40% of those who are at risk do not self-identify or seek services for substance-abuse problems on their own (Raschko, 1990). Unfortunately, **physicians have a difficult time identifying alcoholism or drug abuse**. In one study only 37% of elderly alcoholics were identified compared with a 60% identification rate in younger patients (Fleming, Barry, Manwell, et al., 1997). This is partly because most older adults live in the community while fewer than 5% live in nursing or personal care homes where supervision and physician contact is greater (Altpeter, Schmall, Rakowski, et al., 1994). In addition, **many manifestations of drug abuse can be attributed to other chronic illnesses** often present in those over 55; and because so many drugs are being used legally, adverse reactions due to the misuse of psychoactive drugs can be masked. Even family members can misattribute the symptoms of drug abuse to the normal effects of aging or the effects of legal prescription drugs.

"We thought dad was getting Alzheimer's because he would forget stuff, seemed addled much of the time, hurt himself in little accidents around the house. We finally looked at how many meds he was taking; Ativan,® hydrocodone with acetaminophen, cough syrup in the winter, and even an antidepressant in addition to his heart meds. When he cut back and eventually stopped taking those drugs, except the heart meds, all those symptoms were gone . . . not just better . . . gone."

38-year-old son of a 68-year-old

To compound these problems, the attitude of society is often one of, "They've lived a full life and made their contribution to society, so why disturb their lives now? If they want to abuse drugs at this age, whom will it harm?" This attitude assumes that the unhindered abuse of psychoactive drugs is desirable. But because **addiction is a progressive illness for the elderly as well as the young**, continued use leads to progressive physiological, emotional, social, relationship, family, and spiritual consequences that users find intolerable. Addiction means unhappiness and a lack of choice, no matter what the age of the addicted person (Gambert & Albrecht, 2005).

Costs mount up for untreated elderly chemical abusers. **Failure to prevent and then treat chemical abuse among this population leads to huge medical costs** in treating high blood pressure, cardiac and liver disease, gastrointestinal problems, and all the other diseases resulting from the abuse of drugs.

PHYSIOLOGICAL CHANGES

"My mother had mental problems and used a number of psychiatric medications. She also self-medicated with alcohol and smoked Pall Malls,® and that's where the problems came in. A number of times, I had to take her to the emergency room and even to Bellevue Hospital once to have

her stomach pumped. The alcoholic cirrhosis, the edema, the injuries from falls, and the confusion seemed a normal part of growing up. Only in my teens did I realize it wasn't normal."

42-year-old male son of alcoholic who was 73 when she died

The human body's **physiological functioning and chemistry are not as efficient in the elderly as they are in young** people and midlife adults. This results in an abnormal response to drugs compared with younger adults. Generally, elderly people's enzymes and other body functions become less active, conditions that impair their ability to inactivate or excrete drugs (Smith, 1995). **This makes drugs more potent in older people.** For example, diazepam (Valium®) is deactivated by liver enzymes, but after the age of 30 the liver slowly loses its ability to make all these enzymes. Thus a 10 milligram (mg) dose of Valium® taken by a 70-year-old will result in an effect equal to a dose of about 30 mg taken by a 21-year-old.

The drugs most commonly abused by the elderly besides alcohol are hydrocodone (Vicodin®), narcotic cough syrups, Darvon® and other opioid analgesics, prescription sedatives (e.g., Klonopin®), and OTC sedatives and sleep aids. One change that has reduced the abuse of psychoactive drugs has been the **increased use of psychiatric medications,** such as fluoxetine (Prozac®), sertraline (Zoloft®), and buspirone (BuSpar®) to treat many of the symptoms that the elderly complain of. Many problems with medications fall into the misuse category. **Another major problem comes from not understanding dosing directions especially when several medications are involved,** often from multiple physicians unaware of a colleague's treatments.

Age does not endow a person with immunity to the negative effects of drugs or chemical dependence.

Patterns of Senior Drug Misuse

It is the consumption of medications in a manner that deviates from the recommended prescribed dose or instructions that causes problems. Common patterns include:

◇ **overuse**—taking more or many different types of drugs than necessary;

◇ **underuse**—failure to take appropriately prescribed drug or correct dosage;

◇ **erratic use**—failure to follow instructions, resulting in missed doses, multiple doses, taking at wrong times or for the wrong condition, taking the wrong drug, or taking a drug by the wrong route of administration or dosing conditions (e.g., before meals);

◇ **contraindicated use**—incorrect drug prescribed for elderly resulting in either severe adverse reaction or inactivity of the drug; and

◇ **abuse and addiction**—continued use of non-prescribed or prescribed drug for nonmedical purposes despite negative consequences (Patterson, Lacro & Jeste, 1999).

Common Drugs of Abuse Among Seniors

Despite the concern paid to the misuse and abuse of prescription, OTC, and illicit drugs by seniors, the use of **alcohol, nicotine, and caffeine** still poses the greatest health problems for the elderly as it does for all age groups.

Nicotine. Whether it's the carcinogenic properties of cigarette smoke, the constricting effect of nicotine on blood vessels, the effect on blood viscosity that increases plaque formation, or the increase in blood pressure, **the unhealthy and deadly effects of smoking on the elderly cannot be overemphasized.** Some 13.6% of those over 50 smoke and share the same negative health risks found in any group of nicotine addicts (SAMHSA, 2006). **About 94% of all 430,000 premature deaths from smoking are in people over 50.** Conversely, all of the major causes of premature death among the elderly—cancer, heart disease, and stroke—are associated with smoking. For example, the **elderly smoker has twice the mortality risk of cardiovascular disease than their nonsmoking peers** (Center for Social Gerontology, 2001).

Caffeine. The majority of seniors use caffeine daily, with an average consumption of 200 mg per day. Current research demonstrates that **caffeine-related toxicity; anxiety, high blood pressure, heart arrhythmias, insomnia, and irritability in susceptible people is seen even at doses as low as 100 mg per day** (one cup of brewed coffee). Caffeine dependence withdrawal headaches are generally seen after 350 to 500 mg per day (two to four lattes or espressos). Caffeine use by seniors has also been correlated to loss of bone density and increased risk of hip fractures (Massey, 1998).

Alcohol. Though things may change by 2011 when the Baby Boom generation starts to turn 65, currently 80% of seniors treated for substance-abuse problems in publicly funded programs listed alcohol as their primary drug problem, making this the most prevalent drug of abuse by seniors. **About 6% to 11% of elderly patients who are admitted to hospitals display symptoms of alcoholism.** This figure goes up to 14% for emergency room admissions, 20% for elderly patients in psychiatric wards, and as high as 49% in some nursing homes, though the latter figure may result from the use of nursing homes as short-term alcoholism treatment facilities (JAMA, 1996). These figures do not include primary diseases that are aggravated by the use of alcohol.

"They don't tell you about all the changes getting old brings. My liver and stomach hurts now whenever I drink, so does my gallbladder, so do my kidneys. But even if they had warned me when I was young, I wouldn't have listened."

62-year-old drinker with cirrhosis

Alcohol abuse and other licit drugs problems are often missed or neglected by medical providers. They are not rigorously documented in elderly patients' medical histories; patients are often confused about the history of their consumption or reluctant to discuss this due to embarrassment. Some health professionals believe that seniors should not be approached on this subject or often neglect to ask relevant questions in the mistaken belief that older patients, especially women, do not drink (Dunne, 1994). **Impaired coordination, fall injuries, confusion, memory problems**, irritability, digestion problems, vitamin/mineral deficiencies, severe liver problems, legal problems, sleep problems and serious interactions with therapeutic medications are consequences of elder alcohol abuse (Institute of Alcohol Studies, 1999).

Thus prevention education and treatment services targeted for the aged are as important as those for adolescents. Other **age-related changes besides the liver significantly affect the way an older person responds to alcohol:** a decrease in body water, an increased sensitivity and decreased tolerance to alcohol, and a decrease in the metabolism of alcohol in the gastrointestinal tract. For these reasons the same amount of alcohol that previously had little effect can now cause intoxication (Smith, 1995).

Over-the-Counter Medications. Seniors are by far the **major consumers of OTC medications and dietary supplements**. The OTC medications most misused and abused by this population consists of sedatives, cold and cough aids, and stimulants.

Sedatives like Unisom,® Sleep-Eze,® Nytol,® and Sominex® principally contain an antihistamine for their sedating effects; those that are liquid also contain alcohol in concentrations much greater than wine. Abuse of these substances by young and old alike is well documented.

Cold, cough, allergy, and even motion sickness medications also contain antihistamines and alcohol and are sometimes abused for their sedating effects.

Stimulants like No-Doz,® Vivarin,® and Keep Alert® and medications for diet control like Xenadrine® usually contain **caffeine, herbal caffeine, or ephedrine** as their active ingredient. Abuse of these medications is rare, but in a health-compromised senior, even minor abuse of these stimulants can cause problems.

Prescription Drugs. Estimates of abuse of these drugs in the elderly range from 5% to 33%. Some research documents that one-third of residents in intermediate care facilities were receiving long-acting medications that are not recommended for use by elderly patients.

Sedative/Hypnotic Medications. Use of benzodiazepines by seniors, 71% in the over-50 and 33% in the over-65 populations, is of particular concern because there has been a correlation of confusion, falls, and hip fractures with their use in the elderly.

Opioid Analgesics. The most rapid increase in diversion of prescription drugs for abuse has occurred with prescription opioid pain medications like oxycodone (**OxyContin**®) and hydrocodone. In 2003, 5% of older adults and 13% of all individuals treated for substance abuse were primarily opioid prescription pain medication or heroin abusers (SAMHSA, 2006). **Hydrocodone (Vicodin,® Lortab,® and Norco®) is the most widely used and abused prescription opiate** among seniors, a dubious distinction that used to belong to codeine-based prescriptions. Since 1990 there has been a 500% increase in the number of emergency department visits due to hydrocodone. Because it is often co-formulated with acetaminophen, the abuse of the combination for the psychic effects of the opioid can cause liver damage from the acetaminophen—a particular problem with seniors.

Seniors, especially those using walking-assistance devices, or "walkers," are **also targeted by younger opioid abusers to pass off forged prescriptions for controlled opioid analgesics**. Seniors are less likely to be questioned or challenged on these prescriptions and receive either cash or medications for their efforts. Though data is lacking regarding age and abuse of opioid prescription cough medications, anecdotal reports indicate that seniors who are prescribed Hycomine,® Tussionex,® or Ambenyl®—or any hydrocodone-, codeine-, or opioid-containing cold and cough medication—regularly and on a continuous basis are likely using for reasons other than just a seasonal cold or allergy.

Illicit Drugs. Current and past data indicate a **low prevalence of illicit-drug use (e.g., heroin, cocaine, meth, and marijuana) by the elderly**. In 1979 almost 14 million (27%) Baby Boomers, then age 21 to 33, reported current (within the previous 30 days) illicit-drug abuse. The prevalence of illicit-drug use sharply and regularly declined in this population over the next 10 to 12 years. During that period illicit-drug use leveled out to an annual prevalence of 5% and has remained stable ever since. Age-comparable individuals from the previous generation have a 3.8% annual prevalence of illicit-drug use. It is expected that as more Baby Boomers survive into old age, a larger number of illicit-drug users will be an increasing part of the elderly population by 2011 (Patterson, Lacro & Jeste, 1999; Korper & Raskin, 2003).

Factors Contributing to Elderly Drug Misuse & Abuse

Aging is associated with a growing burden of disease that disproportionately exposes the elderly to prescription and OTC medications. This coupled with age-related physiological changes and medication problems places seniors at greater risk for drug-abuse problems (Patterson, Lacro & Jeste, 1999). **Abuse of alcohol or drugs by the elderly causes many health problems, such as liver disease, increased blood pressure, some forms of cancer, increased likelihood of falls, incontinence, cognitive impairment, hypothermia, emotional problems, and self-neglect.** All too often health professionals and even family members regard such problems as merely signs of aging and ignore the potential for drug or alcohol abuse (Institute of Alcohol Studies, 1999; Fleming, Barry, Manwell, et al., 1997; Altpeter, Schmall, Rakowski, et al., 1994). Many side effects or adverse reactions from the use of many legal prescriptions for various illnesses can mask the signs and symptoms of alcohol or drug abuse, making diagnosis difficult in the elderly.

Compared with younger adults, substance-abuse disorders present more often as medical or neuropsychiatric problems in the elderly. **Current diagnostic criteria for substance**

abuse are based on younger populations and may not be applicable for seniors. The criteria of increased alcohol or drug tolerance with progressive increased consumption, for example, may be invalid in seniors because of age-associated changes in pharmacokinetics and physiology that may alter their drug tolerance. For instance, a similar amount of alcohol or a benzodiazepine sedative may lead to a greater degree of intoxication in an elderly person compared with a young adult due to decreased metabolism and thus less tolerance brought about by such age-related changes (Patterson, Lacro & Jeste, 1999).

Physicians often fail to do a thorough history of alcohol or substance abuse (including caffeine and nicotine) in the elderly because there may be other more urgent medical problems to address. Some may also believe that it is harmful to address and intervene in an elderly person's established pattern of drinking or drug abuse. Seniors, like other drug abusers, may be in denial about their addiction or at least reluctant to disclose any alcohol or drug abuse (Institute of Alcohol Studies, 1999).

"Drug use and misuse among the elderly continues to be a neglected area of research in the field of social gerontology. Standard textbooks, for example, devote little or no attention to the topic."

(*Petersen & Thomas, 1975*)

Though written more than three decades ago, this statement unfortunately remains current as substance misuse by the elderly continues to be minimized in our culture.

◇ **Of total hospital admissions for the elderly, 20% are directly due to prescription or OTC drug reactions exclusive of alcohol and illicit-drug admissions.**

◇ About 20% of seniors who were regular drinkers exceeded recommended limits; 5% to 12% of men and 1% to 2% of women are problem drinkers (Dunne, 1994).

◇ Up to 80% of senior arrests are for drunkenness.

PREVENTION ISSUES

Primary Prevention

Because social drinkers and even abstainers can develop late-onset alcoholism, often in response to age-related problems, **older people need to be reeducated about the dangers of excessive use of alcohol and other psychoactive drugs.** Seniors need to receive information and counseling about ways to manage the problems associated with growing older without using psychoactive drugs at all or at least, in the case of alcohol, in moderation. Community volunteerism, an active social life, and continuing education are ways to encourage primary prevention. Information about primary prevention, customized for the elderly, needs to be given to those who provide services to this population, such as nurses, physicians, and social workers.

Secondary Prevention

Secondary prevention for the elderly focuses on **recognition of early stages of alcoholism or drug abuse and appropriate intervention tactics.** Frequently, there is **strong denial by this age group** because many of this generation see alcohol and other drug abuse as a sin or moral failure. Drug abuse tends to be hidden mainly because of the seclusion and solitude many live in, so a mobile professional staff and vigorous outreach programs are necessary. Home visits are particularly effective. It is **important to recognize alcoholism and addiction as primary diseases that must be treated.**

In addition to healthcare workers' recognizing signs of addiction, friends and family of older adults along with drivers and volunteers from senior centers who see older adults on a regular basis and are intimately acquainted with their habits and daily routines should also be aware of signs. Other venues and activities where problems can be identified are clubs, health fairs, congregate meal sites, and senior day care programs.

Tertiary Prevention

Treatment frequently involves different procedures from those used with younger clients. This age group is not responsive to abrupt, coercive, confrontational therapies. **The pace of therapy has to be slow, patient, and reassuring.** Bringing in the entire family to create an understanding and sympathetic support group helps. Detoxification needs more time as does the period for recovery, often two years or more. Thereafter outpatient counseling, peer group work, and a protective environment (safe from alcohol and other drugs) provide continuing care and reinforce recovery (Center for Substance Abuse Prevention, 1998). The least-intrusive yet medically sound treatment options are recommended not only to resolve elderly patients' alcohol or other drug problems but also to move them into specialized treatment by helping them overcome their denial or resistance to change.

CONCLUSIONS

The major challenge of prevention efforts for all ages is to provide accurate measurements of the long-term effectiveness of the strategies involved, not just short-term assessments of how much they learned; learning without action has little impact on the problem. Studies cannot conclusively show the effectiveness of a campaign because so many factors are involved and it can be hard to connect inevitable trends in society with specific efforts. To do nothing, however, is worse. A second, seemingly successful, recent direction is the use of massive drug/alcohol prevention advertising campaigns that are more effective, more honest, and more pervasive than earlier efforts. The reasoning is that if multiple ads and marketing campaigns can get people to eat unhealthy food, drink beer, and smoke cigarettes, why can't they do the opposite.

There is profound disagreement about drugs and drug policy in our society. Some see all drugs as inherently evil substances that must be regulated by laws. Some see drug use as a matter of choice (free choice in the case of legal drugs and eventual decriminalization and even legalization in the case of illicit drugs). Some see drug abuse as a pathological disease requiring treatment. Whatever the view, there is much hope for current and future effective prevention strategies.

CURRENT PROMISING DIRECTIONS

As we begin the twenty-first century, prevention is seen as a shared responsibility. The most promising approaches are the ones in which various segments of a community work in unison–youth, merchants, police, professionals, schools, parents, the government, and the media. An entire community arrives at a consensus about what it must do to prevent drug abuse, then agrees on the specific models that would best serve individuals and the community as a whole.

People are at risk throughout their lives. **If they are going to be exposed from cradle to grave, prevention efforts also must extend over a lifetime.**

◇ **Early primary prevention can treat a pregnant mother who uses drugs so that the child is not born addicted.** Prenatal care programs can provide parenting skills, teaching her to give unconditional love, showing the importance of holding her baby, and making her aware of other resources available to her. Toddlers can be given activities that increase bonding with their parents or caregivers. If the child has been exposed to drugs in the womb, rigorous early care can minimize long-term effects.

◇ **The family is a crucial prevention delivery system in childhood.** Parents may decide not to drink or use especially during their child-rearing years and model life-enhancing behaviors.

◇ **Grammar schools can integrate prevention into the curriculum.** Developmental skills can be taught, including resistance and decision-making skills. Students can be taught how to process moral dilemmas and how to talk about feelings.

◇ **By middle school** many children stop listening to adults and start listening to other children and often begin smoking, drinking, and using drugs. **Peer educator programs can identify natural leaders who will serve as models,** leaders, teachers, and guides for in-school peer prevention efforts.

◇ **In high school and college, prevention must assume a higher level of sophistication to counter experimentation, social use, and habituation** because there is greater exposure to drugs. Prevention at this level must make a continual effort involving curriculum infusion, normative education, support services, environmental change, policy formulation and enforcement as well as alternatives to alcohol and other drug use in social occasions.

◇ **For the workforce, prevention needs to be continued through EAPs.** They must be proactive and provide ongoing prevention, refer-

ral, and treatment opportunities. Prevention education should be provided in the normal course of job training. Pre-employment testing seems to be quite useful.

◇ Programs should be developed that address and **publicize many of the health risks of drug use, such as increased potential of sexually transmitted diseases, including HIV and hepatitis C** from needle use, as well as heart disease from cigarettes, stimulants, and overeating.

◇ **For older people preretirement training sessions and grief counseling can help prevent alcohol and other drug use.** Outreach programs need to take the prevention message to the people who are housebound or are not part of the school-workplace-community avenues of access.

◇ **Finally, prevention must be adapted to the needs of specific audiences.** A program for a rural midwestern town is not appropriate for a school in inner-city Los Angeles. Secondary prevention designed for experimenters who need to know effects of drugs might actually stimulate experimentation in a primary audience. Because no single prevention program can demonstrate universal reproducible results, modifications of existing programs must be made to fit particular situations.

CHAPTER SUMMARY

Introduction

1. Psychoactive drugs affect people at all ages from the crack-affected baby to the elderly woman who borrows a friend's prescription painkiller. Thus prevention programs should be carried out throughout people's lives.

PREVENTION

Concepts of Prevention

2. The goals of prevention are to prevent abuse before it begins (primary prevention), stop it where it has begun (secondary prevention), and treat people where abuse and addiction have taken hold (tertiary prevention).

3. The three main methods of prevention are supply reduction,

demand reduction, and harm reduction.

4. About one-third of the National Drug Control Budget is aimed at demand reduction.

5. Historically, prevention has wavered between temperance and prohibition.

6. In the 1920s and 1930s, Prohibition did reduce problems associated with alcohol, although it was repealed 14 years after being

put into law due to the need for taxes and the public's desire to drink.

7. Scare tactics, drug information programs (knowledge-based), skill-building and resiliency programs, environmental change programs, normative education, and public health model programs are some of the prevention tactics that have been tried.

8. The public health model alters the relationship among the host (the actual user), the environment (the social climate), and the agent (the psychoactive drug) to control addiction.

9. The most effective prevention programs involve the family, support, skills training, therapy, and parenting programs.

Prevention Methods

10. Supply reduction by law enforcement and other government agencies (e.g., interdiction and limiting precursor chemicals), augmented by the passage of antidrug laws, is aimed at reducing the supply of drugs on the streets.

11. The prison population has tripled since 1980 to 2.3 million. The effectiveness of supply reduction is open to debate due to cost and high drug availability.

12. Demand reduction tries to reduce people's desire for drugs either through primary, secondary, or tertiary prevention (which includes treatment). These methods are also called *universal*, *selective*, and *indicated prevention*.

13. Evidence-based principles for substance-abuse prevention give direction to prevention programming such as using approaches that have been shown to be effective.

14. Primary prevention for drug-naive people aims at preventing experimentation and social use or, at worst, delaying the age of first use. Though it is the most

important level of demand reduction, it receives the least funding.

15. Secondary prevention seeks to halt drug use once it has begun, through education, intervention, and skill building.

16. Tertiary prevention, usually some form of treatment, seeks to stop further damage from drug abuse and addiction. Through intervention, individual and group therapy, medical intervention, cue extinction, and promotion of a healthy lifestyle, recovery is encouraged.

17. Treatment results in a $4 to $20 savings for each dollar spent.

18. The primary goal of harm reduction is not abstinence but rather reduction of the harm that addicts do to themselves and to society through their use of drugs.

19. Drug substitution programs, designated-driver programs, controlled use, and outreach needle-exchange programs are some examples of harm reduction. These programs conflict with zero-tolerance government programs.

Challenges to Prevention

20. The social and health problems from alcohol, tobacco, and prescription drugs cause more problems than do illicit drugs.

21. The legality of alcohol and tobacco, along with heavy advertising, limits the effectiveness and the credibility of many prevention programs.

22. Prevention that works takes time, must be carried on throughout people's lifetimes, and must be adequately funded.

FROM CRADLE TO GRAVE

Patterns of Use

23. About 8% of Americans ages 12 and up used illicit drugs in the past month.

24. Whites and African Americans had an equal level of illicit-drug use; African Americans were

least likely to have a drinking problem.

25. The age of first use of drugs has gotten lower particularly since 1992. Caffeine, cigarettes, inhalants, and alcohol are generally the first drugs used. The earlier people begin drug use, the more likely they are to develop problems.

26. Neither level of intelligence, income, nor social class protects one from abuse and addiction.

Pregnancy & Birth

27. Almost 18.6% of fetuses are exposed just to alcohol and another 17% to marijuana, and 17.6% to tobacco.

28. Fetal alcohol syndrome (FAS) is the third most common birth defect and the leading cause of mental retardation in the United States.

29. Drugs can aggravate health problems in the pregnant woman, such as diabetes, anemia, sexually transmitted diseases (STDs), high blood pressure plus infections caused by infected needles or from infected partners.

30. Eighty percent of children with AIDS are born to mothers who use drugs intravenously or have sex with an infected user.

31. Pregnant addicts often have no prenatal care and often live a chaotic lifestyle, which can also hurt their fetuses.

32. Major problems for the fetus from drug use during pregnancy include a higher rate of miscarriage, blood vessel damage, severe infant withdrawal symptoms, and a much higher risk of sudden infant death syndrome (SIDS).

33. Drugs are particularly dangerous to the fetus because its defense mechanisms (e.g., drug-neutralizing metabolic system, immune system, and body organs) are not yet developed, so each surge of effects from a drug the mother takes gives multiple surges to the defenseless fetus.

34. The period of maximum fetal vulnerability is the first 12 weeks

of pregnancy, but vulnerability extends through birth.

35. The problems of drug abuse during pregnancy last well beyond the birth of the baby. Withdrawal, intoxication, and developmental delays are commonplace.

36. The majority of drug-exposed babies who receive prenatal, perinatal, and postnatal care manage to catch up in their development to non-drug-exposed children.

37. Fetal alcohol spectrum disorders (FASD) include a number of conditions such as fetal alcohol syndrome.

38. FAS is the third most common cause of mental retardation in the United States. It is measured by mental and physical defects.

39. Other cognitive deficits such as ARND (alcohol-related neuro-developmental disorder) and ARBD (alcohol-related birth defects) are even more prevalent than FAS. ARND manifests as mental problems; ARBD as physical problems.

40. Cocaine and amphetamines cause increased blood pressure and heart rate in both the mother and the fetus. Stroke and premature placental separation also occur. Infants go through withdrawal symptoms such as agitation.

41. Opioids cause physical addiction to the fetus and full-blown withdrawal symptoms at birth. HIV and hepatitis C infections are also common with intravenous (IV) heroin users.

42. Heavy marijuana use (which usually goes undetected) can cause abnormal responses to light, and the neonates usually weigh slightly less. Heavy smoking, prescription drug use, and over-the-counter (OTC) drug use (often including caffeine or ephedrine) also affect the fetus.

43. Prevention includes careful screening for drug use, drug education, and addiction treatment along with pre-, peri-, and postnatal care.

Youth & School

44. Alcohol, tobacco, and marijuana are still the major drug problems in high schools and colleges.

45. The levels of substance abuse among youth in the United States are among the highest of any developed country.

46. Substance abuse adds 10% to the cost of elementary and secondary school education.

47. A sense of invulnerability, the lag time between initial drug use and severe consequences, and especially delayed emotional maturation are major problems with psychoactive drug use in junior high, high school, and college.

48. More than half of juvenile male arrestees tested positive for one or more illegal drugs.

49. Identifying risks and teaching resiliency are two important prevention strategies for students.

50. A strong sense of family, established personal positions on drugs, a strong spiritual sense, active community involvement, and attachment to non-drug using adult role models help prevent drug abuse and addiction.

51. Primary, secondary, and tertiary prevention must be continued throughout school and beyond.

52. Heavy drinking and secondhand drinking (e.g., disruptive dorm mates) are the two biggest drug problems in college.

53. The drinking culture in colleges (rite of passage) is hard to change.

54. Normative assessment (understanding and disseminating the real levels of abuse), having non-alcohol activities, and providing alcohol- and drug-free dormitories are good college-level prevention techniques.

55. In students' minds, they exaggerate the bad effects but really exaggerate the positive effects of drugs. College prevention efforts should keep these ideas in mind.

56. As college students move to sophomore, junior, and senior years, their drinking and drug use slows down.

Love, Sex & Drugs

57. Viagra,® Cialis,® and Levitra® have changed the attitudes toward human sexuality.

58. Those who use psychoactive drugs to achieve sexual gratification are usually looking for a quick sensation rather than enduring emotions.

59. Physical effects of drugs on sex include hormonal changes, blood flow and blood pressure changes, nerve stimulation or desensitization, and changes in muscle tension—all of which affect sexual response.

60. When drugs are used over the long term, the desired effects start to lessen and the side effects, including depression, lack of interest, and inability to achieve an erection or orgasm, increase.

61. Drugs affect desire, excitation, and orgasm often in diverse and contradictory ways.

62. Most of the effects on sexuality are from the drugs' disruption of serotonin, dopamine, and norepinephrine.

63. Alcohol's affects on physical sexual functioning are closely related to blood alcohol concentration (BAC). The mental effects are less strictly dose related and have more to do with the user's psychological makeup.

64. There has been a cultural link among love, sex, and alcohol. Initially, alcohol lowers inhibitions and often increases aggressiveness. Long-term abuse causes a decrease in performance.

65. Cocaine and amphetamines in low doses can stimulate desire, but in high doses they make orgasm more difficult. In females they can either increase or decrease desire and orgasm, but in high doses a decrease is much more likely.

66. Tobacco use is glamorized in movies and encouraged by financial incentives.

67. Opioids generally suppress sexual activity. Sixty percent of users report a general decrease of desire; 90% report decreased desire while they were high.

68. Sedative-hypnotics enhance desire by lowering inhibitions and inducing relaxation. With abuse, sexual dysfunction and apathy become more common.

69. Because of the distortion of the senses involved with psychedelics, their effect on sexual experience can be very unpredictable. Marijuana's effects on sexuality have more to do with mind-set and setting.

70. MDMA (ecstasy) calms users, gives them warm feelings toward others, and induces a heightened sensual awareness. Long-term or excess use can deplete serotonin and reduce sexual functioning.

71. Volatile nitrites (inhalants) prolong and enhance orgasm.

72. Early use of psychotropic medications, such as antidepressants, may enable patients to engage in sexual activities that their depression or psychosis kept them from doing. Antidepressants have been linked to decreased desire as well as problems with erection and orgasm.

73. The search for a true aphrodisiac that increases desire and not just the ability to have an erection may be illusory because sexuality is more a matter of mental attitude than physical sensation.

74. By lowering inhibitions, distorting judgment, and increasing aggressive impulses, alcohol and other drugs contribute to sexual assault and violence, particularly in those predisposed to such acts. It makes a predator more aggressive and a victim more vulnerable.

75. Worldwide 333 million cases of sexually transmitted diseases occurred last year.

76. The use of contaminated needles and the increased incidence of high-risk sexual behavior due to drug abuse (including trading sex for drugs) have increased the incidence of STDs.

77. The most common STDs are chlamydia (the most common), gonorrhea, syphilis, trichomonas, pelvic inflammatory disease, venereal warts, and particularly AIDS.

78. AIDS is a disease that destroys the immune system, so the user is susceptible to any infection. Drugs also lower the body's defenses indirectly. One million Americans are living with human immunodeficiency virus (HIV); worldwide the number living with HIV is 39.5 million.

79. Other diseases and infections caused by dirty needles include hepatitis B and C, cotton fever, endocarditis, abscesses, malaria, tuberculosis, and syphilis. Hepatitis C infects more than 4 million Americans. About 75% of IV drug users test positive for hepatitis B.

80. The best AIDS prevention program is substance-abuse treatment and education about the dangers of sharing needles and engaging in high-risk sexual practices. Free needle exchange and other harm-reduction techniques can be of great benefit.

81. With care (if affordable), those with HIV can live 10 to 20 years or more.

Drugs at Work

82. Drug abuse in the workplace costs American business more than $200 billion per year in loss of productivity and increases in medical and legal costs.

83. The most effective answer to drug abuse in the workplace seems to be employee assistance programs (EAPs).

84. Studies show that good EAPs have decreased absenteeism 60% to 85% and on-the-job accidents 45% to 75%.

85. Positive drug tests in industry and business have fallen over the years. Part of the reason is that the pervasiveness of pre-employment testing keeps many drug users from even applying to a company that does tests.

86. About 8.2% of full-time employees are current illicit-drug users; 8.4% reported heavy alcohol use.

87. Most drug abusers work full-time. Drug use increases medical and legal costs, absenteeism, and on-the-job accidents while decreasing productivity.

Drugs in the Military

88. Drug education, zero tolerance, and drug testing have drastically reduced drug use in the military.

89. The military has a zero-tolerance policy bolstered by 3 million drug tests each year.

90. Alcohol use is still a problem in the armed forces, with a heavy drinking rate of 17.1%.

91. Each branch of the service has its own alcohol and drug program.

Drug Testing

92. The major uses of drug testing are pre-employment testing, testing to see whether a client in treatment or on probation is being abstinent, and testing in jobs that involve public safety. Some other reasons are for—cause testing, random testing, and post-accident testing.

93. Drugs can be tested for in the urine, blood, hair, saliva, and sweat.

94. The drugs most often tested for are alcohol, amphetamines, cannabinoids, cocaine, opioids (illicit and prescription), and PCP. Benzodiazepines, barbiturates, methadone, MDMA are also tested for.

95. The major types of drug tests are thin layer chromatography (TLC), enzyme-multiplied immunoassay technique (EMIT), gas chromatography/mass spectrometry (GC/MS), and hair analysis. Saliva, sweat, and breath are also used for testing. Breath tests are especially used for alcohol.

96. The important aspects of testing are the length of time it takes for drugs to leave the body, the accuracy of the various methods, and

the consequences of false positives and false negatives.

97. It takes two to three hours for most drugs to enter the urine and be detectable (latency). Alcohol, the exception, takes 30 minutes.

98. False-negative test results can be as damaging as false positives. For this reason a medical review officer (MRO) is used to rule out testing errors.

99. The best chance for a reliable drug-testing program includes direct observation of the sample being given and a rigid chain of custody.

100. Failure to recognize a serious addiction can be more serious than damage to one's reputation from a false positive.

Drugs & the Elderly

101. There is excessive use of prescription drugs by the elderly:

83% take at least one drug per day.

102. Physicians have a difficult time identifying alcoholism and drug abuse in the elderly.

103. Drug abuse is responsible for filling up many of our hospital beds.

104. The most commonly abused drugs are alcohol, nicotine, caffeine, prescription painkillers, prescription sedatives, and OTC medications. Illicit drugs are much less of a problem with the elderly than with younger people.

105. Overuse, underuse, erratic use, contraindicated use, abuse, and addiction are the ways drugs can be misused.

106. As people get older, their bodies become less able to neutralize and metabolize psychoactive drugs.

107. Drug abuse in the elderly is often overlooked. Continuing education, recognition of the signs of abuse, and appropriate treatment need to be directed at the elderly.

Conclusions

108. Prevention professionals need to figure out which programs work.

109. Prevention has no simple answer, and no one program that will work for everyone.

110. Prevention programs need to be tailored to specific age groups and further refined for ethnic, cultural, gender, and other target groups.

REFERENCES

Aaron, P. & Musto, D. F. (1981). Temperance and prohibition in America: A historical overview. In M. Moore & D. Gerstein, eds. *Alcohol and Public Policy: Beyond the Shadow of Prohibition.* Washington, DC: National Academy Press.

Adger, H., Jr. (1998). Children in alcoholic families: Family dynamics and treatment issues. In A. W. Graham & T. K. Schultz, eds. *Principles of Addiction Medicine* (2nd ed., pp. 1111-14). Chevy Chase, MD: American Society of Addiction Medicine, Inc.

Agency for Health Care Administration. (1999). *Drug Abuse Hospitalization Costs Study, May 1999. State of Florida.* http://www.floridahealthstat.com/publications/drugabuse.pdf (accessed May 18, 2007).

Alano, M. A., Ngougmna, E., Ostrea, E. M., Jr. & Konduri, G. G. (2001). Analysis of nonsteroidal anti-inflammatory drugs in meconium and its relation to persistent pulmonary hypertension of the newborn. *Pediatrics, 107*(3), 519-23.

Altpeter, M., Schmall, V., Rakowski, W., Swift, R. & Campbell, J. (1994). *Alcohol and Drug Problems in the Elderly: Instructor's Guide.* Providence,

RI: Center for Alcohol and Addiction Studies.

Ames, G. M., Cunradi, C. B., Moore, R. S. & Stern, P. (2007). Military culture and drinking behavior among U. S. Navy careerists. *Journal of Studies on Alcoohol and Drugs, 68*(3), 336-44.

Amornwichet, P., Teeraratkul, A., Simonds, R. J., Naiwatanakul, T., Chantharojwong, N., Culnane, M., et al. (2002). Preventing mother-to-child HIV transmission: The first year of Thailand's national program. *JAMA, 288*(2), 245-48.

Anglin, M. D., Prendergast, M. & Farabee, D. (1998) *The Effectiveness of Coerced Treatment for Drug-Abusing Offenders.* ONDCP Conference of Scholars and Policy Makers. http://www.ncjrs.org/ondcppubs/treat/consensus/anglin.pdf (accessed May 17, 2007).

Anthony, J. & Hetzer, J. (1991). Syndrome of drug abuse and dependence. In L. N. Robins & D. A. Regier, eds. *Psychiatry Disorders in America.* New York: The Free Press, Macmillan.

Armstrong, M. A., Gonzales Osejo, V., Lieberman, L., Carpenter, D. M., Pantoja, P. M. & Escobar, G. J. (2003). Perinatal substance abuse intervention in obstetric clinics decreases adverse

neonatal outcomes. *Journal of Perinatology, 23*(1), 3-9.

Arrestee Drug Abuse Monitoring [ADAM]. (2003). *Annual Report, 2000.* National Institute of Justice. http://www.ncjrs.gov/pdffiles1/nij/193013.pdf (accessed May 17, 2007).

Associated Press. (April 18, 2007). Student aid denied with drug use.

Augood, C., Duckitt, K. & Templeton, A. A. (1998). Smoking and female infertility: A systematic review and meta-analysis. *Human Reproduction, 13*(6), 1532-39.

Bateman, D. A. & Heagarty, M. C. (1989). Passive freebase cocaine ("crack") inhalation by infants and toddlers. *American Journal of Diseases of Children, 143*(1), 25-27.

Bates, C. & Wigtil, J. (1994). *Skill-Building Activities for Alcohol and Drug Education.* Boston: Jones and Bartlett Publishers, Inc.

Beck, J. & Rosenbaum, M. (1994). *Pursuit of Ecstasy: The MDMA Experience.* Albany: State University of New York Press.

Behnke, M., Eyler, F. D., Garvan, C. W. & Wobie, K. (2001). The search for congenital malformations in newborns with fetal cocaine exposure. *Pediatrics, 107*(5), E74.

Blume, S. B. & Zilberman, M. (2005). Alcohol and women. In J. H. Lowinson, P. Ruiz, R. B. Millman & J. G. Langrod, eds. *Substance Abuse: A Comprehensive Textbook* (4th ed., pp. 1049-64). Baltimore: Williams & Wilkins

Boston Globe. (June 27, 2003). Canada plans injection site for drug users. *San Francisco Chronicle*, p. D1.

Botvin, G. J. & Griffin. (2005). School-based programs. In J. H. Lowinson, P. Ruiz, R. B. Millman & J. G. Langrod, eds. *Substance Abuse: A Comprehensive Textbook* (4th ed., pp. 1211-29). Baltimore: Williams & Wilkins.

Brecht, M. L. (2005). Natural history of methamphetamine abuse and long-term consequences. *NIDA/CEWG*, 39-40.

Browne, M. L., Bell, E. M., Druschel, C. M., Gensburg, L. J., Mitchell, A. A., Lin, A. E., et al. (2007). Maternal caffeine consumption and risk of cardiovascular malformations. *Birth Defects Research, Part A: Clinical and Molecular Teratology*. Prepublication.

Bry, B. H., McKeon, P. & Pandina, R. J. (1982). Extent of drug use as a function of number of risk factors. *Journal of Abnormal Psychology, 91*(4), 273-79.

Buffum, J. C. (1982). Pharmacosexology: The effects of drugs on sexual function, a review. *Journal of Psychoactive Drugs, 14*(1-2), 5-44.

Buffum, J. C. (1988). Substance abuse and high-risk sexual behavior: Drugs and sex—the dark side. *Journal of Psychoactive Drugs, 20*(2), 165-68.

Burns, L., Mattick, R. P., Lim, K. & Wallace, C. (2007). Methadone in pregnancy: Treatment retention and neonatal outcomes. *Addiction, 102*(2), 264-70.

Cahoon-Young, B. (1997). Prevalence of hepatitis C virus in women: Who's getting it, why, and co-infection with HIV. Perspective on the epidemiology. *Treatment and Interventions for the Hepatitis C Virus*. San Francisco: Haight Ashbury Free Clinics.

Camenga, D. R., Klein, J. D. & Roy, J. (2006). The changing risk profile of the American adolescent smoker: Implications for prevention programs and tobacco interventions. *Journal of Adolescent Health, 39*(1), 120.e1-10.

Campbell, D. & Graham, M. (1988). *Drugs and Alcohol in the Workplace: A Guide for Managers*. New York: Facts On File.

Center for Social Gerontology. (2001). *Fact Sheet on Tobacco and Older Persons*. http://www.tcsg.org (accessed May 18, 2007).

Center for Substance Abuse Prevention. (1998). *Substance Abuse Among Older Adults*, CSAT Treatment Improvement Protocol No. 26. Rockville, MD: Author.

Centers for Disease Control [CDC]. (1999). *Mother-to-Child (Perinatal) HIV Transmission and Prevention*. http://www.cdc.gov/hiv/resources/factsheets/PDF/perinatl.pdf (accessed May 18, 2007).

Centers for Disease Control. (2005). *Update: Syringe Exchange Programs*. http://www.cdc.gov/mmwr/preview/mmwrhtml/mm5427a1.htm (accessed May 2, 2007).

Centers for Disease Control. (2006A). *Cases of HIV and AIDS in the United States and Dependent Areas, 2005*. http://www.cdc.gov/hiv/topics/surveillance/resources/reports/2005report/default.htm (accessed May 18, 2007).

Centers for Disease Control. (2006B). *2004 Surgeon General's Report: The Health Consequences of Smoking*. http://www.cdc.gov/tobacco/data_statistics/sgr/sgr_2004/index.htm#full (accessed May 18, 2007).

Centers for Disease Control. (2006C). *Trends in Reportable Sexually Transmitted Diseases in the United States, 2005*. http://www.cdc.gov/std/stats/trends2005.htm (accessed May 18, 2007).

Centers for Disease Control. (2006D). *Sexually Transmitted Diseases: Treatment Guidelines 2006*. http://www.cdc.gov/std/treatment/2006/toc.htm (accessed May 18, 2007).

Centrella, M. (1994). Physician addiction and impairment current thinking: A review. *Journal of Addictive Diseases, 13*(1), 91-105.

Chasnoff, I. J., Anson, A., Hatcher, R., Stenson, H., Iaukea, K. & Randolph, L. A. (1998). Prenatal exposure to cocaine and other drugs. Outcome at four to six years. *Annals of the New York Academy of Sciences, 846*, 314-28.

Chasnoff, I. J., McGourty, R. F., Bailey, G. W., Hutchins, E., Lightfoot, S. O., Pawson, L. L., et al. (2005). The 4P's Plus screen for substance use in pregnancy: Clinical application and outcomes. *Journal of Perinatology, 25*(6), 368-74.

Chasnoff, I. J., Neuman, K., Thornton, C. & Callaghan, M. A. (2001). Screening for substance use in pregnancy: A practical approach for the primary care physician. *American Journal of Obstetrics and Gynecology, 184*(4), 752-58.

Cherukuri, R., Minkoff, H., Feldman, J., Parekh, A. & Glass, L. (1988). A cohort study of alkaloidal cocaine ("crack") in pregnancy. *Obstetrics and Gynecology, 72*(2), 145-51.

Chu, K., Block, S. & Shell, A. (2007, April 17). Employers grapple with medical marijuana use. *USA Today*, p. 1B.

Clay, R. A. (2006). Incarceration vs. treatment: Drug courts help substance abusing offenders. *SAMHSA News, 14*(2). http://ncadistore.samhsa.gov/catalog/productDetails.aspx?ProductID=17460 (accessed May 19, 2007).

Cone, E. J., Presley, L., Lehrer, M., Seiter, W., Smith, M., Kardos, K. W., et al. (2002). Oral fluid testing for drugs of abuse: Positive prevalence rates by Intercept immunoassay screening and GC-MS-MS confirmation and suggested cutoff concentrations. *Journal of Analytical Toxicology, 26*(8), 541-46.

Cook, P. C., Petersen, R. C. & Moore, D. T. (1994). *Alcohol, Tobacco, and Other Drugs May Harm the Unborn*. Rockville, MD: U.S. Department of Health and Human Services, Public Health Service.

Crowe, L. & George, W. (1989). Alcohol and sexuality. *Psychological Bulletin, 105*, 374-86.

DASIS. (2006). *Older Adult Alcohol Admissions: 2003*. http://oas.samhsa.gov/2k6/olderAdultsTX/olderAdultsTX.pdf (accessed May 18, 2007).

Day, N. L., Richardson, G. A., Goldschmidt, L., Robles, N., Taylor, P. M., Stoffer, D. S., et al. (1994). Effect of prenatal marijuana exposure on the cognitive development of offspring at age three. *Neurotoxicology and Teratology, 16*(2), 169-75.

Derlet, R. & Albertson, T. (2002). *Toxicity, Methamphetamine*. http://www.emedicine.com/EMERG/topic859.htm (accessed May 18, 2007).

Des Jarlais, D. C., Hagan, H. & Friedman, S. R. (2005). Epidemiology and emerging public health perspectives. In J. H. Lowinson, P. Ruiz, R. B. Millman & J. G. Langrod, eds. *Substance Abuse: A Comprehensive Textbook* (4th ed., pp. 913-21). Baltimore: Williams & Wilkins.

De Wit, D. J., Offord, D. R. & Wong, M. (1997). Patterns of onset and cessation of drug use over the early part of the life course. *Health Education and Behavior, 24*(6), 746-58.

Dielman, T. E. (1995). School-based research on the prevention of adolescent alcohol use and misuse: Methodological issues and advances. In G. M. Boyd, J. Howard & R. A. Zucker, eds. *Alcohol Problems Among Adolescents: Current Directions in Prevention Research*. Hillsdale, NJ: Lawrence Erlbaum Associates.

Drug Enforcement Administration [DEA]. (2003A). *FAQs About the Illicit Drug*

Anti-Proliferation Act. http://www. usdoj.gov/dea/ongoing/anti-proliferation_act.html (accessed May 17, 2007).

Drug Enforcement Administration. (2003B). *Guidelines for a Drug-Free Workforce.* http://www.usdoj.gov/dea/demand/dfmanual/index.html (accessed May 18, 2007).

Drug Enforcement Administration. (2006A). Drug paraphernalia. http://www.usdoj.gov/dea/concern/paraphernaliafact.html (accessed May 1, 2007).

Drug Enforcement Administration. (2006B). *National Drug Threat Assessment 2007.* http://www.usdoj.gov/dea/concern/18862/index.htm#Contents (accessed May 17, 2007).

Dunne, F. J. (1994). Misuse of alcohol or drugs by elderly people. *British Medical Journal, 308*(6929), 608-9.

Eggert, L. L. (1996). *Reconnecting Youth: An Indicated Prevention Program.* National Conference on Drug Abuse Prevention Research. http://www.drugabuse.gov/MeetSum/CODA/Youth.html (accessed May 18, 2007).

El-Bassel, N., Schilling, R. F., Gilbert, L., Faruque, S., Irwin, K. L. & Edlin, B. R. (2000). Sex trading and psychological distress in a street-based sample of low-income urban men. *Journal of Psychoactive Drugs, 32*(3), 259-67.

Employee Assistance Professionals Association. (1990). Standards for employee assistance programs. *Exchange, 20*(10).

Englehart, P. F. & Barlow, L. (2005). The workplace. In J. H. Lowinson, P. Ruiz, R. B. Millman & J. G. Langrod, eds. *Substance Abuse: A Comprehensive Textbook* (4th ed., pp. 1331-45). Baltimore: Williams & Wilkins.

Ennett, S. T., Tobler, N. S., Ringwalt, C. L. & Flewelling, R. L. (1994). How effective is drug abuse resistance education? A meta-analysis of Project DARE outcome evaluations. *American Journal of Public Health, 84*(9), 1394-401.

Erowid. (2007). *Drug testing basics.* http://www.erowid.org/psychoactives/testing/testing_info1.shtml (accessed May 22, 2007).

Eyler, F. D., Behnke, M., Conlon, M., Woods, N. S. & Wobie, K. (1998). Birth outcome from a prospective, matched study of prenatal crack/cocaine use: II. Interactive and dose effects on neurobehavioral assessment. *Pediatrics, 101*(2), 237-41.

Fang, C. T., Chang, Y. Y., Hsu, H. M., Twu, S. J., Chen, K. T., Lin, C. C., et al. (2007). Life expectancy of patients with newly diagnosed HIV infection in the era of highly active antiretroviral ther-apy. *Monthly Journal of the Association of Physicians, 100*(2), 97-105.

Fantuzzi, G., Aggazzotti, G., Righi, E., Facchinetti, F., Bertucci, E., Kanitz, S., et al. (2007). Preterm delivery and exposure to active and passive smoking during pregnancy: A case-control study from Italy. *Paediatric and Perinatal Epidemiology, 21*(3), 194-200.

Feacham, R. G. A. (1995). Valuing the Past . . . Investing in the Future. Evaluation of the National HIV/AIDS Strategy 1993-94 to 1995-96. Canberra, Australia: Australian Government Publishing Service.

Federal Trade Commission. (2006). *Cigarette Report for 2004 and 2005.* http://www.ftc.gov/opa/2007/04/cigaretterpt.shtm (accessed May 19, 2007).

Finnegan, L. P. & Ehrlich, S. M. (1990). Maternal drug abuse during pregnancy: Evaluation and pharmacotherapy for neonatal abstinence. *Modern Methods of Pharmacological Testing in the Evaluation of Drugs of Abuse, 6,* 255-63.

Finnegan, L. P. & Kandall, S. R. (2005). Maternal and neonatal effects of alcohol and drugs. In J. H. Lowinson, P. Ruiz, R. B. Millman & J. G. Langrod, eds. *Substance Abuse: A Comprehensive Textbook* (4th ed., pp. 805-39). Baltimore: Williams & Wilkins.

Fleming, M. F., Barry, K. L., Manwell, L. B., Johnson, K. & London, R. (1997). Brief physician advice for problem alcohol drinkers. A randomized controlled trial in community-based primary care practices. *JAMA, 277*(13), 1039-45.

Frank, D. A., Augustyn, M., Knight, W. G., Pell, T. & Zuckerman, B. (2001). Growth, development, and behavior in early childhood following prenatal cocaine exposure: A systematic review. *JAMA, 285*(12), 1613-25.

French, M. T., Zarkin, G. A., Bray, J. W. & Hartwell, T. D. (1999). Costs of employee assistance programs: Comparison of national estimates from 1993–1995. *Journal of Behavioral Health Services Research, 26*(1), 95-103.

Fried, P. A. (1995). The Ottawa Prenatal Prospective Study (OPPS): Methodological issues and findings—it's easy to throw the baby out with the bath water. *Life Sciences, 56*(23-24), 2159-68.

Fried, P. A., O'Connell, C. M. & Watkinson, B. (1992). 60- and 72-month follow-up of children prenatally exposed to marijuana, cigarettes, and alcohol: Cognitive and language assessment. *Journal of Developmental and Behavioral Pediatrics, 13*(6), 383-91.

Fried, P. A. & Smith, A. M. (2001). A literature review of the consequences of pre-natal marijuana exposure. An emerging theme of a deficiency in aspects of executive function. *Neurotoxicology and Teratology, 23*(1), 1-11.

Fried, P. A., Watkinson, B. & Gray, R. (1998). Differential effects on cognitive functioning in 9- to 12-year-olds prenatally exposed to cigarettes and marijuana. *Neurotoxicology and Teratology, 20*(3), 293-306.

Fried, P. A., Watkinson, B. & Siegel, L. S. (1997). Reading and language in 9- to 12-year-olds prenatally exposed to cigarettes and marijuana. *Neurotoxicology and Teratology, 19*(3), 171-83.

Fulroth, R., Phillips, B. & Durand, D. J. (1989). Perinatal outcome of infants exposed to cocaine and/or heroin in utero. *American Journal of Diseases of Children, 143*(8), 905-10.

Gambert, S. R. & Albrecht III, C. R. (2005). The elderly. In J. H. Lowinson, P. Ruiz, R. B. Millman & J. G. Langrod, eds. *Substance Abuse: A Comprehensive Textbook* (4th ed., pp. 1038-47). Baltimore: Williams & Wilkins.

Gerstein, D. R., Johnson, R. A., Harwood, H., Fountain, D., Suter, N. & Malloy, K. (1994). *Evaluating Recovery Services: The California Drug and Alcohol Treatment Assessment (CALDATA).* Sacramento, CA: California Department of Alcohol and Drug Programs.

Gold, M. S. & Jacobs, W. S. (2005). Cocaine (and crack): Clinical aspects. In J. H. Lowinson, P. Ruiz, R. B. Millman & J. G. Langrod, eds. *Substance Abuse: A Comprehensive Textbook* (4th ed., pp. 218-51). Baltimore: Williams & Wilkins.

Goldberg, R. J. (1998). Selective serotonin reuptake inhibitors: Infrequent medical adverse effects. *Archives of Family Medicine, 7*(1), 78-84.

Gomby, D. S. & Shiono, P. H. (1991). *The Future of Children.* Los Altos, CA: Center for the Future of Children.

Gourivetch, M. N. & Arnsten, J. H. (2005). Medical complications of drug use. In J. H. Lowinson, P. Ruiz, R. B. Millman & J. G. Langrod, eds. *Substance Abuse: A Comprehensive Textbook* (4th ed., pp. 840-62). Baltimore: Williams & Wilkins.

Grant, B. F. (2000). Estimates of U.S. children exposed to alcohol abuse and dependence in the family. *American Journal of Public Health, 90*(1), 112-15.

Gupta, P. C. & Ray, C. S. (2003). Smokeless tobacco and health in India and South Asia. *Respirology, 8*(4), 419-31.

Hands off. (August 1, 1998). Hands off pregnant drug users. *USA Today,* p. 1D.

Hankin, J. R. (2002). Fetal alcohol syndrome prevention research. *Alcohol Research & Health, 26*(1), 58-65.

Hansen, W. B. & Graham. J. W. (1991). Preventing alcohol, marijuana, and cigarette use among adolescents: Peer pressure resistance training vs. establishing conservative norms. *Preventive Medicine, 20*(3), 414-30.

Harris, N. S., Thompson, S. J., Ball, R., Hussey, J. & Sy, F. (2002). Zidovudine and perinatal human immunodeficiency virus type 1 transmission: A population-based approach. *Pediatrics, 109*(4), E60.

Harvard University. (1998). Cocaine before birth. *The Harvard Mental Health Letter, 15*(6), 1-4.

Hazelden Foundation. (1993). *Refusal Skills.* Center City, MN: Author.

Hazelden Foundation. (2006). *Substance Abuse Among the Elderly: A Growing Problem.* http://www.hazelden.org/web/public/ade60220.page (accessed May 18, 2007).

Health Canada. (2006). *No new injection sites for addicts until questions answered says Minister Clement.* http://www.hc-sc.gc.ca/ahc-asc/media/nr-cp/2006/2006_85_e.html (accessed May 22, 2007).

Hechtman, L. (1989). Teenage mothers and their children: Risks and problems: A review. *Canadian Journal of Psychiatry, 34*(6), 569-75.

Henderson, D. J., Boyd, C. J. & Whitmarsh, J. (1995). Women and illicit drugs: Sexuality and crack cocaine. *Health Care for Women International, 16*(2), 113-24.

Holland, J. (2001). *Ecstasy: The Complete Guide.* Rochester, VT: Park Street Press.

Hubbard, R. L., Craddock, S. G. & Anderson, J. (2003). Overview of 5-year follow-up outcomes in the Drug Abuse Treatment Outcome Studies (DATOS). *Journal of Substance Abuse Treatment, 25*(3), 125-34.

Huo, D. & Ouellet, L. J. (2007). Needle exchange and injection-related risk behaviors in Chicago: A longitudinal study. *Journal of Acquired Immune Deficiency Syndromes, 45*(1), 108-14.

IMS Health. (2007). *IMS Reports U.S. Prescription Sales Jump 8.3 Percent in 2006, to $274.9 Billion.* http://www.imshealth.com/ims/portal/front/articleC/0,2777,6599_3665_80415465,00.html (accessed May 18, 2007).

Institute of Alcohol Studies. (1999). *Alcohol and the Elderly.* http://www.ias.org.uk/resources/factsheets/elderly.pdf (accessed May 18, 2007).

Jaffe, J. H. & Shopland, D. R. (1995). Tobacco: Medical complications. In J. H. Jaffe, ed. *Encyclopedia of Drugs and Alcohol* (Vol. 2, pp. 1045-46). New York: Simon & Schuster Macmillan.

Jastak, J. T. (1991). Nitrous oxide and its abuse. *Journal of the American Dental Association, 122*(2), 48-52.

Johnson, S. D., Phelps, D. L. & Cottler, L. B. (2004). The association of sexual dysfunction and substance use among community epidemiological sample. *Archives of Sexual Behavior, 33*(1), 55-63.

Jones, K. L. & Smith, D. W. (1973). Recognition of the fetal alcohol syndrome in early infancy. *Lancet, 2*(7836), 999-1001.

Joseph, H. & Langrod, J. (2005). The homeless. In J. H. Lowinson, P. Ruiz, R. B. Millman & J. G. Langrod, eds. *Substance Abuse: A Comprehensive Textbook* (4th ed., pp. 1141-68). Baltimore: Williams & Wilkins.

Journal of the American Medical Association [JAMA]. (1996). Alcoholism in the elderly. Council on Scientific Affairs. *JAMA, 275*(10), 797-801.

Juliana, P. & Goodman, C. (2005). Children of substance-abusing parents. In J. H. Lowinson, P. Ruiz, R. B. Millman & J. G. Langrod, eds. *Substance Abuse: A Comprehensive Textbook* (4th ed., pp. 1013-20). Baltimore: Williams & Wilkins.

Kahila, H., Saisto, T., Kivitie-Kallio, S, Haukkamaa, M. & Halmesmaki, E. (2007). A prospective study on buprenorphine use during pregnancy: effects on maternal and neonatal outcome. *Acta Obstetrica et Gynecologica Scandinavica, 86*(2), 185-90.

Kaminer, Y. (1994). Adolescent substance abuse. In M. Galanter & H. D. Kleber, eds. *Textbook of Substance Abuse Treatment.* Washington, DC: The American Psychiatric Press.

Kandall, S. R. (1993). *Improving Treatment for Drug-Exposed Infants* (Treatment Improvement Protocol Series). Rockville, MD: Center for Substance Abuse Treatment.

Kandall, S. R., Gaines, J., Habel, L., Davidson, G. & Jessop, D. (1993). Relationship of maternal substance abuse to sudden infant death syndrome in offspring. *Journal of Pediatrics, 123*(1), 120-26.

Karacic V., Skender, L., Brcic, I. & Bagaric, A. (2002). Hair testing for drugs of abuse: A two-year experience. *Arhiv za Higijenu Rada i Toksikologiju, 53*(3), 213-20.

Kintz, P. (1996). *Drug Testing in Hair.* Boca Raton, FL: CRC Press.

Kintz, P., Bernhard, W., Villain, M., Gasser, M., Aebi, B. & Cirimele, V. (2005). Detection of *Cannabis* use in drivers with the drugwipe device and by GC-MS after Intercept device collection. *Journal of Analytical Toxicology, 29*(7), 724-27.

Kitashima, M. (1997). Lesson from my life. *Resiliency in Action, 2*(3), 30-36.

Kline, M. D. (1989). Fluoxetine and anorgasmia. *American Journal of Psychiatry, 146*(6), 804-5.

Klein, L. & Goldenberg, R. L. (1990). Prenatal care and its effect on pre-term birth and low birth weight. In I. R. Markets & J. E. Thompson, eds. *New Perspectives on Prenatal Care* (pp. 511-13). New York: Elsevier.

Klette, K. L., Kettle, A. R. & Jamerson, M. H. (2006). Prevalence of use for AMP, MAMP, MDA, MDMA, MDEA, in military entrance processing stations specimens. *Journal of Analytical Toxicology, 30*(5), 319-22.

Knapp, C. M., Ciraulo, D. A. & Jaffe, J. H. (2005). Opiates: Clinical aspects. In J. H. Lowinson, P. Ruiz, R. B. Millman & J. G. Langrod, eds. *Substance Abuse: A Comprehensive Textbook* (4th ed., pp. 180-94). Baltimore: Williams & Wilkins.

Korper, S. P. & Raskin, I. E. (2003). *The Impact of Substance Use and Abuse by the Elderly: The Next 20 to 30 Years.* http://www.oas.samhsa.gov/aging/chap1.htm (accessed May 18, 2007).

Kumpfer, K. L. (1994). *Promoting Resiliency to AOD Use in High Risk Youth.* Rockville, MD: Center for Substance Abuse Prevention.

Kumpfer, K. L., Goplerud, E. & Alvarado, R. (1998). Assessing individual risks and resiliencies. In A. W. Graham, T. K. Schultz, M. F. Mayo-Smith, R. K. Ries & B. B. Wilford, eds. *Principles of Addiction Medicine* (3rd ed., pp. 1157-78). Chevy Chase, MD: American Society of Addiction Medicine, Inc.

Lacy, B. W. & Ditzler, T. F. (2007). Inhalant abuse in the military: An unrecognized threat. *Military Medicine, 172*(4), 388-92.

Lee, S. J. (2006). *Overcoming Crystal Meth Addiction.* New York: Marlowe & Company.

Leinwand, D. (July 12, 2006). More schools test for drugs. *USA Today,* p. 1A.

Lender, E. M. & Martin, J. K. (1987). *Drinking in America.* New York: Free Press.

Lester, B. M., Tronick, E. Z., LaGasse, L., Seifer, R., Bauer, C. R., Shankaran, S., et al. (2002). The Maternal Lifestyle Study: Effects of substance exposure during pregnancy on neurodevelopmental outcome in 1-month-old infants. *Pediatrics, 110*(6), 1182-92.

LifeSkills Training. (2003). *Life Skills*. http://www.lifeskillstraining.com (accessed May 18, 2007).

Littlefield, J. (2003). *Preventing Adolescent Alcohol Misuse*. http://ag.arizona.edu/pubs/general/resrpt1999/alcoholuse.pdf (accessed May 18, 2007).

Lumeng, J. C., Cabral, H. J., Gannon, K., Heeren, T. & Frank, D. A. (2007). Prenatal exposures to cocaine and alcohol and physical growth patterns to age 8 years. *Neurotoxicology and Teratology*. Prepublication.

Lyman, D. R., Milich, R., Zimmerman, R., et al. (1999). Project DARE: No effects at 10-year follow-up. *Journal of Consulting and Clinical Psychology, 67*(4), 590-93.

Macdonald, D. I., DuPont, R. L. & Ferguson, J. L. (2003). The role of the medical review officer. In A. W. Graham, T. K. Schultz, M. F. Mayo-Smith, R. K. Ries & B. B. Wilford, eds. *Principles of Addiction Medicine* (3rd ed., pp. 977-86). Chevy Chase, MD: American Society of Addiction Medicine, Inc.

Marnell, T., ed. (1997). *Drug Identification Bible* (3rd ed.). Denver: Drug Identification Bible.

Martin, J. C. (1992). The effects of maternal use of tobacco products or amphetamines on offspring. In T. B. Sonderegger, ed. *Perinatal Substance Abuse: Research Findings and Clinical Implications*. Baltimore: The Johns Hopkins University Press.

Massey, L. K. (1998). Caffeine and the elderly. *Drugs and Aging, 13*(1), 43-50.

Mathias, R. (2000). *Putting Science-Based Drug Abuse Prevention Programs to Work in Communities. NIDA Notes, 14*(6). http://www.drugabuse.gov/NIDA_Notes/NNVol14N6/Putting.html (accessed May 18, 2007).

Mattson, S. N., Schoenfeld, A. M. & Riley, E. P. (2001). Teratogenic effects of alcohol on brain and behavior. *Alcohol Research & Health, 25*(3), 185-91.

May, P. A. (1996). Research issues in the prevention of fetal alcohol syndrome and alcohol-related birth defects. *Research Monograph 32, Women and Alcohol: Issues for Prevention Research*. Bethesda, MD: National Institute on Alcohol Abuse and Alcoholism.

May, P. A. & Gossage, J. P. (2001). Estimating the prevalence of fetal alcohol syndrome: A summary. *Alcohol Research & Health, 25*(3), 159-67.

Mayes, L. C., Grillon, C., Granger, R. & Schottenfeld, R. (1998). Regulation of arousal and attention in preschool children exposed to cocaine prenatally. *Annals of the New York Academy of Sciences, 846*, 126-43.

Mello, N. K., Mendelson, J. H. & Teoh, S. K. (1993). An overview of the effects of alcohol on neuroendocrine function in women. In S. Zakhari, ed. *Alcohol and the Endocrine System*. NIAAA Research Monograph No. 23, NIH Pub. 93-3533. Bethesda, MD: National Institute on Alcohol Abuse and Alcoholism.

Meston, C. M. & Gorzalka, B. B. (1992). Psychoactive drugs and human sexual behavior: The role of serotonergic activity. *Journal of Psychoactive Drugs, 24*(1), 1-40.

Metzger, D. S., Woody, G. E., McLellan, A., O'Brien, C. P., Druley, P., Navaline, H., et al. (1993). Human immunodeficiency virus seroconversion among intravenous drug users in and out of treatment: An 18-month prospective follow-up. *Journal of Acquired Immune Deficiency Syndromes, 6*(9), 1049-56.

Milberger, S., Biederman, J., Faraone, S. V. & Jones, J. (1998). Further evidence of an association between maternal smoking during pregnancy and attention deficit hyperactivity disorder: Findings from a high-risk sample of siblings. *Journal of Clinical Child Psychology, 27*(3), 352-58.

MMWR. (2007). Use of niacin in attempts to defeat urine drug testing—five states, January-September, 2006. *Morbidity and Mortality Weekly Report, 56*(15), 365-66.

Monitoring the Future. (2007). *Monitoring the Future: Overview of Key Findings, 2006*. http://www.monitoringthefuture.org/pubs/monographs/overview2006.pdf (accessed May 17, 2007).

Morganthaler, J. & Joy, D. (1994). *Better Sex Through Chemistry: A Guide to the New Prosexual Drugs*. Petaluma, CA: Smart Publications.

Morrow, C. E., Culbertson, J. L., Accornero, V. H., Xue, L., Anthony, J. C. & Bandstra, E. S. (2006). Learning disabilities and intellectual functioning in school-aged children with prenatal cocaine exposure. *Developmental Neuropsychology, 30*(3), 905-31,

Moskowitz, J. (1989). The primary prevention of alcohol problems. A critical review of the research literature. *Journal of Studies on Alcohol, 50*(1), 54-88.

Mumola, C. (1998). *Substance Abuse and Treatment, State and Federal Prisoners, 1997*. Washington, DC: Bureau of Justice Statistics.

National Center on Addiction and Substance Abuse [CASA]. (2001). *Malignant Neglect: Substance Abuse and America's Schools*. http://www.casacolumbia.org/absolutenm/templates/Press Releases.aspx?articleid=110&zoneid= 48 (accessed May 19, 2007).

National Center on Addiction and Substance Abuse. (2002). *Dangerous Liaisons: Substance Abuse and Sexual Behavior*. http://www.casacolumbia.org/absolutenm/templates/ChairmanStatements.aspx?articleid=246&zoneid=31 (accessed May 19, 2007).

National Center on Addiction and Substance Abuse. (2006). *CASA* 2006 Teen Survey Reveals: Teen Parties Awash in Alcohol, Marijuana and Illegal Drugs—Even When Parents Are Present*. http://www.casacolumbia.org/absolutenm/templates/PressReleases.aspx?articleid=451&zoneid=56 (accessed May 18, 2007).

National Center on Addiction and Substance Abuse. (2007). *Wasting the Best and the Brightest: Substance Abuse at America's Colleges and Universities*. http://www.casacolumbia.org/absolutenm/templates/PressReleases.aspx?articleid=477&zoneid=65 (accessed May 19, 2007).

National Criminal Justice Reference System [NCJRS]. (2007). *Drug Courts: Facts and Figures*. http://www.ncjrs.gov/spotlight/drug_courts/facts.html (accessed May 17, 2007).

National Institute on Drug Abuse [NIDA]. (1994). *Annualized Estimates from the National Pregnancy and Health Survey*. Washington, DC: Author. http://www.drugabuse.gov/NIDA_Notes/NNVol10N1/Pregnancytable.html (accessed May 19, 2007).

National Institute on Drug Abuse. (1998). *NIDA InfoFacts: Costs to Society*. http://www.nida.nih.gov/Infofax/costs.html (accessed May 18, 2007).

National Institute on Drug Abuse. (1999). *NIDA InfoFacts: Rohypnol and GHB*. http://www.nida.nih.gov/Infofax/RohypnolGHB.html (accessed May 18, 2007).

National Institute on Drug Abuse. (2000). *NIDA Community Drug Alert Bulletin-Hepatitis*. http://www.drugabuse.gov/HepatitisAlert/HepatitisAlert.html (accessed May 19, 2007).

National Institute on Drug Abuse. (2003). *Preventing Drug Abuse Among Children and Adolescents*. http://www.drugabuse.gov/Prevention/applying.html (accessed May 18, 2007).

National Research Council. (1995). *Preventing HIV Transmission. The Role of Sterile Needles and Bleach*. Washington, DC: National Academy Press.

Noble, A., Vega, W. A., Kolody, B., Porter, P., Hwang, J., Merk, G. A., et al. (1997). Prenatal substance abuse in California: Findings from the Perinatal Substance

Exposure Study. *Journal of Psycho-active Drugs, 29*(1), 43-53.

Novick, D. M., Reagan, K. J., Croxson, T. S., Gelb, A. M., Stenger, R. J. & Kreek, M. J. (1997). Hepatitis C virus serology in parenteral drug users with chronic liver disease. *Addiction, 92*(2), 167-71.

NREPP. (2007). *SAMHSA's National Registry of Evidence Based Programs and Practices.* http://www.nrepp. samhsa.gov/ (accessed May 23, 2007).

N-SSATS. (2006). *National Survey of Substance Abuse Treatment Services (N-SSATS) 2005.* http://www.dasis.samhsa. gov/webt/state_data/US05.pdf (accessed May 17, 2007).

Nurco, D. N., Hanlon, T. E., Bateman, R. W. & Kinlock, T. W. (1995). Drug abuse treatment in the context of correctional surveillance. *Journal of Substance Abuse Treatment, 12*(1), 19-27.

O'Brien, R., Cohen, S., Evans, G. & Fine, J. (1992). *The Encyclopedia of Drug Abuse* (2nd ed.). New York: Facts On File.

Oei, J. & Lui, K. (2007). Management of the newborn infant affected by maternal opiates and other drugs of dependency. *Journal of Paediatrics and Child Health, 43*(1-2), 9-18.

Office of National Drug Control Policy [ONDCP]. (2000). *Evidence-Based Principles for Substance Abuse Prevention.* http://www.ncjrs.gov/ond-cppubs/publications/prevent/evidence_based_eng.html (accessed May 12, 2007).

Office of National Drug Control Policy. (2006). *National Drug Control Strategy: 2007 Annual Report.* Bethesda, MD: National Drug Clearinghouse. http://www.whitehousedrugpolicy.gov/ publications/policy/ndcs07/chap1.html (accessed May 17, 2007).

Office of National Drug Control Policy. (2007). *White House Drug Czar Releases National Drug Control Strategy.* http://www.whitehousedrug-policy.gov/news/press03/021003.html (accessed May 17, 2007).

Pagliaro, A. M. & Pagliaro, L. A. (2003). Alcohol and other drug use during pregnancy. In A. W. Graham, T. K. Schultz, M. F. Mayo-Smith, R. K. Ries & B. B. Wilford, eds. *Principles of Addiction Medicine* (3rd ed., pp. 1247-58). Chevy Chase, MD: American Society of Addiction Medicine, Inc.

Paria, B. C., Das, S. K. & Dey, S. K. (1995). The preimplantation mouse embryo is a target for cannabinoid ligand-receptor signaling. *Proceedings of the National Academy of Sciences, 92*(21), 9460-44.

Paria, B. C., Zhao, X, Wang, J., Das, S. K. & Dey, S. K. (1999). Fatty-acid amide hydrolase is expressed in the mouse uterus and embryo during the periimplantation period. *Biology of Reproduction, 60*(5), 1151-57.

Parents' Resource Institute for Drug Education. (2002). *PRIDE Questionnaire Report: 2001-02 National Summary Grades 6 Through 12.* http:// www.pridesurveys.com/main/support-files/natsum01.pdf (accessed May 18, 2007).

Partnership for a Drug-Free America. (2005). *PATS Parents 2004 Report.* http://www.drugfree.org/Portal/DrugIss ue/Research/PATS_Parents_2004_Repo rt/National_Study_Reveals_Drug-Experienced_Parents (accessed May 19, 2007).

Patterson, T. L., Lacro, J. P. & Jeste, D. V. (1999). Abuse and misuse of medications in the elderly. *Psychiatric Times, XVI4.*

PBIS. (2007). *Positive Behavioral Interventions & Supports. School-Wide PBS: Tertiary Prevention.* http://www. pbis.org/tertiaryPrevention.htm#whatis (accessed May 18, 2007).

Perkins, H. W. & Craig, D. W. (2002). Alcohol education project. http://alco-hol.hws.edu (accessed May 18, 2007).

Perkins H. W., Meilman P. W., Leichliter J. S., Cashin, J. R. & Presley, C. A. (1999). Misperceptions of the norms for the frequency of alcohol and other drug use on college campuses. *Journal of American College Health, 47*(6), 253-58.

Petersen, D. M. & Thomas, C. W. (1975). Acute drug reactions among the elderly. *Journal of Gerontology, 30*(5), 552-56.

Peugh, J. & Belenko, S. (2001). Alcohol, drugs and sexual function: A review. *Journal of Psychoactive Drugs, 33*(3), 223-32.

Physicians' Desk Reference. (2007). *Physicians' Desk Reference* (61st ed.). Montvale, NJ: Medical Economics Co.

Plans to link. (October 11, 1999). Plans to link welfare benefits to drug testing spark outcry. *Alcoholism and Drug Abuse Weekly,* pp. 1-2.

Plessinger, M. A. & Woods, J. R., Jr. (1998). Cocaine in pregnancy: Recent data on maternal and fetal risks. *Obstetrics and Gynecology Clinics of North America, 25*(1), 99-118.

Polymeru, A. (2007). *Alcohol and Drug Prevention in Colleges and Universities.* http://www.mentorfoundation.org/up-loads/UK_Prevention_Colleges_and_ Universities.pdf (accessed May 18, 2007).

Poteet-Johnson, D. J. & Dias, P. J. (2003). Office assessment of the substance-using adolescent. In A. W. Graham, T. K. Schultz, M. F. Mayo-Smith, R. K. Ries & B. B. Wilford, eds. *Principles of Addiction Medicine* (3rd ed., pp. 1523-34). Chevy Chase, MD: American Society of Addiction Medicine, Inc.

Pumariega, A. J., Kilgus, M. D. & Rodriguez, L. (2005). Adolescents. In J. H. Lowinson, P. Ruiz, R. B. Millman & J. G. Langrod, eds. *Substance Abuse: A Comprehensive Textbook* (4th ed., pp. 1021-37). Baltimore: Williams & Wilkins.

Quest Diagnostics. (2003). *Drug Testing Index.* http://www.questdiagnostics. com/employersolutions/dti/2007_03/dti _index.html (accessed May 18, 2007).

Quinn, T. C. (1996). Global burden of the HIV pandemic. *Lancet, 348*(9020), 99-106.

Raschko, R. (1990). "Gatekeepers" do the case finding in Spokane. *Aging, 361,* 38-40.

Reyna, V. F. & Farley, F. (January 2007). Is the teen brain too rational? *Scientific American Mind,* pp. 58-65.

Rhem, K. T. (2001). *Drug, Alcohol Treatment Available to DoD Beneficiaries.* American Forces Press Service. http://www.defenselink.mil/ specials/drugawareness/afpsstory.html (accessed May 18, 2007).

Richardson, G. A. (1998). Prenatal cocaine exposure: A longitudinal study of development. *Annals of the New York Academy of Sciences, 846,* 144-52.

Richardson, G. A., Day, N. L. & Goldschmidt, L. (1995). Prenatal alcohol, marijuana, and tobacco use: Infant mental and motor development. *Neurotoxicology and Teratology, 17*(4), 479-87.

Robins, L. N. (1993). The sixth Thomas James Okey Memorial Lecture. Vietnam veterans' rapid recovery from heroin addiction: A fluke or normal expectation? *Addiction, 88*(8), 1041-54.

Roizen, J. (1997). Epidemiological issues in alcohol-related violence. In M. Galanter, ed. *Recent Developments in Alcoholism* (Vol. 13). New York: Plenum Press.

Rosen, R. C. (1991). Alcohol and drug effects on sexual response: Human experimental and clinical studies. *Annual Review of Sex Research, 2,* 119-79.

Rosenberg, K. P., Bleiberg, K. L., Koscis, J. & Gross, C. (2003). A survey of sexual side effects among severely mentally ill patients taking psychotropic medications: Impact on compliance. *Journal of Sex and Marital Therapy, 29*(4), 289-96.

RTI International. (1999). *RTI Worldwide Survey Reveals Reduced Usage of Alcohol, Tobacco, and Illegal Drugs by U.S. Military Personnel.* http://www.rti. org/page.cfm?nav=391&objectid=AB12 BFB4-F306-4667-9CCDF72168A77F27 (accessed May 18, 2007).

Rusche, S. (1995). Prevention movement. In J. H. Jaffe, ed. *Encyclopedia of Drugs and Alcohol* (Vol. II, pp. 856-61). New York: Simon & Schuster Macmillan.

Rush, B. (1814). *An Inquiry into the Effect of Ardent Spirits upon the Human Body and Mind with an Account of the Means and of the Remedies for Curing Them* (8th rev. ed). Brookfield, MA: E. Merriam & Co.

Rush, D. & Callahan, K. R. (1989). Exposure to passive cigarette smoking and child development: A critical review. *Annals of the New York Academy of Sciences, 562*, 74-100.

Russel, S. (June 27, 2003). Scientists urge worldwide AIDS vaccine effort. *San Francisco Chronicle*, p. A3.

SafeState. (2006). *Drug and Alcohol Abuse Prevention*. http://safestate.org/index.cfm?navId=10 (accessed May 18, 2007).

Saitz, R. (2003). Overview of medical and surgical complications. In A. W. Graham, T. K. Schultz, M. F. Mayo-Smith, R. K. Ries & B. B. Wilford, eds. *Principles of Addiction Medicine* (3rd ed., pp. 1157-78). Chevy Chase, MD: American Society of Addiction Medicine, Inc.

Schmid, P. C., Paria, B. C., Krebsbach, R. J., Schmid, H. H. & Dey, S. K. (1997). Changes in anandamide levels in mouse uterus are associated with uterine receptivity for embryo implantation. *Proceedings of the National Academy of Sciences, 94*(8), 4188-92.

Seifert, S. A. (1999). Substance use and sexual assault. *Substance Use & Misuse, 34*(6), 935-45.

Sharp, C. W. & Rosenberg, N. L. (2005). Inhalants. In J. H. Lowinson, P. Ruiz, R. B. Millman & J. G. Langrod, eds. *Substance Abuse: A Comprehensive Textbook* (4th ed., pp. 336-66). Baltimore: Williams & Wilkins.

Shen, W. W. & Sata, L. S. (1983). Neuropharmacology of the male sexual function. *Journal of Clinical Pharmacology, 3*(4), 265-66.

Sher, K. J. (1997). Psychological characteristics of children of alcoholics. *Alcohol Health and Research World, 21*(3), 247-54.

Simoni-Wastila, L. & Yang, H. K. (2006). Psychoactive drug abuse in older adults. *American Journal of Geriatric Pharmacotherapy, 4*(4), 380-94.

Smith, J. W. (1995). Medical manifestations of alcoholism in the elderly. *International Journal of the Addictions, 30*(13-14), 1749-98.

Smith, D. E., Wesson, D. R. & Apter-Marsh, M. (1984). Cocaine- and alcohol-induced sexual dysfunction in patients with addictive diseases. *Journal of Psychoactive Drugs, 16*(4), 359-61.

Smith, D. E., Wesson, D. R. & Calhoun, S. R. (1995). Rohypnol: Quaalude of the nineties? *CSAM News. Newsletter of the California Society of Addiction Medicine, 22*(2).

Smith, L. M., LaGasse, L. L., Derauf, C., Grant, P., Shah, R., Arria, A., et al. (2006). The Infant Development, Environment, and Lifestyle Study: Effects of prenatal methamphetamine exposure, polydrug exposure, and poverty on intrauterine growth. *Pediatrics, 118*(3), 1149-56.

SmithKline Beecham Clinical Laboratories. (1997). *SmithKline Beecham Drug Testing Index, 1997*. Collegeville, PA: Author.

Smoking. (May 14, 2007). Smoking will net movies stronger ratings. *Los Angeles Times*, p. A1.

Sokol, R. J. & Clarren, S. K. (1989). Guidelines for use of terminology describing the impact of prenatal alcohol on the offspring. *Alcoholism: Clinical & Experimental Research, 13*(4), 597-98.

Spadoni, A. D., McGee, C. L., Fryer, S. L. & Riley, E. P. (2007). Neuroimaging and fetal alcohol spectrum disorders. *Neuroscience and Biobehavioral Reviews, 31*(2), 239-45.

Streissguth, A. (1997). *Fetal Alcohol Syndrome*. Baltimore: Brookes Publishing Co.

Substance Abuse and Mental Health Services Administration. (1997). *Drug Use Among U.S. Workers*. http://www.samhsa.gov/oas/wkplace/workpla6.htm#E8E6 (accessed Month, 00, 200X).

Substance Abuse and Mental Health Services Administration [SAMHSA]. (1999A). *Substance Abuse and Mental Health Statistics Source Book, 1998*. Rockville MD: National Clearinghouse for Alcohol and Drug Information.

Substance Abuse and Mental Health Services Administration. (1999B). *Worker Drug Use and Workplace Policies and Programs: Results from the National Household Survey on Drug Abuse*. Rockville, MD: National Clearinghouse for Alcohol and Drug Information.

Substance Abuse and Mental Health Administration. (2000). *Patterns of Alcohol Use Among Adolescents and Associations with Emotional and Behavioral Problems*. Rockville, MD: National Clearinghouse for Alcohol and Drug Information.

Substance Abuse and Mental Health Services Administration. (2006). *Results from the 2005 National Household Survey on Drug Abuse*. http://www.oas.samhsa.gov/nsduhLatest.htm (accessed May 19, 2007).

Substance Abuse and Mental Health Services Administration. (2007). *Drugs in the Workplace*. http://dwp.samhsa.gov/DrugTesting/Files_Drug_Testing/FactSheet/factsheet041906.aspx (accessed May 19, 2007).

Tobacco tax has desired effect. (January 14, 2000). *Medford Mail Tribune*, p. 6A.

UNAIDS. (2006) *December 06 AIDS Epidemic Update*. http://data.unaids.org/pub/EpiReport/2006/2006_EpiUpdate_en.pdf (accessed May 18, 2007).

UNAIDS. (2007). *Russian Federation: Epidemiological Fact Sheets on HIV/AIDS*. http://www.unaids.org/en/Regions_Countries/Countries/russian_federation.asp (accessed May 18, 2007).

University of California at San Francisco. (2004). *How Does HIV Prevention Work on Different Levels?* CAPS Fact Sheet. http://www.caps.ucsf.edu/pubs/FS/levels.php (accessed May 18, 2007).

U.S. Bureau of the Census. (2004). *U.S. Interim Projections by Age, Sex, Race, and Hispanic Origin*. http://www.census.gov/ipc/www/usinterimproj (accessed May 19, 2007)

U.S. Department of Education (2006). *Guide to U.S. Department of Education Programs*. http://www.ed.gov/programs/gtep/gtep.pdf (accessed May 18, 2007).

U.S. Department of Justice [DOJ]. (2002). *Drugs and Crime Facts*. Bureau of Justice statistics. http://www.ojp.gov/bjs/pub/pdf/dcf.pdf (accessed May 17, 2007).

U.S. Department of Justice. (2006). *Prisoners in 2005*. http://www.ojp.usdoj.gov/bjs/pub/pdf/p05.pdf (accessed May 17, 2007).

U.S. Department of Justice. (2007). *Probation and Parole Statistics*. http://www.ojp.usdoj.gov/bjs/pandp.htm (accessed May 19, 2007).

U.S. Department of Labor [USDL]. (1990). *What Works: Workplaces Without Drugs*. Rockville, MD: Author.

U.S. Department of Labor. (2006). *General Workplace Impact*. http://www.dol.gov/asp/programs/drugs/workingpartners/stats/wi.asp (accessed May 18, 2007).

U.S. Department of Labor. (2007). *Drug Test Results Reveal Continued Decline in Worker Meth and Marijuana Use*. http://www.dol.gov/asp/programs/drugs/workingpartners/whatsnew/2007-04-004.htm (accessed May 18, 2007).

U.S. Department of State. (2007). *International Narcotics Control Strategy Report*. http://www.state.gov/p/inl/

rls/nrcrpt/2007 (accessed May 17, 2007).

U.S. Medicine. (2004). *Heavy Drinking, Smoking Increases in Military, Drug Use Is Down.* http://www.usmedicine.com/article.cfm?articleID=859&issueID=62 (accessed May 18, 2007).

Vereby, K. G., Meenan, G. & Buchan, B. J. (2005). Diagnostic laboratory: Screening for drug abuse. In J. H. Lowinson, P. Ruiz, R. B. Millman & J. G. Langrod, eds. *Substance Abuse: A Comprehensive Textbook* (4th ed., pp. 564-77). Baltimore: Williams & Wilkins.

Walsh, J. M. (2007). New technology and new initiatives in U.S. workplace testing. *Forensic Science International.* Prepublication.

Warner, E. A. (2003). Laboratory diagnosis. In A. W. Graham, T. K. Schultz, M. F. Mayo-Smith, R. K. Ries & B. B. Wilford, eds. *Principles of Addiction Medicine* (3rd ed., pp. 337-48). Chevy Chase, MD: American Society of Addiction Medicine, Inc.

Weaver, M. F. (2005). Perinatal addiction. In A. W. Graham, T. K. Schultz, M. F. Mayo-Smith, R. K. Ries & B. B. Wilford, eds. *Principles of Addiction Medicine* (3rd ed., pp. 1231-46). Chevy Chase, MD: American Society of Addiction Medicine, Inc.

Wechsler, H., Kelley, K., Weitzman, E. R., SanGiovanni, J. P. & Seibring, M. (2000). What colleges are doing about student binge drinking: A survey of college administrators. *Journal of American College Health, 48*(5), 219-26.

Wechsler, H., Lee, J. E., Kuo, M., Seibring, M., Nelson, T. F. & Lee, H. (2002). Trends in college binge drinking during a period of increased prevention efforts: Findings from 4 Harvard School of Public Health College Alcohol Study surveys: 1993-2001. *Journal of American College Health, 50*(5), 203-17.

Weinberg, B. A. & Bealer, B. K. (2001). *The World of Caffeine.* New York: Routledge Press.

Weir, E. (2000). Substance abuse among physicians. *Canadian Medical Association Journal, 162*(12), 1730.

Werblin, J. M. (1998). High on sex. *Professional Counselor, 13*(6), 33-37.

White, W. L. (1998). *Slaying the Dragon: The History of Addiction Treatment and Recovery in America.* Bloomington, IL: Chestnut Health Systems/Lighthouse Institute.

White, J., Nicholson, T., Duncan, D. & Minors, P. (2002). A demographic profile of employed users of illicit drugs. In M. A. Rahim, R. T. Golembiewski & K. D. Mackenzie, eds. *Current Topics in Management* (Vol. 6). Amsterdam: Elsevier Science Ltd.

Wilsnack, S. C., Klassen, A. D., Schur, B. E. & Wilsnack, R. W. (1991). Predicting onset and chronicity of women's problem drinking: A five-year longitudinal analysis. *American Journal of Public Health, 81*(3), 305-18.

Wodak, A. & Lurie, P. (1997). A tale of two countries: Attempts to control HIV among injecting drug users in Australia and the United States. *Journal of Drug Issues, 27*(1), 117-34.

Wolff, K., Farrell, M., Marsden, J., Monteiro, M. G., Ali, R., Welch, S., et al. (1999). A review of biological indicators of illicit drug use, practical considerations and clinical usefulness. *Addiction, 94*(9), 1279-98.

World Health Organization [WHO]. (2005). *Sexually Transmitted Diseases. WHO Information Fact Sheets.* http://www.who.int/inf-fs/en/fact110.html (accessed May 15, 2007).

World Health Organization. (2007). *Global AIDS Epidemic Continues to Grow.* http://www.who.int/hiv/mediacentre/news62/en/index.html (accessed May 19, 2007).

Worth, D. (1991). American women and polydrug abuse. In P. Roth, ed. *Alcohol and Drugs Are Women's Issues* (Vol. 1). Metuchen, NJ: Women's Action Alliance and the Scarecrow Press.

Wright, H. I., Gavaler, J. S. & Thiel, D. H. (1991). Effects of alcohol on the male reproductive system. *Alcohol Health and Research World, 15*(2), 110-14.

Young, N. K. (1997). Effects of alcohol and other drugs on children. *Journal of Psychoactive Drugs, 29*(1), 23-42.

Zakhari, S., ed. (1993). *Alcohol and the Endocrine System.* NIAAA Research Monograph No. 23, NIH Pub. No. 93-3533. Bethesda, MD: National Institute on Alcohol Abuse and Alcoholism.

Zhu, J. H. & Stadlin, A. (2000). Prenatal heroin exposure. Effects on development, acoustic startle response, and locomotion in weanling rats. *Neurotoxicology and Teratology, 22*(2), 193-203.

Zuckerman, B., Frank, D. A., Hingson, R., Amaro, H., Levenson, S. M., Kayne, H., et al. (1989). Effects of maternal marijuana and cocaine use on fetal growth. *New England Journal of Medicine, 320*(12), 762-68.

Treatment

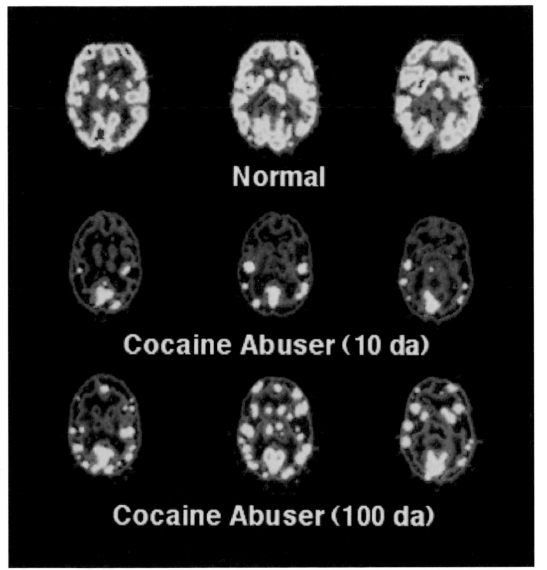

Normal

Cocaine Abuser (10 da)

Cocaine Abuser (100 da)

*T*hese positron emission tomography (PET) scans of a normal person's brain and a heavy cocaine user's brain show how long recovery can take and why it is so difficult. The yellow signifies normal brain function. In a nonuser yellow and even red is abundant. In the cocaine abuser, 10 days after quitting, there is significantly less yellow and therefore less normal brain function. At 100 days there is some additional normal activity, but not nearly as active as it should be. It can take a year for a long-term cocaine abuser who becomes abstinent to approach anywhere near normal brain function.
Photo courtesy of Nora Volkow (Volkow, Hitzemann, Wang, et al., 1992)

- **Introduction:**
  ◊ **A Disease of the Brain.** The most prevalent mind disorder is substance abuse. It causes more illness, death, and social disruption than any other brain disease. Substance abuse also costs our society more financial loss than any other medical condition.
  ◊ **Current Issues in Treatment:**
    - There is a rapidly expanding use of medications to treat detoxification, control withdrawal symptoms, lessen craving, and promote short- and long-term abstinence.
    - Advanced imaging methods and other new diagnostic techniques are being used to visualize anatomical or functional anomalies of the human brain that result in or from addiction and even to predict treatment outcomes.
    - Clinicians are developing more-effective tools to diagnose addiction that can better match clients to specific treatment interventions.
    - There is increased emphasis on evidence-based best practices in treatment with decreased appreciation of practice-based clinical management.
    - Increasing research supports coerced treatment (e.g., drug courts) as being just as effective if not more so in promoting abstinence and recovery from drug addiction when compared with voluntary treatment admissions.
    - There is a lack of resources to provide the treatment that has been proven effective.
    - The conflict between abstinence-oriented recovery and harm reduction philosophies of treatment continues. Historically, the United States has vacillated among temperance, individual abstinence, and societal prohibition.
- **Treatment Effectiveness.** Steady improvements in positive treatment outcomes show 12-month continuous recovery rates ranging up to 80%, resulting in $4 to $39 savings for every $1 spent on treatment. It also reduces crime by 75%.
- **Principles & Goals of Treatment.** Certain principles for effective treatment include having a wide variety of treatment programs readily available, using medications in conjunction with individual and group therapy, and treating any coexisting conditions and not just the addiction itself. Goals include motivating clients toward abstinence and reconstructing their lives in ways that exclude drug abuse.
- **Selection of a Program.** Use of developing addiction assessment tools helps treatment professionals match the client to the best program. American Society of Addiction Medicine Patient Placement Criteria uses six problem area dimensions to determine which of four levels of care is best suited for the client. Providing a wide range of treatment approaches plus customizing treatment for culture, gender, ethnicity, and other traits dramatically improves outcomes.
- **Beginning Treatment.** Breaking through denial is the crucial first step in treatment. Hitting bottom, especially when health, family, work, financial, or legal problems are involved, often gets the user into treatment. Direct intervention with an intervention specialist is also used to get the person into treatment.
- **Treatment Continuum.** Once addiction has occurred, treatment and recovery become a lifetime process.
  ◊ **Detoxification** uses medical care, emotional support, and medications to control withdrawal symptoms, reduce craving, and help the client begin abstinence.
  ◊ **Initial abstinence** uses counseling, anticraving medications, drug substitution, and desensitization techniques to rebalance body chemistry, continue abstinence, and prevent relapse due to environmental triggers.
  ◊ **Long-term abstinence** involves participation in continued counseling and groups to prevent relapse and begin changing living habits.
  ◊ **Recovery** is a lifelong process that involves rebuilding one's lifestyle to live sober and drug-free.
  ◊ **Outcome and follow-up** studies are used to judge the effectiveness of treatment programs.
- **Individual vs. Group Therapy.** Individual counseling, peer groups, 12-step groups, facilitated group therapy, and educational groups are all used in treatment.
- **Treatment & the Family.** Treatment should involve the whole family. The problems of codependency, enabling, and being the child of an alcoholic/addict must be addressed.
- **Adjunctive & Complementary Treatment Services.** Abuse and addiction of substances have a negative impact on the user's family and on his or her physical, emotional, social, and spiritual well-being. Treatment that effectively addresses all of these components is being encouraged to increase positive outcomes.
- **Drug-Specific Treatment.** Certain psychoactive drugs call for specialized medical and counseling treatment techniques (e.g., methadone maintenance, stimulant-abuse groups, or dual-diagnosis groups). A behavioral addiction like gambling is treated with many of the same techniques that are used for substance addiction. Office-based opiate addiction treatment using buprenorphine has ushered in a new era of opiate addiction treatment.
- **Target Populations.** Treatment should be culturally specific (i.e., ethnicity, gender, and language) because needs vary between men and women, old and young, and among Black, White, Hispanic, Asian, and American Indian people.
- **Treatment Obstacles.** Developmental arrest, lack of cognition, conflicting goals, relationship/family strife, insurmountable debt/financial problems, employment needs, associations with dysfunctional peers in a drug-infested environment, poor follow-through, and lack of facilities are the main problems in treatment.
- **Medical Intervention Developments.** More than 60 medications are being developed, focusing on detoxification, replacement or agonist therapies, antagonist or vaccine effects, anticraving effects, and restoration of homeostasis.

As Marijuana Use Rises, More People Are Seeking Treatment for Addiction

Alcoholism drug doubted

TREATMENT STUDY

Campral no better than placebo; now is counseling and behavioral therapy, including Alcoholics Anonymous. "I think results of this kind

The study looked at various combinations of Campral, naltrexone cluding those taking a placebo, substantially

PEOPLE ARE AWARE of the addictive potential

Mayor promises drug treatment on demand

Helping the Addict Who Relapses

BY EMIL CHIAUZZI

87 percent of my patients.

They also overlooked negative emotions, such as irritability, uncertainty

Baltimore has new way to treat addicts

Methadone cuts will spur crime

Local addicts about to be eliminated

Bend officials weigh pros, cons of needle

Acupuncture helps treat drug addicts, doctors report

Methadone alternative has no high

By Donna Leinwand
USA TODAY

Baltimore officials are launching a plan they hope will change the way thousands of heroin addicts in the city are treated and free up space in local treatment programs for other addicts.

New appetite regulator approved

Addicts would get treatment, not jail

By CHARL

Gamblers overwhelm state treatment program

The Associated Press

PORTLAND — Record number of Oregonians are seeking treatment for gambling addictions, threatening to overflow the free treatment program, officials say.

last year on all forms of gambling — an average of $447 per adult.

About one in four seeking treatment said gambling cost them a marriage or other significant relationship.

Meth addicts fill up 'detox'

INTRODUCTION

"One of the reasons you came into recovery was to get away from your old life. Being in the recovery program must be something that you want and desire; and once you start desiring it, it sets a fire in your heart and in your mind and you start being more productive and being more aware of how your life was and how beautiful your life can be."

46-year-old recovering addict

"Treatment is effective. Scientifically based drug addiction treatments typically reduce drug abuse by 40% to 60%. These rates are not ideal, of course, but they are comparable to compliance rates seen with treatment for other chronic diseases, such as asthma, hypertension, and diabetes. Moreover, treatment markedly reduces undesirable consequences of drug abuse and addiction, such as unemployment, criminal activity, and HIV/AIDS or other infectious diseases, whether or not patients achieve complete abstinence."

Alan I. Leshner, Ph.D., former director, National Institute on Drug Abuse

By 2005 treatment outcomes studies of the Matrix Model and other treatment programs were demonstrating up to 87% one-year continual sobriety rates from treatment of methamphetamine and other drugs, which is a better compliance rate than that obtained from treating most other chronic diseases (Hser, Evans & Huang, 2005).

A DISEASE OF THE BRAIN

Mental illnesses, nervous system diseases, brain tumors, and physical head traumas come to mind when one thinks of pathological conditions of the human mind; but in reality **chemical dependency and addiction are more prevalent than other brain diseases and have a much greater impact on the fabric of society**. For example, from the ages of 18 to 54, the one-year prevalence rate of:

◇ anxiety disorders is 16.4%;

◇ mood disorders (major depression, bipolar disease, and affective disorders) is about 7.1%;

◇ schizophrenia is about 1.3%;

◇ any mental disorder is about 26%

(National Institute of Mental Health, 2007; U.S. Public Health Service, 1999).

This compares with:

◇ **22 million Americans (9.1% of those aged 12 or older) who abused or were dependent on either alcohol or an illicit drug** during the past year (18.6 million on alcohol only, 6.8 million on an illicit drug only, 3.3 million on both alcohol and an illicit drug);

◇ **nicotine addiction that occurs in about 29% of the population over the age of 12;** and

◇ **gambling addiction that affects 2% to 6% of adults**

(Kessler, McGonagle, Zhao, et al., 1994; National Institute on Alcohol Abuse and Alcoholism, 2000; Substance Abuse and Mental Health Services Administration [SAMHSA], 2006A).

Chemical dependency may also be the number one continuing public physical health problem in the United States.

◇ More than 440,000 Americans die prematurely every year due to nicotine addiction (and another 53,000 from secondhand smoke);

◇ another 130,000 die prematurely from alcohol dependence, abuse, overdose, or associated diseases;

◇ 6,000 to 10,000 die of cocaine, heroin, and methamphetamine overdose or dependence;

◇ 35% to 40% of all hospital admissions are related to nicotine-induced health problems; and

◇ 25% of all hospital admissions are related to alcohol-induced health problems

(Centers for Disease Control [CDC], 2001, 2002; SAMHSA, 2006B).

These figures are startling when compared with other major health problems such as AIDS, prostate or breast cancer, and even stroke, many of which are often the result of drug abuse and addiction.

Psychoactive drug abuse also has profound effects on social systems, family relationships, crime, violence, mental health, and a dozen other areas of daily life. Certainly, if we could reduce the impact of addiction, it would have a major affect on the quality of life in the United States and around the world.

CURRENT ISSUES IN TREATMENT

Seven aspects of chemical dependency and behavioral addictions treatment dominate research, clinical practice, and discussion.

1. **There is a rapidly expanding use of medications to treat detoxification, control withdrawal symptoms, reduce craving, and promote short- and long-term abstinence.**
Because addictive use of substances alters brain chemistry, there are increasing efforts to find medications that can correct or lessen the impact of those chemical and structural changes. These include:

◇ **drugs to lessen withdrawal symptoms** (e.g., phenobarbital for alcohol withdrawal and antipsychotics to control stimulant-induced psychosis);

◇ **drugs to lessen craving** (bromocriptine and bupropion for stimulants; naltrexone, buprenorphine, and clonidine for heroin; and naltrexone and acamprosate for alcohol);

◇ **substitute medications that are less damaging** than the primary substance of abuse, including methadone, levomethadyl acetate (LAAM, no longer available in the United States), and, more recently, buprenorphine;

◇ **nutritional supplements** to stimulate neurotransmitter production imbalanced by drug use; and

◇ **antidepressants** to increase serotonin activity and relieve depression and cravings.

2. **Researchers are increasing the use of imaging systems and other new diagnostic techniques to visualize the structural and physiological effects of addiction on the human brain.**
Until the advent of sophisticated imaging techniques, gene identification technologies, and sensitive neurochemical measurement methodologies, addiction was easy to deny because compulsion was considered a behavioral disorder with few if any physical indicators that could be examined. New imaging techniques have **identified multiple brain circuit systems involved in addiction** (e.g., reward, motivation, memory/learning, and control) and have been able to display those changes (Volkow, Fowler & Wang, 2003). Four common imaging techniques are used to examine changes in the central nervous system (CNS) (Meuller, 1999):

◇ **CAT (computerized axial tomography)** scans use X-rays to show structural changes in brain tissues due to drugs.

◇ **MRI (magnetic resonance imaging)** uses the positioning of magnetic nuclei to give two- and three-dimensional images of brain structures in great detail. It can record subtle alterations of brain tissues due to psychoactive drug use or brain anomalies that indicate a susceptibility to drug abuse. For example, an MRI study at the University of Southern California showed a smaller prefrontal cortex (11% smaller on average) in those prone to rage and violence, a diagnostic technique that proved as accurate as psychological testing techniques (Raine, Lencz, Bihrle, et al., 2000). There are variations of MRI techniques, as well: magnetic resonance spectroscopy (31P MRS) measures abnormal brain activity due to chronic drug use, and **fMRI (functional MRI)** records blood flow changes caused by drugs.

◇ **PET (positron emission tomography)** scans use the metabolism of radioactively labeled chemicals that have been injected into the bloodstream to measure glucose metabolism, blood flow, and oxygenation. This visualizes the effects of naturally occurring neurotransmitters that are affected by drugs.

◇ **SPECT (single photon emission computerized tomography)** scans also use radioactive tracers to measure cerebral blood flow and brain metabolism to show how a brain functions (or doesn't function) when using drugs; they are similar to PET scans but are less expensive and easier to use

(Mathias, 1999).

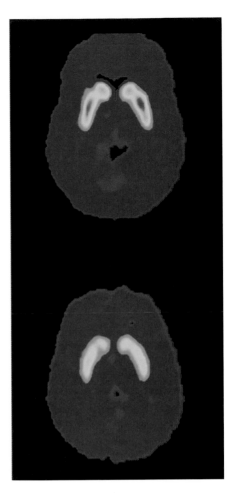

This PET scan imaging project was designed to look for dopamine receptors. It found that extra dopamine receptors added a protective factor to subjects who had a family history of alcoholism. The top scan of a nondrinker with a strong family history of alcoholism shows excess receptors (red and bright yellow). The bottom scan of an alcoholic with no family history of alcoholism shows a shortage of dopamine receptors (dull yellow and no red). This is just one of the many important uses of brain imaging to study addiction.
(Volkow, Wang, Begleiter, et al., 2006)

••••••••••••••••••••••••••••••••••

"There's so much these scans and looking at the brain can offer the field of addiction. We can show children, teenagers, and adults that drugs have an impact on their brains. It's much more powerful than showing them a picture of fried eggs and bacon. It's very helpful when confronting denial to actually sit in front of a computer

screen with somebody who has been using drugs, and they say, 'Oh, there are really no problems.' And you can say, 'Let's look at yours.' And what I've seen—it's really turned many people around."

Daniel Amen, M.D., founder, Amen Clinic for Behavioral Medicine

3. **Development of more-effective tools to diagnose addiction can better match clients to specific treatment interventions.**

Research on questionnaires and techniques that can be used to objectively identify and evaluate the severity of alcohol or other drug-abuse problems have resulted in the validation of several dozen diagnostic tools. These range from simple four-question self-report instruments like the **CAGE test** to the comprehensive 200-item **Addiction/Alcohol Severity Index**. Unquestionably vital for accurate research data, valid diagnostic criteria have become increasingly helpful in matching clients to an appropriate level of treatment interventions that can result in better outcomes and make optimal use of the limited resources available. Possibly the **most widely used** and probably the most practical of these is the **American Society of Addiction Medicine Patient Placement Criteria (ASAM PPC)**. Accurate assessment and placement tools actually provide patient advocacy for appropriate treatment interventions. Utilization of such tools results in individualized, assessment-driven, appropriate, and cost-controlled treatment. As patients progress in recovery, reevaluation of their treatment needs by these assessment tools also provides for flexible use of services across a broad continuum of care (Mee-Lee & Shulman, 2003).

4. **There is an increased emphasis on evidence-based best practices in treatment, with decreased appreciation of practice-based clinical management.**

Driven by the view that substance-abuse treatment has long been based on personal experiences, intuition, particular styles of communication, and even folklore, *evidence-based best practices* has become the new paradigm and buzzword of both substance-abuse

treatment and prevention professionals. **The overall goal of evidence-based practice efforts is to ensure that treatment consistently provides the best potential for positive outcomes.** Because there is a current lack of sufficient treatment resources, evidence-based practices are meant to provide the most cost- and time-effective treatment services. There is no consensus, however, on what constitutes or fully validates an evidence-based practice nor on how much or even what kind of evidence is needed.

A useful understanding of these issues has been offered by the **Iowa Practice Improvement Collaborative** with the development of a **13-point criteria measure for evidence-based practice**:

1. At least one randomized clinical trial has shown the practice to be effective.

2. The practice has demonstrated effectiveness in several replicated research studies using different samples, at least one of which is comparable to the treatment population of the region or agency.

3. The practice either targets behaviors or shows good effect on behaviors that are generally present.

4. The practice can logistically be applied in similar regions and population density areas.

5. The practice is feasible: it can be used in a group format, is attractive to third-party payers, is low cost, and has training available.

6. The practice is manualized or sufficiently operationalized for staff use. Its key components are clearly laid out.

7. The practice is well accepted by providers and clients.

8. The practice is based on a clear and well-articulated theory.

9. The practice has associated methods of ensuring fidelity (consistency of delivery of the treatment over time and not alterable or practiced in different ways by staff over time).

10. The practice can be evaluated.

11. The practice shows good retention rates for clients.

12. The practice addresses cultural diversity and different populations.

13. The practice can be used by staff with a wide diversity of backgrounds and training

(Iowa Practice Improvement Collaborative, 2003).

The Substance Abuse and Mental Health Services Administration (SAMHSA) has created an inventory of recommended prevention and treatment interventions known as the **National Registry of Evidence-Based Programs and Practices (NREPP)**. This registry currently describes more than 160 programs as model, effective, or promising. In the spring of 2006, the NREPP was expanded and revised to include program listings for treatment of mental health as well as addictive disorders (at *www.modelprograms.samhsa.gov*) (National Registry of Evidence-Based Programs and Practices, 2007).

The downside of the increased emphasis on evidence-based best practices is the decreased appreciation of practice-based treatments. Many and especially the most effective of these evidence-based practices were developed and have been in practice long before there was any process for validating them or even before there was such a concept (Alcoholics Anonymous, Narcotics Anonymous, and the 12-step fellowship model). Perhaps there are a vast number of other outstanding practice-based interventions and programs that are yet to be validated and that have no means to do so. It would be a great loss to the recovery field if such programs were abandoned for lack of validation resources.

5. **Increasing research supports coerced treatment (e.g., drug courts) as being just as effective if not more so in promoting positive outcomes as voluntary treatment.**
Coerced treatment is that which comes about through mandated participation via the criminal justice system (CJS) through drug courts, mandatory sentencing, probation/parole stipulations, or state or federal legislation requiring compulsory treatment. Defendants who complete a drug court program can have their charges dis-

missed or probation sentences reduced. **Currently, all 50 states operate drug court programs.** In 2000 about 508 drug courts were operating in the United States, with 281 more in the planning stage. By 2006, 1,753 drug courts were in operation with another 212 in the planning stage (Clay, 2006). Of the more than 100,000 people who had entered drug courts, 50% to 65% graduated or remain active participants. These courts keep felony offenders in treatment at about double the retention rate of community drug programs. Two reasons why, are that there is much closer supervision and there is the threat of incarceration (Belenko, 2001; National Criminal Justice Reference Service, 2007).

Recent findings of the five-year **Drug Treatment Alternative-to-Prison (DTAP) program** in New York uphold several previous studies in demonstrating the effectiveness of coerced-treatment outcomes. The DTAP study demonstrated significant **reductions in the re-arrest rate (33%), reconviction rate (45%), and return-to-prison rate (87%)** compared with prisoners who had not participated in the program. Also 92% of DTAP participants were employed upon completion of the program, whereas only 26% were employed before their arrest (Anglin, Prendergast & Farabee, 1998; National Center on Addiction and Substance Abuse [CASA], 2003). These reports further document **great cost savings from treatment compared with the cost of incarceration for the same length of time.** Such findings combined with the success of drug courts and other initiatives led to the passage of Proposition 36 in California and similar legislation in a number of other states, such as Maryland and New Mexico, that mandated treatment for nonviolent drug-addicted criminal offenders.

The growing number of coerced-treatment initiatives may actually result in an adverse effect on treatment availability. The downturn in the U.S. economy during the early 2000s resulted in the loss of a number of substance-abuse treatment programs. Many treatment slots are currently funded by these new coerced-treatment initiatives and reserved for those involved with the criminal justice system, which fur-

ther **reduces treatment availability for addicts who are not involved with the law** even though some of the legislation says that CJS treatment slots will not replace any non-CJS slots.

6. **There is a lack of resources to provide the treatment that has been proven effective.**
According to one report, **states spend an average of about 13% of their budgets to battle the effects of drug, alcohol, and cigarette abuse** (especially the costs of incarceration, drug courts, and probation for drug offenses). Unfortunately, only 4% of that amount is for treatment and prevention in spite of the fact that many states have done outcome studies to assess the cost-effectiveness of treatment (CASA, 2001). Studies show that **for every $1 spent on treatment, $4 to $39 are saved, mostly in prison costs, lost time on the job, health problems, and extra social services** (Gerstein, Johnson, Harwood, et al., 1994; Hubbard, Craddock & Anderson, 2003). Other research has shown the greatly increased effectiveness of matching treatment modalities to each client's needs (McLellan, Grissom, Zanis, et al., 1997; Nielsen, Nielsen & Wraae, 1998). Finally, studies have shown that the more services such as healthcare, psychological care, and social support that are available, the better the outcome (Fiorentine, 1999). The problem is that because of limited community, state, and federal resources; more reliance on managed care; and a general reluctance to spend money on treatment for drug addicts, **cities, counties, and states cannot provide sufficient treatment even for those who desperately want it**. In San Francisco and Baltimore, two cities where the concept of treatment on demand was seriously studied, waiting lists for treatment slots remain excessively high. In 2003 because of budget cuts, the state of Oregon (through the Oregon Health Plan) stopped paying for drug-abuse treatment programs such as methadone maintenance. Other states are trying to avoid cutting their methadone and drug treatment programs because they know that that would cost more in the long run (Kettler, 2003).

Despite the vast amount of rigorous scientific research validating the effectiveness and the benefits of treating addiction, the number of substance abusers treated remained fairly constant from 1992 (1,527,930 treatment admissions) through 2000 (1,599,703 treatment admissions) in spite of a greater need. For example, national data estimates 12 million to 14 million alcoholics in 2000, of which only about 724,000 received treatment (SAMHSA, 2003). That works out to a mere 5% of the total.

The 2002 National Survey on Drug Use and Health noted that 18.6 million Americans age 12 or older reported needing treatment for alcohol problems; of these only 8% received treatment at a specialized facility. Similarly, 7.7 million persons needed treatment for an illicit-drug problem, and only 18% of those received treatment according to the same survey (Morton & Aleman, 2005; SAMHSA, 2003). When considered in the context of an **actual decrease in national substance-abuse treatment facilities from 15,230 in 1999 to only 13,367 in 2005**, the data clearly validates that there is a continued lack of treatment resources (SAMHSA, 2006C). In addition, coverage by health insurers is rare. Employer-provided health benefits for drug addiction treatment fell 50% to 75% between 1988 and 1998 compared with an 11.5% decline for general health insurance (Galanter, Keller, Dermatis, et al., 2000).

In September 1996 the Mental Health Parity Act was signed into law, but it excluded substance-abuse provisions despite the strong relationship between substance-abuse treatment and mental health care. Several bills have now been introduced in Congress to bring parity to substance-abuse treatment benefits analogous to what has been done for mental health care, but no such legislation has even come close to enactment (Morton & Aleman, 2005).

7. **The conflict between abstinence-oriented recovery and harm reduction as philosophies of treatment continues.**

Most treatment professionals believe that users who have crossed the line into uncontrolled use of drugs or compulsive behaviors can refuse the first drink, injection, or bet but find it increasingly difficult to refuse the second. These treatment personnel believe that abstinence is absolutely necessary for recovery because the very definition of addiction is based on the concept of loss of control. In various studies **the Haight Ashbury Free Clinics found that when a client slipped (e.g., had a drink, took one hit, or smoked one cigarette), it turned into a full relapse in 95% of the cases** (O'Malley, Jaffe, Chang, et al., 1992). The full relapse might take an hour, a day, a month, or occasionally longer to reoccur, but in 19 out of 20 users who have crossed the line into addiction, it will eventually happen. Even in 1879 a recovering alcoholic and temperance lecturer, Luther Bensen, was aware of his susceptibility to uncontrolled use:

"Moderation? A drink of liquor is to my appetite what a red-hot poker is to a keg of dry powder.... When I take one drink, even if it is but a taste, I must have more, even if I knew hell would burst out of the earth and engulf me the next instant."

Luther Bensen (Bensen, 1879)

Conversely, there is a growing group of drug-abuse treatment personnel who believe that harm reduction is a viable treatment alternative. The problem with evaluating the effectiveness of harm reduction is that it means different things to different groups. One definition of harm reduction is "a willingness to work for incremental changes rather than to require complete behavior change" (Morris, 1995). Another is "any steps taken by drug users to reduce the harm of their behavior" (Marlatt, 1995; Marlatt & Tapert, 1993).

Harm reduction includes:

◇ **drug replacement therapy** (such as methadone maintenance instead of heroin use or methylphenidate maintenance instead of cocaine use);

◇ **needle exchange**, safe injecting sites, and naloxone distribution to opiate addicts;

◇ **designated nondrinking/non-drug-using driver** and wet hostels or sobering stations;

◇ **the substitution of "less harmful" drugs for "more harmful" ones** (e.g., marijuana instead of heroin);

◇ **testing illegal drugs for users** so they don't use a dangerous misrepresented substance or additive;

◇ **drug decriminalization/legalization** through legislation; and

◇ the most controversial technique, **controlled drinking/drug use through behavior modification**.

Numerous studies have been done on controlled drinking, and again the problem is definitions that obscure reported data. What constitutes controlled drinking? Was the patient an alcoholic or a problem drinker before starting treatment? Is the patient's self-reporting of the amount being drunk and the consequences accurate (Peele, 1995)? **Long-term follow-up strongly suggests that true controlled drinking does not work** (Bottlender, Spanagel & Soyka, 2007; Vaillant, 1995). For some, harm reduction consists of individual techniques that will help advance the addict to full (abstinent) recovery; to others, harm reduction is an all-encompassing philosophy of treatment and drug use.

Finally, it is **difficult to measure treatment outcome**. Is it measured in days of abstinence, amount of drug used, reduction in hospital visits, improvement in marital and other relationships, or amount of money saved by society? This lack of consensus can further aggravate the argument (Drucker, Nadelmann, Newman, et al., 2005).

More on Abstinence vs. Harm Reduction (temperance, to abstinence, to prohibition)

In his excellent book *Slaying the Dragon*, on the history of addiction treatment in the United States, William White shows that this controversy has been around for at least 235 years. The Temperance movement started at the end of the eighteenth century as America emerged from its revolution against England and coincidentally changed its drinking habits. From 1792 to 1830, per-capita consumption went from 2.5 gallons of pure alcohol per year to an unbelievable 7.1 gallons, or two standard drinks for every man, woman, and child every day of the year

(Cherrington, 1920). (In 2004 per-capita consumption was back down to 2.23 gallons.) **The initial goal of the Temperance movement was just to limit the amount drunk, but as consumption and public drunkenness increased that goal shifted from temperance to abstinence**, that is, complete avoidance by the alcoholic of any and all alcoholic beverages (White, 1998). Even then many people thought of alcoholism as a disease.

"The remedy we would suggest, particularly to those whose appetite for drink is strong and increasing, is a total abstinence from the use of all intoxicating liquors. This may be deemed a harsh remedy, but the nature of the disease absolutely requires it."

From an 1811 temperance pamphlet (Dascus, 1877)

A large segment of the **Temperance movement then expanded the goal to make society as a whole abstinent (Prohibition)**, not just those who couldn't limit their consumption. This way alcohol would simply not be available, at least not legally.

"Our main object is not to reform inebriates, but to induce all temperate people to continue temperance, by practicing total abstinence. The drunkards, if not reformed, will die, and the land be free."

Dr. Justin Edwards, 1824 (Dorchester, 1884)

This shift from simply treating the addict to reforming society confused the perception of the problem of how to treat alcoholism and addiction. The question became, **"Should a substance that triggers uncontrolled harmful use in 5% to 10% of the population (25% to 50% for tobacco) be banned, permitted, or controlled?"** In wanting to allow controlled use of a psychoactive substance by those with a substance-abuse problem, some advocates of harm reduction ignore the nature of addiction.

"Most of us have been unwilling to admit we were real alcoholics. No person likes to think he is bodily and mentally different from his fellows. Therefore, it is not surprising that our drinking careers have been

characterized by countless vain attempts to prove we could drink like other people. The idea that somehow, someday he will control and enjoy his drinking is the great obsession of every abnormal drinker. The persistence of this illusion is astonishing. Many pursue it into the gates of insanity or death."

Alcoholics Anonymous Big Book (Alcoholics Anonymous [AA], 1934, 1976)

Conversely some advocates of abstinence and/or prohibition overreact to any use of a psychoactive substance, even in the 90% of the population with a lower susceptibility to uncontrolled use. In many of the arguments on the subject, **both sides confuse ideas about the effectiveness of abstinence-based treatment and effective harm reduction techniques with arguments about freedom, politics, and morality.**

The recent advocacy of harm reduction started in the late 1980s and early 1990s in response to the inaccessibility of treatment to many segments of society (e.g., those infected with the HIV virus, hepatitis C, and other diseases who continued to spread the infections or reinfect themselves through dirty needles, contaminated drugs, and unsafe sex). **Needle-exchange programs, free condoms, food incentives, and social service referral information enabled outreach workers to come in contact with homeless street kids, illicit-drug users, prostitutes, and others living on the fringes of society to engage them in prevention efforts** that would slow the spread of these diseases. The contact also gave the outreach workers an opportunity to engage them in drug treatment or, at the very least, increase their awareness of drug abuse and addiction.

The harm reduction workers were willing to accept small changes in drug use status to protect the addict and society from further infection. As in the past, **the harm reduction concept became an end in itself for certain treatment personnel rather than a transitory step for clients on the way to abstinence and full recovery**. Interest in harm reduction also

Patients at a Keeley Institute who were addicted to alcohol and other drugs would go for a four-week cure. Part of the treatment was daily injections of a secret formula to help subdue the pains of withdrawal and keep the patient in treatment. Though the formula was kept secret, various laboratories suggested that the medicine contained a number of ingredients, some of which were psychoactive. These included alcohol, strychnine, willow bark, ginger, ammonia, belladonna, atropine, hyoscine, scopolamine, coca, opium, and morphine.

Courtesy of the Keeley Collection. © 2000 Illinois State Historical Library.

came from healthcare insurers and managed care systems that saw it as a more economical way to cover their obligations to provide treatment for chemical dependency problems (Morris, 1995).

One item that has added to the controversy surrounding harm reduction is confusion about the difference between abuse and addiction. The key is that there is a qualitative difference between those two levels of drug use, not just a quantitative difference. **Many of the successes of harm reduction have been in users who had not crossed that line into loss of control that is the hallmark of addiction**, so harm reduction in some of those cases was sustainable. But even there, because addiction is a progressive disease and intensifies with use, continued abuse will often become addiction. **Many treatment centers effectively employ an abstinence-based philosophy of treatment that also incorporates many harm reduction techniques.** The rest of this chapter reflects that philosophy.

TREATMENT EFFECTIVENESS

Even though chemical dependency is the number one health and social problem in the United States and possibly the world, it is also the most treatable. Several studies have confirmed that **treatment outcomes for drug and alcohol abuse result in long-term abstinence along with tremendous health, social, and spiritual benefits to the patient.**

"Everything that I am and everything that I have in me is invested in what I'm doing today in recovery— everything."
56-year-old recovering heroin addict

What is often overlooked when local, state, and federal governments vote on how much money should be allotted for treatment is the undeniable fact that treatment saves money—large sums of money (Figure 9-1).

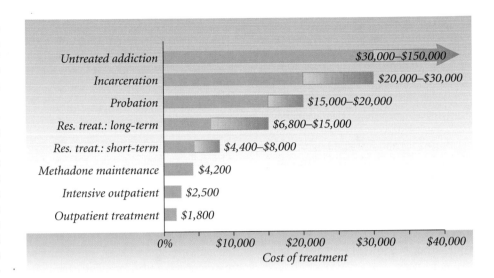

Figure 9-1 •
The cost of treatment for an addict utilizing outpatient treatment is less than one-tenth the cost of incarceration.
(Estimates by authors)

TREATMENT STUDIES

California Drug and Alcohol Treatment Assessment Study

Studies conducted by the Rand Corporation and the Research Triangle Institute support the findings of the California Drug and Alcohol Treatment Assessment (CALDATA) Study, the most comprehensive and rigorous study on treatment outcome conducted by the state of California and duplicated by several other states. All of these studies monitored the effect of treatment on several hundred thousand addicts and alcoholics in a variety of programs.

The CALDATA Study monitored 1,850 individuals for three to five years following treatment. Continuous abstinence in these patients approached 50% of all those treated. It further demonstrated that crime was abated in 74% of those treated and that **the state enjoyed actual savings of $7 for every $1 spent on treatment**. For more-expensive programs, there was a savings of $4, and for the inexpensive programs the savings were $12. California spent $209 million on treatment between October 1991 and September 1992 and saved an estimated $1.5 billion, much due to crime reduction and reduced use of healthcare facilities. The

only downside was that those in recovery lost income while undergoing treatment and their financial condition did not improve immediately afterward. The study also looked at a number of variables that, when examined, supported many concepts and practices in the treatment field.

◇ **Treatment was most effective when patients were treated continuously for at least six to eight months.**

◇ Shorter periods of time resulted in poorer outcomes, whereas longer treatment duration resulted in better outcomes. There was a point of diminishing returns.

◇ **Group therapy was shown to be much more effective than individual therapy.**

◇ **Drug of choice also seemed to affect outcomes.** For example, those who listed alcohol as their primary drug of choice had treatment outcomes twice as effective as those who listed heroin. Cocaine users' outcomes fell between those two drugs.

◇ **Better treatment outcomes were linked to program modifications directed at being culturally consistent with a specific target**

population. For example, programs that targeted women and added child care services to their treatment programs had much better outcomes than generic treatment programs for women. Those programs that added transportation services had better outcomes than those that had just child care. Every additional innovation that was target-group specific improved the outcome of treatment (Gerstein, Datta, Ingels, et al., 1997; Mecca, 1997).

Drug Abuse Treatment Outcome Study

Another study of the effectiveness of treatment, the Drug Abuse Treatment Outcome Study (DATOS), tracked 10,010 drug abusers in 100 treatment facilities in 11 cities, who began treatment from 1991 to 1993. The study compared pre- and post-treatment drug use, criminal activity, employment, and thoughts of suicide (Hubbard, Craddock & Anderson, 2003). The four common types of drug-abuse treatment studied were outpatient methadone programs, long-term (several months) residential programs, short-term (up to 30 days) inpatient programs, and outpatient drug-free programs. Researchers found that **the use of all drugs after treatment was reduced 50% to 70%.** The final level of drug use after treatment was about the same for all four programs. **Short- and long-term residential programs seemed to have the greatest effect.** As expected, low retention rates were most prevalent in clients with greater problems (Meuller & Wyman, 1997). Unfortunately, most patients said they did not receive the services they thought they needed. The study also found a decrease in the number of services offered over the past decade (Etheridge, Craddock, Dunteman, et al., 1995).

Treatment Episode Data Sets

To supply **descriptive information about the flow of admissions to substance-abuse treatment providers,** the Treatment Episode Data Sets (TEDS) survey, part of the Drug and Alcohol Services Information System (DASIS), collects data from all 50 states, the District of Columbia, and Puerto Rico. The information is available through publications or online at *http://www.dasis. samhsa.gov/teds05/tedshi2k5_web.pdf.*

National Survey of Substance Abuse Treatment Services

The National Survey of Substance Abuse Treatment Services (N-SSATS) is an annual **survey of all drug treatment facilities in the United States, public and private**. Unlike the TEDS survey, which focuses on the clients who enter treatment, the N-SSATS examines the facilities themselves and their assessment services, continuing care, transitional services, community outreach, and other services. It is available in publications or online at *http://www. oas.samhsa.gov/DASIS/2k5nssats.cfm.*

Treatment Research Institute, University of Pennsylvania

Economic Benefits of Drug Treatment: A Critical Review of the Evidence for Policy Makers, released in February 2005, validates cost-effectiveness of substance-abuse treatment. This meta-analysis of more than 1,000 addiction treatment outcome studies conducted over nearly two decades documented cost savings ranging from 33¢ to $39 for every $1 spent in all studies analyzed. Meta-analysis is a systematic evaluation of a number of individual studies for the purpose of integrating the findings. None of the studies evaluated in this meta-analysis could document any loss from money invested in drug-abuse treatment. The main economic benefit recognized by this major study occurred from decreased crime (including incarceration and victimization costs) and post-treatment reduction in healthcare costs (Belenko, Patapis & French, 2005).

TREATMENT & PRISONS

On December 31, 2005:

◊ **2,193,798 Americans were in federal, state, and local prisons (11% of whom were women)** and

◊ **more than 5 million were on parole or probation**

(U.S. Department of Justice [DOJ], 2006B).

In addition:

◊ **about 57% of federal inmates and 20% of state inmates were serving a sentence for a drug offense;** 11.5% were arrested for a drug-abuse violation (about 1.6 million arrests, 1.2 million for possession);

◊ **40% to 65% committed their crime while under the influence of alcohol or drugs;**

◊ of those on probation, 24% were for a drug law violation and 17% were for driving while intoxicated; and

◊ average time served increased from 22 months to 27 months

(DOJ, 2006B).

The percentage of arrestees testing positive for drugs (not including alcohol) is many times higher than the percentage of drug use in the general population. Despite the high percentage of drug problems among the inmate population, **treatment slots are available for only about 10% of those who have serious drug habits,** although 94% of federal prisons, 56% of state prisons, and 33% of jails provide some on-site substance-abuse treatment to inmates (DOJ, 2006B; SAMHSA, 2000). Various studies of inmate populations with drug problems found that a comparatively low percentage have had contact with the treatment community. There are more programs in prisons than in jails (Peters, Matthews & Dvoskin, 2005).

By 2005, 6.9 million adults were involved with the criminal justice system; 5 million of these were under probation or parole supervision, the rest incarcerated (DOJ, 2007). The Bureau of Justice Statistics estimated that about 70% of state and 57% of federal prisoners used drugs regularly prior to incarceration (National Institute on Drug Abuse [NIDA], 2006). In 2002, 52% of incarcerated women and 44% of incarcerated men met the criteria for alcohol or drug dependence (Karberg & James, 2005). A survey of juvenile detainees found that 56% of boys and 40% of girls tested positive for drug use at the time of their arrest (DOJ, 2006A).

Earlier studies of prisoners and those involved with the CJS have shown that **drug-abuse treatment re-**

duces recidivism dramatically when the treatment is linked to community services rather than strictly in-jail services (DOJ, 2003). Because the cost of keeping a felon in jail runs between $25,000 and $40,000 per year (not including assistance for the felon's family, compensation for human and property damage, and a dozen other liabilities), the savings for keeping people out of prison are significant. In contrast, outpatient treatment costs between $1,800 and $4,000 per year, depending on the treatment approach (Office of National Drug Control Policy, 2001).

Despite the plethora of data demonstrating a high incidence of CJS participants having drug or alcohol problems and the effectiveness of treatment, the Bureau of Justice Statistics reported that **fewer than 17% of incarcerated offenders with drug problems had received treatment while in prison**. About 50% had received treatment while under any correctional supervision (jail, probation, parole) (DOJ, 2005).

"In California during the early nineties, we built nine new prisons, but we built no new universities and actually suffered a decrease in drug treatment slots due to reduced funding. Yet 80% to 85% of our prisoners listed a drug problem as a major reason for their offense. I think we have our priorities backward."
California education consultant

PRINCIPLES & GOALS OF TREATMENT

PRINCIPLES OF EFFECTIVE TREATMENT

In a 1999 publication by the National Institutes of Health (NIH), *Principles of Drug Addiction Treatment,* 13 principles of effective treatment were listed. These are applicable to any treatment facility, program, or therapy:

1. **No single treatment is appropriate for all individuals.** Matching treatment settings, interventions, and services to each individual's particular problems and needs is critical to his or her ultimate success in returning to productive functioning in the family, the workplace, and society.

2. **Treatment needs to be readily available.** Because individuals who are addicted to drugs may be uncertain about entering treatment, taking advantage of opportunities when they are ready for treatment is crucial. Potential applicants can be lost if treatment is not immediately available or readily accessible.

3. **Effective treatment attends to multiple needs of the individual, not just his or her drug use.**

4. **An individual's treatment and services plan must be assessed continually** and modified as necessary to ensure that the plan meets the person's changing needs.

5. **Remaining in treatment for an adequate period of time is critical for treatment effectiveness.** Research indicates that for most patients the threshold of significant improvement is reached at about three months in treatment.

6. **Counseling (individual and/or group) and other behavioral therapies are critical components of effective treatment for addiction.**

7. **Medications are an important element of treatment for many patients**, especially when combined with counseling and other behavioral therapies. Methadone, LAAM, naltrexone, bupropion, and a number of other medications can help with detoxification as well as short- and long-term abstinence. In 2002 the use of LAAM was associated with cardiac arrhythmias, so it is subsequently not being used as much as buprenorphine combined with naloxone (Suboxone®) for the treatment of opiate addiction (Schwetz, 2001).

8. **Addicted or drug-abusing individuals with coexisting mental disorders should have both disorders treated in an integrated way.**

9. **Detoxification is only the first stage of addiction treatment and by itself does little to change long-term drug use.**

10. **Treatment need not be voluntary to be effective.** Sanctions or enticements in the family, employment setting, or CJS can

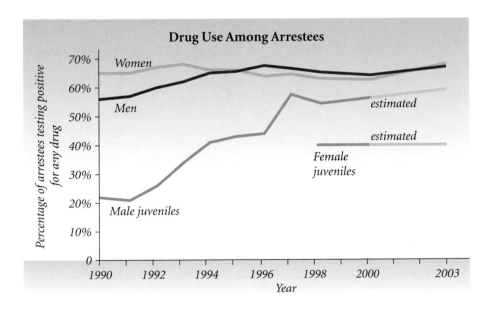

Drug Use Among Arrestees

Women
Men
Male juveniles
estimated
estimated
Female juveniles

Percentage of arrestees testing positive for any drug

70%
60%
50%
40%
30%
20%
10%
0

1990 1992 1994 1996 1998 2000 2003
Year

Figure 9-2 •

Testing at jails and prisons is for illicit drugs and excludes alcohol. Besides alcohol the most common drugs found in arrestees are marijuana and cocaine.

(Arrestee Drug Abuse Monitoring Program, 2006)

significantly increase both treatment entry and retention rates and the success of drug treatment interventions.

11. **Possible drug use during treatment must be monitored continuously.** The objective monitoring of a patient's drug and alcohol use during treatment, such as through urinalysis or other tests, can help the patient withstand urges to use drugs.

12. **Treatment programs should provide assessment for HIV/AIDS, hepatitis B and C, tuberculosis, and other infectious diseases as well as counseling to help patients modify or change behaviors that place themselves or others at risk of infection.**

13. **Recovery from drug addiction can be a long-term process and frequently requires multiple episodes of treatment.** Participation in self-help programs during and following treatment is often helpful in maintaining abstinence.

(National Institute on Drug Abuse, 1999).

The problem is that **fully implementing most of the concepts is costly.** Many local, state, and federal governments and healthcare systems are unable or reluctant to commit the necessary funds to provide a full range of services.

PRINCIPLES OF DRUG-ABUSE TREATMENT FOR CJS POPULATIONS

More than 30 years of research by the National Institute on Drug Abuse (NIDA) on drug-abuse treatment for individuals involved with the CJS (criminal justice system) has yielded a similar set of 13 principles, which was established in July 2006:

1. **Drug addiction is a brain disease that affects behavior.**

2. **Recovery from drug addiction requires effective treatment** followed by management of the problem over time.

3. **Treatment must last long enough to produce stable behavioral changes.**

4. **Assessment is the first step in treatment.**

5. **Tailoring services to fit the needs** of the individual is an important part of effective drug-abuse treatment for the CJS population.

6. **Drug use during treatment should be carefully monitored with drug testing.**

7. Treatment should target factors that are associated with criminal behavior, such as attitudes and beliefs that support a criminal lifestyle and behavior ("criminal thinking").

8. CJS supervision should **incorporate treatment planning** for drug-abusing offenders, and treatment providers should be aware of correctional supervision requirements.

9. **Continuity of care is essential** for drug abusers reentering the community.

10. **A balance of rewards and sanctions** encourages prosocial behavior and treatment participation.

11. Offenders with co-occurring drug-abuse and mental health problems often require an integrated treatment approach.

12. **Medications are an important part of treatment** for many drug-abusing offenders.

13. Treatment planning for drug-abusing offenders who are living in or reentering the community should **include strategies to prevent and treat serious, chronic medical conditions** such as HIV/AIDS, hepatitis B and C, and tuberculosis (NIDA, 2006).

Drug-abuse treatment for CJS populations continues to expand, fueled by successes of the drug court and state-mandated sentencing alternatives. A specific set of treatment principles targeted for CJS participants is beneficial and culturally relevant as the unique needs of this population continues to be identified.

GOALS OF EFFECTIVE TREATMENT

Most treatment experts agree that the two most important goals for treatment outcome are, first, to motivate clients toward abstinence from their drugs of abuse and, second, to reconstruct their lives once their focus is redirected away from substance abuse. Integrating harm reduction into these goals would mean the willingness to accept incremental behavioral changes that reduce the harm that addiction is causing.

To accomplish these and other goals, several elements need to be addressed through an understanding that **addiction treatment is a lifelong process for the addict.** Treatment merely motivates, initiates, and provides some tools that help addicts ultimately obtain uninterrupted abstinence from their addiction throughout their lives.

"Well, basically, I'd like to stay off drugs. I'd like to get my family life together again and have a relationship with my children—a good one—and, if nothing else, I'd just like to know that when I do die, I did have a life, you know, aside from being just another dope fiend in the gutter."
34-year-old recovering crack addict, mother of three

Primary Goals

Motivation Toward Abstinence. Components of these efforts consist of education, counseling, and involvement with 12-step or self-help programs. This might include harm reduction approaches like methadone maintenance, whereby an addict is provided with an alternate medically controlled drug to promote abstinence from the street drug of choice.

Creating a Drug-Free Lifestyle. This covers all aspects of an addict's life, including the ability to address social/environmental issues, like homelessness, relationships, family, and friends, to develop drug-free life interactions. Addicts are connected to drug-free activities such as clean-and-sober dances or camping; and, most important, they learn relapse prevention skills such as stress reduction, cue resistance, coping, decision-making, and conflict resolution.

Supporting Goals

Enriching Job or Career Functioning. Often neglected in treatment, job and career constitute a major portion of someone's life. This goal is accomplished through vocational services, management of personal finances, and maintenance of a drug-free workplace.

Optimizing Medical Functioning. Besides treatment of withdrawal and other acute medical problems associated with addiction, many addicts have undiagnosed or existing medical problems that have been neglected through their use of drugs. The comprehensive treatment program includes the ability to assess and treat such conditions.

Optimizing Psychiatric & Emotional Functioning. Many studies suggest that greater than 50% of all substance abusers also have a coexisting psychiatric condition. Identification and appropriate treatment of psychiatric problems are essential elements of the modern treatment program (*see Chapter 10*).

Addressing Relevant Spiritual Issues. Although the inclusion of spirituality or religious beliefs in addiction treatment is controversial, the most effective long-term treatments of addiction are the spiritually based 12-step Alcoholics Anonymous (AA) and other anonymous programs. Many other treatment programs in operation base their interventions on the 12-step traditions. Thus it has become essential for programs to at least help clarify this issue with their clients and provide appropriate referrals (Schuckit, 1994, 2000). A large number of empirical studies demonstrate a 60% to 80% correlation of better addiction treatment outcome to spiritual participation (Carter, 1998; Sterling, Weinstein, Losardo, et al., 2007).

"I don't have hopes of living forever. I never have. I mean, to be my age is a complete shock to me, so it's not about that; the issue is about the quality of life."

40-year-old recovering heroin addict

SELECTION OF A PROGRAM

Most program selections occur spontaneously based on cost, familiarity, location, and convenience of access. The current era of managed healthcare has made accurate diagnoses and pretreatment assessments essential to validate the least intrusive yet appropriate level of treatment that promotes better health and recovery. **Acceptable evidence-based assessment tools are now mandated to match addicts to an appropriate level of care** at treatment programs with evidence-based treatment interventions to qualify for insurance or even publicly funded reimbursement for the services provided.

DIAGNOSIS

Various diagnostic tools can be used to help verify, support, or clarify the potential diagnosis of chemical addiction (Lewis, Dana & Blevins, 2001; Winters, 2003). The following are some of the more common ones used.

◇ The **American Psychiatric Association's** *Diagnostic and Statistical Manual of Mental Disorders (DSM-IV-TR)* delineates substance use from substance-induced disorders. Use is divided into substance abuse and dependence, which relies on the pattern and the duration of drug use and descriptions of negative impacts on social or occupational functioning to determine abuse. Pathological effects of tolerance or withdrawal symptoms confirm a diagnosis of dependence (American Psychiatric Association [APA], 2000).

◇ The **Selective Severity Assessment (SSA)** evaluates 11 physiologic signs (e.g., pulse, temperature, and tremors) to confirm the severity of the addict's addiction.

◇ The **National Council on Alcoholism Criteria for Diagnosis of Alcoholism (NCA CRIT)** and its **Modified Criteria (MOD-CRIT)** assesses 35 items through a structured interview to outline two bases on which to make the diagnosis of alcoholism:

- physical and clinical parameters, and
- behavioral, psychological, and attitudinal impact.

◇ The **Addiction Severity Index (ASI)** represents **the most comprehensive and lengthy criteria** for the diagnosis of chemical dependency; 200 items cover six areas that are affected by substance use and abuse. There is also ASI-Lite (a shortened version of the ASI with 22 fewer questions) and T-ASI, which is modified for the assessment of teen drug use.

◇ The **Michigan Alcoholism Screening Test (MAST)**, a simple diagnostic aid, uses just 25 yes/no questions that are primarily directed at the negative life effects of alcohol on the user (*see Chapter 5*). There is also the Brief Michigan Alcohol Screening Test (B-MAST), with just 10 questions, as well as various other modifications: the MAST/AD screens for alcohol and drugs; the M-SAPS is a substance-abuse problem scale; and the SMAST-G is a short version of MAST for geriatric assessment.

◇ The **CAGE Questionnaire** is the simplest assessment tool for problem drinking and consists of just four questions:
  1. Have you felt the need to **c**ut down on your drinking?
  2. Do you feel **a**nnoyed by people complaining about your drinking?
  3. Do you ever feel **g**uilty about your drinking?
  4. Do you ever drink an **e**ye-opener in the morning to relieve the shakes?

  Two or more affirmative responses suggest that the client is a problem drinker (Allen, Eckardt & Wallen, 1988).

◇ **AUDIT** = 10-item screen: frequency, daily amount, incidence of six or more drinks, inability to stop, inability to fulfill normal expectations, eye-opener, guilt/remorse, blackouts/brownouts, suffered or injured someone while drinking, and others suggest moderating your drinking. A score of 8 or more indicates hazardous drinking.

◇ **CRAFFT** = driving a **c**ar while high, use to **r**elax, use **a**lone, **f**orget things while high, family and/or friends ask you to cut down, and have gotten into trouble while on alcohol or drugs.

◇ **RAPS4** (Rapid Alcohol Assessment Screen) = four items: guilt, blackouts, failing normal expectations, and eye-opener.

◇ **SAAST** (Self-Administered Alcoholism Screening Test) = 35 yes/no questions.

◇ **T-ACE** = tolerance, annoyed, cut down, and eye-opener.

◇ **TWEAK** = tolerance (just begin to feel drug effects after three or more drinks or hits, able to hold six or more drinks or hits) = 2; worried = 2; eye-opener = 1; amnesia = 1; kut down = 1. A score of 3 or more indicates a problem.

◇ **DAST** (Drug Abuse Screening Test), a five-minute, 20-item scale that can be used for screening, treatment planning, and post-treatment outcome evaluation. The DAST assesses the consequences of drug use and has been validated against the DSM-III and DSM-IV diagnostic criteria.

◇ **PESQ** (Personal Experience Screening Questionnaire), targeted for adolescents, has 18 questions, takes 25 minutes, and screens for both drugs and alcohol. It examines problem onset, psychological and social functioning, problem severity, and frequency of use, and it can detect "faking."

◇ **4P's Plus** was developed by Dr. Ira Chasnoff of the Children's Research Triangle in Chicago, Illinois. It is being proffered as a universal prescreening tool of all pregnancies for potential alcohol/nicotine, substance-abuse, and domestic-violence problems. The P questions evaluate: **p**arental history of alcohol or drug problems; **p**artner's use of alcohol or drugs; **p**ast personal history of alcohol use; and use of either tobacco or alcohol during the month preceding **p**regnancy (also validated for 28 days after delivery). Any use of tobacco or alcohol 30 days before pregnancy or within 28 days after delivery indicates the need for further assessment or intervention.

◇ **ASAM PPC-2R (American Society of Addiction Medicine Patient Placement Criteria Revised)** is designed to address co-occurring disorders, adolescent criteria, and residential levels of care. **It evaluates six dimensions of problem areas and illness severity**:
1. acute intoxication/withdrawal potential;
2. biomedical conditions and complications;
3. emotional, behavioral, or cognitive conditions and complications;
4. readiness to change;
5. relapse, continued use, or continued problem potential; and
6. recovery environment.

to match patients to four levels of care:
1. outpatient treatment;
2. intensive outpatient/partial hospitalization;
3. residential/inpatient treatment; and
4. medically managed intensive inpatient treatment.

As patients progress in their recovery treatment efforts, the assessment can be redone to move them into different levels of care that match their current needs.

Though time-consuming, the ASAM PPC-2R provides the most accurate and acceptable evaluation for the insurance and third-party payment industries. It also provides an effective way to match substance abusers to the appropriate yet least intrusive level of treatment that promotes better health and recovery.

TREATMENT OPTIONS

"Let the experiment be fairly tried; let an institution be founded; let the means of cure be provided; let the principles on which it is to be founded be extensively promulgated and, I doubt not, all intelligent people will be satisfied of its feasibility; . . . let the principle of total abstinence be rigorously adopted and enforced; . . . let appropriate medication be afforded; . . . let the mind be soothed; . . . let good nutrition be regularly administered—this course, rigorously

The U.S. government's attitude toward most treatment methods at the end of World War I limited the facilities available for addicts. In 1929 the government allocated funds for two "narcotics farms" to house and rehabilitate addicts who had been convicted of violating federal drug laws or those who wished to commit themselves voluntarily. The Lexington, Kentucky, Narcotics Farm opened in 1935; the second facility, in Fort Worth, Texas, opened in November 1938. The Lexington facility shown in this picture had about 1,000 inmates. Treatment could last up to a year or more. A study of effectiveness showed that 90% to 96% of addicts returned to active addiction, most within six months of discharge.
Courtesy of the U.S. Department of Health and Human Services Program Support Center (White, 1998)

adopted and pursued, will restore nine out of 10 in all cases."

Dr. Samuel Woodward, 1833 (Grinrod, 1840, 1886)

A nineteenth-century expert on mental health, Dr. Samuel Woodward thought that society should support recovery because addiction is a complex interaction among social, biological, and toxic factors. Given these multiple influences, treatment has evolved along various paths, all of which enjoy some success. Because each person is unique and the level of addiction different, however, **no treatment has proven to be universally effective for everyone**. Often, effective treatment requires a variety of techniques in a number of settings.

"Someone asked me, 'Where would you go to get off drugs? Where would you feel comfortable?' If I had everything I needed, lifetime supplies, and I was shipwrecked on an island, that would be fine."

22-year-old recovering methamphetamine abuser

A wide range of options exists for the treatment of alcohol or other chemical addiction. The range is:

◇ from "cold turkey" or "white knuckle" dry-outs to medically assisted detoxification;

◇ from expensive medical or residential approaches to free peer groups, 12-step programs, or social model group therapy;

◇ from outpatient treatment, to halfway houses, to residential programs;

◇ from long-term residential treatment (two years or more) to seven-day hospital detoxification with aftercare; and

◇ from methadone maintenance, replacement therapies, or other harm reduction techniques to acupuncture, aversion therapies, or a dozen other treatment modalities.

"I believed there were only AA and NA [Narcotics Anonymous] for my 'crank' use and I knew—I just knew these wouldn't work. Then after a

particularly nasty run, which I thought I kept from my probation officer, he gave me a choice of getting into treatment or going back to prison. I was startled when he handed me a full-page list of different places I could go. There was a medical program. There was an NA program made up of speed freaks like myself. There was a mental health program near my apartment. There were places I could go to live while kicking. The only problem was waiting for an open slot."

35-year-old recovering "crank" addict

In many studies on the effectiveness of different types of programs, the process of treatment self-selection is sometimes forgotten. This means that **addicts will often end up in a program that works and drop out of those that feel uncomfortable, are not relevant to their problem, or that they are not ready for** based on the stage of their addiction. So a statistic might read, "this program is effective for only 10% of all addicts," and that's true as far as it goes. However, it could read, "this type of program works for 10% of the addicted population, and luckily there are a dozen other programs and if each one is effective with only 10% of the population, we can offer recovery to most addicts." It also means that we can't put all treatment hopes in just one type of therapy, be it drug replacement therapy, motivational interviewing, a therapeutic community, or 12-step programs. A simile would be that treatment for a heart condition could be diet change, coronary artery bypass, angioplasty, or, in the extreme, a heart transplant.

Types of Facilities

Medical model detoxification programs can be inpatient, residential, or outpatient. The treatment in such programs is **supervised and managed by medical professionals**. **Medications can be administered** in conjunction with traditional recovery-oriented counseling and educational approaches. These are usually the **most expensive types of programs**, but they

have the advantage of being able to do a more comprehensive assessment and treatment of the addict's overall physical and mental health. Inpatient medical model programs can cost $3,000 to $25,000, depending on the length of stay (three to 28 days) and the amenities provided. Outpatient medical model programs range from $1,500 to $5,000, depending primarily on the length of treatment (one to six months).

Residential/inpatient treatment is generally short-term (one to 28 days) and can be either **medically supervised** (ASAM Level III) or **medically managed** (ASAM Level IV). This consists of intensive counseling, drug education, and other recovery activities while clients are housed in the facility at all times (Mee-Lee & Shulman, 2003).

Partial hospitalization and day treatment are outpatient medical model programs that involve the client in therapeutic activities for four to six hours per day while the client lives at home. ASAM Placement Criteria require that clients participate in a minimum of 20 hours per week in a structured program to meet this level of treatment (Mee-Lee & Shulman, 2003). These programs provide medical services for detoxification and for medically assisted recovery with medications that treat withdrawal symptoms, modify craving, or help prevent relapse. Counseling and drug education are part of these programs. **Intensive outpatient programs** (six- to eight-hour-per-week) are a modification of this model.

Methadone maintenance and other replacement therapies are also considered outpatient medical model programs. **Methadone maintenance costs $4,000 to $6,000 per year** (Barnett, 1999; O'Donnell & Trick, 2006). Buprenorphine in the form of Suboxone® is becoming an alternate form of replacement therapy for opioid addiction. In 2006 a month's supply of Suboxone® at a dose of 16 milligrams (mg) per day cost about $287.50. Thus the price of Suboxone® alone would be about $3,480 per year; then one would have to factor in the medical and clinical costs of providing this form of therapy, which would result in a much greater cost than methadone maintenance.

Office-based medical detoxification and maintenance treatment for

opiate abusers can now be provided by qualified private medical practitioners. The Food and Drug Administration (FDA) approved the Drug Addiction Treatment Act of 2000, which legalized the prescribing to opiate addicts of Schedule III, IV, and V controlled substances by physicians specially certified with the Drug Enforcement Administration (DEA). Prior to the new law, controlled substances for the treatment of addiction were restricted to registered clinics. This restriction threatened the confidentiality of treatment because anyone seen at such a facility could be assumed to be an addict. It also exposed patients to other drug users and often required undue travel by many addicts. Although physicians must undergo special training to become certified to treat addicts in their offices, there is some concern that medical treatment detached from immediate, on-site counseling, education, social, and other services for addicts will be ineffective in promoting recovery. **This new type of treatment is also known as** *office-based opiate addiction treatment,* **or** *O-BOAT.*

Social model detoxification programs are nonmedical (no or minimal medical staff presence) and can be either residential or outpatient. These programs are short-term (seven to 28 days) and are aimed at providing a safe and sober environment for addicts to rebalance the body and brain chemistry that was disrupted by drug abuse. This enables them to then enter a full recovery program.

Social model recovery programs (also called **outpatient drug-free programs**) use a wide variety of approaches to move a client toward recovery. Because social model programs are totally nonmedical, clients usually must be abstinent from drugs for 72 hours before they will be admitted. Approaches include cognitive-behavioral therapy, insight-oriented psychotherapy, problem-solving groups, and 12-step programs. Clients may stay in such programs for months or longer (Dodd, 1997). This model includes **outpatient programs** ranging from weekly education and early intervention (ASAM Level 0.5), to weekly counseling (Level I), to **intensive outpatient programs** (Level II) consisting

of a minimum of three sessions per week of three to four hours duration. The total length of outpatient therapy can vary from one to several months.

Therapeutic communities (TCs) are generally long-term (one- to three-year) self-contained residential programs that provide full rehabilitative and social services under the direction of the facility (NIDA, 2002B). These include daily counseling, drug education, vocational and educational rehabilitation, and case management, including referrals to social and health services. Many counselors, administrators, and role models in TCs are ex-addicts. The goals of this type of program are:

◊ habilitation or rehabilitation of the total individual;

◊ changing negative patterns of behavior and thinking as well as feelings that predispose drug use; and

◊ development of a drug-free lifestyle (Institute of Medicine, 1990).

The three major stages of treatment in a TC are: (1) **induction and early treatment**, usually during the first 30 days, including learning TC policies and procedures, beginning to understand addiction, and committing to the recovery process; (2) **primary treatment**; and (3) **reentry into the community at large** (NIDA, 2002B).

Because of funding limitations and availability, variations of the long-term (one- to three-year) TC concept have developed; these include short-term communities (3 to 6 months), modified therapeutic communities (6 to 9 months), adolescent therapeutic communities for juveniles that focus on the specific problems of youth, and jail-based TCs (Crowe & Reeves, 1994). There are also day treatment TCs that are less intensive than residential TCs but more intensive than the usual outpatient drug treatment program. The keys are maintaining a community approach and the principle of self-help.

Because addicts are often put off by having to make such a long commitment to being isolated from society, many programs divide the treatment into three- to six-month phases that permit making commitments to each phase of treatment rather than the full one to three years all at one time.

Halfway houses permit addicts to keep their jobs and outside contacts while being involved in a residential treatment program. Addicts receive educational and therapeutic interactions after work hours and live within the relative safety of the facility, where drugs and alcohol are prohibited and external triggers (cues) are minimized. Weekends or nonworking days are reserved for more-intensive program work that continues for a long duration (one to three years).

Several **new religious movements and faith-based treatment initiatives also use halfway house or inpatient treatment programs** to treat addiction; these include Teen Challenge and Espiritismo. Some are controversial because some critics say that joining a religious movement is exchanging one compulsion for another; the other side says that a spiritual awakening is necessary for true recovery and that such a program can provide that structure (Langrod, Muffler, Abel, et al., 2005).

Sober-living and transitional-living programs are generally for clients who have completed a long-term residential program. They consist of **apartments or cooperatives for groups of recovering addicts** with strong house rules to maintain a clean-and-sober living environment that is supportive of each person's recovery effort. Minimal-to-moderate treatment structure is provided for those living arrangements, and programs merely monitor compliance to protocols that allow the addicts to reenter the broader society with a drug-free lifestyle.

Harm reduction programs, discussed earlier in this chapter, consist mainly of pharmacotherapy maintenance approaches (also called *replacement therapy* or *agonist maintenance treatment*), particularly methadone maintenance clinics. Another harm reduction program that is less successful is controlled drinking or drug use taught through behavioral training programs. There are also education programs that teach how to minimize problems from drug use; **partial detox clinics** that help addicts lower their drug tolerance to minimize damage to the user; **sobering stations** that provide a safe place for addicts and alcoholics to sleep off their inebriation or hangover; and even **designated driver programs** that seem to sanction heavy drinking by some (Morris, 1995).

Admissions

In 2005, 1.849 million people were treated in various programs and facilities. It is estimated that another 2 million hardcore users also needed treatment and possibly another 3 million to 4 million problematic users needed some kind of care. The totals mean that in 2005 about 7.5 million Americans had serious enough drug and alcohol problems to need treatment.

BEGINNING TREATMENT

It is vital to remember that addiction is a dysfunction of the mind caused by actual biochemical changes in the central nervous system. We are born with most of the brain cells we will ever have (including the reservoir of immature stem cells); brain cells are unlike tissues such as skin cells, which are totally replaced every eight days or so (Snyder, Park, Flax, et al., 1997). Thus the brain cell disease of addiction is a chronic progressive process that can be treated and arrested but not reversed to any great extent nor cured. Most recovery professionals recognize that **recovery is a lifelong process because the brain cells have been permanently changed**. Addicts (those who have lost control of their drug use) must refrain from ever abusing and, in most cases, even using small amounts of any psychoactive drug if they want to avoid relapsing into addiction.

"Friday I was feeling good. I even went to a meeting. I'd been in this program for two years. I thought I could have one drink to relax with some friends I ran into. I had about five Scotches and ended up using coke all night long in a hotel with two prostitutes. I went through about $700 and was broke, and then I stole $150 from my roommate. I was ripped off a couple of times buying stuff, and at the end of it I was tweaked and I still wanted more."

24-year-old recovering crack cocaine user

RECOGNITION & ACCEPTANCE

Treatment starts with the addict's recognition and acceptance of his or her addiction. This **self-diagnosis often requires the addict to hit bottom or be the subject of an intervention** with an assessment to support and validate the need for treatment. **Addicts and alcoholics rarely accept the diagnosis of their addiction from others** even if the one making the

---

TABLE 9–1   ADMISSIONS TO DRUG TREATMENT BY PRIMARY SUBSTANCE OF ABUSE, 1992–2005

Primary Substance	1992	1996	2000	2004	2005
Alcohol	**898,021**	**832,844**	**821,450**	**756,629**	**723,646**
alcohol only	562,778	473,536	458,623	417,863	398,656
alcohol w/secondary drug	335,243	359,308	362,777	338,746	324,990
Opiates	**181,876**	**240,971**	**302,044**	**329,797**	**322,232**
heroin		224,366	273,889	266,013	254,345
hydrocodone, OxyContin®		16,605	28,155	63,784	67,887
Cocaine	**267,292**	**263,896**	**234,610**	**259,349**	**256,491**
smoked cocaine	183,282	195,751	170,616	187,337	185,236
nonsmoked cocaine	84,010	68,145	63,994	72,012	71,256
Marijuana/hashish	**92,414**	**192,918**	**249,687**	**300,792**	**292,250**
Stimulants (amphetamine, methamphetamine)	**22,117**	**52,964**	**86,390**	**152,673**	**170,470**
Sedative-hypnotics/tranquilizers	**8,350**	**7,848**	**10,098**	**13,054**	**12,400**
Hallucinogens	**3,437**	**2,839**	**3,213**	**2,407**	**2,057**
PCP	**2,833**	**2,504**	**2,868**	**3,262**	**2,807**
Inhalants	**2,918**	**1,974**	**1,362**	**1,238**	**1,372**
Over-the-counter medications	**522**	**550**	**788**	**882**	**762**
Other	**3,007**	**3,737**	**12,431**	**8,701**	**8,354**
None reported	**45,143**	**40,686**	**45,224**	**57,146**	**56,707**
TOTAL ADMISSIONS	**1,527,930**	**1,643,731**	**1,770,165**	**1,885,930**	**1,849,548**

(SAMHSA, 2006B)

TABLE 9–2   ONE-DAY CENSUS OF CLIENTS IN TREATMENT—BY FACILITY OWNERSHIP & TYPE OF CARE

Year	Private Profit	Private Nonprofit	State/Local Govt.	Federal Govt.	Tribal Govt.	Total	Inpatient Treatment	Outpatient Treatment
1980	17,997	284,483	150,376	25,977	N/C	**478,833**	N/A	N/A
1984	60,191	395,831	164,232	45,595	N/C	**665,849**	N/A	N/A
1990	113,522	451,951	172,290	27,025	3,041	**767,829**	93,888	673,941
1995	179,337	575,002	198,579	46,861	9,348	**1,009,127**	144,842	864,285
2000	242,184	552,092	153,989	40,549	12,082	**1,000,896**	109,349	891,547
2005	302,595	596,633	139,098	36,194	8,529	**1,081,048**	119,243	961,805

In 2005:

◇ 68% of all clients were male;

◇ 4.9% of female clients were pregnant;

◇ close to half of all clients resided in urban areas;

◇ one-fourth of all clients were intravenous (IV) drug users at the time of admission;

◇ 12% were under 20 years old;

◇ 67% were between 21 and 44 years old;

◇ 20% were between 45 and 64 years old;

◇ 0.6% were older than 65

(SAMHSA, 2006C).

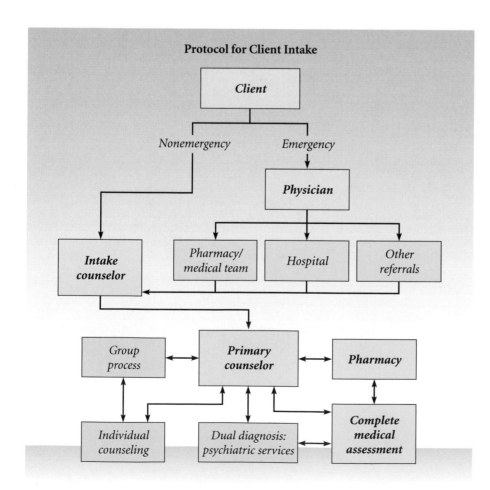

Protocol for Client Intake

assessment is a health professional. Only after an addict accepts the addiction can he or she embrace the lifelong continuum of recovery. **Coerced treatment via criminal justice sanctions can actually help addicts realize that they have hit bottom.**

Hitting Bottom

Addiction is a progressive illness that leads to severe life impairment and dysfunction when left to proceed without disruption.

"It really took my soul. I really feel it took my soul. As a human being, it's

Figure 9-3 •

This is the protocol structure for a typical clinic (outpatient medical model program; an M.D. needs to be available). It emphasizes the complexity of treating a compulsive drug user who comes in for treatment, particularly if other problems, such as medical complications, mental problems (dual diagnosis), or HIV disease, are involved. The limiting factor for many clinics is their budget.

important to have a soul, and I think I was just a hollow shell. It took my family, it took my kids, it took my self-esteem, which is probably the most important facet of all because without that everything else was just temporary anyway."
Recovering heroin abuser

The earlier addiction is recognized, accepted, and treated, the more likely the addict will have a rewarding life and good health. Hitting bottom doesn't have to be life threatening; it can simply be hopelessness.

"I got up and I looked at my pipe. And then I said, 'No,' and I put it down and I put it in the trash—I didn't break it—and I rocked myself and I said, 'No dope, no dope, no dope,' and I rocked myself until I could not rock myself any more."
Recovering crack addict

There are two vital things to keep in mind about hitting bottom. The first is that **every individual has a different sense of what hitting bottom is.** For some, losing their job is bottoming out; for others it is the loss of their relationship or their children. The other thing to remember is that **one does not have to hit bottom to accept that he or she has a chemical dependency problem and participate in treatment.** It is much healthier to enter and embrace treatment before one suffers great losses in life.

Denial

Overcoming denial is the essential first step in all treatment; it is also the most difficult. Denial is the universal defense mechanism experienced not only by addicts but also by their families, friends, and associates. Denial prevents or delays the proper recognition and acceptance of a chemical dependency or compulsive behavioral problem. **Denial is a refusal to acknowledge the negative impact that the drug use is having on one's life.** It is also assigning the reason for negative consequences to other causes

YEAH, YEAH. WE ALL TRY TO DENY IT, DEWEY, BUT THE FIRST STEP TOWARD RECOVERY IS TO ADMIT THAT YOU'RE HOOKED.

Bass rehab.

IN THE BLEACHERS
© Steve Moore.
Reprinted by permission of Universal Press Syndicate. All rights reserved.

rather than to the drug use or compulsive behavior.

One compounding problem is that many professionals are unwilling to make the diagnosis or they just don't recognize the signs and symptoms. In particular, **the medical profession has a tendency to deny or overlook addiction.** How often or how thoroughly does a physician inquire about a patient's alcohol or other drug use history? How often is a caffeine intake assessment done by a physician who is treating anxiety and insomnia in a patient? A study of physician awareness in Boston found that about 45% of 1,440 patients with substance-abuse problems said that their physician was unaware of their illness (Saitz, Mulvey, Plough, et al., 1997). A July 2005 survey conducted by the National Center on Addictions and Substance Abuse at Columbia University found that more than 50% of physicians reported receiving no training in identifying addiction and 75% of physicians and 50% of pharmacists had received no training since professional school in identifying prescription drug abuse or diversion of prescription drugs (CASA, 2005). Uninsured clients, those with a history of medical illness, and those who had been previously treated for substance

abuse or mental illness were even more unlikely to be diagnosed correctly by their physician (Saitz, Mulvey, Plough, et al., 1997).

"I woke up after passing out in a friend's home, and they had taken my money away from me, and they had posted somebody at the door, and my mother came and said, 'I will not watch your children for you while you go out and party. If you do something about your problem, I'll take care of your kids for a week.' That was the first time anybody had said to me I had a problem, and that was the first time anybody said, 'Stop. You can't do this anymore.'"
37-year-old recovering speed user

Breaking Through Denial

Denial plus the toxic effects that psychoactive drugs have on judgment and memory make the **addict likely to be the last person to recognize and accept her or his addiction.** Usually, those closest to the addict—the family or spouse—have the best chance to make the earliest recognition of addiction (not just use) and to help the person break through denial. Besides close relatives, others able to recognize addiction include friends, co-workers, employers, ministers, medical professionals, the IRS, and the law. On the other hand, **addiction is the only illness that requires a self-diagnosis for treatment to be effective.** Normally, when physicians tell patients that they have high blood pressure, they accept that diagnosis without question and make changes in their lives to improve their health. But when addicts are first confronted with their addiction, they almost always deny any drug problem and continue to abuse drugs.

There are several ways to break through denial.

◇ **Legal Intervention.** The threat of loss of freedom, property, relationships, and professional licensure, among others, forces users to accept that they have a problem with drugs. Legal requirements may mandate treatment; incarceration limits drug use and promotes abstinence in prisons where drug trafficking is supposed to be kept to a minimum. Some prison personnel, however, estimate that, if tested, 10% to 30% of inmates in many prisons would test positive for an illicit psychoactive drug.

◇ **Workplace Intervention.** Poor performance and the threat of the loss of one's livelihood can break through denial. Strong employee assistance programs work with the at-risk employee, often using a "last chance agreement" to participate successfully in treatment or resign from the job.

◇ **Physical Health Problems.** Deteriorating health and doctors' warnings can make a user consider drug problems as a possible cause or complicating factor. The existence of lung cancer, high blood pressure, or heart, liver, kidney, and other diseases caused by drug toxicity can be a powerful tool to confront a patient's denial of addiction.

◇ **Pregnancy.** Concern over one's neonate (developing fetus) has been another strong motivator to accept the need for sobriety.

◇ **Mental Health Problems.** Emotional and mental traumas like depression, anger, and mental confusion that affect day-to-day functioning can also act as warning signals.

◇ **Financial Difficulties.** Problems such as paying bills, buying food, or covering the rent, which are affected by escalating drug costs, force the user to deal drugs, turn to other crimes, or cut back on use, thus compelling the user to recognize the financial damage of addiction

(Heather, 1989; Miller & Hester, 1989).

Table 9-3 shows the sources of referral for people who have entered substance-abuse treatment. Some interesting observations: first is that, over-

all, about one-third are self-referred and another one-third are referred by the criminal justice system, usually court-ordered treatment; the percentage of self-referrals for marijuana is only one-half of the number of referrals for other drugs (SAMHSA, 2003).

"My dad's an alcoholic. I've tried so many things just to get him into treatment, but no matter how much I try, he just doesn't listen. So I'm not gonna let him take me down from my recovery. I just told him, you know, 'Forget it. And if you want to be with me, you're going to have to be clean.' And he only loves two things and that's me and my brother. And if we take one of those away, he might want to quit."

15-year-old recovering polydrug abuser

Intervention

Strategies have been developed to attack the denial in drug abusers and addicted people and help them recognize their dependence on drugs. Generally referred to as *interventions,* these strategies have been documented since the late 1800s to effectively bring addicts into treatment and hold them there. There are now specialists who help organize and implement interventions. The current style of formal intervention was developed by Dr. Vernon Johnson in the 1960s and refined by a number of treatment professionals.

TABLE 9–3   ADMISSIONS BY SOURCE OF REFERRAL IN THE UNITED STATES IN 2005

Source of Referral	All Admissions	Alcohol Only	Alcohol w/ Other Drug	Heroin	Crack Cocaine	Other	Marijuana	Methamphetamine
Total admissions	1,849,548	398,856	324,990	254,345	185,236	27,752	292,250	152,368
Individual (self)	**33.6%**	28.4%	31.3%	59.3%	37.6%	31.7%	15.9%	23.8%
Criminal justice/DUI	**36.1%**	41.5%	35.0%	14.2%	26.4%	33.7%	56.7%	49.2%
Substance-abuse provider	**10.2%**	8.6%	12.7%	14.7%	15.4%	11.7%	5.5%	5.1%
Other healthcare provider	**7.0%**	8.8%	8.1%	5.1%	8.0%	7.6%	4.6%	4.6%
School (educational)	**1.1%**	0.7%	0.9%	0.2%	0.1%	0.3%	4.0%	0.4%
Employer/EAP	**0.7%**	1.2%	0.9%	0.3%	0.5%	1.5%	1.0%	0.4%
Other community referral	**11.2%**	11.0%	11.2%	6.44%	12.0%	13.5%	12.4%	16.5%

(SAMHSA, 2006B)

"Intervention is a process by which the harmful, progressive, and destructive effects of chemical dependency are interrupted and the chemically dependent person is helped to stop using mood-altering chemicals and to develop new, healthier ways of coping with his or her needs and problems. It implies that the person need not be an emotional or physical wreck (or hit bottom) before such help can be given."

Vernon E. Johnson, founder, Johnson Institute
(Johnson, 1986)

Generally, a formal **intervention should be tried after informal interventions have failed** or if a professional feels that the wall of denial is too great. Most intervention strategies consist of the following elements.

Love. An intervention should always start and end with an expression of love and genuine concern for the well-being of the addicted person. Multiple participants should be recruited from various aspects of the addict's life—all of whom share a sense of true affection for the user but recognize the progressive impairment of the addiction and are bold enough to commit to participating in the intervention. Generally, this intervention team consists of two or more of the following: family members, close friends and co-workers, other recovering addicts, a clergy or community leader, and a lead facilitator.

Facilitator. A professional intervention specialist or a knowledgeable chemical dependency treatment professional is selected to organize the intervention, educate the participants about addiction and treatment options, train and assist team members in the preparation of their statements, and support or confirm the diagnosis of addiction. The team meets and prepares its intervention without revealing its activities to the user.

Intervention Statements. Each team member prepares a statement that he or she will make to the addicted person at the intervention.

Each statement consists of four parts:

◇ a declaration of how much they love, care for, and respect the user;
◇ specific incidents they have personally witnessed or experienced related to the addiction and the pain they have personally experienced because of the incidents;
◇ personal knowledge that the incidents occurred not because of the user's intent but because of the drug's effects on the user's behavior; and
◇ reassurance of their love, concern, and respect for the user with a strong request that he or she recognize and accept the illness and enter treatment immediately.

Anticipated Defenses & Outcomes. The facilitator prepares the team to deal with expected defense mechanisms like denial, rationalization, minimization, anger, and accusations. The team also prepares for all logistics (reserving a program or hospital admission, packing clothing and toiletries, and covering work and home duties) so that the user will have no excuse to delay entering treatment immediately should a successful intervention ensue. The team also prepares for contingencies and alternative treatments other than the ones they selected should the addict refuse to accept their first recommendation. It is important that the user accept one of the treatment options selected by the team and not delay entry by saying he or she wants a different program. In making arrangements, team members should be knowledgeable about the addicted person's specific needs, his or her resources to afford treatment, the specific components and deficiencies of available treatments, and the ultimate client goal of the potential programs.

Intervention. Timing, location, and surprise are crucial components of the actual intervention. A neutral, nonthreatening, and private location must be secured. It should occur at a time (usually early Sunday morning) when the user is most likely to be sober and not under the influence of a drug. The evidence presented in statements should include current incidents. A reliable plan should be developed to get the addicted person to the location that does not cause him or her to suspect what is about to occur. Finally, the facilitator should prepare the order of the statements that have been rehearsed by the team prior to the intervention.

Contingency. Successful or not, **it is important for the intervention team members to continue to meet after the intervention** to process their experiences. This also provides the opportunity for team members (especially family members) to explore their own support or treatment needs for issues such as codependency, enabling, or adult children of addicts syndrome.

Despite the inherent risks of anger or rejection that may result from an unsuccessful intervention, the potential benefits from these strategies far outweigh the risks. At a very minimum, the pathological effects of secrecy that pervade an addiction have been brought out to all those who are most affected by it, allowing an opportunity for successful treatment or supportive services for all who participate.

TREATMENT CONTINUUM

"I know it sounds strange, but the best thing that ever happened to me was that I became an addict. That's because my addiction forced me into treatment and the recovery process, and through recovery I found what was missing in my life."
Nurse with 20 years of recovery time

The chronic, progressive, and relapsing nature of addiction is a depressing and degrading process. Results of a Beck's Depression Inventory evaluation of patients entering treatment at the Haight Ashbury Detox Clinic demonstrated that 34% to 38% tested for maximum depression. Admission interviews also demonstrated that 30% to 34% had made at least one suicide gesture prior to seeking help for their addiction. Fortunately, recovery is a spiritually uplifting and motivating process through which individuals gain a sense of purpose, community, and meaning in their lives. **Recovery is gradual, and a client undergoes several changes no matter which therapy is used: detoxification, initial abstinence, long-term abstinence (sobriety), and continuous recovery.** It is necessary that the addict become and remain abstinent through all phases of treatment to be successful; slips and relapses are part of the addiction process, however, and often occur during treatment. For this reason **relapse needs to be accepted but not excused in recovery.** Clients should not be made to feel ashamed after a relapse and should be welcomed back into treatment. **The relapse should then be aggressively processed by the client and the counselor or therapist to recognize its causes and identify strategies that may help to prevent future ones.** Harm reduction education and alternatives should be included during this processing of slips and relapses. Slips should be targeted most for prevention of relapse as first use is much more avoidable then continued use after a slip. The four steps to recovery are the ones used at programs that have the resources and the ability to work with recovering clients over an extended period of time.

DETOXIFICATION

The first step is to get the drug out of the body if the client is still using. The user's biochemistry has become so unbalanced that only abstinence will give it time to metabolize the drug and begin to normalize the brain's neurochemical balance. Detoxification will also help normalize clients' thinking processes so that they can participate fully in their own recovery. **It takes about a week to completely excrete a drug such as cocaine and perhaps another four weeks to 10 months until the body chemistry settles down.** Certain drugs, including marijuana, benzodiazepines, and PCP, take longer to be excreted from the body. Some treatment programs will assist in the detox phase, but most require several days of abstinence prior to admis-

sion to ensure that the patient is no longer at risk of suffering dangerous withdrawal symptoms, such as seizures, particularly when alcohol or sedatives are involved. **Social or nonmedically supervised programs require that clients go through either a medical detoxification or be 72 hours clean and sober** on their own before being admitted for recovery treatment. This is to minimize the potential for a medical emergency withdrawal problem once the client has entered social model treatment.

"My mother swore off the gin and the Valium® for my wedding. She was too good to her word. She started withdrawing and having convulsions at my reception and almost died in the ambulance. It put somewhat of a damper on the honeymoon."
23-year-old bride

The initial detoxification often includes a process called "white knuckling" in which addicts or abusers stop taking the drug on their own and suffer through physical and mental withdrawal symptoms. It can also be done on a normal outpatient basis, an intense outpatient basis, at a residential facility that is medically supervised, or at a medically managed inpatient facility that can provide treatment in the emergency room of a hospital if the client is in crisis (Chang & Kosten, 2005). **Medically or chemically assisted detoxification is aimed at minimizing withdrawal symptoms** that can cause life-endangering effects or an immediate relapse.

For those facilities that assist in detoxification, **assessment of the severity of addiction is important to determine if medical detoxification is necessary** and if so which facility should be used. The level of intoxication, the potential for severe withdrawal symptoms, the presence of other medical or psychological problems, the patient's response to treatment recommendations, the potential for relapse, and the environment for recovery—all need to be determined.

Severe physical dependence on depressants, major medical or psychiatric

complications, and pregnancy are all indications for initiating detoxification in a hospital-based program.

"Something told me I had to stop, so I did. And I stopped by myself for seven days straight. I didn't know what I was going through. I was having flashes, I heard people talking to me, and I was sweating. I had the shakes real bad, so I called S. F. General Hospital. They gave me poison control and they transferred me to the Haight Ashbury Clinic."
23-year-old recovering cocaine addict

Medication Therapy for Detoxification

A variety of specific medications are used during the detoxification phase to ease the symptoms of withdrawal and minimize the initial drug cravings. *(There is more thorough coverage of potential treatment medications at the end of this chapter.)*

◊ **Clonidine** (Catapres®) dampens the withdrawal symptoms of opioids, alcohol, and even nicotine addiction.

◊ **Phenobarbital** is used to prevent withdrawal seizures and other symptoms associated with alcohol and sedative-hypnotic dependence.

◊ **Methadone**, a long-acting opioid, is one of four federally approved medications for opioid addiction treatment (for detoxification and maintenance). The other three are buprenorphine, LAAM, and naltrexone.

◊ **Buprenorphine** (Subutex® and Suboxone®) can be used for short-term opioid detoxification or long-term maintenance.

◊ **Naltrexone (ReVia®) blocks the effects of opioids.** The addict will have no response to heroin if he or she happens to slip while in treatment. It is also FDA approved for use to prevent craving in recovering alcoholics.

◊ **Psychiatric medications**, which include antipsychotics such as haloperidol (Haldol®), **antidepressants** such as desipramine and imipramine (Tofranil®), and selective serotonin reuptake inhibitor (SSRI) antidepressants such as sertraline (Zoloft®) and fluoxetine (Prozac®), have been used in the initial detoxification of cocaine, amphetamine, and other stimulant addictions.

◊ **Bromocriptine** (Parlodel®), **amantadine** (Symmetrel®), and **L-Dopa**® have been used to treat the craving associated with cocaine and stimulant drug dependence.

◊ **Acomprosate** is prescribed to decrease alcohol cravings. It is more effective when used in combination with naltrexone along with psychosocial interventions (Boothby & Doering, 2005).

◊ **Varenicline (Chantix®) and bupropion (Zyban®)** are used to lessen withdrawal and curb craving of nicotine addiction.

◊ **Nicotine patches (Nicoderm® and ProSTEP®)** are approved to treat the withdrawal symptoms of tobacco, whereas nicotine-laced gum (Nicorette®) helps lessen craving.

◊ **Disulfiram (Antabuse®) helps prevent alcoholism relapse by creating unpleasant side effects if alcohol is used.** It has had limited use because of medication compliance problems, but the recent increase in CJS-mandated and CJS-coerced treatment has renewed interest in its use for alcohol dependence (Blanc & Daeppen, 2005).

◊ Finally, a number of **amino acids** are used individually or in combination to try to alleviate withdrawal and craving symptoms. The theory is that the brain uses these amino acids to make neurotransmitters that were depleted by the drug addiction. It is believed that the imbalance or depletion of neurotransmitters is the cause of many of the withdrawal symptoms and the intense craving. Common amino acids used for this purpose are tyrosine, taurine, tryptophan, d,1-phenylalanine, lecithin, and glutamine.

Psychosocial Therapy

Medical intervention alone is rarely effective during the detoxification phase. Indeed most programs forgo medical treatment if the addict is not in any physiological or psychological danger from drug withdrawal. **Intensive counseling and group work have proven to be the most effective** measures of engaging addicts in a recovery process and should be the main focus of all phases of treatment despite the many medical innovations being developed.

Psychosocial client interactions during detoxification are usually intense (daily encounters in an outpatient program) and highly structured for a four- to 12-week duration. **The aim of this treatment phase is to break down residual denial and engage the client in the full recovery process.** This is accomplished through mandated participation in educational sessions, task-oriented group work, therapy sessions, peer recovery groups, 12-step programs, and individual counseling.

Treatment focuses on **helping the addict to learn about the disease concept of addiction**, the harmful effects of the disease, and the intensity of detoxification symptoms. Clients also receive information about their treatment and any medications used in detoxification. They also develop their recovery or treatment plan with their primary counselor and initiate activities to accomplish their goals during the detoxification phase. Some programs have also **begun to use structured treatment manuals** that have a developed curriculum for each phase of treatment, with individual daily lesson plans, exercises, and homework assignments.

"I knew I could do it myself. I tried those programs in AA. I stopped using drugs a million times and I never needed one of those programs."
Heroin addict dying from AIDS

INITIAL ABSTINENCE

Once the addict has been detoxified, **body chemistry must be allowed to regain balance**. Continued abstinence during this phase is best promoted by addressing both the continuous craving for drugs and the aspects of the addict's life that may present a risk of relapse.

During the early part of this treatment stage, brain chemistry is out of balance. **Depletion of brain neurotransmitters brought about by the drug use results in a type of drug hunger known as endogenous craving.** Anticraving medications, such as those used during the detoxification phase, can be continued during the initial abstinence phase when more—traditional approaches—voluntary isolation from environmental triggers or cues (e.g., bars, co-users, and drug paraphernalia), counseling, and 12-step meetings—are ineffective in controlling the episodic drug hunger.

Medical approaches like **Antabuse®** for alcoholism, naltrexone for opioids and alcohol, and various amino acids have been used. They may help rebalance the brain chemistry, continue to suppress and/or reverse the pleasurable effects of drugs, or decrease the drug craving—all of which helps encourage the addict to stay clean (Gatch & Lal, 1998; O'Brien, 1997).

Research into a cocaine vaccine and a true alcohol antagonist may lead to treatments for these addictions in the same manner that naltrexone is often effective in preventing readdiction to opioids and craving for alcohol.

In addition to endogenous craving, two other symptoms that begin in and continue through later stages of treatment also pose a powerful threat to continued sobriety: post-acute withdrawal symptoms and environmentally cued or triggered craving.

Post-Acute Withdrawal Symptoms & Cognitive Impairments

Continued abstinence can lead to post-acute withdrawal symptoms (PAWS), **a group of emotional and physical symptoms that appear after major withdrawal symptoms have abated.** The syndrome can persist for six to 18 months or even longer—up to 10 years for some—and may contribute to interrupted abstinence or relapse. It is believed that PAWS **result from a combination of brain neuron damage caused by drug use and the psychological stress of living drug- and alcohol-free** after many years of a drug-using lifestyle. The syndrome usually begins within seven to 14 days of abstinence and peaks in intensity over three to six months. Symptoms often occur at regular intervals and without apparent outside stressors. The patterns can be on payday schedules (every two weeks or monthly), during holidays, or even annually on recovery birthdays. These times seem to be associated with patterns of past drug use or stressful events. Six major types of problem symptoms are most often associated with PAWS:

◇ **Sleep disturbances:** difficulty falling or staying asleep, restlessness, and vivid and disturbing nightmares.

◇ **Memory problems:** short-term memory is most impaired, often making it difficult to learn new skills or process new information.

◇ **Inability to think clearly:** difficulty with concentration, rigid and repetitive thinking, and impairment of abstract reasoning (non-concrete, theoretical, or philosophical thinking); thoughts become confused and chaotic during stressful situations; decreased problem-solving skills, even with usually simple problems; overall intelligence is not affected, and the thinking impairment is episodic and not continuous.

◇ **Anxiety and hypersensitivity to stress:** chronic stress with inability to differentiate between low-stress and high-stress situations; inappropriate reaction to situations and difficulty managing stress; all other symptoms of PAWS syndrome become worse during high-stress situations.

◇ **Inappropriate emotional reactions and mood swings:** overreaction to emotions, resulting is increased stress that then leads to an emotional shutdown or numbness and inability to feel any emotions.

◇ **Physical coordination difficulties:** hand/eye coordination issues; and problems with balance, dizziness, and slow reflexes.

Further, most recovering addicts experience inadequacy, incompetence, embarrassment, lowered self-esteem, and great shame while experiencing PAWS. These are all negative moods states that make them extremely vulnerable to relapse (Gorski & Miller, 1986).

An increase of cognitive deficits during early recovery (impairments of learning, attention, perception, information processing, memory, temporal or time processing, cognitive inflexibility, problem solving, abstract thinking, and even physical coordination) also lasts for several months after initiation of abstinence from drug or alcohol abuse (Taleff, 2004).

"More often than not, it is imperative that a man's brain be cleared before he is approached, as he has then a better chance of understanding and accepting what we have to offer."
Alcoholics Anonymous Big Book, 1939

Environmental Triggers, Relapse Prevention & Cue Extinction

"When I'm smelling the marijuana here in the building where I live and I smell the 'primos' (which is crack cocaine laced with marijuana), the cravings do come back. And what I do is I call my sponsor, I go to a NA and AA meeting, and I mostly talk to my sponsor and I tell her what I'm feeling, and I pray to God to give me the strength not to go out to buy me any kind of drugs to use."
38-year-old recovering polydrug abuser

Environmental triggers or cues often precipitate drug cravings. These triggers have been classified into two broad categories: intrapersonal and interpersonal factors. **Intrapersonal states or internal influences** that have the greatest impact are negative emotional and physical states or internally motivated attempts to regain control and use. **Interpersonal factors or external influences** include relationship conflicts, social pressures, lack of support systems, negative life events, and so-called slippery people, places, and things (Carter & Tiffany, 1999; Marlatt, 1995). Some other factors that can lead to relapse are exhaustion, dishonesty, impa-

tience, argumentativeness, depression, frustration, self-pity, cockiness, complacency, expecting too much from others, letting up on disciplines, use of any mood-altering drugs, and overconfidence (Pharmacist Rehabilitation Organization, 1999). Addicts have discovered this by themselves and long ago developed handy acronyms like **HALT** (**h**ungry, **a**ngry, **l**onely, **t**ired) and **RID** (**r**estless, **i**rritable, **d**iscontent) to remind themselves of the triggers that lead to relapse.

Relapse prevention has become the focus of almost every treatment program. There are a number of strategies and themes that are used in this process.

◇ Addicts must understand the process of relapse and **learn to recognize their personal triggers**, which can be anything from drug odors, seeing friends who use, having money in one's pocket, and even hearing a song about drugs.

◇ Addicts must **develop behaviors to avoid external cues**. These include avoiding old neighborhoods and dealers, changing one's circle of friends, limiting the amount of money that's carried, and not going into bars or gatherings where drugs are readily available.

◇ Addicts must learn to cope with or **be prepared with an automatic reflex strategy to prevent them from using when their craving is activated by internal or external cues.** These include networking with the support system they have put together, going to a 12-step meeting, using their developed coping skills for negative emotional states and cognitive distortions, doing something that reminds them of their addiction problems or their reasons for wanting to stay clean, remembering their last binge, creating a balanced lifestyle, and possibly using anticraving medications (Daley & Marlatt, 2005).

It is important to note that **drug craving is a true psychological response that is manifested by actual physiological changes** of increased heart rate and blood pressure, sweating, dilation of the pupils, specific electrical

Environmental cues that trigger drug craving can include paraphernalia, drug-using partners, old neighborhoods, and especially money.

© 2002 CNS Productions, Inc.

● ●

changes in the skin, and even an immediate drop of two degrees or more in body temperature.

Deconditioning techniques, stress reduction exercises, expressing one's feelings, working out, long walks, and cold showers are all strategies that addicts use to dissipate the craving response when it arises. A technique such as **Dr. Anna Rose Childress's Desensitization Program retrains brain cells to not react when confronted by environmental cues**. The procedure involves exposing an addict to progressively stronger environmental cues over 40 to 50 sessions in a controlled setting. This technique gradually decreases response to the cues until there are no physiological signs of a craving response even when the addict is exposed to heavy triggers. Every time an addict refrains from using while craving a drug, it lessens the response to the next trigger experience. **Desensitization has also been called cue extinction** (Childress, McClellan, Ehrman, et al., 1988; Childress, Mozley, McElgin, et al., 1999).

"I did it myself. Every day I would take out my Librium® pills and look at them, touch them, and even smell

them. Then I would put them back in the bottle because I knew I couldn't ever use them again. After a while I lost interest in them altogether."
44-year-old female recovering benzodiazepine addict

Psychosocial Support

Initial abstinence is also the phase during which addicts start to put their lives back in order, working on all the things they neglected while indulging their addiction. A comprehensive analysis of an addict's medical health, psychiatric status, social problems, and environmental needs must be conducted and a plan developed to address all issues presented.

Most important, **addicts need to build a support system that will give continuing advice, help, and information** when they return to job and home and are subjected to all of the pressures and environmental triggers that led to addiction. Support groups and 12-step programs along with involvement in group therapy and continued recovery counseling have been demonstrated to have the most positive treatment outcomes during the initial abstinence phase.

Acupuncture

The use of acupuncture to relieve withdrawal symptoms and reduce craving has been on the increase in the past 30 years since it was first observed to reduce opium withdrawal symptoms (Wen & Cheung, 1973). The hypothesis as to why acupuncture works is that **by stimulating the peripheral nerves, messages are sent to the brain to release natural (endogenous) endorphins that promote a feeling of well-being** (Birch, 2001). Acupuncture has also been shown to alter levels of other neurotransmitters, specifically serotonin and norepinephrine, as well as the hormones prolactin, oxytocin, thyroxin, corticosteroid, and insulin (Boucher, Kiresuk & Trachtenberg, 2003; Steiner, Hay & Davis, 1982). Besides opioid detoxification, acupuncture has been used to reduce craving for alcohol and stimulants with varying results. As with all initial abstinence and detoxification techniques, it is not effective when used as the sole treatment or modality. It can also be used with detox medication (Han, Trachtenberg & Lowinson, 2005). The problem with acupuncture is that because it is not a replacement therapy for other modalities, it can be expensive, adding an additional therapeutic cost to the treatment process, and **its effects last for only a short time, often requiring multiple daily treatments** to relieve symptoms during detoxification and initial abstinence.

LONG-TERM ABSTINENCE

The pivotal component of this phase occurs when an addict finally admits and accepts her or his addiction as lifelong and surrenders to the long-term, one-day-at-a-time treatment process. **Continued participation in group, family, and 12-step programs is the key to maintaining long-term abstinence from drugs. The addict must accept that addiction is chronic, progressive, incurable, and potentially fatal and that relapse is always possible.**

"I know that I have another relapse in me. I don't know if I have another recovery in me."
7-year member of Alcoholics Anonymous

It is also vital for recovering addicts to accept that their condition is chemical dependency or drug compulsivity and not just alcoholism, or cocainism, or opioidism. Individuals who manifest addiction to a particular drug, such as cocaine, are well advised to **abstain from the use of all psychoactive substances**, especially alcohol. A seemingly benign flirtation with marijuana will probably lead to other drug hungers and relapse. It is a common clinical observation that **compulsive drug abusers often switch intoxicants only to find the symptoms of addiction resurfacing through another addictive agent.** Drug switching does not work with recovery-oriented treatment. A study of men and women in treatment found that 80% had a problem with two or more substances during their lifetimes, either concurrently or sequentially (Carrol, 1980). Even abstention from smoking or chewing tobacco can help in the recovery process (Wiley Interscience, 2001). Years of experience and clinical practice indicate a need to also be wary of compulsive behaviors (e.g., gambling, overeating, sexual addiction, and compulsive shopping) if one is in recovery from drug or alcohol addiction.

RECOVERY

"Can we cure addiction? Absolutely not! This is because addiction has caused unrecoverable changes, alterations, and deaths to brain cells. Brain cells are not readily regenerated like other cells, so the changes caused by drug abuse are permanent. What we can do is arrest the illness, teach new living techniques, rewire the brain to bypass those addicted cells, and give the addict in recovery a worthwhile life. Although addiction can't be cured, it can be effectively prevented and treated."

Darryl Inaba, Pharm.D., clinical director, Genesis Recovery Center

Treatment and a continued focus on abstinence are not enough to ensure recovery and a positive lifestyle. **Recovering addicts also need to re-**structure their lives and find things they enjoy doing that give them satisfaction and natural highs instead of the artificial highs they came to seek through drugs.** Without this they may have sobriety but will not have recovery. This integral phase of treatment has been validated experimentally by Dr. George Vaillant, professor of Psychiatry at Harvard University. In studies in 1983, he indicated **four components necessary to change an ingrained habit of alcohol dependence**. In the following list, the generic term *drug* is substituted for Dr. Vaillant's specific reference to alcohol:

◊ offering the client or patient a non-chemical substitute dependency for the drug, such as exercise;

◊ reminding her or him ritually that even one episode of drug use can lead to pain and relapse;

◊ repairing the social, emotional, and medical damage done; and

◊ restoring self-esteem.

Continued and lifelong participation in the fellowship of 12-step programs along with the concerted effort to seek out natural, healthy, nondrug rewarding experiences is the formula with which most recovering addicts have found success in achieving their treatment goals (Vaillant, 1995).

"I found in sobriety that I love people. I found in sobriety that I have real feelings. I found in sobriety that I have real emotions. I found in sobriety that there's a world of people out there in society that's willing, that's been there all along for me, to assist me. I just never knew it."

56-year-old recovering heroin addict

Natural Highs

"Getting high on life is a skill and just like any other skill-athletic, artistic, musical, or professional—the more you practice it, the more you can improve."

George Obermeier, drug educator

Because psychoactive drugs create sensations or feelings that have natural counterparts in the body, **human beings can create virtually all of the sensations and feelings they try to get through drugs** by concentrating on the feelings they experience from natural life situations. Athletic competition releases the same neurotransmitters as cocaine and methamphetamine. Experiencing a second wind or the runner's high from jogging comes from opiate receptor activation by endorphins. Traveling or experiencing new environments activates the novelty center, the same area of the brain that marijuana affects. Being in touch with the natural or drug-free highs available to the brain is an essential part of living.

OUTCOME & FOLLOW-UP

Promoted primarily by government and other funding sources to justify spending for addiction treatment, **client outcomes and follow-up evaluations have become a major element in treatment program activities**. What is often lost by this process is an opportunity for treatment programs to be flexible and utilize the data obtained to modify their treatment protocols and interventions to promote better outcomes for clients.

Because addiction is by nature a chronic, multivaried, and relapsing condition, **there is a need to develop outcome measures that evaluate different phases of the recovery process**, including long-term follow-up.

Indicators most often evaluated by treatment facilities to determine successful addiction treatment include:

◊ prevalence of drug slips and relapses (duration of continuous sobriety);

◊ retention in treatment;

◊ completion of a treatment plan and its phases;

◊ family functioning;

◊ social and environmental adjustments;

◊ vocational or educational functioning, including personal finance management; and

◊ criminal activity or legal involvement.

It is reassuring to note that, in general, **all types of addiction treatment have demonstrated positive client outcomes when evaluated by rigorous scientific methods** (Belenko, Patapis & French, 2005; Gerstein, Datta, Ingels, et al., 1997; Mecca, 1997).

"These abscesses came through my addiction to heroin. Never cleaned my arm, let alone my body. Now I care about myself."
35-year-old recovering addict

INDIVIDUAL VS. GROUP THERAPY

There are two main integrated components of addiction treatment: psychosocial therapy and medical (especially medication) therapy. Recent developments in understanding the neurobiological process of addiction have resulted in an explosive growth of medication treatments and the new medical specialty of addiction medicine called *addictionology*. It is important to remember, however, that **medical treatments are not effective unless they are integrated with psychosocial therapies**. There are two general types of counseling therapies: individual and group. Most treatment facilities use a combination of both methods.

INDIVIDUAL THERAPY

Individual therapy is usually conducted by credentialed chemical dependency counselors. **They deal with clients on a one-on-one basis to explore the reasons for their continued use of psychoactive substances and to identify all areas of intervention needs with the aim of changing behavior.** This may lead to a referral for specialized treatment, such as psychiatry, medical care, and family counseling. The therapist helps addicts gain perspective on their usage and identify and use tools that will keep them abstinent from drugs. The most common individual therapies are **cognitive—behavioral therapy, reality therapy, aversion therapy, psychodynamic therapy, art therapy, assertiveness training, motivational interviewing or enhancement, and social skills training** (Stevens-Smith & Smith, 2004).

A treatment plan is developed with the client, and individual **treatment may continue from one month to several years**. Although the majority of treatment is based on group and peer interaction, individual treatment may be more effective for certain types of clients and drugs (e.g., heroin and sedatives).

A drug counselor and a heroin addict in a counseling session at the Haight Ashbury Detox Clinic in San Francisco:

Addict: "When I'm going through withdrawal, it's a physical thing, and then after I'm clean, I have the mental problem having to say no every time I get money in my hands: 'Should I or shouldn't I? No, I shouldn't. Go ahead, one more time won't hurt.' After I've passed withdrawal, and I pass by areas where I used to hang out, and I see other people nodding, in my mind, I start feeling like I'm sick again. I want to stay clean."
Counselor: "You can stay clean for a while. Is that what you want? You want to stay clean for a while or for the rest of your life?"
Addict: "I want to stay clean permanently."
Counselor: "Permanently drug-free?"
Addict: "But I can do it without attending those [Narcotics Anonymous] meetings."
Counselor: "All by yourself?"
Addict: "I mean with the medication that I take."
Counselor: "But the medications are only going to last you 21 days. They'll help you for a little while with the withdrawal of getting off heroin, but what are you going to do when the urges come up?"
Addict: "I guess I'll deal with that when the time comes."
Counselor: "So you're just going to wait for it? You're going to wait for the urges to come on and start using then?"
Addict: "Nah, I can deal with it."
Counselor: "You're being highly uncooperative. As a matter of fact, we're going to stop the medications today because we know you're still using heroin and we can't have you using on the program."
Addict: "I need those medications."
Counselor: "What for? It's just another drug. What you're doing is using it like another drug. I'd like for you to come back to get into that group meeting we have at three o'clock. Also I want you to go to an NA meeting every day. I want you to go to these meetings and participate. Talk every opportunity you can. And also what I want you to do is bring back the signed participation card that you attended. I want you to do that. That's just part of the requirement of being in the program. See, I'm going to assume that you want to stop using drugs."

Addict: "Why can't I just get the detoxification drugs?"
Counselor: "Because we're not just a medication program. It's a counseling and full recovery program too."

It is also observed that **individual treatment is less threatening for many individuals** and therefore can be used in the short term to introduce addicts to the treatment process.

Motivational Interviewing and Motivational Enhancement Therapy

One of the most utilized counseling techniques in substance-abuse treatment is motivational interviewing coupled with a **stages-of-change model.** The technique uses a nonconfrontational style to involve clients in their own recovery process and help them to change ambivalence about drug use into motivation to make changes that lead to abstinence and recovery. As in 12-step recovery groups, where people look to their own higher power for direction and strength, people make the successful major changes when their motivation is internal rather than external. The counselor **guides clients through the stages of change by helping them reach decisions for themselves rather than by forcing or overdirecting them.** This technique helps clients "release the potential for change that exists in every person." The objective is to have clients advocate for their own positive lifestyle changes.

The general principles of motivational interviewing are to:

◇ **express empathy**—seeing the world through the clients' eyes and developing empathy is a way to develop a rapport with them; reflective listening and acceptance help the counselor understand the clients;
◇ **roll with resistance**—resistance is not challenged or argued with but rather used to help explore the clients' ideas; using that momentum rather than fighting it decreases resistance;

◇ **develop discrepancy**—the counselor helps the clients recognize discrepancies between where they are and where they want to be and to see how their current actions will not lead them to their goals; and
◇ **support self-efficacy**—by empowering clients to choose their own options, the counselor encourages them to make changes.

(Miller & Rollnick, 2002).

Motivational interviewing techniques are used within the framework of the stages-of-change model. This requires the counselor to match motivational tasks to each client's stage of change:

◇ **Precontemplation** is the stage at which clients do not admit they have a problem and are not thinking about change although others may perceive the behaviors that need changing. The counselor's task is to raise doubt and increase a client's perception of risks and problems with current behavior.
◇ **Contemplation** is the stage at which clients begin thinking that there may be a problem and if they should change. The counselor can tip the balance and evoke reasons to change, show the risks of not changing, and strengthen a client's self-efficacy for change of current behavior.
◇ **Determination (or preparation)** is the stage at which the client decides to do something to change behavior; it is a conscious decision. The counselor can help the client determine the best course of action to take in seeking change.
◇ **Action** is the stage of actively doing something; the client chooses a strategy for change and pursues it, taking steps to put that decision into action. The counselor helps the client take those steps toward change.
◇ **Maintenance** is the stage of actively working on and maintaining change strategies. The counselor helps the client renew the process of contemplation, determination, and action without becoming stuck or demoralized because of relapse

(Miller & Rollnick, 2002; Prochaska & Di Clemente, 1994).

GROUP THERAPY

There are several types of group therapy. They are facilitated, peer, 12-step, educational, targeted, and topic specific. Generally, **a major focus of group therapy is having clients help each other break the isolation that chemical dependency induces** so that they know they are not alone. Addicts are able to gain experience and understanding from one another about their addiction and learn different ways to combat craving to help prevent further drug impairment or relapse. As peers they are also able to confront one another on issues that may lead to relapse or continued use.

"The group keeps me honest with myself. I get to look at a lot of things and behaviors that are going on with me and I try to keep in the now. I keep thinking about staying clean today, and the group keeps me focused on my goal of each day trying to stay clean."
Recovering crack cocaine user

Facilitated Groups

Facilitated group therapy usually consists of six or more clients who meet with one or more therapists or counselors on a daily, weekly, or monthly basis. Therapists facilitate the group by actively leading it, bringing up topics to be discussed, encouraging participants to disclose major life issues, prompting others to provide feedback, and processing all issues with their clinical insight. The facilitator helps establish a group culture wherein sharing, trust, and openness become natural to the participants.

Stimulant-abuse peer group that uses confrontational techniques and a facilitator:

William: "I have two sets of friends. People I use with and people who don't use at all. We've got together and had dinner and so forth."
Facilitator: "That's real safe for you, William. Listen to me, William. They don't know what to look for.

They don't know what to expect, and you can manipulate them real easy."

Maria: "The same thing happened to me. You still think you can sit around with alcoholics, with people who drink, like you think you can hang around with dope dealers?"

William: "So the only people I can associate with are people in recovery?"

Maria: "I had to give up my sister."

William: "Okay, admit it. Everybody out there doesn't have a problem."

Maria: "But you do."

William: "That's true."

Facilitator: "Let me ask you a question. Can you see your ears?"

William: "No."

Facilitator: "So that means we can see something you can't see, right? Okay. So far, this group, with your issues, we're batting a thousand. Yes or no?"

William: "Yes."

Peer Groups

Peer group therapy consists of therapists playing a less active role in the dynamics. **They observe interaction and are available to process any conflicts or areas of need but do not direct or lead the process.**

Drug-abuse recovery peer group:

John: "I didn't want to come here this morning and then to come here and be faced with, 'Well, you gotta think whether you really want to be here.' It's like I'm ready and I'm scared."

Counselor: "What's scaring you?"

John: "I feel like I'm failing myself."

Bob: "When did you fail before?"

John: "When have I failed before? Oh, I would say the last time was when I got busted buying crack. Just going out there is failing. Knowing I shouldn't be doing that."

Bob: "You gotta put that out there. You gotta deal with that."

John: "The thing is I'm scared of when I'm going to snap again."

Self-Help Groups & Alcoholics Anonymous (12-step group)

The concept of abstinence-based self-help groups goes back hundreds of years in America to fraternal temperance societies and reform clubs where recovering alcoholics could go to maintain their abstinence through discussion, prayer, and social activities. **One of the earliest groups was the Washingtonian Revival started in 1840** by six members of a drinking club in Baltimore, Maryland. They started a weekly temperance meeting and, instead of debates, drinking games, and speeches, their main activity was sharing their experiences, starting with confessions of a debasing lifestyle caused by their excessive drinking. New members, still in the throes of their addiction, were encouraged to tell their own story and sign a pledge of abstinence. This working-class movement spread its message rapidly, and chapters formed across the country. At the peak of the Washingtonian movement, more than 600,000 pledges were signed. Some meetings had thousands of participants, almost like a revival. The women's auxiliary was called the Martha Washington Society. The Washingtonian program of recovery was closely mirrored by that of Alcoholics Anonymous, which was created 90 years later.

The Washingtonian Revival program of recovery came to include public confession, public commitment, visits from older members, economic assistance, continued participation in experience sharing, acts of service toward other alcoholics, and sober entertainment.

The demise of the movement seven years after its inception was somewhat of a mystery, although everybody had an explanation—that they mostly ignored spirituality in the movement, that they had a weak organizational structure, that they were too sensationalistic, that they didn't have a sustainable recovery program, and that prosperity made them less essential. The example

of the Washingtonians, however, encouraged other fraternal temperance societies and reform clubs, including the Order of the Good Samaritans, the Order of Good Templars, the Black Templars, the Independent Order of Rechabites, and Osgood's Reformed Drinkers Club. There was continuing debate over whether Prohibition was the real answer to alcoholism. Over the next 50 years, many types of organizations were tried, such as those with a religious basis like rescue missions and the Salvation Army (White, 1998).

It was the evolution and the refinement of these groups coupled with the end of Prohibition, the closing down of many drying-out institutions and treatment hospitals, and the beginning of the Great Depression that eventually led in the 1930s to **Alcoholics Anonymous, the most widespread recovery movement in history. AA is a peer group concept based on 12 steps of recovery. These groups have no professional therapist or facilitator present to interact with their members.** Each group is independent, and members rely on one another's knowledge and successes to help curb alcohol and other drug use. The parent group provides literature, suggestions for meeting format, and general structure. The core book, *Alcoholics Anonymous* (usually referred to as *The Big Book*), was written by Bill Wilson (a recovering alcoholic) and Dr. Bob Smith (a physician), the founders of AA, along with 100 recovering alcoholics who tell their stories (Trice, 1995).

"When I went to my first meeting, a 30-year-old beautician was running her story about how her drinking started, the pain she suffered because of it, and what happened to change her. I was a 49-year-old male with my own business, and yet her story was my story. Her reaction to alcohol was the same as mine. Her helplessness after the first drink was mine. Her denial was mine. Her divorce was mine. Her reactions to life's problems were mine. The familiarity and the sheer power of her running her story

These three Narcotics Anonymous logos, from left to right are from the Western Area, Southern Utah, and Texas Tri County Area. Narcotics Anonymous, founded in 1953, has more than 35,000 weekly meetings in 116 countries; about 80% of these weekly meetings are in the United States. This compares with Alcoholics Anonymous, which has more than 100,000 weekly meetings and 2 million current members.

have kept me in the group for five and a half years. In AA they say, 'We only have our stories and all we can do is tell what worked for us to stay sober.'"
54-year-old recovering alcoholic

Some of the other 12-step groups that have formed include Narcotics Anonymous (NA), Crystal Meth Anonymous (CMA), Cocaine Anonymous (CA), Marijuana Anonymous (MA), Gamblers Anonymous (GA), Overeaters Anonymous (OA), Sexaholics Anonymous (SA), and Debtors Anonymous (DA).

In addition Al-Anon (for families of alcoholics), Adult Children of Alcoholics (ACoA), and Alateen (for teenagers with alcoholic relatives) use the 12-step process to help those immediately affected by the behavior of addicts and alcoholics. All 12-step programs are free. They pay their minimal costs through voluntary donations. **The only requirement for membership is a desire to stop the addiction.**

"We're not here to help you stop your addiction. We're here to help you if you want to stop your addiction."
Popular sign at AA meetings

The 12-step process engages addicts at their level of addiction; breaks the isolation, guilt, and pain; and shows them they are not alone. The process also fully supports the idea that addiction is a lifelong disease (or allergy, as originally defined in Alcoholics Anonymous) that

must be dealt with for the remainder of a person's life. It promotes a program of honesty, open-mindedness, and willingness (**HOW**) to change. Those are the key elements in sustaining lifelong abstinence from drugs, alcohol, and other addictive behaviors. It breaks down denial and supplies a structure through which people can continue to work on their addiction. **The 12-step programs are based on the concept of solving problems through personal spiritual change**, a concept articulated by the Oxford Group, a popular spiritual movement of the 1920s and 1930s and harking back to the Washingtonian Revival groups of the 1840s (AA, 1934, 1976; Miller, 1998; Nace, 2005).

Spirituality & Recovery

Spiritual and faith-based treatment interventions have a long and positive tradition in the recovery community but continue to generate controversy in a culture that promotes freedom of religion yet separation of church and state. Many empirical studies and research reviews document a **60% to 80% correlation between religion or spirituality and better health** in diverse medical areas of prevention, treatment, and recovery for a wide range of mental and physical conditions. These studies compare treatment outcomes of those who are engaged in spiritual or religious practices with those who are not and consistently find better health outcomes and improved quality of life: physical health, affective mental states, sus-

tained recovery from drug and alcohol abuse, coping skills, immune system improvement, lowering blood pressure, better cardiac status, decreasing problems from cerebral vascular disease, more hope, and reduced suicidal ideation in the spiritually engaged (Koenig, George & Peterson, 1998; Koenig, McCullough & Larson, 2001; Powell, 2003).

Spiritual programs rely on belief and faith to help restore health and abstinence from drugs or alcohol. **Use of nonscientific language and religious passages can be more acceptable than the complex clinical and psychological language of recovery. Scripture can also be condemning and judgmental, however, which is difficult for chemically dependent people because they are often already experiencing much undue shame and guilt.** There is also a concern of a "spiritual bypass"—the misuse of faith to avoid taking responsibility for some past behaviors and to avoid making difficult psychological changes. There can also be limitations on who can participate in faith-based programs due to limited and exclusive perceptions of spirituality (Brubaker, 2006; Tangenberg, 2005). Despite such controversies, the evidence is clear that when recovery treatment includes spiritual interventions, it results in positive treatment outcomes. Spirituality should therefore be included as part of the treatment process for substance use disorders. What may now be needed is a more multidimensional view of spirituality by the recovery community.

"People misunderstand spirituality. They mistake it for religion. Spirituality is people's personal relationship with their higher power as they define him, her, or it. Religion is the way they practice their spirituality. My higher power is God as I learned of Him in my youth. For others their higher power could be an ideal, a philosophy, the goodness within themselves, a great person they met in their lives, the stars, or the members of the 12-step group itself. It's something greater than themselves

that they can turn to to get help for their smothering addiction and to reconstruct their lives. It's only when they give up the need to try to control everything in their lives and give up control to their higher power that they gain the power to overcome their addiction and say no to the first drink."

51-year-old ex-priest who gives talks on spirituality and his recovery from alcoholism

Although most 12-step groups understand and accept spirituality, some users cannot accept the idea of a higher power. For those people *The Big Book* of Alcoholics Anonymous says to take what you want and leave the rest.

The 12 Steps of Alcoholics Anonymous

Step 1: **We admitted we were powerless over alcohol [cocaine, cigarettes, food, gambling] and that our lives had become unmanageable.**

Step 2: Came to believe that a power greater than ourselves could restore us to sanity.

Step 3: Made a decision to turn our will and our lives over to the care of God as we understood Him.

Step 4: Made a searching and fearless moral inventory of ourselves.

Step 5: Admitted to God, to ourselves, and to another human being the exact nature of our wrongs.

Step 6: Were entirely ready to have God remove all these defects of character.

Step 7: Humbly asked Him to remove our shortcomings.

Step 8: Made a list of all persons we had harmed and became willing to make amends to them all.

Step 9: Made direct amends to such people wherever possible, except when to do so would injure them or others.

Step 10: Continued to take personal inventory and when we were wrong, promptly admitted it.

Step 11: Sought through prayer and meditation to improve our conscious contact with God as we understood Him, praying only for knowledge of

His will for us and the power to carry that out.

Step 12: **Having had a spiritual awakening as the result of these steps, we tried to carry this message to alcoholics and to practice these principles in all our affairs.**

In a study of 12-step programs at the University of California at Los Angeles (UCLA) by Dr. Robert Fiorentine and his colleagues, it was found that participation in meetings after completing treatment increased the abstinence rate twofold and presumably the recovery rate (Figure 9-4) (Fiorentine, 1999). The same study found that increasing counseling sessions (at least four group sessions and one individual session more per month) reduced drug use by 40%.

"I'm not the same person that I was when I entered this fellowship. Through my recovery and the 12 steps, I have found meaning and purpose in

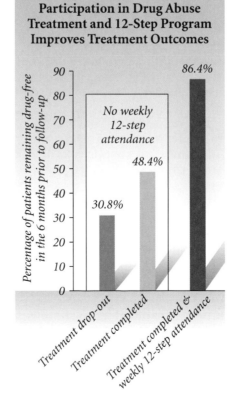

Participation in Drug Abuse Treatment and 12-Step Program Improves Treatment Outcomes

Figure 9-4 •

Weekly attendance at 12-step meetings after treatment almost doubles the abstinence rate of patients (48% vs. 86.4%).

my life. It feels especially good with my kids because they know that I'm here for them. There's no catch-up anymore. I keep my promises. The challenge of a sober parent is keeping promises."

Recovering heroin addict

The 12 steps can work for any addictive behavior. This is because the roots of addiction lie first in the immediate character and current lifestyle of the user and second in the use of psychoactive substances.

There are also secular versions of the peer group process used in 12-step groups. These groups do not believe that a higher power is necessary for recovery.

A group like **Rational Recovery** believes that if you learn to like yourself for who you are, you will not need to drink or use other drugs. They believe that all addictions come from the same roots. Their approach is based on rational emotive therapy developed by Albert Ellis.

Another group, **Secular Organization for Sobriety**, also makes no distinction among the various chemical addictions. Their goal is sobriety, one day at a time, like AA's and NA's goal.

Women for Sobriety (WFS) does have a spiritual basis but feels that AA principles work better for men. WFS emphasizes the power of positive emotions. **Men for Sobriety (MFS)** has also been formed (Horvath, 2005).

Educational Groups

These groups focus primarily on providing information about the addictive process in recovery. **Trained counselors provide the education and often bring in other experts to promote individual lesson plans** to help addicts gain knowledge about their conditions.

Homework assignments are often included to help addicts understand the information. A variety of workbooks and manuals have been written to assist in this process. They also teach relapse prevention, coping skills, and even support therapy. Research during the development of the Matrix Model for stimulant-abuse problems indicate that a manual-based educational process

Cornered   by Baldwin

7-15 © 2002 Mike Baldwin / Dist. by Universal Press Syndicate www.cornered.com
cornered@comic.com

HYPOCHONDRIACS
ANONYMOUS

"First step is the hardest. You've got to admit that you don't have a problem."

may work even better than a formal counseling process to promote and sustain recovery (Anglin & Rawson, 2000).

Targeted Groups

These groups can be part of a formal program or a nonfacilitated peer group and are **directed at specific populations of users**. Such targeted groups include men's groups, women's groups, gay and lesbian groups, physician groups, dual-diagnosis groups, bad girls groups (targeted at prostitutes), professional groups (e.g., healthcare professionals and attorneys), and priest/minister/rabbi groups (targeted at the clergy). The key to the success of any group is its ability to develop a group culture that provides relevant, meaningful, acceptable, and insightful knowledge for its participants.

Topic-Specific Groups

Whereas target groups are aimed at certain cultures, topic-specific groups are aimed at certain issues (e.g., AIDS recovery, early recovery, relapse pre-

vention, recovery maintenance, relationships, and codependency). The advantage of these groups is that **they allow the participants to focus on key issues that are a threat to their continued recovery**.

Most studies indicate that **group therapies seem to promote better outcomes and sustain abstinence more than individual therapies**. Specifically, alcohol and cocaine addictions are more responsive to the group process than to individual counseling. From an administrative standpoint, group processes are also much more cost-effective.

Ten Common Errors Made in Group Treatment by Beginning Counselors or Substance-Abuse Workers

(Adapted from Geoffrey L. Greif, D.S.W., associate dean and professor, University of Maryland)

1. **Failure to have a realistic view of group treatment.**

    Preconceived expectations about the effectiveness of group therapy may

cause a new therapist to become impatient with the group's progress; the reality is that each group progresses at a different rate from, extremely slowly to explosive movement.

    Possible solution: Supervision teaches the therapist to adopt a longer-term perspective. In addition, a thorough understanding of the behaviors caused by the specific drug, the way the other groups in the agency function, and the cultural backgrounds and gender-related behaviors of the members make for more-realistic expectations.

2. **Self-disclosure issues and the failure to drop the "mask" of professionalism.**

    New leaders are often challenged by the group members, who test the therapist's understanding and/or personal experience with substance abuse.

    Possible solution: A response to any challenge by group members needs to be prepared in advance because too much disclosure by the therapist of personal experience can be as bad as too little disclosure. Leaders need to accept the humanity of their clients as well as disclosing their own.

3. **Agency culture issues and personal style.**

    Different methods of running groups can confuse clients and make them feel trapped between styles. Group culture vs. facility culture can cause dissonance.

    Possible solution: The therapist needs to make his or her approach consistent with agency style. Personal styles of treatment that are not contradictory to other counselors' styles should be developed with the help of the supervisor and more-experienced therapists.

4. **Failure to understand the stages of therapy.**

    Groups pass through specific stages during the recovery process, and failure to see the progression can hamper the group process.

    Possible solution: There must be a thorough understanding of the various stages of recovery and how to respond with appropriate and timely exercises and thoughts.

5. Failure to recognize countertransference issues.

Often an inexperienced group leader or therapist will let personal feelings about group members show through or affect their performance, particularly if age, gender, ethnic background, or lifestyle is different.

Possible solution: The novice therapist must be aware of and accept such feelings as a normal part of the therapist/client relationship—they should just avoid acting on those feelings in a nontherapeutic manner.

6. Failure to clarify group rules.

The biggest mistake is failure to clarify group rules (e.g., confidentiality, coming to the group high, arriving late, meeting outside of groups, and making personal attacks on other members).

Possible solution: Posting the rules at every session or a written handout that gives clear explanations of the procedures followed by a discussion of the rules will give the group a solid base of understanding.

7. Failure to do group therapy by focusing on individual problem-solving.

In trying to please individual members of the group by giving insightful and helpful suggestions for problems unrelated to recovery issues, the therapist can weaken the group.

Possible solution: Focus the group on providing advice, information, help, and support to address recovery-related issues rather than individual unrelated problems. This gives meaning, purpose, and power to the group.

8. Failure to plan in advance.

When the leader decides to wing it and doesn't know quite what the group will be doing, less is accomplished.

Possible solution: The therapist should have a plan for each session and possibly a backup plan so that the group never feels directionless. A structured curriculum with a set number of sequential lesson plans that can also serve as benchmarks for the group's progress toward recovery can also be helpful.

9. Failure to integrate new members into the group.

If a new member enters the group, integrating him or her into the established flow can slow the group down. Conversely, if new members are instantly integrated, they don't have time to develop naturally and feel part of the group.

Possible solution: The therapist can use the opportunity to have the group reevaluate its progress and recommit to the group.

10. Failure to understand interactions in the group as a metaphor for drug-related issues occurring in the group member's family of origin.

A new therapist may believe that reactions among group members that are based on a client's familial relationships are true reactions. They might not realize the source of the reactions and so lose an opportunity to use that information to help the client.

Possible solution: The therapist needs to take the time to establish strong bonds with group members so that issues and insights raised by group interactions can be used to help the clients.

TREATMENT & THE FAMILY

"I got put into treatment and got out of treatment, you know. I just bullshitted my whole way through treatment. I told them what they wanted to hear and got out and just relapsed again because my dad was like, 'Here, you want to smoke some weed? You want to drink a beer?' It's kinda hard to say no when your dad's sitting there asking you. It makes you feel like it's okay."

15-year-old recovering polydrug abuser

About one-fourth of the U.S. population is part of a family that is affected by an addictive disorder in a first-degree relative; up to 90% of active addicts live at home with a family or with a significant other (Parran, Liepman & Farkas, 2003). **Addiction is a family disease. Abuse of drugs and alcohol has a greatly impact on all members of an addict's family** regardless of whether they also abuse psychoactive substances (Schenker & Minayo, 2004). Analysis of employed addicts and alcoholics demonstrates that their families use the employer's health insurance much more than the families of nonaddicts. This is indicative of the great emotional, physical, and social strain that addicts place on their families.

"Addicts don't have families, they have hostages."

John DeDomenico, family therapist, Haight Ashbury Detox Clinic

Despite this well-established relationship, **the family is often ignored and neglected in the treatment of addictive disease**. This has resulted in family members' seeking treatment on their own through traditional family and mental health services or through self-help family treatment systems like Tough Love, Al-Anon, and Nar-Anon. More important, continued stress from family problems or troubled family members makes it difficult for the recovering addict to remain abstinent.

"A family is ruled by its sickest member."

Moss Hart, dramatist

GOALS OF FAMILY TREATMENT

Treatment of addicts and their families has four major goals:

1. **Acceptance by all family members that addiction is a treatable disease and not a sign of moral weakness.** The addict also needs to accept this point.

2. **Establishing and maintaining a drug-free family system.** This often includes treatment of the spouse's drug problems or those of the addict's children.

3. **Developing a system for family communication and interaction.** This must continue to reinforce the addict's recovery process. It is accomplished by integrating family therapy into addiction treatment.

4. **Processing the family's readjustment.** This is a necessary step after cessation of drug and alcohol abuse.

"I burnt every bridge that I've got with pretty much everybody in my whole life. The family sessions here are helping a little bit, you know. My mom comes in—my stepdad doesn't want anything to do with me but my mom comes in; we're working, we're listening, you know. We're not just fighting anymore. She's not yelling at the top of her lungs. I'm not telling her to f*** off anymore. We're actually working together. It feels good. I might be able to get a life."

18-year-old male recovering polydrug abuser

DIFFERENT FAMILY APPROACHES

Family therapists employ a wide variety of tools and techniques to accomplish these goals once all family members have been motivated to participate. The following are some of the more common models.

Family Systems Approach

This model explores and recognizes how a family regulates its internal and external environments, making note of how these interactional patterns change over time. Three major focus areas of this approach are daily routines, family rituals (e.g., holidays), and short-term problem-solving strategies. **The drug or drinking problem is seen as an integral part of the functioning of all members of the family**, not just the person with the problem. Some family systems therapists use 12-step groups as part of their therapy, and many feel that correcting family relationships corrects much of the substance-abuse problem.

Family Behavioral Approach

This approach operates under the concept that interactional behaviors are learned and perpetuated by reinforcements for continuing the behavior. Thus the therapist works with the family to recognize those family behaviors associated with drug use; to categorize the interactions as either negative or positive in reinforcing drug use; and then to **provide specific interventions to support and reinforce those behav**iors that promote a drug-free family system. Some of the specific strategies used are couples sessions, homework, self-monitoring exercises, communication training, and the development of negotiating and problem-solving skills. A couple might even enter into a behavior change agreement (O'Farrell & Cowles, 1989). Some who use the behavioral approach focus more on working with the nonabusing spouse.

Family Functioning Approach

This approach first helps the addict or treatment program classify the family system into one of four different types. It then uses the classification as a guide for the therapeutic intervention that is best suited to the functioning of that family system.

1. **Functional family systems** are those in which the family of the addict has maintained healthy interactions. Interventions in this system are targeted directly at the addict. Other family members receive limited education and advice to support the addict's recovery.

2. **Neurotic or enmeshed family systems** usually require intensive family treatment aimed at restructuring the way the family interacts.

3. **Disintegrated family systems** call for a separate yet integrated treatment of addicts and their families. The family may attend Al-Anon while an alcoholic is engaged in an intensive medical detoxification program. Though the addict is separated in treatment, this approach needs to be integrated at some point into the common goal of maintaining a drug-free lifestyle.

4. **Absent family systems** are those in which family members are not available for treatment.

Social Network Approach

This approach focuses mainly on the treatment of the addict but also establishes a concurrent and integrated support network for the family members to assist them with the problems caused by the addiction. Through participation in multiple family support or therapy groups, **the family breaks** their isolation and develops skills that help them support the recovery effort of their addicted member.

TOUGHLOVE® Approach

Though controversial, this movement has grown on the West Coast. The *TOUGHLOVE®* approach addresses the major obstacle of denial in both the addict and his or her family. When the addict refuses to accept or deal with dysfunctional drug-using behavior, the family members seek treatment and support from other families experiencing similar problems. **The family learns to establish limits for their interaction with the addict.** This has even included kicking the addict out of the home and severing all contact until the addict agrees to treatment.

OTHER BEHAVIORS

"Even though it was my dad that drank 'til he got sick, doing the intervention was harder for me than for him. I knew he denied his drinking. I didn't realize that I did too even though I didn't drink myself and that I had almost as many problems as he did."

31-year-old adult child of an alcoholic

The stress of living with an alcoholic or a drug abuser causes dysfunctional behaviors in the nonusing family members. The most prevalent conditions are codependency, enabling, and manifesting symptoms caused by being children of addicts or adult children of alcoholics.

Codependency

Just as addicts are dependent on a substance, **codependents are mutually dependent on the addicts to fulfill some need of their own**. For example, a wife may be dependent on her husband's maintaining his addiction so that she can retain her power over the relationship. So long as he's addicted, she has an excuse for her own shortcomings and problems. In this way it creates dysfunction in the addict because it promotes the addiction. Codependency can also be extremely subtle. For example, a person who has been abstinent from alcohol for a week or so has a spouse who offers a drink as a reward for the abstinence. In this kind of household, **the chances of recovery are greatly reduced unless the codependents are willing to accept their role in the addictive process and submit to treatment themselves** (Gorski, 1993; Liepman, Keller, Botelho, et al., 1998).

"I was clean for 16 months. My husband had only been clean for six weeks. And I tried to show him that being clean and sober does work because my husband, he's not an alcoholic, he basically just smokes crack. And I think he saw what the program was doing for me and that I wasn't going back out or relapsing and buying drugs for him. [In the past] he would sit here and think I would get up and feel sorry for him and go, 'Okay, honey, you're craving, let's get high together.'"

38-year-old recovering polydrug abuser

Enabling

When a family becomes dependent on the addiction of a family member, **there is a strong tendency to avoid confrontation about the addictive behavior and a subconscious effort to actively perpetuate the addiction,** often led by a person who benefits from that addiction-the chief enabler. Although enablers may be disgusted with the addict and the addictive behavior, they continue to pay off drug debts, pay rent, provide money, or even continue emotional support for a practicing addict. As with codependents, **the enablers need to accept the role they are playing in this cycle and seek therapy** so that they can be more effective in the addict's recovery.

Children of Addicts & Adult Children of Addicts

Many studies have found coping problems in a large percentage of the children of addicts and alcoholics. About 11 million children of alcoholics are under the age of 18, and about 3 million of those will develop alcoholism, other drug problems, and seri-

LES PAPAS.

Un fils modèle.

The etching by Henri Daumier is titled The Fathers *while the caption reads "A model son."*

ous coping problems (Windle, 1999). (These statistics also mean that about three-fourths of the children of alcoholics do not develop addiction or serious coping problems.)

Many children of addicts take on predictable maladaptive behavioral roles within the family that "co" the addiction and often continue on into their adult personalities. In addict families, the roles taken on by the children are usually one or more of the following:

◊ **Model child.** These children are high achievers and are overly responsible. They become chief enablers of addicted parents by taking over their roles and responsibilities.

◊ **Problem child.** These children experience continual multiple personal problems and often manifest early drug or alcohol addiction. They demand and get most of what attention is left from parents and siblings.

◊ **Lost child.** These children are withdrawn, "spaced-out," and disconnected from the life and the emotions around them. Often avoiding any emotionally confronting issues, they are unable to form close friendships or intimate bonds with others.

◊ **Mascot child or family clown.** These children use another avoidance strategy, which is to make everything trivial by minimizing all serious issues. They are well liked and easy to befriend but are usually superficial in all relationships, even those with their own family members.

What is important to remember about children of addicts or alcoholics is that **although they may not abuse drugs, their behavior and emotional reactions can be as dysfunctional as those of an addict.** Often they learn very early on that they cannot control the addiction of their parent, so they often resort to trying to control all other aspects of their lives, leading to strained and inappropriate relationships later in life.

Adult children of addicts or alcoholics also:

◊ are **isolated and afraid** of people and authority figures;

◊ are **approval seekers** who lose identity in the process;

◊ **are frightened by angry people** and personal criticism;

◊ **become or marry alcoholics** or find another compulsive person to fulfill abandonment needs;

◊ feel guilty when standing up for themselves instead of giving in to others;

◊ become addicted to excitement and stimulation;

◊ confuse love and pity, and tend to love people who can be pitied and rescued;

◊ repress feelings from traumatic childhoods and lose the ability to feel or express feelings;

◊ judge themselves harshly and have low self-esteem; and

◊ are reactors rather than initiators.

(Hawkins, 2003; Sher, 1997).

Adult Children of Alcoholics is a 12-step program to help adult children of alcoholics work through the emotional baggage that followed them into adulthood (ACoA, 2007). ACoA and other similar groups try to help members:

◊ understand the disease of addiction and alcoholism because understanding is the beginning of forgiveness;

◊ put themselves at the top of their priority list;

◊ detach with love;

◊ feel, accept, and express feelings and build self-esteem; and

◊ learn to love themselves, thus making it possible for them to love others in healthy ways.

ADJUNCTIVE & COMPLEMENTARY TREATMENT SERVICES

Drug abuse and addiction along with behavioral addictions have a negative impact on the sufferer's physical, emotional, familial, social, and spiritual well-being. Addicts and alcoholics suffer from higher rates of AIDS, viral hepatitis (A, B and C), heart disease, mental illness, emotional disorders, and other physical and psychiatric illnesses compared with nonaddicts. All of these issues represent serious health and quality-of-life problems for addicts. The traditional role of addiction treatment has been to **help identify these various needs and then case-manage addicts toward appropriate treatment or service providers**.

Recent concepts believe that treatment that effectively addresses all of these components through a comprehensive, integrated, and "wrap-around" service delivery design within the same program results in increased positive outcomes. Treatment campuses with a variety of integrated services, the merger of county mental health and substance-abuse services departments into a single behavioral health department, and the "any door" or "no wrong door" substance-abuse treatment ac-

cess initiatives—all are examples of this growing movement toward a single, comprehensive addiction treatment system. The recent interest and growth of faith-based or spiritual substance-abuse treatment initiatives are also part of this development. The U.S. Department of Health and Human Services created the HHS Center for Faith-Based and Community Initiatives to help incorporate nonprofit religious and secular organizations in preventing and treating drug abuse and addiction.

DRUG-SPECIFIC TREATMENT

POLYDRUG ABUSE

Experience at treatment centers across the United States shows that although addicts may identify a drug of choice, they are more often than not polysubstance abusers who are using a wide range of substances either concurrently or intermittently. The profile of alcoholics, for example, often includes sedatives, methamphetamine, cocaine, marijuana, and even opioids in addition to the abuse of alcohol. **Treatment programs need to be aggressive about identifying the total drug profile of their clients.** Heroin addicts will often minimize or lie about their use of alcohol even though their drinking may be at a more problematic level than their use of heroin. **Many substance abusers also practice a behavioral addiction such as gambling, compulsive eating, or even Internet addiction simultaneously** with their drug use or sequentially during their recovery.

"I have cleaned up off of dope though I've been a drug addict for 23 years. And I have no desire whatsoever to do drugs, but alcohol is still there and I do it out of boredom."
42-year-old recovering heroin addict with AIDS

A recent twin study found high levels of co-morbidity for abuse/dependence for six different substances (marijuana, cocaine, hallucinogens, sedatives, stimulants, and opiates) and only low levels for single substances.

Each twin's environment, not heredity, was more influential in the specific drug of choice (Kendler, Jacobson, Prescott, et al., 2003). **Addiction must be addressed as chemical dependency rather than a drug-specific problem.** Treatment is effective in promoting recovery, preventing relapse, and preventing a switch to alternate drug addictions.

"The cravings were just continuous. It was just like—if I was coming off of speed, I wanted heroin. If I was coming off heroin, I wanted to snort cocaine; and if I was coming off that, I wanted to stay numb. I wanted to just go from one drug to another."
38-year old recovering polydrug abuser

Given the similarity of the roots of addiction, each drug still has unique effects and problems that should be specifically addressed.

STIMULANTS (cocaine & amphetamines)

The differences between treatments for amphetamine and cocaine abusers indicate that **methamphetamine abusers were more likely to be male, Caucasian, and gay or bisexual.** They were also more likely than cocaine abusers to engage in unsafe sex, share needles, be HIV-positive, have a psychiatric diagnosis, and be on psychiatric medications (Copeland & Sorensen, 2001). On the other hand, cocaine abusers were similar to meth abusers in adherence to treatment protocols and recovery rates, suggesting that a stimulant-abuse program can probably handle both drugs together rather than have separate protocols and groups.

The profile of the **typical U.S. methamphetamine abuser in 2006 was a white male between the ages of 19 and 40.** In younger users (eighth- and tenth-graders), however, and in some parts of the West (especially Hawaii and southern California), an equal if not slightly greater number of meth abusers are women (National Drug Intelligence Center, 2007). Further, the vast majority of the known users in Hawaii are of Asian or Pacific Islander decent. There is also a high incidence of abuse among the gay male population of the San Francisco Bay Area. It is interesting that Mexico is also experiencing a rapid growth in abuse of methamphetamine, and some counties in California are seeing a significant population of Hispanic abusers.

Although admissions for treatment of cocaine abuse have decreased since 1994, some 256,000 people were admitted for cocaine treatment in 2005, which represents 14% of the 1.85 million treated for substance-abuse problems that year. Of those treated 72% were primarily smokable or "crack" cocaine abusers. Although there was a 250% increase in admissions for methamphetamine and amphetamine abuse in the same period, about 170,000 people were treated for this problem in 2005, or about 9% of all substance-abuse treatments (SAMHSA, 2006B).

A wide range of drug-induced psychiatric symptoms often accompanies stimulant abuse. Acute paranoia, schizophrenia, major depression, and bipolar disorders are often the initial presentations by a stimulant addict, particularly at the end of a long run. These symptoms require psychiatric intervention to prevent harm and to **assess whether they are caused by the drug itself or whether the mental illnesses are preexisting** and will remain a problem after detoxification and initial abstinence.

Besides psychiatric symptoms, other key effects to watch out for in cocaine or amphetamine abusers who are detoxifying are prolonged craving, anergia (exhaustion), anhedonia (lack of an ability to feel pleasure), and euthymia (a feeling of elation that occurs three to five days after stopping use). Euthymia makes users feel that they never were addicted and that they don't need to be in treatment. Anergia and anhedonia begin to overtake the euthymia about two weeks after starting detoxification, and these feelings, particularly the total lack of ability to feel pleasure, often lead to relapse (Gawin, Khalsa & Ellinwood, 1994).

Detoxification & Initial Abstinence

After detoxification and treatment for any psychotic and life-threatening symptoms, such as extremely high blood pressure, high body temperature, high and irregular heart rate, and even seizures, **the vast majority of stimulant abusers respond positively to traditional drug-counseling approaches.** Evidence-based best practices have demonstrated that cognitive-behavioral therapies (CBT) and behavioral therapies like the Matrix Model along with 12-step-oriented individual counseling are useful for cocaine- or stimulant-abuse treatment (Kleber, 2006).

Stimulant addicts who do not initially respond to these traditional approaches require a more intensive medical approach to bridge the detoxification/withdrawal period prior to their engagement in recovery. No medication has yet received FDA approval for the treatment of cocaine or methamphetamine dependence, though several are in FDA Investigational New Drug (IND) development. **A variety of drugs are medically used to treat various symptoms of stimulant detoxification and initial abstinence.**

◇ **Antidepressant agents,** such as SSRI drugs like fluoxetine (Prozac®) and citalopram (Celexa®) or other newer ones such as mirtazapine (Remeron®), nefazodone (Serzone®), and venlafaxine (Effexor®), are widely used. These affect serotonin, the neurotransmitter in the brain that deals with both depression and mood.

◇ **Antipsychotic medications** are used to buffer the effects of unbalanced dopamine, which can mimic a psychosis. These drugs include risperidone (Risperdal®), olanzapine (Zyprexa®), ziprasidone (Geodon®), quetiapine (Seroquel®), haloperidol (Haldol®), and others. These are also called **neuroleptic medications.**

◇ **Sedatives** are prescribed very carefully on a short-term basis to treat anxiety or sleep disturbance problems; these include phenobarbital, chloral hydrate, buspirone (BuSpar®), and, less often, flurazepam (Dalmane®), chlordiazepoxide (Librium®), and even diazepam (Valium®).

◇ **Nutritional approaches** aimed at enhancing the production of those neurotransmitters that have been depleted by heavy stimulant use help decrease craving and counteract many of the withdrawal symptoms seen in stimulant addiction. Tyrosine, phenylalanine, and tryptophan are proteins used by brain cells to manufacture the dopamine, adrenaline, and serotonin that was depleted by stimulant abuse. Their effectiveness has not been proven with conclusive studies.

◇ **Dopamine agonists** like bromocriptine (Parlodel®), amantadine (Symmetrel®), and levodopa (combined with carbidopa in Sinemet®) activate the dopamine receptors in the brain to **suppress withdrawal symptoms and initial craving for stimulants**. Abuse of both cocaine and amphetamines depletes brain dopamine levels, which results in craving and other symptoms of withdrawal.

◇ **Others include modafinil (Provigil®)**, a stimulant drug used to treat narcolepsy and sleep disorders, which is also used to treat stimulant cravings. Antiepileptic seizure drugs like **topiramate (Topamax®)** block sodium ion channels on brain cells and are also used to decrease craving for stimulant drugs.

Long-Term Abstinence

A lot of research is currently being put into the treatment of craving and particularly stimulant craving. Two major types of craving have been addressed: endogenous craving and environmentally triggered craving.

To counter endogenous craving, believed to be caused by the depletion of dopamine activity at the nucleus accumbens of the limbic system, **many medications (as mentioned above) have been used to stimulate dopamine release**, thereby diminishing long-term craving for stimulants. Acupuncture is also used to stimulate dopamine release. Animal research suggests that the dopamine imbalance may last for up to 10 months after cessation of cocaine or amphetamine use (Ricaurte, Seiden & Schuster, 1984).

Environmentally triggered craving is particularly intense in stimu-lant addiction. It is more likely to lead to relapse than endogenous craving and must be treated with intense counseling, group sessions, or desensitization techniques. This type of craving may last throughout one's life, but evidence indicates that **continued abstinence weakens the craving response**. This weakening can lead to the extinction of craving caused by environmental triggers.

In an investigation funded by the National Institute on Drug Abuse of 1,600 cocaine-dependent patients with moderate-to-severe problems, researchers found that an absolute minimum of three months of treatment was needed to achieve lasting results (eight months maximized effectiveness). About two and a half times more patients relapsed after leaving short-term treatment (38% relapsed) than those leaving long-term residential treatment (15% relapsed) (Simpson, Joe, Fletcher, et al., 1999).

Cocaine aversion therapy is a very recent and very interesting strategy to treat cocaine dependence. This is the potential **use of disulfiram to induce aversive physical consequences if cocaine is used** (similar to how it is used to treat alcohol dependence). Disulfiram, the oldest FDA-approved addiction treatment drug, was found to induce aversive effects-increased heart rate, blood pressure, anxiety, paranoia, and restlessness—when taken simultaneously with cocaine. This effect has been shown to reduce cocaine use by those in cocaine recovery treatment. Although many cocaine abusers also abuse alcohol, the cocaine effect has been shown to be unrelated to its effect on alcohol metabolism. Researchers speculate that both disulfiram and cocaine increase dopamine effects at a wide variety of locations in the brain, resulting in a synergistic action of negative symptoms. Early research also seems to indicate that the averse effects occur more in men than in women (Carroll, Fenton, Ball, et al., 2004; Nich, McCance-Katz, Petrakis, et al., 2004; Whitten, 2005).

TOBACCO

Increasingly more **treatment centers for drug and alcohol addictions are including treatment for nicotine addiction as part of their program**. Many believe that full recovery from addiction is made more difficult if the recovering client still smokes. The traditional view has been that giving up tobacco might hinder recovery from what they consider more-dangerous drugs. In fact, recovery rates seem to improve among those who also give up smoking (Gulliver, Kamholz & Helstrom, 2006; Wiley Interscience, 2001). More than 80% of alcoholics and drug addicts smoke compared with 25% of the non-addicted population.

The only guaranteed successful therapy involving tobacco is to never smoke, chew, or use it in any form. Abstinence is necessary because many of the neurological and neurochemical alterations that cause nicotine addiction are permanent. This means that even 10 years after cessation of smoking, a single cigarette can trigger the nicotine craving.

The failure rate for most therapies to stop smoking is extremely high. About 70% of all smokers want to quit, and 46% try each year (CDC, 2000). In the past the focus in treatment was the psychological components of the smoking habit. Those approaches, however, didn't fully take into account the lifetime nature of nicotine addiction and therefore recovery. They tried to apply short-term fixes (e.g., 21-day smoking-cessation programs) to a long-term problem.

Recently, in recognition of the very real alterations in brain chemistry that trigger nicotine craving during withdrawal, **the treatment community has focused on pharmacological treatments**. The five-month success rate with the various pharmacological treatments in one study were: nicotine patch, 17.7%; nicotine inhaler, 22.8%; nicotine gum, 23.7%; bupropion SR (Zyban®), 30.5%; nicotine spray, 30.5%; and a combination of two or more, 28.6% (CDC, 2000). Nicotine lozenges were found to have about the same success rate as nicotine gum in British studies of their use to treat nicotine addiction (Cambell, 2003). Varenicline (Chantix®), approved for nicotine addiction treatment in 2006, has an initial success rate in Europe of 44% and a 22% to 23% sustained (up to one year) nicotine abstinence efficacy (Jorenby,

Hays, Rigotti, et al., 2006; Oncken, Gonzales, Nides, et al., 2006). The average smoker tries to quit five to seven times before succeeding.

Nicotine Replacement Treatment

Because the main mechanism that causes craving is the drop in blood levels of nicotine that then triggers withdrawal symptoms such as irritability, anxiety, drowsiness, and light-headedness, research has been aimed at nicotine replacement systems. **The purpose of these systems is to slowly reduce the blood plasma nicotine levels to the point where cessation will not trigger severe withdrawal symptoms** that will cause the smoker to relapse (Thompson & Hunter, 1998). This pharmacological technique of using low, controlled dosages of a substance to prevent withdrawal and not reinforce the addiction is called **antipriming**.

The five types of nicotine replacement systems are transdermal nicotine patches, nicotine gum, nicotine sprays, nicotine nasal inhalers, and nicotine lozenges. One of the main advantages of all of these systems is that users are no longer damaging their lungs with some of the 4,000 chemicals found in cigarette smoke. This alone could save almost 200,000 lives per year in the United States alone. The main problem is that **if relapse prevention, counseling, and self-help groups are not used in conjunction with nicotine replacement therapy, the chances of smokers' returning to their old habits are high** (Hurt, Ebbert, Gays, et al., 2003).

Nicotine Patches. By 1999 all four FDA-approved nicotine patches (Nicotrol,® Nicoderm CQ,® ProSTEP,® and Habitrol®) were available as over-the-counter (OTC) or nonprescription medications. These nicotine-infused adhesive patches are applied to the skin. Patches can be worn intermittently (daytime only) or continuously. Most of them contain enough nicotine to last 24 to 72 hours. **The advantages of patches are the steady rate of release of nicotine, the ease of compliance, and the lack of toxic effects to tissues in the mouth, lungs, and digestive track.** The disadvantages are the cost, the inability to alter the amount being

With 47 million Americans addicted to cigarettes, the potential market for devices and drugs, such as a nicotine patch, to help kick the habit is huge.
© 1999 CNS Productions, Inc.

• •

absorbed, and the four to six hours it takes for a patch to raise the nicotine level enough to dull nicotine craving. Also, if the user starts smoking while wearing the patch, extremely high and dangerous plasma levels of nicotine can result.

Nicotine Gum. Nicotine gums, such as Nicorette,® have the advantage of slowing the rise in nicotine levels that smoking brings. **The 10-second nicotine rush of an inhaled cigarette gives way to the 15- to 30-minute slow rise that nicotine gum provides when absorbed through the gums** and other mucosal tissues. A slower rise means that craving, which is triggered by the sudden drop in nicotine levels after smoking, doesn't occur. The 15- to 30-minute rise, however, is considerably faster than the four to six hours it takes for a transdermal patch to work, so the user has more control over the dose.

The disadvantages are that the user can cram a lot of gum into the mouth or not use it at all; the gum can irritate mucosal tissues; and an oral habit is maintained (users are still putting something in their mouths when the craving hits or when they are agitated).

Nicotine Nasal Spray. Nicotrol® nasal spray is self-administered and **reaches the brain in 3 to 5 minutes, thereby providing more instant relief** to the nicotine craving and giving more control to the user. Disadvantages include irritation to the nasal passages and reinforcement of nicotine addiction.

Nicotine Inhalers. The Nicotrol® inhaler gives the **fastest relief for nicotine craving** without involving the inhalation of all the other toxic chemicals present in cigarette smoke. The problem seems to be that misuse can produce plasma levels similar to those produced by smoking, thereby perpetuating the addictive process.

Nicotine Lozenges. Ariva® mint-favored tobacco lozenges actually contain up to 60% powdered tobacco (1 mg nicotine). Such a lozenge is **more a source of nicotine when one is in a smoke-free environment (e.g., on a long airplane flight) than it is a smoking-cessation product**. It was actually marketed without FDA approval as a tobacco product before the American Medical Association and other groups filed a petition with the FDA to regulate it along with nicotine water.

Treating the Symptoms

The purpose of symptomatic treatment is to **reduce the anxiety, depression, and craving associated with nicotine withdrawal** that trigger relapse. Though **only varenicline (Chantix®) and bupropion (Zyban®) have FDA approval to treat nicotine withdrawal and craving**, a number of other medications are being used for these indications. Benzodiazepines, buspirone, fluoxetine (Prozac®) or other antidepressants, mecamylamine, propranolol, naltrexone, and naloxone—all have been used to try to alleviate the symptoms of nicotine withdrawal. Even clonidine, often used to control symptoms of heroin or alcohol withdrawal, has been used effectively to control withdrawal from nicotine (Rustin, 1998).

Treating the Behaviors

Most behavioral therapies (CBT, motivational enhancement therapy, and brief therapy) used for smoking cessation include one-on-one counseling, group therapy, educational approaches, aversion therapy, hypnotism, and acupuncture. These have a **one-year success rate of 15% to 30%, with best results achieved when they are combined with pharmacological interventions**. Many of the techniques used in stimulant-abuse recovery are directly applicable to quitting smoking. These include:

◇ desensitizing the smoker to environmental cues that trigger craving;
◇ practicing alternate methods of calming oneself when under stress or going through withdrawal;
◇ avoiding environments and situations, such as bars, where smoking is rampant;
◇ finding other ways of getting the small rush or mild euphoria that nicotine provides;
◇ teaching the smoker the physiology of nicotine use and addiction along with the medical consequences of smoking or chewing tobacco; and
◇ teaching the smoker the extraordinary benefits of quitting
(Kleber, 2006).

OPIOIDS

The vast majority of treatment admissions for opioid abuse lists heroin as the primary drug of abuse, 254,345 out of 322,232 opioid admissions (SAMHSA, 2006B). Heroin admissions had actually declined in proportion to synthetic and nonprescription methadone treatment admissions in 2005, with a small but significant increase in treatment of diverted prescription opioid pain medications. Most heroin abusers also use prescription opioids to prevent withdrawal or tide them over until they can get heroin.

Along with treatment for nicotine addiction, **treatment for opioid addiction has the highest rate of relapse**. This is partially because **physical withdrawal from opioids is more severe than withdrawal from stimulants**. For this reason most opioid abusers who want to recover must be involved in a detoxification and treatment program. In addition, because 83% of admissions for injection drug-abuse treatment were opiate abusers, additional health problems due to needle-borne infections complicate the recovery process (SAMHSA, 2006B).

Detoxification

Methadone, LAAM (no longer available in the United States), and **buprenorphine** are the FDA-approved medications for opioid detoxification. **These drugs are substituted for heroin or the opioid being abused and then gradually tapered to minimize withdrawal.** Programs also use clonidine—or combine it with promethazine, hydroxyzine, benzodiazepines, anticholinergics, non-steroidal anti-inflammatory drugs, or even mild opioids like Darvon®—to manage the symptoms of opioid withdrawal and detoxify the addict. This allows addicts to have less fear of the pain of withdrawal and less pain during withdrawal, and it encourages them to stay in treatment. Rapid opioid detoxification and anesthesia-assisted rapid opioid detoxification with naloxone or naltrexone combined with clonidine or a variety of other medications is an alternate but not recommended detoxification strategy for opioid dependence (Kleber, 2006).

"The physical part of the treatment for opioid addiction is only a tiny portion of the process. It's what happens after you get off, after you detox, that's important. Everyone around you is using, and in a lot of cases you may have financial problems. You may not even have a place to stay. There are other kinds of things that build up and cause you to use again."
Drug counselor

Initial Abstinence & Long-Term Abstinence

A **long-lasting opioid antagonist, such as naltrexone (ReVia®), is used after detoxification** to ensure abstinence because it decreases craving for the drug and also blocks opioids from activating brain cells. Also now available as Vivitrol,® an injectable suspension for alcohol addiction treatment, naltrexone in this formulation does not provide sustained blood levels that could be effective in treating opioid addiction. Depo-naltrexone, an injectable pellet that can provide adequate blood levels of the drug to treat opioid dependence, is in current development.

As with all other treatments, initial abstinence and long-term abstinence are **supported by participating in individual counseling sessions, group sessions, or self-help groups** such as Narcotics Anonymous. Behavioral therapies like CBT, contingency management, and psychodynamic psychotherapy and family therapy have been used effectively to treat opioid addiction (Kleber, 2006). **During the first four to eight weeks of abstinence, daily attendance in these programs is crucial** in maintaining a drug-free state when the craving is strongest. As successful treatment continues, fewer sessions are necessary.

Recovery

Because opioid addiction is so time-consuming and involving, **the key to recovery from heroin or other opioid addiction is learning a new lifestyle**. Instead of waking up every morning with the need to raise $100 to $200 to support a heavy habit, instead of nodding off or feeling drugged, and instead of trying to get clean needles to avoid HIV infection, addicts must learn how to enjoy nondrug activities. They have to learn how to have a relationship and even how to get a driver's license.

"I'm not used to having a room. For the last two years, I was on the streets. I spent $200 a day on heroin and couldn't even manage to find enough money to get a room at the end of the night. That's pretty sick. I've never

actually had a checking account and such because I started using and dealing heroin when I was 12 and I always had to hide my finances."

42-year-old recovering heroin addict

Other Opioid Treatment Modalities

When the FDA approved methadone, LAAM, and buprenorphine for opioid detoxification, it also approval these medications for opioid replacement therapy.

Methadone. There has recently been an effort to expand the use of methadone in the treatment of heroin and other opioid addictions. A consensus statement by the National Institutes of Health **recommended less regulation for dispensing methadone**, wider dispensing authority for trained physicians rather than just at methadone clinics, and improved training in medical schools for physicians on how to diagnose and treat opiate addiction (National Institutes of Health [NIH], 1997).

Much controversy has swirled around the concept of opiate or opioid substitution ever since morphine addiction became a problem in the nineteenth century. Because of the large number of morphine addicts following the Civil War, opiate maintenance clinics multiplied. At this time morphine was used in China to treat opium addiction. In the early 1900s, heroin was used to treat morphine addiction in Europe. This practice of using opiates to treat opiate addiction was ended in the United States (though it continued in England and other countries) in the 1920s and not revived until **methadone maintenance was developed in the late 1960s in New York City** by Vincent Dole and Marie Nyswander (Dole & Nyswander, 1965; Payte, 1997). This treatment modality eventually spread to hundreds of methadone maintenance clinics nationwide in the 1970s and 1980s. **In 2005, 1,069 methadone maintenance clinics provided treatment for more than 200,000 heroin addicts** (DASIS, 2006; NIH, 1997).

The theory is that methadone, a synthetic opiate, while **not as intense**

Methadone is usually dispensed in juice and drunk on the spot to make sure it is being taken properly and is not being diverted to street sales.

© 1999 CNS Productions, Inc.

• •

as heroin, is longer lasting and thus will keep the user from having heroinlike withdrawal symptoms for 36 to 48 hours**. Heroin, on the other hand, causes withdrawal symptoms in just a few hours, so the user goes through the roller coaster of highs and lows and the pain of withdrawal on a daily basis (Lowinson, Marion, Joseph, et al., 2005). Balancing the dose is a continuing problem with the use of methadone, requiring constant monitoring for symptoms of withdrawal.

With methadone maintenance, the highs and the lows that promote addiction are avoided. The user doesn't have to hustle money to pay for a habit, get drugs and needles on the street, or be exposed to a high-risk lifestyle. With HIV and hepatitis C infection rates in IV heroin users as high as 80%, this method of harm reduction

has certain benefits. These include forcing the addict to come to a certain location every day, where counseling, medical care, and other services are available, thus reducing the harm addicts do to themselves and others (Payte & Zweben, 1998).

The controversy over methadone maintenance arises because **many chemical dependency treatment personnel believe that drug abuse should not be treated with another addicting drug on a long-term basis**. Because many users seek treatment after only a short period of addiction while their dose is still relatively low, the immediate use of methadone further ingrains their opioid addiction. In fact, one study has shown that a higher dose of methadone is more effective in reducing illegal opioid and heroin use than a moderate dose, thus imprinting the reliance on the opioid (Strain, Bigelow, Liebson, et al., 1999). Many methadone users have conflicted feelings about use of this harm reduction technique.

"I got on methadone. It was great. It let me hold a job down, methadone did, and I wasn't sick; but still for me, that's not a program to be on for me. It's like a millstone around your neck. You have to be there every day. Sometimes you take your dose home. If you want to go on a vacation, you get permission. And later on, on the program, I started using heroin while I'm using methadone. And that became a problem. I actually had two habits."

45-year-old recovering heroin addict

It is important to remember that methadone is a strong opioid that will cause withdrawal symptoms if stopped.

"When you're kicking methadone, God, that's the worst one to kick. Your bones'd be aching. You can't hardly get out of bed if you're on a big dosage. And there are very few places where you can cold turkey off methadone. Very few places. They bring it to jail if you get locked up 'cause that would be

cruel and unusual punishment if they cut you off of methadone."
45-year-old recovering heroin addict

Pro-methadone advocates cite close to 50 years of numerous rigorous studies that demonstrate the effectiveness of methadone maintenance with positive outcomes for society as well as for the addict. Keeping addicts from their harmful lifestyle through replacement therapy is more important than focusing on total recovery from opioid addiction, which is extremely difficult. Methadone therapy has been shown to reduce crime, medical/emotional illness, and other work, education, or social problems by providing access to stabilized doses of a legal drug.

LAAM. Levomethadyl acetate (formerly named levo acetyl alpha methadol) is an **opioid agonist replacement therapy that is longer acting than methadone.** Orlam,® the trade name of this drug, **will remain active in the body for up to three days,** so users further avoid the daily withdrawals and the ups and downs of heroin addiction. They also do not have to go to a clinic every day. It was said to also be potentially less euphoric and thus less prone to abuse, with milder withdrawal symptoms than methadone. By 2001 its **use was connected to severe heart arrhythmias,** so the FDA required a so-called black box warning about this in its package information insert (Schwetz, 2001). The manufacturer of Orlam,® Roxanne Laboratories, then voluntarily ceased production of the medication in 2003, and LAAM is no longer available in the United States.

Buprenorphine. In October 2002 the FDA approved high-dose sublingual tablets of buprenorphine (Subutex® and Suboxone®) for use in the treatment of opioid addiction. Buprenorphine is an opioid agonist-antagonist, which means that **at low doses it is a powerful opioid, almost 50 times as powerful as heroin; but, strangely, at doses above 8 to 16 mg, it blocks the opioid receptors.** It enables an addict to be started on methadone then switched to buprenorphine as a transition to a true antagonist like naltrexone.

Subutex® is used during the early part of detoxification; **Suboxone®** is used thereafter and also during the maintenance phase of treatment. Suboxone® combines naloxone with buprenorphine to prevent injection misuse of the medication. Buprenorphine can be used for either long-term detoxification or short-term maintenance that will permit greater stabilization for patients **detoxifying from methadone maintenance.** Methadone-maintained clients have been effectively switched to buprenorphine after their methadone dose has been reduced. There is some evidence of buprenorphine abuse in the United States and Europe because it is indeed a powerful opioid. In India and Nepal, buprenorphine is the most abused opioid, even more than heroin.

As mentioned earlier, the biggest change in terms of opioid treatment is that **physicians will be allowed to treat patients with buprenorphine in their offices rather than only at drug treatment clinics.** With office-based opiate addiction treatment, the prescribing physicians must complete special training courses, treat no more than 30 patients at a time, and **refer patients to appropriate counseling and support services although there is no requirement for follow-through** (NIDA, 2002A). Qualified physicians then get an *X* appended to their DEA registration numbers, identifying them as able to write valid prescriptions for buprenorphine. In December 2006 the 30-patient limit of the 2000 Drug Addiction Treatment Act was amended to allow certified physicians who had submitted intent petitions to treat up to 100 patients at a time with buprenorphine.

"We believe that increased access to treatment for all substance abusers is vital in dealing with the problems of addiction. The potential that buprenorphine will be used without the full range of treatment interventions that are necessary for successful recovery, however, is frightening. Addicts need counseling, peer interactions, education, nutritional support, and lifestyle changes that will

not be available if a physician relies only on a medical intervention."
Darryl Inaba, Pharm.D., clinical director, Genesis Recovery Center

SEDATIVE-HYPNOTICS (barbiturates & benzodiazepines)

The majority of tranquilizer and sedative abusers tend to be older, White (85% to 89%), and female (59% to 60%). Most enter treatment through self-referral. About 41% of primary tranquilizer treatment admissions and 33% of sedative admissions reported concurrent use of alcohol; 18% reported concurrent use of marijuana (SAMHSA, 2003).

If not medically managed, withdrawal from sedative-hypnotic addiction can result in life-threatening seizures. Thus **intensive medical assessment and medically managed treatment is a necessity when treating people who have become addicted to sedative-hypnotics** such as secobarbital ("reds"), Xanax® (alprazolam), other benzodiazepines, and even muscle relaxants like Soma® (carisoprodol) (Hayner, Galloway & Wiehl, 1993).

Detoxification

"Coming off of Xanax,® it is so intense. Your whole body twitches; your muscles twitch. You want to just pull your hair out. You are bitchy and snappy, and I'd gone as far as thinking that I'd see something that is really not there. You think that everybody is against you. I got to the point that I was so bad that I was throwing up trying to come off of it. I couldn't sleep . . . sweats. It is one of the most horrendous feelings."
40-year recovering prescription drug abuser

Though no medications have been approved to treat sedative-hypnotic addiction specifically, **substitution therapy (using a drug that is cross-tolerant with another drug) is needed to detoxify dependency on these substances.** Although many drugs in this class can be used to accomplish detoxification, **outpatient programs often use phenobarbital because of its long duration of action** and more-specific antiseizure activity. A dose of phenobarbital sufficient to prevent withdrawal symptoms without causing major drowsiness or sedation is established as a baseline to begin detoxification. Butabarbital is also used as an alternative to phenobarbital in the detox process. Phenytoin (Dilantin®), carbamazepine (Tegretol®), or gabapentin (Neurontin®) may be added to either medication therapy to further prevent seizures.

The **initial detoxification from sedative-hypnotics requires intensive and daily medical management** that also provides the opportunity to get the addict into counseling and social services that are vital to recovery once detoxification is completed.

Initial Abstinence

Continued abstinence from sedatives **requires intensive participation in group, individual, and educational counseling** as well as specific self-help groups or NA. Many sedative addicts, and especially those addicted to benzodiazepines, complain of bizarre and prolonged symptoms such as taste or visual distortions for several months after detoxification. Also many experience inappropriate rage or anger during the early months of abstinence that requires skilled mental health intervention.

After detoxification some sedative-hypnotic **addicts experience the reemergence of withdrawal-like symptoms even though they have remained totally abstinent. This reaction can occur anywhere from one to several months after detoxification** and may occasionally require medical intervention. Two controversial explanations have been offered to account for this phenomenon. One asserts that long-acting benzodiazepines, like diazepam (Valium®) or alprazolam (Xanax®), produce active metabolites that persist in the body, resulting in additional withdrawal symptoms once their levels decrease, even after several months of abstinence from the parent drug. Another explanation asserts that these are not true withdrawal symptoms but merely the reemergence of an

original anxiety disorder that was controlled by the use of sedatives. Under this second explanation, psychiatrists need to initiate maintenance pharmacotherapy treatment to address the underlying psychiatric problems. **Because many antianxiety medications are abusable sedative-hypnotics, switching to nonbenzodiazepine alternatives, particularly SSRIs like Zoloft,® is preferable. BuSpar® (buspirone), a low-abuse-potential serotonergic agent, can also be used.** If benzodiazepines must be used to treat anxiety in a chemically dependent person, skillful medical management is needed to prevent excessive inappropriate use or relapse to sedative-hypnotic addiction (Dickinson, Mayo-Smith & Eickelberg, 2003).

Flumazenil (Mazicon®) is an effective benzodiazepine antagonist currently available only in injectable form. Though it is used mainly to treat benzodiazepine overdoses, there is a growing interest in its use to treat craving in alcohol and stimulant abusers. Future developments may lead to effective oral and long-acting benzodiazepine or

barbiturate antagonists to help those addicted to sedative-hypnotics continue initial abstinence similar to the way naltrexone is used to treat opiate addiction.

Recovery

Continued participation in self-help groups like Benzodiazepine Anonymous, Pills Anonymous, and Narcotics Anonymous has been the most effective means of promoting continuous abstinence and recovery in sedative-hypnotic addicts.

As with cocaine and other addictions, sedative-hypnotic addicts are vulnerable to environmental cues that trigger drug hunger and relapse throughout their lifetimes. Treatment that includes cue or trigger recognition, avoidance tools, and coping mechanisms is vital in addressing sedative-hypnotic addiction.

ALCOHOL

Alcohol alone was the primary substance of abuse for almost 21.5% of all treatment admissions in the

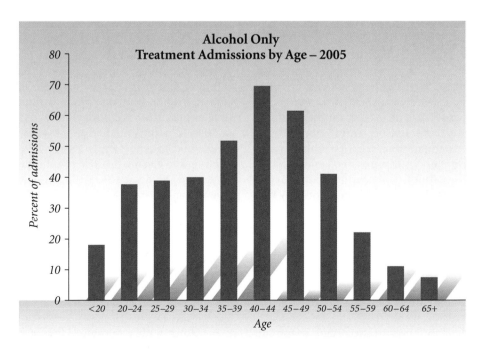

Figure 9-5 •

Because alcohol dependence takes longer to develop than dependence on other drugs, admissions for treatment grow later in the life of an alcoholic, peaking after the age of 45. When another drug is involved, even though alcohol is the primary drug, problems and the need for treatment occur sooner.

(SAMHSA, 2006B)

United States in 2005. Alcohol with a secondary drug was 17.5% of all treatment admissions. The total for alcohol was therefore 39%. The average age of those with alcohol only as their problem was 39 compared with 35 who were admitted for alcohol and a secondary drug problem. **Marijuana was the most common secondary drug (61%),** then crack cocaine (24%), powder cocaine (20%), methamphetamine (9%), and heroin (8%) (SAMHSA, 2006B).

Denial

Denial on the part of the compulsive drinker is the biggest hindrance to beginning treatment. One reason why denial is so common with the use of alcohol is the long time it can take for social or habitual drinking to advance to abuse and addiction (10 years on the average) (Schuckit, 2000). Denial also occurs because alcoholics have no memory of the negative effects they experienced while in an alcoholic blackout. Thus they don't believe that alcohol has really harmed them. Further, **alcohol impairs judgment and reason in all users, making them less likely to associate any problem with their drinking.**

Detoxification

Both acute intoxication and initial withdrawal from alcohol **can be medically dangerous** and should be monitored in a safe environment like a *sobering station,* where trained professionals can respond quickly and appropriately to any emergency. In alcohol-dependent persons, **acute intoxication usually lasts for only 4 to 8 hours, and withdrawal begins within 4 to 12 hours after cessation of use**.

For a heavy drinker or an alcoholic, physical withdrawal is very uncomfortable. Symptoms such as sweating, increased heart rate, increased respiratory rate, and gastrointestinal complaints can often be handled by aspirin, rest, liquids, and any one of hundreds of hangover cures that have been handed down from generation to generation. Minor alcohol withdrawal is most often handled at home unless **delirium tremens (confusion, agitation, hallucinations, un-controllable tremors, and paranoia) or seizure activity necessitates admission to a hospital**. Symptoms are likely to peak in intensity by 48 to 72 hours and are greatly diminished by five days. On the other hand, lesser symptoms, including mildly elevated blood pressure, dizziness, disturbed sleep, and moodiness, also known as *post-acute withdrawal symptoms,* can last for weeks or months.

Up to 10% of untreated alcohol withdrawals and even up to 3% of medically treated episodes include severe, potentially life-threatening symptoms such as seizure activity that require medical management with a variety of sedating drugs, such as barbiturates, benzodiazepines (e.g., chlordiazepoxide [Librium®]), paraldehyde, chloral hydrate, and the phenothiazines. Because several of these drugs are addictive, they should be used sparingly and on a very short-term basis. Normally, tapering is done on a 5- to 7-day basis but can be extended to 11 to 14 days. If untreated, the delirium tremens and seizure activity can be fatal in up to 35% of those who experience the condition (Hillbom & Hjelm-Jager, 1984; Kleber, 2006).

There are a number of alcohol withdrawal assessment tools that can be used to help determine its severity and guide the appropriate medical or clinical intervention. One example is the Clinical Institute Withdrawal Assessment for Alcohol (CIWA-A) scale. This tool quantifies physical signs and patient complaints of withdrawal into a score that determines the type and the degree of medical treatment needed to prevent occurrence of life-endangering seizure or other medical problems during alcohol detoxification. The Addiction Research Foundation provides guidelines on the use of the CIWA-A scale with a medication protocol when patients score 10 or more points on the scale (Addiction Research Foundation, 2007).

Along with emergency medical care, **withdrawal and detoxification should include emotional support and basic physical care, such as rest and efforts to restore physiologic homeostasis** with fluids, thiamin, folic acid, multivitamins, minerals, amino acids, electrolytes, and fructose.

Evidence-based best practices indicate the effectiveness of motivational enhancement, behavioral, cognitive-behavioral, 12-step-facilitation, group, or psychodynamic interpersonal therapies along with participation in self-help groups like AA for all phases of alcohol dependence treatment. Many of the problems will begin to abate with detoxification, but **for the long-term drinker some damage is irreversible**: liver disease, enlarged heart, cancer, and nerve damage, among others (Kleber, 2006; Schuckit, 2000; Wiehl, Hayner & Galloway, 1994).

Initial Abstinence

A common treatment for initial abstinence is the use of Antabuse® (disulfiram), a drug that will make people ill if they drink alcohol. This is used for six months or longer to help get alcoholics through initial abstinence when they're most likely to relapse. Medication non-compliance has always been the main drawback of disulfiram treatment. **The growth of CJS-mandated treatments has increased its use in recent years.** A more important part of this process is **encouraging alcoholics to go to AA meetings or other support groups** in addition to individual therapy. One procedure is to have the user go to 90 AA meetings within 90 days (called a "90/90 contract").

In 1996 **naltrexone (ReVia®) was approved by the FDA for the treatment of alcohol addiction** during the first three months of recovery; it decreased alcohol relapse by 50% to 70% when combined with a comprehensive treatment program. Unfortunately, naltrexone can potentially be hard on the liver, and it would block the effects of opioid pain medications during an emergency. It therefore needs to be used under strict supervision. **Acamprosate (Campral®) has had modest treatment effects in lowering craving** and keeping clients in treatment (Boothby & Doering, 2005). Rigorous studies of its effectiveness to prevent drinking compared with naltrexone, disulfiram, and placebo, however, found acamprosate no more effective than a placebo in reducing alcohol use (Anton, O'Malley, Ciraulo, et al., 2006).

A number of other drugs are being tried, including topiramate (Topamax®), which blocks dopamine so the alcohol doesn't stimulate the reward/reinforcement pathway (Ross, 2003). Blocking dopamine also seems to help in weight loss and binge-eating disorder (McElroy, Hudson, Capece, et al., 2007).

Interestingly, recent research showed that cannabinoids play a role in modulating the reinforcing effects of alcohol and other abused drugs by affecting the nucleus accumbens.

As the alcohol clears from the system, the clinician needs to **evaluate the client for psychiatric problems (especially depression and anxiety) that have developed or were preexisting**. Attempts at suicide should also be considered because the **lifetime risk of suicide in alcoholics is 10%**.

Long-Term Abstinence & Recovery

In treatment one often encounters someone known as a "dry drunk." This means that the person is not actually drinking alcohol but still has the behavior and the mind-set of an alcoholic. Thus the purpose of this stage of treatment, besides avoiding relapse, is to **begin healing the confusion, immaturity, and emotional scars that kept the person drinking for so many years**.

Many treatment centers advertise 30-day drying-out programs, implying that detoxification is the key to recovery rather than a small initial step in a long process. As with all addictions, working on recovery throughout one's lifetime is necessary to prevent relapse. Research demonstrates that alcohol and all drugs of addiction induce changes in the brain that remain long after a person enters sobriety. These changes include increased dendrites and receptors that are primed to respond to drinking triggers and cues through long-term memory processes, so **the recovering alcoholic is always susceptible to relapse** (Harvard, 2007; Hyman, Malenka & Nestler, 2006). Thus developing a relapse prevention plan—identifying the tools needed and implementing those resources to maintain continuous sobriety—is vital during this phase of

treatment Clinicians/authors like Terry Gorski and Ernie Larsen have developed excellent texts that can be of great assistance to both the recovering alcoholic and the treatment professional with the relapse prevention process (Gorski & Miller, 1986; Larsen, 1985).

PSYCHEDELICS

For all arounders such as LSD, MDMA, "'shrooms," and ketamine, **the overwhelming majority of users in treatment are male, White, and under the age of 24**. For **marijuana smokers, the majority who are in treatment are male and under the age of 24** but more evenly divided ethnically (SAMHSA, 2006B).

Many psychedelics mimic mental conditions, such as schizophrenia, so **the clinician or intake counselor can make only a tentative diagnosis when first seeing the patient until the drug has had time to clear**, usually without medication. Antipsychotic drugs, sedatives, and other medications are sometimes used, however, to stabilize clients if they seem a danger to themselves. Although some tissue dependence (physical addiction) is seen with GHB (gamma hydroxybutyrate), PCP, ketamine, and marijuana abuse, most all arounders do not result in daily compulsive chronic abuse. **Treatment for the abuse of psychedelics is therefore most often focused on the substance-induced disorders (intoxication or mental disorders), family dynamics, and social consequences** that result from the abuse.

Bad Trips (acute anxiety reactions)

The amount of LSD or other psychedelic taken, the surroundings, and the user's mental state and physical condition—all determine the reaction to psychedelics. Because of the effect of psychedelics on the emotional center of the brain, a user is open to the extremes of euphoria and panic. Inexperienced and even experienced users who take too high a dose of LSD or other psychedelic can feel **acute anxiety, paranoia, and fear over loss of control, or feelings of grandeur leading to dangerous behaviors**.

"In the eighth grade I started doing acid and drinking a lot; and when I was about 15, I took too much acid one night and I tripped out and I cut my arm. Got a big old scar on my arm and took off my clothes and ran down the street naked. Just tripped out. So then I went to rehab after that. I spent four days in the hospital."
Former LSD user

There are two things to remember when using the ARRRT talk-down technique to manage a bad trip. (Table 9-4).

◇ First, if the user seems to be experiencing severe medical, physical, or even emotional reactions that are not responding to the talk-down, medical intervention is needed. Get the person to a hospital or bring in emergency medical personnel

TABLE 9–4 TREATMENT FOR BAD TRIPS

The Haight Ashbury Detox Clinic developed the following **ARRRT guidelines** in dealing with a person experiencing a bad trip:

A Acceptance. First gain the user's trust and confidence.

R Reduction of stimuli. Get the user to a quiet, nonthreatening environment.

R Reassurance. Educate the user that he is experiencing a bad trip and assure him that he is in a safe place, among safe people, and that he will be all right.

R Rest. Help the user relax using stress reduction techniques that promote a calm state of mind.

T Talk-down. Discuss peaceful, nonthreatening subjects with the user, avoiding any topic that seems to create more anxiety or a strong reaction.

experienced in treating that kind of reaction.

◇ Second, although most psychedelic bad-trip reactions are responsive to ARRRT, PCP and ketamine may cause unexpected and sudden violent or belligerent behavior. Exercise caution in approaching a "bum tripper" suspected of being under the influence of these drugs.

The best treatment for someone on a bad trip is to talk him or her down in a calm manner without raising your voice or appearing threatening. Avoid quick movements and let the person move around so there is no feeling of being trapped.

The condition known as **hallucinogen persisting perception disorder (HPPD)** is the recurrence of some of the symptoms of the hallucinogen even when none has been taken. One treatment that has been tried with some success is the use of high-potency benzodiazepines such as clonazepam, which reduced the symptoms of HPPD (Lerner, Gelkopf, Skladman, et al., 2003).

Marijuana, LSD, and some of the club drugs (MDMA, ecstasy, GHB, and ketamine) have created addictive behaviors in users. Though this is most often **treated with traditional counseling, education, and self-help groups, marijuana and GHB also cause true tissue dependence** that results in withdrawal symptoms that may require medical management (especially so with GHB dependence). The GHB withdrawal syndrome is similar to that encountered in alcohol dependence (inclusive of delirium tremens and seizure activity) and in benzodiazepine or sedative-hypnotic addiction with a long duration of symptoms. Its treatment should therefore be medically managed with similar interventions and cautions as employed to treat alcohol or sedative hypnotic dependence (Miotto & Roth, 2001). Chronic daily abuse of LSD and MDMA is more like a stimulant addiction because tolerance to the psychedelic effects occurs within only a few days.

MARIJUANA

Since the 1980s **there has been a steady increase in the number of peo-**

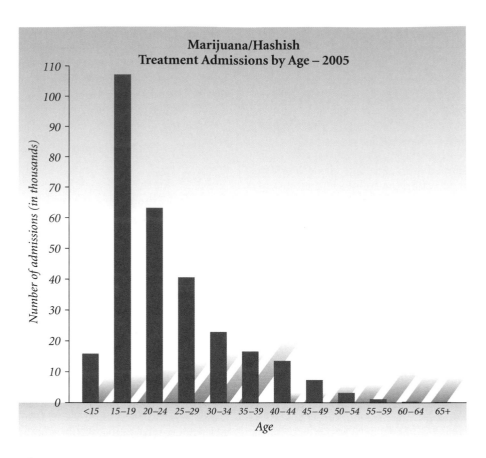

Marijuana/Hashish Treatment Admissions by Age – 2005

Figure 9-6 •

The vast majority of those entering treatment for marijuana dependence are under the age of 20 because more than half of the referrals for treatment are court mandated; only 17% are self-referred.

(SAMHSA, 2006B)

ple entering treatment for marijuana dependence. Although much of the growth has been because of court-mandated treatment referrals (Figure 9-6), which account for 56% of admissions, there is also an increase of those who are self-referred into treatment for marijuana abuse (SAMHSA, 2006B). Thus through the eyes of marijuana smokers as well as the eyes of the law, there is a growing problem with marijuana dependence. For many observers these facts seem to challenge the continued perception that marijuana is a benign drug.

The other reason for the increase in marijuana-associated dependence is the wider availability, at the street level, of marijuana with higher levels of THC. In much the same way that the refinement of opium to heroin or of coca leaves to pure cocaine overloaded the reward/reinforcement pathway and altered brain chemistry, the 8% to 14%

or more average THC content of sinsemilla has put the long-term user at risk (even though many users say, "Well I just take fewer puffs," but tolerance still develops more quickly). Clinical experience and a growing body of research have shown that **marijuana can cause a true addiction syndrome encompassing both physical and emotional dependence**.

"I ain't gonna say I can quit anytime. But if I had to stop, I could stop. I ain't gonna say I could quit. I can't go cold turkey just like that. I could go maybe three days without and then I smoke a joint. And then maybe I go like three or four days without, and then maybe I'll smoke a joint, but that'd take some work."

33-year-old chronic marijuana abuser

The physical withdrawal symptoms, though uncomfortable, rarely require medical treatment. They consist of major sleep and appetite disturbances, headaches, irritability, anxiety, emotional depression, and even mild tremors or muscular discomfort. Craving persists for several months to years after abstinence. One of the main reasons people deny that these withdrawal symptoms do occur is that **their onset is often delayed for several days or weeks after cessation of use**. Marijuana has a wide distribution in body tissues and especially in fat, enabling it to persist in the system over a prolonged period of time. Urine tests of chronic marijuana users remain positive sometimes for three weeks to several months.

"After I stopped smoking, it took me about three or four months before I really came out of the fog and really started getting a grasp of what was going on around me . . . and another month or so after that is when I really started to understand that I could do this. And then I started really enjoying it."

28-year-old recovering compulsive marijuana smoker

Treatment for marijuana abuse or addiction is evolving along the same lines as that developed for alcohol misuse except that there are **no specific recommended pharmacotherapies for marijuana withdrawal or dependence**. Psychosocial interventions, education, and peer support have been the most effective in helping people abstain and prevent relapse. **Motivational enhancement therapy and the development of coping skills along with intensive relapse prevention therapy appear to be effective psychosocial interventions** (Kleber, 2006). Currently, treatment for marijuana addiction is made difficult because much of society still views "pot" as nonproblematic, and users in particular view those in treatment as overreacting to their use of the drug. This often undermines the treatment process. Further, 12-step programs and other peer support systems, invaluable in the treatment of other drug dependencies, have not yet evolved fully for marijuana dependence though Marijuana Anonymous is growing worldwide.

Current research on anandamide, the neurotransmitter most affected by marijuana, is giving clues to the nature of marijuana's effects on the body and mind, possibly leading to drugs to assist in short- and long-term abstinence. There is already an anandamide antagonist called *SR141716A* that has been used to study the marijuana withdrawal syndrome because the drug will almost instantly block all effects of marijuana, at least temporarily. The chemical name is rimonabant, and the trade names for the product being developed are Acomplia® and Zimulti.® **The approved uses for this anandamide antagonist will be for weight-loss, anti-diabetes, smoking-cessation, and metabolic syndrome.** Though available in Europe and Mexico, it is not expected to be FDA approved in the United States until late 2007.

INHALANTS

The treatment of those who abuse inhalants involves **immediate removal from exposure to the substance** to prevent them from aggravating its dangerous effects, such as lack of oxygen to the brain, damage to the respiratory system, and injuries from accidents. Initial treatment for the delirium that can be caused by inhalants also consists of reassurance and a quiet, nonstimulating environment. **Patients must then be monitored for potential adverse psychiatric conditions** that may require the use of antipsychotic medications targeted to treat psychoses and suicidal depression. Many inhalants can also produce physical dependence that is similar to the that which occurs with sedative-hypnotics. Clients should be monitored for withdrawal seizures and treated with appropriate anticonvulsant medication when warranted.

Each inhalant has its own physical toxic effects and may lead to heart, liver, lung, kidney, and even blood diseases. **The symptoms must be evaluated and treated.** These substances are reinforcing and can cause psychic dependence and often require long-term psychosocial interventions targeted to prevent relapse into addiction.

Because most inhalants are easily accessible to adolescents, the majority of abusers are under the age of 20. Almost one-third of inhalant treatment admissions had used inhalants by the age of 12 and another one-third by the age of 13 (SAMHSA, 2006B). What this means in treatment is that there are major developmental problems that must be addressed. Treatment specialists talk about the need to habilitate rather than rehabilitate the "huffer."

About two-thirds of inhalant abusers admitted for treatment reported use of other drugs as well, primarily alcohol and marijuana. These figures emphasize the need to evaluate all "huffers" for possible addiction to other drugs.

TREATMENT FOR BEHAVIORAL ADDICTIONS

It has become increasingly recognized that behavioral addictions, which result from a genetic predisposition to addiction, an environment that further predisposes one to compulsive behaviors, and pleasurable reinforcement from the activity itself, follow similar brain pathways as drug addiction. **Behavioral addictions require the same intensity of intervention and treatment as substance-abuse disorders.** Behavioral addictions include compulsive gambling, sexual addiction, compulsive Internet use, compulsive shopping, and eating disorders (anorexia, bulimia, and binge eating)

Because many behavioral addictions have not been studied and treated to the same extent as drug abuse and addiction, there is a scarcity of research data, treatment facilities, and qualified treatment personnel. Besides treatment at mental health facilities, **the front line of treatment has been the evolution of self-help and 12-step support groups for these nonchemical addictions**.

Compulsive Gambling

Americans lost $60 billion to $70 billion last year in slot and poker machines; at poker, dice, and roulette tables; in sports betting; and on 38 state lotteries. The number of compulsive gamblers has grown dramatically with the increase in games of chance that are now found in every state except Utah and Hawaii. **The sheer availability of gambling facilities has contributed to the large increase of problem and pathological gamblers and to multiple relapses during treatment.** In one of the few before-and-after studies, the percentage of Iowans reporting a gambling problem at some time in their lives went from 1.7% in 1989 to 5.4% in 1995 after gambling's introduction, and it's probably even more today—a three- to fourfold increase (Harden & Swardson, 1996). In a different study, the number of pathological gamblers was estimated at 3.6 million in 2002 due to the proliferation of gambling outlets (Califano, 2001). Even the gaming industry estimates that 25% to 40% of its revenue comes from that 6% to 8% who are compulsive or problem gamblers. The figures are probably much higher for certain types of gambling (e.g., poker machines in Oregon, where it is estimated that 7% of the population spends 60% to 80% of the money generated by this type of gambling). The other problem with gambling statistics is the **perception by even addicted gamblers that "It's only a cash flow problem, not an addiction."**

"I was at a Gamblers Anonymous meeting in Reno and about 50 people were there. The longest abstinence in that meeting was just four months. In meetings I've been to in other states, many people have years of abstinence. The only difference I see is that in Reno gambling is everywhere, and the triggers are everywhere, and the temptation is everywhere."
44-year-old recovering compulsive gambler

With so many compulsive gamblers, there is a **startling lack of facilities to treat this addiction**. Until a few years ago, many states didn't have a single gambling addiction specialist. By 2007, 17 states had provisions and paid for treatment of pathological gambling although the number treated is only a fraction of the total. Society has been slow to recognize compulsive gambling as a compulsion as powerful as any drug addiction.

Compulsive gambling has been described as one of the purest addictions because the only substance involved is money. **Until a devastating bottom has been reached, most gamblers are reluctant to seek treatment let alone admit that they have a problem.** Outside interventions, especially those triggered by legal problems (e.g., arrest for embezzlement or declaring bankruptcy), are usually necessary (Brubaker, 1997).

"I bought some furniture on credit from a company and financed it real good. Made a few payments, and they sent me a letter saying you can get more credit, so immediately I got both, sold all my furniture and then I went and bought more and sold all of that just so I could keep gambling."
74-year-old recovering sports gambler

The Charter Hospital of Las Vegas, which treats compulsive gamblers, reports **withdrawal symptoms similar to those of alcoholism: restlessness, irritability, anger, abdominal pain, headaches, diarrhea, cold sweats, insomnia, tremors, apprehension about well-being, and above all an intense desire to return to gambling**.

"I don't want to sit here and tell anybody anything that's unrealistic. I miss gambling. I miss it still. It brought a sense of—like a power or a satisfaction. I'm learning how to treat it and how to deal with it but that doesn't mean it's over."
42-year-old relapsing compulsive gambler

The standard assessment test for compulsive gambling is the **South Oaks Gambling Screen**, usually accompanied by an in-depth assessment and a formal diagnosis. Treatment options developed over the past 30 years include self-help groups such as Gamblers Anonymous (Blume & Tavares, 2005).

"The problem primarily is that there are no physical gross indicators to a lay person like hangovers, or gross intoxication, or bodily changes, or

measurable body fluids that a doctor likes to find. They are mostly psychological and sociological and, of course, financial. And without that kind of history, we usually don't even get to a diagnosis."
Joseph Pursch, M.D., psychiatrist

Gamblers Anonymous parallels the 12-step program used by Alcoholics Anonymous. It also employs sponsors, group meetings, commitment to complete abstinence, contact numbers, and support to help the gambler particularly through the initial 90-day phase. Additional support groups include Gam-Anon for the families of compulsive gamblers and Gam-A-Teen, a group for children of pathological gamblers.

"Going to GA groups helps me—seeing people who have gone through the same struggles and seeing how every one of them wishes they had quit when they were my age so they didn't have to go through the struggles."
21-year-old recovering compulsive gambler

One of the keys to treating compulsive gamblers is **enabling them to overcome irrational thoughts (magical thinking) about their chances of winning** because many of them cannot accept the fact that gambling games at casinos, lotteries, racetracks, and in poker machines are meant to take their money. The more they gamble, the more they will lose; and if they get ahead, they will compulsively put that money back into the game. Almost all pathological gamblers think that they can overcome the computer chips in slot machines and the inevitable laws of chance.

"I don't think about those odds. What entices me to stay is I'll see other people winning and I'll think, well, my machine hasn't paid out. It's about time that it will."
53-year-old compulsive gambler

The other key in treatment is to get a pathological gambler to recognize that it's the action at a gaming table or the "zoning out" at a machine that is sought, not really the money.

Outpatient, inpatient, and residential treatment programs are available (but scarce), though insurance companies seldom pay for a primary diagnosis of compulsive gambling. It usually takes a diagnosis of a mood disorder or other coexisting condition to get insurance coverage for treatment. Frequently, compulsive gamblers have already lost their jobs and insurance coverage before they seek help for their addiction. In the past few years, 17 states that have government-controlled lotteries, gambling machines, and scratch-off games are recognizing their responsibility in providing treatment for compulsive gamblers. Connecticut spends the most money for treatment. Next is Oregon, which passed a bill allotting 1% of its net gambling revenues, or almost $4 million in 2006, to treatment. California, with 12 times the population, allots much less.

Even with gambling, several addictions are always involved. **Gambling often coexists, replaces, or follows alcoholism, compulsive spending, and a few other disorders.** Many alcoholics switched to gambling when they quit drinking, and it quickly became as compulsive as the alcohol (McElroy, Soutullo & Goldsmith, 2003). More than 50% of pathological gamblers are also alcohol or substance abusers (Ibanez, Blanco & Donahue, 2001). All addictions should be treated simultaneously because relapse to one substance or behavior will often trigger another addiction.

*"I just got my 14-year chip at my Monday AA meeting just in time to go to my GA meeting. I'd always gambled, but boy, it took off about three years after I quit the alcohol. It's been harder to get any time without those f****** poker machines."*

63-year-old "dry" compulsive gambler

Although no medication has been approved to treat pathological gambling, there is interest in pharmacological interventions for this and other behavioral addictions. A new drug, **nalmefene (Revex®) may help reduce urges in pathological gamblers.** The drug is not yet approved for the treatment of gambling addiction and is actually in development more to treat alcohol and nicotine dependence. A recent study of its effectiveness to reduce gambling in pathological gamblers found that 59.2% rated much improved or very much improved compared with 34% of those on placebo (Grant, Potenza, Hollander, et al., 2006). Other studies confirmed these results and also found that lower doses of the medications (25 mg per day) were just as effective and caused fewer side effects.

Treatment of pathological gambling is therefore psychosocial; long-term peer support groups that include the **cognitive-behavioral approaches used to treat chemical dependencies and participation in GA are effective** (Petry, 2005).

It should also be noted that results of two fairly comprehensive national surveys have found that **among individuals with a lifetime history of *DSM-IV-TR*** pathological gambling, 36% to 39% did not experience any gambling-related problems in the past year, even though only 8% to 12% had ever sought either formal treatment or attended GA meetings. About one-third of the individuals with pathological gambling disorder in these two nationally representative U.S. samples were characterized by natural recovery. Pathological gambling may not always follow a chronic and persistent course (Slutske, 2006).

Eating Disorders

"Losing weight is easy. I've probably lost 1,000 pounds over the years . . . but I've gained 1,055.

46-year-old compulsive eater

One of the keys to effective treatment of all three eating disorders— anorexia, bulimia, and binge eating—is early intervention. The longer the disorder continues, the more deeply ingrained the behavior becomes and the more physiological and psychological damage occurs. A number of steps are recommended for treating eating disorders:

◇ **Diagnose and treat any medical complications**—hospitalize if necessary.

◇ Encourage the client to **exercise and eat a balanced diet** and educate him or her as to the components of proper nutrition (Barclay, 2002).

◇ Use cognitive and other therapies to **change false attitudes and perceptions** of body image and eating.

◇ Encourage attendance at **Overeaters Anonymous or other 12-step groups** to get support.

◇ Use behavioral and group therapies to encourage weight gain in anorexics or weight loss in bulimics and overeaters.

◇ Enhance self-esteem, independence, and development of a stronger identity.

◇ Treat and educate the whole family.

In addition to the general guidelines, each of the three eating disorders has its own unique problems to address.

Anorexia. Most severely ill anorexic patients must be hospitalized because of the excessive weight loss, disturbed heart rhythms, extreme depression, and often-suicidal ideation. It usually takes **10 to 12 weeks for full nutritional recovery.** The hospital or home care includes medical treatment and nutritional stabilization requiring weight gain of 1 or 2 lbs. per week even if the patient or family is resistant to gaining weight. Exercise is also recommended. **The complexities of anorexia require a team approach**: physicians for medical complications, dietitians, therapists, counselors, and trained nurses to ensure good outcomes. Unfortunately, most health insurance covers only 15 days.

For the hospitals and clinics that treat this eating disorder, the rate of full recovery is about 40%. **In one study the recovery rate among 84 anorexic women after 12 years was 54%** based on the restarting of menstruation (41% based on the criterion of general well-being); the mortality rate was 11% (Helm, Munster & Schmidt, 1995). The first priority in treatment is, of course, preventing permanent damage and/or death by starvation. Severely ill patients are monitored for body weight, serum electrolytes, and diet as the patient is returned to normal nutrition.

For an adolescent a weight gain of 4 oz. (0.1 kg) per day is the goal. The staff usually monitors each patient for two to three hours after eating to prevent self-induced vomiting. Fluoxetine (Prozac®), other antidepressants, and monoamine oxidase (MAO) inhibitors have been tried to help patients **improve eating behavior by treating the underlying depression**. Generally though, antidepressant drugs have had marginal effects in aiding recovery (APA, 2006; Jacobi, Dahme & Rustenbach, 1997).

One of the first problems in treatment is convincing the patient that anorexia is potentially fatal. Often it is a parent who brings a young woman to treatment. The client will think that her anorexic body weight is normal or even heavier than normal. Programs involve stabilizing the patient and psychological counseling to alert the anorexic to the problem and its causes; to devalue an overemphasis on thinness, weight, dieting, and food; to build self-esteem; and to promote healthy behaviors. They also involve family therapy to provide the family with understanding, support, and the ability to cope.

Bulimia. **Clients with bulimia usually have more long-term health problems than those with anorexia**, such as atherosclerosis and diabetes; these problems rarely require hospitalization but **often necessitate continuing medical care**. As with other eating disorders, bulimia is **best treated in its early stages**. Unfortunately, people with bulimia often are in a normal weight range, so their problem may escape detection for years. After diagnosis a decision is made to treat an individual in a hospital or on an outpatient basis.

Because of the multiple problems involved, a **multidisciplinary integrated treatment is generally used**.

◇ An **internist** advises on medical problems.
◇ A **nutritionist** provides help with diet and eating patterns.
◇ A **psychotherapist** provides emotional support and counseling and may begin therapy that involves changing attitudes and behaviors.

◇ A **psychopharmacologist** may counsel on which psychoactive medications might be effective. In recent years antidepressants have been used, especially SSRIs along with MAO inhibitors (Goldbloom, 1997; Kleber, 2006).

The Karolinska Institute in Stockholm found that conditioning methods that focused on physical symptoms, not on psychological problems, were the most effective treatment for those with bulimia as well as for anorexics. When patients were trained to eat, recognize satiation, avoid excessive exercise after eating (as in exercise bulimia disorder), and some other behavioral conditioning, remission rates were 75% (Bergh, Brodin, Lindberg, et al., 2002).

Family and group therapies are extremely useful for providing understanding and emotional support to the patient. Group therapy may be a great relief to a person who doesn't need to keep the disorder secret any longer. Family, friends, and colleagues can help an ill person start and complete treatment and then provide the encouragement to make sure the disorder does not reoccur. There are also self-help and peer support groups organized specifically for bulimia, but these are currently less effective than groups for compulsive overeating.

Binge-Eating Disorder (and compulsive overeating). Many people with these disorder have unsuccessfully attempted to control it; more than 90% of dieters return to their original weight or greater within two years. Professional treatment personnel generally recognize that both **physiological and psychological causes underlie the disorder** and address those issues while initiating a weight-loss program. Common treatment methods include:

◇ counseling sessions that focus on **changing attitudes and ideals**;
◇ psychiatric treatment that **examines underlying traumas**;
◇ **behavioral therapy** to help monitor and control responses to stress and environmental cues and to change eating habits;
◇ **pharmacological treatment** with antidepressants (e.g., Zoloft® or

Paxil®), the opioid blocker naltrexone, the antiseizure medication topiramate (Topamax®), or a dozen other drugs (*see* "Pharmaceutical Treatments for Obesity" later in this chapter); and
◇ surgical intervention. **Surgery is really more of an intervention for the consequences of compulsive overeating than a treatment for the disorder itself**; some 20% of patients continue or soon return to excessive eating and weight gain after the procedure.

Bariatric or gastric bypass surgery for obesity has become increasing popular despite a number of complications, such as gallstones, abdominal hernias, nutritional deficiencies, and the need for repeat surgeries. Also about 30% develop alcoholism perhaps due to increased alcohol absorption or from the transference of their food addiction to a chemical one (Spencer, 2006). **Self-help groups, such as OA, OA-HOW** (*HOW* stands for *honesty, open-mindedness* and *willingness*), and **GreySheeters Anonymous** reassure people who overeat that they are not alone and provide examples, support, and specific programs for positive changes (Kleber, 2000).

Unlike alcohol and other drug dependencies where total abstinence is possible, abstinence from all food is of course impossible. The treatment goal is to learn to **manage one's intake and to avoid foods that trigger binges**, such as refined sugars, chocolate, or carbohydrates. Binge foods are substances that provide a person with much greater emotional relief than other foods, and they vary from person to person.

Prevention efforts aimed at the environment are being pursued.

◇ A number of school systems such as in Los Angeles have banned sugared/caffeinated soft drinks from school grounds. The FDA wants to require all food sold in schools to meet good-nutrition standards.
◇ More-detailed labeling is now required by law; it lets consumers know the amount of calories, sugar, fats, sodium, trans fats, and other

nutritional ingredients in anything they eat.

◇ A lawsuit was filed against fast-food restaurants because of the high-fat, high-sugar content of most of their foods and the unavailability of healthy foods. This is reminiscent of the many lawsuits filed against tobacco companies for selling a dangerous product. The fast-food lawsuit was dismissed.

Pharmaceutical Treatments for Obesity

In the 1950s and 1960s, legal amphetamines (dexedrine and methadrine) were the diet drugs of choice. Since then illegal amphetamines and then methamphetamines have remained available. In the 1980s and 1990s, it was a variety of amphetamine congeners, weaker versions of amphetamines, including a combination of diet pills called "fen-phen," that were used. Fen-phen became the target of massive lawsuits due to alleged heart damage from the drugs. In addition, **many of the stimulants used as diet aids proved to have an addictive component, creating more problems than they solved**. Rapid tolerance to their anorexic effects was another problem because weight gain would quickly return unless the dose was continually increased, often to near-toxic levels. In the 2000s it is Meridia® (sibutramine, an antidepressant), Xenical® (orlistat, a fat blocker that was granted OTC status in February 2007), Ionamin® or Adipex-P® (phentermine HCL, a Schedule IV stimulant appetite suppressant), and a dozen other substances with varying pharmacological actions.

A promising line of research opened in 1999 when a Japanese researcher discovered **ghrelin, a hormone that is secreted by the stomach and the small intestine to signal hunger**. When people diet, the level of this hormone increases, signaling the body that it is starving; hunger is increased, metabolism is made more efficient, and the up-and-down cycle of dieting is intensified (Cummings, Weigle, Frayo, et al., 2002). A number of drug companies are looking into the **development of a vaccine that would block the effects of this hormone and stop**

the sensation of hunger to assist dieting (Carlson & Cummings, 2006).

Some of the other drugs in the developmental pipeline include Axokine® (modified ciliary neurotropic factor, or CNTF), an injectable drug that makes the user feel full, and Acomplia® or Zimulti® (rimonabant), a cannabinoid antagonist to suppress a CNS receptor that regulates food intake).

There are also a vast number of herbal and alleged "natural" weight-loss pills that are heavily marketed on television, on the Internet, and in other media:

◇ One-A-Day WeightSmart,® containing multivitamins, green tea extract, cayenne pepper, caffeine, and guarana, is claimed to increase metabolic rate.

◇ Hoodia gordonii, a South African cactuslike plant is said to suppress appetite by chemicals that fool the brain into thinking that the stomach is full.

◇ CortiSlim® contains magnolia bark, which is said to be antistress, to inhibit the brain's release of cortisol and therefore reduce fat and the desire to eat.

◇ Xenadrine EFX® contains the amino acid tyrosine (a precursor to dopamine in the brain), green tea extract, and various other herbs that are claimed to increase energy, metabolism, and wakefulness, with decreased appetite and calories.

◇ TrimSpa® contains Hoodia gordonii, caffeine, theobromine, and synephrine, which is touted to decrease appetite and block fat.

In January 2007 the Federal Trade Commission fined the makers of Xenadrine EFX,® CortiSlim,® One-A-Day WeightSmart,® and TrimSpa® $25 million for making false and deceptive advertising claims about their products that were not scientifically verified (De La Cruz, 2007).

In addition, other psychoactive medications such as cocaine, coffee, ephedrine-based medications, and especially cigarettes have been tried, often with initial successes that are trumpeted in newspapers and medical TV shows, but later do not seem as efficient or ef-

fective. **Many substances will work initially, but prolonged use seems to make them lose their effectiveness** due to the body's physiological adaptation (e.g., tolerance and a raising of the body's metabolic set point), and the side effects of certain stimulants can be significant. In general, **diet pills (especially amphetamines and amphetamine congeners) are recommended only for short-term use**, so careful monitoring by physicians and review boards is very important.

Sexual Addiction

There are a number of theories about the etiology of sexual addiction, ranging from brain chemistry abnormalities, to sociocultural stresses, to childhood sexual abuse, to cognitive-behavioral theories, to psychoanalytic theories, and to combinations of more than one theory. One theory of some aspects of sexual addiction suggests that predisposed individuals experience an intense form of sexual stimulation when young, identify it with a parent (usually the mother), and come to anticipate that such sexual behavior can provide pleasure or relieve pain or tension. The experience is often in conjunction with covert or overt seduction. Because of this relationship to early childhood sexual experiences, the **treatment inevitably has to deal more with childhood development rather than just the mechanics of the addiction**. The treatment often includes **behavior modification (e.g., aversion therapy); cognitive-behavioral therapy; group, family, or couple therapy; psychodynamic psychotherapy; motivational interviewing; and medications** (often to reduce the sex drive) (Goodman, 2005). Again the concurrent use of addictive substances is more prevalent than in the general population because predisposing factors in all addictions are so similar and because psychoactive drugs are often used to affect sexuality (e.g., to lower inhibitions or enhance arousal). Recovery from sexual addiction, like recovery from drug addiction, is a lifelong process.

Sexaholics Anonymous. Like compulsive gambling, sexual addiction is difficult to treat. **The sense of being**

alone in their addiction or what they consider a unique behavior is alleviated when sexaholics realize that there are millions of others with the same problems.

"When we came to SA, we found that in spite of our differences, we shared a common problem—the obsession of lust, usually combined with a compulsive demand for sex in some form. We identified with one another on the inside. Whatever the details of our problem, we were dying spiritually— dying of guilt, fear, and loneliness. As we came to see that we shared a common problem, we also came to see that for us, there is a common solution—the Twelve Steps of Recovery practiced in a fellowship and on a foundation of what we call sexual sobriety."

Sexaholics Anonymous, 1989

The main issues that need to be addressed are the **feelings of shame, guilt, anxiety, and depression that are associated with sexual addiction**. Those issues can be addressed in therapy groups, in individual therapy, and at Sexaholics Anonymous and Sex Addicts Anonymous meetings. Unlike recovery from a drug addiction, complete abstinence from sex is almost impossible, so the goal becomes abstinence from compulsive destructive sexual behaviors. Associated behaviors that need to be addressed are control problems, secrecy, isolation, distorted thinking, and emotional distancing.

Internet Addiction

Internet addiction crosses the line into other computer-related addictions: cybersexual addiction, cyberrelationship addiction, online gambling and day trading, information overload (compulsive Web surfing), computer addiction (game playing), or any combination of the above (Netaddiction, 2000). Along with compulsive gambling, Internet addiction is the fastest-growing addiction, exploding from virtually nonexistent 10 years ago.

Because it is so new, treatment personnel and treatment facilities are rare. Because the Internet has become so much a part of life and work situations, it is hard to give up use altogether, particularly if it's part of one's job. **The usual abstinence model is often impossible to follow, so a harm reduction model is usually necessary.**

Richard Davis of York University, who has studied Internet addiction extensively, has **10 suggestions to help alleviate this condition:**

1. **Move your computer to a different room** to change a number of environmental cues that you have become used to.
2. **Never go online alone.** Always go online with someone else in the room (or at least in the house).
3. **Create an Internet usage log.** The actual hours of use are often a surprise to users.
4. **Tell people about your problem.** It is necessary to break the isolation caused by excessive Internet activity.
5. Do regular exercise. This will overcome sedentary habits of sitting in front of a computer and improve general health.
6. Never use an alias. Be yourself online.
7. Take an Internet holiday, anywhere from one day to several days or even a week.
8. Stop dwelling and obsessing on Internet use.
9. Help someone else control their Internet addiction.
10. Get professional help (e.g., a psychotherapist, counselor, or mentor) (Davis, 2001).

Internet addiction has grown rapidly in China, where a recent report found that almost **14% of Chinese teens have been determined to be compulsive Internet users**. The Chinese government has initiated a nationwide campaign to combat this dependence and has funded the development of **eight tough-love military prison-like in-patient rehabilitation clinics across the country**. Parents must pay upward of $1,300 per month (about 10 times the average Chinese salary) for the treatment of their children by these "clinics," which includes counseling, military discipline, medications, hypnosis, and even aversive electrical shock (Cha, 2007).

TARGET POPULATIONS

Even though the roots of addiction are similar among all people, treatment works better if it's tailored to specific groups based on gender, sexual orientation, age, ethnicity, job, and even economic status.

MEN VS. WOMEN

Male treatment admissions outnumbered female admissions more than 2 to 1 (68% male, 32% female). Men were more likely to enter treatment through the criminal justice system (SAMHSA, 2006C). In general, **women substance abusers will progress to addiction more rapidly than men**, die at a younger age, and be less likely to ask for and/or receive help.

Research by Dr. Lynne O'Conner of the Wright Institute in California discovered that the process of addiction and especially recovery varies dramatically for men and women. **Men are often external attributers, blaming negative life events like addiction on things outside their control, whereas women are more often internal attributers, blaming problems on themselves.** When this is extended to their views of addiction, men often blame a wide variety of external forces for their dependence on drugs, whereas women often blame themselves for being bad or crazy or immoral.

The counseling and intervention used in treatment have focused on early confrontation to break down addicts'

denial and make them accept their condition. While appropriate for men, this treatment approach with many women merely reinforces their guilt and shame and often prevents them from engaging in treatment or compels them to leave treatment early. **Treatment approaches that are more supportive and less confrontational result in better outcomes for women.**

Women are usually the primary child care provider in a family, so for a woman to be able to participate in treatment, child care must be included. It has also been found that women lack transportation more often than their male counterparts. Therefore providing bus tokens, vans, car-pooling, or other means of transportation to women clients also results in higher success rates. About 60% of treatment facilities offer such services as transportation assistance, transitional employment, family counseling, individual therapy, and relapse prevention to help female clients (SAMHSA, 2006B). A survey of 400 women in recovery attending a conference, Women Healing: Restoring Connections, found that the **three greatest barriers to their seeking addiction treatment** were:

◇ an **inability to admit the problem** or simply not recognizing their addiction (39%);
◇ a **lack of emotional support** for treatment from family members (32%); and
◇ **inadequate child care** while in treatment.

The conference was presented by the Betty Ford Center, the Caron Foundation, and the Hazelden Foundation.

YOUTH

Early onset drug use is the single best predictor of future drug problems in an individual (Adlaf, Paglia, Ivis, et al., 2000). Individuals who experiment with nicotine, alcohol, and marijuana before the age of 12 are much more likely to experience major addiction problems than those who wait until they are 18 or 19 to do so. **Individuals who delay their first use of these substances until after the age of 25, rarely develop chemical dependency**

problems. Several factors may account for this observation. The adolescent:

◇ has less body water/fat than adults;
◇ has immature enzyme metabolism systems;
◇ if genetically vulnerable to addiction, manifests the condition shortly after beginning use;
◇ is more vulnerable to environmental stressors and drug availability; and
◇ has had less time to develop life skills and healthy coping mechanisms.

Research has also focused on the adolescent's brain and hormones. After birth **the brain develops slowly from back to front cortices and is not fully mature until age 25**. Because this includes vital components of the reward/reinforcement pathway, such as the ventral medial prefrontal cortex that coordinates executive functioning and impulse controls, **the adolescent is less able to control compulsive drug use**. At puberty (age 12 to 14), sexual hormones kick in and affect brain chemistry, creating emotional mood swings that are conducive to drug use as well (Giedd, Blumenthal, Jeffries, et al., 1999; Wallis & Dell, 2004). Decreased activity in the left ventral medial prefrontal cortex has been observed in both chemical dependency and impulse control disorders. This affects temporal processing, the ability to make and carry out long-term planning, as well *delay discounting,* the modern term used to describe an inability to delay gratification (Bickel, Kowal & Gatchalian, 2006). Teens have problems recognizing consequences that are not immediate. The idea that a three-month flirtation with cocaine will necessitate a lifetime of recovery is beyond their scope. Because the adolescent's temporal horizon is so immediate or present oriented, **treatment should be molded around goals that are achievable within a short period of time and rewarded or reinforced immediately**.

Young people are often viewed as having the perception of invulnerability to drugs and other risky behaviors. They are therefore thought to be in much greater denial about their addiction than adults. To the contrary, growing evidence indicates that because of their immature prefrontal cortex, risk taking may be hardwired into the adolescent brain. **Teens have been shown to actually overestimate the true risks of their potential actions as compared with adults. What makes them more vulnerable to take risks is that their perception of the potential benefits of the activity outweighs even their exaggerated perceptions of the risks involved.** Perhaps treatment and prevention efforts should devote more energy to downplaying benefits of alcohol/drug use or explaining that the benefits of drug taking are much less rewarding than what most believe them to be (Reyna & Farley, 2007). Normative assessment exercises with youth have helped expose many misperceptions about benefits obtained from risky behaviors like alcohol or drug consumption.

Finally, studies confirm that **young people are much less willing to accept guidance or intervention from adults but are more willing to listen to their peers** (Pumariega, Kilgujs & Rodriguez, 2005). Both of these factors call for youth programs targeted around peer interaction and guidance to other youth. **Normal adult programs do not work with young people. Specific youth-directed programs must be provided.**

Trends in Adolescent Substance Abuse

The second millennia started with a renaissance of youth interest in marijuana and psychedelics (ecstasy and salvia divinorum), but alcohol remains the drug of choice in youth, and there is a growing use of nicotine despite the much publicized negative consequences from its use.

Generation X.   Raves have spread to diverse settings and a wide variety of age groups. **Club drugs have become very popular in the college, high school, and even middle school populations.** An estimated 11.5 million Americans have used ecstasy (MDMA) as of 2005. Among eighth-, tenth-, and twelfth-graders, MDMA use increased progressively through the 1990s, peaked

in 2001, and has been in decline ever since allegedly because of decreased availability (Monitoring the Future, 2007).

Generation Rx.   By 2006 there was a sharp **increase in the abuse of prescription and OTC medications, especially by adolescents** (CASA, 2005; Partnership for a Drug Free America [PATS], 2006). This shift **from "Generation X"** of the rave and club drug scene **to "Generation Rx,"** adolescents and young adults who share and mix their diverted prescription and OTC drugs at "pharming parties," presents many problems. Approximately 30% of all hospital emergency room deaths and 80% of drug mentions during an emergency room encounter involve prescription drugs (CASA, 2005). The 15 million to 17 million Americans who admit to abusing prescription drugs, doubles the numbers of a decade earlier (CASA, 2005).

A strong association between the abuse of street drugs and alcohol has been noted in those teens who abuse prescription drugs. One study found that teens who abused prescription drugs were 21 times more likely than those who didn't to abuse cocaine, 12 times more likely to do heroin, 5 times more likely to abuse marijuana, and twice as likely to use alcohol (CASA, 2006).

OLDER AMERICANS

The number of elderly Americans, enabled by medical advances, continues to grow disproportionately to the general population. At present **37 million Americans are 65 years or older.** That figure will increase to 54 million by the year 2030 fueled mostly by the Baby Boom generation; by 2050, 85 million Americans, about 20% of the projected population, will be over the age of 65 (U.S. Census Bureau, 2007). As this population grows, the problems with drug overuse, abuse, and addiction will increase along with the need for more treatment slots. Though members of the Baby Boom generation (born 1946 to 1964) witnessed the greatest incidence of adolescent illicit-drug abuse during the 1960s and 1970s (they moved away from it in the 1980s and 1990s), it is projected that **most of the

problems for this generation (which begins to turn 65 by 2011) will result from the abuse of legal prescription drugs, OTC drugs, and alcohol.** The abuse of prescription and OTC drugs has already doubled in the adult population and tripled in the adolescent population since 2000 (Korper & Raskin, 2003; Patterson, Lacro & Jeste, 1999). About 22% of all seniors use a potentially abusable prescription drug, with opioid painkillers comprising about two-thirds of that total (Simoni-Wastila, Zuckerman, Singhal, et al., 2006).

Data from a publicly funded treatment program in 2005 demonstrated that **80% of seniors treated for substance-abuse problems identified alcohol as their main drug.** The remaining 20% reported using the following substances, compared with other age groups seeking treatment:

◇ opiates (heroin or prescription pain medications), 5% compared with 13% for other age groups;

◇ cocaine, 4% compared with 14%;

◇ marijuana, 3% compared with 18%; and

◇ stimulants (methamphetamine and others), 1% compared with 6% (SAMHSA, 2006C).

Only 17% of those treated for alcohol reported a secondary illicit substance of abuse compared with 52% of other age groups in treatment during 2003 (SAMSHA, 2006B).

It is often **difficult for healthcare professionals to spot drug and alcohol abuse.** In many cases, it is not part of the assessment when the patient presents with a physical problem.

Factors That Contribute to Elderly Drug Misuse and Abuse

1. **The growing prevalence of illness exposes the elderly to more prescription drugs.**

2. **Physical resiliency declines with age, so psychoactive drugs will have a greater effect on the older user.**

3. There are many **attitudes and misconceptions** on the part of physicians and the general public that affect care:

◇ Seniors don't abuse drugs or alcohol.

◇ It's too late to address addiction at this age.

◇ Seniors have earned the right to abuse drugs; addiction is pleasurable.

◇ By age 65 a person is either too smart or has already matured/burnt out of abusing alcohol or drugs.

◇ At age 65 there is not enough time left in a person's life to develop a severe alcohol or drug-abuse problem.

4. **There is inadequate medical training of health professionals on geriatric medication and chemical dependency issues.**

5. **There are age-related physiological changes that potentiate the effects and alcohol/drug toxicity.** Physicians and drug treatment personnel must be aware that with increased age there is:

◇ decreased gastrointestinal acid secretion, motility, and blood flow;

◇ decreased lean body mass and total body water and thus less dilution of a drug;

◇ decreased plasma albumin to bind and keep drugs from being too toxic;

◇ decreased hepatic blood flow and increased hepatic cell/function damage;

◇ decreased metabolism due to fewer and less efficient liver enzymes and decreased stomach enzymes (Korper and Raskin, 2003);

◇ half to two-thirds the metabolic rate of middle-aged individuals;

◇ decreased kidney function; and

◇ increased receptor site sensitivity; alcohol and depressants depress brain function more in the elderly, impairing coordination and memory, leading to falls and general confusion (Institute of Alcohol Studies, 2007).

6. **There is a lack of adequate social and support services for seniors.** They need the support to combat not only their dependence or abuse but also:

◇ isolation and loneliness;

◇ retirement, ageism, and inactivity;

◇ rejection, disrespect, and abandonment by family and the community;

◇ relationship problems, death of partner and friends, and survivor guilt;

◇ decreased overall satisfaction with quality of life;

◇ financial or housing stress;

◇ coming to terms with chronic illnesses, persistent pain, or impending death;

◇ loss of physical appearance and abilities; and

◇ frustration over memory loss and decreased cognitive ability.

7. The community enables elders to manage their own alcohol/drug-abuse problems and to avoid medical detection and legal problems.

Also, many older Americans view addiction as a character flaw rather than a disease, **so they are less likely to seek help for any problematic use of alcohol or other drugs**. Worse, medical professionals often ignore signs of alcoholism or addiction in the elderly out of respect or a mistaken belief that they are less likely to be addicted. Signs of addiction are often misinterpreted as part of the aging process or a reaction to prescription medications that are common among the elderly. Also, because of less physical resiliency in those over 55, **problematic use of alcohol or other drugs occurs at lower dosages than with younger people.** The House Select Committee on Aging has reported that about 70% of hospitalized elderly persons show evidence of alcohol-related problems (although they might be in the hospital for some other condition). It is estimated that about 2.5 million older adults are addicted to alcohol, drugs, or both; this is out of a population of more than 60 million Americans over the age of 55 (U.S. Census Bureau, 2007).

Treatment of the Elderly Alcohol or Drug Abuser

At present **there are few treatment programs aimed specifically at older Americans**, but as the percentage of seniors increases and the Baby Boomers begin to retire, the need will grow. As with other demographics, **older Americans with a substance-abuse problem seem to do better in therapy groups with others their own age although mixed groups will work.** Of nine centers set up by NIDA to study addiction, one has been designated specifically to investigate this problem in older Americans. It is located at the University of Florida in Gainesville.

Though substantial work has been done to validate diagnostic criteria and treatment of alcohol abuse in the elderly, most substance-abuse diagnoses and treatment strategies are neither age-specific nor sensitive enough to effectively accommodate the unique biological and social condition of the elderly substance abuser (Korper and Raskin, 2003). Still, outcome-focused investigations demonstrate that older alcohol- and substance-abusing adults who receive treatment specific to their needs achieve positive health outcomes. This treatment may take longer because **alcohol and other drug withdrawal may be more severe in the elderly, but detoxification can be managed safely** in this population (NHSDA Report, 2001).

Available evidence indicates that the traditional range of treatment modalities (such as residential, outpatient, social model, and medical model) and the spectrum of interventions (group, individual, peer, brief therapy, motivational counseling, cognitive-behavioral therapies, family, spiritual, and others) that are effective in treating younger drug and alcohol abusers are also effective in the elderly patient if age-related innovations are made to make them more medically and culturally sensitive to the unique needs of this population (NHSDA Report, 2001). For instance, **elder substance abusers may suffer a greater degree of cognitive impairment** (e.g., problems with verbal abstraction), and research suggests that this is associated with poorer prognosis in treatment. Treatment that addresses this consideration can improve participation and outcomes in elderly patients. Groups, posters, informational brochures, and even waiting-area reading material that is focused on seniors can also promote increased participation and positive outcomes (Patterson, Lacro & Jeste, 1999).

ETHNIC GROUPS

According to the U.S. Census Bureau, **one-third of the U.S. population is non-White (African American, Hispanic, Asian, etc.)** (U.S. Census Bureau, 2007). This does not include first-, second-, and even third-generation Whites whose cultural traditions are still very influential in their lives. Recognition of cultural variances among groups provides better treatment outcomes. Studies verify that **treatment specifically targeted to different ethnic and cultural groups promotes continued abstinence better than general treatment programs** (Madray, Brown & Primm, 2005; Perez-Arce, Carr & Sorensen, 1993). Cultural competency and culturally consistent treatment are now key components of successful programming. It is imperative to note that culture includes a diverse constellation of vital elements: customs, values, rituals, norms, religious beliefs, and ideals. You can't base a culture on the color of the skin, on the region of the world, or even on a common language spoken. The more specific the program is in addressing an identified group's cultural needs, the more effective it will be (Rounds-Bryant, Motivans & Pelissier, 2003).

African American

Non-Hispanic African Americans made up 22.1% of the admissions to publicly funded substance-abuse treatment facilities although they constitute only 12% of the U.S. population. Men outnumbered women by 3 to 1. African-American female admissions were more likely to involve hard drugs (alcohol, 8.9% of admissions; cocaine, 29.7%; opiates, 10.6%) than were African-American male admissions (alcohol, 28% of admissions; cocaine, 52.1%; opiates, 17.7%). African Americans also had significant treatment admissions for marijuana (22% male and 6.6% female for all 2005 admissions), hallucinogens (11.4% male, 5.5% female), and PCP (36.2% male, 14.1% female) (SAMHSA, 2006B).

A recent study looked at retention rates in drug treatment programs in the Los Angeles County area. There were lower completion rates among African-American clients (17.5%) compared with White (26.7%) clients (Jacobson, Robinson & Bluthenthal, 2007). The reasons for this disparity are only partially explainable because of economic status. There is, in general, a surprising lack of research examining the discrepancies among different ethnic groups especially when it comes to treatment.

The following ideas as to the **differences in the treatment/intervention needs of inner-city African-American substance abusers** are the result of years of experience working with the African-American community in San Francisco by members of the Haight Ashbury Detox Clinic and the Black Extended Family Program at Glide Memorial Church (Smith, Buxton, Bilal, et al., 1993).

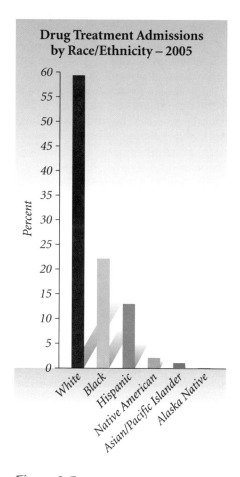

Figure 9-7 •

The racial composition of admissions to drug treatment programs has remained fairly consistent since 1992 and proportionally is somewhat different from the actual composition of the U.S. population. Whites are 72% of the U.S. population but only 59.3% of admissions to drug programs, whereas African Americans are 12% of the population but 22.1% of admissions (SAMHSA, 2006B).

Higher Pain Threshold. Historically, African Americans have developed a high pain threshold to help them survive in a harsh and painful environment. Unfortunately, this **greater tolerance for suffering delays a cry for help, leading to more-severe addiction and other life problems before entering treatment**. One solution to lowering the pain threshold and getting addicts to treatment sooner is educating the African-American community about the true impact of drugs.

◇ In some urban areas, an alarmingly high number of African-American babies are born drug affected.

◇ African-American teenagers have a greater chance of dying from drug-related crime than they do from being hit by a car.

◇ There are more African-American men in their twenties who are in jail for drug-related offenses than are in college.

◇ **Because African-American women are using crack at a greater rate than any other drug except alcohol, their family structure is dissolving at an alarming rate.**

◇ Many urban neighborhoods with a high African-American population have an extremely high infant mortality rate due to drug use by pregnant women who abuse or are addicted.

Drugs as an Economic Resource. Few economic windfalls are available to inner-city African-American communities. Reducing drug dealing here means a loss of income to many families. This is in contrast to the European American community, where drug/alcohol abuse usually drains the finances of families.

The true economics of the process need to be taught. For example, once the dealer becomes a user, the economic drain starts. Other members of the community are devastated and become dysfunctional; crime is brought to their own backyards.

"Most African Americans come into recovery by way of the criminal justice system, very late in the whole process of addiction, and are compelled to come to programs like Glide or Haight Ashbury by the courts. So you have a whole different attitude from people who have hit rock bottom and decided they've got to seek help. The kids are more concerned about just finishing their term and finishing whatever sentence they have and getting out. They don't want to deal with counselors. They don't want to deal with advice. So what you've got is a chance, at that point, to try to hook them into some kind of system that allows them to get back into society with a greater chance of success."

Youth drug counselor

Crime Leads to Chemical Dependency. Most often crime is the first entry into the chemical dependency subculture rather than drug use itself as is true in the White community. Often in the African-American community, the pattern is to make sales first and then sample the wares later.

Strong Sense of Boundaries. Intervention is viewed as an inappropriate imposition or violation of one's space. There is resistance from within the community to approaching someone with a chemical dependency problem because that would violate the person's boundaries or turf, but not approaching someone also perpetuates denial.

These problems are the most difficult to address. They need a major attitudinal change; that is, is it better to respect one's turf or to attempt intervention and try to do something about the problem?

Chemical Dependency: Primary or Secondary Problem? Minority communities often cite underemployment, poor housing, and lack of social/recreational resources as the primary problems instead of chemical dependency. This perpetuates denial and pre-

vents many addicts from getting into treatment early. **Drug users must understand that no other issues can be tackled successfully without tackling recovery first.** The community needs to accept chemical dependency as a primary problem.

"Recovery is a lifetime process. That's a very difficult thing for African Americans to focus on. We're sprinters. We're real good at the 50-yard dash and the 100-yard dash and we have a feeling that, Okay, it's a drug problem. Once I stop using and I put it behind me, I can forget it and go about my business. But no, recovery is a lifetime process, and you have to think more in terms of being a marathoner."

Rafiq Bilal, former director, Black Extended Family Program

Conspiracy Theory. The belief that the rapid spread of crack (and AIDS) into the African-American community is deliberate genocide, is very widely held among African Americans. Given the history of slavery, segregation, and de facto segregation, this is understandable. Whether or not the conspiracy theory is true, addiction is still a disease that must be treated in the individual as well as in society as a whole.

Revelations. In the African-American community, organized spirituality has been key to promoting recovery. Treatment programs based in church settings have been shown to be more effective than more-traditional treatment settings. In one study in Arkansas's Mississippi River Delta region, one-third of a group of drug users had consulted with clergy, and everyone reported significant religiosity. The clergy members who were interviewed, however, said they were not as prepared or knowledgeable as they should be in the field of substance abuse (Sexton, Carlson, Siegal, et al., 2006).

"The African-American community is very spiritually oriented whether from involvement with the church or from historical associations. Most

interesting is a recovery pattern of consecutive periods of clean time/ relapse, clean time/relapse, until a revelation or 'snapping' occurs that results in a continuous sustained recovery effort. This is different from the more classic expanding periods of sobriety leading toward more-sustained long-term recovery."

Rafiq Bilal, former director, Black Extended Family Program

The Black Extended Family Program under the guidance of the Reverend Cecil Williams uses the concept and the emotional force of the extended family to help keep people in treatment and give them an alternative to the lonely life of the addict. This concept reestablishes family, spirituality, and self-worth, qualities that have been weakened by drug use. The **Terms of Resistance,** a 10-step equivalent of the 12 steps, was developed by Reverend Williams in 1992:

1. I will gain control over my life.
2. I will stop lying.
3. I will be honest with myself.
4. I will accept who I am.
5. I will feel my real feelings.
6. I will feel my pain.
7. I will forgive myself and forgive others.
8. I will rebirth a new life.
9. I will live my spirituality.
10. I will support and love my brothers and sisters

(Smith, Buxton, Bilal, et al., 1993).

Hispanic

In 2005 the U.S. Census Bureau estimated that **42.7 million (14.4%) of the U.S. population was of Hispanic origin,** including those currently living in Puerto Rico (a U.S. territory) and undocumented Hispanics living in the United States. These populations were estimated to be 3.4 million and 5 million, respectively. In Los Angeles, California, Hispanics represents 47% of the population, and in San Diego they are 25%. The breakdown is approximately **58.5% Mexican**

American, 9.6% Puerto Rican, 4.8% Central American, 3.8% South American, 3.5% Cuban American, 2.2% Dominican, and 17.6% other Hispanic groups (Ruiz, 2005).

◇ **In 2005, 253,000 (13.7%) of all those in substance-abuse treatment in the United States were classed as being of Hispanic origin.** This percentage matches the Hispanic percentage of the general population.

◇ These admissions comprised Mexican (39.4%), Puerto Rican (29.2%), Cuban (3.6%) and other, non-specified (12.4%) individuals.

◇ The most common primary substances of abuse among Hispanics who presented themselves for treatment were alcohol (23.3%), opiates (27.1%), and marijuana (13.4%). The admissions for opiate abuse were twice that of non-Hispanic groups.

◇ Hispanic admissions were 77% male and 23% female compared with 68.1% male and 31.9% female among non-Hispanic admissions (SAMHSA, 2006B).

Great disparities exist for Hispanic substances abusers. Even though the 2006 estimated Hispanic population was 14.4% of the U.S. population, 44% to 45% of federal drug offenders and a greater number of first-time offenders were of Hispanic origin. Lifetime state or federal drug incarceration probability for Hispanics is four times that of Whites, and per-capita incarceration for Hispanic males is twice that of White males (DOJ, 2006A).

With Hispanics it is important to understand the cultural diversity and the differences among groups as well as the similarities. The most common similarities are Spanish language, Catholic background, Indian or African traits, Iberian heritage, and strong family structure. The differences are the number of years or generations they have lived in the United States; the country of origin (the three most prevalent being Mexico, Puerto Rico, and Cuba); their level of education; and their economic status (e.g., are they Mexican migrant workers who immigrate to sur-

vive poverty and help their family back home; are they upper-class Mexicans or Costa Ricans looking to protect their wealth; are they middle- and upper-class Cubans who fled Fidel Castro a generation ago and have become a driving force in the Florida economy; or are they lower-, middle-, and upper-class Puerto Ricans [American citizens] who have moved to the East Coast to find a better life for their families?).

After addressing any emergency physical or mental health needs, **the first thing a treatment facility has to determine is the level of acculturation of any Hispanic clients coming in for treatment.** For example, how well do they speak English; are they newly arrived immigrants; how integrated are they in the predominantly White society; are they first-, second-, or third-generation Hispanics who have stayed aware of their cultural heritage and kept in contact with friends and relatives in their country of origin; or are they caught between two cultures without a solid home base?

In New York the rapid influx of Puerto Ricans in the fifties, sixties, and seventies often caused a fragmentation of the extended family system, a polarization between generations, a loss of many aspects of the Puerto Rican culture, and an identity crisis. These stressors, along with language differences, were found responsible (in a New York State survey) for increases in substance abuse. With Cuban Americans, however, the rapid integration into American society has resulted in a level of drug use about half that of the Mexican-American and Puerto Rican communities (Ruiz & Langrod, 2005).

What this means in terms of treatment is that **programs must be flexible, have a diverse staff with a preponderance of Spanish-speaking and/or bilingual and bicultural counselors and administrators, and be willing to treat the whole family because family is so significant in Hispanic cultures.** Because Hispanic-American families have excellent networking systems, these systems can be used extensively in the treatment process. In addition, the treatment facility should be aware of the distinct and clear roles that each family member plays in the Hispanic family dy-

namic. This is in contrast to many White families, where the roles of each member can be quite variable.

The core aspects of Hispanic cultures are *dignidad, respeto, y carino*— dignity, respect, and love. Even the concept of urine testing can be a touchy subject because the request for a urine test implies a lack of trust. Another aspect of Hispanic cultures is the strong role that spirituality plays. In addition to a Catholic heritage, some Hispanic cultures have nonorthodox religious beliefs, such as spiritualism, Santería, Brujería, and Curanderism. Pentecostal and Jehovah's Witness churches are also increasing in Hispanic communities.

"Some of the recent Mexican immigrants I've worked with who have an alcohol problem didn't start drinking heavily until they came to this country at the age of 25 or 30. At home they had to care for their families and had little money. Here they are separated from their families and have more money, and so the use of alcohol and other drugs escalates. The other thing I've found is that even if a Hispanic client speaks perfect English, the fact that I'm bilingual and bicultural increases participation in treatment."

Hispanic drug counselor

Asian & Pacific Islander

There are more than 11 million Asians and Pacific Islanders (APIs) living in the United States, and this figure is expected to grow to 41 million by 2050. In California they represent 9.6% of the state's population (about 3.2 million); in New York, 3.9% (693,000); in Hawaii, 61.8% (685,200); in Texas, 1.9% (320,000); and in Illinois, 2.5% (285,000) (U.S. Census Bureau, 2007).

As with Hispanic populations, **Asians and Pacific Islanders represent a wide variety of cultures.** The differences include:

◇ a variety of distinct and separate ethnic groups (such as Japanese, Filipino, Cambodian, Indian, and Samoan);

◇ a variety of languages (such as Korean, Chinese, Tagalog, and hundreds more);

◇ a variety of religions (from Buddhism and Hinduism to Animism, Islam, and Christianity);

◇ a variety of strong cultural characteristics based on thousands of years of history;

◇ a great variety of cultures even among immigrants from the same country (e.g., Cantonese, Shanghaiese, and Taiwanese—all from China); and

◇ different levels of acculturation depending on the number of generations they have been in the United States. (For example, many Chinese Americans and Japanese Americans stretch back four or five generations, whereas the newer immigrants, such as Laotians, Vietnamese, Koreans, Hmong, and Thai, go back only one or two generations (Tsuang, 2005).

The similarities are:

◇ they live along the Pacific Rim;

◇ **they have a strong regard for family with usually enmeshed family systems;**

◇ **they generally have a high respect for education;**

◇ **they are less demonstrative or open in their communication about personal issues;**

◇ they are more reserved about expressing accomplishments because they feel this would be a form of arrogant boasting; and

◇ **they are reluctant to discuss health issues or death** because they superstitiously believe that it would make those problems occur.

These and other similarities affect treatment.

Key issues for API populations include immigration, acculturation, and intergenerational conflicts. The **difficulties of a new language**, the pressures of being a minority, and the feelings of loss, grief, separation, and isolation as they adjust to a new country—all can act as risk factors for drug abuse. The loss of traditional cul-

tural values during the process of assimilation can lead to drinking and other drug use to deal with that stress; and, finally, the younger generation adapts more quickly to their new culture, leading to conflicts with their parents over traditional values (SAMHSA, 2002).

Asian Americans respond more to credentialed professionals than to peer counselors and prefer individual counseling to group counseling. They rely more on their own responsibility to handle their addiction rather than a higher power or external control. They also feel that if they were to complain about their issues, they would be imposing on others. They feel that saving face and individual honor are important, so they are less responsive and will avoid confrontation. They prefer alternative ways of expressing their feelings, such as creative or expressive arts therapy. They also require a strong incorporation of family therapy. Finally, they have strongly developed gender roles, so **separate male and female groups are more effective than mixed groups**.

Entry into treatment for Asian Americans usually occurs late because an admission of addiction is an admission of loss of control. Another problem is that addicts live for the addiction and for themselves rather than for the family and the community, so their addiction and individualism makes them less likely to respond to usual interventional techniques. Finally, **the sense of family shame often keeps the family enabling and rescuing the addict repeatedly rather than insisting he get into treatment**. On the other hand, the strong sense of family makes for greater compliance with protocols once treatment, which incorporates family therapy, has commenced. **Programs for Asian Americans must involve the family in any treatment, or the odds of success are greatly lowered.**

Available Programs.   Because of the wide variety of Asian-American cultures, the historical importance and availability of certain drugs, and the wide geographic distribution in cities and states of various groups, **treatment personnel must do surveys of their neighborhoods to make treatment**

relevant. For example, the use of treatment services by Asian Americans in San Francisco in the 1980s was extremely low. This was misinterpreted to mean that Asian Americans had fewer drug problems than other ethnic groups. Community reports, however, found as high an incidence of drug abuse in the Asian community as in other ethnic groups, the difference being that the Asian Americans' drugs of choice were sedatives, particularly street Quaaludes® and Soma® (sedating muscle relaxant), which weren't addressed in most treatment programs. When San Francisco Bay Area treatment services developed a specific, culturally consistent Asian-American program incorporating family therapy, treatment of sedative abuse, and personnel who were bicultural and bilingual, it resulted in a dramatic increase of Asian Americans coming into treatment at a level consistent with their overall population in the region.

The most commonly used drugs in API communities vary:

◇ Chinese—tobacco and alcohol;

◇ Japanese—alcohol, marijuana, tobacco, crack cocaine, and methamphetamine;

◇ Koreans—alcohol (whiskey and rice wine) and crack cocaine;

◇ Filipino—alcohol, marijuana, and cocaine;

◇ Vietnamese—tobacco, marijuana, and alcohol; and

◇ Cambodian—alcohol, tobacco, crack cocaine, and smokable methamphetamine

(SAMHSA, 2002).

By 2005 Asians/Pacific Islanders in treatment for substance-abuse problems in the United States consisted of 32.6% for alcohol abuse, 28.7% for methamphetamine and other stimulants, 19.1% for marijuana, 9.6% for heroin and other opiates, 7.1% for cocaine, 0.1% sedative-hypnotics, and 0.1% for PCP and other hallucinogens (SAMHSA 2006B).

American Indian

Most American Indians are located in 27 states, with more than half living in Arizona. American

Indian groups have a wide variety of cultural traditions. For example, the five eastern nations (tribes) of Oklahoma, who are literate and successful, have low rates of alcoholism. This is in comparison with some western mountain tribes who, in one study, were found to have a rate of alcoholism seven times the national average. **Overall 58.5% of American Indian/ Alaska Native treatment admissions were for alcohol compared with 39.2% for the general population** (SAMHSA, 2006B). In addition, drugs with a historical context, such as tobacco and peyote, are used more often in ceremonies than as recreational drugs, so the introduction of different drugs, particularly alcohol and inhalants, with no cultural tradition of restricted use, has caused numerous problems (Foulks, 2005).

Bicultural and bilingual treatment personnel greatly increase the chances of successful treatment. Many nations incorporate cultural traditions in healing, including talking circles, purification ceremonies, sweat lodges, meditative practices, shamanistic ceremonies, and even community "sings."

Detoxification centers, halfway houses, outpatient programs, and hospital units have been funded by the Indian Health Service and certain state and county governments. Because more than 60% of American Indians live away from traditional communities in multi-ethnic urban areas, however, treatment centers in those locales should have the same diversity of bilingual and bicultural personnel for American Indians as they do for other ethnic and cultural groups.

Talking circles have been used for hundreds of years in various American Indian tribes as a way to solve problems and heal community members. The process is similar to peer groups, though instead of round-robin talking with no interruptions, there is crosstalk and questions. The sessions usually last two or three hours, though they can last much longer.

"On reservations you get locked into a community where you don't grow and there is a minimum of interaction

with other groups. There is virtually no middle class. You have a group who are highly religious who do not drink at all, you have a few who work for the Bureau of Indian Affairs or in limited industry and drink sparingly, and you have another group that lives to drink and drinks to live. There's not enough work, nothing to do, and often nothing to look forward to for many in this group. You're just another Indian and you're not to be trusted. You have to want to be more than just another drunken Indian.

"We have to be proud of who we are before we can reach recovery. In the Native American community, the family is very tight. Everyone is your cousin or aunt or uncle. A sense of pride in your people is part of the core of spirituality that helps us survive. As part of this, we've always looked to elders for guidance. The elders would talk to you about your drinking [a form of intervention] to get you to make changes in your life. The elders have a variety of approaches. They might even do a tough-love approach and tell alcoholics to leave the reservation, finish their drinking, and come back when they are sober; or they might tell them to get honest with themselves and make a sobriety pledge to the medicine man or in a pipe ceremony.

"We have a variety of tribes that I deal with here in Montana, such as Sioux, Northern Cheyenne, Blackfoot, and Crow. Each one has its own traditions. Unfortunately, a number of clinic directors on reservations who are brought in from the outside have trouble understanding the traditions, so they rely more on standard psychosocial therapy, which is not as effective and breeds distrust. Adding to this is the fact that, for many Native

Americans, hitting bottom is not as big a trigger for self-referral into treatment as it is in the Anglo community. Often they are not aware of what bottom is. It takes intervention or court mandate to make changes. On the other hand, once they get recovery, they are much less likely to let go. I tell them that alcoholism is like the raven that has stolen your shadow. If your shadow is gone, your spirituality is gone. Be proud of who you are."
Bob Clarkson, American Indian drug and alcohol counselor

"Great Spirit, grant me the serenity of a dove to accept the things I cannot change, the courage of an eagle to change the things I can, and the wisdom of an owl to know the difference."
American Indian version of the Serenity Prayer used in Alcoholics Anonymous

OTHER GROUPS

There are numerous groupings of Americans who require targeted treatment. **Whether they are substance abusers who have physical disabilities, gays or lesbians, homeless, mentally challenged, or a dozen other groups, the key to effective treatment seems to be involvement with peer groups** who have experienced the lifestyle, the problems, the prejudices, the shunning, the joys, and the problems with self-esteem or relationships and can speak and help based on personal experience.

The common point that needs to be recognized is that addiction is addiction. To imagine that problems with addictive behavior would disappear if only some other conditions or problems were taken care of is a sure path to continued addictive behavior. On the other hand, the other problems such as racism and mental instability have to be addressed and treated at the same time because **many of the roots of compulsive use lie in a subconscious effort to avoid or cope with the pain experienced in these conditions or lifestyles.**

Physically Disabled

Americans with disabilities represent a much-neglected group of chemically dependent people. Some of the more common disabilities are blindness, deafness, head or brain injury (50,000 per year), and spinal cord injury (10,000 to 15,000 new cases per year). Despite passage of the Americans with Disabilities Act in 1990, most programs remain inaccessible to many with mobility, visual, or hearing impairments. In addition, there is very little interdisciplinary training for working with physically disabled substance abusers. One problem that occurs is that **the counselor can over focus on the physical disability and miss signs and symptoms of relapse and additional problems or focus too strongly on the addiction and not take into account the extra stress caused by the disability.** Conversely, the rehabilitation professional might feel unqualified or leery of handling substance-abuse problems or might not even recognize the signs and symptoms. In addition society's attitude toward people with disabilities can promote the concept of learned helplessness and dependency on others and subsequently on drugs. One irony of substance abuse in people with physical disabilities is that substance use is a factor in up to 68% of traumatic disabling injuries (Heinemann & Rawal, 2005). A thorough medical and drug history is helpful in judging whether the substance abuse predated the disability, was triggered by it, or occurred independently of it. **Because physical disabilities often involve pain, there is an increased use of prescription medications that can be abused.**

"I used my disability to the fullest extent of the law. I could go in on the scooter, put on some make-up, and coerce them out of anything. I had one doctor going for several months, and I remember that I was taking so much Vicodin® at the time that I was throwing up and I would tell him that I had headaches and that caused me to throw up, so he would continue to give me the pain medication that would make me throw up. I was down to around 98 pounds at the end of that run. I have been doing that for 17 years, in and out of rehab five times."
58-year-old wheelchair-bound woman in recovery

Again it is a preexisting susceptibility to addiction or the increased need for pain relief that usually indicates that the person with a physical disability will have a dependence problem with pain medications (Schnoll, 1993).

In a study of 96 people with long-term spinal cord injuries, 43% used prescription medications with abuse potential, and one-fourth of those, or about 10% of the total, reported misusing the medications. **The group that regularly misused the prescription medications was less accepting of their disability and more depressed.** Another study found that the existence of a preexisting substance-abuse problem made it more likely that the client would not participate fully in rehabilitation, thereby slowing recovery and increasing stress (Heinemann, 1993).

Lesbian, Gay, Bisexual & Transgender

There has been a lack of research on substance abuse in the gay and lesbian communities, so the studies that have been done are not exhaustive, merely suggestive. Even the population of the lesbian, gay, bisexual, and transgender (LGBT) community is difficult to determine. One study estimates that in the United States, 9.8% of men and 5% of women report same-gender sexual behavior since puberty, whereas 2.8% of men and 1.4% of women report a homosexual or bisexual identity (Michaels, 1996). The studies that have been done put the incidence of drug and alcohol use in the gay community significantly higher than in the general population (Bickelhaupt, 1995; SAMHSA, 2001). Circuit parties—erotically charged, two-day dance events attended by up to 25,000 self-identified gay and bisexual men—were originally developed to raise HIV/AIDS awareness, but in some cases have become venues where HIV is more likely to be transmitted (Ghaziani & Cook, 2005). Crystal meth has become the drug of choice (along with alcohol) at gay clubs and circuit parties. At a Los Angeles clinic, 1 out of 3 gay or bisexual men who tested positive for HIV admitted to using this powerful methamphetamine, a percentage three times greater than a similar survey found four years earlier (Lee, 2006).

A directory of gay and lesbian AA groups listed more than 800 meetings in the United States in the mid-nineties. **Various studies have estimated that 20% to 35% of gay men and lesbians are heavy alcohol users (compared with 10% to 12% of heterosexuals** (Cabaj, 2005; Hughes & Wilsnack, 1997; Skinner, 1994; Skinner & Otis, 1996). Marijuana was also used at a significantly higher level, almost one-third more than in the general population (Kelly, 1991). Besides alcohol, marijuana, and crystal meth, a sample of gay men found them 21 times more likely to use nitrite inhalants and four to seven times more likely to use hallucinogens, painkillers, sedatives, and tranquilizers (Freese, Obert, Dickow, et al., 2000).

The high incidence of HIV and AIDS in the gay male community is aggravated by drug or alcohol use for two reasons: the use of drugs lowers inhibitions and leads to unsafe sex, and the use of contaminated needles spreads the HIV virus quickly. This problem is aggravated by a **social life that often involves bars or other settings that promote drug and alcohol use** (D'Augelli, 1996).

"I'd been using drugs for years and years, but when I found out I was positive, I said, 'Oh, I'm going to die,' and I just started slamming dope faster and harder, and I did that for two years; and when I wasn't dead, I said, 'Wait a minute, I'm not dying, I gotta keep going with my life.' And I started realizing that I could get clean, and I could stay as healthy as I could, and I could make something out of my life."
Gay recovering substance abuser with AIDS

Though sexual minorities must suffer society's hostility, indifference, fear, or misunderstanding and be subject to extra stress, **it is still the roots** of addiction that are the greater influence—genetics tempered by childhood stresses and inflamed by drug use.

"When I first came here, I was so nervous about being gay, one of the minority in the group 'cause there's a lot more straight men, but I really like it now because I can work on my issues about being heterophobic—I get fears around heterosexuals. I stereotype straight guys: Oh, they all hate me and they all think I'm less of a man. And I get to find out that's not true, and I get to find out that if someone does have that, then that's theirs. It ain't mine."

Gay recovering polydrug abuser

Societal homophobia, heterosexism, and internalized homophobia (the fear and hatred of one's own homosexuality) are often some of the greatest barriers to long-term sobriety and recovery (Kominars, 1995). In recent years there has been a decrease in these feelings mostly due to a decrease in societal homophobia, which might lead to better recovery outcomes for sexual minorities (Cabaj, 2005). A number of polls of Americans, however, found that homosexuality remains unacceptable to a large segment of the population. This can make LGBT clients reluctant to speak about their sexual orientation. This reluctance leaves out pieces of the personality puzzle for treatment personnel (SAMHSA, 2001). For example, **defining the client's family and involving them in treatment can be difficult**. Has the family of origin rejected their son, or daughter, or sibling? What is the structure of the family?

Relapse prevention is particularly difficult when one's lifestyle puts him or her in contact with people who are still drinking and using marijuana or crystal meth. Often the social contact and events in the LGBT community are an important aspect of coping with the homophobia and isolation that comes from the straight community, and, unfortunately, alcohol, crystal meth, and

other drugs are often a part of this scene (Lee, 2006).

Treatment programs such as the Matrix Model developed at UCLA or various inpatient programs that focus on meth and specific communities are proving that meth treatment is effective when it is focused, intensive, and extended over a sufficient period of time (up to two years for outpatient treatment).

TREATMENT OBSTACLES

Denial and lack of financial or treatment resources have always constituted the biggest obstacles to addiction treatment. But as the treatment of addictive disease continues to evolve, other significant obstacles are being identified that require intervention for successful treatment outcomes.

DEVELOPMENTAL ARREST & COGNITIVE IMPAIRMENTS

The use of psychoactive drugs can delay users' emotional development and keep them from learning how to deal with life's problems. In terms of treatment, the counselors or other professionals must identify the level of development in the individual: they must be aware of how much of what they or others are teaching is being understood. In addition, if a client is not fully detoxified or is not given time to start functioning normally, even the most sophisticated treatment can fall on deaf ears. More-extensive assessment is one way to overcome these problems.

Much research now confirms that abuse of most psychoactive drugs results in actual **damage to brain cells or brain functioning that results in cognitive deficits especially during the first several months of abstinence and recovery**. For example, methamphetamine abuse causes major damage to the hippocampus and other limbic cortices (Thompson, Hayashi, Simon, et al., 2004) as well as a 24% loss in dopamine transporter mechanisms (Volkow, Chang, Wang, et al., 2001). The prefrontal cortex involved in the executive functions of the brain also exhibits functional anomalies in the

chemically dependant brain, resulting in **30% to 80% of substance abusers' having mild to severe cognitive impairments** (Grossman & Onken, 2003).

Thus there is a neurocognitive basis for the observed problems of denial, attention, memory, learning, temporal processing, goal setting or "delayed discounting" (inability to appreciate delayed gratification), problem solving, decision making, abstract thinking, and other cognitive functions in recovering addicts that often lead to slips and relapses. Most treatment protocols employ psychoeducational or cognitive-behavioral components that require goal setting and planning, sustained attention, response inhibition, skill acquisition, problem solving, and decision-making skills—the same cognitive abilities that are most impaired in many substance abusers. Current treatment interventions may be inadequate for substance abusers with cognitive deficits. **Many clients may not be able to comprehend the interventions that are presented to them during early recovery.** This leads to early dropout, chronic relapses, and poorer long-term treatment outcomes.

Cognitive impairment findings in substance abusers have led to a recommendation **that cognitive status examinations be conducted upon admission and then repeated** at regular intervals during treatment to direct the level and the intensity of treatment interventions. One treatment approach then focuses on accelerating cognitive recovery of brain function. **Cognitive performance has been shown to improve with continued abstinence and recovery, but these skills are needed earlier in the treatment process if one is to make the most practical and cost-effective use of treatment.** Successive relapses often get worse, resulting in increasing harm, guilt, and loss. Clients can be given work assignments or participate in sessions designed to improve identified deficits. Examples of this would be specific sessions targeted for memory training or problem-solving skills development. Environmental interventions like the use of unambiguous cues to prompt or discourage specific behaviors can also help those with memory impairment (Grossman & Onken, 2003).

Another approach is to **modify existing treatment protocols to the cognitive abilities of the client** based on cognitive status examinations. Such treatment adaptations could include: decreased length of counseling sessions, increased frequency of sessions, repeated presentation of therapeutic material, multimodality (visual, workbook, audio, and experiential) presentations, memory aids (calendars, appointment books, association cues, and mnemonics), stress management to improve attention and concentration, use of simple language, immediate feedback to clarify misunderstandings and reward progress, and homework assignments to reinforce learning exercises. When practical, the length of a treatment episode can also be increased so that **more-difficult and abstract concepts are presented later in treatment when cognitive processing has improved. Three to six months of continuous abstinence has been associated with the return of many but not all cognitive abilities.**

FOLLOW-THROUGH (monitoring)

Nothing is more indicative of poor treatment outcome than early program dropout or lack of compliance to the treatment protocol. Ironically, the client confidentiality that is so vital to the addiction treatment process has contributed to the problem of poor treatment compliance. Clients who have not or will not release information about their treatment progress can be noncompliant to protocols without the awareness of families, employers, or others until more destruction has resulted from their resumed addiction.

Professional licensing boards (medical, nursing, and legal) now mandate the release of confidentiality as a condition of retaining a license when addicts who are professionals are delivered to treatment after their addiction has been discovered. **This has also been adopted by many CJS referral sources such as drug courts**, probation, or paroled-mandated treatment. Further, federal confidentiality laws were amended to permit the processing of an irrevocable release of information for CJS referrals. Other releases can be canceled at any time at the mandate of the client. This practice, though ensuring better program compliance, created another obstacle for the treatment professional: How could a therapist engage an addict in deep and sensitive issues about the addiction without being viewed as an extension of the licensing board, the family, or law enforcement? To address this obstacle, some licensing boards and employee assistance programs now employ a program monitor who oversees the progress of an addict in treatment to ensure compliance to program protocols.

CONFLICTING GOALS

An individual addict's treatment goal may conflict with a program's goal. Some addicts may enter treatment merely to be able to better manage their abuse of drugs or to qualify for certain social benefits. Most treatment programs insist on an immediate commitment from their clients to a drug-free lifestyle. This difference between goals leads to a poor treatment outcome.

Program goals may conflict with society's goals for treating addicts. Programs naturally focus on the care of their clients, using interventions that they hope will lead their clients to the best possible life outcome. Society is more interested in supporting programs that decrease the social costs of addiction (e.g. crime, health costs, accidents, and violence).

The problems of **conflicting goals are best managed by the development of clear program objectives and goals and better assessment and matching of clients to programs**. Although these concepts seem straightforward and easy to practice, only now is investment in these two areas beginning to occur.

TREATMENT RESOURCES

The biggest obstacle continues to be lack of treatment resources. On a national basis, individuals who apply for treatment are put on a waiting list of two weeks to three months or longer before they can get into treatment. Studies have shown that **for every 100 people put on waiting list, 66% will never make it into treatment**. A study of heroin addicts put on a waiting list for comprehensive methadone maintenance therapy in Baltimore, Maryland, documented that only 20.8% were available to access treatment when space opened for them to enter treatment, an attrition rate of 79.2% (Schwartz, Highfield, Jaffe, et al., 2006). What happens to those potential clients is a matter of deep concern. Many die from drugs or from suicide while waiting for treatment (O'Boyle & Brandon, 1998). Most become more heavily involved in drugs potentially due to a "demotion" on Prochaska and Di Clemente's scale of readiness to change, which means that any delay in accessing treatment results in a loss of motivation. A high proportion may also end up in the criminal justice system. Because treatment has been shown to be very effective, it is a national tragedy that we continue to have long protracted waiting periods for clients wanting to access treatment. The national Treatment Episode Data Set documents that almost 1.9 million individuals received treatment for alcohol- or substance-abuse problems in 2005. This means that only 1 of every 15 to 25 projected substance abusers was treated in that year (SAMHSA, 2006B).

MEDICAL INTERVENTION DEVELOPMENTS

INTRODUCTION

Drug replacement therapies, medical pharmacotherapy, chemically assisted detoxification, drug-assisted recovery, antipriming medications, drug restoration of homeostasis, medicated "resetting" of the brain, and other medical interventions currently in development to treat drug addiction would have been considered oxymoronic in the field of recovery a few short years ago. These terms are still considered heresy by many chemical dependency treatment clinicians and recovering addicts as both recognize that the use of psychoactive drugs is the problem to begin with and often results in relapse.

Cornered   by Baldwin

4-10 © 2003 Mike Baldwin / Dist. by Universal Press Syndicate www.cornered.com
cornered@comlc.com

"Do a double-blind test. Give the new drug to rich patients and a placebo to the poor. No sense getting their hopes up. They couldn't afford it even if it works."

Advances in the understanding of the neuropharmacology of addiction during the 1990s Decade of the Mind, led to a virtual flood of medication developments targeted to treat chemical dependencies. By 2000 the number of new drugs being developed to treat addictions was second only to those in development to treat other mental health disorders and far outnumbered the drugs being developed to treat infections, heart disease, cancer, AIDS, and other illnesses. Chemical dependency treatment specialists now need to broaden their understanding and acceptance of medical therapies as they are certain to be incorporated into addiction treatment in the near future.

MEDICATIONS APPROVED TO TREAT SUBSTANCE USE DISORDERS

The FDA has approved several medications to be used by physicians to treat substance use disorders (SUDs).

For Alcohol Dependence

Disulfiram (Antabuse®) was approved in 1948 and is one of the oldest medications sanctioned to specifically treat an addiction. It modifies the liver's metabolism of alcohol, resulting in a toxic buildup of acetaldehyde when alcohol is drunk. **Aversive consequences (flushing, nausea, vomiting, dizziness, and rapid heart beat) occur immediately, discouraging further use of alcohol in the recovering alcoholic.** Coerced treatment (CJS imposed) is creating a bit of a comeback for this medication as compliance to taking it is increased. Disulfiram is also being looked at as a treatment for cocaine and other stimulant abuse as it was recently discovered that dysphoria and other adverse effects occur when stimulants are taken by disulfiram-treated clients. The effect is seen more in male than female clients and is independent of its effects on alcohol metabolism (Carrol, Fenton, Ball, et al., 2004; Nich, McCance-Katz, Petrakis, et al., 2004; Whitten, 2005).

Naltrexone (ReVia®) was first approved in 1984 to treat cravings of opiate addiction. In December 1994 the drug was also **approved to treat alcohol craving.** Precisely how naltrexone decreases cravings for alcohol is unknown. The drug blocks opiates from acting in the brain; this includes the brain's own naturally occurring opioid neurotransmitters, endorphins. Some speculate that this **disrupts activation of the reward/reinforcement pathway of the brain** to curb craving.

Acamprosate (Campral®) was approved to **treat craving in alcoholism** in July 2004. It had been **used effectively in Europe for this indication since 1989.** Although its mechanism of action is unknown, it modulates the GABA (gamma-aminobutyric acid) type A and B receptors as well as the NMDA glutamate receptor—all of which are disrupted by alcohol consumption. Acamprosate is thought to stabilize these receptors to moderate the craving response. Though studies prior to its FDA approval and its history of effective use in Europe indicated significant effectiveness to decrease alcohol craving, post-FDA approval studies have shown it to be less effective than naltrexone or disulfiram alone or when used in combination with those medications in preventing slips and relapses (Anton, O'Malley, Ciraulo, et al., 2006).

Naltrexone injectable suspension (Vivitrol®) received FDA approval **for treatment of alcohol craving** in 2005.

Though naltrexone oral tablets had already been approved to treat alcohol craving in 1984, Vivitrol® is a new formulation of the medication that permits its use by **monthly injection to ensure that the medication is not being neglected** and therefore reduces patient compliance problems. Recovering alcoholics taking the oral ReVia® form of this medication often discontinued its use on their own after a few months, which often resulted in a relapse. Injected into a muscle once a month, the suspension also results in sustained but lower blood levels of the drug, which is thought to produce fewer side effects than the oral medication.

For Nicotine Addiction

Varenicline (Chantix®) was approved in May 2006 to treat tobacco addiction. It is a partial agonist of the nicotinic acetylcholine receptor. This action then **blocks the ability of nicotine to activate the receptor, which slows the release of dopamine to decreases nicotine craving**.

Bupropion or amfebutamone (Zyban® or Wellbutrin®) was approved by the FDA in December 1996 as the **first oral pill to treat nicotine craving**. This medication is a dopamine and norepinephrine reuptake inhibitor, but its precise mechanism of decreasing cravings for nicotine is not yet known. Bupropion is also medically used as an antidepressant medication.

Nicotine gum by prescription was approved in 1984, and in 1996 **Nicorette®** gum was approved for nonprescription availability for **nicotine replacement therapy**. From 1991 to 1992, four **transdermal patch delivery systems** for nicotine were approved; two of these—**Nicotrol®** and **Nicoderm CQ®**—became nonprescription products by 1996, and the other two—**ProSTEP®** and **Habitrol®**—were approved for OTC sales by 1999. By November 2002 nicotine was also available for tobacco cessation treatment via nasal spray (Nicotrol,® 1996), inhaler (Nicotrol,® 1998), and lozenges (Ariva,® 2002). Nicotine replacement therapy is used to substitute for more-harmful tobacco smoking as well as a form of addiction treatment called **anti-priming therapy**.

For Opiate/Opioid Addiction

Buprenorphine (Suboxone® and Subutex®) was approved in October 2002 for **opioid detoxification and replacement therapy**. Suboxone® combines naloxone with buprenorphine to prevent injection misuse of the medication. It is a powerful partial opioid mu receptor agonist at low to moderate doses but soon reaches a "ceiling effect" when dosages are increased and then becomes an opioid antagonist at high doses. **Physicians are granted DEA permission to use this medication for opioid addiction at their offices** rather than having to be part of an approved treatment clinic (office-based opioid addiction treatment, or **O-BOAT**).

Naltrexone (ReVia® and Trexan®) was approved by the FDA in 1984 to treat opioid dependence. It is an **opioid receptor antagonist that blocks the actions all opioids**. This means that even if a heroin addict slips and injects heroin or uses any other opioid such as Vicodin,® OxyContin,® or Darvon,® he will have no reaction to it while on naltrexone. It has also been found to decrease craving for a wide variety of addictive substances and is used to prevent relapses.

LAAM (Orlam®) was approved as a **replacement therapy for opioid addiction** in July 1993. It is longer acting than methadone and could therefore be dosed trice-weekly instead of daily. It was said to also be potentially **less euphoric and thus less prone to be abused** with milder withdrawal symptoms than methadone. The manufacturer of LAAM voluntarily ceased production of the medication in 2003 due to concerns that it caused cardiac arrhythmias, so LAAM is no longer available in the United States.

Methadone (Dolophine,® Methadose,® Tussol,® and Adanon®) was approved in the 1960s for **detoxification and replacement therapy of heroin addiction**. Methadone remains the standard medication used to treat opioid dependence. Because it is orally acting and has a long duration of action (prevents withdrawal symptoms for 24 hours or longer), **it is a successful harm reduction strategy** with close to 50 years of research demonstrating its ability to reduce medical and legal complications of opioid addiction.

For Stimulant Drug Addiction

There are no medications that are FDA approved for the specific indication of treating methamphetamine or cocaine dependence. Many FDA-approved **medications are being used to treat the symptoms** associated with stimulant addiction withdrawal, however, and several drugs are in development to treat this condition. **Abuse of stimulant drugs disrupts the same brain neurotransmitters that are imbalanced in depression and thought disorders**, so antidepressant (e.g., sertraline, bupropion, trazodone, and imipramine) and neuroleptic (e.g. haloperidol, respiridon, and olanzapine) medications are frequently used to treat symptoms of stimulant withdrawal. Dopaminergic medications (e.g., L-Dopa, amantadine, and bromocriptine) have also been used to dampen cravings for stimulant drugs.

For Sedative-Hypnotic Dependence

Addiction to barbiturates, benzodiazepines, other sedative-hypnotics, muscle relaxants, some inhalants, GHB, and even alcohol **can result in fatal seizures during withdrawal and must therefore be medically managed**. Though no medications have been FDA approved to specifically treat this condition, many drugs approved to treat seizure disorders (e.g., phenobarbital, various benzodiazepines, phenytoin, carbamazepine, and gabapentin) are currently used effectively to treat sedative-hypnotic drug dependence. A benzodiazepine antagonist, flumazenil (Mazicon® and Ro-Mazicon®), approved by the FDA for overdose treatment, may be of benefit in the treatment of alcohol, benzodiazepine, and other depressant drug addictions.

MEDICATIONS IN DEVELOPMENT TO TREAT SUBSTANCE USE DISORDERS

The different types of medications being developed to treat various SUDs can also be classified based on the targeted stage of recovery or by their effects on the nervous system and rest of the body (O'Brien, 1997; Senft, 1991; Vocci, 1999).

Detoxification

Medications that moderate or eliminate the withdrawal syndrome in addicts have been shown to be effective in engaging them in long-term treatment. Some examples of this detox development include clonidine and lofexidine (anti-hypertension medications) to treat opioid withdrawal; selegiline, propranolol (a beta blocker), and SSRI antidepressants (paroxetine) for cocaine and stimulant addiction; and phenobarbital or lorazepam for alcohol or sedative-hypnotic dependence (O'Brien, 1997; Vocci, 1999).

Rapid Opioid Detoxification

This strategy uses various medications to manage opioid withdrawal symptoms in combination with naloxone or naltrexone, opioid antagonists that force the rapid onset of the abstinence syndrome. Opioid addicts experience few symptoms and are quickly able to return to their daily lives without suffering prolonged withdrawal. Medications used to alleviate the naloxone/naltrexone forced onset of opioid withdrawal include:

◊ clonidine, a medication that dampens brain hyperactivity associated with withdrawal; physical detoxification from opioid tissue dependence is accomplished in two to three days;

◊ midazolam, a benzodiazepine sedative that is said to accomplish opioid detoxification in 24 hours; and

◊ lorazepam or midazolam combined with clonidine, used while an addict is anesthetized with propofol (a common anesthetic).

Detoxification of an opioid addict is alleged to occur within only six to eight hours. These methods of rapid detoxification are medically dangerous and require intensive medical management. Further, it is very important to remember that the techniques accomplish only physical detoxification and do not address the long-term behavioral and emotional components of addiction (Bartter & Gooberman, 1996; Byrne, 1998; Cucchia, Monnat, Spagnoli, et al., 1998; Dyer, 1998; Lorenzi, Marsili, Boncinelli, et al., 1999; Sneft, 1991).

Replacement or Agonist Effects

Controversy over whether this type of therapy is more harm reduction than recovery remains very heated in the addiction treatment community. Few can deny the effectiveness of methadone replacement therapy, however, in producing positive benefits both for the addict (reduced morbidity and mortality while increasing overall life functioning) and for society (cost-effectiveness and reduction in crime) (Ball & Ross, 1991). **Positive results from methadone maintenance have stimulated the search for other replacement or agonist therapies. Methylphenidate and pemoline for cocaine and stimulant dependence and SSRI antidepressants and GHB for alcohol and sedative-hypnotic addiction** are examples of replacement therapies in development to treat addictive disorders (O'Brien, 1997; Vocci, 1999). Propoxyphene and tramadol as opioid replacement therapies have also been investigated.

Antagonist (blocking) Medications or Vaccines

Medications or vaccines that block the effects of addictive drugs without inducing their own major psychoactive effects are widely accepted as recovery-oriented treatment approaches. **While taking these types of agents, addicts will be unable to experience the effects of an abused drug should they have a slip.** This destroys the addict's motivation for using and promotes continued abstinence. Significant examples of this treatment approach are the development of depo-naltrexone and depo-buprenorphine injections for **opioid addiction** and UH-232 or NGB-2904 for **cocaine addiction**. A cocaine vaccine, TA-CD, which produces antibodies for cocaine, as well as **two vaccines for nicotine—CYT-002-NicQb (Nicotine-Qbeta) and NicVAX®**—to prevent these drugs from getting to the brain are also in development (Carrera, Ashley, Parsons, et al., 1995; Fox, Kantak, Edwards, et al., 1996; Heading, 2007; O'Brien, 1997; Vocci, 1999; Xi, Newman, Gilbert, et al., 2006). An **alcohol/benzodiazepine antagonist—imidazobenzodiazepine, or Ro 15-4513,** researched more than 20 years ago is again in investigation as a treatment for alcohol or benzodiazepine addiction (Wallner, Hanchar & Olsen, 2006).

Mixed Agonist-Antagonist

A single medication can have an agonist effect at one receptor site and an antagonist effect at another site. Or a combination of drugs are used together that work independently at different receptor sites to accomplish the same overall agonist-antagonist goal. The agonist component of this approach is targeted to prevent withdrawal, while the antagonist effects prevent craving by blocking any further drug use. Examples of this approach are the developments of butorphanol in opioid addiction, cyclazocine in cocaine dependence, and the combination of low-dose nicotine with mecamylamine to treat nicotine addiction. Rapid opioid detoxification described previously also employs this technique of combining agonist with antagonist medication to treat heroin and other opioid addictions (O'Brien, 1997; Rose, Behm, Westman, et al., 1994).

Anticraving & Anticued Craving

Craving or drug hunger is now an established component of addiction. Negative emotional states (e.g., *h*ungry, *a*ngry, *l*onely, *t*ired—*HALT;* *r*estless, *ir*ritable, *d*iscontent—*RID;* and depression) as well as imbalances of brain chemistry due to drug use result in endogenous craving. Environmental cues or triggers (e.g., drug odors, white powders, paraphernalia, crack houses, drug-using acquaintances) also induce craving and a great potential for relapse. **Medications that can check or curb the endogenous craving and/or environmentally cued craving responses have been dramatic developments in treating addictions** (O'Brien, 1997). Naltrexone has been fully approved as an anticraving treatment for alcoholism and is in development to see if it also blocks cocaine and opioid craving (O'Brien, 1997; O'Malley, Jaffe, Chang, et al., 1992; Volpicelli, Alterman, Hayashida, et al., 1992). A concern regarding potential liver toxicity with naltrexone has limited its use in treating alcohol dependence. Nalmefene, another opioid antagonist, has been shown to reduce alcohol craving without any liver toxicity and is now being developed to treat alcohol addiction (Mason, Ritvo, Morgan, et al., 1994; O'Brien, 1997).

Baclofen, a nonopioid muscle relaxant, also exhibits alcohol anticraving effects through modulation of GABA and dopamine neurotransmitters. It is also in development to block cravings for cocaine and opioid dependence (O'Brien, 1997).

Mecamylamine appears to block environmentally cued craving of cocaine and is currently in development for this indication, along with its development as a nicotine anticraving medication (Reid, Mickalian, Delucchi, 1998).

Bupropion, approved for the treatment of nicotine craving, is also in development as a cocaine and methamphetamine anticraving medication. Bupropion research demonstrated that it prevented nicotine craving in patients who did not have symptoms of depression, which indicates that it lessens craving by another unknown mechanism. Similarly, SSRI antidepressants like paroxetine decrease alcohol use in even nondepressed alcoholics (O'Brien, 1997).

The craving response is physiologically similar to the body's stress reaction. This has led researchers to study drugs that can antagonize corticotropin-releasing factor (CRF), which triggers the stress reaction in the brain. The hypothesis is that craving can be prevented by blocking the body's stress reaction. Ketoconazole and CP154,526 inhibit the release of CRF in the brain and are being developed to treat cocaine craving. Metyrapone inhibits the synthesis of body corticoids, which are also involved in the stress reaction. It is also being developed to treat cocaine craving (Vocci, 1999).

Metabolism Modulation

Medications like disulfiram (Antabuse®) that can alter the metabolism of an abused drug to render it ineffective or cause noxious reactions when the abused drug is taken are also being developed. The effectiveness of disulfiram relies on the compliance of the alcoholic to take it in support of the stated desire for abstinence. Historically, Antabuse® has therefore had limited success in treating alcoholism due to compliance problems. The increase of coerced-treatment practices like drug courts and probation stipulations during the past decade, however, has improved disulfiram treatment compliance and increased positive outcomes (O'Brien, 1997; Fuller, Branchey, Brightwell, et al., 1986). This has raised interest in the metabolism modulation approach (Vocci, 1999). One such development is with butyrylcholinesterase (BChE), which increases the metabolism of cocaine to render it ineffective when abused (Dickerson & Janda, 2005).

Restoration of Homeostasis

The homeostasis paradigm for drug addiction was first proposed by C. K. Himmelsbach in 1941 (Littleton, 1998). Abuse of addictive drugs imbalances brain chemistry that then reinforces the need to continue using the drug. This is known as allostasis. **Medications and nutrients that restore brain chemical imbalances are theorized to restore homeostasis and mitigate the need for continued drug use.** Drugs that have dopamine-activating effects in the brain (e.g., selegiline, amantadine, and pergolide) and antidepressants that increase serotonin in the brain (e.g., desipramine, nefazodone, paroxetine, sertraline, and venlafaxine) are being developed to treat cocaine and alcohol addiction by restoring brain chemical homeostasis (Vocci, 1999).

Amino Acid Precursor Loading

This strategy consists of administering protein supplements (e.g., tyrosine, taurine, d,l phenylalanine, glutamate, and tryptophan) to addicts in an effort to **increase the brain's production of its neurochemicals to restore homeostasis.** Though this technique has not yet been validated by rigorous research, many treatment programs report good patient treatment compliance and positive outcomes when amino acid precursor loading is added to the treatment process for cocaine, amphetamine, alcohol, and opioid dependence (Blum, 1989).

Modulation of Drug Effects & Antipriming

A fairly recent development is the **use of medications that can modulate or blunt the pleasure-reinforcing effects of addictive drugs.** Research demonstrates that risk of relapse is great when a recovering addict is primed or uses an addictive substance. Subreinforcing doses of abused substances or drugs that can block this priming action can decrease relapse. This antipriming strategy is behind the development of low-dose nicotine delivery systems, such as the nicotine patch, gum, spray, and inhaler, to treat nicotine addiction (Vocci, 1999).

Two classes of drugs being looked at for their ability to blunt the reinforcing effects of abused drugs are the calcium and sodium ion channel blockers.

Calcium channel-blocking medications prevent calcium ions from entering brain cells. This then **blocks the release of dopamine** and prevents the reinforcing effects of cocaine, opioids, and alcohol from occurring. Nimodipine, amlodipine, nifedipine, and isradipine are all calcium channel blockers being developed to treat addiction to cocaine, opioids, and alcohol (Vocci, 1999; Shulman, Jagoda, Laycock, et al., 1998).

Sodium ion channel blockers include such medications as riluzole, phenytoin, and lamotrigine, which interfere with neuron transmission by blocking the cells' uptake of sodium, enhancing the effects of GABA. Increased GABA activity results in **muting cocaine's reinforcing effects.** Cyclazocine, a mixed opioid agonist-antagonist, also reduces cocaine reinforcement by interfering with cocaine's action on presynaptic neurons' sodium ion channels (Vocci, 1999).

Drugs with Unknown Strategies

◇ Psychedelic drugs like **ibogaine and ketamine are said to be effective in treating cocaine and opioid addiction** even though the early use of ibogaine to treat opioid addiction resulted in some fatalities.

◇ Dextromethorphan (DM), a nonprescription anticough medication, is being studied to treat opioid addiction. DM has been shown to be a weak glutamate agonist, but its mechanism to decrease opiate withdrawal symptoms, craving, and relapse is unclear.

◇ Cycloserine, an antibiotic for the treatment of tuberculosis, is being studied for its ability to decrease opioid use by some unknown mechanism.

◇ Anticonvulsant medications like topiramate, valproate, and carbamazepine appear to diminish cocaine's craving and "kindling" effects.

◇ Topamax® (topiramate) is also said to decrease the craving and priming effects of alcohol abuse.

◇ "Smart drugs," also known as *nootropic agents,* are believed to increase brain activity by unknown mechanisms and are also being tested to treat cocaine and stimulant addiction. Camitine/coenzyme Q10, ginkgo biloba, pentoxifylline, Hydergine,® and piracetam are current nootropics being studied for use in cocaine addiction treatment.

◇ Tiagabine and gabapentin are anticonvulsant medications used in the treatment of epilepsy. They are believed to increase brain GABA while decreasing glutamate activity, but their ability to decrease alcohol, methamphetamine, or cocaine relapse occurs by some yet-to-be-discovered mechanism (Vocci, 1999; O'Brien, 1997).

◇ Disulfiram, the oldest FDA-approved addiction treatment drug, causes aversive effects—increased heart rate, blood pressure, anxiety, paranoia, and restlessness—when taken simultaneously with cocaine. Similar to its use for alcohol addiction, disulfiram has been shown to reduce cocaine abuse by causing unpleasant effects if those being treated with the drug use cocaine. Although many cocaine abusers also abuse alcohol, this cocaine effect has been shown to be unrelated to its effect on alcohol metabolism. Researchers speculate that this may have something to do with the dopamine-enhancing effects of both drugs in the brain, but the adverse effects seem to occur more in men than in women (Carroll, Fenton, Ball, et al., 2004; Nich, McCance-Katz, Petrakis, 2004; Whitten, 2005).

These and other clinical observations of drugs that lessen addiction or relapse liability indicate that there is a lot more to be learned about the addicted brain.

Other Strategies

Some companies, such as Drug Abuse Sciences, Inc., are developing *time-release delivery systems* for naltrexone (Naltrel®), methadone (METHALiz®), and buprenorphine (Buprel®). The aim of this development is to improve treatment compliance by having medications injected into the body on a monthly basis.

Patented medical protocols to treat addiction is a recent development in chemical dependency treatment. An example of this is the Prometa® protocol for medical treatment of alcohol and stimulant drug dependence. **Prometa employs FDA-approved medications (though not approved to treat addiction) in a rigid short-term protocol to abate drug hunger and promote recovery.** Medications like flumazenil (Mazicon® and Ro-Mazicon®) are administered in a hospital over two or three days along with gabapentin (Neurontin®) and hydroxyzine (Vistaril®), which are continued over the next 30 days. Another example is the Healing Visions Clinic on the Caribbean Island of St. Kitts. This medical protocol uses ibogaine and other medications over three to seven days for treatment of opioid and other addictions. Ibogaine is banned in the United States.

Packaged clinical protocols to treat addiction are another new development. **These are copyrighted and sold to treatment providers to help facilitate clinical interventions and promote better outcomes. An example of this is the Matrix Model for cocaine, methamphetamine, and other stimulant drug addictions.** Individual treatment manuals, educational resources, and video presentations organized around a 90- to 120-day clinical process that encourages recovery are included in the copyrighted packet for use by addiction treatment providers.

Many other manuals and packaged protocols are marketed, and they provide valuable tools for addicts to help them address recovery issues like relapse prevention, PAWS, cognitive impairment, environmental cues, cravings, and family and other issues that can trigger slips and addiction relapse. PAWS (sleep, memory, thinking, anxiety, emotional, and reflex coordination problems) can last for several months to years of abstinence. An increased documentation of cognitive deficits during early recovery (impairments of learning, attention, perception, information processing, memory, temporal or time processing, cognitive inflexibility, problem solving, abstract thinking, and even physical coordination) also lasts for several months after initiation of abstinence from drug or alcohol abuse (Taleff, 2004). Treatment manuals and packaged clinical protocols can be very helpful during the cognitively impaired early recovery process.

THE NEW DRUG DEVELOPMENT PROCESS

The FDA has established a rigorous structured process for the approval of new drugs to treat specific therapeutic indications or the approval of existing drugs to be used for new therapeutic applications. This consists of three steps and four phases.

Step 1: Preclinical Research & Development

This step and phase consists of the initial chemical development of a drug along with animal studies to determine the general effects, toxicity, and projected abuse liability of the substance. If these results indicate that the drug is useful and marketable, the drug's sponsor will apply for an Investigational New Drug number that will permit human research on the substance to be conducted.

Step 2: Clinical Trials

Step 2 comprises three phases that study the efficacy and the safety of the drug in humans.

◇ **Phase I: Initial Clinical Stage.** A small number of human subjects are used to establish drug safety, dosage range for effective treatment, and the occurrence of side effects or adverse reactions.

◇ **Phase II: Clinical Pharmacological Evaluation Stage.**

Double-blind studies (neither the researcher nor the test subject knows if they have received the actual test drug or a placebo) are used to evaluate the effects of the drug, determine side effects, and gauge the effectiveness of its use in treating a specific medical condition.

◊ **Phase III: Extended Clinical Evaluation.** The new drug is made available to a large number of researchers and patients with the indicated medical condition to further evaluate its safety, effectiveness, recommended dosage, and side effects.

Step 3: Permission to Market

If the drug successfully completes Steps 1 and 2 to demonstrate acceptable efficacy and safety, the FDA can allow the drug to be marketed under its patented name. The process from Step 1 to Step 3 takes up to 12 years to complete. After the drug is marketed, the FDA continues to monitor it for adverse or toxic reactions because it can take years for some negative effects to manifest and be identified. This post-marketing scrutiny is often referred to as "Phase IV" because of the FDA's ability to remove the drug from the market at any time if negative effects outweigh the benefits of using the drug.

CHAPTER SUMMARY

Introduction

1. The most prevalent disease of the brain is addiction. Annually it causes more than a half million deaths and intense social disruption. The vast majority of deaths are from the legal drugs: tobacco and alcohol.

2. Current issues in treatment include:
   ◊ the rapidly expanding use of medications to treat detoxification, control craving, and assist relapse prevention; medications include drugs to lessen withdrawal symptoms, anticraving drugs, antidepressants, substitute medications (e.g., methadone), and nutritional supplements;
   ◊ the use of imaging and other new diagnostic techniques to visualize the physiological effects of drugs; CAT (computerized axial tomography), MRI (magnetic resonance imaging), PET (positron emission tomography), and SPECT (single photon emission computerized tomography) are four of the methods used;
   ◊ the increase of more-effective tools to diagnose addiction and better match clients to levels of treatment;
   ◊ the growing emphasis on evidence-based treatment interventions;
   ◊ the lack of resources to provide treatment (studies have shown that treatment is effective, but governments do not allot enough money to provide sufficient treatment);
   ◊ the use of coerced treatment, such as drug courts, to mandate care for abusers and addicts and thus reduce re-arrest rates and cut costs; and
   ◊ the conflict between abstinence-oriented recovery and harm reduction as philosophies of treatment; most treatment modalities say abstinence is absolutely necessary to recovery, whereas harm reduction advocates say that incremental changes are acceptable.

Treatment Effectiveness

3. Treatment is effective. It has a 50% success rate according to the DATOS and CALDATA studies.

4. Each $1 spent on treatment saves at least $4 to $39 in costs related to unchecked addiction.

5. Prison costs $25,000 to $40,000 per inmate per year compared with $1,800 to $4,000 for outpatient treatment or methadone maintenance.

6. Almost two-thirds of arrestees test positive for psychoactive drugs, particularly cocaine and marijuana.

7. There is a shortage of treatment slots for inmates in jails and prisons.

Principles & Goals of Treatment

8. The National Institutes of Health listed 13 principles of effective treatment (e.g., no single treatment is appropriate for all individuals, treatment needs to be readily available, and effective treatment attends to multiple needs of the individual). Similar principles have been established for treatment of individuals involved with the criminal justice system (CJS), starting with the principle that addiction is a "brain disease that affects behavior."

9. The two primary treatment goals are motivation toward abstinence and creating a drug-free lifestyle. The secondary goals have to do with creating a better lifestyle by improving job, medical, psychiatric, emotional, and spiritual functioning.

Selection of a Program

10. No single type of treatment is effective for everyone; it must be tailored to the individual.

11. Diagnosis of the type and the level of addiction is ascertained through interviews and a wide variety of diagnostic tests, particularly the Addiction Severity Index (ASI). The ASAM PPC-2R assesses six dimensions of drug involvement and matches these to one of four appropriate levels of treatment.

12. Treatment options include medical model detoxification, social model

detoxification, social model recovery, therapeutic communities, halfway houses, sober-living or transitional-living programs, partial hospitalization, and harm reduction programs.

13. About 1.9 million clients are treated each year for drug abuse. About 1,081,000 are in treatment on any given day.

14. About 5.5 million more hardcore and heavy substance abusers need treatment.

15. More than 70% of those in treatment are male.

Beginning Treatment

16. Recovery is a lifelong process because brain chemistry is permanently altered by drug abuse.

17. Recognition and acceptance of addiction by the client is crucial to recovery.

18. Breaking through denial is the critical first step to beginning treatment.

19. Denial can be overcome when the addict hits bottom or through a direct intervention (e.g., legal system, family, workplace supervisor, or physician). It is important to recognize that the earlier an addict starts treatment, the better the positive outcomes. An addict does not have to hit bottom to engage in treatment.

20. The two major sources of referral are self-referral and legal referrals by the criminal justice system.

21. The elements of a formal intervention are love, a facilitator, intervention statements, anticipated defenses and outcomes, the intervention itself, and contingency plans.

Treatment Continuum

22. Treatment starts with detoxification and escalates through initial abstinence, long-term abstinence, and recovery.

23. It takes about a week for drugs to clear from the body and four weeks to 10 months for brain and body chemistry to settle down.

24. Drugs can be cleared and kept from the system through abstinence, medication therapy, and psychosocial therapy.

25. Recovery medications include clonidine, buprenorphine, naltrexone, phenobarbital, methadone, antipsychotics, antidepressants, varenicline, bupropion, and others.

26. Intensive counseling and group therapy are necessary to aid detoxification.

27. Initial abstinence is supported through anticraving medications (e.g., naltrexone, bromocryptine, and nicotine replacements), individual counseling, and group therapy.

28. Environmental triggers cause relapse. Cue extinction (desensitization) is one way to avoid relapse. Another is learning automatic responses to cravings.

29. Relapse prevention is the key to initial abstinence. Post-acute withdrawal symptoms (PAWS) may persist for several months or years.

30. Psychosocial support to help clients put their lives back in order is crucial: job support, physical and mental health problems support, and housing searches.

31. Acupuncture can help calm withdrawal symptoms and reduce craving to some extent.

32. Addicts must accept that treatment for addiction is a lifelong process and that chemical dependency extends to a variety of substances, not just the drug of choice.

33. Long-term abstinence uses individual and group therapy and 12-step programs to prolong abstinence.

34. Recovery entails restructuring one's life, not just staying abstinent.

35. Human beings can experience naturally all of the highs they seek through drugs.

36. Follow-up is important not just to satisfy government funding agencies but to know which programs work.

37. Follow-up helps tailor programs to match the client and identify clients who need to be treated again for a relapse.

INDIVIDUAL VS. GROUP THERAPY

38. Individual therapy conducted by a trained counselor helps the recovering addict address specific personal issues and identify needs.

39. Some individual therapies include cognitive-behavioral therapy, reality therapy, psychodynamic therapy, motivational interviewing, and aversion therapy.

40. Motivational interviewing and motivational enhancement therapy are nonconfrontational therapies to resolve a client's ambivalence about wanting recovery; they use the stages-of-change model to alter the client's behavior.

41. Group therapy can be used to break the isolation of chemical dependency. The types of groups include facilitated, peer, 12-step, educational, topic-specific, and targeted.

42. Various 12-step programs, such as Alcoholics Anonymous (AA), Narcotics Anonymous (NA), and Overeaters Anonymous (OA), use sponsors, spirituality, and the power of people telling their own stories to teach a clean-and-sober lifestyle. Including spirituality in the treatment process can improve positive outcomes.

43. There are a number of errors that novice counselors make in groups (e.g., unrealistic view of group treatment, self-disclosure confusion, and failure to plan in advance).

Treatment & the Family

44. Addiction affects the addict's family as well, so good treatment should involve the whole family.

45. There are a number of family treatment approaches, including the family systems approach, the family behavioral approach, and tough love.

46. Codependency and enabling, whereby family members support the addict in his or her addiction, must be addressed in treatment.

47. In families with adult addicts, the children take on certain roles:

model child, problem child, lost child, and family clown.

48. Adults who were raised in addictive households carry many of their problems into adulthood and must face those problems in treatment.

49. Groups such as Al-Anon, Nar-Anon, and ACoA help support and educate the families and friends of alcoholics and addicts.

Adjunctive & Complementary Treatment Services

50. Besides abstinence, treatment must include services to handle physical, emotional, family, social, and spiritual deficits.

Drug-Specific Treatment

51. Most people coming in for treatment are polydrug abusers (including behavioral addictions), even though they have a drug of choice.

52. Stimulant abuse often initially presents treatment professionals with drug-induced symptoms of psychosis and paranoia.

53. Cognitive-behavioral therapies (CBT) and anticraving medications help overcome anergia, euthymia, and craving during stimulant abstinence.

54. Endogenous (internal) stimulant craving is caused by neurochemical imbalances and bad thinking. Exogenous craving is caused by environmental cues.

55. More and more drug treatment centers include smoking cessation as part of recovery. CBT with anticraving medications like varenicline or bupropion have been shown to be effective for nicotine addiction.

56. Because smoking addiction involves nicotine craving, nicotine replacement therapies (e.g., nicotine patches) help taper tobacco craving.

57. Heroin and other opioid treatments usually need medications to alleviate withdrawal during detoxification.

58. Methadone maintenance is a harm reduction therapy that substitutes a controlled opioid for an illicit, problem-causing street opioid. Buprenorphine is also used for detoxification and abstinence maintenance and can be prescribed by certified doctors from their offices. Naltrexone blocks relapses and craving in opioid addiction.

59. Sedative-hypnotic withdrawal can be life-threatening unless assisted with medical therapy that includes an antiseizure medication like phenobarbital. Withdrawal symptoms can last for weeks or even months.

60. Denial is the biggest hindrance to beginning treatment particularly for alcohol abusers. Physical withdrawal can be but is usually not life-threatening.

61. Peer groups and 12-step programs are vital to both long-term abstinence and recovery from alcoholism or any other addiction.

62. Talk-downs with emotional support and time for the drug to leave the body are the usual treatments for bad trips due to LSD and other psychedelics. Antipsychotic or antianxiety medications are also used when needed.

63. There has been a steady increase in people going into treatment for marijuana. The majority of referrals are court ordered.

64. The majority of inhalant abusers are under 20 years old compared with older abusers of other drugs.

65. The treatment for behavioral addictions is similar to that for drug addiction.

66. Sufficient facilities and personnel for treating compulsive gamblers are sorely lacking.

67. Early intervention for eating disorders is very important in treating anorexia, bulimia, and compulsive overeating.

68. Sexual addiction is most often treated by getting at the psychodynamic roots of the compulsion.

69. Internet addiction includes cybersexual addiction, cyberrelationship addiction, information overload, and computer addiction (playing games).

Target Populations

70. Treatment must be tailored to specific groups based on gender, sexual orientation, age, ethnic group, job, and even economic status.

71. Treatment for men should be different than for women. Men often blame external forces, whereas women often blame themselves for their addiction.

72. Youth are less willing to accept guidance, so youth-directed programs that use peer support seem to work best. Youth are more vulnerable to the toxic effects of drugs and suffer cognitive deficits because the frontal cortices are still developing into young adulthood.

73. Older Americans are a fast-growing segment of those with a substance-abuse problem and are often reluctant to seek treatment because they view addiction as a character flaw rather than a disease. Elders suffer cognitive deficits that need assessment and consideration during the treatment process.

74. Treatment for different ethnic groups works better with culture-specific treatment protocols.

75. African-American, Hispanic, Asian-American/Pacific Islander, and American Indian treatment often requires strong family involvement and accessing the spiritual roots of each community.

76. Little research has been done on treatment for those with physical disabilities. Too much focus is on the handicap and not enough on the addiction.

77. There is also a lack of research for the lesbian, gay, bisexual, and transgender (LGBT) communities. The use of alcohol and drugs lowers inhibitions and abets the spread of disease, including HIV. Homophobia and heterophobia complicate substance-abuse treatment.

Treatment Obstacles

78. Being aware of the emotional maturity of clients, doing follow-ups to make sure that clients are

complying with the program, resolving conflicting goals, and making sure there are enough treatment slots to meet demand are vital to the effectiveness of treatment programs. Assessing and addressing cognitive deficits caused by drug toxicity, immature brain structures, and old age have become a major focus of treatment.

MEDICAL INTERVENTION DEVELOPMENTS

79. The fastest-growing field in treatment is the development of new medications. Disulfiram, naltrexone (oral and injection), and acamprosate are approved to treat alcoholism. Various nicotine replacement therapies (gum, patch, spray, inhaler, and lozenges), bupropion, and varenicline are approved to treat tobacco addiction. Methadone, naltrexone, and buprenorphine are approved to treat heroin and opioid dependence. Drugs are being developed for: detoxification, replacement therapy (agonist effects), antagonist effects, vaccines, mixed agonist-antagonist effects, anticraving, metabolism modulation, restoration of homeostasis, and modulation of drug effects and antipriming.

80. There are three steps in the new drug development process, including preclinical research and development, clinical trials, and permission to market.

REFERENCES

ACoA. (2007). *Adult Children of Alcoholics World Service Organization.* http://www.adultchildren.org (accessed May 2, 2007).

Addiction Research Foundation. (2007). *Clinical Institute Withdrawal Assessment for Alcohol.* http://www.medres.utoronto.ca/Assets/Education/Clinical+Tools/CIWA.pdf (accessed May 2, 2007).

Adlaf, E. M., Paglia, A., Ivis, F. J. & Ialomiteanu, A. (2000). Nonmedical drug use among adolescent students: Highlights from the 1999 Ontario Student Drug Use Survey. *Canadian Medical Association Journal, 162*(12): 1677-80.

Alcoholics Anonymous [AA]. (1934, 1976). *Alcoholics Anonymous.* New York: Alcoholics Anonymous World Services, Inc.

Allen, J. P., Eckardt, M. J. & Wallen, J. (1988). Screening for alcoholism: Techniques and issues. *Public Health Reports, 103*(6), 586-92.

American Psychiatric Association [APA]. (2000). *Diagnostic and Statistical Manual of Mental Disorders* (4th ed., text revisions [DSM-IV-TR]). Washington, DC: Author.

American Psychiatric Association. (2006). Treatment of patients with eating disorders (3rd ed.). *American Journal of Psychiatry, 163*(suppl. 7), 4-54.

Anglin, M. D., Prendergast, M. & Farabee, D. (1998). *The Effectiveness of Coerced Treatment for Drug-Abusing Offenders,* ONDCP Conference of Scholars and Policy Makers. http://www.ncjrs.org/ondcppubs/treat/consensus/anglin.pdf (accessed May 2, 2007).

Anglin, M. D. & Rawson, R. A. (2000). The CSAT methamphetamine treatment project: What are we trying to accomplish? *Journal of Psychoactive Drugs, 32*(2), 209-10.

Anton, R. F., O'Malley, S. S., Ciraulo, D. A., Cisler, R. A., Couper, D., Donovan, D. M., et al. (2006). Combined pharmacotherapies and behavioral interventions for alcohol dependence. *JAMA, 295*(17), 2003-17.

Arrestee Drug Abuse Monitoring Program. (2006). *Drug and Alcohol Use and Related Matters Among Arrestees: 2003.* http://www.ncjrs.gov/nij/adam/ADAM2003.pdf (accessed May 2, 2007).

Ball, J. C. & Ross, A., eds. (1991). *The Effectiveness of Methadone Maintenance Treatment.* New York: Springer-Verlag.

Barclay, L. (2002). New treatment achieves 75% remission in eating disorders. *Proceedings of the National Academy of Sciences, 99*(14), 9486-91.

Barnett P. G. (1999). The cost-effectiveness of methadone maintenance as a health care intervention. *Addiction 94*(4), 479-88.

Bartter, T. & Gooberman L. L. (1996). Rapid opiate detoxification. *American Journal of Drug and Alcohol Abuse, 22*(4), 489-95.

Belenko, S. (2001). *Research on Drug Courts: A Critical Review.* New York: National Center on Addiction and Substance Abuse.

Belenko, S., Patapis, N. & French M. T. (2005). *Economic Benefits of Drug Treatment: A Critical Review of the Evidence for Policy Makers.* Missouri Foundation for Health. http://www.tresearch.org/resources/specials/2005Feb_EconomicBenefits.pdf (accessed May 2, 2007).

Bensen, L. (1879). *Fifteen Years in Hell: An Autobiography.* Indianapolis, IN: Douglas & Carlon.

Bergh, C., Brodin, U., Lindberg, G. & Sodersten, P. (2002). Randomized controlled trial of a treatment for anorexia and bulimia nervosa. *Proceedings of the National Academy of Sciences, 99*(14), 9486-91.

Bickel, W. K., Kowal, B. P. & Gatchalian, K. M. (2006). Understanding addiction as a pathology of temporal horizon. *Behavior Analyst Today, 7*(1), 32-46.

Bickelhaupt, E. E. (1995). Alcoholism and drug abuse in gay and lesbian persons: A review of incidence studies. In R. J. Kus, ed. *Addiction and Recovery in Gay and Lesbian Persons.* New York: Harrington Park Press.

Birch, S. (2001). An overview of acupuncture in the treatment of stroke, addiction, and other health problems. In G. Stux & R. Hammerschlag, eds. *Clinical Acupuncture: Scientific Basis.* New York: Springer.

Blanc, M. & Daeppen, J. B. (2005). Does disulfiram still have a role in alcoholism treatment? *Review of Swiss Medicine 29*(1), 1732-33.

Blum, K., et al. (1989). Cocaine therapy: The reward-cascade link. *Professional Counselor, 27.*

Blume, S. B. & Tavares, H. (2005). Pathological gambling. In J. H. Lowinson, P. Ruiz, R. B. Millman & J. G. Langrod, eds. *Substance Abuse: A Comprehensive Textbook* (4th ed., pp. 374-86). Baltimore: Williams & Wilkins.

Boothby, L. A. & Doering, P. L. (2005). Acamprosate for the treatment of alcohol dependence. *Clinical Therapeutics* 27(6), 695-714.

Bottlender, M., Spanagel, R. & Soyka, M. (2007). One drink, one drunk-controlled drinking by alcoholics? 3-year outcome after intensive outpatient treatment. *Psychotherapie, Psychosomatik, Mezidiniche Psychologie, 57*(1), 32-38.

Boucher, T. A., Kiresuk, T. J. & Trachtenberg, A. I. (2003). Alternative therapies. In A. W. Graham, T. K. Schultz, M. F. Mayo-Smith, R. K. Ries & B. B. Wilford, eds. *Principles of Addiction Medicine* (3rd ed., pp. 509-32). Chevy Chase, MD: American Society of Addiction Medicine, Inc.

Brubaker, M. (1997). *Compulsive Gambling and Recovery.* New Orleans, LA: Brubaker Consulting.

Brubaker, M. D. (2006). Wrestling with angels: Faith-based programs can assist recovery, but create barriers for some. *Addiction Professional, 4*(3), 12-16.

Byrne, A. (1998). Rapid intravenous detoxification in heroin addiction. *British Journal of Psychiatry, 172,* 451.

Cabaj, R. P. (2005). Gays, lesbians, and bisexuals. In J. H. Lowinson, P. Ruiz, R. B. Millman & J. G. Langrod, eds. *Substance Abuse: A Comprehensive Textbook* (4th ed., pp. 1129-40). Baltimore: Williams & Wilkins.

Califano, J. A. (2001). *High Stakes: Substance Abuse and Gambling.* National Center on Addiction and Substance Abuse. http://www.casacolumbia.org/absolutenm/templates/ChairmanStatements.aspx?articleid=244&zoneid=31 (accessed May 2, 2007).

Cambell, I. (2003). Nicotine replacement therapy in smoking cessation (editorial). *Thorax, 58*(6), 464-65.

Carlson M. J. & Cummings D. E. (2006). Prospects for an anti-ghrelin vaccine to treat obesity. *Molecular Interventions, 6*(5), 249-52.

Carrera, M. R., Ashley, J. A., Parsons, L. H., Wirsching, P., Koob, G. F. & Janda, K. D. (1995). Suppression of psychoactive effects of cocaine by active immunization. *Nature, 378*(6558), 727-30.

Carrol, J. F. (1980). Uncovering drug abuse by alcoholics and alcohol abuse by addicts. *International Journal of the Addictions, 15*(4), 591-95.

Carroll, K. M., Fenton, L. R., Ball, S. A., Nich, C., Frankforter, T. L., Shi, J., et al. (2004). Efficacy of disulfiram and cognitive behavioral therapy in cocaine-dependent outpatients: A randomized placebo-controlled trial. *Archives of General Psychiatry, 61*(3): 264-72.

Carter, T. M. (1998). The effects of spiritual practices on recovery from substance abuse. *Journal of Psychiatric and Mental Health Nursing, 5*(5), 409-13.

Carter, B. L. & Tiffany, S. T. (1999). Meta-analysis of cue-reactivity in addiction research. *Addiction, 94*(3), 327-40.

Centers for Disease Control [CDC]. (2000). *Treating Tobacco Use and Dependence.* U.S. Public Health Service. http://www.surgeongeneral.gov/tobacco/smokesum.htm (accessed May 2, 2007).

Centers for Disease Control. (2001). *Cigarette Smoking-Related Mortality. Tobacco Information and Prevention Source.* http://www.cdc.gov/tobacco/research_data/health_consequences/mortali.htm (accessed May 2, 2007).

Centers for Disease Control. (2002). *MMWR—Annual Smoking-Attributable Mortality, Years of Potential Life Lost, and Economic Costs—United States, 1995–1999.* http://www.cdc.gov/mmwr/preview/mmwrhtml/mm5114a2.htm (accessed May 2, 2007).

Cha, A. E. (February 23, 2007). China prescribes tough love for Internet addicts. *Medford Mail Tribune,* p. 10A.

Chang, G. & Kosten, T. R. (2005). Detoxification. In J. H. Lowinson, P. Ruiz, R. B. Millman & J. G. Langrod, eds. *Substance Abuse: A Comprehensive Textbook* (4th ed., pp. 579-86). Baltimore: Williams & Wilkins.

Cherrington, E. (1920). *The Evolution of Prohibition in the United States.* Westerville, OH: The American Issue Press.

Childress, A. R., McClellan, A. T., Ehrman, R. & O'Brien, C. P. (1988). Classically conditioned responses in opioid and cocaine dependence: A role in relapse? In B. A. Ray, ed. *Learning Factors in Substance Abuse,* NIDA Research Monograph 84. Rockville, MD: National Institute on Drug Abuse.

Childress, A. R., Mozley, P. D., McElgin, W., Fitzgerald, J., Reivich, M. & O'Brien, C. P. (1999). Limbic activation during cue-induced cocaine craving. *American Journal of Psychiatry, 156*(1), 11-18.

Clay, R. A. (2006). Incarceration vs. Treatment, *SAMSA News, 14*(2). http://www.samhsa.gov/SAMHSA_NEWS/VolumeXIV_2/MarchApril2006.pdf (accessed May 4, 2007).

Copeland, A. L. & Sorensen, J. L. (2001). Differences between methamphetamine users and cocaine users in treatment. *Drug and Alcohol Dependence, 62*(1), 91-95.

Crowe, A. H. & Reeves, R. (1994). *Treatment for Alcohol and Other Drug Abuse: Opportunities for Coordination.* Technical Assistance Publication Series #11. Rockville, MD: Substance Abuse and Mental Health Services Administration.

Cucchia, A. T., Monnat, M., Spagnoli, J., Ferrero, F. & Bertschy, G. (1998). Ultra-rapid opiate detoxification using deep sedation with oral midazolam: Short and long-term results. *Drug and Alcohol Dependency, 52*(3), 243-50.

Cummings, D. E., Weigle, D. S., Frayo, R. S., Breen, P. A., Ma, M. K., Dellinger, E. P., et al. (2002). Plasma ghrelin levels after diet-induced weight loss or gastric bypass surgery. *New England Journal of Medicine, 346*(21), 1623-30.

D'Augelli, A. R. (1996). Lesbian, gay, and bisexual development during adolescence and young adulthood. In R. P. Cabaj & T. S. Stein, eds. *Textbook of Homosexuality and Mental Health* (pp. 267-88). Washington, DC: American Psychiatric Press.

Daley, D. C. & Marlatt, G. A. (2005). Relapse prevention. In J. H. Lowinson, P. Ruiz, R. B. Millman & J. G. Langrod, eds. *Substance Abuse: A Comprehensive Textbook* (4th ed., pp. 772-85). Baltimore: Williams & Wilkins.

Dascus, J. (1877). *Battling with the Demon: The Progress of Temperance.* Saint Louis, MO: Scammell & Company.

DASIS. (2006). *Facilities Operating Opioid Treatment Programs: 2005.* http://oas.samhsa.gov/2k6/OTP/OTP.pdf (accessed May 2, 2007).

Davis, R. A. (2001). Freedom from e-slavery: Tips on Getting Your Life Back. http://www.internetaddiction.ca (accessed May 2, 2007).

De La Cruz, D. (January 4, 2007). FTC fines weight-pill marketers. *Medford Mail Tribune,* p. A1.

Dickerson, T. J. & Janda, K. D. (2005). Recent advances for the treatment of cocaine abuse: Central nervous system immunopharmacotherapy. *AAPS Journal, 7*(3), E579-E586.

Dickinson, W. E., Mayo-Smith, R. K. & Eickelberg, S. J. (2003). Management of sedative-hypnotic intoxication and withdrawal. In A. W. Graham, T. K. Schultz, M. F. Mayo-Smith, R. K. Ries & B. B. Wilford, eds. *Principles of Addiction Medicine* (3rd ed., pp. 1497-503). Chevy Chase, MD: American Society of Addiction Medicine, Inc.

Dodd, M. H. (1997). Social model of recovery: Origin, early features, changes, and future. *Journal of Psychoactive Drugs, 29*(2), 133-39.

Dole, V. P. & Nyswander, M. E. (1965). A medical treatment for diacetylmorphine (heroin) addiction: A clinical trial with methadone hydrochloride. *JAMA, 193*(8), 646-50.

Dorchester, D. (1884). *The Liquor Problem in All Ages.* New York: Phillips & Hunt.

Drucker, E., Nadelmann, E., Newman, R. G., Wodak, A., McNeely, J. & Malinowska-Semprucht, K. (2005). Harm reduction: Pragmatic drug policies for public health and safety. In J. H. Lowinson, P. Ruiz, R. B. Millman & J. G. Langrod, eds. *Substance Abuse: A Comprehensive Textbook* (4th ed., pp. 1229-50). Baltimore: Williams & Wilkins.

Dyer, C. (1998). Addict died after rapid opiate detoxification. *British Medical Journal, 316*(7126), 170.

Etheridge, R. M., Craddock, S. G., Dunteman, G. H. & Hubbard, R. L. (1995). Treatment services in two national studies of community-based drug abuse treatment programs. *Journal of Substance Abuse, 7*(1), 9-26.

Fiorentine, R. (1999). After drug treatment: Are 12-step programs effective in maintaining abstinence? *American Journal of Drug and Alcohol Abuse, 25*(1), 93-116.

Foulks, E. F. (2005). Alcohol use among American Indians and Alaskan Natives. In J. H. Lowinson, P. Ruiz, R. B. Millman & J. G. Langrod, eds. *Substance Abuse: A Comprehensive Textbook* (4th ed., pp. 1119-27). Baltimore: Williams & Wilkins.

Fox, B. S., Kantak, K. M., Edwards, M. A., Black, K. M., Bollinger, B. K., Botka, A. J., et al. (1996). Efficacy of a therapeutic cocaine vaccine in rodent models. *Nature Medicine, 2*(10), 1129-32.

Freese, T. E., Obert, J., Dickow, A., Cohen, J. & Lord, R. H. (2000). Methamphetamine abuse: Issues for special populations. *Journal of Psychoactive Drugs, 32*(2), 177-82.

Fuller, R. K., Branchey, L., Brightwell, D. R., Derman, R. M., Emrick, C. D., Iber, F. L., et al. (1986). Disulfiram treatment of alcoholism. A Veterans Administration cooperative study. *JAMA, 256*(11), 1449-55.

Galanter, M., Keller, D. S., Dermatis, H. & Egelko, S. (2000). The impact of managed care on substance abuse treatment: A report of the American Society of Addiction Medicine. *Journal of Addictive Diseases, 19*(3), 13-34.

Gatch, M. B. & Lal, H. (1998). Pharmacological treatment of alcoholism. *Progress in Neuro-Psychopharmacology and Biological Psychiatry, 22*(6), 917-44.

Gawin, F. H., Khalsa, M. E. & Ellinwood, E., Jr. (1994). Stimulants. In M.

Galanter & H. D. Kleber, eds. *Textbook of Substance Abuse Treatment* (pp. 111-39). Washington, DC: American Psychiatric Press.

Gerstein, D. R., Datta, A. R., Ingels, J. S., Johnson, R. A., Rasinski, K. A., Schildhaus, S., et al. (1997). *National Treatment Improvement Evaluation Study (NTIES) Final Report.* Rockville, MD: Center for Substance Abuse Treatment.

Gerstein, D. R., Johnson, R. A., Harwood, H., Fountain, D., Suter, N. & Malloy, K. (1994). *Evaluating Recovery Services: The California Drug and Alcohol Treatment Assessment (CALDATA).* Sacramento, CA: California Department of Alcohol and Drug Programs (Executive Summary: Publication No. ADP94-628).

Ghaziani, A. & Cook, T. D. (2005). Reducing HIV infections at circuit parties. *IAPAC Monthly, 11*(4), 100-108.

Giedd, J. N., Blumenthal, J., Jeffries, N. O., Castellanos, F. X., Liu, H., Zijdenbos, A., et al. (1999). Brain development during childhood and adolescence: A longitudinal MRI study. *Nature Neuroscience, 2*(10): 861-63.

Goldbloom, D. S. (1997). Pharmacotherapy of bulimia nervosa. *Medscape Women's Health, 2*(1), 4.

Goodman, A. (2005). Sexual addiction. In J. H. Lowinson, P. Ruiz, R. B. Millman & J. G. Langrod, eds. *Substance Abuse: A Comprehensive Textbook* (4th ed., pp. 504-39). Baltimore: Williams & Wilkins.

Gorski, T. T. (1993). *Addictive Relationships: Why Love Goes Wrong in Recovery.* Independence, MO: Herald House Independence Press.

Gorski, T. & Miller, M. (1986). *Staying Sober: A Guide for Relapse Prevention.* Independence, MO: Herald House Independence Press.

Grant, J. E., Potenza, M. N., Hollander, E., Cunningham-Williams, R., Nurminen, T., Smits, G., et al. (2006). Multicenter investigation of the opioid antagonist nalmefene in the treatment of pathological gambling. *American Journal of Psychiatry, 163*(2), 303-12.

Grinrod, R. (1840, 1886). *Bacchus: An Essay on the Nature, Causes, Effects and Cure of Intemperance.* Columbus, OH: J & H Miller.

Grossman, D & Onken, L., organizers. (2003). *Summary of NIDA Workshop: Developing Behavioral Treatments for Drug Abusers with Cognitive Impairments.* htpp://www.drugabuse. gov/whatsnew/meetings/cognitiveimpairment.html (accessed May 2, 2007).

Gulliver, S. B., Kamholz, B. W. & Helstrom, A. W. (2006). Smoking cessation and alcohol abstinence: What does the data tell us? *Alcohol Research & Health, 29*(3), 208-12.

Han, J., Trachtenberg, A. I. & Lowinson, J. H. (2005). Acupuncture. In J. H. Lowinson, P. Ruiz, R. B. Millman & J. G. Langrod, eds. *Substance Abuse: A Comprehensive Textbook* (4th ed., pp. 743-62). Baltimore: Williams & Wilkins.

Harden, B. & Swardson, A. (March 4, 1996). Addiction: Are states preying on the vulnerable? *Washington Post,* p. A1.

Harvard. (January 2007). Addiction and the problem of relapse. *Harvard Mental Health Letter.*

Hawkins, H. (2003). Adolescent risk and protective factors. In A. W. Graham, T. K. Schultz, M. F. Mayo-Smith, R. K. Ries & B. B. Wilford, eds. *Principles of Addiction Medicine* (3rd ed., pp. 1497-503). Chevy Chase, MD: American Society of Addiction Medicine, Inc.

Hayner, G., Galloway, G. & Wiehl, W. O. (1993). Haight Ashbury Free Clinics' drug detoxification protocols—Part 3: Benzodiazepines and other sedative-hypnotics. *Journal of Psychoactive Drugs, 25*(4), 331-35.

Heading, C. E. (2007). Drug evaluation CYT-002-NicQb, a therapeutic vaccine for the treatment of nicotine addiction. *Current Opinion in Investigational Drugs, 8*(1), 71-77.

Heather, N. (1989). Brief intervention strategies. In R. K. Hester & W. R. Miller, eds. *Handbook of Alcoholism Treatment Approaches* (pp. 93-116). Boston: Allyn and Bacon.

Heinemann, A. W. (1993). An introduction to substance abuse and physical disability. In A. W. Heineman, ed. *Substance Abuse & Physical Disability* (pp. 3-9). Binghamton, NY: The Haworth Press, Inc.

Heinemann, A. W. & Rawal, P. H. (2005). Disability and rehabilitation issues. In J. H. Lowinson, P. Ruiz, R. B. Millman & J. G. Langrod, eds. *Substance Abuse: A Comprehensive Textbook* (4th ed., pp. 1169-86). Baltimore: Williams & Wilkins.

Helm, P., Munster, K. & Schmidt, L. (1995). Recalled menarche in relation to infertility and adult weight and height. *Acta Obstetricia et Gynecolegica Scandinavica, 74*(9), 718-22.

Hillbom, M. E. & Hjelm-Jager, M. (1984). Should alcohol withdrawal seizures be treated with anti-epileptic drugs? *Acta Neurologica Scandinavica, 69*(1), 39-42.

Horvath, A. T. (2005). Alternative support groups. In J. H. Lowinson, P. Ruiz, R. B. Millman & J. G. Langrod, eds. *Substance Abuse: A Comprehensive Textbook* (4th ed., pp. 599-608). Baltimore: Williams & Wilkins.

Hser, J. L., Evans, E. & Huang, Y. C. (2005). Treatment outcomes among women and men methamphetamine abusers in California. *Journal of Substance Abuse Treatment, 28*(1), 77-85.

Hubbard, R. L., Craddock, S. G. & Anderson, J. (2003). Overview of 5-year follow-up outcomes in the drug abuse treatment outcome studies (DATOS). *Journal of Substance Abuse Treatment 25*(3), 125-34.

Hughes, T. L. & Wilsnack, S. C. (1997). Use of alcohol among lesbians. *American Journal of Orthopsychiatry, 67*(1), 20-36.

Hunt, G., Evens, K., Wu, E. & Reyes, A. (2005). Asian American youth, the dance scene and club drugs. *Journal of Drug Issues, 35*(4), 695-731.

Hurt, R. D., Ebbert, J. O., Gays, J. T. & Dale, L. C. (2003). Pharmacologic interventions for tobacco dependence. In A. W. Graham, T. K. Schultz, M. F. Mayo-Smith, R. K. Ries & B. B. Wilford, eds. *Principles of Addiction Medicine* (3rd ed., pp. 801-814). Chevy Chase, MD: American Society of Addiction Medicine, Inc.

Hyman, S. E., Malenka, R. C. & Nestler, E. J. (2006). Neural mechanisms of addiction: The role of reward-related learning and memory. *Annual Review of Neuroscience, 29,* 565-98.

Ibancz, A., Blanco, C., Donahue, E., Lesiur, H. R., Perez de Castro, I., Fernandez-Piqueras, J., et al. (2001). Psychiatric comorbidity in pathological gamblers seeking treatment. *American Journal of Psychiatry, 158*(10), 1733-35.

Institute of Alcohol Studies. (2007). *Alcohol and the Elderly.* http://www.ias.org.uk/resources/factsheets/elderly.pdf (accessed May 2, 2007).

Institute of Medicine. (1990). *Treating Drug Problems (Vol. 1).* Washington, DC: The National Academies Press. http://books.nap.edu/books/0309042852/html/index.html (accessed May 2, 2007).

Iowa Practice Improvement Collaborative. (2003). *Evidence-Based Practices: An Implementation Guide for Community-Based Substance Abuse Treatment Agencies.* Iowa City, IA: Iowa Practice Improvement Collaborative.

Jacobi, C., Dahme, B. & Rustenbach, S. (1997). Comparison of controlled psy-cho- and pharmacotherapy studies in bulimia and anorexia nervosa. *Psychotherapie, Psychosomatic, Medizinische, Psychologie, 47*(9-10), 346-64.

Jacobson, J. O., Robinson, P. L. & Bluthenthal, R. N. (2007). Racial disparities in completion rates from publicly funded alcohol treatment: Economic resources explain more than demographics and addiction severity. *Health Services Research, 42*(2), 773-94.

Johnson, V. E. (1986). *Intervention.* Minneapolis, MN: Johnson Institute Books.

Jorenby, D. E., Hays, J. T., Rigotti, N. A., Azoulay, S., Watsky, E. J., Williams, K. E., et al. (2006). Efficacy of varenicline, an alpha4beta2 nicotinic acetylcholine receptor partial agonist, vs. placebo or sustained-release bupropion for smoking cessation. *JAMA, 296*(1), 56-63.

Karberg, J. C. & James, D. J. (2005). *Substance Dependence, Abuse and Treatment of Jail Inmates 2002.* U.S. Department of Justice, Office of Justice Programs, Washington, DC, 2005.

Kelly, J., ed. (1991). *San Francisco Lesbian, Gay and Bisexual Alcohol and Other Drugs Needs Assessment Study: Vol. I.* Sacramento, CA: EMT Associates, Inc.

Kendler, K. S., Jacobson, K. C., Prescott, C. A. & Neale, M. C. (2003). Specificity of genetic and environmental risk factors for use and abuse/dependence of cannabis, cocaine, hallucinogens, sedatives, stimulants, and opiates in male twins. *American Journal of Psychiatry 160*(4), 687-95.

Kessler, R. C., McGonagle, K. A., Zhao, S., Nelson, C. B., Hughes, M., Eshleman, S., et al. (1994). Lifetime and 12-month prevalence of DSM-III-R psychiatric disorders in the United States. Results from the National Comorbidity Survey. *Archives of General Psychiatry, 51*(1), 8-19.

Kettler, B. (February 5, 2003). Methadone cuts will spur crime. *Medford Mail Tribune,* p. 1A.

Kleber, H. D. (2000). Practice guideline for the treatment of patients with eating disorders (revision). *American Journal of Psychiatry, 157*(suppl. 1), 1-39.

Kleber, H. D. (2006). *Practice Guidelines for the Treatment of Patients with Substance Use Disorders* (2nd ed.). Arlington, VA: American Psychiatric Association.

Koenig, H. G., George, L. K. & Peterson, B. L. (1998). Religiosity and remission of depression in medically ill older patients. *American Journal of Psychiatry, 155*(4), 536-42.

Koenig, H. K., McCullough, M. E. & Larson, D. B. (2001). *Handbook of Religion and Health.* Oxford: Oxford University Press.

Kominars, S. B. (1995). Homophobia: The heart of the darkness. In R. J. Kus, ed. *Addiction and Recovery in Gay and Lesbian Persons.* New York: Harrington Park Press.

Korper, S. P. & Raskin, I. E. (2003). *The Impact of Substance Use and Abuse by the Elderly: The Next 20 to 30 Years.* SAMHSA. http://www.oas.samhsa.gov/aging/chap1.htm (accessed May 2, 2007).

Langrod, J. G., Muffler, J., Abel, J., Richardson, J. T., Curet, E., Joseph, H., et al. (2005). Faith-based approaches. In J. H. Lowinson, P. Ruiz, R. B. Millman & J. G. Langrod, eds. *Substance Abuse: A Comprehensive Textbook* (4th ed., pp. 763-71). Baltimore: Williams & Wilkins.

Larsen, E. (1985). *Stage II Recovery: Life Beyond Addiction.* New York: Harper Collins Publisher.

Lee, S. J. (2006). *Overcoming Crystal Meth Addiction.* New York: Marlowe & Company.

Lerner, A. G., Gelkopf, M., Skladman, I., Rudinski, D., Nachshon, H. & Bleich, A. (2003). Clonazepam treatment of lysergic acid diethylamide-induced hallucinogen persisting perception disorder with anxiety features. *International Clinical Psychopharmacology, 18*(2), 101-5.

Lewis, J. A., Dana, R. Q. & Blevins, G. A. (2001). *Substance Abuse Counseling* (3rd ed.). Belmont, CA: Wadsworth Publishing.

Liepman, M. R., Keller, D. M., Botelho, R. J., Monroe, A. D. & Sloane, M. A. (1998). Understanding and preventing substance abuse by adolescents: A guide for primary care clinicians. *Primary Care, 25*(1), 137-62.

Littleton, J. (1998). Neurochemical mechanisms underlying alcohol withdrawal. *Alcohol Health and Research World, 22*(1), 13-24.

Lorenzi, P., Marsili, M., Boncinelli, S., Fabbri, L. P., Fontanari, P., Zorn, A. M., et al. (1999). Searching for a general anaesthesia protocol for rapid detoxification from opioids. *European Journal of Anaesthesiology, 16*(10), 719-27.

Lowinson, J. H., Marion, I., Joseph, H., Langrod, J., Salsitz, J., Payte, J. T., et al. (2005). Methadone maintenance. In J. H. Lowinson, P. Ruiz, R. B. Millman & J. G. Langrod, eds. *Substance Abuse: A Comprehensive Textbook* (4th ed., pp. 616-33). Baltimore: Williams & Wilkins.

Madray, C., Brown, L. S., Jr. & Primm, B. J. (2005). African Americans: Epidemiology, prevention, and treatment issues. In J. H. Lowinson, P. Ruiz, R. B. Millman & J. G. Langrod, eds. *Substance Abuse: A Comprehensive Textbook* (4th ed., pp. 1093-1103). Baltimore: Williams & Wilkins.

Marlatt, G. A. (1995). Relapse prevention: Theoretical rational and overview of the model. In G. A. Marlatt & J. Gorden, eds. *Relapse Prevention: A Self-Control Strategy in the Maintenance of Behavior Change.* New York: Guilford Publications.

Marlatt, G. A. & Tapert, S. F. (1993). Harm reduction: Reducing the risks of addictive behaviors. In J. S. Baer, G. A. Marlatt & R. J. McMahon, eds. *Addictive Behaviors Across the Lifespan* (pp. 243-71). Newbury Park, CA: Sage Publications.

Mason, B. J., Ritvo, E. C., Morgan, R. O., Salvato, F. R., Goldberg, G., Welch, B., et al. (1994). A double-blind, placebo-controlled pilot study to evaluate the efficacy and safety of oral nalmefene HCL for alcohol dependence. *Alcoholism, 18*(5), 1162-67.

Mathias, R. (1999). The basics of brain imaging. *NIDA Notes, 11*(5). http://www.nida.nih.gov/NIDA_Notes/NNVol11N5/Basics.html (accessed May 4, 2007).

McElroy, S. L., Hudson, J. I., Capece, J. A., Beyers, K., Fisher, A. C. & Rosenthal, N. R. (2007). Topiramate in the treatment of binge eating disorder associated with obesity: A placebo-controlled study. *Biological Psychiatry, 61*(9), 1039-48.

McElroy, S. L., Soutullo, C. A. & Goldsmith, R. J. (2003). Other impulse control disorders. In A. W. Graham, T. K. Schultz, M. F. Mayo-Smith, R. K. Ries & B. B. Wilford, eds. *Principles of Addiction Medicine* (3rd ed., pp. 33-46). Chevy Chase, MD: American Society of Addiction Medicine, Inc.

McLellan, A. T., Grissom, G. R., Zanis, D., Randall, M., Brill, P. & O'Brien, C. P. (1997). Problem-service "matching" in addiction treatment: A prospective study in four programs. *Archives of General Psychiatry, 54*(8), 730-35.

Mecca, A. M. (1997). Blending policy and research: The California outcomes study. *Journal of Psychoactive Drugs, 29*(2), 161-63.

Mee-Lee, D. & Shulman, G. D. (2003). The ASAM placement criteria and matching patients to treatment. In A. W. Graham, T. K. Schultz, M. F. Mayo-Smith, R. K. Ries & B. B. Wilford, eds. *Principles of*

Addiction Medicine (3rd ed., pp. 453-66). Chevy Chase, MD: American Society of Addiction Medicine, Inc.

Meuller, M. D. (1999). NIDA-supported researchers use brain imaging to deepen understanding of addiction. *NIDA Notes, 11*(5). http://www.nida.nih.gov/NIDA_Notes/NNVol11N5/Deepen.html (accessed May 4, 2007).

Meuller, M. D. & Wyman, J. R. (1997). Study sheds new light on the state of drug abuse treatment nationwide (DATOS). *NIDA Notes, 12*(5). http://www.nida.nih.gov/nida_notes/NNVol12N5/Study.html (accessed May 2, 2007).

Michaels, S. (1996). The prevalence of homosexuality in the United States. In R. P. Cabaj & T. S. Stein, eds. *Textbook of Homosexuality and Mental Health* (pp. 43-63). Washington, DC: American Psychiatric Press.

Miller, W. R. (1998). Researching the spiritual dimensions of alcohol and other drug problems. *Addiction, 93*(7), 979-90.

Miller, W. R. & Hester, R. K. (1989). Treating alcohol problems: Toward an informed eclecticism. In R. K. Hester & W. R. Miller, eds. *Handbook of Alcoholism Treatment Approaches* (pp. 3-13). Boston: Allyn and Bacon.

Miller, W. & Rollnick, S. (2002). *Motivational Interviewing* (2nd ed.). New York: Guilford Publications.

Miotto, K. & Roth, B. (2001). *GHB Withdrawal Syndrome.* Texas Commission on Alcohol and Drug Abuse. http://www.erowid.org/chemicals/ghb/ghb_addiction2.pdf (accessed May 2, 2007).

Monitoring the Future. (2007). *Monitoring the Future, 2006.* http://www.monitoringthefuture.org/pubs/monographs/overview2006.pdf (accessed May 2, 2007).

Morris, S. (1995). *Harm reduction vs. disease model: Challenge for educators.* Presented at the conference of the International Coalition of Addiction Studies Educators (INCASE), Boston, MA.

Morton, J. D. & Aleman, P. (April 2005). Trends in employer-provided mental health and substance abuse benefits. *Monthly Labor Review,* 25-35.

Nace, E. P. (2005). Alcoholics Anonymous. In J. H. Lowinson, P. Ruiz, R. B. Millman & J. G. Langrod, eds. *Substance Abuse: A Comprehensive Textbook* (4th ed., pp. 587-98). Baltimore: Williams & Wilkins.

National Center on Addiction and Substance Abuse [CASA]. (2001). Shoveling Up: The Impact of Substance Abuse on State Budgets. http://www.

casacolumbia.org/absolutenm/templates/ChairmanStatements.aspx?articleid=239&zoneid=31 (accessed May 2, 2007).

National Center on Addiction and Substance Abuse. (2003). *Crossing the Bridge: An Evaluation of the Drug Treatment Alternative-to-Prison (DTAP) Program.* http://www.casacolumbia.org/supportcasa/item.asp?cID=12&PID=88 (accessed May 2, 2007).

National Center on Addiction and Substance Abuse. (2005). *Under the Counter: The Diversion and Abuse of Controlled Prescription Drugs in the U.S.* http://www.casacolumbia.org/absolutenm/articlefiles/380-under_the_counter_-_diversion.pdf (accessed May 2, 2007).

National Criminal Justice Reference Service. (2007). *Drug Courts-Facts and Figures.* http://www.ncjrs.gov/spotlight/drug_courts/facts.html (accessed May 2, 2007).

National Drug Intelligence Center. (2007). *National Drug Threat Assessment.* http://www.usdoj.gov/ndic/pubs21/21137/21137p.pdf (accessed May 2, 2007).

National Institute of Mental Health. (2007). *Statistics.* http://www.nimh.nih.gov/healthinformation/statisticsmenu.cfm (accessed May 2, 2007).

National Institute on Alcohol Abuse and Alcoholism. (2000). *10th Special Report to the U.S. Congress on Alcohol and Health.* http://pubs.niaaa.nih.gov/publications/10report/intro.pdf (accessed May 2, 2007).

National Institute on Drug Abuse [NIDA]. (1999). *Principles of Drug Addiction Treatment.* NIH Publication No. 99-4180 http://www.nida.nih.gov/PODAT/PODATindex.html (accessed April 24, 2007).

National Institute on Drug Abuse. (2002A). Buprenorphine approval expands options for addiction treatment. *NIDA Notes, 17*(4). http://www.nida.nih.gov/NIDA_notes/NNVol17N4/Buprenorphine.html (accessed May 4, 2007).

National Institute on Drug Abuse. (2002B). *Research Report Series-Therapeutic Community.* http://www.drugabuse.gov/ResearchReports/Therapeutic/Therapeutic3.html (accessed May 2, 2007).

National Institute on Drug Abuse. (2006). *Principles of Drug Abuse Treatment for Criminal Justice Populations.* NIDA, NIH Publication No. 06-5316. http://www.drugabuse.gov/PODAT_CJ (accessed May 2, 2007).

National Institutes of Health [NIH]. (1997). *Effective Medical Treatment of Heroin Addiction. NIH Consensus Statement.*

Bethesda, MD: National Institutes of Health.

National Registry of Evidence-Based Programs and Practices. (2007). *SAMHSA Model Programs*. http://www.modelprograms.samhsa.gov (accessed May 2, 2007).

Netaddiction. (2000). Center for Internet Addiction Recovery. http://www.netaddiction.com (accessed May 2, 2007).

NHSDA Report. (2001). Substance use among older adults. http://www.oas.samhsa.gov/2k1/olderadults/olderadults.htm (accessed May 4, 2007).

Nich, C., McCance-Katz, E. F., Petrakis, I. L., Cubells, J. F., Rounsaville, B. J. & Carroll, K. M. (2004). Sex differences in cocaine-dependent individuals' response to disulfiram treatment. *Addictive Behaviors, 29*(6), 1123-28.

Nielsen, B., Nielsen, A. S. & Wraae, O. (1998). Patient-treatment matching improves compliance of alcoholics in outpatient treatment. *Journal of Nervous and Mental Disease, 186*(12), 752-60.

O'Boyle, M. & Brandon, E. A. (1998). Suicide attempts, substance abuse, and personality. *Journal of Substance Abuse Treatment, 15*(4), 353-56.

O'Brien, C. P. (1997). A range of research-based pharmacotherapies for addiction. *Science, 278*(5335), 66-70.

O'Donnell, C. & Trick M. (2006). *Methadone Maintenance Treatment and the Criminal Justice System, NASADAD*. http://www.nasadad.org/resource.php?base_id=650 (accessed May 4, 2007).

O'Farrell, T. J. & Cowles, K. S. (1989). Marital and family therapy. In R. K. Hester & W. R. Miller, eds. *Handbook of Alcoholism Treatment Approaches* (pp. 183-205). Boston: Allyn and Bacon.

O'Malley, S. S., Jaffe, A. J., Chang, G., Schottenfeld, R. S., Meyer, R. E. & Rounsaville, B. (1992). Naltrexone and coping skills therapy for alcohol dependence. *Archives of General Psychiatry, 49*, 881-87.

Office of National Drug Control Policy. (2001). *Drug Treatment in the Criminal Justice System*. http://www.whitehousedrugpolicy.gov/publications/factsht/treatment/index.html (accessed May 2, 2007).

O'Malley, S. S., Jaffe, A. J., Chang, G., Schottenfeld, R. S., Meyer, R. E. & Rounsaville, B. (1992). Naltrexone and coping skills therapy for alcohol dependence. *Archives of General Psychiatry, 49*(11) 881-87.

Oncken, C., Gonzales, D., Nides, M., Rennard, S., Watsky, E., Billing, C. B., et al. (2006). Efficacy and safety of the novel selective nicotinic acetylcholine receptor partial agonist, varenicline, for smoking cessation. *Archives of Internal Medicine, 166*(15):1571-77.

Parran, T. V., Liepman, M. R. & Farkas, K. (2003). The family in addiction. In A. W. Graham, T. K. Schultz, M. F. Mayo-Smith, R. K. Ries & B. B. Wilford, eds. *Principles of Addiction Medicine* (3rd ed., pp. 395-402). Chevy Chase, MD: American Society of Addiction Medicine, Inc.

Partnership for a Drug Free America [PATS]. (2006). *The Partnership Attitude Tracking Study*. http://www.drugfree.org/Files/Full_Teen_Report (accessed May 4, 2007).

Patterson, T. L., Lacro, J. P. & Jeste, D. V. (1999). Abuse and misuse of medications in the elderly. *Psychiatric Times, XVI4*.

Payte, J. T. (1997) Methadone maintenance treatment: The first thirty years. *Journal of Psychoactive Drugs, 29*(2), 149-53.

Payte, J. T. & Zweben, J. E. (1998). Opioid maintenance therapies. In A. W. Graham, T. K. Schultz, M. F. Mayo-Smith, R. K. Ries & B. B. Wilford, eds. *Principles of Addiction Medicine* (3rd ed., pp. 33-46). Chevy Chase, MD: American Society of Addiction Medicine, Inc.

Peele, S. (1995). Controlled drinking vs. abstinence. In J. H. Jaffe, ed. *Encyclopedia of Drugs and Alcohol* (Vol. 1, pp. 92-97). New York: Simon & Schuster Macmillan.

Perez-Arce, P., Carr, K. D. & Sorensen, J. L. (1993). Cultural issues in an outpatient program for stimulant abusers. *Journal of Psychoactive Drugs, 25*(1), 35-44.

Peters, R. H., Matthews, C. O. & Dvoskin, J. A. (2005). Treatment in prisons and jails. In J. H. Lowinson, P. Ruiz, R. B. Millman & J. G. Langrod, eds. *Substance Abuse: A Comprehensive Textbook* (4th ed., pp. 707-21). Baltimore: Williams & Wilkins.

Petry, N. M. (2005). *Pathological Gambling: Etiology, Comorbidity, and Treatment*. Washington, D.C.: American Psychological Association.

Pharmacist Rehabilitation Organization. (1999). A checklist of symptoms leading to relapse. *Pharmacists Rehabilitation Organization Newsletter, 3*(1), 1-2.

Powell, A. (2003). Psychiatry and Spirituality—The Forgotten Dimension. http://www.rcpsych.ac.uk/pdf/powell_19_11_03_2%20.pdf (accessed May 2, 2007).

Prochaska, D. R. & Di Clemente, C. C. (1994). *Transtheoretical Approach: Crossing Traditional Boundaries of Therapy*. Melbourne, FL: Krieger Publishing Company.

Pumariega, A. J., Kilgujs, M. D. & Rodriguez, L. (2005). Adolescents. In J. H. Lowinson, P. Ruiz, R. B. Millman & J. G. Langrod, eds. *Substance Abuse: A Comprehensive Textbook* (4th ed., pp. 1021-37). Baltimore: Williams & Wilkins.

Raine, A., Lencz, T., Bihrle, S., LaCasse, L. & Colletti, P. (2000). Reduced prefrontal gray matter volume and reduced autonomic activity in antisocial personality disorder. *Archives of General Psychiatry, 57*(2), 119-27.

Reid, M. S., Mickalian, J. D., Delucchi, K. L., Hall, S. M. & Berger, S. P. (1998). An acute dose of nicotine enhances cue-induced cocaine craving. *Drug and Alcohol Dependence, 49*(2), 95-104.

Reyna, V. F. & Farley, F. (2007). Is the teen brain too rational? *Scientific American Mind, 17*(6), 58-65.

Ricaurte, G. A., Seiden, L. S. & Schuster, C. R. (1984). Further evidence that amphetamines produce long-lasting dopamine neurochemical deficits by destroying dopamine nerve fibers. *Brain Research, 303*(2), 359-64.

Rose, J. E., Behm, F. M., Westman, E. C., Levin, E. D., Stein, R. M. & Ripka, G. V. (1994). Mecamylamine combined with nicotine skin patch facilitates smoking cessation beyond nicotine patch treatment alone. *Clinical Pharmacology and Therapeutics, 56*(1), 86-99.

Ross, E. (May 16, 2003). Epilepsy drug helps alcoholics quit drinking. *Medford Mail Tribune*, p. 1A.

Rounds-Bryant, J. L., Motivans, M. A. & Pelissier, B. (2003). Comparison of background characteristics and behaviors of African-American, Hispanic, and White substance abusers treated in federal prison: Results from the TRIAD Study. *Journal of Psychoactive Drugs, 35*(3), 333-41.

Ruiz, P. (2005). Hispanics' mental health care plight. *Behavioral Health, 25*(6), 17-20.

Ruiz, P. & Langrod, J. G. (2005). Hispanic Americans. In J. H. Lowinson, P. Ruiz, R. B. Millman & J. G. Langrod, eds. *Substance Abuse: A Comprehensive Textbook* (4th ed., pp. 1103-12). Baltimore: Williams & Wilkins.

Rustin, T. A. (1998). Incorporating nicotine dependence into addiction treatment. *Journal of Addictive Diseases, 17*(1), 83-108.

Saitz, R., Mulvey, K. P., Plough, A. & Samet, J. H. (1997). Physician unawareness of serious substance abuse. *American Journal of Drug and Alcohol Abuse, 23*(3), 343-54.

Schenker, M. & Minayo, M. C. (2004). The importance of family in drug abuse treatment: A literature review. *Cadernos de Saude Publica, 20*(3), 649-59.

Schnoll, S. (1993). Prescription medication in rehabilitation. In A. W. Heineman, ed. *Substance Abuse & Physical Disability* (pp. 79-91). Binghamton, NY: The Haworth Press, Inc.

Schuckit, M. A. (1994). Goals of treatment. In M. Galanter & H. D. Kleber, eds. *Textbook of Substance Abuse Treatment* (pp. 3-10). Washington, DC: American Psychiatric Press.

Schuckit, M. A. (2000). *Drug and Alcohol Abuse* (5th ed.). New York: Kluwer Academic/Plenum Publishers.

Schwartz, R. P., Highfield, D. A., Jaffe, J. H., Brady, J. V., Butler, C. B., Rouse, C. O, et al. (2006). A randomized controlled trial of interim methadone maintenance. *Archives of General Psychiatry, 63*(1), 102-9.

Schwetz, B. (2001). From the FDA: Labeling changes for Orlam. *Journal of the American Medical Association, 285*(21), 2705.

Senft, R. A. (1991). Experience with clonidine-naltrexone for rapid opiate detoxification. *Journal of Substance Abuse Treatment, 8*(4), 257-59.

Sexton, R. L., Carlson, R. G., Siegal, H., Leukefeld, C. G. & Booth B. (2006). The role of African-American clergy in providing informal services to drug users in the rural South: Preliminary ethnographic findings. *Journal of Ethnic Substance Abuse, 5*(1), 1-21.

Sher, K. J. (1997). Psychological characteristics of children of alcoholics. *Alcohol Health & Research World, 21*(3), 247-54.

Shulman, A., Jagoda, J., Laycock, G. & Kelly, H. (1998). Calcium channel-blocking drugs in the management of drug dependence, withdrawal and craving. A clinical pilot study with nifedipine and verapamil. *Australian Family Physician, 27*(suppl. 1), S19-S24.

Simoni-Wastila, L., Zuckerman, I. H., Singhal, P. K., Briesacher, B. & Hsu, V. D. (2006). National estimates of exposure to prescription drugs with addiction potential in community-dwelling elders. *Substance Abuse, 26*(1), 33-42.

Simpson, D. D., Joe, G. W., Fletcher, B. W., Hubbard, R. L. & Anglin, M. D. (1999). A national evaluation of treatment outcomes for cocaine dependence. *Archives of General Psychiatry, 56*(6), 507-14.

Skinner, W. F. (1994). The prevalence and demographic predictors of illicit and licit drug use among lesbians and gay men. *American Journal of Public Health, 84*(8), 1307-10.

Skinner, W. F. & Otis, M. D. (1996). Drug and alcohol use among lesbian and gay people in a southern U.S. sample. *Journal of Homosexuality, 30*(3), 59-92.

Slutske, W. S. (2006). Natural recovery and treatment-seeking in pathological gambling: Results of two U.S. national surveys. *American Journal of Psychiatry, 163*(2), 297-302.

Smith, D. E., Buxton, M. E., Bilal, R. & Seymour, R. B. (1993). Cultural points of resistance to the 12-step recovery process. *Journal of Psychoactive Drugs, 25*(1), 97-108.

Sneft, R. A. (1991). Experience with clonidine-naltrexone for rapid opiate detoxification. *Journal of Substance Abuse Treatment, 8*(4), 257-59.

Snyder, E., Park, K. I., Flax, J. D., Liu, S., Rosario, C. M., Yandava, B. D., et al. (1997). Potential of neural "stem-like" cells for gene therapy and repair of the degenerating central nervous system. *Advanced Neurology, 72,* 121-32.

Spencer J. (July 18, 2006). After weight-loss surgery, some find new addictions. Report of Melodie Moorehead at American Society for Bariatric Surgery Association. *Wall Street Journal,* p. 1A.

Steiner, R. P., Hay, D. L. & Davis, A. W. (1982). Acupuncture therapy for the treatment of tobacco smoking addiction. *American Journal of Chinese Medicine, 10*(1-4), 107-21.

Sterling, R. C., Weinstein, S., Losardo, D., Raively, K., Hill, P., Petrone, A., et al. (2007). A retrospective case control study of alcohol relapse and spiritual growth. *American Journal on Addictions, 16*(1), 56-61.

Stevens-Smith, P. & Smith, R. L. (2004). *Substance Abuse Counseling: Theory & Practice* (3rd ed). Upper Saddle River, NJ: Prentice-Hall College Division.

Strain, E. C., Bigelow, G. E., Liebson, I. A. & Stitzer, M. L. (1999). Moderate- vs. high-dose methadone in the treatment of opioid dependence. *JAMA, 281*(11), 1000-5.

Substance Abuse and Mental Health Services Administration [SAMHSA]. (2000). *Substance Abuse Treatment in Adult and Juvenile Correctional Facilities.* DHHS Publication No. SMA DO-3380. Rockville, MD: Author.

Substance Abuse and Mental Health Services Administration. (2001). *A Provider's Introduction to Substance Abuse Treatment for Lesbian, Gay, Bisexual, and Transgender Individuals.* DHHS Publication No. SMA 01-3498. Rockville, MD: Center for Substance Abuse Treatment.

Substance Abuse and Mental Health Services Administration. (2002). *Communicating Appropriately with Asian and Pacific Islander Audiences.* http://ncadi.samhsa.gov/govpubs/MS701 (accessed May 2, 2007).

Substance Abuse and Mental Health Services Administration. (2003). *National Household Survey on Drug Abuse, 2002.* Series H-22, DHHS Publication No. SMA 03-3836. Rockville, MD: Author.

Substance Abuse and Mental Health Services Administration. (2006A). *2005 National Survey on Drug Use and Health.* http://www.oas.samhsa.gov/nsduh/2k5nsduh/2k5results.pdf (accessed May 2, 2007).

Substance Abuse and Mental Health Services Administration. (2006B). *Treatment Episode Data Sets, 2005.* http://www.dasis.samhsa.gov/teds05/tedshi2k5_web.pdf (accessed May 2, 2007).

Substance Abuse and Mental Health Services Administration. (2006C). *National Survey of Substance Abuse Treatment Services (N-SSATS), 2005.* http://www.dasis.samhsa.gov/05nssats/nssats2k5web.pdf (accessed May 4, 2007).

Swan, R. (2006). Feelin' their thizzle: How the culture of ecstasy has changed as the drug moved from raves to hip-hop. *East Bay Express, 28*(23), 15-25.

Taleff, M. J. (2004). Alcohol-caused impairment and early treatment. *Counselor, Magazine for Addiction Professionals, 5*(1), 76-77.

Tangenberg, K. M. (2005). Twelve-step programs and faith-based recovery. In C. Hilarski, ed. *Addiction, Assessment, and Treatment with Adolescents, Adults, and Families.* Binghamton, NY: The Haworth Press, Inc.

Thompson, G. H. & Hunter, D. A. (1998). Nicotine replacement therapy. *Annals of Pharmacotherapy, 32*(10), 1067-75.

Thompson, P. M., Hayashi, K. M., Simon, S. L., Geaga, J. A., Hong, M. S., Sui, Y., et al. (2004). Structural abnormalities in the brains of human subjects who use methamphetamine. *Journal of Neuroscience, 24*(26), 6028-36.

Trice, H. M. (1995). Alcoholics Anonymous. In J. H. Jaffe, ed. *Encyclopedia of Drugs and Alcohol* (Vol. 1, pp. 85-92). New York: Simon & Schuster Macmillan.

Tsuang, J. W. (2005). Asian Americans and Pacific Islanders. In J. H. Lowinson, P. Ruiz, R. B. Millman & J. G. Langrod, eds. *Substance Abuse: A Comprehensive Textbook* (4th ed., pp. 1103-12). Baltimore: Williams & Wilkins.

U.S. Census Bureau. (2007). *U.S. Interim Projections by Age, Sex, Race, and*

Hispanic Origin. http://www.census. gov/ipc/www/usinterimproj (accessed May 2, 2007).

U.S. Department of Justice [DOJ]. (2003). *Arrestee Drug Abuse Monitoring.* http://www.ncjrs.gov/pdffiles1/nij/1930 13.pdf (accessed May 2, 2007).

U.S. Department of Justice. (2005). *Substance Dependence, Abuse, and Treatment of Jail Inmates, 2002.* Bureau of Justice Statistics. http://www.ojp. gov/bjs/pub/pdf/sdatji02.pdf (accessed May 2, 2007).

U.S. Department of Justice. (2006A). *Criminal Offenders Statistics.* http:// www.ojp.usdoj.gov/bjs/crimoff.htm#recidivism (accessed May 4, 2007).

U.S. Department of Justice. (2006B). *Prison and Jail Inmates at Midyear 2005.* http://www.ojp.usdoj.gov/bjs/ pub/pdf/pjim05.pdf (accessed May 2, 2007).

U.S. Department of Justice. (2007). *Probation and Parole Statistics.* http://www.ojp.usdoj.gov/bjs/pandp.htm (accessed May 2, 2007).

U.S. Public Health Service. (1999). *Mental Health: A Report of the Surgeon General.* http://www.surgeongeneral. gov/library/mentalhealth/home.html (accessed May 2, 2007).

Vaillant, G. E. (1995). *The Natural History of Alcoholism Revisited.* Cambridge, MA: Harvard University Press.

Vocci, F. (October 1999). *Medications in the pipeline.* Paper presented at the CSAM Conference, Addiction Medicine: State of the Art, Marina Del Rey, CA.

Volkow, N. D., Chang, L., Wang, G. J., Fowler, J. S., Franceschi, D., Sedler, M., et al. (2001). Loss of dopamine transporters in methamphetamine abusers recovers with protracted abstinence. *Journal of Neuroscience, 21*(23), 9414-18.

Volkow, N. D., Fowler, J. S. & Wang, G. J. (2003). The addicted brain: Insights from imaging studies. *Journal of Clinical Investigation, 111*(10), 1444-51.

Volkow, N. D., Hitzemann, R., Wang, G. J., Fowler, J. S., Burr, G., Pascani, K., et al. (1992). Decreased brain metabolism in neurologically intact healthy alcoholics. *American Journal of Psychiatry, 149*(8), 1016-22.

Volkow, N. D., Wang, G. J., Begleiter, H., Porjesz, B., Fowler, J. S., Telang, F., et al. (2006). High levels of dopamine D$_2$ receptors in unaffected members of alcoholic families: Possible protective factors. *Archives of General Psychiatry, 63*(9), 999-1008.

Volpicelli, J. R., Alterman, A. I., Hayashida, M. & O'Brien, C. P. (1992). Naltrexone in the treatment of alcohol dependence. *Archives of General Psychiatry, 49*(11), 876-80.

Wallis, C. & Dell, K. (May 10, 2004). What makes teens tick. *Time.* http://www. time.com/time/magazine/article/ 0,9171,994126,00.html (accessed May 2, 2007).

Wallner, M., Hanchar, H. J. & Olsen, R. W. (2006). Low-dose alcohol actions on alpha4beta3delta GABAA receptors are reversed by the behavioral alcohol antagonist Ro15-4513. *Proceedings of the National Academy of Sciences, 103*(22), 8540-45.

Wen, H. L. & Cheung, S. Y. C. (1973). Treatment of drug addiction by acupuncture and electrical stimulation. *Asian Journal of Medicine, 9,* 23-24.

White, W. L. (1998). *Slaying the Dragon: The History of Addiction Treatment and Recovery in America.* Bloomington, IL: Chestnut Health Systems/Lighthouse Institute.

Whitten, L. (2005). Disulfiram reduces cocaine abuse. *NIDA Notes, 20*(2), 4-5.

Wiehl, W. O., Hayner, G. & Galloway, G. (1994). Haight Ashbury Free Clinics' drug detoxification protocols-Part 4: Alcohol. *Journal of Psychoactive Drugs, 26*(1), 57-59.

Wiley Interscience. (2001). Programs including nicotine addiction as part of treatment. *Alcoholism & Drug Abuse Weekly, 13*(38), 1-3.

Windle, M. T. (1999). *Alcohol Use Among Adolescents.* Thousand Oaks, CA: Sage Publications.

Winters, K. C. (2003). Assessment of alcohol and other drug use behaviors among adolescents. In *Assessing Alcohol Problems: A Guide for Clinicians and Researchers* (2nd ed.). NIH Publication No. 03-3745, 101-23.

Xi, Z. X., Newman, A. H., Gilbert, J. G., Pak, A. C., Peng, X. Q., Ashby, C. R., Jr., et al. (2006). The novel dopamine D3 receptor antagonist NGB 2904 inhibits cocaine's rewarding effects and cocaine-induced reinstatement of drug-seeking behavior in rats. *Neuropsychopharmacology, 31*(7), 1393-405.

Mental Health
& Drugs

*SHOUT (woodcut) © 2004 Artemio
Rodriguez. Used with permission*

MENTAL HEALTH & DRUGS

- **Introduction.** About one-third of adults with any mental disorder, such as depression, schizophrenia, bipolar disorder, or anxiety disorder, also have a co-occurring substance use disorder. Conversely, between 50% and 70% of substance abusers also have a co-occurring mental disorder.
  - ◊ The neurotransmitters, receptor sites, and other brain mechanisms involved in mental and emotional problems and illnesses are the same ones affected by psychoactive drugs.
  - ◊ Substance-related disorders are divided into substance use disorders (SUDs) and substance-induced disorders.
- **Determining Factors.** Heredity, environment, and the use of psychoactive drugs affect mental health in much the same way as they affect SUDs like substance abuse and addiction.

DUAL DIAGNOSIS (CO-OCCURRING DISORDERS)

- **Definition.** Co-occurring disorders are defined as "the existence in an individual of at least one independent major mental disorder as well as an independent alcohol or drug use disorder." The number of individuals suffering from both a substance-abuse problem and a mental illness is growing. The decrease of inpatient mental facilities has magnified this problem.
- **Epidemiology.** There is a high incidence of mental imbalances among drug users, and, conversely, many people with mental/emotional problems use drugs, often to self-medicate.
- **Patterns of Dual Diagnosis.** A mental illness can be pre-existing or substance induced (temporary or permanent). Drug use can aggravate a mental illness or mask it.
- **Making the Diagnosis.** Because the direct effects as well as the withdrawal effects of drugs can mimic mental illnesses, initial diagnoses need to be "rule-out" diagnoses.
- **Mental Health vs. Substance Abuse.** The previous distrust between these two treatment communities has partly given way to cooperation and recognition of the duality of drug abuse and mental illness.
- **Psychiatric Disorders.** Thought (psychotic), affective (mood), anxiety, and personality disorders are the most common psychiatric problems. These include schizophrenia, major depression, bipolar disorder, post-traumatic stress disorder, panic disorder, and borderline personality disorder.
- **Treatment.** Mental illness and substance-related disorders must be treated simultaneously, or treatment will not be as effective. Treatment can include individual therapy, group therapy, self-help groups, and psychiatric medications. Treatment takes place in a variety of facilities, from outpatient to residential.
- **Psychopharmacology.** Antidepressants, antipsychotics, mood stabilizers, and antianxiety drugs are the principal medications used to control mental illnesses.

The authors are indebted to Pablo Stewart, M.D., clinical professor of psychiatry at the University of California at San Francisco School of Medicine, for his invaluable guidance and contributions in co-writing this chapter.

Brain discovery may offer hope for attention disorders

Different locations govern distraction

Deciphering a brain

friend's face out of a crowd. Other is more advanced times' debts

Report warns of drugs' risk to elderly

OLDER TYPES OF ANTI-PSYCHOTICS

FDA urged to add health advisory

Many Diagnoses of Depression May Be Misguided, Study Says

By BENEDICT CAREY

U.S. soldiers' mental health needs unmet panel finds

By LISA C....

Serotonin gene variant may cause depression

for the American Psychiatric Association, said, "I think the concern this study raises ... that we do need to be very

Drug, alcohol abusers likelier to suffer mental ills, study says

More kids on anti-psychotic drugs

for behavioral drugs grow

...hotic medication for children have increased ...ccording to a new study.

prescriptions given to the same child, but he said that is unlikely and noted his findings echo results from smaller studies.
The study appears in the ...h April edition of the

Kids and depression: Are drugs the answer?

Adequate care rare for mental illness

Mental illness linked to short life

Anti-psychotics and obesity could be facto...

Flawed gene linked to manic-depression

mon m...
s expec...
l study...
Gener...
o recei...
as wh...

A flawed gene that appears to promote manic-depression, or bipolar disorder, has been identified by scientists. The finding eventually could help point the way to new treatments. A ...

Mouse gene change leads to anxiety, taste for alcohol

Researchers are looking for new biological methods to treat alcoholism and anxiety disorders in people

By JAMIE TALAN
LA TIMES-WASHINGTON POST SERVICE

gene has other important behavioral effects. Understanding how these biological systems work could lead to new ways to treat alcoholism and anxiety disorders, said Subhash Pandey, associate professor of psychiatry and director of neuroscience alcoholism research at the University of Illinois

FDA approves stronger warning on antidepressants

'Black box' will alert young adult patients

By Denise Gellene
LOS ANGELES TIMES

The Food and Drug Administration approved on Wednesday the

The FDA's action requires drug companies to submit proposed labeling and updated medication guides within 30 days. A total of 36 drugs would display the new warn-

Eli Lilly and Co. sai... make informed tre...

MENTAL HEALTH & DRUGS

INTRODUCTION

The National Comorbidity Survey, a once-in-a-decade mental health study, found that **almost half of all Americans will develop a mental disorder at some time in their lives**—half of those cases by the age of 14 and three-quarters by the age of 24:

◇ 46.4% will have at least one mental disorder,

◇ 27.7% will have two or more mental disorders, and

◇ 17.3% will have three or more mental disorders.

The different classes of disorders consisted of: anxiety disorders, 28.8%; mood disorders, 20.8%; impulse-control disorders, 24.8%; and substance use disorders, 14.6%. Median age of onset is much earlier for anxiety and impulse-control disorders (11 years) than for substance use (20 years) and mood disorders (30 years) (Kessler, Berglund, Demler, et al., 2005).

"I didn't think that I was a mentally ill person. I thought, Well, I'm a drug addict and I'm an alcoholic, and if I don't drink and I don't use, then it should just be a simple matter of just changing my entire life; and I felt a little bit overwhelmed by the thought."
35-year-old male with major depression

Of the 40 million Americans who experience any mental disorder such as schizophrenia, major depression, bipolar disorder, an anxiety disorder, or a personality disorder in the course of a year, about 7 million to 10 million also experience a substance-related disorder (National Institute of Mental Health [NIMH], 1999; Substance Abuse and Mental Health Services Administration [SAMHSA], 2002A).

BRAIN CHEMISTRY

The interconnection between mental/emotional health and drug use is so pervasive that understanding this link gives a valuable insight into the functioning of the human mind at all

levels. The reason for the link is that **the neurotransmitters affected by psychoactive drugs are the same ones involved in mental illness. Many people with mental problems are drawn to psychoactive drugs in an effort to rebalance their brain chemistry and control their agitation, depression, or other mental problems. The opposite is also true. For some people who abuse drugs, their chemistry becomes unbalanced enough to aggravate a pre-existing mental illness or mimic the symptoms of one** (Barondes, 1993; Zimberg, 1999).

"I wound up preferring the heroin because I felt relaxed when I would snort it. I felt like I didn't have any troubles. I felt like I had some peace of mind, and the drugs that were up, like speed and cocaine, made me feel really anxious."

Recovering drug abuser with major depression

This connection between mental health and drug use can be seen in the **similarity between the symptoms of psychiatric disorders and the direct effects of psychoactive drugs or their withdrawal symptoms**. For example:

◊ cocaine or amphetamine intoxication mimics mania, anxiety, or psychosis;

◊ cocaine or amphetamine withdrawal looks like major depressive disorder or generalized anxiety disorder;

◊ the manic effects of cocaine or amphetamine followed by the exhaustion of withdrawal mimic a bipolar illness that includes manic delusions and then depression;

◊ excessive use of alcohol causes a depressed mood, a lack of interest in surroundings, and a disruptive sleep pattern characteristic of a major depressive disorder; and

◊ psychedelic drugs (e.g., mescaline and LSD) mimic the delusional hallucinations associated with a psychotic or thought disorder (Goldsmith & Ries, 2003).

CLASSIFICATION OF SUBSTANCE-RELATED DISORDERS

Substance-related disorders are classified in the *Diagnostic and Statistical Manual of Mental Disorders* (*DSM-IV-TR*) as mental disorders (American Psychiatric Association [APA], 2000). They are divided into two general categories:

1. **Substance use disorders (SUDs)** involve patterns of drug use and are divided into substance dependence and substance abuse. (Note that the word *addiction* is not used.)

   ◊ **Substance dependence** is defined in the *DSM-IV-TR* as **a maladaptive pattern of substance use leading to clinically significant impairment or distress** as manifested by three or more of the following: tolerance; withdrawal; the need for larger amounts; unsuccessful efforts to cut down use; an expenditure of large amounts of time to get, use, and think about the drug; important social, employment, or recreational activities are limited or curtailed; and continued use despite adverse consequences.

   ◊ **Substance abuse** is defined as "recurrent substance use that results in disruption of work, school, or home obligations; recurrent use in physically hazardous situations; recurrent legal problems; and **continued use despite adverse consequences**.

2. **Substance-induced disorders** include **conditions that are caused by the use of the specific substances**. These conditions usually disappear after a period of abstinence, although some of the damage can last weeks, months, years, and even a lifetime. Substance-induced **disorders include intoxication, withdrawal, and certain mental disorders** (e.g., delirium, dementia, amnestic disorder, psychotic disorder, mood disorder, anxiety disorder, sexual dysfunction, and sleep disorder). The substances specifically defined in the *DSM-IV-TR* include alcohol, am-

phetamines, *Cannabis,* cocaine, hallucinogens, inhalants, opioids, PCP, and sedative-hypnotics.

DETERMINING FACTORS

The three main factors that affect the central nervous system's balance and therefore a human being's susceptibility to mental illness as well as addiction are **heredity, environment, and the use of psychoactive drugs** (Brady, Myrick & Sonne, 2003; Brehm & Khantzian, 1997). For example, nearly every neurochemical system involved in depression is also found to be abnormal in substance use and substance-induced disorders (McDowell, 1999).

HEREDITY & MENTAL BALANCE

How does heredity affect our mental health? Research has already shown a **close link between heredity and schizophrenia, bipolar disorder, de-**pression, and even anxiety. The risk of a child's developing schizophrenia is somewhere between 0.5% and 1% if the child has no close-order relatives with schizophrenia. On the other hand, if the child has a close relative who has schizophrenia, the risk jumps 15- to 30-fold (Gottesman, 1991).

"My great uncle's got schizophrenia and my nephew's got schizophrenia. He's got it really bad because he can't control his fits. I didn't think about that growing up, only when I started hearing the voices. Then I thought, Hmm, just like my nephew."

28-year-old male with schizophrenia

Studies suggest that genetic influences that make a person susceptible to schizophrenia are those that control certain brain structures and particularly those that control synaptic activity. Glutamate transmission along with dopamine and GABA signaling are involved (Matyas, 2006).

Some individuals are born with a brain chemistry that makes them sus-ceptible to certain mental illnesses. **If the genetically susceptible brain chemistry is then stressed by a hostile environment or, to a lesser extent, psychoactive drug use, that person has an increased likelihood of developing mental illness.** If there is a very heavy genetic susceptibility, it may not take as severe an environmental stress. If there's a low genetic susceptibility, it will take a much stronger environmental or chemical stress to trigger the illness. Even with a high susceptibility and strong environmental stresses, mental illness may not develop. Statistics show that even if there is a close relative with major depression, five out of six children or siblings will not develop that illness (Goodwin, 1990; Kendler & Diehl, 1993).

"In my family my mom, my aunt, and my grandmother were diagnosed as manic depressive [bipolar disorder]. It runs in the family. It didn't have anything to do with drugs. It was just a lack of something in the brain."

16-year-old male in treatment for bipolar disorder

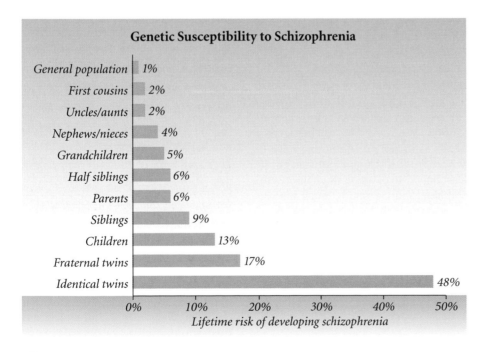

Genetic Susceptibility to Schizophrenia

General population	1%
First cousins	2%
Uncles/aunts	2%
Nephews/nieces	4%
Grandchildren	5%
Half siblings	6%
Parents	6%
Siblings	9%
Children	13%
Fraternal twins	17%
Identical twins	48%

Lifetime risk of developing schizophrenia

Figure 10-1 •
The risk of developing schizophrenia if a genetic relation has the disease varies with the number of shared genes. Second-degree relatives, such as nieces, share only 25% of one's genes, a parent shares 50%, and an identical twin shares 100%.
(Gottesman, 1991)

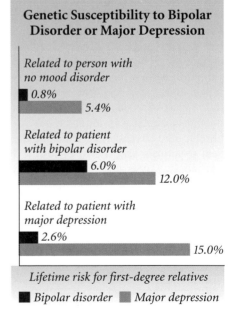

Genetic Susceptibility to Bipolar Disorder or Major Depression

Related to person with no mood disorder
0.8%
5.4%

Related to patient with bipolar disorder
6.0%
12.0%

Related to patient with major depression
2.6%
15.0%

Lifetime risk for first-degree relatives
■ Bipolar disorder   ■ Major depression

Figure 10-2 •
The risk of developing depression or bipolar disorder is greatly increased if a first-degree relative (parent, sibling, or child) has the disease.
(Goodwin, 1990)

Genetic links for behavioral disorders, such as binge-eating disorder, compulsive gambling, and even attention-deficit disorder, have been found in twin surveys. Identical twins raised by two different sets of foster parents often exhibit the same character traits and behaviors regardless of their different environments (Zickler, 1999).

It is important to remember that heredity affects susceptibility to drug or behavioral addiction in much the same pattern that heredity affects susceptibility to mental illness. **A high genetic susceptibility does not mean that that mental illness or addiction will occur, only that there is a greater chance that it will occur.**

"Both my parents were alcoholics. My brother's an addict and an alcoholic. I basically followed in my father's footsteps—the drinking, the running around, losing wives, kids, all that."
38-year-old recovering alcoholic with major depression

The relationship among heredity, mental illness, and psychoactive drugs can be seen by examining the connections among the neurotransmitter dopamine, the drug cocaine, and schizophrenia. Heredity can affect the formation of dopamine receptor sites and the ability of the brain to produce dopamine. Schizophrenia seems to be caused in part by the brain's having too much dopamine. Cocaine stimulates the release of dopamine, so long-term or high-dose use can induce a schizophrenic-like psychosis. **With both the real psychosis and the drug-induced psychosis, excess dopamine seems to be a key element** (Blum, Braverman, Holder, et al., 2000).

ENVIRONMENT & MENTAL BALANCE

There is ongoing debate about which factor—genetics or environment—is more important. The prevailing consensus had swung toward genetics, but some research is showing how environment and drug use can alter genetic factors. The same environmental factors that can induce a susceptibility to drug abuse can induce mental/emotional problems (Rusk & Rusk, 2007). **The**

neurochemistry of people subject to extreme stress can be disrupted and unbalanced to a point that their reactions to normal situations are different from those of most other people.** For example, continued stress depletes norepinephrine and that can cause depression. Such persons may react to stressful situations by running away, falling apart, becoming extremely angry, or using psychoactive drugs. The stressors they respond to don't even have to be dramatic. They can merely be normal family expectations. For such individuals, a mother saying, "It's eleven o'clock—I wish you'd get out of bed," can result in extreme anger that further disrupts the child's balance, thought processes, and, therefore, behavior (Barondes, 1993).

"My parents had a troubled marriage and they'd fight and argue, and my mother would be beaten. I think maybe some of the rage and some of the anger manifested itself into the schizophrenia or just triggered it. After my schizophrenia became really prominent, I noticed that little things, like on-the-job stress, would get to me and I'd move on because it would trigger all sorts of problems."
28-year-old with a dual diagnosis

Abuse and sexual molestation can be major negative environmental factors. Well over 50% of the young adults who are psychotic and have a problem with drugs experienced at least one form of abuse when they were children, and the rate is much greater for women than for men. In addition, more than 75% of female addicts suffered incest, molestation, or physical abuse as a child or an adult (SAMHSA, 2002A; Zweben, 1996).

"My dad beat my mom when he was under the influence of alcohol. He was an alcoholic. He also beat my older sister and me. When he came home, I was always running and hiding. A few years after he left the family, I was molested. I was screwed up, but when

I went into the service I found that the marijuana and the heroin I abused in 'Nam kept my emotions under control."
Vietnam veteran with post-traumatic stress disorder

PSYCHOACTIVE DRUGS & MENTAL BALANCE

Along with heredity and environment, the use of psychoactive drugs can deplete, increase, mimic, or otherwise disrupt the neurochemistry of the brain. This disruption of brain chemistry by drugs can lead to mental illness (often temporary), drug addiction, or both.

If a nervous system is affected by enough psychoactive drugs, any individual may develop mental/emotional problems, but it is the predisposed brain that is much more likely to have prolonged or permanent difficulties. There is no set time for this to occur. The process may take years or, as in the case of psychedelic drugs, just one use can release an underlying psychopathology (Smith & Seymour, 2001). **The brain that is not predisposed is the one most likely to return to its predrug functioning during abstinence.**

"Apparently, through three generations of my family and our alcohol drinking or opium smoking, I inherited a tendency to manic depression that wouldn't awaken under just alcohol abuse. It took a more exotic drug, one that was a little bit beyond the range of a northern European family, to bring out my illness—and that was marijuana."
45-year-old with bipolar disorder

The type of drug has a great impact on symptoms of co-occurring disorders. For example, women with a dual diagnosis of cocaine abuse and post-traumatic stress disorder (cocaine/PTSD) had greater occupational impairment, less monthly income, more legal problems (e.g., greater number of arrests for prostitution), and greater social impairment (e.g., unmarried and with fewer friends) than those

This illustration, The Extraction of the Stone of Madness by Pieter Brueghel, the Elder, is a satire of ways to treat mental illness. It shows that even 300 years ago people thought that mental illness was caused by something physical inside the brain. Compare this with the modern view of many clinicians that mental illness can be treated by changing the neurochemistry inside the brain through psychotropic medications.
Courtesy of the National Library of Medicine, Bethesda, MD

who had an alcohol/PTSD dual diagnosis. On the other hand, those with an alcohol/PTSD dual diagnosis were more likely to have serious accidents and extraordinarily stressful life events. Rates of major depression and social phobia were also higher among this group than in the cocaine/PTSD group (Back, Sonne, Killeen, et al., 2003).

Every time a psychoactive substance enters the brain, it changes the equilibrium, and the neurochemistry has to adjust. When exposure to that drug has ended, the brain does not always return to its original balance. For example, **a brain predisposed to major depression can aggravate that mental problem by heavy abuse of alcohol and sedative-hypnotics or withdrawal from stimulant drugs** (Drake & Mueser, 1996, 2002). **A brain predisposed to schizophrenia can be activated and a psychotic episode triggered by psychedelic abuse.** One mental disorder, hallucinogen persisting perception disorder (HPPD), is marked by the transient recurrence of disturbances of perception (flashbacks) similar to those experienced while actually using a hallucinogen. The symptoms are disturbing and can cause impairment in everyday functioning. They may disappear in a few months or may last for years.

DUAL DIAGNOSIS (CO-OCCURRING DISORDERS)

DEFINITION

Increasing numbers of individuals are under treatment for co-occurring disorders, which are defined as **the existence in an individual of at least one mental disorder along with an alcohol or drug use disorder.** This means that a cocaine abuser might also have a psychosis even when not using the drug. An alcoholic might be severely depressed even when clean-and-sober. A further example is a person with a preexisting attention-deficit/hyperactivity disorder (ADHD) who has become dependent on methamphetamine and self-medicates his condition. Although *co-occurring disorders* is the most common term in the substance-abuse and mental health fields, other terms, such as *comorbidity, double trouble, substance-abusing mentally ill (SAMI), mentally ill chemical abuser (MICA),* and especially *dual diagnosis,* have also been used (SAMHSA, 2002B). In this chapter **we use *co-occurring disorders* and dual diagnosis interchangeably.**

"After more than 30 years of use, when I gave up the codeine and the Valium® in treatment, I started to remember the pain. You know, the first thing that flashed through my mind was my uncle's face when he was hurting me real bad when I was 10. I hadn't remembered it for 32 years."
45-year-old female with major depression

"The previous patient is a case where the diagnosis becomes clearer the longer she is clean-and-sober. She appears to have suffered from a major depressive disorder, but there's also evidence of a post-traumatic stress disorder. The symptoms for the PTSD did not emerge until she was able to remain clean-and-sober for a period of time. Her treatment would necessarily include the simultaneous addressing of her substance abuse and mental health problems."
Pablo Stewart, M.D.

The mental health conditions most often diagnosed as part of a dual diagnosis fall into **two categories**: preexisting and substance induced. Examples of **pre-existing mental disorders** are:

◇ **thought disorders** (psychotic disorders), such as schizophrenia;

◇ **mood disorders** (affective disorders), such as major depressive disorder and bipolar disorder; and

◇ **anxiety disorders**, such as panic disorders, obsessive-compulsive disorders, post-traumatic stress disorder, and ADHD

(APA, 2000; Friedmann, Saitz & Samer, 2003; Levin, Sullivan & Donovan, 2003; Lilenfeld & Kaye, 1996; McElroy, Soutullo, Goldsmith, et al., 2003; Salloum & Daley, 1994; Schuckit, 2000).

Examples of **substance-induced mental disorders** are:

◇ **stimulant-induced psychotic disorders**,

◇ **alcohol-induced mood disorders**, and

◇ **marijuana-induced delirium**.

"I have this illness, mental illness, with manic depression, and when I take the alcohol, my functioning isn't as clear cut, not as sharp as, say, the average person who isn't suffering any mental problems."
52-year-old with a dual diagnosis

It is important to distinguish between having symptoms of mental illness and actually having a major psychiatric disorder. Everyone feels blue and sad sometimes. Everyone has the capacity for grief and loneliness, but this does not mean that a person is medically depressed, requiring medication or psychiatric treatment. It's really **a question of severity and persistence of the symptoms** (APA, 2000; Woody, 1996; Zimberg, 1999). The connection between substance abuse and mental disorders is real. One study found that the chance of major depression combined with alcoholism in women was substantially higher and probably was mainly the result of genetic factors, but environment still had an influence (Kendler, Heath, Neale, et al., 1993).

It is common for people who are abusing substances to present with symptoms of a personality disorder, particularly borderline or antisocial personality disorders. As a person achieves and maintains sobriety, however, **the majority of the symptoms of the personality disorder will often dissipate** unless the person has a pre-existing condition. There is much debate as to the actual prevalence of personality disorders.

EPIDEMIOLOGY

In an earlier study published in *Journal of the American Medical Association*, **44% of alcohol abusers and 64.4% of other substance abusers actually admitted for treatment had, in addition to their drug problem, at least one serious mental illness** (Regier, Farmer, Rae, et al., 1990). In another study, in Taiwan, about 60% of those seeking treatment for heroin addiction had at least one Axis I psychiatric disorder (Chiang, Chan, Chang, et al., 2007). Certain drugs increase the likelihood of mental

illness. For example, three-fourths of cocaine abusers had a diagnosable mental disorder as did half of all compulsive marijuana users. The majority of the mental illnesses were caused by substances, although some users were self-medicating their pre-existing psychiatric disorders with street drugs (Dennison, 2005; Kessler, Berglund, Demler, et al., 2005).

"I believe I had depression all along, even before I started using, and so through alcohol, marijuana, and even heroin, I was treating that depression."
24-year-old with a dual diagnosis

Conversely, 29% to 34% of all mentally ill people had a problem with either alcohol or other drugs (Merikangas, Stevens & Fenton, 1996; Regier, Farmer, Rae, et al., 1990). The overlap is even greater with certain mental disorders: 61% of people with bipolar disorder and 47% of people with a thought disorder also had a problem with substance abuse. Finally, in prisons the prevalence of a psychiatric illness when the prisoner had an addictive disorder was a remarkable 81%.

Unfortunately, **of the 7 million to 13 million people who do have co-occurring disorders**, about 23% received mental health care only and 9% received substance-abuse treatment only, leaving just 8% who received both and 60% who received none (Watkins, Burnam, Kung, et al., 2001).

PATTERNS OF DUAL DIAGNOSIS

Which substance is used and how it is used help determine the two general patterns of dual diagnosis.

PRE-EXISTING MENTAL ILLNESS

One kind of dual diagnosis involves **the person who has a clearly defined mental illness and then gets involved in drugs** (e.g., the teen with major depression who discovers amphetamines). Here the **drugs are often used to self-medicate symptoms of the mental illness.**

"My mom asked my little brother if he thought I'd been depressed a lot in my life, and he said I'd been depressed ever since he could remember. The speed got me out of it except when I was coming down."

16-year-old male

The presence of a pre-existing mental illness does not prevent the user from developing a substance-abuse condition. Therefore **mentally ill people often have a concurrent substance-abuse problem that does not involve self-medication**. An example of this would be a schizophrenic who also suffers from alcoholism.

SUBSTANCE-INDUCED MENTAL ILLNESS

This type of dual diagnosis happens when there isn't a pre-existing problem. **As a result of substance abuse and/or withdrawal, the user develops psychiatric problems** because the toxic effects of the drug disrupt the brain chemistry (Drake & Mueser, 1996; Ziedonis, Steinberg, Simelson, et al., 2003). The **imbalance in the brain chemistry in this type of diagnosis is usually temporary, and with abstinence the mental illness will disappear** within a few weeks to a year (Smith & Seymour, 2001). A significant number of these problems, however, manifest as unresolved and chronic mental illnesses. This is more likely to occur in those with a pre-existing susceptibility to mental illness.

"My initial flip-out was in 1986 after snorting 'crank' for six weeks straight, about half a gram a day. I started hearing voices and thinking that my phones were tapped. Friends brought me to the psychiatric hospital, where I was treated with antipsychotic medication. My diagnosis was methamphetamine-induced psychotic disorder."

28-year-old with a dual diagnosis

Substance-induced mental disorders include delirium, dementia, per-

sisting amnestic disorder, psychotic disorder, mood disorder, anxiety disorder, sexual dysfunction, sleep disorder, and hallucinogen persisting perception disorder.

"This speed run's only been 13 days, but I get these sores and I get paranoid and real crazy. After I come down, it'll be weird. It will take weeks to get back into shape. And all that other crap will disappear."

43-year-old heavy intravenous (IV) methamphetamine addict

MAKING THE DIAGNOSIS

ASSESSMENT

When people see a friend or relative acting oddly and having trouble coping with everyday life over a pro-

longed period, they don't know whether to ascribe that difficulty to relationship problems, trouble at home, drug use, or mental illness. Substance-abuse and mental health professionals have the same problem, as is evident from the variations in diagnoses of the many mental health disorders cited earlier in this chapter. Thus when assessing mental illness in a substance abuser, a general rule used by treatment professionals is that **the initial diagnosis should be a "rule-out" diagnosis. This means that several possible diagnoses will be considered during the period of assessment.**

"The doctor told me that a person who drank for 25 years like me would probably take a year to clear. That was one reason why I never figured out that I was manic depressive. I didn't notice it. I figured I was depressed because I was drunk all the time."

35-year-old male with a dual diagnosis

Because many psychiatric symptoms can be the result of drug toxicity and/or withdrawal, it is incorrect to immediately assume that all of these symptoms are due to a pre-existing mental illness. **The prudent clinician addresses all symptoms but avoids making a specific psychiatric diagnosis until the drug abuser has had time to get sober** and beyond drug withdrawal (Senay, 1997; Shivani, Goldsmith & Anthenelli, 2002).

"I was on opiates and antidepressants, and I would have very severe respiratory problems at night, got no sleep, wanted to crawl out of my skin. I was paranoid. I thought that everybody was against me, and it probably took me a good two weeks of being in treatment to be completely through withdrawals. The nice thing about coming into treatment is they do taper you. They help you through those first few days of withdrawal when you feel like you want to die."

38-year-old pharmaceutical opiate abuser

Factors that may influence the diagnosis include:

◇ the particular pattern of substance use,

◇ the presence of a pre-existing mental illness,

◇ the evidence of any self-medication,

◇ the age of onset of any psychiatric symptoms, and

◇ the relationship of the psychiatric symptoms to the substance use.

Reasons for Increased Diagnoses

There are several possible reasons why the number of dual-diagnosis clients on the streets seems dramatically higher in the 1990s and 2000s than during the 1960s and 1970s:

◇ The **number of inpatient mental health facilities has diminished** (Figure 10-3) due to decreasing mental health budgets, decreasing mental health coverage by HMOs and other insurance programs, and

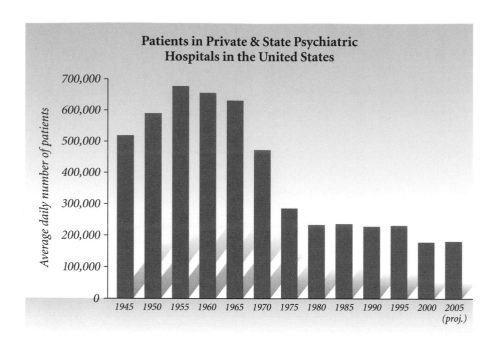

Figure 10-3 •

The psychiatric hospital census has gone down while the number of people diagnosed with mental illnesses has gone up.

occasionally misguided government policies on mental health support.

◇ There is a **proliferation of substances of abuse**, particularly stimulants. Because cocaine, methamphetamines, and psycho-stimulants are more toxic to brain chemistry than most substances (except inhalants and alcohol), people with fragile brain chemistry are more likely to be pushed over the edge into chronic neurochemical imbalance and mental illness (Keller & Dermatis, 1999).

◇ The **increasing number and greater expertise of licensed professionals** working in the field of chemical dependency treatment have resulted in a greater recognition and documentation of dual diagnosis.

◇ The **increasing awareness of substance abuse and its effects by mental health workers** has resulted in their increased recognition of it as an important co-occurring condition.

◇ Managed care and diagnosis-related group payments for treat-

ment services usually provide more financial incentives for the treatment of multiple medical and psychiatric problems than for just addiction treatment (Guydish & Muck, 1999). These **payment structures can pressure some clinicians to overdiagnose mental illness in the substance abuser** (Smith, Lawlor & Seymour, 1996; Soderstrom, Smith, Dischinger, et al., 1997).

For these reasons an increasing number of people with psychiatric disorders have been forced to deal with their problems on an outpatient basis or on their own. Being detached from hospital supervision, clients are more likely to exhibit poor control of their prescribed medication, thus aggravating their mental problems and making them more likely to turn to street drugs for relief.

All of these factors have also led to increases in mentally ill homeless people, whose problems are exacerbated by the lack of a support system. The number of homeless (sheltered and unsheltered) in the United States in any given week is estimated at 754,000 (Department of Housing and Urban Development, 2007). Approximately one-half to two-thirds of this homeless population meets diagnostic criteria for substance dependence. **At least 25% of the total homeless population also suffers from pre-existing mental illness. Of the mentally ill homeless, more than 70% suffer from substance dependence** (Crome, 1999; Rahav, Rivera, Nuttbrock, 1995).

"I had used heroin to control my depression sort of as a mood stabilizer, so withdrawing from it caused an even worse depression. When I came out of the sort of fog from the first five days of not having it, I felt better, but the pink cloud feeling vanished quite quickly and was replaced with the depression that I was used to."
45-year-old with major depression

UNDERSTANDING THE DUAL-DIAGNOSIS PATIENT

Understanding and adapting to the treatment complexities of the client with a mental health problem and a substance-abuse problem is a challenge for treatment professionals.

"When I went into the hospital, I would tell them I had a problem, that I was on Valium® and codeine. The first thing they would then give me was a shot of Valium.® I told them that Valium® addiction was one of my problems. They still gave it to me."
40-year-old female with a dual diagnosis

In the past, inability to treat a person who manifested both substance-abuse and mental problems, combined with an outright refusal to develop treatment strategies for the dual-diagnosis client, resulted in inappropriate and potentially dangerous interactions with clients. **They were often shuffled aimlessly back and forth between the mental health care system and the substance-abuse treatment system without receiving adequate care from either.** Even though there's been an increase in facilities that address the dual-diagnosis client, inap-

propriate care is all too often still the rule rather than the exception. Budget considerations and a lack of expertise have much to do with this problem.

Substance-abuse treatment facilities do not usually want these patients because they see them as too disorganized and too disruptive or, in many cases, too inattentive to participate in group therapy, which is frequently the core element of treatment. **Psychiatric treatment centers also avoid these patients because they're perceived as substance abusers, disruptive, and manipulative.** They also frequently relapse into active substance abuse that interferes with medications used to treat mental illnesses (Wu, Kouzis & Leaf, 1999).

MENTAL HEALTH VS. SUBSTANCE ABUSE

The following list comprises 12 differences that have existed between the mental health (MH) treatment community and the substance-abuse (SA) treatment community. Although certain difficulties persist, these two communities are moving toward a closer working relationship. An increasing number of facilities employ both mental health and substance-abuse treatment staff and take a team approach to treatment. They offer on-site treatment for the dual-diagnosis client or at least provide a cross-referral team approach to a separate mental health treatment provider.

1. **MH treatment providers used to say, "Control the underlying psychiatric problem, and the drug abuse will disappear." SA treatment providers used to say, "Get the patient clean-and-sober, and the mental health problems will resolve themselves."** While these statements have some validity, both disciplines are recognizing that perhaps one-third to three-fourths of their clients are legitimately dually diagnosed and require concurrent treatment of both the substance-abuse and the mental health problems.

2. **In the MH system, partial recovery from one's problems is more**

readily acceptable than in SA programs, where most professionals believe that lifelong abstinence from all abused drugs, including alcohol and marijuana, is necessary. This abstinence and a supporting program of recovery coupled with a rigorous SA treatment are necessary for ongoing recovery in a dual-diagnosis client.

3. **Clients are more reluctant to seek help from the MH system than from SA treatment programs.** This is probably because of the stigma attached to mental illness. Clients and their families hope that the problem is only addiction from which they believe they can recover more fully than they can from mental illness. With women substance abusers, so much stigma and negative stereotypes are attached to their condition that many seek mental health treatment to actually address their chemical dependency problem.

"I tell members of my family that I'm in a halfway house for drug addiction as opposed to mental health because it seems with drug addiction I can get better, but with mental health, people see it as a chronic long-term problem."
19-year-old dually diagnosed male with major depression

4. **MH relies more on medication to treat the client whereas SA programs tend to be divided between promoting a drug-free philosophy and substituting a less-damaging drug such as methadone in a harm reduction maintenance program.** Increasingly, medically oriented SA programs, as opposed to social model SA programs, utilize medications to help clients detoxify before getting them into a long-term drug-free philosophy.

"I refused to take any psychiatric medication for a long time. I thought you had to be really crazy to take it, and I thought that this was a big conflict that would limit my recovery. If I take medication, I'm a drug addict.

But I'm glad I'm taking it now. I'm able to sleep and think better."

35-year-old with major depression

5. **MH uses case management, shepherding clients from one service to another, whereas SA programs have traditionally emphasized self-reliance** because they neither want to enable clients nor make clients transfer their dependence to the program. In spite of that, case management is being used in many SA treatment programs. Traditional SA treatment staff now utilize outside resources to provide a more holistic treatment approach. SA programs that do not have in-house mental health treatment capacity should refer their dual-diagnosis clients to outside agencies to receive appropriate mental health care simultaneous with their SA treatment.

6. **MH has traditionally utilized a supportive psychotherapeutic approach, whereas many SA programs continue to use confrontation techniques** that many MH professionals think are inappropriate. A major conflict often occurs when a patient is not responding to traditional SA treatment because he also suffers from a psychiatric disorder. **One can't use the same behavioral threshold to terminate a dual-diagnosis patient from treatment as one would with someone who suffers only from substance abuse.** In programs that provide dual-diagnosis services, the staff needs to learn to recognize psychiatric symptoms that can often interfere with SA treatment. It is inappropriate to discharge patients from treatment who are psychiatrically unstable.

7. **Both the MH system and the SA system have problems with sharing information** because of confidentiality laws and regulations. In general, however, MH shares information with allied fields more readily than does SA.

8. In **MH the treatment team is composed of professionally prepared individuals**: social workers, nurses, psychiatrists, psychologists, and licensed counselors. **In some SA programs, recovering substance abusers often make up the bulk of the treatment staff.** Personal recovery does not prepare someone to professionally treat substance abusers, and most states now require special training and credentialing to be able to work with addicts, although "having been there" does engender an instant credibility among substance abusers. All staff working with mentally ill substance abusers also require specialized professional preparation to adequately treat these difficult patients.

9. **MH relies on scientifically based treatment approaches. SA programs often rely on the philosophy "what works for me will work for you."** No longer can traditional SA treatment programs rely solely on self-experience and tradition. MH staff, however, can learn much from traditional SA treatment especially as it applies to spirituality in recovery.

"All I can tell someone is, 'I have a problem. I don't know which way you're going to deal with it or tackle it, but I have a problem, and I can't function, and I need help.'"

Dual-diagnosis patient with major depression

10. **MH pays a lot of attention to the idea of preventing the client from getting worse. In the past, SA programs, taking their cue from early 12-step fellowship beliefs, had a tendency to allow people to hit bottom to break through their denial.** Most SA programs now see that approach as outmoded and dangerous. To engage people in treatment, they rely more on motivational interviewing, a way to help people recognize and do something about their problems. It is particularly useful with people who are reluctant to change or are ambivalent about changing (Miller & Rollnick, 2000; Pantalon & Swanson, 2003). The dual-diagnosis client needs support throughout the change process, much more so than the single-diagnosis client (Finnell, 2003).

11. **In MH, treatment is individualized, whereas many traditional SA programs tend to be "one size fits all."** Best practices dictate that appropriate techniques from both disciplines be utilized with the dual-diagnosis patient because both conditions require simultaneous treatment. Traditional education approaches used in SA treatment must be integrated into individualized mental health treatment plans.

12. **MH and SA education during treatment are structured and knowledge based, but SA education also places importance on long-held traditions and peer experiences.** Expanding information from scientific discoveries of the brain and its functioning has increased the understanding and the knowledge of both MH and SA. Many of these discoveries support the long-standing traditions of chemical dependency treatment, and peer experiences remain a valuable relapse prevention resource.

Although the situation may be improving from the perspective of the MH treatment community, dual diagnosis has represented an almost insurmountable challenge to the clinical expertise of the staff of SA programs. Their assessment skills and even their underlying concept of recovery or sobriety have been challenged by patients with a dual diagnosis. It can be difficult to differentiate pre-existing mental illness from a substance-induced mental illness. **Patients are often misdiagnosed with mental illness early in the treatment or assessment processes, resulting in their being referred to MH programs that all too often reject them because of their concurrent SA problems.**

SA programs often resist developing the expertise needed to diagnose and treat MH problems. Fiscal and other limited-resource problems prevent the expansion of their services to meet the needs of dual-diagnosis clients, creating a tendency to establish

MH problems as an exclusionary criteria for treatment admission or continued treatment in many SA programs. Even SA programs with expertise in mental health often mistake psychoactive substance-induced mental illness for proof that there is an existing psychiatric diagnosis.

RECOMMENDATIONS

"Our consumers do not have the opportunity to separate their addiction from their mental illness, so why should we do so administratively and programmatically?"
(Osher, 2001)

Research over the past decade confirms that **the dual-diagnosis patient must be treated for both disorders simultaneously.** They are best treated **in a single program when appropriate resources are available** (Kosten & Ziedonis, 1997). Where programs equipped to handle dual-diagnosis cases are not available, **SA programs need to establish links with MH service providers and vice versa** so that they can work together in providing the client with their combined treatment expertise. This is particularly important because when patients are admitted for treatment for psychiatric problems, they are more willing to acknowledge coexisting SA problems and more receptive to facing the need for additional treatment (RachBeisel, Dixon & Gearon, 1999).

Each discipline needs to recognize that MH and SA treatments are both long-term propositions; and therefore **they need to establish both short-term and long-range services to address the problems of dual diagnosis** (Minkoff & Regner, 1999). Recent research also suggests that incorporating behavioral (motivational) approaches to substance-abuse treatment is more effective for the dual-diagnosis client because the structure is better suited to overcoming cognitive difficulties that accompany schizophrenia and certain other mental illnesses (Drake, Mercer-McFadden, Mueser, et al., 1998). Most important, some research has found that **intensive case management was associated with the greatest improvement in dual-diagnosis clients.** A smaller

but measurable improvement was also shown with standard aftercare and outpatient psychoeducational groups (Dumaine, 2003). A recent study found that existing effective treatments for reducing psychiatric symptoms also tend to work in dual-diagnosis patients and, conversely, existing effective treatments for reducing substance use also decrease substance use in dual-diagnosis patients (Tiet & Mausbach, 2007).

MULTIPLE DIAGNOSES

As the substance-abuse treatment community becomes more aware of other simultaneous disorders that complicate the treatment of addiction, it must be willing to accept new challenges, such as:

◇ **multiple drug (polydrug) abuse;**
◇ **other medical disorders** such as chronic pain syndrome, fibromyalgia, hepatitis, epilepsy, cancer, heart and kidney disease, diabetes, sickle cell anemia, and even sexual dysfunction; and
◇ **triple diagnosis** (dual diagnosis complicated by the presence of HIV disease).

"One of the biggest things that caused me the most anxiety is, you know, I'm HIV positive and I really started having problems with sleep. I found that out and I was really torn between cleaning up and staying clean or just going out and using. I felt like, Well, I'm going to die anyway, a nasty horrible death, and I had nightmares and then my feelings surfaced to a point where a lot of other feelings came up about old stuff."
Recovering HIV-positive alcohol abuser with a general anxiety disorder

The literature is very clear that **when people are dually diagnosed, they must achieve sobriety from all drugs of abuse, not just their drug of choice.** This means that recovering heroin addicts, for example, need to refrain from alcohol and marijuana use even though they have never had a stated problem with these substances.

Research using the Addiction Severity Index links successful substance-abuse treatment with addressing a person's medical problems. **Substance-abuse treatment therefore must be linked to appropriate medical care for clients to achieve any degree of long-term sobriety.** This includes the treatment of legitimate pain syndromes that may require narcotic analgesics. Substance-abuse treatment programs need to creatively incorporate the treatment of legitimate pain syndromes into their overall approaches.

Of special significance is the **epidemic growth of hepatitis C and other severe liver diseases in chemically dependent patients**. The prevalence of hepatitis C in IV drug users is now much greater than that of HIV, emphasizing the need to avoid hepatotoxic drugs, especially alcohol.

In addition, a variety of medical disabilities such as hearing or mobility impairment, social concerns including cultural attitudes toward chemical dependency and mental health treatment, and language barriers may also provide impediments to successful treatment of those with multiple diagnoses.

Although not a disability issue, women, particularly those who are pregnant and/or parenting, have special treatment needs. For example, women process psychiatric medications differently than men and will have higher plasma levels for a given dose of a prescribed drug and therefore need lower doses (Zweben, 1996). In addition, programs that treat the pregnant woman's addiction or her mental illness are usually organized separately, thus the pregnant addict with a mental illness can receive conflicting information (Grella, 1996). Finally, the health risks to the fetus or newborn are greatly increased because both drug use and mental illness interfere with the normal nurturing qualities of a mother (Mallouh, 1996). **These problems require the development of future drug programs that are holistic, use several modalities, and are multidisciplinary** to meet the challenge of the evolving complicated clinical needs of the chemically dependent patient (Gourevitch & Arnsten, 2005).

Triple diagnosis is defined as the presence of an HIV infection in the

dual-diagnosis client. Persons with AIDS, an AIDS-related condition, or an HIV-positive blood test or who are a partner of someone with AIDS require additional treatment expertise and specific services to effectively address their chemical dependency.

As the AIDS epidemic has progressed out of the gay and IV drug-using populations and into the cocaine- and other drug-using heterosexual populations, **triple diagnosis is straining health department resources and further complicating treatment** (Wechsberg, Desmond, Inciardi, et al., 1998).

"When we looked at the first 49 consecutive HIV-infected patients who came in to our substance-abuse services at San Francisco General Hospital, the bottom line was that 84% had some Axis I psychiatric diagnosis. A third had depressive disorders, and another third had anxiety disorders. And 18% had organic brain syndromes, mild-to-moderate dementia, or organic psychosis."

Steven L. Batki, M.D., psychiatrist, medical director, San Francisco General Hospital Substance Abuse Services

According to the National Treatment Improvement Evaluation Study, **dual-diagnosis patients were more likely to share a needle, have sex for money, have sex with an IV drug user, and report being raped** than someone with no psychiatric co-occurring disorder. Dual-diagnosis clients should be targeted for more-intense HIV interventions to avoid adding AIDS to their difficulties (Dausey & Desai, 2003; Parry, Blank & Pithey, 2007).

NOTE: The following sections will examine the different kinds of psychiatric disorders; discuss the relationships among heredity, environment, and psychoactive drugs as related to mental illness and drug addiction; and then examine the various treatments available for the mentally ill substance-abusing patient, particularly the use of psychotropic medications in therapy.

PSYCHIATRIC DISORDERS

"A neurotic is the person who builds a castle in the air. A psychotic is the person who lives in it. And a psychiatrist is the person who collects the rent."

Anonymous

Overall about 21% of the U.S. population is affected by one or more mental disorders during a given year (Table 10-1). Anxiety disorders are the most prevalent, followed by mood disorders (especially depression). Schizophrenia is extremely debilitating but occurs much less frequently than anxiety or mood disorders (NIMH, 1999).

PRE-EXISTING MENTAL DISORDERS

Although there are hundreds of mental illnesses as classified by the mental health community, the following are the principal ones that are most often associated with co-occurring disorders.

Thought Disorder (schizophrenia)

Schizophrenia is a chronic psychotic illness that affects approximately 0.5 to 1.5% of the population. There are many other psychiatric illnesses that have psychotic symptoms as part of their presentation. These include but are not limited to schizoaffective disorder, schizophreniform dis-

TABLE 10–1   BRAIN DISORDERS IN AMERICANS (ONE-YEAR PREVALENCE)

Diagnosis	Percentage of Adults 18 to 54	Percentage of Adults 55 & Older	Percentage of Children & Adolescents
Schizophrenia	**1.3%**	**0.6%**	**1.2%**
Mood disorders	**7.1%**	**4.4%**	**6.2%**
bipolar I disorder	1.1%	0.2%	
major depressive episode	5.3%	3.8%	
unipolar major depression	5.3%	3.7%	
Anxiety disorders	**16.4%**	**11.4%**	**13.0%**
obsessive-compulsive disorder	2.4%	1.5%	
panic disorder	1.6%	0.5%	
simple phobia	8.3%	7.3%	
social phobia	2.0%		
generalized anxiety disorder	3.4%		
post-traumatic stress disorder	3.6%		
agoraphobia	4.9%	4.1%	
Any brain disorder (one person might have multiple disorders)	**21.0%**	**19.8%**	**20.9%**

(NIMH, 1999; Shaffer, Fisher, Dulcan, et al., 1996)

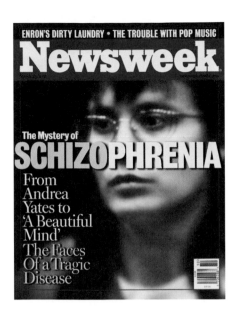

order, paranoid type, bipolar disorder with psychotic features, major depressive disorder with psychotic features, delusional disorder, and substance-induced psychotic disorder.

A thought disorder such as schizophrenia is believed to be mostly inherited. It is characterized by:

◇ **hallucinations** (false visual, auditory, or tactile sensations and perceptions),

◇ **delusions** (false beliefs),

◇ **inappropriate affect** (an illogical emotional response to a given situation),

◇ **ambivalence** (difficulty making even the simplest decisions),

◇ **poor association** (difficulty connecting thoughts and ideas),

◇ **impaired ability to care for oneself,**

◇ **autistic symptoms** (a pronounced detachment from reality),

◇ **disorganized speech,**

◇ **poor job performance,** and

◇ **strained social relations.**

Depending on the subtype, one or more of the signs must be present for at least one month (or, for some, six months) for the diagnosis to be made (APA, 2000). Delusions and hallucinations are the key symptoms.

"I was hearing voices, and the voices wouldn't go away, and they followed

me wherever I went. I got into creating scenarios as to who they were and what they were doing."
28-year-old male with schizophrenia

Schizophrenia usually strikes individuals in their late teens or early adulthood and can be with them for life, although occasionally there is spontaneous remission. Schizophrenia is extremely destructive to those with the illness as well as to their friends and families.

When diagnosing schizophrenia, clinicians try to determine which psychoactive drugs the patient is using. When these are not taken into consideration, clinicians may end up with a false or incomplete diagnosis. Clinicians can accomplish this assessment by taking a thorough medical history, interviewing close friends and family, and/or using urinalysis or hair analysis. Unfortunately, a large percentage of drug and alcohol problems are still missed.

Several abused drugs mimic schizophrenia and psychosis, producing symptoms that can be easily misdiagnosed:

◇ **Cocaine and amphetamines can cause a toxic psychosis** (especially when used to excess) that is almost indistinguishable from a true paranoid psychosis.

◇ **Steroids can also cause a psychosis.** Steroid-induced paranoia can be indistinguishable from true paranoia.

◇ **Uppers, such as MDMA** (ecstasy) and related stimulant/hallucinogens, **and even marijuana can cause paranoia**.

◇ The **psychedelics,** such as LSD, peyote (mescaline), psilocybin, and PCP, **disassociate users from their surroundings**, so hallucinogenic abuse can also be mistaken for a thought disorder.

◇ **Alcohol abuse** causes thiamin (vitamin B_1) deficiency, which results in brain damage known as Wernicke's encephalopathy and Korsakoff's psychosis (Wernicke-Korsakoff syndrome).

◇ Also, **withdrawal from downers can be mistaken for a thought disorder because of extreme agitation.**

Many of the drug-induced psychiatric symptoms should disappear as the body's drug levels subside upon detoxification and treatment (Delgado & Moreno, 1998; Senay, 1997, 1998).

Major Depressive Disorder

Mood disorders (affective disorders) include major depressive disorder, bipolar affective disorder, and dysthymia (mild depression). They are the second most prevalent psychiatric disorders after anxiety disorders. **Almost 15% of Americans will experience a major depressive disorder in their lifetime; 8.6% in any one-year period** (Kessler, Berglund, Demler, et al., 2003). It has been estimated that depression costs employers $44 billion per year. Depressed people may make it to work, but their performance is substandard. And though more Americans are seeking help for their depression, only one-fourth of the total are receiving adequate help (Stewart, Ricci, Chee, et al., 2003).

Major depression is characterized by depressed mood, diminished interest and diminished pleasure in most activities, disturbances of sleep patterns and appetite, decreased ability to concentrate, feelings of worthlessness, and suicidal thoughts (APA, 2000). All of these symptoms may persist without any life situation to provoke them. For example, a patient with major depression may win a lot of money in a lottery and respond to it by staying depressed. For the diagnosis of major depression, **these feelings must occur every day, most of the day, for at least one week running.** Causes such as medical illness or drug abuse would probably rule out a diagnosis of major depression as would natural reactions to a divorce, a strained relationship, or the death of a loved one. These conditions, however, can cause the susceptible individual to develop major depression.

"The depression just came when it wanted to come. I just sat there and thought about something and I got depressed. The anger came because every male that has ever been in my life has beaten me or used me, you know, mentally and physically—not sexually thank goodness."
17-year-old male with major depression

Excessive alcohol use, stimulant withdrawal (cocaine or amphetamine), and the comedown or resolution phase of a psychedelic (LSD or ecstasy) result in temporary drug-induced depression that is almost indistinguishable from that of major depression but will clear in time with the completion of withdrawal or comedown. Depression and/or anxiety found in substance abusers are, in about 80% of the cases, due to the drugs and not to a pre-existing mental disorder (Nunes, Donovan, Brady, et al., 1994).

Bipolar Affective Disorder

Bipolar affective disorder (formerly called "manic depression") is **characterized by alternating periods of depression, normalcy, and mania.** The depression phase is described above. The depression is as severe as that which occurs in major depression. If untreated, **many bipolar patients have frequent suicide attempts**.

The mania, on the other hand, is characterized by:

◇ **a persistently elevated, expansive, and irritated mood;**

◇ **inflated self-esteem or grandiosity;**

◇ **decreased need for sleep;**

◇ **the pressure to keep talking** and being more talkative than usual;

◇ **flight of ideas;**

◇ **distractibility;**

◇ an increase in goal-directed activity or psychomotor agitation; and

◇ **excessive involvement in pleasurable activities** that have a high potential for painful consequences (e.g., drug abuse, gambling, or inappropriate sexual advances often leading to unsafe sex) (APA, 2000).

These symptoms can be severe enough to cause marked impairment in job, social activities, and relationships.

"The manic feeling is a real feeling of elation and euphoria. There's that grinding angry sort of—I don't really get angry and violent, well I did in jail, but I don't really want to hurt anybody or anything. And as far as being depressed goes, I can really say I've only been depressed about three times, once to the point of being suicidal."
30-year-old male with bipolar disorder

Bipolar affective disorder usually begins in a person's twenties and affects men and women equally. Many researchers believe that this disease is genetic. **Toxic effects of stimulant or psychedelic abuse will often resemble a bipolar disorder.** Users experience swings from mania to depression, depending on the phase of the drug's action, the surroundings, and their own subconscious feelings and beliefs. More than half of those with a bipolar diagnosis (56%) have an alcohol use disorder (Regier, Farmer, Rae, et al., 1990; Sonne & Brady, 2002). Integrated group therapy, a new treatment developed specifically for patients with bipolar disorder and substance dependence, seems to be effective in treating this condition (Weiss, Griffin, Kolodziej, et al., 2007).

OTHER PSYCHIATRIC DISORDERS

Anxiety Disorders

Anxiety disorders are the most common psychiatric disturbances seen in medical offices. About 16% of adults (18 to 54 years old) will experience an anxiety disorder in a given year (NIMH, 1999). There are a number of anxiety disorders.

Post-Traumatic Stress Disorder. PTSD is a **persistent reexperiencing of a traumatic event** that involved actual or threatened death or a serious threat or injury (e.g., combat, a physical/sexual assault, or a motor vehicle accident) to one's physical integrity. The event can be experienced personally or witnessed. Associated symptoms include intense fear and horror as well as persistent avoidance of stimuli associated with the trauma and persistent symptoms of increased arousal (e.g., sleep problems, irritability, anger, and hypervigilance). This disorder can be chronic in nature and very disabling (Reilly, Clark, Shopshire, et al., 1994). One study estimated that **20% to 25% of those in treatment for substance use disorders may have PTSD** (Brady, 1999). At Veterans Administration (VA) hospitals, treatment centers, and domiciliaries, the incidence of PTSD among substance abusers is even higher (Ruzek, 2003). PTSD is twice as common in women as in men, often due to physical and sexual abuse. A recent Veterans Affairs multisite study found that people with PTSD who used cocaine were worse off on presentment for treatment and took longer to recover (Najavits, Harned, Gallop, et al., 2007).

"I broke down after about six months over in Vietnam, and I was in charge of a gun crew. And when I broke down from seeing the deaths and all the abuse over there, some people's lives were lost. I'm responsible and it hurts. When I was medically evacuated back to the States, I immediately jumped into alcohol and heroin."
Vietnam veteran with PTSD

Panic Disorder. This is another common anxiety disorder. **It consists of recurrent unexpected panic attacks.** The person also has a persistent concern about having additional attacks, worries about the implications of having an attack, and changes behavior due to the attacks. **A panic attack is a discreet period of intense fear or discomfort in the absence of real danger** that is accompanied by at least four of the following 13 somatic or cognitive symptoms: **palpitations, sweating, trembling or shaking, sensations of shortness of breath** or smothering, feeling of choking, chest pain or discomfort, nausea or abdominal distress, dizziness or lightheadedness, derealization or depersonalization, fear of losing control or of going crazy, fear of dying, paresthesias (numbness), and chills or hot flushes. The attack has a sudden onset and builds to a peak rapidly (usually in 10 minutes or less); it is often accompanied by a sense of imminent danger or impending doom and an urge to escape (APA, 2000).

"I'd be waiting for my prescription at a drugstore and someone would just look at me and all of a sudden my whole

body just went inside itself and I started shaking. My heart was racing. I couldn't say anything. I was just in total panic. I couldn't move. My mind kept saying there's nothing to be scared of, but I couldn't control it. I had no idea what really triggered it. My husband would come up and hold me and sit there and say, 'Breathe.' And after a couple of minutes, I would be all right and I would use one of my pills for anxiety, Lorazepam,® a benzodiazepine. I think that my use of cocaine over a period of several years messed up my neurochemistry, particularly my adrenaline system."

50-year-old female with a panic disorder

Panic attacks can occur in someone who has a panic disorder or a major depressive disorder as well as in a cardiac patient experiencing tachycardia. Panic attacks can also be induced by stimulants, psychedelics, and marijuana.

Other anxiety disorders include:

◇ **agoraphobia** without a history of panic disorder (a generalized fear of open spaces);

◇ **social phobia**, the fear of being seen by others as acting in a humiliating or embarrassing way (e.g., fear of eating in public);

◇ **simple phobia**, an irrational fear of a specific thing or place; and

◇ **obsessive-compulsive disorder**, uncontrollable intrusive thoughts and irresistible and often distressing actions, such as checking that a door is locked or repeated hand washing.

"I had a number of obsessions. The obvious one right now is my hair. I cut my hair obsessively in a crew cut, constantly, by my own hand. The thought would just come into my mind. It was something I didn't really have control over. I would smoke marijuana almost as compulsively as I cut my hair."

Client with an obsessive-compulsive disorder

Generalized Anxiety Disorder (GAD). GAD is defined by unrealistic worry about several life situations that lasts for six months or longer. It is another common anxiety disorder along with several miscellaneous disorders such as acute stress disorder (APA, 2000).

Sometimes it is extremely difficult to differentiate among the anxiety disorders. Many are defined more by symptoms than by specific names. Some of the more common symptoms of anxiety disorders are shortness of breath, muscle tension, restlessness, stomach irritation, sweating, palpitations, hypervigilance, difficulty concentrating, and excessive worry. **Often anxiety and depression are mixed together.** Some physicians think that many anxiety disorders are really an outgrowth of depression (Nitenson & Gastfriend, 2003).

Toxic effects of stimulant drugs and withdrawal from opioids, sedatives, and alcohol (downers) also cause symptoms similar to those described in anxiety disorders and can be easily misdiagnosed as such (Nunes, Donovan, Brady, et al., 1994). In one study of college students, the odds of having an anxiety disorder were much greater if alcohol abuse and dependence were present; and the odds of having alcohol dependence were also greater if an anxiety disorder was present (Kushner, Sher & Erickson, 1999). The effect of excessive caffeine, especially in susceptible individuals, should not be overlooked.

Dementias

These are **problems of brain dysfunction brought on by physical changes in the brain** caused by aging, miscellaneous diseases, injury to the brain, or psychoactive drug toxicities. Alzheimer's disease, in which older people suffer the unusually rapid death of brain cells, resulting in memory loss, confusion, loss of emotions, and gradually the ability to care for themselves, is one example of this mental disorder. Mental confusion from heavy marijuana use and various prescription drugs may mimic symptoms of this disorder.

Developmental Disorders

These disorders, usually first diagnosed in infancy, childhood, or adolescence, include **mental retardation, autism, communication disorders, and attention-deficit/hyperactivity disorders.** (*See Chapter 3 for more information on ADHD.*) Heavy and frequent use of psychedelics like LSD or PCP can be mistaken for developmental disorders.

Somatoform Disorders

These disorders have **physical symptoms without a known or discoverable physical cause and are likely to be psychological,** such as hypochondria (abnormal anxiety over one's health accompanied by imaginary symptoms). Cocaine, amphetamine, and other stimulant psychosis create a delusion that the user's skin is infested with bugs when no infestation exists.

Personality Disorders

These disorders, such as antisocial and borderline personality disorders, are characterized by inflexible behavioral patterns that lead to substantial distress or functional impairment.** Most patients with such personality disorders act out, that is, exhibit behavioral patterns that have an angry, hostile tone; that violate social conventions; and that result in negative consequences. **Anger is intrinsic to personality disorders as are chronic feelings of unhappiness and alienation from others, conflicts with authority, and family discord. These disorders frequently coexist with substance abuse** and are particularly hard to treat because of the acting out, which may include relapsing to drug use or creating a major disruption in the treatment setting (Dimeoff, Comtois & Linehan, 2003; Schuckit, 1986; Smith & Seymour, 2001). In children and adolescents, conduct disorder and oppositional defiant disorder are predictors of alcohol and drug use problems (Clark, Vanyukov & Cornelius, 2002).

Eating Disorders

Eating disorders (bulimia, anorexia, and binge eating) often co-occur with substance use disorders and other psychiatric and personality disorders. **Weak impulse control is often found in eating disorders and substance use** disorders, a possible common etiology along with genetic factors for both conditions (Grillo, Sinha & O'Malley, 2002). Eating disorders are often found in conjunction with major depression and PTSD (Dansky, Brewerton & Kilpatrick, 2000).

Pathological Gambling

Pathological gambling, an impulse-control disorder, is more common in clients who abuse or are dependent on alcohol. Gamblers will often drink in conjunction with their gambling trips to casinos or bars. Methamphetamine abuse is also found in many compulsive gamblers because it enables them to remain in the casino or at a poker machine for hours at a time. **Often a recovering alcoholic or addict will switch addictions and become just as pathological about gambling** as he or she was about drinking or using other drugs (Grant, Kushner & Kim, 2002).

Other Disorders

There are dozens of other mental disorders, including adjustment disorders, sleep disorders, sexual and gender identity disorders, and factitious disorders that can exist independently or in combination with other mental disorders and drug use disorders.

SUBSTANCE-INDUCED MENTAL DISORDERS

Among patients who suffer from a dual diagnosis, **the majority of the mental health problems encountered are caused by substance use rather than being pre-existing.** As mentioned, a clinically sound approach in dealing with these patients is to first assume that the mental illness is substance induced until proven otherwise (Shivani, Goldsmith & Anthenelli, 2002).

Alcohol-Induced Mental Illness

Impulse-Control Problems. People who abuse alcohol often demonstrate impulse-control problems. These problems include but are not limited to **violence, unsafe sex, other high-risk behaviors, and even suicide.** These behaviors are not due to an independent impulse-control disorder if they occur only in the context of alcohol use.

Sleep Disorders. Sleep problems are a common symptom that clinicians use to establish the presence of a mental disorder. Alcohol, however, significantly contributes to a person's sleep problems. These include difficulty staying asleep as well as early-morning awakening. Alcohol causes sleep problems due to its powerful suppression of REM sleep. **Sleep problems induced by alcohol can last for months after a person attains stable sobriety.** If a person's sleep problems occur in the context of alcohol use, they may not indicate the presence of an independent mental disorder.

Anxiety. Alcohol is a minor tranquilizer that has antianxiety properties. When a person's alcohol intake exceeds the body's ability to metabolize it, however, the person will experience alcohol withdrawal upon cessation. **Symptoms of alcohol withdrawal include increased pulse rate, body temperature, and blood pressure as well as a variety of anxiety-like symptoms.** These alcohol-induced anxiety symptoms will dissipate over a period of two to three days. The clinician needs to take into consideration the patient's alcohol use prior to diagnosing an independent anxiety disorder.

Depression. **Studies indicate that up to 45% of alcoholics present with concurrent symptoms of major depressive disorder. After four weeks of sobriety, however, only 6% of alcoholics will persist with these depressive symptoms** (Brown & Schuckit, 1988). Therefore a clinician cannot make the diagnosis of major depressive disorder in a person who is drinking alcohol until after at least four weeks of sobriety. There are conflicting data in the literature regarding the association between major depressive disorder and a history of alcoholism. Some authors suggest that recovering alcoholics are at four-fold risk of developing major depressive disorder (Hasin & Grant, 2002), although the mechanism of this association has not been identified. **Treatment with antidepressant medication is contraindicated in people who are drinking alcohol.**

"It's an egg-and-chicken situation because when I sober up I could say I

was like a depressed personality. I have a problem of depression. Then I found that alcohol totally matched my needs. Then I drank a long time, so I start seeking stimulants. Then I found cocaine; it totally matched my needs. I think my problem comes first before my drug use, but at first when I drank it was total self-medication for my depression.
34-year-old female with major depression

Psychosis. This clinical syndrome is marked by the **development of psychotic symptoms after many decades of heavy drinking.** These symptoms exist in the absence of intoxication and withdrawal. This syndrome has gone by a variety of names in the past, with the most current one being **alcohol-induced psychotic disorder.** Any and all psychotic symptoms can be seen with this disorder; they include but are not limited to auditory and visual hallucinations, delusional thought content, and ideas of reference. Of note, alcohol-induced psychotic disorder is extremely responsive to treatment with antipsychotic medication, although the actual mechanism is unclear. Clinicians should be cautioned to avoid the use of antipsychotic medication during periods of acute alcohol withdrawal. Conversely, alcohol use disorder is the most common co-occurring disorder found in clients with schizophrenia (Drake & Mueser, 2002).

Dementia. The neurotoxic effects of alcohol are well established. Alcohol abuse can cause a dementia-like syndrome with prominent cognitive deficits. Alcohol-induced dementia can mimic other similar conditions such as Alzheimer's disease. **The patient with alcohol-induced dementia, even in its most severe form, can regain some cognitive functioning in sobriety,** although the process may take up to a year. The clinician should be mindful that patients in early recovery from alcoholism will often present with severe memory problems that can interfere with their treatment. Thoughtful clinicians need to be aware of this fact and modify their treatment approaches accordingly.

Stimulant-Induced Mental Illness

Impulse-Control Problems. As is seen with alcohol abuse, **stimulant abusers also demonstrate impulse-control problems**. These behaviors are not due to an independent impulse-control disorder if they occur only in the context of stimulant use.

Mania. The person who is acutely intoxicated with stimulants can present in an identical fashion as someone who is in the acute manic phase of a bipolar disorder. The clinician should be cautioned not to assume that this manic-like behavior is solely attributable to a bipolar disorder if it occurs only in the context of stimulant abuse. **If the maniclike symptoms are solely due to the use of stimulants, they will completely resolve upon cessation of intoxication.** Antimanic medications such as depakote and lithium are not indicated for stimulant-induced manic disorder; the syndrome is best treated by helping the patient achieve stable abstinence.

Panic Disorder. The use of **stimulants can induce a panic attack**. The panic focus in the brain increases in size with each stimulant-induced panic attack. (Panic focus is that part of the brain from which panic attacks originate. Excess drug use turns neighboring cells into more panic cells. It is very similar to what is called a "seizure focus.") At a certain point, which is unique to the individual, this panic focus can take on a life of its own—**a person can go on to have a chronic panic disorder even if they never use stimulants again**.

Depression. Depression is caused by an imbalance of neurotransmitters, like serotonin. Stimulant drugs, such as methamphetamine, cause a temporary imbalance of these neurochemicals. **This imbalance can last up to 10 weeks after a person stops using stimulants.** During this period the person will present with depressed mood, anhedonia (lack of ability to feel pleasure), suicidality, anxiety, and sleep disturbance-symptoms identical to those of someone suffering from a major depressive disorder. **If the symptoms of depression are caused by stimulant withdrawal, antidepressants may help with the symptoms only during the initial detoxification phase** of treatment and probably should not be continued on a long-term basis as in the treatment of major depression. The proper treatment approach for those suffering from stimulant-induced mood disorder is monitoring their suicidality while engaging them in substance-abuse treatment.

In the early days of the crack cocaine epidemic of the mid-1980s, there was great enthusiasm for the use of antidepressants to treat stimulant abuse. Although the initial reports were very promising, when this treatment approach was studied in a double-blind research design, the initial benefits were not replicated.

Anxiety. As with alcohol-induced anxiety, this can also be induced by stimulant abuse. **Stimulant-induced anxiety disorders occur in the context of both acute intoxication and withdrawal.** Again, the proper treatment of stimulant-induced anxiety includes engaging people in substance-abuse treatment.

Psychosis. It is a well-known medical fact that stimulants can cause both short- and long-term psychotic symptoms. Not everyone who abuses stimulants will experience psychotic symptoms. **Individuals who do have psychotic symptoms will almost surely reexperience those symptoms each time they use; and as abuse continues, the duration of the effects will increase.** Medical literature (especially from Japan, which has had many stimulant epidemics) reports that psychotic symptoms can last up to five years after cessation of use. There are a few reports of symptoms lasting a lifetime. Although this five-year figure represents one end of the spectrum, it is certainly **common for people to experience psychotic symptoms for many months after cessation of stimulant abuse.** Proper treatment includes the use of antipsychotic medications in these individuals. The exact dosing and duration of treatment with antipsychotic medications depends on the severity of the stimulant-induced psychotic disorder.

Cognitive Impairment. With the advent of neuroimaging, investigators have been able to demonstrate that **stimulant abuse causes both transient and permanent damage to the brain**. This brain damage (loss of hippocampus and other limbic grey matter) is responsible for the cognitive impairment often seen in stimulant abusers.

Marijuana-Induced Mental Illness

In many circles marijuana is felt to be a benign substance. Upon closer scrutiny, however, it has been shown to be a potent psychoactive substance. This is especially problematic given the easy availability of higher-potency marijuana. **The higher concentration of the active ingredient THC is thought to be responsible for the psychiatric syndromes noted in marijuana users.**

Delirium. The use of the term *delirium* is often connected to a person who is ranting and raving; however, the essential feature of a marijuana-induced delirium is a **disturbance of consciousness that is accompanied by a change in cognition** that cannot be better accounted for by a pre-existing or evolving dementia. Most people suffering from a delirium are not readily recognizable by the general public or by the clinician who's not adept at diagnosing subtle neurocognitive problems. This is also true of the person who's experiencing the delirium. Marijuana is thought to be responsible for causing delirium in some chronic users. This delirium looks like the typical "stoners" (people who use marijuana on a regular basis) who are spaced out, detached, and oblivious to the world around them. These individuals often have **difficulty with memory, multitasking, and other simple cognitive processes**. The current thinking is that it **may take three months or even longer for this delirium to clear after a person stops using marijuana**.

Psychosis. Again, due in part to the high concentrations of THC currently available, it is not uncommon for people intoxicated on marijuana to experience psychotic symptoms, which include but are not limited to **paranoia and auditory and visual hallucinations**. These **symptoms tend to be transient and occur only while the person is high**. There are increased reports, however, of **hallucinogen persisting perceptual disorder (HPPD)** occurring in marijuana abusers, with symptoms lasting for several months even with no further exposure to the substance. If the psychotic symptoms persist after cessation of use, the clinician should be alerted to consider alternate explanations for the psychotic symptoms.

Panic. As with stimulant abuse, **marijuana can induce a panic attack in the intoxicated user**. The role of marijuana in causing a chronic panic disorder, as is seen in stimulant abuse, has not been studied. It would follow that people who continue to experience marijuana-induced panic attacks would increase the size of the panic focus.

Amotivational Syndrome. As stated in Chapter 6, the traditional notion is that marijuana makes you unmotivated. The reality of this is still unclear. **Does marijuana make you amotivational, or do amotivational people tend to smoke marijuana?** To date there have not been any good scientific studies explaining the relationship between marijuana and amotivational syndrome.

Other Drug-Induced Mental Illnesses

Most psychoactive substances can induce transitory or more-enduring psychiatric syndromes. But remember: **the incidence of substance-induced psychiatric symptoms is much greater than the incidence of pre-existing psychiatric problems (and symptoms)**. For example, during the active phase of alcohol and drug abuse, many patients present with symptoms of personality disorders; but with treatment and stabilization, most symptoms tend to disappear. Of particular concern lately is the emergence of psychiatric syndromes secondary to the psychostimulant MDMA (ecstasy). Although it has not been rigorously studied to date, it appears that ecstasy can cause both mood and psychotic problems in susceptible individuals. Because many psycho-stimulants release serotonin, **symptoms of serotonin syndrome should be considered when treating psychoses related to their use**.

TREATMENT

The close association of unbalanced brain chemistry in mental illness with the distorting brain effects of heredity, environment, and psychoactive drug use suggests that **treatment of mental illness and/or addiction should be directed toward rebalancing brain chemistry**.

REBALANCING BRAIN CHEMISTRY

Heredity & Treatment

As of yet we cannot alter a person's genetic code. We can't change a person with alcoholic marker genes that signal a susceptibility to alcoholism, drug addiction, or other addictive behavior. We can't decrease the genetic vulnerability of a teenager with a mother and a grandmother who have schizophrenia. **We can, however, alert some people that they are more at risk for a certain mental illness, drug addiction, or other compulsive behavior due to their heredity** (Blum, Braverman & Holder, 2000). Current research in gene therapy that is aimed toward altering genetic factors could be a giant step in controlling inherited mental illnesses. We are getting closer to being able to manipulate individual genes (gene therapy) for this purpose. Some researchers are focusing on the evolving science of **pharmacogenomics**, the study of how an individual's genetic inheritance affects the body's response to psychoactive drugs, with the aim of someday being able to **choose the treatment and the medication that is most compatible with the person's genetic profile** (Human Genome Project, 2007).

Environment & Treatment

Currently, heredity can't be altered, so **human beings can attempt to improve their environment thereby al-**

tering brain chemistry to better handle both their mental illness and drug abuse. People can leave an abusive relationship, avoid their drug-using associates, get enough sleep, avoid situations that make them angry, seek out new friends in self-help groups, avoid isolation, and make sure they get good nutrition. If people change where and how they live, they can avoid the stressors and the environmental cues that keep them in a state of turmoil, continually unbalance their neurochemistry, and make them more likely to abuse drugs and intensify their mental illness.

Psychoactive Drugs & Treatment

We are currently in the midst of a psychopharmacologic revolution. New treatments are available to patients to alleviate their suffering. **It is imperative that all substance-abuse treatment providers familiarize themselves with the basics of psychopharmacology, as it is the cornerstone of mental health treatment.** This notion may be contrary to the beliefs of many people who have been in the field for a while; however, the success of many of these therapies may help people let go of some of their prejudices regarding psychopharmacology.

Oftentimes patients are torn between which substance to use.

"I took both alcohol and lithium for my manic depression. The difference is that one is faster working. The alcohol works quickly; the lithium takes time to get there. But the alcohol caused other problems in my life in addition to my depression. I think I'll stick to the lithium."

52-year-old female

There is an **ever-expanding group of drugs called psychotropic or psychiatric medications (e.g., antidepressants, antipsychotics or neuroleptics, mood stabilizers, and antianxiety drugs)** that are prescribed by physicians to try to counteract the neurochemical imbalance caused by mental illness or addiction and that help the dual-diagnosis client lead a less destructive life. (The various psychotropic medications are examined in detail later in this chapter.)

Starting Treatment

With many dual-diagnosis clients, it is hard to know where to start treatment. Do you treat the mental illness or the addiction first, or do you treat them both right from the beginning? Best practice currently is to **address both problems simultaneously, that is, stabilize both the substance and mental health problems in an attempt to make the most accurate assessment possible.** This includes acute stabilization of the homicidal or suicidal patient as well as detoxification from drug dependence. It should be noted, however, that formal treatment can proceed only after a thorough diagnostic assessment.

"It is often difficult to know where to start with a dually diagnosed patient. Upon initial evaluation it is almost impossible to know which came first, the substance abuse or mental illness. My approach to these very difficult patients is to assume that all psychiatric symptoms are substance induced until proven otherwise."

Pablo Stewart, M.D.

Impaired Cognition

A very common but underappreciated condition of dual-diagnosis clients is significant cognitive impairment. Unfortunately, many clinicians involved in treatment believe that once dually diagnosed individuals forgo the booze or drugs, they should be able to engage in treatment, but that's not always the case. **A study of a number of dual-diagnosis clients at a public hospital found that the majority was mildly-to-severely cognitively impaired and had difficulty participating in treatment.** Reviewing screening exams on neurocognitive function at a VA hospital, researchers found that approximately 50% of the patients were mildly-to-severely impaired (Blume, Davis & Schmaling, 1999).

For the treatment provider, this means that the patient often appears normal but is suffering from significant cognitive impairment. For example, the patient can repeat what he hears, but the information and the therapy don't sink in. **It may take weeks or months after detoxification for reasoning, memory, and thinking to come back to a point where the dual-diagnosis individual can begin to fully engage in treatment.** As the patient remains in treatment, teaching strategies must be tailored to the person's ability to process the information that the doctor and the staff are providing.

The most common cognitive impairments associated with substance use disorders consist of problems with attention, memory, understanding, learning, use and meaning of words, and judgment. Abuse of drugs also causes temporal processing problems, which consist of poor understanding of time planning, processing goals over time, and delayed discounting (inability to appreciate delayed gratification).

Developmental Arrest

Drug abuse and mental illness often result in the arresting of emotional development. Consider a young man in his late teens or early twenties who is intelligent and fully grown but has been using drugs since the age of 12 and has also had emotional and mental problems. This type of patient comes to treatment with all kinds of difficulties. One of the worst problems is that he suffered developmental arrest at age 12, the point at which most people begin to work through issues and stresses in their lives. Most people mature through all the struggles and go on to become adults; but those who use drugs, who have avoided difficult emotions, and have not gone through that process of maturation will still experience all the emotions that they avoided five or six years earlier.

"It's all those issues as a child that I seemed to take into my adulthood and they come out. I'd get my buttons pressed. Someone gets me a little pissed off. You know, I really thought when I came into recovery I wouldn't be angry

anymore. Well it took me almost three years in treatment to realize that anger is a legitimate feeling. It's how I deal with it today and how I used to deal with it. That's what I'm learning about."

30-year-old with a dual diagnosis

Many dual-diagnosis clients have the character traits that are normal in children but abnormal in adults, making treatment extremely difficult. Dr. Burt Pepper, a psychiatrist who treats young dual-diagnosis clients, lists 11 of these characteristics:

1. They have a **low frustration tolerance**.

2. They **can't work persistently for a goal** without constant encouragement and guidance, partially because of their low tolerance for frustration.

3. They **lie to avoid punishment**.

4. They have mixed feelings about independence and dependence and then, **feeling hostile about dependency**, they test limits.

5. **They test limits constantly** because they haven't learned them yet or have rejected them.

6. **Their feelings are expressed as behaviors.** They cry, run away, and hit rather than talk, reason, explain, or apologize.

7. **They have a shallow labile affect, which means a shallowness of mood.** Give a kid a toy, he'll laugh; take it away, he'll cry.

8. They have a **fear of being rejected**. Extreme rejection sensitivity can even be expressed as paranoid schizophrenia.

9. Some live only in the present, but most of the older teens or young adults live in the past. **Most dual-diagnosis clients have no hope for the future** possibly because they remember the past too well or have trouble thinking.

10. **Denial is a common characteristic in young children.** One form is a refusal to deal with unpleasant but necessary duties. Another form is an unwillingness to stop something that's pleasurable, like kids playing roughhouse until one gets badly hurt.

11. **They feel *Either you're for me or against me***, a black-and-white approach to every judgment in life, with no modulation or moderation.

These characteristics are also very common in people being treated solely for chemical dependency. This situation suggests that developmental assessment must be performed on clients; that is, **treatment providers need to appreciate where a person is in his or her developmental process and address treatment accordingly**. An example might be that a person was unable to establish basic trust, a developmental step that is usually accomplished in early childhood. Treatment would have to be directed to help this person establish basic trust before addressing more-advanced developmental issues.

The above difficulties are all chronic or even lifelong problems that cannot be treated with short-term therapy. **These are problems of living, of living sober, and of living with the symptoms of the mental illness.** The best treatment consists of addressing all of the issues that the individual client brings to the treatment setting.

Psychotherapy, Individual Counseling & Group Therapy

"Look into the depths of your own soul and learn first to know yourself, then you will understand why this illness was bound to come upon you and perhaps you will thenceforth avoid falling ill."

Sigmund Freud, 1924

Psychotherapy is a very effective way of treating a person with both mental illness and substance-abuse illness. Psychotherapy can be applied in either an individual or a group manner. **Group therapy has become the standard for both substance-abuse and mental illness treatments** (Zweben, 2003), however the exact strategies for employing psychotherapy for mental illness are not the focus of this chapter.

The therapist should be cautioned that **the primary treatment of severe mental illness is psychopharmacology and not psychotherapy, whereas the opposite may be true for treating substance use disorders**, at least for the current era. Because of this paradox, many patients are often allowed to suffer needlessly during the course of psychotherapy when they actually need medication. This is not to imply that the clinician doesn't talk to the patient while he or she is being stabilized on medication.

In the recent past, the psychotherapeutic approach for substance-abuse disorders focused on working through the substance abuser's denial. It was strongly believed that a person could not get clean-and-sober if he did not deal with his denial about the illness. Although this psychotherapeutic strategy was very appealing to clinicians, it did little for the substance abuser. Current thinking regarding the proper use of psychotherapy in substance use disorders includes a **phase model**.

The first phase of a psychotherapeutic approach for a dual-diagnosis client is achieving abstinence. This is a period of at least six months during which the therapist emphasizes supportive psychotherapeutic techniques. These techniques include relapse prevention work, education on stress reduction and mental illness, and abstinence psychotherapy. During this phase the wise therapist avoids confronting the patient about his or her denial.

The next phase is called maintaining abstinence. This period occurs after the patient has between six and 24 months of sobriety. During this phase the therapist begins introducing notions of denial and other maladaptive defense mechanisms.

At the end of this phase, **psychotherapy for the substance abuser is indistinguishable from any other psychodynamically oriented treatment** except for the increased emphasis on education, abstinence from addictive drugs and psychotherapy along with psychotropic medications when appropriate (Davis, Klar & Coyle, 1991; Zimberg, 1994).

Group discount therapy

PSYCHOPHAR-MACOLOGY

The field of medicine that addresses the use of medications to help correct or control mental illnesses and drug addiction is called *psychopharmacology*. The scope of this branch of medicine has grown rapidly in the past 15 years, producing hundreds of new medications and greatly expanding this approach to mental illness.

Quite often the dual-diagnosis patient does need medication for psychiatric disorders, such as **antidepressants and mood stabilizers for mood disorders, antipsychotic (neuroleptic) medications for thought disorders, and antianxiety medications for anxiety disorders**. These medications should be prescribed only after a thorough assessment. Care should also be taken in the use of these medications given the individual's difficulty in dealing with drugs. The clinician has to make sure that the medication used for the psychiatric problem does not aggravate or complicate the substance-abuse problem.

Medications are used on a short-term, medium-term, or even lifetime basis to try to rebalance the brain chemistry that became unbalanced either through hereditary anomalies, environmental stress, and/or the use of psychoactive drugs and compulsive behaviors. These medications are used in conjunction with individual or group therapy and with lifestyle changes.

Previously, one of the biggest debates in treatment centers was about the reliance on psychiatric medications. Some clinicians looked at medications only as a last resort. Others felt that meds should be the first step in treatment. Due to recent advances in the mental and substance-abuse fields, psychiatric medications are much more acceptable to treatment providers.

The various **psychiatric medications currently in use affect the manner in which neurotransmitters work** in different ways:

◊ They can **increase the presynaptic release** of neurotransmitters (methylphenidate).

◊ They can **block the neurotransmitter** from connecting with a given receptor site (antipsychotics).

◊ They can **inhibit the reuptake** of neurotransmitters by the presynaptic neuron, thus increasing the amount of neurotransmitter available in the synapse. (Selective serotonin reuptake inhibitors [SSRIs] such as Prozac® and Zoloft® work in this way on serotonin.)

◊ They can **inhibit the metabolism** of neurotransmitters (Nardil® and MAO inhibitors), thereby enhancing the action of norepinephrine or dopamine.

◊ They can **enhance the effect** of existing neurotransmitters. (Benzodiazepines such as Valium® increase the effects of GABA.)

Besides manipulating brain chemistry, **some drugs act directly to control symptoms**. For example, beta blockers (Inderal®) calm the sympathetic nervous system that controls heart rate, blood pressure, and other functions that can go out of control in a panic attack or drug withdrawal state.

One problem with psychiatric medications is that it's **very hard to design a drug that will work only on a certain neurotransmitter in a particular way**. Advances have occurred in this regard. For example, the new atypical antipsychotics are designed to work on the specific dopamine receptors involved in psychotic symptoms. Even with these advance medications, however, there is some overlap to dopamine receptors in other parts of the central nervous system not involved in the psychotic process. Therefore there will always be side effects even with these newer medications. **It is imperative to constantly monitor each patient's reactions to the drug and adjust the dose accordingly.** A careful review of the purpose of the drug along with possible side effects and a specific plan of use should be fully explained to each patient.

"The medication that we are talking about giving you in this treatment program is really designed to correct some of the damage that you did to your body and to your mind with the drugs or damage that had been happening as a result of some emotional or psychological problem. It does not mean you're sick, it does not mean you're defective, and it does not mean you're weak. It just means that your biochemistry somehow got out of balance, and the medications that we're recommending, especially the antidepressant medications, are to rebalance those chemicals and bring you to a point where you can fully and effectively function and then begin to work on your other problems."

Stanley Yantis, M.D., psychiatrist, consulting with a dual-diagnosis client

PSYCHIATRIC MEDICATIONS VS. STREET DRUGS

One of the advantages of physician-prescribed psychiatric medications over street drugs is that generally, except for the benzodiazepines and stimulants, they are not addicting. In fact **the treatment of anxiety, depression, and other mental problems through psychiatric medications can relieve many of the reasons and the triggers for drug abuse**. A study of the risk of substance use disorders in boys who were treated with methylphenidate and other ADHD treatment drugs found a significant decrease in the risk of having drug use problems as adults compared with patients who were not treated (Biederman, Wilens, Mick, et al., 1999).

Sometimes being prescribed psychiatric medications can cause problems for dual-diagnosis clients because they are often taught to stay away from all drugs during recovery. The treatment profession has developed and distributed pamphlets to the various recovery fellowships, explaining the need for psychiatric medications in many dual-diagnosis patients in recovery. Nevertheless there are well-meaning members of these fellowships who insist that no one taking these medications is really recovering. The patient may be talked into flushing his or her medications down the toilet with potentially adverse psychiatric results. Consequently, it is essential that those responsible for treating dual-diagnosis clients understand and support those clients through the potential problems of early recovery (Buxton, Smith & Seymour, 1987; Center for Substance Abuse Treatment, 1995).

When using street drugs, patients feel a false sense of control over which drugs they ingest, inject, or otherwise self-administer. The same patients, when receiving medication from a doctor, often express the feeling that they are not in control of their lives. Thus many are more apt to rely on street drugs rather than on psychiatric medications for relief of their emotional problems. It is up to the physician to work with the patient regarding any and all issues raised by the use of prescription medications.

"Before I came to the clinic, I thought that using antidepressants was taboo. I wanted to use street drugs but not any of these clinical ones. There's a stigma to it. I used marijuana to deal with my depression, and I could take it when I felt I needed it, not a pill that I had to take every so often as prescribed by my psychiatrist."

35-year-old with depression and a problem with marijuana

Table 10-2 is a compilation of many of the ideas that have been covered in these pages regarding the relationships among brain chemistry, drug addiction, and mental illness. When studying the table, notice how many different neurotransmitters are affected by a single street drug especially cocaine or alcohol. Also note the physical and mental traits that are affected by a neurotransmitter and how a street drug affects those functions (Lavine, 1999; Physician's Desk Reference [PDR], 2007).

We discuss the drugs under the heading of the mental illness that they are generally used to treat (Table 10-2). There is some overlap, for example, when a drug used for depression, such as Prozac,® is also used to treat obsessive-compulsive disorder, or when the antipsychotic Seroquel® is also used for bipolar disorder.

DRUGS USED TO TREAT DEPRESSION

Many in the psychiatric field feel that **depression is caused by an abnormality in the production of the neurotransmitters serotonin and norepinephrine (noradrenaline)** plus a few others. Antidepressants are usually meant to increase the amount of serotonin or norepinephrine available to the brain to correct this imbalance. The number of people receiving outpatient treatment for depression has more than tripled since 1987. During that same period, the number of clients receiving psychotherapy dropped about 15%, so the primary treatment for those suffering from depression is medication rather than psychotherapy.

The newer antidepressants (such as Prozac,® Paxil,® Zoloft,® Wellbutrin,®

Remeron,® Serzone,® Celexa,® Cymbalta,® and Effexor®) work through a variety of mechanisms mostly by increasing the levels of certain neurotransmitters, including dopamine, norepinephrine and especially serotonin.

Selective Serotonin Reuptake Inhibitors

Fluoxetine (Prozac®) was the first and most popular of the newer antidepressants; it has received a large amount of publicity both pro and con since its release in 1988. It seems quite effective in the treatment of depression, with fewer side effects than tricyclic antidepressants or the MAO inhibitors. It is also used to treat obsessive-compulsive disorder, panic disorder, and eating disorders.

Fluoxetine, sertraline (Zoloft®), citalopram (Celexa®), paroxetine (Paxil®), and fluvoxamine (Luvox®) are classified as SSRIs, which **increase the amount of serotonin available to the nervous system**. The amount needed to be effective varies widely from patient to patient and has to be adjusted. It generally **takes two to four weeks for the full effects to be felt**. The most common side effects are insomnia, nausea, diarrhea, headache, and nervousness. **Most of the side effects are mild** and go away in a few weeks.

Recently, the federal Food and Drug Administration (FDA) warned against the use of paroxetine (Paxil®) for those under age 18 due to a slightly increased risk of suicide. The drug is not approved for pediatric use, but some physicians had been prescribing it anyway. The FDA did approve fluoxetine (Prozac®) for pediatric use (U.S. Food and Drug Administration, 2003).

One potential problem with SSRIs is that when used in conjunction with street drugs that stimulate the release of serotonin (e.g., methamphetamine), they can lead to what is called **serotonin syndrome**. Caused by excess serotonin, the **symptoms include elevated body temperature, shivering and tremors, mental changes, rigidity, autonomic nervous system instability, and occasionally death**. The use of SSRIs by people who abuse stimulants (e.g., cocaine and amphetamine)

TABLE 10–2   THE RELATIONSHIPS AMONG NEUROTRANSMITTERS, THEIR FUNCTIONS, STREET DRUGS, MENTAL ILLNESS & PSYCHIATRIC MEDICATIONS

Neurotransmitter	Normal Functions	Street Drugs That Disrupt the Neurotransmitter	Associated Mental Illnesses	Some Examples of Medications to Rebalance Neurotransmitters
Serotonin	Mood stability, appetite, sleep control, sexual activity, aggression, self-esteem	Alcohol, nicotine, amphetamine, cocaine, PCP, LSD, MDMA (ecstasy)	Anxiety disorders (e.g., PTSD, panic disorder, obsessive-compulsive disorder, generalized anxiety disorder); mood disorders (e.g., bipolar disorder, major depressive disorder, depression)	Selective serotonin reuptake inhibitors, or **SSRIs** (e.g., Prozac,® Zoloft,® Paxil,® Celexa®); serotonin and norepinephrine reuptake inhibitors, or **SNRIs** (Cymbalta,® Effexor®); **Tricyclic** and other antidepressants (e.g., Elavil,® Desyrel,® Remeron,® Serzone®); atypical antianxiety agent (BuSpar®)
Dopamine	Muscle tone/control, motor behavior, energy, reward mechanisms, attention span, pleasure, mental stability, hunger/thirst/sexual satiation	Cocaine, nicotine, PCP, amphetamine, caffeine, LSD, marijuana, alcohol, opioid	Psychotic disorders (e.g., schizophrenia, schizoaffective disorder); Parkinson's disease	Antipsychotics or dopamine antagonists (e.g., Risperdal,® Clozaril,® Zyprexa,® Abilify,® Invega®); anti-Parkinson's or dopamine agonist (e.g., L-dopa, amantadine, bromocriptine)
Norepinephrine, epinephrine	Energy, motivation, eating, heart rate, blood pressure, dilation of bronchi, assertiveness, alertness, confidence	Cocaine, nicotine, marijuana, MDMA, 2CB, CBR	Anxiety disorders, attention span, pleasure, narcolepsy	Bupropion, desipramine, methylamphetamine, caffeine, mood disorders, methylphenidate, clonidine, beta blockers, SNRIs (see serotonin)
Endorphin, enkephalin	Pain control, reward mechanisms, stress control (physical and emotional)	Heroin, OxyContin,® opioids, PCP, alcohol, marijuana, salvorin A	Psychotic disorders, mood disorders	Agonist = methadone, LAAM, buprenorphine; antagonist = naltrexone, nalmefene
GABA (gamma aminobutyric acid)	Inhibitor of many neurotransmitters, muscle relaxant, control of aggression, arousal	Alcohol, marijuana, barbiturates, PCP, benzodiazepines	Anxiety, sleep disorders, narcolepsy, seizure disorders	Benzodiazepines, glutamine, THC, Neurontin,® Lyrica®
Acetylcholine	Memory, learning, muscular reflexes, aggression, attention, blood pressure, heart rate, sexual behavior, mental acuity, sleep, muscle control	Marijuana, nicotine, alcohol, PCP, cocaine, amphetamine, LSD	Alzheimer's disease, schizophrenia, tremors	Vistaril,® Artane,® Cogentin,® Benadryl,® tacrine (Cognex®), donepezil (Aricept®), rivastigmine (Exelon®), galantamine (Reminyl®), mecamylamine (Inversine®)
Cortisone, corticotrophin	Immune system, healing, stress	Heroin, cocaine	Schizophrenia, depression, insomnia, anxiety	Corticosteroids (e.g., Prednisone,® cortisone), ACTH, cortisol; ketoconazole inhibits ACTH
Histamine	Sleep, inflammation of tissues, stomach acid, secretion, allergic response	Antihistamines, opioids	Bipolar depressive illness	Antihistamines (e.g., Benadryl,® Chlortrimeton,® Vistaril,® Allegra,® Phenergan,® Claritin®)
Anandamide, 2AG	Natural function is still unknown but several receptors still discovered	Marijuana, hashish	Not known, possibly compulsive overeating	Marijuana antagonist rimonabant (Acomplia,® Zimulti®)

can result in severe stimulant toxicity, meaning people are much more susceptible to the medical and psychiatric side effects of the stimulants (e.g., convulsions, psychosis, and severe manic-like behavior).

Depressive mood disorder resistant to SSRI treatment led to the development of medications that enhanced the activity of other specific neurotransmitters. **Serotonin-norepinephrine reuptake inhibitors (SNRIs)** specifically inhibit the reuptake of serotonin and norepinephrine (e.g., venlafaxine [Effexor®] and duloxetine [Cymbalta®]). **Selective norepinephrine-dopamine reuptake inhibitors (NDRIs)** include bupropion (Wellbutrin®

Cornered

by Mike Baldwin

8-31 © 2005 Mike Baldwin / Dist. by Universal Press Syndicate www.cornered.com
cornered@comic.com

BALDWIN

"In a perfect world, you wouldn't suffer from depression and I wouldn't profit from it. But we don't live in a perfect world. OK, well, maybe I do."

and Zyban®). Selective norepinephrine reuptake inhibitors (NRIs) include reboxetine (Edronax® and Vestra®). Many more are in development.

Tricyclic Antidepressants

Tricyclic antidepressants were once the main medications used to treat depression, but over the past 15 years the newer antidepressants have proved to have fewer toxic effects and side effects. SSRIs and others are now the preferred medications for depression.

Tricyclic antidepressants, such as imipramine (Tofranil®) and desipramine (Norpramin®), are thought to **block reabsorption of serotonin and norepinephrine by the sending neuron**, thereby increasing the activity of those biochemicals at the receiving neuron. This blocking effect in turn **forces the synthesis of more of these neurochemicals** via eventual downregulation of their autoreceptors. The delay of autoreceptor down-regulation and the synthesis of extra serotonin account for the observed lag time in effecting a change in the patient's mood. **It usually takes two to six weeks for a patient to respond to the drug therapy** (Meyer & Quenzer, 2005).

The tricyclics are very effective in treating patients with chronic symptoms of depression. **People without depression do not get a lift from tricyclic antidepressants** as they do with a stimulant. In fact, most of these medications actually cause drowsiness.

"The antidepressants did not get me high as far as what I could feel. It wasn't like feeling drunk or stoned. You don't get that sensation. The high I got is more like a lift, a mood lift. It's the difference between being lethargic and sad or active and happy."

41-year-old male with depression

The tricyclic antidepressants, available mainly as pills, can be dangerous if taken in overdose. Monitoring for dosage compliance as well as **constant feedback from the patient about the effects and the side effects is necessary to ensure safety and treatment efficacy**. Major side effects are dry mouth, blurred vision, inhibited urina-

tion, hypotension, cardiac instability, seizures, and sleepiness (Zwillich, 1999).

"I went off antidepressants. And after a month, six weeks, I began getting depressed again but I had to be convinced that I was depressed again. And they said, 'You really should go back on medication,' and I didn't want to admit that I didn't want to be on medication. I wanted to exist without it."

35-year-old with major depression

These drugs are also dangerous to the heart when mixed with street drugs or alcohol. Of note, **tricyclics are rarely prescribed for depressive disorders due to the overwhelming superiority of the newer antidepressant medications**.

Monoamine Oxidase Inhibitors

Monoamine oxidase (MAO) inhibitors such as phenelzine (Nardil®), tranylcypromine (Parnate®), and isocarboxazid (Marplan®) are also used to treat depression. These very strong drugs **work by blocking an enzyme (monoamine oxidase) that metabolizes the neurotransmitters norepinephrine and serotonin. This in essence raises the level of these neurotransmitters.** MAO inhibitors have several potentially dangerous side effects, however, so care and close monitoring are necessary. They do give fairly quick relief from a major depression or panic disorder, but the user must be on a special diet and remain aware of the possibility of high blood pressure, headaches, and several other side effects. Combined use of MAO inhibitors with stimulants, depressants, and alcohol can be fatal. There are also a number of over-the-counter drugs that should not be taken with MAO inhibitors (PDR, 2007). As with the tricyclic antidepressants, MAO inhibitors are rarely used due to the severity of their side-effect profile.

Stimulants

In the past amphetamine or amphetamine congeners including Dexedrine,® Biphetamine,® Desoxyn,®

Ritalin,® and Cylert® were used to treat depression. They work by increasing the amount of norepinephrine and epinephrine in the central nervous system. They are mood elevators when used in moderation, but **because tolerance develops rapidly and the mood lift proved to be too alluring, misuse and addiction developed fairly quickly**. The overuse led to various physical and mental problems such as agitation, aggression, paranoia, and psychosis. Stimulants are no longer indicated for the treatment of depression. Ritalin,® Adderall,® and Concerta® are prescribed for patients with attention-deficit/hyperactivity disorder. In the recovering dual-diagnosis client with ADHD and a substance-abuse problem, stimulants are also contraindicated. Psychiatrists are now prescribing nonstimulant medication such as buproprion and atomoxetine (Strattera®) to treat ADHD.

DRUGS USED TO TREAT BIPOLAR DISORDER

The main drug used for the treatment of bipolar disorder over the past 30 years has been lithium. Other medications have been developed during this time that include carbamazepine (Tegretol®), valproic acid (Depakene®), divalproex sodium (Depakote®), oxcarbazepine (Trileptal®), gabapentin (Neurontin®), and topiramate (Topamax®). Each of these medications is well tolerated by patients and very effective in the treatment of bipolar disorder. Each has a very distinct side-effect profile as well and requires a thorough medical evaluation prior to initiation. Quetiapine (Seroquel®), an antipsychotic drug, was also approved to treat bipolar disorder in 2007. **All of these drugs are used as mood stabilizers** even though some were initially designed for other purposes.

Lithium

Lithium is a naturally occurring mineral that **helps stabilize both the highs and the lows of bipolar disorder**. It is more effective, however, in stabilizing the highs. Although it is generally safe, it carries some potentially serious side effects such as hypothyroidism and requires close

medical monitoring. A patient can expect to see **clinical improvement in as soon as two weeks after initiation of the medication**. As with the other psychiatric medications, **the use of street drugs and alcohol is contraindicated in patients taking lithium**.

"The way manic depression works, at least for me, is the medicine can control about 20% of it. The other 80% is me. I have to learn how to control my moods with my mind because the medication is only a small part."
40-year-old with bipolar disorder

Many of the drugs currently used to treat bipolar disorder are also anti-seizure medications. As in seizure disorders, these medications help the bipolar patient by stabilizing the misfiring neurons. Each of these medications has its own unique set of medical side effects, requires close monitoring, and, like lithium, should not be taken with street drugs or alcohol. Other drugs such as valproate are used in conjunction with or instead of lithium because many clients do not like the side effects of lithium. Compliance among dual-diagnosis bipolar patients was better with valproate than with lithium (Weiss, Greenfield, Najavits, 1998).

DRUGS USED TO TREAT PSYCHOSES (ANTIPSYCHOTICS OR NEUROLEPTICS)

In the early 1950s, a new class of drugs, **phenothiazines, was found to be effective in controlling the symptoms of schizophrenia**. Some of the drugs, such as chlorpromazine (Thorazine®), thioridazinc (Mellaril®), fluphenazine (Prolixin®), and prochlorperazine (Compazine®), were initially referred to as "major tranquilizers" to differentiate them from barbiturates and benzodiazepines, which were called "minor tranquilizers." **Newer antipsychotics—nonphenothiazines like haloperidol (Haldol®), risperidone (Risperdal®), olanzapine (Zyprexa®), clozapine (Clozaril®), loxapine (Loxitane®), and molindone (Moban®)**—have become widely used. They act like phenothiazines and have similar side effects. Even newer an-

tipsychotics are being developed. In 2002 aripiprazole (Abilify®), a dopamine system stabilizer, was approved (Stahl, 2001A&B). In 2007 an active metabolite of risperidone (Risperdal®) called paliperidone (Invega®) was approved to treat schizophrenia. Both block dopamine and serotonin receptors, but their exact mechanism of action is unknown (Medication Monitor, 2007).

Researchers found that one of the major causes of psychotic symptoms in schizophrenia is an excess of dopamine. Most of the **antipsychotic medications work by blocking the dopamine receptors in the brain**, thereby inhibiting the effects of the excess dopamine. Generally, antipsychotic drugs work to alleviate the psychotic symptoms but do not cure the illness itself. This is true for all of the mental illnesses that have psychoses associated with them. The antipsychotic drugs are not without potentially serious side effects. The main difference among many of the antipsychotic drugs is their side-effect profile.

The main side effects of antipsychotics have to do with the blockage of dopamine. In Table 10-2 you can see that dopamine controls muscle tone and motor behavior. **By blocking the dopamine, symptoms such as involuntary movement and the inability to sit still are common.** Parkinsonian syndrome (mainly a tremor but also slowed movements and the loss of facial expression), akathisia (agitation, jumpiness exhibited by 75% of patients), akinesia (temporary loss of movement and apathy), and even the more serious tardive dyskinesia (involuntary movements of the jaws, head, neck, trunk, and extremities) are the most common complications when using these medications. Often anticholinergic medications, such as Cogentin® and Artane,® and even an antihistamine like Benadryl® are given to block side effects.

There are other potentially serious side effects associated with antipsychotics. **Although these medicines are relatively safe, extreme care should be taken before they are prescribed.**

Another commonly encountered side effect of antipsychotic medications is sedation; **patients on antipsychotics may seem drugged**. Sedation is an unwanted side effect and is not the primary purpose of prescribing antipsychotic medications. There are times, however, when the astute clinician will take advantage of this side effect when treating the agitated psychotic patient. These drugs are dangerous when used as sleeping pills by patients who are not psychotic; and they should never be used only to control an agitated patient or as a sleep aid.

There is a trend toward using atypical antipsychotics such as **risperidone (Risperdol®)** in the acutely psychotic patient. Because the antipsychotic drugs do not have an immediate effect on the patient's psychotic symptom, **it may take several weeks to achieve full antipsychotic effect**. During this time the patient should be treated with the lowest dose possible that is still exerting a clinical effect. After several weeks at this low dose, the amount may be slowly increased if the patient retains intractable psychotic symptoms. If after four to six weeks at this higher dose the patient's symptoms remain unchanged, the clinician usually switches to a different type of antipsychotic. The patient's dose of antipsychotic medication can usually be safely lowered after the symptoms are better under control. This approach is particularly important in treating elderly patients.

Clozapine (Clozaril®) is usually effective in the 30% of patients who do not respond to standard antipsychotic drug therapy, although weekly blood tests are necessary to monitor the side effects of clozapine, which make its use very expensive. Newer atypical antipsychotics, like risperidone (Risperdal®), olanzapine (Zyprexa®), aripiprazole (Abilify®), and paliperidone (Invega®), do not require blood tests but are still more expensive than the older antipsychotics. Current best practice promotes the use of atypical antipsychotics over their less expensive predecessors.

More than 33.5 million prescriptions were written for antipsychotic medications in the United States in 2001, up 34% from the previous two years. Even more dramatic is the **sixfold increase in the number of children taking antipsychotics** from 1993 to 2002 (from 201,000 to 1,224,000)

(Cooper, Hickson, Fuchs, et al., 2004; Olfson, Blanco, Liu, et al., 2006; Thomas, 2002).

Patients with a pre-existing psychotic illness such as schizophrenia or schizoaffective disorder often self-medicate with street drugs in an attempt to control their symptoms. The street drugs commonly used include heroin as well as other opiates, alcohol, marijuana, or sedative-hypnotics. Because all of these street drugs have dangerous toxic effects when combined with antipsychotic drugs, patients are exhorted to cease using them while under psychiatric treatment (Breier, Su, Saunders, et al., 1997).

"I would drink alcohol with some of these pills that I was taking, and I would really black out, and I would lose consciousness, pass out, and it was pretty bad; and I would have different types of side effects like blotchy skin, and it was bad, really, really, bad."
28-year-old addict with schizophrenia and bipolar disorder

DRUGS USED TO TREAT ANXIETY DISORDERS

For generalized anxiety disorder as well as some of the other anxiety disorders, the **benzodiazepines are widely used**. The most commonly prescribed are alprazolam (Xanax®), clonazepam (Klonopin®), diazepam (Valium®), chlordiazepoxide (Librium®), and clorazepate (Tranxene®). Developed in the early 1960s, the benzodiazepines were considered safe substitutes for barbiturates and meprobamate (e.g., Miltown®). They act very quickly, particularly Valium.® **The calming effects are apparent within 30 minutes.** Some of the benzodiazepines are long acting (diazepam, chlordiazepoxide, clorazepate, clonazepam, prazepam, and halazepam), and some are short acting (triazolam, lorazepam, and temazepam). These drugs work by facilitating inhibition by GABA, the major inhibitory neurotransmitter. **Many physicians avoid prescribing any benzodiazepine on a chronic basis**, asserting that these sedative-hypnotics should be used only for a

brief period of time to stabilize anxiety or to medicate sleep problems.

The main problem with benzodiazepines is that they are habit forming, even at clinical doses, and do have dangerous withdrawal symptoms. They should be avoided in treating the dual-diagnosis patient for whom they can re-trigger drug abuse. There are many other medications that can be safely used with the dual-diagnosis patient. These include BuSpar® and the beta blockers. **Recently, SSRI antidepressants such as Paxil® have been approved for use in anxiety disorder** (Ikeda, 1994; PDR, 2007).

With SSRIs and for almost all psychiatric medications, care should be taken when stopping the medication.

"I went off the Paxil.® I stopped immediately instead of tapering off of them, and I had headaches; and again I was just really angry. My anxiety level—that is what I was taking it for—just shot up to the roof. I thought a couple of times I was having a heart attack. I went to my doctor, and he told me flat out that you cannot just stop taking the Paxil,® that you will have huge withdrawal symptoms."
38-year-old with a dual diagnosis

Buspirone (BuSpar®) is one of the only other drugs labeled for generalized anxiety disorder. It is a serotonin modulator that **blocks the transmission of excess serotonin, one of the causes of the symptoms of many forms of anxiety**. It also mimics serotonin, so it can substitute for low levels of serotonin, a feature used by some doctors to treat depression. It takes one to two weeks to work and is not nearly as dramatic, initially, as the benzodiazepines, so many patients are reluctant to use it. It has the advantage of minimal side effects and has not been shown to be habit forming.

As stated, the SSRIs such as Paxil® and Zoloft® are currently indicated for use in anxiety disorders. These drugs have a direct antianxiety effect and are not used just with depressed patients who also have anxiety symptoms.

Drugs for Obsessive-Compulsive Disorder

For obsessive-compulsive disorder (OCD), almost every type of psychotropic medication has been tried, usually with relatively poor results. Anafranil® (clomipramine) has recently been used with reasonable results. SSRIs and SNRIs like paroxetine, sertraline, fluoxetine, and venlafaxine have also been used.

Drugs for Panic Disorder

Several drugs are used to control panic attacks and panic disorder. Previously, benzodiazepines were the primary drug of choice for the treatment of panic disorders. As noted previously, benzodiazepine-type medication should be avoided in the patient with a dual diagnosis. **Current treatment recommendations include the use of SSRI antidepressant medications.** These are very effective in the treatment of panic and generally have a favorable side-effect profile. These medications must be taken daily and are not designed to treat a person with an acute panic attack.

Other frequently used medications in the treatment of panic are the beta blockers like propranolol. They help control both the physical and the psychological symptoms associated with panic. Care should be taken when using beta blockers as they can have serious cardiac side effects in certain patients.

COMPLIANCE & FEEDBACK

The biggest problem with psychiatric medications (and with any prescription medication) is compliance with the physician's instructions. If patients aren't getting the desired effects, they will often alter the dosage on their own, simply stop taking the medication, or combine it with other drugs, causing dangerous interactions.

"I stopped taking it and got so depressed I took the remnants of both prescriptions, which was 1,000 milligrams [mg] of Seroquel® and 1,500 mg of Zoloft.® I took all at one time because I became so depressed. My fiancée and I had a fight, and I wanted to kill myself."

38-year-old male with a dual diagnosis

Because insurance coverage for office visits can be limited as are publicly funded treatment slots, **a patient might see a physician only once a month or less even at the beginning of use of a psychiatric medication**, when feedback is necessary to select the right drug and adjust the dose. The physician and the client must work in tandem for the greatest success. At the Haight Ashbury Detox Clinic, the clients have to come in almost every day.

"This clinic has been a lifesaver for me. I'm able to come in every day and talk to a therapist about how I'm feeling, but also I'm able to talk to doctors and a pharmacist about how the medications are working, so they're able to make adjustments, modifications, changes on a daily basis, which has really helped me stabilize my moods and thoughts."

35-year-old at the Haight Ashbury Detox Clinic with schizoaffective disorder

TABLE 10–3   PSYCHIATRIC MEDICATIONS

MAJOR DEPRESSION (antidepressants)

Selective serotonin reuptake inhibitors (SSRIs): citalopram (Celexa®), fluoxetine (Prozac,® Sarafem®), fluvoxamine (Luvox®), paroxetine (Paxil®), sertraline (Zoloft®), escitalopram (Lexapro®)

Tricyclic antidepressants: *tertiary amine tricyclics*-amitriptyline (Elavil,® Endep®), clomipramine (Anafranil®), doxepin (Sinequan,® Adapin®), imipramine (Tofranil,® Janimine®), trimipramine (Surmontil®); *secondary amine tricyclics*-desipramine (Norpramin,® Pertofrane®), nortriptyline (Aventyl,® Pamelor®), protriptyline (Vivactil®); *tetracyclics*-amoxapine (Asendin®), maprotiline (Ludiomil®)

Norepinephrine-dopamine reuptake inhibitors (NDRIs): bupropion (Wellbutrin®), bupropion SR (Wellbutrin SR,® Zyban®)

Serotonin-norepinephrine reuptake inhibitors (SNRIs): venlafaxine (Effexor®), venlafaxine XR (Effexor XR®), duloxetine (Cymbalta®)

Serotonin modulators: nefazodone (Serzone®), trazodone (Desyrel®)

Norepinephrine reuptake inhibitors (NRIs): reboxetine (Edronax,® Vestra®)

Norepinephrine-serotonin modulators: mirtazapine (Remeron®)

Monoamine oxidase (MAO) inhibitors: phenelzine (Nardil®), tranylcypromine (Parnate®), selegiline (Eldepryl®)

Stimulants used as antidepressants: amphetamine/methamphetamine (Adderall,® Dexedrine,® Biphetamine,® Desoxyn®), methylphenidate (Ritalin,® Concerta®), pemoline (Cylert®)

BIPOLAR AFFECTIVE DISORDER (mood stabilizers)

Lithium: Eskalith,® Lithobid,® carbamazepine (Tegretol®), valproic acid (Depakene®), divalproex sodium (Depakote®), olanzapine (Zyprexa®), oxcarbazepine (Trileptal®), gabapentin (Neurontin®), topiramate (Topamax®), aripiprazole (Abilify®), Quetiapine (Seroquel®)

(continued)

TABLE 10–3 PSYCHIATRIC MEDICATIONS (*continued*)

THOUGHT DISORDERS (antipsychotics)

Butyrophenones: haloperidol (Haldol®)

Dibenzoxazepines: loxapine (Loxitane®), molindone (Moban,® Lidone®)

Heterocyclics: chlorprothixene (Taractan®), triflupromazine (Vesprin®)

Phenothiazines: chlorpromazine (Thorazine®), prochlorperazine (Compazine®)

Piperazines: acetophenazine (Tindal®), fluphenazine (Prolixin,® Permitil®), perphenazine (Trilafon,® Etrafon®), trifluoperazine (Stelazine®)

Piperidines: mesoridazine (Serentil®), pimozide (Orap®), piperacetazine (Quide®), thioridazine (Mellaril®)

Thioxanthenes: thiothixene (Navane®)

Atypical antipsychotics: aripiprazole (Abilify®), clozapine (Clozaril®), olanzapine (Zyprexa®), quetiapine (Seroquel®), risperidone (Risperdal®), ziprasidone (Geodon®), paliperidone (Invega®)

Drugs used to treat extrapyramidal side effects of antipsychotics: amantadine (Symmetrel®), benztropine (Cogentin®), diphenhydramine (Benadryl®), propranolol (Inderal®), trihexyphenidyl (Artane®)

GENERALIZED ANXIETY DISORDER (anxiolytics)

Benzodiazepines: *short-acting (2- to 4-hour duration of action)*-alprazolam (Xanax®), lorazepam (Ativan®), oxazepam (Serax®), temazepam (Restoril®), triazolam (Halcion®); *long-acting (6- to 24-hour duration of action)*-chlordiazepoxide (Librium®), clonazepam (Klonopin®), clorazepate (Tranxene®), diazepam (Valium®), halazepam (Paxipam®), prazepam (Centrax®)

Nonbenzodiazepines: buspirone (BuSpar®), citalopram (Celexa®), paroxetine (Paxil®), venlafaxine (Effexor®)

OBSESSIVE-COMPULSIVE DISORDER (OCD)

Clomipramine (Anafranil®), fluoxetine (Prozac®), fluvoxamine maleate (Luvox®), sertraline (Zoloft®), venlafaxine (Effexor®)

PANIC DISORDER

First-line drugs (medications that should be tried first to control panic): SSRIs (Zoloft,® Prozac,® Paxil®), alprazolam (Xanax®), clonazepam (Klonopin®), desipramine (Norpramin,® Pertofrane®), imipramine (Tofranil®)

Beta blockers: atenolol (Tenormin®), propranolol (Inderal®)

Others: MAO inhibitors, e.g., phenelzine (Nardil®) and tranylcypromine (Parnate®)

SOCIAL PHOBIA

Beta blockers: atenolol (Tenormin®), propranolol (Inderal®)

POST-TRAUMATIC STRESS DISORDER

First-line drugs: SSRIs (Zoloft,® Paxil®)

Second-line drugs: beta blockers (atenolol, pindolol [Visken®], propranolol)

SLEEP DISORDER

Benzodiazepines: clonazepam (Klonopin®), clorazepate (Tranxene®), estazolam (ProSom®), flurazepam (Dalmane®), oxazepam (Serax®), quazepam (Doral®), temazepam (Restoril®), triazolam (Halcion®), zaleplon (Sonata®), zolpidem (Ambien®)

Nonbenzodiazepines: amitriptyline (Elavil®), chloral hydrate, diphenhydramine (Benadryl®), doxepin (Sinequan®), eszopiclone (Lunesta®), trazodone (Desyrel®), ramelteon (Rozerem®)

ATTENTION-DEFICIT/HYPERACTIVITY DISORDER (ADHD)

Stimulants: amphetamine (Adderall,® Adderall XR®), pemoline (Cylert®), dextroamphetamine (Dexedrine,® DextroStat,® Dexedrine Spansule®), dexmethylphenidate (Focalin®), methylphenidate (Ritalin,® Methylin,® Metadate,® Concerta®)

Nonstimulant: atomoxetine (Strattera®)

(Keltner & Folks, 1997; Marangell, Silver, Martinez, et al., 2002; PDR, 2007)

MENTAL HEALTH & DRUGS

MENTAL HEALTH & DRUGS

Introduction

1. Almost half of all Americans will develop a mental disorder at some time in their lives.

2. Of the 40 million Americans with a mental illness, 7 million to 10 million also have a substance-related disorder.

3. The neurotransmitters that are involved in mental illness are the same ones involved in drug abuse and addiction.

4. The direct effects of many psychoactive drugs as well as the withdrawal effects mimic many mental illnesses.

5. Substance-related disorders include substance use disorders (substance dependence and substance abuse) and substance-induced disorders (e.g., amphetamine psychosis and alcohol depression).

6. Substance dependence is defined as a maladaptive pattern of substance use leading to clinically significant impairment or distress.

Determining Factors

7. Heredity, environment, and psychoactive drugs affect susceptibility to mental illness in much the same way as they affect susceptibility to drug abuse and dependence.

8. The risk of developing a mental illness depends to a great extent on heredity. The risk of a person's developing schizophrenia if he or she has a close relative with schizophrenia jumps from 1% to about 15%; for major depression it jumps from 5% to 15%; for a bipolar illness, it jumps from 1% to 12%.

9. Genetic links also exist for behavioral disorders such as gambling and compulsive overeating.

10. Environmental influences, such as extreme stress, can unbalance neurochemistry to a point that increases susceptibility to mental illness.

11. Physical and sexual abuse in childhood is very common (50% to 75%) in those who are psychotic.

12. Psychoactive drugs can alter neurochemistry and aggravate pre-existing mental illnesses, mimicking the symptoms of mental illness.

13. Someone who is predisposed to depression or schizophrenia can trigger the illness by using psychoactive drugs.

DUAL DIAGNOSIS (CO-OCCURRING DISORDERS)

Definition

14. Dual diagnosis is defined as the existence in an individual of at least one mental disorder along with an alcohol or drug use disorder.

15. Pre-existing mental disorders used to define dual diagnosis include thought or psychotic disorders (schizophrenia), mood or affective disorders (major depression and bipolar affective disorder), and anxiety disorders (panic disorder and post-traumatic stress disorder [PTSD]).

16. Substance-induced mental disorders include stimulant-induced psychotic disorders and alcohol-induced mood disorders. The symptoms usually disappear with abstinence if there is no pre-existing mental disorder.

17. It is important to distinguish between having symptoms of mental illness and actually having a major psychiatric disorder.

18. It is common for drug abusers to present with symptoms of a personality disorder (e.g., antisocial personality disorder or borderline personality disorder). The symptoms can usually be minimized with abstinence.

Epidemiology

19. About 44% of alcohol abusers and 64.4% of substance abusers admitted for treatment also have a serious mental illness. Conversely, 29% to 34% of mentally ill people have a problem with either alcohol or other drugs.

20. Seven million to 13 million people have co-occurring disorders.

Patterns of Dual Diagnosis

21. One type of dual diagnosis is the person who has a clearly defined mental illness and then gets involved in drugs.

22. The second type of dual diagnosis is the direct result of substance abuse or withdrawal, where the abuser develops psychiatric problems that are usually temporary but occasionally persist and evolve into a chronic mental health problem.

Making the Diagnosis

23. The initial diagnosis should be a "rule-out" diagnosis, where several possible diagnoses are considered. The clinician should avoid a specific diagnosis until the client has had time to get sober.

24. A number of factors influence the diagnosis, including the pattern of substance use, any pre-existing mental illness, and evidence of any self-medicating.

25. The number of dual-diagnosis patients has increased due to the diminishing number of mental health care facilities, the proliferation of substances of abuse, the increasing numbers and greater expertise of licensed professionals in the field, and the pressures from managed care to diagnose a reimbursable illness.

26. There is a higher percentage of mental illness and dual diagnosis among the homeless.

27. Patients were often shuffled back and forth between the mental health care system and the substance-abuse treatment system.

Mental Health vs. Substance Abuse

28. Five of the 12 main differences between the mental health (MH)

treatment community and the substance-abuse (SA) treatment community are:

◊ MH used to say, "Control the psychiatric problem, and the drug abuse will disappear." SA used to say, "Get the patient clean-and-sober, and the mental health problem will disappear." Concurrent treatment is necessary for one-third to three-fourths of the clients, depending on the survey.

◊ In MH partial recovery is more acceptable, whereas in SA most believe that lifetime abstinence is possible.

◊ MH often uses psychiatric drugs to treat the dual-diagnosis patient, whereas SA promotes a drug-free philosophy or occasionally a drug substitution method (e.g., methadone maintenance).

◊ MH has a supportive psychotherapeutic approach philosophy, whereas SA often uses a confrontative philosophy.

◊ MH keeps the client from getting worse, whereas SA has a tendency to let people hit bottom to break through denial.

29. Health professionals must reconcile the two philosophies of treatment to develop programs that treat both illnesses (mental illness and addiction) rather than rejecting them.

30. Multiple diagnoses can include polydrug abuse, medical diseases, hepatitis C, chronic pain, and/or other medical conditions in addition to a dual-diagnosis client.

31. A triple diagnosis is defined as HIV, drug abuse, and a mental illness. The explosive growth of triple diagnoses is straining health department resources. Comprehensive drug treatment programs that have multiple treatment capabilities are necessary.

Psychiatric Disorders

32. Overall about 21% of the U.S. population is affected by mental disorders during a given year, with anxiety disorders the most prevalent.

33. A thought disorder, such as schizophrenia, is characterized by hallucinations, delusions, an inappropriate affect, poor association, and an impaired ability to care for oneself. It usually strikes individuals in their late teens and early adulthood. Several abused drugs can mimic schizophrenia, particularly stimulants and psychedelics.

34. Major depression is characterized by a depressed mood, diminished interest and pleasure in most activities, sleep and appetite disturbances, feelings of worthlessness, and thoughts of suicide. About 15% of Americans will experience a major depressive disorder in their lifetime. Excessive alcohol use and stimulant drug withdrawal can cause temporary drug-induced depression.

35. A bipolar affective disorder is characterized by alternating periods of depression, normalcy, and mania. Excess stimulant or psychedelic abuse will often resemble a bipolar disorder.

36. Anxiety disorders, the most common psychiatric disturbances, include post-traumatic stress disorder (PTSD), generalized anxiety disorder, panic disorder, agoraphobia, social phobia, simple phobia, and obsessive-compulsive disorder. Often anxiety and depression are mixed together.

37. Other mental illnesses include dementias (e.g., Alzheimer's disease), developmental disorders (e.g., ADHD), somatoform disorders (e.g., hypochondria), personality disorders, eating disorders, and compulsive gambling.

38. Substance-induced mental disorders are much more prevalent in dual-diagnosis patients than pre-existing psychiatric disorders.

39. Alcohol-induced mental illnesses include impulse-control problems, sleep disturbances, anxiety, depression, psychosis, and dementia.

40. Stimulant-induced mental illnesses include impulse-control problems, mania, panic disorder, depression, anxiety, psychosis, and cognitive impairment.

41. Marijuana-induced mental illnesses include delirium, psychosis, panic, and amotivational syndrome.

Treatment

42. Clients can be alerted to any genetic predisposition to addiction. Environment can be changed to reduce stressors and drug-using cues. Psychiatric medications can be used to rebalance the neurochemistry of mental illness.

43. The main psychiatric medications are antipsychotics, antidepressants, mood stabilizers, and antianxiety drugs.

44. The drug dependence or abuse and the mental health problem must be stabilized and then treated simultaneously.

45. Impaired cognition and developmental arrest make treatment of dual-diagnosis patients difficult. Many people seeking treatment are much younger emotionally than they are physically.

46. Group therapy has become the standard for substance-abuse and mental illness treatments. Psychopharmacology is the primary form of clinical treatment for mental illness.

47. The three phases of psychotherapy for dual diagnosis treatment are achieving abstinence, maintaining abstinence, and continuing psychotherapy along with psychiatric medication.

Psychopharmacology

48. The major classes of psychiatric drugs are antidepressants and mood stabilizers for mood disorders, antipsychotics (neuroleptics) for thought disorders (psychoses), and antianxiety medications for anxiety disorders. They can be used on a short-term, medium-term, and even lifetime basis.

49. Psychiatric medications manipulate brain chemistry in a variety of ways and relieve symptoms of mental illness. Because they can also cause undesirable and severe

side effects, they should be closely monitored.

50. To feel in control of their lives, many people with mental illnesses try to self-medicate with street drugs or alcohol.

51. Drugs used to treat depression are: selective serotonin reuptake inhibitors (SSRIs) such as Prozac,® Zoloft,® Paxil,® and Celexa®; serotonin-norepinephrine reuptake inhibitors (SNRIs) such as Effexor® and Cymbalta®; norepinephrine-dopamine reuptake inhibitors (NDRIs) such as Wellbutrin® and Zyban®; norepinephrine reuptake inhibitors (NRIs) such as Edronax® and Vestra®; tricyclic antidepressants such as Elavil® and Tofranil®; monoamine oxidase (MAO) inhibitors such as Nardil® and Parnate®; and stimulants such as Adderall® and Concerta.®

52. The main drug used to treat a bipolar disorder is lithium. Carbamazepine (Tegretol®), topiramate (Topamax®), quetiapine (Seroquel®), gabapentin (Neurontin®), and divalproex sodium (Depakote®) are also used.

53. Some of the drugs used to treat psychoses, such as schizophrenia, are haloperidol (Haldol®), clozapine (Clozaril®), risperidone (Risperdal®), aripiprazole (Abilify®), paliperidone (Invega®), olanzapine (Zyprexa®), and the phenothiazines, such as chlorpromazine (Thorazine®). Mostly they control dopamine levels in the brain.

54. The principal drugs used to treat anxiety are the benzodiazepines (e.g., Valium® and Xanax®) and the nonbenzodiazepine buspirone (BuSpar®). Normally, the benzodiazepines begin acting within 30 minutes, whereas buspirone requires one to two weeks before its full effects are realized. SSRIs and other antidepressants have also been useful in treating anxiety disorders in SUD patients.

REFERENCES

American Psychiatric Association [APA]. (2000). *Diagnostic and Statistical Manual of Mental Disorders* (4th ed., text revision [*DSM-IV-TR*]). Washington, DC: Author.

Back, S. E., Sonne, S. C., Killeen, T., Dansky, B. S. & Brady, K. T. (2003). Comparative profiles of women with PTSD and comorbid cocaine or alcohol dependence. *American Journal of Drug & Alcohol Abuse, 29*(1), 169-89.

Barondes, S. H. (1993). *Molecules and Mental Illness.* New York: Scientific American Library.

Biederman, J., Wilens, T., Mick, E., Spencer, T. & Faraone, S. V. (1999). Pharmacotherapy of attention-deficit/hyperactivity disorder reduces risk for substance use disorder. *Pediatrics, 104*(2), e20.

Blum, K., Braverman, E. R., Holder, J. M., Lubar, J. F., Monastra, V. J., Miller, D., et al. (2000). Reward deficiency syndrome: A biogenetic model for the diagnosis and treatment of impulsive, addictive, and compulsive behaviors. *Journal of Psychoactive Drugs, 32*(suppl.), i-iv, 1-112.

Blume, A. W., Davis, J. M. & Schmaling, K. B. (1999). Neurocognitive dysfunction in dually diagnosed patients: A potential roadblock to motivating behavior change. *Journal of Psychoactive Drugs, 31*(2), 111-15.

Brady, K. T. (1999). Treatment of PTSD and substance use disorders. Paper presented at the 152nd annual meeting of the American Psychiatric Association, Washington, DC.

Brady, K. T., Myrick, H. & Sonne, S. (2003). Comorbid addiction and affective disorders. In A. W. Graham, T. K. Schultz, M. F. Mayo-Smith, R. K. Ries & B. B. Wilford, eds. *Principles of Addiction Medicine* (3rd ed., pp. 1277-86). Chevy Chase, MD: American Society of Addiction Medicine, Inc.

Brehm, N. M. & Khantzian, E. J. (1997). Psychodynamics. In J. H. Lowinson, P. Ruiz, R. B. Millman & J. G. Langrod, eds. *Substance Abuse: A Comprehensive Textbook* (3rd ed., pp. 90-100). Baltimore: Williams & Wilkins.

Breier, A., Su, T. P., Saunders, R., Carson, R. E., Kolachana, B. S., de Bartolomeis, A., et al. (1997). Schizophrenia is associated with elevated amphetamine-induced synaptic dopamine concentrations. *Proceedings of the National Academy of Sciences, 94*(6), 2569-74.

Brown, S. A. & Schuckit, M. A. (1988). Changes in depression among abstinent alcoholics. *Journal of Studies on Alcohol, 49*(5), 412-17.

Buxton, M. E., Smith, D. E. & Seymour, R. B. (1987). Spirituality and other points of resistance to the 12-step recovery process. *Journal of Psychoactive Drugs, 19*(3), 275-86.

Center for Substance Abuse Treatment. (1995). *Assessment and Treatment of Patients with Coexisting Mental Illness and Alcohol and Other Drug Abuse.* DHHS Publication No. (SMA) 95-3061.

Rockville, MD: U.S. Department of Health and Human Services. http://www.ncbi.nlm.nih.gov/books/bv.fcgi?rid=hstat5.chapter.29713 (accessed May 23, 2007).

Chiang, S. C., Chan, H. Y., Chang, Y. Y., Sun, H. J., Chen, W. J. & Chen, C. K. (2007). Psychiatric comorbidity and gender difference among treatment-seeking heroin abusers in Taiwan. *Psychiatry and Clinical Neurosciences, 61*(1), 105-11.

Clark, D. B., Vanyukov, M. & Cornelius, J. (2002). Childhood antisocial behavior and adolescent alcohol use disorders. *Alcohol Research & Health, 26*(2), 109-15.

Cooper, W. O., Hickson, G. B., Fuchs, C., Arbogast, P. G. & Ray, W. A. (2004). New users of antipsychotic medications among children enrolled in TennCare. *Archives of Pediatrics and Adolescent Medicine, 158*(8), 753-59.

Crome, I. B. (1999). Substance misuse and psychiatric comorbidity: Toward improved service provision. *Drugs: Education, Prevention and Policy, 6*(2), 151-74.

Dansky, B. S., Brewerton, T. D. & Kilpatrick, D. G. (2000). Comorbidity of bulimia nervosa and alcohol use disorders: Results from the National Women's Study. *International Journal of Eating Disorders, 27*(2), 180-90.

Dausey, D. J. & Desai, R. A. (2003). Psychiatric comorbidity and the prevalence of HIV infection in a sample of patients in treatment for substance abuse. *Journal of Nervous and Mental Disease, 191*(1), 10-17.

Davis, K., Klar, H. & Coyle, J. T. (1991). *Foundations of Psychiatry*. Philadelphia: Harcourt Brace Jovanovich, Inc.

Delgado, P. L. & Moreno, F. A. (1998). Hallucinogens, serotonin, and obsessive-compulsive disorder. *Journal of Psychoactive Drugs, 30*(4), 359-66.

Dennison, S. J. (2005). Substance use disorders in individuals with co-occurring psychiatric disorders. In J. H. Lowinson, P. Ruiz, R. B. Millman & J. G. Langrod, eds. *Substance Abuse: A Comprehensive Textbook* (4th ed., pp. 904-12). Baltimore: Williams & Wilkins.

Department of Housing and Urban Development. (2007). *Annual Homeless Assessment Report to Congress*. http://www.huduser.org/Publications/pdf/ahar.pdf (accessed May 22, 2007).

Dimeoff, L. A., Comtois, K. A. & Linehan, M. M. (2003). Co-occurring addictive and borderline personality disorder. In A. W. Graham, T. K. Schultz, M. F. Mayo-Smith, R. K. Ries & B. B. Wilford, eds. *Principles of Addiction Medicine* (3rd ed., pp. 1359-70). Chevy Chase, MD: American Society of Addiction Medicine, Inc.

Drake, R. E., Mercer-McFadden, C., Mueser, K. T., McHugo, G. J. & Bond, G. R. (1998). Review of integrated mental health and substance abuse treatment for patients with dual disorders. *Schizophrenia Bulletin, 24*(4), 589-608.

Drake, R. E. & Mueser, K. T. (1996). Alcohol-use disorder and severe mental illness. *Alcohol Health & Research World, 20*(2), 87-93.

Drake, R. E. & Mueser, K. T. (2002). Co-occurring alcohol use disorder and schizophrenia. *Alcohol Research & Health, 26*(2), 99-102.

Dumaine, M. L. (2003). Meta-analysis of interventions with co-occurring disorders of severe mental illness and substance abuse: Implications for social work practice. *Research on Social Work Practice, 13*(2), 142-65.

Finnell, D. S. (2003). Use of the Transtheoretical Model for individuals with co-occurring disorders. *Community Mental Health Journal, 39*(1), 3-15.

Friedmann, P. D., Saitz, R. & Samer, J. H. (2003). Linking addiction treatment with other medical and psychiatric treatment systems. In A. W. Graham, T. K. Schultz, M. F. Mayo-Smith, R. K. Ries & B. B. Wilford, eds. *Principles of Addiction Medicine* (3rd ed., pp. 497-508). Chevy Chase, MD: American Society of Addiction Medicine, Inc.

Goldsmith, R. J. & Ries, R. K. (2003). Substance-induced mental disorders. In A. W. Graham, T. K. Schultz, M. F. Mayo-Smith, R. K. Ries & B. B. Wilford, eds. *Principles of Addiction Medicine* (3rd ed., pp. 1263-76). Chevy Chase, MD: American Society of Addiction Medicine, Inc.

Goodwin, M. D. (1990). *Manic-Depressive Illness*. London: Oxford University Press.

Gottesman, I. I. (1991). *Schizophrenia Genetics: The Origins of Madness*. New York: W. H. Freeman and Co.

Gourevitch, M. N. & Arnsten, J. H. (2005). Medical complications of drug use. In J. H. Lowinson, P. Ruiz, R. B. Millman & J. G. Langrod, eds. *Substance Abuse: A Comprehensive Textbook* (4th ed., pp. 840-62). Baltimore: Williams & Wilkins.

Grant, J. E., Kushner, M. G. & Kim, S. W. (2002). Pathological gambling and alcohol use disorder. *Alcohol Research & Health, 26*(2), 143-50.

Grella, C. E. (1996). Background and overview of mental health and substance abuse treatment systems: Meeting the needs of women who are pregnant or parenting. *Journal of Psychoactive Drugs, 28*(4), 319-43.

Grillo, C. M., Sinha, R. & O'Malley, S. S. (2002). Eating disorders and alcohol use disorders. *Alcohol Research & Health, 26*(2), 151-60.

Guydish, J. & Muck, R. (1999). The challenge of managed care in drug abuse treatment. *Journal of Psychoactive Drugs, 31*(3), 193-95.

Hasin, D. S. & Grant, B. F. (2002). Major depression in 6,050 former drinkers: Association with past alcohol dependence. *Archives of General Psychiatry, 59*(9), 794-800.

Human Genome Project. (2007). *Pharmacogenomics*. http://www.ornl.gov/sci/techresources/Human_Genome/medicine/pharma.shtml (accessed May 22, 2007).

Ikeda, R. (1994). Prescribing for chronic anxiety disorders. *Journal of Psychoactive Drugs, 26*(1), 75-76.

Keller, D. S. & Dermatis, H. (1999). Current status of professional training in the addictions. *Substance Abuse, 20*(3), 123-40.

Keltner, N. L. & Folks, D. G. (1997). *Psychotropic Drugs*. St. Louis: Mosby-Year Book, Inc.

Kendler, K. S. & Diehl, S. R. (1993). The genetics of schizophrenia: A current genetic-epidemiological perspective. *Schizophrenia Bulletin, 19*, 261-95.

Kendler, K. S., Heath, A. C., Neale, M. C., Kessler, R. C. & Eaves, L. J. (1993).

Alcoholism and major depression in women. A twin study of the causes of comorbidity. *Archives of General Psychiatry, 50*(9), 690-98.

Kessler, R. C., Berglund, P., Demler, O., Jin, R., Koretz, D., Merikangas, K. R., et al. (2003). The epidemiology of major depressive disorder: Results from the National Comorbidity Survey Replication (NCS-R). *JAMA, 289*(23), 3095-105.

Kessler, R. C., Berglund, P., Demler, O., Jin, R., Merikangas, K. R. & Walters, E. E. (2005). Lifetime prevalence and age-of-onset distributions of DSM-IV disorders in the National Comorbidity Survey Replication. *Archives of General Psychiatry, 62*(6), 593-602.

Kessler, R. C., McGonagle, K. A., Zhao, S., Nelson, C. B., Hughes, M., Eshleman, S., et al. (1994). Lifetime and 12-month prevalence of DSM-III-R psychiatric disorders in the United States. Results from the National Comorbidity Survey. *Archives of General Psychiatry, 51*(1), 8-19.

Kosten, T. R. & Ziedonis, D. M. (1997). Substance abuse and schizophrenia: Editors' introduction. *Schizophrenia Bulletin, 23*(2), 181-86.

Kushner, M. G., Sher, K. J. & Erickson, D. J. (1999). Prospective analysis of the relation between DSM-III anxiety disorders and alcohol use disorders. *American Journal of Psychiatry, 156*(5), 723-32.

Lavine, R. (1999). Roles of the psychiatrist and the addiction medicine specialist in the treatment of addiction. *San Francisco Medicine, 72*(4), 20-22.

Levin, F. R., Sullivan, M. A. & Donovan, S. J. (2003). Co-occurring addictive and attention deficit/hyperactivity disorder and eating disorders. In A. W. Graham, T. K. Schultz, M. F. Mayo-Smith, R. K. Ries & B. B. Wilford, eds. *Principles of Addiction Medicine* (3rd ed., pp. 1321-46). Chevy Chase, MD: American Society of Addiction Medicine, Inc.

Lilenfeld, L. R. & Kaye, W. H. (1996). The link between alcoholism and eating disorders. *Alcohol Health & Research World, 20*(2), 94-99.

Mallouh, C. (1996). The effects of dual diagnosis on pregnancy and parenting. *Journal of Psychoactive Drugs, 28*(4), 367-80.

Marangell, L. B., Silver, J. M., Martinez, J. M. & Yudofsky, S. C. (2002). *Psychopharmacology*. Washington, DC: American Psychiatric Publishing, Inc.

Matyas, T. (2006). Gene polymorphism and gene expression in schizophrenia. *Psychiatria Hungarica, 21*(6), 404-12.

McDowell, D. M. (1999). Evaluation of depression in substance abuse. Paper presented at the 152nd annual meeting of the American Psychiatric Association, Washington, DC.

McElroy, S. L., Soutullo, C. A., Goldsmith, R. J. & Brady, K. T. (2003). Co-occurring addictive and other impulse-control disorders. In A. W. Graham, T. K. Schultz, M. F. Mayo-Smith, R. K. Ries & B. B. Wilford, eds. *Principles of Addiction Medicine* (3rd ed., pp. 1347-58). Chevy Chase, MD: American Society of Addiction Medicine, Inc.

Medication Monitor. (2007). Updates on advances in therapy, 2007. *APHA Drug Info Line, 8*(1), 7.

Merikangas, K. R., Stevens, D. & Fenton, B. (1996). Comorbidity of alcoholism and anxiety disorders: The role of family studies. *Alcohol Health & Research World, 20*(2), 100-6.

Meyer, J. S. & Quenzer, L. F. (2005). *Psychopharmacology: Drugs, the Brain, and Behavior.* Sunderland, MA: Sinauer Associates, Inc.

Miller, W. & Rollnick, S. (2000). *Motivational Interviewing.* New York: Guilford Publications.

Minkoff, K. & Regner, J. (1999). Innovations in integrated dual diagnosis treatment in public managed care: The Choate dual diagnosis case rate program. *Journal of Psychoactive Drugs, 31*(1), 3-12.

Najavits, L. M., Harned, M. S., Gallop, R. J., Butler, S. F., Barber, J. P., Thase, M. E., et al. (2007). Six-month treatment outcomes of cocaine-dependent patients with and without PTSD in a multisite national trial. *Journal of Studies on Alcohol and Drugs, 68*(3), 353-61.

National Institute of Mental Health [NIMH]. (1999). *Mental Health: A Report of the Surgeon General.* http://www.samhsa.gov/reports/congress2002/execsummary.htm (accessed May 22, 2007).

Nitenson, N. & Gastfriend, D. R. (2003). Co-occurring and anxiety disorders. In A. W. Graham, T. K. Schultz, M. F. Mayo-Smith, R. K. Ries & B. B. Wilford, eds. *Principles of Addiction Medicine* (3rd ed., pp. 1287-96). Chevy Chase, MD: American Society of Addiction Medicine, Inc.

Nunes, E. V., Donovan, S. J., Brady, R. & Quitkin, F. M. (1994). Evaluation and treatment of mood and anxiety disorders in opioid-dependent patients. *Journal of Psychoactive Drugs, 26*(2), 147-53.

Olfson, M., Blanco, C., Liu, L., Moreno, C. & Laje, G. (2006). National trends in the outpatient treatment of children and adolescents with antipsychotic drugs. *Archives of General Psychiatry, 63*(6), 679-85.

Osher, F. C. (2001). Co-occurring addictive and mental disorders. In R. W. Manderscheid & M. J. Henderson, eds. *Mental Health, United States, 2000.* DHHS Publication No. (SMA) 01-3537. Rockville, MD: Center for Mental Health Services. http://mentalhealth.samhsa.gov/publications/allpubs/SMA01-3537/chapter10.asp (accessed May 23, 2007).

Pantalon, M. V. & Swanson, A. J. (2003). Use of the University of Rhode Island Change Assessment to measure motivational readiness to change in psychiatric and dually diagnosed individuals. *Psychology of Addictive Behaviors, 17*(2), 91-97.

Parry, C. D., Blank, M. B. & Pithey, A. L. (2007). Responding to the threat of HIV among persons with mental illness and substance abuse. *Current Opinion in Psychiatry, 20*(3), 235-41.

Physician's Desk Reference [PDR]. (2007). *Physicians Desk Reference* (57th ed.). Montvale, NJ: Medical Economics Company, Inc.

RachBeisel, J., Dixon, L. & Gearon, J. (1999). Awareness of substance abuse problems among dually diagnosed psychiatric inpatients. *Journal of Psychoactive Drugs, 31*(1), 53-57.

Rahav, M., Rivera, J. J., Nuttbrock, L., Ng-Mak, D., Sturz, E. L., Link, B. G. et al. (1995). Characteristics and treatment of homeless, mentally ill, chemical-abusing men. *Journal of Psychoactive Drugs, 27*(1), 93-103.

Regier, D. A., Farmer, M. E., Rae, D. S., Locke, B. Z., Keith, S. J., Judd, L. L., et al. (1990). Comorbidity of mental disorders with alcohol and other drug abuse. Results from the Epidemiologic Catchment Area (ECA) Study. *JAMA, 264*(19), 2511-18.

Reilly, P. M., Clark, H. W., Shopshire, M. S., Lewis, E. W. & Sorensen, D. J. (1994). Anger management and temper control: Critical components of post-traumatic stress disorder and substance abuse treatment. *Journal of Psychoactive Drugs, 26*(4), 401-7.

Rusk, T. N. & Rusk N. (2007). Not by genes alone: New hope for prevention. *Bulletin of the Menninger Clinic, 71*(1), 1-21.

Ruzek, J. I. (2003). Concurrent post-traumatic stress disorder and substance use disorder among veterans. In P. Ouimette & P. J. Brown, eds. *Trauma and Substance Abuse.* Washington, DC: American Psychological Association.

Salloum, I. M. & Daley, D. C. (1994). *Understanding Major Anxiety Disorders and Addiction.* Center City, MN: Hazelden Foundation.

Schuckit, M. A. (1986). Genetic and clinical implications of alcoholism and affective disorder. *American Journal of Psychiatry, 143*(2), 140-47.

Schuckit, M. A. (2000). *Drug and Alcohol Abuse.* New York: Kluwer Academic/Plenum Publishers.

Senay, E. C. (1997). Diagnostic interview and mental status examination. In J. H. Lowinson, P. Ruiz, R. B. Millman & J. G. Langrod, eds. *Substance Abuse: A Comprehensive Textbook* (3rd ed., pp. 364-368). Baltimore: Williams & Wilkins.

Senay, E. C. (1998). *Substance Abuse Disorders in Clinical Practice.* New York: W. W. Norton & Company.

Shaffer, D., Fisher, P., Dulcan, M. K., Davies, M., Piacentini, J., Schwab-Stone, M. E., et al. (1996). The NIMH Diagnostic Interview Schedule for Children, Version 2.3. *Journal of the American Academy of Child and Adolescent Psychiatry, 35*(7), 865-77.

Shivani, R., Goldsmith, J. & Anthenelli, R. M. (2002). Alcoholism and psychiatric disorders: Diagnostic challenges. *Alcohol Research & Health, 26*(2), 90-98.

Smith, D. E., Lawlor, B. & Seymour, R. B. (1996). Healthcare at the Crossroads. *San Francisco Medicine, 69*(6).

Smith, D. E. & Seymour, R. B. (2001). *The Clinician's Guide to Substance Abuse.* Center City, MN: Hazelden/McGraw-Hill.

Soderstrom, C. A., Smith, G. S., Dischinger, P. C., McDuff, D. R., Hebel, J. R., Gorelick, D. A., et al. (1997). Psychoactive substance use disorders among seriously injured trauma center patients. *JAMA, 277*(22), 1769-74.

Sonne, S. C. & Brady, M. D. (2002). Bipolar disorder and alcoholism. *Alcohol Research & Health, 26*(2), 103-8.

Stahl, S. M. (2001A). Dopamine system stabilizers, aripiprazole, and the next generation of antipsychotics: Part 1, "Goldilocks" actions at dopamine receptors. *Journal of Clinical Psychiatry, 62*(11), 841-42.

Stahl, S. M. (2001B). Dopamine system stabilizers, aripiprazole, and the next generation of antipsychotics: Part 2, illustrating their mechanism of action. *Journal of Clinical Psychiatry, 62*(12), 923-24.

Stewart, W. F., Ricci, J. A., Chee, E., Hahn, S. R. & Morganstein, D. (2003). Cost of lost productive work time among U.S. workers with depression. *JAMA, 289*(23), 3135-44.

Substance Abuse and Mental Health Services Administration [SAMHSA]. (2002A). *Report to Congress on the Prevention and Treatment of Co-Occurring Substance Abuse Disorders and Mental Disorders.* http://www.samhsa.gov/reports/congress2002/foreword.htm (accessed May 22, 2007).

Substance Abuse and Mental Health Services Administration. (2002B). *Women, Co-Occurring Disorders and Violence Study.* http://www.samhsa.gov/reports/congress2002/chap4slebp.htm (accessed May 22, 2007).

Thomas, K. (July 23, 2002). Surge in antipsychotic drugs given to kids draws concern. *USA Today,* p. D8.

Tiet, Q. Q. & Mausbach, B. (2007). Treatment for patients with dual diagnosis: A review. *Alcoholism: Clinical and Experimental Research, 31*(4), 513-36.

U.S. Food and Drug Administration. (2003). *FDA Approves Prozac for Pediatric Use to Treat Depression and OCD.* http://www.fda.gov/bbs/topics/ANSWERS/2003/ANS01187.html (accessed May 22, 2007).

Watkins, K. E., Burnam, A., Kung, F. Y. & Paddock, S. (2001). A national survey of care for persons with co-occurring mental and substance use disorders. *Psychiatric Services, 52*(8), 1062-68.

Wechsberg, W. M., Desmond, D., Inciardi, J. A., Leukefeld, C. G., Cottler, L. B. & Hoffman, J. (1998). HIV prevention protocols: Adaptation to evolving trends in drug use. *Journal of Psychoactive Drugs, 30*(3), 291-98.

Weiss, R. D., Greenfield, S. F., Najavits, L. M., Soto, J. A., Wyner, D., Tohen, M., et al. (1998). Medication compliance among patients with bipolar disorder and substance use disorder. *Journal of Clinical Psychiatry, 59*(4), 172-74.

Weiss, R. D., Griffin, M. L., Kolodziej, M. E., Greenfield, S. F., Najavits, L. M. & Daley, D. C., et al. (2007). A randomized trial of integrated group therapy vs. group drug counseling for patients with bipolar disorder and substance dependence. *American Journal of Psychiatry, 164*(1), 100-107.

Woody, G. E. (1996). The challenge of dual diagnosis. *Alcohol Health & Research World, 20*(2), 76-80.

Wu, L. T., Kouzis, A. C. & Leaf, P. J. (1999). Influence of comorbid alcohol and psychiatric disorders on utilization of mental health services in the National Comorbidity Survey. *American Journal of Psychiatry, 156*(8), 1230-36.

Zickler, P. (1999). Twin studies help define the role of genes in vulnerability to drug abuse. *NIDA Notes, 14*(4). http://www.nida.nih.gov/NIDA_Notes/NNVol14N4/Twins.html (accessed May 23, 2007).

Ziedonis, D., Steinberg, M. L., Simelson, D. & Wyatt, S. (2003). Co-occurring disorders and psychotic disorders. In A. W. Graham, T. K. Schultz, M. F. Mayo-Smith, R. K. Ries & B. B. Wilford, eds. *Principles of Addiction Medicine* (3rd ed., pp. 1297-320). Chevy Chase, MD: American Society of Addiction Medicine, Inc.

Zimberg, S. (1994). Individual psychotherapy: Alcohol. In M. Galanter & H. D. Kleber, eds. *The American Psychiatric Press Textbook of Substance Abuse Treatment* (pp. 263-73). Washington, DC: American Psychiatric Press, Inc.

Zimberg, S. (1999). A dual diagnosis typology to improve diagnosis and treatment of dual disorder patients. *Journal of Psychoactive Drugs. 31*(1), 47-51.

Zweben, J. E. (1996). Psychiatric problems among alcohol and other drug dependent women. *Journal of Psychoactive Drugs, 28*(4), 345-66.

Zweben, J. E. (2003). Integrating psychosocial services with pharmacotherapies in the treatment of co-occurring disorders. In A. W. Graham, T. K. Schultz, M. F. Mayo-Smith, R. K. Ries & B. B. Wilford, eds. *Principles of Addiction Medicine* (3rd ed., pp. 1371-80). Chevy Chase, MD: American Society of Addiction Medicine, Inc.

Zwillich, T. (1999). Beware of long-term effects of antidepressants. *Clinical Psychiatry News, 27*(9), 16.

G L O S S A R Y

A

AA *See* Alcoholics Anonymous

abruptio placentae Premature separation of the placenta from the wall of the uterus often due to cocaine or amphetamine use during pregnancy.

abscess A chronic, localized, pus-filled infection common in injection drug users because of their use of infected needles, repeated attempts to get the needle into a vein, or the irritating effects of the drug on the skin and body tissues.

absinthe A potent herb liquor containing wormwood, anise, and fennel that initially causes stimulation and euphoria but in large doses can be toxic.

absorption The transfer of alcohol or other drug from the point of ingestion, injection, or inhalation until it enters the bloodstream.

abstinence The act of refraining from the use of alcohol and any other drug. It also refers to stopping addictive behaviors, such as overeating and gambling.

abuse The continuation of any drug use or compulsive behavior despite adverse consequences; the step before addiction occurs.

academic model of addiction A theory of addiction that says it is caused by the body's adaptation to continued use of psychoactive drugs.

Acapulco gold Marijuana grown near Acapulco, Mexico, that is usually gold in color.

acculturation Acceptance and adoption of customs and mores of one culture by another.

acetaminophen A nonaspirin analgesic and antipyretic; often used in combination with opioids, such as codeine or hydrocodone; over-the-counter trade names include Tylenol® and Datril.®

acetone A volatile solvent abused as an inhalant; minute traces are found naturally in the body.

acetylaldehyde The first substance that is formed when alcohol is metabolized by the enzyme alcohol dehydrogenase in the liver; it is more toxic than alcohol.

acetylcholine (ACH) The first neurotransmitter to be discovered, it works at the nerve/muscle interfaces. It also affects memory, learning, aggression, alertness, blood pressure, heart rate, sexual behavior, and mental acuity.

ACH *See* **acetylcholine**

acid Lysergic acid diethylamide (LSD).

acne rosacea An alcohol-caused skin disease marked by swelling and inflammation of the face, especially the nose.

ACoA *See* **Adult Children of Alcoholics**

acquaintance rape Sexual assault by a person who is known to the victim, often a relative, neighbor, or even a date.

acquired immune deficiency syndrome (AIDS) A disease/syndrome caused by HIV and characterized by vulnerability to opportunistic infections.

acromegaly Abnormal bone growth; it can be caused by human growth hormone.

ACTH *See* **adrenocorticotropic hormone**

active transport The process by which a drug that is water-soluble hitchhikes across the blood-brain barrier by attaching to protein molecules.

acupuncture A 3,000-year-old treatment modality that uses needle insertion at nerve intersections to help heal. It has recently been used for heroin detoxification.

acute tolerance Instant tolerance (adaptation of the body) to a toxic dose of a drug. Also called *tachyphylaxis.*

addiction A progressive disease process characterized by loss of control over use, obsession with use, continued use despite adverse consequences, denial that there are problems, and a powerful tendency to relapse.

Addiction Severity Index (ASI) A structured interview that assesses six areas affected by substance use and abuse to assess substance dependence or alcoholism.

adenosine An inhibitory neurotransmitter affected (blocked) by caffeine.

ADHD *See* **attention-deficit/hyperactivity disorder**

adhesive patch *See* **skin patch**

adrenaline The principal stimulant neurohormone of most species; it stimulates heart rate and blood pressure, dilates bronchial muscles, and alerts the senses. *See* **epinephrine**.

adrenocorticotropic hormone (ACTH) Stimulates the adrenal cortex, causing the secretion of cortisol (an anti-inflammatory substance) and other glucocorticoids.

Adult Children of Alcoholics (ACoA) A 12-step self-help program to help adult children of alcoholics deal with the emotional turmoil caused by the addiction.

adulterant A pharmacologically inactive substance used to dilute a drug.

adulteration The dilution of a drug to increase its volume; used by street dealers to increase profits.

aerosol Liquid (usually a medicine) that is dispersed in the form of a fine mist.

affect How a person's mood is expressed (e.g., flat affect, blunted affect, or shallow affect).

affective disorder Any mood or emotional disorder (e.g., depression or bipolar affective disorder).

aftercare The services that are provided to recovering addicts after they leave a residential treatment program.

agonist A drug that initiates an effect when it imitates a neurotransmitter rather than blocks it (e.g., morphine).

agonist maintenance treatment   A harm reduction program (e.g., methadone maintenance) that consists of pharmacotherapy maintenance approaches coupled with counseling.

agoraphobia   A pervasive mental disorder characterized by an irrational fear of leaving home or a familiar setting and venturing outdoors or into a public place; often associated with panic attacks.

agua rica   A partially processed form of cocaine base in solution. Cocaine is often smuggled in this form.

AIDS   *See* **acquired immune deficiency syndrome**

Al-Anon   A 12-step self-help organization to aid the friends and relatives of alcoholics.

Alateen   A 12-step self-help organization for teenagers affected by an alcoholic parent or friend; it helps them deal with the pain and the disruption in their lives.

alcohol   An organic chemical created naturally by the fermentation of sugar, starch, or other carbohydrate. It can also be synthesized from ethylene or acetylene.

alcohol dehydrogenase   The principal enzyme in the liver that metabolizes alcohol.

alcohol-induced disorders   A diagnostic category in *DSM-IV-TR* under alcohol-related disorders that describes a group of psychiatric symptoms caused by alcohol intoxication or alcohol withdrawal, including alcohol-induced withdrawal, amnesia, psychotic disorder, and mood disorders.

alcohol-related birth defects (ARBD)   Any number of physical abnormalities that are caused by excess alcohol drinking during pregnancy without the facial deformities seen with fetal alcohol syndrome.

alcohol-related disorders   A diagnostic category in *DSM-IV-TR* that includes alcohol use disorders and alcohol-induced disorders.

alcohol-related neurodevelopmental disorder (ARND)   Nervous system abnormalities caused by excess drinking during pregnancy without the facial deformities seen with fetal alcohol syndrome.

alcoholic hepatitis   Inflammation and impairment of liver function caused by excess use of alcohol. *Also see* **hepatitis**.

Alcoholics Anonymous (AA)   The first 12-step self-help alcoholism recovery group, founded in 1934 by Bill Wilson and Dr. Bob Smith; tens of thousands of chapters exist worldwide.

alcoholism   Addiction to alcohol; a progressive disease characterized by loss of control over use, obsession with use, continued use despite adverse consequences, denial that there is a problem, and a powerful tendency to relapse.

ale   A beer with a slightly more bitter taste and a higher alcohol content than lager beer; uses the top fermentation process. The alehouse or pub and the use of ale rather than lager are prominent features of British life.

alkaloid   Any nitrogen-containing plant compound with pharmacological (often psychoactive) activity (e.g., morphine, cocaine, and nicotine).

alkanes   A class of hydrocarbons that are gases at room temperature; includes methane, butane, and propane.

allele gene   A paired gene whose difference from a normal gene may be responsible for one of the 3,500 chromosomally linked human diseases. Normally, the alleles have the same function (e.g., two alleles control eye color, but one is for blue eyes and the other is for brown eyes). In terms of addiction, one allele may be responsible for normal alcohol metabolism while the other does the same job but does it poorly, so the alcohol has a greater effect.

allergic reaction   An abnormal reaction to a substance; severe reactions such as anaphylactic shock caused by cocaine can be fatal.

allergy   A view of the effects of the substances of addiction, such as alcohol and methamphetamine, which causes an intense craving in someone who has altered his brain chemistry and become addicted.

alkanes   A class of hydrocarbons, including methane, butane, and propane, that can be inhaled.

allostasis   A process for achieving homeostasis through a number of physiological or behavioral changes rather than through the normal homeostatic process of small alterations in just a few body functions.

alpha alcoholism   *See* **Jellinek, E. M.**

alprazolam (Xanax®)   A popular benzodiazepine used to relieve anxiety.

alveoli   Tiny sacs at the end of the bronchioles in the lungs, where inhaled air or vaporized drugs are transferred to blood via the capillaries.

altered state of consciousness   A nonordinary state of perception that can be caused by psychoactive drugs.

Alzheimer's disease   The most widespread form of senile dementia; an organic disease marked by the progressive deterioration of mental functions.

Amanita muscaria   A hallucinogenic mushroom that is often prepared in liquid form and drunk. Also called *fly agaric*.

American Indians   Refers to indigenous people of North and South America who predated the colonizing European settlers of the fifteenth through nineteenth centuries. They are thought to have crossed over the Bering Strait from Asia 10,000 to 20,000 years ago. Also called *Native Americans*.

American Society of Addiction Medicine (ASAM)   A society of physicians dedicated to increasing access to and improving the quality of addiction medicine.

amine   A nitrogen atomic group attached to a carbon molecule (e.g., amino acids and amphetamines).

amino acid precursor loading   A medical intervention technique to ingest protein supplements and amino acids to build up neurotransmitter supplies.

amino acids   Organic nitrogen compounds that are the building blocks of proteins; some serve as neurotransmitters.

amotivational syndrome   A lack of desire to complete tasks or to succeed; sometimes attributed to the long-term effects of marijuana.

amphetamine $C_6H_5CH_2CH(NH_2)CH_3$; a nervous system stimulant that is closely related in structure and action to ephedrine and other sympathomimetic amines.

amphetamines   A class of powerful stimulants based on the amphetamine molecule that was first synthesized in 1887 and manufactured in the 1930s; the word is also used to include various methamphetamines. Amphetamines are prescribed for narcolepsy, ADHD, and, until the early 1970s, obesity and depression.

Ample Misuse Prevention Study (AMPS)   A prevention program similar to DARE that consists of a four-session curriculum for fifth- and sixth-graders; it also develops peer resistance skills.

AMPS   *See* **Ample Misuse Prevention Study**

amygdala   Part of the limbic system, or emotional center of the brain, that coordinates the actions of the autonomic and endocrine systems and is involved in regulating basic emotions.

anabolic   Anything that builds up the body (e.g., converting protein from amino acids to help build muscles).

anabolic-androgenic steroid   A steroid that builds muscles and strength; pharmacologically similar to testosterone; it also induces male sexual characteristics.

analeptic   Any stimulant drug.

analgesic   A painkiller that works by changing the perception of the pain rather than truly deadening the nerves as an anesthetic would.

analogues   *See* **designer drugs**

anandamide   An abundant neurotransmitter whose effects are similar to the effects of the THC in marijuana.

anaphylactic reaction   A severe overreaction or even fatal shock from the effects of a drug.

androstenedione   A natural hormone found in all animals and some plants. It is a metabolite of DHEA, a precursor of testosterone; used in sports to enhance recovery and muscle growth from exercise.

androgenic   Having a masculinizing effect.

anergia   A total lack of energy and motivation often caused by excess stimulant use.

anesthetic   A substance that causes the loss of the ability to feel pain or other sensory input (e.g., ether and halothane).

"angel dust"   *See* **phencyclidine**

anhedonia   The lack of the ability to feel pleasure, often caused by overuse of cocaine or amphetamines.

anorectic   A person with the eating disorder anorexia nervosa; a substance that reduces appetite.

anorexia nervosa   An eating disorder marked by a refusal to eat and a fear of maintaining a minimum normal weight.

anorexic   *See* **anorectic**

Antabuse®   *See* **disulfiram**

antagonist   A drug that blocks the normal transmission of messages between nerve cells by blocking the receptor sites that would normally be attached to certain neurotransmitters.

anterograde amnesia   Impairment of memory for events occurring after the onset of amnesia; inability to form new memories; often caused by the use of drugs such as flunitrazepam (Rohypnol®), alcohol, or some benzodiazepines.

antianxiety drug   *See* **anxiolytics**

antibody   An immunoglobulin molecule that recognizes and attacks foreign substances in the body such as viruses and bacteria.

anticholinergics   A class of mild deliriant drugs found in certain hallucinogenic plants (e.g., belladonna, henbane, mandrake, and datura). The active substances (scopolamine, atropine, and hyoscyamine) interfere with the action of acetylcholine, causing psychedelic reactions.

antidepressants   A series of drugs that are used to treat depression mostly by boosting the levels of serotonin in the brain (e.g., tricyclic antidepressants and selective serotonin reuptake inhibitors such as fluoxetine (Prozac®) and sertraline (Zoloft®).

antihistamines   Any drug that stops the inflammatory actions of histamines; used for congestion and allergies.

anti-inflammatories   Any substance, such as cortisone, that reduces inflammation.

antipriming   The use of medications to modulate or blunt the pleasurable reinforcing effects of psychoactive drugs.

antipsychotics   Drugs, such as phenothiazines, that are used to treat schizophrenia and other psychoses. Others include haloperidol, clozapine, risperidone (Risperdal®), quetiapine fumarate (Seroquel®), aripiprazole (Abilify®), and loxapine. Also called *neuroleptics.*

antiretroviral therapy   The use of antiretroviral drugs in combination with others to control the replication of HIV, the virus responsible for AIDS.

antisocial personality disorder   A psychiatric condition characterized by a person's disregards the rights and the feelings of others, feels no remorse, needs instant gratification, cannot learn from mistakes, cannot form personal relationships, and is often involved in risk taking, drug abuse, pathological lying, and criminality.

antitussives   Any medication that relieves coughing, such as hydrocodone or codeine.

anxiety   A state of intense fear and apprehension; symptoms include higher pulse, faster respiration, and excess sweating. Long-term anxiety can increase one's susceptibility to drugs use because some drugs (e.g., alcohol, heroin, and prescription sedatives) can control the symptoms of anxiety.

anxiety disorders   A series of mental disorders marked by excessive anxiety, fear, worry, and avoidance, including panic attacks, panic disorder, agoraphobia, obsessive-compulsive disorder, post-traumatic stress disorder, and generalized anxiety disorder.

anxiolytics   Drugs that are prescribed to treat anxiety disorders, including benzodiazepines, barbiturates, buspirone, and the Z-hypnotics.

AOD   An acronym for *alcohol and other drugs;* used in the drug-abuse prevention field.

aphrodisiac   A substance, such as sildenafil citrate (Viagra®), that increases sexual desire and/or performance.

apoptosis   Programmed cell death identified by an orderly series of biochemical events that often occur with drug use.

aqua vitae A medieval name for distilled liquor-literally "water of life"-when alcohol was thought to have unique medicinal and rejuvenation properties.

ARBD *See* **alcohol-related birth defects**

ARND *See* **alcohol-related neurodevelopmental disorder**

arrhythmia Irregularity of heartbeat (loss of rhythm) that can be lethal; often caused by drug use.

ARRRT Stands for *acceptance, reduction of stimuli, reassurance, rest, and talk-down*—steps for treatment of a bad psychedelic experience.

ASAM *See* **American Society of Addiction Medicine**

ASAM PPC-2R A screening test for co-occurring disorders, adolescent criteria, and residential levels of care. It evaluates six dimensions of problem areas and illness severity to match patients to four levels of care.

ASI *See* **Addiction Severity Index**

asthma medications A series of respiratory medications that include anti-inflammatory agents, decongestants, and bronchodilators to control asthma. Their use is restricted in sports competitions, but medical use is allowed.

astrocytes Star-shaped glial cells in the brain that support surrounding neurons.

ataxia Inability to coordinate muscular activity, often caused by brain disorders or drug use.

atherosclerosis Fat and plaque deposits on the lining of blood vessels, caused by high blood pressure, stress, smoking, and cocaine or methamphetamine use. It is often the cause of heart attacks, heart failure, and heart disease. Also called *hardening of the arteries.*

atropine (hyoscyamine) An active ingredient of the belladonna plant; an anticholinergic alkaloid and hallucinogen that can cause tachycardia and pupil dilation.

attention-deficit/hyperactivity disorder (ADHD) A disorder with several subtypes characterized by one or more of the following: inattention, impulsivity, and hyperactivity; it begins in childhood and may extend into adulthood.

Audit A 10-item screening exam for alcohol abuse.

autonomic nervous system Part of the peripheral nervous system that controls involuntary functions such as circulation, body temperature, and breathing.

autoreceptor A specialized neurotransmitter receptor on the button of a sending neuron that senses how much neurotransmitter is in the synaptic gap and then signals the cell to produce more or less of that neurotransmitter.

aversion therapy A form of therapy that inflicts pain as the client uses a substance, to encourage abstinence (e.g., some smoking-cessation programs give clients an electric shock when they smoke).

axon Part of the nerve cell that conducts the impulse away from the cell body to the terminals; they can be 40 to 50 centimeters long.

ayahuasca A hallucinogenic beverage brewed from the *Banisteriopsis caapi* bush by the Peruvian Chama Indians.

azidothymidine, zidovudine (AZT) HIV inhibitor medication used for control of HIV disease and AIDS.

AZT *See* **azidothymidine, zidovudine**

B

BAC *See* **blood alcohol concentration**

Bacchus Roman god of wine; same as Dionysus, the Greek god of wine.

"bad trip" An unpleasant or dangerous panic reaction to a psychedelic such as LSD.

"bagging" Putting an inhalant, such as model airplane glue, in a plastic bag and inhaling the fumes.

"balloons and crackers" The use of a pin or other cracking device to puncture a can of nitrous oxide or other inhalant; a balloon is placed over the end of the can, and the vapors collected in the balloon are then inhaled.

barbiturates A class of sedative-hypnotic drugs derived from the barbituric acid molecule (e.g., phenobarbital, butalbital, and secobarbital (Seconal®).

basal ganglia A group of neurons at the base of the cerebral hemispheres that help control involuntary muscle movement.

base A form of cocaine that can be smoked. The cocaine in cocaine hydrochloride has been freed from the hydrochloride molecule. *Crack* is freebase cocaine.

basing The process of transforming cocaine hydrochloride into smokable cocaine freebase and the practice of smoking cocaine base.

"basuco" A brownish puttylike intermediate product of cocaine refinement that can be smoked (usually in cigarettes); popular in coca-growing countries.

bee pollen A combination of plant pollen with nectar and bee saliva that is used to increase endurance; can cause severe allergic reactions.

beer An alcohol beverage that is brewed by fermenting malted grains (usually barley) and hops, an aromatic herb. Beer includes ale, bock beer, pilsner beer, malt liquor, stout, porter, and lager.

behavior modification A treatment technique based on the idea that psychological problems are learned and therefore can be unlearned.

behavioral tolerance Use of parts of the brain that are not affected by a drug to compensate for the other parts of the brain that are.

belladonna A hallucinogenic plant whose active ingredients (hyoscyamine, atropine, and scopolamine) cause intoxication, hallucinations, and drugged sleep. Also called *nightshade.*

benzodiazepines A group of minor tranquilizers, such as clonazepam (Klonopin®) and alprazolam (Xanax®), that calm anxiety, relax muscles, and induce sleep.

benzoylecgonine One of the metabolites of cocaine that can be found in the urine long after cocaine is no longer present in the body.

beta alcoholism *See* **Jellinek, E. M.**

beta blockers A class of drugs that calm the body's heart rate, respiration, and tension by blocking epinephrine (adrenaline) at the heart and in the brain; often used to control panic attacks; used illegally in sports such as riflery, diving, and archery.

betel nut   A nut from the areca palm tree that is chewed by 200 million people, particularly in Asia, for its mild stimulant effects.

bhang   An Indian name for the leaves and the stems of *Cannabis* (marijuana) plants; it is a mild form of marijuana that can be prepared for smoking, drinking, or ingestion.

Big Book   The main book of Alcoholics Anonymous; it contains the philosophy of AA and autobiographical stories of recovering alcoholics; used extensively in AA meetings.

binding sites   *See* **receptor sites**

"bindle"   A piece of paper folded like a miniature envelope to hold a small amount of a drug, such as 1 gram of cocaine.

binge   Using large amounts of a drug in a short period of time (e.g., cocaine binge). It can also refer to a behavioral addition (e.g., gambling or eating binge).

binge drinking   Drinking large amounts of alcohol at one sitting; artificially defined as five or more drinks for men and four or more drinks for women in one drinking session.

binge-eating disorder   Recurring episodes of binge eating without resorting to vomiting or other methods used by the bulimic or anorexic to avoid gaining weight.

bioavailability   The degree to which a drug becomes available to the target tissue after administration.

biotransformation   Metabolic transformation of drugs that enter the bloodstream to metabolites.

Biphetamine®   A trade name for a capsule containing two forms of amphetamines, used mostly in the 1950s, 1960s, and 1970s.

bipolar affective disorder   A mental illness characterized by mood swings between excessive elation and severe depression, with periods of normalcy. Also called *manic depression.*

"black tar" heroin   A black or brown form of heroin produced in Mexico. It varies from hard to sticky, has 20% to 80% purity, and is water-soluble. It is more popular on the West Coast of the United States than in the East.

blackout   Loss of awareness and recall without unconsciousness due to intoxication by alcohol or other drugs (amnesia while under the influence of drugs).

blood alcohol concentration (BAC)   The concentration of alcohol in the blood; used legally to identify drunk drivers (e.g., 8 parts alcohol per 10,000 parts blood equals a BAC of 0.08, which is the legal limit in all states). Most countries have a lower legal BAC for drivers.

blood-brain barrier   Tightly sealed cells lining the blood vessel walls in the brain; prevents most toxins, bacteria, and pathogens from reaching the brain. Psychoactive drugs breach this barrier.

blood doping   Transfusing extra blood before an endurance sporting event to increase the oxygen-carrying capacity of the circulatory system.

"blotter acid"   A form of LSD; a drop of the drug is absorbed on a small piece of blotter paper and swallowed or placed on the tongue and absorbed.

"blow"   Street name for cocaine hydrochloride powder that is snorted.

bock beer   A stronger, darker, and sweeter variety of lager that has a shelf life of six weeks; a seasonal beer made from the residue in vats; traditionally ready for consumption with the coming of spring.

"body packer"   A smuggler who swallows balloons or condoms usually filled with heroin or cocaine and then defecates the drugs after clearing customs.

"bong"   A water pipe used to smoke marijuana. The smoke is cooled and made less harsh as it passes through the water.

borderline personality disorder (BPD)   An Axis II mental illness characterized by sharp shifts in mood, impulsivity (often self-destructive), anger, alienation, and unstable self-image; BPD patients are often drawn to drug use and are very difficult to treat.

BPD   *See* **borderline personality disorder**

brain imaging techniques   Methods of making images of the brain and brain functions without dissection or death. Techniques include CAT, PET, SPECT, MRI, fMRI, and beta scans.

brainstem   Located at the top of the spinal cord, this section of the hindbrain is the sensory switchboard for the mind. It is often affected by hallucinogens. Contains the medulla and reticular formation.

brand name   *See* **trade name**

breathalyzer   A machine that can measure the blood alcohol concentration by analyzing the exhaled breath of a drinker.

bromide   Hydrogen bromide salts formerly used (before barbiturates) as sedatives, hypnotics (sleeping pills), and anticonvulsants.

bromocriptine   Medication that increases dopamine in the brain; helps initial detoxification from cocaine or amphetamines.

bromo-dragonFLY (ABDF)   A recently synthesized hallucinogenic drug related to the phenethylamine family. Its effects are similar to LSD but are much longer acting, sometimes for days.

brownout   Like an alcohol blackout except the drinker has partial recall of events.

bruxism   Clenching of the teeth that can be caused by stimulants, particularly methamphetamines and MDMA.

Buerger's disease   Circulatory disease that can be caused by smoking. It can result in amputation of a limb.

buccal   Having to do with the cheek; absorption site for several drugs that are used orally (e.g., chewing tobacco and coca leaf).

bufotenine   A hallucinogenic substance found in the skin secretions of several toads and in some plants.

bulimia nervosa   An eating disorder characterized by binge eating followed by weight-control techniques that include vomiting, excessive exercise, laxatives, and starvation.

buprenorphine   A drug that can help block both withdrawal symptoms and the effects of heroin; it is useful in detoxification and maintenance programs; it can be prescribed in a doctor's office.

bupropion (Zyban®)   An antidepressant that raises the levels of norepinephrine and dopamine to reduce craving; used in smoking-cessation programs.

"businessman's special"   *See* **dimethyltryptamine**

buspirone (BuSpar®)   An antianxiety drug that was created to avoid affecting parts of the brain that can lead to addiction.

BuSpar®   *See* **buspirone**

butanol (butyl alcohol)   A synthetic alcohol used in many industrial processes.

"button"   The round top of a peyote cactus that is harvested for its psychoactive ingredient mescaline.

butyl nitrite   An inhalant that causes a brief rush by dilating blood vessels in the heart and the head, followed by dizziness, headaches, and giddiness.

C

caffeine   A stimulant alkaloid of the chemical class called *xanthines,* found in coffee, tea, chocolate, and colas.

caffeinism   Intoxication due to caffeine use, characterized by restlessness, insomnia, nervousness, diuresis (increased excretion of urine), and gastrointestinal problems.

CAGE Questionnaire   A four-question test for problem drinking used frequently in medical settings. *CAGE* stands for *cut down, annoyed, guilty,* and *eye-opener.*

CALDATA   *See* **California Alcohol and Drug Treatment Assessment**

California Alcohol and Drug Treatment Assessment (CALDATA)   The most comprehensive study of treatment effectiveness done in California; it showed that each $1 spent in treatment saves at least $7 in reduced costs (e.g., because of incarceration, missed work, and burglaries).

cAMP   *See* **cyclic adenosine monophosphate**

CAMP   *See* **Campaign Against Marijuana Planting**

Campaign Against Marijuana Planting (CAMP)   A multi-jurisdictional law enforcement campaign to search out and destroy illegal marijuana fields and plants; its implementation is being resisted by some counties.

cyclic adenosine monophosphate (cAMP)   A neurotransmitter involved in the development of opioid tolerance and tissue dependence.

Cannabis   The botanical genus of all plants that contain marijuana or hemp. *C. indica* contains the most THC (psychoactive ingredient) of all the species; a short shrub. *C. ruderalis* has a low THC content. *C. sativa* is the most common species; can be high in hemp fiber content or THC content; often 10 to 20 feet tall.

cannabinoids   Any of the psychoactive chemicals found in *Cannabis* plants, including THC, the major psychoactive ingredient, cannabinol, and cannabidiol.

cannabinol (CBN)   A non-psychoactive cannabinoid found in the *Cannabis* plant; it is an oxidation product of THC.

capillary   The tiniest blood vessel in the circulatory system; absorbs drugs from mouth, gums, intestinal wall, nose, lungs, or other points of contact.

carbohydrates   The most abundant biological molecules and the main plant energy source for animals and humans; refined carbohydrates act like a psychoactive drug in food addicts and compulsive overeaters.

carbon monoxide   A poisonous gas that is one of the toxic byproducts of smoking tobacco. Its chemical symbol is CO instead of the nontoxic CO_2 (carbon dioxide) that we exhale and breathe every day.

carcinogen   Any substance or pathogen that can cause cancer.

cardiomyopathy   A general diagnostic term for a primary noninflammatory disease of the heart muscle; an enlarged, flabby, and inefficient heart often caused by excessive, chronic drinking.

cardiovascular   Relating to heart and blood vessels (e.g., the cardiovascular system).

catecholamine   A class of neurotransmitters that are particularly affected by psychoactive drugs, especially stimulants (e.g., epinephrine, norepinephrine, and dopamine).

cathinone   The active stimulant alkaloid ingredient, along with cathine, in the plant stimulant called *khat.*

CBN   *See* **cannabinol**

CD   *See* **chemical dependency**

CD4+ cell   An immune cell, such as a lymphocyte, that is found in the blood and helps regulate immune functions. Also called *T-helper cell.*

central nervous system (CNS)   The brain and the spinal cord.

cerebellum   The large part of the hindbrain that affects motor systems, coordination of movement, and muscle tone.

cerebral cortex   The outer part of the new brain (cerebrum) that enfolds the old brain. The gray matter is 1 to 4 millimeters thick. It reasons, thinks, processes sensory input, and initiates voluntary movement.

cerebral hemispheres   The two halves of the cerebrum that make up the cerebral cortex and the basal ganglia. Each half controls the sensory input and the motor functions of the opposite half of the body.

cerebrum   The largest part of the brain; consists of the cerebral cortex (gray matter) and the thicker white matter that connects the cerebral cortex to the rest of the brain.

charas   Indian word for the resin of the *Cannabis* (marijuana) plant that is made into hashish.

chasing   Continuing to gamble to recoup previous losses; takes place during the losing phase that most often occurs in problem and compulsive gamblers; the four phases are winning, losing, desperation, and giving up.

"chasing the dragon"   Heating heroin on a piece of metal foil and inhaling the smoke through a straw.

chemical dependency (CD)   Physical and/or psychological dependence on one or more psychoactive drugs. *Also see* **addiction**.

chemotherapy   Use of medications or chemicals to control disease, usually cancer.

chewing tobacco   Tobacco leaves that are processed to be chewed, allowing the nicotine-laden tobacco juice to be absorbed by capillary blood vessels in the mouth, mostly in the gums.

"chillum"   A cone-shaped clay, wood, or stone pipe used to smoke bhang, ganja, or charas (various parts of a *Cannabis* plant); widely used in India.

"China white"   (1) Refined and unusually pure heroin from Southeast Asia, mostly from the Golden Triangle. (2) Synthetic heroin (e.g., alpha-methylfentanyl).

"chipper"   One who uses drugs such as heroin, occasionally; a sporadic heroin user.

"chiva"   Spanish street name for Mexican tar heroin.

chlamydia   The most common sexually transmitted disease in the United States; the presence of the infection is marked by a fluid discharge from the genitals or rectum.

chloral hydrate   A drug used after the mid-1800s as a sedative, an anticonvulsant, and a hypnotic; used in a "Mickey" to knock out and shanghai sailors.

cholinergic   Pertaining to receptor sites and other neuronal structures involved in the synthesis, production, storage, and function of the neurotransmitter acetylcholine.

chromatography   Drug-testing process; gas chromatography and thin layer chromatography are the main uses.

chromosome   Rod-shaped structures made of DNA and protein in the nuclei of cells. Each of the 46 chromosomes (in 23 pairs) in one cell contains more than 1,000 genes (our genetic code).

"chronic"   (1) Slang for marijuana. (2) Potent marijuana. (3) Crack smoked with a marijuana cigarette.

chronic obstructive lung disease (COPD)   Progressive degeneration of the air sacs in the lungs (e.g., emphysema and chronic bronchitis); often caused by smoking tobacco or, less often, marijuana.

cirrhosis   A serious progressive liver disease that scars the liver, often caused by heavy chronic alcohol abuse as well as by hepatitis B and C.

clonazepam (Klonopin®)   A popular benzodiazepine sedative. People in methadone maintenance use it to increase the high from methadone.

clonidine   Anti-hypertensive medication used to help block withdrawal symptoms from heroin, alcohol, sedatives, and even nicotine.

club drugs   Drugs used at music parties, often called *raves,* that include MDMA (ecstasy), ketamine, GHB, GBL, and nitrous oxide.

CNS   *See* **central nervous system**

co-occurring disorders   The simultaneous occurrence of an interrelated mental disorder and a substance use disorder. Also called *dual diagnosis.*

coca (*Erythroxylum coca*)   The leaves of this shrub contain 0.5% to 1.5% cocaine and are chewed for a mild stimulation; 95% of all coca is grown in South America.

coca paste   The first extract of the refinement process that converts coca leaf to cocaine; often smoked (mostly in South America); often contains sulfuric acid and other toxic impurities.

cocada   A wad of coca leaves and soda lime formed into a ball; chewed by natives of the Andes Mountains.

cocaethylene   A toxic metabolite of cocaine formed by the use of alcohol and cocaine; causes more-severe cardiovascular effects and often more anger than cocaine

alone.

cocaine   The active ingredient of the coca bush. This alkaloid, first extracted by Albert Niemann in 1859, is a powerful, fast-acting stimulant.

cocaine freebase   A smokable form of cocaine made by releasing the hydrochloride molecule from cocaine hydrochloride; has a lower vaporization point than snorting cocaine.

cocaine hydrochloride   The refined extract from the coca bush. This white powder is used as a topical anesthetic for surgery and misused by addicts for snorting or injecting.

cocaine psychosis   A drug-induced mental illness; symptoms include extreme paranoia and hallucinations; similar to methamphetamine psychosis.

codeine   An extract of opium discovered in 1832. Between 0.5% and 2.5% of opium is codeine. This opiate analgesic is used to control mild pain, coughs, and diarrhea. Also called *methyl morphine.*

codependency   "A pattern of painful dependence on another person's compulsive behaviors and on approval from others in an attempt to find safety, self-worth, and identity" (Scottsdale definition). Codependents judge their self-worth by relying on other's opinions of them, so they try too hard to please, have low self-esteem, are very impulsive, and are in denial.

cognition   Accurate appraisal of one's surroundings through perceiving, thinking, and remembering; often disrupted during drug use, detoxification, and initial abstinence.

"cold turkey"   Detoxification from a drug, such as heroin, without the use of lower medications to ease the withdrawal symptoms.

coke   Street name for cocaine.

"coke bugs"   Imaginary insects that a long-term cocaine abuser thinks are crawling under the skin; they often cause abusers to scratch themselves bloody. Similar to "meth bugs."

collapsed vein   A blood vessel that collapses on itself due to repeated injections or other traumas.

competency-building program   Training in self-esteem, in socially acceptable behavior, and in decision-making, self-assertion, problem-solving, and vocational skills.

compulsion   An uncontrolled need to perform certain acts, often repetitively, to forget painful thoughts or unacceptable ideas (e.g., obsessive-compulsive disorder).

compulsive behaviors   These include compulsive gambling, anorexia, bulimia, overeating, sexual addiction, compulsive shopping, and codependency. Drug addiction is a compulsive behavior.

compulsive gambling   A progressive impulse-control disorder characterized by: a preoccupation with and a compulsion to bet increasing amounts of money on games of chance; continued gambling despite financial, work-related, and relationship problems; compulsion to chase losses; use of illegal acts or lying to get money with which to bet; and extreme denial that there is a problem.

computer games addiction   Compulsion to play games,

both online and through stand-alone systems.

computer relationship addiction Excessive searching through the Internet for relationships that can lead to cyber-affairs.

confabulation Repetition of false memories.

confrontation A counseling technique used individually or in a group that challenges a client's denial. This technique is crucial in treatment because most addicts are reluctant or afraid to change.

congeners (1) A chemical relative of another drug. (2) By-products of fermentation (organic alcohols and salts) that add flavor and bite to alcoholic beverages.

congenital abnormalities Birth defects in a newborn infant.

Conquistadors The soldiers who accompanied Spanish explorers and missionaries, mostly to the Americas, to search for wealth and to exploit and colonize new territories.

contact high (1) A nondrugged person emotionally experiencing a druglike experience from being around or in contact with drug users. (2) Getting high from skin absorption of a drug such as LSD. (3) Actually inhaling enough drugs (marijuana, cocaine, or heroin) to be affected in an environment where other people are smoking drugs.

controlled drinking a controversial harm reduction technique that permits some drinking rather than abstinence as a way to limit alcohol abuse.

controlled drugs Psychoactive substances that are strictly regulated (scheduled) according to the Controlled Substances Act of 1970; Schedule 1 includes cocaine, heroin, and marijuana.

Controlled Substances Act of 1970 The comprehensive drug control law passed to reduce the growing availability and use of psychoactive drugs in the United States.

convulsions Involuntary muscle spasms, often severe, that can be caused by stimulant overdose or by depressant withdrawal.

COPD *See* **chronic obstructive lung disease**

coronary arteries Arteries that directly supply the heart with blood; blocked coronary arteries are often the cause of heart attacks.

corpus callosum The group of nerve fibers that connects the two cerebral hemispheres of the cerebrum.

cortex The outer part of an organ (e.g., cerebral cortex, the outer part of the brain).

corticosteroids A class of drugs related to cortisol, a hormone normally produced by the body; helps control allergic reactions; relieves inflammation and pain and can create a sense of physical well-being; different from anabolic steroids.

corticotropin A neurotransmitter involved in the immune system, healing, and stress.

cortisone A steroidlike metabolite of hydrocortisone, a compound that reduces inflammation.

cotton fever A blood poisoning or infection caused by injecting cotton fibers, pyrogens, or bacteria when using heroin, cocaine, or amphetamines intravenously. Symptoms include chills and fever.

countertransference When a therapist or counselor lets personal feelings influence how he or she treats a client.

crack Slang for cocaine that is made into smokable form by transforming cocaine hydrochloride to freebase cocaine, using baking soda, heat, and water.

"crank" Street name for methamphetamine sulfate but often applied to any methamphetamine.

crash The comedown from a high (usually a stimulant high) in which energy is depleted by the drug (e.g., methamphetamine or cocaine), causing the user to stay awake for days. Depression, anergia, and anhedonia are common.

craving The powerful desire to use a psychoactive drug or engage in a compulsive behavior. It is manifested in physiological changes such as sweating, anxiety, raised heart rate, a drop in body temperature, pupil dilation, and stomach muscle movements.

creatine A nutritional supplement; this compound is synthesized in the body from amino acids or extracted from fish and meat; helps muscle energy metabolism, allowing someone who is working out to recover faster.

critical dose A threshold level of drinking below which most neurobehavioral effects are not seen.

cross-dependence Occurs when an individual becomes addicted or tissue-dependent on one drug, resulting in biochemical and cellular changes that support an addiction to other drugs.

cross-tolerance The development of tolerance to other drugs by the continued exposure to a similar drug (e.g., tolerance to heroin translates to tolerance to morphine, alcohol, and barbiturates).

"crystal" Used mostly to denote other amphetamines particularly dextromethamphetamine ("ice"), a smokable form of methamphetamine.

cue extinction *See* **desensitization**

cybersexual addiction Excessive use of online pornography or sex-related chat rooms to set up virtual or real sexual relationships.

cycling Alternating use of different steroids over set periods of time to minimize side effects and maximize desired strength- and muscle-enhancing effects.

cystic acne An inflammation of oil glands in the skin, characterized by eruptions and scarring; often caused by prolonged use of anabolic-androgenic steroids.

cytokines A neurochemical that transmits messages between cells in the immune system; they can kill neurons.

D

Drug Abuse Resistance Education (DARE) A drug and violence prevention curriculum, usually taught in the fifth grade by police officers. It has been revising its curriculum to counter criticism of its effectiveness.

DARE *See* **Drug Abuse Resistance Education**

date rape Sexual assault by a date rather than by a stranger. This and acquaintance rape are the most common types of rapes.

date-rape drug Drugs like flunitrazepam (Rohypnol®), a strong sedative-hypnotic that can induce amnesia, and

GHB are slipped into a drink so that a date can be assaulted while in a stupor and not remember what happened. It is now banned in the United States.

DATOS *See* **Drug Abuse Treatment Outcome Study**

datura Hallucinogenic plant used throughout history; it contains the alkaloids hyoscyamine and scopolamine and disrupts the action of acetylcholine.

DAWN *See* **Drug Abuse Warning Network**

DEA *See* **Drug Enforcement Administration**

decriminalization Eliminating criminal penalties for drug possession or use and replacing them with fines or other civil penalties.

dehydration A deficiency of water in the body that can be aggravated by some drugs (e.g., GHB, creatine, MDMA, and methamphetamine), particularly when exercising or dancing.

dehydroepiandrosterone (DHEA) A hormone supplement used by some athletes to try to increase testosterone levels.

delirium tremens (DTs) Severe withdrawal symptoms from high-dose chronic alcohol use; symptoms include visual and auditory hallucinations, trembling, and convulsions; sometimes results in death.

deliriants Drugs that cause hallucinations, delusions, and confusion (e.g., ketamine, nutmeg, datura, belladonna, and deadly nightshade).

delta-9 tetrahydrocannabinol The main active ingredient in marijuana. Also called *THC.*

delta alcoholism *See* **Jellinek, E. M.**

delusion A mistaken idea that is not swayed by reason, often involving the senses.

demand reduction A strategy to reduce drug use by lessening people's desire to begin use through prevention, treatment, and education.

dementia Intellectual impairment, found in some older people, often in those with Alzheimer's disease; includes loss of memory and abstract thinking, personality changes, and impaired social skills.

Demerol® *See* **meperidine**

dendrites Tiny fibers that branch out from nerve cells to receive messages from other nerve cells. Many drugs act on the ends of the dendrites and affect this message transmission.

denial The inability or unwillingness to perceive one's dependence on a drug; a defense mechanism manifested by drug abusers and addicts.

deoxyribonucleic acid (DNA) An organic substance found in the chromosomes of all living cells that stores and replicates hereditary information. The other type of nucleic acid is ribonucleic acid (RNA).

dependence (1) Physiological adaptation to a psychoactive drug to the point where abstinence triggers withdrawal symptoms and readministration of the drug relieves those symptoms. (2) Psychological need for a psychoactive drug to induce desired effects or avoid negative emotions or feelings. (3) Reliance on a substance (or a compulsive behavior).

depersonalization A mental state when there is a loss of the feeling of reality or of one's self; can be caused by several psychoactive drugs, particularly hallucinogens.

depressants Psychoactive drugs, such as alcohol, sedative-hypnotics, opiates, or muscle relaxants, that decrease the actions in the brain, resulting in depressed respiration, heart rate, muscle strength, and other functions. Also called *downers.*

depression A psychological mood disorder characterized by such symptoms as depressed mood, feelings of hopelessness, sleep disturbances, and even suicidal feelings.

depressive symptoms Feelings of sadness caused by grief, medical conditions, or reactions to stress; they are usually short-lived compared with depressive disorders, which can last for many months or years.

desensitization A therapy technique that first exposes drug addicts to drug cues and drug-using situations that increase craving and then desensitizes them through education, biofeedback, or talk-down. Also called *cue extinction.*

designer drugs Drugs formulated by street chemists that are similar to controlled drugs. There are designer amphetamines that act partly like psychedelics (e.g., MDMA and MDA) and designer heroin (e.g., MPPP). Also called *analogues.*

detection period The time frame after using a drug in which the substance can be detected by drug testing.

detoxification A drug therapy technique for eliminating a drug from the body. It can take a few hours to two weeks or more, depending on type of drug and length of use. Detoxification can also be done without medications. It is the first step in most treatment protocols for addiction.

developmental arrest The slowing or stopping of emotional development in a drug user, an abused child, or a child with other psychological problems.

dextroamphetamine A strong amphetamine stimulant sold as Dexedrine® and Eskatrol.®

dextromethamphetamine Smokable methamphetamine. Also called *"crystal," "ice," "glass,"* and *"shabu."*

dextromethorphan (DXM) A nonprescription opioid cough suppressant found in more than 140 medications; very high doses can cause psychedelic effects.

developmental disorders Mental disorders, such as mental retardation and ADHD, first diagnosed in childhood.

DHEA *See* **dehydroepiandrosterone**

diacetylmorphine Chemical name for heroin. *See* **heroin.**

Diagnostic and Statistical Manual of Mental Disorders (DSM-IV-TR) A publication of the American Psychiatric Association that classifies mental illnesses.

diathesis-stress theory of addiction A theory that says a predisposition to addiction caused by hereditary and environmental factors, such as stress, is triggered and later aggravated by excessive drug use.

diazepam (Valium®) The most popular benzodiazepine of the 1960s, 1970s, and 1980s. It is classified as a sedative-hypnotic.

diencephalon An area of the brain located beneath the cerebral cortex, consisting of the thalamus and the hypothalamus.

diet pills Any substance that reduces appetite; most often amphetamine congeners, such as dexfenfluramine (Redux®) and fenfluramine (Pondimin®), or amphetamines such as methamphetamine hydrochloride (Desoxyn®).

diffusion　The tendency of drug molecules to spread from an area of high concentration to an area of low concentration.

diluent　Usually, a pharmacologically inactive substance used to dilute or bind together potent drug substances. Street drugs can contain active diluents like quinine and aspirin.

dimethyl sulfoxide (DMSO)　A liquid that is easily absorbed through the skin and often used to transport other drugs, such as steroids, through the skin.

dimethyltryptamine (DMT)　A short-acting hallucinogenic drug found in several plants (yopo beans and epena) as well as in the skin secretions of some frogs; also synthesized in the laboratory as a white, yellow, or brown powder. Also called *businessman's special* because of its short duration of action.

"dirty basing"　A process of making smokable (freebase) cocaine using baking soda alone, without ether, resulting in a product that contains many diluents and impurities.

disease concept　This model maintains that addiction is a chronic, progressive, relapsing, incurable, and potentially fatal condition that is mostly a consequence of genetic irregularities in brain chemistry. The addiction is set in motion by drug use in a susceptible host in an environment conducive to drug misuse. Loss of control and compulsive use quickly follow.

disinhibition　The loss of inhibitions that control behavior, making the person more likely to perform formerly unthinkable or difficult actions (e.g., drinking alcohol makes a person more likely to overcome shyness and talk to others).

dispositional tolerance　Cellular and chemical changes in the body that speed up the metabolism of foreign substances (e.g., the creation of extra cytocells and mitochondria in the liver to handle larger and larger amounts of alcohol).

distillation　A chemical process that vaporizes the alcohol in fermented beverages and then collects the concentrated distillate. It can raise the percentage of alcohol in a beverage from 12% (in wine) to 40% (in brandy).

distribution　The transportation of a drug through the circulatory system to other tissues and organs.

disulfiram (Antabuse®)　A drug used to help prevent alcoholism relapse by triggering unpleasant side effects if alcohol is drunk.

"ditch weed"　Low-grade marijuana that is often found along the roadside in ditches. It was more plentiful when hemp was grown all over the United States.

diuresis　Excess excretion of water due to excess intake or drug use.

diuretic　A drug that decreases the amount of water in the body by increasing the frequency and the quantity of urination; often used to make one's competing weight in sports or to control blood pressure.

diversion　(1) Diverting prescription drugs from legal sources into the illegal market, mostly opiates and sedative-hypnotics. (2) Putting a first-time drug offender in a treatment program rather than jail.

DMSO　*See* **dimethyl sulfoxide**

DMT　*See* **dimethyltryptamine**

DNA　*See* **deoxyribonucleic acid**

DOB (2,5-dimethoxy-4-bromoamphetamine)　A synthetic illegal stimulant/hallucinogen.

DOM (2,5-dimethoxy-4-bromo-amphetamine)　A long-lasting synthetic hallucinogen. Also known in the 1960s as *STP* and classified as a phenylalkylamine psychedelic.

dopamine　A major neurotransmitter almost always affected by psychoactive drugs; it acts at the nucleus accumbens in the reward/reinforcement pathway to produce euphoria and a desire to repeat the drug-using activity; it also helps control voluntary muscle movement.

dopaminergic reward pathway　Sometimes referred to as the *reward/reinforcement pathway,* through which a psychoactive drug triggers a rush and euphoria.

dose-response curve　A graph that shows the relationship between the amount of drug taken and the effects observed in or reported by the user.

double trouble　The existence of a substance use disorder and a mental disorder. Also called *dual diagnosis* and *co-occurring disorders.*

down regulation　The reduction in the number of receptor sites for a specific neurotransmitter, caused by continued use of a drug (e.g., ecstasy overuse causes a reduction in the number of serotonin receptors, inducing the need for greater amounts of the drug).

dragonfly　*See* **bromo-dragonFLY**

DRD$_2$A$_1$ allele gene　The first gene discovered that signals a tendency to alcoholism and other addictions; it signals a shortage of dopamine receptors in the nucleus accumbens.

driving under the influence (DUI)　Drunk driving or driving under the influence of another psychoactive drug.

Driving Under the Influence of Intoxicants (DUII)　A program in the state of Oregon for resolving a conviction for DUI or DWI charges.

driving while intoxicated (DWI)　Drunk driving or driving under the influence of another psychoactive drug.

dronabinol (Marinol®)　A synthetic THC.

Drug Abuse Treatment Outcome Study (DATOS)　Research done between 1991 and 1993 to study the effectiveness of treatment.

Drug Abuse Warning Network (DAWN)　A federally funded data collection system that gathers information on drug fatalities, ER incidents, and use patterns from medical examiners and emergency rooms.

drug courts　Courts that offer alternatives to incarceration for drug offenses by first- and occasionally second-time offenders; coerced treatment is the main alternative.

drug distribution　*See* **distribution**

drug diversion　*See* **diversion** (1)

drug diversion programs　Programs used by drug courts to treat first-time drug users and keep them from advancing to abuse and addiction.

Drug Enforcement Administration (DEA)   The federal agency charged with policing drug abuse, particularly the supply reduction part of prevention.

drug-free workplace   A federal government mandate to keep drugs out of the workplace, often through drug testing.

drug hunger   A strong craving for a particular drug.

drug interaction   The alteration of the effect of one drug by the presence of another drug. *Also see* **synergism**.

drug testing   Examining the blood, breath, urine, saliva, or hair of people to determine if they are using drugs.

drug therapy   (1) The use of medications to detoxify a drug abuser, to reduce craving, or to substitute a less damaging drug for a damaging one. (2) Any medical treatment that involves the use of medications.

dry drinking culture   A culture that restricts the availability of alcohol and taxes it more heavily (e.g., Denmark and Sweden); it is often characterized by binge drinking.

dry drunk   An alcoholic who has quit drinking but is not in recovery; craves alcohol constantly and generally has alcoholic personality traits such as insensitivity to others, a rigid outlook, dissatisfaction, and a lack of insight or self-examination but has learned to resist the impulse rather than change the lifestyle.

DSM-IV-TR   *See Diagnostic and Statistical Manual of Mental Disorders*

DTs   *See* **delirium tremens**

dual diagnosis   A substance abuser with a coexisting mental illness. Also called *comorbidity, MICA* (mentally ill substance abuser), *double trouble,* and *co-occurring disorders.*

DUI   *See* **driving under the influence**

DUII *See* **Driving Under the Influence of Intoxicants**

DWI *See* **driving while intoxicated**

DXM   *See* **dextromethorphan**

dysphoria   a general malaise marked by mild-to-moderate depression, restlessness, and anxiety; less severe than major depression.

dysthymia   A depressive mood disorder that is not as serious as major depression but can last for years (at least two years).

E

EAP   *See* **employee assistance program**

eating disorders   Include anorexia nervosa, bulimia nervosa, binge-eating disorder, and compulsive overeating.

ecstasy   A synthetic analog of the methamphetamine molecule that causes some psychedelic effects. Also called *MDMA, X,* and *XTC. See* **MDMA**.

ECT   *See* **electroconvulsive therapy**

edema   Accumulation of excess water and other fluids in the tissues of the body.

EEG   *See* **electroencephalography**

effective dose   The dose of a drug that causes a desired effect 50% of the time; 25% of the people tested require a higher dosage for the desired effect, and 25% require a lower dosage.

EIA   *See* **enzyme immunoassay**

"eight ball"   One-eighth of an ounce of a drug, usually heroin, cocaine, marijuana, or methamphetamine; a common amount used for sale by street dealers.

electroconvulsive therapy (ECT)   The use of electric shocks to the brain approximately three times a week for two to six weeks to treat depression; developed in Italy in 1938. Also called *shock therapy.*

electroencephalography (EEG)   A technique that detects and measures patterns of electrical activity emanating from the brain by placing electrodes on the scalp.

elimination   The physiologic metabolism and excretion of drugs and other substances from the body.

embalming fluid   *See* **formaldehyde**

embolism   Blockage in a blood vessel, caused by blood clots, additives in drugs, and other foreign matter, such as cotton, associated with intravenous drug use.

embryogenesis   The process of embryo formation in the womb.

emergency medical technician (EMT)   A licensed medical technician who goes out on ambulance calls.

EMIT   *See* **enzyme multiplied immunoassay techniques**

emphysema   A lung disease caused by smoking or by environmental pollutants (e.g., asbestos) that gradually destroy the bronchioles of the lungs and their ability to take in air.

employee assistance program (EAP)   A company-provided counseling service to help employees with substance abuse and other personal problems. Usually, these services are outsourced to a professional treatment group.

EMT   *See* **emergency medical technician**

enabling   Actions by anyone, especially a spouse, relative, or friend, that allow addicts or abusers to continue their addictive behavior. It includes denial, codependence, paying off debts, lying to protect the user, or providing money.

endocarditis   Bacterial infection of the heart valves that can be fatal; often induced by infected needles during IV drug use.

endogenous craving   Craving for a drug caused by neurochemical changes in the brain such as depletion of dopamine resulting from cocaine abuse. The other craving, *exogenous craving,* is caused by external environmental triggers (cued craving).

endogenous opioids   Opioids that originate or are produced within the body, including endorphins, enkephalins, and dynorphins; antonym for *exogenous opioids* (e.g., heroin and opium).

endorphins   Neurotransmitters that resemble opioids. They naturally suppress pain and induce euphoria. Heroin, morphine, and other opioids mimic the effects of endorphins.

energy drinks   A new phenomenon in the stimulant soft-drink market; they usually contain caffeine, vitamins, minerals, sugar, and amino acids. Brands include Red Bull® and Rockstar.®

enkephalins   Naturally occurring opioid peptides that are part of the endorphins and have shorter or fewer amino acids in their molecular structure.

enteric division   The third part of the autonomic nervous system that controls smooth muscles in the gut.

environment   Any external influence on a person, including relationships, school, work, living location, nutrition, availability of drugs, advertising, and kinds of friends. One of the three main factors most influential in forming a susceptibility to drug dependency; the other two factors are heredity and the use of drugs or the acting out of a compulsive behavior.

enzyme   A natural chemical that causes a chemical change in other substances (catalyst) without changing itself. Enzymes are often involved in the metabolism of drugs.

enzyme immunoassay (EIA)   In drug testing, the use of antibodies to seek out specific drugs.

enzyme multiplied immunoassay techniques (EMIT)   A sensitive urine drug test rapidly and easily performed. Specific antigens are created for drugs that then react to their presence in a urine or blood sample.

ephedra   The active ingredient of the ephedra bush, found mostly in China; the synthesized version of this stimulant is called *ephedrine*. Also called *ma huang*.

ephedrine   An alkaloid stimulant extracted from the ephedra bush. It can also be synthesized in labs. It forces the release of norepinephrine, dopamine, and epinephrine in the brain's nerve cells. Because it can be used to manufacture methamphetamines and methcathinone, its importation is strictly controlled. Ephedrine is used as a bronchodilator in the lungs and a vasoconstrictor in the nose, so it is found in many over-the-counter drugs, such as pseudoephedrine (Sudafed®).

ephedrone   *See* **methcathinone**

epinephrine   The body's own natural stimulant neurotransmitter (adrenaline); a catecholamine, often released by stimulants.

epsilon alcoholism   *See* **Jellinek, E. M.**

EPO   *See* **erythropoietin**

ergogenics   Any drug that increases performance and strength in athletes or bodybuilders.

ergot   A toxic fungus that contains lysergic acid; used in the synthesis of LSD; found on rye, wheat, and other grasses.

ergotism   Poisoning by ergot, often characterized by gangrene, numbness, and burning sensations.

erythropoietin (EPO)   A synthetic hormone that stimulates the production of oxygen-laden red blood cells; has potentially fatal side effects. It has been widely used in athletic events, particularly endurance events such as cycling.

Erythroxylum coca   The botanical name for the coca bush, the source of cocaine. It is grown mainly in South America but also in Indonesia. Other, less prevalent plants include *Erythroxylum ipadu, Erythroxylum novotraterse,* and *Erythroxylum truxillense.*

estrogen   A hormone responsible for most feminine characteristics. Found in both men and women but in greater concentration in women (e.g., estradiol, formed by the ovary, placenta, testes, and possibly adrenal cortex, can be synthe-

sized). Its production is often affected by drugs.

ethanol (C_2H_6O)   The main psychoactive ingredient in beer, wine, and distilled liquors; usually made from fermented grains, fruits, or carbohydrate-based vegetables such as potatoes and rice. Also called *ethyl alcohol*.

ether   A volatile liquid, it was the first anesthetic. It was discovered in 1730 and called *anodyne*. Ether was used as a medicine, a drink, and an inhalant; often used for intoxication because it was thought to be less harmful than alcohol.

ethyl alcohol   *See* **ethanol**

etiology   The study of the causes of a disease, including addiction.

euphoria   A feeling of well-being, excitement, and extreme satiation, caused by many psychoactive drugs and certain behaviors, such as gambling and sex.

euphoriant   A substance that causes euphoria (e.g., cocaine, amphetamine, and heroin).

euthymia   A temporary elation; mental peace; less intense than euphoria; often occurs at the beginning of recovery from drug abuse. Also called *pink cloud*.

evolutionary perspective   A theory that looks at physiological changes in the brain as survival adaptations.

excise taxes   Taxes on tobacco and alcohol.

excretion   The elimination of water and waste products, including drugs and their metabolites, due to metabolism through urination, sweating, exhalation, defecation, and lactation.

exogenous   Produced or originating outside the body (e.g., exogenous opioids such as heroin and morphine).

experimentation   The first stage of drug use wherein the person is curious but uses the drug only sporadically and there are no negative consequences.

F

facilitator   A professional intervention specialist or a knowledgeable chemical dependence treatment professional who arranges and participates in an intervention to break through an addict's denial and get him or her into treatment.

factitious disorder   A mental disorder in which an individual voluntarily produces the signs and the symptoms of diseases to become a patient in a medical setting.

FAE   *See* **fetal alcohol effects**

false negative   A negative result on a drug test when the person should really test positive for drugs. It is often caused by operator error.

false positive   A positive result on a drug test when the person should test negative for drugs. False positives can be corrected through retesting and examination by a medical review officer.

family intervention   *See* **intervention**

FAS   *See* **fetal alcohol syndrome**

FASD   *See* **fetal alcohol spectrum disorders**

fat-soluble   Capable of being absorbed by fat. Most psychoactive drugs are absorbed by the brain because the brain has a high fat content.

fatty liver   The accumulation of fatty acids in the liver that begins to occur after just a few days of heavy drinking.

fen-phen The combination of dexfenfluramine and phentermine prescribed for weight control; target of a massive lawsuit due to heart damage caused by the drug combo. Also called *phen-fen*.

fenfluramine A drug that reduces appetite.

fentanyl (1) A powerful synthetic opiate used to control severe pain and as an anesthetic in surgery. It is 100 times stronger than morphine; often abused in the medical community. (2) A street drug called *China white,* used as a substitute for heroin, that uses the same basic formulation as pharmaceutical fentanyl.

fermentation A chemical process that uses yeast to convert sugar (usually found in grains, starches, and fruit) into alcohol.

fetal alcohol effects (FAE) Symptoms and physical defects in the fetus from the mother's alcohol use during pregnancy that are not as severe as those found in fetal alcohol syndrome.

fetal alcohol spectrum disorders (FASD) Refers to the full range of disorders caused by alcohol use during pregnancy: ARBD, ARND, FAE, and FAS.

fetal alcohol syndrome (FAS) Birth defects caused by a mother's excessive use of alcohol while pregnant. Signs of FAS include retarded growth, facial deformities, and delayed mental development.

fetus A formed yet unborn human (from the eighth week after conception to birth).

fibrosis The formation of scar tissue that can be caused by alcohol and other caustic substances.

fight/flight center An area of the old brain and the peripheral nervous system that helps us react to danger by increasing alertness, releasing adrenaline, and raising heart rate and respiration. It is initially triggered by emotional memories and instinctual drives in the amygdala and the hippocampus. Also called *fright/fight/flight/fornication center.*

FIPSE Acronym for *Fund for the Improvement of Post-Secondary Education.*

first-pass metabolism The processing of a substance as it passes through the gut and the liver for the first time.

flashback A remembrance of the intense effects of a drug, such as LSD or PCP, that is triggered by a memory, by encountering environmental cues, or by a residual amount of the drug being released, usually from fat cells.

flunitrazepam (Rohypnol®) A potent sedative-hypnotic, currently banned in the United States, that can cause relaxation, sleepiness, and amnesia; sometimes used in cases of date rape.

fluoxetine (Prozac®) An extremely popular antidepressant medication that is classified as a selective serotonin reuptake inhibitor. It increases the action of serotonin in the brain by preventing its reabsorption.

fly agaric *See Amanita muscaria*

fMRI *See* **functional magnetic resonance imaging**

formaldehyde A chemical used to preserve dead bodies. It has been used as an inhalant; it is also added to marijuana and then smoked-called *"clickers"* or *"clickems."* This material has also been used to help manufacture other illicit drugs such as PCP. Also called *embalming fluid.*

formication A cocaine- or methamphetamine-induced sensation that makes users think that bugs are crawling under their skin.

fortified wine Wine whose alcohol concentration is raised to approximately 20% by adding pure alcohol or brandy.

freebase Cocaine that can be smoked (as opposed to cocaine hydrochloride, which is snorted or injected).

freebasing Transforming cocaine hydrochloride into cocaine freebase, using ether or another flammable solvent so that it can be smoked. This method processes out impurities.

French Connection A French heroin distribution syndicate headed by Jean Jehan; it was the main supplier of refined heroin to the United States from the 1930s to 1973, when it was supposedly broken up by an international law enforcement coalition.

functional magnetic resonance imaging (fMRI) A method of imaging the brain that shows blood flow to give information on motor, sensory, visual, and auditory functions.

G

GABA *See* **gamma-aminobutyric acid**

GAD *See* **generalized anxiety disorder**

gamma alcoholism *See* **Jellinek, E. M.**

gamma-aminobutyric acid (GABA) This inhibitory neurotransmitter is one of the main neurochemicals in the brain.

gamma hydroxybutyrate (GHB) Synthetic version of a natural metabolite of the neurotransmitter GABA; used as a sleep inducer. It is popular among bodybuilders because it improves the muscle-to-fat ratio. It is also touted as a natural psychedelic and used as a party drug.

ganja (ghanga) Indian word for a preparation of the leaves and the flowering tops of the *Cannabis* plant; less potent than charas, the resin, but more potent than bhang, the leaves and stems.

gas chromatography/mass spectrometry (GC/MS) The most accurate method of drug testing for both type of drug and amount. It is supposed to be 99.9% accurate.

gastritis Inflammation of the gastrointestinal system, particularly the stomach, that can be caused by drinking.

gateway drug Any drug whose use supposedly leads to the use of stronger psychoactive drugs. The three most often mentioned are alcohol, tobacco, and marijuana.

GBL A chemical found in paint strippers and other substances that are transformed into GHB, a sedative that is used as a club drug.

GC/MS *See* **gas chromatography/mass spectrometry**

generalized anxiety disorder (GAD) A mental illness that consists of unrealistic worries about several life situations that lasts for six months or longer.

generic name The chemical name or description of a drug as opposed to the brand or trade name (e.g., *oxycodone* is the generic name while *OxyContin®* is the trade name).

genetic marker Any gene that makes a person more susceptible to the effects of a drug if he or she uses that drug (e.g., a marker gene for alcoholism that indicates slow metabolism of alcohol).

genetic predisposition A genetic susceptibility to use drugs addictively that comes into play when the person starts using psychoactive drugs. Also called *genetic susceptibility.*

genetic susceptibility *See* **genetic predisposition**

genotype The genetic makeup of an individual; the totality of his or her inherited traits.

GHB *See* **gamma hydroxybutyrate**

Gin Epidemic A period in English history (1710 to 1750) during which the availability of gin led to widespread public drunkenness and health problems.

ginseng A plant whose root has been used in Asian herbal medicine for 4,000 years; advocates say it prolongs endurance; studies say it doesn't.

glaucoma An eye disease that increases intraocular pressure. Marijuana is promoted as a medicine that can relieve that pressure.

glial cells Cells in the brain that surround neurons and hold them in place, supply nutrients and oxygen, insulate the neurons from one another, destroy pathogens, and remove dead neurons.

glucose A simple sugar found in fruits and plants that converts to alcohol when activated by yeast.

glutamate The most common excitatory neurotransmitter in the brain; NMDA receptors for glutamate are most densely concentrated in the cerebral cortex (especially the hippocampus), amygdala, and basal ganglia. Also called *glutamic acid.*

glutamic acid *See* **glutamate**

glutamine One of 20 amino acids encoded by the standard genetic code; it is used as a nutritional supplement to rebalance neurochemistry and neurotransmitter formation.

glutethimide A short-acting hypnotic that used to be a popular drug of abuse, usually in combination with codeine. It was sold as Doriden.®

Golden Crescent An area of the Middle East that produces large amounts of opium; includes parts of Pakistan, Iran, and especially Afghanistan.

Golden Triangle Formerly the major illicit opium-producing area in the world, now a distant second to the Golden Crescent; includes parts of Myanmar (Burma), Thailand, and Laos.

gonorrhea A common sexually transmitted infection usually marked by discharge from the genitals or rectum and pain when urinating.

"goof balls" (1) Street name for glutethimide (Doriden®); a popular drug of abuse in the 1960s, 1970s, and 1980s. (2) The combination of speed and heroin.

gram (gm) A metric unit of weight often used to measure drugs; 28.35 grams equals 1 ounce; 1,000 grams equals a kilogram, or 2.2 pounds.

"grass" Slang for marijuana.

gray matter The outer surface of the cerebral cortex and parts of the base of the cerebral hemispheres that consists mostly of dendrites and cell bodies.

group therapy The use of several clients in a group setting to help one another break the isolation of addiction, increase knowledge, and practice recovery skills. There are different types of group therapy: facilitated, peer, 12-step, educational, topic-specific, and targeted.

growth hormone *See* **human growth hormone**

gutka A mixture of betel nut, tobacco, lime, and flavorings sold mostly in India; it's chewed, and the stimulant juice is absorbed by the mucosa.

gynecomastia Enlargement of male breasts, often from the excess use of androgenic steroids that metabolize to an estrogen; steroid using athletes often report this effect.

gyrus (gyri) Ridges of convoluted rounded brain tissue of the cerebral hemispheres.

H

HAART *See* **highly active anti-retroviral therapy**

habit A term for addiction (i.e., "he has a habit").

habituation A level of drug use just before abuse, where the substance (or behavior) is used on a regular, habitual basis but does not yet have regular serious consequences. There is some loss of control.

half-life The time it takes for a substance to lose half of its pharmacologic or physiologic activity through metabolism and excretion.

halfway house A residential treatment facility where the addict is allowed to work and have outside contacts while enrolled in a treatment program.

hallucination A sensory experience that doesn't relate to reality, such as seeing a creature or an object that doesn't exist; a common effect of mescaline, psilocybin, PCP, and occasionally LSD (illusions are more common with LSD).

hallucinogen A substance that produces hallucinations (e.g., LSD, mescaline, peyote, DMT, psilocybin, and potent marijuana); a term often used interchangeably with *psychedelic, psychotomimetic,* and *psychotogenic.*

hallucinogen persisting perception disorder (HPPD) A mental condition triggered by memories or environmentally cued remembrances of a past intense experience with a drug such as LSD, PCP, or marijuana.

HALT Stands for *hungry, angry, lonely,* and *tired;* it helps addicts in recovery to remember these triggers that could lead to relapse.

hangover Alcohol withdrawal symptoms that occur 8 to 12 hours after stopping drinking. They include headache, dizziness, nausea, thirst, and dry mouth. The causes are usually the direct effects of alcohol and its additives. Hangover is distinguished from withdrawal, which is more severe and of longer duration.

hard drugs Used in the past to refer to strong Schedule I drugs such as heroin, cocaine, and amphetamines; rarely used nowadays.

harm reduction   A tertiary prevention and treatment technique that tries to minimize the medical and social problems associated with drug use rather than making abstinence the primary goal (e.g., needle exchange and methadone maintenance).

Harrison Narcotics Act   One of the first U.S. laws that controlled the importation, manufacture, distribution, and sale of narcotics; enacted in 1914.

hash oil   An extract of marijuana (made using solvents) that is added to food or to marijuana cigarettes. Its THC content can be as high as 20% to 80%.

hashish   The potent sticky resin of the marijuana plant that is often pressed into cakes and smuggled. The THC content is anywhere from 8% to 40%.

HCG   *See* **human chorionic gonadotropin**

HCV   Stands for *hepatitis C virus. See* **hepatitis C**.

heavy drinking   Defined as drinking five or more drinks in one sitting at least five times a month.

"head shop"   A store that sells drug paraphernalia such as rolling papers, roach clips, water pipes, and crack pipes.

hemp   A generic term often used to describe *Cannabis* plants that are high in fiber content and low in THC content.

henbane (*Hyoscyamus niger*)   A hallucinogenic plant containing the alkaloids scopolamine, hyoscyamine, and atropine.

hepatitis   Liver disease that can inflame or kill liver cells. It is caused by a virus or by a toxic substance, such as alcohol. The most common strains of viral hepatitis are A, B, C, D, and E. Depending on the strain, they can be transmitted through contaminated needles, exchange of body fluids, or feces. Hepatitis B and C are the most common strains in injection drug users. *Also see **alcoholic hepatitis.***

hepatitis B   A common form of hepatitis that is transmitted by contaminated blood, semen, vaginal secretions, and saliva. It is the ninth leading killer in the world. Often transmitted by high-risk sex and contaminated needles; 75% of IV drug users have been infected with hepatitis B.

hepatitis C   A form of viral hepatitis found, in some studies, in 70% to 80% of injection drug users. It is a major cause of liver failure and liver cancer. Four million Americans are infected.

Herbal Ecstasy®   A commercial over-the-counter stimulant that contains herbal ephedrine and herbal caffeine.

heredity   The transmission of physical and even mental characteristics through genes, chromosomes, and DNA.

heroin (diacetylmorphine)   A powerful opiate analgesic derived from morphine. It was discovered in 1874 and soon became the object of abuse and addiction.

herpes simplex   Common sexually transmitted disease usually marked by intermittent painful blisters or sores on the genitals and/or mouth.

hexing herbs   Members of the nightshade family of plants (e.g., belladonna, henbane, mandrake, and datura) that contain scopolamine, hyoscyamine, and atropine.

HGH   *See* **human growth hormone**

highly active anti-retroviral therapy (HAART)   HIV treatment regimen that targets viral enzymes; uses three medications that must be taken according to a strict schedule.

high-risk behavior   Dangerous behavior (e.g., unprotected sex, violence, and risk taking) that can lead to injury or infection. It is often caused when drugs lower inhibitions or impair reasoning.

hippocampus   An area of the primitive midbrain in the temporal lobe that is responsible for emotional memories and conversion of short-term memories to long-term ones. It compares sensory input with experience to decide how to react.

histamine   A natural amine in the body that stimulates gastric secretions, constricts bronchi, and dilates capillaries, usually to bring healing to an injured area of the body. Antihistamines control the inflammation.

"hit"   A dose of a drug.

HIV   *See* **human immunodeficiency virus**

homeostasis   The balance of functions and chemicals in the body as well as the process by which that balance is maintained; responsible for the development of tissue dependence, tolerance, and subsequent withdrawal from psychoactive drugs.

hops   An aromatic herb that comes from the dried cones of the *Humulus lupulus* vine, used in the brewing of virtually all beers; provides the bitter "hoppy" taste of beer.

hormone   A biochemical manufactured by an organ that can alter body function (e.g., pituitary gland).

HPPD   *See* **hallucinogen persisting perception disorder**

"huffer"   Slang for an inhalant user or abuser.

"huffing"   Putting a solvent-soaked rag, sock, or other material over or in one's mouth or nose and inhaling.

human chorionic gonadotropin (HCG)   A drug used to restart testosterone production in the body after long-term or high-dose anabolic steroid use. It can be toxic.

human immunodeficiency virus (HIV)   The virus that causes AIDS.

human growth hormone (HGH)   A substance produced by the body that stimulates body growth and muscle size. It is used illicitly in sports but can have dangerous side effects; can now be synthesized rather than extracted from cadavers.

hydrocodone (Lortab,® Vicodin®)   The most widely abused opiate-based painkiller; prescribed for moderate-to-severe pain.

hydromorphone (Dilaudid®)   A synthetic opiate analgesic prescribed for moderate-to-severe pain.

hydrophilic   The property of attracting or interacting with water molecules; alcohol is hydrophilic.

hyoscyamine   *See* **atropine**

hyperplasia   Precancerous changes in the bronchial tubes of the lungs characterized by abnormal and increased cell growth; often caused by smoking tobacco.

hypertension   High blood pressure; can be caused by stimulant use (and sometimes psychedelics) or by withdrawal from depressants.

hyperthermia Abnormally high body temperature; can be caused by MDMA, methamphetamines, and other party drugs especially when coupled with heavy dancing or exercise.

hypnotic A drug that induces sleep (e.g., some benzodiazepines, barbiturates, bromides, Z-hypnotics, and large amounts of alcohol).

hypodermic needle A device consisting of a hollow needle attached to a syringe that is used for injecting a fluid into the body intramuscularly (in a muscle), intravenously (in a vein), or subcutaneously (under the skin).

hypoglycemia A condition of extremely low glucose level in the blood; often found in people with eating disorders. It causes symptoms of lethargy, lightheadedness, and hunger.

hypothalamus Part of the brain that controls the autonomic nervous system and maintains the body's balance. It also controls the hormonal system and is located near the top of the brainstem.

hypoxia Very low level of oxygen in the blood or tissues; can be caused by inhalant abuse.

I

iatrogenic addiction Addiction caused by medical treatment (e.g., liberal use of opiate analgesics in a hospital setting or by a physician that leads to opiate addiction).

ibogaine A long-acting psychedelic from the iboga shrub that when used in high doses acts like a hallucinogen; in low doses it acts as a stimulant; it is currently being researched as a treatment for heroin addiction.

ibuprofen A nonopiate pain reliever or nonsteroidal anti-inflammatory drug that controls pain, fever, and inflammation.

"ice" Street name for dextromethamphetamine, (actually dextro isomer methamphetamine base); also called *"crystal" meth,* a crystalline form of amphetamine that is smokable. It has slightly milder physical effects than methamphetamine hydrochloride but more-severe mental effects.

illusion A mistaken perception of a real stimulus (e.g., a rope is mistaken for a snake; the colors on a wall seem to be flowing).

immune system A complex system of white blood cells, macrophages, and other cellular and genetic components that defend the body against foreign organisms.

immunosuppression A decrease in the effectiveness of the body's disease-fighting mechanisms; can be caused by the use of certain drugs, by HIV, or by other infectious agents.

immunoassay Testing for drugs using drug antigens. *See* **enzyme multiplied immunoassay techniques**.

impairment Physical and mental dysfunction due to psychoactive drugs or other addictive behaviors.

imprinting A process whereby memories, such as survival memories, are impressed onto nerve cells in the brain.

indica A species of *Cannabis* that is high in THC content. *See* **Cannabis**.

individual counseling One-on-one interaction between a therapist, counselor, or other treatment specialist and a client with emotional or mental problems to help him or her understand and cope with the illness.

indole psychedelics A class of hallucinogens that includes LSD, psilocybin mushrooms, ibogaine, DMT, and yage.

information addiction A form of Internet addiction that involves excessive surfing of the Web, looking for data and information.

ingestion Taking food, liquid, drugs, or medications into the stomach via the mouth.

inhalant Any vaporized, misted, or gaseous substance that is inhaled and absorbed through the capillaries in the alveoli of the lungs; smoked drugs are classified differently.

inhibition Controlling and restraining instinctual, unconscious, or conscious drives especially if they conflict with society's rules.

inhibitory neurotransmitter A neurotransmitter, such as GABA or serotonin, that keeps a neurotransmitter from relaying a message.

inpatient treatment A seven- to 28-day (or more) program in a hospital or other residential facility that focuses on detoxification, therapy, and education.

insufflation A term for snorting a drug, such as cocaine, heroin, or methamphetamine.

insulin A hormone secreted by the pancreas to help control blood-sugar levels; diabetics need to use oral medications to force the pancreas to release more insulin or use it more efficiently; they can also give themselves injections of insulin.

interdiction A supply reduction technique of intercepting drugs before they are distributed to dealers or users.

interferons A class of proteins that increase cells' resistance to infection. Interferon is the main treatment of hepatitis C.

Internet addiction A compulsion to overuse various services available on the Internet; it includes cybersexual addiction, computer-relationship addiction, net compulsions, information addiction, online gambling, and computer games addiction.

intervention A planned attempt to break through addicts' or abusers' denial and get them into treatment. Interventions most often occur when legal, workplace, health, relationship, or financial problems have become intolerable. Also called *family intervention.*

intoxication Functional impairment; loss of physical and mental processes due to substance use. It can be acute due to high-dose use or chronic due to continuous lower-dose use. In both cases it is most often caused by the drug's effect on the central nervous system.

intramuscular injection Injecting a drug into a muscle. It takes three to five minutes for the drug to reach the brain and have an effect.

intravenous injection Injecting a drug directly into a vein. It takes 15 to 30 seconds for the drug to reach the brain.

inverse tolerance Continuous use changes brain chemistry to the point that the same dose suddenly starts causing a more intense reaction. The user becomes more sensitive to the drug's effects as use continues. Also called *kindling* and *sensitization*.

ion   An electrically charged atom.

isopropyl alcohol   *See* **propanol**.

J

Jellinek, E. M. (1890-1963)   Famed researcher of alcoholism, founder of the Center of Alcohol Studies, and cofounder of the National Council on Alcoholism. His well-known *The Disease Concept of Alcoholism* delineated five levels of alcoholism: alpha (problem drinking), beta (problem drinking with health problems), gamma (loss of control with severe health and social consequences), delta (long-term heavy drinking), and epsilon (periodic) alcoholism. These terms are not used nowadays, but the categorical descriptions are.

jimsonweed   A hallucinogenic plant of the *Datura* family; contains the anticholinergic substances hyoscyamine, scopolamine, and atropine.

joint   Slang for a marijuana cigarette.

"Jones"   (1) Withdrawal from chronic heroin use; symptoms include chills, sweating, and body agony. (2) Term for any compulsive or addictive behavior (e.g., "Internet Jones").

"juice"   Street name for methadone, PCP, or steroids.

"junk"   Heroin or any psychoactive drug.

junkie   Someone who is addicted to a psychoactive drug, especially heroin.

K

Kaposi's sarcoma   A form of cancer that usually erupts as purple splotches on the skin. It is considered an opportunistic disease that is one of the signs of AIDS.

Keeley Institute   A series of 118 treatment centers in the United States that treated alcoholics, drug addicts, and tobacco smokers between 1880 and 1920.

ketamine   An anesthetic that produces catatonia and deep analgesia; side effects include excess saliva, dysphoria, and hallucinations. Its chemistry and effects are very similar to PCP. Used as a recreational club drug.

khat   A 10- to 20-foot shrub whose active ingredient is cathinone; a mild-to-medium stimulant. It is brewed in a tea, or the leaves can be chewed and the active ingredient absorbed. It is popular in Somalia, East Africa, Yemen, and other Middle Eastern countries.

kilogram (kg)   A metric unit of weight that equals 2.2 pounds.

kindling   *See* **inverse tolerance**

Klonopin®   *See* **clonazepam**

"knockout drops"   Old street name for chloral hydrate, a sedative-hypnotic.

kola nut   The seeds of the *Cola nitida* tree found in Africa; they contain a high concentration of caffeine.

Korsakoff's psychosis   *See* **Korsakoff's syndrome**

Korsakoff's syndrome   A disease that most often affects heavy, long-term drinkers, partly due to a thiamine (B_1) deficiency; symptoms include short-term memory failure, confusion, emotional apathy, and disorientation. Also called *Korsakoff's psychosis.*

"krystal"   Street name for PCP; not to be confused with the street names "crystal" and "crystal meth" that denote methamphetamine.

L

LAAM   *See* **levomethadyl acetate**

lag phase   The time between first use of a drug and the development of problematic use.

latency   The delay between the time a person uses a drug and the time it appears in urine, blood, saliva, or other fluid and can be tested.

laudanum   A popular opium preparation, first compounded by Paracelsus in the sixteenth century and popularized at the end of the nineteenth century, mostly in patent medicines; used to relieve pain, produce sleep, and allay irritation.

laughing gas   Nitrous oxide; an anesthetic that was originally used and abused in the nineteenth century for its intoxicating effect. Today it is often used at raves or other parties.

legal high   Intoxication by a legal drug, such as alcohol or a prescribed medication; tobacco and caffeine use are also considered legal highs.

legalization   A prevention concept that decriminalizes the cultivation, manufacture, distribution, possession, and use of drugs to reduce crime, drug dealing, and disease.

lethal dose   The amount of a drug that will kill the user. It can vary radically, depending on purity, sensitivity of the user, tolerance, and other factors.

leukoplakia   White oral mucous that persists in the mouth and is sometimes a sign of HIV disease or tobacco use.

levomethadyl acetate (LAAM)   A long-acting opiate used as an alternative to methadone for heroin addiction treatment; now used only experimentally in the United States.

LGBT   Stands for *lesbian, gay, bisexual,* and *transgender.*

"lid"   Traditionally an ounce of marijuana; now any amount in a baggie is often called a "lid."

LifeSkills Training (LST)   A prevention program for grades 7 to 10 that focuses on increasing social skills and reducing peer pressure to drink.

ligand   A compound that binds to a receptor; the part of a neurotransmitter or peptide that slots into a receptor on a nerve cell's receiving dendrite.

limbic system   The emotional center in the central nervous system's midbrain. It includes the amygdala, hippocampus, thalamus, fornix, mammillary body, olfactory bulb, and supracallosal gyrus. It sets the emotional tone of the mind, stores intense emotional memories, alters moods and emotions, controls sleep, processes smells, and modulates the libido.

"line"   A thin line of cocaine hydrochloride, about 2 inches long, that is snorted.

lipid solubility   The ability of a substance to be dissolved in a fatty substance. Many psychoactive drugs have a high lipid (fat) solubility.

lipophilic   Having a high lipid (fat) solubility.

lithium (carbonate)   The main drug used to treat bipolar affective disorder.

liver   The largest gland in the body (2 to 4 pounds); metabolizes protein and carbohydrates and most psychoactive drugs that pass through the blood, especially alcohol.

look-alikes   Legal drugs made with caffeine, ephedrine, or other legal substances to look like hard-to-get sedatives or illegal stimulants.

loss of control   The point in drug use where the user becomes unable to limit or stop use.

lost child   The child of an alcoholic or addict who is extremely shy and deals with problems by avoidance.

LSD   *See* **lysergic acid diethylamide**

lysergic acid diethylamide (LSD)   An extremely potent psychedelic (hallucinogen) synthesized in 1938 that causes illusions, delusions, hallucinations, and stimulation. It was originally made from rye mold.

LST   *See* **LifeSkills Training**

M

ma huang   An ancient Chinese tea that contains ephedra, a plant stimulant. *Also see* **ephedra.**

mace   The outer shell of nutmeg; has psychedelic qualities.

macrophage   *See* **phagocyte**

"magic mushrooms"   Hallucinogenic mushrooms, usually containing psilocybin or psilocin.

magnetic resonance imaging (MRI) scan   A technique of imaging the brain that relies on magnetic waves rather than X-rays. Its three-dimensional images have been used to visualize the neurological effects of psychoactive drugs.

"mainlining"   Using a drug, usually heroin, intravenously.

major depression   A mental illness characterized by a depressed mood and sleep disturbances without a life situation causing it.

major tranquilizer   Antipsychotic drug.

malt   A grain, usually barley, that is sprouted in water, then dried and crushed; the resulting malt is used to brew beer; also used in whiskeys as well as in cereals.

malt liquor   A beerlike beverage with a slightly higher alcohol content (6% to 9%) than normal lager beer (4% to 5%).

mandrake (*Mandragora*)   A bush found in Europe and Africa that contains anticholinergic psychedelics; popular in ancient and medieval times with shamans, witches, and medicine men.

mania   A period of hyperactivity, poor judgment, rapid thoughts, and quick speech; it can lead to a diagnosis of bipolar affective disorder (manic-depressive illness).

manic depression   *See* **bipolar affective disorder**

MAO inhibitor   *See* **monoamine oxidase (MAO) inhibitors**

marijuana   The common name for *Cannabis* plants that have high levels of psychoactive ingredients, especially THC. Also refers to the psychoactive portions of the *Cannabis* plant such as the resin and the flowering tops.

Marinol®   *See* **dronabinol**

mascot child/family clown   The child of an alcoholic or addict who tries to ease tension by being funny; this child has trouble maturing.

MAST   *See* **Michigan Alcoholism Screening Test**

MDA (3,4-methylenedioxyamphetamine)   A synthetic hallucinogen that became popular in the 1960s.

MDMA (3,4-methylenedioxymethamphetamine)   Commonly called *X* or *ecstasy,* a psycho-stimulant first synthesized in the early 1900s and popularized in the 1980s and 1990s.

medial forebrain bundle   A nerve pathway involved in reward and satiation. It extends through the ventral tegmental area, the lateral hypothalamus, the nucleus accumbens, and the frontal cortex.

medical intervention   The use of medications to treat a substance-related or mental disorder. This is usually done in combination with group/individual therapy or other treatment techniques.

medical marijuana   Marijuana that is used for medical rather than recreational purposes. It is the focus of much current debate about legalizing marijuana.

medical model   (1) Using medications to treat addiction because addiction is caused by irregularities of brain cells and brain chemistry. (2) In mental health, the concept that mental illnesses are caused by a disease process and by changes in brain chemistry.

medical model detoxification program   Use of medications and other medical therapies for detoxification under the direction of medical professionals.

medical review officer (MRO)   A physician who reviews positive drug test results to see if there is any other explanation or mitigating circumstances.

medulla   The part of the brain that controls heart rate, breathing, and other involuntary functions.

mentally ill chemical abuser (MICA)   *See* **dual diagnosis**

meperidine (Demerol®)   An opioid analgesic like morphine, prescribed for moderate-to-severe pain.

meprobamate (Miltown®)   A long-acting sedative developed in the 1950s to replace long-acting barbiturates. Commonly called *"mother's little helper."*

mescal   Toxic seed from the mescal tree that at nonpoisonous doses can cause hallucinations.

mescaline   The hallucinogenic alkaloid of the peyote cactus; has been found in other cacti (e.g., San Pedro cactus) and has also been synthesized.

mesocortex   A subdivision of the cerebral cortex, sometimes called the midbrain, that contains the limbic system.

mesolimbic dopaminergic reward pathway   A nerve pathway in the limbic system of the brain that carries reward messages to the nucleus accumbens and the frontal cortex; thought to play a crucial role in addiction.

metabolism   The body's mechanism for processing, using, inactivating, and eventually eliminating foreign substances, such as food or drugs, from the body.

metabolism modulation   The technique of using medications that alter metabolism of an abused drug to render it ineffective.

metabolite   The byproduct of drug metabolism that can also have psychoactive effects on the brain; often used as a marker in drug tests.

methadone   A long-acting synthetic opiate used orally to treat heroin addiction; also used to treat pain.

methadone maintenance   A treatment and harm reduction technique that keeps a heroin addict on methadone for long periods of time, even a lifetime. It helps addicts avoid infections from needle use, the need to break the law to support their habit, and the desire to return to the heroin lifestyle.

methamphetamine freebase   An altered form of methamphetamine called *"snot."* When methamphetamine is altered to the dextro isomer, methamphetamine base is called *"glass," "batu,"* and *"shabu."* Both forms of methamphetamine base are smoked.

methamphetamine hydrochloride   An intense psychoactive stimulant based on the amphetamine molecule; used for injecting, ingesting, and snorting. Also called *meth* and *"crystal."*

methamphetamine sulfate   A methamphetamine compound that is supposedly slightly harsher than methamphetamine hydrochloride. Also called *"crank."*

methanol   Wood alcohol; used as a toxic industrial solvent; it can be synthesized. Also called *methyl alcohol.*

methaqualone (Quaalude®)   A sedative that was widely abused in the 1960s, 1970s, and early 1980s for its disinhibitory and intoxicating effects. It is now only available illegally and is usually counterfeited with a benzodiazepine or antihistamine.

methcathinone   A synthetic stimulant that is chemically related to the natural stimulant cathinone found in the khat bush. Also called *ephedrine.*

methyl alcohol   *See* **methanol**

methylphenidate (Ritalin,® Attenta,® Concerta®)   An amphetamine congener stimulant used to treat attention-deficit/hyperactivity disorder and narcolepsy. It has been abused on the street. Also called *"pellets."*

"Mexican brown"   Heroin processed from poppies grown in Mexico; it is brown due to crude refining techniques.

mic   *See* **microgram**

MICA   Stands for *mentally ill chemical abuser. See* **dual diagnosis**

Michigan Alcoholism Screening Test (MAST)   An assessment test of 25 questions that are primarily directed at the negative life effects of alcohol on the user.

microgram (mic)   One millionth of a gram; a dose of LSD is 25 to 300 mics.

Miltown®   *See* **meprobamate**

Mini Thins®   Small, thin tablets that contain pseudoephedrine; used by street chemists to make methamphetamine or methcathinone.

minor tranquilizers   Antianxiety medications.

misuse   (1) An unusual or illegal use of a prescription, usually for drug diversion purposes. (2) Any nonmedical use of a drug or substance.

mixed drinking culture   A mixed wet and dry drinking culture in which binge drinking is common; much drinking is done away from meals (e.g., England, Canada, and the United States).

MODCRIT   One of the National Council on Alcoholism's assessment tests for alcoholism.

model child   The hardworking child of an alcoholic or addict who often takes over the duties of the dysfunctional parent or parents.

monoamine oxidase (MAO) inhibitors   Psychiatric drugs used to treat depression by raising the levels of norepinephrine and serotonin; can have severe side effects; have very dangerous cross-reactions with other drugs and even foods.

morning glory   A common garden plant that contains lysergic acid amide. The seeds are soaked and the liquid drunk, sometimes causing mild hallucinations.

morphine   A powerful analgesic extracted from opium sap that contains 10% morphine. Extracted and isolated in 1803, it set the stage for the refinement of other psychoactive substances present in many plant and even animal secretions.

motivational interviewing   A nonconfrontational style of treatment to involve clients in their own recovery process and help them convert ambivalence about drug use into motivation to make changes.

MPPP   A chemical found in the designer drug meperidine (Demerol®). *Also see* **MPTP**.

MPTP   The residue of the chemical used to make MPPP; it causes brain damage to dopamine-producing neurons and produces the "frozen addict," who can't move muscles voluntarily; similar to Parkinson's disease. *Also see* **MPPP**.

MRI   *See* **magnetic resonance imaging**

MRO   *See* **medical review officer**

mucous membranes   Moist tissues lining various structures of the body, including the bronchi, esophagus, stomach, gums, larynx, tongue, nasal passages, small intestine, vagina, and rectum. Drugs can be absorbed on these tissues.

"mule"   Someone who smuggles drugs in their luggage, clothing, or body. *Also see* **"body packer."**

multiple diagnosis   The presence of drug addiction in combination with two or more other ailments (e.g., polydrug diagnoses and diabetes).

"munchies"   A strong desire to eat excessively that is caused by marijuana use.

muscarine   A neurological toxin found in the *Amanita muscaria* mushroom that acts as a parasympathetic nervous system stimulant.

muscle relaxants   Central nervous system depressants prescribed to treat muscle tension and pain. Also called *skeletal muscle relaxants.*

muscling   Injecting a drug into a muscle. It takes three to five minutes for the drug to reach the central nervous system.

Muslims   Followers of Islam who are forbidden alcohol and most other psychoactive drugs by their religion.

mutation   An alteration in a gene caused by radiation, chemicals, or medications.

Myanmar   The modern name for Burma in Southeast Asia, one of the main growing areas for the opium poppy and more recently "yaa baa," or speed.

mycology   The science of the study of fungi, especially mushrooms.

N

N-SSATS   *See* **National Survey of Substance Abuse Treatment Services**

NA   *See* **Narcotics Anonymous**

naloxone (Narcan®)   Opioid antagonist that blocks the effects of heroin or other opiates; used to treat overdoses and to help prevent relapse during treatment.

naltrexone (Revia,® Vivitrol®)   Opioid antagonist that blocks the effects of heroin or other opiates; used to help prevent relapse during treatment.

naproxen (Aleve®)   A pain reliever (analgesic); also relieves fever.

"narc"   Narcotics control officer who sometimes works undercover.

Narcan®   *See* **naloxone**

narcolepsy   A sleep disorder characterized by sudden periods of sleep during the day and sleep paralysis or interrupted sleep at night; often treated with amphetamines.

narcotic   From the Greek *narkotikos,* meaning "benumbing"; originally used to describe any derivative of opium but came to refer to any drug that induced sleep or stupor. In 1914 it became a legal term for those drugs that were believed to be highly abused, such as cocaine and opiates.

Narcotics Anonymous (NA)   A 12-step self-help program created in 1947 and developed along the lines of Alcoholics Anonymous but focusing on people addicted to drugs.

National Survey of Substance Abuse Treatment Services (N-SSATS)   An annual survey of all drug treatment facilities in the United States, public and private.

Native American Church   A religious sect of about 250,000 American Indians that uses the hallucinogenic peyote cactus as a sacrament for their rites that combine elements of Christianity and vision-quest ritual.

Native Americans   *See* **American Indians**

natural high   A feeling of elation and satisfaction that is induced without the use of psychoactive drugs (e.g., parachuting, sexual activity, or running).

NCA CRIT   One of the National Council on Alcoholism's assessment tests for alcoholism.

NCADD   Stands for *National Council on Alcoholism and Drug Dependence.*

necrosis   Cell death or tissue death, often caused by drinking. It is a less orderly process than apoptosis, which is programmed cell death.

needle exchange   A harm reduction technique in which outreach workers supply addicts with clean hypodermic needles to prevent the spread of disease.

"needle freak"   An IV drug user who prefers the use of a syringe as a method of drug delivery; someone who has become addicted to using a needle to inject drugs.

negative reinforcement   A hypothesis about learning that says we learn an action when the response lets us avoid a negative stimulus or removes the negative circumstance (e.g., the threat of severe withdrawal from heroin reinforces the continued use of the drug).

neocortex   Processes information from the rest of the brain or from the senses. Also called *new brain.*

neonatal   Refers to the period immediately after birth through the first 28 days of life. Also called *newborn.*

neonatal abstinence syndrome   Withdrawal symptoms in a drug-exposed infant that appear when he or she is born and becomes free of the mother's drug-laden blood.

neuroleptics   *See* **antipsychotics**

neuron   The basic building block of the nervous system, consisting of the cell body, the axon, the dendrites, and the terminals. Also called *nerve cell.*

neurosis   An older term that refers to any mental imbalance that causes distress; it hinders a person's ability to adapt to his or her environment, although the person can still think rationally and function. This is in contrast to a psychosis, which is marked by a loss of touch with reality.

nerve cell   *See* **neuron**

neuropathy   Any condition that affects any segment of the nervous system. The most common form of peripheral neuropathy usually affects the feet and the legs; often a numbness caused by diabetes.

neurotransmitters   Chemicals that are synthesized within the body that transmit messages between nerve cells. The activity of these chemicals is strongly affected by psychoactive drugs.

newborn   *See* **neonatal**

new brain   *See* **neocortex**

"nexus"   (1) Street name for 2CB, a hallucinogenic drug. (2) Street name for methcathinone, a synthetic stimulant.

NIAAA   Stands for *National Institute on Alcohol Abuse and Alcoholism.*

"nickel bag"   Five dollars worth of a drug, such as heroin; inflation has made it hard to find.

Nicotiana tabacum   The most widely used genus and species of plant that produces smoking and smokeless tobacco.

nicotine   The active stimulant alkaloid of the tobacco plant; it mainly affects the natural neurotransmitter acetylcholine.

nicotine replacement therapy   A treatment technique that supplies a smoker with lower and lower doses of nicotine (through patches, inhalers, and gum) to alleviate withdrawal symptoms.

nicotinic receptors   A type of cholinergic receptor that is affected by nicotine.

NIDA   Stands for *National Institute on Drug Abuse.*

nightshade   *See* **belladonna**

NIH   Stands for *National Institutes of Health.*

nitrites   Synthetic drugs (butyl, amyl, and isobutyl nitrite) that are used as inhalants; originally used to treat heart pain (angina); the effects include a rush and mild euphoria followed by headaches, dizziness, and giddiness. Also called *volatile nitrites.*

nitrous oxide *See* **laughing gas**

nitrosamines Chemicals produced from nitrites and secondary amines when heated or subjected to highly acidic conditions. Nitrites are found in tobacco and food products, especially beer, fish, or meat and cheese products preserved with nitrite pickling salt. Many nitrosamines are considered carcinogenic. Tobacco smoke is considered one of the major causes of lung and other cancers.

NMDA receptors A subtype of glutamate receptors; they play a key role in many physiologic processes.

nonpurposive withdrawal Consists of objective physical signs that are directly observable during withdrawal (e.g., seizures, sweating, goose bumps, vomiting, diarrhea, and tremors).

nonsteroidal anti-inflammatory drugs (NSAIDs) Drugs used to control inflammation and lessen pain (e.g., Motrin® and Advil®).

nootropic drugs So-called smart drugs that are supposed to improve mental ability, particularly for the elderly. They are often composed of mild over-the-counter stimulants (e.g., ephedrine and protein neurotransmitter precursors like lecithin and d,l phenylalanine).

norepinephrine A neurotransmitter that prepares the body for physical activity; it affects energy release, appetite, motivation, attention span, heart rate, blood pressure, dilation of bronchi, assertiveness, alertness, and confidence.

normative assessment A prevention technique that teaches people that the true extent of drug use is less than they think; the idea is to lessen the pressure they might feel to use.

NORML Stands for *National Organization for the Reform of Marijuana Laws,* the major political organization trying to legalize marijuana.

"nose candy" Street name for cocaine hydrochloride that is snorted.

NSAIDs *See* **nonsteroidal anti-inflammatory drugs**

nucleus accumbens septi The focus of the reward/reinforcement pathway nerve pathway in the limbic system of the brain that carries reward messages; it produces a surge of pleasure and a message to repeat the action when activated. It is activated by most psychoactive drugs and is thought to play a crucial role in addiction.

nutmeg A spice that contains MDA and can therefore cause psychedelic and stimulant effects.

nutritional supplements Substances that include food extracts, vitamins, and minerals; used in treatment to build strength, facilitate synthesis of neurotransmitters within the body, and encourage better athletic performance.

nystagmus Involuntary tics of the eye pupils as they move or even when they are not moving; often caused by drug use, especially PCP and alcohol. Eye movements are used by law enforcement personnel to determine if a driver is intoxicated.

O

O-BOAT *See* **office-based opiate addiction treatment**

OA *See* **Overeaters Anonymous**

obsessive-compulsive disorder (OCD) An anxiety disorder characterized by disturbing obsessive thoughts that can be resolved only by acting out some compulsive behavior, such as hand washing.

obsessive-compulsive personality disorder A personality disorder marked by excessive neatness, rigid ways of relating to others, perfectionism, and a lack of spontaneity.

occipital lobe Part of the cerebrum involved in vision; found at the rear of each hemisphere.

OCD *See* **obsessive-compulsive disorder**

office-based opiate addiction treatment (O-BOAT) A new treatment protocol that allows certain licensed physicians to prescribe buprenorphine in their offices rather than only in a drug clinic setting.

Office of National Drug Control Policy (ONDCP) The cabinet-level coordinating agency for drug control activities in the United States.

old brain *See* **primitive brain**

ololiqui A variety of the morning glory plant whose seeds contain lysergic acid amide, a weak psychedelic.

ONDCP *See* **Office of National Drug Control Policy**

opiates (1) Any refined extract of the opium poppy (e.g., codeine and morphine) or semisynthetic derivatives of opium (e.g., heroin and hydromorphone). (2) A generic term that refers to any natural refinement, semisynthetic derivative, or synthetic drug that resembles the actions of opium extracts.

opioids Synthetic opiates (e.g., fentanyl, meperidine [Demerol®], methadone, and propoxyphene [Darvon®]); sometimes used as a generic term for all opiates and opioids.

opium A drug that consists of the sap of the opium poppy; used legally for analgesia, cough suppression, and diarrhea control and illegally for euphoria and pain suppression.

Opium Wars Two wars in the 1800s, mostly between England and China, that were fought for the British right to sell opium in China.

opportunistic infection An infection that causes illness in a person with a damaged immune system; often found in AIDS patients (e.g., Kaposi's sarcoma).

oral gratification Satisfaction or pleasure obtained by placing something (e.g., tobacco or food) in the mouth.

organic mental disorders Mental illnesses caused by physical changes in the brain due to injury, diseases, or drugs and chemicals.

organic solvents Hydrocarbon-based compounds refined from petroleum that are used as fuels, aerosols, and solvents. Often inhaled for their psychoactive effects, they include gasoline, paints, paint thinners, nail polish remover, and acetone.

OTC Stands for *over-the-counter. See* **over-the-counter drugs.**

outpatient treatment Programs in which the client lives at home but receives therapy and support from a facility (such as a drug-treatment center), therapist, or therapy group.

outreach Programs in which therapists or treatment workers go into the community to identify and assist drug abusers and addicts rather than wait for them to come into a treatment facility.

over-the-counter (OTC) drugs   Drugs and medications that can be obtained without a prescription and are legally sold in retail stores.

overdose   The accidental or deliberate use of more drug than the body can handle; causes severe medical consequences, including coma and death.

Overeaters Anonymous (OA)   A 12-step self-help group for compulsive overeaters.

oxycodone   A semisynthetic derivative of codeine that is abused by chewing, crushing, and injecting or by crushing and sniffing the formulation and inducing a heroin-like high.

OxyContin®   A time-release version of oxycodone (Percodan®). *See* **oxycodone**.

P

pancreatitis   Inflammation of the pancreas, often caused by heavy drinking.

panic attacks   Short episodes (10 to 20 minutes) of intense anxiety, nervousness, heart palpitations, sweating, and shortness of breath due to anxiety, certain prescription medications, and use of stimulant drugs, including cocaine and amphetamines; withdrawal from depressant drugs can also induce an attack.

panic disorder   An anxiety disorder characterized by multiple panic attacks (sudden repeated episodes of intense anxiety, panic, and confusion).

Papaver somniferum   The botanical name for the opium poppy.

paraldehyde   A sedative developed in 1882 that was used to control symptoms of alcohol withdrawal.

paranoia   Irrational suspicions that someone or something is out to harm you; often induced by psychoactive drugs.

paranoid psychosis   Irrational fears that someone or something is out to get you; the condition can be mimicked by drug use, particularly strong cocaine or amphetamine use.

paraphernalia   Drug-using equipment such as syringes, glass pipes, and water pipes.

paraquat   An herbicide that has been used to destroy illegal marijuana crops.

parasympathetic nervous system   Part of the autonomic nervous system that acts to balance the sympathetic nervous system (i.e., the sympathetic system speeds up heart rate and breathing while the parasympathetic system slows it down); the parasympathetic system mostly uses acetylcholine, whereas the sympathetic system mostly uses norepinephrine.

paregoric   A tincture of opium and alcohol used since the early eighteenth century mainly for diarrhea.

parenteral drug use   Injecting a substance into a vein or muscle or under the skin.

paresthesias   One of the symptoms of panic attacks; it refers to numbness.

parietal lobe   The area of the cerebral cortex that receives information from surface body receptors; found in the middle of the cerebral hemispheres.

Parkinson's disease   A disease caused by the destruction of

one of the dopamine-producing areas of the brain, the basal ganglia; symptoms include tremors, rigidity, and a mask-like face.

paroxetine (Paxil®)   An antidepressant that is a selective serotonin reuptake inhibitor.

passive smoking   Inhaling exhaled smoke from nearby smokers. *Also see* **secondhand smoke**.

passive transport   Movement of a drug from an area of high concentration to an area of low concentration.

"pasta"   Spanish for cocaine paste.

paste   An intermediate product of cocaine refinement that contains impurities, such as kerosene and sulfuric acid. This light-brown doughy substance can be smoked, often in countries that grow or refine the coca leaf.

patent medicines   Medicines that were very popular in the eighteenth, nineteenth, and early twentieth centuries that promised cures for almost any ailment. They often contained opium, cocaine, marijuana, and alcohol. Their unregulated distribution was responsible for the creation of thousands of opium, morphine, and cocaine abusers and addicts.

Paxil®   *See* **paroxetine**

PCP   *See* **phencyclidine**

peer facilitator   A recovering addict and/or alcoholic who acts as a mentor, adviser, or confidante to help a drug abuser recover. Also called *sponsor.*

peer group   A group of people with similar interests; peer pressure can encourage drug use.

pelvic inflammatory disease (PID)   A common sexually transmitted disease; an infection of the uterus, fallopian tubes, and ovaries.

peptides   A compound of two or more amino acids that can form into neurotransmitters.

performance-enhancing drugs   A broad category of drugs and substances used to increase energy, endurance, and strength (e.g., steroids, human growth hormone, and erythropoietin).

periaqueductal gray area   An area at the base of the brain that blocks or inhibits incoming pain messages.

perinatal   Pertaining to the time before, during, or after birth.

peripheral nervous system   One of the two major divisions of the human nervous system (which comprises the autonomic and somatic systems); the other part of the complete system is the central nervous system.

perseveration   Uncontrollable repetition of a response even after the stimulus has ceased.

personality disorders   Abnormal and rigid behavior patterns that begin in childhood, often last a lifetime, and are often self-defeating. They include paranoid, antisocial, narcissistic, borderline, and obsessive-compulsive personality disorders.

"pep pills"   Old street name for amphetamines.

PET scan   *See* **positron emission tomography (PET) scan**

peyote   A small cactus found in northern Mexico and the U.S. Southwest that contains the hallucinogen mescaline.

peyotl   The Native American name for peyote.

phagocyte An immune cell that seeks out and destroys foreign microorganisms, viruses, and dead cells. Also called *macrophage.*

phantasticants A term once used for hallucinogens.

"pharm parties" A party where young people bring prescription drugs they have taken from their parents' medicine cabinets or bought from illicit sources.

pharmacodynamics The study of the effects of drugs on living organisms and the mechanisms of their actions.

pharmacodynamic tolerance A defense mechanism of the brain that causes neurons to become less sensitive to the effects of psychoactive drugs.

pharmacokinetics The science that examines the movement of drugs within the body, including uptake, absorption, transportation, diffusion, and elimination.

pharmacology The science of drug action in the body. It includes pharmacodynamics, pharmacokinetics, pharmacotherapeutics, and toxicology.

phencyclidine (PCP) A psychedelic drug first used as an anesthetic for people and then for animals, but the side effects were too outlandish. As a street drug, starting in the 1960s, it was smoked, snorted, swallowed, and injected; it distorted sensory messages, deadened pain, and suppressed inhibitions. Excessive use can cause catatonia, coma, and convulsions.

phen-fen *See* **fen-phen**

phenothiazines A class of psychiatric medications developed in the early 1950s and used to treat schizophrenia. Also called *neuroleptics* and *antipsychotics.*

phenotype The totality of a person as determined by genetic and environmental factors as opposed to genotype, which focuses only on genetics.

phenylalkylamine psychedelics A class of psychedelics that are chemically related to adrenaline and amphetamine (e.g., peyote and MDMA).

phenylethylamines *See* **psycho-stimulants**

phenylpropanolamine A decongestant and mild appetite suppressant that is used in many over-the-counter medications to treat the symptoms of colds and allergies. This is also an active ingredient in look-alike stimulants.

pheromones Natural human hormones found in sweat that increase sexual desire and stimulation by their odor.

physical dependence *See* tissue dependence

PID *See* **pelvic inflammatory disease**

pilsner beer Any light lager beer; originated in Pilsen, Czechoslovakia. It has a high wheat content from the malted barley.

placebo A nonactive substance (e.g., sugar pill) that is given to a patient to let him think he is getting a real medication. It's used as a control to test the effects of an active medication.

placebo effect A symptomatic response to a nonactive substance caused by the user's emotional and mental expectations rather than by a true pharmacological reaction.

placental barrier The membrane between the mother's and fetus's blood supplies that allows the absorption of nutrients by the embryo while trying to keep toxic substances

out. Psychoactive drugs cross this barrier.

polydrug abuse The use of several drugs either in succession or at one time to achieve a certain effect; most drug abusers are polydrug abusers.

poppers Street name for the nitrite inhalants: amyl, butyl, cyclohexyl, isopropyl, and isobutyl.

positron emission tomography (PET) scan A brain imaging technique that uses the action of glucose to show brain activity.

postsynaptic The end of the dendrite of a nerve cell that's on the receiving side of a neural message.

post-traumatic stress disorder (PTSD) Persistent reexperiencing of the memory of a stressful event outside of usual human experience (e.g., combat, sexual molestation, physical abuse, or a car crash).

"pot" Street name for marijuana.

potentiation An exaggerated effect caused by using two drugs together; a synergistic effect.

potency The pharmacological activity of a given amount of drug.

"pothead" Street name for a marijuana abuser or addict.

precursor Any physiologically inactive substance that is converted to an active enzyme, drug, hormone, neurotransmitter, or other precursor by chemical processes.

predisposition A susceptibility to overreact to the use of a drug; heredity and environment along with drug use can activate this tendency to abusive and addictive use of psychoactive drugs.

prefrontal cortex The front tip of the brain that is involved in executive functions, including planning complex cognitive behaviors, moderating social behavior, determining good and bad, and expressing personality.

prevention A group of social, medical, psychological, economic, or legal measures used to lessen the actual impact of drug abuse and addiction.

primary prevention A series of prevention techniques aimed at nonusers to promote abstinence, delay drug use, increase drug education, and promote healthy alternatives.

primitive brain The area surrounded by the reasoning cerebrum: brainstem, cerebellum, and mesocortex. It handles instincts, automatic body functions, and basic emotions and cravings. A version of it is found in all animals. Also called *old brain.*

"primo" (1) Marijuana and crack smoked together. (2) Really potent drugs.

problem child The child of an alcoholic or addict who experiences multiple personal problems.

problem drinking A pattern of drinking, similar to abuse, in which the drinker is experiencing serious life problems due to drinking but has not yet had a definitive diagnosis of alcoholism.

prodrug Any drug that becomes active when metabolized by the body (e.g., the amino acid tyrosine is converted to the active neurotransmitter dopamine in the brain).

prohibition A supply reduction technique that prohibits the importation, sale, or use of a drug. It is carried out through laws and interdiction.

Prohibition A specific period in American history (1920 to 1933) when the sale and manufacture of alcohol was prohibited through the Eighteenth Amendment.

proof A measure of the amount of pure alcohol in an alcoholic beverage. In America 100% pure alcohol generally equals 200 proof, so 50% alcohol equals 100 proof.

propanol Used in shaving lotion, shellac, antifreeze, and lacquer. Also called *rubbing alcohol* and *isopropyl alcohol.*

protease inhibitors Drugs that help repress HIV reproduction by inhibiting an HIV enzyme (protease). Drugs such as indinavir, nelfinavir, and ritonavir are used in combination with other drugs for antiretroviral therapy.

proteins Large molecules comprising long chains of amino acids. They are involved in metabolic reactions and other biological functions. They also help maintain the cell's structure.

protracted withdrawal Experiencing craving, side effects, and withdrawal symptoms long after being detoxified from a psychoactive drug; usually due to environmental cues that stimulate memories of use. It can also be caused by withdrawal, release of small amounts of the drug from fat storage, or release of accumulated toxic metabolites in the body.

Prozac® *See* **fluoxetine**

pseudoephedrine An isomer of ephedrine that is used in the illicit manufacture of methamphetamines; found in many over-the-counter products such as bronchodilators.

psilocin An active hallucinogenic ingredient of the *Psilocybe* mushroom.

Psilocybe A genus of mushrooms that contain the hallucinogenic substances psilocybin and psilocin (e.g., *Psilocybe cubensis* and *Psilocybe cyanescens*).

psilocybin An active hallucinogenic substance found in *Psilocybe* mushrooms. It is converted to psilocin in the body.

psyche The psychological makeup of a person; the soul.

psychedelic A common term for any drug that can induce illusions, delusions, and/or hallucinations (e.g., LSD, MDMA, psilocybin, ketamine, PCP, and, for some, marijuana).

psychic dependence *See* **psychological dependence**

psycho-stimulants Laboratory variations of the amphetamine molecule (e.g., MDA and MDMA) that cause stimulatory and psychedelic effects. Also called *phenylethylamines.*

psychoactive drug Any substance that directly alters the normal functioning of the central nervous system when it is injected, ingested, smoked, snorted, or absorbed into the blood.

psychological dependence Drug-caused altered state of consciousness that reinforces dependence on the drug. This is different from tissue dependence. Also called *psychic dependence.*

psychopharmacology The field of medicine that addresses the use of medications to help correct or control mental illnesses and drug addiction.

psychosis A psychiatric disorder that grossly distorts a person's thinking and behavior, making it difficult to recognize reality and cope with life. Schizophrenia, bipolar affective disorder, and organic brain disorders are the main causes of this disorder.

psychotherapy A technique of treatment for emotional, behavioral, personality, and psychiatric disorders based principally on verbal communication and interventions with a patient as opposed to physical and chemical interventions.

psychotic Of or relating to psychosis or the behavior associated with psychosis.

psychotomimetic A drug that can induce behavioral and psychological changes that mimic psychosis.

psychotropic drugs Drugs used to treat mental illnesses (e.g., antidepressants, antipsychotics, and anxiolytics).

P-300 waves A brain wave involved in information processing that has been shown to be less active in alcoholics and in sons of alcoholics who have not begun to drink; it shows less responsiveness to sensory stimuli, particularly auditory stimuli.

PTSD *See* **post-traumatic stress disorder**

P₂P Stands for *phenyl-2-propanol,* a chemical used to make methamphetamine.

public health model A model for prevention that holds that there is an interaction among a host (the user), the environment, and the agent (the drug); the model is designed to understand and alter the relationships among these three factors to control addiction.

pupilometer A device for measuring the size of the pupil, a technique used to detect drug use.

Pure Food and Drug Act One of the first laws (1906) that prohibited interstate commerce in misbranded food and drugs and required accurate labeling.

purging Self-induced vomiting; often used by those with bulimia to maintain weight.

purity A measure of the freedom from contaminants in a sample of a drug.

purposive withdrawal Withdrawal symptoms falsely reported by the addict to get drugs from a doctor; psychosomatic symptoms triggered by the expectation that symptoms will occur.

Q

Quaalude® *See* **methaqualone**

"quick drunk" A description of the instant effects of volatile solvents.

quid A ball of chewed drug (coca leaf or tobacco) that is kept in the mouth to allow the active ingredient to be absorbed by the capillaries in the mouth. Also called *chaw* or *plug.*

R

radio immunoassay (RIA) A method of drug testing that uses antibodies to seek out drugs in biofluids.

random testing A method of drug testing with short or no notification; used by many sports organizations.

rapid eye movement (REM) sleep   A natural part of the sleep cycle. REM sleep is interrupted by the use of some psychoactive drugs such as alcohol.

rapid opioid detoxification   A technique of rapidly inducing opioid withdrawal using naloxone or naltrexone and then mitigating the withdrawal symptoms with other medications.

Rational Recovery   A self-help recovery group that uses a cognitive-behavioral approach to treatment and recovery.

rave   A music party—held in a nightclub, in a rented warehouse, in the desert, or even outdoors in a field-where drugs, particularly psychedelics (e.g., LSD, ecstasy [MDMA], GHB, and ketamine), are readily available.

receptor   A protein found on the dendrites or cell body of neurons and other cells that receives and then binds specific neurotransmitters; this process of "slotting in" to the receptor transmits neural messages.

receptor sites   Structural protein molecules on the receiving neuron that receive messages from terminals on the sending neuron by way of neurotransmitters that slot into the receptor sites. Also called **binding sites**.

recovery   The final step in drug treatment following abstention, initial abstinence, and long-term abstinence. Clients have changed their lifestyle and have overcome their major physical and mental dependence on psychoactive drugs or addictive behaviors. They are committed to abstinence, have accepted their addictive disease, and are committed to a continued drug-free lifestyle.

recreational drugs   These legal and illegal drugs include alcohol, tobacco, marijuana, cocaine, methamphetamines, LSD, heroin, and even caffeine. Also called *social drugs* and *street drugs*.

recreational drug use   A level of drug use after experimentation; people seek out the drug to experience certain effects, but there is no established pattern of use and it has a relatively small impact on their lives; use is sporadic, infrequent, and unplanned. Also called *social drug use*.

"reefer"   An old term for a marijuana cigarette. Also called **joint**.

rehabilitation   Restoring an abuser or addict to an optimum state of physical and psychological health through therapy, social support, and medical care.

reinforcement   A learning process whereby a person receives a reward for a certain action. That reward, in turn, increases the likelihood that the person will repeat that action. Negative reinforcement uses the concept that a person will learn to avoid an action if the consequences are painful.

relapse   Reoccurrence of drug use and addictive behavior after a period of abstinence or recovery.

relapse prevention   A treatment technique that focuses on preventing the recovering addict from using again.

relationship addiction   A desire to have a compulsive relationship with one or more persons.

REM   *See* **rapid eye movement (REM) sleep**

repressed memories   A Freudian term for a memory that is in the unconscious and not available to the conscious mind; a favorite target for psychotherapy.

resiliency   The ability of an individual to resist drug use and abuse; the resistance qualities are formed by hereditary and environmental influences at home, in school, and in the community.

resiliency program   A prevention technique that involves building on natural strengths that people already have available within themselves.

resin   The psychoactive secretions of the *Cannabis* plant on the outer portions of the plant and on the flowering buds.

resistance skills training   A prevention technique that involves training an individual to resist peer pressure and the use of psychoactive drugs.

restoration of homeostasis   The technique of using medications and nutrients to restore brain chemical imbalances.

reticular activating system   The part of the brainstem involved in maintaining consciousness; it can be blocked by several drugs, including anesthetics.

reuptake ports   Sites on the axon terminals of neurons that reabsorb neurotransmitters that have been released into the synaptic gap. These sites can be blocked to increase the amount of neurotransmitter available to the receptor sites.

reverse tolerance   A turnaround in the body's ability to handle greater and greater amounts of a drug (e.g., aging or excessive alcohol abuse reduces the liver's ability to handle alcohol, so a chronic alcoholic in his forties or fifties might be able to handle only a few drinks instead of the case of beer he could consume 20 years earlier).

Revia®   *See* **naltrexone**

reward deficiency syndrome   A theory of addiction that proposes a common biological substrate and pathway for drug and behavioral addictions. It further proposes that a person's hereditary inability to experience reward due to a scarcity of dopamine receptor sites in the reward/reinforcement pathway makes the person more likely to search for more-intense experiences to trigger this pathway.

reward/reinforcement pathway   *See* **nucleus accumbens septi**

rhabdomyolysis   Muscle damage.

RIA   *See* **radio immunoassay**

RID   Stands for *restless, irritable, and discontent;* reminds addicts of the triggers that lead them into relapse.

"rig"   Syringe or hypodermic needle.

risk factors   Hereditary and environmental factors that put adolescents and adults at risk to abuse drugs (e.g., physical and mental abuse, a family history of drug abuse, living in poverty, and a lack of self-esteem).

risk-focused prevention   Programs that identify a person's risks to use drugs (e.g., physical or sexual abuse) and teach the person to deal with them.

Ritalin®   *See* **methylphenidate**

"rock"   (1) A piece of crack cocaine. (2) Slang for crack.

Rohypnol®   *See* **flunitrazepam**

"roid"   Street name for an anabolic steroid.

"roid rage" Sudden outbursts of anger caused by excessive steroid use. The rage goes away when the drug is stopped.

"rolling" The Generation X term referring to the practice of concealing an ecstasy tablet in the middle of a Tootsie Roll.®

rubbing alcohol *See* **propanol**

rush A sense of elation or intense satisfaction caused by some psychoactive drugs. The sensations can be mimicked by natural highs, such as thrill seeking, meditation, and fasting.

S

SA *See* **Sexaholics Anonymous**

sacrament A visible sign of an inward grace; a rite, drug, or object used in a ritual such as baptism or the Eucharist (which involves bread and wine). Historically, a number of psychoactive drugs have been used as sacraments in religious services.

Salvia divinorum A psychedelic plant whose effects have been likened to PCP. Salvinorin A is thought to be the key psychoactive ingredient, although how this extract works in the brain is not understood and no receptor sites have yet been identified as the site of action.

SAMHSA Stands for *Substance Abuse and Mental Health Services Administration.*

satiation centers Parts of the brain that tell us when we satisfy a craving of the old brain, such as thirst or hunger. Also called *on/off switches* or *"stop" switch.*

scheduled drugs Drugs that are controlled by the Controlled Substances Act of 1970. Illegal drugs such as cocaine, heroin, and methamphetamines are Schedule I. Strong drugs used medicinally are Schedule II (e.g., morphine, meperidine [Demerol®], and methylphenidate [Ritalin®]).

schizophrenia A mental illness (psychosis) characterized by hallucinations, delusional and inappropriate behavior, poor contact with reality, and an inability to cope with life. Excessive use of strong stimulants, especially methamphetamine, can mimic the symptoms of schizophrenia.

scopolamine An alkaloid found in certain plants (e.g., deadly nightshade) that can induce sleep. Also called *truth serum.*

second messenger A neurotransmitter that attaches itself to another neuron to limit or increase the release of neurotransmitters (e.g., the release of endorphins to inhibit the release of substance P, a pain transmitter).

secondhand drinking The effect of heavy drinking on nondrinkers (e.g., unwanted sexual advances or vomit in the dormitory hallway).

secondhand smoke Cigarette or cigar smoke that is inhaled by a nonsmoker while in the presence of smokers. About 50,000 premature deaths each year are attributed to secondhand smoke.

secondary prevention A strategy to identify those who are beginning to experiment with drugs and prevent them from using or having problems with drugs.

Secular Organization for Sobriety (SOS) A 12-step self-help group for agnostics and atheists.

sedative A drug that eases anxiety and relaxes the body and the mind. Also called *tranquilizers* and *muscle relaxants.*

sedative-hypnotic Any drug that relaxes and soothes the body and the mind, eases anxiety, or induces sleep. The two main categories are benzodiazepines (e.g., alprazolam [Xanax®] and clonazepam [Klonopin®]) and barbiturates (e.g., phenobarbital). More recently, the Z-hypnotics have become popular.

select tolerance The variable development of tolerance for different effects of a drug (i.e., as the user develops a tolerance for desired mental effects, he or she may be developing less tolerance to other lethal effects of that drug, thus making overdose more likely).

selective serotonin reuptake inhibitors (SSRIs) A group of antidepressants that increase the levels of serotonin in the central nervous system (e.g., paroxetine [Paxil®] and sertraline [Zoloft®]).

Selective Severity Assessment Test One of the main diagnostic tests for addiction; evaluates 11 physiologic signs of addiction.

sensitization *See* **inverse tolerance**

serotonin An inhibitory neurotransmitter involved in mood stability, especially depression, anxiety, sleep control, self-esteem, aggression, and sexual activity.

sertraline (Zoloft®) An SSRI antidepressant.

set A person's mood and mental state when taking a drug.

setting The location at which a drug is taken; ambience is important in determining the overall effect of a psychoactive drug such as LSD.

Sexaholics Anonymous (SA) A 12-step self-help group for sex addicts.

sexual addiction Sexual behavior over which the addict has no control; includes masturbation, serial affairs, phone sex, excessive use of pornography, and the use of prostitutes.

sexually transmitted diseases (STDs) Infections transmitted as the result of sexual contact with an infected person (e.g., chlamydia, gonorrhea, syphilis, trichomonas, HIV disease, genital herpes, and hepatitis B and C). Also called *venereal disease.*

"shabu" Slang for smokable methamphetamine. *See* **ice.**

shaman A medicine man or priest who uses magic or spiritual forces to cure illness, communicate with spirits, and control the future. Shamans often use psychoactive drugs to help them reach the desired mental state or trance.

shamanic Any religion that believes that only a shaman is capable of communicating with the supernatural and influencing those forces.

"shoot up" To inject oneself with a drug.

"shooting gallery" A building or room where illicit drugs are regularly injected.

SIDS *See* **sudden infant death syndrome**

sildenafil citrate (Viagra®) A medication to treat erectile dysfunction.

simple phobia Irrational fear of a specific thing or place.

single photon emission computer tomography (SPECT)

scan   A brain imaging technique that measures cerebral blood flow and brain metabolism; enables clinicians and researchers to study how a brain functions before, during, and after drug use; can also image brain function of people with neurological diseases or syndromes, such as Alzheimer's or ADHD.

sinsemilla   A technique for growing high-potency marijuana that consists of keeping female marijuana plants from being pollinated by male ones, thus greatly increasing the THC content to as high as 30% or more.

skeletal muscle relaxants   *See* **muscle relaxants**

skin patch   A drug-soaked adhesive patch that releases drugs slowly (over a period of days) through contact absorption (e.g., nicotine patch).

"skin popping"   Injecting a drug under the skin rather than into a vein or muscle.

"skittles"   Slang for dextromethorphan tablets.

"smack"   Slang for heroin.

small intestine   The portion of the digestive tract between the stomach and the large intestine that absorbs ingested food, liquids, and drugs through the capillaries lining its walls.

smokeless tobacco   Chewing tobacco or snuff; any tobacco that is not smoked.

"sniffing"   Breathing in an inhalant through the nose directly from the container.

"snorting"   Inhaling a drug through the nose to let the capillaries in the mucosal membranes absorb the drug; it takes 5 to 10 minutes for a drug to reach the brain when it is snorted.

snuff   (1) Powdered tobacco that is absorbed through nasal membranes when it is snorted. (2) A term for finely chopped tobacco leaves that are put into the buccal membrane of the mouth for absorption (e.g., Copenhagen® and Skoal®).

sobriety   A term for abstinence from drugs or alcohol (being sober); the concept is used mostly in Alcoholics Anonymous and other 12-step groups.

social drinking   A level of drinking between experimentation and habituation; drinking is sporadic, infrequent, and not patterned (e.g., moderate drinking at social occasions rather than by oneself).

social drug use   *See* **recreational drug use**

social model recovery program   A nonmedical outpatient drug treatment program that uses a number of therapies.

social phobia   Fear of being seen by others as acting in a humiliating or embarrassing way (e.g., fear of eating in public).

soda doping   Ingesting sodium bicarbonate 30 minutes prior to exercise to supposedly delay fatigue.

sodium ion channel blockers   A class of medications that interfere with neuron transmission to mute cocaine's or another drug's effects.

soft drugs   An outdated general term for drugs like marijuana, alcohol, and tobacco that implies that they are less intense than hard drugs (e.g., cocaine, heroin, and amphet-

amines). Soft drugs cause more social and public health problems than so-called hard drugs.

soma   ancient term for *Amanita muscaria*, an hallucinogenic mushroom.

Soma®   Trade name for carisoprodol, a skeletal muscle relaxant drug.

somatic system   Part of the peripheral nervous system that transmits sensory messages to the central nervous system and then transmits responses to muscles, organs, and other tissues.

somatoform disorders   Mental illnesses in which psychological conflicts manifest themselves as physical symptoms.

somatotype   A person's body type; particularly influenced by genetics. The three somatotypes are endomorphic, mesomorphic, and ectomorphic.

SOS   *See* **Secular Organization for Sobriety**

SPECT   *See* **single photon emission computer tomography (SPECT) scan**

speed   Street name for any amphetamine or methamphetamine.

speedball   A drug combination of an upper and a downer (usually heroin and cocaine or heroin and methamphetamine) that is injected, snorted, eaten, or smoked.

"speed freaks"   Old street name for methamphetamine abusers.

spirituality   An individual's personal relationship with his or her higher power; awareness or acceptance that one is part of a greater purpose or existence than just his or her own worldly existence; a crucial aspect of 12-step groups.

spit tobacco   A term for smokeless tobacco, including chewing tobacco and snuff.

"spraying"   Slang for spraying an inhalant directly into the nose or mouth.

SSRIs   *See* **selective serotonin reuptake inhibitors**

Saint Anthony's Fire   A name for ergot poisoning. Ergot is a rye or wheat fungus that contains lysergic acid amine, a hallucinogen. One of the symptoms is a burning sensation of the skin.

stacking   Using two or more steroids at one time to increase effectiveness.

stages-of-change model   This model used in treatment delineates five predictable and identifiable stages one goes through in the process of making life changes: precontemplation, contemplation, determination (or preparation), action, and maintenance.

stash   (1) A hiding place for an illegal drug supply. (2) A supply of illegal drugs.

STDs   *See* **sexually transmitted diseases**

stellate cell   A star-shaped liver cell that stores vitamin A compounds and fat molecules; alcohol and biochemicals released from other liver cells can cause scar tissue.

"step on"   Adulterating a drug with the addition of cheap or inactive substances to increase the amount available for sale.

steroids   *See* **anabolic-androgenic steroid**

stimulant   Any substance—including cocaine, amphetamines, diet pills, coffee, khat, betel nuts, ephedra, and tobacco—that forces the release of epinephrine and norepinephrine, the body's own stimulants.

stout   A top-fermented variety of ale that is very dark and sweet, mostly associated with Ireland.

street drugs   Illegal psychoactive drugs, such as cocaine, heroin, and marijuana.

stress   The body's reaction to illness and environmental forces. It produces psychological strain and physiological changes, including the release of cortisol, rapid respiration and heart rate, constricted blood vessels, and the release of hormones.

subcutaneous   Under the skin; a route of drug administration.

sublingual   Under the tongue; a route of drug administration where the drug is absorbed by mucous membranes.

substance abuse   Continued use of a psychoactive drug despite adverse consequences.

substance dependence   Maladaptive pattern of substance use (e.g., addiction).

substance P   The neurotransmitter that transmits pain from neuron to neuron.

substance-induced disorders   Disorders caused by the actual use of psychoactive drugs (e.g., methamphetamine psychosis).

substance-related disorders   The overall classification for drug disorders that is divided into substance use disorders and substance-induced disorders.

substance use disorder   A classification of substance-related disorders defined by the pattern of drug use, including substance dependence and substance abuse.

substantia nigra   Part of the extrapyramidal system in the brain that helps control muscle movements.

substitution therapy   Using a drug that is cross-tolerant with another to detoxify a user who has become physically dependent.

sudden infant death syndrome (SIDS)   A sudden and often unexplainable death of an otherwise healthy infant; often connected to drug use during pregnancy.

Summer of Love   A period in 1967 when the hippie movement flourished, characterized by drug use and free love.

supply reduction   A prevention approach that uses such techniques as interdiction of illegal drugs, drug use laws, legal penalties, and crop eradication to reduce the supply of drugs available to users, abusers, and addicts.

suppository   A drug-infused device used for introduction of the substance into an orifice of the body such as the rectum.

supraphysiological   Relating to a dose of any substance (neurotransmitter, hormone, or other naturally occurring agent) that is more potent than would normally occur.

susceptibility   A person's individual vulnerability to use drugs addictively or engage in compulsive behaviors; it is based on heredity, environment, and drug use or acting out. These factors make one more likely to use and another to resist use.

sympathetic nervous system   Part of the autonomic nervous system; it helps control involuntary body functions, including digestion, blood circulation, and respiration; it works with the parasympathetic nervous system to balance body functions.

synapse   The process of nerve cell communication through the release of neurotransmitter chemicals that cross the synaptic gap to transmit a message from one nerve cell to another.

synaptic gap   The tiny gap between the terminal of the sending nerve cell and the dendrite or body of the receiving cell.

synergism   An exaggerated effect that occurs when two or more drugs are used at the same time. One reason why this effect occurs is because the liver or body is busy metabolizing one drug while the other slips through unchanged.

synesthesia   An effect of hallucinogens that converts one sensory input to another (e.g., colors are heard and sounds are seen).

synthesis   The process of making drugs in the laboratory with chemicals and artificial techniques rather than extracting them from plants or animals. Biochemicals can also be synthesized internally by the body.

syphilis   A sexually transmitted disease with three levels of infection severity; less common since the discovery of penicillin and other antibiotics.

T

T-cells   A type of white blood cell (lymphocyte) that helps fight infection. Low numbers of T-cells signal an impaired immune system, possibly caused by an HIV infection.

tachycardia   Rapid beating of the heart caused by cardiovascular disease or drugs, especially stimulants.

tachyphylaxis   *See* **acute tolerance**

tar   A by-product of smoking that is carcinogenic.

tar heroin   A black or dark brown heroin originally grown and processed in Mexico. It contains many impurities but can be 20% to 80% pure. It is water-soluble. Tar heroin is now processed in Africa and South America as well.

tardive dyskinesia   A nerve disorder caused by antipsychotic drugs; symptoms include involuntary facial tics and tongue movements.

TCE   *See* **trichloroethylene**

TEDS   *See* **Treatment Episode Data Sets**

temperance   A philosophy of light-to-moderate drinking that is an alternative to abstinence or prohibition.

temporal lobe   The part of the cerebral cortex involved in emotions, language, sensory processing, and memory.

teratogen   A drug that produces a birth defect when taken during pregnancy.

terminals   Small buttons at the ends of nerve cells that release neurotransmitters.

tertiary prevention   A prevention strategy aimed at drug abusers and addicts to reduce harm to themselves and to society. Intervention, treatment, and harm reduction techniques are used.

testosterone   The most potent male hormone, formed mainly in the male testes; the major naturally occurring anabolic steroid.

tetrahydrocannabinol (THC)   The main psychoactive ingredient of marijuana; mimics the natural neurotransmitter anandamide.

"Texas shoeshine" Spray paint containing toluene and abused as an inhalant.

Thai sticks Marijuana buds glued to bamboo shoots; a potent packaging of marijuana.

thalamus Part of the diencephalon deep inside the brain that helps relay information to the cerebral cortex.

THC *See* **tetrahydrocannabinol**

theobromine An alkaloid from the cacao plant that is similar to caffeine; used as a diuretic, heart stimulant, muscle relaxant, and vasodilator.

theophylline An active alkaloid found in tea leaves along with caffeine; used as a diuretic, heart stimulant, muscle relaxant, and vasodilator.

therapeutic community Any long-term (one- to three-year) residential inpatient program that provides full rehabilitative and social services for addicts and alcoholics.

therapeutic drugs Drugs, including anti-inflammatories, painkillers, and muscle relaxants, that are used for specific medical problems.

therapeutic index The effective dose of a drug vs. the lethal or dangerous side effects of that drug; the ratio of the lethal dose to the effective dose.

therapy The treatment of addiction or other problem through a variety of methods, including individual counseling and group therapy, that is conducted by a licensed or credentialed professional.

theriac An opium-based cure-all that was developed almost 2,000 years ago. It has undergone many changes in formulation, but the opium remains.

thin layer chromatography (TLC) A moderately precise drug-testing method for the urine of a suspected drug user.

threshold dose The minimum amount of a drug that produces a desired effect.

tissue dependence The biological adaptation of body cells and functions due to excessive drug use. Also called *physical dependence.*

titration Adjusting the dose of a drug to achieve a desired effect.

TLC *See* **thin layer chromatography**

toad secretion *See* **bufotenine**

tobacco The cured leaves of *Nicotinia tabacum* or other tobacco plant. It is the source of nicotine and can be smoked, chewed, or used as snuff.

tolerance The increasing ability of the body to metabolize or consume greater and greater amounts of a drug or other foreign substance.

toluene A liquid hydrocarbon solvent that is used as an intoxicating inhalant. It is found in many household products and glues.

topical anesthetic A solution, ointment, or gel containing a substance that deadens sensations in the skin, mucous membranes, or conjunctiva (e.g., cocaine, lidocaine, and procaine).

TOUGHLOVE® A treatment approach that requires an addict's family to set strict limits on behavior to break through denial and change behavior.

toxic substance A substance that is poisonous when given in certain amounts. Many toxins are poisonous at low doses.

toxicology The study of toxic substances.

tracking The ability of the eyes to follow a moving object.

tracks Needle scars on an injection drug user's body, especially the arms.

trade name A drug company's name for its patented medication. Also called *brand name.*

trailing phenomenon A drug-induced visual distortion (usually from marijuana or LSD) in which the user sees a trail following a moving object.

tranquilizers Drugs that have antianxiety or antipsychotic properties but don't induce sleep; also prescribed as muscle relaxants.

transdermal A method of drug delivery whereby a drug-infused patch is adhered to the skin so that the drug can be absorbed through the skin.

treatment The use of various techniques and therapies to change maladaptive patterns of behavior and restore a client to full health.

Treatment Episode Data Sets (TEDS) A federal survey that supplies descriptive information about admissions to substance-abuse treatment providers.

trichloroethylene (TCE) A common organic solvent found in correction fluids, paints, and spot removers.

tricyclic antidepressants A class of psychiatric medications that increase the activity of serotonin to elevate mood and counter depression (e.g., amitriptyline).

triggers Any object or action that activates craving in a recovering drug user (e.g., the sight of white powder, money, a syringe, or a former neighborhood or drug-using partner).

triple diagnosis The coexistence of drug addiction, a major mental illness, and AIDS or other physical illness.

trismus Jaw muscle spasm.

truth serum *See* **scopolamine**

tryptophan An amino acid that is a precursor of serotonin.

tuberculosis A bacterial disease that can affect and damage any organ but most often the lungs.

"tweak" (1) Street name for methamphetamine. (2) Unusual hyperactive behavior and emotions caused by excess amphetamine use.

12-step programs Self-help groups based on Alcoholics Anonymous and the 12 steps of recovery. Their purpose is to change addicts' thinking and behavior and enhance their spirituality.

twin studies Long-term studies of adopted twins either raised together or separately to determine the influence of heredity on a person.

U

uppers Stimulants.

urethritis Inflammation of the urinary tract, often caused by excessive use of steroids.

urinalysis Analysis of urine to test for drug use.

U.S. Household Survey A survey of drug use and attitudes in the United States done by the Substance Abuse and Mental Health Services Administration, Office of Applied Studies.

V

Valium® *See* **diazepam**

vasoconstriction Constriction of blood vessels, often due to drugs, especially stimulants like cocaine and methamphetamines.

vasodilation Dilation of blood vessels; can be caused by alcohol or other drugs.

venereal disease *See* **sexually transmitted diseases (STDs)**

ventral tegmental area (VTA) The origin of a prominent dopamine pathway that ascends to various parts of the limbic system, particularly the nucleus accumbens; it is part of the reward/reinforcement pathway.

ventricle A natural cavity in the brain, heart, or other organ. The brain's ventricles are filled with cerebrospinal fluid.

vesicle The microscopic sacs in the terminals of nerve cells that store neurotransmitters until they are released into the synaptic gap.

Viagra® *See* **sildenafil citrate**

Vicodin® *See* **hydrocodone**

Vitas vinifera The most common species of grape used to make wine; comes in more than 5,000 varieties.

Vivitrol® *See* **naltrexone**

volatile nitrites *See* **nitrites**

volatile solvents Petroleum distillates that are abused as inhalants.

Volstead Act The 1920 law that prohibited the sale and public consumption of alcohol. *See* **Prohibition**.

VTA *See* **ventral tegmental area**

W

WCTU *See* **Women's Christian Temperance Union**

"weed" Street name for marijuana.

Wernicke's encephalopathy A central nervous system disease caused by excessive long-term drinking and linked to thiamin deficiency; symptoms include delirium, loss of balance, tremors, and visual impairment; often seen in combination with Korsakoff's syndrome.

wet drinking culture A culture where daily drinking is sanctioned and is integrated into everyday life, often with meals (e.g., France and Italy).

Wets Anti-Prohibitionists active in the United States in the 1920s and 1930s, working toward the repeal of the Volstead Act.

WFS *See* **Women for Sobriety**

Whippets® Small metal canisters containing nitrous oxide (laughing gas). They are sold as whipped cream propellants but abused as an inhalant.

whiskey A distilled alcoholic beverage made from a mash of fermented grains, including rye, barley, corn, oats, and wheat; usually contains about 40% alcohol (80 proof).

white matter Brain matter composed mostly of axons, glial cells, and myelin.

"whites" Street name for amphetamine sulfate (Benzedrine®) tablets originally prescribed for weight control.

wine An alcohol beverage made from the fermented juice of grapes; can be made from other fruits and vegetables (e.g., rice wine, plum wine, and apple wine). Alcohol content of wine is usually 10% to 14% but can go as high as 16%.

"wired" Intoxicated with a stimulant (e.g. cocaine or methamphetamine).

withdrawal The body's attempt to rebalance itself after prolonged use of a psychoactive drug. The symptoms range from mild (caffeine withdrawal) to severe (heroin withdrawal) to life threatening (benzodiazepine withdrawal). The onset and the duration of symptoms are generally predictable.

Women for Sobriety (WFS) A self-help group therapy organization for female alcoholics.

Women's Christian Temperance Union (WCTU) Women's crusade to close saloons and promote temperance; founded in 1874, it had a peak membership of 500,000.

"works" Syringe, cotton, and other paraphernalia used to inject heroin and other drugs.

X

Xanax® *See* **alprazolam**

xanthines A class of alkaloids found in 60 plants (e.g., *Coffea Arabica, Thea sinensis, Theobroma cacao,* and *Cola nitida*). The most prominent xanthine is caffeine.

XTC *See* **ecstasy**

Y

yage A hallucinogenic psychedelic drink made from the ayahuasca vine of South America.

yeast A fungus that exists in soil, fruits, some vegetables, and animal excreta; used to ferment carbohydrates, especially sugars, into alcohol and to make bead rise.

yohimbe tree The source of yohimbine, a stimulant brewed in water as a tea or used in tablet or liquid form as an aphrodisiac.

Z

zero tolerance A prevention philosophy that allows no tolerance or second chances for drug use; often used in schools.

Z-hypnotics Benzodiazepine-like medications, including zopiclone (Imovane®), zolpidem (Ambien®), and zaleplon (Sonata®). Eszopiclone (Lunesta®) is also considered a Z-hypnotic.

Zoloft® *See* **sertraline**

Zyban® *See* **bupropion**

INDEX